THE BIG RED
BOOK OF
SPANISH
VOCABULARY

30,000 Words including
Cogn~~ates Roots and S~~uffixes

Scott Thomas | **Gaby Thomas**
Rose Nash Ph.D. | **Dorothy Richmond**

*New York Chicago San Francisco Lisbon London Madrid Mexico City
Milan New Delhi San Juan Seoul Singapore Sydney Toronto*

The *McGraw·Hill* Companies

Library of Congress Cataloging-in-Publication Data

Thomas, Daniel Scott.
    The big red book of Spanish vocabulary : 30,000 words including cognates, roots, and
suffixes / Daniel Scott Thomas ... [et al.].
        p.   cm.
    Includes index.
    ISBN 0-07-144725-3 (alk. paper)
    1. Spanish language—Glossaries, vocabularies, etc.   I. Title.

PC4680.T46   2005
468.2′421—dc22   2005047982

      6 7 8 9 0   QDB/QDB   3 2 1

ISBN 0-07-144725-3

Interior design by Terry Stone

McGraw-Hill books are available at special quantity discounts to use as premiums and sales
promotions, or for use in corporate training programs. For more information, please write to the
Director of Special Sales, Professional Publishing, McGraw-Hill, Two Penn Plaza, New York, NY
10121-2298. Or contact your local bookstore.

Also in this series:

Gordon and Stillman: *The Big Red Book of Spanish Verbs*
Weibel: *The Big Red Book of Spanish Idioms*

This book is printed on acid-free paper.

Contents

Acknowledgments

First, we'd like to thank our friends and family, who often helped us to clarify our definitions and strengthen this vocabulary guide. Second, we'd like to thank Nicholas J. Brown, author of the *Russian Learner's Dictionary*, and Rob Watt, whose *Concordance* software we used to develop the Frequency Table. Both gave us valuable insight in the initial stages of the project. Third, we'd like to thank our editor, Christopher Brown, for his vision to unite these separate vocabulary guides into one volume, for his practical and patient advice, and for his constant encouragement. Finally, we wish to give special thanks to our friend Chris Hadden from Redmond, Washington, who graciously used his extensive computer expertise at all hours of the day and night to help us with the technical aspects of putting this guide together.

—Scott Thomas and Gaby Thomas

Many experts contributed to the preparation of the cognate section of this book. I am especially grateful to the following: Dr. Eugene Albert, Dr. Richard M. de Andino, Anders E. Augustson, Dr. Joan Fayer, Carl Victor Freedman, Marcie Guttman, Milton Kaplan, Emilio Lopez Irrizary, Dan Knapp, Professor Edith Lebed, Dr. James McCoy, Dr. Eugene V. Mohr, Professor Roberta Raymond, Dr. Felix Schweizer, Chris Roberts, and Stevens M. Wright.

—Rose Nash, Ph.D.

I would like to thank several people for their contributions to the suffix section of this book: Dr. Carol A. Klee, Associate Professor of Spanish at the University of Minnesota; Dr. James M. May, Professor of Classics at St. Olaf College in Northfield, Minnesota; Mitchell E. Blatt, M.D.; Joe Thurston; Michael Ross; and Lola Lorenzo.

—Dorothy Devney Richmond

Using This Vocabulary Book

The Big Red Book of Spanish Vocabulary is composed of four distinct, yet inter-related, dictionaries whose purpose is to enable you to greatly expand your Spanish vocabulary quickly, in an organized and efficient manner, whether you are a beginning, intermediate, or advanced language student. These four dictionaries cover cognates, roots, suffixes, and frequency of use, and are described in detail below.

1. Thesaurus of Spanish Cognates

Computer-*computadora*, famous-*famoso*, entertainment-*entretenimiento*, and inform-*informar* are examples of a large group of words known as *true cognates*—words that look alike and have the same meanings. They account for one-third to one-half of the average educated person's active vocabulary (estimated at 10,000 to 15,000 words) and because of their striking similarities enable language students to learn a large number of words very quickly. This cognate thesaurus takes advantage of this fact and serves to bridge the two languages by listing thousands of such terms categorized for easy learning.

The thesaurus is arranged so that the groups in the first section deal with subjects of general interest, while the later groups are more specialized and technical. Each topic in the thesaurus has its own appropriate format. For example, a complex topic such as Mathematics needs many headings and subheadings to properly organize all the specialized terms used in that field, while a simpler topic like Personal Names needs very few. Regardless of however many headings and subheadings there are, they are arranged so that the general terms for that topic come first, followed by more specific categories.

The specific entries are set up like the following:

TRAVEL AND TOURISM

GENERAL TERMS

attraction	atracción *nf*
class	clase *nf*
destination	destino *nm*
exploration	exploración *nf*
line	línea *nf*
tourism	turismo *nm*
transit	tránsito *nm*
transportation	tra(n)sportación *nf*
vacation *nsg*	vacaciones *nfpl*

ASPECTS OF TOURISM

types of vacations

cruise	crucero *nm*
excursion	excursión *nf*
expedition	expedición *nf*
odyssey	odisea *nf*
peregrination	peregrinación *nf*
safari	safari *nm*
trekking	trekking *nm*
visit	visita *nf*
voyage	viaje *nm*

The English term is listed first, followed by the Spanish along with its corresponding part of speech. Brief notes may be added to the entries for clarification, as is the case in *tra(n)sportación*, in which the parenthesis surrounding a letter in the middle of a word indicates an optional letter, and *vacation*, which is singular in English but plural in Spanish.

One further point worth mentioning is that there are, of course, times when the Spanish cognate is not the only translation of the English cognate. But even in these cases, the cognate is useful for communication. Take, for example, in the topic Clothing, the entry "zipper = zíper *nm*." Some Spanish speakers refer to a zipper as *cremallera* or *cierre*, but they will always recognize and understand *zíper*.

Finally, the thesaurus is organized into the following sections:

- The first section covers everyday vocabulary—familiar, easy-to-remember words that you can put to use immediately.
- The main section of the thesaurus covers special-interest vocabulary and includes one hundred topics organized into nineteen separate theme groups covering a multitude of subjects ranging from art, electricity, and communications to aviation, geography, and sports.
- The final section is devoted to some of the more common false and semi-false cognates—words that look alike but have different meanings in English and Spanish. One common example is "library" (*biblioteca*) and *librería* ("bookstore"). These cases of "mistaken identity" are important in language learning because by knowing them, students will be able to avoid errors in translation.

2. Dictionary of Spanish Roots

If you only had a limited amount of time in which to learn the following words, which group of words would you find easier to study?

Group 1: *castigar* (to punish), *periódico* (newspaper), *pescar* (to fish), *alimentar* (to nourish), *mandar* (to order), and *raya* (stripe, line).

Group 2: *comer* (to eat), *comida* (food), *comedor* (dining room), *comestibles* (groceries), *malcomer* (to eat poorly), and *comilón* (big eater or glutton).

In this Root Dictionary, over 14,000 words have been organized into more than 2,000 word families based on similar origins, such as those listed in Group 2 above, and developed on the concept that it is indeed easier to learn related words than it is to learn unrelated terms. Each family of words listed in the dictionary consists of words having the same root underlying each of the entries. By ordering them in this manner, word study becomes more organized and easier to manage.

Sometimes, of course, you may be assigned or take it upon yourself to learn a list of words like those in Group 1 above—words with no readily apparent connection. In that case, you could consult the Root Dictionary where you would find two words related to *castigar*, five words related to *periódico*, seven words related to *raya*, eleven words related to *pescar*, thirteen words related to *alimentar*, and fifteen words related to *mandar*. By learning their related terms, you could leverage the study of those six original words into fifty-three with only a small amount of additional effort.

Each entry in the dictionary has the following format:

especial special
 especializarse *vr* to specialize
 especificar *vt* [-ificar 3190] to specify
 especialista *nmf* [-ista 1556] specialist
 especialización *nf* specialization
 especificación *nf* specification
 especialmente *av* [-mente 1147] especially
 específicamente *av* [-mente 3996] specifically
 especial *aj* [-cial 250] special
 especializado *aj* specialized
 específico *aj* [-ico(2) 1801] specific

Please note the following.

- The most commonly used word in a grouping—the headword—is listed alphabetically within the dictionary and appears in bold.
- Beneath this headword, the related words are listed according to part of speech. Verbs are listed first, followed by nouns, pronouns, adverbs, and adjectives.
- Only words in common usage have been included, thus allowing the learner to use the words included here with confidence.
- Entries are cross-referenced to both the Guide to Spanish Suffixes and the Spanish Frequency Table. The cross-references to the Guide to Spanish Suffixes are solely to terms that appear as examples in that guide. There are, of course, many other entries in the Root Dictionary (without cross-references) that contain a suffix described in the Guide to Spanish Suffixes but that are not exemplified.

3. Guide to Spanish Suffixes

Far more than most modern languages, Spanish relies on suffixes to denote parts of speech, modify the word root, or even convey subtle nuances of meaning. This guide will help expand your vocabulary and comprehension through mastery of the most common Spanish word endings.

Familiarity with the logic of Spanish word endings promotes a geometric increase in vocabulary for each new term learned. For example, most students learn *el papel* (paper) during the first weeks of study, but learning the suffixes resulting in such terms as *la papelería* (stationery shop), *la papelera* (waste basket; paper case), *el papelero* (paper-maker; stationer), *el papeleo* (paper work; red-tape), and *el papelito* (small piece of paper) often comes much later. The suffixes involved, *-ería, -era, -ero, eo,* and *-ito,* will often be helpful in expanding the use of other basic terms as you learn them.

You will find that, armed with a basic knowledge of Spanish terms—such as those covered in most first-year courses—and an awareness of Spanish suffixes, you will be able both to recognize and create new terms, and you will become more self-reliant and less threatened by Spanish literature and conversation.

This Guide to Spanish Suffixes contains over 130 Spanish suffixes, chosen on the basis of their frequent recurrence throughout the language. Some endings are far more common than others but all are found in words you will encounter in everyday usage.

The specific entries are presented in the following manner:

-lento (-lenta)

Meaning: *like; relating to; full of*
English equivalent: *-lent*
Found in: *adjectives*

Spanish adjectives ending with *-lento* have at their base a noun and indicate that the person or thing described has characteristics of that noun. When describing a feminine noun, these adjectives take the ending *-lenta.*

Formed Word	English Equivalent	Related to	English Equivalent
corpulento [R]	corpulent; fat; fleshy	**el cuerpo**	body
flatulento	flatulent; windy	**el flato**	flatus; wind
fraudulento	fraudulent	**el fraude**	fraud
friolento [R]	chilly; sensitive to cold	**el frío**	cold; coldness; coolness
pulverulento	powdery; dusty	**el polvo**	powder; dust
sanguinolento [R]	bloody; dripping blood	*(Lat.)* **sanguis**	blood
suculento	succulent	**el suco**	sap; juice
violento [R 2363]	violent	**la violencia**	violence
virulento	virulent	**el virus**	virus

The suffixes are arranged alphabetically, along with the important features of each particular ending: its meaning; its English equivalent (when one exists); and the part(s) of speech of the words formed. This basic information is followed by a short paragraph that discusses the meaning of the particular suffix, how words employing it are formed, and interesting features and/or unusual constructions characteristic of that particular ending.

Next you will find an illustrative list of words exhibiting the suffix. Each Spanish entry is accompanied by its English equivalent and the stem to which it is related (many of which the learner will recognize), as well as that stem's English equivalent. When a term refers to a person, only the masculine form is given in order to emphasize the word; however, formation of its feminine counterpart always is discussed in the paragraph preceding the list. In addition, the Spanish entries are cross-referenced to both the Dictionary of Spanish Roots and the Spanish Frequency Table, as appropriate.

Most of the formed terms in this Guide to Spanish Suffixes are related to other Spanish terms; however, some words come directly from Latin or Greek. When this is the case, these terms are noted accordingly. In addition, when a term appears that is used only in a specific context (e.g., technically or colloquially), this also is noted.

4. Spanish Frequency Table

When learning Spanish, one worthy and reasonable goal is to be able to read and understand "everyday Spanish" such as one would find in a daily newspaper and to be able to converse on the topics reported—topics such as national and international events, sports, society, religion, and entertainment. But how does one know which words make up "everyday Spanish"? And how does one decide which are the most important ones to study?

The Spanish Frequency Table was compiled to answer these questions. It was drawn from a sample of over 10,000,000 words found in a daily Spanish-language newspaper in Mexico, *El Siglo de Torreón*, a periodical written in everyday Spanish. From that sample, a list of over 5,000 words was formed and ordered according to frequency—on the assumption that, in general, the more common a word is, the more important it is to learn.

Although such a list cannot aim to be definitive, several questions arise relating to its formation and usefulness for the learner:

- **Will the Spanish be representative of the Spanish spoken around the world?** In the newspaper chosen, the Spanish is international: *El Siglo* uses several news agencies as sources, including Reuters, the *New York Times, El Universal, La Jornada,* and *Notimex.*
- **How does one deal with various word forms such as plurals and verb conjugations?** Variant forms of the same word are counted together under a single heading to obtain a more appropriate frequency count. For example, *voy, vas, va, vamos, vaís, van,* etc. are counted as forms of *ir,* "to go" (*fue* is the one exception to this as it can mean either "went" from *ir* or "was" from *ser.*)

• **What about the temporal nature of news events, so that the frequency of a word (such as a country's name) may change from year to year depending on circumstances?** Editorial judgment was used in deciding which terms should be included and which words should be left out because their ranking seemed unduly high because of current events unlikely to repeat in later years (for example, *talibán* is a word that was excluded).

Words in the Frequency Dictionary appear in the following format:

[11] **por** *prep* for; in place of; instead of; by; during
(the preposition *para* is also often used to
mean "for") □ *por ejemplo* for example; *por
la mañana* during the morning ■ **Él trabaja
por mí. He works instead of me. Me gusta el
libro escrito por Carlos Cuauhtémoc Sánchez.**
I like the book written by Carlos Cuauhtémoc
Sánchez. **Linda vive por la iglesia.** Linda lives
by the church.

Entries include frequency rank, headword, part of speech, and definitions. Sometimes, as in the above example, other explanatory information is included:

□ Indicates a set expression or common phrase that uses the term
■ Indicates sample sentence(s). Examples are provided for the top 1,000 terms to demonstrate the proper use of the word in context.
▶ Indicates a similar word form, where the only difference between the entries may be the presence or absence of an accent or a feminine or masculine ending.

The words listed can be approached in a number of ways: studied in the order presented; accessed by using the index to find the frequency ranking of a particular word; or referred to as a checklist in order to monitor one's progress in learning Spanish vocabulary. Many learners will find it useful to fill in some gaps that they have in their vocabulary development.

There is one additional detail students may find interesting. In the one hundred newspapers sampled to create the Spanish Frequency Table, the most frequently encountered Spanish word is the word meaning "the," *el* and its various forms *la, los,* and *las.* These occurred 909,735 times—almost 10 percent of the total—while the word ranked 5000, *agujero,* meaning "hole," occurred only 97 times, an average of about once a day or once every 100,000 words. It can be argued whether it is really more important to know number 4639, *subasta* (auction), than number 4723, *pastilla* (pill). Their relative importance, of course, depends on circumstances—such as whether you have a headache or not! But, in the end, learners who master the 5,000 words in this dictionary will have no trouble reading nearly every word of a Spanish language newspaper and will be able to converse freely on a wide variety of topics.

Additional Approaches for Expanding Your Vocabulary

One characteristic of this guide to studying vocabulary is that you can start where you like and ultimately wind up with a powerful vocabulary. You may choose to begin your study with cognates, suffixes, or roots or to sequentially follow the frequency list because each section has been written to help you leverage your time. In the paragraphs below you will find a few suggestions on how to use the vocabulary guides.

- **Thesaurus of Spanish Cognates:** In the beginning of this dictionary is the topic Everyday Vocabulary. Here you will find familiar, easy-to-remember words that you can put to use immediately, including a basic list of more than one hundred high-frequency cognates, common short-form words we use in informal speech, Latin expressions, greetings and exclamations, and loanwords that English and Spanish have given to each other. If you have a special interest, look at the topics by theme group. Also, take a good look at the false and semi-false cognates in the section on Common False Cognates. Learning these will help you avoid mistakes in translation.
- **Dictionary of Spanish Roots:** When studying a vocabulary list, look up the words in this dictionary. You will be able to learn many more related words with only a little more effort and this extra effort will help solidify the meaning of the original list word in your own mind .
- **Guide to Spanish Suffixes:** At the end of this guide to suffixes is a list of the suffixes arranged according to their part of speech. This chart also contains the corresponding English equivalent (when there is one) and the meaning of the suffix in English. You may want to use this list as a checklist to monitor your progress in learning Spanish suffixes.
- **Spanish Frequency Table:** Measuring progress on the essentials of a language is a useful and often overlooked element in language study—both for the motivational surge that is encouraged and for the practical aspect of knowing what is missing in one's language study. Whether you are a beginning, intermediate, or advanced Spanish student, you may want to use this list to monitor your progress in learning Spanish vocabulary and as a list of useful words to know and use. By the way, as you study words in the Dictionary of Spanish Roots and the Guide to Spanish Suffixes, note that they are cross-referenced to the Spanish Frequency Table, enabling you to quickly find the entry and mark your progress.

- **Index:** Each Spanish entry in the Dictionary of Spanish Roots, Guide to Spanish Suffixes, and Spanish Frequency Table is included in the Index. An entry followed by a complete Spanish word indicates its place in the Dictionary of Spanish Roots; a dash followed by a suffix indicates where to find the word in the Guide to Spanish Suffixes; and a number indicates its rank and location in the Spanish Frequency Table.

Abbreviations and Grammatical Notes

aj	adjective
av	adverb
conj	conjunction
intj	interjection
nf	feminine noun
nf(el)	feminine noun used with masculine definite article in the singular
nm	masculine noun
nmf	masculine or feminine noun
npl	plural (English) noun
nsg	singular (English) noun
(obs.)	obsolete or historical word
pl	plural
prep	preposition
pron	pronoun
vt	transitive verb
vi	intransitive verb
vr	reflexive verb

1. In definitions, commas are used between words that amplify the meaning of the word and help make the definition more clear. Semicolons are used to indicate a separate definition of the word that may be similar but is distinct.
2. Adjectives are listed in their masculine form.
3. Nouns that can be either masculine or feminine are listed with *,-a* to indicate a change for the feminine form.
4. Nouns that can be either masculine or feminine that end in *-ón* in the masculine, such as *enojón* or *comilón*, are listed with the *,-a* as well, although the accent mark is not used in the feminine, e.g. *enojona* and *comilona*.

Thesaurus of Spanish Cognates

The Wide World of Words

EVERYDAY VOCABULARY

100-PLUS HIGH-FREQUENCY WORDS

accept	aceptar *vt*
action	acción *nf*
affect	afectar *vt*
air	aire *nm*
appear	aparecer *vi*
bank	banco *nm*
basic	básico *aj*
basis	base *nf*
case	caso *nm*
cause	causa *nf*
center	centro *nm*
central	central *aj*
character	carácter *nm*
class	clase *nf*
clear	claro *aj*
combine	combinar(se) *vt(r)*
common	común *aj*
condition	condición *nf*
contain	contener *vt*
contribute	contribuir *vti*
control	control *nm*
cooperate	cooperar *vi*
copy	copia *nf*
create	crear *vt*
day	día *nm*
decide	decidir *vti*
depend	depender *vi*
descend	descender *vi*
describe	describir *vt*
detail	detalle *nm*
difference	diferencia *nf*
different	diferente *aj*
difficult	difícil *aj*
direct	directo *aj*
double	doble *aj*
enter	entrar *vi*
equal	igual *aj*
error	error *nm*
exception	excepción *nf*
exist	existir *vi*

familiar	familiar *aj*
family	familia *nf*
famous	famoso *aj*
favor	favor *nm*
fine	fino *aj*
force	forzar *vt*
form	forma *nf*
general	general *aj*
group	grupo *nm*
hour	hora *nf*
human	humano, -a *aj, nmf*
idea	idea *nf*
important	importante *aj*
individual	individual *aj*
inform	informar *vt*
interest	interés *nm*
line	línea *nf*
list	lista *nf*
moment	momento *nm*
move	mover(se) *vt(r)*
name	nombre *nm*
necessary	necesario *aj*
new	nuevo *aj*
number	número *nm*
obtain	obtener *vt*
obvious	obvio *aj*
occupy	ocupar *vt*
operate	operar *vti*
opportunity	oportunidad *nf*
part	parte *nf*
pass	pasar *vti*
pause	pausa *nf*
perfect	perfecto *aj*
period	período, periodo *nm*
permit	permitir *vt*
person	persona *nf*
piece	pieza *nf*
plan	plan *nm*
point	punto *nm*
popular	popular *aj*
position	posición *nf*
possible	posible *aj*
practical	práctico *aj*
prefer	preferir *vt*
prepare	preparar *vt*
presence	presencia *nf*
present	presentar *vt*
price	precio *nm*
private	privado *aj*

probable	probable *aj*	stereo	estéreo *aj, nm*
problem	problema *nm*	taxi	taxi *nm*
produce	producir *vt*	TV	tele *nf*
program	programa *nm*		
progress	progreso *nm*		

prove	probar *vt*
public	público *aj, nm*
pure	puro *aj*
quality	calidad *nf*
quantity	cantidad *nf*
reality	realidad *nf*
reason	razón *nf*
recognize	reconocer *vt*
reduce	reducir *vt*
repeat	repetir *vt*
rich	rico *aj*
secret	secreto *aj, nm*
separate	separado *aj*
service	servicio *nm*
situation	situación *nf*
social	social *aj*
special	especial *aj*
state	estado *nm*
study	estudiar *vti*
style	estilo *nm*
symbol	símbolo *nm*
system	sistema *nm*
time	tiempo *nm*
total	total *aj, nm*
type	tipo *nm*
typical	típico *aj*
unite	unir(se) *vt(r)*
united	unido *aj*
use	uso *nm*
value	valor *nm*
visit	visita *nf*

greetings and exclamations

ah!	¡ah!
aha!	¡ajá!
ahem!	¡ejem!
ahoy!	¡ahó!
amen!	¡amén!
atchoo!	¡achís!
attention!	¡atención!
ay!	¡ay!
bah!	¡bah!
bingo!	¡bingo!
blah, blah, blah!	¡bla, bla, bla!
boo!	¡bú!
boo-hoo!	¡buuah!
bravo!	¡bravo!
brrr!	¡brrr!
ciao!	¡chao!
eh?	¿eh?
ha-ha!	¡ja-ja!
hallelujah!	¡aleluya!
halt!	¡alto!
hello!	¡hola!, ¡aló!
hey!	¡eh!
ho ho ho!	¡jo, jo!
no!	¡no!
oh no!	¡ay no!
OK!, okay!	¡okey!
sh!	¡sh!
ugh!	¡uf!
whoopee!, yippee!	¡yupi!
yah!	¡ja, ja!
yoo-hoo!	¡juju!
yum yum!	¡ñam ñam!

CONVERSATIONAL FORMS

clipped words in both languages

auto	auto *nm*
bike	bici *nm*
cello	chelo *nm*
fax	fax *nm*
isle	isla *nf*
math *nsg*	mates *nfpl*
memo	memo *nm*
mount	monte *nm*
polio	polio *nm*
porn, porno	porno *aj, nu*
prof	profe *nm*
sax	saxo *nm*
schizo	esquizo, -a *nmf*

imitation and baby talk

bow-wow	guau-guau *nm*
choo-choo	chu-cu-chu(cu) *nm*
click	clic *nm*
crack (sound)	crac *nm*
ding-dong	din don *nm*
ticktock	tictac *nm*
zigzag	zigzag *nm*

LOAN WORDS

from Spanish

banana	banana *nf*
barrio	barrio *nm*
bravado	bravata *nf*
burro	burro, -a *nmf*

cafeteria	cafetería *nf*
cocoa	cacao *nm*
fiesta	fiesta *nf*
flamenco	flamenco *nm*
gringo	gringo, -a *nmf*
hacienda	hacienda *nf*
lasso	lazo *nm*
machismo	machismo *nm*
mosquito	mosquito *nm*
mulatto	mulato, -a *aj, nmf*
patio	patio *nm*
pimiento	pimiento *nm*
pinto	pinto *nm*
poncho	poncho *nm*
potato	patata *nf*
rodeo	rodeo *nm*
siesta	siesta *nf*
taco	taco *nm*
tobacco	tabaco *nm*
tomato	tomate *nm*
tornado	tornado *nm*

from English

baseball	béisbol, baseball *nm*
clip	clip *nm*
cocktail	cóctel *nm*
hamburger	hamburguesa *nf*
hobby	hobby *nm*
jersey	jersey *nm*
jockey	jockey, yoquei *nmf*
junkie	yonqui *nmf*
knockout	nocaut, noqueo *nm*
leader	líder *nm*
meeting	mitin *nm*
microchip	microchip *nm*
pancake	panqueque *nm*
park	parquear *vt*
sandwich	sandwich *nm*
scooter	escúter *nm*
sexy	sexy *aj*
smog	esmog *nm*
snob	snob, esnob *nmf*
stop	stop *nm*
test (multiple-choice)	test *nm*
ticket	ticket *nm*
yuppie, yuppy	yupi *nmf*
zipper	zíper *nm*

LATIN EXPRESSIONS

a priori	a priori *av*
ad infinitum	ad infinitum *av*
alter ego	álter ego *nm*
curriculum vitae	curriculum vitae *nm*
et cetera	etcétera *av*
ex officio	ex oficio *aj*
in absentia	in absentia *av*
in situ	in situ *av*
in vitro	in vitro *aj*
ipso facto	ipso facto *av*
modus operandi	modus operandi *nm*
modus vivendi	modus vivendi *nm*
per capita	per cápita *av*
pro forma	pro forma *aj, av*
pro rata	prorrata *av*
sine qua non	sine qua non *aj*
status quo	statu quo *nm*
sui generis	sui generis *aj*

(*See also* **USING LANGUAGE**)

DICTIONARIES

GENERAL TERMS

alphabetical order	orden alfabético *nm*
dictionary	diccionario *nm*
entry	entrada *nf*
glossary	glosario *nm*
indicator	indicador *nm*
information	información *nf*
lexicography	lexicografía *nf*
lexicon (book)	lexicón *nm*
lexicon (words)	léxico *nm*
list	lista *nf*
specialized	especializado *aj*
standard	estándar *aj*
term	término *nm*
terminology	terminología *nf*
usage	uso *nm*
vocabulary	vocabulario *nm*

KINDS OF DICTIONARIES

standard

bilingual	bilingüe *aj*
monolingual	monolingüe *aj*
multilingual	multilingüe *aj*

specialized

biographical	biográfico *aj*
etymological	etimológico *aj*
frequency	de frecuencias *nfpl*
geographical	geográfico *aj*
phraseological	fraseológico *aj*
pronouncing	de pronunciación *nf*
rhetorical	retórico *aj*
rhyming	de rimas *nfpl*

| technical | técnico *aj* |
| thematic | temático *aj* |

DICTIONARY INFORMATION

type

grammatical	gramatical *aj*
orthographic	ortográfico *aj*
phonetic	fonético *aj*
semantic	semántico *aj*

phonetic and orthographic

accentuation	acentuación *nf*
pronunciation	pronunciación *nf*
syllabi(fi)cation	silabeo *nm*
variants	variante *nf*

grammatical and semantic

definition	definición *nf*
equivalent	equivalente *nm*
irregular form	forma irregular *nf*
part of speech	parte de la oración *nf*

word combinations

acronym	acrónimo *nm*
compound	compuesto *nm*
expression	expresión *nf*
idiomatic expression	expresión idiomática *nf*
locution	locución *nf*
phrasal verb	verbo con partícula *nm, nf*
proverb	proverbio *nm*
set phrase	frase hecha *nf*

usage labels

archaic	arcaico *aj*
colloquial	coloquial *aj*
dialectal	dialectal *aj*
diminutive	diminutivo *aj, nm*
euphemism	eufemismo *nm*
figurative	figurado *aj*
formal	formal *aj*
historical	histórico *aj*
humorous	humorístico *aj*
ironic	irónico *aj*
literary	literario *aj*
neologism	neologismo *nm*
obsolete	obsoleto *aj*
pejorative	peyorativo *aj, nm*
poetic	poético *aj*
rare	raro *aj*
technical	técnico *aj*
vulgar	vulgar *aj*

typographical indicators

italics *npl*	itálica *nf*
letter	letra *nf*
number	número *nm*
parentheses	paréntesis *nmpl*
symbol	símbolo *nm*

other information

abbreviation	abreviatura *nf*
antonym	antónimo *nm*
etymology	etimología *nf*
example in context	ejemplo en contexto *nm*
synonym	sinónimo *nm*

PERSONS

compiler	compilador(a), recopilador(a) *nmf*
etymologist	etimólogo, -a *nmf*
lexicographer	lexicógrafo, -a *nmf*
user	usuario, -a *nmf*

(*See also* **TERMS IN SEMANTICS** under **USING LANGUAGE**; *THE GREEK ALPHABET* under **WRITING**)

BOOKS AND LIBRARIES

GENERAL TERMS

collection	colección *nf*
copyright	copyright *nm*
edition	edición *nf*
publication	publicación *nf*
tome	tomo *nm*
volume	volumen *nm*

ASPECTS OF BOOKS

types of books

ABC-book	abecedario *nm*
almanac	almanaque *nm*
anecdote collection	anecdotario *nm*
annual	anuario *nm*
anthology	antología *nf*
atlas	atlas *nm*
catalog(ue)	catálogo *nm*
codex (obs)	códice *nm*
compendium	compendio *nm*
condensation	condensación *nf*
dictionary	diccionario *nm*
directory	directorio *nm*
dissertation	disertación *nf*

encyclopedia	enciclopedia *nf*
fable collection	fabulario *nm*
guidebook	guía *nf*
hymnal	himnario *nm*
manual	manual *nm*
pharmacopeia	farmacopea *nf*
psalmody	salmodia *nf*
reference	referencia *nf*
reprint	reimpresión *nf*
schoolbook	libro escolar *nm*
telephone directory	guía telefónica *nf*
textbook	libro de texto *nm*
thesaurus	tesauro *nm*
treatise	tratado *nm*

parts of books

addendum	adenda *nf*
appendix	apéndice *nm*
bibliography	bibliografía *nf*
chapter	capítulo *nm*
colophon (obs)	colofón *nm*
contents	contenido *nm*
cover	cubierta *nf*
dedication	dedicatoria *nf*
epigraph	epígrafe *nm*
errata *npl*	fe de erratas *nf, nfpl*
fascicle	fascículo *nm*
folio	folio *nm*
frontispiece	frontispicio *nm*
illustration	ilustración *nf*
index	índice *nm*
introduction	introducción *nf*
margin	margen *nm*
notes	notas *nfpl*
page	página *nf*
passim	passim *av*
preface	prefacio *nm*
recto	recto *nm*
rubric	rúbrica *nf*
subtitle	subtítulo *nm*
text	texto *nm*
title	título *nm*
verso	verso *nm*

words describing books

absorbing	absorbente *aj*
best-seller	bestseller *nm*
informative	informativo *aj*
interesting	interesante *aj*
rare	raro *aj*
valuable	valioso *aj*

book preparation

correction	corrección *nf*
formatting	formateado *nm*
galley	galerada *nf*
idea	idea *nf*
manuscript	manuscrito *nm*
pagination	paginación *nf*
printing	imprenta *nf*
word processor	procesador de palabras *nm, nfpl*

other terms

ex libris	ex libris *nm*
line	línea *nf*
paper	papel *nm*
royalties	royalties *nmpl*
trilogy	trilogía *nf*

ASPECTS OF LIBRARIES

types of libraries

circulating	circulante *aj*
community	comunitario *aj*
Library of Congress	Biblioteca del Congreso *nf, nm*
mobile	móvil, movible *aj*
private	privado *aj*
public	público *aj*
school	escolar *aj*
specialized	especializado *aj*

holdings

archives *npl*	archivo *nm*
audiovisual	audiovisual *aj*
microfiche	microficha *nf*
microfilm	microfilm(e) *nm*
video	video *nm*

tools and equipment

catalog(ue)	catálogo *nm*
cubicle	cubículo *nm*
photocopier	fotocopiadora *nf*

other terms

acquisition	adquisición *nf*
cataloging, cataloguing	catalogación *nf*
classification	clasificación *nf*
donation	donativo *nm*

PERSONS

archivist	archivero, -a, archivista *nmf*
author	autor(a) *nmf*

bibliographer	bibliógrafo, -a *nmf*
bibliomaniac	bibliómano, -a *nmf*
bibliophile	bibliófilo, -a *nmf*
cataloger, cataloguer	catalogador(a) *nmf*
coauthor	coautor(a) *nmf*
editor	editor, -a *nmf*
encyclopedist	enciclopedista *nmf*

JOURNALISM

GENERAL TERMS

article	artículo *nm*
bulletin	boletín *nm*
communiqué	comunicado *nm*
event	evento *nm*
information	información *nf*
media	medios *nmpl*
news *nsg*	noticias *nfpl*
news flash	flash informativo *nm*
press	prensa *nf*
press conference	conferencia de prensa *nf*
publication	publicación *nf*
Pulitzer Prize	Premio Pulitzer *nm*
reporting	reportaje *nm*
sensationalism	sensacionalismo *nm*

ASPECTS OF JOURNALISM

news media

daily (newspaper)	diario *nm*
pamphlet	panfleto *nm*
periodical	periódico *nm*
radio	radio *nm*
tabloid	tabloide *nm*
television	televisión *nf*

newspaper sections

classified (ads)	clasificado *aj*
comics, comic strip	tira cómica *nf*
employment	empleo *nm*
entertainment	entretenimiento *nm*
financial	financiero *aj*
obituaries	obituarios *nmpl*
personals	anuncios personales *nmpl*
sports	deportivo *aj*
TV listings *npl*	programación de TV *nf*

articles

column	columna *nf*
commentary	comentario *nm*
dispatch	despacho *nm*
documentary	documental *nm*

editorial	editorial *nm*
interview	entrevista *nf*
review	revista *nf*
testimonial	testimonial *nm*

news-gathering and reporting

censorship	censura *nf*
confidential	confidencial *aj*
coverage	cobertura *nf*
current	corriente *aj*
dateline	data *nf*
distortion	distorsión *nf*
divulge	divulgar *vt*
freelance	free-lance *aj*
illustration	ilustración *nf*
incident	incidente
libel	libelo *nm*
objectivity	objetividad *nf*
photograph	fotografía *nf*
privacy	privacidad *nf*
suppression	supresión *nf*

other terms

chronicle	crónica *nf*
circulation	circulación *nf*
concern	concernir *vt*
edition	edición *nf*
folio	folio *nm*
gazette	gaceta *nf*
newsprint	papel de prensa *nm, nf*
number	número *nm*
printed matter *nsg*	impresos *nmpl*
publicity	publicidad *nf*
serial	serial *nm*
subscription	su(b)scripción *nf*

PERSONS

article writer	articulista *nmf*
celebrity	celebridad *nf*
censor	censor *nmf*
columnist	columnista *nmf*
commentator	comentarista *nmf*
correspondent	corresponsal *nmf*
diarist	diarista *nmf*
editorial writer	editorialista *nmf*
interviewer	entrevistador(a) *nmf*
pamphleteer	panfletista *nmf*
paparazzi	paparazzi *nmpl*
photographer	fotógrafo, -a *nmf*
publicist	publicista *nmf*
reporter	reportero, -a *nmf*

subscriber	su(b)scriptor(a) *nmf*
distort	distorsionar *vt*

(*See also* **AMATEUR RADIO**; **TELEVISION AND VIDEO**)

LITERATURE

GENERAL TERMS

belles-lettres	bellas letras *nfpl*
criticism	crítica *nf*
expression	expresión *nf*
genre	género *nm*
humanities	humanidades *nfpl*
influence	influencia *nf*
license	licencia *nf*
literature	literatura *nf*
manner	manera *nf*
plagiarism	plagio *nm*
poem	poema *nm*
potpourri	popurrí *nm*
tetralogy	tetralogía *nf*
trilogy	trilogía *nf*

ASPECTS OF LITERATURE

genres

allegory	alegoría *nf*
drama	drama *nm*
epic	épica *nf*
erotica	literatura erótica *nf*
escapism	escapismo *nm*
fiction	ficción *nf*
juvenile	juvenil *aj*
narration	narración *nf*
nonfiction	no ficción *nf*
poetry	poesía *nf*
prose	prosa *nf*
scatology	escatología *nf*

elements

action	acción *nf*
anticlimax	anticlímax *nm*
character	carácter *nm*
climax	clímax *nm*
composition	composición *nf*
conflict	conflicto *nm*
description	descripción *nf*
dialog(ue)	diálogo *nm*
form	forma *nf*
hiatus	hiato *nm*
imagery *nsg*	imágenes *nfpl*
intrigue	intriga *nf*

location	localización *nf*
lyricism	lirismo *nm*
motivation	motivación *nf*
point of view	punto de vista *nm*
story	historia *nf*
structure	estructura *nf*
style	estilo *nm*
theme	tema *nm*
time	tiempo *nm*
treatment	tratamiento *nm*
unity	unidad *nf*

styles and themes

adventure	aventura *nf*
avant-garde	vanguardia *nf*
classicism	clasicismo *nm*
contemporary	contemporáneo *aj*
didactic	didáctico *aj*
epistolary	epistolario *nm*
esoteric	esotérico *aj*
Faustian	faustiano, fáustico *aj*
futurism	futurismo *nm*
Gothic (novel)	gótico *aj*
historical	histórico *aj*
Kafkaesque	kafkaiano, kafkiano *aj*
modernism	modernismo *nm*
naturalism	naturalismo *nm*
neoclassicism	neoclasicismo *nm*
pastoral	pastoral, pastoril *aj*
picaresque	picaresca *aj*
realism	realismo *nm*
romanticism	romanticismo *nm*
surrealism	surrealismo *nm*
symbolism	simbolismo *nm*
Utopian	utópico *aj*

parts of a work

canto	canto *nm*
epilog	epílogo *nm*
episode	episodio *nm*
extract	extracto *nm*
passage	pasaje *nm*
prologue	prólogo *nm*

humor in literature

caricature	caricatura *nf*
comedy	comedia *nf*
farce	farsa *nf*
humor	humor *nm*
irony	ironía *nf*
parody	parodia *nf*
sarcasm	sarcasmo *nm*
satire	sátira *nf*

FORMS OF FICTION

comic book	comic *nm*
detective novel	novela policial *nf*
fable	fábula *nf*
fantasy	literatura fantástica *nf*
folklore	folklore, folclore *nm*
legend	leyenda *nf*
mystery	misterio *nm*
narrative	narrativa *nf*
novel	novela *nf*
novelette	novela corta *nf*
parable	parábola *nf*
romance	romance *nm*
saga	saga *nf*
science fiction	ciencia ficción *nf*

FORMS OF DRAMA

melodrama	melodrama *nm*
miracle	milagro *nm*
morality	moralidad *nf*
passion	pasión *nf*
soliloquy	soliloquio *nm*
tragedy	tragedia *nf*
tragicomedy	tragicomedia *nf*

FORMS OF POETRY

ballad	balada *nf*
couplet	copla *nf*
elegy	elegía *nf*
epigram	epigrama *nm*
epode	epodo, epoda *nm, nf*
haiku	hai kai *nm*
idyll, idyl	idilio *nm*
octave	octava *nf*
ode	oda *nf*
paean	peán *nm*
quatrain	cuarteta *nf*
requiem	réquiem *nm*
rondel, rondelle	rondel *nm*
sonnet	soneto *nm*

FORMS OF FACTUAL PROSE

argument	argumento *nm*
autobiography	autobiografía *nf*
biography	biografía *nf*
commentary	comentario *nm*
critique	crítica *nf*
diary	diario *nm*
dissertation	disertación *nf*
essay	ensayo *nm*
exposition	exposición *nf*

history	historia *nf*
monograph	monografía *nf*
rhetoric	retórica *nf*
synopsis	sinopsis *nf*
thesis	tesis *nf*
treatise	tratado *nm*

SHORT FORMS OF WIT OR WISDOM

adage	adagio *nm*
anecdote	anécdota *nf*
aphorism	aforismo *nm*
apothegm	apotegma *nm*
epigram	epigrama *nm*
epigraph	epígrafe *nm*
epitaph	epitafio *nm*
epithet	epíteto *nm*
homily	homilia *nf*
maxim	máxima *nf*
proverb	proverbio *nm*

FICTIONAL CHARACTERS

generic characters

antagonist	antagonista *nmf*
antihero	antihéroe *nm*
hero	héroe *nm*
heroine	heroína *nf*
ingenue, ingénue	ingenua *nf*
innocent	inocentón *nm*
narrator	narrador(a) *nmf*
persona	persona *nf*
protagonist	protagonista *nmf*
romantic	romántico, -a *nmf*
superhero	superhéroe *nm*
villain	villano, -a *nmf*

science fiction

alien	alienígena *nmf*
android	androide *nm*
humanoid	humanoide *nmf*
Martian	marciano, -a *nmf*
robot	robot *nm*

folklore and legend

elf	elfo, elfina *nm, nf*
genie	genio *nm*
gnome	gnomo, nomo *nm*
houri	hurí *nf*
incubus	incubo *nm*
jinn, jinni	genio *nm*
monster	monstruo *nm*
ogre	ogro *nm*

roc	rocho, ruc *nm*
vampire	vampiro, vampiresa *nm, nf*

famous fictional characters

Aladdin	Aladino *nm*
Faust	Fausto *nm*
Lilliputian	liliputiense *nmf*
Mephistopheles	Mefistófeles *nm*
Merlin the Magician	Merlín el Mago *nm*
Quasimodo	Cuasimodo *nm*
Scheherezade	Sherezade *nf*
Superman	Supermán *nm*

TERMS IN POETRY

basic terms

figure of speech	figura retórica *nf*
line	línea *nf*
meter	metro *nm*
metrics	métrica *nf*
pause	pausa *nf*
poetics	poética *nf*
rhythm	ritmo *nm*
scansion	escansión *nf*
verse	verso *nm*
verse (Bible)	versículo *nm*

major categories

dramatic	dramático *aj*
lyric	lírico *aj*
narrative	narrativo *aj*

kinds of verse

alexandrine	alejandrino *aj*
blank	blanco *aj*
free verse	verso libre *nm*
heroic	heroico *aj*
masculine	masculino *aj*
sestet	sextilla *nf*
strophe	estrofa *nf*
trope	tropo *nm*

kinds of rhythm

anapest	anapesto *nm*
dactyl	dáctilo *nm*
dimeter	dímetro *nm*
distich	dístico *nm*
heptameter	heptámetro *nm*
hexameter	hexámetro *nm*
iamb	yambo *nm*
monometer	monómetro *nm*
octometer	octómetro *nm*

pentameter	pentámetro *nm*
spondee	espondeo *nm*
tercet	terceto, tercerilla *nm, nf*
tetrameter	tetrámero *nm*
triplet	terceto *nm*
trochaic	trocaico *aj*
trochee	troqueo *nm*

figures of speech

allusion	alusión *nf*
hyperbole	hipérbole *nf*
metaphor	metáfora *nf*
metonymy	metonimia *nf*
personification	personificación *nf*
simile	símil *nm*

sound patterns

acrostic	acróstico *nm*
alliteration	aliteración *nf*
anacrusis	anacrusis *nf*
anaphora	anáfora *nf*
assonance	asonancia *nf*
caesura	cesura *nf*
consonance	consonancia *nf*
echo	eco *nm*
hemistich	hemistiquio *nm*
onomatopoeia	onomatopeya *nf*
rhyme	rima *nf*

classical poems

Aeneid	Eneida *nf*
Iliad	Ilíada *nf*
Odyssey	Odisea *nf*

PERSONS

writers and storytellers

author	autor(a) *nmf*
biographer	biógrafo, -a *nmf*
coauthor	coautor(a) *nmf*
critic	crítico, -a *nmf*
diarist	diarista *nmf*
dramatist	dramaturgo, -a *nmf*
essayist	ensayista *nmf*
fabulist	fabulista *nmf*
folklorist	folklorista, folclorista *nmf*
humorist	humorista *nmf*
imagist	imaginista *nmf*
ironist	ironista *nmf*
literati	literatos *nmpl*
novelist	novelista, novelador, -a *nmf*

parodist	parodista *nmf*
plagiarist	plagiario, -a *nmf*
poet	poeta *nmf*
poet laureate	poeta laureado, -a *nmf*
poetaster	poetastro, -a *nmf*
poetess (obs)	poetisa *nf*
rhymester	rimador(a) *nmf*
romanticist	romántico, -a *nmf*
satirist	satírico, -a *nmf*
stylist	estilista *nmf*
surrealist	surrealista *nmf*
symbolist	simbolista *nmf*
versifier	versificador(a) *nmf*

historical storytellers

bard	bardo *nm*
skald	escaldo *nm*
troubadour	trovador *nm*

Pleasures and Pastimes

ENTERTAINMENT

GENERAL TERMS

buffoonery	bufonería *nf*
celebration	celebración *nf*
distraction	distracción *nf*
diversion	diversión *nf*
entertainment	entretenimiento *nm*
festivity	festividad *nf*
frivolity	frivolidad *nf*
hilarity	hilaridad *nf*
humor	humor *nm*
joking	jocoso *aj*
jovial	jovial *aj*
pastime	pasatiempo *nm*
pleasure	placer *nm*
recreation	recreación, recreo *nf, nm*
relax	relajarse *vr*
spectacle	espectáculo *nm*

FORMS OF ENTERTAINMENT

participatory

banquet	banquete *nm*
camping	camping *nm*
cards	cartas *nfpl*

collection	colección *nf*
computer	computadora *nf*
crossword	crucigrama *nm*
excursion	excursión *nf*
feast	festín *nm*
fiesta	fiesta *nf*
gag	gag *nm*
gardening	jardinería *nf*
hobby	hobby *nm*
jigsaw puzzle	puzzle *nm*
masquerade	mascarada *nf*
miniature golf	minigolf *nm*
numismatics	numismática *nf*
origami	origami *nm*
philately	filatelia *nf*
photography	fotografía *nf*
picnic	picnic *nm*
tourism	turismo *nm*

spectator

acrobatics	acrobacia *nf*
attraction	atracción *nf*
ballet	ballet *nm*
burlesque	burlesco *nm*
cinema	cíne *nm*
circus	circo *nm*
comedy	comedia *nf*
comics, comic strip	tira cómica *nf*
concert	concierto *nm*
farce	farsa *nf*
hypnotism	hipnotismo *nm*
imitation	imitación *nf*
magic	magia *nf*
mimicry	mímica *nf*
pantomime	pantomima *nf*
parade (military)	parada *nf*
parody	parodia *nf*
pyrotechnics	pirotenia *nf*
retrospective	retrospectiva *nf*
revue	revista *nf*
rodeo	rodeo *nm*
show	show *nm*
striptease	striptease *nm*
television	televisión *nf*
trick	truco *nm*
variety show *nsg*	variedades *nfpl*
vaudeville	vodevil *nm*
ventriloquism, ventriloquy	ventriloquia *nf*
video	video *nm*

participatory or spectator

art	arte *nf(el)*
dance	danza *nf*

dramatics	arte dramático *nm*
music	música *nf*
radio	radio *nm*
sports	deportes *nmpl*

events and celebrations

carnival	carnaval *nm*
cavalcade	cabalgata *nf*
centennial	centenario *nm*
exhibition	exhibición *nf*
exposition	exposición *nf*
fair	feria *nf*
festival	festival *nm*
function	función *nf*
gala	gala *nf*
jubilee	jubileo *nm*

PLACES

cabaret	cabaret *nm*
casino	casino *nm*
club	club *nm*
discoteque	discoteca *nf*
fairground	ferial *nm*
hippodrome	hipódromo *nm*
museum	museo *nm*
nightclub	club nocturno *nm*
park	parque *nm*
theater	teatro *nm*
zoo	zoo *nm*

TOOLS AND EQUIPMENT

binoculars	binoculares *nmpl*
camcorder	camcórder *nm*
camera	cámara *nf*
carousel, carrousel	carrusel *nm*
confetti	confeti *nm*
festoon	festón *nm*
giant (in a parade)	gigantón *nm*
kaleidoscope	caledoscopio *nm*
marionette	marioneta *nf*
mask	máscara *nf*
tent	tienda *nf*
trampoline	trampolín *nm*
trapeze	trapecio *nm*

PERSONS

acrobat	acróbata *nmf*
amateur	amateur *nmf*
artist	artista *nmf*
buffoon	bufón *nm*
chorine, chorus singer	corista *nmf*

clown	clown *nm*
collector	coleccionista *nmf*
comedian, comedienne	comediante *nmf*
comic	cómico, -a *nmf*
contortionist	contorsionista *nmf*
geisha	geisha *nf*
Harlequin	Arlequín *nm*
humorist	humorista *nmf*
illusionist	ilusionista *nmf*
imitator	imitador(a) *nmf*
magician	mágico, -a *nmf*
master of ceremonies	maestro de ceremonias *nm, nfpl*
mime	mimo *nm*
musician	músico, -a *nmf*
numismatist	numismatista *nmf*
parodist	parodista *nmf*
philatelist	filatelista *nmf*
radio ham	radioaficionado, -a *nmf*
spectator	espectador(a) *nmf*
trapeze artist	trapecista *nmf*
troupe	troupe *nf*
ventriloquist	ventríloquo, -a *nmf*

(*See also* **DANCING**; *entertainment* under **MAGIC**; **MUSIC**; **THEATER PERFORMANCE**; **VISUAL ARTS**)

SPORTS

GENERAL TERMS

athlete	atleta *nmf*
athletics	atletismo *nm*
competition	competencia *nf*
Olympics	Olimpiada *nf*
sport	deporte *nm*
sports	deportismo *nm*
sportsmanship	deportividad *nf*

ASPECTS OF SPORTS

types of sport

amateur	amateur *aj*
intramural	intramuros *aj*
martial	marcial *aj*
professional	profesional *aj*

places

arena	arena *nf*
astrodome	astródomo *nm*
bowling alley	bowling *nm*
camp, encampment	campamento *nm*
casino	casino *nm*

coliseum	coliseo *nm*
golf course	cancha de golf *nf*
gym, gymnasium	gimnasio *nm*
hippodrome	hipódromo *nm*
ring	ring *nm*
stadium	estadio *nm*
tennis court	cancha de tenis *nf, nm*
velodrome	velódromo *nm*

contests

beat (record)	batir *vt*
championship	campeonato *nm*
cup	copa *nf*
derby	derby *nm*
equal (record)	igualar *vt*
favorite	favorito *aj*
match	match *nm*
photo finish	fotofinish *nf*
record	récord *nm*
set	set *nm*
tournament	torneo *nm*
trophy	trofeo *nm*

other terms

disqualification	descalificación *nf*
encampment	campamento *nm*
league	liga *nf*
prelims	preliminares *nmpl or nfpl*
rally	rally *nm*
sponsorship	esponsorización *nf*
training	entrenamiento *nm*

COMMON SPORTS

ball/racket sports

badminton	bádminton *nm*
baseball	béisbol *nm*
basketball	básquetbol *nm*
bowling *nsg*	bolos *nmpl*
cricket	criquet *nm*
croquet	croquet *nm*
football	fútbol *nm*
golf, golfing	golf *nm*
handball	handball *nm*
hockey	hockey *nm*
jai alai	jai alai *nm*
lacrosse	lacrosse *nm*
miniature golf	minigolf *nm*
polo	polo *nm*
rugby	rugby *nm*
tennis	tenis *nm*
volleyball	vóleibol, voleibol *nm*

water sports

aquatics	deportes acuáticos *nmpl*
boating	paseo en bote *nm*
canoeing	canotaje *nm*
regatta	regata *nf*
yachting	navegación en yate *nf, nm*

other sports

acrobatics	acrobacia *nf*
alpinism	alpinismo *nm*
archery	tiro de arco *nm*
camping	camping *nm*
chase (hunting)	caza *nf*
cross-country	cross-country *nm*
curling	curling *nm*
cycling	ciclismo *nm*
equitation	equitación *nf*
falconry	halconería *nf*
mountaineering	montañismo *nm*
obstacle race	carrera de obstáculos *nf, nmpl*
skiing	esquí *nm*
sprint	sprint, esprint *nm*

Olympic events

decathlon	decatlón *nm*
hepathlon	hepatlón *nm*
marathon	maratón *nm*
pentathlon	pentatlón *nm*

martial arts

boxing	boxeo *nm*
jousting *npl*	justas *nfpl*
judo	judo *nm*
jujitsu	jiu-jitsu *nm*
karate	karate *nm*
kung fu	kung fu *nm*
pugilism	pugilato *nm*

fitness

aerobics	aeróbica *nf*
calisthenics	calistenia *nf*
exercise	ejercicio *nm*
gymnastics	gimnasia, gimnástica *nf*
isometrics	isometría *nf*
isotonics	isotonía *nf*
tai chi	tai ji *nm*
yoga	yoga *nm*

RULES AND ACTIONS IN SPORTS

specific actions

base	base *nf*
batting	bateo *nm*
block	bloqueo *nm*
dribble	drible *nm*
inning	inning *nm*
knockout	nocaut, noqueo *nm*
parry	parar *vt*
pass	pase *nm*
service	servicio *nm*
slalom	slalom *nm*
strategy	estrategia *nf*
tierce	tercera *nf*
tumble	tumbo *nm*
volley	volea *nf*

other terms

concede	conceder *vt*
conversion	conversión *nf*
count	cuenta *nf*
defense	defensa *nf*
doubles (tennis)	dobles *nmpl*
fault	falta *nf*
foul	foul *nm*
goal	gol *nm*
intercept	interceptar *vt*
line	línea *nf*
lineup	alineación *nf*
offense	ofensiva *nf*
par	par *nf*
penalty	penalty *nm*
quarterfinal	cuarto de final *nm*
time out	tiempo muerto *av*

EQUIPMENT

boats

canoe	canoa *nf*
caravel	carabela *nf*
catamaran	catamarán *nm*
kayak	kayac *nm*
motorboat	motora *nf*
sailboat	bote de vela *nm, nf*
yacht	yate *nm*

vehicles

bicycle	bicicleta *nf*
motorcycle	moto, motocicleta *nf*
racing car	carro de carreras *nm, nfpl*

skilift	telesquí *nm*
toboggan	tobogán *nm*

other equipment

apparatus *npl*	aparatos *nmpl*
baseball (object)	pelota de béisbol *nf, nm*
bat	bate *nm*
boat	bote *nm*
bunker	búnker *nm*
discus	disco *nm*
football (object)	balón de fútbol *nm*
golf club	palo de golf *nm*
javelin	jabalina *nf*
mashie	mashie *nm*
mask	máscara *nf*
monoski	monoesquí *nm*
muleta	muleta *nf*
parallel bars	barras paralelas *nfpl*
plastron	plastrón *nm*
puck	puck *nm*
putter	putter *nm*
racket	raqueta *nf*
ski	esquí *nm*
snorkel	esnórquel *nm*
tee	tee *nm*
tent	tienda *nf*
trampoline	trampolín *nm*
trapeze	trapecio *nm*
volleyball (object)	balón de voleibol *nm*

PERSONS

athletes

acrobat	acróbata *nmf*
alpinist	alpinista *nmf*
archer	arquero *nm*
batter	bateador *nm*
bowler	jugador(a) de bolos *nmf, nmpl*
boxer	boxeador *nm*
canoeist	canoero, -a *nmf*
cyclist	ciclista *nmf*
discus thrower	discóbolo *nm*
golfer	golfista *nmf*
gymnast	gimnasta *nmf*
jockey	jockey, yoquei *nmf*
linesman	juez de línea *nm, nf*
matador	matador *nm*
party (hunting)	partida *nf*
pro	profesional *nmf*
pugilist	pugilista *nmf*
skier	esquiador(a) *nmf*

transmission and reception

antenna	antena *nf*
coaxial	coaxial *aj*
contrast	contraste *nm*
definition	definición *nf*
dial	dial *nm*
direction	dirección *nf*
iconoscope	iconoscopio *nm*
installation	instalación *nf*
interference	interferencia *nf*
readjust	reajustar *vt*
reconnection	reconexión *nf*
selector	selector *nm*
service	servicio *nm*
static	estático *aj, nm*

TOOLS AND EQUIPMENT

remote control	control remoto *nm*
videocamera	videocámara *nf*
videocassette	videocasete *nm*
videodisc, videodisk	videodisco *nm*
videotape	videocinta *nf*
suppressor	supresor *nm*
camcorder	camcórder *nm*
camera	cámara *nf*
converter	convertidor *nm*
decoder	decodificador, descodificador *nm*
receiver	receptor *nm*
teleprompter	teleprompter *nm*
television set	televisor *nm*
transmitter	tra(n)smisor *nm*
tube	tubo *nm*
video library	videoteca *nf*

PERSONS

audience	audiencia *nf*
cameraman	cameraman, camarágrafo, -a *nmf*
commentator	comentarista *nmf*
dialog writer	dialoguista *nmf*
director	director(a) *nmf*
distributor	distribuidor(a) *nmf*
producer	productor(a) *nmf*
subscriber	suscriptor(a), subscriptor(a) *nmf*
talent	talento *nm*
television viewer	televidente *nmf*

(*See also* **ASPECTS OF FILM-MAKING** under **MOVIES**; *ASPECTS OF PERFORMANCE ART* under **THEATER PERFORMANCE**)

MOVIES
GENERAL TERMS

cinema	cine *nm*
cinematography	cinematografía *nf*
distribution	distribución *nf*
editing	edición *nf*
festival	festival *nm*
filming	filmación *nf*
matinee, matinée	matiné *nf*
nomination	nominación *nf*
Oscar	Oscar *nm*
studio	estudio *nm*

ASPECTS OF FILM-MAKING

elements of a film

action	acción *nf*
background music	música de fondo *nf, nm*
characterization	caracterización *nf*
dialog(ue)	diálogo *nm*
narration	narración *nf*
scene	escena *nf*
sound	son, sonido *nm*
suspense	suspenso *nm*
title	título *nm*

filming and editing techniques

animation	animación *nf*
flashback	flashback *nm*
interruption	interrupción *nf*
montage	montaje *nm*
panorama	panorama *nm*
sequence	secuencia *nf*
special effects	efectos especiales *nmpl*
strobe lighting	iluminación estroboscópica *nf*
trick photography	trucaje *nm*
voice-over	voz superpuesta *nf*

screen processes

CinemaScope	CinemaScope *nm*
cinerama	cinerama *nm*
Technicolor	tecnicolor *nm*

popular characters

cowboy	cowboy *nm*
detective	detective *nmf*
gangster	gángster *nm*
mad scientist	científico loco *nm*
sex symbol	sex symbol *nmf*

popular genres

adventure	aventura *nf*
biography	biografía *nf*
fantasy	fantasía *nf*
farce	farsa *nf*
horror	horror *nm*
musical	musical *nm*
romance	romance *nm*

other terms

adaptation	adaptación *nf*
censorship	censura *nf*
projection	proyección *nf*
subtitles	subtítulos *nmpl*
version	versión *nf*

TOOLS AND EQUIPMENT

camera	cámara *nf*
dolly	dolly *nm*
film	filme *nm*
film library	filmoteca *nm*
projector	proyector *nm*
telephoto (lens)	telefoto *nm*
wide-angle lens	gran angular *nm*

PERSONS

actor	actor *nmf*
actress (obs)	actriz *nf*
animator	animador(a) *nmf*
cameraman	cameraman, camarágrafo, -a *nmf*
censor	censor *nmf*
cinema buff	cinéfilo, -a *nmf*
cinematographer	cinematógrafo, -a *nmf*
composer	compositor(a) *nmf*
critic	crítico, -a *nmf*
decorator	decorador(a) *nmf*
designer	diseñador(a) *nmf*
director	director(a) *nmf*
distributor	distribuidor(a) *nmf*
editor	editor, -a *nmf*
exhibitor	exhibidor(a) *nmf*
extra	extra *nmf*
idol	ídolo *nm*
producer	productor(a) *nmf*
projectionist	proyeccionista *nmf*
talent scout	cazatalentos *nmf*

(*See also* **LITERATURE**; **PHOTOGRAPHY**; **TELEVISION AND VIDEO**; **THEATER PERFORMANCE**)

PHOTOGRAPHY

GENERAL TERMS

camera	cámara *nf*
exposure	exposición *nf*
film	filme *nm*
photograph	fotografía *nf*
photographer	fotógrafo, -a *nmf*
photography	fotografía *nf*
subject	sujeto *nm*

ASPECTS OF PHOTOGRAPHY

types of still photography

aerial photo	aerofoto, áereofoto *nf*
daguerrotype (obs)	daguerrotipo *nm*
hologram	holograma *nm*
microfilm	microfilm(e) *nm*
photo	foto *nf*
photomontage	fotomontaje *nm*
tintype (obs)	ferrotipo *nm*
transparency	transparencia *nf*

taking photographs

advance (film)	avanzar *vt*
angle	ángulo *nm*
aperture	abertura *nf*
color	color *nm*
composition	composición *nf*
direction	dirección *nf*
distance	distancia *nf*
focus	foco *nm*
image	imagen *nf*
line	línea *nf*
overexposure	sobreexposición *nf*
photocomposition	fotocomposición *nf*
photogenic	fotogénico *aj*
pose	pose *nf*
time	tiempo *nm*
underexposure	subexposición *nf*

tools and equipment

airbrush	aerógrafo *nm*
album	álbum *nm*
box camera	cámara de cajón *nf, nm*
carrousel	carrusel *nm*
diaphragm	diafragma *nm*
exposure meter	exposímetro *nm*
filter	filtro *nm*
flash	flash *nm*
lens	lente *nm or nf*
panchromatic (film)	pancromático *aj*
photometer	fotómetro *nm*

projector	proyector *nm*
reflex (camera)	reflejo *aj*
roll (of film)	rollo *nm*
stereoscope	estereoscopio *nm*
stroboscope	estroboscopio *nm*
tripod	trípode *nm*
zoom lens	zoom *nm*

processing film

actinic (rays)	actínico *aj*
contrast	contraste *nm*
definition	definición *nf*
densitometer	densitómetro *nm*
desensitizer	desensibilizador *nm*
detail	detalle *nm*
emulsifier	emulsor *nm*
emulsion	emulsión *nf*
fixer, fixative	fijador *nm*
fixing bath	baño fijador *nm*
grain	grano *nm*
latent (image)	latente *aj*
matte	mate *aj*
negative	negativo *nm*
paper	papel *nm*
pellicle	película *nf*
positive	positivo *nm*
proof	prueba *nf*
reducer	reductor *nm*
reproduction	reproducción *nf*
retouching	retoque *nm*
solution	solución *nf*
thermometer	termómetro *nm*
tone	tono *nm*
unexposed	no expuesto *aj*

(*See also* **MOVIES**; **TELEVISION AND VIDEO**)

AMATEUR RADIO

GENERAL TERMS

AM	AM *nf*
amateur	amateur *aj*
band	banda *nf*
emergency	emergencia *nf*
FM	FM *nf*
license	licencia *nf*
message	mensaje *nm*
radio	radio *nm*
radio broadcasting	radiodifusión *nf*
radio station	radioemisora *nf*
radiotelephone	radioteléfono *nm*
signal	señal *nf*
station	estación *nf*
transmission	tra(n)smisión *nf*

ASPECTS OF AMATEUR RADIO

types of licenses

expert	experto *aj*
general	general *aj*
novice	novato *aj*
technician	técnico, -a *nmf*

components

amplifier	amplificador *nm*
antenna	antena *nf*
circuit	circuito *nm*
converter	convertidor *nm*
dial	dial *nm*
dipole	dipolo *nm*
dynode	dinodo *nm*
microphone	micrófono *nm*
modulator	modulador *nm*
oscillator	oscilador *nm*
receiver	receptor *nm*
rectifier	rectificador *nm*
resistor	resistencia *nf*
selector	selector *nm*
suppressor	supresor *nm*
transformer	tra(n)sformador *nm*
transistor	transistor *nm*
transmitter	tra(n)smisor *nm*
transponder	transpondedor *nm*

measurements

audiofrequency	audiofrecuencia *nf*
hertz	hertz, hertzio, hercio *nm*
kilocycle (obs)	kilociclo *nm*
kilohertz (kHz)	kilohercio *nm*
megahertz (MHz)	megahertzio *nm*

other terms

amplitude	amplitud *nf*
antistatic	antiestático *aj*
audio	audio *nm*
bandwidth	amplitud de banda *nf*
diplex	diplex, díplex *aj*
directional	direccional *aj*
echo	eco *nm*
fidelity	fidelidad *nf*
frequency	frecuencia *nf*
heterodyne	heterodino *nm*
interference	interferencia *nf*
modulation	modulación *nf*
multiband	multibanda *nf*
multiplex	multiplex *nm*
omnidirectional	omnidireccional *aj*

radiofrequency	radiofrecuencia *nf*
radiolocation	radiolocalización *nf*
reception	recepción *nf*
response	respuesta *nf*
static	estático *nm*
volume	volumen *nm*

PERSONS

audience	audiencia *nf*
disc-jockey	disc-jockey *nmf*
operator	operador(a) *nmf*
radio ham	radioaficionado, -a *nmf*
radio listener	radioescucha, radioyente *nmf*

(*See also FORMS OF TELECOMMUNICATION* under **COMMUNICATIONS**; *programs and programming* under **TELEVISION AND VIDEO**)

PERSONAL COMPUTERS

GENERAL TERMS

application	aplicación *nf*
code	código *nm*
communications	comunicaciones *nfpl*
computer	computadora *nf*
cybernetics	cibernética *nf*
electronic	electrónico *aj*
hardware	hardware *nm*
information	información *nf*
interface	interface, interfaz *nf*
listing	listado *nm*
logic	lógica *nf*
PC	PC *nm or nf*
program	programa *nm*
software	software *nm*
system	sistema *nm*

TYPES OF COMPUTERS

analog(ue)	análogo *nm*
dedicated	dedicado *aj*
digital	digital *aj*
hybrid	híbrido *aj*
laptop	laptop *nm*
microcomputer	microcomputadora *nf*
minicomputer	minicomputadora *nf*
multimedia	multimedia *aj*
personal	personal *aj*
portable	portátil *aj*
robot	robot *nm*
supercomputer	supercomputadora *nf*

HARDWARE TERMS

accelerator	acelerador *nm*
access (time)	acceso *nm*
accessory	accesorio *nm*
adapter	adaptador *nm*
architecture	arquitectura *nf*
auxiliary (memory)	auxiliar *aj*
bus	bus *nm*
cache	cache *nm*
cartridge	cartucho *nm*
CD	CD *nm*
chip	chip *nm*
circuit	circuito *nm*
compact disc	disco compacto *nm*
compatible	compatible *aj*
connector	conector *nm*
console	consola *nf*
converter	convertidor *nm*
CPU	CPU *nf*
cursor	cursor *nm*
disk drive	unidad de disco *nf, nm*
disk, diskette	disco *nm*
display	display *nm*
dot-matrix printer	imprimador matricial *nm*
expand	expandir *vt*
external (modem)	externo *aj*
floppy disk	floppy *nm*
font	fuente *nf*
format	formatear *vt*
function (key)	función *nf*
hard disk	disco duro *nm*
integrated (circuit)	integrado *aj*
intelligent (terminal)	inteligente *aj*
interpreter	intérprete *nm*
inverter	inversor *nm*
laser (printer)	láser *nm*
memory	memoria *nf*
microchip	microchip *nm*
microcircuit	microcircuito *nm*
microprocessor	microprocesadora *nf*
miniaturization	miniaturización *nf*
modem	modem *nm*
monitor	monitor *nm*
optical (scanner)	óptico *aj*
peripheral	equipo periférico *nm*
port	puerto *nm*
printer	impresor *nm*
processor	procesador *nm*
RAM	RAM *nf*
real time	tiempo real *nm*
register	registro *nm*
resolution	resolución *nf*

ROM	ROM *nf*
scanner	escáner *nm*
semiconductor	semiconductor *nm*
synthesizer	sintetizador *nm*
terminal	terminal *nm*
touch-sensitive (screen)	sensible al tacto *aj, nm*
tower	torre *nf*
tractor	tractor *nm*
transducer	transductor *nm*
unit	unidad *nf*

SOFTWARE TERMS

algorithm	algoritmo *nm*
alphanumeric	alfanumérico *aj*
ASCII	ASCII *nm*
assembler (language)	ensamblador *nm*
BASIC	BASIC *nm*
binary	binario *aj*
block	bloque *nm*
calculation	cálculo *nm*
character	carácter *nm*
COBOL	COBOL *nm*
compiler	compilador *nm*
configuration	configuración *nf*
corrupt	corromper *vt*
counter	contador *nm*
data *nsg* or *npl*	datos *nmpl*
database	base de datos *nf*
decimal	decimal *nm*
decode	descodificar *vt*
delimiter	símbolo delimitador *nm*
descriptor	descriptor *nm*
DOS	DOS *nm*
error	error *nm*
formatting	formateado *nm*
FORTRAN	FORTRAN *nm*
graphics	gráficos *nmpl*
hex, hexadecimal	hexadecimal *nm*
icon	icono *nm*
index	índice *nm*
initialize	inicializar *vt*
install	instalar *vt*
instruction	instrucción *nf*
interrogation	interrogación *nf*
iteration	iteración *nf*
language	lenguaje *nm*
macro	macro, macroinstrucción *nm, nf*
macrocode	macrocodificación *nf*
message	mensaje *nm*
module	módulo *nm*

numeric(al)	numérico *aj*
parameter	parámetro *nm*
procedure	procedimiento *nm*
processing	procesamiento *nm*
programming, programing	programación *nf*
quantifier	cuantificador *nm*
routine	rutina *nf*
sequence	secuencia *nf*
signal	señal *nf*
simulation	simulación *nf*
symbol	símbolo *nm*
syntax	sintaxis *nf*
tabulation	tabulación *nf*
validate	validar *vt*
variable	variable *aj, nf*
virtual	virtual *aj*
word processing	procesamiento de palabras *nm, nfpl*

COMMUNICATIONS

cyberspace	ciberespacio *nm*
fax	fax *nm*
interactive	interactivo *aj*
interconnect	interconectar *vt*
Internet	Internet *nm*
local (network)	local *aj*
on-line, on line	en línea *aj, av*
parity	paridad *nf*
protocol	protocolo *nm*
remote	remoto *aj*
server	servidor *nm*
time sharing	tiempo compartido *nm*

MEASUREMENTS

baud	baudio *nm*
bit	bitio *nm*
byte	byte *nm*
gigabyte	gigabyte *nm*
hertz	hertz, hertzio, hercio *nm*
kilobaud	kilobaudio *nm*
kilobit	kilobitio *nm*
kilobyte	kilobyte *nm*
kilohertz (kHz)	kilohercio *nm*
megabyte	megabyte *nm*
megahertz (mHz)	megahercio *nm*
nanosecond	nanosegundo *nm*

PERSONS

analyst	analista *nmf*
codifier	codificador *nmf*

operator	operador(a) *nmf*
programmer, programer	programador(a) *nmf*
user	usuario, -a *nmf*

(*See also* **ELECTRICITY AND ELECTRONICS**)

TRAVEL AND TOURISM

GENERAL TERMS

attraction	atracción *nf*
class	clase *nf*
destination	destino *nm*
exploration	exploración *nf*
line	línea *nf*
tourism	turismo *nm*
transit	tránsito *nm*
transportation	tra(n)sportación *nf*
vacation *nsg*	vacaciones *nfpl*

ASPECTS OF TOURISM

types of vacations

cruise	crucero *nm*
excursion	excursión *nf*
expedition	expedición *nf*
odyssey	odisea *nf*
peregrination	peregrinación *nf*
safari	safari *nm*
trekking	trekking *nm*
visit	visita *nf*
voyage	viaje *nm*

lodging

hostel	hostería *nf*
hotel	hotel *nm*
motel	motel *nm*
pension	pensión *nf*
reception	recepción *nf*
suite	suite *nf*

long-distance transportation

airline	aerolínea *nf*
auto, automobile	auto *nm*
boat	bote *nm*
car	carro *nm*
caravan	caravana *nf*
express (train)	expreso *aj, nm*
omnibus	ómnibus *nm*
train	tren *nm*
transatlantic ocean liner	transatlántico *nm*

local transportation

air taxi	aerotaxi *nm*
auto, automobile	automóvil *nm*
bus, autobus	bus, autobús *nm*
funicular	funicular *nm*
gondola	góndola *nf*
limousine	limusina *nf*
metro	metro *nm*
monorail	monorriel *nm*
taxi, taxicab	taxi, taxímetro *nm*
tramway	tranvía *nf*
trolley	trole *nm*

travel arrangements

agency	agencia *nf*
cancellation	cancelación *nf*
charter	chárter *nm*
itinerary	itinerario *nm*
lodging	alojamiento *nm*
pack	empacar *vt*
passage	pasaje *nm*
reservation	reservación *nf*
tariff	tarifa *nf*

classes of travel

deluxe	de lujo *aj*
economy class	clase económica *nf*
first-class	de primera clase *aj*
luxury	de lujo *aj*
second-class	de segunda clase *aj*
third-class	en tercera clase *aj*
tourist	de turista *aj*

documents

passport	pasaporte *nm*
ticket (baggage)	ticket *nm*
traveler's check	cheque de viajero *nm*
visa	visa *nf*

starting and ending

airport	aeropuerto *nm*
carousel, carrousel	carrusel *nm*
disembark	desembarcarse *vr*
embark	embarcarse *vr*
excess (baggage)	exceso *nm*
port	puerto *nm*
station	estación *nf*
terminal	terminal *nm*
terminus	terminal *nm*

seeing the sights

guidebook	guía *nf*
map	mapa *nm*

route	ruta *nf*
ruins	ruinas *nfpl*

PERSONS

chauffeur	chófer *nm*
cicerone	cicerone *nmf*
coachman	cochero *nm*
conductor	conductor(a) *nmf*
globetrotter	trotamundos *nmf*
gondolier	gondolero *nm*
guide	guía *nmf*
hotelkeeper	hotelero, -a *nmf*
passenger	pasajero, -a *nmf*
porter	portero *nm*
taxi driver	taxista *nmf*
tourist	turista *nmf*
transient	transeúnte *aj, nmf*
vagabond	vagabundo, -a *aj, nmf*
visitor	visitante *nmf*
voyager	viajero, -a *nmf*

(*See also* **AVIATION AND SPACE TRAVEL**; **BOATS AND SHIPS**; **LAND TRANSPORTATION**)

The Arts

ART AND AESTHETICS

GENERAL TERMS

aesthetics, esthetics	estética *nf*
creation	creación *nf*
criterion	criterio *nm*
flowering	florecimiento *nm*
formalism	formalismo *nm*
genre	género *nm*
ideal	ideal *aj, nm*
influence	influencia *nf*
manner	manera *nf*
masterpiece	obra maestra *nf*
patronage	patrocinio *nm*
purism	purismo *nm*
quality	calidad *nf*
realism	realismo *nm*
style	estilo *nm*
symbolism	simbolismo *nm*
technique	técnica *nf*

PRINCIPLES OF BEAUTY

contrast	contraste *nm*
design, designing	diseño *nm*
form	forma *nf*
harmony	armonía *nf*
proportion	proporción *nf*
symmetry	simetría *nf*
unity	unidad *nf*

ATTRIBUTES OF THE ARTIST

artistry	talento artístico *nm*
creativity	creatividad *nf*
imagination (inventiveness)	imaginativa *nf*
inspiration	inspiración *nf*
inventiveness	inventiva *nf*
originality	originalidad *nf*
prolific	prolífico *aj*
talent	talento *nm*

THE ENJOYMENT OF ART

appreciation	apreciación *nf*
contemplation	contemplación *nf*
criticism	crítica *nf*
effect	efecto *nm*
experience	experiencia *nf*
idealism	idealismo *nm*
interpretation	interpretación *nf*
pleasure	placer *nm*
satisfaction	satisfacción *nf*
sensation	sensación *nf*
sensibility	sensibilidad *nf*
subjectivism	subjetivismo *nm*
value	valor *nm*

MAJOR STYLES

baroque	barroco *aj*
classicism	clasicismo *nm*
contemporary	contemporáneo *aj*
expressionism	expresionismo *nm*
futurism	futurismo *nm*
impressionism	impresionismo *nm*
modern	moderno *aj*
neoclassicism	neoclasicismo *nm*
postimpressionism	postimpresionismo *nm*
rococo	rococó *aj, nm*
romanticism	romanticismo *nm*

PERSONS

aesthete, esthete	esteta *nmf*
artist	artista *nmf*
connoisseur	conocedor(a) *nmf*
dilettante	diletante *nmf*

| formalist | formalista *aj, nmf* |
| genius | genio *nm* |

MUSIC

GENERAL TERMS

acoustics	acústica *nf*
classical	clásico *aj*
composition	composición *nf*
dynamics	dinámica *nf*
execution	ejecución *nf*
instrument	instrumento *nm*
instruments *npl*	instrumental *nmsg*
literature	literatura *nf*
music	música *nf*
musicology	musicología *nf*
percussion	percusión *nf*
piece	pieza *nf*
popular	popular *aj*
potpourri	popurrí *nm*
practice	practicar *vt*
repertory	repertorio *nm*
sacred	sacro *aj*
symbol	símbolo *nm*
talent	talento *nm*
temperament	temperamento *nm*
theory	teoría *nf*
vocal	vocal *aj*

COMPOSITIONS

religious forms

cantata	cantata *nf*
chorale	coral *nm*
Gregorian chant	canto gregoriano *nm*
hymn	himno *nm*
mass	misa *nf*
motet	motete *nm*
oratorio	oratorio *nm*
passion	pasión *nf*
requiem	réquiem *nm*
spiritual	espiritual *nm*

dance forms

arabesque	arabesco *nm*
bourrée	bourrée *nm*
danza	danza *nf*
galop	galopa *nf*
gavotte	gavota *nf*
gigue	giga *nf*
mazurka	mazurca *nf*
minuet	minué, menueto *nm*
polka	polca *nf*

polonaise	polonesa *nf*
saraband(e)	zarabanda *nf*
tango	tango *nm*
tarantella	tarantela *nf*
waltz	vals *nm*

theatrical forms

ballet	ballet *nm*
grand opera	gran ópera *nf*
musical comedy	comedia musical *nf*
opera	ópera *nf*
opera buffa	ópera bufa *nf*
operetta	opereta *nf*
zarzuela	zarzuela *nf*

other forms

– vocal –

air	aire *nm*
aria	aria *nf(el)*
madrigal	madrigal *nm*
recitative	recitativo *nm*
round	ronda *nf*

– instrumental –

bagatelle	bagatela *nf*
barcarole, barcarolle	barcarola *nf*
canon	canon *nm*
capriccio	capricho *nm*
chaconne	chacona *nf*
chamber music	música de cámara *nf*
concerto	concierto *nm*
divertimento	divertimento *nm*
etude, étude	estudio *nm*
fantasia	fantasía *nf*
fugue	fuga *nf*
improvisation	improvisación *nf*
impromptu	impromptu *nm*
interlude	interludio *nm*
intermezzo	intermezzo *nm*
invention	invención *nf*
lament	lamento *nm*
march	marcha *nf*
nocturne	nocturno *nm*
overture	obertura *nf*
partita	partita *nf*
passacaglia	pasacalle *nm*
prelude	preludio *nm*
rhapsody	rapsodia *nf*
rondo	rondó *nm*
scherzo	scherzo *nm*
sonata	sonata *nf*
sonatina	sonatina *nf*
suite	suite *nf*
symphony	sinfonía *nf*

theme and variations	tema y variaciones *nm,* *nfpl*
toccata	tocata *nf*

— vocal or instrumental —

ballad	balada *nf*
folk music (modern)	música folk *nf*
folk music (traditional)	música folclórica *nf*
serenade	serenata *nf*
tune	tonada *nf*

INSTRUMENTS

sound sources

acoustic(al)	acústico *aj*
digital	digital *aj*
electric	eléctrico *aj*
electronic	electrónico *aj*

keyboard instruments

accordion	acordeón *nm*
celesta	celesta *nf*
clavichord	clavicordio *nm*
organ	órgano *nm*
piano	piano *nm*
spinet	espineta *nf*

string instruments

autoharp	autoarpa *nf*
balalaika	balalaica *nf*
banjo	banjo *nm*
cello	chelo *nm*
contrabass	contrabajo *nm*
dulcimer	dulcémele *nm*
guitar	guitarra *nf*
harp	arpa *nf*
mandolin	mandolina *nf*
ukulele	ukelele *nm*
viola	viola *nf*
violin	violín *nm*
violoncello	violonc(h)elo *nm*
zither	cítara *nf*

wind instruments

bassoon	bajón *nm*
bugle	bugle *nm*
clarinet	clarinete *nm*
contrabassoon	contrabajón *nm*
cornet	corneta *nf*
flute	flauta *nf*
harmonica	armónica *nf*
oboe	oboe *nm*
ocarina	ocarina *nf*

piccolo	piccolo *nm*
saxophone	saxófono *nm*
trombone	trombón *nm*
trumpet	trompeta *nf*
tuba	tuba *nf*

percussion instruments

— drums and cymbals —

bongo	bongó, bongo *nm*
conga *nsg*	congas *nfpl*
cymbal	címbalo *nm*
gong	gong *nm*
timbal	timbal *nm*
timpani	tímpanos *nmpl*
tom-tom	tam-tam *nm*
tympani	tímpanos *nmpl*

— keyboard-related —

concertina	concertina *nf*
marimba	marimba *nf*
melodeon	melodión, melodina *nm,* *nf*
vibraphone	vibráfono *nm*
xylophone	xilófono *nm*

— small instruments —

castanet	castañeta, castañuela *nf*
maracas	maracas *nfpl*
triangle	triángulo *nm*

Asian instruments

gamelan	gamelán *nm*
koto	koto *nm*
samisen	samisén *nm*
sitar	sitar *nm*

other instruments

barrel organ	organillo *nm*
carillon	carillón *nm*
clarion	clarín *nm*
harmonium	armonio *nm*
synthesizer	sintetizador *nm*
theramin	teramín *nm*

MUSIC THEORY

basic concepts

atonality	atonalidad *nf*
chord	acorde *nm*
harmony	armonía *nf*
interval	intervalo *nm*
melody	melodía *nf*
modality	modalidad *nf*
mode	modo *nm*
notation	notación *nf*

note	nota *nf*
polyphony	polifonía *nf*
polytonality	politonalidad *nf*
rhythm	ritmo *nm*
scale	escala *nf*
tempo	tempo *nm*
texture	textura *nf*
tonality	tonalidad *nf*
tone	tono *nm*

kinds of scales

chromatic	cromático *aj*
diatonic	diatónico *aj*
major	mayor *aj*
minor	menor *aj*
modal	modal *aj*
pentatonic	pentatónico *aj*

notes of the diatonic scale

do	do *nm*
fa	fa *nm*
la	la *nm*
mi	mi *nm*
re	re *nm*
sol	sol *nm*
ti	si *nm*
dominant	dominante *aj, nf*
subdominant	subdominante *aj, nf*
supertonic	supertónica *nf*
tonic	tónica *nf*

intervals

augmented	aumentado *aj*
diminished	disminuido *aj*
octave	octava *nf*
perfect	perfecto *aj, nm*
semitone	semitono *nm*
unison	unísono *nm*

chords

arpeggio	arpegio *nm*
augmented	aumentado *aj*
consonant	consonante *aj*
diminished	disminuido *aj*
dissonant	disonante *aj*
major	mayor *aj*
minor	menor *aj*
triad	tríada *nf*

textures

homophonic	homofónico *aj*
monophonic	monofónico *aj*
polyphonic	polifónico *aj*

harmonic devices

cadence	cadencia *nf*
consonance	consonancia *nf*
dissonance	disonancia *nf*
modulation	modulación *nf*
progression	progresión *nf*
resolution	resolución *nf*
suspension	suspensión *nf*

polyphonic devices

contrary (motion)	contrario *aj*
counterpoint	contrapunto *nm*
imitation	imitación *nf*
inversion	inversión *nf*
parallel (motion)	paralelo *aj*
retrograde (motion)	retrógrado *aj*

melodic devices

augmentation	aumento *nm*
diminution	diminución *nf*
figure	figura *nf*
leitmotif, leitmotiv	leitmotivo *nm*
motif	motivo *nm*
obbligato	obligado *nm*
pause	pausa *nf*
repetition	repetición *nf*
sequence	secuencia *nf*
syncopation	síncopa *nf*
theme	tema *nm*
transposition	transporte *nm*

notation

accidental	accidental *nm*
enharmonic	enharmónico *nm*
natural	nota natural *nf*
septuplet	septillo *nm*
sextuplet	sextillo *nm*
triplet	tresillo *nm*

parts of compositions

coda	coda *nf*
exposition	exposición *nf*
finale	final *nm*
introduction	introducción *nf*
movement	movimiento *nm*
part	parte *nf*
passage	pasaje *nm*
transition	transición *nf*

other terms

alto (instrument)	alto *aj*
bass (register)	bajo *aj*
binary (form)	binario *aj*

clef	clave *nf*
contrapuntal	de contrapunto
diapason	diapasón *nm*
discordant	discordante, discorde *aj*
gamut	gama *nf*
harmonization	armonización *nf*
orchestration	orquestación *nf*
register	registro *nm*
sol-fa, solfeggio	solfeo *nm*
tessitura	tesitura *nf*
transcription	tra(n)scripción *nf*

PERFORMANCE TERMS

dynamics

crescendo	crescendo *nm*
decrescendo	descrescendo *nm*
diminuendo	diminuendo *av, nm*
forte	forte *av, nm*
fortissimo	fortísimo *aj, av*
pianissimo	pianísimo *av*
piano	piano *av, nm*

tempo

adagio	adagio *nm*
agitato	agitado *aj*
allegretto	alegreto *aj, av*
allegro	alegro *aj, av, nm*
andante	andante *av, nm*
duple (time)	duplo *aj*
largo	largo *aj, av*
lento	lento *aj, nm*
moderato	moderato *av*
presto	presto *aj, av, nm*

execution

a capella	a capella *aj, av*
arrangement	arreglo *nm*
brio	brío *nm*
cantabile	cantábile *nm*
entrance	entrada *nf*
falsetto	falsete *nm*
intonation	entonación *nf*
legato	ligado *aj, av*
ligature	ligadura *nf*
monotone	monótono *aj*
phrasing	fraseo *nm*
pizzicato	pizzicato *aj, av*
sotto voce	sotto voce *av*
staccato	staccato *aj*
vibrato	vibrato *nm*

embellishment

anticipation	anticipación *nf*
appoggiatura	apoyatura *nf*
flourish	floreo *nm*
mordent	mordente *nm*
tremolo	trémolo *nm*
trill	trino *nm*

places and events

concert	concierto *nm*
concert hall	sala de conciertos *nf, nmpl*
conservatory	conservatorio *nm*
recital	recital *nm*
studio	estudio *nm*

other terms

accompaniment	acompañamiento *nm*
antiphonal	antifonal *aj*
bel canto	bel canto, canto bello *nm*
instrumentation	instrumentación *nf*
interpretation	interpretación *nf*
libretto	libreto *nm*
selection	selección *nf*
solo	solo *nm*
timbre	timbre *nm*
vocalization	vocalización *nf*

POPULAR MUSIC TERMS

blues	blues *nm*
boogie-woogie	bugui-bugui *nm*
bop	bop *nm*
calypso	calipso *nm*
discoteque	discoteca *nf*
jazz	jazz *nm*
ragtime	ragtime *nm*
rap	rap *nm*
reggae	reggae *nm*
rock	rock *nm*
rock'n'roll	rocanrol *nm*
salsa	salsa *nf*
swing	swing *nm*

MUSICAL ACOUSTICS

absolute (pitch)	absoluto *aj*
amplify	amplificar *vt*
fundamental	tono fundamental *nm*
harmonic	armónico *aj, nm*
harmonics *npl*	armonía *nfsg*
partial	tono parcial *nm*
quadraphonic	cuadrifónico *aj*

resonance	resonancia *nf*
stereophonic	estereofónico *aj*
sympathetic (vibration)	simpático *aj*
vibrate	vibrarse *vr*

TOOLS AND EQUIPMENT

baton	batuta *nf*
cassette	cassete, casete *nm or nf*
CD	CD *nm*
compact disc	disco compacto *nm*
component	componente *nm*
console	consola *nf*
metronome	metrónomo *nm*
music cabinet	musiquero *nm*
pedal	pedal *nm*
piston	pistón *nm*
plectrum	plectro *nm*
podium	podio *nm*
resonator	resonador *nm*
stereo	estéreo *nm*
stylus	estilo *nm*

PERSONS

vocal performers

alto (female)	contralto *nf*
alto (male)	alto *nm*
baritone	barítono *nm*
basso	bajo *nm*
basso profundo	bajo profundo *nm*
chorister	corista *nmf*
coloratura	coloratura *nf*
contralto	contralto *nf*
diva	diva *nf*
folk singer	cantante de música folk *nmf*
opera singer	operista *nmf*
serenader	él que da serenatas *nm*
soprano	soprano *nm, nmf*
tenor	tenor *nm*

instrumental performers

accompanist	acompañante *nmf*
accordionist	acordeonista *nmf*
bassoonist	bajonista *nmf*
cellist	chelista, violonc(h)elista *nmf*
clarinetist	clarinete, clarinetista *nmf*
cornetist	corneta *nmf*
flutist	flautista *nmf*
guitarrist	guitarrista *nmf*

harpist	arpista *nmf*
oboist	oboísta *nmf*
organist	organista *nmf*
percussionist	músico de percusión *nmf, nf*
pianist	pianista *nmf*
saxophonist	saxofonista *nmf*
timpanist	timbalero, -a *nmf*
trombonist	trombón *nm*
tympanist	timbalero, -a *nmf*
violinist	violinista *nmf*
violist	viola *nmf*
violoncellist	violonc(h)elista *nmf*
xylophonist	xilofonista *nmf*

performance groups

band	banda *nf*
chamber orchestra	orquesta de cámara *nf*
choir	coro *nm*
chorus	coro *nm*
duet	dueto *nm*
duo	dúo *nm*
octet	octeto *nm*
orchestra	orquesta *nf*
philharmonic	orquesta filarmónica *nf*
quartet, quartette	cuarteto *nm*
quintet, quintette	quinteto *nm*
septet	septeto *nm*
sextet, sextette	sexteto *nm*
trio	trío *nm*

other persons

arranger	arreglista *nmf*
choirmaster	director(a) de coro *nmf, nm*
composer	compositor(a) *nmf*
concert artist	concertista *nmf*
concertmaster	concertino *nm*
director	director(a) *nmf*
instrumentalist	instrumentista *nmf*
interpreter	intérprete *nmf*
librettist	libretista *nmf*
maestro	maestro *nm*
musician	músico, -a *nmf*
musicologist	musicologista *nmf*
protégé(e)	protegido, -a *nmf*
soloist	solista *nmf*
virtuoso	virtuoso, -a *nmf*
vocalist	vocalista *nmf*

OBSOLETE AND HISTORICAL TERMS

gramophone	gramófono *nm*
lyre	lira *nf*

phonograph	fonógrafo *nm*
psaltery	salterio *nm*
tabor, tabour	tamboril *nm*
virginal	virginal *nm*

(*See also* **ART AND AESTHETICS**; *historical storytellers* under **LITERATURE**)

DANCING

GENERAL TERMS

gesture	gesto *nm*
line	línea *nf*
movement	movimiento *nm*
music	música *nf*
rhythm	ritmo *nm*

TYPES OF DANCE

theatrical

acrobatic	acrobático *aj*
ballet	ballet *nm*
exhibition	exhibición *nf*
modern	moderno *aj*

social

ballroom	salón de baile *nm*
folkloric	folklórico, folclórico *aj*
popular	popular *aj*
recreational	recreativo *aj*

other classifications

aerobic	aeróbico *aj*
ceremonial	ceremonial *aj*
narrative	narrativo *aj*
religious	religioso *aj*
ritual	ritual *aj*

NAMES OF DANCES

modern dances

bolero	bolero *nm*
break dancing	break *nm*
cancan	cancán *nm*
cha-cha-cha	cha-cha-chá *nm*
conga	conga *nf*
contredanse	contradanza *nf*
danza	danza *nf*
fandango	fandango *nm*
flamenco	flamenco *nm*
foxtrot	foxtrot *nm*
galop	galopa *nf*
go-go	gogó *nf*

habanera	habanera *nf*
horah	hora *nf*
hula	hula *nf*
jig	giga *nf*
limbo	limbo *nm*
mambo	mambo *nm*
maxixe	machicha *nf*
mazurka	mazurca *nf*
merengue	merengue *nm*
one-step	one-step *nm*
polka	polca *nf*
polonaise	polonesa *nf*
quadrille	cuadrilla *nf*
rumba, rhumba	rumba *nf*
samba	samba *nm or nf*
shimmy	shimmy *nm*
tango	tango *nm*
tarantella	tarantela *nf*
waltz	vals *nm*

historical dances

allemande	alemanda *nf*
bourrée	bourrée *nm*
chaconne	chacona *nf*
cotillion	cotillón *nm*
galliard	gallarda *nf*
gavotte	gavota *nf*
minuet	minué, minuete *nm*
passepied	paspié *nm*
pavan(e)	pavana *nf*
saraband(e)	zarabanda *nf*

TERMS IN BALLET

arabesque	arabesco *nm*
attitude	actitud *nf*
choreography	coreografía *nf*
corps de ballet	cuerpo de baile *nm*
pas	paso *nm*
pirouette	pirueta *nf*
points	puntas de pie *nfpl*
position	posición *nf*
tutu	tutú *nm*

PERSONS

ballerina	bailarina *nf*
balletomane	aficionado, -a al ballet *nmf*
choreographer	coreógrafo, -a *nmf*
dancer	danzante *nmf*

(*See also* **ENTERTAINMENT**; **MUSIC**; **THEATER PERFORMANCE**)

THEATER PERFORMANCE

GENERAL TERMS

acting	actuación *nf*
audition	audición *nf*
cancellation	cancelación *nf*
dramatics	arte dramático *nm*
histrionics *npl*	histrionismo *nm*
mount	montar *vt*
piece	pieza *nf*
production	producción *nf*
program	programa *nm*
represent	representar *vt*
stellar (role, performance)	estelar *aj*
theatricals	funciones teatrales *nfpl*

ASPECTS OF PERFORMANCE ART

types of theater art

amateur	amateur *aj*
avant-garde	vanguardista *aj*
classical	clásico *aj*
community	comunitario *aj*
experimental	experimental *aj*
marionette	marioneta *nf*
professional	profesional *aj*
repertory	repertorio *nm*
Shakespearean, Shakespearian	shakesperiano *aj*
theater of the absurd	teatro del absurdo *nm*

kinds of productions

adaptation	adaptación *nf*
burlesque	burlesco *nm*
comedy	comedia *nf*
drama	drama *nm*
dramatization	dramatización *nf*
farce	farsa *nf*
improvisation	improvisación *nf*
melodrama	melodrama *nm*
musical	comedia musical *nf*
opera	ópera *nf*
operetta	opereta *nf*
pantomime	pantomima *nf*
pastiche	pastiche *nm*
revue	revista *nf*
spectacle	espectáculo *nm*
variety	variedad *nf*
vaudeville	vodevil *nm*

elements of performance

act	acto *nm*
choreography	coreografía *nf*

cyclorama	ciclorama *nm*
declamation	declamación *nf*
decor, décor	decorado *nm*
entrance	entrada *nf*
epilog	epílogo *nm*
intermission	intermedio *nm*
interpretation	interpretación *nf*
mask	máscara *nf*
matinee, matinée	matiné *nf*
prologue	prólogo *nm*
scene	escena *nf*

places

amphitheater	anfiteatro *nm*
arch	arco *nm*
arena	arena *nf*
auditorium	auditorio *nm*
gallery	galería *nf*
open-air theater	teatro al aire libre *nm*
opera house	ópera *nf*
proscenium	proscenio *nm*
theater	teatro *nm*
theater-in-the-round	teatro circular *nm*

audience response

acclaim	aclamación *nf*
applause	aplauso *nm*
boo	abuchear *vti*
bravo!	¡bravo! *intj*
ovation	ovación *nf*

PERSONS

individuals

actor	actor *nm*
actress	actriz *nf*
agent	agente *nmf*
character	carácter *nm*
declaimer	declamador(a) *nmf*
designer	diseñador(a) *nmf*
director	director(a) *nmf*
dramatist	dramaturgo, -a *nmf*
dramaturge	dramaturgo *nmf*
impresario	empresario *nm*
ingénue	ingenua *nf*
interpreter	intérprete *nmf*
mime	mimo *nmf*
protagonist	protagonista *nmf*
technician	técnico, -a *nmf*
tragedian	trágico *nm*
tragedienne	trágica *nf*

groups

chorus	coro *nm*
claque	claque *nf*
company	compañía *nf*
duo	dúo *nm*
public	público *nm*
spectator	espectador(a) *nmf*
applaud	aplaudir *vti*
electrify	electrizar *vt*

(*See also* **spectator** under **ENTERTAINMENT**;
FORMS OF DRAMA under **LITERATURE**)

VISUAL ARTS

GENERAL TERMS

art	arte *nf(el)*
arts and crafts	artes y oficios *nfpl*, *nmpl*
authentic	auténtico *aj*
collection	colección *nf*
color	color *nm*
copy	copia *nf*
design, designing	diseño *nm*
expression	expresión *nf*
figure	figura *nf*
genuine	genuino *aj*
materials	materiales *nmpl*
medium	medio *nm*
object	objeto *nm*
original	original *aj, nm*
piece	pieza *nf*
representation	representación *nf*
style	estilo *nm*
symbol	símbolo *nm*

FORMS OF VISUAL ART

calligraphy	caligrafía *nf*
ceramics	cerámica *nf*
cloisonné	cloisonné *nm*
decor, decoration	decoración *nf*
graphics	diseño gráfico *nm*
lithography	litografía *nf*
origami	origami *nm*
painting	pintura *nf*
photography	fotografía *nf*
sculpture	escultura *nf*
tapestry	tapiz *nm*
taxidermy	taxidermia *nf*
xylography	xilografía *nf*

CREATING AND DISPLAYING ART

art objects

adornment	adorno *nm*
antiques	antigüedades *nfpl*
aquarelle (watercolor)	acuarela *nf*
aquatint	acuatinta *nf*
arabesque	arabesco *nm*
bas-relief	bajorrelieve *nm*
bronze	bronce *nm*
bust	busto *nm*
caricature	caricatura *nf*
china	china *nf*
collage	collage *nm*
curio	curiosidad *nf*
diorama	diorama *nm*
diptych	díptico *nm*
engraving	grabado *nm*
figurine	figura *nf*
filigree	filigrana *nf*
flower arrangement	arreglo floral *nm*
fresco	fresco *nm*
icon, ikon	icono *nm*
illustration	ilustración *nf*
inscription	inscripción *nf*
lithograph	litografía *nf*
Madonna	Madona
mask	máscara *nf*
medallion	medallón *nm*
mezzotint	mezzotinto *nm*
miniature	miniatura *nf*
mobile	móvil *nm*
molding	molde *nm*
montage	montaje *nm*
monument	monumento *nm*
mosaic	mosaico *nm*
mural	mural *nm*
nude	desnudo *nmf*
obelisk	obelisco *nm*
ornament	ornamento *nm*
pedestal	pedestal *nm*
photograph	fotografía *nf*
porcelain	porcelana *nf*
poster	póster *nm*
pot	pote *nm*
relief	relieve *nm*
replica	réplica *nf*
rosette	roseta *nf*
sculpture	escultura *nf*
statuary	estatuaria *nf*
statue	estatua *nf*
statues *npl*	estatuaria *nf*
statuette	estatuilla *nf*

study	estudio *nm*
tapestry	tapicería *nf*
tattoo	tatuaje *nm*
triptych	tríptico *nm*
urn	urna *nf*
xylograph (woodcut)	xilografía *nf*

design

asymmetry	asimetría *nf*
composition	composición *nf*
contour	contorno *nm*
contrast	contraste *nm*
delineation	delineación *nf*
dissymmetry	disimetría *nf*
figuration	figuración *nf*
illumination	iluminación *nf*
image	imagen *nf*
imagery	imaginería *nf*
line	línea *nf*
mannerism	manerismo *nm*
mass	masa *nf*
motif	motivo *nm*
movement	movimiento *nm*
ornamentation	ornamentación, ornato *nf, nm*
perspective	perspectiva *nf*
plane	plano *nm*
profile	perfil *nm*
repetition	repetición *nf*
silhouette	silueta *nf*
space	espacio *nm*
symmetry	simetría *nf*
texture	textura *nf*
tonality	tonalidad *nf*
volume	volumen *nm*

tools, materials, techniques

abrasive	abrasivo *aj, nm*
acrylic	acrílico *aj*
adhesive	adhesivo *aj, nm*
airbrush	aerógrafo *nm*
alabaster	alabastro *nm*
armature	armazón *nf*
brushstroke	brochazo *nm*
chisel	cincel *nm*
color	colorido *nm*
colorant	colorante *nm*
fixative	fijador *nm*
gesso	yeso *nm*
glazed	glaseado *aj*
gouache	gouache *nm*
graphite	grafito *nm*

gum arabic	goma arábiga *nf*
gutta-percha	gutapercha *nf*
lac, lacquer	laca *nf*
latex	látex *nm*
linseed	linaza *nf*
macrame, macramé	macramé *nm*
mannequin, manikin	maniquí *nmf*
marble	mármol *nm*
matte	mate *aj*
metal	metal *nm*
modeling	modelado *nm*
mold	molde *nm*
mucilage	mucílago *nm*
muffle	mufla *nf*
oil	óleo *nm*
paint	pintura *nf*
palette	paleta *nf*
paste	pasta *nf*
pastel	pastel *nm*
patina	pátina *nf*
pigment	pigmento *nm*
plastic	plástico *aj, nm*
pose	pose *nf*
solvent	solvente *nm*
spatula	espátula *nf*
stencil	esténcil *nm*
stylus	estilo *nm*
talc	talco *nm*
tempera	témpera *nf*
terra-cotta	terracota *nf*
touch	toque *nm*
varnish	barniz *nm*

places

gallery	galería *nf*
museum	museo *nm*
salon	salón *nm*
studio	estudio *nm*

COLOR TERMS

general

colorant	colorante *nm*
coloration	coloración *nf*
coloring (substance)	colorante *nm*
coloring (design)	colorido *nm*
discoloration	descoloración, decoloramiento *nf, nm*
polychromy	policromía *nf*
prism	prisma *nm*
spectrum	espectro *nm*
Technicolor	tecnicolor *nm*

classifications

complementary	complementario *aj*
monochrome	monocromo *aj, nm*
polychrome	policromo *aj*
primary	primario *aj*
secondary	secundario *aj*

qualities

contrast	contraste *nm*
intensity	intensidad *nf*
purity	pureza *nf*
tint	tinte *nm*

pigments and dyes

anil	añil *nm*
carmine	carmín *nm*
ocher	ocre *nm*
sienna	siena *nm*
vermilion, vermillion	bermellón *nm*

other color names

amber	ámbar *nm*
aquamarine	aguamarina *nf*
azure	azul celeste *nm*
beige	beige *nm*
canary-yellow	amarillo canario *aj*
cerise	(color) cereza *nf*
chocolate	(color) chocolate *nm*
coffee	(color) café *nm*
copper	(color) cobre *nm*
cream	(color) crema *nf*
ebony	(color de) ébano *nm*
emerald	verde esmeralda *nf*
garnet	granate *nm*
henna	henna, alheña *nf*
indigo	azul índigo *nm*
jade	verde jade *nm*
khaki	caqui, kaki *nm*
lemon	amarillo limón *nm*
lilac	lila *nf*
magenta	magenta *nf*
mauve	malva *nf*
mustard	mostaza *nf*
ocher	ocre *nm*
olive	(color) verde olivo *nm*
orange	(color) naranja *nf*
purple	púrpura *nf*
ruby	rojo rubí *nm*
sapphire	azul zafiro *nm*
scarlet	rojo escarlata *nm*
sepia	sepia *nf*
tobacco	atabacado *aj*
turquoise	turquesa *aj, nf*

ultramarine	ultramarino *aj, nm*
violet	violeta *aj, nm*

description

amber	ambarino *aj*
chromatic	cromático *aj*
colored	coloreado *aj*
colorful	lleno de colorido *aj*
colorless	incoloro *aj*
coppery	cobrizo *aj*
delicate	delicado *aj*
discolored	descolorido *aj*
emerald	esmeraldino *aj*
mixed	mixto *aj*
monochromatic	monocromático *aj*
multicolored	multicolor *aj*
neutral	neutro *aj*
olive-colored	oliváceo *aj*
opalescent	opalescente *aj*
pastel	pastel *aj*
polychromatic	policromado *aj*
purple, purplish	purpúreo *aj*
rose-colored	rosado *aj*
vibrant	vibrante *aj*

STYLES AND GENRES

abstract	abstracto *aj*
Art Deco	Art Decó *nm*
avant-garde	vanguardia *nf*
baroque	barroco *aj*
bucolic	bucólico *aj*
Byzantine	bizantino *aj*
Chinese	chinesco *aj*
contemporary, contemporaneous	contemporáneo *aj*
cubism	cubismo *nm*
Dadaism	dadaísmo *nm*
dexterous, dextrous	diestro *aj*
elaborate	elaborado *aj*
erotica	arte erótico *nm*
Fauvism	fauvismo *nm*
Gothic	gótico *aj, nm*
Greco-Roman, Graeco-Roman	grecorromano *aj*
grotesque	grotesco *aj*
kitsch	kitsch *nm*
minimalism	minimalismo *nm*
modernism	modernismo *nm*
Moorish	morisco *aj*
naturalism	naturalismo *nm*
op art	op-art *nm*
ornate	ornado *aj*
pastoral	pastoral, pastoril *aj*

photorealism	fotorealismo *nm*
pointillism	puntillismo *nm*
pop art	arte popular *nf(el)*
pre-Columbian	pre-colombino *aj*
Pre-Raphaelite	prerrafaelita *aj, nmf*
primitive	primitivo *aj*
realism	realismo *nm*
Renaissance	Renacimiento *nm*
rococo	rococó *aj, nm*
surrealism	surrealismo *nm*

PERSONS

animator	animador(a) *nmf*
artisan	artesano, -a *nmf*
artist	artista *nmf*
Bohemian	bohemio, -a *aj, nmf*
calligrapher	calígrafo, -a *nmf*
caricaturist	caricaturista *nmf*
ceramicist, ceramist	ceramista *nmf*
classicist	clasicista *nmf*
colorist	colorista *nmf*
cubist	cubista *nmf*
decorator	decorador(a) *nmf*
designer	diseñador(a) *nmf*
engraver	grabador(a) *nmf*
illuminator	iluminador(a) *nmf*
illustrator	ilustrador(a) *nmf*
impressionist	impresionista *nmf*
lithographer	litógrafo, -a *nmf*
maestro	maestro *nm*
miniaturist	miniaturista *nmf*
model	modelo *nmf*
modeler	modelador(a) *nmf*
painter	pintor(a) *nmf*
postimpressionist	postimpresionista *nmf*
realist	realista *nmf*
sculptor	escultor(a) *nmf*
stylist	estilista *nmf*
surrealist	surrealista *nmf*
symbolist	simbolista *nmf*

(*See also* **ART AND AESTHETICS**)

ARCHITECTURE

GENERAL TERMS

architectura	arquitectura *nf*
complex	complejo *nm*
construction	construcción *nf*
edifice	edificio *nm*
engineering	ingeniería *nf*
erect	erigir *vt*

exterior	exterior *nm*
facilities	facilidades *nfpl*
foundation	fundamento *nm*
front	frente *nm*
interior	interior *nm*
mass	masa *nf*
materials	materiales *nmpl*
model	modelo *nm*
order	orden *nm*
plan	plan *nm*
plane	plano *nm*
remodelling	remodelación *nf*
renovation	renovación *nf*
scale	escala *nf*
site	sitio *nm*
space	espacio *nm*
structure	estructura *nf*
style	estilo *nm*
texture	textura *nf*

TYPES OF CONSTRUCTION

dwellings

bungalow	bungalow *nm*
castle	castillo *nm*
chalet	chalé, chalet *nm*
condominium	condominio *nm*
hacienda	hacienda *nf*
igloo	iglú *nm*
palace	palacio *nm*
residence	residencia *nf*
teepee	tipi *nm*
villa	villa *nf*
yurt	yurt *nm*

religious

basilica	basílica *nf*
cathedral	catedral *nf*
cloister	claustro *nm*
convent	convento *nm*
hermitage	ermita *nf*
monastery	monasterio *nm*
mosque	mezquita *nf*
oratory	oratorio *nm*
pagoda	pagoda *nf*
priory	priorato *nm*
synagog(ue)	sinagoga *nf*
temple	templo *nm*
tomb	tumba *nf*

military and penal

| citadel | ciudadela *nf* |
| fort | fuerte *nm* |

fortress	fortaleza *nf*
penitentiary	penitenciaría *nf*
prison	prisión *nf*

public use

auditorium	auditorio *nm*
hospital	hospital *nm*
hotel	hotel *nm*
motel	motel *nm*
museum	museo *nm*
observatory	observatorio *nm*
planetarium	planetario *nm*
school	escuela *nf*

other construction

aquaduct	acueducto *nm*
astrodome	astródomo *nm*
campanile	campanario *nm*
catacombs	catacumbas *nfpl*
cenotaph	cenotafio *nm*
cistern	cisterna *nf*
dike	dique *nm*
garage	garaje *nm*
monument	monumento *nm*
obelisk	obelisco *nm*
palisade	palizada *nf*
pyramid	pirámide *nf*
silo	silo *nm*
sphinx	esfinge *nf*
terrace	terraza *nf*
viaduct	viaducto *nm*

ARCHITECTURAL FEATURES
parts of buildings

alcove	alcoba *nf*
annex	anexo *nm*
anteroom	antesala *nf*
corridor	corredor *nm*
duct	conducto *nm*
elevator	elevador *nm*
entrance	entrada *nf*
lavatory	lavatorio *nm*
patio	patio *nm*
salon	salón *nm*
veranda	veranda *nf*
vestibule	vestíbulo *nm*

structural

abacus	ábaco *nm*
apse	ábside *nm*
arcade	arcada *nf*

arch	arco *nm*
architrave	arquitrabe *nm*
atrium	atrio *nm*
balcony	balcón *nm*
balustrade	balaustrada *nf*
base	base *nf*
campanile	campanario *nm*
chimney	chimenea *nf*
colonnade	columnata *nf*
column	columna *nf*
crossing	crucero *nm*
cupola	cúpula *nf*
dado	dado *nm*
dome	domo *nm*
entablature	entablamento *nm*
gallery	galería *nf*
geodesic dome	domo geodésico *nm*
jamb	jamba *nf*
loggia	logia *nf*
mansard	mansarda *nf*
mastaba	mastaba *nf*
minaret	minarete *nm*
monolith	monolito *nm*
narthex	nartex *nm*
nave	nave *nf*
patio	patio *nm*
pavilion	pabellón *nm*
peristyle	peristilo *nm*
pillar	pilar *nm*
porch	porche *nm*
portal	portal *nm*
portico	pórtico *nm*
pylon	pilón *nm*
rotunda	rotonda *nf*
stela, stele	estela *nf*
tower	torre *nf*
transept	transepto *nm*
turret	torreón *nm*
veranda	veranda *nf*
ziggurat	zigurat *nm*

MAJOR ARCHITECTURAL STYLES

baroque	barroco *aj*
Byzantine	bizantino *aj*
colonial	colonial *aj*
Corinthian	corintio *aj*
Doric	dórico *aj*
Georgian	georgiano *aj*
Gothic	gótico *aj*
Ionic	jónico *aj*
Islamic	islámico *aj*

Modernism	modernismo *nm*
post-Modernism	posmodernismo *nm*
Renaissance	Renacimiento *nm*
rococo	rococó *aj, nm*
Romanesque	románico *aj*
Tudor	tudor *aj*

MATERIALS, TOOLS, EQUIPMENT

adhesive	adhesivo *aj, nm*
adobe	adobe *nm*
aluminum	aluminio *nm*
angle iron	angular *nm*
asphalt	asfalto *nm*
block	bloque *nm*
brush	brocha *nf*
bulldozer	bulldozer *nm*
cement	cemento *nm*
cementite	cementita *nf*
ceramics	cerámica *nf*
chisel	cincel *nm*
concrete	concreto *aj, nm*
cork	corcho *nm*
creosote	creosota *nf*
excavator	excavadora *mf*
fiberglass	fibra de vidrio *nf*
granite	granito *nm*
gravel	grava *nf*
insulation	aislamiento *nm*
latex	látex *nm*
macadam	macadán *nm*
marble	mármol *nm*
masonry	masonería *nf*
mastic	mástique *nm*
mortar	mortero *nm*
mortise	mortaja *nf*
oxyacetylene (torch)	oxiacetilénico *aj*
paint	pintura *nf*
panel	panel *nm*
paneling	paneles *nmpl*
pickax	piqueta *nf*
pile	pilar *nm*
pincer	pinza *nf*
plastic	plástico *aj, nm*
plumb	plomo *nm*
plumbing	plomería *nf*
plummet	plomada *nf*
post	poste *nm*
pulley	polea *nf*
punch	punzón *nm*

rock chips	rocalla *nf*
sandpaper	papel de lija *nm*
stake	estaca *nf*
stucco	estuco *nm*
terra-cotta	terracota *nf*
terrazzo	terrazo *nm*

TERMS IN CONSTRUCTION

air conditioning	aire acondicionado *nm*
carpentry	carpintería *nf*
conduit	conducto *nm*
excavation	excavación *nf*
generator	generador *nm*
installation	instalación *nf*
joint	junta *nf*
lamination	laminación *nf*
lot	lote *nm*
occupancy	ocupación *nf*
painting	pintura *nf*
permit	permiso *nm*
prefabrication	prefabricación *nf*
reinforce	reforzar *vt*
specification	especificación *nf*
support	soporte *nm*
suspension	suspensión *nf*
vacant	vacante *aj*
ventilation	ventilación *nf*
zoning	zonificación *nf*

PERSONS

architect	arquitecto, -a *nmf*
carpenter	carpintero, -a *nmf*
constructor	constructor(a) *nmf*
contractor	contratista *nmf*
decorator	decorador(a) *nmf*
electrician	electricista *nmf*
engineer	ingeniero, -a *nmf*
master	maestro, -a *aj, nmf*
occupant	ocupante *nmf*
painter	pintor(a) *nmf*
plumber	plomero *nm*

(*See also* **TECHNOLOGY**)

Knowledge, Faith, and the Paranormal

PHILOSOPHY

GENERAL TERMS

abstraction	abstracción *nf*
causality	causalidad *nf*
concept	concepto *nm*
doctrine	doctrina *nf*
ethic	ética *nf*
existence	existencia *nf*
fate	fatalidad *nf*
form	forma *nf*
hypostasis	hipóstasis *nf*
ism	ismo *nm*
medieval, mediaeval	medieval *aj*
modern	moderno *aj*
monad	mónada *nf*
morality	moralidad *nf*
object	objeto *nm*
philosophy	filosofía *nf*
postulate	postulado *nm*
reality	realidad *nf*
Socratic	socrático *aj*
universal	universal *aj, nm*

BRANCHES OF PHILOSOPHY

major fields

aesthetics, esthetics	estética *nf*
epistemology	epistemología *nf*
ethics	ética *nf*
logic	lógica *nf*
metaphysics	metafísica *nf*

other fields

cosmology	cosmología *nf*
etiology	etiología *nf*
ontology	ontología *nf*
semiotics	semiótica *nf*
teleology	teleología *nf*

WESTERN PHILOSOPHIES

ancient philosophy

Aristotelianism	aristotelismo *nm*
atomism	atomismo *nm*
cynicism	cinismo *nm*
Epicureanism	epicureísmo *nm*
hedonism	hedonismo *nm*
logos	logos *nm*
Neoplatonism	neoplatonismo *nm*
peripatetic	peripatético *aj*
Platonism	platonismo *nm*
skepticism	escepticismo *nm*
stoicism	estoicismo *nm*

medieval philosophy

Gnosticism	(g)nosticismo *nm*
scholasticism	escolasticismo *nm*

modern philosophy

constructivism	constructivismo *nm*
empiricism	empirismo *nm*
existentialism	existencialismo *nm*
materialism	materialismo *nm*
mentalism	mentalismo *nm*
nihilism	nihilismo *nm*
obscurantism	oscurantismo *nm*
phenomenology	fenomenología *nf*
positivism	positivismo *nm*
pragmatics	pragmática *nf*
pragmatism	pragmatismo *nm*
rationalism	racionalismo *nm*
transcendentalism	tra(n)scendentalismo *nm*
utilitarianism	utilitarismo *nm*

political philosophies

anarchism	anarquismo *nm*
authoritarianism	autoritarismo *nm*
conservatism	conservadurismo, conservatismo *nm*
liberalism	liberalismo *nm*
nonviolence	no violencia *nf*
pluralism	pluralismo *nm*

other philosophical theories

animalism	animalismo *nm*
determinism	determinismo *nm*
dualism	dualismo *nm*
idealism	idealismo *nm*
individualism	individualismo *nm*
instrumentalism	instrumentalismo *nm*
mechanism	mecanismo *nm*
monism	monismo *nm*
moralism	moralismo *nm*
nativism	nativismo *nm*
naturalism	naturalismo *nm*
objectivism	objetivismo *nm*
parallelism	paralelismo *nm*
realism	realismo *nm*
relativism	relativismo *nm*

solipsism	solipsismo *nm*
spiritualism	espiritualismo *nm*
subjectivism	subjetivismo *nm*
vitalism	vitalismo *nm*

ORIENTAL PHILOSOPHIES

Buddhism	budismo *nm*
Confucianism	confucianismo *nm*
Hinduism	hinduismo *nm*
Islam	islam *nm*
Jainism	jainismo, yainismo *nm*
nirvana	nirvana *nf*
Taoism	taoísmo *nm*
yang	yang *nm*
yin	yin *nm*

TERMS IN LOGIC

general

analytics	analítica *nf*
argument	argumento *nm*
category	categoría *nf*
cause	causa *nf*
consequence	consecuencia *nf*
copula	cópula *nf*
dialectics	dialéctica *nf*
effect	efecto *nm*
fallacy	falacia *nf*
figure	figura *nf*
genus	género *nm*
logic	lógica *nf*
method	método *nm*
modality	modalidad *nf*
mode	modo *nm*
proposition	proposición *nf*
quantifier	cuantificador *nm*
rationality	racionalidad *nf*
reason	razón *nf*
relationship	relación *nf*
sophism	sofisma *nm*
species	especie *nf*
symbol	símbolo *nm*
system	sistema *nm*
validity	validez *nf*

operations

connection	conexión *nf*
contradiction	contradicción *nf*
conversion	conversión *nf*
deduction	deducción *nf*
disjunction	disyunción *nf*
implication	implicación *nf*
induction	inducción *nf*

nexus	nexo *nm*
opposition	oposición *nf*
predication	predicación *nf*
rationalization	racionalización *nf*
reasoning	razonamiento *nm*

statements

antecedent	antecedente *nm*
assertion	aserción, aserto *nf, nm*
axiom	axioma *nm*
conclusion	conclusión *nf*
corollary	corolario *nm*
formula	fórmula *nf*
homology	homología *nf*
inference	inferencia *nf*
lemma	lema *nm*
paradox	paradoja *nf*
particular	particular *aj, nm*
precept	precepto *nm*
predicate	predicado *nm*
premise	premisa *nf*
syllogism	silogismo *nm*
tautology	tautología *nf*

other terms

analyze	analizar *vt*
apparent	aparente *aj*
coherence	coherencia *nf*
coherent	coherente *aj*
conditional	condicional *aj*
construct	constructo *nm*
contrary	contrario *aj, nm*
convert	convertir *vt*
erroneous	erróneo *aj*
formal	formal *aj*
implicit	implícito *aj*
incompatible	incompatible *aj*
invalid	inválido *aj*
negative	negativo *aj*
ramification	ramificación *nf*
relational	relacional *aj*
spurious	espurio *aj*

PERSONS

Aristotelian	aristotélico *aj, nm*
Cartesian	cartesiano, -a *aj, nmf*
casuist	casuista *nmf*
constructivist	constructivista *aj, nmf*
dialectician	dialéctico, -a *nmf*
empiricist	empírico, -a *nmf*
Epicurean	epicureo, -a *nmf*
existentialist	existentialista *nmf*
fatalist	fatalista *nmf*

hedonist	hedonista *nmf*
Hegelian	hegeliano, -a *aj, nmf*
iconoclast	iconoclasta *nmf*
instrumentalist	instrumentista *nmf*
Kantian	kantiano, -a *aj, nmf*
logician	lógico, -a *nmf*
moralist	moralista *nmf*
nihilist	nihilista *nmf*
philosopher	filósofo *nmf*
positivist	positivista *nmf*
pragmatist	pragmatista *nmf*
rationalist	racionalista *nmf*
realist	realista *nmf*
skeptic	escéptico, -a *nmf*
sophist	sofista *nmf*
spiritualist	espiritista *nmf*
stoic	estoico, -a *nmf*
superman	superhombre *nm*
utilitarian	utilitarista *aj, nmf*

(*See also* beliefs and *doctrines* under **RELIGION**)

RELIGION

GENERAL TERMS

adoration	adoración *nf*
celebration	celebración *nf*
ceremony	ceremonia *nf*
charity	caridad *nf*
conscience	conciencia *nf*
credo, creed	credo *nm*
cult	culto *nm*
deity	deidad *nf*
dissent	disenso *nm*
divinity	divinidad *nf*
doctrine	doctrina *nf*
ecstasy	éxtasis *nm*
ex cathedra	ex cátedra *av*
faith	fe *nf*
glory	gloria *nf*
intolerance	intolerancia *nf*
martyrdom	martirio *nm*
morality	moralidad *nf*
mystery	misterio *nm*
observance	observancia *nf*
pardon	perdón *nm*
persecution	persecución *nf*
piety	piedad *nf*
religion	religión *nf*
rite	rito *nm*
ritual	ritual *aj, nm*
sacred	sagrado, sacro *aj*
spiritual	espiritual *aj*

supernatural	sobrenatural *aj*
theology	teología *nf*

ASPECTS OF RELIGION

types of religion

animism	animismo *nm*
atheism	ateísmo *nm*
demonism	demonismo *nm*
monotheism	monoteísmo *nm*
pantheism	panteísmo *nm*
polytheism	politeísmo *nm*

doctrines

agnosticism	agnosticismo *nm*
anabaptism	anabaptismo *nm*
apologetics	apologética *nf*
asceticism	ascetismo *nm*
caste	casta *nf*
celibacy	celibato *nm*
clericalism	clericalismo *nm*
creationism	creacionismo *nm*
deism	deísmo *nm*
dispensation	dispensa *nf*
dogma	dogma *nm*
dualism	dualismo *nm*
ecumenism	ecumenismo *nm*
ethics	ética *nf*
evangelism	evangelismo *nm*
fetishism	fetichismo *nm*
fundamentalism	fundamentalismo *nm*
Gnosticism	(g)nosticismo *nm*
heterodoxy	heterodoxia *nf*
humanism	humanismo *nm*
karma	karma *nf*
messianism	mesianismo *nm*
monasticism	monaquismo, monacato *nm*
Mosaic law	ley mosaica *nf*
mysticism	misticismo *nm*
omnipotence	omnipotencia *nf*
orthodoxy	ortodoxia *nf*
paganism	paganismo *nm*
Pietism	pietismo *nm*
ritualism	ritualismo *nm*
Satanism	satanismo *nm*
schism	cisma *nm*
scholasticism	escolasticismo *nm*
sectarianism	sectarismo *nm*
secularism	secularismo *nm*
spiritism	espiritismo *nm*
spiritualism	espiritualismo *nm*
syncretism	sincretismo *nm*

theocracy | teocracia *nf*
theosophy | teosofía *nf*

beliefs

Assumption | Asunción *nf*
destiny | destino *nm*
exoneration | exoneración *nf*
expiation | expiación *nf*
immanence, immanency | inmanencia *nf*
immortality | inmortalidad *nf*
incarnation | encarnación *nf*
inferno | infierno *nm*
limbo | limbo *nm*
miracle | milagro *nm*
nirvana | nirvana *nf*
perdition | perdición *nf*
possession | posesión *nf*
predestination | predestinación *nf*
providence | providencia *nf*
purgatory | purgatorio *nm*
redemption | redención *nf*
reincarnation | reencarnación *nf*
resurrection | resurrección *nf*
salvation | salvación *nf*
sanctity | santidad *nf*
savior | salvador(a) *nmf*
superstition | superstición *nf*
theism | teísmo *nm*
transcendence | tra(n)scendencia *nf*
transfiguration | tra(n)sfiguración *nf*
transmigration | tra(n)smigración *nf*
transubstantiation | transubstanciación *nf*
trinity | trinidad *nf*

prediction in religion

preordination | preordinación *nf*
prophecy | profecía *nf*
revelation | revelación *nf*
sign | señal *nf*

holy places

abbey | abadía *nf*
altar | altar *nm*
baptistery, baptistry | baptisterio, bautisterio *nm*
cathedral | catedral *nf*
chapel | capilla *nf*
cloister | claustro *nm*
confessional | confesionario *nm*
convent | convento *nm*
mission | misión *nf*
monastery | monasterio *nm*

mosque | mezquita *nf*
pagoda | pagoda *nf*
paradise | paraíso *nm*
priory | priorato *nm*
sacristy | sacristía *nf*
sanctuary | santuario *nm*
synagog(ue) | sinagoga *nf*
temple | templo *nm*

religious titles

abbess | abadesa *nf*
abbot | abad *nm*
archbishop | arzobispo *nm*
archdeacon | archidiácono *nm*
bishop | obispo *nm*
chaplain | capellán *nm*
Dalai Lama | Dalai Lama *nm*
deacon | diácono *nm*
deaconess | diaconisa *nf*
dervish | derviche *nm*
fakir | faquir *nm*
friar | fraile *nm*
imam | imán *nm*
lama | lama *nm*
mahatma | mahatma *nm*
metropolitan | metropolitano *nm*
ordinary | ordinario *nm*
pastor | pastor *nm*
pontiff | pontífice *nm*
Pope | papa *nm*
prelate | prelado *nm*
primate | primado *nm*
prior | prior *nm*
prioress | priora *nf*
rabbi | rabí *nm*
rector | rector *nm*
reverend | reverendo *nm*
vicar | vicario *nm*

organizations and offices

archdiocese | archidiócesis, arquidiócesis *nf*
benefice | beneficio *nm*
bishopric | obispado *nm*
college | colegio *nm*
consistory | consistorio *nm*
deaconry | diaconado, diaconato *nm*
diocese | diócesis *nf*
episcopate | episcopado *nm*
order | orden *nf*
papacy, popedom | papado *nm*
parish | parroquía *nf*

prelacy	prelacia *nf*
rabbinate	rabinato *nm*
synod	sínodo *nm*
Vatican	Vaticano *nm*
vicarage	vicaría *nf*

scholarship and translation

alteration	alteración *nf*
concordance	concordancia *nf*
demonology	demonología *nf*
emendation	enmienda *nf*
eschatology	escatología *nf*
hagiography	hagiografía *nf*
index	índice *nm*
martyrology	martirologio *nm*
midrash	midrash *nm*
seminary	seminario *nm*
yeshiva	yeshiva *nf*

other terms

apostasy	apostasía *nf*
celestial	celestial *aj*
devout	devoto *aj*
interdict, interdiction	interdicto *nm*
octave	octava *nf*
omniscient	omnisciente *aj*
practice	practicar *vt*
prebend	prebenda *nf*
temporal	temporal *aj*

NAMES

founders of religions

Abraham	Abrahán *nm*
Buddha	Buda *nm*
Christ	Cristo *nm*
Confucius	Confucio *nm*
Jesus Christ	Jesucristo *nm*
Luther	Lutero *nm*
Mohammed, Muhammad	Mahoma *nm*
Moses	Moisés *nm*
Zarathustra	Zaratustra *nm*
Zoroaster	Zoroastro *nm*

major world religions

Buddhism	budismo *nm*
Christianity	cristiandad *nf*
Confucianism	confucianismo *nm*
Hinduism	hinduismo *nm*
Islam	islam *nm*
Judaism	judaísmo *nm*

Shinto	sintoísmo *nm*
Taoism	taoísmo *nm*

other religions and groups

Anglicanism	anglicanismo *nm*
Bahaism	bahaísmo *nm*
Brahmanism	brahmanismo *nm*
Calvinism	calvinismo *nm*
Catholicism	catolicismo *nm*
Congregationalism	congregationalismo *nm*
Jansenism	jansenismo *nm*
Lutheranism	luteranismo *nm*
Methodism	metodismo *nm*
Mormonism	mormonismo *nm*
Orthodox Church	Iglesia ortodoxa *nf*
Protestantism	protestantismo *nm*
Quakerism	cuaquerismo *nm*
Scientology	cientología *nf*
Sikhism	sikhismo *nm*
Unification Church	Iglesia de la Unificación *nf*
Unitarianism	unitarismo *nm*
Voodoo	vudú *nm*
Zoroastrianism	zoroastrismo *nm*

deities

Allah	Alá *nm*
Brahma	Brahma *nm*
Creator	Creador *nm*
Jehovah	Jehová *nm*
Krishna	Krisna *nm*
Messiah	Mesías *nm*
Redeemer	Redentor *nm*
Shiva	Siva *nm*
Vishnu	Visnú, Vishnú *nm*
Yahweh, Yahveh	Jahvé *nm*

holy cities

Bethlehem	Belén *nm*
Jerusalem	Jerusalén *nf*
Mecca	Meca *nf*
Rome	Roma *nf*
Zion (obs)	Sión *nm*

sacred books

Bhagavad-Gita	Bhagavad-Gita *nf*
Bible	Biblia *nf*
Kamasutra	Kama-Sutra
Koran	Corán, Alcorán *nm*
Talmud	Talmud *nm*
Torah	Tora *nm or nf*
Veda	Veda *nm*

holidays and celebrations

Advent	Adviento *nm*
Chanukah, Hanukkah	Janucá *nm*
Epiphany	Epifanía *nf*
Pentecost	Pentecostés *nm*
Purim	purim *nm*
Ramadan	Ramadán *nm*
Yom Kippur	Yom Kippur *nm*

PRACTICES AND TRADITIONS

rites and ceremonies

ablutions	ablución *nf*
absolution	absolución *nf*
apotheosis	apoteosis *nf*
baptism	bautismo, bautizo *nm*
bar mitzvah	bar mitzvah *nm*
bat mitzvah	bat mitzvah *nm*
beatification	beatificación *nf*
canonization	canonización *nf*
catechism	catecismo *nm*
circumcision	circuncisión *nf*
communion	comunión *nf*
confession	confesión *nf*
confirmation	confirmación *nf*
consecration	consagración *nf*
contemplation	contemplación *nf*
conversion	conversión *nf*
deification	deificación *nf*
diabolism	diabolismo *nm*
excommunication	excomunión *nf*
exorcism	exorcismo *nm*
festival	festival *nm*
flagellation	flagelación *nf*
funeral	funeral *nm*
genuflection	genuflexión *nf*
glorification	glorificación *nf*
idolatry	idolatría *nf*
immersion	inmersión *nf*
indulgence	indulgencia *nf*
invocation	invocación *nf*
jubilee	jubileo *nm*
liturgy	liturgia *nf*
mass	misa *nf*
meditation	meditación *nf*
mortification	mortificación *nf*
occultism	ocultismo *nm*
offering	ofrenda *nf*
Offertory	ofertorio *nm*
ordination	ordenación *nf*
penitence	penitencia *nf*
procession	procesión *nf*
propitiation	propiciación *nf*

purification	purificación *nf*
repentance	arrepentimiento *nm*
response	respuesta *nf*
Sabbath	sábado *nm*
sacrament	sacramento *nm*
sacrifice	sacrificio *nm*
sanctification	santificación *nf*
service	servicio *nm*
supplication	súplica, suplicación *nf*
vespers	vísperas *nfpl*

eating and drinking

abstinence	abstinencia *nf*
dietary (laws)	dietético *aj*
feast	fiesta *nf*
kosher	kosher *aj*
libation	libación *nf*
renunciation	renuncia *nf*
seder	seder *nm*
vegetarianism	vegetarianismo *nm*

birth and death

cremation	cremación *nf*
extreme unction	extremaunción *nf*
reliquary	relicario *nm*
vigil	vigilia *nf*

objects, charms, symbols

calix	cáliz *nm*
chalice	cáliz *nm*
cross	cruz *nf*
crucifix	crucifijo *nm*
Eucharist	eucaristía *nf*
fetish	fetiche *nm*
Holy Grail (obs)	Santo Grial *nm*
Host	hostia *nf*
hyssop (obs)	hisopo *nm*
icon, ikon	icono *nm*
idol	ídolo *nm*
incense	incienso *nm*
menorah	menorá *nf*
oblation	oblación *nf*
paschal	pascual *aj*
paten	patena *nf*
phallus	falo *nm*
pulpit	púlpito *nm*
pyx	píxide *nf*
rosary	rosario *nm*
tabernacle (on altar)	tabernáculo *nm*
talisman	talismán *nm*
torii	torii *nm*
totem	tótem *nm*

clothing and appearance

alb	alba *nf(el)*
habit	hábito *nm*
miter	mitra *nf*
mozetta, muzetta	muceta *nf*
pallium	palio *nm*
phylactery	filacteria *nf*
scapular	escapulario *nm*
tallit, tallith	taled *nm*
tiara	tiara *nf*
tonsure	tonsura *nf*
vestment	vestidura, vestimenta *nf*

sins and crimes

adultery	adulterio *nm*
anathema	anatema *nm*
attrition	atrición *nf*
blasphemy	blasfemia *nf*
corruption	corrupción *nf*
deicide (god killing)	deicidio *nm*
envy	envidia *nf*
fornication	fornicación *nf*
gluttony	glotonería *nf*
heresy	herejía *nf*
impenitence	impenitencia *nf*
impiety	impiedad *nf*
infidelity	infidelidad *nf*
nonobservance	inobservancia *nf*
offense	ofensa *nf*
peccadillo	pecadillo *nm*
profanation	profanación *nf*
sacrilege	sacrilegio *nm*
sodomy	sodomía *nf*
temptation	tentación *nf*
transgression	tra(n)sgresión *nf*

prayers

amen	amén *intj*
benediction	bendición *nf*
breviary	breviario *nm*
doxology	doxología *nf*
grace	gracia *nf*
Hallelujah	aleluya *nf*
litany	letanía *nf*
mantra	mantra *nm*
paternoster	paternóster *nm*

other language uses

allegory	alegoría *nf*
bull	bula *nf*
encyclical	encíclica *nf*
homily	homilia *nf*
parable	parábola *nf*

scripture	escritura *nf*
sermon	sermón *nm*

music and art

canon	canon *nm*
chant	canto *nm*
choir	coro *nm*
Gregorian (chant)	gregoriano *aj*
halo	halo *nm*
hymn	himno *nm*
hymnal	himnario *nm*
intone	entonar *vt*
introit	introito *nm*
Kyrie	kirie *nm*
Madonna	Madona
oratorio	oratorio *nm*
passion	pasión *nf*
psalm	salmo *nm*
psalmody	salmodia *nf*
recessional	himno recesional *nm*
spiritual	espiritual *nm*

supernatural beings

angel	ángel *nm*
cherub	querubín *nm*
Christ	Cristo *nm*
Creator	Creador *nm*
demon	demonio *nm*
devil	diablo *nm*
seraph	serafín *nm*
spirit	espíritu *nm*

MEMBERS OF RELIGIOUS GROUPS

larger groups

Bahai	bahai *nmf*
Buddhist	budista *aj, nmf*
Catholic	católico, -a *aj, nmf*
Christian	cristiano, -a *aj, nmf*
Confucianist	confucianista, confuciano, -a *aj, nmf*
Hindu	hindú *aj, nmf*
Islamite	islamita *nmf*
Jew	judío, -a *nmf*
Mohammedan	mahometano, -a *aj, nmf*
Moslem, Muslim	musulmán, -ana *aj, nmf*
Protestant	protestante *aj, nmf*

Protestants

Adventist	adventista *aj, nmf*
Anabaptist	anabaptista *aj, nmf*
Anglican	anglicano, -a *aj, nmf*

Baptist	bautista *aj, nmf*
Calvinist	calvinista *aj, nmf*
Congregationalist	congregacionalista *aj, nmf*
Coptic	copto, -a *aj, nmf*
Episcopalian	episcopalista *aj, nmf*
Huguenot (obs)	hugonote *aj, nmf*
Lutheran	luterano, -a *aj, nmf*
Mennonite	menonita *aj, nmf*
Methodist	metodista *aj, nmf*
Pentecostal	pentecostal *aj, nmf*
Presbyterian	presbiteriano, -a *aj, nmf*
Puritan (obs)	puritano, -a *aj, nmf*
Quaker	cuáquero, -a *aj, nmf*

Jews

Ashkenazi	askenazi *aj, nmf*
Conservative	conservador(a) *aj, nmf*
Hasidism	hasidismo, jasidismo *nm*
Orthodox	ortodoxo *aj*
Reconstructionist	reconstruccionista *aj*
Reform, Reformed	reformado *aj*
Sephardi	sefardí, sefardita *nmf*

Muslims

Hizbollah	hezbolá *nmf*
mujaheddin, mujahedeen	mujahedín, muyahidin *nmpl*
Shiite	chiíta, shií *aj, nmf*
Sufi	sufí *nm*
Sunni	suní, sunita *aj, nmf*

Catholic orders

Augustinian	agustino, -a *nmf*
Benedictine	benedictino *nm*
Capuchin	capuchino *nm*
Carmelite	carmelita *nmf*
Dominican	dominico *nm*
Franciscan	franciscano *aj, nm*
Jacobin	jacobino *nm*
Jesuit	jesuita *nf*
Trappist	trapense *nm*

other groups

Brahman, Brahmin	brahmán, brahmín *nm*
Druse, Druze	druso, -a *aj, nmf*
Mormon	mormón, -ona *aj, nmf*
Rastafarian	rastafariano, -a *aj, nmf*
Rosicrucian	rosacruz *aj, nmf*
Scientologist	cientológo, -a *nmf*
Sephardim	sefardíes *nmfpl*
Sikh	Sikh *aj, nmf*
Unitarian	unitario, -a *aj, nmf*
Universalist	universalista *aj, nmf*

Zen (Buddhist)	zen *nm*
Zoroastrian	zoroástrico, -a *nmf*

HISTORICAL TERMS

persecution against Jews

anti-Semitism	antisemitismo *nm*
Diaspora	diáspora *nf*
ghetto	gueto, ghetto *nm*
Holocaust	Holocausto *nm*
Inquisition	Inquisición *nf*
pogrom	pogromo *nm*

other terms

Counter-Reformation	Contrarreforma *nf*
Crusade	cruzada *nf*
Puritanism (obs)	puritanismo *nm*
Reformation	Reforma *nf*

PERSONS

groups

clergy	clero *nm*
congregation	congregación *nf*
denomination	denominación *nf*
laity	laicado *nm*
sect	secta *nf*

scholars

acolyte	acólito *nm*
cabalist	cabalista *nmf*
catechumen	catecúmeno, -a *nmf*
hagiographer	hagiógrafo, -a *nmf*
novitiate	noviciado, -a *nmf*
seminarian	seminarista *nmf*
Talmudist	talmudista *nmf*
theologian	teólogo *nm*

special-purpose practitioners

baptizer	bautista *nmf*
cantor	cantor(a) *nmf*
clergyman	clérigo *nm*
clergywoman	clériga *nf*
cleric	clérigo, -a *nmf*
confessor	confesor(a) *nmf*
curate	cura *nm*
ecclesiastic	eclesiástico, -a *nmf*
evangelist	evangelista, evangelizador(a) *nmf*
exorcist	exorcista *nmf*
guardian	guardián, -ana *nmf*
guru	gurú, guru *nmf*
inquisitor (obs)	inquisidor(a) *nmf*
lector	lector *nm*

legate	legado *nm*
liturgist	liturgista *nmf*
Magus (obs)	mago *nm*
minister	ministro, -a *nmf*
missionary	misionero, -a *nmf*
monk	monje *nm*
muezzin	muecín *nm*
nuncio	nuncio *nm*
officiant	oficiante *nm*
patron saint	patrono, -a *nmf*
prophet	profeta *nm*
psalmist	salmista *nmf*
rabbi	rabino *nm*
shaman	shamán, chamán *nm*
spiritualist	espiritista *nmf*
yogi	yogui *nmf*

RELATED TERMS

Ashkenazi	askenazita *aj*
Biblical	bíblico *aj*
Christianize	acristianizar *vt*
Hasidic	hasídico *aj*
Islamic	islámico *aj*
Jewish	judío *aj*
Judaic	judaico *aj*
Judaica *nsg*	cosas judaicas *nfpl*
Judeo-Christian	judeocristiano *aj*
Mormon	mormónico *aj*
Sephardic	sefardí *aj*
Talmudic	talmúdico *aj*

(*See also* religious phenomena under **MAGIC**)

MAGIC

GENERAL TERMS

arcane	arcano *aj*
extrasensory	extrasensorial *aj*
fantasy	fantasía *nf*
magic	mágico *aj, nm*
occult	oculto *aj*
paranormal	paranormal *aj*
prediction	predicción *nf*
pseudoscience	pseudociencia *nf*
supernatural	sobrenatural *aj*
superstition	superstición *nf*
surreal	surrealista *aj*

FORMS OF MAGIC

pseudosciences

alchemy	alquimia *nf*
astrology	astrología *nf*
chiromancy	quiromancia *nf*
graphology	grafología *nf*
parapsychology	parasicología *nf*
phrenology	frenología *nf*
physiognomy	fisionomía *nf*
psychokinesis	psicocinesis *nf*
telekinesis	telequinesis *nf*
telepathy	telepatía *nf*
theosophy	teosofía *nf*

entertainment

cards	cartas *nf*
disappearance	desaparición *nf*
escape	escape *nm*
hypnosis	hipnosis *nf*
illusion	ilusión *nf*
levitation	levitación *nf*
mentalism	mentalismo *nm*
prestidigitation	prestidigitación *nf*
trick	truco *nm*

prediction

aeromancy	aeromancia *nf*
augur (obs)	augur *nm*
augury	augurio *nm*
clairvoyance	clarividencia *nf*
divination	adivinación *nf*
geomancy	geomancia *nf*
numerology	numerología *nf*
oracle (obs)	oráculo *nm*
precognition	precognición *nf*
premonition	premonición *nf*
presage	presagio *nm*
prescience	presciencia *nf*
presentiment	presentimiento *nm*
prevision	previsión *nf*
pyromancy	piromancia *nf*
vaticination	vaticinio *nm*

phenomena

apparition	aparición *nf*
astral (spirit)	astral *aj*
avatar	avatar *nm*
charisma	carisma *nm*
manifestation	manifestación *nf*
metempsychosis	metempsicosis *nf*
mystery	misterio *nm*
mysticism	misticismo *nm*
occultism	ocultismo *nm*
taboo	tabú *nm*
theurgy	teurgia *nf*
trance	trance *nm*
vision	visión, vista *nf*

visitation	visitación *nf*
voodoo	vudú *nm*

communication with the dead

evocation	evocación *nf*
necromancy	nigromancía *nf*
Ouija board	tablera de ouija *nf*
spiritism	espiritismo *nm*

other terms

black magic	magia negra *nf*
enchantment	encantamiento *nm*
enigma	enigma *nm*
metamorphosis	metamorfosis *nf*
phantasmagoria	fantasmagoria *nf*
vampirism	vampirismo *nm*

TOOLS AND EQUIPMENT

words and actions

abracadabra!	¡abracadabra! *nm*
hex	hechizo *nm*
invocation	invocación *nf*
open sesame!	¡ábrete sésame! *nm*
ritual	ritual *nm*

objects and symbols

amulet	amuleto *nm*
crystal ball	bola de cristal *nf, nm*
fetish	fetiche *nm*
pentacle	pentáculo *nm*
periapt	periapto *nm*
swastika	esvástica *nf*
talisman	talismán *nm*
tarot	tarot *nm*
tea leaves	hojas de té *nfpl, nm*

substances

aura	aura *nf(el)*
ectoplasm	ectoplasma *nm*
elixir	elíxir *nm*
incense	incienso *nm*
philter	filtro *nm*
potion	poción *nf*

supernatural beings

genie	genio *nm*
incubus	incubo *nm*
jinn, jinni	genio *nm*
phantasm, phantom	fantasma *nm*
poltergeist	poltergeist *nm*
specter	espectro *nm*

spirit	espíritu *nm*
vampire	vampiro, vampiresa *nm, nf*
zombie, zombi	zombie, zombi *nmf*

TERMS IN ASTROLOGY

signs of the Zodiac

Aquarius	Acuario *nm*
Aries	Aries *nm*
Cancer	Cáncer *nm*
Capricorn	Capricornio *nm*
Gemini	Géminis *nmpl*
Leo	Leo *nm*
Libra	Libra *nf*
Pisces	Piscis *nm*
Sagittarius	Sagitario *nm*
Scorpio	Escorpio *nm*
Taurus	Tauro *nm*
Virgo	Virgo *nm*

PERSONS

astrologer	astrólogo, -a *nmf*
chiromancer	quiromantico, -a *nmf*
clairvoyant	clarividente *nmf*
enchanter/enchantress	encantador(a) *nmf*
exorcist	exorcista *nmf*
fakir	faquir *nm*
illusionist	ilusionista *nmf*
magician	mágico, -a *nmf*
magus (obs)	mago *nm*
medium	médium *nmf*
mentalist	mentalista *nmf*
mystic	místico, -a *nmf*
occultist	ocultista *nmf*
parapsychologist	parasicólogo, -a *nmf*
phrenologist	frenólogo *nmf*
prophet	profeta/profetisa *nmf*
shaman	shamán, chamán *nm*
spiritualist	espiritista *nmf*
visionary	visionario, -a *aj, nmf*

(*See also creatures* under **THE BIBLE**; *folklore and legend* under **LITERATURE**; *supernatural beings* under **RELIGION**)

Daily Living

THE CITY

GENERAL TERMS

city	ciudad *nf*
county	condado *nm*
district	distrito *nm*
diversity	diversidad *nf*
location	localización *nf*
megalopolis	megalópolis *nf*
metropolis	metrópoli *nf*
municipality	municipio *nm*
ordinance	ordenanza *nf*
population	población *nf*
suburbia *nsg*	suburbios *nmpl*
urban	urbano *aj*

URBAN PROBLEMS

congestion	congestión *nf*
crime	crimen *nm*
delinquency	delincuencia *nf*
density (population)	densidad *nf*
education	educación *nf*
graffiti *nsg* or *npl*	graffiti *nmpl*
illumination	iluminación *nf*
planning	planificación *nf*
pollution	polución *nf*
poverty	pobreza *nf*
privacy	privacidad *nf*
prostitution	prostitución *nf*
race relations	relaciones raciales *nfpl*
recreation	recreación, recreo *nf, nm*
recycling	reciclaje *nm*
smog	esmog *nm*
traffic	tráfico *nm*
transportation	tra(n)sportación *nf*
unemployment	desempleo *nm*
urban renewal	renovación urbana *aj*
zoning	zonificación *nf*

SECTIONS OF THE CITY

major categories

commercial	comercial *aj*
industrial	industrial *aj*
residential	residencial *aj*

nonspecific locations

locale	local *nm*
locality	localidad *nf*
site	sitio *nm*
subterranean	subterráneo *aj*

particular sections

barrio	barrio *nm*
center	centro *nm*
Chinatown	barrio chino *nm*
ethnic (neighborhood)	étnico *aj*
ghetto	gueto, ghetto *nm*
plaza	plaza *nf*
private (property)	privado *aj*
public (property)	público *aj*
subdivision	subdivisión *nf*
suburb	suburbio *nm*

PLACES

streets and traffic

alley	callejón *nm*
avenue	avenida *nf*
boulevard	bulevar *nm*
crossing	cruce *nm*
crossover	cruzamiento *nm*
crossroads	encrucijada *nf*
island	isleta *nf*
passage	pasaje *nm*
tunnel	túnel *nm*

business

airport	aeropuerto *nm*
barbershop	barbería *nf*
bazaar, bazar	bazar *nm*
casino	casino *nm*
florist shop	floristería *nf*
hotel	hotel *nm*
laundromat	lavadoras automáticas *nfpl*
market	mercado *nm*
marketplace	plaza del mercado *nf, nm*
motel	motel *nm*
restaurant	restaurante *nm*
supermarket	supermercado *nm*

education

college	colegio *nm*
kindergarten	kindergarten *nm*
school	escuela *nf*
university	universidad *nf*

recreation

aquarium	acuario *nm*
club	club *nm*
gym, gymnasium	gimnasio *nm*
museum	museo *nm*
nightclub	club nocturno *nm*
park	parque *nm*
pavilion	pabellón *nm*
stadium	estadio *nm*
theater	teatro *nm*
zoo	zoo *nm*

dwellings

apartment	apartamento *nm*
apartment hotel	apart(h)otel, apartotel *nm*
bungalow	bungalow *nm*
condominium	condominio *nm*
dormitory	dormitorio *nm*
duplex	dúplex *nm*
hacienda	hacienda *nf*
lodge	logia *nf*
mansion	mansión *nf*
orphanage	orfanato, orfelinato *nm*
palace	palacio *nm*
penthouse	penthouse *nm*
residence	residencia *nf*

religion

chapel	capilla *nf*
mosque	mezquita *nf*
synagog(ue)	sinagoga *nf*
temple	templo *nm*

beautification

fountain	fuente *nf*
monument	monumento *nm*
tomb	tumba *nf*

other places

cemetery	cementerio *nm*
clinic	clínica *nf*
funeral home	funeraria *nf*
garage	garaje *nm*
hospital	hospital *nm*
station	estación *nf*
viaduct	viaducto *nm*

PUBLIC TRANSPORTATION

bus	autobús, bus *nm*
express (train)	expreso *aj*
interurban (train)	interurbano *aj*
local (train)	local *aj*
metro	metro *nm*
taxicab, taxi	taxi *nm*
train	tren *nm*
tramway	tranvía *nf*
trolley	trole *nm*
trolleybus	trolebús *nm*
monorail	monorriel *nm*

PERSONS

individuals

cosmopolite	cosmopolita *nmf*
councilman	concejal *nm*
councilwoman	consejala *nf*
guard (museum, park)	guarda *nmf*
indigent	indigente *nmf*
inhabitant	habitante *nmf*
planner	planificador(a) *nmf*
policeman	policía *nm*
policewoman	policía *nf*
prostitute	prostituta *nf*
resident	residente *aj, nmf*
suburbanite	suburbano, -a *nmf*
taxi driver	taxista *nmf*
tourist	turista *nmf*
vagrant	vago, -a *nmf*

groups

council (municipal govt.)	concejo *nm*
minority	minoría *nf*
police	policía *nf*
underclass	clase marginada *nf*

(*See also* **ARCHITECTURE**; **AUTOMOBILES**)

HOME FURNISHINGS

GENERAL TERMS

color scheme	combinación de colores *nf, nmpl*
decor, decoration	decoración *nf*
exterior	exterior *aj, nm*
interior	interior *aj, nm*
ornamentation	ornamentación *nf*
style	estilo *nm*

KINDS OF FURNITURE

colonial	colonial *aj*
comfortable	confortable *aj*
functional	funcional *aj*

metal	metal *nm*
modern	moderno *aj*
plastic	plástico *aj*
rattan	rota *nf*
sectional *aj*	por secciones *nfpl*
varnished	barnizado *aj*

ITEMS

living room

console	consola *nf*
convertible sofa	sofá-cama *nm*
cushion	cojín *nm*
divan	diván *nm*
music cabinet	musiquero *nm*
ottoman	otomana *nf*
sofa	sofá *nm*
television	televisión *nf*

bedroom and bathroom

bidet	bidé *nm*
cabinet	gabinete *nm*
clock radio	radiodespertador *nm*
commode (chest)	cómoda *nf*
eiderdown (quilt)	edredón *nm*
towel	toalla *nf*
towel rack	toallero *nm*
urinal	orinal, urinario *nm*

windows and lighting

candelabrum	candelabro *nm*
candlestick	candelero *nm*
curtain	cortina *nf*
jalousie	celosía *nf*
lamp	lámpara *nf*

floors and walls

flowered (wallpaper, drapes)	floreado *aj*
linoleum	linóleo *nm*
painting	pintura *nf*
paneling *nsg*	paneles *nmpl*
paper (walls)	empapelar *vt*
parquet	parqué *nm*
plaque	placa *nf*
tapestry	tapiz *nm*
vinyl	vinilo *nm*

outdoors

barbecue	barbacoa *nf*
grill	grill *nm*
hammock	hamaca *nf*

appliances

air conditioner	acondicionador de aire *nm*
coffeepot	cafetera *nf*
dehumidifier	deshumedecedor *nm*
freezer	freezer *nm*
humidifier	humedecedor, humectador *nm*
microwave	microonda *nf*
stove	estufa *nf*
washing machine	máquina de lavar *nf*

PERSONS

carpenter	carpintero *nm*
domestic	doméstico, -a *nmf*
electrician	electricista *nmf*
interior decorator	interiorista *nmf*
plumber	plomero *nm*

(*See also* **ARCHITECTURE**; *tools and equipment* under **FOOD AND NUTRITION**)

FOOD AND NUTRITION

ASPECTS OF FOOD CONSUMPTION

places to buy or eat food

cafeteria	cafetería *nf*
canteen	cantina *nf*
commissary	comisario *nm*
fruit store/stand	frutería *nf*
oyster bar	ostrería *nf*
pizzeria	pizzería *nf*
refectory	refectorio *nm*
restaurant	restaurante *nm*
supermarket	supermercado *nm*

tastes, textures, quality

acerb	acerbo *aj*
acrid	acre *aj*
contaminated	contaminado *aj*
creamy	cremoso *aj*
delicious	delicioso *aj*
exotic	exótico *aj*
fresh	fresco *aj*
fruity	afrutado, frutoso *aj*
grainy, granular	granulado *aj*
greasy	grasiento *aj*
insipid	insípido *aj*
juicy	jugoso *aj*
lemony	a limón *aj*
mentholated	mentolado *aj*

pap *nsg*	papilla, papas *nf, nfpl*
piquant	picante *aj*
pure	puro *aj*
rancid	rancio *aj*
saccharine	sacarino *aj*
salty, salted	salado *aj*
savory	sabroso *aj*
seasoned	sazonado *aj*
spicy	especiado *aj*
succulent	suculento *aj*
sugary	azucarado *aj*
tutti-frutti	tutti-frutti *nm*
vinegary	avinagrado, vinagroso *aj*

other general terms

additive	aditivo *aj, nm*
ambiance, ambience	ambiente *nm*
appetite	apetito *nm*
comestibles	comestibles *nmpl*
culinary	culinario *aj*
digestion	digestión *nf*
gastronomy	gastronomía *nf*
menu	menú *nm*
nutrition	nutrición *nf*
provisions	provisiones *nfpl*
savor	sabor *nm*
tempting	tentador *aj*

KINDS OF FOOD

meals

banquet	banquete *nm*
barbecue	barbacoa *nf*
buffet	buffet, bufet, bufé *nm*
feast	festín *nm*
picnic	picnic *nm*

major categories

casserole	cacerola *nf*
cereal	cereal *nm*
condiment	condimento *nm*
confection	confección *nf*
dressing	aderezo *nm*
extract	extracto *nm*
fruit	fruta *nf*
grain	grano *nm*
legume	legumbre *nf*
omelet	omelette *nf*
organic	orgánico *aj*
pasta	pasta *nf*
produce	producto *nm*
salad	ensalada *nf*

sandwich	sandwich *nm*
sauce	salsa *nf*
seasoning	sazón *nf*
soup	sopa *nf*
spice	especia *nf*
vegetable	vegetal *nm*
vegetarian	vegetariano *aj*

soups

bouillabaisse	bullabesa *nf*
condensed soup	sopa condensada *nf*
consommé	consomé *nm*
gazpacho	gazpacho *nm*
goulash	gulash *nm*
gumbo	quingombó *nm*
potage	potaje *nm*
puree, purée	puré *nm*

meat and poultry

beefsteak	biftec, bistec *nm*
capon	capón *nm*
corned beef	corned beef *nm*
croquette	croqueta *nf*
entrecote	entrecot *nm*
fricassee	fricasé *nm*
ham	jamón *nm*
hamburger	hamburguesa *nf*
pastrami	pastrami *nm*
pemican, pemmican	pemicán *nm*
pork	puerco *nm*
ragout	ragú *nm*
salami	salami *nm*
scallop	escalope *nm*
taco	taco *nm*
tournedos	turnedó *nm*

seafood

albacore	albacora *nf*
anchovy	ancho(v)a *nf*
carp	carpa *nf*
caviar	caviar *nm*
halibut	halibut *nm*
oyster	ostra *nf*
perch	perca *nf*
pompano	pámpano *nm*
salmon	salmón *nm*
sardine	sardina *nf*
sturgeon	esturión *nm*
trout	trucha *nf*
tuna	atún *nm*

dairy

brie	brie *nm*
Camembert	camembert *nm*

cheese	queso *nm*
condensed milk	leche condensada *nf*
cream	crema *nf*
evaporated milk	leche evaporada *nf*
fondue	fondue *nf*
Gruyère	gruyere *nm*
homogenized milk	leche homogeneizada *nf*
mozzarella	mozzarella *nf*
pasteurized milk	leche past(e)urizada *nf*

pasta

lasagna, lasagne	lasaña *nf*
macaroni *nsg*	macarrones *nmpl*
ravioli *nsg*	ravioles *nmpl*
rissotto *nsg*	risotto *nm*
spaghetti *nsg*	espaguetis *nmpl*

bread and cereal

brioche	brioche *nm*
croissant	croissant *nm*
crouton	crutón *nm*
farina	harina *nf*
pabulum	pábulo *nm*
pumpernickle	pumpernickel *nm*
rice	arroz *nm*
semolina	sémola *nf*
toast	tostada *nf*
tortilla	tortilla *nf*

vegetables

asparagus	espárrago *nm*
bamboo	bambú *nm*
broccoli	brécol, brócoli *nm*
cauliflower	coliflor *nf*
chayote	chayote, cayote *nm*
endive	endibia, endivia *nf*
escarole	escarola *nf*
jicama	jícama *nf*
kohlrabi	colirrábano *nm*
lentil	lenteja *nf*
potato	patata *nf*
salsify	salsifí *nm*
shallot	chalote *nm*
soybean	soja *nf*
spinach *nsg*	espinacas *nfpl*
taro	taro *nm*
tofu	tofu *nm*
tomato	tomate *nm*

fruits

acerola	acerola *nf*
banana	banana *nf*
bergamot	bergamota *nf*
calabash	calabaza *nf*

cantaloupe, cantaloup	cantalupo *nm*
chayote	chayote *nm*
cherry	cereza *nf*
citron	cidra *nf*
citrus	cítrico *aj*
coconut, cocoanut	coco *nm*
date	dátil *nm*
fig	higo *nm*
guava	guayaba *nf*
kiwi	kiwi *nm*
kumquat	kuncuat *nm*
lemon	limón *nm*
lime	lima *nf*
mandarine	mandarina *nf*
mango	mango *nm*
melon	melón *nm*
nectarine	nectarina *nf*
olive	oliva *nf*
orange	naranja *nf*
papaya	papaya *nf*
pear	pera *nf*
pineapple	piña *nf*
plantain	plátano *nm*
pomegranate	granada *nf*
rhubarb	ruíbarbo *nm*
tamarind	tamarindo *nm*

nuts

almond	almendra *nf*
betel	betel *nm*
Brazil	brasil *nm*
litchi	lichi *nm*
macadamia	macadamia *nf*
pecan	pacana *nf*
pine nut	piñón *nm*
pistachio	pistacho *nm*
sesame	sésamo *nm*

sweet foods

bonbon	bombón *nm*
caramel	caramelo *nm*
chocolate	chocolate *nm*
compote	compota *nf*
crepe, crêpe	crep, crêpe *nm*
doughnut	dona, donut *nf, nm*
flan	flan *nm*
frangipani	franchipaniero *nm*
halva, halvah	halva *nf*
jelly	jalea *nf*
macaroon	macarrón *nm*
marmalade	mermelada *nf*
marzipan	mazapán *nm*
meringue	merengue *nm*

mousse	mousse *nf*
pancake	panqueque *nm*
penuche	panocha *nf*
praline	praliné *nm*
pudding	pudín, budín *nm*
sugar	azúcar *nm or nf*
tapioca	tapioca *nf*
tart	tarta *nf*
torte	torta *nf*
truffle	trufa *nf*

sauces, spices, syrups, flavorings

anise	anís *nm*
bechamel	bechamel, besamel *nf*
bolognese	boloñesa *nf*
caraway	alcaravea *nf*
cardamom	cardamomo *nm*
cayenne	cayena *nf*
chickory	achicoria *nf*
chutney	chutney *nm*
clove	clavo *nm*
coriander	coriandro *nm*
cumin	comino *nm*
curry	curry, cari *nm*
ginger	jengibre *nm*
hollandaise	holandesa *nf*
ketchup, catsup	catsup *nm*
mace	macis *nf*
marjoram	mejorana *nf*
mint	menta *nf*
molasses	melaza *nf*
mustard	mostaza *nf*
oregano	orégano *nm*
paprika	paprika *nf*
pimento, pimiento	pimiento *nm*
roux	roux *nm*
saccharin	sacarina *nf*
saffron	azafrán *nm*
salt	sal *nf*
sassafras	sasafrás *nm*
sorghum	sorgo *nm*
tarragon	estragón *nm*
vanilla	vainilla *nf*
vinegar	vinagre *nm*

fats and oils

lard	lardo *nm*
margarine	margarina *nf*
oleo, oleomargarine	oleomargarina *nf*

dressings

mayonnaise	mayonesa *nf*
vinaigrette	vinagreta *nf*

popular ethnic dishes

chili, chilli	chile *nm*
chop suey	chop suey *nm*
chow mein	chow mein *nm*
couscous	cuscús, couscous *nm*
gnocchi	ñoquis *nmpl*
moussaka	mousaka, moussaka *nf*
pizza	pizza *nf*
soufflé	suflé *nm*
tamale	tamal *nm*

other foods

canapé	canapé *nm*
chicle	chicle *nm*
filet, fillet	filete *nm*
fritter	fritada, fritura *nf*
granulated (sugar)	granulado *aj*
menthol	mentol *nm*
paste	pasta *nf*
peel	peladura *nf*
pulp	pulpa *nf*

PROCESSED FOODS

additives

agar, agar-agar	agar, agar-agar *nm*
antioxidant	antioxidante *nm*
coloring	colorido *nm*
emulsifier	emulsor *nm*
gelatin, gelatine	gelatina *nf*
pectin	pectina *nf*
stabilizer	estabilizante *nm*
supplement	suplemento *nm*

processes

curing	curación *nf*
dehydration	deshidratación *nf*
fermentation	fermentación *nf*
hydrogenation	hidrogenación *nf*
irradiation	irradiación *nf*
packaging	empaque *nm*
pasteurization	past(e)urización *nf*
reconstitution	reconstitución *nf*

PREPARATION AND CONSUMPTION

tools and equipment

beater	batidora *nf*
bottle-opener	abrebotellas *nm*
brazier	brasero *nm*
caldron	calderón *nm*
colander	colador *nm*

food processor	procesador de alimentos *nm*
freezer	freezer *nm*
grill	grill *nm*
jar	jarra *nf*
kebab, kebob	kebab *nm*
liquefier	licuadora *nf*
microwave	microonda *nf*
mold	molde *nm*
pot	pote *nm*
pressure cooker	olla a presión *nf*
recipe	receta *nf*
refrigerator	refrigerador *nm*
sandwich toaster	sandwichera, sandwichero *nf, nm*
separator	separador *nm*
spatula	espátula *nf*
spice rack	especiero *nm*
stove	estufa *nf*
toaster	tostadora *nf*
utensil	utensilio *nm*
yogurt maker	yogurtera *nf*

recipe instructions

base	base *nf*
beat	batir *vt*
blanch	blanquear *vt*
clarify	clarificar *vt*
consistency	consistencia *nf*
dress	aderezar *vt*
eviscerate	eviscerar *vt*
fillet	cortar en filetes *vt, nmpl*
fry	freír *vt*
garnish	guarnecer *vt*
glaze	glasear *vt*
ingredient	ingrediente *nm*
leaven, leavening	levadura *nf*
macerate	macerar *vt*
peel	pelar *vt*
puree, purée	hacer un puré con *vt*
refrigerate	refrigerar *vt*
salt	salar *vt*
scald	escaldar *vt*
season	sazonar *vt*
toast	tostar *vt*

food service

china	china *nf*
china closet	chinero *nm*
fruit bowl	frutero *nm*
plate	plato *nm*
platter	platón *nm*
porcelain	porcelana *nf*

portion	porción *nf*
salad bowl	ensaladera *nf*
saltcellar, saltshaker	salero *nm*
self-service	autoservicio *nm*
soup plate/tureen	sopera *nf*
sugar bowl	azucarera *nf*

eating and digestion

aroma	aroma *nm*
consumption	consumo *nm*
devour	devorar *vt*
famished	famélico *aj*
gustatory	gustativo *aj*
mastication	masticación *nf*
metabolism	metabolismo *nm*
satiation	saciedad *nf*
subsistence	subsistencia *nf*
voracious (appetite)	voraz *aj*

religious and historical terms

ambrosia	ambrosía *nf*
kosher	kosher *aj*
manna	maná *nm*
paschal	pascual *aj*
victuals (obs)	vituallas *nfpl*

NUTRITION

general terms

amino acid	aminoácido *nm*
calorie	caloría *nf*
carbohydrate	carbohidrato *nm*
casein	caseína *nf*
diet	dieta *nf*
dietetics	dietética *nf*
gluten	gluten *nm*
glycogen	glicógeno *nm*
malnutrition	desnutrición *nf*
mineral	mineral *nm*
nutrient	nutriente *nm*
nutriment	nutrimiento *nm*
protein	proteína *nf*
vanillin	vainillina *nf*
vitamin	vitamina *nf*

vitamins

ascorbic (acid)	ascórbico *aj*
niacin (Vitamin B)	niacina *nf*
retinol (Vitamin A)	retinol *nm*
riboflavin	riboflavina *nf*
thiamine, thiamin	tiamina *nf*

minerals

calcium	calcio *nm*
iodine	yodo *nm*
magnesium	magnesio *nm*
phosphorus	fósforo *nm*
potassium	potasio *nm*
sodium	sodio *nm*

sugars

dextrose	dextrosa *nf*
fructose	fructosa *nf*
glucose	glucosa *nf*
lactose	lactosa *nf*
maltose	maltosa *nf*
sucrose	sacarosa *nf*

fats

cholesterol	colesterol *nm*
glycerol	glicerol *nm*
lecithin	lecitina *nf*
lipid, lipide	lípido *nm*
triglyceride	triglicérido *nm*
balanced (diet)	balanceado *aj*
macrobiotic	macrobiótico *aj*
polyunsaturated (fat)	poliinsaturado *aj*

PERSONS

chef	chef, jefe *nmf*
connoisseur	conocedor(a) *nmf*
dietician	dietista *nmf*
Epicurean	epicureo, -a *nmf*
gastronome	gastrónomo, -a *nmf*
glutton	glotón, -ona *nmf*
gourmet	gourmet *nmf*
nutritionist	nutricionista *nmf*
oyster vender	ostrero, -a *nmf*
picnicker	participante del picnic *nmf*
vegetarian	vegetariano, -a *nmf*

(*See also major food crops* under **AGRICULTURE**; **BEVERAGES**)

BEVERAGES

GENERAL TERMS

alcohol	alcohol *nm*
beverage	bebida *nf*
distillery	destilería *nf*
elixir	elíxir *nm*
libation	libación *nf*
liquor	licor *nm*
potion	poción *nf*
prohibition (obs)	prohibición *nf*

ALCOHOLIC BEVERAGES

kinds of drinks

aperitif, apéritif	aperitivo *nm*
cordial	cordial *nm*
liqueur	licor *nm*
wine	vino *nm*

wines

Burgundy	borgoña *nf*
cabernet	cabernet *nm*
cava	cava *nf*
champagne	champán, champaña *nm, nf*
Chianti	quianti *nm*
claret	clarete *nm*
Madeira	madeira *nf*
Malaga	málaga *nf*
moselle	vino del Mosela *nm*
muscatel	moscatel *nm*
must	mosto *nm*
port	oporto *nm*
Riesling	riesling *nm*
rosé	rosado *nm*
sherry	jerez *nm*
vermouth	vermut, vermú *nm*

liqueurs

absinth(e)	absenta *nf*
anisette	licor de anís *nm*
brandy	brandy *nm*
cognac	coñac, coñá *nm*
curaçao	curasao, curazao *nm*
grenadine	granadina *nf*
julep	julepe *nm*
kirsch	kirsch *nm*
kümmel	kummel, cúmel *nm*
maraschino	marrasquino *nm*

mixed drinks

cocktail	cóctel *nm*
daiquiri	daikiri, daiquiri *nm*
manhattan	manhattan *nm*
margarita	margarita *nf*
martini	martini *nm*
punch	ponche *nm*
sangria	sangría *nf*

other alcoholic beverages

gin	ginebra *nf*
ginger beer	cerveza de jengibre *nf*, *nm*
kvass	kwas, kvas *nm*
mescal	mezcal *nm*
ouzo	ouzo *nm*
rum	ron *nm*
sake	sake, saki *nm*
Scotch	whisky escocés *nm*
tequila	tequila
vodka	vodka *nf*
whiskey, whisky	whisky, whiski, güisqui *nm*

drinking practices

abstinence	abstinencia *nf*
intemperance	intemperancia *nf*
moderation	moderación *nf*
sobriety	sobriedad *nf*

public places

bar	bar *nm*
cafe, café	café *nm*
coffee bar	cafetín *nm*
tavern	taberna *nf*

TERMS RELATING TO WINE

aroma	aroma *nf*
bouquet	bouquet, buqué *nm*
enology	enología *nf*
fortified	fortificado *aj*
sec	seco *aj*
select	selecto *aj*
vineyard	viña, viñedo *nf, nm*
wine merchant	vinatero, -a *nmf*
wine shop/trade	vinatería *nf*
winery	vinería *nf*

NON-ALCOHOLIC BEVERAGES

cappuccino	capuchino *nm*
chocolate	chocolate *nm*
cider	sidra *nf*
cocoa	cacao *nm*
cocoa	cocoa *nf*
coffee	café *nm*
coke	coque, Coca-cola *nm*
cola	cola *nf*
espresso	café exprés *nm*
ginger ale	refresco de jengibre *nm*
juice	jugo *nm*
lemonade	limonada *nf*

malted	malteado *aj*
mineral water	agua mineral *nm*
mocha	moca *nf*
nectar	néctar *nm*
orangeade	naranjada *nf*
punch	ponche *nm*
quinine (water)	quinina *nf*
sarsparilla (tea)	zarzaparrilla *nf*
seltzer	agua de Seltz *nf(el)*
soda, soda water	soda *nf*
tea	té *nm*

DESCRIPTIVE TERMS

adulterated	adulterado *aj*
alcoholic	alcohólico *aj*
carbonated	carbonatado *aj*
decaffeinated	descafeinado *aj*
diluted	diluido *aj*
distilled	destilado *aj*
effervescent	efervescente *aj*
fermented	fermentado *aj*
nonalcoholic	no alcohólico *aj*
potable	potable *aj*
refreshing	refrescante *aj*
spumy	espumoso *aj*
tepid	tibio *aj*

CONTAINERS AND ACCESSORIES

barrel	barril *nm*
bottle	botella *nf*
carafe	garrafa *nf*
chalice	cáliz *nm*
cocktail shaker	coctelera *nf*
coffeepot, coffee maker	cafetera *nf*
cork	corcho *nm*
corkscrew	sacacorchos *nm*
decanter	decantador *nm*
extractor	extractor *nm*
ice cube	cubito de hielo *nm*
punchbowl	ponchera *nf*
samovar	samovar *nm*
teapot	tetera *nf*
thermos	termo *nm*
wineglass	copa para vino *nf, nm*

PERSONS

abstainer	abstemio, -a *nmf*
designated driver	conductor designado *nmf*

dipsomaniac	dipsómano, -a *nmf*
distiller	destilador(a) *nmf*
enologist	enólogo, -a *nmf*
vintner	vinatero, -a *nmf*

(*See also* **FOOD AND NUTRITION**)

AUTOMOBILES

GENERAL TERMS

auto, automobile	auto, automóvil *nm*
automotive (industry)	automotor, automotriz *aj*
automotive (vehicles)	automovilístico *aj*
car	carro *nm*
gas, gasoline	gasolina *nf*
luxury	de lujo *aj*
maintenance	mantenimiento *nm*
model	modelo *nm*
repair	reparación *nf*
traffic	tráfico *nm*
vehicle	vehículo *nm*

ASPECTS OF AUTOMOBILES

models

compact	coche compacto *nm*
convertible	convertible *nm*
coupe, coupé	cupé *nm*
Jeep	jeep *nm*
new	nuevo *aj*
sedan	sedán *nm*
sports	deportivo *aj*
used	usado *aj*

parts and equipment

accelerator	acelerador *nm*
battery	batería *nf*
block (engine)	bloque *nm*
cable	cable *nm*
carburetor	carburador *nm*
catalytic converter	catalizador *nm*
chassis	chasis *nm*
controls	controles *nmpl*
cylinder	cilindro *nm*
differential	diferencial *nm*
disk	disco *nm*
emergency (brake)	emergencia *nf*
generator	generador *nm*
glove compartment	guantera *nf*
hubcap	tapacubos *nm*
hydraulic (brake)	hidráulico *aj*
ignition	ignición *nf*

indicator	indicador *nm*
instrument	instrumento *nm*
manual (gearshift)	manual *aj*
motor	motor *nm*
odometer	odómetro *nm*
panel	panel *nm*
pedal	pedal *nm*
piston	pistón *nm*
pump	bomba *nf*
radial (tire)	radial *aj*
radiator	radiador *nm*
silencer	silenciador *nm*
thermostat	termostato *nm*
transmission	transmisión *nf*
valve	válvula *nf*

maintenance and repairs

adjustment	ajuste *nm*
air	aire *nm*
alignment	alineación *nf*
antifreeze	anticongelante *nm*
charge (battery)	carga *nf*
check (brakes)	chequear *vt*
compression	compresión *nf*
garage	garaje *nm*
gas station	gasolinera *nf*
grease	grasa *nf*
inflate (tires)	inflar *vt*
lubrication	lubricación *nf*
performance	performance *nf*
pressure	presión *nf*

driving

acceleration	aceleración *nf*
accident	accidente *nm*
avenue	avenida *nf*
bifurcation	bifurcación *nf*
block (street)	bloquear *vt*
bottleneck	embotellamiento *nm*
circular (route)	circular *aj*
collision	colisión *nf*
congestion	congestión *nf*
crossing	cruce *nm*
crossroads	encrucijada *nf*
curve	curva *nf*
deceleration	deceleración *nf*
direct (route)	directo *aj*
direction	dirección *nf*
intersection	intersección *nf*
island	isla *nf*
kilometer distance	kilometraje *nm*
license	licencia *nf*

median	mediana *nf*
mileage	distancia en millas *nf,* *nfpl*
obstruction	obstrucción *nf*
overpass	paso superior *nm*
parking lot	parking *nm*
parking meter	parquímetro *nm*
pavement	pavimento *nm*
ramp	rampa *nf*
route	ruta *nf*
second gear	segunda *nf*
signal	señal *nf*
speed limit	límite de velocidad *nm,* *nf*
stop (sign)	stop *nm*
traction	tracción *nf*
traffic island	isleta *nf*
tunnel	túnel *nm*
underpass	paso inferior *nm*

PERSONS

accident victim	accidentado, -a *nmf*
garage attendant	garajista *nmf*
motorist	motorista *nmf*
passenger	pasajero, -a *nmf*

(*See also* **streets and traffic** under **THE CITY**; **LAND TRANSPORTATION**; **TRAVEL AND TOURISM**)

WORK

GENERAL TERMS

career	carrera *nf*
employ, employment	empleo *nm*
equipment	equipo *nm*
ergonomics	ergonomía *nf*
industry	industria *nf*
labor	labor *nf*
NAFTA	NAFTA *nm*
occupation	ocupación *nf*
pension	pensión *nf*
permit	permiso *nm*
post	puesto *nm*
profession	profesión *nf*
retirement	retiro *nm*
Social Security	Seguro Social *nm*
speciality, specialty	especialidad *nf*
syndicalism	sindicalismo *nm*
vacation *nsg*	vacaciones *nfpl*
vocation	vocación *nf*
working class	clase obrera *nf*

ASPECTS OF EMPLOYMENT

leading fields of work

agriculture	agricultura *nf*
commerce	comercio *nm*
manufacturing	manufactura *nf*
services	servicios *nmpl*
transportation	tra(n)sportación *nf*

factors affecting work

absenteeism	absentismo *nm*
automation	automación, automatización *nf*
economy	economía *nf*
experience	experiencia *nf*
recession	recesión *nf*
retirement plan	plan de retiro *nm*
technology	tecnología *nf*
vacancy	vacante *nf*

labor relations

arbitration	arbitraje *nm*
conciliation	conciliación *nf*
contract	contrato *nm*
incentive	incentivo *nm*
negotiation	negociación *nf*
nepotism	nepotismo *nm*
pact	pacto *nm*
removal	remoción *nf*
supervision	supervisión *nf*
working conditions	condiciones de trabajo *nfpl, nm*

wages

honorarium *nsg*	honorarios *nmpl*
minimum wage	sueldo mínimo *nm*
net income	ingreso neto *nm*
pay	paga *nf*
payday	día de paga *nm, nf*
remuneration	remuneración *nf*
salary	salario *nm*
stipend	estipendio *nm*

places

department	departamento *nm*
office	oficina *nf*
plant	planta *nf*

basis of employment

daily *aj*	por día *nm*
full-time *aj*	a tiempo completo *nm*
hourly *aj*	por horas *nfpl*
part-time *aj*	a tiempo parcial *nm*

permanent *aj*	permanente *aj*
temporary *aj*	temporal *aj*

terms describing workers

capable	capaz *aj*
competent	competente *aj*
efficient	eficiente *aj*
experienced *aj*	con experiencia *nf*
industrious	industrioso *aj*
qualified	calificado *aj*
salaried	asalariado *aj*
undocumented	indocumentado *aj*
unqualified	no calificado *aj*

terms describing work

arduous	arduo *aj*
fatiguing	fatigoso *aj*
interesting	interesante *aj*
remunerative	remunerador *aj*
routine	rutinario *aj*
sedentary	sedentario *aj*

other terms

apprenticeship	aprendizaje *nm*
assumption (duties)	asunción *nf*
collaboration	colaboración *nf*
sinecure	sinecura *nf*
sustenance	sustento *nm*
uniform	uniforme *nm*

PERSONS

groups

administration	administración *nf*
personnel	personal *nm*
picket line	piquete *nm*

individuals

apprentice	aprendiz, -iza *nmf*
arbitrator	árbitro, -a *nmf*
collaborator	colaborador(a) *nmf*
colleague	colega *nmf*
conciliator	conciliador(a) *nmf*
coordinator	coordinador(a) *nmf*
director	director(a) *nmf*
employee	empleado, -a *nmf*
employer	empleador, -a *nmf*
factotum (handyman)	factótum *nm*
functionary	funcionario, -a *nmf*
inferior	inferior *nmf*
inspector	inspector(a) *nmf*
itinerant worker	obrero, -a itinerante *nmf*

negotiator	negociador(a) *nmf*
office worker	oficinista *nmf*
officer	oficial *nmf*
operative	operario, -a *nmf*
pensioner	pensionado, -a, pensionista *nmf*
professional	profesional *aj, nmf*
specialist	especialista *nmf*
subordinate	subordinado, -a *nmf*
superintendent	superintendente *nmf*
superior	superior *nmf*
supervisor	supervisor(a) *nmf*

(*See also* **BUSINESS**; **ECONOMICS**)

Keeping the Body Beautiful

CLOTHING

GENERAL TERMS

accessory	accesorio *nm*
design	diseño *nm*
dictates (of fashion)	dictados *nmpl*
mode	moda *nf*
ornament	ornamento *nm*
pair	par *nm*
style	estilo *nm*
vogue	boga *nf*

ASPECTS OF CLOTHING

functions of clothing

communication	comunicación *nf*
decoration	decoración *nf*
entertainment	entretenimiento *nm*
modesty	modestia *nf*
protection	protección *nf*

types of clothing

appropriate	apropiado *aj*
ceremonial	ceremonial *aj*
formal	formal *aj*
informal	informal *aj*
maternity *aj*	de maternidad *nf*
sports	deportivo *aj*
theatrical	teatral *aj*
traditional	tradicional *aj*

cleaning

air out	airear *vt*
detergent	detergente *aj, nm*
laundry	lavandería *nf*
ticket (laundry)	ticket *nm*

ARTICLES OF CLOTHING

headwear

crown	coronilla *nf*
fez	fez *nm*
helmet	yelmo *nm*
kepi	quepis, kepis *nm*
mantilla	mantilla *nf*
plumed	con plumas *aj*
shako	chacó *nm*
toque	toca *nf*
turban	turbante *nm*
visor	visera *nf*

footwear

boot	bota, botín *nf, nm*
bootee	botita *nf*
laces	lazos *nmpl*
moccasin	mocasín *nm*
platform	plataforma *nf*
sandal	sandalia *nf*

undergarments and sleepwear

corselet, corslet	coselete *nm*
corset	corsé *nm*
lingerie	lencería *nf*
negligee, negligée, negligé	negligé *nm*
pajamas	pijama, piyama *nm*
pantyhose	medias panti(e)s *nmpl, nfpl*

outerwear

blazer	blazer *nm*
blouse	blusa *nf*
blouse (long)	blusón *nm*
bolero	bolero *nm*
caftan	caftán *nm*
cape	capa *nf*
cardigan	cárdigan *nm*
domino	dominó *nm*
guayabera	guayabera *nf*
jacket	chaqueta *nf*
mantle	manto *nm*
miniskirt	minifalda *nf*
mitten	mitón *nm*
pants	pantalones *nmpl*

parka	parka *nf*
poncho	poncho *nm*
sweater	suéter *nm*
uniform	uniforme *nm*

other garments

bikini	bikini, biquini *nm or nf*
coordinates	coordinados *nmpl*
jeans	jeans *nmpl*
jellabah	chilaba *nf*
kimono	kimono, quimono *nm*
leotard	leotardo *nm*
overalls	overol *nm*
sari	sari *nm*
sarong	sarong *nm*
tunic	túnica *nf*
tutu	tutú *nm*

historical clothing

armor	armadura *nf*
brassard	brazal *nm*
chiton	quitón *nm*
mail	malla *nf*
pantaloons	pantalones *nmpl*
tabard	tabardo *nm*
toga	toga *nf*
tricorne (hat)	tricornio *nm*

ACCESSORIES AND ORNAMENTS

bandoleer, bandolier	bandolera *nf*
boa	boa *nf*
bracelet	brazalete *nm*
brooch	broche *nm*
clip-on (earrings)	de clip *nm*
coronet	corona *nf*
diadem	diadema *nf*
laces	lazos *nmpl*
mask	máscara *nf*
monocle	monóculo *nm*
parasol	parasol *nm*
pendant	pendiente *nm*
serape	sarape *nm*
shawl	chal *nm*
stole	estola *nf*
veil	velo *nm*

SEWING TERMS

stitches

basting	baste *nm*
bias	bies *nm*
double	doble *aj*
zigzag	zigzag *nm*

design features

appliqué	aplicación *nf*
band	banda *nf*
button	botón *nm*
filigree	filigrana *nf*
fringe	franja *nf*
miter	mitra *nf*
peplum	peplo *nm*
pleat	pliegue *nm*
raglan	raglán *aj, nm*
zipper	zíper *nm*

tools and equipment

bobbin	bobina *nf*
elastic	elástico *aj, nm*
mannequin, manikin	maniquí *nmf*
pattern	patrón *nm*
sewing machine	máquina de coser *nf*
stiletto	estilete *nm*
Velcro	velcro *nm*

measurements and sizes

centimeter	centímetro *nm*
cup	copa *nf*
meter	metro *nm*
yard	yarda *nf*
yardage	medida en yardas, tela *nf*

fabric patterns

flowered	floreado *aj*
geometric	geométrico *aj*
intricate	intrincado *aj*

other terms

crochet	crochet, croché *nm*
knot	nudo *nm*
palm (glove)	palma *nf*
reverse (side of fabric)	revés *nm*
roll (of fabric)	rollo *nm*
texture	textura *nf*
button shop	botonería *nf*

PERSONS

arbiter	árbitro *nm*
button dealer	botonero, -a *nmf*
designer	diseñador(a) *nmf*
model	modelo *nmf*
modiste	modista *nmf*
transvestite	transvestido, -a *nmf*

(*See also clothing fabrics* under *ASPECTS OF TEXTILES*; **GEMS AND JEWELRY**; *uniform* under **THE MILITARY ESTABLISHMENT**; *clothing and appearance* under **RELIGION**)

COSMETICS AND GROOMING

GENERAL TERMS

barbershop	barbería *nf*
beauty salon	salón de belleza *nm, nf*
cosmetic	cosmético *aj, nm*
cosmetology	cosmética *nf*
substance	sustancia *nf*
treatment	tratamiento *nm*

ASPECTS OF SKIN AND HAIR CARE

treatments

coloring	coloración *nf*
depilation	depilación *nf*
douche	ducha *nf*
electrolysis	electrólisis *nf*
face lift	lifting *nm*
facial	tratamiento facial *nm*
laser	láser *nm*
liposuction	liposucción *nf*
manicure	manicura *nf*
massage	masaje *nm*
pedicure	pedicura *nf*
peeling	peeling *nm*
permanent	permanente *nf*
sauna	sauna *nf*
shiatsu	shiatsu *nm*
styling	estilización *nf*
tattoo	tatuaje *nm*

substances

aloe	áloe, aloe *nm*
antiperspirant	antisudoral *nm*
astringent	astringente *aj, nm*
balm	bálsamo *nm*
brilliantine	brillantina *nf*
calamine (lotion)	calamina *nf*
camphor ice	cerato de alcanfor *nm*
citronella	citronela *nf*
cologne	colonia *nf*
conditioner	acondicionador *nm*
cream	crema *nf*
deodorant	desodorante *nm*
depilatory	depilatorio *nm*
emollient	emoliente *nm*
eucalyptus (oil)	eucalipto *nm*
gargle	gargarismo *nm*

gel	gel *nm*
glycerin(e)	glicerina *nf*
henna	alheña *nf*
humectant	humectante *nm*
lanolin	lanolina *nf*
lavender	lavanda *nf*
lotion	loción *nf*
lubricant	lubricante *nm*
mask	máscara *nf*
mousse	mousse *nf*
perfume	perfume *nm*
peroxide	peróxido *nm*
petrolatum	petrolato *nm*
pomade	pomada *nf*
shampoo	champú *nm*
spray	espray *nm*
talcum powder	talco *nm*
tint	tinte *nm*
unguent	ungüento *nm*

tools and equipment

roller	rulo, rulero *nm*
toupee	tupé *nm*
towel	toalla *nf*

other terms

Afro	afro *nm*
apply (makeup)	aplicar *vt*
hypoallergenic	hipoalergénico *aj*
manageable (hair)	manejable *aj*
medicated	medicinal *aj*
retouch	retocarse *vt*

PERSONS

barber	barbero, -a *nmf*
cosmetologist	cosmetólogo, -a *nmf*
hair stylist	estilista *nmf*
manicurist	manicuro, -a *nmf*
masseur	masajista *nm*
masseuse	masajista *nf*
plastic surgeon	cirujano plástico *nmf*

(*See also* NUTRITION under **FOOD AND NUTRITION**; *fitness* under **SPORTS**)

GEMS AND JEWELRY

GENERAL TERMS

facet	faceta *nf*
gem	gema *nf*
glyptography	gliptografía *nf*
jewelry	joyería *nf*
mounting	montura *nf*

precious	precioso *aj*
semiprecious	semiprecioso *aj*

TYPES OF GEMS

precious

diamond	diamante *nm*
emerald	esmeralda *nf*
ruby	rubí *nm*
sapphire	zafiro *nm*

semiprecious

agate	ágata *nf*
carnelian	carniola, cornalina *nf*
garnet	granate *nm*
jade	jade *nm*
jasper	jaspe *nm*
lapis lazuli	lapislázuli *nm*
onyx	ónice, ónix, ónique *nm*
opal	ópalo *nm*
pearl	perla *nf*
sardonyx	sardónica, sardónice *nf*
turquoise	turquesa *nf*

other jewelry materials

alabaster	alabastro *nm*
amber	ámbar *nm*
amethyst	amatista *nf*
aquamarine	aguamarina *nf*
coral	coral *nm*
nacre	nácar *nm*
topaz	topacio *nm*
tourmaline	turmalina *nf*
zircon	circón, zircón *nm*

other terms

artificial	artificial *aj*
brillant	brillante *nm*
cameo	camafeo *nm*
carbuncle (ruby)	carbúnculo, carbunclo *nm*
cultured (pearl)	cultivado *aj*
iridescence	iridescencia *nf*
natural (pearl)	natural *aj*
opalescence	opalescencia *nf*
solitaire	solitario *nm*
transparent	tra(n)sparente *aj*

PERSONS

diamond cutter	diamantista *nmf*
glyptographer	gliptógrafo, -a *nmf*

jeweler, jeweller	joyero, -a *nmf*
lapidary	lapidario, -a *nmf*

(*See also* **ACCESSORIES AND ORNAMENTS** under **CLOTHING**)

The Inner Self

FEELINGS AND EMOTIONS

EMOTIONAL STATES

happy

anxious (eager)	ansioso *aj*
content, contented	contento *aj*
euphoric	eufórico *aj*
exuberant	exuberante *aj*
gratified	gratificado *aj*
jovial	jovial *aj*
jubilant	jubiloso *aj*
satisfied	satisfecho *aj*

unhappy

anguished	angustiado *aj*
contrite	contrito *aj*
depressed	deprimido *aj*
desolate	desolado *aj*
despairing	desesperanzado *aj*
desperate	desesperado *aj*
disconsolate	desconsolado *aj*
discontented	descontento *aj*
dissatisfied	insatisfecho *aj*
envious	envidioso *aj*
inconsolable	inconsolable *aj*
lugubrious	lúgubre *aj*
melancholic, melancholy	melancólico *aj*
miserable	miserable *aj*
somber	sombrío *aj*
tormented	atormentado *aj*

afraid

alarmed	alarmado *aj*
apprehensive	aprensivo, aprehensivo *aj*
horror-stricken	horrorizado *aj*
panicky	pánico *aj*
terrified	aterrorizado *aj*
timorous	timorato *aj*
vulnerable	vulnerable *aj*

upset, annoyed

confused	confundido *aj*
disconcerted	desconcertado *aj*
disoriented	desorientado *aj*
distracted	distraído *aj*
frustrated	frustrado *aj*
impatient	impaciente *aj*
irritated	irritado *aj*
perplexed	perplejo *aj*
tense	tenso *aj*

angry

exasperated	exasperado *aj*
furious	furioso *aj*
indignant	indignado *aj*
infuriated	enfurecido *aj*
irate	iracundo *aj*
jealous	celoso *aj*
livid	lívido *aj*
offended	ofendido *aj*
provoked	provocado *aj*
rabid	rabioso *aj*
resentful	resentido *aj*

FEELINGS

pleasant

affection	afecto *nm*
amity	amistad *nf*
animation	animación *nf*
calmness	calma *nf*
camaraderie	camaradería *nf*
certainty	certeza, certidumbre *nf*
composure	compostura *nf*
confidence	confianza *nf*
consolation	consuelo *nm*
contentment	contento *nm*
delight	deleite *nm*
desire	deseo *nm*
effusion	efusión *nf*
enchantment	encanto *nm*
enthusiasm	entusiasmo *nm*
euphoria	euforia *nf*
exaltation	exaltación *nf*
excitement	excitación *nf*
expectation *nsg*	expectativas *nfpl*
exuberance	exuberancia *nf*
exultation	exultación *nf*
fascination	fascinación *nf*
felicity	felicidad *nf*
fervor	fervor *nm*
gratification	gratificación *nf*
gratitude	gratitud *nf*

hilarity	hilaridad *nf*
intimacy	intimidad *nf*
joviality	jovialidad *nf*
jubilation	júbilo *nm*
nostalgia	nostalgia *nf*
passion	pasión *nf*
pensive	pensativo *aj*
pleasure	placer *nm*
satisfaction	satisfacción *nf*
serenity	serenidad *nf*
solace	solaz *nm*
solemnity	solemnidad *nf*
solitude	soledad *nf*
surprise	sorpresa *nf*
tranquility	tranquilidad *nf*
zeal	celo *nm*

unpleasant

abandonment	abandono *nm*
abhorrence	aborrecimiento *nm*
abnegation	abnegación *nf*
abomination	abominación *nf*
acrimony	acrimonia *nf*
alarm	alarma *nf*
ambivalence	ambivalencia *nf*
anguish	angustia *nf*
animadversion	animadversión *nf*
animosity	animosidad *nf*
antagonism	antagonismo *nm*
antipathy	antipatía *nf*
anxiety	ansiedad *nf*
apathy	apatía *nf*
apprehension	aprensión *nf*
aversion	aversión *nf*
boredom	aburrimiento *nm*
confusion	confusión *nf*
consternation	consternación *nf*
contrition	contrición *nf*
depression	depresión *nf*
desolation	desolación *nf*
despair, desperation	desesperación *nf*
detestation	detestación *nf*
disaffection	desafecto *nm*
discontent	descontento *nm*
disdain	desdén *nm*
disenchantment	desencanto *nm*
disorientation	desorientación *nf*
displeasure	desplacer *nm*
disquiet, disquietude	inquietud *nf*
dissatisfaction	insatisfacción *nf*
distraction	distracción *nf*

doubt	duda *nf*
enmity	enemistad *nf*
envy	envidia *nf*
exacerbation	exacerbación *nf*
exasperation	exasperación *nf*
frenzy	frenesí *nm*
frustration	frustración *nf*
fury	furia *nf*
futility	futilidad *nf*
horror	horror *nm*
hostility	hostilidad *nf*
humiliation	humillación *nf*
impatience	impaciencia *nf*
indecision	indecisión *nf*
indignation	indignación *nf*
inferiority	inferioridad *nf*
inhibition	inhibición *nf*
insecurity	inseguridad *nf*
intimidation	intimidación *nf*
ire	ira *nf*
irritation	irritación *nf*
jealousy	celosía *nf*
malevolence	malevolencia *nf*
malice	malicia *nf*
melancholy	melancolía *nf*
misery	miseria *nf*
monotony	monotonía *nf*
nervousness	nerviosidad *nf*
odium	odio *nm*
panic	pánico *nm*
provocation	provocación *nf*
rage	rabia *nf*
rancor	rencor *nm*
recrimination	recriminación *nf*
repentance	arrepentimiento *nm*
repugnance	repugnancia *nf*
repulsion	repulsión *nf*
resentment	resentimiento *nm*
resignation	resignación *nf*
revenge	venganza *nf*
revulsion	revulsión *nf*
rivalry	rivalidad *nf*
strangeness	extrañeza *nf*
tedium	tedio *nm*
tension	tensión *nf*
terror	terror *nm*
torment	tormento *nm*
uncertainty	incertidumbre *nf*
unreality	irrealidad *nf*
vacillation	vacilación *nf*
vehemence	vehemencia *nf*
vengeance	venganza *nf*

CHARACTER TRAITS

ELEMENTS OF PERSONALITY

aptitude	aptitud *nf*
attitude	actitud *nf*
attribute	atributo *nm*
character	carácter *nm*
emotion	emoción *nf*
habit	hábito *nm*
idiosyncrasy	idiosincrasia *nf*
intellect	intelecto *nm*
morale	moral *nf*
preconception	preconcepción *nf*
predilection	predilección *nf*
predisposition	predisposición *nf*
self-expression	autoexpresión *nf*
self-image	autoimagen *nf*
sentiments	sentimientos *nmpl*
talent	talento *nm*
temperament	temperamento *nm*
tendencies	tendencias *nfpl*
volition	volición *nf*

QUALITIES

desirable

affability	afabilidad *nf*
altruism	altruismo *nm*
amiability	amabilidad *nf*
aplomb	aplomo *nm*
ardor	ardor *nm*
aspiration	aspiración *nf*
avidity	avidez *nf*
benevolence	benevolencia *nf*
charisma	carisma *nm*
circumspection	circunspección *nf*
civic-mindedness	civismo, civilidad *nm, nf*
commiseration	conmiseración *nf*
compassion	compasión *nf*
cordiality	cordialidad *nf*
courage	coraje *nm*
courtesy	cortesía *nf*
credibility	credibilidad *nf*
curiosity	curiosidad *nf*
decency	decencia *nf*
dedication	dedicación *nf*
deference	deferencia *nf*
determination	determinación *nf*
dexterity	destreza *nf*
dignity	dignidad *nf*
diligence	diligencia *nf*
discretion	discreción *nf*

dynamism	dinamismo *nm*
effervescence	efervescencia *nf*
elegance	elegancia *nf*
empathy	empatía *nf*
ethics	ética *nf*
expressivity	expresividad *nf*
fidelity	fidelidad *nf*
fortitude	fortaleza *nf*
gallantry	galantería *nf*
generosity	generosidad *nf*
heroism	heroísmo *nm*
honesty	honestidad, honradez *nf*
honor	honor, honra *nm, nf*
hospitality	hospitalidad *nf*
humanitarianism	humanitarismo *nm*
humility	humildad *nf*
humor	humor *nm*
idealism	idealismo *nm*
imagination (inventiveness)	imaginativa *nf*
impartiality	imparcialidad *nf*
imperturbability	imperturbabilidad *nf*
individuality	individualidad *nf*
infallibility	infalibilidad *nf*
ingenuity	ingenio *nm*
integrity	integridad *nf*
inventiveness	inventiva *nf*
invulnerability	invulnerabilidad *nf*
judgment	juicio *nm*
largess(e)	largueza *nf*
leadership	liderazgo, liderato *nm*
loyalty	lealtad *nf*
magnanimity	magnanimidad *nf*
maturity	madurez *nf*
mercy	merced *nf*
modesty	modestia *nf*
munificence	munificencia *nf*
naturalness	naturalidad *nf*
nobility	nobleza *nf*
obedience	obediencia *nf*
objectivity	objetividad *nf*
optimism	optimismo *nm*
patience	paciencia *nf*
perseverance	perseverancia *nf*
persistence	persistencia *nf*
perspicacity	perspicacia *nf*
persuasiveness	persuasiva *nf*
philanthropy	filantropía *nf*
pity	piedad *nf*
placidity	placidez *nf*
precociousness, precocity	precocidad *nf*
promptness	prontitud *nf*

prudence	prudencia *nf*	disobedience	desobediencia *nf*
rectitude	rectitud *nf*	docility	docilidad *nf*
refinement	refinamiento *nm*	duplicity	duplicidad *nf*
respect	respeto *nm*	egocentrism	egocentrismo *nm*
respectability	respetabilidad *nf*	egoism	egoísmo *nm*
reverence	reverencia *nf*	egotism	egotismo *nm*
sagacity	sagacidad *nf*	elitism	elitismo *nm*
self-criticism	autocrítica *nf*	excitability	excitabilidad *nf*
self-determination	autodeterminación *nf*	exclusivism	exclusivismo *nm*
self-discipline	autodisciplina *nf*	exhibitionism	exhibicionismo *nm*
self-sufficiency	autosuficiencia *nf*	fallibility	falibilidad *nf*
sensibility	sensibilidad *nf*	falsity	falsedad, falsía *nf*
sincerity	sinceridad *nf*	fanaticism	fanatismo *nm*
sociability	sociabilidad *nf*	ferocity	ferocidad *nf*
solicitude	solicitud *nf*	frankness	franqueza *nf*
sophistication	sofisticación *nf*	hypocrisy	hipocresía *nf*
spontaneity	espontaneidad *nf*	ignorance	ignorancia *nf*
stability	estabilidad *nf*	immaturity	inmadurez *nf*
subtlety	sutileza *nf*	immodesty	inmodestia *nf*
tact	tacto *nm*	immorality	inmoralidad *nf*
tenacity	tenacidad *nf*	impassivity	impasibilidad *nf*
tolerance	tolerancia *nf*	impersonality	impersonalidad *nf*
urbanity	urbanidad *nf*	impertinence	impertinencia *nf*
valor	valentía, valor *nf, nm*	impetuosity	impetuosidad *nf*
values	valores *nmpl*	implacability	implacabilidad *nf*
veracity	veracidad *nf*	impracticability	impracticabilidad *nf*
vigilance	vigilancia *nf*	imprudence	imprudencia *nf*
virtue	virtud *nf*	impudence	impudencia *nf*
virtuosity	virtuosismo *nm*	inaccessibility	inaccesibilidad *nf*
		inadaptability	inadaptabilidad *nf*
		inadequacy	inadecuación *nf*

undesirable

affectation	afectación *nf*	inconstancy	inconstancia *nf*
aggression,	agresividad *nf*	incorrigibility	incorregibilidad *nf*
aggressiveness		incredibility	incredibilidad *nf*
amorality	amoralidad *nf*	incredulity	incredulidad *nf*
arbitrariness	arbitrariedad *nf*	indecency	indecencia *nf*
arrogance	arrogancia *nf*	indecorum	indecoro *nm*
audacity	audacia *nf*	indelicacy	falta de delicadeza *nf*
avarice	avaricia *nf*	indifference	indiferencia *nf*
banality	banalidad *nf*	indiscretion	indiscreción *nf*
belligerence	beligerancia *nf*	indolence	indolencia *nf*
brusqueness	brusquedad *nf*	inefficiency	ineficacia *nf*
brutality	brutalidad *nf*	inelegance	inelegancia *nf*
capriciousness	capricho *nm*	ineptitude	ineptitud *nf*
condescension	condescendencia *nf*	ineptness	inepcia, ineptitud *nf*
cowardice	cobardía *nf*	inexperience	inexperiencia *nf*
cruelty	crueldad *nf*	ingenuousness	ingenuidad *nf*
cynicism	cinismo *nm*	(naivete)	
defiance	desafío *nm*	ingratitude	ingratitud *nf*
depravity	depravación *nf*	inhumanity	inhumanidad *nf*
discourtesy	descortesía *nf*	insincerity	insinceridad *nf*
dishonesty	deshonestidad *nf*	insolence	insolencia *nf*
disloyalty	deslealtad *nf*	instability	inestabilidad *nf*

intemperance	intemperancia *nf*
intolerance	intolerancia *nf*
intransigence	intransigencia *nf*
irrationality	irracionalidad *nf*
irresolution	irresolución *nf*
irresponsibility	irresponsabilidad *nf*
irreverence	irreverencia *nf*
masochism	masoquismo *nm*
mediocrity	mediocridad *nf*
obstinacy	obstinación *nf*
opportunism	oportunismo *nm*
partiality	parcialidad *nf*
passivity	pasividad *nf*
pedantry	pedantería *nf*
perversity	perversidad *nf*
pessimism	pesimismo *nm*
pomposity	pomposidad *nf*
pretense, pretension	pretensión *nf*
provincialism	provincialismo *nm*
pugnacity	pugnacidad *nf*
pusillanimity	pusilanimidad *nf*
racism	racismo *nm*
rapacity	rapacidad *nf*
rebelliousness	rebeldía *nf*
reticence	reticencia *nf*
self-destruction	autodestrucción *nf*
servility	servilismo *nm*
sexism	sexismo *nm*
snobbery, snobbishness	snobismo, esnobismo *nm*
stupidity	estupidez *nf*
subjectivity	subjetividad *nf*
submissiveness	sumisión *nf*
superficiality	superficialidad *nf*
timidity	timidez *nf*
vainglory	vanagloria *nf*
vanity	vanidad *nf*
villainy	villanía *nf*
voracity	voracidad *nf*
vulgarity	vulgaridad *nf*
vulnerability	vulnerabilidad *nf*

depends on point of view

acquiescence	aquiescencia *nf*
ambition	ambición *nf*
austerity	austeridad *nf*
conformity	conformidad *nf*
eccentricity	excentricidad *nf*
eclecticism	eclecticismo *nm*
frugality	frugalidad *nf*
inflexibility	inflexibilidad *nf*
innocence	inocencia *nf*
intellectualism	intelectualismo *nm*

intrepidity	intrepidez *nf*
introspection	introspección *nf*
lenience, leniency	lenidad *nf*
liberality	liberalidad *nf*
nonconformity	disconformidad *nf*
normalcy, normality	normalidad *nf*
permissiveness	permisividad *nf*
propensity	propensión *nf*
reserve	reserva *nf*
sentimentalism	sentimentalismo *nm*
suggestibility	sugestibilidad *nf*
temerity	temeridad *nf*

(*See also* **PSYCHOLOGY**)

SENSE IMPRESSIONS

GENERAL TERMS

acuity	acuidad *nf*
audible	audible *aj*
auditory	auditivo *aj*
discernment	discernimiento *nm*
discriminate	discriminar *vt*
distinguish	distinguir *vti*
emotion	emoción *nf*
olfactory	olfatorio *aj*
palate	paladar *nm*
perception	percepción *nf*
sensation	sensación *nf*
sensory	sensorial, sensorio *aj*
sensual, sensuous	sensual *aj*
sentiment	sentimiento *nm*
sound	son, sonido *nm*
tactile	táctil *aj*
touch	toque *nm*
vision	visión, vista *nf*
visual	visual *aj*

THE SENSE OF VISION

common light sources

candle	candela *nf*
lamp	lámpara *nf*
lantern	linterna *nf*
neon	neón *nm*
torch	antorcha *nf*

light associations

brilliant	brillante *aj*
clear	claro *aj*
incandescent	incandescente *aj*
invisible	invisible *aj*
iridescent	iridescente, irisado *aj*

lucid	lúcido *aj*
luminescent	luminescente *aj*
luminous	luminoso *aj*
opalescent	opalescente *aj*
opaque	opaco *aj*
phosphorescent	fosforescente *aj*
visible	visible *aj*

pleasant sights

art	arte *nf(el)*
decoration	decoración *nf*
garden	jardín *nm*
panorama	panorama *nm*
scene	escena *nf*
spectacle	espectáculo *nm*
splendor	esplendidez, esplendor *nf, nm*
vista	vista *nf*

unpleasant sights

chaos	caos *nm*
commotion	conmoción *nf*
disorder	desorden *nm*
monstrosity	monstruosidad *nf*
sordidness	sordidez *nf*
squalor	escualidez *nf*

other terms

appearance	aparición *nf*
color	color *nm*
evanescent	evanescente *aj*
illumination	iluminación *nf*
illusion	ilusión *nf*
luster	lustre *nm*
obscure	oscuro *aj*
reflection	reflejo *nm*
semitransparent	semitransparente *aj*
silhouette	silueta *nf*
translucent	tra(n)slúcido *aj*
transparent	tra(n)sparente *aj*

THE SENSE OF HEARING

pleasant sounds

euphonious	eufónico *aj*
harmonious	armonioso *aj*
mellifluous	melifluo *aj*
melodious	melodioso *aj*
murmur	murmullo *nm*
musical	musical *aj*
resonant	resonante *aj*
sonorous	sonoro *aj*

unpleasant sounds

alarm	alarma *nf*
cacophony	cacofonía *nf*
clamor	clamor *nm*
crack	crac *nm*
pandemonium	pandemonio, pandemónium *nm*
rasping	raspadura *nf*
stentorian	estentóreo *aj*
strident	estridente *aj*

imitative sounds

choo-choo	chu-cu-chu(ca) *nm*
click	clic *nm*
ding dong	din don *nm*
echo	eco *nm*
ticktock	tictac *nm*
tintinabulation	tintineo *nm*

other terms

acoustic(al)	acústico *aj*
inaudible	inaudible *aj*
megaphone	megáfono *nm*
repercussion	repercusión *nf*
reverberation	reverberación, reverbero *nf, nm*
silence	silencio *nm*
sound	sonar *vi*
subsonic	subsónico *aj*
supersonic	supersónico *aj*
tone	tono *nm*
tumult	tumulto *nm*
tumultuous	tumultuoso *aj*
ululate	ulular *vi*
voice	voz *nf*

THE SENSE OF TOUCH

kinds of touch

breeze	brisa *nf*
caress	caricia *nf*
embrace	abrazo *nm*
gummy	gomoso *aj*
manipulation	manipulación, manipuleo *nf, nm*
palpation	palpación *nf*

other terms

balm	bálsamo *nm*
mastic	mástique *nm*
mucilage	mucílago *nm*
tangible	tangible *aj*
voluptuous	voluptuoso *aj*

THE SENSE OF SMELL

pleasant

aroma	aroma *nm*
bouquet	bouquet, buqué *nm*
essence	esencia *nf*
fragrance	fragancia *nf*
perfume	perfume *nm*
potpourri	popurrí *nm*
sandalwood	sándalo *nm*
tuberose	tuberosa *nf*
violet	violeta *nf*

unpleasant

acrid	acre *aj*
fetid, foetid	fétido *aj*
fetidness	fetidez *nf*
nauseating	nauseabundo *aj*
putrid	pútrido, putrefacto *aj*
rancid	rancio *aj*

other terms

deodorant	desodorante *nm*
odor	olor *nm*
pungent	pungente *aj*

GENERAL PHYSICAL SENSATIONS

agility	agilidad *nf*
comfort	confort *nm*
energetic	enérgico *aj*
inactivity	inactividad *nf*
languid	lánguido *aj*
languor	languidez *nf*
lassitude	lasitud *nf*
lethargy	letargo, aletargamiento *nm*
phlegmatic	flemático *aj*
relaxation	relajación *nf*
robustness	robustez *nf*
sensuousness	sensualidad *nf*
stress	estrés *nm*
stupefaction	estupefacción *nf*
stupor	estupor *nm*
tension	tensión *nf*
trembling	temblor *nm*
vigor	vigor *nm*
vitality	vitalidad *nf*
vivacity	vivacidad, viveza *nf*

(*See also* **tastes**, **textures**, **quality**, under **FOOD AND NUTRITION**; *TERMS IN WAVE PHYSICS* under **PHYSICS**; *PHYSIOLOGY* under **THE HUMAN BODY**)

ACTIONS AND ACTORS

DESIRABLE

adaptable	adaptable *aj*
admirable	admirable *aj*
adorable	adorable *aj*
adventurous	aventurero *aj*
agreeable	agradable *aj*
altruistic	altruista *aj*
ambitious	ambicioso *aj*
amiable	amable *aj*
amicable	amigable *aj*
attentive	atento *aj*
attractive	atractivo, atrayente *aj*
benevolent	benévolo *aj*
calm	calmo *aj*
capricious	caprichoso *aj*
captivating	cautivador *aj*
cautious	cauteloso, cauto *aj*
charitable	caritativo *aj*
communicative	comunicativo *aj*
compassionate	compasivo *aj*
competent	competente *aj*
conciliatory	conciliador *aj*
conscientious	concienzudo *aj*
considerate	considerado *aj*
cooperative	cooperativo *aj*
cordial	cordial *aj*
cosmopolitan	cosmopolita *aj*
courteous	cortés *aj*
creative	creativo *aj*
credible	creíble *aj*
cultivated, cultured	culto *aj*
curious	curioso *aj*
decent	decente *aj*
deferential	deferente *aj*
deliberate	deliberado *aj*
devoted	devoto *aj*
dignified	digno *aj*
diligent	diligente *aj*
diplomatic	diplomático *aj*
discreet	discreto *aj*
distinguished	distinguido *aj*
dynamic	dinámico *aj*
efficient	eficiente *aj*
elegant	elegante *aj*
enchanting	encantador *aj*
experienced	experimentado *aj*
expert	experto, -a *aj, nmf*
faithful	fiel *aj*
fascinating	fascinador, fascinante *aj*
flexible	flexible *aj*
gallant	galante *aj*

generous	generoso *aj*
grateful	agradecido *aj*
gregarious	gregario *aj*
heroic	heroico *aj*
honest	honesto, honrado *aj*
honorable	honorable, honrado *aj*
hospitable	hospitalario *aj*
humane	humano *aj*
humanitarian	humanitario *aj*
humble	humilde *aj*
humorous	humorístico *aj*
idealistic	idealista *aj*
illustrious	ilustre *aj*
imaginative	imaginativo *aj*
impartial	imparcial *aj*
incorruptible	incorruptible *aj*
indefatigable	infatigable *aj*
indulgent	indulgente *aj*
influential	influyente *aj*
informed	informado *aj*
ingratiating	congraciador *aj*
innovative	innovador *aj*
inquisitive (mind)	inquisitivo *aj*
intellectual	intelectual *aj*
intelligent	inteligente *aj*
interested	interesado *aj*
intrepid	intrépido *aj*
intuitive	intuitivo *aj*
inventive	inventivo aj
irreproachable	irreprochable aj
just	justo aj
laudable	laudable aj
laudatory	laudatorio aj
logical	lógico aj
loyal	leal aj
magnanimous	magnánimo aj
methodical	metódico aj
meticulous	meticuloso aj
model	modelo aj
modest	modesto aj
moral	moral aj
motivated	motivado aj
munificent	munificente, munífico aj
noble	noble aj
normal	normal aj
obedient	obediente aj
objective	objetivo aj
observant	observador aj
passionate	apasionado aj
patient	paciente aj
peaceful	pacífico aj
permissive	permisivo aj

perspicacious	perspicaz aj
persuasive	persuasivo aj
philanthropic	filantrópico aj
philosophical	filosófico aj
placid	plácido aj
pleasant, pleasing	placentero aj
precocious	precoz aj
presentable	presentable aj
prestigious	prestigioso aj
prudent	prudente aj
punctilious	puntilloso aj
quixotic	quijotesco aj
rational	racional aj
reasonable	razonable aj
receptive	receptivo aj
refined	refinado aj
reflective	reflexivo aj
respectful	respetuoso aj
responsible	responsable aj
reverent	reverente aj
romantic	romántico, -a aj, nmf
sagacious	sagaz aj
scrupulous	escrupuloso aj
selective	selectivo aj
self-directed	autodirigido aj
self-sufficient	autosuficiente aj
serene	sereno aj
serious	serio *aj*
sociable	sociable *aj*
solicitous	solícito *aj*
spontaneous	espontáneo *aj*
stable	estable *aj*
stimulating	estimulante *aj*
tactful *aj*	de mucho tacto *nm*
tolerant	tolerante *aj*
tranquil	tranquilo *aj*
unconventional	poco convencional *aj*
unpretentious *aj*	sin pretenciones *nfpl*
urbane	urbano *aj*
valiant	valiente *aj*
valorous	valeroso *aj*
versed	versado *aj*
vigilant	vigilante *aj*
virtuous	virtuoso *aj*

UNDESIRABLE

aberrant	aberrante *aj*
abhorrent	aborrecible *aj*
abnormal	anormal *aj*
absurd	absurdo *aj*
affected	afectado *aj*
aggressive	agresivo *aj*
alarming	alarmante *aj*

antisocial	antisocial *aj*
atrocious	atroz *aj*
audacious	audaz *aj*
belligerent	beligerante *aj*
boring	aburrido, aburridor *aj*
brusque	brusco *aj*
brutal, brutish	brutal *aj*
calculating	calculador *aj*
compulsive	compulsivo *aj*
condescending	condescendiente *aj*
contumacious	contumaz *aj*
conventional	convencional *aj*
corrupt	corrupto, corrompido *aj*
counterproductive	contraproducente *aj*
cowardly	cobarde *aj*
crass	craso *aj*
criminal	criminal *aj, nmf*
critical	crítico *aj*
cruel	cruel *aj*
cynical	cínico *aj*
decadent	decadente *aj*
defiant	desafiante *aj*
degenerate	degenerado, -a *aj, nmf*
denigrating	denigrante *aj*
deplorable	deplorable *aj*
depraved	depravado *aj*
destructive	destructor *aj*
detestable	detestable *aj*
diabolic(al)	diabólico *aj*
dictatorial	dictatorial *aj*
disagreeable	desagradable *aj*
disciplined	disciplinado *aj*
discourteous	descortés *aj*
disdainful	desdeñoso *aj*
dishonorable	deshonroso *aj*
disloyal	desleal *aj*
disobedient	desobediente *aj*
disorganized	desorganizado *aj*
disrespectful	irrespetuoso *aj*
dissolute	disoluto *aj*
docile	dócil *aj*
dogmatic	dogmático *aj*
domineering	dominante *aj*
eccentric	excéntrico, -a *aj, nmf*
effusive	efusivo *aj*
egocentric	egocéntrico *aj*
egoistic(al), egotistic(al)	egoísta, egotista *aj*
exasperating	exasperante *aj*
extravagant	extravagante *aj*
extremist	extremista *aj, nmf*
false	falso *aj*
flagrant	flagrante *aj*

frenetic	frenético *aj*
frivolous	frívolo *aj*
frugal	frugal *aj*
furtive	furtivo *aj*
gluttonous	glotón *aj*
horrendous	horrendo *aj*
horrible	horrible *aj*
hostile	hostil *aj*
humorless *aj*	sin sentido del humor *nm*
hypercritical	hipercrítico *aj*
hypocritical	hipócrita *aj*
ignoble	innoble *aj*
ignominious	ignominioso *aj*
ignorant	ignorante *aj*
illogical	ilógico *aj*
immature	inmaduro *aj*
immoderate	inmoderado *aj*
immodest	inmodesto *aj*
immoral	inmoral *aj*
imperious	imperioso *aj*
impertinent	impertinente *aj*
impetuous	impetuoso *aj*
impractical	impráctico *aj*
improper	impropio *aj*
imprudent	imprudente *aj*
impulsive	impulsivo *aj*
inane	inano *aj*
incapable	incapaz *aj*
incautious	incauto *aj*
incompetent	incompetente *aj*
inconsiderate	desconsiderado *aj*
inconsistent	inconsistente *aj*
incorrigible	incorregible *aj*
indecent	indecente *aj*
indefensible	indefendible *aj*
indelicate	indelicado *aj*
indiscreet	indiscreto *aj*
indolent	indolente *aj*
indomitable	indomable, indómito *aj*
inefficient	ineficaz *aj*
inept	inepto *aj*
inexcusable	inexcusable *aj*
infantile	infantil *aj*
ingenuous	ingenuo *aj*
inhibited	inhibido *aj*
inhospitable	inhospitalario *aj*
inhumane	inhumano *aj*
iniquitous	inicuo *aj*
insatiable	insaciable *aj*
insecure	inseguro *aj*
insidious	insidioso *aj*
insincere	insincero *aj*

insolent	insolente *aj*	pugnacious	pugnaz *aj*
insubordinate	insubordinado *aj*	puritanical	puritano *aj*
insufferable	insufrible *aj*	pusillanimous	pusilánime *aj*
insulting	insultante *aj*	questionable	cuestionable *aj*
intolerable	intolerable *aj*	racist	racista *aj, nmf*
intolerant	intolerante *aj*	rancorous	rencoroso *aj*
intractable	intratable *aj*	rapacious	rapaz *aj*
intransigent	intransigente *aj*	rebellious	rebelde *aj*
irrational	irracional *aj*	repellent	repelente *aj*
irresponsible	irresponsable *aj*	reprehensible	reprensible *aj*
irritable	irritable *aj*	reproachful	reprobador *aj*
irritating	irritante *aj*	repugnant	repugnante *aj*
lascivious	lascivo *aj*	repulsive	repulsivo *aj*
malevolent	malévolo *aj*	reserved	reservado *aj*
malicious	malicioso *aj*	reticent	reticente *aj*
manipulative	manipulador *aj*	ridiculous	ridículo *aj*
mannered	amanerado *aj*	rigid	rígido *aj*
masochistic	masoquista *aj*	sadistic	sádico *aj*
materialistic	materialista *aj*	sanctimonious	santurrón *aj*
menacing	amenazador *aj*	sarcastic	sarcástico *aj*
moralizing	moralizador *aj*	sardonic	sardónico *aj*
morbid	mórbido *aj*	satanic	satánico *aj*
nefarious	nefario *aj*	savage	salvaje *aj, nmf*
neurotic	neurótico, -a *aj, nmf*	scandalous	escandaloso *aj*
objectionable	objetable *aj*	self-destructive	autodestructor *aj*
obsequious	obsequioso *aj*	senseless	insensato *aj*
obsessive	obsesivo *aj*	servile	servil *aj*
obstinate	obstinado *aj*	sexist	sexista *aj, nmf*
odious	odioso *aj*	shocking	chocante *aj*
offensive	ofensivo *aj*	simplistic	simplista *aj*
officious	oficioso *aj*	sinister	siniestro *aj*
opprobious	oprobioso *aj*	snobbish	esnobista *aj*
ostentatious	ostentoso *aj*	solitary	solitario *aj*
otiose	ocioso *aj*	strange	extraño *aj*
overcritical	criticón *aj*	strict	estricto *aj*
parasitic	parásito *aj*	stupid	estúpido *aj*
parsimonious	parsimonioso *aj*	submissive	sumiso *aj*
partial	parcial *aj*	subnormal	subnormal *aj*
passionless	poco apasionado *aj*	subversive	subversivo, -a *aj, nmf*
pedantic	pedante, pedantesco *aj*	superficial	superficial *aj*
pedestrian	pedestre *aj*	surreptitious	subrepticio *aj*
perfidious	pérfido *aj*	suspicious	sospechoso *aj*
persistent	persistente *aj*	tactless	falto de tacto *aj, nm*
perverse	perverso *aj*	timid	tímido *aj*
pessimistic	pesimista *aj*	tormenting	atormentador *aj*
pitiless	despiadado *aj*	tyrannical	tiránico, tirano *aj*
pompous	pomposo *aj*	ultraconservative	ultraconservador(a) *aj, nmf*
possessive	posesivo *aj*		
pretentious	pretencioso *aj*	unacceptable	inaceptable *aj*
promiscuous	promiscuo *aj*	unceremonious	inceremonioso *aj*
provincial	provincial *aj*	uncivil	incivil *aj*
provocative	provocador *aj*	uncivilized	incivilizado *aj*
puerile	pueril *aj*	uncontrollable	incontrolable *aj*

uncultured	inculto *aj*
uncuous	untuoso *aj*
undesirable	indeseable *aj*
undisciplined	indisciplinado *aj*
uneducated	ineducado *aj*
ungovernable	ingobernable *aj*
ungrateful	ingrato *aj*
unimaginative	poco imaginativo *aj*
unintelligent	ininteligente *aj*
unjust	unjusto *aj*
unlettered	iletrado *aj*
unpardonable	imperdonable *aj*
unscrupulous	inescrupuloso *aj*
unsociable	insociable *aj*
unsocial	insocial *aj*
unsportsmanlike	antideportivo *aj*
vacuous	vacuo *aj*
vain	vanidoso *aj*
vainglorious	vanaglorioso *aj*
vengeful	vengativo *aj*
vicious	vicioso *aj*
vile	vil *aj*
villainous	villano *aj*
vindictive	vindicativo *aj*
violent	violento *aj*

(*See also* **ROLES AND RELATIONSHIPS**)

EXPERIENCES

BENEFICIAL

acclaim	aclamación *nf*
accolade	acolada *nf*
admiration	admiración *nf*
adulation	adulación *nf*
advantage	ventaja *nf*
affection	afecto *nm*
amenity	amenidad *nf*
applause	aplauso *nm*
approbation	aprobación *nf*
approval	aprobación *nf*
assent	asentimiento, asenso *nm*
benefit	beneficio *nm*
caprice	capricho *nm*
celebrity	celebridad *nmf*
compliment	cumplido *nm*
cooperation	cooperación *nf*
eminence	eminencia *nf*
encomium	encomio *nm*
esteem	estima *nf*
eulogy	elogio *nm*
fame	fama *nf*
glamour, glamor	glamour *nm*

homage	homenaje *nm*
honors	honores *nmpl*
laurels	laureles *nmpf*
popularity	popularidad *nf*
prestige	prestigio *nm*
recognition	reconocimiento *nm*
recommendation	recomendación *nf*
reconciliation	reconciliación *nf*
renown	renombre *nm*
respect	respeto *nm*
tribute	tributo *nm*
veneration	veneración *nf*

HARMFUL

abuse	abuso *nm*
accident	accidente *nm*
adversity	adversidad *nf*
affront	afrenta *nf*
altercation	altercado *nm*
calamity	calamidad *nf*
confinement	confinamiento *nm*
confrontation	confrontación *nf*
connivance	connivencia *nf*
debacle	debacle *nf*
defamation	difamación *nf*
degradation	degradación *nf*
demoralization	desmoralización *nf*
denigration	denigración *nf*
deprivation	privación *nf*
deterioration	deterioro *nm*
detriment	detrimento *nm*
difficulty	dificultad *nf*
dilemma	dilema *nm*
disadvantage	desventaja *nf*
disapproval	desaprobación *nf*
discord	discordia *nf*
discredit	descrédito *nm*
discrimination	discriminación *nf*
disfigurement	desfiguración *nf*
dishonor	deshonra *nf*
disillusion	desilusión *nf*
disorganization	desorganización *nf*
dispossession	desposeimiento *nm*
dispute	disputa *nf*
disservice	deservicio *nm*
domination	dominación *nf*
enslavement	esclavización *nf*
expropriation	expropiación *nf*
falsification	falsificación *nf*
favoritism	favoritismo *nm*
fiasco	fiasco *nm*
furor	furor *nm*
ignominy	ignominia *nf*

inconvenience	inconveniente *nm*
indignity	indignidad *nf*
indoctrination	adoctrinamiento *nm*
inequity	inequidad *nf*
infamy	infamia *nf*
iniquity	iniquidad *nf*
injustice	injusticia *nf*
insistence	insistencia *nf*
intrusion	intrusión *nf*
lamentation	lamentación *nf*
limitation	limitación *nf*
machination	maquinación *nf*
maltreatment	maltrato, maltratamiento *nm*
menace	amenaza *nf*
misfortune	infortunio *nm*
mistreatment	maltrato *nm*
mutilation	mutilación *nf*
neglect, negligence	negligencia *nf*
obscurity	o(b)scuridad *nf*
obsession	obsesión *nf*
oppression	opresión *nf*
opprobium	oprobio *nm*
ostracism	ostracismo *nm*
palliative	paliativo *nm*
paperwork	papeleo *nm*
perfidy	perfidia *nf*
persecution	persecución *nf*
prejudice	prejuicio *nm*
preoccupation (worry)	preocupación *nf*
pretext	pretexto *nm*
protestation	protestación *nf*
reprimand	reprimenda *nf*
reproach	reproche *nm*
repudiation	repudiación, repudio *nf, nm*
restriction	restricción *nf*
ridicule	ridículo *nm*
ruin	ruina *nf*
scandal	escándalo *nm*
servitude	servidumbre *nf*
stigma	estigma *nm*
subjugation	subyugación *nf*
subterfuge	subterfugio *nm*
suffering	sufrimiento *nm*
suppression	supresión *nf*
suspicion	sospecha *nf*
temptation	tentación *nf*
tribulation	tribulación *nf*
ultimatum	ultimátum *nm*
unpopularity	impopularidad *nf*

(*See also* CULTURAL ANTHROPOLOGY under **ANTHROPOLOGY**)

Forms of Address

PERSONAL NAMES

FEMININE NAMES

Biblical origin

Deborah	Debora *nf*
Esther	Éster *nf*
Eve	Eva *nf*
Josephine	Josefa *nf*
Judith	Judit *nf*
Mary	María *nf*
Rachel	Raquel *nf*
Ruth	Rut *nf*
Sarah	Sara *nf*

Greek or Latin origin

Alexandra	Alejandra *nf*
Barbara	Bárbara *nf*
Beatrice	Beatriz *nf*
Catherine	Catalina *nf*
Cecily	Cecilia *nf*
Clara	Clara *nf*
Clementine	Clementina *nf*
Constance	Constanza *nf*
Daphne	Dafne *nf*
Diana	Diana *nf*
Dorothy	Dorotea *nf*
Ellen	Elena *nf*
Emily	Emilia *nf*
Florence	Florencia *nf*
Gloria	Gloria *nf*
Helen	Helena *nf*
Inez	Inés *nf*
Irene	Irena *nf*
Julia	Julia *nf*
Juliana	Juliana *nf*
Juliet	Julieta *nf*
Lucy	Lucía *nf*
Madeline	Magdalena *nf*
Margaret	Margarita *nf*
Patricia	Patricia *nf*
Pauline	Paulina *nf*
Regina	Regina *nf*
Rose	Rosa *nf*
Sophia	Sofía *nf*
Theresa	Teresa *nf*
Veronica	Verónica *nf*
Victoria	Victoria *nf*
Virginia	Virginia *nf*

Germanic origin

Adele	Adela *nf*
Alice	Alicia *nf*
Amelia	Amalia *nf*
Bridgit	Brígida *nf*
Caroline	Carolina *nf*
Edith	Edita *nf*
Ernestine	Ernestina *nf*
Frances	Francisca *nf*
Frieda	Frida *nf*
Gertrude	Gertrudís *nf*
Henrietta	Enriqueta *nf*
Louise	Luisa *nf*
Matilda	Matilde *nf*

other origins

Ann, Anne, Anna	Ana *nf*
Bernadette	Bernarda *nf*
Charlotte	Carlota *nf*
Christine	Cristina *nf*
Elizabeth	Isabela *nf*
Isabella	Isabel *nf*
Joan	Juana *nf*
Leonore	Leonora *nf*
Lorraine	Lorena *nf*
Martha	Marta *nf*
Rosalind	Rosalinda *nf*
Susan	Susana *nf*

MASCULINE NAMES

Biblical origin

Aaron	Arón *nm*
Abraham	Abrahán *nm*
Adam	Adán *nm*
Benjamin	Benjamín *nm*
Daniel	Daniel *nm*
David	David *nm*
Emmanuel, Imanuel	Emanuel, Imanuel *nm*
Ezekiel	Ezequiel *nm*
Ezra	Esdras *nm*
Gabriel	Gabriel *nm*
Isaac	Isaac *nm*
Jacob	Jacobo *nm*
James	Jaime *nm*
John	Juan *nm*
Joseph	José *nm*
Joshua	Josué *nm*
Luke	Lucas *nm*
Mark	Marcos *nm*
Matthew	Mateo *nm*
Michael	Miguel *nm*
Nathan	Natán *nm*

Noah	Noé *nm*
Paul	Pablo *nm*
Peter	Pedro *nm*
Raphael	Rafael *nm*
Samuel	Samuel *nm*
Saul	Saúl *nm*
Simon	Simón *nm*
Solomon	Salomón *nm*
Thomas	Tomás *nm*
Timothy	Timoteo *nm*

Greek or Latin origin

Alexander	Alejandro *nm*
Ambrose	Ambrosio *nm*
Andrew	Andrés *nm*
Anthony	Antonio *nm*
Bartholomew	Bartolomé *nm*
Benedict	Benito *nm*
Cecil	Cecilio *nm*
Christopher	Cristóbal *nm*
Claud, Claude	Claudio *nm*
Clement	Clemente *nm*
Dennis	Dionisio *nm*
Emil	Emilio *nm*
Eugene	Eugenio *nm*
George	Jorge *nm*
Giles	Gil *nm*
Gregory	Gregorio *nm*
Hadrian	Adriano *nm*
Horace	Horacio *nm*
Ignatius	Ignacio *nm*
Jerome	Jerónimo *nm*
Julian	Julián *nm*
Julius	Julio *nm*
Laurence, Lawrence	Lorenzo *nm*
Leo	Leo *nm*
Leonard	Leonardo *nm*
Lucius	Lucio *nm*
Marcus	Marcos *nm*
Martin	Martín *nm*
Nicholas	Nicolás *nm*
Patrick	Patricio *nm*
Philip	Felipe *nm*
Stephen	Esteban *nm*
Theodore	Teodoro *nm*
Victor	Victor *nm*
Vincent	Vicente *nm*

Germanic origin

Adolf	Adolfo *nm*
Albert	Alberto *nm*
Alphonso	Alfonso *nm*
Bernard	Bernardo *nm*

Charles	Carlos *nm*
Ernest	Ernesto *nm*
Ferdinand	Fernando *nm*
Francis	Francisco *nm*
Frederick	Federico *nm*
Gerald	Geraldo *nm*
Gerard	Gerardo *nm*
Godfrey	Godofredo *nm*
Harold	Haroldo *nm*
Henry	Enrique *nm*
Lewis, Louis	Luis *nm*
Ralph	Raúl *nm*
Raymond	Ramón, Raimundo *nm*
Reginald	Reginaldo *nm*
Richard	Ricardo *nm*
Robert	Roberto *nm*
Rudolph	Rudolfo *nm*
Walter	Gualterio *nm*
William	Guillermo *nm*

other origins

Adrian	Adriano *nm*
Alan	Alano *nm*
Alfred	Alfredo *nm*
Arthur	Arturo *nm*
Augustine	Agustín *nm*
Calvin	Calvino *nm*
Edward	Eduardo *nm*
Ellis	Elías *nm*
Herbert	Herberto *nm*
Hugh	Hugo *nm*
Maurice	Moricio *nm*
Oliver	Oliverio *nm*
Stanley	Estanislao *nm*

RELATED TERMS

alias	alias *av, nm*
anonymity	anonimato *nm*
autograph	autógrafo *nm*
eponym	epónimo *nm*
family name	nombre de familia *nm, nf*
fictitious name	nombre ficticio *nm*
first name	nombre de pila *nm*
identity	identidad *nf*
incognito	incógnito *aj, av*
nom de plume	nombre de pluma *nm, nf*
onomastics	onomástica *nf*
patronymic	patronímico *nm*
pseudonym	(p)seudónimo *nm*

(*See also* **THE BIBLE**; **HISTORY**; **RELIGION**)

TITLES

GENERAL TERMS

designation	designación *nf*
domain	dominio *nm*
honorific	honorífico *aj*
rank	rango *nm*
title	título *nm*

KINDS OF TITLES

political

ambassador	embajador(a) *nmf*
Chancellor	canciller *nm*
congressman	congresista *nm*
congresswoman	congresista *nf*
consul	cónsul *nm*
emir	emir *nm*
emperor	emperador *nm*
empress	emperatriz *nf*
Excellency	Excelencia *nmf*
governor	gobernador(a) *nmf*
khan	kan *nm*
minister	ministro, -a *nmf*
premier	primer ministro *nmf*
president	presidente *nmf*
prime minister	primer ministro *nm*
prime minister	primera ministra *nf*
regent	regente *nmf*
secretary	secretario, -a *nmf*
senator	senador(a) *nmf*
sultan	sultán *nm*
sultana	sultana *nf*
vice-president	vicepresidente *nmf*

royal

archduchess	archiduquesa *nf*
archduke	archiduque *nm*
baron	barón *nm*
baroness	baronesa *nf*
baronet	baronet *nm*
count	conde *nm*
countess	condesa *nf*
duchess	duquesa *nf*
duke	duque *nm*
Lord	lord *nm*
Majesty	Majestad *nmf*
marquis	marqués *nm*
marquise	marquesa *nf*
noble, nobleman	noble *nm*
noble, noblewoman	noble *nf*
peer	par *nmf*

peeress   paresa *nf*
prince   príncipe *nm*
princess   princesa *nf*
raja(h)   rajá *nm*
rani   rani *nf*
sheik(h)   jeque *nm*

professional

counselor   consejero, -a *nmf*
doctor   doctor(a) *nmf*
emeritus   emérito *aj*
professor   profesor(a) *nmf*

other titles

chamberlain   chambelán *nm*
comrade   camarada *nf*
dame   dama *nf*
majordomo   mayordomo *nm*

OFFICES, RANKS, DOMAINS

ambassadorship   embajada *nf*
barony   baronía *nf*
caliphate   califato *nm*
captaincy   capitanía *nf*
chancellery   cancillería *nf*
commissariat   comisariato *nm*
consulship   consulado *nm*
duchy   ducado *aj*
dukedom   ducado *aj*
emirate   emirato *nm*
empire   imperio *nm*
generalship   generalato *nm*
governorship   gobierno *nm*
khanate   kanato *nm*
ministry   ministerio *nm*
peerage   paría *nf*
presidency   presidencia *nf*
princedom   principado *nm*
professorship   profesorado *nm*
rabbinate   rabinato *nm*
regency   regencia *nf*
secretariat   secretaría *nf*
senatorship   senaduría *nf*
sergeancy   sargentía *nf*
sheikdom   principado de jeque *nm*
sultanate   sultanato *nm*
vice-presidency   vicepresidencia *nmf*

(*See also PERSONS* under **LAW**; *PERSONS* under
RELIGION; *PERSONS* under **THE MILITARY
ESTABLISHMENT**)

ROLES AND RELATIONSHIPS

GENERAL TERMS

companionship   compañerismo *nm*
company   compañía *nf*
comradeship   camaradería *nf*
individual   individuo *nm*
personality   personalidad *nf*
relationship   relación *nf*
role, rôle   rol *nm*

RELATIONSHIPS

friendly

admirer   admirador(a) *nmf*
ally   aliado, -a *nmf*
associate   asociado, -a *nmf*
benefactor   benefactor(a) *nmf*
collaborator   colaborador(a) *nmf*
colleague   colega *nmf*
companion   compañero, -a *nmf*
comrade   camarada *nmf*
confidant   confidente *nmf*
consoler   consolador(a) *nmf*
disciple   discípulo, -a *nmf*
emulator   emulador(a) *nmf*
fan   fan *nmf*
liberator   liberador, libertador *nm*
protector   protector(a) *nmf*
protégé(e)   protegido, -a *nmf*
provider   proveedor(a) *nmf*
receiver   recibidor(a) *nmf*
recipient   receptor(a) *nmf*
redeemer   redentor(a) *nmf*
spouse   esposo, -a *nmf*
sympathizer   simpatizante *nmf*
visitor   visitante *nmf*

unfriendly

accuser   acusador(a) *nmf*
adversary   adversario, -a *nmf*
antagonist   antagonista *nmf*
attacker   atacante *nmf*
avenger   vengador(a) *nmf*
competitor   competidor(a) *nmf*
contender   contendiente *nmf*
critic   crítico, -a *nmf*
defamer   difamador(a) *nmf*
denigrator   denigrador(a),
                 denigrante *nmf*
detractor   detractor(a) *nmf*
enemy   enemigo, -a *nmf*
exploiter   explotador(a) *nmf*

expropriator	expropiador(a) *nmf*
flagellator	flagelador(a) *nmf*
manipulator	manipulador(a) *nmf*
opponent	oponente *nmf*
oppressor	opresor(a) *nmf*
persecutor	perseguidor(a) *nmf*
rival	rival *nmf*
tormenter, tormentor	atormentador(a) *nmf*
victim	víctima *nf*

same status

double	doble *nmf*
equal	igual *nmf*
peer	par *nmf*
substitute	sustituto, -a *nmf*

ROLES

peacemakers

arbitrator	árbitro, -a *nmf*
conciliator	conciliador(a) *nmf*
coordinator	coordinador(a) *nmf*
intermediary	intermediario, -a *nmf*
judge	juez *nmf*
mediator	mediador(a) *nmf*
moderator	moderador, -a *nmf*
negotiator	negociador(a) *nmf*
pacifier	pacificador(a) *nmf*

trouble-makers

agitator	agitador(a) *nmf*
alarmist	alarmista *nmf*
instigator	instigador(a) *nmf*
intruder	intruso, -a *nmf*
malcontent	malcontento, -a *nmf*
obstructionist	obstruccionista *nmf*
rebel	rebelde *nmf*
renegade	renegado, -a *nmf*
subversive	subversivo, -a *nmf*
traitor	traidor(a) *nmf*

advisers

counselor	consejero, -a *nmf*
guide	guía *nmf*
instructor	instructor(a) *nmf*
leader	líder *nm*
mentor	mentor(a) *nmf*
monitor	monitor(a) *nmf*
trainer	entrenador(a) *nmf*
tutor	tutor(a) *nmf*

jokesters

buffoon	bufón *nm*
comedian	comediante *nmf*

comedienne	comedianta *nf*
comic	cómico, -a *nmf*
humorist	humorista *nmf*
master of ceremonies	maestro de ceremonias *nm, nfpl*
parodist	parodista *nmf*

thinkers

analyzer	analizador(a) *nmf*
genius	genio *nm*
intellectual	intelectual *nmf*
pragmatist	pragmatista *nmf*
prodigy	prodigio *nm*
rationalist	racionalista *nmf*
skeptic	escéptico, -a *nmf*
strategist	estratega *nmf*
visionary	visionario, -a *nmf*

doers

adventurer	aventurero, -a *nmf*
creator	creador(a) *nmf*
designer	diseñador(a) *nmf*
initiator	iniciador(a) *nmf*
innovator	innovador(a) *nmf*
inventor	inventor(a) *nmf*
organizer	organizador(a) *nmf*
originator	originador(a) *nmf*
pioneer	pionero, -a *nmf*
planner	planificador(a) *nmf*
producer	productor(a) *nmf*

givers

altruist	altruista *nmf*
contributor	contribuyente *nmf*
donor	donador(a), donante *nmf*
humanitarian	humanitario, -a *nmf*
philanthropist	filántropo, -a *nmf*
volunteer	voluntario, -a *nmf*

mavericks

disputant, disputer	disputador(a) *nmf*
dissident, dissenter	disidente *nmf*
independent	independiente *nmf*
individualist	individualista *nmf*
nonconformist	anticonformista *nmf*
objector	objetor(a) *nmf*
revolutionary	revolucinario, -a *nmf*

advocates

activist	activista *nmf*
apologist	apologista *nmf*
champion	campeón, -ona *nmf*
defender	defensor(a) *nmf*

enthusiast	entusiasta *nmf*
partisan	partidario, -a *nmf*
patron	patrocinador(a) *nmf*
promoter	promotor(a) *nmf*
propagandist	propagandista *nmf*

PERSONALITY TYPES

eccentric

bohemian	bohemio, -a *nmf*
eccentric	excéntrico, -a *nmf*
eclectic	ecléctico, -a *nmf*
fanatic	fanático, -a *nmf*
hermit	ermitaño, -a *nmf*

haters

homophobe	homofóbo, -a *nmf*
misanthrope	misántropo, -a *nmf*
misogynist	misógino *nm*
neo-Nazi	neonazi *nmf*
racist	racista *nmf*
supremacist	supremacista *nmf*
xenophobe	xenófobo, -a *nmf*

pleasure-seekers

aesthete, esthete	esteta *nmf*
connoisseur	conocedor(a) *nmf*
cosmopolitan, cosmopolite	cosmopolita *nmf*
epicure	epicúreo, -a *nmf*
esthete, aesthete	esteta *nmf*
gourmet	gourmet *nmf*
hedonist	hedonista *nmf*
libertine	libertino, -a *nmf*
sensualist	sensualista *nmf*
sybarite	sibarita *nmf*
voluptuary	voluptuoso, -a *nmf*

self-centered

egotist	egotista *nmf*
exhibitionist	exhibicionista *nmf*
megalomaniac	megalómano, -a *nmf*
opportunist	oportunista *nmf*

bullies

brute	bruto, -a *nmf*
masochist	masoquista *nmf*
mutilator	mutilador(a) *nmf*
opressor	opresor(a) *nmf*
ruffian	rufián *nm*
sadist	sádico, -a *nmf*
savage	salvaje *nmf*

vandal	vándalo, -a *nmf*
villain	villano, -a *nmf*

narrow-minded

chauvinist	chovinista *nmf*
dogmatist	dogmatista *nmf*
extremist	extremista *nmf*
ideologue	ideólogo, -a *nmf*
jingo, jingoist	jingoísta *nmf*
moralizer	moralizador(a) *nmf*
purist	purista *nmf*
radical	radical *nmf*
reactionary	reaccionario, -a *nmf*

liars

adulator	adulador(a) *nmf*
charlatan	charlatán, -ana *nmf*
defrauder	defraudador(a) *nmf*
falsifier	falsificador(a) *nmf*
hypocrite	hipócrita *nmf*
impostor	impostor(a) *nmf*
prevaricator	prevaricador(a) *nmf*
sycophant	sicofante *nm*

immoral

corrupter	corruptor(a) *nmf*
decadent	decadente *nmf*
degenerate	degenerado, -a *nmf*
pervert	pervertido, -a *nmf*
reprobate	réprobo, -a *nmf*
seducer	seductor(a) *nmf*
sociopath	sociópata *nmf*
tempter	tentador(a) *nmf*

martinets

authoritarian	autoritario, -a *nmf*
autocrat	autócrata *nmf*
demagog(ue)	demagogo, -a *nmf*
despot	déspota *nmf*
dictator	dictador(a) *nmf*
tyrant	tirano, -a *nmf*

other persons—good

expert	experto, -a *nmf*
hero	héroe *nm*
heroine	heroína *nf*
idealist	idealista *nmf*
notable	notable *nmf*
optimist	optimista *nmf*
perfectionist	perfeccionista *nmf*
personage	personaje *nm*
realist	realista *nmf*
reformer	reformador(a) *nmf*
restorer	restaurador(a) *nmf*

other persons—bad

boob	bobo, -a *nmf*
conformist	conformista *nmf*
coward	cobarde *nmf*
cynic	cínico, -a *nmf*
dilettante	diletante *nmf*
idiot	idiota *nmf*
ignoramus	ignorante *nmf*
monopolizer	monopolizador(a) *nmf*
offender	ofensor(a) *nmf*
pariah	paria *nmf*
pessimist	pesimista *nmf*
sexist	sexista *nmf*
snob	snob, esnob *nmf*
vagabond	vagabundo, -a *nmf*

(*See also* PERSONS under **ENTERTAINMENT**; *PERSONS* under **FAMILY**; *PERSONS* under **JOURNALISM**; *PERSONS* under **USING LANGUAGE**; *PERSONS* under **LAW**; *PERSONS* under **MAGIC**; *PERSONS* under **MONEY AND FINANCE**; *PERSONS* under **ORGANIZATIONS AND MEETINGS**; *PERSONS* under **POLITICS AND GOVERNMENT**; *PERSONS* under **THE MILITARY ESTABLISHMENT**; *individuals* under **WORK**)

Society and Culture

FAMILY

GENERAL TERMS

family	familia *nf*
generation	generación *nf*
lineage	linaje *nm*
matrimony	matrimonio *nm*

CLASSIFICATION

marriage terms

ceremony	ceremonia *nf*
certificate	certificado *nm*
conjugal	conyugal *aj*
connubial	connubial *aj*
courting	cortejo *nm*
domesticity	domesticidad *nf*
marital	marital *aj*
marriage of convenience	matrimonio de conveniencias *nm, nfpl*
matrimonial	matrimonial *aj*
mixed	mixto *aj*
morganatic	morganático *aj*
nubile	núbil *aj*
nuptials	nupcias *nfpl*
plural	plural *aj*
prenuptial	prenupcial *aj*
proposal	propuesta *nf*

types of families

communal	comunal *aj*
equalitarian	igualitario *aj*
extended	extendido *aj*
interracial	interracial *aj*
matriarchal	matriarcal *aj*
nuclear	nuclear *aj*
patriarchal	patriarcal *aj*
polygamous, polygynous	polígamo *aj*
traditional	tradicional *aj*

family groups

clan	clan *nm*
dynasty	dinastía *nf*
tribe	tribu *nf*

marriage practices

consanguinity	consanguinidad *nf*
endogamy	endogamia *nf*
exogamy	exogamia *nf*
monogamy	monogamia *nf*
polyandry	poliandria *nf*
polygamy	poligamia *nf*
polygyny	poliginia *nf*

lineage terms

extraction	extracción *nf*
genealogy	genealogía *nf*
heredity, heritage	herencia *nf*
matrilineal *aj*	por línea materna *nf*
mulatto	mulato, -a *aj, nmf*
origin	origen *nm*
patrilineal	patrilineal *aj*
primogeniture	primogenitura *nf*
putative	putativo *aj*

parents

adoptive	adoptivo *aj*
biological	biológico *aj*
maternal	materno *aj*
paternal	paterno *aj*

children

adopted	adoptado *aj*
fraternal (twins)	fraternal *aj*
identical (twins)	idéntico *aj*
natural	natural *aj*
progeny	progenie *nf*
quadruplet	cuatrillizo, -a *nmf*
quintuplet	quintillizo, -a *nmf*
septuplet	septillizo, -a *nmf*
sextuplet	séxtuple *nmf*
triplet	trillizo, -a *nmf*

other terms

affinity	afinidad *nf*
cohabitation	cohabitación *nf*
collateral	colateral *aj*
concubinage	concubinato *nm*
consort	consorte *nmf*
filial	filial *aj*
harem	harén *nm*
seraglio	serrallo *nm*

LEGAL ASPECTS

possible grounds for divorce

abandonment	abandono *nm*
abuse	abuso *nm*
addiction	adicción *nf*
adultery	adulterio *nm*
alcoholism	alcoholismo *nm*
alienation	alienación *nf*
bigamy	bigamia *nf*
cruelty	crueldad *nf*
impotence	impotencia *nf*
incest	incesto *nm*
incompatibility	incompatibilidad *nf*
insanity	insania *nf*
neglect	negligencia *nf*
separation	separación *nf*

family crimes

fratricide (act)	fratricidio *nm*
infanticide (act)	infanticidio *nm*
matricide (act)	matricidio *nm*
parricide (act)	parricidio *nm*

other terms

adoption	adopción *nf*
alimony *nsg*	alimentos *nmpl*
annulment	anulación *nf*
custody	custodia *nf*
disinherit	desheredar *vt*
divorce	divorcio *nm*

illegitimacy	ilegitimidad *nf*
inheritance	herencia *nf*
intestate	intestado *aj*
legitimate	legítimo *aj*
patrimony	patrimonio *nm*
repudiation	repudio *nm*
succession	sucesión *nf*
surviving	sobreviviente *aj*

SEXUAL ASPECTS

consummation	consumación *nf*
extramarital	extramatrimonial *aj*
family planning	planificación familiar *nf*
fidelity	fidelidad *nf*
incestuous	incestuoso *aj*
infidelity	infidelidad *nf*
misogamy	misogamia *nf*
pair	pareja *nf*
pair off	emparejarse *vr*
paternity	paternidad *nf*
premarital	premarital *aj*
refuge	refugio *nm*
sex	sexo *nm*

PERSONS

adulterer	adúltero, -a *nmf*
adultress	adúltera *nf*
bastard	bastardo, -a *aj, nmf*
bigamist	bígamo, -a *nmf*
concubine	concubina *nf*
descendant	descendiente *nmf*
divorcé	divorciado *nm*
divorcée	divorciada *nf*
family member	familiar *nmf*
fratricide (killer)	fratricida *nm*
genealogist	genealogista *nmf*
heir	heredero, -a *nmf*
infanticide (killer)	infanticida *nmf*
ma, mama, momma	mamá *nf*
matriarch	matriarca *nf*
matricide (killer)	matricida *nmf*
matron	matrona *nf*
mom, mommy	mamita *nf*
orphan	huérfano, -a *nmf*
pa, papa, pop, poppa	papá, papi, papito *nm*
parricide (killer)	parricida *nmf*
paterfamilias	paterfamilias *nm*
patriarch	patriarca *nm*
polygamist	polígamo, -a *nmf*
primogenitor	primogenitor *nm*
progenitor	progenitor(a) *nmf*

second-born	segundogénito, -a *aj*, *nmf*	physical	físico *aj*
		preschool	preescolar *aj*
second son	segundón *nm*	special	especial *aj*
spouse	esposo, -a *nmf*	vocational	vocacional *aj*
successor	sucesor(a) *nmf*		
widow	viuda *nf*		
widower	viudo *nm*		

types of schools

(*See also* **SEXUALITY**)

academy	academia *nf*
accredited	acreditado *aj*
coeducational	coeducacional *aj*
college	colegio *nm*
correspondence	correspondencia *nf*
elementary	elemental *aj*
extension	de extensión *nf*
graduate	graduado *aj*
institute	instituto *nm*
intermediate	intermedio *aj*
kindergarten	kindergarten *nm*
laboratory	laboratorio *nm*
medical	de medicina
military	militar *aj*
normal (obs)	normal *aj*
postgraduate	pos(t)graduado *aj*
preparatory	preparatorio *aj*
primary	primario *aj*
private	privado *aj*
professional	profesional *aj*, *nmf*
progressive	progresivo *aj*
public	público *aj*, *nm*
reform	reforma *nf*
religious	religioso *aj*
secondary	secundario *aj*
seminary	seminario *nm*
technological	tecnológico *aj*
university	universidad *nf*

EDUCATION

GENERAL TERMS

academe	mundo académico *nm*
academic	académico *aj*
calendar	calendario *nm*
class	clase *nf*
course	curso *nm*
curriculum	currículo *nm*
discipline	disciplina *nf*
edification	edificación *nf*
education	educación *nf*
erudition	erudición *nf*
examination	examen *nm*
graduation	graduación *nf*
institution	institución *nf*
instruction	instrucción *nf*
lesson	lección *nf*
materials	materiales *nmpl*
matriculation	matrícula *nf*
method	método *nm*
program	programa *nm*
school	escuela *nf*
specialization	especialización *nf*
study	estudio *nm*
test	test *nm*

major disciplines

arts	artes *nfpl*
humanities	humanidades *nfpl*
languages	lenguas *nfpl*
literature	literatura *nf*
mathematics	matemática(s) *nf(pl)*
sciences	ciencias *nfpl*

SPECIALIZATIONS

didactics	didáctica *nf*
heuristics	heurística *nf*
methodology	metodología *nf*
pedagogy	pedagogía *nf*

kinds of courses

advanced	avanzado *aj*
computer-assisted	asistido por computadora *aj*, *nf*
interdisciplinary	interdisciplinario *aj*
introductory	introductorio *aj*
prerequisite	requisito *nm*
programmed, programed	programado *aj*
repeated	repetido *aj*

ASPECTS OF EDUCATION

general types

adult	adulto *aj*
alternative	alternativo *aj*
bilingual	bilingüe *aj*, *nmf*
formal	formal *aj*
general	general *aj*
informal	informal *aj*
liberal	liberal *aj*, *nmf*

seminar	seminario *nm*
short course	cursillo *nm*

methods of learning

analysis	análisis *nm*
conditioning	condicionamiento *nm*
demonstration	demostración *nf*
memorize	memorizar *vt*
repetition	repetición *nf*
Socratic	socrático *aj*
transfer, transference	tra(n)sferencia *nf*
trial and error	ensayo y error *nm*

school calendar

grade	grado *nm*
sabbatical	sabático *aj*
semester	semestre *nm*
trimester	trimestre *nm*
vacation *nsg*	vacaciones *nfpl*

degrees and graduation

baccalaureate	bachillerato *nm*
cum laude	cum laude *av*
diploma	diploma *nm*
dissertation	disertación *nf*
doctorate	doctorado *nm*
honorary	honorario *aj*
magna cum laude	magna cum laude *av*
master's degree	maestría *nf*
summa cum laude	summa cum laude *av*
thesis	tesis *nf*

other terms

absent	ausente *aj*
credit	crédito *nm*
department	departamento *nm*
extracurricular	extracurricular *aj*
extramural	extramural *aj*
faculty	facultad *nf*
honorarium *nsg*	honorarios *nmpl*
intramural	intramuros *aj*
objective	objetivo *nm*
orientation	orientación *nf*
place	plaza *nf*
Sorbonne	Sorbona *nf*
stipend	estipendio *nm*
unit	unidad *nf*

TESTS AND EXAMINATIONS

kinds of tests

aptitude	aptitud *nf*
competency	competencia *nf*
diagnostic	diagnóstico *aj*

evaluation	evaluación *nf*
intelligence	inteligencia *nf*
interest	interés *nm*
multiple-choice *aj*	de opción múltiple *nf*
personality	personalidad *nf*
predictive *aj*	que predice
reasoning	razonamiento *nm*
recognition	reconocimiento *nm*
standardized	estandarizado *aj*
subjective	subjetivo *aj*
true-or-false	cierto o falso *aj*

kinds of exams

doctoral	doctoral *aj*
final	final *aj*
oral	oral *aj*
preliminary	preliminar *aj*
semifinal	semifinal *aj*

other terms

admission	admisión *nf*
demerit	demérito *nm*
norm	norma *nf*
percentile	percentil *nm*
psychometrics	(p)sicometría *nf*
validation	convalidación *nf*
validity	validez *nf*

TOOLS AND MATERIALS

atlas	atlas *nm*
audiovisual	audiovisual *aj*
calculator	calculadora *nf*
compass	compás *nm*
computer	computadora *nf*
dictionary	diccionario *nm*
exercises	ejercicios *nmpl*
map	mapa *nm*
pointer	puntero *nm*
schoolbook	libro escolar *nm*
textbook	libro de texto *nm*
transparency	transparencia *nf*

PERSONS

groups

professors *npl*	profesorado *nm*
student body	estudiantado *nm*

individuals

academician	académico, -a *nmf*
bachelor	bachiller *nm*
collegian	colegiado, -a *nmf*
consultant	consultor(a) *nmf*

counselor	consejero, -a *nmf*
dean	decano *nm*
doctor	doctor(a) *nmf*
educator	educador(a) *nmf*
examinee	examinando, -a *nmf*
examiner	examinador, -a *nmf*
graduate	graduado, -a *nmf*
instructor	instructor(a) *nmf*
matriculant	matriculador(a) *nmf*
mentor	mentor(a) *nmf*
monitor	monitor(a) *nmf*
pedagog(ue)	pedagogo *nm*
postgraduate	pos(t)graduado, -a *nmf*
professor	profesor(a) *nmf*
professor emeritus	profesora emérita *nf*
professor emeritus	profesor emérito *nm*
rector	rector *nm*
registrar	registrador(a) *nmf*
seminarian	seminarista *nmf*
student	estudiante *nmf*
tutor	tutor(a) *nmf*

ORGANIZATIONS AND MEETINGS

GENERAL TERMS

election	elección *nf*
group	grupo *nm*
invitation	invitación *nf*
membership	membresía *nf*
organization	organización *nf*
parliamentary law	reglamento parlamentario *n*
participation	participación *nf*
procedure	procedimiento *nm*
voting	votación *nf*

ASPECTS OF ORGANIZATIONS

establishment

auspices	auspicios *nmpl*
charter	carta *nf*
constitution	constitución *nf*
found	fundar *vt*

types

affiliation	afiliación, afiliada *nf*
association	asociación *nf*
circle	círculo *nm*
club	club *nm*
commission	comisión *nf*
committee	comité *nm*

consortium	consorcio *nm*
council (advisory)	consejo *nm*
delegation	delegación *nf*
foundation	fundación *nf*
fraternal	fraternal *aj*
legislature	legislatura *nf*
lodge	logia *nf*
parliament	parlamento *nm*
senate	senado *nm*
society	sociedad *nf*
subcommittee	subcomité *nm*

actions and procedures

action	acción *nf*
agenda	agenda *nf*
amendment	enmienda *nf*
approve	aprobar *vti*
clarification	aclaración *nf*
declaration	declaración *nf*
deliberation	deliberación *nf*
disband	desbandar(se) *vt(r)*
discussion	discusión *nf*
dissolution	disolución *nf*
inauguration	inauguración *nf*
initiate	iniciar *vt*
introduce	introducir *vt*
memo, memorandum	memorándum *nm*
motion	moción *nf*
mutatis mutandis	mutatis mutandis *av*
objection	objeción *nf*
officiate	oficiar *vt*
pending	pendiente *aj*
point of order	cuestión de orden *nf, nm*
present (a motion)	presentar *vt*
preside	presidir *vti*
privilege	privilegio *nm*
proposal	propuesta *nf*
ratification	ratificación *nf*
recess	receso *nm*
resolution	resolución *nf*
second (the motion)	secundar *vt*
suspend	suspender *vt*

voting

abstention	abstención *nf*
acclamation	aclamación *nf*
plenum	pleno *nm*
plurality	pluralidad *nf*
quorum	quórum *nm*
unanimous	unánime *aj*

other terms

auditorium	auditorio *nm*
congregate	congregarse *vr*
disunity	desunión *nf*
exclusivist	exclusivista *aj*
factious (groups)	faccioso *aj*
platform	plataforma *nf*
tribune	tribuna *nf*

KINDS OF MEETINGS

small groups

colloquy	coloquio *nm*
consultation	consulta, consultación *nf*
encounter	encuentro *nm*
interview	entrevista *nf*
tête-à-tête	tête-à-tête *nm*
visit	visita *nf*

large groups

assembly	asamblea *nf*
colloquium	coloquio *nm*
conclave	cónclave *nm*
congress	congreso *nm*
convention	convención *nf*
convocation	convocatoria *nf*
debate	debate *nm*
meeting (political)	mitin *nm*
plenary	plenario *aj*
reception	recepción *nf*
session	sesión *nf*
symposium	simposio *nm*

small or large

class	clase *nf*
conference	conferencia *nf*
reunion	reunión *nf*
seminar	seminario *nm*

TERMS IN DEBATING

affirmative	afirmativo *nm*
argue	argumentar *vi*
decision	decisión *nf*
moderate	moderar *vt*
negative	negativo *nm*
opposing	opuesto *aj*
opposition	oposición *nf*
proposition	proposición *nf*
question	cuestión *nf*
resolve	resolver *vt*

PERSONS

officers

president	presidente *nmf*
secretary	secretario, -a *nmf*
treasurer	tesorero, -a *nmf*
vice-president	vicepresidente *nmf*

members

associate member	miembro no numerario *nmf*
founding member	fundador(a) *nmf*
full member	miembro de número *nmf*
honorary member	miembro honorario *nmf*
lifetime member	miembro vitalicio *nmf*

other persons

abstainer	abstencionista *nmf*
conventioneer	convencionista *nmf*
delegate	delegado, -a *nf*
founder	fundador(a) *nmf*
initiate	iniciado, -a *nmf*
mason, Mason	masón *nm*
member	miembro *nm*
moderator (debate)	moderador, -a *nmf*
objector	objetor(a) *nmf*
observer	observador(a) *nmf*
opponent	oponente *nmf*
organizer	organizador(a) *nmf*
panelist	miembro del panel *nm*
parliamentarian	parlamentario, -a *nmf*
participant	participante, partícipe *nmf*
representative	representante *nmf*
Rotarian	rotario, -a *nmf*

(*See also* **POLITICS AND GOVERNMENT**)

SOCIOLOGY

GENERAL TERMS

caste	casta *nf*
class	clase *nf*
community	comunidad *nf*
culture	cultura *nf*
group dynamics *npl*	dinámica de grupo *nf, nm*
institution	institución *nf*
population	población *nf*
social change	cambio social *nm*
social welfare	bienestar social *nm*
socialization	socialización *nf*

sociology	sociología *nf*
status	estatus *nm*
status symbol	símbolo de estatus *nm*
stratum	estrato *nm*
structure	estructura *nf*

SPECIALIZATIONS

criminology	criminología *nf*
demography	demografía *nf*
deviance	desviación *nf*
economics	economía *nf*
psychology	(p)sicología *nf*
social work	asistencia social *nf*
sociobiology	sociobiología *nf*
sociolinguistics	sociolingüística *nf*
statistics	estadística *nf*

ASPECTS OF SOCIOLOGY

social studies

civics	educación cívica *nf*
geography	geografía *nf*
history	historia *nf*

population statistics

census	censo *nm*
control	control *nm*
ethnicity	identidad étnica *nf*
explosion	explosión *nf*
immigration	inmigración *nf*
marital status	estado civil *nm*
minority	minoría *nf*
race	raza *nf*
rural	rural *aj*
urban	urbano *aj*
vital statistics	estadísticas demográficas *nfpl*

factors in social status

celebrity	celebridad *nf*
fame	fama *nf*
family	familia *nf*
fortune	fortuna *nf*
image	imagen *nf*
influence	influencia *nf*
possessions	posesiones *nfpl*
power	poder *nm*
prestige	prestigio *nm*
reputation	reputación *nf*
role, rôle	rol *nm*

conducting surveys

data *nsg* or *npl*	datos *nmpl*
estimate	estimado *nm*
interview	entrevista *nf*
map	mapa *nm*
margin of error	margen de error *nm*
norm	norma *nf*
opinion poll	encuesta de opinión *nf*
prediction	predicción *nf*
preference	preferencia *nf*
questionnaire	cuestionario *nm*
study	estudio *nm*
subject	sujeto *nm*

frequent survey topics

abuse	abuso *nm*
crime	crimen *nm*
drugs	drogas *nfpl*
government	gobierno *nm*
lifestyle	estilo de vida *nm, nf*
politics	política *nf*
prejudice	prejuicio *nm*
race relations	relaciones raciales *nfpl*
sex	sexo *nm*
treatment	trato *nm*
unemployment	desempleo *nm*
violence	violencia *nf*

PERSONS

high status

cosmopolite	cosmopolita *nmf*
debutante, débutante	debutante *nf*
elite, élite	élite *nf*
socialite	persona de alta sociedad
yuppie, yuppy	yupi *nmf*

low status

beatnik (obs)	beatnik *nmf*
hippy, hippie (obs)	hippy *nmf*
homeless person	persona sin hogar *nf, nm*
sociopath	sociópata *nmf*

other persons

demographer	demógrafo, -a *nmf*
informant	informante *nmf*
interviewer	entrevistador(a) *nmf*
social scientist	científico, -a social *nmf*
sociologist	sociólogo, -a *nmf*
statistician	estadístico, -a *nmf*

(*See also* **URBAN PROBLEMS** under **THE CITY**)

ANTHROPOLOGY

GENERAL TERMS

anthropology	antropología *nf*
civilization	civilización *nf*
culture	cultura *nf*
humanity, humankind	humanidad *nf*
race	raza *nf*
society	sociedad *nf*

SPECIALIZATIONS

anthropometry	antropometría *nf*
archeology	arqueología *nf*
ethnography	etnografía *nf*
ethnology	etnología *nf*
linguistics	lingüística *nf*
sociology	sociología *nf*

PHYSICAL ANTHROPOLOGY

human development

adaptation	adaptación *nf*
cephalic index	índice cefálico *nm*
evolution	evolución *nf*
hominid	homínido, -a *aj, nmf*
homo sapiens	homo sapiens *nm*
mammal	mamífero *nm*
primate	primate *nm*
vertebrate	vertebrado *aj, nm*

prehistoric humans

Cro-Magnon	cromañón *nm*
Neanderthal	neandertal *nm*
pithecanthropus	pitecántropo, -a *nmf*

racial type

Caucasoid	caucasoide *aj*
Mongoloid	mongoloide *aj*
Negroid	negroide *aj*

CULTURAL ANTHROPOLOGY

basic concepts

conformity	conformidad *nf*
diversity	diversidad *nf*
ethnocentrism	etnocentrismo *nm*
functionalism	funcionalismo *nm*
migration	migración *nf*
multiculturalism	multiculturalismo *nm*
orthogenesis (obs)	ortogénesis *nf*
relativism	relativismo *nm*
stereotype	estereotipo *nm*

kinds of culture

advanced	avanzado *aj*
contemporary	contemporáneo *aj*
counterculture	contracultura *nf*
decadent	decadente *aj*
ethnic	étnico *aj*
indigenous	indígena *aj*
international	internacional *aj*
material	material *aj*
matriarchal	matriarcal *aj*
national	nacional *aj*
nonmaterial	no material *aj*
patriarchal	patriarcal *aj*
popular	popular *aj*
primitive	primitivo *aj*
subculture	subcultura *nf*
tribal	tribal *aj*

elements of developed cultures

arts	artes *nfpl*
conventions	convenciones *nfpl*
customs	costumbres *nfpl*
decorum	decoro *nm*
education	educación *nf*
etiquette	etiqueta *nf*
family	familia *nf*
folklore	folklore, folclore *nm*
government	gobierno *nm*
institution	institución *nf*
invention	invención *nf*
language	lenguaje *nm*
religion	religión *nf*
symbols	símbolos *nmpl*
technology	tecnología *nf*
tradition	tradición *nf*
values	valores *nmpl*

cultures in contact

acculturation	aculturación *nf*
Americanization	americanización *nf*
assimilation	asimilación *nf*
culture shock	choque de culturas *nm*
diffusion	difusión *nf*
Europeanization	europeización *nf*
exodus	éxodo *nm*
insularity	insularidad *nf*
latinize	latinizar *vt*
xenophilia	afición a lo extranjero *nf*
xenophobia	xenofobia *nf*

Affairs of State

LAW

GENERAL TERMS

appeal	apelación *nf*
argument	argumento *nm*
attestation	atestación, atestado *nf, nm*
bar	barra *nf*
capacity	capacidad *nf*
case	caso *nm*
cause	causa *nf*
charge	cargo *nm*
circumstance	circunstancia *nf*
claim	reclamación, reclamo *nf, nm*
code	código *nm*
codex	códice *nm*
codification	codificación *nf*
competence	competencia *nf*
compliance	cumplimiento *nm*
contingency	contingencia *nf*
costs	costas *nfpl*
counsel	consejo *nm*
court	corte *nf*
crime	crimen *nm*
decision	decisión *nf*
decree	decreto *nm*
defense	defensa *nf*
deposition	deposición *nf*
dictum	dictamen *nm*
discovery	descubrimiento *nm*
document	documento *nm*
documentation	documentación *nf*
domain, dominion	dominio *nm*
domicile	domicilio *nm*
equity	equidad *nf*
expenses	expensas *nfpl*
forum	foro *nm*
habeas corpus	habeas corpus *nm*
ignorance (of the law)	ignorancia *nf*
impediment	impedimento *nm*
injustice	injusticia *nf*
innocence	inocencia *nf*
instance	instancia *nf*
intent	intención *nm*
interpretation	interpretación *nf*
judicature	judicatura *nf*
jurisdiction	jurisdicción *nf*
jurisprudence	jurisprudencia *nf*

justice	justicia *nf*
law	ley *nf*
legal	legal *aj*
legitimate	legítimo *aj*
licit	lícito *aj*
litigation	litigio *nm*
majority (age)	mayoría *nf*
malice	malicia *nf*
mandate	mandato *nm*
motive	motivo *nm*
noncompliance	incumplimiento *nm*
null	nulo *aj*
obligation	obligación *nf*
occupancy	ocupación *nf*
offer	oferta *nf*
opinion	opinión *nf*
order	orden *nf*
ordinance	ordenanza *nf*
practice	práctica *nf*
process	proceso *nm*
promulgation	promulgación *nf*
proof	prueba *nf*
protection	protección *nf*
public domain	dominio público *nm*
recourse	recurso *nm*
regulations	reglamento *nmsg*
rehabilitation	rehabilitación *nf*
representation	representación *nf*
statute	estatuto *nm*
technicality	tecnicismo *nm*
tribunal	tribunal *nm*
violation	violación *nf*
violence	violencia *nf*

TYPES OF LAW

public

administrative	administrativo *aj*
constitutional	constitucional *aj*
criminal	criminal *aj*
international	internacional *aj*
maritime	marítimo *aj*
martial	marcial *aj*
mercantile	mercantil *aj*
penal	penal *aj*

civil

canon	canónico *aj*
civil	civil *aj*
commercial	comercial *aj*
contract	de contrato *nm*
corporation	de corporación *nf*
family	de familia *nf*
labor	laboral *aj*

patent	de patente *nf*
property	de propiedad *nf*

historical

Justinian	justiniano *aj*
Mosaic	mosaico *aj*
Napoleonic	napoleónico *aj*
Roman	romano *aj*

ASPECTS OF LEGAL PRACTICE

kinds of courts

appellate	de apelación *nf*
circuit	circuito *nm*
district	distrito *nm*
federal	federal *aj*
municipal	municipal *aj*
Supreme Court	Corte Suprema *nf*
traffic	de tráfico *nm*

rights

access	acceso *nm*
consortium	consorcio *nm*
constitutional	constitucional *aj*
herbage	herbaje *nm*
inalienable	inalienable *aj*
prerogative	prerrogativa *nf*
privacy	privacidad *nf*
privilege	privilegio *nm*
proprietary	propietario *aj*
reversion	reversión *nf*
riparian	ribereño *aj*
suffrage	sufragio *nm*
tenancy	tenencia *nf*
use	uso *nm*
usufruct	usufructo *nm*

terms in law enforcement

apprehend (a criminal)	aprehender *vt*
arrest	arresto *nm*
clandestine (operation)	clandestino *aj*
cordon	cordón *nm*
criminology	criminología *nf*
dactylography	dactilografía *nf*
detection	detección *nf*
felony	felonía *nf*
Interpol	Interpol *mf*
investigation	investigación *nf*
patrol	patrulla *nf*
polygraph	polígrafo *nm*
reconstruct (a crime)	reconstruir *vt*
secret (police)	secreto *aj*

judicial actions

adoption	adopción *nf*
amnesty	amnistía *nf*
annulment	anulación *nf*
asylum	asilo *nm*
citation	citación *nf*
detainer	orden de detención *nf*
expropriation	expropiación *nf*
extradition	extradición *nf*
immunity	inmunidad *nf*
inquest	encuesta *nf*
instigation	instigación *nf*
interdict, interdiction	interdicto *nm*
interlocutory (decree)	interlocutorio *aj*
judgment	orden judicial *nf*
legalization	legalización *nf*
moratorium	moratoria *nf*
naturalization	naturalización *nf*
novation	novación *nf*
nullification	anulación *nf*
prescription	prescripción *nf*
prohibition	prohibición *nf*
proscription	proscripción *nf*
replication (reply)	réplica *nf*
requisition	requisitoria *nf*
rescission	rescisión *nf*
revocation	revocación *nf*
sanctuary	santuario *nm*
subrogation	subrogación *nf*
transfer, transference	tra(n)sferencia *nf*
validation	validación *nf*
vitiate	viciar *vt*

documents

affidavit	afidávit *nm*
article	artículo *nm*
certificate	certificado *nm*
clause	cláusula *nf*
codicil	codicilo *nm*
covenant	convenio *nm*
holograph	(h)ológrafo *nm*
instrument	instrumento *nm*
license	licencia *nf*
memorandum	memorándum *nm*
petition	petición *nf*
power of attorney	poder notarial *nm*
title	título *nm*
verification	verificación *nf*

legal argumentation

adduce	aducir *vt*
allegation	alegato *nm*

confutation	confutación *nf*
objection	objeción *nf*
protest	protesta *nf*
refutation	refutación *nf*

evidence

admissible	admisible *aj*
conclusive	concluyente *aj*
corroboration	corroboración *nf*
cumulative	cumulativo *aj*
fraudulent	fraudulento *aj*
irrelevance, irrelevancy	irrelevancia *nf*
moral	moral *aj*
pertinence	pertinencia *nf*
preponderance	preponderancia *nf*
prima facie	prima facie *av*
probative, probatory	probatorio *aj*
relevant	relevante *aj*
stipulation	estipulación *nf*
testimony	testimonio *nm*

other terms

abjure	abjurar *vt*
abolish	abolir *vt*
abrogate	abrogar *vt*
abuse	abusar *vi*
alienate (property)	alienar *vt*
appropriate	apropiar(se) *vt(r)*
arbitration	arbitraje *nm*
attenuating	atenuante *aj*
authority	autoridad *nf*
contravene	contravenir *vt*
desist	desistir *vi*
exempt	exento *aj*
exert (authority)	ejercer *vt*
fictitious (name)	ficticio *aj*
forensic	forense *aj*
fungible	fungible *aj*
inoperative	inoperante *aj*
instruct (the jury)	instruir *vt*
intention	intencionalidad *nf*
interrogatory	interrogatorio *nm*
invalid	inválido *aj*
mandamus	mandamiento *nm*
mediation	mediación *nf*
pending	pendiente *aj*
peremptory	perentorio *aj*
precedent	precedente *nm*
prejudicial	perjudicial *aj*
proceeding	procedimiento *nm*
quasi contract	cuasicontrato *nm*
ratify (a contract)	ratificar *vt*
receivership	receptoría *nf*

reclaim (rights)	reclamar *vt*
renunciation (of a claim)	renuncia *nf*
sequestration	secuestración *nf*
summary (judgment)	sumario *aj*

CRIMES AND MISDEMEANORS

kinds of crimes

capital	capital *aj*
financial	financiero *aj*
military	militar *aj*
nonviolent	no violento *aj*
political	político *aj*
premeditated	premeditado *aj*
sex	de sexo
violent	violento *aj*

violent

aggravated (assault)	con agravante *nm*
assassination	asesinato *nm*
banditry	bandidaje *nm*
cannibalism	canibalismo *nm*
fratricide (act)	fratricidio *nm*
gangsterism	gangsterismo *nm*
genocide	genocidio *nm*
homicide (act)	homicidio *nm*
infanticide (act)	infanticidio *nm*
lynching	linchamiento *nm*
robbery	robo *nm*
terrorism	terrorismo *nm*
vandalism	vandalismo *nm*

financial

bankruptcy	bancarrota *nf*
connivance	connivencia *nf*
extortion	extorsión *nf*
tax evasion	evasión fiscal *nf*
usury	usura *nf*

sex crimes

bestiality	bestialidad *nf*
incest	incesto *nm*
pedophilia	pedofilia *nf*
prostitution	prostitución *nf*
seduction	seducción *nf*
sodomy	sodomía *nf*

political and military

assassination	asesinato *nm*
collaboration (with enemy)	colaboracionismo *nm*
desertion	deserción *nf*

espionage	espionaje *nm*
insubordination	insubordinación *nf*
insurrection	insurrección *nf*
misconduct	mala conducta *nf*
sabotage	sabotaje *nm*
sedition	sedición *nf*
treason	traición *nf*

language crimes

calumny	calumnia *nf*
defamation	difamación *nf*
libel	libelo *nm*
obscenity	obscenidad *nf*
perjury	perjurio *nm*
plagiarism	plagio *nm*
subornation	soborno *nm*

crimes on the high seas

mutiny	motín *nm*
piracy	piratería *nf*

miscellaneous crimes

collusion	colusión *nf*
complicity	complicidad *nf*
conspiracy	conspiración *nf*
contumacy	contumacia *nf*
delinquency	delincuencia *nf*
discrimination	discriminación *nf*
fraud	fraude *nm*
incitement	incitación *nf*
infraction	infracción *nf*
kleptomania	cleptomania *nf*
negligence	negligencia *nf*
obstruction	obstrucción *nf*
possession	posesión *nf*
slavery	esclavitud *nf*
suicide (act)	suicidio *nm*
vagrancy	vagancia *nf*

legal defenses

accident	accidente *nm*
alibi	alibí *nm*
coercion	coerción *nf*
consent	consentimiento *nm*
incapacity	incapacidad *nf*
incompetence	incompetencia *nf*
insanity	insania *nf*
insolvency	insolvencia *nf*
justification	justificación *nf*
necessity	necesidad *nf*
prevention	prevención *nf*
reasonable (doubt)	razonable *aj*
self-defense	autodefensa *nf*

other terms

accusation	acusación *nf*
admission	admisión *nf*
brutal	brutal *aj*
coercive	coercitivo *aj*
commit	cometer *vt*
confession	confesión *nf*
conviction	convicción *nf*
culpability	culpabildad *nf*
exculpation	exculpación *nf*
forced (entry)	forzado *aj*
incendiary	incendiario *aj*
incrimination	incriminación *nf*
indemnity	indemnidad *nf*
infringe	infringir *vi*
interrogation	interrogación *nf*
involuntary (manslaughter)	involuntario *aj*
justifiable (homicide)	justificable *aj*
perpetration	perpetración *nf*
plot	complot *nm*
presumption	presunción *nf*
punishable	punible *aj*
responsibility	responsabilidad *nf*
self-incrimination	autoincriminación *nf*
transgression	tra(n)sgresión *nf*
verdict	veredicto *nm*
vindication	vindicación *nf*

PUNISHMENT

kinds of punishment

compensation	compensación *nf*
condemnation	condena *nf*
confiscation	confiscación *nf*
corporal	corporal *aj*
damages	daños *nmpl*
deportation	deportación *nf*
detention	detención *nf*
electrocution	electrocución *nf*
execution	ejecución *nf*
exile	exilio *nm*
incapacitation	privación de la capacidad *nf*
incarceration	encarcelación *nf*
internment	internamiento *nm*
penalty	pena *nf*
punitive	punitivo *aj*
reprimand	reprimenda *nf*
sanction	sanción *nf*
sentence	sentencia *nf*
torture	tortura *nf*

places of punishment

calaboose	calabozo *nm*
cell	celda *nf*
correctional institution	correccional *nm or nf*
penitentiary	penitenciaría *nf*
prison	prisión *nf*
reformatory	reformatorio *nm*
stockade	estacada *nf*

other terms

clemency	clemencia *nf*
commutation	conmutación *nf*
corrective	correctivo *aj, nm*
impunity	impunidad *nf*

PERSONS

offenders

accomplice	cómplice *nmf*
accused	acusado, -a *nmf*
assassin	asesino, -a *nmf*
bandit	bandido, -a *nmf*
bigamist	bígamo, -a *nmf*
collaborationist	colaboracionista *nmf*
conspirator	conspirador(a) *nmf*
convict	convicto, -a *nmf*
criminal	criminal *nmf*
culprit	culpable *nmf*
defrauder	defraudador(a) *nmf*
delinquent	delincuente *nmf*
deportee	deportado, -a *nmf*
detainee	detenido, -a *nmf*
extortionist	autor(a) de extorsiones *nmf, nfpl*
felon	felón *nm*
fratricide (killer)	fratricida *nmf*
fugitive	fugitivo, -a *nmf*
gangster	gángster *nm*
homicide (killer)	homicida *nmf*
insurrectionist	insurrecto, -a *nmf*
kleptomaniac	cleptómano, -a *nmf*
libeler, libelist	libelista *nmf*
Mafioso	mafioso *nm*
offender	ofensor(a) *nmf*
pedophile	pedofilo, -a *nmf*
perjurer	perjuro, -a *nmf*
perpetrator	perpetrador(a) *nmf*
pirate	pirata *nmf*
plagiarist	plagiario, -a *nmf*
prisoner	prisionero, -a *nmf*
saboteur	saboteador(a) *nmf*
suborner	sobornador(a) *nmf*
suspect	sospechoso, -a *nmf*

terrorist	terrorista *aj, nmf*
trafficker	traficante *nmf*
transgressor	tra(n)sgresor(a) *nmf*
vagrant	vago, -a *nmf*
vandal	vándalo, -a *nmf*

law enforcement personnel

agent	agente *nmf*
commissioner	comisionado, -a *nmf*
criminalist	criminalista *nmf*
criminologist	criminalista *nmf*
custodian	custodio, -a *nmf*
deputy	diputado, -a *nmf*
detainer	detentador(a) *nmf*
detective	detective *nmf*
inspector	inspector(a) *nmf*
interrogator	interrogador(a) *nmf*
investigator	investigador(a) *nmf*
judge	juez *nmf*
jurist	jurista *nmf*
juror	jurado *nmf*
Justice of the Peace	juez/jueza de paz *nmf, nf*
magistrate	magistrado *nmf*
matron	matrona *nf*
penologist	penalista *nmf*
policeman/ policewoman	policía *nmf*
public defender	defensor(a) de oficio *nmf, nm*

other individuals

accuser	acusador(a) *nmf*
adjuster	ajustador(a) *nmf*
administrator	administrador(a) *nmf*
adversary	adversario, -a *nmf*
advocate	abogado, -a *nmf*
appellant	apelante *nnf*
arbitrator	árbitro, -a *nmf*
beneficiary	beneficiario, -a *nmf*
claimant	reclamante *nmf*
client	cliente *nmf*
codifier	codificador(a) *nmf*
corroborator	corroborante *nmf*
cosignatory	cosignatario, -a *nmf*
deponent	deponente *nmf*
divorcé	divorciado *nm*
divorcée	divorciada *nf*
executor	ejecutor(a) *nmf*
expert	experto, -a *nmf*
heir	heredero, -a *nmf*
informant	informante *nmf*
instigator	instigador(a) *nmf*

juvenile	juvenil *nmf*
legatee	legatario *nm*
legislator	legislador(a) *nmf*
litigant, litigator	litigante *nmf*
mediator	mediador(a) *nmf*
minor	menor *nmf*
notary	notario, -a *nmf*
occupant	ocupador(a) *nmf*
official	oficial *nmf*
ombudsman	ombudsman *nm*
party (legal person)	parte *nf*
person	persona *nf*
petitioner	peticionario, -a *nmf*
possessor	poseedor(a) *nmf*
principal	principal *nm*
promulgator	promulgador(a) *nmf*
registrar	registrador(a) *nmf*
sheriff	sheriff *nmf*
victim	víctima *nf*
vigilante	vigilante *nmf*

groups

clientele	clientela *nf*
judiciary	judicatura *nf*
jury	jurado *nm*
Mafia	Mafia *nf*
militia	milicia *nf*
police	policía *nf*

(*See also* LEGAL TERMS under BUSINESS; *legal aspects* under DEATH; *LEGAL ASPECTS* under FAMILY)

THE MILITARY ESTABLISHMENT

GENERAL TERMS

action	acción *nf*
ally	aliado *nm*
combat	combate *nm*
command	mando, comando *nm*
conflict	conflicto *nm*
defense	defensa *nf*
enemy	enemigo *nm*
equipment	equipo *nm*
hostilities	hostilidades *nfpl*
martial	marcial *aj*
military	militar *aj*
offense	ofensiva *nf*
order	orden *nf*
protocol	protocolo *nm*
rank	rango *nm*

service	servicio *nm*
uniform	uniforme *nm*

FIELDS IN MILITARY SCIENCE

ballistics	balística *nf*
communications	comunicaciones *nfpl*
counterespionage	contraespionaje *nm*
counterintelligence	contrainteligencia *nf*
cryptography	criptografía *nf*
electrothermics	electrotermia *nf*
engineering	ingeniería *nf*
espionage	espionaje *nm*
intelligence	inteligencia *nf*
logistics	logística *nf*
strategy	estrategia *nf*
tactics	táctica *nf*

ASPECTS OF MILITARY LIFE

groups

armada	armada *nf*
auxiliaries	tropas auxiliares *nfpl*
battalion	batallón *nm*
battery	batería *nf*
brigade	brigada *nf*
cadre	cuadro *nm*
cavalry	caballería *nf*
Coastguard, the *nsg*	guardacostas, los *nmpl*
company	compañía *nf*
contingent	contingente *nm*
corps	cuerpo *nm*
detachment	destacamento *nm*
division	división *nf*
echelon	escalón *nm*
escort	escolta *nf*
file	fila *nf*
fleet	flota *nf*
forces	fuerzas *nfpl*
group	grupo *nm*
infantry	infantería *nf*
junta	junta *nf*
legion	legión *nf*
military police	policía militar *nf*
military *nsg*	militares *nmpl*
militia	milicia *nf*
National Guard	Guardia Nacional *nf*
party (reconaissance)	partida *nf*
patrol	patrulla *nf*
regiment	regimiento *nm*
section	sección *nf*
squadron	escuadrón *nm*
troop	tropa *nf*

unit	unidad *nf*
vanguard	vanguardia *nf*

places

armory	armería *nf*
banquette	banqueta *nf*
barracks	barraca *nf*
base	base *nf*
bastion	bastión *nm*
blockhouse	blocao *nm*
camp, encampment	campamento *nm*
citadel	ciudadela *nf*
command post/area	comandancia *nf*
commissary	comisario *nm*
concentration camp	campo de concentración *nm*
decree	decreto *nm*
emplacement	emplazamiento *nm*
fort	fuerte *nm*
fortification	fortificación *nf*
fortress	fortaleza *nf*
front	frente *nm*
garrison	guarnición *nf*
guardhouse (guards' quarters)	cuartel de la guardia *nm, nf*
latrine	letrina *nf*
parade	parada *nf*
parapet	parapeto *nm*
park	parque *nm*
Pentagon	Pentágono *nm*
perimeter	perímetro *nm*
post	puesto *nm*
prison	prisión *nf*
prison camp	campo de prisioneros *nm, nmpl*
quarters *npl*	cuartel *nm*
sector	sector *nm*
silo (missile)	silo *nm*
stockade	estacada *nf*
tent	tienda *nf*
trench	trinchera *nf*

ranks and titles

admiral	almirante *nm*
aide-de-camp	edecán *nm*
brigadier	brigadier *nm*
captain	capitán, -ana *nmf*
chaplain	capellán *nm*
Chief-of-Staff	jefe del estado mayor *nmf, nm*
colonel	coronel(a) *nmf*
commodore	comodoro *nm*
degrade	degradar *vt*
general	general(a) *nmf*
generalissimo	generalísimo *nm*
lieutenant	lugarteniente *nmf*
major	mayor *nm*
marshall	mariscal *nm*
rear admiral	contraalmirante *nm*
sergeant	sargento *nm*

offices

admiralty	almirantazgo *nm*
captaincy	capitanía *nf*
colonelcy, colonelship	coronelato *nm*
generalship	generalato *nm*
lieutenantship	lugartenencia *nf*
sergeancy	sargentía *nf*

type of service

career	carrera *nf*
compulsory	compulsorio *aj*
conscription	conscripción *nf*
enlistment	alistamiento *nm*
recruitment	reclutamiento *nm*
regular	regular *aj*
reserves	reservas *nfpl*
voluntary	voluntario *aj*

crimes

atrocity	atrocidad *nf*
desertion	deserción *nf*
mutiny	motín *nm*
rapine	rapiña *nf*
torture	tortura *nf*

uniform

bandoleer, bandolier	bandolera *nf*
decoration	condecoración *nf*
helmet	yelmo *nm*
insignia	insignias *nfpl*
kepi	quepis, kepis *nm*
khaki	caqui, kaki *nm*
medal	medalla *nf*
plume (helmet)	plumero *nm*
shako	chacó *nm*

protocol

attention!	¡atención! *intj*
countermarch	contramarcha *nf*
countersign	contraseña *nf*
halt!	¡alto! *vi*
review	revista *nf*
safe-conduct	salvoconducto *nm*
salute	saludo *nm*
salvo	salva *nf*

other terms

bivouac	vivaque *nm*
depredation	depredación *nf*
march	marcha *nf*
martial law	ley marcial *nf*
morale	moral *nf*
obedience	obediencia *aj*
ration	ración *nf*
regimentation	regimentación *nf*
rigors	rigores *nmpl*

TACTICS AND COMBAT

kinds of wars

biological	biológico *aj*
conventional	convencional *aj*
defensive	defensivo *aj*
guerrilla	guerrilla *nf*
mechanized	mecanizado *aj*
naval	naval *aj*
nonnuclear	no nuclear *aj*
nuclear	nuclear *aj*
offensive	ofensiva *nf*
psychological	(p)sicológico *aj*
terrorism	terrorismo *nm*
undeclared	no declarado *aj*

beginnings of wars

alert	alerta *aj, av, nf*
declaration	declaración *nf*
hostile encounter	encuentro, encuentronazo *nm*
insurrection	insurrección *nf*
invasion	invasión *nf*
mobilization	movilización *nf*
preparedness	estado de preparación *nm, nf*
rebellion	rebelión *nf*

during wars

battle	batalla *nf*
campaign	campaña *nf*
censorship	censura *nf*
deescalation	desescalada *nf*
escalation	escalada *nf*
flank	flanco *nm*
formation	formación *nf*
line	línea *nf*
maneuver	maniobra *nf*
mission	misión *nf*
mount (offensive)	montar *vt*
operation	operación *nf*
position	posición *nf*

reinforcements	refuerzos *nmpl*
replacement	reemplazo *nm*
salient	saliente *nm*
stratagem	estratagema *nf*
tactic	táctica *nf*

ends of wars

armistice	armisticio *nm*
capitulation	capitulación *nf*
captivity	cautiverio, cautividad *nm, nf*
cease-fire	cese del fuego *nm*
conquest	conquista *nf*
demilitarization	desmilitarización *nf*
demobilization	desmovilización *nf*
devastation	devastación *nf*
disarmament	desarme *nm*
fraternization	confraternización *nf*
pacification	pacificación *nf*
peace	paz *nf*
reparations	reparaciones *nfpl*
subjugation	subyugación *nf*
surrender	rendición *nf*
triumph	triunfo *nm*
victory	victoria *nf*

offensive actions

advance	avance *nm*
ambush	emboscada *nf*
assault	asalto *nm*
attack	ataque *nm*
blockade	bloqueo *nm*
bombing, bombardment	bombardeo *nm*
capture	captura *nf*
counterattack	contraataque *nm*
embargo	embargo *nm*
imprison	aprisionar *vt*
incursion	incursión *nf*
infiltration	infiltración *nf*
interception	interceptación *nf*
occupation	ocupación *nf*
penetration	penetración *nf*
pillage	pillaje *nm*
sabotage	sabotaje *nm*
sacking	saqueo *nm*

defensive actions

barricade	barricada *nf*
camouflage	camuflaje *nm*
counteroffensive	contraofensiva *nf*
evacuation	evacuación *nf*
retirement	retirada *nf*

retreat	retreta *nf*
submersion	sumersión *nf*

descriptive words

bellicose	belicoso *aj*
combative	combativo *aj*
conquering (hero)	conquistador *aj*
ferocious	feroz *aj*
impregnable	impregnable *aj*
indefensible	indefendible *aj*
invincible	invencible *aj*
invulnerable	invulnerable *aj*
paramilitary	paramilitar *aj*
triumphant	triunfante *aj*
valiant	valiente *aj*
victorious	victorioso *aj*

other terms

booty	botín *nm*
combat fatigue	fatiga de combate *nf*
contraband	contrabando *nm*
expeditionary	expedicionario *aj*
antimilitarist	antimilitarista *aj*

WEAPONS AND EQUIPMENT

general terms

ammunition	munición *nf*
armaments *npl*	armamento *nm*
arms	armas *nfpl*
arsenal	arsenal *nm*
munitions	municiones *nfpl*

types of weapons

amphibious	anfibio *aj*
antiaircraft	antiaéreo *aj*
antiballistic	antibalístico *aj*
antimissile	antiproyectil *aj*
antipersonnel	antipersonal *nm*
antisubmarine	antisubmarino *aj*
artillery	artillería *nf*
atomic	atómico *aj*
bacteriological	bacteriológico *aj*
ballistic	balístico *aj*
chemical	químico *aj*
gas	gas *nm*
strategic	estratégico *aj*
tactical	táctico *aj*

vessels, vehicles, aircraft

bomber	bombardero *nm*
convoy	convoy *nm*
corvette	corbeta *nf*
cruiser	crucero *nm*
destroyer	destructor *nm*
frigate	fragata *nf*
galley	galera *nf*
helicopter	helicóptero *nm*
interceptor	interceptor, interceptador *nm*
minelayer	minador *nm*
minesweeper	dragaminas *nm*
reconnaissance	reconocimiento *nm*
submarine	submarino *aj, nm*
tank	tanque *nm*
torpedo boat	torpedero *nm*
transport	transporte *nm*
troop carrier	transporte de tropas *nm, nfpl*
troop tren	tren militar *nm*

hand weapons

automatic weapon	arma automática *nf(el)*
bayonet	bayoneta *nf*

other weapons

bomb	bomba *nf*
cannon	cañón *nm*
cruise missile	misil de crucero *nm*
mine	mina *nf*

other equipment

baggage	bagaje *nm*
bunker	búnker *nm*
impedimenta	impedimenta *nf*
launcher (missile)	lanzamisiles *nm*
launcher (rocket)	lanzacohetes *nm*
mask (gas)	máscara *nf*
materiel, matériel	material *nm*
paraphernalia	parafernalia *nf*

HISTORICAL TERMS

archery	tiro de arco *nm*
armor	armadura *nf*
brassard	brazal *nm*
catapult	catapulta *nf*
cavalier	caballero *nm*
cavalry	caballería *nm*
centurion	centurión *nm*
cohort	cohorte *nf*
corsair	corsario *nm*
cors(e)let	coselete *nm*
dragoon	dragón *nm*

duel	duelo *nm*
galleon	galeón *nm*
gauntlet	guantelete *nm*
gladiator	gladiador *nm*
halberd	alabarda *nf*
harquebus	arcabuz *nm*
hussar	húsar *nm*
janissary	jenízaro *nm*
kamikaze	kamikaze *nm*
laurels	laureles *nmpl*
mace	maza *nf*
mail	malla *nf*
musket	mosquete *nm*
musketeer	mosquetero *nm*
musketry	mosquetería *nf*
panoply	panoplia *nf*
petard	petardo *nm*
phalanx	falange *nm*
pretorian, praetorian	pretoriano *aj, nm*
samurai	samurai *nm*

PERSONS

adjutant	ayudante *nmf*
adversary	adversario, -a *nmf*
aggressor	agresor(a) *nmf*
aide	ayudante *nmf*
allies	aliados *nmpl*
archenemy, arch-enemy	archienemigo *nm*
archer	arquero, -a *nmf*
artilleryman	artillero, -a *nmf*
assailant	asaltante *nmf*
attacker	atacador *nm*
belligerent	parte beligerante *nf*
bombardier	bombardero *nm*
cadet	cadete *nmf*
cannoneer	cañonero *nm*
captive	cautivo, -a *aj, nmf*
captor	captor(a) *nmf*
cavalryman	soldado de caballería *nm, nf*
chief	jefe *nmf*
civilian	civil *aj, nmf*
coastguard	guardacostas *nmf*
collaborator	colaboracionista *nmf*
combatant	combatiente *nmf*
commandant, commander	comandante *nmf*
commando	comando *nm*
conqueror	conquistador(a) *nmf*
conscript	conscripto *nm*
counterspy	contraespía *nmf*
cryptographer	criptógrafo, -a *nmf*

defender	defensor(a) *nmf*
deserter	desertor *nm*
duelist	duelista *nmf*
engineer	ingeniero, -a *nmf*
evacuee	evacuado, -a *nmf*
gendarme	gendarme *nm*
grenadier	granadero *nm*
guard	guardia *nmf*
guerrilla (person)	guerrillero *nm*
hero	héroe *nm*
infantryman	infante *nm*
infiltrator	infiltrado, -a *nmf*
insurgent	insurgente *aj, nmf*
invader	invasor(a) *nmf*
lancer	lancero *nm*
legionnaire	legionario *nm*
liberator	liberador, libertador *nm*
marine	marino *nm*
mercenary	mercenario, -a *nmf*
militant	militante *aj, nmf*
militarist	militarista *nmf*
militiaman	miliciano *nm*
mutineer	amotinado, -a *nmf*
nonbelligerant	no beligerante *aj, nmf*
officer	oficial *nmf*
orderly	ordenanza *nmf*
pacifist	pacifista *nmf*
partisan	partisano, -a *nmf*
personnel	personal *nm*
pillager	pillador *nm*
prisoner	prisionero, -a *nmf*
propagandist	propagandista *nmf*
rearguard	retaguardia *nf*
rebel	rebelde *nmf*
recruit	recluta *nmf*
refugee	refugiado, -a *nmf*
relief	relevo *nm*
renegade	renegado, -a *aj, nmf*
reservist	reservista *nmf*
saboteur	saboteador(a) *nmf*
sapper	zapador *nm*
sentinel	centinela *nm*
sentry	centinela *nm*
soldier	soldado *nmf*
spy	espía *nmf*
strategist	estratega *nmf*
tactician	táctico *nm*
terrorist	terrorista *aj, nmf*
veteran	veterano, -a *nmf*
subjugate	subyugar, sojuzgar *vt*

(*See also* **CAUSES OF DEATH BY KILLING** under **DEATH**)

POLITICS AND GOVERNMENT

GENERAL TERMS

administration	administración *nf*
autonomy	autonomía *nf*
ballot	balota *nf*
capital (city)	capital *nf*
capitol (building)	capitolio *nm*
charter	carta *nf*
constitution	constitución *nf*
diplomacy	diplomacia *nf*
election	elección *nf*
emigration	emigración *nf*
geopolitics	geopolítica *nf*
government	gobierno *nm*
immigration	inmigración *nf*
independence	independencia *nf*
movement	movimiento *nm*
official	oficial *aj*
party	partido *nm*
patriotism	patriotismo *nm*
peace	paz *nf*
political science *nsg*	ciencias políticas *nfpl*
politics	política *nf*
power	poder *nm*
regime	régimen *nm*
reign	reinado *nm*
status	estado *nm*
system	sistema *nm*
veto	veto *nm*
vote	voto *nm*

ORGANIZATION

forms of government

anarchy	anarquía *nf*
coalition	coalición *nf*
constitutional	constitucional *aj*
democracy	democracia *nf*
dictatorship	dictadura *nf*
matriarchy	matriarcado *nm*
monarchy	monarquía *nf*
patriarchy	patriarcado *nm*
republic	república *nf*

scope of government

de facto	de facto *aj, av*
domestic	doméstico *aj*
federal	federal *aj*
global	global *aj*
international	internacional *aj*
interregnum	interregno *nm*
local	local *aj*

national	nacional *aj*
provincial	provinciano *aj*
provisional	provisional *aj*
state	estatal *aj*

ruling groups

aristocracy	aristocracia *nf*
autarchy	autarquía *nf*
autocracy	autocracia *nf*
bureaucracy	burocracia *nf*
dynasty	dinastía *nf*
gerontocracy	gerontocracia *nf*
gynecocracy	ginecocracia *nf*
meritocracy	meritocracia *nf*
ochlocracy	oclocracia *nf*
oligarchy	oligarquía *nf*
plutocracy	plutocracia *nf*
technocracy	tecnocracia *nf*
theocracy	teocracia *nf*

entities

colony	colonia *nf*
confederacy	confederación *nf*
confederation	confederación *nf*
county	condado *nm*
dependency	dependencia *nf*
dominion	dominio *nm*
duchy	ducado *aj*
emirate	emirato *nm*
empire	imperio *nm*
federation	federación *nf*
khanate	kanato *nm*
mandate	mandato *nm*
nation	nación *nf*
prefecture	prefectura *nf*
principality	principado *nm*
protectorate	protectorado *nm*
province	provincia *nf*
regency	regencia *nf*
reservation (Indian)	reserva *nf*
state	estado *nm*
territory	territorio *nm*

FUNCTIONING

rights and freedoms

civil rights	derechos civiles *nmpl*
equality	igualdad *nf*
justice	justicia *nf*
liberty	libertad *nf*
press	prensa *nf*
protection	protección *nf*
religion	religión *nf*

government responsibilities

censure	censura *nf*
census	censo *nm*
civil defense	defensa civil *nf*
intelligence	inteligencia *nf*
legislation	legislación *nf*
national security	seguridad nacional *nf*
police	policía *nf*
public health	salud pública *nf*
regulation	regulación *nf*

legislative bodies

assembly	asamblea *nf*
Soviet (obs)	soviet *nm*
commissariat	comisaría *nf*
congress	Congreso *nm*
diet	dieta *nf*
junta	junta *nf*
legislature	legislatura *nf*
parliament	parlamento *nm*
presidium, praesidium	presidio *nm*
senate	senado *nm*

official announcements

declaration	declaración *nf*
decree	decreto *nm*
edict	edicto *nm*
manifesto	manifiesto *nm*
memorandum	memorándum *nm*
proclamation	proclama, proclamación *nf*
propaganda	propaganda *nf*
resolution	resolución *nf*
ultimatum	ultimátum *nm*

international relations

accord	acuerdo *nm*
alignment	alineamiento *nm*
alliance	alianza *nf*
annexation	anexión *nf*
bilateral	bilateral *aj*
breach	brecha *nf*
cede	ceder *vt*
compact	pacto *nm*
concordat	concordato *nm*
consulate	consulado *nm*
containment	contención *nf*
credentials	credenciales *nfpl*
embargo	embargo *nm*
embassy	embajada *nf*
extraterritoriality	extraterritorialidad *nf*

foreign aid	ayuda externa *nf*
mission	misión *nf*
multilateral	multilateral *aj*
multinational	multinacional *aj*
negotiation	negociación *nf*
neutrality	neutralidad *nf*
pact	pacto *nm*
passport	pasaporte *nm*
protocol	protocolo *nm*
ratification	ratificación *nf*
reciprocity	reciprocidad *nf*
recognition	reconocimiento *nm*
SALT *nsg*	SALT *npl*
treaty	tratado *nm*
unification	unificación *nf*
unilateral	unilateral *aj*
visa	visa *nf*

immigration and emigration

Americanization	americanización *nf*
asylum	asilo *nm*
exile	exilio *nm*
expatriation	expatriación *nf*
nationality	nacionalidad *nf*
naturalization	naturalización *nf*
repatriation	repatriación *nf*

influences on government

activism	activismo *nm*
consensus	consenso *nm*
ideology	ideología *nf*
initiative	iniciativa *nf*
lobby	lobby *nm*
plebiscite	plebiscito *nm*
pressure group	grupo de presión *nm, nf*
public opinion	opinión pública *nf*
referendum	referéndum *nm*

opposition to government

agitation	agitación *nf*
assassination	asesinato *nm*
civil disobedience	desobediencia civil *nf*
defection	defección *nf*
dissension	disensión *nf*
dissidence	disidencia *nf*
disturbances	disturbios *nmpl*
espionage	espionaje *nm*
insurrection	insurrección *nf*
pamphlet (political)	panfleto *nm*
protest	protesta *nf*
purge	purga *nf*
rebellion	rebelión *nf*
resistance	resistencia *nf*

revolution	revolución *nf*
sabotage	sabotaje *nm*

ceremonies and events

coronation	coronación *nf*
crowning	coronamiento *nm*
inauguration	inauguración *nf*

symbols

swastika	esvástica *nf*
crown	corona *nf*
emblem	emblema *nm*
heraldry	heráldica *nf*
national anthem	himno nacional *nm*
seal	sello *nm*
standard (flag)	estandarte *nm*
throne	trono *nm*

pejorative descriptions

authoritarian	autoritario *aj*
bureaucratic	burocrático *aj*
chauvinistic	chovinista *aj*
corrupt	corrupto *aj*
despotic	despótico *aj*
dictatorial	dictatorial *aj*
extremist	extremista *aj*
inefficient	ineficiente *aj*
jingoistic	jingoísta *aj*
oppressive	opresivo *aj*
radical	radical *aj*
repressive	represivo *aj*
tyrannical	tiránico *aj*

other terms

bicameral	bicameral *aj*
bipartisan	bipartidista *aj*
constituent (assembly)	constituyente *aj*
discretionary (powers)	discrecional *aj*
presentation	presentación *nf*
session	sesión *nf*
unicameral	unicameral *aj*

MOVEMENTS AND PHILOSOPHIES

absolutism	absolutismo *nm*
anarchism	anarquismo *nm*
capitalism	capitalismo *nm*
centrism	centrismo *nm*
coexistence	coexistencia *nf*
collectivism	colectivismo *nm*
communism	comunismo *nm*
conservatism	conservadurismo, conservatismo *nm*
expansionism	expansionismo *nm*

extremism	extremismo *nm*
federalism	federalismo *nm*
feminism	feminismo *nm*
imperialism	imperialismo *nm*
internationalism	internacionalismo *nm*
isolationism	aislacionismo *nm*
liberalism	liberalismo *nm*
Marxism	marxismo *nm*
materialism	materialismo *nm*
mercantilism	mercantilismo *nm*
militarism	militarismo *nm*
nationalism	nacionalismo *nm*
nihilism	nihilismo *nm*
nonintervention	no intervención *nf*
nonproliferation	no proliferación *nf*
nonviolence	no violencia *nf*
obstructionism	obstruccionismo *nm*
pacifism	pacifismo *nm*
paternalism	paternalismo *nm*
pluralism	pluralismo *nm*
populism	populismo *nm*
privatization	privatización *nf*
protectionism	proteccionismo *nm*
radicalism	radicalismo *nm*
regionalism	regionalismo *nm*
revanchism	revanchismo *nf*
revisionism	revisionismo *nm*
separatism	separatismo *nm*
socialism	socialismo *nm*
suffrage	sufragio *nm*
totalitarianism	totalitarismo *nm*
Zionism	sionismo *nm*

U.S. POLITICS

constitution

amendment	enmienda *nf*
article	artículo *nm*
preamble	preámbulo *nm*

branches of government

executive	ejecutivo *aj*
judicial	judicial *aj*
legislative	legislativo *aj*

cabinet departments

agriculture	agricultura *nf*
commerce	comercio *nm*
defense	defensa *nf*
education	educación *nf*
interior	interior *nm*
treasury	tesorería *nf*

other government agencies

CIA	CIA *nf*
FBI	FBI *nm*
Medicare	Medicare *nm*
Social Security	Seguro Social *nm*

election terms

acceptance (speech)	aceptación *nf*
Americanism	americanismo *nm*
arena	arena *nf*
campaign	campaña *nf*
contribution	contribución *nf*
convention	convención *nf*
count (of votes)	recuento *nm*
Democratic Party	Partido Democrático *nm*
electoral college	colegio electoral *nm*
eligible	eligible *aj*
meeting	mitin *nm*
nomination	nominación *nf*
opposition	oposición *nf*
platform	plataforma *nf*
politicking	politiqueo *nm*
primary	elección primaria *nf*
recount	recuento *nm*
Republican Party	Partido Republicano *nm*
residency	residencia *nf*
strategy	estrategia *nf*
voting	votación *nf*

other terms

historical record	historial *nm*
representation	representación *nf*
statehood	condición de estado *nf, nm*

BRITISH AND EUROPEAN POLITICS

abdication	abdicación *nf*
accession	accesión *nf*
House of Commons	Cámara de los Comunes *nf*
House of Lords	Cámara de los Lores *nf*
royal family	familia real *nf*

UNITED NATIONS TERMS

aggression	agresión *nf*
atomic energy	energía atómica *nf*
colonialism	colonialismo *nm*
crisis	crisis *nf*
disarmament	desarme *nm*
displacement (refugees)	desplazamiento *nm*
emergent, emerging (nation)	emergente *aj*
General Assembly	Asamblea General *nf*
hegemony	hegemonía *nf*
humanitarian aid	ayuda humanitaria *nm*
intervention	intervención *nf*
militancy	militancia *nf*
neocolonialism	neocolonialismo *nm*
neutrality	neutralidad *nf*
nonaligned	no alineado *aj*
nonproliferation	no proliferación *nf*
pacifism	pacifismo *nm*
partition	partición *nf*
peacekeeping	mantenimiento de la paz *nm, nf*
peacetime	época de paz *nf*
proliferation	proliferación *nf*
propaganda	propaganda *nf*
sanctions	sanciones *nfpl*
Secretariat	Secretaría *nf*
security	seguridad *nf*
Security Council	Consejo de Seguridad *nm, nf*
self-determination	autodeterminación *nf*
simultaneous interpretation	interpretación simultánea *nf*
superpower	superpotencia *nf*
supremacy	supremacia *nf*
UNESCO	UNESCO *nf*
UNICEF	UNICEF *nm or nf*
volunteer forces	fuerzas voluntarias *nfpl*
World Bank	Banco Mundial *nm*

HISTORICAL TERMS

United States

abolition	abolición *nf*
antebellum	antes de la Guerra Civil
antislavery	antiesclavista *aj*
colonial	colonial *aj*
confederacy	confederación *nf*
emancipation	emancipación *nf*
prohibition	prohibición *nf*
reconstruction	reconstrucción *nf*
segregation	segregación *nf*
slavery	esclavitud *nf*

Soviet Union

Bolshevism	bolchevismo *nm*
destalinization	desestalinización *nf*
glasnost	glasnost *nm*
gulag	gulag *nm*
KGB	KGB *nf*

Leninism	leninismo *nm*
Politburo	Politburó *nm*
Soviet	soviético *aj*
Stalinism	stalinismo *nm*

former empires

Austria-Hungary	Austria-Hungría
Byzantine	bizantino *aj*
Ottoman	otomano *aj*
Roman	romano *aj*

other historical terms

apartheid	apartheid *nm*
crusade	cruzada *nf*
Falangism	falangismo *nm*
fascism	fascismo *nm*
feudalism	feudalismo *nm*
Gestapo	Gestapo *nf*
guillotine	guillotina *nf*
Hapsburg	hapsburgo, Habsburgo *aj, nm*
Jacobean	jacobino *aj*
League of Nations	Sociedad de Naciones *nf*
Machiavelli	Maquiavelo
Maoism	maoísmo *nm*
Nazism, Naziism	nazismo *nm*
palatinate	palatinado *nm*
peonage	condición de peón *nf, nm*
Restoration	Restauración *nf*
tribune	tribuno *nm*
triumvirate	triunvirato *nm*
Tudor	tudor, Tudor *aj, nm*
Versailles	Versalles *nf*

PERSONS

groups

bloc	bloque *nm*
cabinet	gabinete *nm*
cell (party)	célula *nf*
commission	comisión *nf*
committee	comité *nm*
council (advisory)	consejo *nm*
delegation	delegación *nf*
electorate	electorado *nm*
faction	facción *nf*
judiciary	judicatura *nf*
leadership	liderazgo, liderato *nm*
legation	legación *nf*
majority	mayoría *nf*

minority	minoría *nf*
nobility	nobleza *nf*
royalty	realeza *nf*

other persons

activist	activista *nmf*
agitator	agitador(a) *nmf*
ally	aliado, -a *nmf*
ambassador	embajador(a) *nmf*
amnestied person	amnistiado, -a *nmf*
anarchist	anarquista *nmf*
anticommunist, anti-Communist	anticomunista *aj, nmf*
aristocrat	aristócrata *nmf*
assassin	asesino, -a *nmf*
assemblyman	asambleísta *nmf*
assemblywoman	asambleísta *nmf*
autocrat	autócrata *nmf*
bureaucrat	burócrata *nmf*
candidate	candidato, -a *nmf*
capitalist	capitalista *nmf*
centrist	centrista *nmf*
chancellor	canciller *nm*
chauvinist	chovinista *aj, nmf*
colonist	colono, -a *nmf*
colonizer	colonizador(a) *nmf*
communist, Communist	comunista *aj, nmf*
compatriot	compatriota *nmf*
congressman	congresista *nm*
congresswoman	congresista *nf*
conscientious objector	objetor(a) de conciencia *nmf, nf*
conservative	conservador(a) *aj, nmf*
consort	consorte *nmf*
consul	cónsul *nm*
councilman	concejal *nm*
councilwoman	concejala *nf*
counterspy	contraespía *nmf*
delegate	delegado, -a *nf*
demagog(ue)	demagogo *nm*
Democrat	demócrata *nmf*
despot	déspota *nm*
dignitary	dignatario, -a *nmf*
diplomat	diplomático *nmf*
displaced person	desplazado, -a *nmf*
dissenter, dissident	disidente *nmf*
egalitarian	igualitario, -a *aj, nmf*
elector	elector(a) *nmf*
emancipator	emancipador(a) *nmf*
emigre	emigrado *nm*

emigree	emigrada *nf*
emissary	emisario, -a *nmf*
emperor	emperador *nm*
empress	emperatriz *nf*
envoy	enviado, -a *nmf*
exile	exil(i)ado, -a *nmf*
expatriate	expatriado, -a *aj, nmf*
extremist	extremista *nmf*
fascist	fascista *aj, nmf*
federalist	federalista *aj, nmf*
feminist	feminista *aj, nmf*
functionary	funcionario, -a *nmf*
governor	gobernador(a) *nmf*
immigrant	inmigrante *aj, nmf*
imperialist	imperialista *aj, nmf*
insurgent	insurgente *aj, nmf*
integrationist	integracionista *nmf*
interventionist	intervencionista *nmf*
isolationist	aislacionista *aj, nmf*
jingo, jingoist	jingoísta *nmf*
laborite	laborista *nmf*
leader	líder *nm*
legislator	legislador(a) *nmf*
liberal	liberal *aj, nmf*
libertarian	libertario, -a *nmf*
martyr	mártir *nmf*
Marxist	marxista *aj, nmf*
matriarch	matriarca *nf*
member	miembro *nmf*
militarist	militarista *nmf*
minister	ministro, -a *nmf*
moderate	moderado, -a *aj, nmf*
monarch	monarca *nm*
monarchist	monarquista *nmf*
nationalist	nacionalista *nmf*
negotiator	negociador(a) *nmf*
neo-Nazi	neonazi *aj, nmf*
nonresident	no residente *aj, nmf*
observer	observador(a) *nmf*
obstructionist	obstruccionista *nmf*
oligarch	oligarca *nm*
pacifist	pacifista *nmf*
pamphleteer	panfletista *nmf*
parliamentarian	parlamentario, -a *nmf*
party member	partidista *nmf*
patriot	patriota *nmf*
plenipotentiary	plenipotenciario *aj, nm*
plutocrat	plutócrata *nmf*
political schemer	politiquero, -a *nmf*
political scientist	politólogo, -a *nmf*
politician	político, -a *nmf*
populist	populista *aj, nmf*

potentate	potentado *nm*
president	presidente *nmf*
president-elect	presidente electo *nm*
pretender	pretendiente *nmf*
prime minister (man)	primer ministro *nm*
prime minister (woman)	primera ministra *nf*
progressive	progresista *aj, nmf*
proletarian	proletario, -a *aj, nmf*
propagandist	propagandista *nmf*
protectionist	proteccionista *aj, nmf*
provocateur	agente provocador *nmf*
radical	radical *nmf*
reactionary	reaccionario, -a *aj, nmf*
rebel	rebelde *nmf*
refugee	refugiado, -a *nmf*
repatriate	repatriado, -a *nmf*
representative	representante *nmf*
Republican	republicano, -a *nmf*
revanchist	revanchista *aj, nmf*
revolutionary	revolucionario, -a *aj, nmf*
royalist	realista *aj, nmf*
saboteur	saboteador(a) *nmf*
secretary	secretario, -a *nmf*
secretary-general	secretario, -a general *nmf*
senator	senador(a) *nmf*
separatist	separatista *aj, nmf*
socialist	socialista *aj, nmf*
sovereign	soberano, -a *aj, nmf*
Sovietologist	sovietólogo, -a *nmf*
spy	espía *nmf*
statesman/ stateswoman	estadista *nmf*
subversive	subversivo, -a *aj, nmf*
sympathizer	simpatizante *nmf*
technocrat	tecnócrata *nmf*
traitor	traidor(a) *nmf*
treasurer	tesorero, -a *nmf*
tyrant	tirano, -a *nmf*
ultraconservative	ultraconservador(a) *aj, nmf*
undersecretary	subsecretario, -a *nmf*
vice-president	vicepresidente *nmf*
voter	votante *nmf*
Zionist	sionista *aj, nmf*

(*See also political and military* under **LAW**; *procedures* under **ORGANIZATIONS AND MEETINGS**; **TITLES**)

Buying and Selling

ECONOMICS

GENERAL TERMS

balance of trade	balanza de comercio *nf*
Benelux	Benelux *nm*
by-product	subproducto *nm*
capital	capital *nm*
class	clase *nf*
collective	colectivo *nm*
collective bargaining	negociación colectiva *nf*
commerce	comercio *nm*
Common Market	Mercado Común *nm*
consumption	consumo *nm*
distribution	distribución *nf*
economy	economía *nf*
ECU, ecu	ECU, ecu *nm*
Federal Reserve Board	Junta de la Reserva Federal
GATT	GATT *nm*
index	índice *nm*
industry	industria *nf*
infrastructure	infraestructura *nf*
intervention	intervención *nf*
labor	laboral *aj*
market	mercado *nm*
mass production	producción en serie *nf*
medium of exchange	medio de pago *nm*
modeling	modelización *nf*
NAFTA	NAFTA *nm*
national (debt)	nacional *aj*
nationalization	nacionalización *nf*
OPEC	OPEC, OPEP *nf*
petrodollar	petrodólar *nm*
product	producto *nm*
production	producción *nf*
property	propiedad *nf*
protective tariff	tarifa proteccionista *nf*
quota	cuota *nf*
sanction	sanción *nf*
service	servicio *nm*
socioeconomic	socioeconómico *aj*
standard of living	estándar de vida *nm, nf*
tariff	tarifa *nf*

SPECIALIZATIONS

consumerism	consumismo *nm*
econometrics	econometría *nf*

macroeconomics	macroeconomía *nf*
microeconomics	microeconomía *nf*

ASPECTS OF ECONOMICS

classes

aristocracy	aristocracia *nf*
bourgeoisie	burguesía *nf*
intelligentsia	inteligentsia *nf*
lumpenproletariat	lumpenproletariado *nm*
proletariat	proletariado *nm*

systems and theories

autarchy	autarquía *nf*
capitalism	capitalismo *nm*
communism	comunismo *nm*
expansionism	expansionismo *nm*
fascism	fascismo *nm*
feudalism	feudalismo *nm*
industrialism	industrialismo *nm*
mercantilism	mercantilismo *nm*
monetarism	monetarismo *nm*
protectionism	proteccionismo *nm*
slavery	esclavitud *nf*
socialism	socialismo *nm*
syndicalism	sindicalismo *nm*
vassalage	vasallaje *nm*

kinds of economies

centralized	centralizado *aj*
controlled	controlado *aj*
free market	de libre mercado *aj*
industrialized	industrializado *aj*
international	internacional *aj*
invisible	invisible *aj*
planned	planificada *aj*
stable	estable *aj*

economic conditions

boom	boom *nm*
deflation	deflación *nf*
depression	depresión *nf*
employment	empleo *nm*
inflation	inflación *nf*
poverty	pobreza *nf*
productivity	productividad *nf*
recession	recesión *nf*
scarcity	escasez *nf*
stagflation	estagflación *nf*
stagnation	estancamiento *nm*
unemployment	desempleo *nm*

PERSONS

bourgeois	burgués, -esa *aj, nmf*
capitalist	capitalista *nmf*
consumer	consumidor(a) *nmf*
economist	economista *nmf*
industrialist	industrial *nmf*
Keynesian	keynesiano, -a *aj, nmf*
Marxist	marxista *aj, nmf*
producer	productor(a) *nmf*
proletarian	proletario, -a *aj, nmf*
protectionist	proteccionista *aj, nmf*

(*See also* **BUSINESS**; **MONEY AND FINANCE**)

BUSINESS

GENERAL TERMS

audit	auditoría *nf*
boycott	boicot, boicoteo *nm*
cancellation	cancelación *nf*
capital	capital *nm*
cargo	carga, cargamento *nf, nm*
commerce	comercio *nm*
competition	competencia *nf*
cost	costo, coste *nm*
credit	crédito *nm*
cycle	ciclo *nm*
demand	demanda *nf*
employment	empleo *nm*
expansion	expansión *nf*
financing	financiamiento, financiación *nm, nf*
fixed (price, interest)	fijo *aj*
freightage (cost)	flete *nm*
gain	ganancia *nf*
inventory	inventario *nm*
market, marketplace	mercado *nm*
moratorium	moratoria *nf*
net (profit)	neto *aj*
operate	operar *vti*
price	precio *nm*
price-fixing	fijación de precios *nf, nmpl*
product	producto *nm*
prohibitive (cost)	prohibitivo *aj*
quality	calidad *nf*
receipt	recibo *nm*
regulations *npl*	reglamento *nm*
representation	representación *nf*
residual (profit)	residual *aj*
service	servicio *nm*

unit	unidad *nf*
value	valor *nm*

KINDS OF BUSINESSES

ownership and organization

cartel	cártel *nm*
company	compañía *nf*
conglomerate	conglomerado *nm*
consortium	consorcio *nm*
cooperative	cooperativa *nf*
corporation	corporación *nf*
firm	firma *nf*
franchise	franquicia *nf*
monopoly	monopolio *nm*
multinational	multinacional *aj, nf*
mutual *nsg*	seguros mutuos *nmpl*
subsidiary	subsidiario *aj, nm*

type of product or service

accounting	contabilidad *nf*
agriculture	agricultura *nf*
banking	banca *nf*
construction	construcción *nf*
consulting	consultoría *nf*
contracting	contratación *nf*
exporting	exportación *nf*
fabrication	fabricación *nf*
importing	importación *nf*
manufacturing	manufactura *nf*
marketing	mercadeo *nm*
mining	minería *nf*
publications	publicaciones *nfpl*
transportation	tra(n)sportación *nf*

RETAIL MARKETING

places

antique shop	anticuario *nm*
bank	banco *nm*
bazaar, bazar	bazar *nm*
boutique	boutique *nf*
concession	concesión *nf*
department store	tienda por departamentos *nf, nmpl*
emporium	emporio *nm*
establishment	establecimiento *nm*
hotel	hotel *nm*
kiosk	kiosco, quiosco *nm*
motel	motel *nm*
perfumery	perfumería *nf*
pharmacy	farmacia *nf*

restaurant	restaurante *nm*
souk	zoco *nm*
supermarket	supermercado *nm*

advertising

announcement	anuncio *nm*
campaign	campaña *nf*
catalog(ue)	catálogo *nm*
circular	circular *nf*
commercial	anuncio comercial *nm*
economical	económico *aj*
exposition	exposición *nf*
logo	logo, logotipo *nm*
promotion	promoción *nf*
slogan	slogan, eslogan *nm*

selling

assortment	surtido *nm*
commission	comisión *nf*
consignment	consignación *nf*
container	contenedor *nm*
discount	descuento *nm*
merchandise *nsg*	mercancias *nfpl*
offer	oferta *nf*
option	opción *nf*
package	paquete *nm*
packaging	empaque *nm*
prospectus	prospecto *nm*
quotation	cotización *nf*
receipt	recibo *nm*
transaction	transacción *nf*

LEGAL TERMS

ad valorem	ad valorem *av*
contraband	contrabando *nm*
contract	contrato *nm*
contractual	contractual *aj*
embargo	embargo *nm*
guarantee	garantía *nf*
obligation	obligación *nf*
patent	patente *nf*
title	título *nm*

OFFICE EQUIPMENT

calendar	calendario *nm*
clip	clip *nm*
computer	computadora *nf*
copier	fotocopiadora *nf*
duplicator	duplicador *aj*
fax	fax *nm*
numbering machine	numeradora *nf*
paper	papel *nm*

photocopier	fotocopiadora *nf*
portfolio	portafolio *nm*
telephone	teléfono *nm*

PERSONS

buyers

clientele	clientela *nf*
consumer	consumidor(a) *nmf*

sellers

coffee merchant	cafetero, -a *nmf*
concessionaire	concesionario *nm*
fruit merchant	frutero, -a *nmf*
lottery ticket seller	lotero, -a *nmf*
merchant	mercante, mercader, merchante *nmf*
proprietor	propietario, -a *nmf*
trafficker	traficante *nmf*
vendor	vendedor(a) *nmf*

other business people

auditor	auditor(a) *nmf*
competitor	competidor(a) *nmf*
consignee	consignatorio, -a *nmf*
consignor	cosignador(a) *nmf*
contractor	contratista *nmf*
directors (board of)	directiva *nf*
executive	ejecutivo *nm*
exporter	exportador(a) *nmf*
fabricator	fabricante *nmf*
importer	importador(a) *nmf*
personnel	personal *nm*
subcontractor	subcontratista *nmf*
supervisor	supervisor(a) *nmf*
consultant	consultor(a) *nmf*
demonstrator	demostrador(a) *nmf*
director	director(a) *nmf*
employee, employe	empleado, -a *nmf*
inspector	inspector(a) *nmf*
producer	productor(a) *nmf*
promoter	promotor(a) *nmf*
rival	rival *aj, nmf*
secretary	secretario, -a *nmf*

(*See also* **ECONOMICS**; **MONEY AND FINANCE**)

MONEY AND FINANCE

GENERAL TERMS

banking	banca *nf*
credit card	tarjeta de crédito *nf*
currency	moneda corriente *nf*

devaluation	devaluación, desvalorización *nf*
finance	finanza *nf*
fiscal	fiscal *aj*
guaranty	garantía *nf*
interest	interés *nm*
monetary	monetario *aj*
par	par *nf*
payment	pago *nm*
per capita	per cápita *av*
per cent	por ciento *av*
realization	realización *nf*
valuables	objetos de valor *nmpl, nm*

FINANCIAL CONDITION

having/making money

accumulate	acumular(se) *vt(r)*
amass	amasar *vt*
compensation	compensación *nf*
fortune	fortuna *nf*
honorarium	honorarios *nmpl*
lucrative	lucrativo *aj*
luxury	lujo *nm*
pension	pensión *nf*
recompense	recompensa *nf*
reimbursement	reembolso *nm*
remuneration	remuneración *nf*
riches	riquezas *nfpl*
salary	salario *nm*
solvency	solvencia *nf*
stipend	estipendio *nm*
subsidy	subsidio *nm*
subvention	subvención *nf*

not having/losing money

bankruptcy	bancarrota *nf*
debt	deuda *nf*
deficit	déficit *nm*
dissipation	disipación *nf*
impoverishment	empobrecimiento *nm*
incur (expense)	incurrir *vt*
indebtedness	adeudo *nm*
insolvency	insolvencia *nf*
parsimony	parsimonia *nf*
pauperism	pauperismo *nm*
penury	penuria *nf*
poor	pobre *aj*
poverty	pobreza *nf*
reversal	revés *nm*
ruin	ruina *nf*

ASPECTS OF MONEY AND FINANCE

banking

account	cuenta *nf*
balance	balance *nm*
bank	banco *nm*
blank (check)	en blanco
CD	CD *nm*
certified (check)	certificado *aj*
check	cheque *nm*
checkbook	chequera *nf*
credit	crédito *nm*
debit	debe, débito *nm*
deposit	depósito *nm*
endorsement	endoso *nm*
floating	flotante *aj*
percentage	porcentaje *nm*
personal (check)	personal *aj*
PIN	PIN *nm*
promissory (note)	promisorio *aj*
redeem	redimir *vt*
refinancing	refinanciamiento *nm*
self-financing	autofinanciamiento *nm*
transaction	transacción *nf*
transfer, transference	tra(n)sferencia *nf*

stock market

appreciation	apreciación *nf*
arbitrage, arbitration	arbitraje *nm*
bond	bono *nm*
calculated (risk)	calculado *aj*
commission	comisión *nf*
convertible	convertible *aj*
correction	corrección *nf*
coupon	cupón *nm*
dilution (of assets)	dilución *nf*
discount rate	tasa de descuento *nf, nm*
dividend	dividendo *nm*
fund	fondo *nm*
futures	futuros *nmpl*
gain	ganancia *nf*
liquid (assets)	líquido *aj*
list	lista *nf*
margin	margen *nm*
negotiable	negociable *aj*
nominal (value)	nominal *aj*
nonnegotiable	no negociable *aj*
obligation	obligación *nf*
offering	ofrenda *nf*
option	opción *nf*
parity	paridad *nf*
preferred	preferente *aj*

price	precio *nm*
principal	principal *nm*
pro rata	prorrata *av*
quotation	cotización *nf*
speculation	especulación *nf*
value	valor *nm*

insurance

– types of insurance –

accident	accidente *nm*
collision	colisión *nf*
hospitalization	hospitalización *nf*
medical	médico *aj*
postal	postal *aj*
property	propiedad *nf*

– other insurance terms –

actuarial	actuarial *aj*
annuity	anualidad *nf*
claim	reclamación *nf*
coverage	cobertura *nf*
damage	daño *nm*
expectancy (life)	expectativa *nf*
indemnity (compensation)	indemnización *nf*
indemnity (exemption)	indemnidad *nf*
lapse	lapso *nm*
mutual	mutuo *aj*
policy	póliza *nf*
premium	primo *nm*
risk	riesgo *nm*

taxes

amortization	amortización *nf*
audit	auditoría *nf*
charity	caridad *nf*
collect	colectar *vt*
deduction	deducción *nf*
depreciation	depreciación *nf*
exclusion	exclusión *nf*
exemption	exención *nf*
intangible	intangible *aj*

other terms

acceptance	aceptación *nf*
cancel (a debt)	cancelar *vt*
charge	cargo *nm*
consolidation (debts)	consolidación *nf*
disposable income *nsg*	ingresos disponibles*nmpl*
gratis	gratis *av*
order (to pay)	orden *nf*
pecuniary	pecuniario *aj*
remit	remitir *vt*

surcharge	sobrecarga *nf*
tribute (obs)	tributo *nm*

MONETARY UNITS

current

balboa	balboa *nm*
bolivar	bolívar *nm*
boliviano	boliviano *nm*
cent	centavo *nm*
centesimo	centésimo *nm*
centime	céntimo *nm*
colon	colón *nm*
cordoba	córdoba *nm*
cruzeiro	cruzeiro *nm*
dinar	dinar *nm*
dollar	dólar *nm*
drachma	dracma *nm*
escudo	escudo *nm*
euro	euro *nm*
florin	florín *nm*
forint	forint *nm*
franc	franco *nm*
guarani	guaraní *nm*
guilder	gulden *nm*
kopeck	copec *nm*
krona	corona *nf*
krone	corona *nf*
krugerrand	krugerrand *nm*
lempira	lempira *nm*
leu	leu *nm*
lev	lev *nm*
lira	lira *nf*
mark	marco *nm*
penny	penique *nm*
peseta	peseta *nf*
peso	peso *nm*
pfennig	pfennig *nm*
piaster, piastre	piastra *nf*
quetzal	quetzal *nm*
rand	rand *nm*
rial	rial *nm*
riyal	riyal *nm*
ruble	rublo *nm*
rupee	rupia *nf*
schilling (Austrian)	chelín *nm*
shekel	shekel, siclo *nm*
shilling (British)	chelín *nm*
sol	sol *nm*
sterling	esterlina *nf*
yen	yen *nm*
yuan	yuan *nm*
zloty	zloty *nm*

historical and obsolete

crown	corona *nf*
denarius	denario *nm*
doubloon	doblón *nm*
ducat	ducado *nm*
guinea	guinea *nf*
napoleon	napoleón *nm*
real	real *nm*
sequin	cequí *nm*
talent	talento *nm*

other terms

bill	billete *nm*
billfold	billetera *nf*
circulation	circulación *nf*
Eurodollar	eurodólar *nm*
inscription	inscripción *nf*
legend (on coin)	leyenda *nf*
piece	pieza *nf*
reverse (of coin)	reverso *nm*
stable (currency)	estable *aj*

PERSONS

accountant	contable, contador(a) *nmf*
actuary	actuario *nm*
adjuster	ajustador(a) *nmf*
analyst	analista *nmf*
auditor	auditor(a) *nmf*
banker	banquero *nmf*
beneficiary	beneficiario, -a *nmf*
billionaire	billonario, -a *nmf*
cashier	cajero, -a *nmf*
cosignatory	cosignatario, -a *nmf*
creditor	acreedor(a) *nmf*
debtor	deudor(a) *nmf*
depositor	depositante *nmf*
endorser	endosador(a), endosante *nmf*
financier	financiero, -a *nmf*
guarantor	garante *nmf*
indigent	indigente *aj, nmf*
magnate	magnate *nmf*
millionaire	millonario, -a *nmf*
multimillionaire	multimillonario, -a *nmf*
numismatist	numismatista *nmf*
speculator	especulador(a) *nmf*
statistician	estadístico, -a *nmf*
treasurer	tesorero, -a *nmf*
usurer	usurero, -a *nmf*

(*See also* **BUSINESS**; *financial* under **LAW**)

Transportation

AVIATION AND SPACE TRAVEL

GENERAL TERMS

aerospace	espacio *nm*
air	aire *nm*
airline	aerolínea *nf*
aviation	aviación *nf*
instrument	instrumento *nm*
pressurized (cabin)	a presión *nf*
satellite	satélite *nm*
solo	volar solo *vi*
space	espacio *nm*
spaceship	nave espacial *nf*

FIELDS OF SPECIALIZATION

aerobatics	acrobacia *nf*
aerodynamics	aerodinámica *nf*
aeromedicine	aeromedicina *nf*
aeronautics	aeronáutica *nf*
altimetry	altimetría *nf*
astronautics	astronáutica *nf*
astronomy	astronomía *nf*
avionics	aviónica *nf*
bioastronautics	bioastronáutica *nf*
cosmogony	cosmogonía *nf*
cosmography	cosmografía *nf*
cosmology	cosmología *nf*
exobiology	biología espacial *nf*
navigation	navegación *nf*
telemetry	telemetría *nf*

ASPECTS OF AIR TRAVEL

places

aerodrome	aeródromo *nm*
airport	aeropuerto *nm*
hangar	hangar *nm*
heliport	helipuerto *nm*
terminal	terminal *nm*
tower	torre *nf*

types of aircraft

aerostat	aeróstato *nm*
air taxi	aerotaxi *nm*
airliner	aeronave *nf*
airplane	aeroplano *nm*
aquaplane	acuaplano *nm*

balloon	balón *nm*		horizon	horizonte *nm*
biplane	biplano *nm*		piloting	pilotaje *nm*
bomber	bombardero *nm*		taxi	taxear *vi*
dirigible	dirigible *nm*		traffic	tráfico *nm*
helicopter	helicóptero *nm*		turbulence	turbulencia *nf*
monoplane	monoplano *nm*		velocity	velocidad *nf*
ornithopter	ornitóptero *nm*			
transport	transporte *nm*			
turbojet	turborreactor *nm*			
turboprop	turbopropulsor *nm*			
zeppelin	zepelín *nm*			

communications systems

loran	lorán *nm*
radar	radar *nm*
shoran	shoran *nm*

parts and equipment

aileron	alerón *nm*
astrodome	astródomo *nm*
autogyro	autogiro *nm*
board	bordo *nm*
cabin	cabina *nf*
chart	carta *nf*
compass	compás *nm*
ejector	eyector *nm*
float	flotador *nm*
fuselage	fuselaje *nm*
gyrostabilizer	giroestabilizador *nm*
interceptor	interceptor *nm*
manifest	manifiesto *nm*
marker	marcador *nm*
mask	máscara *nf*
oxygen	oxígeno *nm*
panel	panel *nm*
retractable (wheels)	retractable *aj*
rotor	rotor *nm*
stabilizer	estabilizador *nm*

TERMS IN SPACE TRAVEL

parts and equipment

capsule	cápsula *nf*
module	módulo *nm*
propellant	propelente *nm*
retrorocket	retrocohete *nm*
umbilical	cordón umbilical *nm*

other terms

destruct	destrucción deliberada *nf*
ejection	eyección *nf*
escape	escape *nm*
exploration	exploración *nf*
extraterrestrial	extraterrestre *aj*
launch	lancha *nf*
mission	misión *nf*
NASA	NASA *nf*
orbit	órbita *nf*
propulsion	propulsión *nf*
sonic	sónico *aj*
space probe	sonda espacial *nf*
space-walk	pasear por el espacio *vi*
station	estación *nf*
stratospheric	estratosférico *aj*
supersonic	supersónico *aj*
zero gravity	gravedad nula *nf*

instruments

altimeter	altímetro *nm*
controls	controles *nmpl*
gyrocompass	girocompás *nm*
gyropilot	giropiloto *nm*
gyroscope	giroscopio *nm*
indicator	indicador *nm*
radio	radio *nm*
tachometer	tacómetro *nm*
telemeter	telemetro *nm*
transmitter	transmisor *nm*

PERSONS

ace	as *nmf*
astronaut	astronauta *nmf*
aviator	aviador(a) *nmf*
captain	capitán, -ana *nmf*
copilot	copiloto *nmf*
cosmonaut	cosmonauta *nmf*
engineer	ingeniero *nmf*
navigator	navegante *nmf*
passenger	pasajero, -a *nmf*

flying and navigation

airway	aerovía *nf*
altitude	altura *nf*
ascent	ascenso *nm*
descent	descenso *nm*
deviation	desviación *nf*
direction	dirección *nf*

pilot	piloto *nmf*
radar operator	radarista *nmf*

(*See also* **METEOROLOGY**)

BOATS AND SHIPS

GENERAL TERMS

aboard	a bordo *av*
boat	bote *nm*
navigation	navegación *nf*
port	puerto *nm*
sailboat	bote de vela *nm, nf*
tonnage	tonelaje *nm*

WATER VESSELS

sailboats

brigantine	bergantín *nm*
caravel	carabela *nf*
catamaran	catamarán *nm*
clipper	clíper *nm*
junk	junco *nm*
ketch	queche *nm*
trimaran	trimarán *nm*
yawl	yola *nf*

military ships

convoy	convoy *nm*
corsair	corsario *nm*
corvette	corbeta *nf*
cruiser	crucero *nm*
destroyer	destructor *nm*
frigate	fragata *nf*
galleon	galeón *nm*
minelayer	minador *nm*
minesweeper	dragaminas *nm*
submarine	submarino *nm*
torpedo boat	torpedero *nm*

other craft

aquaplane	acuaplano *nm*
barge	barcaza *nf*
bathyscaph(e)	batiscafo *nm*
bathysphere	batisfera *nf*
canoe	canoa *nf*
cargo boat	carguero *nm*
cutter	cúter *nm*
derelict	derrelicto *nm*
gondola	góndola *nf*
hydrofoil	hidrofoil *nm*
hydroplane	hidroplano *nm*
kayak	kayac *nm*

launch	lancha *nf*
motorboat	motora *nf*
pirogue	piragua *nf*
rowboat	bote de remos *nm, nmpl*
sampan	sampán *nm*
skiff	esquife *nm*
tanker	tanquista *nf*
yacht	yate *nm*

groups of ships

armada	armada *nf*
fleet	flota *nf*
flotilla	flotilla *nf*
squadron	escuadra *nf*

parts and sections

board	bordo *nm*
cabin	cabina *nf*
galley	galera *nf*
keel	quilla *nf*
lateen	latina *aj*
mast	mástil *nm*
poop deck	castilla de popa *nf*
porthole	portilla *nf*
prow	proa *nf*
stabilizer	estabilizador *nm*
superstructure	superestructura *nf*

NAVIGATION

kinds of navigation

celestial navigation	navegación astronómica *nf*
loran	lorán *nm*
radar	radar *nm*
radio navigation	radionavegación *nf*
sonar	sónar *nm*

tools and equipment

anchor	ancla, áncora *nf*
bowline	bolina *nf*
buoy	boya *nf*
chart	carta *nf*
compass	compás *nm*
dredger	draga *nf*
float	flotador *nm*
gyrocompass	girocompás *nm*
gyropilot	giropiloto *nm*
gyroscope	giroscopio *nm*
gyrostabilizer	giroestabilizador *nm*
hydrophone	hidrófono *nm*
line	línea *nf*
marker	marcador *nm*

monitor	monitor *nm*
periscope	periscopio *nm*
pontoon	pontón *nm*
sextant	sextante *nm*
tachometer	tacómetro *nm*

plotting

deviation	desviación *nf*
distance	distancia *nf*
point	punto *nm*
position	posición *nf*
route	ruta *nf*
sounding	sondeo *nm*
time	tiempo *nm*
wind	viento *nm*

measurements

knot	nudo *nm*
league	legua *nf*
octant	octante *nm*
quadrant	cuadrante *nm*

waterways

canal	canal *nm*
channel	canal *nm*
coast, seacoast	costa *nf*
lake	lago *nm*
ocean	océano *nm*
river	río *nm*

starting and ending

anchorage (action)	anclaje *nm*
anchorage (place)	ancladero *nm*
arrival	arribo *nm*
disembarcation (cargo)	desembarque *nm*
embarcation	embarcación, embarco *nf, nm*
launching	lanzamiento *nm*

other terms

afloat	a flote *av*
ahoy	ahó *intj*
careen	carena, carenadura *nf*
circumnavigation	circunnavegación *nf*
crosscurrent	contracorriente *nf*
displacement	desplazamiento *nm*
flotation	flotación *nf*
radio beacon	radiofaro *nm*
salvage	salvamento *nm*
submersion	sumersión *nf*
undercurrent	corriente submarina *nf*
unnavigable	innavegable *aj*
waterline	línea de flotación *nf*
windward	barlovento *aj, av*

MARITIME TRADE TERMS

cabotage	cabotaje *nm*
cargo	carga, cargamento *nf, nm*
embargo	embargo *nm*
freightage (cost)	flete *nm*
manifest	manifiesto *nm*
merchant marine	marina mercante *nf*
quarantine	cuarentena *nf*

PERSONS

aquanaut	acuanauta *nmf*
captain	capitán, -ana *nmf*
chief	jefe *nmf*
commodore	comodoro *nm*
gondolier	gondolero *nm*
launcher	lanzador(a) *nmf*
marine	marino, -a *nmf*
mariner	marinero, marino *nm*
navigator	navegante *nmf*
officer	oficial *nmf*
pilot	piloto *nmf*
pirate	pirata *nmf*
stevedore	estibador *nm*

(*See also **crimes on the high seas** under **LAW**; **directional winds** under **METEOROLOGY**; **water sports** under **SPORTS***)

LAND TRANSPORTATION

GENERAL TERMS

beast of burden	bestia de carga *nf*
motor vehicle	vehículo automotor *nm*
traffic	tráfico *nm*
transportation	tra(n)sportación *nf*
vehicle	vehículo *nm*

MEANS OF TRANSPORTATION

motor-driven vehicles

ambulance	ambulancia *nf*
automobile	automóvil *nm*
bus	autobús, bus *nm*
car	carro *nm*
elevated railroad	ferrocarril elevado *nm*
funicular	funicular *nm*
limousine	limusina *nf*
metro	metro *nm*
monorail	monorriel *nm*
motorcycle	moto, motocicleta *nf*
omnibus	ómnibus *nm*

taxi, taxicab	taxi, taxímetro *nm*
trailer	trailer *nm*
train	tren *nm*
tramway	tranvía *nf*
trolley	trole *nm*
trolleybus	trolebús *nm*

human-driven vehicles

bicycle	bicicleta *nf*
cart	carreta *nf*
litter (obs)	litera *nf*
scooter	escúter *nm*
ski	esquí *nm*
toboggan	tobogán *nm*
tricycle	triciclo *nm*
unicycle	monociclo *nm*
velocipede	velocípedo *nm*

animal-driven vehicles

caravan	caravana *nf*
carriage	carruaje *nm*
phaeton (obs)	faetón *nm*
troika	troica *nf*

mechanical devices

carrousel (baggage)	carrusel *nm*
elevator	elevador *nm*
escalator	escalera *nf*
skilift	telesquí *nm*

animals

ass	asno, -a *nmf*
buffalo	búfalo *nm*
camel	camello *nm*
elephant	elefante *nm*
llama	llama *nf*
mule	mulo, -a *nmf*
yak	yac *nm*

(*See also* **AUTOMOBILES**; *streets and traffic* under **THE CITY**; **TRAVEL AND TOURISM**)

Living Things Great and Small

PLANTS

GENERAL TERMS

agriculture	agricultura *nf*
androgyny	androginia *nf*

coloration	coloración *nf*
conservation, conservancy	conservación *nf*
cultivation	cultivo *nm*
deforestation	desforestación *nf*
flora	flora *nf*
florescence	florescencia *nf*
forestation	forestación *nf*
garden	jardín *nm*
gardening	jardinería *nf*
habitat	habitat *nm*
nature	naturaleza *nf*
plant	plantar *vt*
reforestation	reforestación *nf*
vegetation	vegetación *nf*
verdure	verdor, verdura *nm, nf*

MAJOR FIELDS OF SPECIALIZATION

agronomy	agronomía *nf*
botany	botánica *nf*
dendochronology	dendocronologia *nf*
dendrology	dendrologia *nf*
ecology	ecología *nf*
floriculture	floricultura *nf*
forestry	ingenería forestal *nf*
horticulture	horticultura *nf*
hydroponics	hidroponía, hidroponia *nf*
lichenology	liquenología *nf*
phytogeography	fitogeografía *nf*
phytopathology	fitopatología *nf*
pomology	pomología *nf*
silviculture	silvicultura *nf*

PLANT CLASSIFICATIONS

angiosperm	angiosperma *nf*
annual	planta anual *nf*
aquatic	acuático, acuátil *aj*
biennial	planta bienal *aj, nf*
bryophyte	briofita *nf*
carnivorous	carnívoro, carnicero *aj*
chaparral	chaparral *nm*
chlorophyte	clorofita *nf*
composite	compuesto *aj, nm*
conifer	conífera *nf*
coniferous	conífero *aj*
cryptogam	criptógama *nf*
cycad	cicadácea *nf*
datura	datura *nf*
deciduous (tree)	deciduo *aj*
epiphyte	epífita *nf*
exotic	exótico *aj*

flowering	floreciente *aj*
foliate	foliado *aj*
fungus	fungo *nm*
gramineous	gramíneo *aj*
gymnosperm	gimnosperma *nf*
herb	hierba *nf*
hermaphrodite	hermafrodita *aj, nmf*
hybrid	híbrido *aj, nm*
insectivore	insectívoro *nm*
legume	legumbre *nf*
lichen	líquen *nm*
lycopod	licopodio *nm*
moss	musgo *nm*
perennial	planta perenne *nf*
phytoplankton	fitoplancton *nm*
pteridophyte	pteridófita *nf*
spermatophyte	espermatófita *nf*
spermatozoid	espermatozoide *nm*
succulent	suculento *nm*
thalophyte	talofita *nf*
vascular	vascular *aj*
xerophyte	xerofita *nf*

NAMES OF PLANTS

trees and shrubs

acacia	acacia *nf*
acanthus	acanto *nm*
ailanthus	ailanto *nm*
almond tree	almendro *nm*
anil	añil *nm*
azalea	azalea *nf*
balsa	balsa *nf*
balsam	abeto balsámico *nm*
banana	banano *nm*
banyan	baniano *nm*
baobab	baobab *nm*
bougainvillea	buganvilla *nf*
box, boxwood	boj *nm*
cacao	cacao *nm*
calabash	calabacero *nm*
camellia	camelia *nf*
camphor	alcanforero, alcanfor *nm*
catalpa	catalpa *nf*
cedar	cedro *nm*
ceiba	ceiba *nf*
cherry	cerezo *nm*
cinchona	chinchona *nf*
citron	cidro *nm*
clove	clavero *nm*
coca	coca *nf*
coconut palm	cocotero *nm*

coffee tree	cafeto *nm*
cola, kola	cola *nf*
cork oak	alcornoque *nm*
croton	crotón *nm*
cypress	ciprés *nm*
date palm	datilera *nf*
ebony	ébano *nm*
elm	olmo *nm*
eucalyptus	eucalipto *nm*
fig	higuera *nf*
forsythia	forsitia *nf*
fruit tree	frutal *nm*
ginkgo	gingco *nm*
guava	guayabo *nm*
guayule	guayule *nm*
gum	goma *nf*
jacaranda	jacarandá *nm*
jasmine	jazmín *nm*
jojoba	jojoba *nf*
juniper	junípero *nm*
kalmia	kalmia *nf*
kamala	kamala *nm*
kapok	capoquero *nm*
kumquat	kuncuat *nm*
laburnum	laburno *nm*
laurel	laurel, lauro *nm*
lemon	limonero *nm*
lilac	lila *nf*
lime	limero *nm*
magnolia	magnolia *nf*
mango	mango *nm*
manzanita	manzanita *nf*
mesquite	mezquita *nf*
mimosa	mimosa *nf*
myrtle	mirto *nm*
ocotillo	ocotillo *nm*
olive	olivo *nm*
orange	naranjo *nm*
palm	palma, palmera *nf*
palmetto	palmito *nm*
papaya	papayo *nm*
pear	peral *nm*
pecan	pacana *nf*
pine	pino *nm*
pineapple	piña *nf*
pistachio	pistacho *nm*
poinciana	poinciana *nf*
pomegranate	granado *nm*
quassia	cuasia *nf*
rhododendron	rododendro *nm*
rosebush	rosal *nm*
sago	sagú *nm*
sandalwood	sándalo *nm*

sapodilla	zapotillo *nm*	marguerite	margarita *nf*
sassafras	sasafrás *nm*	narcissus	narciso *nm*
sequoia	secoya *nf*	nicotiana	nicotiana *nf*
spiraea	espirea *nf*	orchid	orquídea *nf*
sumac(h)	zumaque *nm*	ornamental	ornamental *aj*
sycamore	sicomoro, sicómoro *nm*	passionflower	pasionaria *nf*
tamarind	tamarindo *nm*	pelargonium	pelargonio *nm*
tamarisk	tamarisco *nm*	peony	peonía *nf*
teak	teca *nf*	petunia	petunia *nf*
tragacanth	tragacanto *nm*	philodendron	filodendro *nm*
tulip tree	tulipanero, tulipero *nm*	phlox	flox *nm*
upas	upas *nm*	pimpernel	pimpinela *nf*
viburnum	viburno *nm*	pyrethrum	piretro *nm*
yucca	yuca *nf*	rose	rosa *nf*
		salvia	salvia *nf*
		saxifrage	saxífraga, saxifragia *nf*

house and garden plants

		snapdragon	boca de dragón *nf*
		spathe	espata *nf*
abutilon	abutilón *nm*	tuberose	tuberosa *nf*
ageratum	agérato *nm*	tulip	tulipán *nm*
amaryllis	amarilis *nf*	verbena	verbena *nf*
anemone	anémona *nf*	violet	violeta *nf*
aspidistra	aspidistra *nf*	zinnia	cinnia *nf*
aster	áster *nm*		
balsam	balsamina *nf*		

wild flowers

begonia	begonia *nf*		
belladonna	belladona *nf*	aconite (plant)	acónito *nm*
bromeliad	bromelia, bromeliacea *nf*	amaranth	amaranto *nm*
		cinquefoil	quinquefolio *nm*
caladium	caladio *nm*	clematis	clemátide *nf*
cattleya	catleya *nf*	edelweiss	edelweiss *nm*
chrysanthemum	crisantemo *nm*	gentian	genciana *nf*
colchicum	cólquico *nm*	hepatica	hepática *nf*
coleus	coleo *nm*	locoweed	loco *nm*
crocus	croco *nm*	scabious	escabiosa *nf*
cyclamen	ciclamen, ciclamino *nm*	solanum	solanácea *nf*
dahlia	dalia *nf*		
delphinium	delfinio *nm*		

herbs

dracaena	drago *nm*		
freesia	fresia *nf*	calendula	caléndula *nf*
fuchsia	fucsia *nf*	cineraria	cineraria *nf*
gardenia	gardenia *nf*	coriander	coriandro *nm*
geranium	geranio *nm*	cumin	comino *nm*
gladiolus	gladiolo *nm*	fritillary	fritilaria *nf*
gloxinia	gloxínea *nf*	ginseng	ginsén, ginseng *nm*
heliotrope	heliotropo *nm*	hellebore	heléboro, eléboro *nm*
hibiscus	hibisco *nm*		
hyacinth	jacinto *nm*	lavender	lavanda *nf*
informal	informal *aj*	marjoram	mejorana *nf*
jonquil	junquillo *nm*	mint	menta *nf*
lily	lirio *nm*	quinoa	quinua *nf*
lobelia	lobelia *nf*	saffron	azafrán *nm*
lotus	loto *nm*	tarragon	estragón *nm*
lupine	lupino *aj*	vanilla	vainilla *nf*

aquatic plants

alga	alga *nf(el)*
diatom	diatomea *nf*
hydrophyte	hidrófita *nf*
kelp	kelp *nm*
papyrus	papiro *nm*
sargasso	sargazo *nm*

succulents

agave	agave *nf*
aloe	áloe, aloe *nm*
cactus	cactus, cacto *nm*
euphorbia	euforbio *nm*
opuntia	opuncia *nf*

grasses

bamboo	bambú *nm*
brome	bromo *nm*
sorghum	sorgo *nm*

other plants

bignonia	bignonia *nf*
bonsai	bonsai *nm*
bryony	brionia *nf*
campanula	campánula *nf*
jalap	jalapa *nf*
liana	liana *nf*
mandrake	mandrágora *nf*
morel	morilla *nf*
myrrh	mirra *nf*
penicillium	penicilium *nm*
ramie	ramio *nm*
rattan	rota *nf*
sphagnum	musgo esfagnáceo *nm*
spikenard	espicanardo, espicanardi *nm*
truffle	trufa *nf*

PERSONS

botanist	botanista, botánico, -a *nmf*
conservationist	conservacionista *nmf*
herbalist	herbalario *nm*
horticulturist	horticultor(a) *nmf*
naturalist	naturalista *nmf*
naturist	naturista *nmf*
rice grower	arrocero *nm*
florist	florista *nmf*
forester	guarda forestal *nmf*
palm farmer	palmero, -a *nmf*
pomologist	pomólogo, -a *nmf*

(*See also major food crops* under **AGRICULTURE**; *natural fibers* under *ASPECTS OF TEXTILES*; *vegetables*; *fruits*; *nuts*; *sauces, spices, syrups* under **FOOD AND NUTRITION**)

ANIMALS

GENERAL TERMS

animal	animal *aj, nm*
beast	bestia *nf*
brute	bruto *aj, nm*
creature	criatura *nf*
fauna	fauna *nf*

SPECIALIZATIONS

anatomy	anatomía *nf*
apiculture	apicultura *nf*
aquaculture	acuacultura *nf*
aviculture	avicultura *nf*
biochemistry	bioquímica *nf*
ecology	ecología *nf*
embryology	embriología *nf*
entomology	entomología *nf*
ethology	etología *nf*
helminthology	helmintología *nf*
herpetology	herpetología *nf*
histology	histología *nf*
ichthyology	ictiología *nf*
morphology	morfología *nf*
neurobiology	neurobiología *nf*
ophiology	ofiología *nf*
ornithology	ornitología *nf*
physiology	fisiología *nf*
sericulture	sericultura *nf*
taxidermy	taxidermia *nf*
zoogeography	zoogeografía *nf*
zoography	zoografía *nf*
zoology	zoología *nf*

CLASSIFICATIONS

acephalous	acéfalo *aj*
amphibious, amphibian	anfibio *aj, nm*
anthropoid	antropoide *aj, nm*
arthropod	artrópodo *nm*
avian	ave *nf(el)*
biped	bípedo *nm*
bivalve	bivalvo *nm*
bovine	bovino *nm*
canine	canino *aj, nm*
carnivore	carnívoro, -a *nmf*

cephalopod	cefalópodo *nm*
cetacean	cetáceo *aj, nm*
chordate	cordado *nm*
constrictor	constrictor *nm*
crustacean	crustáceo *nm*
ctenophore	ctenóforo *nm*
cyclostome	ciclóstoma *nm*
decapod	decápodo *nm*
domesticated	domesticado *aj*
echinoderm	equiodermo *nm*
edentate	edentado *aj, nm*
equine	equino *aj, nm*
exotic	exótico *aj*
feline	felino *aj, nm*
feral	feral *aj*
gallinaceous	gallináceo *aj*
herbivore	herbívoro, -a *nmf*
hermaphrodite	hermafrodita *aj, nmf*
hibernating	hibernante *aj*
hybrid	híbrido *aj, nm*
hymenopteran	himenóptero *aj, nm*
insect	insecto *nm*
insectivore	insectívoro *nm*
invertebrate	invertebrado *aj, nm*
lepidoptera	lepidópteros *nmpl*
lupine	lupino *aj*
mammalian	mamífero *nm*
marsupial	marsupial *aj, nm*
migratory	migratorio *aj*
mollusk	molusco *nm*
omnivore	omnívoro, -a *nmf*
ophidian	ofidio *aj, nm*
oviparous	ovíparo *aj*
pachyderm	paquidermo *nm*
parasite	parásito *nm*
piscatorial	piscatorio *aj*
porcine	porcino *aj*
predator	predador *nm*
primate	primate *nm*
prosimian	prosimio *aj, nm*
protozoan,	protozoo, protozoario
protozoon	*nm*
quadruped	cuadrúpedo *nm*
reptile	reptil *nm*
rodent	roedor *nm*
rorqual	rorcual *nm*
ruminant	rumiante *aj, nm*
satyr, satyrid	sátiro *nm*
saurian	saurio *aj, nm*
simian	simio, -a *nmf*
tetrapod	tetrápode *nm*
ungulate	ungulado *nm*
univalve	univalvo *aj, nm*

venomous	venenoso *aj*
vertebrate	vertebrado *aj, nm*
viviparous	vivíparo *aj*
zooid	zooide *nm*
zoophyte	zoófito *nm*

MAMMALS

primates

baboon	babuino *nm*
chimpanzee	chimpancé *nm*
gibbon	gibón *nm*
gorilla	gorila *nf*
human	humano, -a *nmf*
lemur	lémur *nm*
macaque	macaco, -a *nmf*
mandrill	mandril *nm*
orangutan	orangután *nm*
tarsier	tarsero *nm*
titi	tití *nm*

felines

angora	angora *nm*
cat	gato *nm*
cheetah	chita *nf*
civet	civeta *nf*
jaguar	jaguar *nm*
kitty	gatito, -a *nmf*
leopard	leopardo *nm*
lion	león *nm*
lioness	lcona *nf*
lynx	lince *nm*
ocelot	ocelote *nm*
panther	pantera *nf*
puma	puma *nf*
tiger	tigre *nm*
tigress	tigresa *nf*
wildcat	gato montés *nm*

canines

basset hound	basset *nm*
beagle	beagle *nm*
boxer (dog)	bóxer *nm*
bull terrier	bulterrier *nm*
bulldog	buldog *nm*
chihuahua	chihuahua *nmf*
cocker spaniel	cocker *nmf*
collie	collie *nmf*
coyote	coyote *nm*
dalmatian	dálmata *nm*
dingo	dingo *nm*
griffon	grifón *nm*
jackal	chacal *nm*

labrador	labrador *nm*
malamute	malamut *nm*
mastiff	mastín *nm*
Pekinese, Pekingese	pequinés, -esa *nmf*
spaniel	spaniel *nm*
terrier	terrier *nm*

equines

arab horse	caballo árabe *nm*
ass	asno, -a *nmf*
burro	burro, -a *nmf*
mule	mulo, -a *nmf*
mustang	mustang, mustango *nm*
onager	onagro *nm*
pinto	pinto *nm*
zebra	cebra *nf*

marsupials

kangaroo	canguro *nm*
koala	koala *nm*
opossum	oposum *nm*
wallaby	wallabi *nm*
wombat	uombat *nm*

ruminants

alpaca	alpaca *nf*
antelope	antílope *nm*
bison	bisonte *nm*
buffalo	búfalo *nm*
camel	camello *nm*
carabao	carabao *nm*
caribou	caribú *nm*
cheviot	cheviot *nm*
dromedary	dromedario *nm*
elk	alce *nm*
gaur	gaur *nm*
gazelle	gacela *nf*
giraffe	jirafa *nf*
gnu	ñu *nm*
guanaco	guanaco *nm*
ibex	íbice *nm*
impala	impala *nf*
karakul	karakul *nm*
kudu	kudu *nm*
llama	llama *nf*
merino	merino *nm*
okapi	okapí *nm*
peccary	pecarí *nm*
vicuna, vicuña	vicuña *nf*
wapiti	wapití *nm*
yak	yac, yak *nm*
zebu	cebú *nm*

rodents

agouti, agouty	agutí *nm*
chinchilla	chinchilla *nf*
gerbil	gerbo *nm*
hamster	hámster *nm*
jerboa	jerbo *nm*
lemming	lemming *nm*
marmot	marmota *nf*
mongoose	mangosta *nf*
nutria	nutria *nf*
paca	paca *nf*
porcupine	puercoespín *nm*
rat	rata *nf*

pachyderms

elephant	elefante *nm*
hippopotamus	hipopótamo *nm*
rhinoceros	rinoceronte *nm*

cetaceans

beluga	beluga *nf*
cachalot	cachalote *nm*
dolphin	delfín *nm*
dugong	dugongo *nm*
manatee	manatí *nm*
narhwal, narwal	narval *nm*

other mammals

armadillo	armadillo *nm*
babirusa, babiroussa, babirussa	babirusa *nf*
echidna	equidna *nf*
ermine	armiño *nm*
hyena	hiena *nf*
leveret	lebrato *nm*
marten	marta *nf*
panda	panda *nmf*
pangolin	pangolín *nm*
tapir	tapir *nm*

BIRDS

flying birds

bulbul	bulbul *nm*
canary	canario *nm*
cardinal	cardenal *nm*
cockatoo	cacatúa *nf*
condor	cóndor *nm*
cuckoo	cuco *nm*
eagle	águila *nf*
falcon	halcón *nm*
gyrfalcon, gerfalcon	gerifalco, gerifalte *nm*
kea	kea *nf*

marabou	marabú *nm*
myna(h)	mainato *nm*
oriole	oriopéndula *nf*
parakeet	periquito *nm*
partridge	perdiz *nf*
phalarope	falaropo, falárope *nm*
pheasant	faisán *nm*
pigeon	pichón *nm*
tanager	tanagra *nf*
toucan	tucán *nm*
tragopan	tragopón *nm*
trogon	trogón *nm*
vireo	vireo *nm*
vulture	buitre *nm*

flightless and aquatic birds

albatross	albatros *nm*
avocet	avoceta *nf*
cassowary	casuario *nm*
cormorant	cormorán *nm*
eider	eider *nm*
emu	emú *nm*
flamingo	flamenco *nm*
goose	ganso, -a *nmf*
guan	guan *nm*
ibis	ibis *nm*
kiwi	kiwi *nm*
merganser	mergánsar, mergo *nm*
pelican	pelicano *nm*
penguin	pingüino *nm*
petrel	petrel *nm*
pullet	pollo, -a *nmf*

INSECTS AND WORMS

acarid	acárido *nm*
acarus	ácaro *nm*
annelid	anélido *aj*
anopheles	anofeles *nm*
aphid	áfido *nm*
arachnid	arácnido *nm*
centipede	ciempiés *nm*
cockroach	cucaracha *nf*
hemiptera	hemíptero *nm*
kermes	quermes, kermes *nm*
mantis	mantis *nf*
millipede	milpiés *nm*
mosquito	mosquito *nm*
phylloxera	filoxera *nf*
planarian	planario *nm*
scarab	escarabajo *nm*
tarantula	tarántula *nf*
termite	termita *nf*
thysanopteran	tisanópter *aj, nm*

trichina	triquina *nf*
trichoptera	tricóptero *nm*
tsetse	tse-tsé *nf*
wasp	avispa *nf*

FISH AND MARINE LIFE

fish

albacore	albacora *nf*
anchovy	ancho(v)a *nf*
angelfish	angelote *nm*
barracuda	barracuda *nf*
bonito	bonito *nm*
bream	brema *nf*
carp	carpa *nf*
goby	gobio *nm*
grenadier	granadero *nm*
halibut	halibut *nm*
herring	arenque *nm*
lamprey	lamprea *nf*
manta ray	manta *nf*
moray	morena *nf*
perch	perca *nf*
piranha	piraña *nf*
pompano	pámpano *nm*
ray	raya *nf*
remora	rémora *nf*
salmon	salmón *nm*
sardine	sardina *nf*
sturgeon	esturión *nm*
tarpon	tarpón *nm*
trout	trucha *nf*
tuna	atún *nm*
turbot	turbo *nm*

marine animals

abalone	abalone *nm*
ameba, amoeba	ameba, amiba *nf*
amphioxus	anfioxo *nm*
anemone	anémone *nf*
argonaut	argonauta *nm*
bryozoan	briozoario *nm*
chiton	quitón *nm*
conch	concha *nf*
conger	congrio *nm*
coral	coral *nm*
cowrie, cowry	cauri *nm*
gastropod	gasterópodo *nm*
hermit crab	ermitaño *nm*
hydra	hidra *nf*
hydroid	hidroideo *nm*
medusa	medusa *nf*
nautilus	nautilo *nm*

oyster	ostra *nf*
paramecium	paramecio *nm*
polyp	pólipo *nm*
scorpion	escorpión *nm*
sepia	sepia *nf*
sponge	esponja *nf*
triton	tritón *nm*
trypanosome	tripanosoma *nm*
vorticella	vorticela *nf*

REPTILES

snakes

anaconda	anaconda *nf*
asp	áspid(e) *nm*
boa	boa *nf*
cobra	cobra *nf*
coral	coral *nm*
moccasin	mocasín *nm*
python	pitón *nm*
serpent	serpiente, sierpe (poetic) *nf*
viper	víbora *nf*

other reptiles

alligator	aligátor *nm*
axolotl	ajolote *nm*
caiman, cayman	caimán *nm*
chameleon	camaleón *nm*
crocodile	cocodrilo *nm*
gecko	geco *nm*
iguana	iguana *nf*
salamander	salamandra *nf*
skink	esquinco, estinco *nm*
tortoise	tortuga *nf*
tuatara	tuatara, tuatera *nf*
turtle	tortuga *nf*

BIOLOGY

GENERAL TERMS

bioactive	bioactivo *aj*
biodegradable	biodegradable *aj*
biodiversity	biodiversidad *nf*
biology	biología *nf*
biomass	biomasa *nf*
biorhythm	biorritmo *nm*
biosphere	biosfera *nf*
biotype	biotipo *nm*
cell	célula *nf*
characteristic	característica *nf*
colony	colonia *nf*
creature	criatura *nf*

culture	cultivo *nm*
ecosystem	ecosistema *nm*
generic	genérico *aj*
germ	germen *nm*
habitat	habitat *nm*
instinct	instinto *nm*
intelligent	inteligente *aj*
microorganism	microorganismo *nm*
molecule	molécula *nf*
nature	naturaleza *nf*
ontogeny	ontogenia, ontogénesis *nf*
organism	organismo *nm*
phylogeny	filogenia *nf*
protoplasm	protoplasma *nm*
soma	soma *nm*
specimen	espécimen *nm*
stimulus	estímulo *nm*
tissue	tejido *nm*
viable	viable *aj*

BRANCHES OF BIOLOGY

major fields

bacteriology	bacteriología *nf*
biophysics	biofísica *nf*
biotechnology	biotecnología *nf*
botany	botánica *nf*
cryobiology	criobiología *nf*
cytology	citología *nf*
ecology	ecología *nf*
embryology	embriología *nf*
entomology	entomología *nf*
ethology	etología *nf*
evolution	evolución *nf*
exobiology	biología espacial *nf*
genetics	genética *nf*
histology	histología *nf*
ichthyology	ictiología *nf*
immunology	inmunología *nf*
limnology	limnología *nf*
marine biology	biología marina *nf*
medicine	medicina *nf*
microbiology	microbiología *nf*
molecular (biology)	molecular *aj*
morphology	morfología *nf*
neurobiology	neurobiología *nf*
ornithology	ornitología *nf*
paleontology	paleontología *nf*
physiology	fisiología *nf*
sociobiology	sociobiología *nf*
systematics	sistemática *nf*
taxonomy	taxonomía *nf*

virology	virología *nf*	physiological	fisiológico *aj*
zoology	zoología *nf*	physique	físico *aj*
		region	región *nf*
		reproduction	reproducción *nf*
		stature	estatura *nf*
		synergy	sinergia *nf*
		temperature	temperatura *nf*
		tone	tono *nm*
		vital (organs)	vital *aj*

related fields

anatomy	anatomía *nf*
bioacoustics	bioacústica *nf*
bioastronautics	bioastronáutica *nf*
biochemistry	bioquímica *nf*
bioclimatology	bioclimatología *nf*
bioecology	bioecología *nf*
bioelectronics	bioelectrónica *nf*
bioengineering	bioingeniería *nf*
biogeography	biogeografía *nf*
biomechanics	biomecánica *nf*
biomedicine	biomedicina *nf*
biometrics	biometría *nf*
biometry	biometría *nf*
bionics	biónica *nf*
bioscopy	biscopía *nf*
chromatography	cromatografía *nf*
cytogenetics	citogenética *nf*
electrophoresis	electroforesia *nf*
eugenics	eugenesia *nf*
mycology	micología *nf*
oology	oología *nf*
parasitology	parasitología *nf*
phenology	fenología *nf*
psychobiology	(p)sicobiología *nf*
somatology	somatalogía *nf*
zymology	cimología *nf*

(*See also* **ANIMALS**; *NUTRITION* under **FOOD AND NUTRITION**; **PLANTS**; *BIOCHEMICALS* under **THE HUMAN BODY**)

Medical Matters

THE HUMAN BODY

GENERAL TERMS

absorption	absorción *nf*
anatomy	anatomía *nf*
apparatus	aparato *nm*
articulation	articulación *nf*
birthmark	marca de nacimiento *nf*
circadian (rhythm)	circadiano *aj*
corporeal	corpóreo *aj*
corpus	cuerpo *nm*
figure	figura *nf*
flaccidity	flaccidez *nf*
orifice	orificio *nm*

STRUCTURE

systems

circulatory	circulatorio *aj*
digestive	digestivo *aj*
endocrine	endocrino *aj*
genitourinary	genitourinario *aj*
lymphatic	linfático *aj*
nervous	nervioso *aj*
parasympathetic	parasimpático *aj*
reproductive	reproductivo *aj*
respiratory	respiratorio *aj*
skeletal	esquelético *aj*

components

adnexa	anexos *nmpl*
appendage	apéndice *nm*
canal	canal *nm*
cartilage	cartílago *nm*
cavity	cavidad *nf*
cord	cordel *nm*
duct	conducto *nm*
fluid	fluido *nm*
gland	glándula *nf*
humor (obs)	humor *nm*
membrane	membrana *nf*
musculature	musculatura *nf*
nerve	nervio *nm*
node	nodo *nm*
nodule	nódulo *nm*
organ	órgano *nm*
passage	pasaje *nm*
sac	saco *nm*
tissue	tejido *nm*
tube	tubo *nm*

major sections

abdomen	abdomen *nm*
bust	busto *nm*
extremities	extremidades *nfpl*
torso	torso *nm*
trunk	tronco *nm*

regions

anal	anal *aj*
cardiopulmonary	cardiopulmonar *aj*
caudal	caudal *aj*
cephalic	cefálico *aj*
cerebrospinal	cerebroespinal *aj*
costal	costal *aj*
dental	dental *aj*
erogenous	erógeno *aj*
facial	facial *aj*
gastrointestinal	gastrointestinal *aj*
gingival	gingival *aj*
gutteral	guteral *aj*
intercostal	intercostal *aj*
intestinal	intestino *aj*
limbic	límbico *aj*
lumbar	lumbar *aj*
pancreatic	pancreático *aj*
pelvic	pélvico *aj*
postnasal	pos(t)nasal *aj*
pubic	púbico *aj*
pulmonary	pulmonar *aj*
rectal	rectal *aj*
renal	renal *aj*
sacroiliac	región sacroilíaca *aj*
sigmoidal	sigmoide, sigmoideo *aj*
spinal	espinal *aj*
suprarenal	suprarrenal *aj*
ulnar	ulnar *aj*
urogenital	urogenital *aj*
ventral	ventral *aj*

relative locations

anterior	anterior *aj*
dorsal	dorsal *aj*
external	externo *aj*
internal	interno *aj*
posterior	posterior *aj*

other terms

intramuscular	intramuscular *aj*
intravenous	intravenoso *aj*
subcutaneous	subcutáneo *aj*
submaxillary	submaxilar *aj*

NAMES OF BODY PARTS

cavities

abdominal	abdominal *aj*
oral	oral *aj*

bones and joints

carpal	carpiano *aj*
clavicle	clavícula *nf*
coccyx	cóccix *nm*
endoskeleton	endoesqueleto *nm*
ethmoid	etmoides *aj, nm*
femur	fémur *nm*
fibula	fíbula *nf*
humerus	húmero *nm*
ilium	ilion *nm*
ischium	isquión *nm*
malleolus	maleólo *nm*
mandible	mandíbula *nf*
maxilla	hueso maxilar *nm*
occiput	occipucio *nm*
parietal	parietal *aj*
pelvis	pelvis *nf*
phalange	falange *nf*
phalanx	falange *nm*
pubis	pubis *nm*
radius	radio *nm*
sacrum	sacro *nm*
scapula	escápula *nf*
skeleton	esqueleto *nm*
sphenoid	esfenoides *nm*
spine	espina, espinazo *nf, nm*
sternum	esternón *nm*
tarsus	tarso *nm*
thorax	tórax *nm*
tibia	tibia *nf*
trapezium	trapecio *nm*
trapezoid	trapezoide *nm*
ulna	ulna *nf*
vertebra	vértebra *nf*
zygoma	cigoma, zigoma *nm*

muscles

abductor	abductor *nm*
adductor	aductor *nm*
biceps	bíceps *nm*
constrictor	constrictor *nm*
diaphragm	diafragma *nm*
deltoid	deltoides *nm*
erector	erector *nm*
extensor	extensor *nm*
flexor	flexor *nm*
frontal	frontal *aj*
gluteus	glúteo *nm*
involuntary	involuntario *aj*
masseter	masetero *nm*
occipital	occipital *aj*
pectoral	pectoral *aj, nm*
quadriceps	cuadriceps *nm*
retractor	retractor *nm*
sphincter	esfinter *nm*
suspensory	suspensorio *aj*

temporal	temporal *aj*
trapezium, trapezius	trapecio *nm*
triceps	tríceps *nm*
zygomatic	cigomatico, zigomatico *aj*

glands

adrenal	suprarrenal *aj*
adrenocortical	adrenocortical *aj*
endocrine	endocrino *aj*
exocrine	exocino *aj*
hypothalamus	hipotálamo *nm*
lachrymal, lacrimal	lacrimal *aj*
lymph	linfa *nf*
mammary	mamario *aj*
pancreas	páncreas *nm*
parathyroid	paratiroides *nf*
parotid	parótida *nf*
pineal	pineal *aj*
pituitary	pituitario *aj*
sebaceous	sebáceo *aj*
thymus	timo *nm*
thyroid	tiroides *nf*
thyroxine	tiroxina *nf*

blood and blood vessels

aorta	aorta *nf*
artery	arteria *nf*
brachial	braquial *aj*
capillary	vaso capilar *nm*
carotid	carótida *aj, nf*
coronary	coronario *aj*
corpuscle	corpúsculo *nm*
erythrocyte	eritrocito *nm*
femoral	femoral *aj*
gamma globulin	gammaglobulina *nf*
globule	glóbulo *nm*
hematic	hemático *aj*
hemoglobin	hemoglobina *nf*
jugular	yugular *aj*
leukocyte	leucocito *nm*
monocyte	monocito *nm*
phagocyte	fagocito *nm*
plasma	plasma *nm*
plexus	plexo *nm*
portal	porta *aj*
Rh-factor	factor Rh *nm*
serum	suero *nm*
thromboplastin	tomboplastina *nf*
vein	vena *nf*

tissues

adenoids	adenoides *nmpl*
adipose	adiposo *aj*

collagen	colágena *nf*
connective	conectivo *aj*
dentin(e)	dentina *nf*
epithelium	epitelio *nm*
erectile	eréctil *aj*
ligament	ligamento *nm*
lymphocyte	linfocito *nm*
membranous	membranoso *aj*
muscle	músculo *nm*
parenchyma	paréquima *nm*
periosteum	periostio *nm*
tendon	tendón *nm*
uvula	úvula *nf*

eye

aqueous	acuoso *aj*
cilia	cilios *nmpl*
cone	cono *nm*
cornea	córnea *nf*
globe	globo *nm*
iris	iris *nm*
ocular	ocular *aj*
pupil	pupila *nf*
retina	retina *nf*
sclera	esclerótica *nf*
vitreous	vítreo *aj*

ear

ampulla	ampolla *nf*
cochlea	cóclea *nf*
Eustachian tube	tubo de Eustaquio *nm*
helix	hélice *nf*
labyrinth	laberinto *nm*
lobule	lobulillo *nm*
mastoid	mastoides *nf*
ossicle	osículo *nm*
petrous	petrosal, petroso *aj*
semicircular	semicircular *aj*
tympanum	tímpano *nm*
vestibule	vestíbulo *nm*

digestive tract

alimentary	alimenticio *aj*
appendix	apéndice *nm*
colon	colon *nm*
diverticulum	divertículo *nm*
duodenum	duodeno *nm*
epiglottis	epiglotis *nf*
esophagus	esófago *nm*
ileum	íleon *nm*
intestine	intestino *nm*
jejunum	yeyuno *nm*
peptic	péptico *aj*

rectum	recto *nm*
salivary	salival *aj*
stomach	estómago *nm*
viscera	vísceras *nfpl*

organs of reproduction

cervix	cerviz *nf*
clitoris	clítoris *nm*
Fallopian	de Falopio
fibroid	fibroide *nm*
genitalia, genitals	genitales *nmpl*
glans	glande *nm*
labia	labios *nmpl*
labium	labio *nm*
ovary	ovario *nm*
oviduct	oviducto *nm*
ovule	óvulo *nm*
ovum	óvulo *nm*
penis	pene *nm*
phallus	falo *nm*
placenta	placenta *nf*
prepuce	prepucio *nm*
prostate	próstata *nf*
pudenda	partes pudendas *nfpl*
scrotum	escroto *nm*
testes	testes *nmpl*
testicle	testículo *nm*
testis	teste *nm*
tubule	túbulo *nm*
umbilicus	ombligo *nm*
uterus	útero *nm*
vagina	vagina *nf*
vesicle	vesícula *nf*
vulva	vulva *nf*

head and brain

Adam's apple	nuez de Adán *nf*
aquiline (nose)	aguileño, aquilino *aj*
buccal	bucal *aj*
cornu	cornu *nm*
corpus callosum	cuerpo calloso *nm*
cortex	corteza *nf*
cranium	cráneo *nm*
encephalon	encéfalo *nm*
fissure	fisura *nf*
follicle	folículo *nm*
fontanel, fontanelle	fontanela *nf*
glottis	glotis *nf*
hemisphere	hemisferio *nm*
lineaments	lineamientos *nmpl*
lobe	lóbulo *nm*
medulla	médula *nf*

meninges	meninges *nm*
mustache, moustache	mostacho *nm*
palate	paladar *nm*
pallium	palio *nm*
peduncle	pedúnculo *nm*
pericranium	pericráneo *nm*
sinus	seno *nm*
thalamus	tálamo *nm*
vocal chords	cuerdas vocales *nfpl*

skin

areola	aréola, areola *nf*
callus	callo *nm*
cutis	cutis *nm*
derm, derma, dermis	dermis *nf*
dermis	dermis *nf*
epidermis	epidermis *nf*
frenum	frenillo *nm*
papilla	papila *nf*
pigment	pigmento *nm*
pore	poro *nm*

lung

alveolus	alvéolo *nm*
bronchia	bronquios *nmpl*
bronchiole	bronquíolo *nm*
diaphragm	diafragma *nm*
larynx	laringe *nf*
nasal	nasal *aj*
pharynx	faringe *nf*
trachea	tráquea *nf*

nerves

autonomic	antónomo *aj*
axon	axón *nm*
center	centro *nm*
cerebellum	cerebelo *nm*
cerebrum	cerebro *nm*
chiasma	quiasma *nm*
dendrite	dendrita *nf*
ganglion	ganglio *nm*
neuron	neurona *nf*
neurotransmitter	neurotransmisor *nm*
nucleus	núcleo *nm*
olfactory	olfatorio *aj*
optic	óptico *aj*
radial	radial *aj*
receptor	receptor *nm*
reflex	reflejo *nm*
sciatic	ciático *aj*
solar plexus	plexo solar *nm*
synapse	sinapsis *nf*

arms and legs

Achilles' tendon	tendón de aquiles *nm*
arch	arco *nm*
axilla	axila *nf*
carpus	carpo *nm*
cuticle	cutícula *nf*
index finger	dedo índice *nm*
meniscus	menisco *nm*
metacarpal	metacarpo *nm*
metatarsus	metatarso *nm*
palm	palma *nf*

heart

atrium	atrio *nm*
auricle	aurícula *nf*
cardiac	cardíaco *aj*
endocardium	endocardio *nm*
myocardium	miocardio *nm*
pericardium	pericardio *nm*
septum	septo, septum *nm*
valve	válvula *nf*
ventricle	ventrículo *nm*

teeth and jaw

bicuspid	bicúspide *aj, nm*
canine	canino *aj, nm*
cementum	cemento *nm*
cingulum	cíngulo *nm*
crown	corona *nf*
cusp	cúspide *nf*
cusp, cuspid	cúspide *nf*
dentine	dentina *nf*
enamel	esmalte *nm*
incisor	incisivo *nm*
molar	molar *nm*
periodontal	periodontal *aj*
premolar	premolar *nm*
pulp	pulpa *nf*

membranes

hymen	himen *nm*
mucous	mocoso *aj*
peritoneum	peritoneo *nm*
pleura	pleura *nf*
velum	velo *nm*

excretory organs

anus	ano *nm*
ureter	uréter *nm*
urethra	uretra *nf*

other terms

dissymmetrical	disimétrico *aj*
isthmus	istmo *nm*
lacuna	laguna *nf*
lumen	lumen *nm*
promonotory	promonotorio *nm*
radicle	radícula *nf*
reticulum	retículo *nm*
transverse	tra(n)sverso *aj*
tricuspid	tricúspide *aj, nf*
vascular	vascular *aj*
vasomotor	vasomotor *aj*
vermiform (appendix)	vermiforme *aj*

PHYSIOLOGY

physical body types

ectomorph	ectomorfo *nm*
endomorph	endomorfo *nm*
mesomorph	mesomorfo *nm*

functions and operations

accommodation	acomodación *nf*
adaptation	adaptación *nf*
ambidextrous	ambidextro *aj*
assimilation	asimilación *nf*
audition	audición *nf*
circulation	circulación *nf*
climacteric	climaterio *nm*
compensation	compensación *nf*
conduction	conducción *nf*
defecation	defecación *nf*
deflection	deflexión *nf*
digestion	digestión *nf*
ejaculation	eyaculación *nf*
elimination	eliminación *nf*
erection	erección *nf*
eructation	eructación, eructo *nf, nm*
evacuation	evacuación *nf*
excitation	excitación *nf*
excitement	excitación *nf*
excretion	excreción *nf*
exhalation	exhalación *nf*
expiration	espiración *nf*
extension	extensión *nf*
fertilization	fertilización *nf*
flection	flexión *nf*
gargling *nsg*	gárgaras, gargarismos *nfpl, nmpl*
gestation	gestación *nf*
ingestion	ingerión *nf*
inhalation	inhalación *nf*

inspiration — inspiración *nf*
involution — involución *nf*
lactation — lactancia *nf*
mastication — masticación *nf*
menopause — menopausia *nf*
menstruation — menstruación *nf*
metabolism — metabolismo *nm*
ovulation — ovulación *nf*
regurgitation — regurgitación *nf*
relaxation — relajación *nf*
respiration — respiración *nf*
salivation — salivación *nf*
secretion — secreción *nf*
senses — sentidos *nmpl*
stimulation — estimulación *nf*
vasoconstriction — vasoconstricción *nf*
vasodilation — vasodilatación *nf*
vision — visión, vista *nf*

movements and body positions

abduction — abducción *nf*
adduction — aducción *nf*
afferent — aferente *aj*
efferent — eferente *aj*
erect — erecto *aj*
gesticulation — gesticulación *nf*
inclination — inclinación *nf*
profile — perfil *nm*
prone — prono *aj*
prostrate — postrar *vt*
recline — reclinarse *vr*
supine — supino *aj*

secretions and body products

bile — bilis *nf*
bilirubin — bilirrubina *nf*
cerumen — cerumen *nm*
chyle — quilo *nm*
chyme — quimo *nm*
dopamine — dopamina *nf*
excrement — excremento *nm*
excreta — excrementos *nmpl*
feces — heces *nfpl*
juice — jugo *nm*
mucus — moco, mucosidad *nm, nf*
pee, peepee — pipí *nm*
phlegm — flema *nf*
saliva — saliva *nf*
sebum — sebo *nm*
semen — semen *nm*
sperm — esperma *nf*

sputum — esputo *nm*
urine — orina *nf*

elements and minerals

calcium — calcio *nm*
carbon — carbono *nm*
carotene — caroteno *nm*
chlorine — cloro *nm*

other terms

appetite — apetito *nm*
corpulence — corpulencia *nf*
diastole — diástole *nf*
electrotonus — electrotono *nm*
endomorphic — endomórfico *aj*
focus — foco *nm*
homeostasis — homeóstasis *nf*
impulse — impulso *nm*
kinesthesia — cinestesia, quin-, kine- *nf*
kinesthetic — cinestético *aj*
lymph — linfa *nf*
metabolic — metabólico *aj*
monocyte — monocito *nm*
motoneuron — motoneurona *nf*
motor — motor *aj*
period — período *nm*
peristalsis — peristalsis *nf*
photokinesis — fotocinesis *nf*
photokinetic — fotocinético *aj*
photopia — fotopía *nf*
phototonus — fototonía *nf*
posture — postura *nf*
potent — potente *aj*
pressure — presión *nf*
pulsation — pulsación *nf*
pulse — pulso *nm*
seminal (fluid) — seminal *aj*
sensory — sensorial, sensorio *aj*
stertorous — estertoroso *aj*
stimulant — estimulante *nm*
sympathetic — simpático *aj*
synergism, synergy — sinergia *nf*
systaltic — sistáltico *aj*
systemic — sistémico *aj*
systole — sístole *nm*
systolic — sistólico *aj*
tactile — táctil *aj*
tampon — tampón *nm*
tonicity — tonicidad *nf*
transmitter — tra(n)smisor *nm*
vomit — vómito *nm*

BIOCHEMICALS

classification

acid	ácido *nm*
carbohydrate	carbohidrato *nm*
enzyme	enzima *nf*
hormone	hormona *nf*
lipid(e)	lípido *nm*
peptide	péptido *nm*
protein	proteína *nf*
vitamin	vitamina *nf*

acids

algin	algina *nf*
amino acid	aminoácido *nm*
deoxyribonucleic	desoxirribonucleico *aj*
lactic	láctico *aj*
nucleic	nucleico *aj*
prostaglandin	prostaglandina *nf*
ribonucleic	ribonucleico *aj*

hormones

adrenaline	adrenalina *nf*
androgen	andrógeno *nm*
corticosteroid	corticosteroide *nm*
corticosterone	corticosterona *nf*
cortisone	cortisona *nf*
epinephrine	epinefrina *nf*
estrogen	estrógeno *nm*
gastrin	gastrina *nf*
insulin	insulina *nf*
oxytocin	oxitocina *nf*
progesterone	progesterona *nf*
prolactin	prolactina *nf*
relaxin	relaxina *nf*
serotonin	serotonina *nf*
steroid	esteroide *nm*
testosterone	testosterona *nf*
thyroxine	tiroxina *nf*

enzymes

cholinesterase	colinesterasa *nf*
diastase	diastasa *nf*
esterase	esterasa *nf*
lactase	lactasa *nf*
lipase	lipasa *nf*
maltase	maltasa *nf*
papain	papaína *nf*
pepsin	pepsina *nf*
protease	proteasa *nf*
ptyalin	tialina *nf*
renin, rennin	renina *nf*
thrombin	trombina, tombasa *nf*
trypsin	tripsina *nf*
zymase	cimasa, zimasa *nf*

peptides

endorphin	endorfina *nf*
interleukin	interleukin *nm*

proteins

albumen	albumen *nm*
albumin	albúmina *nf*
casein	caseína *nf*
collagen	colágena *nf*
fibrin	fibrina *nf*
fibrinogen	fibrinógeno *aj*
gelatin(e)	gelatina *nf*
globulin	globulina *nf*
interferon	interferona *nf*
keratin	queratina *nf*
zein	ceína, zeína *nf*

vitamins

biotin	biotina *nf*
niacin	niacina *nf*
pantothenic	pantoténico *aj*
retinol	retinol *nm*
riboflavin	riboflavina *nf*
thiamin(e)	tiamina *nf*

sugars

dextrose	dextrosa *nf*
fructose	fructosa *nf*
glucose	glucosa *nf*
glycogen	glicógeno *nm*
lactose	lactosa *nf*
maltose	maltosa *nf*

lipids

cholesterol	colesterol *nm*
triglyceride	triglicérido *nm*
antiserum	antisuero *nm*
bioassay	bioensayo *nm*
biocatalyst	biocatalizador *nm*
pectin	pectina *nf*

other substances

agglutinin	aglutinina *nf*
antioxidant	antioxidante *nm*
creatine	creatina *nf*
dopamine	dopamina *nf*
heparin	heparina *nf*
histamine	histamina *nf*
melanin	melanina *nf*

urea	urea *nf*
xanthine	xantina *nf*

(*See also* **BIOLOGY**; *NUTRITION* under **FOOD AND NUTRITION**; **DRUGS**)

MEDICAL PRACTICE

GENERAL TERMS

antibody	anticuerpo *nm*
antisepsis	antisepsia *nf*
antiseptic	antiséptico *aj, nm*
autopsy	autopsia *nf*
bank (blood, bone, eye)	banco *nm*
biofeedback	biorreacción *nf*
biomedical	biomédico *aj*
caduceus	caduceo *nm*
case	caso *nm*
coma	coma *nm*
complication	complicación *nf*
consultation	consulta, consultación *nf*
contamination	contaminación *nf*
cure	cura *nf*
decontamination	descontaminación *nf*
diagnosis (act)	diagnósis *nf*
diagnosis (conclusion)	diagnóstico *nm*
dose	dosis *nf*
Hippocratic	hipocrático *aj*
internship	internado *nm*
license	licencia *nf*
medical	médico *aj*
medicine	medicina *nf*
operation	operación *nf*
panacea	panacea *nf*
patient	paciente *nmf*
physical	físico *aj*
placebo	placebo *nm*
prevention	prevención *nf*
prognosis	pronóstico *nm*
reciprocity	reciprocidad *nf*
remedy	remedio *nm*
residency	residencia *nf*
socialized medicine	medicina estatal *nf*
specialty	especialidad *nf*
symptom	síntoma *nm*
symptomatology	sintomatología *nf*
syndrome	síndrome *nm*
therapy	terapia *nf*
treatment	tratamiento *nm*

BRANCHES OF MEDICINE

major fields

aeromedicine	aeromedicina *nf*
allergy	alergia *nf*
cardiology	cardiología *nf*
dermatology	dermatología *nf*
endocrinology	endocrinología *nf*
epidemiology	epidemiología *nf*
family (medicine)	familiar *aj*
gastroenterology	gastroenterología *nf*
geriatrics	geriatría *nf*
gynecology	ginecología *nf*
hematology	hemotología *nf*
internal (medicine)	interno *aj*
laryngology	laringología *nf*
neonatology	neonatología *nf*
nephrology	nefralogía *nf*
neurology	neurología *nf*
nuclear (medicine)	nuclear *aj*
obstetrics	obstetricia *nf*
occupational (medicine)	ocupacional *aj*
oncology	oncología *nf*
ophthalmology	oftalmología *nf*
orthopedics	ortopedia *nf*
otolaryngology	otolaringología *nf*
otorhinolaryngology	otorrinolaringología *nf*
pathology	patología *nf*
pediatrics	pediatría *nf*
physiatrics, physiatry	fisiatría *nf*
proctology	proctología *nf*
psychiatry	(p)siquiatría *nf*
rheumatology	reumatología *nf*
sports medicine	medicina deportiva *nf*
surgery	cirugía *nf*
therapeutics	terapéutica *nf*
urology	urología *nf*
veterinary medicine	veterinaria *nf*

subspecialties

anesthesiology	anestesiología *nf*
bacteriology	bacteriología *nf*
etiology	etiología *nf*
forensic medicine	medicina forense *nf*
immunology	inmunología *nf*
neuropathology	neuropatalogía *nf*
odontology	odontología *nf*
osteopathy	osteopatía *nf*
pharmacology	farmacología *nf*
podiatry	podiatría *nf*
prosthetics	protética *nf*
radiology	radiología *nf*

therapeutics	terapéutica *nf*
topology	topología *nf*
toxicology	toxicología *nf*
virology	virología *nf*

related fields

anatomy	anatomía *nf*
audiology	audiología *nf*
biochemistry	bioquímica *nf*
biomedicine	biomedicina *nf*
chiropody	quiropedia *nf*
dietetics	dietética *nf*
histology	histología *nf*
hygienics	higiene *nf*
immunochemistry	inmunoquímica *nf*
immunogenetics	inmunogenética *nf*
macrobiotics	macrobiótica *nf*
microbiology	microbiología *nf*
optometry	optometría *nf*
osteology	osteología *nf*
physiology	fisiología *nf*
psychopharmacology	(p)sicofarmacología *nf*
public health	salud pública *nf*
radiography	radiografía *nf*
roentgenology	roentgenología *nf*
serology	serología *nf*

DIAGNOSIS

general symptoms and conditions

adiposity	adiposidad *nf*
analgesia	analgesia *nf*
colic	cólico *nm*
congestion	congestión *nf*
consciousness	conciencia *nf*
constriction	constricción *nf*
convulsion	convulsión *nf*
crepitation	crepitación *nf*
debility	debilidad *nf*
dehydration	deshidratación *nf*
delirium	delirio *nm*
diarrhea	diarrea *nf*
distension, distention	distensión *nf*
dyspepsia	dispepsia *nf*
edema	edema *nm*
expectoration	expectoración *nf*
exudation	exudación *nf*
fatigue	fatiga *nf*
fever	fiebre *nf*
fibrillation	fibrilación *nf*
flatulence	flatulencia *nf*

hemorrhage	hemorragia *nf*
hypothermia	hipotermia *nf*
icterus (jaundice)	ictericia *nf*
indigestion	indigestión *nf*
inflammation	inflamación *nf*
irritation	irritación *nf*
lassitude	lasitud *nf*
lethargy	letargo, aletargamiento *nm*
lumbago	lumbago *nm*
nausea	náusea *nf*
neuralgia	neuralgia *nf*
pallor	palidez *nf*
palpitation	palpitación *nf*
paroxysm	paroxismo *nm*
phlegm	flema *nf*
pulse	pulso *nm*
purulence	purulencia *nf*
pus	pus *nm*
pustulation	pustulación *nf*
retention (of fluids)	retención *nf*
shock	choque *nm*
somnolence	somnolencia *nf*
spasm	espasmo *nm*
stress	estrés *nm*
stricture	estrictura *nf*
stupor	estupor *nm*
syncope	síncope *nm*
tic	tic *nm*
tumefaction	tumefacción *nf*
tumescence	tumescencia *nf*
turgescence	turgencia *nf*
ulceration	ulceración *nf*
urgency	urgencia *nf*
vomiting	el vomitar *nm*

diagnostic fields

angiography	angiografía *nf*
arteriography	arteriografía *nf*
audiometry	audiometría *nf*
bronchoscopy	broncoscopia *nf*
cardiography	cardiografía *nf*
celioscopy	celioscopia *nf*
cystoscopy	ciscoscopia *nf*
dosimetry	dosimetría *nf*
endoscopy	endoscopia *nf*
fluoroscopy	fluoroscopia *nf*
gastroscopy	gastroscopia *nf*
laparoscopy	laparoscopia *nf*
mammography	mamografía *nf*
pyelography	pielografía *nf*
radioscopy	radioscopia *nf*
retinoscopy	retinoscopia *nf*

sigmoidoscopy	sigmoidoscopia *nf*
tomography	tomografía *nf*

devices

arthroscope	artroscopio *nm*
audiometer	audiómetro *nm*
bronchoscope	broncoscopio *nm*
cystoscope	ciscoscopio *nm*
dosimeter	dosímetro *nm*
electrocardiograph	electrocardiógrafo *nm*
electroencephalograph	electroencefalógrafo *nm*
endoscope	endoscopio *nm*
fluoroscope	fluoroscopio *nm*
gastroscope	gastroscopio *nm*
kymograph	quimógrafo *nm*
laparoscope	laparoscopio *nm*
laryngoscope	laringoscopio *nm*
manometer	manómetro *nm*
microscope	microscopio *nm*
otoscope	otoscopio *nm*
radiograph	radiografía *nf*
retinoscope	retinoscopio *nm*
scanner	escanógrafo *nm*
sigmoidoscope	sigmoidoscopio *nm*
speculum	espéculo *nm*
spirograph	espirógrafo *nm*
spirometer	espirómetro *nm*
stethoscope	estetoscopio *nm*
thermometer	termómetro *nm*
X ray	rayo X *nm*

charts and pictures

angiogram	angioscopio *nm*
arteriogram	arteriograma *nm*
audiogram	audiograma *nm*
echocardiogram	ecocardiograma *nm*
electrocardiogram	electrocardiograma *nm*
electroencephalogram	electroencefalograma *nm*
mammogram	mamograma *nm*
pyelogram	pielograma *nm*
tomogram	tomograma *nm*

techniques and procedures

amniocentesis	amniocentesis *nf*
auscultation	auscultación *nf*
biopsy	biopsia *nf*
dissection	disección *nf*
evaluation	evaluación *nf*
examination	examen *nm*
history	historia *nf*
observation	observación *nf*
palpation	palpación *nf*

percussion	percusión *nf*
sperm count	cuenta espermática *nf*
tuberculin test	prueba tuberculina *nf*
ultrasound	ultrasonido *nm*
urinalysis	urinálisis *nf*

other diagnostic terms

anomaly	anomalía *nf*
astatic	astático *aj*
asymptomatic	asintomático *aj*
atonic	atónico *aj*
autogenous	autógeno *aj*
autoimmune, auto-immune	autoinmuno *aj*
benign	benigno *aj*
conscious	consciente *aj*
degeneration	degeneración *nf*
facies	facies *nf*
flux	flujo *nm*
infected	infecto *aj*
inoperable	inoperable *aj*
irreversible	irreversible *aj*
mimesis	mimética *nf*
normal	normal *aj*
predisposition	predisposición *nf*
reversible	reversible *aj*
Rhesus (factor)	rhesus *aj*
sign	señal *nf*
state	estado *nm*
unconscious	inconsciente *aj*
vital (signs, function)	vital *aj*

TREATMENT

prevention

checkup	chequeo *nm*
chlorination	clorinación *nf*
defenses	defensas *nfpl*
douche	ducha *nf*
exercise	ejercicio *nm*
fluoridation	fluorización *nf*
fumigation	fumigación *nf*
holistic	holístico *aj*
hygiene	higiene *nf*
immunity	inmunidad *nf*
immunization	inmunización *nf*
inoculation	inoculación *nf*
nutrition	nutrición *nf*
precaution	precaución *nf*
prophylaxis	profilaxis *nf*
purge	purga *nf*
quarantine	cuarentena *nf*
relaxation	relajación *nf*

sanitation	saneamiento *nm*
vaccination	vacunación *nf*
vaccine	vacuna *nf*

medications

antibiotic	antibiótico *nm*
bactericide	bactericida *nm*
cure-all	curalotodo *nm*
fungicide	fungicida *nm*
lithium	litio *nm*
microbicide	microbicida *nf*
sedation	sedación *nf*
suppository	supositorio *nm*
unguent	ungüento *nm*

other treatments

acupuncture	acupuntura *nf*
aeration	aeración *nf*
alleviation	alivio *nm*
allopathy	alopatía *nf*
aromatherapy	aromaterapia *nf*
artificial respiration	respiración artificial *nf*
balneotherapy	balneoterapia *nf*
biotherapy	bioterapia *nf*
catharsis	catarsis *nf*
chelation	quelación *nf*
chemotherapy	quimioterapia *nf*
compress	compresa *nf*
compression (to stop bleeding)	compresión *nf*
curettage	curetaje *nm*
decompression	descompresión *nf*
defibrillation	defibrilación *nf*
desensitization	desensibilización *nf*
detoxification	desintoxicación *nf*
dialysis	diálisis *nf*
diathermy	diatermia *nf*
diet	dieta *nf*
drugs	drogas *nfpl*
electrotherapy	electroterapia *nf*
enema	enema *nf*
fomentation	fomento *nm*
galvanism	galvanismo *nm*
gamma ray	rayo gamma *nf*
gene therapy	terapia génica *nf*
homeopathy	homeopatía *nf*
hospitalization	hospitalización *nf*
hydrotherapy	hidroterapia *nf*
hyperbaric (chamber)	hiperbárico *aj*
hypnotherapy	hipnoterapia *nf*
immunotherapy	inmunoterapia *nf*
infrared (radiation)	infrarrojo *aj*
infusion	infusión *nf*

inhalation	inhalación *nf*
injection	inyección *nf*
intensive (care)	intensivo *aj*
irrigation	irrigación *nf*
isolation	aislamiento *nm*
lavage	lavado *nm*
localization	localización *nf*
manipulation	manipulación, manipuleo *nf, nm*
massage	masaje *nm*
mecanotherapy	mecanoterapia *nf*
medication (medicine)	medicamento *nm*
medication (treatment)	medicación *nf*
oxygen	oxígeno *nm*
pacemaker	marcapasos *nm*
perfusion	perfusión *nf*
phlebotomy	flebotomía *nf*
phototherapy	fototerapia *nf*
physiotherapy	fisioterapia *nf*
puncture	punción *nf*
radiotherapy	radioterapia *nf*
regimen	régimen *nm*
resuscitation	resucitación *nf*
stimulation	estimulación *nf*
surgery	cirugía *nf*
traction	tracción *nf*

healing terms

agglutination	aglutinación *nf*
cicatrix (scar)	cicatriz *nf*
coagulation	coagulación *nf*
coagulum	coágulo *nm*
coalescence	coalescencia *nf*
convalescence	convalecencia *nf*
crisis	crisis *nf*
critical	crítico *aj*
recovery (consciousness)	recobro *nm*
recuperation	recuperación *nf*
rehabilitation	rehabilitación *nf*

SELECTED SPECIALIZED FIELDS

allergy

allergen	alérgeno *nm*
histamine	histamina *nf*
hypersensitive	hipersensible *aj*
pollinosis	polinosis *nf*
reaction	reacción *nf*
rhinitis	rinitis *nf*

gynecology and obstetrics

abortion	aborto *nm*
amenorrhea, amenorrhoea	amenorrea *nf*
amniotic	amniótico *aj*
Caesarean section	cesárea *nf*
canal (birth)	canal (parto) *nm*
cervicitis	cervicitis *nf*
climacteric	climaterio *nm*
colostrum	calostro *nm*
conception	concepción *nf*
condom	condón *nm*
confinement	confinamiento *nm*
contraception	contracepción *nf*
contraceptive	contraceptivo, anticonceptivo *aj, nm*
contraction	contracción *nf*
decidua	decidua *nf*
diaphragm	diafragma *nm*
dilatation	dilatación *nf*
ectopia	ectopia *nf*
endometriosis	endometriosis *nf*
episiotomy	episiotomía *nf*
estrogen	estrógeno *nm*
fertility	fertilidad *nf*
fetal, foetal	fetal *aj*
fetus	feto *nm*
fibroid	fibroide *nm*
gravida	mujer grávida *nf*
impregnate	empreñar *vt*
in vitro (fertilization)	en vitro *aj*
induce (labor)	inducir *vt*
infertility	infertilidad *nf*
insemination	inseminación *nf*
intrauterine	intrauterino *aj*
lochia	loquios *nmpl*
maternity	maternidad *nf*
menopause	menopausia *nf*
menorrhagia	menorragia *nf*
multipara	multípara *nf*
multiple (births)	múltiple *aj*
neonatal	neonatal *aj*
oxytocin	oxitocina *nf*
parturition	parto *nm*
pessary	pesario *nm*
pica	pica *nf*
placenta	placenta *nf*
postnatal	postnatal *aj*
postpartum	de posparto
potency	potencia *nf*
premature	prematuro *aj*

presentation	presentación *nf*
progesterone	progesterona *nf*
puerperal	puerperal *aj*
sterility	esterilidad *nf*
sterilization	esterilización *nf*
toxemia	toxemia *nf*
tubal	tubárico *aj*
umbilical	umbilical *aj*
vaginitis	vaginitis *nf*
virility	virilidad *nf*

oncology

carcinogenic	cancerígeno *aj*
carcinoma	carcinoma *nm*
lymphoma	linfoma *nf*
malignancy	malignidad *nf*
metastasis	metástasis *nf*
neoplasm	neoplasma, neoplasia *nm, nf*
remission	remisión *nf*
sarcoma	sarcoma *nm*

ophthalmology

achromatopsia	acromatopsia *nf*
amblyopia	ambliopía *nf*
ametropia	ametropía *nf*
astigmatism	astigmatismo *nm*
bifocal	bifocal *aj*
bifocals	lentes bifocales *nmpl or nfpl*
binocular	binocular *aj*
blepharoptosis	blefaroptosis *nf*
cataract	catarata *nf*
conjunctivitis	conjunctivitis *nf*
daltonism (color-blindness)	daltonismo *nm*
diopter	dioptría *nf*
diplopia	diplopia *nf*
emmetropia	emetropía *nf*
exophthalmos, exophthalmus	exoftalmía *nf*
focal	focal *aj*
focus	foco *nm*
glaucoma	glaucoma *nm*
hyperopia	hipermetropía *nf*
iritis	iritis *nf*
keratitis	queratitis *nf*
leukoma, leucoma	leucoma *nm*
myopia	miopía *nf*
nebula	nébula *nf*
nyctalopia	nictalopía *nf*
nystagmus	nistagmo *nm*
ophthalmia	oftalmia *nf*

ophthalmic	oftálmico *aj*
ophthalmoscope	oftalmoscopio *nm*
photophobia	fotofobia *nf*
presbyopia	presbiopía *nf*
retinitis	retinitis *nf*
retinopathy	retinopatía *nf*
scleritis	escleritis *nf*
scotoma	escotoma *nm*
strabismus	estrabismo *nm*
trachoma	tracoma *nm*
trifocal	trifocal *aj*
uveitis	uveítis *nf*

psychiatry

Alzheimer's Disease	enfermedad de Alzheimer *nf*
amnesia	amnesia *nf*
autism	autismo *nm*
catalepsy	catalepsia *nf*
catatonia	catatonía *nf*
delirium	delirio *nm*
dementia	demencia *nf*
echolalia	ecolalia *nf*
electroshock	electrochoque *nm*
hyperactivity	hiperactividad *nf*
hypnotherapy	hipnoterapia *nf*
hysteria	histeria, histerismo *nf, nm*
idiocy	idiotez *nf*
infantilism	infantilismo *nm*
mania	manía *nf*
manic-depressive	maniacodepresivo, -a *aj, nmf*
narcoanalysis	narcoanálisis *nf*
narcosynthesis	narcosíntesis *nf*
paranoia	paranoia *nf*
psychosis	(p)sicosis *nf*
psychotic	(p)sicótico *aj*
schizophrenia	esquizofrenia *nf*
senility	senilidad/senilismo *nm*
trance	trance *nm*

TERMS IN SURGERY

general terms

anesthesia	anestesia *nf*
asepsis	asepsia *nf*
aseptic	aséptico *aj*
cauterization	cauterización *nf*
donor	donador(a), donante *nmf*
effusion	efusión *nf*
enterostomy	enterostomía *nf*

excision	excisión *nf*
exploration	exploración *nf*
group (blood)	grupo *nm*
hemostasis	hemostasis *nf*
implant	implante *nm*
incision	incisión *nf*
intravenous	intravenoso *aj*
ligation	ligación *nf*
oxygenation	oxigenación *nf*
postoperative	posoperatorio *aj*
premedication	medicación previa *nf*
procedure	procedimiento *nm*
prosthesis	prótesis *nf*
resection	resección *nf*
scarify	escarificar *vt*
section	sección *nf*
sequela	secuela *nf*
taxis	taxis *nf*
transfusion	tra(n)sfusión *nf*

types of surgery

ambulatory	ambulatorio *aj*
cosmetic	cosmético *aj, nm*
electrosurgery	electrocirugía *nf*
emergency	emergencia *nf*
explorative, exploratory	exploratorio *aj*
invasive	invasor *aj*
microsurgery	microcirugía *nf*
neurosurgery	neurocirujía *nf*
orthopedic	ortopédico *aj*
plastic surgery	cirugía plástica *nf*
reconstructive	reconstructivo *aj*
rectal	rectal *aj*
thoracic	torácico *aj*

types of anesthesia

caudal	caudal *aj*
conduction	conducción *nf*
cryoanesthesia	crioanestesia *nf*
epidural	epidural *aj*
general	general *aj*
hypnosis	hipnosis *nf*
hypothermia	hipotermia *nf*
local	local *aj*
peridural	peridural *aj*
spinal	espinal *aj*

surgical procedures

adenectomy	adenectomía *nf*
amputation	amputación *nf*
angioplasty	angioplastía *nf*
appendectomy	apendectomía *nf*

arthrocentesis   artrocentesis *nf*
arthroplasty   artroplastia *nf*
arthroscopy   artroscopia *nf*
bypass   bypass *nm*
castration   castración *nf*
cholecystectomy   colecistectomía *nf*
circumcision   circuncisión *nf*
colostomy   colostomía *nf*
craniotomy   craniotomía *nf*
cryosurgery   criocirugía *nf*
cystectomy   ciscectomía *nf*
gastrectomy   gastrectomía *nf*
hysterectomy   histerectomía *nf*
implantation   implantación *nf*
laparotomy   laparotomía *nf*
liposuction   liposucción *nf*
lobectomy   lobectomía *nf*
lobotomy   lobotomía *nf*
mammoplasty   mamoplastia *nf*
mastectomy   mastectomía *nf*
nephrectomy   nefrectomía *nf*
nephrotomy   nefrotomía *nf*
oophorectomy   ooforectomia *nf*
ovariectomy   ovariectomía *nf*
pneumonectomy   neumonectomía *nf*
psychosurgery   (p)sicocirugía *nf*
rhinoplasty   rinoplastia *nf*
sterilization   esterilización *nf*
sterilize   esterilizar *vt*
tonsillectomy   tonsilectomía *nf*
tracheotomy   traqueotomía *nf*
transplant   trasplante *nm*
vasectomy   vasectomía *nf*

TOOLS AND EQUIPMENT

adhesive (tape)   adhesivo *aj, nm*
ambulance   ambulancia *nf*
aspirator   aspirador *nm*
atomizer   atomizador *nm*
autoclave   autoclave *nf*
bandage   venda, vendaje *nf, nm*
cannula   cánula *nf*
catgut   catgut *nm*
catheter   catéter *nm*
cautery   cauterio *nm*
curet, curette   cureta *nf*
depressor   depresor *nm*
dilator   dilator *nm*
disinfectant   desinfectante *nm*
ether   éter *nm*
forceps   fórceps *nm*
gauze   gasa *nf*

hemostat   hemóstato *nm*
hypodermic   inyección hipodérmica *nf*
incubator   incubadora *nf*
instruments   instrumental *nmsg*
laser   láser *nm*
mask   mascarilla *nf*
microtome   micrótomo *nm*
monitor (device)   monitor *nm*
pipette   pipeta *nf*
respirator   respirador *nm*
resuscitator   resuscitator *nm*
retractor   retractor *nm*
scalpel   escalpelo *nm*
sphygmomanometer   esfigmomanómetro *nm*
sponge   esponja *nf*
sterilizer   esterilizador *nm*
suture   sutura *nf*
syringe   jeringa *nf*
thermometer   termómetro *nm*
tourniquet   torniquete *nm*
trephine   trefina *nf*
xyster   xister *nm*

MEDICAL FACILITIES

asylum   asilo *nm*
clinic   clínica *nf*
dispensary   dispensario *nm*
hospice   hospicio *nm*
hospital   hospital *nm*
infirmary   enfermería *nf*
laboratory   laboratorio *nm*
leprosarium   leprosería *nf*
pharmacy   farmacia *nf*
polyclinic   policlínica, policlínico *nf, nm*
sanatorium, sanitarium   sanatorio *nm*
solarium   solana, solario *nf, nm*

PERSONS

health professionals

abortionist   abortista *nmf*
allergist   alergista *nmf*
allopath   alópata *nmf*
ambulance driver   ambulanciero, -a *nmf*
anesthesiologist   anestesiólogo, -a *nmf*
anesthetist   anestetista *nmf*
audiologist   audiólogo, -a *nmf*
cardiologist   cardiólogo *nmf*

chiropodist	quiropodista *nmf*
chiropractor	quiropráctico, -a *nmf*
clinician	clínico, -a *nmf*
consultant	consultor(a) *nmf*
dermatologist	dermatólogo *nmf*
dietician	dietista *nmf*
diplomate	diplomada, -a *nmf*
doctor	doctor(a) *nmf*
druggist	droguero, droguista *nmf*
embryologist	embriólogo, -a *nmf*
endocrinologist	endocrinólogo, -a *nmf*
epidemiologist	epidemiólogo, -a *nmf*
gastroenterologist	gastroenterologista *nmf*
geriatrician	geriatra *nmf*
gynecologist	ginecólogo, -a *nmf*
hematologist	hematólogo, -a *nmf*
histologist	histólogo, -a *nmf*
homeopath	homeópata *nmf*
hygienist	higienista *nmf*
hypnotist	hipnotizador(a), hipnotista *nmf*
immunologist	inmunólogo, -a *nmf*
intern	interno, -a *nmf*
internist	internista *nmf*
kinesologist	cinesiólogo, -a, kines-, quine- *nmf*
neurologist	neurólogo *nmf*
neurosurgeon	neurocirujano, -a *nmf*
obstetrician	obstetra *nmf*
oculist	oculista *nmf*
odontologist	odontólogo, -a *nmf*
oncologist	oncologista *nmf*
ophthalmologist	opftalmólogo *nmf*
optician	óptico, -a *nmf*
optometrist	optometrista *nmf*
orthopedist	ortopedista *nmf*
osteopath	osteópata *nmf*
otolaringologist	otolaringólogo, -a *nmf*
paramedic	auxiliar médico/médica *nmf*
pathologist	patólogo, -a *nmf*
pediatrician	pediatra *nmf*
pharmacist	farmacéutico, -a *nmf*
pharmacologist	farmacólogo, -a *nmf*
physiologist	fisiólogo, -a *nmf*
physiotherapist	fisioterapeuta *nmf*
podiatrist	podólogo, -a *nmf*
proctologist	proctólogo *nm*
psychiatrist	(p)siquiatra *nmf*
radiologist	radiólogo, -a *nmf*
specialist	especialista *nmf*
surgeon	cirujano, -a *nmf*
technician	técnico, -a *nmf*

therapist	terapeuta *nmf*
toxicologist	toxicólogo, -a *nmf*
urologist	urólogo, -a *nmf*
veterinarian	veterinario, -a *nmf*
virologist	virólogo, -a *nmf*

patients

addict	adicto, -a *nmf*
alcoholic	alcohólico, -a *nmf*
amnesiac, amnesic	amnésico, -a *aj, nmf*
amputee	amputado, -a *nmf*
anorexic	anoréxico, -a *nmf*
aphasic	afásico, -a *aj, nmf*
asthmatic	asmático, -a *aj, nmf*
convalescent	convaleciente *aj, nmf*
cretin	cretino, -a *nmf*
diabetic	diabético, -a *aj, nmf*
drug addict	drogadicto, -a *nmf*
epileptic	epiléptico, -a *aj, nmf*
hemophiliac	hemofílico, -a *nmf*
hypochondriac	hipocondríaco, -a *nmf*
hypothyroid	hipotiroide, hipotiroideo, -a *nmf*
idiot	idiota *nmf*
insomniac	insomne *nmf*
invalid	inválido, -a *nmf*
leper	leproso, -a *nmf*
mute	mudo, -a *nmf*
outpatient	paciente externo *nmf*
paraplegic	parapléjico, -a *nmf*
quadriplegic	cuadripléjico, -a *aj, nmf*
recipient (transplant)	receptor *nmf*
schizophrenic	esquizofrénico, -a *aj, nmf*
somnambulist	somnambulista *nmf*
spastic	espástico, -a *aj, nmf*

HISTORICAL TERMS

affection (= disease)	afección *nf*
consumption (= tuberculosis)	consunción *nf*
lancet (= scalpel)	lanceta *nf*
ligature (= suture)	ligadura *nf*
mesmerism (= hypnotism)	mesmerismo *nm*
mongolism (= Down's syndrome)	mo(n)golismo *nm*
phthisis (= tuberculosis)	tisis *nf*

St. Vitus' dance   baile de San Vito *nm*
(= chorea)
trepanation   trepanación *nf*
(= drilling)

PHYSICAL DISORDERS

GENERAL TERMS

abnormality	anormalidad *nf*
affliction	aflicción *nf*
defect	defecto *nm*
incubation	incubación *nf*
indisposition	indisposición *nf*
infection	infección *nf*
latency	latencia *nf*
malady	mal *nm*
malaise	malestar *nm*
pathogenesis	patogénesis *nf*
stasis	estasis *nf*
transmit (disease)	transmitir *vt*
virulence	virulencia *nf*

TYPES OF ILLNESS

etiology

bacterial	bacteriano *aj*
cardiovascular	cardiovascular *aj*
circulatory	circulatorio *aj*
communicable (disease)	comunicable *aj*
congenital	congénito *aj*
contagious	contagioso *aj*
coronary	coronario *aj*
debilitating	debilitante *aj*
degenerative	degenerativo *aj*
dietary	dietético *aj*
functional	funcional *aj*
fungal	fungal, fungino *aj*
genetic	genético *aj*
geriatric	geriátrico *aj*
hereditary	hereditario *aj*
hormonal	hormonal *aj*
immunogenic	inmunógeno, inmunizador *aj*
immunological	inmunológico *aj*
infectious	infeccioso *aj*
inflammatory	inflamatorio *aj*
malignant	maligno *aj*
mental	mental *aj*
metabolic	metabólico *aj*
nervous	nervioso *aj*
nutritional	nutritivo *aj*
occupational	ocupacional *aj*

oncological	oncológico *aj*
organic	orgánico *aj*
parasitic	parasitario *aj*
pediatric	pediátrico *aj*
pernicious	pernicioso *aj*
psychogenic	(p)sicógeno *aj*
psychosomatic	(p)sicosomático *aj*
respiratory	respiratorio *aj*
systemic	sistémico *aj*
venereal	venéreo *aj*
verminous	verminoso *aj*
viral	virulento *aj*

other terms

acute	agudo *aj*
catastrophic	catastrófico *aj*
chronic	crónico *aj*
curable	curable *aj*
endemic	endémico *aj*
epidemic	epidémico, epidemial *aj*
grave	grave *aj*
incurable	incurable *aj*
pandemic	pandémico *aj*
rabid	rabioso *aj*
terminal	terminal *aj*
treatable	tratable *aj*
untreatable	no tratable *aj*

CAUSES OF ILLNESS

infectious diseases

bacillus	bacilo *nm*
bacteria	bacterias *nfpl*
bacteriophage	bacteriófago *nm*
coccus	coco *nm*
fungus	hongo *nm*
germ	germen *nm*
gonococcus	gonococo *nm*
microorganism	microorganismo *nm*
pathogen	microbio patógeno *nm*
protozoan, protozoon	protozoario *nm*
retrovirus	retrovirus *nm*
rickettsia	ricketsia *nf*
spirochete	espiroqueta *nf*
staphylococcus	estafilococo *nm*
streptococcus	estreptococo *nm*
virus	virus *nm*

other causes

accident	accidente *nm*
avulsion	avulsión *nf*
carcinogen	agente cancerígeno *nm*

chemical	químico *nm*	malaria	malaria *nf*
collapse	colapso *nm*	mononucleosis	mononucleosis *nf*
decrepitude	decrepitud *nf*	paratyphoid fever	fiebre paratifoidea *nf*
dysfunction	disfunción *nf*	pneumonia	neumonía *nf*
embolus	émbolo *nm*	psoriasis	psoriasis *nf*
exacerbation	exacerbación *nf*	rabies	rabia *nf*
heredity	herencia *nf*	rheumatism	reumatismo *nm*
hypersensitivity	hipersensibilidad *nf*	rubella, rubeola	rubéola *nf*
immunodeficiency	inmunodeficiencia *nf*	scabies	escabies *nf*
insufficiency	insuficiencia *nf*	scarlet fever	escarlatina *nf*
irritant	agente irritante *nm*	scrofula	escrófula *nf*
malnutrition	desnutrición *nf*	tetanus	tétano(s) *nm*
obesity	obesidad *nf*	trichinosis	triquinosis *nf*
oncogene	oncogén *nm*	tuberculosis	tuberculosis *nf*
parasite	parásito *nm*	tularemia	tularemia *nf*
radiation	radiación *nf*	typhoid fever	fiebre tifoidea *nf*
recrudescence	recrudecimiento *nm*	typhus	tifus, tifo *nm*
toxin	toxina *nf*	undulant fever	fiebre ondulante *nf*
trauma	trauma *nm*		
tubercle	tubérculo *nm*		
venom	veneno *nm*		
vitamin deficiency	déficit vitamínico *nm*		

means of transmission

inflammatory

air	aire *nm*	adenitis	adenitis *nf*
animals	animales *nmpl*	appendicitis	apendicitis *nf*
contact	contacto *nm*	arthritis	artritis *nf*
contagion	contagio *nm*	bronchitis	bronquitis *nf*
contaminant	contaminador,	bursitis	bursitis *nf*
	contaminante *nm*	cellulitis	celulitis *nf*
		colitis	colitis *nf*
		cystitis	cistitis *nf*

NAMES OF DISORDERS

infection, contagious diseases

abscess	absceso *nm*	dermatitis	dermatitis *nf*
anthrax	ántrax *nm*	diverticulitis	diverticulitis *nf*
athlete's foot	pie de atleta *nm*	encephalitis	encefalitis *nf*
bubonic plague	peste bubónica *nf*	encephalomyelitis	encefalomielitis *nf*
cholera	cólera *nm*	endocarditis	endocarditis *nf*
croup	crup *nm*	enteritis	enteritis *nf*
dengue	dengue *nm*	gastritis	gastritis *nf*
diphtheria	difteria *nf*	gastroenteritis	gastroenteritis *nf*
dysentery	disentería *nf*	hepatitis	hepatitis *nf*
elephantiasis	elefantiasis *nf*	laryngitis	laringitis *nf*
erysipelas	erisipela *nf*	mastitis	mastitis *nf*
grippe	gripe *nf*	mastoiditis	mastoiditis *nf*
herpes	herpes *nm*	meningitis	meningitis *nf*
HIV	virus VIH, virus del sida *nm*	myelitis	mielitis *nf*
		myocarditis	miocarditis *nf*
		nephritis	nefritis *nf*
impetigo	impétigo *nm*	neuritis	neuritis *nf*
influenza, flu	influenza *nf*	osteoarthritis	osteoartritis *nf*
leprosy	lepra *nf*	osteomyelitis	osteomielitis *nf*
lupus	lupus *nm*	pericarditis	pericarditis *nf*
		peritonitis	peritonitis *nf*
		pharyngitis	faringitis *nf*
		phlebitis	flebitis *nf*
		polio, poliomyelitis	poliomielitis *nf*
		prostatitis	prostatitis *nf*

sinusitis	sinusitis *nf*
stomatitis	estomatitis *nf*
tendonitis	tendonitis *nf*

metabolic

catabolism	catabolismo *nm*
diabetes	diabetes *nf*
gout	gota *nf*
obesity	obesidad *nf*
polydipsia	polidipsia *nf*
polyphagia	polifagia *nf*
porphyria	porfiria *nf*
steatorrhea	esteatorrea *nf*
xanthoma	xantoma *nm*

digestive

anorexia	anorexia *nf*
bulimia	bulimia *nf*
dysphagia	disfagia *nf*
halitosis	halitosis *nf*
hemorrhoids	hemorroides *nfpl*
reflux	reflujo *nm*

heart

angina	angina *nf*
arrhythmia	arritmia *nf*
attack	ataque *nm*
bradycardia	bradicardia *nf*
cardiomegaly	cardiomegalia *nf*
rheumatic fever	fiebre reumática *nf*
tachycardia	taquicardia *nf*
thrombosis	trombosis *nf*

skin

acne	acné *nm*
albinism	albinismo *nm*
callus	callo *nm*
contusion	contusión *nf*
cyst	quiste *nm*
eczema	eczema *nm*
eruption	erupción *nf*
erythema	eritema *nf*
excoriation	excoriación *nf*
laceration	laceración *nf*
lesion	lesión *nf*
papilloma	papiloma *nm*
pemphigus	pénfigo *nm*
tinea	tiña *nf*
ulcer	úlcera *nf*
uticaria	uticaria *nf*

blood

anemia	anemia *nf*

angioma	angioma *nm*
anoxemia, anoxia	anoxemia, anoxia *nf*
atheroma	ateroma *nm*
bacteremia	bacteremia *nf*
cyanosis	cianosis *nf*
embolism	embolia *nf*
hematuria	hematuria *nf*
hemolysis	hemolisis *nf*
hemophilia	hemofilia *nf*
hemoptysis	hemoptisis *nf*
hypertension	hipertensión *nf*
hypoglycemia	hipoglicemia *nf*
ischemia, ischaemia	isquemia *nf*
leukemia	leucemia *nf*
purpura	purpura *nf*
thrombus	trombo *nm*

muscles

ataxia	ataxia *nf*
clonus	clonus, clono *nm*
dystrophy	distrofia *nf*
myasthenia	myastenia *nf*
trismus	trismo *nm*

brain

cephalalgia	cefalalgia, cefalea *nf*
cerebral palsy	parálisis cerebral *nf*
concussion	concusión *nf*
epilepsy	epilepsia *nf*
glioma	glioma *nm*
hydrocephalus, hydrocephaly	hidrocefalia *nf*
hydrophobia	hidrofobia *nf*

poisoning

atropism	atropismo *nm*
autointoxication	autointoxicación *nf*
barbiturism	barbiturismo *nm*
botulism	botulismo *nm*
caffeinism	cafeinismo *nm*
intoxication	intoxicación *nf*
phosphorism	fosforismo *nm*
ptomaine	tomaína *nf*
salmonella	salmonela *nf*
septicemia	septicemia *nf*

language disorders

agraphia	agrafia *nf*
alalia	alalia *nf*
alexia	alexia *nf*
aphasia	afasia *nf*
aphonia	afonía *nf*

cataphasia	catafasia *nf*
coprolalia	coprolalia *nf*
dyslexia	dislexia *nf*
echolalia	ecolalia *nf*
muteness	mudez *nf*

sleep disorders

apnea	apnea *nf*
insomnia	insomnio *nm*
narcolepsy	narcolepsia *nf*
somnambulism	somnambulismo *nm*

other illnesses

acidosis	acidosis *nf*
acromegaly	acromegalia *nf*
addiction	adicción *nf*
adenopathy	adenopatía *nf*
alcoholism	alcoholismo *nm*
alkalosis	alcalosis *nf*
Alzheimer's disease	enfermedad de Alzheimer *nf*
anaphylaxis	anafilaxis *nf*
aneurysm, aneurism	aneurisma *nm*
anhydrosis	anhidrosis *nf*
ankylosis	anquilosis *nf*
anosmia	anosmia *nf*
aplasia	aplasia *nf*
apoplexy	apoplejía *nf*
arteriosclerosis	arteriosclerosis *nf*
arthralgia	artralgia *nf*
asbestosis	asbestosis *nf*
asphyxia, asphyxiation	asfixia *nf*
asthenia	astenia *nf*
asthma	asma *nf(el)*
atherosclerosis	aterosclerosis *nf*
atrophy	atrofia *nf*
avitaminosis	avitaminosis *nf*
beriberi	beriberi *nm*
bilharzia	bilharziosis *nf*
brucellosis	brucelosis *nf*
bubo	bubón, buba *nm, nf*
cachexia	caquexia *nf*
calcification	calcificación *nf*
calculus	cálculo *nm*
canalization	canalización *nf*
cancer	cáncer *nm*
carbuncle	carbunclo *nm*
catarrh	catarro *nm*
chancre	chancro *nm*
chancroid	chancroide *nm*
chlamydia	clamidia *nf*
chondroma	condroma *nm*
chorea	corea *nf*

cirrhosis	cirrosis *nf*
claudication	claudicación *nf*
combat fatigue	fatiga de combate *nf*
coryza	coriza *nf*
crapulence	crápula *nf*
cretinism	cretinismo *nm*
cystic fibrosis	fibrosis cística *nf*
cystocele	ciscocele *nf*
decalcification	descalcificación *nf*
deformity	deformidad *nf*
delirium tremens	delírium tremens *nm*
disfigurement	desfiguración *nf*
dislocation	dislocación *nf*
dismemberment	desmembramiento *nm*
diuresis	diuresis *nf*
drug addiction	drogadicción *nf*
dyspnea, dyspnoea	disnca *nf*
dysuria	disuria *nf*
emphysema	enfisema *nm*
enuresis	enuresis *nf*
epistaxis	epistaxis *nf*
epithelioma	epitelioma *nm*
eructation	eructación, eructo *nf, nm*
fibrosis	fibrosis *nf*
fistula	fístula *nf*
fracture	fractura *nf*
furuncle (boil)	furúnculo *nm*
gangrene	gangrena *nf*
giantism, gigantism	gigantismo *nm*
glycosuria	glicosuria, glucosuria *nf*
gonorrhea	gonorrea *nf*
hematoma	hematoma *nm*
hemiplegia (stroke)	hemiplejía *nf*
hernia	hernia *nf*
herpes	herpes *nm*
hirsutism	hirsutismo *nm*
hydrops, hydropsy	hidropesía *nf*
hyperacidity	hiperacidez *nf*
hypercholesterolemia	hipercolesterolemia *nf*
hyperglycemia	hiperglicemia *nf*
hyperplasia	hiperplasia *nf*
hyperthermia	hipertermia *nf*
hyperthyroidism	hipertiroidismo *nm*
hypertrophy	hipertrofia *nf*
hyperventilation	hiperventilación *nf*
hypotension	hipotensión *nf*
hypothyroidism	hipotiroidismo *nm*
hypoxia	hipoxia *nf*
inanition	inanición *nf*
incontinence	incontinencia *nf*
infarct, infarction	infarto *nm*
keloid	queloide *nm*

kyphosis	cifosis *nf*	spina bifida	espina bífida *nf*
Legionnaires' disease	enfermedad del legionario *nf*	syphilis	sífilis *nf*
		tinnitus	tinnitus *nm*
lipoma	lipoma *nm*	torticolis (stiff neck)	tortícolis *nm*
lordosis	lordosis *nf*	tumor	tumor *nm*
macrocephaly	macrocefalia *nf*	varicose veins	varices, várices nfpl
melanism	melanismo, melanosis *nm, nf*	vertigo	vértigo *nm*
melanoma	melanoma *nm*		
microcephaly	microcefalía *nf*		

DRUGS

GENERAL TERMS

migraine	migraña *nf*	abuse	abuso *nm*
myxedema, myxoedema	mixedema *nm*	adulterant	sustancia adulterante *nf*
narcosis	narcosis *nf*	antidote	antídoto *nm*
narcotism	narcotismo *nm*	contraindication	contraindicación *nf*
necrosis (gangrene)	necrosis *nf*	drug addiction	drogadicción *nf*
nephralgia	nefralgia *nf*	drugstore	droguería *nf*
nephrolith (kidney stone)	nefrólito *nm*	effect	efecto *nm*
		formulary	formulario *nm*
neurasthenia	neurastenia *nf*	generic	genérico *aj*
neuroma	neuroma *nm*	incompatibility	incompatibilidad *nf*
neuropathy	neuropatía *nf*	intolerance	intolerancia *nf*
obstruction	obstrucción *nf*	medicine	medicina *nf*
occlusion	oclusión *nf*	mixture	mixtura *nf*
osteoporosis	osteoporosis *nf*	overdose	sobredosis *nf*
otalgia	otalgia *nf*	patent medicine	medicamento patentado *nm*
palsy	perlesía *nf*		
paralysis	parálisis *nf*	pharmaceutical	farmacéutico *aj, nm*
paresis	paresis, paresia *nf*	pharmacist	farmacéutico, -a *nmf*
pellagra	pelagra *nf*	pharmacologist	farmacólogo, -a *nmf*
perforation	perforación *nf*	pharmacology	farmacología *nf*
plethora	plétora *nf*	pharmacopeia	farmacopea *nf*
pleurisy	pleuresía *nf*	pharmacy	farmacia *nf*
pneumoconiosis	neumoconiosis *nf*	potent	potente *aj*
pneumothorax	neumotórax *nm*	preparation	preparación, preparado *nf, nm*
polyp	pólipo *nm*		
polyuria	poliuria *nf*	psychopharmacology	(p)sicofarmacología *nf*
prolapse	prolapso *nm*	reaction	reacción *nf*
prostatism	prostatismo *nm*	sensitivity	sensibilidad *nf*
prostration	postración *nf*	specific	específico *nm*
ptosis	ptosis *nf*	substance	sustancia *nf*
pustule	pústula *nf*	synergy	sinergia *nf*
quadriplegia	cuadriplejía *nf*	synthetic	sintético *aj*
radiation sickness	radiotoxemia *nf*	tolerance	tolerancia *nf*
rickets	raquitismo *nm*	toxicity	toxicidad *nf*
rupture	ruptura *nf*		
scald, scalding	escaldadura *nf*		
schistosomiasis	esquistosomiasis *nf*		
sciatica	ciática *nf*		

CLASSES OF DRUGS

scleroma	escleroma *nm*	analgesic	analgésico *aj, nm*
sclerosis	esclerosis *nf*	anaphrodisiac	anafrodisíaco *aj, nm*
scoliosis	escoliosis *nf*	anesthetic	anestético *aj, nm*
silicosis	silicosis *nf*		

antacid	antiácido *aj, nm*	
anthelmintic	antihelmíntico *aj, nm*	
antibacterial	antibacteriano, antibactérico *aj*	
antibiotic	antibiótico *aj, nm*	
anticoagulant	anticoagulante *aj, nm*	
anticonvulsant	anticonvulsivante *aj, nm*	
antihistamine	antihistamínico *nm*	
antimalarial	antipalúdico *aj*	
antipyretic	antipirético *aj, nm*	
antiseptic	antiséptico *aj, nm*	
antiserum	antisuero *nm*	
antispasmodic	antiespasmódico *aj, nm*	
antitoxin	antitoxina *nf*	
antitussive	antitusígeno *aj*	
antiviral	antiviral *aj*	
aphrodisiac	afrodisíaco *aj, nm*	
astringent	astringente *aj, nm*	
bactericide	bactericida *nm*	
bronchodilator	broncodilatador *nm*	
calefacient	remedio calefaciente *nm*	
cardiovascular	cardiovascular *aj*	
carminative	carminativo *aj, nm*	
contraceptive	contraceptivo, anticonceptivo *aj, nm*	
counterirritant	contrairritante *nm*	
decongestant	descongestivo *nm*	
disinfectant	desinfectante *nm*	
diuretic	diurético *nm*	
emetic	emético *aj, nm*	
expectorant	expectorante *nm*	
gargle	gargarismo *nm*	
germicide	germicida *nf*	
hormones	hormonas *nfpl*	
immunosuppresives	inmunosupresivos *nmpl*	
laxative	laxante *aj, nm*	
medicinal	medicinal *aj*	
narcotic	narcótico *aj, nm*	
purgative	purgante, purgativo *aj, nm*	
relaxant	relajante *nm*	
salts	sales *nfpl*	
soporific	soporífero *nm*	
spermicide	espermicida, espermaticida *nm*	
steroid	esteroide *nm*	
stimulant	estimulante *nm*	
vaccine	vacuna *nf*	
vermicide	vermicida *nm*	
vitamins	vitaminas *nfpl*	

COMMON MEDICINAL DRUGS

antibiotics

ampicillin	ampicilina *nf*
aureomycin	aureomicina *nf*
bacitracin	bacitracina *nf*
calomel	calomelanos, calomel *nm*
cyclosporine	ciclosporina *nf*
erythromycin	eritromicina *nf*
gramicidin	gramicidina *nf*
iodine	yodo *nm*
mercurochrome	mercurocromo *nm*
penicillin	penicilina *nf*
streptomycin	estreptomicina *nf*
sulfa	sulfa *nf*
sulfonamide	sulfonamida *nf*
Terramycin	terramicina *nf*
tetracycline	tetraciclina *nf*

cardiovascular drugs

antiarrhythmic	antiarrítmico *aj*
antihypertensive	antihiperténsico *aj*
beta (blocker)	beta *nf*
cardiotonic	cardiotónico *aj*
digitalis	digital *nf*
reserpine	reserpina *nf*
vasoconstrictor	vasoconstrictor *nm*
vasodilator	vasodilatador *nm*

analgesics

acetaminophen	acetaminofen *nm*
anodyne	anodino *aj, nm*
aspirin	aspirina *nf*
camphorated oil	aceite alcanforado *nm*
codeine	codeína *nf*
ibuprofen	ibuprofen *nm*
liniment	linimento *nm*
menthol	mentol *nm*
morphine	morfina *nf*
opiate	opiata *nf*
paregoric	elixir paregórico *nm*

anesthetics

benzocaine	benzocaíne *nf*
chloroform	cloroformo *nm*
ether	éter *nm*
nitrous oxide	óxido nitroso *nm*
Novocain (= procaine)	novocaína *nf*
procaine	procaína *nf*

stimulants

adrenalin(e)	adrenalina *nf*

analeptic	analéptico *aj, nm*
benzedrine	bencedrina *nf*
(= amphetamine)	
caffein(e)	cafeína *nf*
camphor	alcanfor *nm*
cocain(e)	cocaína *nf*
elixir	elíxir *nm*
ephedrine	efedrina *nf*
epinephrine	epinefrina *nf*
nicotine	nicotina *nf*
tonic	tónico *nm*

antianxiety drugs

antidepressant	antidepresivo *aj, nm*
antipsychotic	antipsicótico *aj*
barbiturate	barbitúrico *nm*
bromide	bromuro *nm*
calmative	calmante *aj, nm*
laudanum	láudano *nm*
sedative	sedante, sedativo *aj, nm*
tranquilizer	tranquilizante *nm*

poisons

arsenic	arsénico *nm*
curare	curare *nm*
nux vomica	nuez vómica *nf*
strychnine	estricnina *nf*

FORMS AND ADMINISTRATION

ampule, ampoule	ampolla, ampolleta *nf*
capsule	cápsula *nf*
cream	crema *nf*
gas	gas *nm*
gel	gel *nm*
inhalant	inhalante *aj, nm*
inhaler	inhalador *nm*
injection	inyección *nf*
liquid	líquido *aj, nm*
lotion	loción *nf*
oral	oral *aj*
pastille	pastilla *nf*
patch	parche *nm*
pill	píldora *nf*
tablet	tableta *nf*

DEATH

GENERAL TERMS

cause	causa *nf*
comfort	confortar *vt*
condolence	condolencia *nf*
console	consolar *vt*

defunct	difunto *aj*
dismember	desmembrar *vt*
expectancy (life)	expectativa *nf*
extinction	extinción *nf*
fatal	fatal *aj*
inter	enterrar *vt*
lethal	letal *aj*
macabre	macabro *aj*
moribund	moribundo *aj*
perish	perecer *vi*
posthumous	póstumo *aj*

CAUSES OF DEATH BY KILLING

individual killing

asphyxiation	asfixia *nf*
assassination	asesinato *nm*
decapitation	decapitación *nf*
electrocution	electrocución *nf*
euthanasia	eutanasia *nf*
execution	ejecución *nf*
fratricide (act)	fratricidio *nm*
harakiri, hara-kiri	haraquiri *nm*
homicide (act)	homicidio *nm*
infanticide (act)	infanticidio *nm*
lynching	linchamiento *nm*
matricide (act)	matricidio *nm*
parricide (act)	parricidio *nm*
regicide (act)	regicidio *nm*
scalp	escalpar *vt*
strangulation	estrangulación *nf*
suffocation	sofocación, sofoco *nf*
suicide (act)	suicidio *nm*

mass killing

atrocity	atrocidad *nf*
bombing	bombardeo *nm*
cannibalism	canibalismo *nm*
cataclysm	cataclismo *nm*
catastrophe	catástrofe *nf*
conflagration	conflagración *nf*
disaster	desastre *nm*
epidemic	epidemia *nf*
gas	gasear *vt*
genocide	genocidio *nm*
holocaust	holocausto *nm*
massacre	masacre *nf*
pestilence	pestilencia *nf*
pogrom	pogromo *nm*

instruments

bomb	bomba *nf*
dagger	daga *nf*

garrote, garotte	garrote *nm*
guillotine	guillotina *nf*
pistol	pistola *nf*
rifle	rifle *nm*

poisons

arsenic	arsénico *nm*
phosgene	fosgeno *nm*
strychnine	estricnina *nf*
venom	veneno *nm*

ASPECTS OF DYING

medical aspects

cadaver	cadáver *nm*
decease	deceso *nm*
embalming	embalsamamiento *nm*
expiration	expiración *nf*
morbidity	morbosidad *nf*
mortality	mortalidad *nf*
survival	supervivencia *nf*

legal aspects

administrator	administrador(a) *nmf*
autopsy	autopsia *nf*
certificate	certificado *nm*
disposition	disposición *nf*
executor	ejecutor(a) *nmf*
exhumation	exhumación *nf*
forensic	forense *aj*
heir/heiress	heredero, -a *nmf*
inheritance	herencia *nf*
inquest	encuesta *nf*
interment	entierro *nm*
intestate	intestado *aj*
legacy	legado *nm*
nuncupative (will)	nuncupativo *aj*
perpetuity	perpetuidad *nf*
testate	testado *aj*
testator	testador(a) *nmf*

religious aspects

cortege, cortège	cortejo *nm*
cremation	cremación *nf*
eschatology	escatología *nf*
eternity	eternidad *nf*
funeral	funeral *nm*
immortality	inmortalidad *nf*
metempsychosis	metempsicosis *nf*
preservation	preservación *nf*
reincarnation	reencarnación *nf*
reliquary	relicario *nm*
resurrection	resurrección *nf*

places

cemetery	cementerio *nm*
crematorium, crematory	crematorio *nm*
crypt	cripta *nf*
funeral home	funeraria *nf*
hospice	hospicio *nm*
hospital	hospital *nm*
mausoleum	mausoleo *nm*
pyre	pira *nf*
sepulcher	sepulcro *nm*
sepulture	sepultura *nf*
tomb	tumba *nf*

historical terms

catacombs	catacumbas *nfpl*
catafalque	catafalco *nm*
cenotaph	cenotafio *nm*
hecatomb	hecatombe *nf*
mastaba	mastaba *nf*
mummy	momia *nf*
necropolis	necrópolis *nf*
ossuary	osario *nm*
pantheon	panteón *nm*

art, music, and language

elegy	elegía *nf*
epitaph	epitafio *nm*
mask	máscara *nf*
memorial	memorial *nm*
necrology	necrología *nf*
obituary	obituario *nm*
oration (funeral)	oración *nf*
requiem	réquiem *nm*
sarcophagus	sarcófago *nm*
stela, stele	estela *nf*

other terms

carrion	carroña *nf*
necromancy	nigromancía *nf*
necrophagia	necrofagia *nf*
necrophilia	necrofilia *nf*
necrophobia	necrofobia *nf*

PERSONS

killers

assassin	asesino, -a *nmf*
cannibal	caníbal *nmf*
exterminator	exterminador(a) *nmf*
fratricide	fratricida *nmf*
homicide	homicida *nmf*
infanticide	infanticida *nmf*

matricide	matricida *nmf*
parricide	parricida *nmf*
regicide	regicida *nmf*
strangler	estrangulador(a) *nmf*
suicide	suicida *nmf*

other persons

consoler	consolador(a) *nmf*
embalmer	embalsamador(a) *nmf*
mortal	mortal *aj, nmf*
organ donor	donante de órgano *nmf*
spiritualist	espiritista *nmf*
survivor	sobreviviente *nmf*
widow	viuda *nf*
widower	viudo *nm*

(*See also* **pesticides** under **AGRICULTURE**; *violent* under **LAW**; *birth and death* under **RELIGION**)

AGE AND AGING

GENERAL TERMS

celebrate (birthday)	celebrar *vt*
gerontocracy	gerontocracia *nf*
life expectancy *nsg*	expectativas de vida *nfpl*
long-lived	longevo *aj*
maturation	maduración *nf*
Medicare	Medicare *nm*
rejuvenation	rejuvenecimiento *nm*
retirement	retiro *nm*
Social Security	Seguro Social *nm*

FIELDS OF SPECIALIZATION

childhood

pediatrics	pediatría *nf*
pedodontics	pedodoncia *nf*
pedology	pedología *nf*

old age

geriatrics	geriatría *nf*
gerontology	gerontología *nf*

ASPECTS OF AGING

stages of life

adolescence	adolescencia *nf*
adulthood	edad adulta *nf*
climacteric	climaterio *nm*
infancy	infancia *nf*
maturity	madurez *nf*
menopause	menopausia *nf*

preadolescence	preadolescencia *nf*
prepubescence	prepubescencia *nf*
puberty	pubertad *nf*
pubescence	pubescencia *nf*
senescence	senectud *nf*

age determination

chronological	cronológico *aj*
emotional	emocional *aj*
mental	mental *aj*
physical	físico *aj*
psychological	(p)sicológico *aj*

legal categories

adult	adulto, -a *aj, nmf*
juvenile	juvenil *aj, nmf*
majority	mayoría *nf*
minor	menor *aj, nmf*
minority	minoría *nf*

geriatic disorders

Alzheimer's disease	enfermedad de Alzheimer *nf*
presbycusis	presbicusis *nf*
presbyopia	presbiopía *nf*
puerilism	puerilismo *nm*
senility	senilidad, senilismo *nm*

PERSONS

adolescent	adolescente *aj, nmf*
babe, baby	bebé *nmf*
centenarian	centenario, -a *aj, nmf*
geriatrician	geriatra *nmf*
gerontologist	gerontologo, -a *nmf*
nonagenarian	nonagenario, -a *nmf*
octogenarian	octogenario, -a *nmf*
pederast	pederasta *nm*
pediatrician	pediatra *nmf*
septuagenarian	septuagenario, -a *aj, nmf*
sexagenarian	sexagenario, -a *aj, nmf*

(*See also* **lineage terms** under **FAMILY**)

Understanding Our Universe

SCIENCE AND THE SCIENCES

GENERAL TERMS

cosmos	cosmos *nm*
energy	energía *nf*
evolution	evolución *nf*
fundamental	fundamento *nm*
matter	materia *nf*
nature	naturaleza *nf*
order	orden *nm*
origin	origen *nm*
relativity	relatividad *nf*
science	ciencia *nf*
state	estado *nm*
system	sistema *nm*
taxonomy	taxonomía *nf*
technology	tecnología *nf*
type	tipo *nm*
universe	universo *nm*

MAJOR SCIENTIFIC FIELDS

basic divisions

applied	aplicado *aj*
pure	puro *aj*

abstract sciences

logic	lógica *nf*
mathematics *nsg*	matemáticas *nfpl*
metaphysics	metafísica *nf*

physical sciences

astronomy	astronomía *nf*
chemistry	química *nf*
geography	geografía *nf*
geology	geología *nf*
meteorology	meteorología *nf*
physics	física *nf*

biological sciences

anatomy	anatomía *nf*
biochemistry	bioquímica *nf*
biology	biología *nf*
botany	botánica *nf*
medicine	medicina *nf*
paleontology	paleontología *nf*
physiology	fisiología *nf*

psychology	(p)sicología *nf*
zoology	zoología *nf*

social sciences

anthropology	antropología *nf*
economics	economía *nf*
history	historia *nf*
linguistics	lingüística *nf*
political science *nsg*	ciencias políticas *nfpl*
sociology	sociología *nf*

technical sciences

biotechnology	biotecnología *nf*
chronometry	cronometría *nf*
microscopy	microscopia, microscopía *nf*
radiology	radiología *nf*
robotics	robótica *nf*
systematics	sistemática *nf*

TERMS IN SCIENTIFIC RESEARCH

analysis	análisis *nm*
chaos	caos *nm*
classification	clasificación *nf*
collection	colección *nf*
conclusion	conclusión *nf*
control	control *nm*
data *nsg* or *npl*	datos *nmpl*
definition	definición *nf*
diagram	diagrama *nm*
discovery	descubrimiento *nm*
dissemination	diseminación *nf*
evidence	evidencia *nf*
experiment	experimento *nm*
formula	fórmula *nf*
generalization	generalización *nf*
hypothesis	hipótesis *nf*
interpretation	interpretación *nf*
investigation	investigación *nf*
laboratory	laboratorio *nm*
mass	masa *nf*
method	método *nm*
methodology	metodología *nf*
model	modelo *nm*
notation	notación *nf*
observation	observación *nf*
principle	principio *nm*
prove	probar *vt*
quantification	cuantificación *nf*
repetition	repetición *nf*
result	resultado *nm*
solution	solución *nf*
supposition	suposición *nf*

theory	teoría *nf*
time	tiempo *nm*
validation	validación *nf*
verification	verificación *nf*

PERSONS

discoverer	descubridor(a) *nmf*
evolutionist	evolucionista *nmf*
genius	genio *nm*
inventor	inventor(a) *nmf*
scientist	científico, -a *nmf*
theoretician	teórico, -a *nmf*

(*See also* TERMS IN LOGIC under **PHILOSOPHY**)

MATHEMATICS

GENERAL TERMS

algorithm	algoritmo *nm*
analysis	análisis *nm*
axiom	axioma *nm*
chaos	caos *nm*
characteristic	característica *nf*
computation (general)	computación *nf*
decrement	decremento *nm*
determinant	determinante *nm*
discontinuity	discontinidad *nf*
domain	dominio *nm*
duality	dualidad *nf*
element	elemento *nm*
equality	igualdad *nf*
equation	ecuación *nf*
example	ejemplo *nm*
expression	expresión *nf*
extract	extraer *vt*
function	función *nf*
gradient	gradiente *nm*
group	grupo *nm*
harmonic	armónico *aj*
homomorphism	homomorfismo *nm*
increment	incremento *nm*
inequality	desigualdad *nf*
infinity	infinidad *nf*
intersection	intersección *nf*
invariant	invariante *nf*
isomorphism	isomorfismo *nm*
lemma	lema *nm*
logarithm	logaritmo *nm*
magnitude	magnitud *nf*
mathematician	matemático, -a *nmf*
mathematics *nsg*	matemáticas *nfpl*
matrix	matriz *nf*
modulus	módulo *nm*

multiple	múltiplo *nm*
notation	notación *nf*
number, numeral	número *nm*
numerical	numérico *aj*
operation	operación *nf*
operator	operador *nm*
order	orden *nm*
parameter	parámetro *nm*
part	parte *nf*
percent	por ciento *nm*
period	período *nm*
point	punto *nm*
postulate	postulado *nm*
problem	problema *nm*
progression	progresión *nf*
proof	prueba *nf*
proportion	proporción *nf*
proposition	proposición *nf*
quantity	cantidad *nf*
residual	variancia residual *nf*
result	resultado *nm*
scalar	escalar *aj*
sign	signo *nm*
solution	solución *nf*
space	espacio *nm*
subgroup	subgrupo *nm*
symbol	símbolo *nm*
tensor	tensor *nm*
theorem	teorema *nm*
three-dimensional	tridimensional *aj*
two-dimensional	bidimensional *aj*
union	unión *nf*
unit	unidad *nf*
unity	unidad *nf*
variation	variación *nf*
vector	vector *nm*

BRANCHES

pure mathematics

algebra	álgebra *nf*
arithmetic	aritmética *nf*
calculus	cálculo *nm*
geometry	geometría *nf*
logic	lógica *nf*
probability	probabilidad *nf*
topology	topología *nf*
trigonometry	trigonometría *nf*

applied mathematics

accounting	contabilidad *nf*
econometrics	econometría *nf*
statistics	estadística *nf*

BASIC CONCEPTS

systems

binary	binario *aj*
decimal	decimal *aj, nm*
duodecimal	duodecimal *aj*
hexadecimal	hexadecimal *aj, nm*
infinitesimal	infinitesimal *aj*
metric	métrico *aj*
scale	escala *nf*
sexagesimal	sexagesimal *aj*
ternary	ternario *aj*

numerals

Arabic	arábigo *aj*
cipher	cifra *nf*
digit	dígito *nm*
reciprocal	número recíproco *nm*
Roman	romano *aj*

types of numbers

abstract	abstracto *aj*
base	base *nf*
cardinal	cardinal *aj*
complex	complejo *aj, nm*
constant	constante *aj, nf*
discrete	discreto *aj*
dual	dual *aj*
finite	finito *aj*
fraction	fracción *nf*
imaginary	imaginario *aj*
index	índice *nm*
infinite	infinito *aj, nm*
integer	número entero
irrational (number)	irracional *aj*
minimum	mínimo *nm*
mixed	mixto *aj*
natural	natural *aj*
negative	negativo *aj*
ordinal	ordinal *aj*
positive	positivo *aj, nm*
prime	primo *aj*
rational	rational *nf*
real	real *aj*
variable	variable *aj, nf*

fractions

cancellation	cancelación *nf*
common	común *aj*
denominator	denominador *nm*
equivalent	equivalente *aj, nm*
improper	impropio *aj*
mantissa	mantisa *nf*
numerator	numerador *nm*
proper	propio *aj*
term	término *nm*
value	valor *nm*

multiples

double	doble *aj, nmf*
duple	duplo *aj*
octuple	óctuplo *aj*
quadruple	cuádruplo *nm*
quintuple	quíntuplo *aj, nm*
sextuple	séxtuplo *aj, nm*
triple	triple *aj*

other quantities

billion	billón *nm*
dozen	docena *nf*
million	millón *nm*
null	nulo *aj*
octillion	octillón *nm*
zero	cero *nm*

groupings

dichotomy	dicotomía *nf*
quadruplet	cuádruplo *nm*
trichotomy	tricotomía *nf*

operations and processes

addition	adición *nf*
calculation	cálculo *nm*
computation (specific)	cómputo *nm*
conversion	conversión *nf*
division	división *nf*
duplication	duplicación *nf*
estimation	estimación *nf*
factorization	división en factores
induction	inducción *nf*
inversion	inversión *nf*
involution	involución *nf*
multiplication	multiplicación *nf*
permutation	permutación *nf*
reduction	reducción *nf*
subtraction	su(b)stracción *nf*
transposition	tra(n)sposición *nf*

ordinal numbers

billionth	billonésimo *aj, nm*
centesimal	centésimo *aj, nm*

millionth	millonésimo *aj, nm*	sequence	secuencia *nf*
sixth	sexto *aj, nm*	series	serie *nf*

TERMS IN ALGEBRA

abscissa	abscisa *nf*
binomial	binomio *aj, nm*
coefficient	coeficiente *nm*
coordinate	coordenada *nf*
exponent	exponente *nm*
formula	fórmula *nf*
monomial	monomio *nm*
ordinate	ordenada *nf*
polynomial	polinomio *nm*
transcendental	tra(n)scendental *aj*
trinomial	trinomio *nm*

TERMS IN ARITHMETIC

cube	cubo *nm*
difference	diferencia *nf*
divide	dividir *vt*
dividend	dividendo *nm*
divisible	divisible *aj*
divisor	divisor *nm*
factor	factor *nm*
indivisible	indivisible *aj*
minuend	minuendo *nm*
minus	menos *nm*
multiplicand	multiplicando *nm*
multiplier	multiplicador *nm*
product	producto *nm*
quotient	cociente *nm*
rest (remainder)	resto *nm*
subtotal	subtotal *nm*
subtrahend	substraendo, sustraendo *nm*
sum	suma *nf*
total	total *aj, nm*

TERMS IN CALCULUS

convergence	convergencia *nf*
deduct	deducir *vt*
derivative	derivada *nf*
differential	diferencial *nf*
differentiation	diferenciación *nf*
divergence	divergencia *nf*
infinitesimal	infinitésimo *nm*
integral	integral *nf*
integration	integración *nf*
limit	límite *nm*

TERMS IN GEOMETRY

branches

analytic	analítico *aj*
Cartesian	cartesiano *aj*
elliptic	elíptico *aj*
Euclidean	euclidiano *aj*
hyperbolic	hiperbólico *aj*
non-Euclidean	no euclidiano
plane	plano *aj, nm*
projective	proyectivo *aj*
solid	sólido *aj, nm*
transformational	tra(n)sformacional *aj*

general terms

area	área *nf(el)*
directrix	directriz *nf*
generate	generar *vt*
compass	compás *nm*
complement	complemento *nm*
congruence	congruencia *nf*
curvature	curvatura *nf*
diagram	diagrama *nm*
dimension	dimensión *nf*
envelope	envolvente *nf*
equidistant	equidistante *aj*
figure	figura *nf*
focus	foco *nm*
generatrix	generatriz *nf*
hypothesis	hipótesis *nf*
incidence	incidencia *nf*
median	mediana *nf*
minute	minuto *nm*
multidimensional	multidimensional *aj*
pi	pi *nf*
rectification	rectificación *nf*
similarity	similitud *nf*
supplement	suplemento *nm*
symmetry	simetría *nf*
trace	traza *nf*
volume	volumen *nm*

geometric figures
– plane –

circle	círculo *nm*
cycloid	cicloide *nf*
decagon	decágono *nm*
ellipse	elipse *nf*
ellipsoid	elipsoide *nm*

epicycle	epiciclo *nm*
epicycloid	epicicloide *nf*
heptagon	heptágono *nm*
hexagon	hexágono *nm*
hyperbola	hipérbola *nf*
hypocycloid	hipocicloide *nf*
octagon	octágono *nm*
oval	óvalo *nm*
parabola	parábola *nf*
pentagon	pentágono *nm*
polygon	polígono *nm*
quadrate	cuadrado *nm*
quadrilateral	cuadrilátero *aj, nm*
semicircle	semicírculo *nm*
spiral	espiral *nf*
triangle	triángulo *nm*
trihedral	triedro *nm*

– solid (regular polyhedra) –

dodecahedron	dodecaedro *nm*
icosahedron	icosaedro *nm*
octahedron	octaedro *nm*
pentahedron	pentaedro *nm*
tetrahedron	tetraedro *nm*

– other 3-dimensional figures –

cone	cono *nm*
conic	sección cónica *nf*
cube	eubo *nm*
cylinder	cilindro *nm*
helix	hélice *nf*
hyperboloid	hipcrboloidc *nf*
parallepiped	paralelepípedo *nm*
polyhedron	poliedro *nm*
prism	prisma *nm*
pyramid	pirámide *nf*
sphere	esfera *nf*
spheroid	esferoide *nm*

– parts of figures –

altitude	altura *nf*
angle	ángulo *nm*
apex	ápice *nm*
apothem	apotema *nf*
arc	arco *nm*
axis	eje(*nm*)
bisection	bisección *nf*
bisector	bisector, bisectriz *nm, nf*
center	centro *nm*
chord	cuerda *nf*
circumference	circunferencia *nf*
curve	curva *nf*
diameter	diámetro *nm*

evolute	evoluta *nf*
hypotenuse	hipotenusa *nf*
involute	involuta *nf*
line	línea *nf*
node	nodo *nm*
octant	octante *nm*
parallel	paralelo *aj, nm*
perimeter	perímetro *nm*
quadrant	cuadrante *nm*
radius	radio *nm*
secant	secante *nf*
section	sección *nf*
sector	sector *nm*
segment	segmento *nm*
sextant	sextante *nm*
tangent	tangente *aj, nf*
transversal	transversal *nf*
trisection	trisección *nf*
vertex	vértice *nm*

kinds of angles

adjacent	adyacente *aj*
alternate	alterno *aj*
acute	agudo *aj*
complementary	complementario *aj*
exterior	exterior *aj*
interior	interior *aj*
obtuse	obtuso *aj*
opposite	opuesto *aj*
supplementary	suplementario *aj*
vertical	vertical *aj, nf*

kinds of triangles

equilateral	equilateral *aj*
isosceles	isósceles *aj*
right	recto *aj*
scalene	escaleno *aj*

kinds of quadrilaterals

parallelogram	paralelogramo *nm*
quadrangle	cuadrángulo *nm*
radian	radián *nm*
rectangle	rectángulo *nm*
rhombus	rombo *nm*
trapezoid	trapecio *nm*

description

circumscribed	circunscrito *aj*
contiguous	contiguo *aj*
geometric(al)	geométrico *aj*
Pythagorean (theorem)	pitagórico *aj*
angular	angular *aj*

circular	circular *aj*
collinear	colineal *aj*
concentric	concéntrico *aj*
congruent	congruente *aj*
coplanar	coplanario *aj*
curved	curvo *aj*
curvilinear	curvilíneo *aj*
cylindrical	cilíndrico *aj*
diagonal	diagonal *aj, nf*
eccentric	excéntrico *aj*
helical	helicoida *aj*
hexagonal	hexagonal *aj*
horizontal	horizontal *aj, nf*
linear	lineal *aj*
normal	normal *aj*
oblique	oblicuo *aj*
oblong	oblongo *aj, nm*
octagonal	octagonal *aj*
oval	oval, ovalado *aj*
parabolic	parabólico *aj*
perpendicular	perpendicular *aj, nf*
quadrangular	cuadrangular *aj*
rectangular	rectangular *aj*
rectilinear	rectilinear *aj*
regular	regular *aj*
rhombic	rombal, rómbico *aj*
semicircular	semicircular *aj*
similar	similar *aj*
symmetrical	simétrico *aj*
tangential	tangencial *aj*
tetrahedral	tetraédrico *aj*
transverse	tra(n)sverso *aj*
triangular	triangular *aj*
trilateral	trilateral *aj*
unidirectional	unidireccional *aj*

TERMS IN STATISTICS

correlation	correlación *nf*
covariance	covariancia *nf*
dependent	dependiente *aj*
deviation	desviación *nf*
extrapolation	extrapolación *nf*
frequency	frecuencia *nf*
independent	independiente *aj*
interpolation	interpolación *nf*
margin of error	margen de error *nm*
median (number)	mediano *aj*
percentile	percentil *nm*
population	población *nf*
quartile	cuartil *nm*
regression	regresión *nf*
variance	variancia *nf*

TERMS IN TRIGONOMETRY

cosecant	cosecante *nf*
cosine	coseno *nm*
cotangent	cotangente *nf*
sine	seno *nm*
spherical	esférico *aj*

TOOLS

abacus	ábaco *nm*
calculator	calculadora *nf*
computer	computadora *nf*
counter	contador *nm*
graph	gráfica *nf*
table	tabla *nf*

PHYSICS

GENERAL TERMS

activity	actividad *nf*
atmosphere	atmósfera *nf*
component	componente *aj, nm*
cosmos	cosmos *nm*
crystal	cristal *nm*
dimension	dimensión *nf*
electric	eléctrico *aj*
element	elemento *nm*
energy	energía *nf*
ether (obs)	éter *nm*
flux	flujo *nm*
formula	fórmula *nf*
gas	gas *nm*
gravity	gravedad *nf*
impact	impacto *nm*
ion	ion *nm*
liquid	líquido *aj, nm*
magnetic	magnético *aj*
mass	masa *nf*
matter	materia *nf*
metal	metal *nm*
molecule	molécula *nf*
motion	moción *nf*
number	número *nm*
pressure	presión *nf*
property	propiedad *nf*
reaction	reacción *nf*
relativity	relatividad *nf*
saturation	saturación *nf*
semiconductor	semiconductor *nm*
solid	sólido *nm*
sound	son, sonido *nm*

space	espacio *nm*
space-time	espacio-tiempo *nm*
stability	estabilidad *nf*
structure	estructura *nf*
temperature	temperatura *nf*
time	tiempo *nm*
transformation	tra(n)sformación *nf*
universe	universo *nm*

BRANCHES OF PHYSICS

major fields

acoustics	acústica *nf*
atomic	atómico *aj*
biophysics	biofísica *nf*
cryogenics	criogenia *nf*
electromagnetism	electromagnetismo *nm*
geophysics	geofísica *nf*
mathematical	matemático *aj*
mechanics	mecánica *nf*
molecular (physics)	molecular *aj*
nuclear (physics)	nuclear *aj*
optics	óptica *nf*
particle	partícula *nf*
plasma	plasma *nm*
quantum (physics)	cuántico *aj*
solid-state	estado sólido *nm*
thermodynamics	termodinámica *nf*

subfields

astronomy	astronomía *nf*
astrophysics	astrofísica *nf*
cosmology	cosmología *nf*
crystallography	cristalografía *nf*
electricity	electricidad *nf*
electrodynamics	electrodinámica *nf*
electrokinetics	electrocinética *nf*
electronics	electrónica *nf*
energetics	energética *nf*
hydrodynamics	hidrodinámica *nf*
hydrostatics	hidrostática *nf*
kinematics	cinemática *nf*
kinetics	cinética *nf*
micrography	micrografía *nf*
micrometry	micrometría *nf*
microscopy	microscopia, microscopía *nf*
pneumatics	neumática *nf*
radiography	radiografía *nf*
spectroscopy	espectroscopia *nf*
thermography	termografía *nf*

CHEMISTRY
GENERAL TERMS

activity	actividad *nf*
anode	ánodo *nm*
catalyst	catalizador *nm*
cathode	cátodo *nm*
chemical	químico *aj, nm*
chemist	químico, -a *nmf*
composition	composición *nf*
equation	ecuación *nf*
equilibrium	equilibrio *nm*
formula	fórmula *nf*
fraction	fracción *nf*
group	grupo *nm*
homology	homología *nf*
isobar	isobara *nf*
mass	masa *nf*
mole	mol *nm*
number	número *nm*
orbit	órbita *nf*
periodic table	tabla periódica *nf*
product	producto *nm*
property	propiedad *nf*
qualitative	cualitativo *aj*
quantitative	cuantitativo *aj*
reaction	reacción *nf*
series	serie *nf*
state	estado *nm*
substance	sustancia *nf*
substrate	substrato *nm*
symbol	símbolo *nm*
valence	valencia *nf*

BRANCHES

major fields

analytical	analítico *aj*
inorganic	inorgánico *aj*
organic	orgánico *aj*
physical	físico *aj*
polymer	polímero *nm*
synthetic	sintético *aj*

interdisciplinary fields

biochemistry	bioquímica *nf*
electrochemistry	electroquímica *nf*
geochemistry	geoquímica *nf*
photochemistry	fotoquímica *nf*
radiochemistry	radioquímica *nf*
thermochemistry	termoquímica *nf*

other specializations

metallurgy	metalurgia *nf*
microchemistry	microquímica *nf*
stereochemistry	estereoquimica *nf*
zymology	cimología *nf*
zymurgy	cimurgia, zimurgia *nf*

BASIC CONCEPTS

components

atom	átomo *nm*
compound	compuesto *nm*
electron	electrón *nm*
element	elemento *nm*
ion	ion *nm*
molecule	molécula *nf*
neutron	neutrón *nm*
nucleus	núcleo *nm*
proton	protón *nm*

composition

dyad	díada *nf*
monad	mónada *nf*
radiocarbon	radiocarbono *nm*
tetrad	tétrade *nm*

forms of matter

allotrope	forma alotrópica *nf*
crystal	cristal *nm*
crystaloid	cristaloide *nm*
gas	gas *nm*
gel	gel *nm*
liquid	líquido *nm*
phase	fase *nf*
solid	sólido *nm*

kinds of substances

additive	aditivo *aj, nm*
aerosol	aerosol *nm*
agent	agente *nm*
amphoteric	anfótero *aj*
antioxidant	antioxidante *nm*
concentrate	concentrado *nm*
cryogen	criógeno *nm*
derivative	derivado *nm*
enzyme	enzima *nf*
extract	extracto *nm*
ferment	fermento *nm*
flowers	flor *nf*
halogen	halógeno *nm*
inductor	inductor *nm*
inhibitor	inhibidor *nm*

isotope	isótopo *nm*
metal	metal *nm*
neutralizer	neutralizador *nm*
oxidant	oxidante *nm*
precipitate	precipitado *nm*
reactant	agente reactor
residue	residuo *nm*
resin	resina *nf*
saturant	substancia saturativa
solute	soluto *nm*

properties

acidity	acidez *nf*
alkalinity	alcalinidad *nf*
atomicity	atomicidad *nf*
basicity	basicidad *nf*
isomerism	isomería *nf*
isomorphism	isomorfismo *nm*
phosphorescence	fosforescencia *nf*
polymerism	polimerismo *nm*
polymorphism	polimorfismo *nm*
salinity	salinidad *nf*
solubility	solubilidad *nf*
volatility	volatilidad *nf*

other terms

equimolecular	equimolecular *aj*
exothermic	exotérmico *aj*
ferrous	ferroso *aj*
inert	inerte *aj*
linear	lineal *aj*
miscible	miscible *aj*
nascent	naciente *aj*
orthorhombic	otorrómbico *aj*
radioactive	radiactivo, radioactivo *aj*
reversible (reaction)	reversible *aj*
stability	estabilidad *nf*

METEOROLOGY

GENERAL TERMS

air	aire *nm*
climate	clima *nm*
clime (poetic)	clima *nm*
direction	dirección *nf*
elements	elementos *nmpl*
equinox	equinoccio *nm*
front	frente *nm*
pattern	patrón *nm*
prediction	predicción *nf*
prognostication	pronóstico *nm*

solstice solsticio *nm*
zone zona *nf*

FIELDS OF SPECIALIZATION

aerology aerología *nf*
bioclimatology bioclimatología *nf*
climatology climatología *nf*
meteorology meteorología *nf*
phenology fenología *nf*

FACTORS DETERMINING WEATHER

altitude altitud *nf*
aridity aridez *nf*
condensation condensación *nf*
current (ocean) corriente *nf*
evaporation evaporación *nf*
humidity humedad *nf*
movement movimiento *nm*
occluded front oclusión *nf*
precipitation precipitación *nf*
pressure presión *nf*
temperature temperatura *nf*
turbulence turbulencia *nf*
wind viento *nm*

ASPECTS OF METEOROLOGY

climates

Arctic ártico *aj*
continental continental *aj*
maritime marítimo *aj*
Mediterranean mediterráneo *aj*
temperate templado *aj*
tropical tropical *aj*

air zones

aerosphere aerosfera *nf*
atmosphere atmósfera *nf*
hydrosphere hidrosfera *nf*
ionosphere ionosfera *nf*
mesosphere mesosfera *nf*
ozonosphere ozonosfera *nf*
stratosphere estratosfera, estratósfera
 nf
thermosphere termosfera *nf*
troposphere troposfera *nf*

cloud types

cirrocumulus cirrocúmulo *nm*
cirrostratus cirrostrato *nm*

cirrus cirro *nm*
cumulonimbus cumulonimbo
 nm
cumulus cúmulo *nm*
nimbostratus nimboestrato *nm*
nimbus nimbo *nm*
stratocumulus estratocúmulo
 nm
stratus estrato *nm*

storms

avalanche avalancha *nf*
cyclone ciclón *nm*
deluge diluvio *nm*
hurricane huracán *nm*
monsoon monzón *nm*
tempest tempestad *nf*
tornado tornado *nm*
torrent torrente *nm*
typhoon tifón *nm*

directional winds

easterly del este
northerly del norte
southerly del sur
westerly del oeste

other winds

anticyclone anticiclón *nm*
breeze brisa *nf*
foehn fohn *nm*
harmattan harmatán *nm*
khamsin kamsín *nm*
mistral mistral *nm*
norther nortada *nf*
simoom simún *nm*
sirroco siroco *nm*
trade winds vientos alisios
 nmpl
vortex vórtice *nm*
zephyr céfiro *nm*

other weather terms

balmy balsámico *aj*
brrr! ¡brrr! *intj*
calm calma *nf*
clear (sky) claro *aj*
clement clemente *aj*
frigid frígido *aj*
global global *aj*
inclement inclemente *aj*
inhospitable inhóspito *aj*

inundation	inundación *nf*
invigorating	vigorizador *aj*
parhelion	parhelia, parhelio *nf, nm*
pluvial	pluvial *aj*
tempestuous	tempestuoso *aj*
torrid	tórrido *aj*
turbulent	turbulento *aj*
variable	variable *aj*
windy	ventoso

AIR QUALITY TERMS

alert	alerta *nf*
inversion	inversión *nf*
miasma	miasma *nm*
ozone	ozono *nm*
pollution	polución *nf*
smog	esmog *nm*

TOOLS, EQUIPMENT, MEASUREMENTS

anemometer	anemómetro *nm*
aneroid (barometer)	aneroide *aj*
barogram	barograma *nm*
barograph	barógrafo *nm*
barometer	barómetro *nm*
centigrade	centígrado *aj, nm*
Fahrenheit	Fahrenheit *aj, nm*
hygrometer	higrómetro *nm*
isobar	isobara *nf*
isogram	isograma *nm*
isotherm	isoterma *nf*
millibar	milibar *nm*
nephoscope	nefoscopio *nm*
psychrometer	psicrómetro *nm*
radiosonde	radiosonda *nf*
satellite	satélite *nm*
thermograph	termógrafo *nm*
thermometer	termómetro *nm*

PERSONS

| climatologist | climatólogo, -a *nmf* |
| meteorologist | meteorólogo, -a *nmf* |

(*See also **flying and navigation*** under **AVIATION AND SPACE TRAVEL**; **GEOGRAPHY**)

Putting Science to Work

TECHNOLOGY

GENERAL TERMS

automation	automación, automatización *nf*
engineering	ingeniería *nf*
equipment	equipo *nm*
industry	industria *nf*
innovation	innovación *nf*
instrument	instrumento *nm*
invention	invento *nm*
machine	máquina *nf*
machinery	maquinaria *nf*
mechanism	mecanismo *nm*
motor	motor *nm*
patent	patente *nf*
progress	progreso *nm*
project	proyecto *nm*
prototype	prototipo *nm*
repair	reparación *nf*
technique	técnica *nf*
technology	tecnología *nf*

ASPECTS OF TECHNOLOGY

new technologies

bionics	biónica *nf*
biotechnology	biotecnología *nf*
desalinization	desalinización *nf*
electronics	electrónica *nf*
electrotechnology	electrotecnia *nf*
nanotechnology	nanotecnología *nf*
radiography	radiografía *nf*
robotics	robótica *nf*
telecommunications	telecomunicaciones *nfpl*

engineering fields

acoustic(al)	acústico *aj*
aeronautical	aeronáutico *aj*
aerospace	aeroespacial *aj*
agricultural	agrícola *aj*
architectural	arquitectónico *aj*
automotive	automotor, automotriz *aj*
biomedical	biomédico *aj*
chemical	químico *aj*
civil	civil *aj*

construction	construcción *nf*
electrical	eléctrico *aj*
electromechanical	electromecánico *aj*
genetics	genética *nf*
hydraulic	hidráulico *aj*
hydroelectric	hidroeléctrico *aj*
industrial	industrial *aj*
manual	manual *aj*
marine	marino *aj*
mechanical	mecánico *aj*
metallurgical	metalúrgico *aj*
military	militar *aj*
mining *aj*	minero, de minas *aj, nfpl*
nuclear	nuclear *aj*
petrochemical	petroquímico *aj*
sanitary	sanitario *aj*
structural	estructural *aj*
transit	de tránsito *nm*

important inventions

adding machine	máquina de sumar *nf*
air brake	freno de aire *nm*
air conditioning	aire acondicionado *nm*
Bunsen burner	mechero Bunsen *nm*
calculator	calculadora *nf*
calendar	calendario *nm*
cash register	caja registradora *nf*
cassette	cassete, casete *nm or nf*
catapult	catapulta *nf*
cellophane	celofán *nm*
cellular telephone	teléfono celular *nm*
celluloid	celuloide *nm*
combination lock	cerradura de combinación *nf*
computer	computadora *nf*
cyclotron	ciclotrón *nm*
derrick	derrick *nm*
diesel	diesel *nm*
dynamite	dinamita *nf*
escalator	escalera mecánica *nf*
fluorescent light	luz fluorescente *nf*
generator	generador *nm*
gyroscope	giroscopio *nm*
hypodermic needle	aguja hipodérmica *nf*
incandescent light	luz incandescente *nf*
inclined plane	plana inclinada *nf*
internal-combustion engine	motor de combustión interna *nm, nf*
knitting machine	máquina de tejer *nf*
linotype	linotipia, linotipo *nf, nm*
locomotive	locomotora *nf*

microphone, mike	micrófono *nm*
microscope	microscopio *nm*
milking machine	máquina de ordeñar *nf*
nuclear reactor	reactor nuclear *nm*
pistol	pistola *nf*
poloroid camera	cámara poloroid *nf*
printing press	prensa, imprenta *nf*
pulley	polea *nf*
pump	bomba *nf*
radar	radar *nm*
radio	radio *nm*
revolver	revólver *nm*
robot	robot *nm*
sewing machine	máquina de coser *nf*
sonar	sónar *nm*
stethoscope	estetoscopio *nm*
telegraph	telégrafo *nm*
telephone	teléfono *nm*
television	televisión *nf*
thermometer	termómetro *nm*
thermostat	termostato *nm*
tractor	tractor *nm*
transistor	transistor *nm*
vending machine	máquina expendedora *nf*
washing machine	máquina de lavar *nf*
X-ray machine	aparato de rayos X *nm*
zipper	zíper *nm*

TECHNICAL TERMS

tools, parts, equipment

automaton	autómata *nm*
calender	calandria *nf*
carburetor	carburador *nm*
compressor	compresor *nm*
condenser	condensador *nm*
connector	conectador *nm*
controller	controlador *nm*
differential	diferencial *nm*
duplex	dúplex *nm*
dynamometer	dinamómetro *nm*
eccentric	excéntrica *nf*
electrodynamometer	electrodinamómetro *nm*
equalizer	igualador *nm*
implement	implemento *nm*
joint	junta *nf*
lute	luten *nm*
machine tool	máquina herramienta *nf*
micrometer	micrómetro *nm*
pallet	paleta *nf*
pantograph	pantógrafo *nm*
pinion	piñón *nm*

piston	pistón *nm*
pivot	pivote *nm*
pulverizer	pulerizador *nm*
purifier	depurador *nm*
rectifier	rectificador *nm*
reducer	reductor *nm*
regenerator	regenerador *nm*
register	registro *nm*
regulator	regulador *nm*
rotary	máquina rotativa *nf*
selector	selector *nm*
servomechanism	servomecanismo *nm*
servomotor	servomotor *nm*
sling	eslinga *nf*
stamper	estampador *nm*
stator	estator *nm*
tubing	tubería *nf*
turbine	turbina *nf*
turbocompressor	turbocompresor *nm*
unit	unidad *nf*
universal (joint)	universal *aj*
valve	válvula *nf*

other terms

alignment	alineación *nf*
articulation	articulación *nf*
assembly	ensamblaje *nm*
calibration	calibración *nf*
coaxial	coaxial *aj*
coupling	acoplamiento *nm*
dismantle	desmantelar *vt*
efficiency	eficiencia *nf*
expansion	expansión *nf*
fulcrum	fulcro *nm*
lubrication	lubricación *nf*
management (of a machine)	manejo *nm*
modular	modular *aj*
mounting	montaje *nm*
penetration	penetración *nf*
performance	performance *nf*
plumb	aplomado *aj*
precision	precisión *nf*
process	proceso *nm*
recycle	reciclar *vt*
refrigeration	refrigeración *nf*
resilience, resiliency	resilencia *nf*
solder, soldering	soldadura *nf*
suction	succión *nf*
synchronous (machine)	sincrónico *aj*
tolerance	tolerancia *nf*
torsion	torsión *nf*
traction	tracción *nf*

treatment	tratamiento *nm*
vibration	vibración *nf*

PERSONS

engineer	ingeniero, -a *nmf*
innovator	innovador(a) *nmf*
inventor	inventor(a) *nmf*
machinist	maquinista *nmf*
mechanic	mecánico, -a *nmf*
repairman	reparador(a) *nmf*
technician	técnico, -a *nmf*

(*See also* **components** under **AMATEUR RADIO**; *TERMS IN CONSTRUCTION* under **ARCHITECTURE**; *parts and equipment* under **AUTOMOBILES**; *TOOLS AND EQUIPMENT* under **MEDICAL PRACTICE**; *TOOLS AND EQUIPMENT* under **MOVIES**; **PERSONAL COMPUTERS**; *TOOLS AND EQUIPMENT* under **TELEVISION AND VIDEO**)

AGRICULTURE

GENERAL TERMS

agrarian	agrario *aj*
agriculture	agricultura *nf*
animal	animal *nm*
conservation	conservación *nf*
cultivation	cultivo *nm*
electrification	electrificación *nf*
fertilizer	fertilizante *nm*
mechanization	mecanización *nf*
pesticide	pesticida *nm*
plant	planta *nf*
produce	producto *nm*
property	propiedad *nf*
rural	rural *aj*

SPECIALIZATIONS

agronomy	agronomía *nf*
hydroponics	hidroponía, hidroponia *nf*
pedology	pedología *nf*
pomology	pomología *nf*

ASPECTS OF FARMING
organization and ownership

collective farm	granja colectiva *nf*
cooperative	cooperativa *nf*
kibbutz	kibbutz *nm*
latifundium	latifundio *nm*
plantation	plantación *nf*
ranch	rancho *nm*

land units

acre	acre *nm*
hectare	hectárea *nf*
parcel	parcela *nf*
tract	tracto *nm*

farming method

diversified	diversificado *aj*
extensive	extensivo, extenso *aj*
intensive	intensivo *aj*

soils and soil conservation

alkaline	alcalino *aj*
arable	arable *aj*
compact	compacto *aj*
drainage	drenaje *nm*
erosion	erosión *nf*
fertile	fértil *aj*
gumbo	gumbo *nm*
humus	humus *nm*
irrigation	irrigación *nf*
loess	loes *nm*
rotation	rotación *nf*
subsoil	subsuelo *nm*
substratum	sustrato *nm*
terrace	terraza *nf*

types of farms

aquaculture	acuacultura *nf*
banana plantation	bananar *nm*
cherry orchard	cerezal *nm*
coca plantation	cocal *nm*
coconut plantation	cocotal *nm*
coffee plantation	cafetal *nm*
floriculture	floricultura *nf*
fruit growing	fruticultura *nf*
horticulture	horticultura *nf*
olive growing	olivicultura *nf*
oyster culture	ostricultura *nf*
silviculture	silvicultura *nf*
tobacco plantation	tabacal *nm*
viniculture	vinicultura *nf*

planting groups

olive grove	olivar *nm*
oyster bed	ostrero *nm*
rice field/paddy	arrozal *nm*
tomato patch	tomatal *nm*
tomato plant	tomatera *nf*
vineyard	viña, viñedo *nf, nm*

types of crops

fiber	fibra *nf*
fruit	fruta *nf*
grain	grano *nm*
tobacco	tabaco *nm*
vegetable	vegetal *nm*

major food crops

alfalfa	alfalfa *nf*
cereal	cereal *nm*
cocoa	cacao *nm*
coffee	café *nm*
copra	copra *nf*
olive (fruit)	oliva *nf*
potato	patata *nf*
raffia	rafia *nf*
rice	arroz *nm*
sesame	sésamo *nm*
sorghum	sorgo *nm*
soy, soybean	soja *nf*
sugar	azúcar *nm or nf*
tea	té *nm*

care of animals

corral	corral *nm*
forage	forraje *nm*
silage	ensilaje *nm*
stable	establo *nm*

pesticides

DDT	DDT *nm*
fumigant	substancia fumigatoria *nf*
fungicide	fungicida *nm*
herbicide	herbicida *nm*
insecticide	insecticida *nm*
Malathion	Malatión *nm*
parathion	paratión *nm*
pyrethrum	piretrina *nf*
rotenone	rotenona *nf*

fertilizers

chemical	químico *aj*
compost	compost *nm*
guano	guano *nm*
organic	orgánico *aj*
potash	potasa *nf*

other terms

clearing (in forest)	claro *nm*
hybrid	híbrido *aj, nm*
parasite	parásito *nm*
pasture	pastura, pasto *nf, nm*
transplant	trasplantar *vt*

TOOLS AND EQUIPMENT

elevator	elevador *nm*
granary	granero *nm*

incubator	incubadora *nf*
separator	separador *nm*
silo	silo *nm*
stake	estaca *nf*
tractor	tractor *nm*

PERSONS

absentee landlord	absentista, ausentista *nmf*
agronomist	agrónomo, -a *nmf*
coffee grower/ merchant	cafetero, -a, cafetelero, -a *nmf*
cowboy	cowboy *nm*
cultivator	cultivador(a) *nmf*
fruit farmer/grower	fruticultor(a) *nmf*
fumigator	fumigador *nm*
gardener	jardinero, -a *nmf*
gaucho	gaucho *nm*
horticulturist	horticultor(a) *nmf*
olive grower	olivarero, -a *nmf*
palm farmer	palmero, -a *nmf*
planter	plantador(a) *nmf*
rancher	ranchero, -a *nmf*
winegrower	vinicultor, -a *nmf*

(*See also* GROWING OF PLANTS under **PLANTS**)

COMMUNICATIONS

GENERAL TERMS

communication	comunicación *nf*
connection	conexión *nf*
contact	contacto *nm*
electronic	electrónico *aj*
interactive	interactivo *aj*
interconnect	interconectar *vt*
message	mensaje *nm*
receive	recibir(se) *vt(r)*
satellite	satélite *nm*

SPECIALIZATIONS

communication theory	comunicología *nf*
information technology	informática *nf*
phototelegraphy	fototelegrafía *nf*
radiocommunication	radiocomunicación *nf*
radiotelegraphy	radiotelegrafía *nf*
radiotelephony	radiotelefonía *nf*
telecommunications	telecomunicaciones *nfpl*
telegraphy	telegrafía *nf*
telephony	telefonía *nf*

FORMS OF TELECOMUNICATION

aerogram	aerograma *nm*
cable	cable *nm*
cablegram	cablegrama *nm*
cellular telephone	teléfono celular *nm*
E-mail, electronic mail	correo electrónico *nm*
fax, facsimile	fax, facsímil *nm*
intercom, interphone	interfono *nm*
postcard	postal *nf*
radio	radio *nm*
radiogram	radiograma *nm*
radiophone	radiófono *nm*
radiotelephone	radioteléfono *nm*
teleconferencing *nsg*	teleconferencias *nfpl*
telegram	telegrama *nm*
telegraph	telégrafo *nm*
telephone	teléfono *nm*
teletype	teletipo *nm*
telex	telex *nm*
video	video *nm*
videoconference	videoconferencia *nf*
videophone	videófono *nm*

RELATED TERMS

mail

airmail	correo aéreo *nm*
certified	certificado *aj*
correspondence	correspondencia *nf*
express	expreso *aj*
franking	franqueo *nm*
paper	papel *nm*
registered	registrado *aj*
stamp	estampilla *nf*
zip code	código postal *nm*

telephone

answering service	servicio de mensajes *nm, nmpl*
busy signal	señal de ocupado *nf*
call blocking	bloqueo de llamadas *nm, nfpl*
dial tone	tono de marcar/discar *nm*
direct dial	discado directo *nm*
extension	extensión *nf*
line	línea *nf*
long-distance *aj*	de larga distancia *nf*
mobile	móvil, movible *aj*
number	número *nm*
person-to-person *av*	de persona a persona *nf*
prefix	prefijo *nm*

public	público *aj*
telephone directory	guía telefónica *nf*

other terms

beep	bip *nm*
diplex	diplex *aj*
intercept	interceptar *vt*
Internet	Internet *nm*
optical fiber	fibra óptica *nf*
simplex	simplex *aj*
teletext	teletex, teletexto *nm*
transmitter	transmisor *nm*

PERSONS

messenger	mensajero, -a *nmf*
radio operator	radiotelegrafista *nmf*
telegraph operator	telegrafista *nmf*
telephone operator	telefonista *nmf*

(*See also* **communication signals** under **LINGUISTIC SCIENCE**)

ELECTRICITY AND ELECTRONICS

GENERAL TERMS

atom	átomo *nm*
charge	carga *nf*
circuit	circuito *nm*
conduction	conducción *nf*
current	corriente *nf*
electrician	electricista *nmf*
electricity	electricidad *nf*
electron	electrón *nm*
electronics	electrónica *nf*
electrotechnology	electrotecnia *nf*
ion	ion *nm*

ASPECTS OF ELECTRICITY

types

alternating	alterno *aj*
direct	directo *aj*
static	estático *aj*
unidirectional (current)	unidireccional *aj*

sources

battery	batería *nf*
cell	célula *nf*
crystal	cristal *nm*
dynamo	dínamo *nm*

electrolyte	electrólito *nm*
galvanism	galvanismo *nm*
generator	generador *nm*
hydroelectricity	hidroelectricidad *nf*
piezoelectricity	piezoelectricidad *nf*
pile	pila *nf*
quartz	cuarzo *nm*
voltaic (cell)	voltaico *aj*

kinds of circuits

cycle	ciclo *nm*
integrated	integrado *aj*
parallel	paralelo *aj*
printed	impreso *aj*
series, serial	en serie *nf*

conduction

anode	ánodo *nm*
arc	arco eléctrico *nm*
cathode	cátodo *nm*
conductor	conductor *nm*
connection	conexión *nf*
contact	contacto *nm*
discharge	descarga *nf*
electrode	electrodo *nm*
electronegative	electronegativo *aj*
electropositive	electropositivo *aj*
flow	flujo *nm*
frequency	frecuencia *nf*
impulse	impulso *nm*
inductance	inductancia *nf*
insulator	aislador, aislante *nm*
negative	negativo *aj*
neutral	neutro *aj*
nonconductor	no conductor *nm*
photoconductivity	fotoconductibilidad *nf*
polarization	polarización *nf*
pole	polo *nm*
positive	positivo *aj*
potential	potencial *nm*
proton	protón *nm*
reactance	reactancia *nf*
reluctance	reluctancia *nf*
resistance	resistencia *nf*
terminal	terminal *nm*

effects

electrolysis	electrólisis *nf*
incandescence	incandescencia *nf*
magnetism	magnetismo *nm*
shock	choque *nm*
short circuit	cortocircuito *nm*

control

capacitance	capacitancia *nf*
circuit breaker	cortacircuitos *nm*
condenser	condensador *nm*
fuse	fusible *nm*
impedance	impedancia *nf*
interrupter	interruptor *nm*
rheostat	reóstato *nm*
solenoid	solenoide *nm*
suppression	supresión *nf*
transformer	transformador *nm*

tools and parts

adapter	adaptador *nm*
alternator	alternador *nm*
armature	armadura *nf*
capacitor	capacitor *nm*
carbon	carbón *nm*
charger	cargador *nm*
commutator	conmutador *nm*
connector	conectador *nm*
converter	convertidor *nm*
cord	cordón *nm*
coupler	acoplador *nm*
dielectric	dieléctrico *aj, nm*
discharger	descargador *nm*
dynamotor	dinamotor *nm*
equalizer	igualador *nm*
exciter	excitador *nm*
extension (cord)	extensión *nf*
filament	filamento *nm*
inductor	inductor *nm*
inverter	inversor *nm*
line	línea *nf*
magneto	magneto *nm*
neutralizer	neutralizador *nm*
oscillator	oscilador *nm*
oscillograph	oscilógrafo *nm*
rectifier	rectificador *nm*
regulator	regulador *nm*
resistor	resistor *nm*
rotor	rotor *nm*
stator	estator *nm*
vibrator	vibrador *nm*

ASPECTS OF ELECTRONICS

specializations

avionics	aviónica *nf*
bioelectronics	bioelectrónica *nf*
microelectronics	microelectrónica *nf*
thermionics	termiónica *nf*

functioning

bias	bias *nm*
distortion	distorsión *nf*
echo	eco *nm*
emission	emisión *nf*
gain	ganancia *nf*
microcircuit	microcircuito *nm*
photoelectron	fotoelectrón *nm*
photoemission	fotoemisión *nf*
response	respuesta *nf*
semiconductor	semiconductor *nm*
signal	señal *nf*
solid-state *aj*	de estado sólido *nm*

tools and parts

amplifier	amplificador *nm*
collector	colector *nmf*
diode	diodo *nm*
dynatron	dinatrón *nm*
dynode	dinodo *nm*
magnetron	magnetrón *nm*
maser	maser *nm*
monitor	monitor *nm*
pentode	pentodo, péntodo *nm*
photomultiplier	fotomultiplicador *nm*
sensor	sensor *nm*
servomechanism	servomecanismo *nm*
stroboscope	estroboscopio *nm*
suppressor	supresor *nm*
tetrode	tetrodo *nm*
transducer	transductor *nm*
transistor	transistor *nm*
triode	tríodo *nm*
tube	tubo *nm*
vacuum (tube)	vacío *nm*

useful applications

burglar alarm	alarma antirrobo *nf*
computer	computadora *nf*
diathermy	diatermia *nf*
electrocardiograph	electrocardiógrafo *nm*
electroencephalograph	electroencefalógrafo *nm*
fax	fax *nm*
fluorescent lamp	tubo fluorescente *nm*
Geiger counter	contador Geiger *nm*
iconoscope	iconoscopio *nm*
intercom	interfono *nm*
laser	láser *nm*
microscope	microscopio *nm*
microwave	microonda *nf*
missile	misil *nm*
multiplex	múltiplex *nm*

neon sign	letrero de neón *nm*
photocell,	fotocélula *nf*
photoelectric cell	
radar	radar *nm*
radio	radio *nm*
sonar	sónar *nm*
spectrograph	espectrógrafo *nm*
telephone	teléfono *nm*
telescope	telescopio *nm*
television	televisión *nf*
thermostat	termostato *nm*
ultrasound	ultrasonido *nm*

MEASUREMENTS

instruments

ammeter	amperímetro *nm*
electrometer	electrómetro *nm*
electroscope	electroscopio *nm*
galvanometer	galvanómetro *nm*
potentiometer	potenciómetro *nm*
voltammeter	voltamperímetro *nm*
voltmeter	voltímetro *nm*
wattmeter	vatímetro *nm*

units of measurement

amperage	amperaje *nm*
ampere	amperio *nm*
coulomb	culombio *nm*
farad	farad, faradio *nm*
gauss	gauss *nm*
joule	julio *nm*
kilohertz	kilohercio *nm*
(abbr: kHz)	
kilovolt	kilovoltio *nm*
kilowatt	kilovatio *nm*
kilowatt-hour	kilovatio-hora *nf*
ohm	ohmio, ohm *nm*
volt	voltio *nm*
voltage	voltaje *nm*
watt	vatio *nm*
watt-hour	vatio-hora *nf*
wattage	vataje *nm*

TEXTILES

GENERAL TERMS

fiber	fibra *nf*
piece goods	géneros en piezas *nmpl,*
	nfpl
sericulture	sericultura *nf*

textile	textil *nm*
texture	textura *nf*
treatment	tratamiento *nm*

ASPECTS OF TEXTILES

types of fibers

animal	animal *aj*
artificial	artificial *aj*
natural	natural *aj*
optical	óptico *aj*
plant	planta *nf*
regenerated	regenerado *aj*
synthetic	sintético *aj*

natural fibers

abaca	abacá *nm*
alpaca	alpaca *nf*
angora	angora *nm*
asbestos	asbesto *nm*
drill	dril *nm*
henequen	henequén *nm*
jute	yute *nm*
kapok	kapoc *nm*
manila	manila *nf*
nutria	nutria *nf*
pita	pita *nf*
raffia	rafia *nf*
ramie	ramina *nf*
sisal	sisal *nm*

artificial fibers

acetate	acetato *nm*
acrylic	acrílico *aj*
cellulose	celulosa *nf*
fiberglass	vidrio fibroso *nm*
nylon	nilón *nm*
olefin	olefina *nf*
polyester	poliester *nm*

clothing fabrics

astrakhan	astracán *nm*
batiste	batista *nf*
brocade	brocado *nm*
calico	calicó *nm*
cambric	cambray *nm*
caracul, karakul	caracul, karakul *nm*
cashmere	cachemira *nf*
chiffon	chiffón *nm*
chintz	chintz, chinz *nm*
crepe	crepé, crespón
	nm

cretonne	cretona *nf*
crinoline	crinolina *nf*
Dacron	dacrón *nm*
damask	damasco *nm*
felt	fieltro *nm*
flannel	franela *nf*
flannelette	franela fina *nf*
fustian	fustán *nm*
gabardine	gabardina *nf*
gauze	gasa *nf*
georgette	georgette *nm*
gingham	guinga *nf*
jersey	jersey *nm*
khaki	caqui *nm*
lamé	lamé *nm*
linen	lino *nm*
madras	madrás *nm*
merino	merino *nm*
mohair	moer *nm*
moire, moiré	moaré *nm*
muslin	muselina *nf*
organdie, organdy	organdí *nm*
Orlon	orlón *nm*
percale	percal *nm*
poplin	popelina *nf*
rayon	rayón *nm*
sateen, satin	satín *nm*
satin	satén, satín *nm*
serge	sarga *nf*
taffeta	tafetán *nm*
tissue	tisú *nm*
toweling	tela de toalla *nf*
tricot	tricot *nm*
tulle	tul *nm*
veiling	tela para velos *nf, nmpl*
velour	velour *nm*
velveteen	velvetón *nm*
zibeline, zibelline	cebellina *nf*

Quantification

MEASUREMENT

GENERAL TERMS

convert	convertir *vt*
dimension	dimensión *nf*
isometric	isométrico *aj*
measure	mensura *nf*

quantity	cantidad *nf*
standard	estándar *aj, nm*
system	sistema *nm*

ASPECTS OF MEASUREMENT

kinds of measures

approximate	aproximado *aj*
direct	directo *aj*
exact	exacto *aj*
indirect	indirecto *aj*
linear	linear, lineal *aj*
liquid	líquido *aj*

requirements

instrument	instrumento *nm*
scale	escala *nf*
unit	unidad *nf*

systems of measurement

analog(ue)	análogo *nm*
British	británico *aj*
decimal	decimal *nm*
metric	métrico *aj*

scales

Celsius	Celsio *nm*
centigrade	centígrado *aj, nm*
Fahrenheit	Fahrenheit *nm*
kelvin	kelvin *nm*

things measured

acreage	medida en acres *nf, nmpl*
area	área *nf(el)*
caliber	calibre *nm*
capacitance	capacitancia *nf*
capacity	capacidad *nf*
cylinder capacity	cilindrada *nf*
density	densidad *nf*
deviation	desviación *nf*
distance	distancia *nf*
electricity	electricidad *nf*
entropy	entropía *nf*
force	fuerza *nf*
frequency	frecuencia *nf*
gravity	gravedad *nf*
humidity	humedad *nf*
intensity	intensidad *nf*
magnitude	magnitud *nf*
mass	masa *nf*
pressure	presión *nf*

temperature	temperatura *nf*
time	tiempo *nm*
tonnage	tonelaje *nm*
velocity	velocidad *nf*
voltage	voltaje *nm*
volume	volumen *nm*

UNITS OF MEASUREMENT

length and distance

centimeter	centímetro *nm*
decameter, dekameter	decámetro *nm*
decimeter	decímetro *nm*
fermi	fermi *nm*
hectometer	hectómetro *nm*
kilometer	kilómetro *nm*
meter	metro *nm*
micromillimeter	micromilímetro *nm*
micron	micrón *nm*
mil	mil *nm*
mile	milla *nf*
millimeter	milímetro *nm*
nanometer	nanómetro *nm*
palm	palmo *nm*
vara	vara *nf*
yard	yarda *nf*

electricity

ampere	amperio *nm*
coulomb	culombio *nm*
farad	farad, faradio *nm*
gauss	gauss *nm*
kilovolt	kilovoltio *nm*
kilowatt	kilovatio *nm*
kilowatt-hour	kilovatio-hora *nf*
megawatt	megavatio *nm*
ohm	ohmio, ohm *nm*
volt	voltio *nm*
watt	vatio *nm*
watt-hour	vatio-hora *nf*

volume

barrel	barril *nm*
cartload	carretada *nf*
centiliter	centilitro *nm*
deciliter	decilitro *nm*
gallon	galón *nm*
hectoliter	hectolitro *nm*
kiloliter	kilolitro *nm*
liter	litro *nm*

magnum	magnum *nm*
milliliter	mililitro *nm*
minim	mínima *nf*
pint	pinta *nf*
quart	cuartilla *nf*
stere	estéreo *nm*
tierce (obs)	tercia *nf*
wagonload	vagón *nm*
cubic (inch/foot/yard)	cúbico *aj*

weight

centigram	centigramo *nm*
decigram	decigramo *nm*
dram	dracma *nf*
grain	grano *nm*
gram	gramo *nm*
hectogram	hectogramo *nm*
kilo	kilo *nm*
kilogram	kilogramo *nm*
milligram	miligramo *nm*
mole	mol *nm*
ounce	onza *nf*
quintal	quintal *nm*
scruple	escrúpulo *nm*
ton	tonelada *nf*
troy	troy *nm*

force

dyne	dina *nf*
erg	ergio *nm*
joule	julio *nm*
kilogram-meter	kilográmetro *nm*
kilojoule	kilojulio *nm*
kiloton	kilotón *nm*
megaton	megatón *nm*

other units

acre	acre *nm*
calorie	caloría *nf*
candela	candela *nf*
cord	cuerda *nf*
decibel	decibel *nm*
diopter, dioptre	dioptría *nf*
hectare	hectárea *nf*
hertz	hertz, hertzio, hercio *nm*
kilocalorie	kilocaloría *nf*
kilohertz	kilohercio *nm*
knot	nudo *nm*

league	legua *nf*
millibar	milibar *nm*

MEASURING TOOLS

altimeter	altímetro *nm*
anemometer	anemómetro *nm*
audiometer	audiómetro *nm*
balance	balanza *nf*
barometer	barómetro *nm*
buret, burette	bureta *nf*
calibrator	calibrador *nm*
calorimeter	calorímetro *nm*
chronometer	cronómetro *nm*
compass	compás *nm*
counterweight	contrapeso *nm*
dynamometer	dinamómetro *nm*
electrometer	electrómetro *nm*
electroscope	electroscopio *nm*
galvanometer	galvanómetro *nm*
gasometer	gasómetro *nm*
hydrometer	hidrómetro *nm*
hygrometer	higrómetro *nm*
inclinometer	inclinómetro *nm*
magnetometer	magnetómetro *nm*
micrometer	micrómetro *nm*
odometer	odómetro *nm*
pedometer	podómetro *nm*
photometer	fotómetro *nm*
potentiometer	potenciómetro *nm*
psychrometer	psicrómetro *nm*
radiocompass	radiocompás *nm*
rheostat	reóstato *nm*
seismometer	sismómetro *nm*
sextant	sextante *nm*
thermometer	termómetro *nm*
voltmeter	voltímetro *nm*
wattmeter	vatímetro *nm*

(*See also* **TOOLS AND MEASUREMENTS** under
GEOGRAPHY; *BASIC CONCEPTS* under
MATHEMATICS; *MEASUREMENTS* under
PERSONAL COMPUTERS)

TIME

GENERAL TERMS

chronometry	cronometría *nf*
duration	duración *nf*
during	durante *prep*

event	evento *nm*
frequency	frecuencia *nf*
occasion	ocasión *nf*
occurrence	ocurrencia *nf*
recurrent	recurrente *aj*
spacing	espaciamiento *nm*
time	tiempo *nm*

ASPECTS OF TIME

kinds of time

biological	biológico *aj*
circadian	circadiano *aj*
free time	tiempo libre *nm*
geological	geológico *aj*
linguistic	lingüístico *aj*
lunar	lunar *aj*
real time	tiempo real *nm*
sidereal	sidéreo *aj*
solar	solar *aj*
time out	tiempo muerto *nm*
universal	universal *aj*

clocks

clepsydra	clepsidra *nf*
clock radio	radiodespertador *nm or nf*
cuckoo	cucú *nm*
digital	digital *aj*
quartz	cuarzo *nm*
ticktock	tictac *nm*

times of the day

antemeridian (ᴀᴍ)	antemeridiano *aj*
daytime	día *nm*
midday	mediodía *nm*
midnight	media noche *nf*
nocturnal	nocturno *aj*
postmeridian (ᴘᴍ)	postmeridiano *aj*

time zones in the U.S.

Central Standard Time	hora central *nf*
Eastern time	hora oficial del Este *nf, nm*
Pacific time	hora del Pacífico *nf, nm*

recurrent events

anniversary	aniversario *nm*
bicentenary, bicentennial	bicentenario *nm*
centenary, centennial	centenario *nm*
decennial	aniversario decenal *nm*
episode	episodio *nm*

equinox	equinoccio *nm*
quindecennial	quindenio *nm*
quinquennial	quinquenio *nm*
Sabbath	sábado *nm*
siesta	siesta *nf*
solstice	solsticio *nm*
tricentennial	tricentenario *nm*
vicissitude	vicisitud *nf*

recording and preserving

almanac	almanaque *nm*
chronicle	crónica *nf*
chronology	cronología *nf*
time capsule	cápsula del tiempo *nf, nm*

other time expressions

hourly (by the hour)	por horas *av*
nowadays *av*	hoy en día *nm*
time sharing	tiempo compartido *nm*
time warp	salto en el tiempo *nm*
time-saving *aj*	que ahorra tiempo *nm*

MONTHS OF THE YEAR

January	enero *nm*
February	febrero *nm*
March	marzo *nm*
April	abril *nm*
May	mayo *nm*
June	junio *nm*
July	julio *nm*
August	agosto *nm*
September	septiembre *nm*
October	octubre *nm*
November	noviembre *nm*
December	diciembre *nm*

EXACT TIME UNITS

nanosecond	nanosegundo *nm*
microsecond	microsegundo *nm*
millisecond	milisegundo *nm*
second	segundo *nm*
minute	minuto *nm*
quarter hour	cuarto de hora *nm, nf*
hour	hora *nf*
day	día *nm*
decade	década, decenio *nf, nm*
century	centuria *nf*
quadrennium	cuadrienio *nm*
decennium	decenio *nm*
millenium	milenio, milenario *nm*

INEXACT TIME UNITS

eon, aeon	eón *nm*
epoch	época *nf*
era	era *nf*
eternity	eternidad *nf*
future	futuro *nm*
instant	instante *nm*
interim	ínterin, interín *nm*
interval	intervalo *nm*
moment	momento *nm*
past	pasado *nm*
pause	pausa *nf*
period	período, periodo *nm*
present	presente *nm*

TOOLS AND EQUIPMENT

calendar	calendario *nm*
chronometer	cronómetro *nm*
chronoscope	cronoscopio *nm*
gnomon (obs)	gnomon *nm*
hour hand	horario *nm*
minute hand	minutero *nm*
pendulum	péndulo *nm*
pointer	puntero *nm*
second hand	segundero *nm*
synchronizer	sincronizador *nm*

TIME ASSOCIATIONS

duration

abrupt	abrupto *aj*
biennial	bienal *aj*
brief	breve *aj*
continual, continuous	continuo *aj*
durable	duradero *aj*
enduring	duradero *aj*
eternal	eterno *aj*
immemorial	inmemorial *aj*
interminable	interminable *aj*
long-lived	longevo *aj*
momentary	momentáneo *aj*
perennial	perenne *aj*
permanent	permanente *aj*
perpetual	perpetuo *aj*
prolonged	prolongado *aj*
provisional	provisional *aj*
temporal	temporal *aj*
temporary	temporario *aj*
tentative	tentativo *aj*
transient	transeúnte *aj*
transitory	transitorio *aj*

frequency

annual	anual *aj*
aperiodic	aperiódico *aj*
bicentenary, bicentennial	bicentenario *aj*
centenary, centennial	centenario *aj*
daily	diario *aj, av*
decennial	decenal *aj*
episodic	episódico *aj*
frequent	frecuente *aj*
hourly	horario *aj*
infrequent	infrecuente *aj*
intermittent	intermitente *aj*
periodic	periódico *aj*
quadrennial	cuadrienal *aj*
quindecennial	quindecenal *aj*
quinquennial	quinquenal *aj*
quotidian	cotidiano *aj*
rarely	raramente *av*
regular	regular *aj*
spasmodic	espasmódico *aj*
sporadic	esporádico *aj*
successive	sucesivo *aj*
tricentennial	tricentenario *aj*
triennial	trienal *aj*

speed

accelerated	acelerado *aj*
gradual	gradual *aj*
rapid	rápido *aj*

relational

antecedent	antecedente *aj*
anticipatory	anticipador *aj*
chronological	cronológico *aj*
consecutive	consecutivo *aj*
contemporary, contemporaneous	contemporáneo *aj*
current	corriente *aj*
final	final *aj*
initial	inicial *aj*
modern	moderno *aj*
obsolete	obsoleto *aj*
original	original *aj*
posterior	posterior *aj*
prehistoric	prehistórico *aj*
present-day *aj*	de hoy día *nm*
previous	previo *aj*
recent	reciente *aj*
remote	remoto *aj*
retroactive	retroactivo *aj*
subsequent	subsecuente *aj*

manner

abortive	abortivo *aj*
acyclic	acíclico *aj*
asynchronous	asíncrono *aj*
concurrent	concurrente *aj*
cyclic(al)	cíclico *aj*
dilatory	dilatorio *aj*
immediate	inmediato *aj*
imminent	inminente *aj*
inevitable	inevitable *aj*
inopportune	inoportuno *aj*
instantaneous	instantáneo *aj*
opportune	oportuno *aj*
predestined	predestinado *aj*
predetermined	predeterminado *aj*
premature	prematuro *aj*
prompt	pronto *aj*
punctual	puntual *aj*
simultaneous	simultáneo *aj*
synchronous	sincrónico *aj*
tardy	tardío *aj*
ultramodern	ultramoderno *aj*
urgent	urgente *aj*

seasons

autumnal	otoñal *aj*
hibernal	hibernal *aj*
vernal	vernal *aj*

other terms

anachronism	anacronismo *nm*
archetype	arquetipo *nm*
cease	cesar *vt*
celerity	celeridad *nf*
coincide	coincidir *vi*
commence	comenzar *vti*
concur	concurrir *vi*
date	datar *vt*
defer	diferir *vt*
intercalate	intercalar *vt*
interruption	interrupción *nf*
lapse	lapso *nm*
moratorium	moratoria *nf*
postpone	posponer *vt*
proximity	proximidad *nf*
retard	retardar *vt*
tempo	tempo *nm*

PERSONS

chronicler	cronista *nmf*
precursor	precursor(a) *nmf*

predecessor	predecesor(a) *nmf*
successor	sucesor(a) *nmf*

SIZE AND DEGREE

GENERAL TERMS

criterion	criterio *nm*
distinction	distinción *nf*
equalization	igualación *nf*
gradation	gradación *nf*
norm	norma *nf*
scale	escala *nf*
standard	estándar *nm*

RATINGS OF THINGS

things rated

complexity	complejidad *nf*
deviation	desviación *nf*
extent	extensión *nf*
importance	importancia *nf*
intensity	intensidad *nf*
magnitude	magnitud *nf*
precision	precisión *nf*
quality	calidad *nf*
quantity	cantidad *nf*
rank	rango *nm*

average

acceptable	aceptable *aj*
adequate	adecuado *aj*
general	general *aj*
intermediate	intermedio *aj*
medial	medial *aj*
median, medium	mediano *aj*
mediocre	mediocre *aj*
moderate	moderado *aj*
natural	natural *aj*
normal	normal *aj*
ordinary	ordinario *aj*
passable	pasable *aj*
proportionate	proporcionado *aj*
reasonable	razonable *aj*
regular	regular *aj*
routine	rutinario *aj*
satisfactory	satisfactorio *aj*
standard	estándar *aj*
typical	típico *aj*
universal	universal *aj*
usual	usual *aj*

nonaverage

aberrant	aberrante *aj*
abnormal	anormal *aj*
acute	agudo *aj*
anomalous	anómalo *aj*
atypical	atípico *aj*
disparity	disparidad *nf*
disproportionate	desproporcionado *aj*
exaggerated	exagerado *aj*
exceptional	excepcional *aj*
extraordinary	extraordinario *aj*
immoderate	inmoderado *aj*
irregular	irregular *aj*
nonstandard	no estándar *aj*
uncommon	poco común *aj*
unique	único *aj*
unnatural	antinatural *aj*
unreasonable	desrazonable *aj*
unusual	inusual *aj*

above the norm

abundant	abundante *aj*
ample	amplio *aj*
appreciable	apreciable *aj*
astronomical	astronómico *aj*
augmented	aumentado *aj*
colossal	colosal *aj*
considerable	considerable *aj*
copious	copioso *aj*
crucial	crucial *aj*
definitive	definitivo *aj*
dominant, dominating	dominante *aj, nf*
elephantine	elefantino *aj*
enormous	enorme *aj*
excellent	excelente *aj*
excessive	excesivo *aj*
exhorbitant	exorbitante *aj*
extensive	extensivo, extenso *aj*
extravagant	extravagante *aj*
gigantic	gigante *aj*
grand	grande *aj*
herculean	hercúleo *aj*
ideal	ideal *aj*
immeasurable	inmensurable *aj*
immense	inmenso *aj*
innumerable	innumerable *aj*
intense	intenso *aj*
macroscopic	macroscópico *aj*
magnificent	magnífico *aj*
majestic	majestuoso *aj*
major	mayor *aj*

marvelous	maravilloso *aj*
massive	masivo *aj*
maxi-	maxi- *pref*
maximal	máximo *aj*
meritorious	meritorio *aj*
monstruous	monstruoso *aj*
monumental	monumental *aj*
much	mucho *aj, av, pron*
necessary	necesario *aj*
optimal, optimum	óptimo *aj*
opulent	opulento *aj*
overestimated	sobreestimado *aj*
overvalued	sobrevalorado *aj*
palatial	palaciego *aj*
precious	precioso *aj*
precise	preciso *aj*
predominant	predominante *aj*
premier	primero *aj*
preponderant	preponderante *aj*
priceless	inapreciable *aj*
principal	principal *aj*
priority	prioridad *nf*
profound	profundo *aj*
profuse	profuso *aj*
prominent	prominente *aj*
regal	regio *aj*
remote	remoto *aj*
resplendent	resplandeciente *aj*
rich	rico *aj*
severe	severo *aj*
significant	significativo *aj*
spacious	espacioso *aj*
spectacular	espectacular *aj*
splendid	espléndido *aj*
stupendous	estupendo *aj*
substantial	su(b)stancial, su(b)stancioso *aj*
sufficient	suficiente *aj*
sumptuous	suntuoso *aj*
super-	super- *pref*
superb	soberbio *aj*
superfine	superfino, extrafino *aj*
superfluous	superfluo *aj*
superior	superior *aj*
superlative	superlativo *aj*
supersensitive	supersensible *aj*
terrific	terrífico *aj*
titanic	titánico *aj*
tremendous	tremendo *aj*
ubiquitous	ubicuo *aj*
ultramodern	ultramoderno *aj*
vast	vasto *aj*

versatile	versátil *aj*
voluminous	voluminoso *aj*

below the norm

concise	conciso *aj*
deficient	deficiente *aj*
diminished	disminuido *aj*
imprecise	impreciso *aj*
inferior	inferior *aj*
infinitesimal	infinitesimal *aj*
insignificant	insignificante *aj*
insufficient	insuficiente *aj*
mere	mero *aj*
microscopic	microscópico *aj*
mini-	mini- *pref*
miniature *aj*	en miniatura *nf*
minimal	mínimo *aj*
minuscule	minúsculo *aj*
minute	minucioso *aj*
modest	modesto *aj*
poor	pobre *aj*
reduced	reducido *aj*
scarce	escaso *aj*
simplified	simplificado *aj*
subsidiary	subsidiario *aj*
substandard	no estándar *aj*
superficial	superficial *aj*
trivial	trivial *aj*
unimportant *aj*	sin importancia *nf*
unnecessary	innecesario *aj*
unsatisfactory	insatisfactorio *aj*

ends of the scale

absolute	absoluto *aj*
apex	ápice *nm*
basic	básico *aj*
complete	completo *aj*
consummate	consumado *aj*
culmination	culminación *nf*
epitome	epítome *nm*
essential	esencial *aj, nm*
extreme	extremado *aj*
fundamental	fundamental *aj*
maximum	máximo *nm*
minimum	mínimo *nm*
perfection	perfección *nf*
quintessence	quintaesencia *nf*
supreme	supremo *aj*
ultimate	último *aj*
ultra-	ultra- *aj*
zero	cero *nm*

other terms

primary	primario *aj*
secondary	secundario *aj*
tertiary	terciario *aj*

(*See also* **overusers**, **underusers** under **USING LANGUAGE**)

COUNTING AND ARRANGEMENT

GENERAL TERMS

arrange	arreglar *vt*
classify	clasificar *vt*
copy	copia *nf*
count	contar(se) *vt(r)*
enumeration	enumeración *nf*
gradation	gradación *nf*
group	agrupar *vt*
grouping	modo de agrupar *nm, vt*
number	número *nm*
order	orden *nm*
organize	organizar *vt*
quantity	cantidad *nf*

ASPECTS OF ORGANIZATION

things to be organized

datum	dato *nm*
detail	detalle *nm*
entry	entrada *nf*
item	ítem *nm*
specific	específico *nm*
statistic	estadística *nf*

kinds of organization

diagram	diagrama *nm*
graph	gráfica *nf*
hierarchy	jerarquía *nf*
index	índice *nm*
list	lista *nf*
scheme	esquema *nm*
sequence	secuencia *nf*
series	serie *nf*
table	tabla *nf*

basic sorting orders

alphabetical	alfabético *aj*
ascending	ascendente *aj*
chronological	cronológico *aj*
descending	descendente *aj*

inverse	inverso *aj*
numerical	numérico *aj*

COUNTING TERMS

inexact quantities

approximate	aproximado *aj*
estimate	estimado *nm*
miscellany	miscelánea *nf*
multitude	multitud *nf*
myriad	miríada *nf*
numerous	numeroso *aj*
plenitude	plenitud *nf*
plethora	plétora *nf*
various	vario *aj*

copies

duplicate	duplicado *aj, nm*
quadruplicate	cuadruplicado *aj, nm*
quintuplicate	quintuplicado *aj, nm*
triplicate	triplicado *aj, nm*

other terms

dozen	docena *nf*
gross	gruesa *nf*
numbering machine	numeradora *nf*
sole	solo *aj*

GROUPING TERMS

things created

category	categoría *nf*
class	clase *nf*
combination	combinación *nf*
compilation	compilación, recopilación *nf*
entirety	entereza *nf*
entity	entidad *nf*
group	grupo *nm*
module	módulo *nm*
totality	totalidad *nf*
type	tipo *nm*
unit	unidad *nf*

boundaries

confines	confines *nmpl*
delimitation	delimitación *nf*
demarcation	demarcación *nf*
limit	límite *nm*
margin	margen *nm*
periphery	periferia *nf*

parts

certain (particular)	cierto *aj, pron*
compartment	compartimiento *nm*
component	componente *aj, nm*
constituent	constitutivo *aj, nm*
part	parte *nf*
portion	porción *nf*
section	sección *nf*
subdivision	subdivisión *nf*
subgroup	subgrupo *nm*

(*See also* BASIC CONCEPTS under **MATHEMATICS**; *performance groups* under **MUSIC**)

All About Language

LINGUISTICS

GENERAL TERMS

acquisition	adquisición *nf*
cognate	cognado *aj, nm*
communication	comunicación *nf*
dialect	dialecto *nm*
discourse	discurso *nm*
expression	expresión *nf*
formation	formación *nf*
grammar	gramática *nf*
grammatical rule	regla gramatical *nf*
language (general)	lenguaje *nm*
language (specific)	lengua *nf*
lexicon	léxico *nm*
linguistics	lingüística *nf*
metalanguage	metalenguaje *nm*
model	modelo *nm*
theory	teoría *nf*
vocabulary	vocabulario *nm*

BRANCHES OF LINGUISTICS

approaches

anthropological	antropólogico *aj*
applied	aplicado *aj*
comparative	comparativo *aj*
contrastive	contrastivo *aj*
diachronic	diacrónico *aj*
historical	histórico *aj*
mathematical	matemático *aj*
synchronic	sincrónico *aj*
theoretical	teorético, teórico *aj*

major fields

morphology	morfología *nf*
phonology	fonología *nf*
semantics	semántica *nf*
syntax	sintaxis *nf*

subfields

discourse analysis	análisis del discurso *nm*
metalinguistics	metalingüística *nf*
neurolinguistics	neurolingüística *nf*
psycholinguistics	(p)sicolingüística *nf*
sociolinguistics	sociolingüística *nf*

related specializations

cryptography	criptografía *nf*
dialectology	dialectología *nf*
epigraphy	epigrafía *nf*
etymology	etimología *nf*
glottochronology	glotocronología *nf*
graphology	grafología *nf*
lexicography	lexicografía *nf*
logography	logografía *nf*
metrics	métrica *nf*
paleography	paleografía *nf*
philology	filología *nf*
phonetics	fonética *nf*
phonics	fónica *nf*
semiology	semiología *mf*
semiotics	semiótica *nf*
stylistics	estilística *nf*

PHONOLOGY

GENERAL TERMS

accent	acento *nm*
articulation	articulación *nf*
homonym	homónimo *nm*
homophone	homófono *nm*
intonation	entonación *nf*
phonemics	fonémica *nf*
phonetics	fonética *nf*
phonology	fonología *nf*
pronunciation	pronunciación *nf*
sound	sonido *nm*
transcription	tra(n)scripción *nf*
variant	variante *nf*
vocal	vocal *aj*
voice	voz *nf*

SPECIALIZATIONS

branches of phonetics

acoustic(al)	acústico *aj*
articulatory	articulatorio *aj*
experimental	experimental *aj*
perceptual	perceptivo *aj*

other specializations

phonics	fónica *nf*
phonography	fonografía *nf*
prosody	prosodia *nf*

GRAMMAR

GENERAL TERMS

class	clase *nf*
conjugation	conjugación *nf*
construction	construcción *nf*
declension	declinación *nf*
form	forma *nf*
formative	formativo *nm*
function	función *nf*
order	orden *nm*
paradigm	paradigma *nm*
part of speech	parte de la oración *nf*
syntax	sintaxis *nf*

ASPECTS OF GRAMMAR

grammatical categories

aspect	aspecto *nm*
case	caso *nm*
comparison	comparación *nf*
gender	género *nm*
number	número *nm*
person	persona *nf*

formatives

affix	afijo *nm*
base	base *nf*
clause	cláusula *nf*
enclitic	enclítico *nm*
inflection	inflexión *nf*
morpheme	morfema *nm*
particle	partícula *nf*
phrase	frase *nf*
prefix	prefijo *nm*
proclitic	proclítico *nm*
suffix	sufijo *nm*
termination	terminación *nf*
variant	variante *aj, nf*

parts of speech

adjective	adjetivo *nm*
adverb	adverbio *nm*
article	artículo *nm*
conjunction	conjunción *nf*
determiner	determinativo *nm*
interjection	interjección *nf*
noun	nombre *nm*
preposition	preposición *nf*
pronoun	pronombre *nm*
substantive	su(b)stantivo *nm*
verb	verbo *nm*

functions

adjunct	adjunto *nm*
antecedent	antecedente *nm*
complement	complemento *nm*
coordination	coordinación *nf*
intensifier	intensificador *nm*
modifier	modificador *nm*
negation	negación *nf*
object	objeto *nm*
qualifier	calificativo *nm*
quantifier	cuantificador *nm*
subordination	subordinación *nf*

NOUNS

number

dual	dual *aj*
plural	plural *aj, nm*
singular	singular *aj, nm*

gender

feminine	femenino *aj, nm*
masculine	masculino *aj, nm*
neuter	neutro *aj, nm*

classification

abstract	abstracto *aj*
animate	animado *aj*
collective	colectivo *aj*
common	común *aj*
compound	compuesto *nm*
concrete	concreto *aj*
countable	contable *aj*
epicene	epiceno *aj*
inanimate	inanimado *aj*
inseparable	inseparable *aj*
mass	masivo *aj*
proper	propio *aj*
separable	separable *aj*
uncountable	no contable *aj*

cases

ablative	ablativo *aj, nm*
accusative	acusativo *aj, nm*
concessive	concesivo *aj, nm*
dative	dativo *aj, nm*
genitive	genitivo *aj, nm*
instrumental	instrumental *aj, nm*
locative	locativo *aj, nm*
nominative	nominativo *aj, nm*
objective	objetivo *aj*
oblique	oblicuo *aj*
partitive	partitivo *aj*
possessive	posesivo *aj, nm*
vocative	vocativo *aj*

VERBS

general terms

copula	cópula *nf*
direct object	complemento directo *aj*
indirect object	complemento indirecto *nm*
mood	modo *nm*
principal parts	partes principales *nfpl*
tense	tiempo *nm*
voice	voz *nf*

classification

auxiliary	auxiliar *aj, nm*
causative	causativo *aj, nm*
copulative	copulativo *aj*
defective	defectivo *aj*
gerund	gerundio *nm*
inchoative	incoativo *aj*
infinitive	infinitivo *nm*
interrogative	interrogativo *aj*
intransitive	intransitivo *aj*
irregular	irregular *aj*
modal	modal *aj*
participle	participio *nm*
phrasal verb	verbo con partícula *nm, nf*
pronominal	pronominal *aj*
reflexive	reflexivo *aj*
regular	regular *aj*
transitive	transitivo *aj*

principal parts

past participle	participio pasado *nm*
past tense	tiempo pasado *nm*
present participle	participio presente *nm*
simple form	forma simple *nf*

person

first person	primera persona *nf*
second person	segunda persona *nf*
third person	tercera persona *nf*

tense

future	futuro *aj, nm*
historical (present)	histórico *aj*
past	pasado *aj, nm*
perfect	perfecto *aj, nm*
pluperfect	plusquamperfecto *aj, nm*
present	presente *aj, nm*
preterit	pretérito *aj, nm*

aspect and mood

active	activo *aj*
emphatic	enfático *aj*
frequentative	frecuentativo *aj, nm*
imperfect	imperfecto *aj, nm*
imperfective	imperfectivo *aj, nm*
indicative	indicativo *aj, nm*
passive	pasivo *aj*
perfective	perfectivo *aj, nm*
potential	potencial *aj, nm*
progressive	progresivo *aj, nm*
subjunctive	subjuntivo *aj, nm*

ADJECTIVES AND ADVERBS

kinds of adjectives

attributive	atributivo *aj*
augmentative	aumentativo *aj*
demonstrative	demostrativo *aj*
diminutive	diminutivo *aj*
possessive	posesivo *aj*
qualifying	calificativo *aj*

kinds of adverbs

conjunctive	conjuntivo *aj*
intensive	intensivo *aj*
interrogative	interrogativo *aj*

degrees of comparison

comparative	comparativo *aj*
positive	positivo *aj*
superlative	superlativo *aj*

OTHER PARTS OF SPEECH

pronouns

demonstrative	demostrativo *aj*
impersonal	impersonal *aj*

indefinite   indefinido *aj*
interrogative   interrogativo *aj*
personal   personal *aj*
reflexive   reflexivo *aj*
relative   relativo *aj*

articles

definite   definido *aj*
indefinite   indefinido *aj*

conjunctions

coordinating   coordinante *aj*
correlative   correlativo *aj*
disjunctive   disyuntivo *aj*
subordinating   subordinante *aj*
reciprocal   recíproco *aj*

TERMS IN SYNTAX

phrases

adjectival   adjetival *aj*
adverbial   adverbial *aj*
appositive   apositivo *aj*
infinitival *aj*   del infinitivo *nm*
periphrastic   perifrástico *aj*
prepositional   preposicional *aj*

clauses

concord   concordia *nf*
conditional   condicional *aj*
coordinate   coordinado *aj*
dependant, dependent   dependiente *aj*
independent   independiente *aj*
subordinate   subordinado *aj*
temporal *aj*   de tiempo *nm*

sentences

affirmative   afirmativo *aj*
complex   complejo *aj*
compound   compuesto *aj*
declarative   declarativo *aj*
declaratory   declaratorio *aj*
direct discourse   estilo directo *nm*
elliptical   elíptico *aj*
exclamatory   exclamatorio *aj*
grammatical   gramaticalmente correcto *aj*
imperative   imperativo *aj*
indirect discourse   estilo indirecto *nm*
interrogative   interrogativo *aj*
negative   negativo *aj*
predicate   predicado *nm*
simple   simple *aj*

subject   sujeto *nm*
ungrammatical   antigramatical *aj*

(*See also* **grammatical and semantic** under **DICTIONARIES**)

WRITING

GENERAL TERMS

alphabet   alfabeto *nm*
diacritic   signo diacrítico *nm*
graphic accent   acento ortográfico *nm*
manuscript   manuscrito *nm*
orthography   ortografía *nf*
punctuation   puntuación *nf*
script   escritura *nf*

SPECIALIZATIONS

calligraphy   caligrafía *nf*
cryptography   criptografía *nf*
decipherment   descifre *nm*
epigraphy   epigrafía *nf*
graphology   grafología *nf*
paleography   paleografía *nf*
philology   filología *nf*
stenotypy   estenotipia *nf*

ASPECTS OF WRITTEN LANGUAGE

forms

abbreviation   abreviatura *nf*
initials   iniciales *nfpl*
inscription   inscripción *nf*
monogram   monograma *nm*
text   texto *nm*

types of writing systems

alphabetic(al)   alfabético *aj*
cuneiform   cuneiforme *aj*
hieroglyphic   jeroglífico *aj*
ideography   ideografía *nf*
logography   logografía *nf*
pictography   pictografía *nf*
stenography   estenografía *nf*
syllabary   silabario *nm*

units

character   carácter *nm*
cryptogram, cryptograph   criptograma *nm*
digraph   dígrafo *nm*
grapheme   grafema *nm*
hieroglyph   jeroglífico *nm*

ideogram, ideograph	ideograma *nm*
letter	letra *nf*
phonogram	fonograma *nm*
pictogram, pictograph	pictograma *nm*
pictograph	pictografía *nf*
stenotype	estenotipo *nm*
symbol	símbolo *nm*

diacritical marks

cedilla	cedilla *nf*
dieresis	diéresis *nf*
tilde	tilde *nm or nf*
vowel point	punto vocálico *nm*

graphic accents

acute	agudo *aj*
breve	breve *nf*
circumflex	circunflejo *aj*
grave	grave *aj*

punctuation

apostrophe	apóstrofo *nm*
capital letter	letra capital *nf*
comma	coma *nf*
contraction	contracción *nf*
paragraph	párrafo *nm*
parenthesis	paréntesis *nm*
period	período, periodo *nm*
suspension	suspensión *nf*

handwriting

cursive script	cursiva *nf*
flourish	floreo *nm*
illegible	ilegible *aj*
legible	legible *aj*

other terms

ABC-book	abecedario *nm*
aleph	álef *nm*
aphaeresis	aféresis *nf*
homograph	homógrafo *nm*
insert (word)	insertar *vt*
lacuna	laguna *nf*
obliteration	obliteración *nf*
palindrome	palíndromo *nm*
Romanization	romanización *nf*
spelling reform	reforma ortográfica *nf*
stylograph	estilógrafo *nf*
transliteration	trasliteración *nf*

ALPHABETS

Arabic	árabe *aj*
Cyrillic	cirílico *aj*
Greek	griego *aj*
Hebrew	hebreo *aj*
phonetic	fonético *aj*
Roman	romano *aj*

HISTORICAL TERMS

scripts

Cherokee	cheroquí *aj, nm*
Egyptian	egipcio, -a *aj, nm*
Gothic	gótico *aj, nm*
Phoenician	fenicio *aj, nm*
Semitic	semítico *aj, nm*
Ugaritic	ugarítico *aj, nm*

other terms

boustrophedon	bustrófedon *nm*
palimsest	palimsesto *nm*
Rosetta stone	piedra de Roseta *nf*
rune	runa *nf*
scribe	escriba *nm*

THE GREEK ALPHABET

alpha	alfa *nf(el)*
beta	beta *nf*
chi	ji *nf*
delta	delta *nf*
epsilon	epsilón *nf*
eta	eta *nf*
gamma	gamma *nf*
iota	iota *nf*
kappa	kappa *nf*
lambda	lambda *nf*
mu	my *nf*
omega	omega *nf*
omicron	ómicron *nf*
phi	phi, fi *nf*
pi	pi *nf*
psi	psi *nf*
rho	rho *nf*
sigma	sigma *nf*
tau	tau *nf*
theta	theta *nf*
upsilon	ípsilon *nf*
xi	xi *nf*
zeta	zeta *nf*

PERSONS

calligrapher	calígrafo, -a *nmf*
copyist	copista *nmf*
cryptographer	criptógrafo, -a *nmf*
decipherer	descifrador, -a *nmf*

graphologist	grafólogo, -a *nmf*
paleographer	paleógrafo, -a *nmf*
philologist	filólogo *nmf*
stenographer	estenógrafo, -a *nmf*
stenotypist	estenotipista *nmf*

(*See also* TERMS IN POETRY under **LITERATURE**)

USING LANGUAGE

GENERAL TERMS

communication	comunicación *nf*
expression	expresión *nf*
fluency	fluidez *nf*
information	información *nf*
message	mensaje *nm*
rhetoric	retórica *nf*
semantics	semántica *nf*
use	uso *nm*

LANGUAGE FUNCTIONS

good purpose

clarification	aclaración *nf*
congratulations	congratulaciones *nfpl*
consultation	consulta *nf*
counsel	consejo *nm*
description	descripción *nf*
elaboration	elaboración *nf*
elucidation	elucidación *nf*
enumeration	enumeración *nf*
exhortation	exhortación *nf*
explication	explicación *nf*
felicitation	felicitación *nf*
hortative, hortatory	hortatorio *aj*
identification	identificación *nf*
interpretation	interpretación *nf*
interrogation	interrogación *nf*
iteration	iteración *nf*
notification	notificación *nf*
persuasion	persuasión *nf*
socialization	socialización *nf*
suggestion	sugerencia *nf*

bad purpose

accusation	acusación *nf*
denunciation	denuncia, denunciación *nf*
evasion	evasión *nf*
excuse	excusa *nf*
falsification	falsificación *nf*
fulmination	fulminación *nf*
insinuation	insinuación *nf*

invective	invectiva *nf*
malediction	maldición *nf*
obscenity	obscenidad *nf*
profanity	profanidad *nf*
vilification	vilipendio *nm*
vituperation	vituperio *nm*

SPECIFIC FORMS

written

addendum	adenda *nf*
annotation	anotación *nf*
bulletin	boletín *nm*
citation	citación *nf*
composition	composición *nf*
concordance	concordancia *nf*
correspondence	correspondencia *nf*
document	documento *nm*
gloss	glosa *nf*
list	lista *nf*
literature	literatura *nf*
manuscript	manuscrito *nm*
marginalia	notas marginales *nfpl*
memo, memorandum	memorándum *nm*
missive	misiva *nf*
note	nota *nf*
postscript	pos(t)data *nf*
printed matter *nsg*	impresos *nmpl*
publications	publicaciones *nfpl*
questionnaire	cuestionario *nm*

spoken

announcement	anuncio *nm*
colloquy	coloquio *nm*
comment, commentary	comentario *nm*
conversation	conversación *nf*
debate	debate *nm*
declamation	declamación *nf*
declaration	declaración *nf*
dialog(ue)	diálogo *nm*
dictation	dictado *nm*
dictum	dictamen *nm*
discourse	discurso *nm*
discussion	discusión *nf*
edict	edicto *nm*
eulogy	elogio *nm*
harangue	arenga *nf*
interlocution	interlocución *nf*
interpolation	interpolación *nf*
interruption	interrupción *nf*
mention	mención *nf*
monolog(ue)	monólogo *nm*

murmurrings	murmullos *nmpl*
observation	observación *nf*
oration (funeral)	oración *nf*
oratory	oratoria *nf*
peroration	peroración *nf*
promise	promesa *nf*
recital (poem)	recital *nm*
recitation	recitado, recitación *nm, nf*
response (question)	respuesta *nf*
rumor	rumor *nm*
salaam	zalema *nf*
salutation	saludo, salutación *nf*
sermon	sermón *nm*
tête-à-tête	tête-à-tête *nm*
verbalization	expresión verbalmente *nf*

written or oral

admonition	admonición, amonestación *nf*
anecdote	anécdota *nf*
blasphemy	blasfemia *nf*
calumny	calumnia *nf*
compliment	cumplido *nm*
diatribe	diatriba *nf*
falsehood	falsedad *nf*
insult	insulto *nm*
name	nombre *nm*
panegyric	panegírico *nm*
proclamation	proclama *nf*
proposal	propuesta *nf*
propaganda	propaganda *nf*
recapitulation	recapitulación *nf*
recommendation	recomendación *nf*
relate	relatar *vt*
repetition	repetición *nf*
retraction (statement)	retractación *nf*

restricted language use

argot	argot *nm*
jargon	jerga, jerigonza *nf*
legalese	jerga legal *nf*
nomenclature	nomenclatura *nf*
vernacular	vernáculo *nm*

DESCRIBING LANGUAGE USE

desirable

articulate	articulado *aj*
clear	claro *aj*
correct	correcto *aj*
eloquent	elocuente *aj*
expressive	expresivo *aj*
intelligible	inteligible *aj*
proper	propio *aj*
succinct	sucinto *aj*

undesirable

ambiguous	ambiguo *aj*
cryptic	críptico *aj*
equivocal (reply)	equívoco *aj*
expletive	palabra expletiva *nf*
grandiloquent	grandilocuente *aj*
improper	impropio *aj*
incoherent	incoherente *aj*
incorrect	incorrecto *aj*
inexpressive	inexpresivo *aj*
insinuating	insinuador *aj*
insulting	insultante *aj*
mordant	mordaz *aj*
obscene	obsceno *aj*
obscure	o(b)scuro *aj*
offensive	ofensivo *aj*
pejorative	peyorativo *aj, nm*
poisonous (fig)	ponzoñoso *aj*
redundant	redundante *aj*
repetitive	repetitivo *aj*
scabrous	escabroso *aj*
turgid	turgente *aj*
unclear	poco claro *aj*
unintelligible	ininteligible *aj*
vague	vago *aj*
vilifying	vilipendiador *aj*
vitriolic	vitriólico *aj*
vociferating	vociferante *aj*
vulgar	vulgar *aj*

incorrect language

barbarism	barbarismo *nm*
corruption	corrupción *nf*
hypercorrection	ultracorrección *nf*
locution	locución *nf*
neologism	neologismo *nm*
pleonasm	pleonasmo *nm*
solecism	solecismo *nm*
vulgarism	vulgarismo *nm*

special usages

acronym	acrónimo *nm*
cliché	cliché *nm*
colloquialism	expresión coloquial *nf*
euphemism	eufemismo *nm*
evasive statement	evasiva *nf*
localism	localismo *nm*
metaphrase	metáfrasis *nf*

palindrome	palíndromo *nm*
regionalism	regionalismo *nm*

other terms

abstract	abstracto *aj*
concrete	concreto *aj*
formal	formal *aj*
indescribable	indescriptible *aj*
ineffable	inefable *aj*
informal	informal *aj*
literal	literal *aj*
nontechnical	no técnico *aj*
onomatopoeic	onomatopéyico *aj*
poetic	poético *aj*
scientific	científico *aj*
technical	técnico *aj*

DESCRIBING LANGUAGE USERS

overusers

bombastic	bombástico *aj*
garrulous	gárrulo *aj*
loquacious	locuaz *aj*
pontificate	pontificar *vi*
repetitious	repetidor *aj*
sententious	sentencioso *aj*
tendentious	tendencioso *aj*
verbiage	verborragía, verborrea *nf*
verbose	verboso *aj*
vituperative	vituperioso *aj*
vociferous	vociferador *aj*

underusers

inarticulate	inarticulado *aj*
laconic	lacónico *aj*
mute	mudo *aj*
silent	silencioso *aj*
taciturn	taciturno *aj*
uncommunicative	poco comunicativo *aj*

other terms

emphatic	enfático *aj*
fluently *av*	con fluidez *nf*
humorous	humorístico *aj*
inoffensive	inofensivo *aj*
ironic(al)	irónico *aj*
sarcastic	sarcástico *aj*
vehement	vehemente *aj*

voice qualities

dulcet	dulce *aj*
mellifluous	melifluo *aj*

resonant	resonante *aj*
strident	estridente *aj*
vibrant	vibrante *aj*

TERMS IN SEMANTICS

kinds of meaning

connotative	connotativo *aj*
contextual *aj*	del contexto *nm*
denotative	denotativo *aj*
figurative	figurado *aj*
inferred	inferido *aj*
lexical	léxico *aj*
notional	nocional *aj*
referential *aj*	de referencia *nf*

other terms

antonym	antónimo *nm*
polysemy	polisemia *nf*
presupposition	presuposición *nf*
significance	significado, significación *nm, nf*
synonomy	sinonimia *nf*
synonym	sinónimo *nm*
term	término *nm*

TERMS IN RHETORIC

allusion	alusión *nf*
amplification	ampliación *nf*
antithesis	antítesis *nf*
apostrophe	apóstrofe *nm*
argumentation	argumentación *nf*
circumlocution	circunlocución *nf*
controvert	controvertir *vt*
diction	dicción *nf*
digression	digresión *nf*
disquisition	disquisición *nf*
dissuasion	disuasión *nf*
elocution	elocución *nf*
figure of speech	figura retórica *nf*
inversion	inversión *nf*
oxymoron	oxímoron *nm*
paraphrase	paráfrasis *nf*
periphrasis	perífrasis *nf*
polemic	polémica *nf*
qualification	calificación *nf*
redefine	redefinir *vt*
refutation	refutación *nf*
reiteration	reiteración *nf*
syllogism	silogismo *nm*
synecdoche	sinécdoque *nm*

PERSONS

annotator	anotador(a) *nmf*
announcer	anunciador(a) *nmf*
arguer	argumentador(a) *nmf*
commentator	comentarista *nmf*
conversationalist	conversador(a) *nmf*
correspondent	correspondiente *nmf*
declaimer	declamador(a) *nmf*
fulminator	fulminador(a) *nmf*
interlocutor	interlocutor(a) *nmf*
interpreter	intérprete *nmf*
lexicographer	lexicógrafo, -a *nmf*
orator	orador(a) *nmf*
pamphleteer	panfletista *nmf*
polemicist	polemista *nmf*
fluency	fluidez *nf*

(*See also* usage labels under **DICTIONARIES**; word games under **GAMES**; **LITERATURE**)

LANGUAGES OF THE WORLD

KINDS OF LANGUAGES

artificial	artificial *aj*
international	internacional *aj*
lingua franca	lengua franca *nf*
modern	moderno *aj*
national	nacional *aj*
native language	lengua materna *nf*
official	oficial *aj*
regional	regional *aj*
second	segundo *aj*

LANGUAGE FAMILIES

major language families

Afro-Asiatic	afroasiático *aj*
Dravidian	dravidiano, dravida *aj*
Indo-European	indoeuropeo *aj*
Malayo-Polynesian	malayopolinesio *aj*
Sino-Tibetan	sinotibetano *aj*
Uralic-Altaic	uralo-altaico, uraloaltaico *aj, nm*

other language families

Altaic	altaico *aj*
Aryan	ario *aj*
Austro-Asiatic	austroasiático *aj*
Austronesian	austronesio *aj*

Bantu	bantú *aj*
Caucasian	caucasiano, caucásico *aj*
Indo-Aryan	indoario *aj*
Indo-Germanic	indogermánico *aj*
Mayan	maya *aj*
Semitic	semítico *aj*
Teutonic	teutónico *aj*
Turkic	turico *aj*

branches of Indo-European

Albanian	albanés *nm*
Armenian	armenio *nm*
Baltic	báltico *nm*
Celtic	celta *nm*
Germanic	germánico *nm*
Greek	griego *nm*
Indo-Iranian	indoiranés *nm*
Romance	romance *nm*
Slavic	eslavo *nm*

LANGUAGE NAMES

major world languages

Arabic	árabe *nm*
Bengali	bengalí *nm*
Chinese	chino *nm*
English	inglés *nm*
French	francés *nm*
Hindi	hindi *nm*
Indonesian	indonesio *nm*
Japanese	japonés *nm*
Korean	coreano *nm*
Portuguese	portugués *nm*
Punjabi	penjabi *nm*
Russian	ruso *nm*
Spanish	español *nm*
Tamil	tamil *nm*
Urdu	urdu *nm*

other European languages

Bulgarian	búlgaro *nm*
Byelorussian	bielorruso *nm*
Castilian	castellano *nm*
Catalan	catalán *nm*
Croatian	croata *nm*
Czech	checo *nm*
Danish	danés, dinamarqués *nm*
Estonian	estonio *nm*
Finnish	finlandés *nm*
Gaelic	gaélico *nm*
Hungarian	húngaro *nm*
Icelandic	islandés *nm*
Irish	irlandés *nm*

Italian	italiano *nm*
Lappish	lapón *nm*
Latvian	latvio *nm*
Lett, Lettish	letón *nm*
Lithuanian	lituano *nm*
Norwegian	noruego *nm*
Polish	polaco *nm*
Rumanian, Romanian	rumano *nm*
Scottish	escosés *nm*
Serbo-Croatian	servocroata *nm*
Swedish	sueco *nm*
Turkish	turco *nm*
Ukrainian	ucraniano *nm*
Yiddish	yid(d)ish *nm*

other Asian languages

Afghan	afgano *nm*
Azerbaijan	azerbaiyano *nm*
Burmese	birmano *nm*
Cambodian	camboyano *nm*
Cantonese	cantonés *nm*
Hawaiian	hawaiano *nm*
Hebrew	hebreo *nm*
Hindi	hindi *nm*
Hindustani	indostaní *nm*
Javanese	javanés *nm*
Khmer	kmer *nm*
Malay	malayo *nm*
Manchu	manchú, manchuriano *nm*
Mandarin	mandarín *nm*
Mongolian	mongol *nm*
Nepali	nepalés *nm*
Persian	persa *nm*
Sinhalese, Singhalese	cingalés *nm*
Tagalog	tagalo *nm*
Thai	tailandés *nm*
Tibetan	tibetano *nm*
Vietnamese	vietnamita *nm*

American Indian languages

Eskimo	esquimal *nm*
Guarani	guaraní *nm*
Navaho, Navajo	navajo *nm*
Quechua	quechua, quichua *nm*

African languages

Afrikaans	africaans *nm*
Amharic	amhárico *nm*
Berber	beréber *nm*
Coptic	copto *nm*
Hausa	hausa *nm*
Swahili	swahili, suajili *nm*

Yoruba	yoruba *nm*
Zulu	zulú *nm*

historical languages

Akkadian	acadio *nm*
Anglo-Saxon	anglosajón *nm*
Aramaic	arameo *nm*
Assyrian	asirio *nm*
Babylonian	babilonio *nm*
Cornish	córnico *nm*
Etruscan	etrusco *nm*
Gothic	gótico *nm*
Greek	griego *nm*
Hamitic	camita *nm*
Hittite	hitita *nm*
Latin	latín *nm*
Mayan	maya *nm*
Phoenician	fenicio *nm*
Phrygian	frigio *nm*
Sanskrit	sánscrito *nm*
Sumerian	sumerio *nm*

regional languages

Basque	vascuence, vasco *nm*
Breton	bretón *nm*
Malagasy	malgache *nm*
Maldivian	maldivo *nm*
Romansch, Romansh	romanche *nm*

mixed and artificial languages

Basic English	inglés básico *nm*
Creole	criollo *nm*
Esperanto	esperanto *nm*
Franglais	franglés *nm*
Spanglish	espanglés *nm*

BORROWINGS

Americanism	americanismo *nm*
Anglicism	anglicismo *nm*
Arabic expression	arabismo *nm*
Argentinian expression	argentinismo *nm*
calque	calco *nm*
Cubanism	cubanismo *nm*
Gallicism	galicismo *nm*
Hebraism	hebreaísmo *nm*
Italianism	italianismo *nm*

PERSONS

Africanist	africanista *nmf*
Arabist	arabista *nmf*
Hebraist	hebraísta *nmf*

Hispanist	hispanista *nmf*
interpreter	intérprete *nmf*
Sinologist	sinólogo, -a *nmf*

(*See also* ETHNIC GROUPS AROUND THE WORLD
under **ANTHROPOLOGY**; **PLACE NAMES:
POLITICAL**)

Our Planet and Its Peoples

GEOGRAPHY

GENERAL TERMS

area	área *nf(el)*
climate	clima *nm*
direction	dirección *nf*
distance	distancia *nf*
elevation	elevación *nf*
formation	formación *nf*
geography	geografía *nf*
global	global *aj*
hemisphere	hemisferio *nm*
horizon	horizonte *nm*
hydrosphere	hidrósfera *nf*
isometric	isométrico *aj*
line	línea *nf*
location	localización *nf*
map	mapa *nm*
pole	polo *nm*
region	región *nf*
zone	zona *nf*

SPECIALIZATIONS

biological geography

biogeography	biogeografía *nf*
ecology	ecología *nf*
oceanography	oceanografía *nf*
phytogeography	fitogeografía *nf*
zoogeography	zoogeografía *nf*

physical geography

climatology	climatología *nf*
cosmography	cosmografía *nf*
geochemistry	geoquímica *nf*
geodesy	geodesia *nf*
geomorphology	geomorfología *nf*

hydrography	hidrografía *nf*
hydrology	hidrología *nf*
oceanology	oceanología *nf*
orography	orografía *nf*
physiography	fisiografía *nf*

other fields

cartography	cartografía *nf*
geopolitics	geopolítica *nf*
meteorology	meteorología *nf*
photogrammetry	fotogrametría *nf*
topography	topografía *nf*
toponymy	toponimia *nf*

ASPECTS OF GEOGRAPHY

physical formations

abyss	abismo *nm*
archipelago	archipiélago *nm*
atoll	atolón *nm*
bank	banco *nm*
bay	bahía *nf*
canyon	cañón *nm*
cape	cabo *nm*
cascade	cascada *nf*
cataract	catarata *nf*
cave	cueva *nf*
cavern	caverna *nf*
cay	cayo *nm*
channel	canal *nm*
continent	continente *nm*
delta	delta *nm*
desert	desierto *nm*
divide	divisoria *nf*
dune	duna *nf*
estuary	estuario *nm*
fiord	fiordo *nm*
grotto	gruta *nf*
gulf	golfo *nm*
iceberg	iceberg *nm*
island, isle	isla *nf*
islet	isleta *nf*
isthmus	istmo *nm*
jungle	jungla *nf*
lagoon	laguna *nf*
lake	lago *nm*
massif	macizo *nm*
mountain	monte, montaña *nm, nf*
oasis	oasis *nm*
ocean	océano *nm*
peak	pico *nm*

peninsula	península *nf*
point	punta *nf*
precipice	precipicio *nm*
promonotory	promonotorio *nm*
rapids	rápidos *nmpl*
reef	arrecife *nm*
river	río *nm*
sandbank	banco de arena *nm, nf*
sandbar	barra de arena *nf*
tributary	tributario *nm*
vale	valle *nm*
valley	valle *nm*
virgin forest	bosque virgen *nm*
volcano	volcán *nm*

regions and zones

agricultural	agrícola *aj*
alpine	alpestre, alpino *aj*
Antarctic	antártico *aj, nm*
Arctic	ártico *aj, nm*
coastal	costero *aj*
desert-like	desértico *aj*
inhabited	habitado *aj*
littoral	litoral *aj, nm*
mountainous	montañoso *aj*
northland	tierra del norte *nf*
overpopulated	superpoblado *aj*
pampa	pampa *nf*
pelagic	pelágico *aj*
populated	poblado *aj*
riverside	ribera *nf*
savanna(h)	sabana *nf*
steppe	estepa *nf*
subcontinent	subcontinente *nm*
taiga	taiga *nf*
tropics	zona tropical *nf*
tundra	tundra *nf*
unexplored	inexplorado *aj*
uninhabited	inhabitado *aj*

directions and locations

antipodes	antípodas *nfpl*
cardinal point	punto cardinal *nm*
east	este *nm*
eastbound	con rumbo al este
easterly	desde/hacia el este
eastern	del este, oriental
easternmost	más al este
eastward	hacia el este
magnetic pole	polo magnético *nm*
midcontinent	medio del continente *nm*

north	norte *nm*
northeast	nordeste *nm*
northeasterly	del nordeste
northeastern	del nordeste
northerly	desde/hacia el norte
northern	del norte
northward	hacia el norte
northwards	hacia el norte
northwest	noroeste *aj, nm*
northwestern	hacia el noroeste
orientation	orientación *nf*
southeast	sudeste *nm*
west	oeste *nm*
westbound	con rumbo al oeste
westerly	del oeste
western	del oeste
westward	hacia el oeste

climates

arid	árido *aj*
continental	continental *aj*
equatorial	ecuatorial *aj*
glacial	glacial *aj*
insular	insular *aj*
oceanic	oceánico *aj*
polar	polar *aj*
subtropical	subtropical *aj*
temperate	templado *aj*
torrid	tórrido *aj*
tropical	tropical *aj*

other terms

confluence	confluencia *nf*
corridor	corredor *nm*
crest (wave)	cresta *nf*
current	corriente *nf*
declivity	declive *nm*
denude	desnudar *vt*
enclave	enclave *nm*
erosion	erosión *nf*
exploration	exploración *nf*
fluvial	fluvial *aj*
frontier	frontera *nf*
geostrophic	geostrófico *aj*
habitat	habitat *nm*
meander	meandro *nm*
territorial	territorial *aj*
turbid (water)	túrbio *aj*
vegetation	vegetación *nf*

CARTOGRAPHY

kinds of maps

aerial map	aeromapa *nm*
celestial	celeste *aj*
contour	contorno *nm*
inventory	inventario *nm*
mobility	movilidad *nf*
nautical	náutico *aj*
physical	físico *aj*
political	político *aj*
population	población *nf*
projection	proyección *nf*
reference	referencia *nf*
relief	relieve *nm*
terrestrial	terrestre *aj*
thematic	temático *aj*
transit	tránsito *nm*
transportation	tra(n)sportación *nf*
world map	mapamundi *nm*

forms of maps

atlas	atlas *nm*
globe	globo *nm*
homolosine	homolosenoidal *aj*
photomap	fotomapa *nm*
plane	plano *aj, nm*
planisphere	planisferio *nm*
terrain	terreno *nm*

imaginary lines

circle	círculo *nm*
equator	ecuador *nm*
latitude	latitud *nf*
longitude	longitud *nf*
meridian	meridiano *nm*
parallel	paralelo *nm*
tropic	trópico *nm*

isometric lines

isobar	isobara *nf*
isogonic	isogónico, isógono *aj*
isogram	isograma *nm*
isotherm	isoterma *nf*

other terms

altitude	altitud *nf*
azimuth	acimut, azimut *nm*
chart	carta *nf*
color	color *nm*
distortion	distorsión *nf*
graphic	gráfico *aj*
index	índice *nm*

scale	escala *nf*
symbol	símbolo *nm*

TOOLS AND MEASUREMENTS

compass	compás *nm*
geocentric	geocéntrico *aj*
inclinometer	inclinómetro *nm*
pantograph	pantógrafo *nm*
theodolite	teodolito *nm*

PERSONS

famous explorers

Columbus	Colón
Magellan	Magallanes
Vespucci	Vespucio

other persons

cartographer	cartógrafo, -a *nmf*
discoverer	descubridor(a) *nmf*
explorer	explorador(a) *nmf*
geographer	geógrafo, -a *nmf*
topographer	topógrafo, -a *nmf*

(*See also* **GEOLOGY**; **METEOROLOGY**)

PLACE NAMES: PHYSICAL

GLOBAL DIVISIONS

hemispheres

Eastern Hemisphere	hemisferio oriental *nm*
Northern Hemisphere	hemisferio boreal *nm*
Southern Hemisphere	hemisferio austral *nm*
Western Hemisphere	hemisferio occidental *nm*

inhabitants

Easterner	habitante del este *nmf*
Northerner	norteño, -a *nmf*
Southerner	sureño, -a *nmf*
Westerner	habitante del oeste *nmf*

CONTINENTS

names

Africa	África
Antarctica	Antártida
Asia	Asia
Australia	Australia
Europe	Europa

North America	Norteamérica	Singapore	Singapur
South America	Sudamérica	Tahiti	Tahití
		Taiwan	Taiwan
		Tasmania	Tasmania

inhabitants

		Tobago	Tobago
African	africano, -a *aj, nmf*	Trinidad	Trinidad
Asian	asiático, -a *aj, nmf*	Zanzibar	Zanzíbar
Australian	australiano, -a *aj, nmf*		
European	europeo, -a *aj, nmf*		

island groups

North American	norteamericano, -a *aj, nmf*	Antilles	Antillas
		Azores	Azores
South American	sudamericano, -a *aj, nmf*	Bahamas	Bahamas
		Balearics	Baleares
		Bermuda	Bermudas

PENINSULAS

		Canaries	Canarias
		Caymans	Caimanes
Arabia	Arabia	Faeros	Feroes
Asia Minor	Asia Menor	Fiji	Fiji, Fiyi
Balkans	Balcanes	Galapagos	Galápagos
Crimea	Crimea	Grenadines	Granadinas
Iberia	Iberia	Hebrides	Hébrides
Indo-China	Indochina	Maldives	Maldivas
Sinai	Sinai	Melanesia	Melanesia
Yucatan	Yucatán	Micronesia	Micronesia
		Philippines	Filipinas
		Polynesia	Polinesia

ISLANDS

		Samoa	Samoa

single islands

		Virgins	Vírgenes
Bali	Bali		
Barbados	Barbados		

inhabitants

Borneo	Borneo		
Corfu	Corfú	Aleutian	Aleuta *aj, nmf*
Corsica	Córcega	Balinese	balinés, -esa *aj, nmf*
Crete	Creta	Barbadian	barbadense *aj, nmf*
Cuba	Cuba	Bermudian	bermudeño, -a *aj, nmf*
Curaçao	Curazao	Canarian	canario, -a *aj, nmf*
Cyprus	Chipre	Corsican	corso, -a *aj, nmf*
Elba	Elba	Cretan	cretense *aj, nmf*
Greenland	Groenlandia	Cuban	cubano, -a *aj, nmf*
Grenada	Granada	Cypriot	chipriota *aj, nmf*
Guadeloupe	Guadalupe	Fijian	fidjiano, -a, fiyiano, -a *aj, nmf*
Guam	Guam		
Ireland	Irlanda	Filipino	filipino, -a *aj, nmf*
Jamaica	Jamaica	Greenlander	groenlandés, -esa *nmf*
Java	Java	Grenadian	granadino, -a *aj, nmf*
Jersey	Jersey	islander	isleño, -a *nmf*
Madagascar	Madagascar	Jamaican	jamaiciano, -a, jamaiquino, -a *aj, nmf*
Majorca	Mallorca		
Minorca	Menorca		
Puerto Rico	Puerto Rico	Javanese	javanés, -esa *aj, nmf*
Rhodes	Rodas	Majorcan	mallorquín, -ina *aj, nmf*
Sardinia	Cerdeña	Maldivian	maldivo, -a *aj, nmf*
Sicily	Sicilia	Melanesian	melanesio, -a *aj, nmf*
		Micronesian	micronesio, -a *aj, nmf*

Polynesian	polinesio, -a *aj, nmf*
Puerto Rican	puertorriqueño, -a *aj, nmf*
Samoan	samoano, -a *aj, nmf*
Sardinian	sardo, -a *aj, nmf*
Sicilian	siciliano, -a *aj, nmf*
Tahitian	tahitiano, -a *aj, nmf*
Taiwanese	taiwanés, -esa *aj, nmf*

WATER FORMATIONS

oceans

Antarctic	Antártico
Arctic	Ártico
Atlantic	Atlántico
Indian	Índico
Pacific	Pacífico

seas

Adriatic	Adriático
Aegean	Egeo
Arabian	Arábigo
Baltic	Báltico
Caribbean	Caribe
Caspian	Caspio
Ionian	Jónico
Mediterranean	Mediterráneo
North Sea	Mar del Norte *nm*

rivers

Amazon	Amazonas
Congo	Congo
Danube	Danubio
Ebro	Ebro
Elbe	Elba
Euphrates	Eufrates
Ganges	Ganges
Jordan	Jordán
Mississippi	Misisipí
Moselle	Mosela
Niger	Níger
Nile	Nilo
Rhine	Rin
Seine	Sena
Thames	Támesis
Tiber	Tíber
Yangtze	Yang-Tsé
Yukon	Yukón
Zambezi	Zambeze

gulfs

| Aden | Adén |
| Bothnia | Botnia |

| Mexico | Méjico, México |
| Persian | Pérsico |

straits and channels

Bosphorus	Bósforo
Dardanelles	Dardanelos
Magellan	Magallanes

bays and capes

Biscay	Vizcaya
Canaveral	Cañaveral
Horn	Hornos

MOUNTAINS

single mountains

Fuji, Fujiyama	Fujiyama
Kilimanjaro	Kilimanjaro
Olympus	Olimpo
Parnassus	Parnaso
Sinai	Sinai
Vesuvius	Vesubio

mountain ranges

Alps	Alpes
Andes	Andes
Apennines	Apeninos
Appalachians	Apalaches
Carpathians	Carpatos
Himalayas	Himalaya
Pyrenees	Pirineos
Rockies	Rocosas
Urals	Urales

PLACE NAMES: POLITICAL

(*Note:* Island countries are listed in **PLACE NAMES: PHYSICAL**)

COUNTRIES

names

Afghanistan	Afganistán
Albania	Albania
Algeria	Argelia
Angola	Angola
Argentina	La Argentina
Armenia	Armenia
Australia	Australia
Austria	Austria
Azerbaijan	Azerbaiyán, Azerbaiján
Bahamas	Bahamas
Bangladesh	Bangladesh

Barbados	Barbados	Jamaica	Jamaica
Belgium	Bélgica	Japan	Japón
Belize	Belice	Jordan	Jordania
Bhutan	Bután	Kenya	Kenya
Bolivia	Bolivia	Kirghizia, Kirghizistan	Kirguizistán
Bosnia	Bosnia	Korea	Corea
Botswana	Botsuana	Kuwait	Kuwait
Brazil	Brasil	Laos	Laos
Bulgaria	Bulgaria	Latvia	Latvia
Burundi	Burundi	Lebanon	Libano
Byelorus, Bielorus	Bielorrusia	Lesotho	Lesotho
Cambodia	Camboya	Liberia	Liberia
Cameroon	Camerún	Libya	Libia
Canada	El Canadá	Liechtenstein	Liechtenstein
Chile	Chile	Lithuania	Lituania
China	La China	Luxemb(o)urg	Luxemburgo
Colombia	Colombia	Malawi	Malawi
Costa Rica	Costa Rica	Malaysia	Malasia
Croatia	Croacia	Mali	Malí
Cuba	Cuba	Malta	Malta
Czech Republic	República Checa	Mauritania	Mauritania
Denmark	Dinamarca	Mexico	Méjico, México
Dominican Republic	La República Dominicana	Monaco	Mónaco
		Morocco	Marruecos
Ecuador	El Ecuador	Mozambique	Mozambique
Egypt	Egipto	Myanmar	Mianmar
El Salvador	El Salvador	Namibia	Namibia
England	Inglaterra	Nepal	Nepal
Estonia	Estonia	New Zealand	Nueva Zeland(i)a
Ethiopia	Etiopía	Nicaragua	Nicaragua
Fiji	Fiji, Fiyi	Nigeria	Nigeria
Finland	Finlandia	Norway	Noruega
France	Francia	Oman	Omán
Gambia	Gambia	Pakistan	Paquistán
Georgia	Georgia	Panama	Panamá
Ghana	Ghana	Papua New Guinea	Papua Nueva Guinea
Great Britain	Gran Bretaña	Paraguay	Paraguay
Greece	Grecia	Peru	Perú
Guatemala	Guatemala	Phillipines	Filipinas
Guinea	Guinea	Poland	Polonia
Guyana	Guyana	Portugal	Portugal
Haiti	Haití	Rumania, Romania	Rumania
Holland	Holanda	Russia	Rusia
Honduras	Honduras	Rwanda	Rwanda
Hungary	Hungría	Saudi Arabia	Arabia Saudita
Iceland	Islandia	Senegal	Senegal
India	La India	Serbia, Servia	Serbia
Indonesia	Indonesia	Sierra Leone	Sierra Leona
Iran	Irán	Slovakia	Eslovaquia
Iraq	Iraq	Somalia	Somalia
Ireland	Irlanda	Spain	España
Israel	Israel	Sri Lanka	Sri Lanka
Italy	Italia	Sudan	Sudán

Surinam	Surinam	Chilean	chileno, -a *aj, nmf*
Swaziland	Suazilandia	Chinese	chino, -a *aj, nmf*
Sweden	Suecia	Colombian	colombiano, -a *aj, nmf*
Switzerland	Suiza	Costa Rican	costarricense,
Syria	Siria		costarriqueño, -a *aj,*
Tadzhikistan	Tayiquistán		*nmf*
Tanzania	Tanzania	Croat, Croatian	croata *aj, nmf*
Thailand	Tailandia	Cuban	cubano, -a *aj, nmf*
Togo	Togo	Czech	checo, -a *aj, nmf*
Tunisia	Túnez	Dane	danés, -esa,
Turkey	Turquía		dinamarqués, -esa
Turkmenistan	Turkmenistán		*nmf*
Uganda	Uganda	Dominican	dominicano, -a *aj, nmf*
Ukraine	Ucrania	Ecuadorean	ecuatoriano, -a *aj, nmf*
United Kingdom	Reino Unido	Egyptian	egipcio, -a *aj, nmf*
United States	Estados Unidos	Englishman	inglés *nm*
Uruguay	Uruguay	Englishwoman	inglesa *nf*
Uzbekistan	Uzbekistán	Estonian	estonio, -a *aj, nmf*
Venezuela	Venezuela	Ethiopian	etíope *aj, nmf*
Vietnam	Vietnam	Fijian	fidjiano, -a, fiyiano, -a
Yemen	Yemen		*aj, nmf*
Zaire	Zaire	Finn	finlandés, -esa *nmf*
Zambia	Zambia	Frenchman	francés *nm*
Zimbabwe	Zimbabwe	Frenchwoman	francesa *nf*

inhabitants

Afghan	afgano, -a *aj, nmf*	Gambian	gambiano, -a *aj, nmf*
Albanian	albanés, -esa *aj, nmf*	Georgian	georgiano, -a *aj, nmf*
Algerian	argelino, -a *aj, nmf*	Ghanaian	ghanés, -esa *aj, nmf*
Angolan	angoleño, -a *aj, nmf*	Greek	griego, -a *aj, nmf*
Argentine,	argentino, -a *aj, nmf*	Guatemalan	guatemalteco, -a *aj,*
Argentinean			*nmf*
Armenian	armenio, -a *aj, nmf*	Guinean	guineo, -a *aj, nmf*
Australian	australiano, -a *aj, nmf*	Guyanese	guyanés, -esa *aj, nmf*
Austrian	austríaco, -a *aj, nmf*	Haitian	haitiano, -a *aj, nmf*
Azerbaijani	Azerbaiyáni *aj, nmf*	Hollander	holandés, -desa *nmf*
Bahamian	bahameño, -a, bahamés,	Honduran	hondureño, -a *aj, nmf*
	-esa *aj, nmf*	Hungarian	húngaro, -a *aj, nmf*
Bangladeshi	bangladesí *aj, nmf*	Icelander	islandés, -esa *nmf*
Barbadian	barbadense *aj, nmf*	Indian	indio, -a *aj, nmf*
Belgian	belga *aj, nmf*	Indonesian	indonesio, -a *aj, nmf*
Belizean	beliceño, -a *aj, nmf*	Iranian	iraní, iranio, -a *aj, nmf*
Bhutanese	butanés, -esa *aj, nmf*	Iraqi	iraquí *aj, nmf*
Bolivian	boliviano, -a *aj, nmf*	Irishman	irlandés *nm*
Bosnian	bosnio, -a *aj, nmf*	Irishwoman	irlandesa *nf*
Botswanan	botsuano, -a *aj, nmf*	Israeli	israelí *aj, nmf*
Brazilian	brasileño, -a *aj, nmf*	Italian	italiano, -a *aj, nmf*
Bulgarian	búlgaro, -a *aj, nmf*	Jamaican	jamaiciano, -a,
Burundian	burundés, -esa *aj, nmf*		jamaiquino, -a *aj,*
Byelorussian	bielorruso, -a *aj, nmf*		*nmf*
Cambodian	camboyano, -a *aj, nmf*	Japanese	japonés, -esa *aj, nmf*
Camerounian	camerunés, -esa *aj, nmf*	Jordanian	jordano, -a *aj, nmf*
Canadian	canadiense *aj, nmf*	Kenyan	keniano, -a *aj, nmf*
		Korean	coreano, -a *aj, nmf*
		Kuwaiti	kuwaití *aj, nmf*

Lao, Laotian	laosiano, -a *aj, nmf*
Latvian	latvio, -a, letón, -ona *aj, nmf*
Lebanese	libanés, -esa *aj, nmf*
Liberian	liberiano, -a *aj, nmf*
Libyan	libio, -a *aj, nmf*
Lithuanian	lituano, -a *aj, nmf*
Luxemb(o)urger	luxemburgués, -esa *aj, nmf*
Malawian	malawiano, -a *aj, nmf*
Malay, Malaysian	malayo, -a *aj, nmf*
Malian	maliense *aj, nmf*
Maltese	maltés, -esa *aj, nmf*
Mauritanian	mauritano, -a *aj, nmf*
Mexican	mejicano, -a *aj, nmf*
Monacan, Monegasque	monagesco, -a *aj, nmf*
Moroccan	marroquí *aj, nmf*
Mozambican	mozambiqueño, -a *aj, nmf*
Namibian	namibio, -a *aj, nmf*
Nepalese, Nepali	nepalés, -esa *aj, nmf*
Netherlander	neerlandés, -esa *nmf*
New Zealander	neocelandés, -esa *nmf*
Nicaraguan	nicaragüense *aj, nmf*
Nigerian	nigeriano, -a *aj, nmf*
Norwegian	noruego *aj, nmf*
Omani	omaní *aj, nmf*
Pakistani	pakistaní, paquistaní *aj, nmf*
Panamanian	panameño, -a *aj, nmf*
Papuan	Papú *aj, nmf*
Paraguayan	paraguayo, -a *aj, nmf*
Peruvian	peruano, -a *aj, nmf*
Phillipine, Filipino	filipino, -a *aj, nmf*
Pole	polaco, -a *nmf*
Portuguese	portugués, -esa *aj, nmf*
Rumanian, Romanian	rumano, -a *aj, nmf*
Russian	ruso, -a *aj, nmf*
Rwandan	rwandés, -esa *aj, nmf*
Salvadoran, Salvadorian	salvadoreño, -a *aj, nmf*
Saudi, Saudi-Arabian	saudita, saudí *aj, nmf*
Senegalese	senegalés, -esa *aj, nmf*
Serb	serbio, -a, servio, -a *nmf*
Serbian	serbio, servio *aj, nm*
Slovak, Slovakian	eslovaco, -a *aj, nmf*
Somali, Somalian	somalí *aj, nmf*
Spaniard	español(a) *nmf*
Sri Lankan	esrilanqués, -esa *aj, nmf*
Sudanese	sudanés, -esa *aj, nmf*
Swede	sueco, -a *nmf*
Swiss	suizo, -a *aj, nmf*

Syrian	sirio, -a *aj, nmf*
Tanzanian	tanzaniano, -a *aj, nmf*
Thai	tailandés, -esa *aj, nmf*
Togolese	togolés, -esa *aj, nmf*
Tunisian	tunecino, -a *aj, nmf*
Turk	turco, -a *nmf*
Ugandan	ugandés, -esa *aj, nmf*
Ukranian	ucrani(a)no, -a *aj, nmf*
Uruguayan	uruguayo, -a *aj, nmf*
Uzbek	uzbeko, -a *aj, nmf*
Venezuelan	venezolano, -a *aj, nmf*
Vietnamese	vietnamita *aj, nmf*
Yemeni, Yemenite	yemení *aj, nmf*
Zairian	zaireño, -a *aj, nmf*
Zambian	zambiano, -a *aj, nmf*
Zimbabwean	zimbabwense *aj, nmf*

CITIES

names

Addis Ababa	Addis-Abeba
Alexandria	Alejandría
Algiers	Argel
Amman	Amán
Astrakhan	Astracán
Athens	Atenas
Avignon	Aviñón
Baghdad	Bagdad
Bangkok	Bangkok
Barcelona	Barcelona
Basel, Basle	Basilea
Bayonne	Bayona
Beijing	Beijing
Belgrade	Belgrado
Berlin	Berlín
Bern, Berne	Berna
Bogota	Bogotá
Bologna	Bolonia
Bruges	Brujas
Brussels	Bruselas
Bucharest	Bucarest
Budapest	Budapest
Cairo	El Cairo
Calcutta	Calcuta
Canton	Cantón
Caracas	Caracas
Cologne	Colonia
Copenhagen	Copenhague
Cordova	Córdoba
Crakow	Cracovia
Damascus	Damasco
Dublin	Dublín

Dunkirk	Dunquerque
Edinburgh	Edimburgo
Frankfort	Francfort
Gaza	Gaza
Geneva	Ginebra
Genoa	Génova
Ghent	Gante
Gibraltar	Gibraltar
Hague, The	La Haya
Havana	La Habana
Hong Kong	Hong-Kong
Honolulu	Honolulú
Istanbul	Estambul
Jakarta	Yakarta
Jerusalem	Jerusalén
Kabul	Kabul
Khartoum	Jartum
Koblenz	Coblenza
Krakow	Cracovia
Lima	Lima
London	Londres
Madrid	Madrid
Marseille	Marsellas
Mecca	La Meca
Milan	Milán
Moscow	Moscú
Naples	Nápoles
Nazareth	Nazaret
New Delhi	Nueva Delhi
New Orleans	Nueva Orleáns
New York	Nueva York
Nice	Niza
Paris	París
Philadelphia	Filadelfia
Prague	Praga
Rangoon	Rangún
Rio de Janeiro	Río de Janeiro
Riyadh	Riad, Riyad
Rome	Roma *nf*
Saint Petersburg	San Petersburgo
Seoul	Seúl
Stockholm	Estocolmo
Strasbourg	Estrasburgo
Taipei	Taipeh
Tangiers	Tánger
Teheran, Tehran	Teherán
Timbuktu	Tombuctú, Timbuctú
Tokyo	Tokio
Tripoli	Trípoli
Tunis	Túnez
Valencia	Valencia
Venice	Venecia

Versailles	Versalles
Warsaw	Varsovia
Washington	Washington

inhabitants

Athenian	ateniense *aj, nmf*
Berliner	berlinés, -esa *nmf*
Cantonese	cantonés, -esa *aj, nmf*
Cordovan	cordobés, -esa *aj, nmf*
Dubliner	dublinés, -esa *nmf*
Florentine	florentino, -a *nmf*
Genevan	ginebrino, -a, ginebrés, -esa *nmf*
Genoese	genovés, -esa *aj, nmf*
Havanan	habanero, -a *nmf*
Londoner	londinense *nmf*
Madrilenian	madrileño, -a *nmf*
Muscovite	moscovita *nmf*
Neapolitan	napolitano, -a *nmf*
New Yorker	neoyorquino, -a *nmf*
Parisian	parisiense *nmf*
Roman	romano, -a *nmf*
Tangerine	tangerino, -a *aj, nmf*
Venetian	veneciano, -a *aj, nmf*

GEOGRAPHICAL REGIONS OF THE WORLD

names

America	América
Asia Minor	Asia Menor
Australasia	Austrolasia
Balkans	Balcanes *nmpl*
Central America	Centroamérica
Eurasia	Eurasia
Hispano-America	Hispanoamérica *nf*
Latin America	Latinoamérica
Occident	Occidente *nm*
Oceania	Oceanía
Orient	Oriente *nm*
Scandinavia	Escandinavia

inhabitants

American	americano, -a *aj, nmf*
Australasian	australasiático, -a *aj, nmf*
Balkan	balcánico, -a *aj, nmf*
Central American	centroamericano, -a *aj, nmf*
Eurasian	eurasiático, -a *aj, nmf*
Latin-American, Latino	latinoamericano, -a *aj, nmf*

Occidental	occidental *aj, nmf*
Oriental	oriental *aj, nmf*
Scandinavian	escandinavo, -a *aj, nmf*

PARTS OF COUNTRIES

names

Alsace	Alsacia
Andalusia	Andalucía
Appalachia *nsg*	los Apalaches *nmpl*
Aragon	Aragón
Arcadia	Arcadia
Balkans	Balcanes
Barbary	Berbería
Bavaria	Baviera
Benelux	Benelux
Bengal	Bengala
Bohemia	Bohemia
Brittany	Bretaña
Burgandy	Borgoña
Castile	Castilla
Catalonia	Cataluña
Caucasus	Cáucaso
Cornwall	Cornualles
Dalmatia	Dalmacia
Flanders	Flandes
Galicia	Galicia
Galilee	Galilea
Gascony	Gascuña
Gaza Strip	franja de Gaza *nf*
Hindustan	Indostán
Kashmir	Cachemira
Lapland	Laponia
Levant	Levante
Lombardy	Lombardía
Macedonia	Macedonia
Manchuria	Manchuria
Moldavia, Moldava	Moldavia, Moldava
Mongolia	Mongolia
Moravia	Moravia
Normandy	Normandía
North Korea	Corea del Norte
Palestine	Palestina
Provence	Provenza
Prussia	Prusia
Punjab	Pendjab
Quebec	Quebec
Saar	Sarre
Savoy	Saboya
Saxony	Sajonia

Scotland	Escocia
Siberia	Siberia
Slovenia	Eslovenia
Tibet	Tibet
Transylvania	Transilvania
Tuscany	Toscana
Tyrol, Tirol	Tirol
Wales	Gales

inhabitants

Alsatian	alsaciano, -a *aj, nmf*
Andalusian	andaluz(a) *aj, nmf*
Arcadian	árcade, arcadio, -a *aj, nmf*
Balkan	balcánico, -a *aj, nmf*
Bavarian	bávaro, -a *aj, nmf*
Bengali, Bengalese	bengalí *aj, nmf*
Bohemian	bohemio, -a *aj, nmf*
Breton	bretón, -a *nmf*
Burgundian	borgoñón, -ona *aj, nmf*
Castilian	castellano, -a *aj, nmf*
Catalan, Catalonian	catalán, -lana *aj, nmf*
Caucasian	caucásico, -a *aj, nmf*
Dalmatian	dálmata *aj, nmf*
French-Canadian	francocanadiense *aj, nmf*
Galician	gallego, -a *aj, nmf*
Gascon	gascón, -ona *aj, nmf*
Hindustani	indostanés, -esa, indostano, -a *aj, nmf*
Lapp, Laplander	lapón, -ona *nmf*
Manchu	manchú, manchuriano, -a *aj, nmf*
Moldavian	moldavo, -a *aj, nmf*
Mongol, Mongolian	mongol *aj, nmf*
Moravian	moravo, -a *aj, nmf*
Norman	normando, -a *aj, nmf*
North Korean	norcoreano, -a *aj, nmf*
Palestinian	palestino, -a *aj, nmf*
Provençal	provenzal *aj, nmf*
Prussian	prusiano, -a *aj, nmf*
Punjabi	penjabo, -a *nmf*
Savoyard	saboyano, -a *aj, nmf*
Saxon	sajón, -ona *aj, nmf*
Scotsman	escosés *nm*
Scotswoman	escosesa *nf*
Siberian	siberiano, -a *aj, nmf*
Slovene, Slovenian	esloveno, -a *aj, nmf*

Tibetan	tibetano, -a *aj, nmf*	Missouri	Misuri
Transylvanian	transilvano, -a *aj, nmf*	New Hampshire	Nueva Hampshire
Tuscan	tuscano, -a *aj, nmf*	New Jersey	Nueva Jersey
Tyrolean	tirolés, -esa *aj, nmf*	New Mexico	Nuevo México
		Pennsylvania	Pensilvania
		Texas	Tejas

U.S. STATES

names

inhabitants

Hawaii	Hawai
Louisiana	Luisiana

Floridian	floridense *aj, nmf*
Hawaiian	hawaiano, -a *aj, nmf*
Texan	tejano, -a *aj, nmf*

Common False Cognates

False cognates, sometimes called "false friends," are words that appear quite similar in English and Spanish but do not have the same meanings. The classic example is *embarazada*, meaning "pregnant" rather than "embarrassed." This list contains the most common false cognates along with a few semi-false cognates—words that sometimes have the same significance but that often have a distinct meaning.

Spanish	Correct Meaning in English	Not to Be Confused with English	Spanish
actual	current	actual	real, verdadero
actualidad	present time	actuality	la realidad
actualmente	currently	actually	realmente, verdaderamente, en realidad
advertencia	warning	advertisement	el anuncio
agenda	a day-planner, personal organizer	agenda	el orden del día
agresivo	physically aggressive	aggressive (go-getter)	audaz, dinámico
aplicación	appliqué	application	la solicitud
aplicar	to apply oneself or to apply something	to apply (for a position)	llenar una solicitúd
apología	eulogy	apology	la disculpa
arena	sand	arena	el gimnasio, el auditorio
argumento	defense of an idea	argument	la discusión, la disputa
armada	navy	army	el ejército
asignatura	school course	signature	la firma
asistencia	attendance	assistance	la ayuda
asistir	to attend	to assist	ayudar
atender	to serve, to pay attention, to attend to (someone)	to attend (to be present)	asistir
aviso	warning, notice	advice	los consejos
bachillerato	high school diploma	bachelor's degree	la licenciatura
basamento	base of a column (architecture)	basement	el sótano
billón	trillion	billion	mil millones
bizarro	gallant, brave, valiant	bizarre	raro, excéntrico
boda	wedding	body	el cuerpo
bordar	to embroider	to board	abordar
calificación	grade (in school)	qualification	la habilidad
campo	field; country, countryside	camp	el campamento
carpeta	file folder, notebook	carpet	la alfombra
carta	letter	cart	la carreta
chocar	to crash	to choke	ahogarse, atragantarse, estrangular
colegio	school	college	la universidad
collar	necklace	collar (of a garment)	el cuello
colorado	red, reddish	colored	colorido
comodidad	comfort	comodity	producto, mercancía, artículo

Spanish	Correct Meaning in English	Not to Be Confused with English	Spanish
complexión	physiological build	complexion	**la tez**
comprometerse	to commit, to promise, to obligate oneself	to compromise (to come to an agreement)	**ponerse de acuerdo**
compromiso	commitment, promise, obligation	compromise (agreement)	**el acuerdo**
conducir	to drive	to conduct	**dirigir**
conductor	driver	conductor	**el/la director,-a**
confidencia	shared secret	confidence (emotional state)	**la confianza**
consistente	thick (liquid)	consistent	**constante**
constipación	cold (disease)	constipation	**el estreñimiento**
constiparse	to have a cold	to be constipated	**estreñirse**
contestar	to answer	to contest	**reclamar, contender**
copa	trophy; wine glass	cup	**la taza**
copia	copy (imitation, reproduction, photocopy)	copy (of a book, magazine, etc.)	**el ejemplar**
coraje	anger	courage	**el valor**
corresponder	to correspond (to match)	to correspond (to write)	**escribir**
correspondiente	corresponding, respective	correspondent (journalist, reporter)	**el/la corresponsal**
cuestión	matter	question	**la pregunta**
culto	religious service; cultured	cult	**la secta**
damnificado	injured, wounded	damned (condemned)	**condenado**
dato	piece of information	date	**la fecha**
decepción	disappointment	deception	**el engaño**
decepcionar	to disappoint	to deceive	**engañar**
defraudar	to disappoint	to defraud	**cometer fraude**
delito	crime	delight	**la delicia**
demandar	to sue	to demand	**exigir**
desgracia	mishap	disgrace	**la deshonra, la vergüenza**
desmayo	fainting	dismay; to dismay	**la consternación; consternar**
despertar(se)	to wake up	desperate	**desesperado**
destituido	removed from office	destitute	**desamparado, indigente**
dirección	address; but may be direction	direction	**la direction, el rumbo**
discusión	argument	discussion	**la plática, la conversación**
discutir	to argue	to discuss	**platicar, conversar**
disgustar	to bother	to disgust	**repugnar**
disgusto	unpleasantness	(to be) disgusted	**(tener) asco, (sentir) repugnancia**
editar	to publish	to edit	**redactar**
editor	publisher	editor	**el/la redactor,-a**
embarazada	pregnant	(to be or feel) embarrassed	**(tener) vergüenza, (dar) pena, (sentir) avergonzado**
embarazar	to impregnate	to embarrass	**avergonzar**
emocionante	exciting	emotional	**conmovido** (*emotionally moved*); **conmovedor** (*emotionally moving*)
emocionarse	to become excited	to become emotional	**conmoverse**
en absoluto	absolutely not	absolutely	**completamente, totalmente**

Spanish	Correct Meaning in English	Not to Be Confused with English	Spanish
excitado	sexually excited	excited	**emocionado**
excitarse	to become sexually excited	to become excited	**emocionarse**
éxito	success	exit	**la salida**
experimentar	to experience	to experiment	**hacer una prueba**
fábrica	factory	fabric	**la tela**
factoría	merchant trading post	factory	**la fábrica**
facultad	(university) department or school	faculty	**profesorado**
familiar	pertaining to family	familiar	**conocido**
fastidioso	annoying	fastidious	**quisquilloso**
fracaso	failure	fracas	**el pleito**
fútbol	soccer	football	**el fútbol americano**
fútil	insignificant, trivial	futile	**inútil**
gala	charm, elegance	gala	**la fiesta, la fiesta de gala**
ganga	bargain	gang	**la pandilla**
genial	brilliant	genial	**cordial**
gracioso	funny	gracious	**gentil, cortés, misericordioso**
guerrilla	guerrilla war	guerrilla	**el guerrillero**
idioma	language	idiom	**el modismo**
ilusión	a hope or dream longed for	illusion	**(algo) irreal**
ingenuidad	naïvete, ingenuousness	ingenuity	**la ingeniosidad**
injuria	insult	injury	**la herida**
injuriar	to insult	to injure	**herir, lastimarse**
intentar	to try	to intend	**tener el propósito de; proponerse**
intoxicado	poisoned	intoxicated	**el borracho**
intoxicar	to poison	to intoxicate	**emborrachar**
introducir	to introduce (something new)	to introduce (person)	**presentar**
jubilación	retirement	jubilation	**el júbilo**
jubilado	retired	jubilant	**jubiloso**
jubilarse	to retire	to be jubilant	**estar jubiloso; estar lleno de júbilo**
largo	long	large	**grande**
lectura	reading	lecture	**el discurso**
librería	bookstore	library	**la biblioteca**
librero	bookcase	librarian	**el/la bibliotecario,-a**
lujuria	lust	luxury	**el lujo**
marrón	dark brown	maroon	**rojo oscuro**
minorista	retail; retailer	minority	**la minoría**
miseria	a small amount	misery	**el sufrimiento, el dolor, la tristeza**
molestar	to bother	to molest (sexually)	**molestar sexualmente**
muslo	thigh	muscle	**el músculo**
nombre	name	number	**el número**
notorio	noticeable	notorious	**de mala reputación**
once	eleven	once	**una vez**
oscuro	dark	obscure	**vago, desconocido**
pariente	family member	parent	**el padre** (*father*); **la madre** (*mother*); **los padres** (*parents*)
patrón	boss; pattern	patron	**el/la cliente,-a**

Spanish	Correct Meaning in English	Not to Be Confused with English	Spanish
pretender	to try	to pretend	**fingir, simular**
prevenir	to foresee; to forewarn	to prevent	**evitar, impedir**
quieto	calm, without movement	quiet	**callado**
quitar	to remove	to quit	**renunciar**
raro	strange	rare	**poco común**
realización	realization (of a plan, dream, etc.)	realization (of a fact or idea), understanding	**el hecho de darse cuenta; comprensión**
realizar(se)	to make real, to accomplish; to become real or completed	to realize (a fact or idea), to come to an understanding	**darse cuenta**
recolección	collection (drive to raise funds or collect goods or materials)	recollection	**el recuerdo**
recordar	to remember; to remind	to record	**grabar**
refrán	proverb, saying	refrain	**el estribillo**
reino	kingdom	reign	**el reinado**
relativo	relative (adjective)	relative (family relation)	**el/la pariente,-a**
relevancia	importance	relevance	**la conexión, la aplicabilidad**
relevante	important	(to be) relevant	**tener que ver**
remover	to stir, move or turn over (while resting or sitting, for example)	to remove	**quitar**
rentable	profitable	rentable	**alquilable, arrendable**
resumir	to sum up	to resume	**empezar de nuevo**
revolver	to revolve; to stir	revolver	**el revólver**
ropa	clothing	rope	**la cuerda**
sano	healthy	sane	**en su juicio, en sus cinco sentidos**
sensible	sensitive	sensible	**sensato, razonable**
sensiblemente	perceptibly	sensibly	**sensatamente**
simpático	nice, kind	sympathetic	**compasivo**
simple	foolish, but may at times be used for simple	simple	**sencillo**
sobre	over; envelope	sober	**sobrio**
sopa	soup	soap	**el jabón**
soportar	to tolerate, to put up with	to support	**sostener**
suceso	event, occurrence	success	**el éxito**
suplir	to substitute	to supply	**suministrar**
tabla	plank	table	**la mesa**
tuna	cactus fruit	tuna	**el atún**
último	last, final	ultimate	**lo máximo**
vaso	glass (for drinking)	vase	**el florero**
verso	verse (type of writing)	verse of scripture or of music	**el versículo** (*of scripture*); **la estrofa** (*of a song*)
vicioso	addicted to vice	vicious	**malvado, bravo**
violador	rapist	violator	**el/la delincuente**
violar	to violate, but also means to rape	to violate	**infringir**

Dictionary of Spanish Roots

This dictionary contains over 14,000 words, organized into more than 2,000 word families based on similar origins. The most commonly used word in a grouping—the headword—is listed alphabetically and appears at the top of the group. Beneath this headword, the related words are listed according to part of speech. Verbs are listed first, followed by nouns, pronouns, adverbs, and adjectives. Entries are cross-referenced to both the Guide to Spanish Suffixes [-suffix] and Spanish Frequency Table [number] where applicable. (Note that there are many entries in this Root Dictionary that contain suffixes described in the Guide to Spanish Suffixes, but cross-references are only included to terms that appear as examples in that section.) For further explanation on the formation and use of this dictionary, please consult the Introduction.

A

abandonar to abandon
abandonar *vt* [859] to abandon
abandono *nm* [-o(1) 3940] abandonment
abandonado *aj* abandoned

abatir to cause suffering; to discourage
abatir *vt* [3013] to cause suffering; to discourage
abatirse *vr* [3013] to suffer a loss; to become discouraged
abatimiento *nm* suffering; discouragement
abatido *aj* suffering; discouraged; demolished

abeja bee
abejón *nm* large bee
abejorreo *nm* buzzing sound made by a bee
abejorro *nm* bumblebee
abeja *nf* [4184] bee

abismo abyss
abismar *vt* to put something in the abyss; to disparage
abismo *nm* abyss
abismal *aj* abysmal

abogado lawyer, advocate
abogar *vi* to defend; to be an advocate for
abogado *nmf* [-ado(2)] lawyer, advocate
abogacía *nf* advocacy; profession of a lawyer

abono payment of an installment
abonador *nmf* person who makes a payment
abono *nm* payment of an installment
abonado *aj* paid
abonador *aj* paying

abordar to board
abordar *vt* [1593] to board
transbordar *vt* to change planes, trains, ships, etc. while on a trip
abordaje *nm* boarding passengers
bordo *nm* [1386] an exterior side of a ship
transbordo, trasbordo *nm* the act of changing planes, trains, etc. while on a trip

aborrecer to hate, to abhor
aborrecer *vt* to hate, to abhor
aborrecimiento *nm* hatred
aborrecible *aj* [-ible] detestable

abrigo overcoat
abrigar *vt* to cover with thick clothing; to protect
desabrigar *vt* to uncover; to expose to the elements
desabrigarse *vr* to uncover oneself
abrigo *nm* [-o(1)] overcoat; shelter, protection
desabrigo *nm* lack of protection
abrigado *aj* covered or protected by a coat or blanket
desabrigado *aj* uncovered or unprotected by a coat or blanket; unprotected

abrir to open
abrir *vt* [266] to open
abrirse *vr* to be opened, to come open
entreabrir *vt* to open partially
reabrir *vt* to reopen
reabrirse *vr* to be reopened
abrecartas *nm* letter opener
abrelatas *nm* can opener
abertura *nf* [-ura(2)] opening

abierto *aj* open
entreabierto *aj* partially open

abrumado overwhelmed
abrumar *vt* to overwhelm
abrumarse *vr* to be overwhelmed
abrumado *aj* overwhelmed
abrumador *aj* overwhelming

absoluto absolute
absolutista *nmf* absolutist
absolutismo *nm* absolutism
absolutamente *av* [-mente 3814] absolutely
absoluto *aj* [-uto 2364] absolute

abstenerse to abstain
abstenerse *vr* to abstain
abstencionista *nmf* one who abstains from voting
abstemio,-a *nmf* teetotaler
abstencionismo *nm* abstention from voting
abstención *nf* abstention
abstinencia *nf* [-encia] abstinence
abstemio *aj* abstaining

abstracto abstract
abstraer *vt* to abstract
abstracción *nf* abstraction
abstracto *aj* abstract

absurdo absurd
absurdo *nm* [3763] nonsense
absurdidad *nf* [-idad] absurdity
absurdo *aj* [3763] absurd

abuelo grandfather
tatarabuelo *nm* great-great-grandfather
tatarabuela *nf* great-great-grandmother
abuelo *nm* grandfather
bisabuelo *nm* great-grandfather
abuela *nf* grandmother
bisabuela *nf* great-grandmother

abundante abundant
abundar *vi* [2574] to abound
sobreabundar *vi* to abound greatly
abundancia *nf* [-ancia] abundance
sobreabundancia *nf* overabundance
abundante *aj* [-ante(1) 4105] abundant
superabundante *aj* very abundant

aburrido boring
aburrir *vt* [4278] to bore
aburrirse *vr* [4278] to be bored, to become bored
aburrimiento *nm* boredom
aburrido *aj* bored

abuso abuse
abusar *vi* [3273] to abuse
abusón,-a *nmf* abuser
abuso *nm* [-o(1) 1821] abuse

abusivo *aj* [-ivo] abusive
abusón *aj* [-ón(2)] abusing

acabar to finish; to exhaust
acabar *vti* [714] to finish; to exhaust
acabarse *vr* [714] to be finished; to be exhausted
acabado *aj* finished; exhausted
inacabable *aj* unending; inexhaustible

academia academy
academia *nf* [1530] academy
académico *aj* [-ico(2) 1848] academic

accidente accident
accidentar *vt* to cause an accident
accidentarse *vr* to have an accident
accidentado,-a *nmf* person involved in an accident
accidente *nm* [773] accident
accidentado *aj* involved in an accident
accidental *aj* accidental

acción action
accionar *vti* to take action
coaccionar *vt* to coerce, to force
reaccionar *vi* [2689] to react
accionista *nmf* shareholder; participant in an enterprise
reaccionario,-a *nmf* reactionary
acción *nf* [-ción 188] action; share of company stock
coacción *nf* coercion
interacción *nf* interaction
reacción *nf* [1873] reaction
retroacción *nf* retroactive action
transacción *nf* [3823] transaction
coactivo *aj* coerced, forced
reaccionario *aj* reactionary
retroactivo *aj* retroactive

aceite oil
aceitar *vt* to oil
enaceitar *vt* to oil; to get oil on
aceitero,-a *nmf* oil merchant
aceite *nm* [1522] oil
aceitera *nf* oil container
aceitero *aj* pertaining to oil
aceitoso *aj* oily

aceituna olive
aceitunero,-a *nmf* olive merchant or grower
aceituno *nm* olive tree
aceituna *nf* olive
aceitunado *aj* olive-colored
aceitunero *aj* pertaining to olives

acelerado accelerated
acelerar *vti* to accelerate
acelerarse *vr* to hurry up (oneself)
desacelerar *vi* to decelerate, to slow down

adaptar

acelerador *nm* accelerator pedal
acelerón *nm* [-ón(1)] quick, sudden acceleration
aceleración *nf* acceleration
desaceleración *nf* [-ción 4520] deceleration
acelerada *nf* acceleration
acelerado *aj* accelerated

acento accent
acentuar *vt* [4972] to accentuate; to accent
acentuarse *vr* to be accentuated; to be accented
acento *nm* accent
acentuación *nf* accentuation
acentuado *aj* accentuated; accented

aceptar to accept
aceptar *vt* [429] to accept
aceptabilidad *nf* acceptability
aceptación *nf* [-ción 3023] acceptance
aceptable *aj* [-able 4780] acceptable
inaceptable *aj* unacceptable

acercar to move close; to draw nearer
acercar *vt* [1513] to move close; to draw nearer
acercarse *vr* [1513] to move closer; to draw nearer
acercamiento *nm* [-miento 3412] photographic or television close-up; act of moving closer
acerca de *av* about

acero steel
acerar *vt* to put steel on something
acero *nm* [3713] steel
acerería *nf* steelwork
acerado *aj* covered with steel

acompañar to accompany
acompañar *vt* [315] to accompany
acompañarse *vr* to accompany each other
acompañante *nmf* [-ante(2) 4486] escort; companion
compañero,-a *nmf* [624] companion; classmate; co-worker
acompañamiento *nm* accompaniment
compañerismo *nm* relationship between or among companions
compañía *nf* [532] company
acompañado *aj* accompanied; escorted
acompañante *aj* [-ante(2) 4486] accompanying
desacompañado *aj* unaccompanied

acordar to make a deal; to come to an accord
acordar *vt* [1355] to make a deal; to come to an accord
acordarse *vr* [1355] to remember
acorde *nm* [4371] chord
acuerdo *nm* [-o(1) 167] agreement
desacuerdo *nm* disagreement
acordado *aj* agreed-upon

acorde *aj* [4371] in-tune
desacorde *aj* discordant; out-of-tune

acto act
activar *vt* [4406] to activate
actuar *vt* [650] to act
desactivar *vt* to deactivate
reactivar *vt* [3573] to reactivate
activista *nmf* [3251] activist
activismo *nm* activism
acto *nm* [700] act
actor *nm* [-or 401] actor
entreacto *nm* intermission
reactivo *nm* reactive chemical
reactor *nm* reactor
activación *nf* activation
actividad *nf* [-idad 260] activity
actriz *nf* [-triz 620] actress
actuación *nf* [-ción 808] performance
inactividad *nf* inactivity
radioactividad *nf* radioactivity
activo *aj* [-ivo 1806] active
inactivo *aj* inactive
radioactivo *aj* radioactive
reactivo *aj* reactive

actual current; up-to-date
actualizar *vt* [-izar 3167] to make current; to bring up-to-date
actualidad *nf* [-idad 1334] present time
actualización *nf* [-ción 3692] modernization
actualmente *av* [-mente 536] currently; nowadays
actual *aj* [430] current; up-to-date

acumular to accumulate
acumular *vt* [1616] to accumulate
acumularse *vr* to be accumulated
acumulador *nm* car battery
cúmulo *nm* pile, group; cumulus cloud
acumulación *nf* accumulation
acumulable *aj* able to be accumulated
acumulador *aj* accumulative

acusar to accuse
acusar *vt* [779] to accuse
acusado,-a *nmf* accused
acusador,-a *nmf* accuser
acusativo *nm* accusative, in grammar
acusación *nf* [-ción 1852] accusation
acusado *aj* accused
acusador *aj* accusing
acusatorio *aj* [-orio(2)] accusatory

adaptar to adapt
adaptar *vt* [2828] to adapt
adaptarse *vr* [2828] to become adapted to
readaptar *vt* to adapt again
readaptarse *vr* to become adapted again to

adaptador *nm* adapter
adaptación *nf* [-ción 4106] adaptation
readaptación *nf* [-ción 4687] the act of adapting to a situation or circumstance again
adaptable *aj* adaptable
adaptado *aj* adapted
inadaptable *aj* not adaptable
inadaptado *aj* not adapted
adecuado adequate
adecuar *vt* [960] to arrange or to adapt for a purpose
adecuarse *vr* to adapt oneself
adecuación *nf* adaptation
adecuado *aj* adequate
inadecuado *aj* [-ado(1) 4720] inadequate
adelante ahead
adelantar *vt* [590] to move forward; to go in
adelantarse *vr* to move oneself forward; to go ahead
adelantamiento *nm* moving forward; progress
adelanto *nm* progress; advancement
delantal *nm* apron
delantero *nm* [-ero(2) 1235] forward person (soccer, etc.)
delantera *nf* front bumper; forward position (soccer, etc.)
adelante *int* come in!
adelante *av* ahead
delante de *av* in front of
adelantado *aj* fast (clock); advanced; ahead of
delantero *aj* [-ero(2) 1235] pertaining to the forward position (soccer, etc.)
adhesión adhesion
adherir *vi* [4487] to adhere
adherirse *vr* to be adhering to; to be stuck to
adhesivo *nm* adhesive
adherencia *nf* adherence
adhesión *nf* adhesion
adherente *aj* adhesive
adhesivo *aj* adhesive
antiadherente *aj* not adhesive
autoadhesivo *aj* self-adhesive
adivinar to guess
adivinar *vt* to guess
adivinador,-a *nmf* fortune teller
adivino,-a *nmf* fortune teller
adivinación *nf* guess; fortune telling
adivinanza *nf* [-anza] riddle
adivinado *aj* guessed; solved
admitir to admit
admitir *vt* [1518] to admit
readmitir *vt* to readmit
admisibilidad *nf* admissibility

admisión *nf* admission
readmisión *nf* readmission
inadmisible *aj* inadmissible
admitido *aj* admitted
adolescencia adolescence
adolescente *nmf* [-ente(2) 1853] adolescent
adolescencia *nf* adolescence
adolescente *aj* [-ente(2) 1853] adolescent
adoptar to adopt
adoptar *vt* [1769] to adopt
adopción *nf* adoption
adoptivo *aj* adoptive
adorar to adore
adorar *vt* [4690] to worship; to adore
adorador,-a *nmf* worshiper
adoración *nf* [-ción] adoration
adorable *aj* [-able] adorable
adorado *aj* adored
adorador *aj* adoring
adorno ornament; decoration
adornar *vt* [3206] to decorate; to adorn; to beautify
ornamentar *vt* to decorate; to adorn; to beautify
adornamiento *nm* adornment; decoration
adorno *nm* [-o(1) 4576] ornament; decoration
ornamento *nm* ornament
ornato *nm* ornament
ornamentación *nf* ornamentation
adornado *aj* adorned; decorated; made beautiful
ornamental *aj* [-al(2)] ornamental
adquirido acquired
adquirir *vt* [892] to acquire
adquisición *nf* [-ción 3040] acquisition
adquirido *aj* acquired
advertir to warn; to notice
advertir *vt* to warn; to notice
advertencia *nf* warning
inadvertencia *nf* inadvertence; lack of warning
advertido *aj* warned
inadvertido *aj* inadvertent; without warning
aéreo aero
aéreo *aj* [-eo(2) 1824] aero
aerobio *aj* aerobic
aerodinámico *aj* aerodynamic
aeromodelista *aj* pertaining to airplane modeling
aeronáutico *aj* aeronautic
aeronaval *aj* air-naval
aerostático *aj* blimp, dirigible
anaerobio *aj* anaerobic
antiaéreo *aj* anti-aircraft
aerodinámica *nf* aerodynamics

aerograma *nf* aerogram
aerolínea *nf* [4133] airline
aeromoza *nf* flight attendant
aeronáutica *nf* aeronautics
aeronave *nf* [4882] airship
aerostática *nf* balloon or blimp flying
aeroclub *nm* airplane flying club
aerodeslizador *nm* hovercraft
aeródromo *nm* aerodrome
aerofaro *nm* airplane signal or warning tower
aerógrafo *nm* airbrush
aeromodelismo *nm* airplane modeling
aeromodelo *nm* airplane model
aeroplano *nm* airplane
aeropuerto *nm* [1163] airport
aerosol *nm* aerosol
aerostato *nm* blimp, dirigible
anaerobio *nm* anaerobic organism
aeromodelista *nmf* airplane model builder
aerobics *nmpl* aerobics, aerobic exercise

afán effort
afanarse *vr* to work hard; to work with effort
afanador,-a *nmf* hard-worker; cleaning person
afán *nm* [3892] effort
afanador *aj* hardworking
afanoso *aj* hardworking

afecto affection
afecto *nm* [3701] affection
desafecto *nm* lack of affection
afección *nf* affection
afecto *aj* [3701] inclined; with a fondness for
afectuoso *aj* affectionate
desafecto *aj* lacking affection, not affectionate

afeitar to shave
afeitar *vt* to shave
afeitarse *vr* to shave oneself
afeitado *nm* shaving
afeitadora *nf* electric shaver
afeitado *aj* shaved

afición fondness
aficionarse *vr* to become fond of
aficionado,-a *nmf* fan
radioaficionado,-a *nmf* fan of radio
afición *nf* [-ción 2279] fondness
aficionado *aj* [-ado(2) 1139] fond of; interested in

afirmar to affirm
afirmar *vt* [337] to affirm
reafirmar *vt* [4253] to reaffirm
afirmación *nf* [-ción 4346] affirmation
afirmativa *nf* affirmative
reafirmación *nf* reaffirmation
afirmativo *aj* affirmative

agarrar to grab; to grasp
agarrar *vt* [3804] to grab; to grasp
agarrarse *vr* to grab hold of; to take hold of
desgarrar *vt* to tear (clothes)
agarrador *nm* potholder
agarrón *nm* fight
desgarro *nm* cut, scratch, wound
desgarrón *nm* violent tearing of clothing
garras *nfpl* claws
agarradera *nf* handle
garra *nf* claw
agarrador *aj* grasping
desgarrado *aj* torn
desgarrador *aj* tearing; clawing

agente agent
agenciar *vt* to procure for someone else
agente *nmf* [-ente(?) 389] agent
agencia *nf* [-encia 850] agency

agitar to shake; to stir; to agitate
agitar *vt* [4864] to shake; to stir; to agitate
agitarse *vr* to be shaken up; to be agitated
agitador,-a *nmf* agitator
agitación *nf* agitation
agitado *aj* agitated

aglomeración accumulation
aglomerarse *vr* to come together; to accumulate
aglomerado *nm* pressed material, particle board
aglomerante *nm* material that hardens (cement, resin, plaster, etc.)
aglomeración *nf* accumulation
aglomerante *aj* hardening

agotar to tire; to exhaust; to run out
agotar *vt* [2895] to tire; to exhaust; to run out
agotarse *vr* [2895] to become tired; to be exhausted; to be out of
agotamiento *nm* tiring; exhaustion; running out of
agotado *aj* tired, exhausted; unavailable
agotador *aj* tiring, exhausting
inagotable *aj* inexhaustible

agregar to add
agregar *vt* [256] to add
agregarse *vr* to join; to be added to
disgregar *vt* to take away; to separate
agregación *nf* aggregation; aggregate
disgregación *nf* separation
agregado *aj* added

agrícola agricultural
agricultor,-a *nmf* [2751] farmer
agro *nm* fertile field
agricultura *nf* [1916] agriculture
agronomía *nf* agronomy
agrario *aj* [1922] agrarian

agrícola *aj* [1435] agricultural
agrónomo *aj* agronomic; farming
agropecuario *aj* [1315] having to do with
agriculture and animal farming

agua water
aguar *vt* to water down
aguarse *vr* (figurative) to throw a wet blanket
on a party, etc.; to become inundated with
water
desaguar *vt* to remove water; to drain
acuarelista *nmf* [-ista] watercolor painter
aguador,-a *nmf* water boy, water girl
aguafiestas *nmf* party pooper; wet blanket
acuario *nm* [3956] aquarium
acueducto *nm* aqueduct
agua *nm* [127] water
aguacero *nm* downpour
aguamiel *nm* mixture of honey and water
aguazal *nm* flooded land
desagüe *nm* draining or removal of water
paraguas *nm* umbrella
paragüero *nm* [-ero(1)] umbrella stand
acuarela *nf* watercolor
acuosidad *nf* wateriness
aguamarina *nf* aquamarine
aguanieve *nf* sleet
acuático *aj* aquatic
acuoso *aj* watery
aguado *aj* flexible; easily bent; overly stretched;
watery

aguantar to tolerate; to put up with
aguantar *vt* [3358] to tolerate; to put up with
aguantarse *vr* [3358] to be able to stand (tolerate)
aguante *nm* tolerance
aguantable *aj* tolerable
inaguantable *aj* intolerable

agudo pointed; sharp
agudizar *vt* to intensify
agudizarse *vr* to become sharpened (senses)
aguijonear *vt* to sting; to prick with a thorn or
other sharp object
agujerar, agujerear *vt* to make holes in
something; to perforate
aguzar *vt* to sharpen; to stimulate
agujetero,-a *nmf* needle maker or seller
aguijón *nm* [-ón(1)] stinger; thorn
agujero *nm* [5000] hole; pincushion
agujetero *nm* pincushion
agudeza *nf* sharpness
aguja *nf* needle
agujeta *nf* shoestring
agudo *aj* [4150] pointed; sharp
agujereado *aj* perforated

águila eagle
aguilucho *nm* eaglet
águila *nf* [2167] eagle
aguileño *aj* with an eagle-like nose

ahogo drowning
ahogar *vt* [4661] to drown
desahogar *vt* to relieve
desahogarse *vr* to be relieved
ahogado *nmf* drowning victim
ahogo *nm* drowning
desahogo *nm* relief
ahogado *aj* drowned
desahogado *aj* relieved; less busy

ahorrar to save
ahorrar *vt* [3293] to save
ahorrarse *vr* to save for oneself (money, time,
effort, etc.)
ahorrador,-a *nmf* saver, person who likes to
save, thrifty person
ahorro *nm* [-o(1) 1987] savings
ahorrador *aj* saving; thrifty
ahorrativo *aj* saving; thrifty

aire air; wind
airearse *vr* to air out
aires *nmpl* airs (of pretension)
aire *nm* [866] air; wind
aireado *aj* ventilated; aired out
airoso *aj* windy; putting on airs

ajustar to adjust
ajustar *vt* [2693] to adjust
ajustarse *vr* [2693] to become adjusted to
desajustar *vt* to put out of adjustment
desajustarse *vr* to be out of adjustment
reajustar *vt* to readjust
ajuste *nm* [2468] adjustment
desajuste *nm* lack of adjustment
reajuste *nm* readjustment
ajustado *aj* tight-fitting, exact-fitting; adjusted
ajustador *aj* adjusting

ala wing
aletear *vi* to flap wings
aleteo *nm* flapping
ala *nf* [3536] wing
aleta *nf* [-eta] fin
alado *aj* winged

alabar to praise
alabar *vt* to praise
alabanza *nf* [-anza] praise

alameda park with trees
álamo *nm* poplar tree
alameda *nf* [-eda] park with trees

alarma alarm
  alarmar *vt* to alarm
  alarmarse *vr* to be alarmed
  alarmista *nmf* alarmist
  alarma *nf* [-a 4237] alarm
  alarmado *aj* alarmed
  alarmante *aj* [-ante(1) 4901] alarming

alba dawn
  alborear *vi* to dawn
  albino,-a *nmf* albino
  albinismo *nm* albinism
  albor *nm* brightness of the dawn
  alba *nf* dawn
  alborada *nf* first rays of sunlight in the
    morning
  albar *aj* white
  albero *aj* white
  albino *aj* albino
  albo *aj* white

alcalde mayor
  alcalde *nm* [578] mayor
  alcaldesa *nf* mayor (woman)
  alcaldía *nf* [-ería(2) 3553] city hall; office of mayor

alcanzar to reach
  alcanzar *vti* [439] to reach
  alcance *nm* [1959] reach
  alcanzable *aj* reachable
  inalcanzable *aj* unreachable

alcohol alcohol
  alcoholizar *vt* to add alcohol to; to spike with
    alcohol
  alcoholizarse *vr* to become drunk
  alcohólico *nmf* [-ico(2) 2856] alcoholic
  alcohol *nm* [1436] alcohol
  alcoholímetro *nm* alcohol-level measuring
    device
  alcoholismo *nm* alcoholism
  alcohómetro *nm* alcohol-level measuring device
  alcoholizado *aj* drunk; inebriated
  alcohólico *aj* [-ico(2) 2856] alcoholic
  antialcohólico *aj* favoring prohibition of alcohol

aldea small town
  aldeano,-a *nmf* person who lives in a small
    town
  aldea *nf* small town
  aldeano *aj* [-ano] small-town

alegría happiness
  alegrar *vt* to make happy
  alegrarse *vr* to be happy; to become happy
  alegrón *nm* great unexpected joy or happiness
  alegría *nf* [-ería(2) 1746] happiness
  alegre *aj* [2260] happy

alentar to encourage
  alentar *vt* [4372] to encourage
  alentarse *vr* to be encouraged
  desalentar *vt* to discourage
  desalentarse *vr* to be discouraged
  desaliento *nm* discouragement
  alentado *aj* encouraged
  alentador *aj* encouraging
  desalentador *aj* discouraging

alfiler pin
  alfiler *nm* pin
  alfilerazo *nm* poke with a pin
  alfiletero *nm* [-ero(1)] box of pins; pincushion

algún some
  algo *pron* [258] some
  alguien *pron* [981] someone
  alguno,-a *pron* something
  algo *av* [258] some; a little
  algún *aj* some

alianza alliance
  aliarse *vr* to ally oneself
  aliado,-a *nmf* ally
  alianza *nf* [-anza 1288] alliance
  aliado *aj* [-ado(2) 2985] allied

alimento food; nourishment
  alimentar *vt* [2168] to feed; to give nourishment
    (also figurative)
  alimentarse *vr* to eat; to nourish oneself (also
    figurative)
  sobrealimentar *vt* to overeat
  alimentador *nm* apparatus used for feeding
    material into a machine, feeder
  alimento *nm* [-o(1) 702] food; nourishment
  alimentación *nf* [-ción 1780] nourishment
  sobrealimentación *nf* overeating
  subalimentación *nf* malnutrition; eating an
    insufficient amount to maintain health
  alimentador *aj* feeding
  alimentario *aj* alimentary; pertaining to feeding
  alimenticio *aj* [-icio 3223] nutritive
  sobrealimentado *aj* overfed
  subalimentado *aj* underfed

alivio relief
  aliviar *vt* [2879] to relieve
  aliviarse *vr* [2879] to be relieved; to be cured
  alivio *nm* relief
  liviandad *nf* lightness (weight)
  aliviador *aj* relieving
  liviano *aj* light (weight)

alma soul
  desalmado,-a *nmf* cruel person; one who is said
    to be without a soul

alma *nf* [1341] soul
desalmado *aj* cruel; without a soul

almacén warehouse
almacenar *vt* [3318] to store
almacenista *nmf* warehouse worker
almacén *nm* warehouse
almacenaje *nm* [-aje(1)] warehousing
almacenamiento *nm* [-miento 4186] warehousing

almirante admiral
almirantazgo *nm* [-azgo] admiralty
almirante *nm* admiral
vicealmirante *nm* vice-admiral

almohadón large pillow
almohadillar *vt* to pad; to stuff with cotton or
  other material
almohadón *nm* large pillow
almohada *nf* pillow
almohadilla *nf* small pillow; cushion
almohadillado *aj* padded; stuffed with cotton or
  other material

almuerzo brunch
almorzar *vi* to eat brunch
almuerzo *nm* [-o(1)] brunch

alojamiento accommodations
alojar *vt* to host; to accommodate
alojarse *vr* to accommodate oneself; to stay
  overnight (at a house, in a hotel, etc.)
desalojar *vi* [4623] to vacate
alojamiento *nm* accommodations
desalojamiento *nm* vacating of a house;
  eviction

alquilar to rent
alquilar *vt* to rent
desalquilarse *vr* to be vacant
alquiler *nm* renter
desalquilado *aj* vacant

alrededor around
alrededores *nmpl* surroundings
alrededor *av* [542] around

alteración alteration
alterar *vt* [2400] to alter
alterarse *vr* [2400] to be altered
alternar *vti* [3231] to alternate
alternador *nm* alternator
alterabilidad *nf* alterability
alteración *nf* [-ción 3124] alteration
alternativa *nf* alternative
alterable *aj* alterable
alterado *aj* changed; altered; upset
alternante *aj* alternating
alternativo *aj* alternative
alterno *aj* alternate

inalterable *aj* unalterable
inalterado *aj* unaltered

alto tall
altibajos *nmpl* highs and lows
altavoz *nm* megaphone; loudspeaker
altímetro *nm* altimeter
altiplanicie *nm* plateau; high plain
altiplano *nm* plateau; high plain
altísimo *nm* the Most High; God
altoparlante *nm* loudspeaker
altanería *nf* arrogance
alteza *nf* highness; excellence; nobility
altisonancia *nf* pompousness, especially in one's
  use of language
altitud *nf* altitude
altivez *nf* arrogance
altiveza *nf* arrogance
altura *nf* [-ura(1) 1272] height
altamente *av* [-mente 3641] highly
altanero *aj* arrogant
altisonante *aj* pompous, especially in one's use
  of language
altivo *aj* arrogant
alto *aj* [233] tall; high

aludir to allude
aludir *vi* to allude
alusión *nf* allusion
aludido *aj* alluded
alusivo *aj* allusive

alumno student
alumno,-a *nmf* [728] student
alumnado *nm* student body

alzar to raise up; to elevate
alzar *vt* [1770] to raise up; to elevate
alzarse *vr* [1770] to rise or tower (buildings,
  mountains); to soar (airplanes, birds); to rise
  up in rebellion
realzar *vt* to elevate the quality; to enhance
alzacuello *nm* ecclesiastical collar
alzamiento *nm* raising; elevating
alza *nf* rise in price
alzada *nf* height of a horse
alzado *aj* conceited; proud

amanecer dawn
amanecer *vi* [4238] to dawn; to be doing
  something or to be somewhere at dawn
amanecer *nm* [4238] dawn

amar to love
amar *vt* [1216] to love
amarse *vr* to love each other
enamorar *vt* [2114] to cause to fall in love
enamorarse *vr* [2114] to fall in love
amado,-a *nmf* beloved

amante *nmf* [-ante(2) 2431] lover, often having a negative connotation
enamorado,-a *nmf* someone who is in love
amor *nm* [397] love
amorcillo *nm* [-illo(2)] cupid
amorío *nm* love affair
desamor *nm* lack of love
enamoramiento *nm* falling in love
amabilidad *nf* kindness
amable *aj* kind
amado *aj* loved, beloved
amante *aj* [-ante(2) 2431] loving
amoroso *aj* [-oso 3294] loving, full of love, tenderhearted
enamoradizo *aj* easily enamored
enamorado *aj* [-ado(2)] in love

amargo bitter
amargar *vt* to make bitter
amargarse *vr* to become bitter
amargado,-a *nmf* bitter person
amargura *nf* [-ura(1)] bitterness
amargado *aj* embittered
amargo *aj* [4674] bitter

amarillo yellow
amarillear *vi* to yellow
amarillista *nmf* journalist who sensationalizes the news; person who engages in yellow journalism
amarillismo *nm* yellow journalism
amarillo *nm* [1807] yellow
amarillez *nf* [ez] yellowness
amarillento *aj* [-iento] yellowish
amarillo *aj* [1807] yellow
amarilloso *aj* yellowish

ambición ambition
ambicionar *vt* to display or to pursue ambition
ambicioso,-a *nmf* ambitious person
ambición *nf* [-ción 4517] ambition
ambicioso *aj* [4453] ambitious

ambiente environment; ambience
ambientar *vt* to create an atmosphere
ambiente *nm* [823] environment; ambience
ámbito *nm* [1983] immediate surroundings or situations affecting someone
ambientación *nf* ambience of a scene created in stories, theater, television, etc.
ambientador *aj* creating an atmosphere (sometimes applied to air fresheners)
ambiental *aj* [2138] environmental

ambos both
ambos *pron* [515] both
ambidextro,-a *nmf* ambidextrous person
ambivalencia *nf* ambivalence

ambidextro *aj* ambidextrous
ambivalente *aj* ambivalent
ambos *aj* [515] both

ambulante able to move
deambular *vt* to wander without purpose or destination
ambulatorio *nm* dispensary
ambulancia *nf* [-ancia 4008] ambulance
ambulante *aj* [-ante(1) 1743] able to move
ambulatorio *aj* pertaining to an illness that does not cause the patient to be bedridden

amenazar to threaten
amenazar *vt* [1862] to threaten
amenaza *nf* [-a 1303] threat
amenazador *aj* threatening
amenazante *aj* threatening

amigo friend
amigacho,-a *nmf* good friend, informally used
amigo,-a *nmf* friend
amigote *nm* [-ote] great friend
amistad *nf* [-tad 753] friendship
amigable *aj* amicable
amigo *aj* [298] friendly
amiguero *aj* easily able to make friends
amistoso *aj* [3125] friendly

amparo protection
amparar *vt* [4535] to protect
ampararse *vr* [4535] to protect oneself
desamparar *vt* to remove protection, to forsake
desamparado,-a *nmf* defenseless person; helpless person; person without protection, widow, orphan
amparo *nm* [-o(1) 1689] protection
desamparo *nm* lack of protection, help, or support
desamparado *aj* defenseless; helpless

amplio ample
ampliar *vt* [1650] to make larger or wider
amplificar *vt* [-ificar] to amplify
amplificador *nm* amplifier
ampliación *nf* [-ción 1791] widening or enlarging; enlargement
ampliadora *nf* photographic enlarger
amplificación *nf* amplification
amplitud *nf* [-itud] amplitude, wideness
ampliado *aj* enlarged; widened
amplificador *aj* amplifying
amplio *aj* [1348] ample

analizar to analyze
analizar *vt* [957] to analyze
psicoanalizar *vt* [-izar] to psychoanalyze
analista *nmf* [1962] analyst
psicoanalista *nmf* psychoanalyst

análisis *nm* [1362] analysis
autoanálisis *nm* self-analysis
psicoanálisis *nm* psychoanalysis
analítico *aj* [-ico(2)] analytical; analytic
analizable *aj* analyzable
analizador *aj* analyzing

análogo analogous
analogía *nf* analogy
análogo *aj* analogous

anatomía anatomy
anatomía *nf* anatomy
anatómico *aj* [-o(3)] anatomical

ancho wide
ancho *nm* [2752] width
anchura *nf* [-ura(1)] wideness
ancho *aj* [2752] wide

anciano old person; elder
anciano,-a *nmf* [2422] old person; elder
ancianidad *nf* old age
anciano *aj* old

andar to walk; to associate with (friends); to be
(out and about); to go out (dating)
andar *vi* [988] to walk; to associate with
(friends); to be (out and about); to go out
(dating)
desandar *vt* to retrace one's steps; to go back
the way one came
andariego,-a *nmf* person who likes to be on the
move
andadas *nfpl* habits
andaderas *nfpl* baby's walker
andadura *nf* walking
andador *aj* walking; fond of walking
andariego *aj* [-iego] walking; referring to a
person who likes to walk

anécdota anecdote
anecdotario *nm* collection of anecdotes
anécdota *nf* [4219] anecdote
anecdótico *aj* anecdotal

ángel angel
ángel *nm* [4518] angel
angelito *nm* little angel
angelote *nm* [-ote] big angel
arcángel *nm* archangel
angelical *aj* angelical; angelic
angélico *aj* [-ico(2)] angelical; angelic

angosto narrow
angostura *nf* narrowness
angosto *aj* narrow

ángulo angle
ángulo *nm* [4056] angle
rectángulo *nm* rectangle

triángulo *nm* triangle
angular *aj* angular
rectangular *aj* rectangular
rectángulo *aj* rectangular
triangular *aj* [-ado(1)] triangular
triángulo *aj* triangular

angustia anguish, distress
angustiar *vt* to cause anguish
angustiarse *vr* to be in anguish; to be distressed
angustia *nf* [-a 4009] anguish; distress
angustiado *aj* anguished; in anguish
angustioso *aj* provoking anguish

anhelo great desire, yearning
anhelar *vti* [4865] to desire passionately, to yearn
anhelo *nm* great desire, yearning
anhelante *aj* greatly desirable

ánimo desire, will
animar *vt* [2225] to encourage
animarse *vr* [2225] to be encouraged
desanimar *vt* to discourage
desanimarse *vr* to be discouraged
reanimar *vt* to reanimate
reanimarse *vr* to be reanimated
animador,-a *nmf* encouraging person; director
of a party; audience prompter for a television
program
ánimo *nm* desire, will
desánimo *nm* discouragement
ánima *nf* soul, spirit
animación *nf* [-ción] animation
reanimación *nf* reanimation
¡ánimo! *int* Come on! Get up! Get going!
animadamente *av* with desire, with will,
purposefully
animado *aj* encouraged
animador *aj* encouraging
anímico *aj* pertaining to the soul
animoso *aj* filled with desire or will; energetic
desanimado *aj* discouraged
inanimado *aj* inanimate

anónimo anonymous
anonimato *nm* anonymity
anónimo *nm* [3613] anonymous work
anónimo *aj* [3613] anonymous

ansia feeling of anxiety
ansiar *vt* to be anxious
ansia *nf* feeling of anxiety
ansiedad *nf* [3735] anxiety
ansiado *aj* desired
ansioso *aj* anxious

antecedente antecedent; previous
anteceder *vt* to precede
antecedentes *nmpl* personal history or records

antecesor,-a *nmf* predecessor, ancestor
antecedente *nm* [2725] antecedent; past; background
antecedente *aj* [2725] record

anteriormente previously
anterioridad *nf* anticipation
anteriormente *av* [-mente 2395] previously
antes *av* [153] before
anterior *aj* [251] previous
antes *aj* [153] before

antiguo ancient
antiguos *nmpl* ancients
antigualla *nf* antique
antigüedad *nf* [4031] antiquity
anticuado *aj* antiquated
anticuario *nm* antique dealer or collector; antique store
antiguo *aj* [1114] ancient
antiquísimo *aj* very ancient

antojarse to make one crave
antojarse *vr* to make one crave
antojo *nm* craving
antojadizo *aj* with cravings

anular to annul
anular *vt* [2986] to annul
anularse *vr* to be annulled
anulación *nf* annulment

anunciar to announce
anunciar *vt* [490] to announce
anunciarse *vr* to be announced
anunciador,-a *nmf* announcer
anuncio *nm* [-o(1) 1997] announcement; advertisement
anunciador *aj* announcing

añadir to add
añadir *vt* [509] to add
añadidura *nf* [-dura] addition
añadido *aj* added

año year
añejar *v* to age (wine)
añejarse *vr* to be aged
aniversario *nm* [-ario(2) 1244] anniversary
anuario *nm* annual, yearbook
añejamiento *nm* aging (wine)
año *nm* [30] year
cumpleaños *nm* [1342] birthday
anualidad *nf* annuity
perennidad *nf* perpetuity
antaño *av* yesteryear
anual *aj* [-al(2) 1159] annual
añejo *aj* aged (wine)
perennal *aj* perennial
perenne *aj* perennial

apagar to turn off
apagar *vt* [3614] to turn off
apagarse *vr* to be turned off
apagavelas *nm* candle snuffer
apagón *nm* [-ón(1)] power outage
apagadizo *aj* [-dizo] with a propensity to lose power
apagado *aj* turned off

aparecer to appear
aparecer *vi* [623] to appear
aparecerse *vr* [623]] to appear
aparentar *vt* to seem
desaparecer *vi* [1095] to disappear
reaparecer *vi* [4323] to reappear
aparecido,-a *nmf* ghost, specter
desaparecido,-a *nmf* missing person
aparición *nf* [-ción 1908] apparition
apariencia *nf* [-encia 3554] appearance
desaparición *nf* [-ción 2472] disappearance
reaparición *nf* reappearance
aparentemente *av* [-mente 3015] apparently
aparente *aj* [-ente(1) 4347] apparent
desaparecido *aj* missing

aparte separately
apartar *vt* [2802] to separate; to save
apartarse *vr* [2802] to separate oneself
apartamento *nm* apartment
apartamiento *nm* separation, withdrawal
aparte *nm* [2220] separate paragraph; an aside in theater or a speech
aparte *av* [2220] separately
apartado *aj* separated; saved; reserved

apelar to appeal
apelar *vi* [4884] to appeal
apelación *nf* appeal
apelable *aj* appealable
apelativo *aj* appellate
inapelable *aj* not appealable

apellido last name
apellidar *vt* to give as a last name
apellidarse *vr* to have as a last name
apellido *nm* [-ido(2) 3331] last name

apertura opening; aperture
apertura *nf* [-ura(1) 1172] opening; aperture
reapertura *nf* reopening

apetito appetite
apetecer *vt* to please one's appetite
aperitivo *nm* appetizer
apetito *nm* [-ito(2) 4808] appetite
apetencia *nf* appetite
inapetencia *nf* lack of appetite
aperitivo *aj* appetizer

apetecible *aj* tempting, desirable, appetizing

apetitoso *aj* appetizing

aplaudir to applaud

aplaudir *vt* [3416] to applaud

aplauso *nm* [3042] applause

aplicar to apply (cream, medicine, etc.)

aplicar *vt* [484] to apply (cream, medicine, etc.)

aplicarse *vr* [484] to apply on oneself (cream, medicine, etc.)

aplicado,-a *nmf* good student

desaplicado,-a *nmf* bad student

aplicación *nf* [-ción 1326] application; appliqué

aplicable *aj* applicable

aplicado *aj* hard-working; studious

desaplicado *aj* lazy; lacking effort

inaplicable *aj* inapplicable

aportar to donate

aportar *vt* [1130] to donate

aporte *nm* donation

aportación *nf* donation; contribution

aposento room, lodging

aposentar *vt* to provide room or lodging

aposentarse *vr* to room or lodge somewhere

aposentamiento *nm* lodging

aposento *nm* room, lodging

apoyar to support

apoyar *vt* [-o(1) 452] to support

apoyo *nm* [229] support

apoyado *aj* supported

aprender to learn

aprender *vt* [913] to learn

aprendiz,-a *nmf* learner

aprendizaje *nm* [3790] learning

apretado tight

apretar *vt* [3390] to tighten; to be tight on; to squeeze

apretujar *vt* to squeeze

apretujarse *vr* to be squeezed into

aprieto *nm* difficult situation; tight spot

apretón *nm* [-ón(1)] squeeze

apretujón *nm* tight squeeze

apretura *nf* narrow place

apretado *aj* tight

aprobar to approve; to pass (a test)

aprobar *vt* [846] to approve; to pass (a test)

desaprobar *vt* to disapprove

reprobar *vt* to fail; to give a failing grade to; to reprove

aprobado *nm* certificate of a passing score; approval

aprobación *nf* [-ción 2144] approval

desaprobación *nf* disapproval

reprobación *nf* failure

aprobado *aj* approved; passed

aprobatorio *aj* [-orio(2)] passing

desaprobador *aj* disapproving; failing

reprobado *aj* failed

aprovechar to take advantage of

aprovechar *vti* [632] to take advantage of an opportunity

aprovecharse *vr* to take advantage of a situation for one's own benefit; to take advantage of someone

desaprovechar *vti* to miss (an opportunity)

aprovechamiento *nm* [-miento 3615] improvement

aprovechable *aj* able to be used or taken advantage of

aprovechado *aj* taken advantage of; well-used

desaprovechado *aj* not taken advantage of; poorly used

aptitud aptitude

inepto,-a *nmf* inept person

aptitud *nf* [-itud] aptitude

ineptitud *nf* [-itud] ineptitude

inepto *aj* inept

apto *aj* apt; capable

apuntar to note; to write down

apuntar *vt* [1003] to note

apuntarse *vr* to sign up for

apuntador,-a *nmf* prompter in theater

apunte *nm* note

apuntado *aj* noted; written down

apurar to hurry

apurar *vt* to hurry

apurarse *vr* to be in a hurry

apurado *aj* in a hurry; hurry

arbitrario arbitrary

arbitrar *vt* to arbitrate

árbitro,-a *nmf* referee; umpire; arbiter

arbitraje *nm* [2762] officiating; arbitration

arbitrariedad *nf* arbitrariness

arbitral *aj* pertaining to officiating or arbitration

arbitrario *aj* [-ario(2)] arbitrary

árbol tree

arbolar *vt* to raise (flag)

enarbolar *vt* to raise (flag)

árbol *nm* tree

arbolado *nm* grove of trees

arbusto *nm* bush

arboladura *nf* masts and related equipment of a ship

arboleda *nf* park filled with trees

arbolado *aj* filled with trees
arbóreo *aj* [-eo(2)] pertaining to trees

archivo file
archivar *vt* to file
archivador,-a *nmf* file clerk
archivero *nm* file cabinet
archivador *nm* file cabinet or box
archivo *nm* [-o(1) 524] file

arco arch
enarcar *vt* to make in the shape of an arch
arco *nm* [2965] arch

arder to sting or burn something
arder *vti* to sting or burn something
ardor *nm* burning; intense fire (also figurative)
ardiente *aj* stinging
ardido *aj* angry, irritated
ardoroso *aj* burning; stinging

arena sand
enarenar *vt* to cover with sand
enarenarse *vr* to be covered with sand
arenal *nm* large area covered with sand
arena *nf* [1629] sand
arenoso *aj* sandy

argumento argument
argüir *vti* to argue
argumentar *vi* [2203] to argue; to give arguments
argumento *nm* [-o(1) 2161] argument
argumentación *nf* argumentation

árido arid, dry
aridecer *vt* to make arid or dry
aridecerse *vr* to become arid or dry
áridos *nmpl* dry goods
aridez *nf* [-ez] aridity
árido *aj* [-ido(1)] arid, dry

aristocracia aristocracy
aristócrata *nmf* aristocrat
aristocracia *nf* aristocracy
aristocrático *aj* aristocratic

arma arm, weapon
armar *vt* [521] to arm; to put together
armarse *vr* to become armed
desarmar *vt* [4650] to disarm; to take apart
rearmar *vt* to rearm
rearmarse *vr* to become rearmed
armero,-a *nmf* arms expert, salesman, or maker
armamento *nm* armament
armero *nm* gun cabinet or locker
desarme *nm* disarmament
rearme *nm* rearmament
arma *nf* [-a 703] arm, weapon
armada *nf* [-ada(1)] navy; battle fleet
armadura *nf* [-dura] armor

armería *nf* [-ería(2)] arms factory or shop; gun store
armado *aj* armed
desarmable *aj* able to be taken apart
desarmado *aj* unarmed; taken apart

armonía harmony
armonizar *vt* to harmonize
armónico *nm* harmonic
armonio *nm* harmonium
armonía *nf* [3504] harmony
armónica *nf* harmonica
armonización *nf* harmonization
armónicamente *av* in harmony
armónico *aj* harmonic
armonioso *aj* harmonious

aroma aroma
aromatizar *vt* to fill with an aroma
aromatizador *nm* air freshener
aroma *nf* [4348] aroma
aromatización *nf* air freshening; the filling of air with an aroma
aromático *aj* aromatic

arqueología archeology
arqueólogo,-a *nmf* archeologist
arqueología *nf* archeology
arqueológico *aj* archeological

arquetipo archetype
arquetipo *nm* archetype
arquetípico *aj* archetypal

arquitecto architect
arquitecto,-a *nmf* [4435] architect
arquitectura *nf* architecture
arquitectónico *aj* architectural

arrancar to pull from the root; to start a race; to start forward
arrancar *vti* [1833] to pull from the root; to start a race; to start forward
arranque *nm* [2406] pulling from the root; violent impulse
arrancada *nf* forward impulse of a horse or a car, etc.
¡arranquen! *int* go! start!
arrancado *aj* pulled up by the roots

arrastrar to drag
arrastrar *vt* [3238] to drag
arrastrarse *vr* [3238] to drag oneself; to crawl
arrastre *nm* dragging
arrastradizo *aj* dragging; crawling
arrastrado *aj* ruined

arrebatar to grab forcefully
arrebatar *vt* [4691] to grab forcefully; to burn too quickly (flame of a stove)

arrebatarse *vr* to become extremely angry

arrebatamiento *nm* grabbing; act of becoming extremely angry

arrebato *nm* grabbing; act of becoming extremely angry

arrebatado *aj* grabbed; extremely angered, infuriated, furious

arrebatador *aj* gripping

arreglar to fix

arreglar *vt* [2358] to fix

arreglarse *vr* [2358] to be fixed; to get oneself ready

desarreglar *vt* to move out of place

arreglista *nmf* musical arranger

arreglo *nm* [-o(1) 1979] arrangement

desarreglo *nm* moving out of place

arreglado *aj* fixed; arranged

desarreglado *aj* moved out of place

arremeter to attack

arremeter *vt* to attack

arremetida *nf* attack

arribar to arrive

arribar *vi* [2567] to arrive

arribo *nm* [-o(1) 3957] arrival of a ship

arribada *nf* arrival of a ship

arrojar to throw forcefully

arrojar *vt* [2145] to throw forcefully

arrojarse *vr* [2145] to hurl oneself

arrojo *nm* throw; hurling of oneself

arrojado *aj* [-ado(1)] thrown; hurled; fearless, intrepid, brave

arroyo creek

arroyar *vt* to form channels of water

arroyo *nm* creek

arroyuelo *nm* small creek

arroz rice

arrocero,-a *nmf* rice grower

arrocero *nm* bag used for holding rice, often used at weddings

arroz *nm* [3224] rice

arrozal *nm* [-al(3)] rice paddy or field

arrocero *aj* pertaining to rice

arte art

arte *nmf* [837] art

artesano,-a *nmf* artisan

artífice *nmf* craftsman

artista *nmf* [-ista 517] artist

artificio *nm* [-icio] skill, ability

artesanía *nf* arts and crafts; crafted object

artesanal *aj* pertaining to arts and crafts

artesano *aj* well-skilled at crafts

artístico *aj* [-ico(2) 1215] artistic

artificioso *aj* made with skill or ability

artículo article

articulista *nmf* article writer; newspaper or magazine reporter

artículo *nm* [-culo 878] article

artificial artificial

artificialmente *av* artificially

artificial *aj* [-cial 4121] artificial

artillería artillery

artillero *nm* artillery soldier

artillería *nf* artillery

asalto assault

asaltar *vt* [3791] to assault

asaltante *nmf* [-ante(2) 4781] assailant

asalto *nm* [-o(1) 2677] assault

asaltante *aj* [-ante(2) 4781] assaulting

asamblea assembly

asambleísta *nmf* one who is part of an assembly

asamblea *nf* [1299] assembly

asesinar to murder

asesinar *vt* [2077] to murder; to assassinate

asesino,-a *nmf* [2829] murderer; assassin

asesinato *nm* [1914] murder

asesino *aj* murdering

asiduo assiduous

asiduidad *nf* diligence; assiduity

asiduo *aj* [-uo] assiduous

asignar to assign

asignar *vt* [2121] to assign to a post or job; to assign money

asignatario,-a *nmf* heir; person who receives money from an inheritance

asignación *nf* [-ción 4600] assigning to a post; assigning of money

asistir to attend

asistir *vti* [596] to attend

asistente *nmf* [-ente(2) 1042] assistant

asistencia *nf* [-encia 1455] attendance

inasistencia *nf* absence

asistente *aj* [-ente(2) 1042] assisting; attending

asistido *aj* attended; assisted

asociación association

asociar *vt* [2032] to associate

asociarse *vr* to be associated

asociado,-a *nmf* associate

asociación *nf* [-ción 631] association

asociado *aj* associated

asociativo *aj* associating

asomar to show oneself

asomar *vi* to show oneself

asomarse *vr* to peer

asombrar   to amaze
  asombrar *vt*   to amaze
  asombrarse *vr*   to be amazed
  asombro *nm*   amazement
  asombrado *aj*   amazed
  asombroso *aj*   amazing

áspero   rough
  aspereza *nf*   roughness
  áspero *aj*   rough

aspirar a   to aspire; to inhale
  aspirar a *vt* [2678]   to aspire; to inhale; to vacuum
  aspirante *nmf* [-ante(2) 2513]   aspirant
  aspiradora *nf* [-dor(2)]   vacuum cleaner
  aspiración *nf* [-ción 3005]   aspiration
  aspirado *aj*   vacuumed; aspirate (letter)
  aspirador *aj*   aspiring
  aspirante *aj* [-ante(2) 2513]   aspiring, desiring

astro   heavenly body
  astrólogo,-a *nmf*   astrologer
  astronauta *nmf*   astronaut
  astrónomo,-a *nmf*   astronomer
  asterisco *nm*   asterisk
  asteroide *nm*   asteroid
  astro *nm* [2737]   heavenly body
  astrolabio *nm*   astrolabe
  astrofísica *nf*   astrophysics
  astrología *nf*   astrology
  astronáutica *nf*   astronautics
  astronave *nf*   spaceship
  astronomía *nf*   astronomy
  asteroide *aj*   asteroid
  astral *aj* [-al(2)]   pertaining to heavenly bodies
  astrológico *aj*   astrological
  astronómico *aj*   astronomical

asumir   to assume (a position or responsibility)
  asumir *vt* [1267]   to assume (a position or responsibility)
  asunción *nf*   assumption

asustar   to frighten
  asustar *vt* [3825]   to frighten
  asustarse *vr* [3825]   to be frightened
  asustadizo *aj* [-dizo]   easily frightened
  asustado *aj*   frightened
  asustón *aj*   frightening

atacar   to attack
  atacar *vt* [1460]   to attack
  contraatacar *vt*   to counter-attack
  atacante *nmf* [-ante(2) 3264]   attacker
  ataque *nm* [522]   attack
  contraataque *nm*   counter-attack
  atacante *aj* [-ante(2) 3264]   attacking

atar   to tie
  atar *vt* [4554]   to tie
  atarse *vr*   to be tied
  desatar *vt* [2919]   to untie; to unleash
  desatarse *vr* [2919]   to be unleashed
  atadero *nm*   hitching post
  atado *nm*   bundle
  atadura *nf*   tying
  atado *aj*   bundled; tied
  desatado *aj*   untied; unleashed

atención   attention
  atender *vt* [442]   to attend to
  desatender *vt*   to neglect; to avoid attending to
  atención *nf* [-ción 379]   attention
  desatención *nf*   neglect
  atención *int* [-ción 379]   attention!
  atentamente *av*   attentively
  atento *aj* [2788]   attentive
  desatento *aj*   neglectful
  inatento *aj*   inattentive

atinar   to hit the target, to hit the bull's-eye
  atinar *vi*   to hit the target, to hit the bull's-eye
  desatinar *vi*   to aim poorly
  desatinado,-a *nmf*   person with poor aim; blundering person
  tino *nm*   aim
  atinadamente *av*   with good aim
  atinado *aj*   on the mark; just right
  desatinado *aj*   off the mark; blundering

atleta   athlete
  atleta *nmf* [2414]   athlete
  atletismo *nm* [-ismo 3528]   track and field
  atlético *aj* [-ico(2) 1827]   athletic

atmósfera   atmosphere
  atmósfera *nf*   atmosphere
  atmosférico *aj*   atmospheric

átomo   atom
  atomizar *vt*   to atomize
  atomizador *nm*   atomizer
  átomo *nm*   atom
  atomización *nf*   atomization
  atómico *aj*   atomic
  subatómico *aj*   subatomic

atraer   to attract
  atraer *vt* [1956]   to attract
  atractivo *nm* [-ivo 1509]   attraction
  atracción *nf* [-ción 4134]   attraction
  atractivamente *av*   attractively
  atractivo *aj* [-ivo 1509]   attractive
  atrayente *aj* [-ente(1)]   attractive

atreverse   to dare
  atreverse *vr*   to dare

atrevimiento *nm* daring, audacity
atrevido *aj* daring
atribuir to attribute
atribuir *vt* [2315] to attribute
atribuirse *vr* to be attributed to
atributo *nm* [-uto] attribute
atribución *nf* attribution
atribuible *aj* attributable
atributivo *aj* attributive
audacia audacity
audacia *nf* [-icia] audacity
audaz *aj* [-az] audacious
audiencia audience
audífono *nm* hearing aid
auditorio *nm* [-orio(1) 1586] auditorium
audición *nf* audition
audiencia *nf* [1939] audience
audible *aj* audible
audiovisual *aj* audiovisual
auditivo *aj* auditory
inaudible *aj* inaudible
inaudito *aj* unheard of
aumentar to augment; to add to; to gain
aumentar *vt* [586] to augment; to add to; to gain
aumento *nm* [-o(1) 857] gain, increase
aumentado *aj* increased, enlarged, added
aumentativo *aj* augmentative (grammatical term)
ausencia absence
ausentarse *vr* to absent oneself
ausente *nmf* person who is not present
ausentismo *nm* absenteeism
ausencia *nf* [-encia 1599] absence
ausente *aj* absent
austero austere
austeridad *nf* austerity
austero *aj* austere
auténtico authentic
autenticar *vt* to authenticate; to give a certificate of authenticity
autentificar *vt* to authenticate; to give a certificate of authenticity
auténtica *nf* certificate of authenticity
autenticación *nf* authentication
autenticidad *nf* authenticity
auténtico *aj* [2301] authentic
automóvil automobile
automovilista *nmf* [-ista 2843] motorist
auto *nm* [904] auto, car
autobús *nm* [2261] bus
autódromo *nm* [3815] auto race track
automotor *nm* engine (train)

automóvil *nm* [1492] automobile
automovilismo *nm* [5002] motoring; automobile construction
autoescuela *nf* driving school
autopista *nf* [4974] highway
automovilístico *aj* [-ico(2) 3677] pertaining to motoring or automobile construction
autónomo autonomous
autonomía *nf* [-ería(2) 3924] autonomy
autonómico *aj* pertaining to autonomy
autónomo *aj* [1221] autonomous
autoridad authority
autorizar *vt* [-izar 1178] to authorize
desautorizar *vt* to take away authority
autoritarismo *nm* authoritarianism
autoridad *nf* [-idad 186] authority
autorización *nf* [-ción 2274] authorization
desautorización *nf* removal of authority
autoritario *aj* [4866] authoritarian
autoritativo *aj* authoritative
autorizable *aj* authorizable
autorizado *aj* authorized
desautorizado *aj* unauthorized
auxilio help
auxiliar *vt* [2173] to help
auxiliador,-a *nmf* helper
auxiliar *nmf* [2173] assistant
auxilio *nm* [-o(1) 2848] help
auxiliador *aj* helpful
auxiliar *aj* [2173] auxiliary
avanzar to advance
avanzar *vi* [789] to advance
avance *nm* [1024] advance
avanzada *nf* group of military scouts
avante *av* ahead
avanzado *aj* advanced
aventajar to gain an advantage
aventajar *vt* to gain an advantage
aventajado *aj* having an advantage; advantageous
desaventajado *aj* behind (in a comparison); disadvantageous
aventura adventure
aventurar *vt* to venture; to risk
aventurarse *vr* to take a risk, to dare
aventurero,-a *nmf* adventurer
aventura *nf* [-a 2213] adventure
aventurado *aj* risky
aventurero *aj* adventurous
avión airplane
aviador,-a *nmf* aviator
avión *nm* [1160] airplane
portaaviones *nf* aircraft carrier

aviación *nf* aviation
avioneta *nf* [-eta] small airplane

aviso warning
avisar *vt* [3678] to warn
aviso *nm* [-o(1) 2234] warning

ayer yesterday
anteayer *av* day before yesterday
ayer *av* [111] yesterday

ayudar to help
ayudar *vt* [495] to help
ayudarse *vr* to help oneself; to help each other
ayudante *nmf* assistant
ayuda *nf* [-a 677] help

azúcar sugar
azucarar *vt* to put sugar in something
azucararse *vr* to be sugared
azúcar *nf* [1377] sugar
azucarero,-a *nmf* expert in sugar production
azucarera *nf* sugar bowl
azucena *nf* white lily; innocent or guileless person
azucarado *aj* sugared
azucarero *aj* [-ero(1)] pertaining to sugar

azul blue
azular *vt* to make blue; to color with blue
azul *nm* [772] blue
azul *aj* [772] blue
azulado *aj* bluish

B

bachiller high school or junior college student
bachiller *nmf* high school or junior college student
bachillerato *nm* [-ato 4867] study at the high school or junior college level

baile dance
bailotear *vi* to dance in an arrhythmic manner
bailar *vi* [1869] to dance
bailarín,-a *nmf* [3529] dancer, especially a ballet dancer; ballerina
bailador,-a *nmf* dancer
ballet *nm* [4620] ballet
bailoteo *nm* arrhythmic dance or movement
baile *nm* [1524] dance
bailante *aj* dancing
bailador *aj* pertaining to dance
bailable *aj* danceable

bajo low
abajarse *vr* to go down

bajar *vt* [1050] to lower
bajarse *vr* [1050] to lower oneself; to get off a vehicle
rebajar *vt* to lower (especially price), to cut or make even lower
rebajarse *vr* to humble oneself
bajo *prep* [172] under
altibajos *nmpl* ups and downs or highs and lows, especially of life
bajista *nmf* bass player
bajío *nm* lowland; sandbank
bajo *nm* [172] lowland; depths; bass instrument; bass player; bass singer
contrabajo *nm* double bass
baja *nf* lowering
bajada *nf* lowering or action of lowering
bajamar *nf* water's edge
bajeza *nf* [-eza] low or vile act, often criminal
rebaja *nf* sale
abajo *av* [1726] below, under
bajamente *av* in a low manner
bajo *av* [172] low
bajista *aj* pertaining to a bearish market; bearish
bajo *aj* [172] low; short
cabizbajo *aj* sad, with head hanging low
rebajado *aj* lowered, often in price

bala bullet
balazo *nm* [-azo(2) 4010] bullet wound
balín *nm* [-ín] BB or pellet
bala *nf* [3177] bullet
balística *nf* ballistics
balístico *aj* ballistic

balancear to balance
balancear *vt* to balance
balancearse *vr* to become balanced
resbalar *vi* to slip, to slide
balance *nm* [3344] balance
balanceo *nm* balance
balancín *nm* rocking chair
resbalón *nm* slip or slide
balanza *nf* [-anza 4949] scale of the balance type
resbaladizo *aj* [-dizo] slippery
resbaloso *aj* slippery

banco bank
desbancar *vt* to break the bank
banco *nm* [648] bank
banca *nf* [2008] bench
bancarrota *nf* [-ote] bankruptcy
bancario *aj* [-ario(2) 1507] bank; pertaining to the bank

bandera flag
 abanderar *vt* to register a ship under a nation's flag
 abanderado,-a *nmf* flag bearer
 bando *nm* [3070] band or group of animals
 bandera *nf* [1400] flag
 banderín *nf* [-ín] small flag or pennant
 banderita *nf* small flag or pennant

banquete banquet
 banquetear *vti* to feast
 banquetero,-a *nmf* person who prepares and serves a banquet
 banquete *nm* [-ete 3806] banquet

baño bath
 bañar *vt* [3627] to bathe
 bañarse *vr* [3627] to bathe oneself
 bañista *nmf* swimmer at a public pool
 bañadero *nm* bathing area for animals
 baño *nm* [-o(1) 1909] bath
 bañera *nf* [-era] bathtub

barato cheap, inexpensive
 abaratar *vt* to lower the price of
 abaratarse *vr* to become lower in price
 abaratamiento *nm* action of lowering the price
 baratija *nf* something that is cheap or cheaply made
 barato *aj* [3306] cheap

barba beard
 barbero *nm* [-ero(3)] barber
 barba *nf* [3662] beard; chin
 barbería *nf* [-ería(1)] barber shop
 barbilla *nf* [-illa] chin
 barbado *aj* bearded
 barbilampiño *aj* beardless, cleanshaven
 barbudo *aj* [-udo] bearded

bárbaro barbaric
 bárbaro,-a *nmf* [3266] barbarian
 barbarismo *nm* barbarianism
 barbaridad *nf* barbarity
 barbarie *nf* culturally ignorant person
 bárbaro *aj* barbaric

barco boat, ship
 desembarcar *vt* to unload
 desembarcarse *vr* to become unloaded
 embarcar *vt* to load a ship
 barco *nm* [3147] boat, ship
 barquero *nm* helmsman
 desembarcadero *nm* wharf
 desembarco *nm* unloading of a ship
 embarcadero *nm* wharf, loading dock
 embarcador *nm* ship loader; dock worker
 embarque *nm* loading of a ship

barca *nf* ship, boat
 embarcación *nf* [4521] medium-sized boat

barón baron
 barón *nm* baron
 baronesa *nf* baroness

barro clay
 barrizal *nm* place filled with clay
 barro *nm* [4436] clay
 barroso *aj* muddy, clay-like

barroco baroque
 barroquismo *nm* the quality of being baroque
 barroco *aj* baroque

base base
 basar *vt* [1351] to base
 basarse *vr* to base oneself
 basamento *nm* base, referring to a construction project
 base *nf* [333] base
 básico *aj* [-ico(2) 1133] basic

bastar to be enough
 bastar *vi* [2221] to be enough
 bastante *av* [1412] enough
 bastante *aj* [1412] enough, sufficient

batalla battle
 batallar *vi* to battle; to struggle; to fight with
 batallador,-a *nmf* fighter; person who battles
 batallón *nm* batallion
 batalla *nf* [-a 2035] battle

batir to beat
 batear *vt* [2946] to bat; to swing a bat
 batir *vt* [4437] to beat
 batirse *vr* [4437] to become beaten (food, mixture)
 bateador,-a *nmf* [2575] batter (sport)
 bate *nm* bat
 batidor *nm* [-dor(1)] beater
 batidor *aj* [-dor(1)] beating
 batiente *aj* beating

beber to drink
 beber *vt* [2239] to drink
 bebedor,-a *nmf* drinker
 bebé *nm* [1338] baby
 bebedero *nm* [-ero(2)] drinking fountain
 bebedizo *nm* [-dizo] drinkable liquid; potable drink
 bebida *nf* [-ido(2) 1426] drink
 bebedor *aj* drinking
 bebible *aj* [-ible] drinkable
 bebido *aj* under the influence of alcohol

bello beautiful, pretty
 embellecer *vt* to beautify

embellecimiento *nm* [-miento] beautification; embellishment
belleza *nf* [-eza 1651] beauty
bello *aj* [1283] beautiful, pretty

beneficio benefit
beneficiar *vt* [1177] to benefit
beneficiarse *vr* [1177] to benefit from
benefactor,-a *nmf* benefactor
beneficiario,-a *nmf* [3319] beneficiary
beneficio *nm* [-icio 690] benefit
beneficencia *nf* beneficence
beneficiado,-a *nf* person who has benefited
beneficioso *aj* beneficial
benéfico *aj* [-ico(2) 3737] beneficial

beso kiss
besar *vt* [3593] to kiss
besarse *vr* to kiss each other
besuquear *vt* to kiss excessively
besucón,-a *nmf* one who kisses excessively
besamanos *nm* hand kissing of royalty
beso *nm* [-o(1) 3320] kiss
besuqueo *nm* [-eo(1)] overly affectionate kiss
besucón *aj* pertaining to over-affectionate kissing

biblioteca library
bibliófilo,-a *nmf* booklover
bibliotecario,-a *nmf* librarian
Biblia *nf* Bible
bibliografía *nf* bibliography
biblioteca *nf* [-teca 2254] library
bíblico *aj* [-ico(2)] biblical
bibliográfico *aj* bibliographic

bien well, fine
bienaventurado,-a *nmf* blessed or fortunate person
bienhechor,-a *nmf* someone who does good things
bien *nm* [130] the good, the fine
bienestar *nm* [2906] wellbeing
benevolencia *nf* benevolence
bienaventuranza *nf* beatitude; blessedness
bienvenida *nf* [3057] welcome
bien *av* [130] well, fine
benevolente *aj* benevolent
benévolo *aj* benevolent
bien *aj* [130] fine, good
bienaventurado *aj* blessed
bienhechor *aj* referring to one who does good
bienintencionado *aj* well-intentioned
bienvenido *aj* welcome

bigote mustache
bigote *nm* mustache
bigotudo *aj* [-udo] mustached

billete bill
billetaje *nm* collection of tickets
billete *nm* bill; *billete de lotería:* lottery ticket
billetero *nm* wallet; someone who sells lottery tickets

biológico biological
biógrafo,-a *nmf* biographer
biólogo,-a *nmf* biologist
bioquímico,-a *nmf* biochemist
antibiótico *nm* antibiotic
autobiografía *nf* autobiography
biofísica *nf* biophysics
biografía *nf* [4975] biography
biología *nf* biology
biopsia *nf* biopsy
bioquímica *nf* biochemistry
microbiología *nf* microbiology
simbiosis *nf* [-osis] symbiosis
antibiótico *aj* antibiotic
autobiográfico *aj* autobiographical
biográfico *aj* biographical
biológico *aj* [-ico(2) 3679] biological
bioquímico *aj* biochemical
microbiológico *aj* microbiological
simbiótico *aj* symbiotic

blanco white
blanquear *vt* [4470] to make something white
blanquearse *vr* to become white
blanco,-a *nmf* a white one
blanqueador,-a *nmf* whitewash; whitener
blanco *nm* [318] the blank or target
blanqueo *nm* [-eo(1)] whitening; whitewashing
Blancanieves *nf* Snow White
blancura *nf* [-ura(1)] whiteness
blanco *aj* [318] white
blancuzco *aj* [-usco] whitish
blanqueador *aj* whitening
blanquecino *aj* [-ino(2)] off-white

blando smooth and soft
ablandar *vt* to soften
reblandecer *vt* to soften (situation)
reblandecerse *vr* to become soft
ablandamiento *nm* the act of softening (thing)
reblandecimiento *nm* the act of softening (situation)
blandura *nf* softness
blando *aj* smooth, soft
blanduzco *aj* partly soft, rather soft

bloque block
bloquear *vt* [2870] to block
desbloquear *vt* to unblock
bloque *nm* [3879] block
bloqueador *nm* sunblock; sunscreen

bloqueo *nm* [-eo(1) 4438] blocking
desbloqueo *nm* unblocking

boca mouth
desembocar *vi* to flow out of the mouth of a river, lake, or road
embocar *vt* to put the lips on the mouthpiece of a wind instrument
boceras *nmf* loudmouth
desbocado,-a *nmf* foul-mouthed person
bocadillo *nm* [-illo(1)] appetizer; snack
bocado *nm* [-ada(3)] a bite of food
boquete *nm* opening
tapabocas *nm* gag
boca *nf* [1619] mouth
bocacalle *nf* entrance to a street; street that flows into a boulevard
bocamanga *nf* cuff of a sleeve
bocanada *nf* mouthful
bocera *nf* food or drink that sticks to the lips
desembocadura *nf* the mouth of a river
embocadura *nf* embouchure, the position of the mouth on the mouthpiece of a musical instrument
desbocado *aj* foul-mouthed

bola round object; bullet
bolear *vt* to volley; to practice with a ball
boliche *nm* bowling
bolígrafo *nm* ball-point pen
bola *nf* [1891] round object; bullet
bolera *nf* bowling alley

bolsillo pocket
bolsear *vt* to steal; to pick someone's pocket; to snatch someone's purse
desembolsar *vt* to take out of a pocket, purse or bag; to pay a debt
embolsar *vt* to put into a pocket, purse or bag
reembolsar *vt* to reimburse
reembolsarse *vr* to become reimbursed
bolsero,-a *nmf* person that makes or sells bags or purses; purse-snatcher; pickpocket
bolsillo *nm* [-illo(1) 4783] pocket
bolso *nm* purse
desembolso *nm* expense
reembolso *nm* reimbursement
bolsa *nf* [1000] purse; bag
reembolsable *aj* reimbursable

bomba¹ bomb
bombardear *vt* to bombard
bombardeo *nm* [-eo(1) 4502] bombardment
bombardero *nm* bomber (airplane)
bombazo *nm* [-azo(1)] bombing; explosion of a bomb
cazabombardero *nm* fighter bomber (airplane)

bomba *nf* [2191] bomb
bomba *aj* [2191] bomb

bomba² pump
bombear *vt* to pump
bombeo *nm* act of pumping
bombero *nm* firefighter
bomba *nf* [2191] pump

bordar to embroider
bordar *vt* to embroider
bordador,-a *nmf* embroiderer
bordado *nm* [4408] embroidery
bordadora *nf* embroidery machine
bordado *aj* [4408] embroidered

borde edge
bordear *vt* to move along the edge
desbordar *vt* to pass or flow over the edge
desbordarse *vr* to overflow
borde *nm* [3764] edge
desbordamiento *nm* overflow
desbordante *aj* overflowing

borrar to erase
borrajear *vt* to scribble notes
borrar *vt* [4057] to erase
borronear *vt* to erase frequently
borrador *nm* [-dor(2)] eraser; rough draft
borrón *nm* act of erasing
borroso *aj* blurred, smeared
imborrable *aj* unforgettable

bosque forest
emboscar *vt* to ambush
bosquimano,-a, bosquimán,-a *nmf* Bushman
guardabosque *nmf* forest ranger
boscaje *nm* small forest
bosque *nm* [1405] forest
emboscada *nf* ambush
boscoso *aj* forested

botella bottle
embotellar *vt* to bottle
embotellador,-a *nmf* bottler
botellazo *nm* [-azo(2)] a hit with a bottle
embotellado *nm* bottling of liquids
embotellamiento *nm* bottling up (e.g., of traffic)
botella *nf* [3159] bottle
embotelladora *nf* bottling plant
embotellado *aj* bottled

botón button, bud
abotonar *vt* to button
abotonarse *vr* to button oneself up
botón *nm* button
botones *nm* bellboy
botonadura *nf* buttons of a piece of clothing as a group

bóveda curved structure
abovedar *vt* to cover a space with a curved structure; to make a curved structure
bóveda *nf* curved structure

bravo fierce, brave
bravucón,-a *nmf* person who is brave only in appearance
braveza *nf* valor
bravuconada *nf* false bravery
bravura *nf* [-ura(1)] valor
bravo *aj* [1410] fierce
bravucón *aj* brave only in appearance

brazo arm
abrazar *vt* [4689] to hug
abrazarse *vr* [4689] to hug each other
abrazo *nm* [-o(1)] hug
antebrazo *nm* forearm
brazal *nm* armband
brazalete *nm* bracelet
brazo *nm* [1358] arm
abrazadera *nf* clamp, brace
braza *nf* butterfly stroke (swimming)
brazada *nf* [-ada(3)] stroke (swimming)

breve brief
abreviar *vt* to abbreviate
breviario *nm* a brief; summary
abreviatura *nf* abbreviation
brevedad *nf* [4903] brevity
abreviado *aj* abbreviated
breve *aj* [1033] brief

brillante brilliant, shiny
abrillantar *vt* to make shiny
brillar *vi* [3894] to shine
abrillantador,-a *nmf* person who shines precious gems; product used for shining
abrillantado *nm* the process of shining something
brillo *nm* [-o(1) 4810] shine
brillantez *nf* brilliance
brillantina *nf* cosmetic used to make hair shine
brillante *aj* [-ante(1) 2342] brilliant, shiny

brindar to toast, to salute with a toast
brindar *vt* [867] to toast, to salute with a toast
brindis *nm* [4032] a toast

brioso full of energy and decision
brío *nm* energy, decision
brioso *aj* full of energy and decision

broma practical joke
bromear *vi* to play a practical joke on someone; to tease
embromar *vt* to play a practical joke on someone; to tease

bromista *nmf* practical joker
broma *nf* [3912] practical joke
bromista *aj* practical joking; given to playing practical jokes

bronce bronze
broncear *vt* to bronze; to tan
broncearse *vr* to become bronzed or suntanned; to get a suntan
bronce *nm* [3680] bronze
bronceador *nm* tanning lotion
bronceado *aj* bronzed; suntanned

brotar to bloom, to germinate, to sprout
brotar *vi* to bloom, to germinate, to sprout
rebrotar *vi* to sprout a branch; to revive
brote *nm* [3178] sprout

bruscamente brusquely
brusquedad *nf* brusqueness
bruscamente *av* brusquely; without subtlety
brusco *aj* brusque

bueno good
bonachón,-a *nmf* someone of good character
buenazo,-a *nmf* kind and peaceful person
bondad *nf* [4928] kindness; goodness
buenaventura *nf* good fortune, good luck
enhorabuena *nf* used as an expression of congratulations
bonachón *aj* of good character
bondadoso *aj* kind
buenazo *aj* of a kind and peaceful nature
bueno *aj* [84] good

burgués bourgeois
aburguesarse *vr* to become part of the bourgeoisie
burgués,-a *nmf* bourgeois
burgo *nm* small town dependent on a larger entity
burguesía *nf* bourgeoisie
burgués *aj* [-és] bourgeois

burla the making fun of someone
burlarse *vr* to make fun of someone
burlón,-a *nmf* one who makes fun of someone else
burla *nf* [-a 4489] the making fun of someone
burlesco *aj* [-esco] burlesque
burlón *aj* [-ón(2)] referring to a person who makes fun of someone

buscar to look for, to seek
buscar *vt* [154] to look for, to seek
rebuscar *vt* to look for again
buscapleitos *nmf* fighter; someone who is always looking for a fight
buscapiés *nm* a type of firecracker
busca *nf* [-a] act of looking for something

búsqueda *nf* [1972] search
rebusca *nf* act of looking for something again
buscada *aj* looked for; sought after

C

caballero gentleman
cabalgar *vi* to ride a horse
descabalgar *vi* to dismount
caballitos *nmpl* carousel
caballista *nmf* horse expert
caballerizo,-a *nmf* worker in a stable
caballero *nm* [1948] gentleman; knight
caballo *nm* [2365] horse
cabalgada *nf* ride on horseback; group of horseback riders
cabalgadura *nf* [-dura] saddle and accessories; riding horse
cabalgata *nf* procession of mounted horsemen
caballería *nf* riding horse
caballeriza *nf* stable
caballerosidad *nf* gentlemanliness
caballar *aj* pertaining to horses; horse-like
caballeresco *aj* [-esco] pertaining to knights
caballeroso *aj* gentlemanly

cabello hair
cabello *nm* [2159] hair
cabellera *nf* [4536] long hair
cabelludo *aj* having a lot of hair

caber to fit
caber *vi* [1276] to fit
cabida *nf* room to fit; capacity for more

cabeza head
cabecear *vi* to nod off
decapitar *vt* to decapitate
descabezar *vt* to decapitate
encabezar *vt* [1047] to head, to lead
cabecilla *nmf* head, leader
cabeceo *nm* [-eo(1)] nodding off
cabezazo *nm* hit with the head
cabezudo *nm* [-udo] person with a large head
encabezamiento *nm* action of leading or heading
reposacabezas *nm* headrest
rompecabezas *nm* jigsaw puzzle
cabecera *nf* [4602] headboard
cabeza *nf* [797] head
cabezota *nf* large head; person with a large head
decapitación *nf* decapitation

cabezón *aj* [-ón(2)] bigheaded, foolish
cabezudo *aj* [-udo] with a large head; bigheaded, foolish

cabra female goat
cabrero,-a *nmf* goatherd
cabrito,-a *nmf* young goat
cabrón *nm* male goat, also used as an offensive term
cabra *nf* [3186] female goat
cabritilla *nf* goatskin from a young goat
cabrío *aj* pertaining to goats

cadáver cadaver
cadáver *nm* [2769] cadaver
cadavérico *aj* pertaining to cadavers; cadaver-like, pale

cadena chain
desencadenar *vt* to remove a chain
desencadenarse *vr* to become free from a chain; to free oneself from a chain; to be unleashed (a series of events)
encadenar *vt* to chain
encadenado,-a *nmf* person in chains
desencadenamiento *nm* freeing from a chain; unleashing of a series of events
encadenamiento *nm* [-miento] chaining
cadena *nf* [1468] chain
encadenado *aj* chained

caer to fall
caer *vi* [447] to fall
caerse *vr* to fall (oneself)
decaer *vi* to decay
recaer *vi* to suffer a relapse (illness)
paracaidista *nmf* parachutist
paracaídas *nm* parachute
paracaidismo *nm* parachuting
caída *nf* [1270] fall
recaída *nf* relapse
alicaído *aj* depressed; weakened
caído *aj* fallen

café café; coffee
descafeinar *vt* to decaffeinate
café *nm* [1367] café; coffee
cafetal *nm* [-al(3)] coffee plantation
cafeto *nm* [-o(2)] coffee plant
cafeína *nf* caffeine
cafetera *nf* [-era 4221] coffee pot
cafetería *nf* [-ería(1)] cafeteria
cafetero *aj* pertaining to coffee
descafeinado *aj* decaffeinated

caja box, case
desencajar *vt* to dislodge, to remove something; to take out

desencajarse *vr* to be dislodged; to be removed from an encased position, to be removed from a tight enclosure

desencajonar *vt* to remove from a drawer

encajar *vt* to encase, to force into another object, to insert

encajarse *vr* to be forced into another object; to be inserted

encajonar *vt* to place in a drawer; (fig) to box in

cajero,-a *nmf* [4603] cashier

cajón *nm* [-ón(3)] drawer

encaje *nm* encasing, forcing of something inside another object

caja *nf* [1935] box, case

cajetilla *nf* [-illa] pack of cigarettes

desencajado *aj* removed, dislodged

encajado *aj* encased; lodged

cálculo calculation; calculus

calcular *vt* [2671] to calculate

calculador *nm* calculator

cálculo *nm* [-culo 4046] calculation; calculus

calculable *aj* [-able] calculable

calculador *aj* calculating

incalculable *aj* incalculable

calidad quality

calificar *vt* [-ificar 1052] to grade; to qualify

descalificar *vt* to disqualify

calificativo *nm* qualifying adverb or adjective

calificación *nf* [-ción 2194] grade

calidad *nf* [513] quality

descalificación *nf* disqualification

calificable *aj* able to qualify

calificado *aj* graded; qualified

calificador *aj* [4122] grading

calificativo *aj* qualifying

incalificable *aj* unable to qualify; shameful, disgraceful

callar to quiet, to silence

acallar *vt* to quiet, to silence

callar *vt* [3765] to quiet, to silence

callarse *vr* [3765] to be quiet, to be silent

callado *aj* quiet, silent

calle street

callejear *vi* to walk the streets

callejón *nm* alley

calle *nf* [214] street

callejuela *nf* [-uelo] short street

callejero *aj* [-ero(2) 3990] pertaining to streets; street-walking

calmar to calm

calmar *vt* [2348] to calm

calmarse *vr* [2348] to be calm

calmante *nm* tranquilizer

calma *nf* calm

calmante *aj* calming, tranquilizing

calmoso *aj* slow or lazy

calor heat

acalorar *vt* to produce heat

acalorarse *vr* to be overheating; to become angry

caldear *vt* to raise the temperature in a place

calentar *vt* [1642] to heat up something

precalentar *vt* to preheat

recalentar *vt* to reheat

sobrecalentarse *vr* to be overheated

sobrecalentar *vt* to overheat

acaloramiento *nm* heated discussion; heated words, anger

caldeamiento *nm* heating

caldero *nm* small cauldron

caldillo *nm* light gravy or broth

caldo *nm* [3506] broth

calentador *nm* heater

calentamiento *nm* heating

calientaplatos *nm* hot plate

calor *nm* [1926] heat

precalentamiento *nm* preheating

caldera *nf* [-era] cauldron

calefacción *nf* heating system

calentura *nf* fever

caloría *nf* [-ería(2) 3507] calorie

acalorado *aj* hot

caldoso *aj* with broth, similar to broth in texture; soupy

calentador *aj* heating

calenturiento *aj* [-iento] feverish

cálido *aj* [-ido(1) 4205] warm

caliente *aj* hot

calórico *aj* fattening; with many calories

caluroso *aj* warm

cama bed

encamar *vt* to put to bed

encamarse *vr* to be bedridden

camillero,-a *nmf* stretcher bearer

camarote *nm* [-ote] berth, cabin in a ship

camastro *nm* [-astro] uncomfortable bed

cama *nf* [2657] bed

camarera *nf* maid; waitress

camilla *nf* [-illa] stretcher

cubrecama *nf* bedspread

recámara *nf* bedroom

encamado *aj* bedridden

camarada comrade

camarada *nmf* comrade

camaradería *nf* camaraderie

cambio change
cambalachear *vt* to exchange
cambiar *vti* [437] to change
cambiarse *vr* to move; to change
descambiar *vt* to undo a change
intercambiar *vt* [3408] to exchange
recambiar *vt* to move or change again
cambista *nmf* moneychanger
cambiazo *nm* fraud
cambio *nm* [-o(1) 202] change
intercambio *nm* [-o(1) 2661] exchange
cambiante *aj* changing
intercambiable *aj* exchangeable

camino road, path
caminar *vi* [1493] to walk
encaminar *vt* [2584] to start someone down a
    path
encaminarse *vr* [2584] to follow a pursuit
caminante *nmf* [-ante(2)] walker
camino *nm* [-ino(1) 663] road, path
caminata *nf* [4351] walk, stroll

camión bus, truck
camionero,-a *nmf* bus driver; truck driver
autocamión *nm* bus; truck
camión *nm* [951] bus; truck
camioneta *nf* [-eta 1398] van; pickup truck

camisa shirt
camisero,-a *nmf* shirt maker or seller
camisón *nm* nightgown
camisa *nf* [4206] shirt
camisera *nf* blouse
camisería *nf* clothing store specializing in shirts
camiseta *nf* [-eta 3187] tee shirt; undershirt
camisola *nf* camisole
descamisado *aj* shirtless; poor or miserable

campana bell
campanear *vi* to ring a bell
campanero,-a *nmf* bell maker; bell ringer
campanario *nm* bell tower
campaneo *nm* [-eo(1)] ringing of a bell
campana *nf* [4868] bell
campanada *nf* one ring of a bell
campanilla *nf* small bell
acampanado *aj* bell-shaped

campeón champion
campeón,-a *nmf* [673] champion
campeonato *nm* [-ato 834] championship
subcampeón *nm* [4946] runner-up, second place
    winner

campo country
acampar *vi* to camp
campear *vi* to lead or take animals to pasture

campesino,-a *nmf* peasant; one who lives in the
    country
campista *nmf* camper
campamento *nm* [4047] camp
campesinado *nm* peasantry
campo *nm* [306] country
descampado *nm* countryside without
    vegetation
acampada *nf* camping
campiña *nf* agricultural field
campero *aj* [-ero(2)] out in the open, in the
    country
campesino *aj* [-ino(2) 597] rural, pertaining to the
    country
campestre *aj* [-estre 1902] rural, pertaining to the
    country
campirano *aj* rural, pertaining to the country
descampado *aj* barren, without vegetation

canal canal
canalizar *vt* [-izar 3029] to build a canal
canalón *nm* gutter
canal *nf* [916] canal
canalización *nf* building of a canal
acanalado *aj* grooved, channeled

cándido candid
candor *nm* candor
candidez *nf* candidness
cándido *aj* [-ido(1)] candid
candoroso *aj* candid

canon religious canon
canonizar *vt* to canonize
canon *nm* religious canon
canonización *nf* [-ción 4334] canonization
canónico *aj* canonical

cansar to tire
cansar *vt* [2528] to tire
cansarse *vr* [2528] to become tired
descansar *vi* [2148] to rest
cansancio *nm* [3925] tiredness
descansadero *nm* resting place
descanso *nm* [-o(1) 1905] rest
incansablemente *av* untiringly
cansado *aj* tired
descansado *aj* rested
incansable *aj* untiring

cantar to sing
cantar *vt* [843] to sing
canturrear *vi* to sing in a low voice or without
    paying much attention; to hum
encantar *vt* [2092] to charm; to enchant
cantante *nmf* [-ante(2) 423] singer
cantor,-a *nmf* singer
cancionero *nm* music book

cantar *nm* [843] singing
canto *nm* [-o(1) 2666] song, chant
canturreo *nm* singing in a low voice or without paying much attention; humming
canción *nf* [520] song
cantata *nf* cantata
cantante *aj* [-ante(2) 423] singing
cantor *aj* singing
encantado *aj* charmed; enchanted

caña cane (plant); fishing pole
cáñamo *nm* hemp
cañamón *nm* hemp seeds
cañaveral *nm* cane field
caña *nf* [3960] cane (plant); fishing pole

cañón cannon
cañonear *vt* to fire a cannon; to bombard
encañonar *vt* to aim a cannon or firearm
cañón *nm* [4785] cannon
cañonazo *nm* hit with a cannonball
encañado *nm* fortified with cannon
cañonero *aj* armed with cannon

caos chaos
caos *nm* [4167] chaos
caótico *aj* [-ico(2)] chaotic

capa cape
capirote *nm* pointed cap
capote *nm* cape with sleeves
capa *nf* [2980] cape
capucha *nf* hood attached to a cape

capacidad capacity
capacitar(se) *vt(r)* [2778] to train
incapacitar *vt* [2778] to incapacitate
recapacitar *vi* to reflect, to think over
capacidad *nf* [-idad 646] capacity, ability
capacitación *nf* [-ción 1686] training
incapacidad *nf* [-idad 4095] incapacity
capaz *aj* [-az 1499] capable
incapacitado *aj* untrained; injured
incapaz *aj* [-az 4461] incapable

capilla chapel
capellán *nm* chaplain; priest
capilla *nf* [2991] chapel

capital capital
capitalizar *vt* to capitalize
capitalista *nmf* [-ista] capitalist
capitalismo *nm* capitalism
capitalización *nf* capitalization
capital *aj* [487] capital
capitalista *aj* [-ista] capitalistic

capitán captain
capitanear *vt* to act as captain; to lead troops
capitán,-a *nmf* [2458] captain

capitana *nf* wife of a captain
capitanía *nf* captaincy

capricho capricious
encapricharse *vr* to act capriciously, to be capricious
caprichoso,-a *nmf* capricious person
capricho *nm* caprice
encaprichamiento *nm* capriciousness
caprichoso *aj* capricious

cara face
carear *vt* to bring face-to-face
caricaturizar *vt* to draw a caricature
encarar *vt* [4607] to face
encararse *vr* [4607] to be facing
caricaturista *nmf* caricaturist; cartoon artist
descarado,-a *nmf* shameless person
careo *nm* [-eo(1)] judicial confrontation
descaro *nm* insolence
cara *nf* [1094] face
carátula *nf* face of a clock
careta *nf* cardboard mask
caricatura *nf* [-ura(2)] caricature; cartoon
descaradamente *av* insolently
descarado *aj* insolent
encarado *aj* referring to facial appearance

carácter character
caracterizar *vt* [-izar 1758] to characterize
caracterizarse *vr* [1758] to be characterized
carácter *nm* [1443] character
característica *nf* characteristic
caracterización *nf* characterization
característicamente *av* characteristically
característico *aj* [-ico(2) 1324] characteristic
caracterizado *aj* characterized

carbón coal; charcoal
carbonizar *vt* to carbonize
carbonizarse *vr* to be carbonized
carbón *nm* [4604] coal; charcoal
carboncillo *nm* charcoal pencil
carbonero *nm* [-ero(2)] charcoal maker or seller
carbono *nm* carbon
supercarburante *nm* high-octane fuel
carbonera *nf* [-era] locker for storing coal or charcoal
carbonería *nf* store specializing in sale of coal or charcoal
carbonización *nf* carbonization
carbonero *aj* [-ero(2)] pertaining to coal or charcoal
carbónico *aj* containing carbon; pertaining to carbon
carbonífero *aj* carboniferous

carcajada guffaw, loud laughter
  carcajearse *vr* to guffaw, to laugh loudly
  carcajada *nf* guffaw, loud laughter

cárcel jail
  desencarcelar *vt* to free from jail
  encarcelar *vt* [4124] to jail, to put in jail
  carcelero,-a *nmf* jailer
  cárcel *nf* [1416] jail
  encarcelación *nf* incarceration

cargo charge; responsibility
  cargar *vt* [1988] to carry; to charge
  cargarse *vr* to be charged; to carry
  descargar *vt* to discharge; to empty
  descargarse *vr* to become discharged; to run
    out of energy
  encargar *vt* [686] to place in charge of; to assign
    a task to
  encargarse *vr* [686] to take charge of
  sobrecargar *vt* to overload, to overburden
  sobrecargarse *vr* to become overcharged with
    energy
  cargador,-a *nmf* person who carries or loads
  descargador,-a *nmf* person who unloads
  encargado,-a *nmf* person in charge
  carga *nm* [-a 1831] load
  cargador *nm* charger
  cargamento *nm* cargo
  cargo *nm* [-o(1) 398] charge; responsibility;
    position
  carguero *nm* cargo ship, freighter
  descargo *nm* unloading
  encargo *nm* task, assignment; act of placing
    someone in charge
  montacargas *nm* freight elevator
  recargo *nm* extra charge or fee, surcharge,
    penalty
  sobrecargo *nm* overload
  cargazón *nf* heaviness
  descarga *nf* [-a 4542] unloading
  recarga *nf* recharging
  sobrecarga *nf* surcharge
  cargado *aj* charged; loaded
  cargador *aj* charging
  encargado *aj* [-ado(2)] in charge
  recargable *aj* rechargeable
  recargado *aj* recharged

cariño care
  acariciar *vt* to caress
  acariciarse *vr* to be caressed; to caress each
    other
  encariñarse *vr* to be fond of
  cariño *nm* [1792] care
  caricia *nf* [-a] caress

  acariciador *aj* caressing
  cariñoso *aj* caring

carne meat; flesh
  descarnar *vt* to remove the meat from a bone
  encarnar *vt* [3964] to incarnate
  encarnarse *vr* to become flesh
  reencarnarse *vr* to be reincarnated
  carnicero,-a *nmf* butcher
  carnero *nm* [4663] male sheep
  carne *nf* [1110] meat; flesh
  carnicería *nf* [-ería(1)] meat market; butcher's
    shop; carnage
  encarnación *nf* [-ción 4245] incarnation
  reencarnación *nf* reincarnation
  carnal *aj* carnal
  carnicero *aj* [-ero(3)] carnivorous
  cárnico *aj* pertaining to meat
  carnívoro *aj* [-ívoro] carnivorous
  carnoso *aj* [-oso] meaty, fleshy
  descarnado *aj* having little or no meat
  encarnado *aj* incarnate

carretera highway
  acarrear *vt* to transport a load; to carry
    consequences
  acarreo *nm* transporting of a load
  carretero *nm* car builder
  carretón *nm* two-wheeled cart or wagon
  carril *nm* [2913] lane
  carro *nm* [971] car; chariot
  carruaje *nm* carriage
  carreta *nf* cart, wagon
  carretada *nf* [-ada(3)] load
  carretera *nf* [970] highway
  carretilla *nf* [-illa] wheelbarrow
  carrocería *nf* body of a car
  carroza *nf* hearse

carta letter
  cartearse *vr* to correspond by letter
  carterista *nmf* [-ista] pickpocket
  cartero,-a *nmf* mail carrier, postman
  abrecartas *nm* letter opener
  cartel *nm* [2011] poster
  carteo *nm* correspondence
  pesacartas *nm* postal scale
  carta *nf* [1201] letter
  cartelera *nf* entertainment guide; marquee
  cartera *nf* [-era 3530] wallet

casa house
  casar *vt* [1709] to marry
  casarse *vr* [1709] to get married
  descasar *vt* to divorce; to annul
  casamentero,-a *nmf* matchmaker
  casamiento *nm* wedding

caserón *nm* [-ón(3)] large house, mansion
casa *nf* [135] house
casona *nf* large house, mansion
casadero *aj* [-ero(2)] of marriageable age
casado *aj* [2009] married
casamentero *aj* matchmaking
casero *aj* [-ero(3)] homemade
malcasado *aj* divorced

castellano Spanish language
castellanizar *vt* to adapt a foreign word to the
  Spanish language
castellano,-a *nmf* Castilian
castellanismo *nm* Spanish word or expression
  adopted for use in another language
castellano *nm* Spanish language
castellano *aj* pertaining to the Spanish
  language; Castilian

castigo punishment
castigar *vt* [2560] to punish
castigo *nm* [-o(1) 2958] punishment

castizo pure
castidad *nf* [-idad] chastity
castizo *aj* [-izo] pure
casto *aj* chaste

casualidad coincidence
casualidad *nf* [-idad] coincidence
casualmente *av* coincidentally, accidentally
casual *aj* coincidental, accidental

catálogo catalog
catalogar *vt* [4733] to catalog, to classify
catálogo *nm* catalog
catalogación *nf* cataloguing, classification

catástrofe catastrophe
catástrofe *nf* catastrophe
catastrófico *aj* catastrophic

cátedra subject of study at a university
catedrático,-a *nmf* professor
cátedra *nf* subject of study at a university

catolicismo Catholicism
católico,-a *nmf* Catholic
catolicismo *nm* Catholicism
católico *aj* [-ico(2) 1548] Catholic

caudal abundance of water
acaudalar *vt* to learn much; to make a fortune
caudal *nm* abundance of water
acaudalado *aj* rich, wealthy
caudaloso *aj* with great abundance

caudillo military leader
acaudillar *vt* to lead a military group
caudillaje *nm* [-aje(1)] military leadership
caudillo *nm* military leader

causa cause
causar *vt* [716] to cause
causa *nf* [-a 518] cause
causalidad *nf* causality
causal *aj* causal
causante *aj* [4298] causing

caza hunt
cazar *vt* [3702] to hunt
cazador,-a *nmf* hunter
cazatalentos *nmf* talent searcher; headhunter
cazabombardero *nm* fighter bomber
cazasubmarinos *nm* submarine chaser
cazatorpedero *nm* destroyer
cacería *nf* hunting
caza *nf* hunting, hunt
cazador *aj* [-dor(1)] hunting

ceder to cede, to yield
acceder *vt* [2587] to accede; to concede
ceder *vti* [2275] to cede, to yield
conceder *vt* [2082] to concede

cegar to blind
cegar *vt* to blind
cegarse *vr* to become blind
cegato,-a *nmf* myopic person
ciego,-a *nmf* blind person
ceguera *nf* blindness
cegador *aj* blinding
cegato *aj* suffering from myopia
ciego *aj* [-o(1) 4262] blind

ceja eyebrow
entrecejo *nm* space between the eyebrows
ceja *nf* eyebrow
cejijunto *aj* with eyebrows close together

celda jail or prison cell; cell of a beehive;
  spreadsheet cell
celda *nf* [4240] jail or prison cell; cell of a
  beehive; spreadsheet cell
celdilla *nf* cell of a beehive

celebrar to celebrate; to laugh at a joke
celebrar *vt* [332] to celebrate; to laugh at a joke
celebrarse *vr* [332] to be celebrated, to have a
  celebration
celebración *nf* [-ción 1591] celebration
celebridad *nf* celebrity
celebrante *aj* [-ante(2)] celebrating
célebre *aj* [4241] well-known, famous

celeste sky blue
celeste *nm* [4187] sky blue
cielo *nm* [2118] sky; heaven
rascacielos *nm* skyscraper
celeste *aj* [4187] sky blue
celestial *aj* celestial, heavenly

celos jealousy
encelar *vt* to make jealous
encelarse *vr* to become jealous
recelar *vt* to be suspicious
celos *nmpl* jealousy
recelo *nm* suspicion
celoso *aj* jealous
receloso *aj* suspicious

célula cell
célula *nf* [2235] cell
celular *aj* [2595] cellular
unicelular *aj* unicellular

cenar to eat dinner, to dine
cenar *vi* to eat dinner, to dine
cena *nf* [-a 2646] dinner

centro center; downtown
centralizar *vt* [-izar] to centralize
centralizarse *vr* to be centralized
centrar *vt* [2764] to center
concentrar(se) *vt(r)* [1565] to concentrate
descentralizar *vt* to decentralize
descentrar *vt* to remove from the center
desconcentrar *vt* to distract
descontrentarse *vr* to become distracted
centrista *nmf* centrist
centrocampista *nmf* halfback (soccer)
centralismo *nm* centralism
centro *nm* [175] center; downtown
concentrado *nm* concentration
central *nf* [-al(2) 672] central
centralización *nf* centralization
concentración *nf* [-ción 2033] concentration
descentralización *nf* decentralization
centrado *aj* centered
central *aj* [-al(2) 672] central
centralista *aj* centralist, someone who favors
  the centralization of power
centralizador *aj* centralizing
céntrico *aj* centrally located
centrípeto *aj* centripetal
centrista *aj* centrist
concentrado *aj* concentrated
concéntrico *aj* concentric
descentrado *aj* not centered
desconcentrado *aj* unfocused, lacking in
  concentration

ceñido tight
ceñir *vt* to tighten; to adjust tightly
ceñirse *vr* to tighten (on oneself); to adjust
  tightly (on oneself); to tighten one's belt (also
  figurative)
desceñir *vt* to loosen
ceñido *aj* tight; adjusted

cera wax
cerumen *nm* earwax
cirio *nm* large wax candle
cera *nf* wax

cerca ncar
cercanía *nf* [-ería(2) 4311] nearby surroundings
cerca *av* [502] near
cercano *aj* [1096] near

cerco fence
cercar *vt* to fence
cercado *nm* [-ado(2)] fenced area
cerco *nm* fence
cerca *nf* [502] fence

cerebro brain
cerebelo *nm* cerebellum
cerebro *nm* [2521] brain
cerebral *aj* [3332] cerebral

cerrar to close
cerrar *vt* [527] to close
encerrar *vt* [3405] to enclose; to lock up
encerrarse *vr* [3405] to be withdrawn
cerrajero,-a *nmf* locksmith
cerrojo *nm* keyhole
cierre *nm* [1290] closing time; zipper
encierro *nm* locking up; enclosing
cerradura *nf* [-dura] keyhole
cerrajería *nf* locksmith's shop
cerrado *aj* closed
encerrado *aj* locked up; enclosed

cesar to cease
cesar *vi* to cease
cese *nm* [4931] cessation
cesación *nf* cessation
incesantemente *av* incessantly
cesante *aj* ceasing
incesante *aj* incessant

charla chatting
charlar *vi* to chat
charlatán,-a *nmf* charlatan
charla *nf* [-a 3717] chatting
charlatanería *nf* charlatanism
charlador *aj* given to chatting
charlatán *aj* engaging in charlatanism

cheque check
cheque *nm* [3333] check
chequera *nf* checkbook

chico small
achicar *vt* to make smaller
achicarse *vr* to become smaller
chico,-a *nmf* boy or girl
chiquillo,-a *nmf* boy or girl; young man or
  woman, term of endearment

chiquitín,-a *nmf* term of endearment for a man or woman
chiquito,-a *nmf* little boy or girl
chicote *nm* [-ote] short piece of rope or string, etc.
chiquillada *nf* group of children
achicado *aj* made smaller
chico *aj* [853] small
chiquitín *aj* very small
chiquito *aj* tiny

chifla whistle
chiflar *vi* to whistle
rechiflar *vi* to whistle insistently
chifla *nf* whistle

chiste joke
chistoso,-a *nmf* funny person
chiste *nm* [4557] joke
chistoso *aj* funny

chocar to crash
chocar *vi* [3196] to crash
choque *nm* [1688] crash

chocolate chocolate
chocolatero,-a *nmf* person who makes or sells chocolate; chocolate lover
chocolate *nm* [3059] chocolate
chocolatín *nm* small bar of chocolate
chocolatera *nf* [-era] pot for making hot chocolate
chocolatería *nf* store specializing in chocolate or hot chocolate; chocolate factory
chocolatero *aj* chocolate loving

ciclo cycle
reciclar *vt* to recycle
ciclista *nmf* [-ista 2178] cyclist
motociclista *nmf* motorcyclist
ciclismo *nm* cycling
ciclo *nm* [1266] cycle
ciclo-cross *nm* motocross bicycling
ciclón *nm* cyclone
motocicleta *nm* [4745] motorcycle
motociclismo *nm* motorcycling
reciclaje *nm* recycling
triciclo *nm* tricycle
bicicleta *nf* [2603] bicycle
cíclico *aj* cyclic
ciclista *aj* [-ista 2178] pertaining to bicycles or bicycling
reciclado *aj* recycled

ciencia science
científico,-a *nmf* scientist
ciencia *nf* [1466] science
científico *aj* [-ico(2) 1531] scientific

ciento one hundred
centenario,-a *nmf* centenarian
centavo *nm* [-avo 2469] cent
centena, centenar *nm* one hundred
centenario *nm* [-ario(2) 3537] century, one hundred years
centésimo *nm* [-ésimo] one-hundredth (fraction)
centigramo *nm* centigram
centilitro *nm* centiliter
centímetro *nm* [2770] centimeter
céntimo *nm* cent
centurión *nm* centurion
cien *nm* [1799] one hundred
cienmilésimo *nm* one hundred thousandth
cienmillonésimo *nm* one hundred millionth
porcentaje *nm* [-aje(1) 1816] percentage
centena *nf* hundred
centuria *nf* century
centenario *aj* [-ario(2) 3537] hundred-year-old
centésimo *aj* [-ésimo] hundredth
centígrado *aj* [4455] centigrade
cien *aj* [1799] one hundred
cienmilésimo *aj* hundred thousandth
cienmillonésimo *aj* hundred millionth
ciento *aj* [134] one hundred
porcentual *aj* [4196] percentage

cierto certain
acertar *vt* [3859] to hit the mark; to be right
certificar *vt* [-ificar 3345] to certify
desacertar *vi* to miss the mark; to be wrong
acertijo *nm* riddle
acierto *nm* hitting the mark
desacierto *nm* missing the mark
certeza *nf* [-eza 3860] certainty; truth
certidumbre *nf* [-dumbre] certainty; truth
certificación *nf* [-ción 4188] certification
incertidumbre *nf* [dumbre 3104] lack of certainty, doubt
ciertamente *av* [-mente 3112] certainly
inciertamente *av* uncertainly; falsely
acertado *aj* on the mark, correct
certero *aj* with good aim
certificado *aj* [3370] certified
cierto *aj* [403] certain; true
desacertado *aj* off the mark, incorrect
incierto *aj* [4791] uncertain; untrue, false

cifra cipher, code; numerical digit
cifrar *vt* to write a code
cifrarse *vr* to summarize or synthesize
descifrar *vt* to decipher or break a code
desciframiento *nm* code breaking
cifra *nf* [-a 977] cipher, code; numerical digit
cifrado *aj* coded

descifrado *aj* solved, cracked, broken (code)
descifrable *aj* decipherable
indescifrable *aj* indecipherable

cigarro cigarette
cigarrero,-a *nmf* cigarette maker or seller
cigarrillo *nm* cigarette
cigarro *nm* [3463] cigarette
cigarrera *nf* cigarette case

cima top
encimar *vt* to place on top
cima *nf* [3565] top
encima *av* [1539] on top of

cimientos foundations
cimentar *vt* to lay a foundation
cimientos *nmpl* foundations
cemento *nm* [4888] cement
cimiento *nm* foundation

cinco five
cincuentón,-a *nmf* fifty-year-old person
cinco *nm* [228] five
cincuenta *nm* [2401] fifty
cincuentavo *nm* [-avo] one-fiftieth (fraction)
cincuentenario *nm* fiftieth anniversary
cincuentena *nf* group of fifty
cinco *aj* [228] five
cincuenta *aj* [2401] fifty
cincuentavo *aj* [-avo] fiftieth
cincuentón *aj* [-ón(2)] fifty-year-old

cine cinema, movie theater
cineasta *nmf* [3392] cinematographer
cinéfilo,-a *nmf* movie lover
cine *nm* [554] cinema, movie theater
cineclub *nm* association for promoting films
cinematógrafo *nm* movie projector
cinematografía *nf* cinematography
cinematográfico *aj* [-ico(2) 2262] cinematographic

cínico cynical
cínico,-a *nmf* cynic
cinismo *nm* cynicism
cínico *aj* cynical

cinto belt
encintar *vt* to tie with a belt or drawstring; to wrap with tape
cinto *nm* belt
cinturón *nm* [4439] seatbelt
cinta *nf* [652] tape
cintura *nf* waist

círculo circle
circular *vti* [1369] to circulate
circuncidar *vt* to circumcise
circundar *vt* to encircle
circunscribir *vt* to circumscribe

circunvalar *vt* to surround
circo *nm* [4953] circus
circuito *nm* [1525] circuit
círculo *nm* [-culo 2745] circle
circunloquio *nm* circumlocution
cortacircuitos *nm* circuit breaker
cortocircuito *nm* short circuit
semicírculo *nm* semicircle
circulación *nf* [-ción 1390] circulation
circular *nf* [1369] circular
circuncisión *nf* circumcision
circunferencia *nf* circumference
circunlocución *nf* circumlocution
circunscripción *nf* circumscription
circunspección *nf* circumspection, prudence
circunstancia *nf* [-ancia 1694] circumstance
circular *aj* [1369] circular
circulatorio *aj* [-orio(2)] circulatory
circunciso *aj* circumcised
circundante *aj* surrounding
circunflejo *aj* circumflex
circunscrito *aj* circumscribed
circunspecto *aj* circumspect, prudent
circunstancial *aj* circumstantial
semicircular *aj* semicircular

citar to cite a source; to make an appointment
citar *vti(r)* [750] to cite a source; to make an appointment
citarse *vr* to make an appointment with each other
citatorio *nm* summons to court
cita *nf* [-a 1469] citation, reference; appointment, date
citación *nf* citation (ticket), summons to court

ciudad city
ciudadano,-a *nmf* [567] citizen
ciudad *nf* [58] city
ciudadanía *nf* [-ería(2) 1035] citizenship
ciudadela *nf* citadel
ciudadano *aj* citizen

civilización civilization
civilizar *vt* to civilize
civilizarse *vr* to become civilized
civilista *nmf* expert in civil law
civismo *nm* civics
civilización *nf* civilization
cívico *aj* [-ico(2) 3285] civic
civil *aj* [608] civil
civilizado *aj* civilized
civilizador *aj* civilizing
incivil *aj* uncivil
incivilizado *aj* uncivilized

claro clear

aclarar *vt* [890] to clarify or explain; to clear up;
   to make lighter
aclararse *vr* to become clear; to clear up
clarear *vt* to make clear or light
clarearse *vr* to become transparent or light
clarificar *vt* to clarify
esclarecer *vt* [4911] to enlighten; to resolve a
   conflict
clarividente *nmf* person able to see and
   understand clearly; person with acute
   perception
esclarecimiento *nm* [-miento] enlightenment;
   resolution of a conflict
aclaración *nf* clarification; explanation
clara *nf* egg white
claridad *nf* [-idad 3268] clarity
clarificación *nf* clarification
clarividencia *nf* ability to see and understand
   clearly; acute perception
claro *int* [472] of course!
claro *av* [472] clearly
aclarado *aj* explained
aclaratorio *aj* [-orio(2)] clarifying, explanatory
clarificador *aj* clarifying
clarividente *aj* able to see and understand
   clearly; having acute perception
claro *aj* [472] clear; bright; light
esclarecido *aj* illuminated; explained

clase class, category

clasificar *vt* [-ificar 1949] to classify, to categorize
clase *nf* [712] class; category
clasificación *nf* [-ción 1854] classification
clasista *aj* relating to socio-economic classes

clásico classic

clasicista *nmf* classicist, expert in classics
neoclásico,-a *nmf* neoclassicist
clasicismo *nm* classicism
clásico *nm* [1462] classic
neoclasicismo *nm* neoclassicism
clasicista *aj* classicist
clásico *aj* [1462] classic
neoclásico *aj* neoclassic

claustro cloister

enclaustrar *vt* to hide; to place in a secret place
enclaustrarse *vr* to be hidden; to be placed in a
   secret place
claustro *nm* cloister
claustrofobia *nf* [-fobia] claustrophobia
enclaustrado *aj* hidden

clavar to nail

clavar *vt* to nail

desclavar *vt* to remove a nail
enclavar *vt* to nail
clavo *nm* nail
sacaclavos *nm* nail remover
clavija *nf* plug
clavado *aj* nailed

clave key; password

clave *nf* [1573] key; password
clave *aj* [1573] key

clérigo cleric

clérigo *nm* cleric
clero *nm* clergy; congregation
clerecía *nf* clergy

cliente client, customer

cliente *nmf* [1561] client, customer
clientela *nf* clientele

clima climate; weather

aclimatar *vt* to acclimate
aclimatarse *vr* to become acclimated
climatizar *vt* [-izar] to control the climate
aclimatación *nf* acclimation
clima *nf* [2251] climate; weather
climatización *nf* control of the climate
climatología *nf* climatology, study of climates
aclimatable *aj* able to be climate-controlled
climático *aj* climatic
climatizado *aj* climate controlled
climatológico *aj* pertaining to the study of
   climates

clínica clinic

clínico,-a *nmf* clinician
clínica *nf* [1515] clinic
clínico *aj* clinical

club club

aeroclub *nm* airplane flying club
cineclub *nm* association for promoting films
videoclub *nm* video rental store

cobardía cowardice

acobardar *vt* to frighten
acobardarse *vr* to cower; to be cowardly
cobarde *nmf* coward
cobardía *nf* [-ería(2)] cowardice
cobardemente *av* cowardly
cobarde *aj* cowardly

cobrar to charge

cobrar *vt* [1080] to charge
cobrarse *vr* to recuperate (regaining money,
   regaining health)
cobrador *nm* bill collector
cobro *nm* [-o(1) 1845] bill collecting
cobrador *aj* bill collecting

cobre copper
  cobre *nm* [4844] copper
  cobrizo *aj* [-izo] copper-colored; copper

coche car
  guardacoches *nmf* parking lot attendant
  lavacoches *nmf* car washer
  coche *nm* [3024] car
  cochero *nm* [-ero(1)] coachman; driver of a carriage
  cochera *nf* garage

cocina kitchen
  cocer *vt* [1970] to boil; to cook
  cocerse *vr* to be boiling; to be cooking
  cocinar *vt* [3286] to cook, to prepare food, to prepare a meal
  cocinero,-a *nmf* cook
  cocido *nm* [-ido(2)] boiling; cooking
  cocina *nf* [-a 1980] kitchen
  cocido *aj* [-ido(2)] cooked

código code
  codificar *vt* to codify
  codificación *nf* codification
  codificador *aj* codifying

cohibido inhibited, reserved
  cohibir *vt* to inhibit
  cohibirse *vr* to behave in an inhibited manner, to behave with restraint
  cohibición *nf* inhibition
  cohibido *aj* inhibited, reserved

cola tail
  colear *vi* to move the tail; to mop
  coleador *nm* mop
  cola *nf* [3197] tail

colaboración collaboration
  colaborar *vi* [1894] to collaborate
  colaboracionista *nmf* collaborator, one who cooperates with the enemy
  colaborador,-a *nmf* [2998] collaborator, one who works or cooperates with another on a project
  colaboración *nf* [-ción 2018] collaboration
  colaborador *aj* collaborating

colección collection
  coleccionar *vt* to make or form a collection
  colectar *vt* to raise funds
  recolectar *vt* [4750] to collect
  coleccionista *nmf* collector
  colección *nf* [2866] collection
  colecta *nf* collection (money)
  recolección *nf* [3832] recollection

colectivo collective
  colectivizar *vt* to form a collective
  colectivo *nm* [-ivo 2619] collective

colectividad *nf* collectivity
colectivización *nf* collectivization
colectivo *aj* [-ivo 2619] collective

colegio secondary school
  colega *nmf* [2917] colleague
  colegial,-a *nmf* secondary school student
  colegio *nm* [1264] secondary school

cólera anger
  encolerizar *vt* to anger; to make angry
  encolerizarse *vr* to become very angry, to become filled with ire
  cólera *nf* anger

colgar to hang
  colgar *vt* [3255] to hang
  colgarse *vr* to be hung
  descolgar *vt* to take down
  descolgarse *vr* to be taken down
  colgante *nm* [-ante(1)] errand; pendant
  colgado *aj* hung
  colgante *aj* [-ante(1)] hanging

colmar to overflow
  colmar *vt* to overflow
  colmado *aj* overflowing

colonia colony
  colonizar *vt* to colonize
  descolonizar *vt* to decolonize
  colonialista *nmf* colonialist
  colonizador,-a *nmf* colonizer, colonist
  coloniaje *nm* colonial period
  colonialismo *nm* colonialism
  colonia *nf* [173] colony; neighborhood
  colonización *nf* colonization
  descolonización *nf* decolonization
  colonial *aj* [-al(2)] colonial
  colonialista *aj* colonialistic, colonialist
  colonizador *aj* colonizing

color color
  colorear *vt* to color
  decolorar *vt* to bleach; to remove color from clothing
  decolorarse *vr* to become bleached; to become lighter in color
  colorista *nmf* painter, colorist
  color *nm* [574] color
  colorado *nm* [-ado(1)] red
  colorante *nm* substance used for coloring, food coloring
  colorete *nm* [-ete] lipstick
  colorido *nm* strong or bright coloring
  decolorante *nm* chemical used for removing color
  descoloramiento *nm* removal of color
  Tecnicolor *nm* Technicolor

coloración *nf* coloration
decoloración *nf* discoloration
colorado *aj* [-ado(1)] red
colorante *aj* coloring
colorista *aj* coloristic
descolorido *aj* discolored, pale
incoloro *aj* colorless
unicolor *aj* of one color

colosal colossal
coloso *nm* colossus
colosal *aj* colossal

columna column
columnista *nmf* columnist
quintacolumnista *nmf* member of a fifth
   column
columna *nf* [?498] column
columnata *nf* colonnade

comarca region, shire
comarca *nf* [723] region, shire
comarcal *aj* regional
comarcano *aj* nearby

combinación combination
combinar *vt* [1870] to combine
combinarse *vr* to be combined
combinado *nm* combination
combinación *nf* [-ción 2926] combination
combinado *aj* combined

combustible combustible
combustible *nm* [2907] combustible material
combustión *nf* combustion
combustible *aj* [2907] combustible
incombustible *aj* incombustible

comedia comedy
comediante *nmf* [-ante(2) 3718] comedian,
   comedienne
cómico,-a *nmf* comic
comedia *nf* [2240] comedy
comicidad *nf* funniness, comicalness
tragicomedia *nf* tragic comedy
cómico *aj* [3703] comic, comical
tragicómico *aj* tragicomic

comentar to comment
comentar *vt* [264] to comment
comentarista *nmf* commentator
comentario *nm* [1345] comment, commentary

comenzar to commence, to begin
comenzar *vt* [313] to commence, to begin
recomenzar *vti* to recommence, to begin again
comienzo *nm* [-o(1) 2881] beginning

comer to eat
carcomer *vt* to gnaw (done by worms)
carcomerse *vr* to be consumed

comer *vt* [841] to eat
comerse *vr* to leave out, to skip something
   written or spoken (word, letter)
malcomer *vi* to eat poorly
comestibles *nmpl* groceries
comensal *nmf* restaurant customer
comilón,-a *nmf* big eater; glutton
comedero *nm* feeding-trough
comedor *nm* dining room
carcoma *nf* woodworm
comida *nf* [-ido(2) 1097] food
comestible *aj* edible
comilón *aj* [-ón(2)] big eating; gluttonous
incomestible *aj* inedible
incomible *aj* inedible

comercial commercial
comercializar *vt* [-izar 3030] to commercialize
comerciar *vi* to engage in business
comerciante *nmf* [-ante(2) 1325] businessman,
   merchant
comercial *nm* [-cial 633] commercial, radio or
   television avertisement
comercio *nm* [-o(1) 685] commerce, business
comercialización *nf* [-ción 2435] commercialization
comercial *aj* [-cial 633] commercial
comerciante *aj* [-ante(2) 1325] business

cometer to commit
acometer *vt* to attack or work on a problem
   vigorously
cometer *vt* [1265] to commit
cometido *nm* [-ido(2) 2068] commitment,
   responsibility
acometida *nf* attacking or working vigorously
   on a problem
acometividad *nf* audacity
comisión *nf* [-sión 265] commission
acometedor *aj* audacious

comisario chief of police or other organization
comisario *nm* chief of police or other
   organization
comisaría *nf* police station

comisión commission
comisionar *vt* [2936] to commission
comisionado,-a *nmf* person commissioned to
   perform a specific task
comisión *nm* [-sión 265] commission
subcomisión *nm* subcommittee
comisionado *aj* commissioned

cómodo comfortable
acomodar(se) *vt(r)* [3601] to arrange
incomodar *vt* to bother, to interrupt
incomodarse *vr* to feel uncomfortable or upset

acomodador,-a *nmf* usher or attendant; restaurant host or hostess
acomodo *nm* arranging; arrangement
acomodación *nf* arranging; arrangement
cómoda *nf* dresser
comodidad *nf* [-idad 4471] comfort
incomodidad *nf* discomfort
cómodamente *av* comfortably
acomodado *aj* arranged; comfortably well-off
cómodo *aj* [4869] comfortable
comodón *aj* fond of comfort
incómodo *aj* [4770] uncomfortable

comparar to compare
comparar *vt* [2205] to compare
comparación *nf* [-ción 2162] comparison
comparable *aj* comparable
comparado *aj* compared
comparativo *aj* comparative
incomparable *aj* incomparable

compás rhythm, beat
compás *nm* rhythm, beat
acompasado *aj* rhythmic; calm

compensar to compensate
compensar *vt* [3913] to compensate
recompensar *vt* to reward
compensación *nf* [-ción 4264] compensation
recompensa *nf* reward
compensador *aj* compensating

competencia competition; competence
competir(se) *vi(r)* [1732] to compete
competidor,-a *nmf* [2647] competitor
incompetente *nmf* incompetent person
competencia *nf* [-encia 523] competition; competence
competición *nf* competition
competitividad *nf* [-idad 3793] competitiveness
incompetencia *nf* incompetence
competente *aj* [-ente(1) 3681] competent
competidor *aj* competing
competitivo *aj* [-ivo 2609] competitive, of high quality
incompetente *aj* incompetent

complejo complex
acomplejar *vt* to give a complex
acomplejarse *vr* to have a complex
acomplejado,-a *nmf* person with a complex
complejo *nm* [1867] complex
complejidad *nf* complexity
acomplejado *aj* having a complex
complejo *aj* [1867] complex

complementar to complement
complementar *vt* [3972] to complement

complementarse *vr* [3972] to complement each other
complemento *nm* [-o(1) 4709] complement
complementario *aj* [3926] complementary

completamente completely
completar *vt* [2169] to complete
completamente *av* [-mente 2184] completely
completo *aj* [985] complete
incompleto *aj* incomplete

complicado complicated
complicar *vt* [1444] to complicate
complicarse *vr* [1444] to be complicated
complicación *nf* [-ción 3232] complication
complicado *aj* complicated

componer to compose; to fix, to repair
componer *vt* [2789] to compose; to fix, to repair
componerse *vr* to recuperate
descomponer *vi* to break (something)
descomponerse *vr* to break down; to decompose
compositor,-a *nmf* [2255] composer
componente *nm* [3566] component
compuesto *nm* [2440] chemical compound
composición *nf* [-ción 3113] composition
compostura *nf* repair
descomposición *nf* breaking down; decomposition
descompostura *nf* breaking down; decomposition
componente *aj* [3566] component
compuesto *aj* [2440] composed; fixed
descompuesto *aj* broken down; decomposed

comprar to buy
comprar *vt* [880] to buy
comprarse *vr* to buy for oneself
comprador,-a *nmf* buyer
compra *nf* [-a 1328] bought item; buying
compraventa *nf* buying and selling

comprender to comprehend; to understand
comprender *vt* [1537] to comprehend; to understand
comprenderse *vr* to understand each other
comprensión *nf* [3942] comprehension
incomprensión *nf* incomprehension
incomprensiblemente *av* incomprehensibly
comprensible *aj* [-ible] comprehensible; understandable
comprensivo *aj* able to understand; understanding
incomprensible *aj* incomprehensible
incomprensivo *aj* unable to understand

común common
mancomunar *vt* to associate or place two people together for a purpose
mancomunarse *vr* to be grouped, associated, or placed together for a common purpose
anticomunista *nmf* anticommunist
comunista *nmf* [-ista 4265] communist
comunismo *nm* communism
comuna *nf* commune
comunidad *nf* [-idad 350] community; fellowship
comunión *nf* communion
mancomunidad *nf* grouping or associating of people for a common purpose
de mancomún *av* according to common agreement
anticomunista *aj* anticommunist
común *aj* [806] common
comunal *aj* communal
comunista *aj* [-ista 4265] communist, communistic
comunitario *aj* [3495] community

comunicar to communicate
comunicar *vt* [1734] to communicate
comunicarse *vr* to communicate with each other; to be in communication (with)
incomunicar *vt* to isolate, to prevent from communicating
incomunicarse *vr* to be isolated; to avoid communication
comunicado *nm* [1380] written public notice
intercomunicador *nm* intercom
comunicación *nf* [-ción 649] communication
incomunicación *nf* isolation
intercomunicación *nf* intercommunication
telecomunicación *nf* [3244] telecommunication
comunicable *aj* communicable; able to be or ought to be communicated
comunicado *aj* [1380] well-connected (hub); easily accessed
comunicante *aj* communicating
comunicativo *aj* communicative, sociable
incomunicado *aj* incommunicado

concebir to conceive
concebir *vt* [4169] to conceive
anticonceptivo *nm* contraceptive
anticoncepción *nf* contraception
concepción *nf* conception
contracepción *nf* contraception
preconcepción *nf* preconception
anticonceptivo *aj* contraceptive
concebible *aj* [-ible] conceivable
inconcebible *aj* inconceivable
preconcebido *aj* preconceived

concepto concept
concebir *vt* [4169] to conceive
conceptuar *vt* to imagine, to form an idea
concepto *nm* [1336] concept
concepción *nf* conception
concebible *aj* [-ible] conceivable
conceptual *aj* conceptual

concierto concert
concertar *vt* to arrange, to make an arrangement
desconcertar *vt* to disconcert
desconcertarse *vr* to become disconcerted
concertista *nmf* concert musician
concierto *nm* [755] concert
desconcierto *nm* act of being disconcerted
concertado *aj* arranged, agreed upon

concluir to conclude
concluir *vt* [462] to conclude
concluirse *vr* to be concluded
conclusión *nf* [-sión 2309] conclusion
concluso *aj* conclusive
concluyente *aj* concluding
inconcluso *aj* inconclusive

concreto concrete
concretar *vt* [1887] to specify, to make concrete, to firm up
concretarse *vr* to speak directly to the most important aspects
concretamente *av* concretely, specifically
concreto *aj* [-o(1) 1967] concrete

concurrir to attend
concurrir *vi* [4538] to attend
concurrente *nmf* member of the audience
concurrencia *nf* [-encia 4648] audience
concurrente *aj* attending
concurrido *aj* attended

concurso tournament, competition
concursar *vi* to compete in a tournament or competition
concursante *nmf* competitor, participant in a tournament
concurso *nm* [-o(1) 1652] tournament, competition

conde count
condado *nm* [4813] area ruled by a count; county
conde *nm* count
vizconde *nm* viscount
condesa *nf* countess
vizcondesa *nf* viscountess
condal *aj* pertaining to a count or area ruled by a count

condenado condemned, damned
  condenar *vt* [2241] to condemn, to damn
  condenarse *vr* to be condemned, to be damned
  condenado,-a *nmf* condemned prisoner
  condena *nf* [-a 3861] sentence
  condenación *nf* condemnation, damnation
  condenado *aj* condemned, damned
condición condition (all meanings)
  acondicionar *vt* to make ready for use
  condicionar *vt* [4519] to place conditions
  reacondicionar *vt* to make ready for use once
    again
  acondicionador *nm* [-dor(2)] hair conditioner
  acondicionamiento *nm* making ready for use
  condicionamiento *nm* placing of conditions
  condición *nf* [-ción 360] condition (all meanings)
  acondicionado *aj* made ready for use
  condicional *aj* conditional
  incondicional *aj* unconditional
conducir to conduct; to drive
  conducir *vt* [882] to conduct; to drive
  conducirse *vr* to conduct oneself; to drive
    oneself
  conductor,-a *nmf* [906] driver
  conducto *nm* [3109] duct, tube
  conductor *nm* [-or] conductor
  salvoconducto *nm* document of safe-conduct
  superconductor *nm* superconductor
  conducción *nf* [-ción 3807] conduction
  conducta *nf* [2170] conduct
  conductibilidad *nf* conductibility
  conductividad *nf* conductivity
  superconductividad *nf* superconductivity
  conductor *aj* [-or] conducting; driving
conejo rabbit
  conejero,-a *nmf* person who raises or sells
    rabbits
  conejillo de indias *nm* (figurative) a "guinea
    pig"
  conejo *nm* [4058] rabbit
  conejera *nf* rabbit warren
  conejero *aj* rabbit-hunting
confederación confederation
  confederar *vt* to form an alliance or
    confederation
  confederarse *vr* to become part of an alliance
    or confederation
  federar *vt* to federate
  confederado,-a *nmf* confederate
  federal *nmf* [144] federal soldier
  federalista *nmf* federalist
  federalismo *nm* federalism
  confederación *nf* [-ción 2196] confederation

federación *nf* [-ción 791] federation
  confederado *aj* confederated
  federado *aj* federated
  federal *aj* [144] federal
  federalista *aj* federalist
conferencia conference; conference call
  conferenciar *vi* to speak at a conference
  conferenciante *nmf* conference speaker
  conferencista *nmf* conference speaker
  conferencia *nf* [-encia 767] conference; conference
    call
confesar to confess
  confesar *vt* [1793] to confess
  confesarse *vr* to make a confession
  confesor,-a *nmf* confessor
  confesionario *nm* [-ario(1)] confessional
  confesor *nm* [-or] priest which listens to
    confessions
  confesional *aj* confessional
  confeso *aj* confessed
  inconfesable *aj* so serious that it is not
    confessable
  inconfeso *aj* not confessed
confianza confidence, trust
  confiar *vi* [1330] to have faith in; to trust
  confiarse *vr* to feel confidence in something or
    someone; to confide in
  confidente,-a *nmf* confidant, confidante
  confianza *nf* [-anza 940] confidence, trust
  confiable *aj* [-able 4394] trustworthy
  confiado *aj* trusting
conflicto conflict
  conflicto *nm* [937] conflict
  conflictivo *aj* [4889] conflicting
conforme in agreement
  conformar *vt* [848] to satisfy
  conformarse *vr* [848] to accept, to resign oneself
    to
  conformista *nmf* conformist
  inconformista *nmf* nonconformist
  conformismo *nm* conformism
  inconformismo *nm* nonconformity
  conformación *nf* conformation; structure, shape
  conformidad *nf* [-idad] conformity
  disconformidad *nf* nonconformity
  conforme *conj* as soon as; in the same way that;
    according to
  conforme *aj* in agreement
  conformista *aj* conformist
  disconforme *aj* not in agreement
  inconformista *aj* nonconformist
confundir to confuse
  confundir *vt* [2918] to confuse

confundirse *vr* to be confused
confusión *nf* [-sión 3085] confusion
confundible *aj* easily confused
confuso *aj* confused
inconfundible *aj* unable to be confused, obvious

congregar to congregate
congregar *vi* [4870] to gather a group together
congregarse *vr* [4870] to congregate with others
congregante *nmf* member of a congregation
congregación *nf* [-ción 4456] congregation

congreso congress
congresista *nmf* member of a congress
congreso *nm* [450] congress

conocer to know (a person or place), to be familiar with (something)
conocer *vt* [104] to know (a person or place), to be familiar with (something)
conocerse *vr* to know each other; to know oneself; to meet (for the first time)
desconocer *vt* [1126] to fail to recognize or remember
reconocer *vt* [341] to recognize
conocedor,-a *nmf* knowledgeable person
conocido,-a *nmf* acquaintance
desconocido,-a *nmf* person who is not an acquaintance or friend, stranger
conocimiento *nm* [-miento 942] knowledge
desconocimiento *nm* ignorance, lack of knowledge
reconocimiento *nm* [-miento 1254] recognition
conocedor *aj* expert
conocido *aj* known, familiar
desconocido *aj* unknown, unfamiliar
irreconocible *aj* unrecognizable
reconocible *aj* recognizable

conquista conquest
conquistar *vt* [2146] to conquer; to win the affections of someone
reconquistar *vt* to reconquer
conquistador,-a *nmf* conqueror
conquista *nf* [-a 3739] conquest
reconquista *nf* reconquest
conquistador *aj* [-dor(1)] conquering
inconquistable *aj* unconquerable

consciente conscious
conciencia *nf* [-encia 1782] consciousness; conscience
inconsciencia *nf* unconsciousness
subconciencia, subsconsciencia *nf* subconscious
concienzudo *aj* conscientious
consciente *aj* [1971] conscious; aware
inconsciente *aj* unconscious

semiconsciente *aj* semiconscious
subconsciente *aj* subconscious

consecuencia consequence
consecuencia *nf* [810] consequence
secuela *nf* [4552] long-term consequence
secuencia *nf* sequence
consecuentemente *av* consequently
consecuente *aj* [-cial] consequent
consecutivo *aj* [1558] consecutive
inconsecuente *aj* inconsequential
secuencial *aj* sequential

consejo counsel, advice
aconsejar *vt* [3691] to counsel, to advise
aconsejarse *vr* to seek counsel or advice
desaconsejar *vt* to counsel against something
consejero,-a *nmf* [1921] counselor
consejo *nm* [461] counsel
aconsejable *aj* advisable
desaconsejado *aj* imprudent, unwise, ill-advised

consentir to consent; to coddle, to pamper
consentir *vt* [4758] to consent; to coddle, to pamper
consentirse *vr* to pamper oneself
consentido,-a *nmf* coddled or pampered person
consenso *nm* [2416] consensus
consentimiento *nm* consent, permission
consensual *aj* consensual
consentido *aj* coddled, pampered

conservar to conserve
conservar *vt* [1656] to conserve
conservarse *vr* [1656] to remain in a certain state of being
conservador,-a *nmf* conservative; political rightist
conservadurismo *nm* [-ismo] conservatism
conserva *nf* [-a 4110] preserves
conservación *nf* [-ción 2563] conservation
conservador *aj* [-dor(1) 3628] conservative

considerar to consider
considerar *vt* [155] to consider
reconsiderar *vt* to reconsider
desconsiderado,-a *nmf* inconsiderate person
consideración *nf* [-ción 2522] consideration
desconsideración *nf* inconsideration
considerable *aj* [-able 2624] considerable
considerado *aj* considered
desconsiderado *aj* inconsiderate

consignar to consign; to assign; to imprison
consignar *vt* [3207] to consign; to assign; to imprison
consignatario,-a *nmf* consignee
consigna *nf* [-a 4539] assignment

consistencia consistency
consistir *vi* [1643] to consist
consistencia *nf* consistency
inconsistencia *nf* inconsistency
consistente *aj* [-ente(1) 3862] consistent
inconsistente *aj* inconsistent

consolador consoling
consolar *vt* to console
consolarse *vr* to be consoled; to console oneself
consuelo *nm* consolation
consolación *nf* consolation
consolador *aj* consoling
desconsolado *aj* not consoled, sad
desconsolador *aj* not consoling
inconsolable *aj* inconsolable

conspirar to conspire
conspirar *vi* to conspire
conspirador,-a *nmf* conspirator
conspiración *nf* conspiracy

constante constant
constar *vi* [3256] to be certain or evident to someone
constatar *vt* [3274] to confirm, to check, to verify
constancia *nf* [-ancia 3897] constancy, stability
constante *nf* [1193] mathematical constant
constatación *nf* confirmation, verification
inconstancia *nf* inconstancy, instability
constantemente *av* [-mente 2746] constantly
constante *aj* [1193] constant
inconstante *aj* inconstant, unstable

constitución constitution
constituir *vt* [1366] to constitute
constituirse *vr* to be constituted
reconstituir *vt* to reconstitute
constituyente *nmf* constituent
reconstituyente *nm* medicinal substance which revitalizes
constitución *nf* [-ción 1712] constitution
inconstitucionalidad *nf* unconstitutionality
anticonstitucional *aj* unconstitutional
constitucional *aj* [1763] constitutional
constitutivo *aj* constituent
constituyente *aj* constituent
inconstitucional *aj* unconstitutional

construir to construct
construir *vt* [825] to construct
reconstruir *vt* [4993] to reconstruct
constructor,-a *nmf* builder
construcción *nf* [-ción 639] construction
constructora *nf* building contractor (company), construction company
reconstrucción *nf* [-ción 4130] reconstruction

constructivo *aj* constructive
constructor *aj* [2217] pertaining to construction

cónsul consul
cónsul *nm* consul
consulado *nm* [-ato 4906] consulate
consular *aj* consular

consultar to consult
consultar *vt* [1937] to consult
consultorio *nm* [-orio(1) 4649] medical or dental office
consulta *nf* [-a 1721] consultation
consultivo *aj* consultative

consumir to consume
consumir *vt* [1929] to consume
consumirse *vr* [1929] to be consumed
consumismo *nm* practice of over-consumption
consumo *nm* [901] consumption
consumición *nf* consumption
consumido *aj* consumed
consumidor *aj* [-dor(1) 1716] consuming

contacto contact
contactar *vt* to contact
contacto *nm* [-o(1) 1590] contact
tacto *nm* sense of touch
táctil *aj* tactile

contagio infection; contagious disease
contagiar *vt* to infect
contagiarse *vr* to become infected
contagio *nm* infection; contagious disease
contagioso *aj* contagious

contar to count
contabilizar *vt* to track income and expenses
contar *vt* [243] to count
descontar *vt* to discount
recontar *vt* to recount
contador,-a *nmf* [4694] accountant
cuentakilómetros *nm* odometer
cuentarrevoluciones *nm* tachometer
descuento *nm* [-o(1) 3025] discount
recuento *nm* recount
contabilidad *nf* [-idad 4759] accounting
contaduría *nf* accountant's office or position
cuenta *nf* [-a 159] bill
contable *aj* [-able 4760] countable
contado *aj* counted; scarce
incontable *aj* uncountable

contemplar to contemplate
contemplar *vt* [1196] to contemplate
contemplador,-a *nmf* person who contemplates
contemplación *nf* contemplation
contemplativamente *av* contemplatively
contemplador *aj* contemplating

contemporáneo contemporary
contemporáneo,-a *nmf* contemporary
contemporaneidad *nf* contemporaneousness
contemporáneo *aj* [-eo(2) 3646] contemporary

contentar to make happy
contentar *vt* [3838] to make content or happy
contentarse *vr* [3838] to be content or happy
descontentar *vt* to make unhappy
contento *nm* [1846] contentment
descontento *nm* discontentment
contento *aj* [1846] content
descontento *aj* discontented

contestar to answer
contestar *vt* [1701] to answer
contestación *nf* answering

contiguo contiguous
contigüidad *nf* contiguity, nearness, proximity
contiguo *aj* [-uo] contiguous

continente continent
continente *nm* [2533] continent
continental *aj* [3914] continental
transcontinental *aj* transcontinental

continuar to continue
continuar *vti* [300] to continue
continuación *nf* [-ción 2280] sequel
continuidad *nf* [-idad 3225] continuity
discontinuidad *nf* lack of continuity
continuamente *av* [-mente 4578] continually
continuador *aj* continuing
continuo *aj* [-uo 3556] continuous
discontinuo *aj* [-uo] discontinuous

contra against
contrariar *vt* to block; to bother or annoy
contra *prep* [88] against
contrario *nm* [-ario(2) 763] obstacle
contrariedad *nf* contrariety
contrario *aj* [-ario(2) 763] contrary; opposing

contraer to contract
contraer *vt* [1098] to contract
contraerse *vr* [1098] to be contracted

contraste contrast
contrastar *vt* to contrast
contraste *nm* [3664] contrast

contrato contract
contratar *vt* [1776] to contract
contratista *nmf* contractor
contrayente *nmf* [-ente(1) 2000] bride or groom
contrato *nm* [-o(1) 1231] contract
subcontrato *nm* subcontract
contratación *nf* [-ción 3308] contracting
contrayente *aj* [-ente(1) 2000] contracting

contribuir to contribute
contribuir *vt* [1450] to contribute
contribuyente *nmf* [-ente(1) 2438] contributor
contribución *nf* [-ción 4170] contribution
contribuyente *aj* [-ente(1) 2438] contributing

convencer to convince
convencer *vt* [1624] to convince
convencerse *vr* to be convinced
convencimiento *nm* convincing
convincente *aj* convincing

conveniente convenient
convenir *vi* [2487] to be convenient to or for
inconveniente *nm* [-ente(1) 4985] problem, annoyance, inconvenience
conveniencia *nf* convenience
inconveniencia *nf* inconvenience
conveniente *aj* [-ente(1) 2568] convenient
inconveniente *aj* [-ente(1) 4985] inconvenient

convento convent
convento *nm* convent
conventual *aj* pertaining to a convent

conversación conversation
conversar *vi* [4111] to converse
conversador,-a *nmf* conversationalist
conversación *nf* [-ción 1968] conversation
conversador *aj* conversing

convertir to convert
convertir *vt* [308] to convert
convertirse *vr* [308] to be converted
reconvertir *vt* to reconvert
converso,-a *nmf* convert
conversión *nf* conversion
convertibilidad *nf* convertibility
reconversión *nf* reconversion
converso *aj* converted
convertible *aj* [-ible] convertible

convicción conviction, certainty
convicto *nmf* convict
convicción *nf* [3973] conviction, certainty
convicto *aj* convicted

convidar to share
convidar *vt* to share
convidado,-a *nmf* invited person
convidado *aj* [-ado(2)] invited

copia copy
copiar *vt* to copy
fotocopiar *vt* to photocopy
copista *nmf* scribe; historically one who copies books by hand
copia *nf* [-a 1974] copy
copiadora *nf* photocopier
fotocopia *nf* photocopy

fotocopiadora *nf* photocopier
copiador *aj* copying

copioso copious
acopiar *vt* to store
acopio *nm* storing
copioso *aj* copious

coraje anger, courage
encorajar *vt* to anger
encorajarse *vr* to become angry
coraje *nf* [3442] anger; courage
corajudo *aj* easily angered

corazón heart
descorazonar *vt* to break someone's heart; to disappoint; to demoralize
descorazonarse *vr* to lose heart
rompecorazones *nmf* heartbreaker
corazón *nm* [832] heart
corazonada *nf* [-ada(2)] feeling or presentiment in one's heart
descorazonador *aj* demoralizing; disheartening; disappointing

cordial cordial
cordialidad *nf* cordiality
cordial *aj* [2877] cordial

coro chorus
coro *nm* [3531] chorus
corista *nmf* member of a chorus, choir member

corona crown
coronar *vt* [2302] to crown
coronarse *vr* to crown oneself; to be crowned
coronamiento *nm* crowning
corona *nf* [-a 1143] crown
coronación *nf* coronation
coronilla *nf* crown of the head

corral corral
acorralar *vt* to corral, to surround, to pin down, to corner
corral *nm* [-al(1) 2813] corral
acorralado *aj* corralled, surrounded, pinned down, cornered

corrección correction
corregir *vt* [2659] to correct
corregirse *vr* to correct oneself; to be corrected
correccional *nmf* juvenile detention center
correctivo *nm* sanction
corrector *nm* correction fluid
corrección *nf* correction
incorrección *nf* error
correctamente *av* correctly
correccional *aj* correctional
correctivo *aj* corrective
correcto *aj* [2192] correct

corrector *aj* correcting
corregible *aj* corrigible
incorrecto *aj* incorrect
incorregible *aj* incorrigible

correr to run; to dismiss, to fire; to expel
correr *vi* [849] to run; to dismiss, to fire; to expel
correrse *vr* to raise or lower (curtains), to open or close (curtains); to slide easily
corretear *vi* to run back and forth
descorrer *vti* to run back the way one came; to draw (curtains)
descorrerse *vr* to draw (curtains)
recorrer *vt* [747] to cover (distance)
corredor,-a *nmf* [1808] runner; broker
corresponsal *nmf* news correspondent
correveidile *nmf* gossip, tale-bearer
correo *nm* [2091] mail
corretaje *nm* brokerage
correteo *nm* running back and forth
descorrimiento *nm* drawing of the curtains
recorrido *nm* journey, trip, distance to be covered
carrera *nf* [204] race; college major
contracorriente *nf* headwind; crosscurrent
correspondencia *nf* correspondence
corresponsalía *nf* post of a correspondent
corrida *nf* [-ido(2) 3481] run
corredizo *aj* sliding
corredor *aj* running
correspondiente *aj* [-ente(1) 863] corresponding

corroborar to corroborate
corroborar *vt* to corroborate
corroboración *nf* corroboration
corroborativo *aj* corroborative

cortar to cut
acortar *vt* to abbreviate; to make smaller or shorter
acortarse *vr* to be abbreviated; to be made smaller or shorter
cortar *vt* [1849] to cut
cortarse *vr* to be cut
entrecortar *vt* to cut in between
recortar *vt* [2989] to cut with attention to detail
cortador,-a *nmf* cutter; person who cuts
cortacircuitos *nm* circuit breaker
cortafuego *nm* firebreak, fuel break
cortaplumas *nm* small knife
cortauñas *nm* nail clippers
corte *nm* [1016] cut
cortocircuito *nm* short circuit
cortometraje *nm* short film
recorte *nm* [1517] detailed cutting
corta *nf* pruning; time for pruning

cortacésped *nf* lawnmower
cortado *aj* cut
cortador *aj* cutting
cortante *aj* cutting
corto *aj* [978] short
entrecortado *aj* broken up (sounds, telephone call); partly cut
recortado *aj* [-ado(1)] cut with attention to detail

cortejo courting
cortejar *vt* to court
cortejo *nm* courting

cortesía courtesy
cortesía *nf* courtesy
descortesía *nf* discourtesy
cortésmente *av* courteously
cortés *aj* courteous
descortés *aj* discourteous

corteza cortex
descortezar *vt* to remove the core or cortex
corteza *nf* cortex

cosecha crop
cosechar *vt* [4153] to reap, to harvest
cosechero,-a *nmf* farmer
cosecha *nf* [-a 2648] crop
cosechadora *nf* [-dor(2)] reaper, harvesting machine
cosechador *aj* reaping, harvesting

coser to sew
coser *vt* [4932] to sew
descoser *vt* to remove sewn threads
descoserse *vr* to be removed (sewn threads)
cosido *nm* sewing
descosido *nm* removal of sewn threads
cosido *aj* sewn
descosido *aj* unstitched, (figurative) indiscreet

cósmico cosmic
cosmonauta *nmf* cosmonaut
cosmos *nm* cosmos
cosmografía *nf* cosmography
cósmico *aj* cosmic
cosmográfico *aj* cosmographic, cosmographical

costa coast
costa *nf* [1073] coast
costear *vt* to navigate the coast

costar to cost
costar *vt* [2236] to cost
costear *vt* to pay
costearse *vr* to pay one's expenses

costumbre custom
acostumbrar *vt* [1715] to accustom
acostumbrarse *vr* [1715] to become accustomed

desacostumbrarse *vr* to become disaccustomed; to lose a habit
malacostumbrar *vt* to spoil (a person)
costumbre *nf* [1843] custom
acostumbrado *aj* accustomed
desacostumbrado *aj* unaccustomed

cráneo cranium, skull
cráneo *nm* [4580] cranium, skull
craneal *aj* cranial

crear to create
crear *vt* [511] to create
procrear *vt* to procreate
recrear *vt* to re-create
recrearse *vr* to recreate, to enjoy oneself
creador,-a *nmf* [2492] creator
procreador,-a *nmf* procreator
Creador *nm* Creator, God
recreo *nm* [-eo(1)] recreation; recess
creación *nf* [-ción 1237] creation
creatividad *nf* [-idad 3993] creativity
procreación *nf* procreation
recreación *nf* recreation
creador *aj* creating
creativo *aj* [-ivo 3470] creative
procreador *aj* procreative
recreativo *aj* enjoyable

crecer to grow
acrecentar *vt* to make larger or bigger; to increase
acrecentarse *vr* to become larger or bigger; to be increased
crecer *vi* [788] to grow
decrecer *vi* to decrease
incrementar *vi* [912] to grow incrementally
incrementarse *vr* to be growing incrementally
acrecentamiento *nm* growth
crecimiento *nm* [-miento 802] growth
decrecimiento *nm* decreasing, decline
incremento *nm* [-o(1) 1071] increment
crecida *nf* rising (of water)
crecido *aj* grown
creciente *aj* [-ente(1) 2711] growing
decreciente *aj* decreasing, declining

creer to believe, to think
acreditar *vt* [2888] to accredit; to vouch for; to guarantee; to extend credit; to give credence to
acreditarse *vr* to achieve a fine reputation
creer *vt* [240] to believe, to think
creerse *vr* to consider oneself, to believe oneself to be (used pejoratively)
desacreditar *vt* to discredit
acreedor *nmf* creditor; deserving or worthy person

creyente *nmf* [-ente(1)]　believer
incrédulo,-a *nmf* unbeliever
crédito *nm* [-ito(2) 752]　credit
credo *nm* creed
descrédito *nm* discredit; loss of one's good
　name
acreditación *nf* accreditation
credencial *nf* [3371] credential
credibilidad *nf* [-idad 4428]　credibility
credulidad *nf* credulity
creencia *nf* [-encia 3482]　belief
incredulidad *nf* incredulity
acreditado *aj* accredited
acreedor *aj* deserving, worthy
credencial *aj* [3371] accrediting
crédulo *aj* credulous
creíble *aj* [-ible] believable
descreído *aj* no longer believing
incrédulo *aj* incredulous; atheistic
increíble *aj* incredible

crepúsculo twilight
crepúsculo *nm* twilight
crepuscular *aj* pertaining to the twilight

criar to raise (a child or animal)
criar *vt* to raise (a child or animal)
criarse *vr* to be raised
malcriar *vt* to spoil
crío *nmf* young child; baby
malcriado,-a *nmf* spoiled child
criadero *nm* place for raising animals
crianza *nf* [-anza] raising
criatura *nf* [-ura(2) 4223] creature
criado *aj* raised
malcriado *aj* spoiled

crimen crime
incriminar *vt* to incriminate
recriminar *vt* to recriminate
criminal *nmf* [2889] criminal
criminalista *nmf* attorney specializing in
　criminal law
crimen *nm* [1407] crime
criminalidad *nf* criminality
criminología *nf* criminology
incriminación *nf* incrimination
recriminación *nf* recrimination
criminal *aj* [2889] criminal

cristal crystal
cristalizar *vi* to crystallize
cristal *nm* [2951] crystal
cristalino *nm* [-ino(2)] lens of the eye
cristalería *nf* glassware
cristalización *nf* crystallization
cristalino *aj* [-ino(2)] crystalline

cristiano Christian
cristianizar *vt* to Christianize; to evangelize the
　Christian faith
cristiano,-a *nmf* Christian
anticristo *nm* Antichrist
cristianismo *nm* Christianity
Cristo *nm* Christ
cristiandad *nf* Christendom
cristiano *aj* [-ano 1877] Christian

crítica criticism
criticar *vt* [1663] to criticize
crítico,-a *nmf* critic
autocrítica *nf* self-criticism
crítica *nf* [-a 2052] criticism
crítico *aj* [-ico(2) 1403] critical
hipercrítico *aj* hypercritical

crónica chronicle
cronometrar *vt* to time
sincronizar *vt* to synchronize
cronista *nmf* chronicler
anacronismo *nm* anachronism
cronometraje *nm* timing
cronómetro *nm* chronometer, stopwatch
crónica *nf* chronicle
cronología *nf* chronology
sincronía *nf* synchrony
sincronización *nf* synchronization
anacrónico *aj* anachronistic
crónico *aj* [-ico(2) 2839] chronic
cronológico *aj* chronological
sincrónico *aj* synchronous

crudo raw
encrudecer *vt* to make raw, especially one's
　nerves, to annoy
encrudecerse *vr* to become annoyed
crudo *nm* [2452] crude oil
crudeza *nf* rawness
crudo *aj* [2452] raw, crude

cruel cruel
crueldad *nf* cruelty
cruel *aj* cruel

cruzar to cross
crucificar *vt* [-ificar] to crucify
cruzar *vt* [1562] to cross (a street); to cross-breed
cruzarse *vr* to cross (a street)
cruce *nm* [3309] crossing
crucero *nm* [2471] intersection
crucifijo *nm* crucifix
crucifixión *nf* crucifixion
crucigrama *nf* crossword puzzle
cruz *nf* [1818] cross
cruzada *nf* crusade

encrucijada *nf* crossroads

crucial *aj* [-cial 4377] having the form of a cross; crucial

crucificado *aj* crucified

cruzado *aj* [-ado(1)] crossed

cuajar to set

cuajar *v* to set (pudding, gelatin, etc.)

cuajada *nf* setting (pudding, gelatin)

cuajado *aj* set (pudding, gelatin, etc.)

cualidad quality, characteristic

cualidad *nf* [2908] quality, characteristic

cualitativo *aj* qualitative

cuanto as much as, as many as, all the

cuantificar *vt* [-ificar] to quantify

cuantos,-as *propl* certain number, some

cuanto *av* as much as

cuantioso *aj* many; much; a lot of

cuantitativo *aj* quantitative

cuanto *aj* as much as, as many as, all the

¿cuánto? *aj* how much, how many

cuarto room

acuartelar *vt* to quarter (soldiers)

acuartelamiento *nm* quartering (of soldiers)

cuartel *nm* [4606] quarters, barracks

cuarto *nm* [385] room

cuartucho *nm* [-ucho] old, ugly, or run-down room

cuartelero *aj* pertaining to quarters

cuatro four

cuadrar *vt* to make square

cuadrarse *vr* to stand at attention

cuadruplicar *vt* to quadruple

cuartear *vt* to divide into fourths

descuartizar *vt* to cut or divide into pieces

encuadrar *vt* to frame

encuadrarse *vr* to be framed

cuarentón,-a *nmf* forty-year-old

cuatrillizo,-a *nmf* quadruplet

catorce *nm* [4261] fourteen

catorceavo *nm* [-avo] one-fourteenth (fraction)

cuadrado *nm* [-ado(1) 2959] square

cuadragésimo *nm* [-ésimo] one-fortieth (fraction)

cuadrante *nm* quadrant

cuadrilátero *nm* quadrilateral; boxing ring

cuadro *nm* [705] square

cuadrúpedo *nm* four-legged animal; quadruped

cuarenta *nm* [3269] forty

cuarentavo *nm* [-avo] one-fortieth (fraction)

cuarteto *nm* quartet

cuartillo *nm* four-person card game

cuarto *nm* [385] one-fourth (fraction)

cuatrimotor *nm* four-engine airplane

cuatro *nm* [184] four

cuatrocientos *nm* four hundred

descuartizamiento *nm* cutting into pieces

encuadramiento *nm* framing

encuadre *nm* framing of a photographic scene

recuadro *nm* box or framed part of a document (in newspaper, form, avertisement)

cuadra *nf* [3539] block

cuadratura *nf* squaring

cuadrícula *nf* series of boxes as on graph paper

cuadrilla *nf* work group or team

cuarentena *nf* group of forty; Lent

catorce *aj* [4261] fourteen

catorceavo *aj* [-avo] fourteenth

cuadrado *aj* [-ado(1) 2959] square

cuadragésimo *aj* [-ésimo] fortieth

cuadricular *aj* with squares (e.g., graph paper)

cuadrilátero *aj* quadrilateral

cuadrúpedo *aj* four-legged, quadruped

cuádruple *aj* quadruple

cuarenta *aj* [3269] forty

cuarentavo *aj* [-avo] fortieth

cuarentón *aj* [-ón(2)] forty-year-old

cuarto *aj* [385] fourth

cuatrillizo *aj* of quadruplets

cuatro *aj* [184] four

cuatrocientos *aj* four hundred

cubierto covered

cubrir *vt* [1037] to cover

cubrirse *vr* to be covered

descubrir *vt* [1015] to discover

descubrirse *vr* to be discovered

encubrir *vt* to cover up, to hide

encubrirse *vr* to be covered up, to be hidden

recubrir *vt* to re-cover

descubridor,-a *nmf* discoverer

encubridor,-a *nmf* person who hides or covers up something from others

cubierto *nm* [2597] table setting

cubrecolchón *nm* mattress cover

descubrimiento *nm* [-miento 3963] discovery

encubrimiento *nm* hiding or covering-up of something

recubrimiento *nm* re-covering

entrecubiertas *nfpl* space between decks

cubierta *nf* cover; deck of a ship; dust jacket of a book

cubrecama *nf* bedspread

sobrecubierta *nf* second lid; dust jacket; covering of the main deck of a ship

encubiertamente *av* secretly

cubierto *aj* [2597] covered

descubierto *aj* discovered

encubierto *aj* covered-up or hidden

cuchillo knife
acuchillar *vt* to cut or stab with a knife
cuchillazo *nm* cut or stab with a knife
cuchillo *nm* [3603] knife
cuchillada *nf* [-ada(2)] knife wound

cuello neck
collar *nm* necklace; collar
cuello *nm* [2792] neck

cuento story
acontecer *vi* to happen, to occur
contar *vt* [243] to tell a story
cuentista *nmf* storyteller; gossip
acontecimiento *nm* [-miento 1238] event
cuento *nm* [-o(1) 2426] story
cuentista *aj* story-telling; gossiping

cuerda cord; rope; string of a musical
  instrument
acordonar *vt* to cordon off
encordonar *vt* to tie with rope or cord
cordaje *nm* strings of a musical instrument
cordel *nm* cord; rope
cordón *nm* drawstring; cord
cuerda *nf* [3927] cord; string of a musical
  instrument
acordonado *aj* cordoned off

cuerno horn
cornear *vt* to wound with a horn
descornar *vt* to remove the horns from an
  animal
corneta *nm* cornet player
corno *nm* musical horn
cuerno *nm* horn
cornada *nf* hit with an animal's horn; horn
  wound
cornamenta *nf* horns of an animal
corneta *nf* cornet
cornucopia *nf* cornucopia, horn of plenty
córneo *aj* with horns; horn-shaped; pertaining
  to the cornea
cornudo *aj* [-udo] with horns

cuerpo body
incorporar *vt* [1879] to incorporate
incorporarse *vr* [1879] to sit up or stand up
  straight; to clear one's throat
reincorporar *vt* to reincorporate
reincorporarse *vr* to sit up or stand up again
anticuerpo *nm* antibody
corpus *nm* corpus
cuerpo *nm* [402] body
corporación *nf* [1309] corporation
corpulencia *nf* corpulence
incorporación *nf* [-ción 4523] incorporation
reincorporación *nf* reincorporation

corporal *aj* [3321] corporal
corporativo *aj* [4579] corporate
corpóreo *aj* [-eo(2)] corporeal
corpulento *aj* [-lento] corpulent
incorporado *aj* incorporated
incorpóreo *aj* incorporeal

cuestión matter; item for discussion
cuestionar *vt* [1572] to discuss a matter
encuestar *vt* to poll
encuestador,-a *nmf* pollster
cuestionario *nm* [-ario(1)] list of questions
cuestión *nf* [1116] matter; item for discussion
encuesta *nf* [-a 2046] poll
cuestionable *aj* questionable
incuestionable *aj* unquestionable

cuidado care
cuidar *vt* [1273] to care for
cuidarse *vr* to be careful
descuidar *vt* [3578] to neglect
descuidarse *vr* [3578] to be careless; to neglect
  oneself; to let oneself go
cuidado *nm* [1293] care
descuido *nm* [-ido(2) 4441] neglect
cuidado *int* [1293] Be careful!
cuidado *aj* [1293] cared for
cuidadoso *aj* [-oso] careful
descuidado *aj* uncared for, neglected

culpa blame
culpar *vt* [3746] to blame
culparse *vr* to take the blame; to blame oneself
disculpar *vt* to excuse
disculparse *vr* to excuse oneself; to apologize
inculpar *vt* to accuse
culpable *nmf* [-able 2534] guilty person
culpa *nf* [-a 2402] blame
culpabilidad *nf* culpability
disculpa *nf* [-a 4764] excuse
inculpación *nf* accusation
culpable *aj* [-able 2534] culpable, guilty
disculpable *aj* excusable
inculpado *aj* accused

cultivar to cultivate
cultivar *vt* [2542] to cultivate (also figurative)
cultivo *nm* [-ivo 1374] cultivation (also figurative)
cultivado *aj* cultivated (also figurative)

cultura culture
inculto,-a *nmf* uncultured or uneducated person
contracultura *nf* counterculture
cultura *nf* [-ura(2) 615] culture
incultura *nf* lack of culture
culto *aj* [4504] cultured, educated
cultural *aj* [1105] cultural
inculto *aj* lacking culture

cumbre hilltop, mountaintop

encumbrar *vt* to elevate something to great heights

encumbrarse *vr* to reach the mountaintop (also figurative); to be conceited

cumbre *nm* [1855] hilltop, mountaintop

encumbramiento *nm* act of elevating; fame, success

encumbrado *aj* elevated; on the mountaintop; successful, famous

cumplir to complete

cumplir *vt* [270] to complete

cumplirse *vr* to be completed, to be carried out

incumplir *vi* [3883] to leave incomplete, to leave unfinished

cumpleaños *nm* [1342] birthday

cumplido *nm* compliment, demonstration of courtesy

cumplimiento *nm* [-miento 2230] completion

incumplimiento *nm* [-miento 3945] lack of completion

cumplido *aj* complete, finished, with fine manners

cumplidor *aj* referring to someone who keeps his word or promises

incumplido *aj* uncompleted, unfinished

cuna cradle

acunar *vt* to rock in a cradle

cuna *nf* cradle

curar to heal, to cure

curar *vt* [-ura(2) 3226] to heal, to cure

curarse *vr* to be healed, to be cured, to recover

curandero,-a *nmf* healer; quack

cura *nf* [-ura(2) 4075] healing; cure

curación *nf* healing

curado *aj* cured

curativo *aj* curative

incurable *aj* incurable

curioso curious

curiosear *vt* to show curiosity, to be curious; to pry

curioso,-a *nmf* curious person

curiosidad *nf* [-idad 4243] curiosity

curioso *aj* [3444] curious

curso course in school; course of a river

cursar *vt* [3863] to take a course

transcurrir *vi* [2572] to pass (time)

cursillista *nmf* participant in a series of theme-centered courses (often religious)

cursillo *nm* brief series of courses centered on a theme

curso *nm* [-o(1) 932] course

transcurso *nm* [3157] passage (of time); period (of time)

curva curve

curvar *vt* to curve

curva *nf* [4034] curve

curvatura *nf* curvature

curvilíneo *aj* curvilinear

curvo *aj* curved

D

daño damage

dañar *vt* [1751] to damage; to hurt

dañarse *vr* to damage oneself; to hurt oneself

daño *nm* [-o(1) 731] damage

dañado *aj* damaged

dañino *aj* [-ino(2)] damaging

dañoso *aj* damaging

danzar to dance

danzar *vti* to dance

danzante *nmf* [-ante(2)] dancer

danzarín,-a *nmf* dancer

danza *nf* [-a 3006] dance

danzante *aj* [-ante(2)] dancing

dar to give

dar *vt* [37] to give

darse *vr* to give oneself; to give up

dadivoso,-a *nmf* giving person, person who likes to give

dador,-a *nmf* giver

dádiva *nf* contribution; what one gives

dadivoso *aj* giving

dado *aj* given

debatir to debate

debatir *vt* to debate

debate *nm* [1943] debate

deber to owe; to ought to; to must

deber *vt* [43] to owe; to must

deberse *vr* to ought to

debe *nm* debit

deber *nm* [43] duty; debit

debidamente *av* [-mente 3704] correctly; suitably

indebidamente *av* incorrectly; unsuitably

debido *aj* correct; suitable

indebido *aj* [4771] incorrect; unsuitable

débil weak

debilitar *vt* [3928] to debilitate

debilitarse *vr* [3928] to become debilitated

débil *nmf* [2805] weak person

debilucho,-a *nmf* very weak person

debilidad *nf* [-idad 3089] weakness
debilitación *nf* debilitation
débil *aj* [2805] weak
debilitador *aj* debilitating
debilucho *aj* very weak
endeble *aj* weak

decadencia decadence
decaer *vi* to decay
decaimiento *nm* decaying
decadencia *nf* decadence
decadente *aj* decadent
decaído *aj* decayed

decidir to decide
decidir *vi* [374] to decide (in general)
decidirse *vr* [374] to decide, to choose a specific course of action, to make a decision, to make up one's mind
decisión *nf* [-sión 464] decision
indecisión *nf* indecision
decididamente *av* decidedly
decidido *aj* decided
decisivo *aj* [-ivo 3975] decisive
indeciso *aj* indecisive

décimo a tenth
decimal *nm* decimal
decímetro *nm* decimeter
décimo *nm* [-ésimo 2179] one-tenth (fraction)
decimoctavo *nm* [-avo] one-eighteenth (fraction)
decimocuarto *nm* [-ésimo] one-fourteenth (fraction)
decimonoveno *nm* [-ésimo] one-nineteenth (fraction)
decimoquinto *nm* [-ésimo] one-fifteenth (fraction)
decimoséptima *nm* one-seventeenth (fraction)
decimosexto *nm* [-ésimo] one-sixteenth (fraction)
decimotercero *nm* one-thirteenth (fraction)
decimal *aj* decimal
décimo *aj* [-ésimo 2179] tenth
decimoctavo *aj* [-avo] eighteenth
decimocuarto *aj* [-ésimo] fourteenth
decimonoveno *aj* [-ésimo] nineteenth
decimoquinto *aj* [-ésimo] fifteenth
decimoséptimo *aj* [-ésimo] seventeenth
decimosexto *aj* [-ésimo] sixteenth
decimotercero *aj* thirteenth

decir to say or tell
bendecir *vt* [2594] to bless
contradecir *vt* to contradict
contradecirse *vr* to contradict oneself
decir *vt* [28] to say or tell
decirse *vr* to be said

desdecirse *vr* to retract a statement or to repent of saying something
dictaminar *vt* to issue a judicial opinion or decision
dictar *vt* [2920] to dictate
interdecir *vt* to interdict
maldecir *vti* to curse
predecir *vt* to predict
malditos *nmpl* cursed ones
bendito,-a *nmf* blessed one
dictador,-a *nmf* dictator
maldiciente *nmf* [-ente(2)] person who curses frequently
decir *nm* [28] saying
diccionario *nm* [-ario(1)] dictionary
dicho *nm* [506] saying
dictado *nm* dictation
dictamen *nm* [2727] judicial opinion or decision
entredicho *nm* prohibition; doubt concerning one's character or reputation
interdicto *nm* interdict
bendición *nf* [-ción 1357] blessing
contradicción *nf* [-ción 4664] contradiction
dicción *nf* [-ción] diction
dictadura *nf* [-ura(2) 4787] dictatorship
interdicción *nf* interdiction
jurisdicción *nf* [2734] jurisdiction
maldición *nf* curse
predicción *nf* prediction
bendito *aj* blessed
benedictino *aj* Benedictine
contradictorio *aj* contradictory
dicharachero *aj* someone who constantly speaks in sayings, funny stories or jokes
dicho *aj* [506] said, expressed; aforesaid
dictatorial *aj* dictatorial
impredecible *aj* unpredictable
indecible *aj* unspeakable
jurisdiccional *aj* jurisdictional
maldecido *aj* cursed
maldiciente *aj* [-ente(2)] frequently cursing
maldito *aj* cursed; damned
sobredicho *aj* aforementioned, aforesaid
susodicho *aj* aforesaid, above mentioned

declarar to declare
declarar *vt* [499] to declare
declararse *vr* to declare one's feelings or intentions
declaración *nf* [-ción 807] declaration
declarado *aj* declared
declaratorio *aj* declaratory

decoración decoration
condecorar *vt* to decorate with an award

decorar *vt* [4378] to decorate
decorador,-a *nmf* decorator
decorado *nm* [-ado(2)] decorative style
condecoración *nf* decoration (of an award)
decoración *nf* decoration
decorado *aj* [-ado(2)] decorated
decorador *aj* decorating
decorativo *aj* decorative

decoro decorum
decoro *nm* decorum
decoroso *aj* with decorum; with dignity

decreto decree
decretar *vt* [3768] to issue a decree
decreto *nm* [-o(1) 2163] decree

dedicar to dedicate
dedicar *vt* [589] to dedicate
dedicarse *vr* [589] to dedicate oneself
dedicación *nf* [-ción 4976] dedication
dedicatoria *nf* dedication, of a gift, book, etc.
dedicado *aj* dedicated

dedo finger
dedal *nm* [-al(1)] thimble
dedo *nm* [2396] finger

deducir¹ to deduce
deducir *vt* to deduce
deducción *nf* deduction
deducible *aj* [-ible] deducible
deductivo *aj* deductive

deducir² to deduct
deducir *vt* to deduct
deducción *nf* deduction
deducible *aj* [-ible] deductible

defecto defect
defecto *nm* [3445] defect
defectuoso *aj* defective

defender to defend
defender *vt* [1011] to defend
defenderse *vr* to defend oneself
defendido,-a *nmf* defendant
defensor,-a *nmf* [1910] defense attorney
defensa *nm* [564] defense player in sport
defensa *nf* [564] bumper; defense
defensiva *nf* defensive
defendible *aj* defendable
defendido *aj* defended
defensivo *aj* [-ivo 1664] defensive
defensor *aj* defense, referring to attorneys
  responsible for the defense of a client
indefendible *aj* indefensible
indefenso *aj* defenseless

deficiencia deficiency
déficit *nm* [2753] deficit

deficiencia *nf* [-encia 2784] deficiency
deficiente *aj* [4559] deficient

definir to define
definir *vt* [860] to define
definirse *vr* to define oneself
definición *nf* [-ción 3403] definition
definitivamente *av* [-mente 1911] definitely
indefinidamente *av* indefinitely
definible *aj* [-ible] definable
definido *aj* defined
definitivo *aj* [-ivo 1592] definitive
indefinible *aj* indefinable
indefinido *aj* indefinite

dejar to leave; to permit, to allow
dejar *vt* [103] to leave; to permit, to allow
dejarse *vr* to let oneself go, neglect oneself; to
  leave oneself open to something
dejado,-a *nmf* abandoned or neglected person;
  abandoned spouse; unkempt person
dejadez *nf* apathy, excessive laziness, lack of
  desire
dejado *aj* abandoned; unkempt

delegado delegate
delegar *vt* to delegate
subdelegar *vt* to subdelegate
delegado,-a *nmf* [1479] delegate
subdelegado,-a *nmf* subdelegate
delegación *nf* [-ción 1180] delegation
subdelegación *nf* subdelegation
delegado *aj* [-ado(2)] delegated
subdelegado *aj* subdelegated

deleite delight
deleitar *vt* [4244] to delight
deleitarse *vr* [4244] to be delighted
deleite *nm* delight
deleitoso *aj* delightful

delgado thin, slim
adelgazar *vi* to get thin
adelgazamiento *nm* slimming down
delgadez *nf* [-ez] thinness, slimness
adelgazador *aj* slimming
delgado *aj* [1274] thin, slim
delgaducho *aj* [-ucho] skinny

delicado delicate
delicadeza *nf* delicacy
indelicadeza *nf* indelicacy
delicado *aj* [2583] delicate

delicioso delicious
delicia *nf* [4457] delight
delicioso *aj* [-oso 3126] delicious; delightful

delirio delirium
delirar *vt* to make delirious

delirio *nm* delirium
delirante *aj* causing delirium; delirious

demanda lawsuit
demandar *vt* [1483] to sue
demandado,-a *nmf* defendant in a lawsuit
demandante *nmf* plaintiff in a lawsuit
demanda *nf* [-a 560] lawsuit

demás others
demás *pron* [761] the other, the others
demasía *nf* abundance, excess
demás *av* [761] besides
demasiado *av* [1202] too much
demás *aj* [761] in excess
demasiado *aj* [1202] excessive

democrático democratic
democratizar *vt* to democratize
demócrata *nmf* [3418] democrat
socialdemócrata *nmf* social democrat
democracia *nf* [1375] democracy
democratización *nf* democratization
demografía *nf* demography
socialdemocracia *nf* social democracy
antidemocrático *aj* undemocratic
democrático *aj* [-ico(2) 989] democratic
demográfico *aj* demographic
socialdemócrata *aj* social democratic

demonio demon
demonio *nm* demon
demonología *nf* demonology
demoníaco *aj* demoniacal
endemoniado *aj* demon-possessed; extremely angry

demostrar to demonstrate
demostrar *vt* [607] to demonstrate
demostrativo *nm* demonstrative (grammar)
demostración *nf* [-ción 4171] demonstration
demostrable *aj* demonstrable
demostrativo *aj* demonstrative

denso dense
condensar *vt* to condense
condensarse *vr* to become condensed
densificar *vt* to make dense
condensador *nm* condenser
condensación *nf* condensation
densidad *nf* [-idad 4736] density
condensado *aj* condensed
denso *aj* dense

dentro inside
adentrarse *vr* to go inside
adentro *av* [4045] inside
dentro de *av* within

denuncia denunciation
denunciar *vt* [1144] to denounce
denunciador,-a *nmf* denouncer
denunciante *nmf* denouncer
denuncia *nf* [-a 870] denunciation
denunciable *aj* referring to something that can be denounced

departamento department
departamento *nm* [655] department
departamental *aj* departmental

depender to depend
depender *vi* [986] to depend
independizar *vt* to grant independence
independizarse *vr* to become independent
independentista *nmf* person who believes in political independence
dependiente,-a *nmf* employee that works directly with the public
dependencia *nf* [-encia 701] dependency
independencia *nf* [-encia 1427] independency
interdependencia *nf* interdependence
independientemente *av* [-mente 3152] independently
dependiente *aj* [-ente(1) 4762] dependent
independiente *aj* [1684] independent

deporte sport
deportista *nmf* [-ista 2378] sports enthusiast
deporte *nm* [741] sport
polideportivo *nm* sport facility
deportividad *nf* good sportsmanship
antideportivo *aj* referring to a poor sport
deportista *aj* [-ista 2378] sport
deportivo *aj* [479] sport

depósito deposit
depositar *vt* [2493] to deposit
depositarse *vr* to be deposited
depositante *nmf* depositor
depositario,-a *nmf* depositor; treasurer
depósito *nm* [-ito(2) 2555] deposit

depresión depression
deprimir *vt* [4541] to depress
deprimirse *vr* [4541] to be depressed
depresor *nm* [-or] device used for depressing a part of the body, a tongue depressor
depresión *nf* [-sión 2569] depression
depresivo *aj* depressing
depresor *aj* [-or] depressing; humiliating
deprimente *aj* [-ente(1)] depressing
deprimido *aj* depressed

derecha right
enderezar *vt* to straighten up
enderezarse *vr* to straighten oneself up
derechista *nmf* political rightist; right winger

ultraderechista *nmf* ultra-right winger
derechazo *nm* hit with the right hand
derecho *nm* [207] straight; right; law
enderezamiento *nm* straightening up, the act of
   straightening up something
derecha *nf* [1260] right
ultraderecha *nf* ultra-right
derecho *av* [207] right
derechista *aj* right wing
derecho *aj* [207] straight
ultraderechista *aj* ultra-right wing

derivar to derive
derivar *vt* [1563] to derive
derivarse *vr* [1563] to be derived
derivado *nm* derivative
deriva *nf* detour or deviation of a ship's course
derivación *nf* derivation
derivada *nf* mathematical function
derivado *aj* derived
derivativo *aj* derivative

derramar to spill
derramar *vt* [3719] to spill
derramarse *vr* to overflow
derramamiento *nm* spilling; overflowing
derrame *nm* spilling

derribar to tear down
derribar *vt* [3794] to tear down
derribo *nm* tearing down

derrota defeat; rout
derrotar *vt* [1286] to defeat
derrota *nf* [-a 990] defeat; rout
derrotado *aj* defeated

derrotero ship's course, direction
derrotarse *vr* to deviate from the course
derrotero *nm* ship's course, direction
derrota *nf* [-a 990] course, path

desarrollo development
desarrollar *vt* [470] to develop
desarrollarse *vr* to develop oneself; to become
   developed
desarrollo *nm* [-o(1) 235] development
subdesarrollo *nm* underdevelopment
superdesarrollo *nm* overdevelopment
desarrollado *aj* developed
subdesarrollado *aj* underdeveloped
superdesarrollado *aj* overdeveloped

desastre disaster
desastrado,-a *nmf* unkempt person
desastre *nm* [2625] disaster
desastroso *aj* disastrous; careless or disheveled
   when referring to a person

desayuno breakfast
ayunar *vi* to fast
desayunarse *vr* to eat breakfast (oneself)
desayunar *vt* to eat breakfast (in general)
ayuno *nm* [-o(1)] fast
desayuno *nm* [-o(1) 3071] breakfast

descender to descend
ascender *vi* [2007] to ascend
condescender *vi* to adapt oneself to another
   person's manner of being
descender *vi* [2999] to descend
ascensión *nmf* ascension
ascensorista *nmf* elevator repairman or builder
descendiente *nmf* descendant
ascendiente *nmf* ancestor
ascenso *nm* [3169] ascent, rising, moving up
ascensor *nm* [-or] elevator
descendimiento *nm* descent
descenso *nm* [2763] descent
condescendencia *nf* [-encia] congeniality; ability
   to adjust to others' personalities
descendencia *nf* [-encia] descendants, lineage
ascendente *aj* ascending
condescendiente *aj* congenial
descendente *aj* descending

desdén disdain
desdeñar *vt* to disdain
desdeñarse *vr* to treat with disdain
desdén *nm* disdain
desdeñable *aj* despicable
desdeñoso *aj* disdainful

desear to desire
desear *vt* [785] to desire
indeseable *nmf* undesirable person
deseo *nm* [-o(1) 1155] desire
deseable *aj* desirable
deseado *aj* desired
deseoso *aj* desirous; filled with desire
indeseable *aj* undesirable

desierto desert
desertar *vt* to desert
desertor,-a *nmf* deserter
desierto *nm* [2867] desert
deserción *nf* desertion
desértico *aj* desert; relating to the desert;
   desert-like
desierto *aj* [2867] desert-like
semidesierto *aj* semi-desert

deslizar to slip or slide
deslizar *vt* to slip or slide
deslizarse *vr* to slip or slide (oneself)
desliz *nm* slip or slide

deslizamiento *nm* slipping or sliding
antideslizante *aj* anti-skidding; anti-slipping

desnudo nude, naked
desnudar *vt* to undress
desnudarse *vr* to undress oneself
desnudista *nmf* nudist
nudista *nmf* nudist
desnudismo *nm* nudism
desnudo *nm* [-o(1) 3373] nude statue or painting
nudismo *nm* nudism
desnudez *nf* nudity
desnudista *aj* nudist
desnudo *aj* [-o(1) 3373] naked, nude
nudista *aj* nudist
semidesnudo *aj* semi-nude, semi-naked

despacho attorney's office; act of dispatching
despachar *vt* to dispatch
despacharse *vr* to eliminate
despacho *nm* [-o(1) 3995] attorney's office; act of dispatching

despacio slow
despacio *av* slowly
despacio *int* slow down
despacioso *aj* slow; slow-moving; slow-going

despertar to wake up
despertar *vt* [2102] to wake up
despertarse *vr* [2102] to be awakened; to wake up
despertador *nm* [-dor(2)] alarm clock
despierto *aj* [4697] awake

desplegar to unfold; to unroll; to spread; to extend
desplegar *vt* [3839] to unfold; to unroll; to spread; to extend
desplegarse *vr* [3839] to be unfolded; to be unrolled; to be spread out; to be extended
plegar *vt* to fold; to roll up
plegarse *vr* to be folded; to be rolled up
replegar *vt* to fold up with many folds; to retreat
replegarse *vr* to be folded up with many folds
despliegue *nm* dismissal of troops from formation
plegado *nm* folding or rolling of something
pliegue *nm* fold; pleat
repliegue *nm* military retreat; double fold or pleat
plegable *aj* able to be folded
plegado *aj* folded; rolled-up

desprender to detach
desprender *vt* [2684] to detach; to separate
desprenderse *vr* to give away; to become detached

desprendimiento *nm* separation
desprendido *aj* generous

destacar to stand out
destacar *vr* [272] to stand out
destacarse *vr* to distinguish oneself
destacado *aj* distinguished

destino destiny
destinar *vt* [1075] to destine
destinatario,-a *nmf* destination; recipient of a package or letter
destino *nm* [1414] destiny
destinado *aj* destined

desvanecer to vanish
desvanecer *vti* to vanish (vi); to blur or soften a photo or picture (vt)
desvanecerse *vr* to faint
desvanecimiento *nm* vanishing; fainting

detalle detail
detallar *vt* [2040] to cover in detail; to do something paying attention to detail
detallista *nmf* person who pays attention to detail; retail seller
detalle *nm* [1199] detail
detalladamente *av* carefully; with attention to detail
detallado *aj* detailed
detallista *aj* paying attention to detail; sometimes used to refer to a person who pays attention to details in a romantic relationship

detestar to detest
detestar *vt* to detest
detestable *aj* detestable

deuda debt
adeudar *vt* to owe something
adeudarse *vr* to go into debt
endeudarse *vr* to go into debt
deudor,-a *nmf* debtor
adeudo *nm* [-o(1) 2614] debt
deuda *nf* [1481] debt
deudor *aj* indebted

devoción devotion
devocionario *nm* [-ario(1)] devotional book
devoción *nf* devotion

día day
día *nm* [52] day
diario *nm* [-ario(1) 427] diary; daily newspaper
telediario *nm* daily television news bulletin
diariamente *av* [-mente 2702] daily
cotidiano *aj* [2726] daily; everyday
diario *aj* [-ario(1) 427] daily
diurno *aj* daytime

diablo devil
  diablillo *nm* little devil, referring to a
    mischievous child
  diablo *nm* [1402] devil
  diablesa *nf* female devil
  diablura *nf* mischievous trick
  endiabladamente *av* devilishly
  diabólico *aj* diabolic
  endiablado *aj* furious
diálogo dialog
  dialogar *vi* [2974] to converse
  diálogo *nm* [-o(1) 1683] dialog
dibujo drawing
  desdibujar *vt* to soften the lines of a drawing or
    painting
  desdibujarse *vr* to remember without great
    detail
  dibujar *vt* [4978] to draw
  dibujarse *vr* to show oneself; to appear as
  dibujante *nmf* [-ante(2)] artist who draws
  dibujo *nm* [-o(1) 3361] drawing
  desdibujado *aj* blurred; indefinite
dicha joy, happiness
  desdichado,-a *nmf* unhappy or joyless person
  desdicha *nf* joylessness, unhappiness
  dicha *nf* [774] joy, happiness
  desdichadamente *av* unfortunately
  desdichado *aj* unfortunate; unhappy
  dichoso *aj* joyful, happy
diente tooth
  dentar *vi* to teethe
  dentellar *vt* to chatter one's teeth
  dentista *nmf* [-ista 4154] dentist
  odontólogo,-a *nmf* dentist
  diente *nm* [1710] tooth
  dentadura *nf* set of teeth
  odontología *nf* dentistry
  dentado *aj* with teeth
  dental *aj* [2349] dental
  desdentado *aj* toothless
  odontológico *aj* dental
dieta diet
  dietista *nmf* dietician
  dieta *nf* [1510] diet
  dietética *nf* dietetics
  dietético *aj* dietetic
diez ten
  diezmar *vt* to tithe
  diecinueve *nm* nineteen
  diecinueveavo *nm* [-avo] one-nineteenth
    (fraction)
  dieciocho *nm* eighteen
  dieciséis *nm* sixteen

dieciseisavo *nm* [-avo] one-sixteenth (fraction)
diecisiete *nm* seventeen
diecisieteavo *nm* [-avo] one-seventeenth
  (fraction)
diez *nm* [814] ten
undécimo *nm* [-ésimo] one-eleventh (fraction)
diecinueve *aj* nineteen
diecinueveavo *aj* [-avo] nineteenth
dieciochesco *aj* related to the eighteenth
  century
dieciocho *aj* eighteen
dieciséis *aj* sixteen
dieciseisavo *aj* [-avo] sixteenth
diecisiete *aj* seventeen
diecisieteavo *aj* [-avo] seventeenth
diez *aj* [814] ten
undécimo *aj* [-ésimo] eleventh
diferencia difference
  diferenciar *vt* to differentiate
  diferenciarse *vr* to differentiate oneself; to be
    different
  diferencial *nm* differential
  diferencia *nf* [-a 765] difference
  diferenciación *nf* differentiation
  indiferencia *nf* indifference
  diferente *av* [-ente(1) 271] different
  diferencial *aj* differential
  diferente *aj* [-ente(1) 271] different
  indiferente *aj* indifferent
difícil difficult
  dificultar *vt* [3898] to make something difficult
  dificultad *nf* [-tad 1720] difficulty
  difícil *aj* [408] difficult
  dificultoso *aj* difficult
difuso diffuse
  difusión *nf* [-sión 2610] diffusion
  radiodifusión *nf* radio broadcasting
  difundir *vt* [2078] to broadcast; to publish; to
    spread
  difuso *aj* diffuse
  difusor *aj* broadcasting; publishing
  difundido *aj* broadcasted
digno worthy
  dignificar *vt* to dignify
  dignatario,-a *nmf* dignitary
  dignidad *nf* [-idad 3240] dignity
  dignamente *av* worthily
  dignificante *aj* dignifying
  digno *aj* [1856] worthy
dilatado dilated
  dilatar *vt* to dilate
  dilatarse *vr* to become dilated
  dilatación *nf* dilation

dilatado *aj* dilated
dilatador *aj* dilating
diligencia diligence
  diligenciar *vt* to carry out or execute a task
  diligencia *nf* diligence
  diligente *aj* diligent
dimensión dimension
  dimensión *nf* [2882] dimension
  dimensional *aj* dimensional
dinámico dynamic
  dinamitar *vt* to dynamite
  dinamitero,-a *nmf* one who works with dynamite
  dinamismo *nm* dynamism
  aerodinámica *nf* aerodynamics
  dinámica *nf* [3414] dynamics
  dinamita *nf* [-ito(2)] dynamite
  aerodinámico *aj* aerodynamic
  dinámico *aj* dynamic
dinero money
  adinerarse *vr* to enrich oneself
  adinerado,-a *nmf* wealthy or rich person
  dineral *nm* [-al(1)] great deal of money
  dinerillo *nm* small amount of money; small coin
  dinero *nm* [422] money
  adinerado *aj* wealthy
Dios God
  endiosar *vt* to make into a god; to deify
  endiosarse *vr* to be overly conceited or prideful in oneself; to make oneself into a god
  semidiós,-a *nmf* demigod
  Dios *nm* [657] God
  dios *nm* [657] god
  endiosamiento *nm* deification
  diosa *nf* goddess
  adiós *int* [3836] goodbye
diplomático diplomatic
  diplomarse *vr* to earn a diploma
  diplomático,-a *nmf* diplomat
  diploma *nf* diploma
  diplomacia *nf* diplomacy
  diplomado *aj* licensed; with diploma
  diplomático *aj* [-ico(2) 2334] diplomatic
dirigir to direct
  dirigir *vt* [342] to direct
  dirigirse *vr* [342] to direct oneself
  teledirigir *vt* to operate by remote control
  directivo,-a *nmf* member of a board of governors
  director,-a *nmf* [180] director
  dirigente *nmf* [-ente(2) 640] leader responsible for a group or activity

subdirector,-a *nmf* sub-director
direccional *nm* directional signal
directo *nm* [1046] straight hit in boxing
directorio *nm* [-orio(1)] directory
dirigible *nm* airship, dirigible
dirección *nf* [-ción 339] direction
directa *nf* drive or high gear of a motor
directiva *nf* directive
directamente *av* [-mente 1735] directly
directivo *aj* [-ivo 699] directive; managing
directo *aj* [1046] direct
dirigente *aj* [-ente(2) 640] directing
dirigible *aj* able to be guided or directed
indirecto *aj* indirect
multidireccional *aj* multi-directional
teledirigido *aj* remote-controlled
unidireccional *aj* one-directional
discernir to discern
  discernir *vt* to discern
  discernimiento *nm* discernment
discípulo disciple
  disciplinar *vt* to discipline
  indisciplinarse *vr* to provoke or cause lack of discipline
  condiscípulo,-a *nmf* fellow student
  discípulo,-a *nmf* disciple
  autodisciplina *nf* self-discipline
  disciplina *nf* [-a 1764] discipline
  indisciplina *nf* lack of discipline
  disciplinado *aj* disciplined
  disciplinario *aj* disciplinary
  indisciplinado *aj* undisciplined
discreto discreet
  discreto,-a *nmf* a discreet person
  indiscreto,-a *nmf* an indiscreet person
  discreción *nf* discretion
  indiscreción *nf* indiscretion
  discrecional *aj* optional, discretionary
  discreto *aj* [4909] discreet
  indiscreto *aj* indiscreet
discutir to argue
  discutir *vt* [1708] to argue
  discurso *nm* [1736] speech
  discusión *nf* [-sión 1923] discussion
  discursivo *aj* pertaining to a speech
  discutible *aj* [-ible] debatable
  indiscutible *aj* indisputable
disertación dissertation
  disertar *vt* to speak at length on a subject
  disertación *nf* dissertation
disfraz disguise; costume
  disfrazar *vt* to disguise

disfrazarse *vr* to disguise oneself
disfraz *nm* disguise; costume

disfrute enjoyment
disfrutar *vt* [764] to enjoy
disfrute *nm* enjoyment

disimulado pretended, feigned
disimular *vt* to pretend, to feign
disimulación *nf* pretense
disimuladamente *av* in a feigned or pretended manner
disimulado *aj* pretended, feigned

disipar to dissipate
disipar *vt* to dissipate; to disappear
disipado *aj* dissipated

disminuir to diminish
disminuir *vt* [980] to diminish
disminución *nf* [2109] diminution; lowering, lessening

disparar to shoot
disparar *vt* [1737] to shoot
dispararse *vr* to shoot oneself
disparador *nm* shooter
disparo *nm* [-o(1) 1461] shot

dispensar to dispense; to excuse or pardon
dispensar *vt* to dispense; to excuse or pardon
dispensario *nm* dispensary
dispensa *nf* dispensation
indispensable *aj* [-able 2455] indispensable

disputar to dispute
disputar(se) *vt(r)* [1222] to dispute; to debate
disputa *nf* [-a 1975] dispute

distancia distance
distanciar *vt* to separate or increase the distance between two things
distanciarse *vr* to distance oneself
distar *vi* to be distant from
equidistar *vi* to be equidistant
distanciamiento *nm* distancing
distancia *nf* [-a 1564] distance
equidistancia *nf* equidistance
distanciado *aj* distant
distante *aj* distant
equidistante *aj* equidistant

distinguir to distinguish
distinguir *vt* [2185] to distinguish
distinguirse *vr* [2185] to distinguish oneself
distintivo *nm* distinguishing mark or sign
distinción *nf* [-ción 4581] distinction
indistintamente *av* indistinctly
distinguido *aj* distinguished
distintivo *aj* distinctive

distinto *aj* [748] distinct
indistinto *aj* indistinct

distraer to distract
distraer *vt* [4561] to distract
distraerse *vr* [4561] to be distracted
distraído,-a *nmf* absent-minded person
distracción *nf* distraction
distraído *aj* distracted

distribución distribution
distribuir *vt* [1881] to distribute
redistribuir *vt* to redistribute
distribuidor,-a *nmf* distributor
distribución *nf* [-ción 1944] distribution
redistribución *nf* redistribution
distribuidor *aj* [-dor(1) 3431] distributing
distributivo *aj* distributive

diverso diverse
divergir *vi* to diverge
diversificar *vt* [-ificar] to diversify
diversificarse *vr* to be diversified
divertir *vt* [1543] to divert; to entertain
divertirse *vr* [1543] to have fun
divergencia *nf* [-encia] divergence
diversidad *nf* [-idad 4112] diversity
diversificación *nf* diversification
diversión *nf* [-sión 3465] diversion
divergente *aj* divergent
diverso *aj* [446] diverse
divertido *aj* fun; funny

dividir to divide
dividir *vt* [1805] to divide
dividirse *vr* to be divided
subdividir *vt* to subdivide
dividendo *nm* dividend
divisor *nm* divisor
divisoria *nm* dividing line
divisibilidad *nf* divisibility
división *nf* [-sión 915] division
subdivisión *nf* subdivision
divisible *aj* divisible
divisor *aj* dividing
divisorio *aj* [-orio(1)] dividing
indivisible *aj* indivisible

divino divine
divinizar *vt* to make something divine
divinidad *nf* divinity
divino *aj* [3915] divine

divorcio divorce
divorciar *vt* [4505] to divorce
divorciarse *vr* [4505] to become divorced
divorciado,-a *nmf* divorcee
divorcio *nm* [-o(1) 3840] divorce
divorciado *aj* divorced

doble double
desdoblar *vt* to unfold
doblar *vt* [4491] to double; to fold; to turn
doblegar *vt* to fold
doblegarse *vr* to fold (giving up, permitting something)
redoblar *vt* to redouble
dobles *nmpl* doubles in sports
doble *nmf* [1025] double
desdoblamiento *nm* unfolding
doblaje *nm* dubbing
doblez *nm* fold; duplicity, double-dealing
redoble *nm* redoubling
doble *nf* [1025] double
doble *av* [1025] double
doblemente *av* doubly
doble *aj* [1025] double

dócil docile
docilidad *nf* docility
dócil *aj* docile

doctor doctor
doctorarse *vr* to earn a doctorate
docto,-a *nmf* expert
doctor,-a *nmf* [556] doctor
doctorado *nm* [-ato] doctorate
doctamente *av* with wisdom and knowledge
docto *aj* expert
doctoral *aj* doctoral

doctrina doctrine
adoctrinar *vt* to indoctrinate
doctrinario,-a *nmf* doctrinaire person
adoctrinamiento *nm* indoctrination
doctrina *nf* doctrine
doctrinal *aj* doctrinal
doctrinario *aj* doctrinaire

documento document
documentar *vt* to document
documentarse *vr* to check in; to check baggage
indocumentado,-a *nmf* undocumented alien
documental *nm* [3747] documentary
documento *nm* [-o(1) 886] document
documentación *nf* [-ción 2858] documentation
documentado *aj* documented
documental *aj* [3747] documentary
indocumentado *aj* [3946] undocumented

dogma dogma
dogmatizar *vt* to teach dogma
dogmático,-a *nmf* dogmatic person
dogma *nm* dogma
dogmatismo *nm* [-ismo] dogmatism
dogmático *aj* dogmatic

dolor pain
adolecer *vi* to suffer

condolerse *vr* to share in suffering
doler *vi* [3579] to hurt
dolerse *vr* to be hurting
dolor *nm* [1019] pain
condolencia *nf* condolence
dolencia *nf* pain
adolorido *aj* painful; hurting
dolorido *aj* painful; hurting
doloroso *aj* [-oso 3115] physically or emotionally painful
indoloro *aj* painless

doméstico domestic
domar *vt* to tame; to domesticate
domesticar *vt* to tame; to domesticate
domador,-a *nmf* one who tames an animal
doméstico,-a *nmf* domestic worker
electrodoméstico *nm* household electrical appliance
doma *nf* taming
domesticación *nf* domestication
domesticable *aj* tamable
doméstico *aj* [2785] domestic
indomable *aj* untamable
indómito *aj* untamable; rebellious

dominar to dominate
dominar *vt* [2197] to dominate
dominarse *vr* to conquer oneself
predominar *vt* [4800] to predominate
condominio *nm* condominium
predominio *nm* predominance
dominación *nf* [-ción] domination
predominación *nf* predomination
dominante *aj* dominant
predominante *aj* predominant

donde where
adonde *av* to where
adónde *av* to where?
adondequiera *av* to wherever
donde *av* where
dónde *av* where?
dondequiera *av* wherever

dorado golden
dorar(se) *vt(r)* [1989] to make something golden
sobredorar *vt* to plate with gold
dorado *nm* golden color; act of making something golden
dorado *aj* golden

dormir to sleep
adormecer *vt* to cause to feel sleepy
adormecerse *vr* to fall asleep (part of the body); to become drowsy
adormilarse *vr* to be drowsy
dormir *vi* [1549] to sleep

dormirse *vr* to be sleeping
dormitar *vi* to nod off, to doze
durmiente *nmf* [-ente(1)] sleeping person
adormecimiento *nm* drowsiness
dormitorio *nm* [-orio(1)] dormitory
adormecedor *aj* causing drowsiness
adormecido *aj* drowsy
dormido *aj* asleep
durmiente *aj* [-ente(1)] sleeping

dos two
doce *nm* [2122] twelve
doceavo *nm* [-avo] one-twelfth (fraction)
dos *nm* [44] two
doscientos *nm* two hundred
docena *nf* [4458] dozen
doce *aj* [2122] twelve
doceavo *aj* [-avo] twelfth
dos *aj* [44] two
doscientos *aj* two hundred

dote gift, talent; dowry
dotar *vt* [3296] to give a dowry; to endow
superdotado,-a *nmf* gifted person
dotación *nf* endowment; dowry
dote *nf* gift, talent; dowry
dotes *nfpl* talents, gifts
dotado *aj* gifted, talented
superdotado *aj* very gifted; very talented

drama drama
dramatizar *vt* to dramatize
dramaturgo,-a *nmf* dramatist
drama *nm* [3665] drama
dramatismo *nm* drama
dramática *nf* dramatics
dramaturgia *nf* dramatics
psicodrama *nf* psycho-drama
dramático *aj* [-ico(2) 3234] dramatic

duda doubt
dudar *vt* [3110] to doubt
duda *nf* [-a 754] doubt
dudoso *aj* [-oso] doubtful
indudable *aj* indubitable

dueño owner
adueñarse *vr* to become an owner
dueño,-a *nmf* [1206] owner

dulce sweet
dulcificar *vt* to sweeten
endulzar *vt* to sweeten
dulcero,-a *nmf* person who sells or makes candy; someone who has a sweet tooth; candy jar
dulce *nm* [1534] sweet; candy
dulzor *nm* sweetness
edulcorante *nm* synthetic sweetener

dulcería *nf* [-ería(1)] candy store
dulzura *nf* [-ura(1)] sweetness
dulce *aj* [1534] sweet
dulcero *aj* sweet-loving
dulzón *aj* over-sweet

duque duke
archiduque *nm* archduke
duque *nm* duke
archiduquesa *nf* archduchess
duquesa *nf* duchess

durante during
durar *vi* [1165] to last
durante *prep* [81] during
duración *nf* [-ción 2505] duration

duro hard
endurecer *vt* to harden
endurecerse *vr* to become hardened
endurecimiento *nm* hardening; hardness
durabilidad *nf* durability
duro *av* [2086] hard
durable *aj* durable
duradero *aj* long-lasting
duro *aj* [2086] hard

E

echar to throw
desechar *vt* [4490] to throw out;
echar *vt* [1343] to throw; to cough up
echarse *vr* to throw oneself
desecho *nm* [-o(1) 3090] throw-away item
desechable *aj* disposable
echado *aj* thrown-out

eclesiástico ecclesiastical
Eclesiastés *nm* Ecclesiastes
eclesiástico *aj* ecclesiastical

económico economic
economizar *vt* to economize
economista *nmf* [-ista 3419] economist
econometría *nf* econometrics
economía *nf* [508] economy; economics
macroeconomía *nf* macroeconomics
económicamente *av* [-mente 4475] economically
económico *aj* [-ico(2) 220] economical
socioeconómico *aj* socioeconomic

edición edition
editar *vt* [3141] to publish
reeditar *vt* to republish
editor,-a *nmf* [1755] publisher (person)
editorialista *nmf* editorial writer
editorial *nm* [2754] editorial

edición *nf* [-ción 1277] edition
editorial *nf* [2754] publishing company
reedición *nf* republication
editor *aj* [-or] editing
editorial *aj* [2754] editorial; related to publishing
inédito *aj* [3474] unpublished

edificar to edify, to build up
edificar *vt* to edify, to build up
reedificar *vt* to build up again, to rebuild
edificio *nm* [-icio 1187] building
edificación *nf* edification
reedificación *nf* rebuilding
edificador *aj* [-dor(1)] edifying
edificante *aj* edifying

educar to educate
educar *vt* [2755] to educate
reeducar *vt* to reeducate
educador,-a *nmf* educator
maleducado,-a *nmf* rude or ill-mannered
  person
coeducación *nf* coeducation
educación *nf* [435] education
reeducación *nf* reeducation
educado *aj* well-mannered; educated
educador *aj* educating
educativo *aj* [-ivo 831] educative
maleducado *aj* rude or ill-mannered

efecto effect
efectuar *vt* [580] to effect, to bring about
efectuarse *vr* [580] to take place
efectivo *nm* [-ivo 1156] cash
efecto *nm* [680] effect
efectividad *nf* [-idad 4266] effectiveness
efectivamente *av* [-mente 3235] effectively
efectivo *aj* [-ivo 1156] effective
inefectivo *aj* ineffective

eficaz efficient
eficacia *nf* [-icia 4077] efficiency
eficiencia *nf* [-encia 3149] efficiency
ineficacia *nf* inefficiency
eficazmente *av* efficiently
eficientemente *av* efficiently
eficaz *aj* [-az 3209] efficient
eficiente *aj* [2411] efficient
ineficaz *aj* inefficient

egoísmo selfishness
egoísta *nmf* selfish person
ególatra *nmf* self-worshiper
ego *nm* ego
egocentrismo *nm* egocentrism
egoísmo *nm* [-ismo] selfishness
egotismo *nm* egotism

egolatría *nf* self-worship; excessive self-
  adoration
egocéntrico *aj* egocentric
egoísta *aj* selfish; egotistical
ególatra *aj* self-adoring

ejecución execution
ejecutar *vt* [2020] to execute
ejecutor,-a *nmf* executor
ejecutivo *nm* [-ivo 659] executive
ejecución *nf* [2740] execution
ejecutivo,-a *aj* executive

ejemplo example
ejemplarizar *vt* to give an example
ejemplificar *vi* to exemplify
ejemplar *nm* [2728] exemplary person
ejemplo *nm* [568] example
ejemplar *aj* [2728] exemplary

ejercer to exercise
ejercer *vt* [1411] to practice a profession or
  position; to exercise (authority)
ejercitar *vt* to exercise
ejercitarse *vr* to get exercise
ejercicio *nm* [-icio 948] exercise
ejército *nm* [-o(1) 998] army

él he
él *pron* he
ella *pron* she
ellas *pron* they (all female)
ello *pron* it; that
ellos *pron* they (at least one male)

elaboración elaboration
elaborar *vt* [1185] to elaborate
elaboración *nf* [-ción 2793] elaboration

eléctrico electric
electrificar *vt* [-ificar] to electrify
electrizar *vt* to give or produce electricity
electrocutar *vt* to electrocute
electrocutarse *vr* to be electrocuted
electricista *nmf* electrician
electrochoque *nm* electric shock
electrodo *nm* electrode
electrodoméstico *nm* electrical appliance
electroimán *nm* electromagnet
electrolito *nm* electrolyte
electrón *nm* electron
electricidad *nf* [-idad 1628] electricity
electrificación *nf* electrification
electrocardiograma *nf* electrocardiogram
electrocución *nf* electrocution
electrólisis *nf* electrolysis
electrónica *nf* electronics
electrostática *nf* electrostatics
eléctrico *aj* [815] electric

electrizante *aj* electrifying
electromagnético *aj* electromagnetic
electrónico *aj* [1317] electronic
electrostático *aj* electrostatic
fotoeléctrico *aj* photoelectric

elegante elegant
elegancia *nf* elegance
elegantemente *av* elegantly
elegante *aj* [3617] elegant

elegir to elect; to choose
elegir *vt* [934] to elect; to choose
reelegir *vt* to reelect
elegidos *nmpl* chosen
electo *nmf* [3346] person elected to office
elector,-a *nmf* [4013] elector
electorado *nm* electorate
elegido *nm* chosen; selected
elección *nf* [-ción 551] election
elegibilidad *nf* eligibility
reelección *nf* [-ción 4899] reelection
electivo *aj* elective
electo *aj* [3346] elect
electoral *aj* [575] electoral
elegido *aj* elected; chosen
elegible *aj* eligible
reelecto *aj* reelected

elemento element
elemento *nm* [274] element
elemental *aj* [-al(2) 4816] elemental

elevado elevated
elevar *vt* [926] to elevate; to raise
elevarse *vr* to become ecstatic
elevador *nm* elevator
elevación *nf* elevation
elevado *aj* elevated
elevador *aj* elevating

eliminar to eliminate
eliminar *vt* [1021] to eliminate
eliminador,-a *nmf* eliminator
eliminación *nf* [-ción 2898] elimination
eliminatoria *nf* eliminatory round of
　competition
eliminador *aj* eliminating
eliminatorio *aj* [-orio(2) 3037] eliminatory

elocuencia eloquence
elocución *nf* elocution
elocuencia *nf* eloquence
elocuente *aj* eloquent

elogio eulogy; praise
elogiar *vt* to eulogize; to praise
elogio *nm* eulogy; praise
elogiable *aj* praiseworthy

emanar to emanate
emanar *vi* [4665] to emanate
emanación *nf* emanation

embajador ambassador
embajador,-a *nmf* [2615] ambassador
embajada *nf* [3007] embassy

embargo embargo
desembargar *vt* to remove an embargo or
　prohibition of commerce
embargar *vt* to embargo; to prohibit commerce
desembargo *nm* removal of an embargo or
　prohibition on commerce
embargo *nm* [-o(1) 170] embargo

embriaguez inebriation, drunkenness
embriagar *vt* to inebriate, to intoxicate
embriagarse *vr* to become inebriated, to
　become intoxicated
embriaguez *nm* inebriation, intoxication,
　drunkenness
embriagado *aj* inebriated, intoxicated, drunk
embriagador *aj* inebriating, intoxicating

eminente eminent
eminencia *nf* [-encia] eminence
preeminencia *nf* preeminence
eminentemente *av* eminently
eminente *aj* eminent
preeminente *aj* preeminent

emitir to emit
emitir *vt* [1306] to emit
emisor *nm* [3648] transmitter
emisión *nf* [-sión 2288] emission
emisora *nf* radio or television broadcasting
　station
emisor *aj* [3648] emitting

emoción emotion
emocionar *vr* [3099] to excite or provoke emotion
emocionarse *vr* to become excited
emoción *nf* [-ción 1705] emotion
emotividad *nf* emotive quality
emocionado *aj* excited; emotional
emocional *aj* [2535] emotional
emocionante *aj* exciting
emotivo *aj* [-ivo 3828] emotive, causing emotion
emocionalmente *av* emotionally

empeño effort; pawning
desempeñar *vt* [2083] to take out of pawn; to
　carry out an obligation or the duties of an
　office or position
desempeñarse *vr* to carry out an obligation or
　the duties of an office or position
empeñar(se) *vt(r)* [4700] to pawn

desempeño *nm* [-o(1) 1998] redemption of a
pawned item; the carrying out of an obligation
of an office or position
empeño *nm* effort; pawning

emplear to employ
desemplear *vt* [4871] to dismiss from
employment
emplear *vt* [2390] to employ
emplearse *vr* to be employed
desempleado,-a *nmf* unemployed
empleado,-a *nmf* [1027] employee
desempleo *nm* [-eo(1) 2059] unemployment
empleo *nm* [-eo(1) 710] employment
pluriempleo *nm* moonlighting
subempleo *nm* underemployment
desempleado *aj* unemployed

empresa enterprise; business
emprender *vt* [2164] to begin a work or business
empresario,-a *nmf* [884] business owner
empresa *nf* [179] enterprise; business
emprendedor *aj* decisive; enterprising
empresarial *aj* [1675] business

empujar to push
empujar *vt* [2536] to push
empuje *nm* push
empujón *nm* [-ón(1)] hard push, shove

encanto charm; spell
desencantar *vt* to disenchant
encantar *vt* [2092] to enchant; to charm
encantador,-a *nmf* enchanting or charming
person
desencantamiento *nm* act of reversing a spell
desencanto *nm* disenchantment
encantamiento *nm* [-miento] act of casting a spell
encanto *nm* charm; spell
encantado *aj* enchanted; charmed
encantador *aj* enchanting; charming

encender to light a fire; to turn on an electrical
device
encender *vt* [2987] to light a fire; to turn on an
electrical device
encenderse *vr* [2987] to become quickly angry
encendedor *nm* lighter
encendido *nm* lighting; turning on; ignition
encendido *aj* on, when referring to an electrical
device; passionately angry

enciclopedia encyclopedia
enciclopedia *nf* encyclopedia
enciclopédico *aj* encyclopedic

encontrar to find
encontrar *vt* [86] to find
encontrarse *vr* to meet up with; to find
(oneself)

reencontrarse *vr* to meet up with again
encontronazo *nm* collision; dispute
encuentro *nm* [-o(1) 419] encounter; chance
meeting
reencuentro *nm* to encounter again
encontrado *aj* found

enemigo enemy
enemistar *vt* to make an enemy
enemistarse *vr* to become an enemy
enemigo,-a *nmf* [1924] enemy
enemistad *nf* [-tad] enmity
enemigo *aj* enemy

energía energy
energía *nf* [692] energy
energético *aj* [-ico(2) 2335] energy-giving
enérgico *aj* [-ico(2)] energetic

enfadar to irritate; to bother
desenfadar *vt* to stop irritating; to appease
desenfadarse *vr* to escape from an irritation or
a bothersome situation
enfadar *vt* to irritate, to bother
enfadarse *vr* to be irritated by
desenfado *nm* escaping from an unpleasant
situation
enfado *nm* anger
desenfadado *aj* appeased; content
enfadadizo *aj* easily angered
enfadado *aj* irritated
enfadoso *aj* irritating

enfermo sick, ill
enfermar(se) *vt(r)* [3466] to become sick
enfermero,-a *nmf* [4192] nurse
enfermo,-a *nmf* sick person
enfermedad *nf* [459] infirmity; sickness
enfermería *nf* hospital
enfermizo *aj* [-izo] easily made sick
enfermo *aj* [-o(1) 1990] sick; ill

engañar to deceive
desengañar *vt* to disillusion
desengañarse *vr* to be disillusioned
engañar *vt* [3246] to deceive
engañarse *vr* [3246] to deceive oneself
desengaño *nm* disillusionment
engaño *nm* [-o(1) 4715] deception
engañadizo *aj* easily deceived
engañoso *aj* deceptive

engendrar to engender
engendrar *vt* to engender
engendro *nm* deformed creature

enigma enigma
enigma *nf* enigma
enigmático *aj* enigmatic

enmienda mending; correction
  enmendar *vt* to mend; to correct; to eliminate errors or defects
  enmendarse *vr* to correct oneself
  enmendadura *nf* mending; correction
  enmienda *nf* mending; correction

enojo anger
  enojar *vt* [4267] to anger
  enojarse *vr* [4067] to become angry
  enojo *nm* [-o(1) 4313] anger
  enojadizo *aj* [-dizo] easily-angered
  enojado *aj* [-ado(1)] angry
  enojón *aj* frequently angry

enorme enormous
  enormidad *nf* enormity
  enormemente *av* enormously
  enorme *aj* [1344] enormous

ensanchar to widen something, to make wider
  ensanchar *vt* to widen something, to make wider
  ensancharse *vr* to become wider
  ensanchamiento *nm* widening
  ensanche *nm* width
  Sancho Panza *nm* the wide-bellied companion of Don Quixote

ensayo essay; rehearsal
  ensayar *vt* to write an essay; to rehearse
  ensayista *nmf* essayist
  ensayo *nm* [-o(1) 3630] essay; rehearsal

enseñar to teach
  enseñar *vt* [1800] to teach
  enseñanza *nf* [-anza 3150] something learned; a teaching; education
  enseñado *aj* taught

entender to understand
  desentenderse *vr* to pretend not to understand
  entender *vt* [861] to understand
  entenderse *vr* to understand each other
  sobrentender *vt* to understand through context
  sobrentenderse *vr* to be understood through context
  entendedor,-a *nmf* understanding person
  entendido,-a *nmf* capable person; person with great understanding
  entendimiento *nm* [-miento 4608] understanding
  malentendido *nm* misunderstanding
  entendido *aj* understood
  entendedor *aj* understanding

enterar to learn of
  enterar *vr* [1703] to inform
  enterarse *vr* to notice; to learn that; to learn of
  enterado *aj* learned, understood

entero entire, whole
  entero *nm* [2215] whole thing, entirety, whole
  entereza *nf* integrity, wholeness
  enteramente *av* entirely
  entero *aj* [2215] entire, whole

entrada entrance
  entrar *vi* [405] to enter
  entrada *nf* [383] entrance; appetizer
  entrante *aj* [3100] entering; next

entrañas entrails; organs inside the abdomen
  desentrañar *vt* to remove the entrails; to get to the bottom of the matter
  entrañar *vt* to go to the depths of something
  entrañas *nfpl* entrails; organs inside the abdomen
  entraña *nf* the center; the nucleus
  entrañablemente *av* intimately
  entrañable *aj* intimate

entregar to give or deliver
  entregar *vt* [387] to give or deliver
  entregarse *vr* to give oneself to something or someone
  entrega *nf* [-a 691] giving or delivering

entusiasta enthusiast
  entusiasmar *vt* [4562] to generate enthusiasm
  entusiasmarse *vr* [4562] to become enthused
  entusiasta *nmf* enthusiast
  entusiasmo *nm* [-asma 2667] enthusiasm
  entusiasta *aj* enthusiastic, referring to people

envidia envy
  envidiar *vt* to envy
  envidia *nf* envy
  envidiosamente *av* enviously
  envidiable *aj* enviable
  envidioso *aj* envious

envolver to wrap; to involve
  desenvolver *vt* to unwrap
  desenvolverse *vr* to act without inhibition
  envolver *vt* [3162] to wrap
  envolverse *vr* [3162] to become involved
  desenvoltura *nf* unwrapping; development of confidence
  envoltura *nf* wrapping
  desenvuelto *aj* unwrapped; confident

episodio episode
  episodio *nm* [2189] episode
  episódico *aj* episodic

equilibrio equilibrium
  desequilibrarse *vr* to lose one's equilibrium
  desequilibrar *vt* to cause loss of balance, to knock or throw off balance
  equilibrar *vt* [3323] to gain equilibrium

equilibrarse *vr* to gain one's equilibrium
desequilibrado,-a *nmf* unbalanced person
equilibrista *nmf* tightrope walker
desequilibrio *nm* loss or lack of balance
equilibrio *nm* [2552] equilibrium
equilibrismo *nm* balancing act
desequilibrado *aj* unbalanced
equilibrado *aj* balanced

equivaler to be equivalent
equivaler *vi* [4173] to be equivalent
equivalencia *nf* equivalence
equivalente *aj* [-ente(1) 2833] equivalent

equivocar to make a mistake
equivocar *vr* [2351] to mistake
equivocarse *vr* to be mistaken
equivocación *nf* mistake
equivocadamente *av* mistakenly
equivocado *aj* wrong
inequívoco *aj* unmistakable

ermita small church isolated from town
ermitaño,-a *nmf* person in charge of a small
  church isolated from town; hermit
eremita *nm* hermit, often isolated for penitence
  and prayer
ermita *nf* small church isolated from town

error error
errar *vi* to err
error *nm* [1060] error
errata *nf* errata
erradamente *av* erroneously; mistakenly
erróneamente *av* erroneously
errado *aj* mistaken
errático *aj* erratic

erudito erudite
erudito,-a *nmf* erudite person
erudición *nf* erudition
eruditamente *av* eruditely
erudito *aj* [-ito(2)] erudite

esbelto svelte, slender
esbeltez *nf* slenderness
esbelto *aj* svelte, slender

escalera ladder
escalar *vt* [4678] to scale or climb
escalonar *v* to advance one stair step at a time
escalador,-a *nmf* rock climber, mountain
  climber
escalafón *nm* organizational level, by seniority
  or position
escalón *nm* stair step
escaleras *nfpl* stairs
escala *nf* [-a 3060] layover
escalada *nf* scaling
escalera *nf* [-era] ladder

escalerilla *nf* small ladder
escalonadamente *av* in a stair-stepped fashion
escalador *aj* rock-climbing, mountain-climbing
escalonado *aj* with stair steps

escándalo scandal; commotion; disturbance
escandalizar *vti* to cause a scandal; to create a
  lot of commotion
escandalizarse *vr* to be disturbed
escándalo *nm* [2087] scandal; commotion;
  disturbance
escandalosamente *av* scandalously; noisily
escandaloso *aj* [-oso] scandalous; with a lot of
  noise

escapar to escape
escapar *vt* [1861] to escape (in general)
escaparse *vr* [1861] to escape (referring to a
  specific person or thing that is escaping)
escape *nm* escape; exhaust
escapada *nf* escapade
escapatoria *nf* means or way of escape

escaparate showcase
escaparatista *nmf* person who decorates
  showcases
escaparate *nm* showcase

escaso scarce
escasear *vi* to be scarce; to run low
escatimar *vt* to spend the minimum necessary
escasez *nf* [-ez 3594] scarcity
escasamente *av* scarcely
escaso *aj* [1559] scarce

escena scene
escenógrafo,-a *nm* scene writer
escenario *nm* [687] stage; set
escena *nf* [1287] scene
escenografía *nf* scenography
escénico *aj* scenic

esclavitud slavery
esclavizar *vt* to enslave
esclavo,-a *nmf* slave
esclavitud *nf* [-itud] slavery
esclavo *aj* slave

esconder to hide
esconder *vt* [2374] to hide
esconderse *vr* [2374] to be hidden
escondite *nm* hiding place
escondrijo *nm* hiding place
escondidas *av* hidden

escopeta shotgun
escopetazo *nm* [-azo(2)] shot with a shotgun
escopeta *nf* shotgun

escribir to write
adscribir *vt* to ascribe; to assign

adscribirse *vr* to be ascribed; to be assigned

circunscribir *vt* to circumscribe; to limit

circunscribirse *vr* to limit oneself

describir *vt* [2069] to describe

escribir *vt* [896] to write

escribirse *vr* to correspond with each other

escriturar *vt* to formalize a contract

inscribir *vt* [2070] to inscribe

inscribirse *vr* [2070] to be inscribed; to enroll; to enlist

prescribir *vt* to prescribe

proscribir *vt* to proscribe, to prohibit

suscribir, subscribir *vt* to subscribe to an opinion; to sign at the bottom of a document (declaration, petition, etc.)

suscribirse, subscribirse *vr* to subscribe to a publication or club

transcribir, trascribir *vt* to transcribe

escribano,-a *nmf* word from antiquity meaning writer

escritor,-a *nmf* [1722] writer

escrito *nm* [1695] written document

escritorio *nm* [-orio(1)] desk

adscripción *nf* ascription

circunscripción *nf* circumscription

descripción *nf* description

escritura *nf* scripture

inscripción *nf* [-ción 2501] inscription; enrollment

prescripción *nf* prescription

suscripción, subscripción *nf* subscription

transcripción, trascripción *nf* transcription

circunscrito *aj* circumscribed

descriptible *aj* describable

descriptivo *aj* [-ivo] descriptive

descrito *aj* described

escrito *aj* [1695] written

indescriptible *aj* indescribable

inscrito *aj* inscribed; enrolled

suscrito, subscrito *aj* subscribed

escrúpulo scruple

escrúpulo *nm* scruple

escrupulosidad *nf* scrupulousness

escrupulosamente *av* scrupulously

escrupuloso *aj* scrupulous

escuchar to hear

escuchar *vt* [645] to hear

radioescucha *nmf* radio listener

escucha *nf* [-a] act of listening

escudo shield

escudar *vt* to shield

escudarse *vr* to shield oneself

escudero *nm* maker of shields; squire

escudo *nm* shield

escudería *nf* office of squire; auto or motorcycle racing team

escuela school

escolar *nmf* [1467] scholar

autoescuela *nf* driving school

escolaridad *nf* level of studies

escuela *nf* [324] school

escolar *aj* [1467] school

escolástico *aj* scholastic

extraescolar *aj* extracurricular

preescolar *aj* [4180] preschool

escueto plain

escuetamente *av* plainly; briefly; precisely

escueto *aj* plain; brief; precise

escultura sculpture

esculpir *vt* to sculpt

escultor,-a *nmf* sculptor

escultismo *nm* sculpting

escultura *nf* [-ura(2)] sculpture

escultural *aj* sculptural

esencial essential

esencial *nm* [-cial 2653] essential item or person

esencia *nf* [-encia 3081] essence

esencialmente *av* essentially

esencial *aj* [-cial 2653] essential

esfera sphere

esférico *nm* [-ico(2) 3180] ball

esferoide *nm* spheroid

esfera *nf* sphere

esférico *aj* [-ico(2) 3180] spherical

espacio space

espaciar *vt* to space; to make space

espaciarse *vr* to separate one thing from another

espaciador *nm* space-bar

espacio *nm* [-icio 612] space

espacial *aj* [-cial 3236] spatial

espacioso *aj* spacious

espada sword

espadachín *nm* sword fighter

espada *nf* sword

espalda back

respaldar *vt* [2339] to back up; to support

respaldarse *vr* to be helped (by) or protected (by)

guardaespaldas *nmf* bodyguard

respaldo *nm* [-o(1) 1965] economic backing; hardcopy; back of a chair, couch, etc.

espalda *nf* [2297] back

espaldilla *nf* disk or bone of the back

espanto fright

espantar *vt* to frighten

espantarse *vr* to be frightened
espantapájaros *nm* scarecrow
espanto *nm* fright
espantadizo *aj* easily frightened
espantoso *aj* [-oso] frightening

español Spanish
españolizar *vt* to introduce Spanish word into a language
españolizarse *vr* to become Spanish
españoles *nmpl* Spaniards
español,-a *nmf* Spaniard
españolista *nmf* fan of Spanish culture
españolismo *nm* [-ismo] affinity for Spanish culture
español *nf* [438] Spanish language
español *aj* [438] Spanish
españolada *aj* appearing to be Spanish

especial special
especializarse *vr* to specialize
especificar *vt* [-ificar 3190] to specify
especialista *nmf* [-ista 1556] specialist
especialización *nf* specialization
especificación *nf* specification
especialmente *av* [-mente 1147] especially
específicamente *av* [-mente 3996] specifically
especial *aj* [-cial 250] special
especializado *aj* specialized
específico *aj* [-ico(2) 1801] specific

especie species
espécimen *nm* specimen
especie *nf* [1392] species
subespecie *nf* subspecies

espectáculo show; spectacle
espectador,-a *nmf* [2514] spectator
espectáculo *nm* [-culo 826] show; spectacle
espectacularmente *av* spectacularly
espectacular *aj* [2329] spectacular

especulación speculation
especular *vi* [4958] to speculate
especulador,-a *nmf* speculator
especulación *nf* [-ción 4872] speculation
especulativo *aj* speculative

espejo mirror
espejear *vt* to look in the mirror
espejismo *nm* mirage
espejo *nm* [3472] mirror

esperar to wait; to hope; to expect
desesperanzarse *vr* to lose hope
desesperanzar *vt* to lack hope
desesperar *vt* [2849] to cause impatience
desesperarse *vr* [2849] to become impatient
esperanzar *vt* to inspire hope

esperanzarse *vr* to become hopeful or full of expectation
esperar *vt* [131] to wait; to hope; to expect
desesperación *nf* [-ción 4155] impatience
desesperanza *nf* [-anza] hopelessness
espera *nf* [-a] wait
esperanza *nf* [-anza 1115] hope
inesperadamente *av* unexpectedly
desesperado *aj* impatient
desesperante *aj* exasperating
esperanzador *aj* hope-inspiring
inesperado *aj* [-ado(1) 4384] unexpected

espeso thick
espesarse *vr* to become thick
espesar *vt* to thicken
espesante *nm* thickener
espesor *nm* density of a liquid; volume of a solid
espesura *nf* [-ura(1)] thickness
espeso *aj* thick

espía spy
espiar *vt* to spy
espía *nmf* spy
contraespionaje *nm* counterespionage
espionaje *nm* espionage

espiga ear, sprig
espigar *vt* to pick (corn, wheat)
espigarse *vr* to grow quickly, to shoot up
espigón *nm* sharp ear or sprig
espiga *nf* ear, sprig
espigado *aj* slender

espina thorn; spine
espinazo *nm* spinal cord
espino *nm* thorny plant about 1 meter tall
espina *nf* thorn; spine
espinilla *nf* shinbone; pimple; blackhead
espinillera *nf* shin guard
espinal *aj* spinal

espíritu spirit
inspirar *vt* [3288] to inspire
expirar *vi* to expire
suspirar *vti* to exhale, to sigh
espiritista *nmf* believer in the spirit world
espiritualista *nmf* [-ista] spiritualist
espiritismo *nm* belief in the spirit world
espíritu *nm* [1991] spirit
espiritualismo *nm* spiritualism
suspiro *nm* sigh, breath
espiritualidad *nf* [-idad] spirituality
expiración *nf* expiration
inspiración *nf* [-ción 3845] inspiration
espiritualmente *av* spiritually

espiritista *aj* relating to those who practice a belief in the spirit world
espiritual *aj* [3199] spiritual
inspirado *aj* inspired
inspirador *aj* inspiring

espléndido splendid
esplendor *nm* splendor
espléndidamente *av* splendidly
espléndido *aj* splendid
esplendoroso *aj* brilliant; bright

espontáneo spontaneous
espontaneidad *nf* spontaneity
espontáneamente *av* spontaneously
espontáneo *aj* spontaneous

esposo husband
desposar *vt* to perform the marriage ceremony
desposarse *vr* to marry each other; to get married
esposar *vt* to put on handcuffs
esposo,-a *nmf* [465] husband; wife
esposas *nfpl* handcuffs
esposa *nf* wife
desposado *aj* recently married
esposado *aj* handcuffed

espuma foam
espumar *vt* to make foam
espumarajo *nm* [-ajo] foamy saliva
espuma *nf* foam
espumilla *nf* creamy pie or cake topping
espumoso *aj* foamy

esqueleto skeleton
esqueleto *nm* skeleton
esquelético *aj* skeletal; skeleton-like

esquema scheme
esquematizar *vt* to make a schematic drawing
esquema *nf* [2029] scheme
esquemático *aj* schematic

esquina corner
esquinero,-a *nmf* piece of furniture built for a corner
esquina *nf* [1432] corner
esquinado *aj* having the form of a corner; with corners

esquivar to avoid; to withdraw
esquivar *vt* to avoid; to withdraw
esquivo *aj* withdrawn; unsociable

establecer to establish
desestabilizar *vt* to disestablish
estabilizar *vt* to stabilize
estabilizarse *vr* to become stabilized
establecer *vt* [358] to establish
establecerse *vr* [358] to be established

preestablecer *vt* to preestablish
restablecer *vt* to reestablish
restablecerse *vr* to be reestablished
estabilizador *nm* stabilizer
establecimiento *nm* [-miento 1788] establishment
restablecimiento *nm* reestablishment
desestabilización *nf* destabilization
estabilidad *nf* [-idad 2576] stability
estabilización *nf* stabilization
inestabilidad *nf* instability
estabilizador *aj* stabilizing
estable *aj* [3101] stable
inestable *aj* unstable
preestablecido *aj* preestablished

estación station; season of the year
estación *nf* [1486] station; season of the year
estacional *aj* seasonal

estadística statistics; statistic
estadístico,-a *nmf* statistician
estadística *nf* statistics; statistic
estadístico *aj* [-ico(2) 2048] statistical

estado state
estado *nm* [-ado(2) 42] state
paraestatal *aj* [3156] semi-official

estallar to explode
estallar *vi* [3297] to explode
estallido *nm* noise of an explosion

estampa stamp
estampar *vt* to stamp
estampado *nm* small printed paper with a religious image
estampa *nf* stamp
estampación *nf* imprinting
estampilla *nf* [-illa] postage stamp
estampado *aj* stamped; printed

estar to be
estar *vi* [22] to be
bienestar *nm* [2906] wellbeing
malestar *nm* [3948] unpleasant feeling

estatua statue
estatua *nf* statue
estatuaria *nf* technique of statue-making
estatuilla *nf* small statue; statuette
estatuario *aj* statue

estéril sterile
esterilizar *vt* to sterilize
esterilizarse *vr* to become sterile
esterilizador *nm* sterilizer
esterilidad *nf* sterility
esterilización *nf* sterilization
estéril *aj* sterile
esterilizador *aj* sterilizing

estético relating to esthetics or the study of beauty
   esteticista *nmf* specialist in cosmetics
   esteticismo *nm* view of the world which emphasizes physical beauty
   estética *nf* aesthetics
   antiestético *aj* ugly
   estético *aj* [-ico(2) 3977] relating to aesthetics or the study of beauty

estilo style
   estilarse *vr* to be in style
   estilizar *vt* to stylize
   estilista *nmf* stylist
   estilo *nm* [1013] style
   estilística *nf* stylistics
   estilización *nf* stylization
   estilístico *aj* stylistic

estimar to esteem; to estimate
   desestimar *vt* to reject
   estimar *vt* [1437] to esteem; to estimate
   estimarse *vr* [1437] to esteem each other
   sobrestimar *vt* to overestimate
   subestimar *vt* to underestimate
   estima *nf* [-a 2506] esteem; estimate
   estimación *nf* [-ción 4380] estimation
   estimable *aj* [-able 2182] estimable
   estimado *aj* estimated
   inestimable *aj* inestimable

estímulo stimulus
   estimular *vt* [2687] to stimulate
   estimulante *nm* stimulant
   estímulo *nm* [-o(1) 3016] stimulus
   estimulante *aj* stimulating

estirar to stretch
   estirar *vt* [4892] to stretch
   estirarse *vr* to stretch oneself
   estirón *nm* [-ón(1)] violent pull
   estirado *aj* presumptuous

estómago stomach
   estómago *nm* [3348] stomach
   estomacal *aj* stomach

estorbar to block
   estorbar *vt* to block
   estorbo *nm* obstruction

estratificar to stratify
   estratificar *vt* to stratify
   estratificarse *vr* to be stratified
   estrato *nm* stratus
   estratificación *nf* stratification
   estratosfera *nf* stratosphere

estrecho narrow
   estrechar *vt* to make narrow; to clasp hands

   estrecharse *vr* to become narrow; to tighten the bonds of friendship
   estrechamiento *nm* narrowing
   estrecho *nm* [3134] strait
   estrechez *nf* lack of width
   estrechura *nf* [-ura(1)] lack of width; narrowness
   estrechamente *av* closely, intimately
   estrecho *aj* [3134] narrow

estrella star
   estrellar *vt* [2642] to cover with stars; to crack
   estrellarse *vr* to crash violently
   estrellato *nm* star status, referring to famous people
   estrellón *nm* type of fireworks that forms a star in the air
   estrella *nf* [660] star
   estrellado *aj* [-ado(1)] star-shaped (e.g., over-easy egg); filled with stars; starry; cracked

estremecer to cause to quiver, shiver, or shudder
   estremecer *vt* to cause to quiver, shiver, or shudder
   estremecerse *vr* to quiver, shiver, or shudder
   estremecimiento *nm* quivering, shivering, shuddering
   estremecedor *aj* causing quivering, shivering, shuddering
   estremecido *aj* quivering, shivering, shuddering

estructura structure
   estructurar *vt* to structure
   reestructurar *vt* to restructure
   estructura *nf* [-a 1648] structure
   infraestructura *nf* [-ura(2) 1634] infrastructure
   reestructuración *nf* [-ción 4967] restructuring
   superestructura *nf* superstructure
   estructural *aj* [3257] structural

estudio study
   estudiar *vt* [1091] to study
   estudiante *nmf* [-ante(2) 1082] student
   estudiantado *nm* student body
   estudio *nm* [-o(1) 314] study
   estudiantina *nf* musical group made up of students
   estudiado *aj* studied
   estudiantil *aj* [-il 3362] relating to students
   estudioso *aj* studious

estupendo stupendous
   estupendamente *av* [-mente] stupendously
   estupendo *aj* stupendous

estúpido extremely stupid (offensive)
   estúpido,-a *nmf* extremely stupid person (offensive)

estupidez *nf* [-ez] stupidity

estúpido *aj* [-ido(1)] extremely stupid (offensive)

eterno eternal

eternidad *nf* [-idad] eternity

eterno *aj* [3200] eternal

ético ethical

ético,-a *nmf* ethicist

ética *nf* ethics

ético *aj* [-ico(2) 2892] ethical

evangelio gospel

evangelizar *vt* to evangelize

evangelista *nmf* evangelist; writer of one of the gospels

evangelio *nm* [3210] gospel

evangelismo *nm* [-ismo] evangelism

evangelización *nf* evangelization

evangélico *aj* [-ico(2)] evangelical

evangelizador *aj* evangelizing

evidente evident

evidenciar *vt* to show evidence; to prove with evidence

evidencia *nf* [-encia 2149] evidence

evidentemente *av* [-mente 4912] evidently

evidente *aj* [2186] evident

evitar to avoid

evitar *vt* [281] to avoid

evitarse *vr* to avoid (for oneself)

inevitablemente *av* unavoidably

evitable *aj* [-able] avoidable

inevitable *aj* [-able 4462] unavoidable

evocar to evoke

evocar *vt* to evoke

evocación *nf* evocation

evolución evolution

evolucionar *vi* [4415] to evolve

evolucionista *nmf* evolutionist, person who subscribes to the theory of organic evolution

evolucionismo *nm* evolutionism

evolución *nf* [3031] evolution

evolucionario *aj* evolutionary

evolucionista *aj* evolutionist

evolutivo *aj* [-ivo] evolutional; evolutionary

exacto exact

exactitud *nf* [-itud] exactitude

inexactitud *nf* [-itud] inexactitude

exactamente *av* [-mente 3151] exactly

exacto *aj* [3605] exact

inexacto *aj* inexact

exagerar to exaggerate

exagerar *vt* [3508] to exaggerate

exageración *nf* exaggeration

exageradamente *av* exaggeratedly

exagerado *aj* exaggerated

exaltar to exalt

exaltar *vt* to exalt

exaltarse *vr* to be exalted

exaltado,-a *nmf* exalted one

exaltación *nf* exaltation

exaltado *aj* exalted

examinar to examine

examinar *vt* [3796] to examine

examinarse *vr* to examine oneself

examinador,-a *nmf* examiner

examen *nm* exam

examinador *aj* examining

excelente excellent

excelso *aj* prominent; superior

excelencia *nf* [-encia 4382] excellence

excelente *aj* [1224] excellent

excepción exception

exceptuar *vt* to make an exception

excepción *nf* [-ción 2423] exception

excepto *av* [4114] except

excepcional *aj* exceptional

exceso excess

exceder *vt* [4625] to exceed

excederse *vr* to exceed one's previous limitations

sobreexceder *vt* to exceed (usually with negative connotation)

excedente *nm* surplus

exceso *nm* [1717] excess

excedente *aj* exceeding

excesivo *aj* [-ivo 2806] excessive

excitar to excite

excitar *vt* to excite

excitarse *vr* to be excited

sobreexcitar *vt* to overexcite

sobreexcitarse *vr* to become overexcited

excitabilidad *nf* excitability

excitación *nf* excitation

sobreexcitación *nf* overexcitement

excitable *aj* excitable

excitante *aj* exciting

exclusivamente exclusively

excluir *vt* [4564] to exclude

exclusivista *nmf* person who practices exclusivism

exclusivismo *nm* exclusivism

exclusión *nf* [-sión 4933] exclusion

exclusiva *nf* exclusive right to produce or sell a product

exclusividad *nf* exclusivity

exclusivamente *av* [-mente 3484] exclusively

exclusive *av* exclusive

exclusivo *aj* [-ivo 2061] exclusive

excursión excursion

excursionismo *nm* practice of taking excursions for educational or recreational purposes

excursión *nf* excursion

exhalar to exhale

exhalar *vt* to exhale

exhalación *nf* exhalation

exhibición exhibition

exhibir *vt* [2316] to exhibit

exhibicionista *nmf* exhibitionist

exhibicionismo *nm* exhibitionism

exhibición *nf* [-ción 2840] exhibition

exigir to demand

exigir *vt* [851] to demand

exigencia *nf* [-encia 2975] demand

exigente *aj* [4582] demanding

existencia existence

coexistir *vi* to coexist

existir *vi* [192] to exist

preexistir *vi* to preexist

existencialista *nmf* existentialist

existencialismo *nm* existentialism

coexistencia *nf* [-encia] coexistence

existencia *nf* [-encia 1724] existence

inexistencia *nf* inexistence

preexistencia *nf* preexistence

existencial *aj* [-cial] existential

existente *aj* [-ente(1) 2507] existent

inexistente *aj* nonexistent

expansión expansion

expandir *vt* to expand

expandirse *vr* to be expanded

expansionismo *nm* expansionism

expansión *nf* [-sión 4078] expansion

expansionista *aj* expansionist

expansivo *aj* [-ivo] expansive

expedición expedition

expedir *vt* [3965] to expedite

expedicionario,-a *nmf* person who travels on an expedition

expedidor,-a *nmf* expeditor

expedición *nf* expedition

expedicionario *aj* expeditionary

expeditivo *aj* [-ivo] expeditious

expedito *aj* expedited

experiencia experience

experimentar *vt* [1820] to experiment

experto,-a *nmf* expert

experimento *nm* [-o(1) 4626] experiment

experiencia *nf* [759] experience

experimentación *nf* experimentation

inexperiencia *nf* inexperience

expertamente *av* expertly

experimentado *aj* experimented

experimental *aj* [-al(2) 3116] experimental

experto *aj* [1505] expert

inexperimentado *aj* untried

inexperto *aj* inexpert

explicar to explain

explicar *vt* [267] to explain

explicarse *vr* to explain oneself

explicitar *vt* to be explicit

explicación *nf* [-ción 2441] explanation

explicable *aj* explicable

explicativo *aj* explicative

explícito *aj* explicit

inexplicable *aj* inexplicable

explosión explosion

explosionar *vti* to explode

explotar *vt* [2561] to explode

explosivo *nm* [-ivo 2859] explosive

explosión *nf* [-sión 2449] explosion

explosivo *aj* [-ivo 2859] explosive

explotar to exploit

explotar *vt* [2561] to exploit

explotador,-a *nmf* exploiter

explotación *nf* [-ción 3181] exploitation

explotable *aj* exploitable

expresión expression

expresar *vt* [552] to express

expresarse *vr* to express oneself

expresionista *nmf* expressionist

expresionismo *nm* expressionism

expresión *nf* [-sión 1802] expression

expresamente *av* expressly

expreso *av* express

expresado *aj* expressed

expresionista *aj* expressionist

expresivo *aj* expressive

inexpresable *aj* inexpressible

inexpresivo *aj* inexpressive

expulsar to expel

expulsar *vt* [1950] to expel

expulsor *nm* ejector

expulsión *nf* [-sión 2883] expulsion

expulsor *aj* expelling

exquisito exquisite

exquisitez *nf* exquisiteness

exquisito *aj* [-ito(2) 3782] exquisite

extender to extend

extender *vt* [1759] to extend

extenderse *vr* [1759] to be extended; to last

extenuar *vt* to exhaust

extenuarse *vr* to be exhausted

extensión *nf* [-sión 2786] extension
extenuación *nf* extenuation
extensamente *av* extensively
extendido *aj* extended
extenso *aj* [3748] extensive
extenuante *aj* extenuating; exhausting

exterior exterior
exteriorizar *vt* to manifest one's ideas or
  thoughts
exterior *nm* [1031] exterior
exterioridad *nf* appearance of things
exteriorización *nf* manifestation of one's ideas
  or thoughts
exteriormente *av* outwardly
exterior *aj* [1031] exterior

externo external
externo,-a *nmf* day student
externamente *av* externally
externo *aj* [2010] external

extinguir to extinguish
extinguir *vt* to extinguish
extinguirse *vr* to be extinguished
extinguidor *nm* fire extinguisher
extintor *nm* fire extinguisher
extinción *nf* extinction
extinto *aj* extinct
inextinguible *aj* inextinguishable

extranjero foreigner
extrañar(se) *vt(r)* [4175] to miss
extranjero,-a *nmf* [725] foreigner
extraño,-a *nmf* stranger
extranjerismo *nm* inclination to prefer foreign
  products or culture
extranjero *nm* foreign country
extrañeza *nf* amazement or surprise
extrañamente *av* strangely
extranjero *aj* foreign
extraño *aj* [1811] strange

extravagante extravagant
extravagancia *nf* extravagance
extravagante *aj* extravagant

extremo extreme
extremar *vt* to adopt an extreme attitude
extremarse *vr* to go to extremes
extremista *nmf* [-ista 4583] extremist
extremismo *nm* extremism
extremaunción *nf* extreme unction, ritual of the
  Catholic church
extremidad *nf* extremity
extremadamente *av* extremely
extremado *aj* extreme
extremista *aj* [-ista 4583] extremist

extremo *aj* [-o(1) 1636] last; furthest
extremoso *aj* immoderate, said of those who
  lack self-control; extreme

F

fábrica factory
fabricar *vt* [3091] to fabricate
prefabricar *vt* to prefabricate
fabricante *nmf* [-ante(2) 3485] factory worker
fábrica *nf* [-a 2993] factory
fabricación *nf* [-ción 4702] fabrication
prefabricación *nf* prefabrication
prefabricado *aj* prefabricated

fabuloso fabulous
fabulista *nmf* fabulist
fábula *nf* fable
fabuloso *aj* [-oso] fabulous

facción faction
facción *nf* faction
faccioso *aj* factious

fácil easy
facilitar *vt* [2030] to facilitate
facilidad *nf* [-idad 2282] facility; ease of doing
  something
facilitación *nf* facilitation
fácilmente *av* [-mente 2718] easily
fácil *aj* [1099] easy

factura invoice
facturar *vt* to invoice
factura *nf* invoice
facturación *nf* invoicing

faja girdle, corset
fajar *vt* to put on a girdle or corset; to tuck in
fajo *nm* bundle
faja *nf* girdle, corset
fajado *aj* tucked in

falda skirt
falda *nf* [4627] skirt
minifalda *nf* mini-skirt
faldero *aj* [-ero(2)] skirt-chasing

fallecer to pass away; to die
desfallecer *vi* to feel like fainting; to weaken
fallecer *vi* [1419] to pass away, to die
desfallecimiento *nm* fainting; discouragement;
  weakness
fallecimiento *nm* [-miento 4739] passing away
desfallecido *aj* fainting; discouraged; weak
fallecido *aj* dead

falso false
  falsificar *vt* [-ificar] to falsify
  falsificador,-a *nmf* liar; forger; one who falsifies
  falsete *nm* falsetto
  falsedad *nf* falsehood
  falsificación *nf* falsification
  falsificador *aj* falsifying
  falso *aj* [1885] false
faltar to miss
  faltar *vt* [1059] to miss
  falta *nf* [-a 263] miss; lack
  falto *aj* lacking
familia family
  familiarizar *vt* [-izar] to familiarize
  familiarizarse *vr* to become familiar with
  familiar *nmf* [375] family member
  familia *nf* [163] family
  familiaridad *nf* familiarity
  familiar *aj* [375] familiar
famoso famous
  afamar *vt* to make famous
  afamarse *vr* to become famous
  difamar *vt* to defame
  infamar *vt* to dishonor; to libel
  famosos *nmpl* famous people
  difamador,-a *nmf* libeler
  difamación *nf* [-ción] defamation
  infamia *nf* infamy; public dishonor
  afamado *aj* famous; famed
  difamador *aj* defaming
  famoso *aj* [-oso 1093] famous
  infame *aj* infamous
farmacia pharmacy
  farmacéutico,-a *nmf* pharmacist
  farmacólogo,-a *nmf* pharmacologist
  fármaco *nm* [4283] drug sold in pharmacies
  farmacia *nf* [-icia 4934] pharmacy
  farmacología *nf* pharmacology
  farmacéutico *aj* pharmaceutical
  farmacológico *aj* pharmacological
faro lighthouse
  aerofaro *nm* airport beacon
  faro *nm* lighthouse
  farol *nm* streetlamp
  farola *nf* large lighthouse
farsa farce
  farsante *nmf* hypocrite; teller of farce
  farsa *nf* farce
  farsante *aj* relating to tellers of farce or hypocrites; hypocritical
fascismo fascism
  antifascista *nmf* antifascist

fascista *nmf* fascist
  antifascismo *nm* antifascism
  fascismo *nm* fascism
  fascista *aj* fascist
fase phase
  desfasar *v* to go out of phase
  desfasarse *vr* to become out of phase
  desfase *nm* maladjustment (usually timing of a mechanical device)
  fase *nf* [1372] phase
  desfasado *aj* out of phase
fastuoso pompous
  fastuosidad *nf* pomposity
  fastuoso *aj* pompous
fatal fatal
  fatalista *nmf* [-ista] fatalist
  fatalismo *nm* fatalism
  fatalidad *nf* [-idad] fatality
  fatalmente *av* fatally
  fatal *aj* [3722] fatal
  fatalista *aj* [-ista] fatalist
fatiga fatigue
  fatigar *vt* to fatigue; to tire
  fatigarse *vr* to become fatigued; to become tired
  fatiga *nf* fatigue
  fatigosamente *av* tiredly
  fatigado *aj* fatigued, tired
  fatigoso *aj* fatiguing
  infatigable *aj* indefatigable, untiring
favor favor
  desfavorecer *vt* to disfavor
  favorecer *vt* [1620] to favor
  favorito,-a *nmf* favorite
  favor *nm* [704] favor
  favoritismo *nm* favoritism
  desfavorable *aj* unfavorable
  favorable *aj* [-able 2036] favorable
  favorecedor *aj* favoring
  favorecido *aj* favored
  favorito *aj* [-ito(2) 1194] favorite
faz face
  antifaz *nf* mask
  faz *nf* face
fe faith
  desconfiar *vi* to lack faith
  fiar *vt* to guarantee; to loan
  fiarse *vr* to have faith in; to trust, to put one's trust in
  fieles *nmpl* the faithful
  desconfiado,-a *nmf* untrustworthy person

fiador,-a *nmf* person who lends money; the guarantor of a loan

infiel *nmf* unfaithful person

fideicomiso *nm* a trust

desconfianza *nf* [-anza 4695] lack of confidence or faith

fe *nf* [1546] faith

fiabilidad *nf* trustworthiness

fianza *nf* [-anza 3842] bail

fidelidad *nf* fidelity

infidelidad *nf* infidelity

infielmente *av* faithlessly

desconfiado *aj* lacking in trust or confidence in someone

fiable *aj* trustworthy

al fiado *av* on credit

fidedigno *aj* trustworthy

fiel *aj* [2382] faithful

infiel *aj* unfaithful

fecha date

fechar *vt* to stamp the date

fechador *nm* date stamp

fecha *nf* [-a 319] date

fecundo fertile

fecundar *vt* to make fertile

fecundizar *vt* to fertilize

fecundación *nf* fecundation

fecundidad *nf* [-idad] fertility

infecundidad *nf* infertility

fecundo *aj* [-undo] fertile

infecundo *aj* [-undo] infertile

feliz happy

felicitar *vt* [2381] to congratulate

felicitarse *vr* to congratulate each other

infeliz *nmf* unhappy person

felicidad *nf* [-idad 1895] happiness

felicitación *nf* [-ción 1838] act of congratulations

infelicidad *nf* unhappiness

feliz *aj* [1068] happy

infeliz *aj* unhappy

femenino feminine

afeminar *vt* to make effeminate

afeminarse *vr* to become effeminate

feminista *nmf* feminist

afeminado *nm* effeminate man; homosexual

afeminamiento *nm* effeminacy

feminismo *nm* feminism

afeminación *nf* effeminacy

femineidad *nf* femininity

feminidad *nf* femininity

afeminado *aj* effeminate

femenino *aj* [2093] feminine

feminista *aj* feminist

fenómeno phenomenon

fenómeno *nm* [1622] phenomenon

fenomenal *aj* phenomenal

feria fair

ferial *nm* place where a fair is held

feria *nf* [1568] fair

ferial *aj* relating to fairs

fermento fermented substance

fermentar *vti* to ferment

fermento *nm* fermented substance

fermentación *nf* fermentation

feroz ferocious

ferocidad *nf* [-idad] ferocity

fiera *nf* savage animal

fiereza *nf* fierceness; cruelty

ferozmente *av* ferociously

feroz *aj* [-az] ferocious

fiero *aj* fierce

ferrocarril train

ferroviario,-a *nmf* train worker

ferrocarril *nm* [2930] train

teleférico *nm* aerial tramway

ferrería *nf* ironworks

ferretería *nf* [-ería(1)] hardware store

férreo *aj* [-eo(2)] of iron; strong; tenacious

ferroviario *aj* relating to trains

fertilidad fertility

fertilizar *vt* [-izar] to fertilize

fertilizante *nm* fertilizer

fertilidad *nf* fertility

fertilización *nf* fertilization

fértil *aj* fertile

fertilizante *aj* fertilizing

fervoroso full of fervor

enfervorizar *vt* to fill with fervor or enthusiasm

fervor *nm* fervor

férvido *aj* ardent; fervent

ferviente *aj* fervent

fervoroso *aj* full of fervor

ficción fiction

ficción *nf* [4416] fiction

ficticio *aj* fictitious

fiebre fever

fiebre *nf* [3394] fever

febril *aj* [-il] relating to fever

fiesta party

festejar *vt* [924] to celebrate

festejos *nmpl* public festivals

aguafiestas *nmf* someone who takes the fun out of a party, party pooper, wet blanket

festejo *nm* [-o(1) 1415] celebration

festín *nm* party or banquet

festival *nm* [-al(1) 1263]   festival
festividad *nf* festivity
fiesta *nf* [473]   party
festivo *aj* holiday; festival

figura figure
configurar *vt* to configure
configurarse *vr* to give shape
desfigurar *vt* to disfigure
figurar *vi* [2822]   to figure in something; to figure as a part of a situation
figurarse *vr* to figure
figurante,-a *nmf* extra that appears in a movie or theatrical production
figurín *nm* figurine
configuración *nf* configuration
figura *nf* [-a 1005]   figure
figuración *nf* mental image
desfigurado *aj* disfigured
figurado *aj* figurative
figurativo *aj* figurative

fijar to fix in a certain place
fijar *vt* [885]   to fix in a certain place
fijarse *vr* to pay attention
prefijar *vt* to establish ahead of time
fijador *nm* hairspray
prefijo *nm* prefix
sufijo *nm* suffix
fijación *nf* holding in place; hold (of hairspray); fixing; fixation; act of paying attention
fijeza *nf* firmness of ideas
fijamente *av* attentively
afijo *aj* affix
fijo *aj* fixed; in a fixed place; immovable

fila line
desfilar *vi* to parade
enfilar *vt* to line up
desfiladero *nm* parade ground; gully
desfile *nm* [2821]   parade
fila *nf* [1605]   line

filiación proof of identification
afiliarse *vr* to become affiliated with
filiarse *vr* to join; to enlist in the army
filiación *nf* proof of identification
filial *nf* [3376]   branch office of an organization
filial *aj* [3376]   filial

filosofía philosophy
filosofar *vi* to philosophize
filósofo,-a *nmf* philosopher
filosofía *nf* [-ería(2) 3917]   philosophy
filosófico *aj* philosophic

fin end
confinar *vt* to confine

confinarse *vr* to confine oneself; to isolate oneself
finalizar *vt* [-izar 1219]   to finalize
finar(se) *vi(r)* [1752]   to die
finalista *nmf* [-ista 4666]   finalist
semifinalista *nmf* semifinalist
confín *nm* boundary; limit, referring to places (cities, counties, nations, etc.)
confinamiento *nm* [-miento]   confinement
fin *nm* [236]   end
final *nm* [-al(2) 203]   ending
infinitivo *nm* infinitive, grammatical term
infinito *nm* [-ito(2)]   infinite
sinfín *nm* something endless; countless number
finalidad *nf* [-idad 1420]   finality
infinidad *nf* [-idad 4142]   infinity
finalmente *av* [-mente 734]   finally
infinitamente *av* infinitely
infinito *av* [-ito(2)]   infinite
finado *aj* dead
final *aj* [-al(2) 203]   final
finalista *aj* [-ista 4666]   finalist
finito *aj* [-ito(2)]   finite
infinitesimal *aj* infinitesimal
infinitivo *aj* infinitive
infinito *aj* [-ito(2)]   infinite
semifinal *aj* [1528]   semifinal

fingir to fake
fingir *vt* to fake
fingirse *vr* to pretend to be something or someone
fintar *vt* to feign
fingimiento *nm* act of faking
finta *nf* fake movement
fingido *aj* faked

firmar to sign
firmar *vt* [928]   to sign
firmante *nmf* signatory, person who signs a document
antefirma *nf* complimentary closing of a letter
firma *nf* [-a 1076]   signature

firme firm
confirmar *vt* [873]   to confirm
confirmación *nf* confirmation
firmeza *nf* firmness
firme *av* [1957]   firm
firmemente *av* firmly
confirmatorio *aj* confirming
firme *aj* [1957]   firm

fiscal fiscal
confiscar *vt* to confiscate
fiscalizar *vt* to rigorously enforce the law

fiscal *nmf* [682] attorney general; district attorney; legal representative of the government

fisco *nm* tax money stored in the treasury

confiscación *nf* confiscation

fiscalía *nf* [-ería(2) 3201] office of the attorney general

fiscalización *nf* [-ción 4667] enforcement of a law

fiscal *aj* [682] fiscal

físico physical

físico,-a *nmf* physicist

fisiólogo,-a *nmf* physiologist

fisioterapeuta *nmf* physiotherapist

geofísico,-a *nmf* geophysicist

físico *nm* [664] physique

astrofísica *nf* astrophysics

biofísica *nf* biophysics

física *nf* physics

fisiología *nf* physiology

fisioterapia *nf* physiotherapy

geofísica *nf* geophysics

físicamente *av* [-mente 4303] physically

físico *aj* [664] physical

fisiológico *aj* physiologic

geofísico *aj* geophysical

flaco thin, skinny

enflaquecer *vt* to make thinner; to discourage

enflaquecerse *vr* to become thinner; to become discouraged

flaquear *vi* to weaken

enflaquecimiento *nm* weight loss (that makes one thinner); thinning down; discouragement

flaco *nm* [4522] skinny person

flacura *nf* [-ura(1)] thinness

flaqueza *nf* [-eza] thinness

enflaquecido *aj* discouraged

flaco *aj* [4522] thin, skinny

flacucho *aj* [-ucho] comically thin

flecha arrow

flechar *vt* to put an arrow in the bow; to shoot an arrow; (figurative) to fall in love suddenly; to be hit with cupid's arrow

flechazo *nm* a hit with an arrow

flecha *nf* [-a 4740] arrow

flor flower

desflorar *vt* to deflower

florear *vt* to flower

florecer *vi* to bloom; to flourish

florista *nmf* [-ista] florist

florecimiento *nm* flourishing

floreo *nm* a compliment

florero *nm* [-ero(1)] vase

desfloración *nf* deflowering

flor *nf* [1554] flower

flora *nf* flora

floración *nf* flowering

florería *nf* flower shop

floresta *nf* grove

floricultura *nf* floriculture

floristería *nf* [-ería(1)] flower shop

floral *aj* floral

floreado *aj* flowered

floreciente *aj* flourishing

florido *aj* [-ido(1) 2257] flowered; filled with flowers

flotar to float

flotar *vi* to float

reflotar *v* to refloat

flotador *nm* float

flote *nm* floating

flota *nf* fleet

flotación *nf* floating

flotante *aj* floating

fluir *to flow*

afluir *vt* to flow into

confluir *vi* to flow or to run together

fluir *vi* [4628] to flow

fluido *nm* fluid

flujo *nm* [2771] flow

reflujo *nm* ebbing; ebb tide

afluencia *nf* [-encia] crowd

confluencia *nf* [-encia 4845] confluence

fluidez *nf* fluidity; fluency (language)

superfluidad *nf* superfluity

afluente *aj* crowding

confluente *aj* coming together

fluido *aj* fluid; fluent (speaking of language)

fluvial *aj* referring to geologic processes involving rivers

foco lightbulb

desenfocar *vi* to go out of focus

enfocar *vt* [2611] to focus

desenfoque *nm* loss of focus

enfoque *nm* [4414] focus

foco *nm* [3349] lightbulb

desenfocado *aj* unfocused; out of focus

focal *aj* focal

fondo bottom; depth

desfondar *vt* to remove the bottom

desfondarse *vr* to have the bottom removed

fondear *vt* to sound, in a nautical sense

desfonde *nm* removal of the bottom

fondeadero *nm* anchorage

fondo *nm* [455] bottom; depth

forjar to forge

forjar *vt* to forge

forjarse *vr* to be forged
forja *nf* forging; forge
forjado *aj* forged

forma form
deformar *vt* to deform
deformarse *vr* to become deformed
formar *vt* [481] to form
formarse *vr* to be formed
reformar *vt* [4025] to reform
reformarse *vr* [4025] to become reformed; to reform oneself
transformar *vt* [2419] to transform
transformarse *vr* [2419] to become transformed
reformista *nmf* reformer
transformista *nmf* quick-change artist
reformatorio *nm* [-orio(1)] reformatory; reform school
reformismo *nm* reformism
transformador *nm* transformer
deformación *nf* deformation
deformidad *nf* deformity
forma *nf* [-a 139] form
formación *nf* [-ción 1653] formation
malformación *nf* malformation
plataforma *nf* [3656] platform
reforma *nf* [-a 588] reform
reformación *nf* reformation
transformación *nf* [-ción 2698] transformation
deforme *aj* deformed
formativo *aj* formative
indeformable *aj* cannot be deformed
reformador *aj* reforming
reformista *aj* reformist
transformable *aj* transformable
transformador *aj* transformative

formal formal
formalizar *vt* to formalize
formalizarse *vr* to become formalize
formalista *nmf* [-ista] formalist
formalismo *nm* formalism
formalidad *nf* formality
informalidad *nf* informality
informalmente *av* informally
formal *aj* [2139] formal
formalista *aj* [-ista] formalist
informal *aj* [3798] informal

fórmula formula
formular *vt* [3797] to formulate
formulario *nm* a blank form to complete a transaction; book of formulas
formulismo *nm* formulism; paperwork
formulación *nf* formulation

fórmula *nf* [-a 1738] formula
formulario *aj* relating to formulas

fortaleza strength
fortalecer *vt* [1581] to strengthen
fortalecerse *vr* [1581] to become strengthened
fortificar *vt* [-ificar] to fortify
fortalecimiento *nm* [-miento 3783] strengthening
fortín *nm* small fort; outpost
fortaleza *nf* [3135] strength
fortificación *nf* fortification
fortalecedor *aj* fortifying, strengthening
fortificante *aj* fortifying
fortísimo *aj* very strong

fortuna fortune
infortunio *nm* misfortune
fortuna *nf* [2660] fortune
afortunado *aj* [-ado(1) 4279] fortunate
desafortunado *aj* unfortunate
fortuito *aj* fortuitous
infortunado *aj* unfortunate

fotografía photography
fotocopiar *vt* to photocopy
fotografiar *vt* to photograph
fotógrafo,-a *nmf* [3997] photographer
foto *nm* [514] photograph
fotómetro *nm* light meter
fotomontaje *nm* photo montage
fotocopia *nf* photocopy
fotocopiadora *nf* photocopier
fotografía *nf* [-ería(2) 1473] photography
fotosíntesis *nf* photosynthesis
fotoeléctrico *aj* photoelectric
fotogénico *aj* photogenic
fotográfico *aj* [-ico(2) 4398] photographic

fracaso failure
fracasar *vi* [3043] to fail
fracasado,-a *nmf* failure (person)
fracaso *nm* [-o(1) 2045] failure
fracasado *aj* failed

frágil fragile
fragilidad *nf* [-idad] fragility
frágil *aj* [4960] fragile

fragmento fragment
fragmentar *vt* to fragment, to break into fragments
fragmentarse *vr* to become fragmented
fragmento *nm* fragment
fragmentación *nf* fragmentation
fragmentario *aj* fragmentary

frase sentence
parafrasear *vt* to paraphrase
frase *nf* [2375] sentence

fraseología *nf* phraseology

paráfrasis *nf* paraphrase

fraternidad fraternity

confraternar *vt* to create bonds of brotherhood

confraternizar *vt* to create bonds of brotherhood

fraternizar *vi* to fraternize

fratricidio *nm* murder of a brother

confraternidad *nf* brotherhood; meeting of friends

fraternidad *nf* [-idad] fraternity

fraternización *nf* fraternization

fratricida *nf* fratricide

fraternal *aj* fraternal

fraterno *aj* fraternal

fratricida *aj* fratricidal

frecuencia frequency

frecuentar *vt* to frequent

frecuencia *nf* [-encia 1500] frequency

frecuentemente *av* [-mente 3631] frequently

frecuentado *aj* frequented

frecuente *aj* [2044] frequent

frente forehead

afrentar *vt* to face

afrentarse *vr* to come face to face with

afrontar *vt* [3492] to face

confrontarse *vr* to confront each other; to come face to face with

enfrentar *vt* [317] to face

enfrentarse *vr* to come face to face with

afrontamiento *nm* confrontation

enfrentamiento *nm* [-miento 1871] confrontation

frente *nm* [282] front of a war

afrenta *nf* affront

confrontación *nf* [-ción 2914] confrontation

frente *nf* [282] forehead

enfrente *av* [3189] facing; in front

fresco fresh

refrescar *vt* to refresh

refrescarse *vr* to become refreshed

fresco *nm* [2001] coolness

frescor *nm* coolness

refresco *nm* [3410] soda, soft drink

fresca *nf* cool drink

frescura *nf* freshness

fresco *aj* [2001] fresh

refrescante *aj* refreshing

frío cold

enfriar *vt* to make cold

enfriarse *vr* to become cold

resfriar *vt* to cool or chill

resfriarse *vr* to catch cold

enfriamiento *nm* cooling

escalofrío *nm* goose bump; shudder

frigorífico *nm* large refrigerator; cold-storage room

frío *nm* [1136] cold

refrigerador *nm* [-dor(2) 4592] refrigerator

resfriado *nm* a cold or chill

resfrío *nm* a cold or chill

frialdad *nf* coldness

frigidez *nf* [-ez] frigidity

refrigeración *nf* refrigeration; air conditioning

enfriador *aj* cooling

escalofriante *aj* producing goose bumps; scary

frígido *aj* [-ido(1)] frigid

frío *aj* [1136] cold

friolento *aj* [-lento] cold-natured

resfriado *aj* chilled; with a cold

frivolidad frivolity

frivolidad *nf* frivolity

frívolo *aj* frivolous

frondoso with foliage

fronda *nf* palm

frondosidad *nf* great amount of foliage

frondoso *aj* with foliage

frontera border

frontera *nf* [1234] border

fronterizo *aj* [erizo 2245] border

fruto fruit

fructificar *vt* to yield or bear fruit

frutero,-a *nmf* fruit seller

frutal *nm* [-al(3)] fruit-bearing plant

frutero *nm* [-ero(1)] fruit bowl or basket

fruto *nm* [2210] fruit; fruits (e.g., of labor)

fruta *nf* [1540] fruit

frutería *nf* [-ería(1)] fruit shop

infructuosamente *av* fruitlessly

fructífero *aj* [-ífero] fruitful

frutal *aj* [-al(3)] fruit-bearing

frutero *aj* [-ero(1)] for the purpose of carrying or storing fruit

infructuoso *aj* unfruitful

fructuoso *aj* fruitful

fuego fire

fogonero,-a *nmf* person who stokes the fire on a train

cortafuego *nm* firebreak; fuel break

fogón *nm* fire for cooking; stove

fogonazo *nm* sudden burst of flame

fuego *nm* [1020] fire

fogata *nf* campfire

fogosidad *nf* passion

fogoso *aj* ardent and passionate

fuera outside

forastero,-a *nmf* outsider; stranger

afueras *nfpl* [2421] outlying areas
afuera *av* [2388] outside
fuera *av* outside
foráneo *aj* [4036] referring to outsiders or non-locals
forastero *aj* alien; foreign

fuerza strength
esforzar *vr* [4442] to force; to make an effort
esforzarse *vr* to force oneself
forzar *vt* [2635] to force
reforzar *vt* [1932] to reinforce
refuerzos *nmpl* reinforcements
esfuerzo *nm* [-o(1) 696] force; effort
fuerte *nm* [436] fort
refuerzo *nm* [3985] reinforcement
fuerza *nf* [-a 352] strength
fuerte *av* [436] strong
esforzado *aj* forced; with effort
forzado *aj* forced, obliged
forzoso *aj* forced, obligatory
forzudo *aj* very strong; muscular
fuerte *aj* [436] strong
reforzado *aj* reinforced

fuga flight
fugarse *vr* to flee
fugitivo,-a *nmf* fugitive
fuga *nf* [-a 1766] flight
fugaz *aj* fleeting; estrella fugaz: shooting star
fugitivo *aj* fugitive

fulgor shining, brightness
fulgurar *vi* to shine exceptionally bright
refulgir *vi* to glitter or shine
fulgor *nm* shining, brightness
refulgencia *nf* radiance
fulgurante *aj* brightly shining
refulgente *aj* radiant

funcionar to function
funcionar *vi* [1040] to function
funcionario,-a *nmf* [283] person who has a position with the government
funcionamiento *nm* [-miento 1835] functioning
función *nf* [674] function
funcional *aj* [4789] functional

fundar to found
fundamentar *vt* to place the foundation
fundar *vt* [2515] to found
fundarse *vr* [2515] to be founded
fundador,-a *nmf* [2231] founder
fundamento *nm* [-o(1) 4176] fundamental
infundio *nm* unfounded rumor
fundación *nf* [-ción 1654] foundation
fundado *aj* founded

fundamental *aj* [1496] fundamental
infundado *aj* unfounded

fundir to found metals; to smelt metals
fundir *vt* to found metals; to smelt metals
fundirse *vr* to be founded or smelted; to meld (ideas, beliefs)
refundir *vt* to refound or remelt metals
fundido *nm* founding or smelting of metals
fundidor *nm* founder or smelter of metals
fundición *nf* founding or smelting of metals
refundición *nf* refounding of metals

fúnebre funeral
funeral *nm* funeral
funeraria *nf* funeral home
fúnebre *aj* funeral
funeral *aj* funeral
funerario *aj* funeral

furia fury
enfurecimiento *nm* act of becoming furious; fury
furor *nm* furor
furia *nf* fury
furibundo *aj* [-undo] furious; angry
furioso *aj* furious

fusil rifle
fusilar *vt* to kill with a rifle
fusil *nm* rifle
fusilamiento *nm* execution by firing squad
fusilero *nm* infantry soldier who is armed with a rifle
subfusil *nm* submachine gun
fusilería *nf* group of soldiers armed with rifles

futuro future
futurista *nmf* futurist
futurismo *nm* futurism
futuro *nm* [-ura(2) 658] future
futura *nf* future wife, fiancée
futurista *aj* futuristic
futuro *aj* [-ura(2) 658] future

G

gabán cape with sleeves and sometimes a hood
gabán *nm* cape with sleeves and sometimes a hood
gabardina *nf* gabardine; a long coat or smock

galán gallant
engalanar *vt* to adorn for a celebration
engalanarse *vr* to adorn oneself for a celebration

galantear *vt* to perform gallant acts of courting; to treat someone extra-special
galán *nm* [3749] gallant man
galanteo *nm* compliment paid in the act of courting
gala *nf* [2696] gala; celebration
galantería *nf* [-ería(2)] gallantry
galanura *nf* elegance in language or style
gallardía *nf* elegance in language or style
galantemente *av* gallantly; in a gallant manner
engalanado *aj* adorned for a celebration
galán *aj* [3749] gallant
galante *aj* gallant; desiring to be treated in a gallant manner
galanteador *aj* performing gallant acts of courting; treating someone extra-special
gallardo *aj* gallant; excellent

gallina hen
gallinero *nm* hen house, chicken coop
gallo *nm* [4430] rooster
gallina *nf* [-ina] hen

gana desire
desganar *vt* to discourage
desganarse *vr* to become uninspired
desgana *nf* lack of desire
gana *nf* desire
desganado *aj* uninspired; without desire

ganado cattle
ganadero,-a *nmf* [2604] cattle rancher
ganado *nm* [1189] cattle
ganadería *nf* [-ería(2) 2481] cattle ranching
ganadero *aj* pertaining to cattle ranching

ganar to win
ganar *vt* [187] to win
ganarse *vr* to earn
ganador *nmf* winner
ganancia *nf* [-ancia 2041] profit, earnings
ganador *aj* winning
ganancioso *aj* profitable

garantía guarantee
garantizar *vt* [-izar 1313] to guarantee
garante *nmf* guarantor
garantía *nf* [1809] guarantee
garante *aj* guaranteeing
garantizado *aj* guaranteed

garganta throat
gargarizar *vt* to gargle
gargajo *nm* phlegm
gargarismo *nm* gargling
garguero *nm* first part of the tracheal tube
gárgaras *nfpl* gargling
garganta *nf* [4443] throat
gargantilla *nf* [-illa] necklace the size of the neck

gas gas
gas *nm* [1445] gas
gasoducto *nm* gas pipe
gasómetro *nm* gas meter
gaseosa *nf* carbonated drink
gasolina *nf* [3046] gasoline
gasolinera *nf* [-era] gasoline station
gaseoso *aj* gaseous

gastar to spend
desgastar *vt* to wear out
desgastarse *vr* to become worn out
gastar *vt* [2054] to spend
gastarse *vr* [2054] to become worn out or used up
malgastar *vt* to spend poorly; to waste
gastador,-a *nmf* spender
malgastador,-a *nmf* spendthrift
desgaste *nm* wearing out
gasto *nm* [-o(1) 780] expense
gastado *aj* spent
gastador *aj* wasteful of money

gato cat
gatear *vi* to crawl
gato *nm* [2523] cat; jack
gata *nf* female cat
a gatas *av* on all fours

gemir to howl, to moan, or to groan
gemir *vi* to howl, to moan, to groan
gemido *nm* howling, moaning, groaning

general¹ general
generalizar *vt* [-izar 3102] to generalize
generalizarse *vr* to become generalized
generalidad *nf* generality
generalización *nf* generalization
generalmente *av* [-mente 2242] generally
general *aj* [146] general
generalizado *aj* generalized

general² general in the army, etc.
general *nm* [146] general in the army, etc.
generalato *nm* [-ato] generals, committee of generals, high command
generalísimo *nm* supreme general

género genre; gender; class; genus
degenerar *vi* to degenerate
homogeneizar *vt* to homogenize
degenerado,-a *nmf* one who suffers from degeneration
genealogista *nmf* genealogist
gene *nm* [4477] gene
género *nm* [1504] genre; gender; class; genus
genocidio *nm* genocide
genotipo *nm* genotype
subgénero *nm* sub-genus

degeneración *nf* degeneration
genealogía *nf* genealogy
generación *nf* [-ción 1190] generation
genética *nf* genetics
heterogeneidad *nf* heterogeneity
homogeneidad *nf* homogeneity
degenerado *aj* degenerated
degenerativo *aj* degenerative
genealógico *aj* genealogical
generacional *aj* generational
genérico *aj* generic
genético *aj* [-ico(2) 3455] genetic
heterogéneo *aj* heterogeneous
homogéneo *aj* homogeneous
unigénito *aj* only-begotten
generoso generous
generosidad *nf* generosity
generoso *aj* [4983] generous
genio genius
ingeniar *v* to use one's creative ability
ingeniarse *vr* to figure out a way to do
   something
ingeniero,-a *nmf* [1889] engineer
genio *nm* genius
ingenio *nm* [3809] creative ability
genialidad *nf* ingenuity; talent
ingeniería *nf* [-ería(2) 3966] engineering
genial *aj* ingenious
ingenioso *aj* clever
geográfico geographical
geofísico,-a *nmf* geophysicist
geógrafo,-a *nmf* geographer
geólogo,-a *nmf* geologist
geofísica *nf* geophysics
geografía *nf* [-ería(2) 4629] geography
geología *nf* geology
geometría *nf* geometry
geopolítica *nf* geopolitics
geométrico *aj* geometric, geometrical
geocéntrico *aj* geocentric
geofísico *aj* geophysical
geográfico *aj* [-ico(2) 4459] geographic,
   geographical
geológico *aj* geologic, geological
geomagnético *aj* geomagnetic
gestación gestation
gestar *v* to gestate
gestarse *vr* to be under development
gestación *nf* gestation
gestión administration, management
gestionar *vt* [3808] to manage a business or
   project
gestor,-a *nmf* administrator, manager

gestión *nf* [1490] administration, management
gestor *aj* administrating, managing
gigante giant
agigantar *vt* to enlarge greatly
agigantarse *vr* to become giant
gigante *nm* [1930] giant
gigantismo *nm* gigantism, overdevelopment of
   the size of the body
agigantado *aj* excessively enlarged
gigante *aj* [1930] giant
gigantesco *aj* [-esco 4874] gigantic
girar to gyrate
girar *vi* [2756] to gyrate
sobregirar *vt* to over-extend one's credit
girasol *nm* sunflower
giro *nm* [-o(1) 2557] gyration; complete turn; 360-
   degree turn; money-order sent by post
giratorio *aj* [-orio(2)] able to gyrate or revolve
gitano gypsy
gitano,-a *nmf* gypsy
gitanada *nf* an act or saying said or done by
   gypsies
gitanería *nf* [-ería(2)] band of gypsies
gitano *aj* gypsy
globo balloon; globe
globo *nm* [3695] balloon; globe
globalmente *av* globally
global *aj* [2049] global
gloria glory
gloriarse *vr* to glorify
glorificar *vt* [-ificar] to glorify
gloria *nf* [-a 3542] glory
glorificación *nf* glorification
glorioso *aj* glorious
glosar to make a glossary
glosar *vt* to make a glossary
glosario *nm* [-ario(1)] glossary
glosa *nf* an entry in a glossary; note on a text
gobierno government
desgobernar *vt* to misgovern
gobernar *vt* [2002] to govern
gobernarse *vr* to govern oneself
gobernador,-a *nmf* [540] governor
gobernante *nmf* [-ante(2) 2473] governor; ruler;
   leader in the government
autogobierno *nm* self-government
gobierno *nm* [-o(1) 82] government
gobernación *nf* [-ción 1825] governance
gobernable *aj* governable
gobernante *aj* [-ante(2) 2473] governing
gubernamental *aj* [1576] governmental
ingobernable *aj* ungovernable
intergubernamental *aj* intergovernmental

golpe a hit, a blow
golpear *vt* [1485] to hit
golpetear *vt* to tap repeatedly; to repeatedly hit but without force
golpista *nmf* participant in the violent overthrow of the government, person who participates in a junta
golpe *nm* [1088] a hit, a blow
golpeteo *nm* hitting; repeated punching
golpismo *nm* violent overthrow of the government, junta
golpazo *nf* [-azo(2)] strong or violent hit
golpiza *nf* violent beating
golpista *aj* relating to violent overthrow of the government, relating to the formation of a junta

gordo fat
engordar *vt* to make something fat
gordo,-a *nmf* fat person
engorde *nm* fattening of animals
gordo *nm* [2814] fat of meat
engorda *nf* fattening of animals
gordura *nf* [-ura(1)] excess of fat; fatness
gordo *aj* [2814] fat; thick

gota drop of liquid
gotear *vt* to sprinkle, to rain lightly
goteo *nm* dripping
gotero *nm* dropper
goterón *nm* [-ón(3)] large drop of rain
gota *nf* [3378] drop of liquid
gotera *nf* leak (usually in roof of house)

gozar to enjoy
gozar *vt* [1969] to enjoy
gozarse *vr* [1969] to enjoy oneself
regocijar *vt* to rejoice (in general)
regocijarse *vr* to rejoice, to be rejoicing; to become full of joy
goce *nm* joy, less commonly used than "gozo"
gozo *nm* [-o(1)] joy, more commonly used than "goce"
regocijo *nm* rejoicing
gozada *nf* great joy
gozoso *aj* [-oso] joyful

gracia grace
agraciar *vt* to favor; to favor with a gift; to grace
agradar *vi* [2847] to please
agradecer *vi* [1996] to thank; to give thanks
desagradar *vt* to displease
desagradecer *vi* to show a lack of gratitude
desgraciar *vt* to disgrace
desgraciarse *vr* to become disgraced
gratificar *vt* to reward

desagradecido,-a *nmf* an ungrateful person
desgraciado,-a *nmf* a disgraced person; wretch
gratuitamente *av* freely
ingrato,-a *nmf* an ungrateful person
agradecimiento *nm* [-miento 4185] thankfulness
agrado *nm* pleasure
desagradecimiento *nm* ungratefulness, ingratitude
desagrado *nm* [-ado(2)] displeasure
gracias *nfpl* [744] thank-you; thanks
desgracia *nf* [-a 3393] disgrace; misery
gracia *nf* [3467] grace
gratificación *nf* reward; tip; bonus to a salary
gratitud *nf* gratitude
ingratitud *nf* ingratitude
desgraciadamente *av* [-mente 3372] unfortunately
ingratamente *av* ungratefully
agraciado *aj* graced; shown favor
agradable *aj* [-able 2047] pleasing; pleasant
agradecido *aj* [-ido(1) 4645] thankful
desagradable *aj* disagreeable; unpleasant; bothersome
desagradecido *aj* [-ido(2)] unthankful
desgraciado *aj* disgraced; miserable
gracioso *aj* funny
gratificador *aj* rewarding
gratificante *aj* rewarding; satisfying
gratuito *aj* [-ito(2) 2140] free
ingrato *aj* ungrateful

grado grade
degradar *vt* to degrade
degradarse *vr* to become degraded
graduar *vt* to graduate (someone); to test (e.g., eyes)
graduarse *vr* to graduate (e.g., from a grade or school)
postgraduado,-a *nmf* post-graduate student
grado *nm* [898] grade
graduado *nm* graduate
degradación *nf* degradation
grada *nf* level; step; inclined plane
graduación *nf* [4630] graduation
degradante *aj* degrading
graduable *aj* able to graduate
graduado *aj* graduate
gradual *aj* gradual
postgraduado *aj* post-graduate

grande big
agrandar *vt* to enlarge; to make something big
agrandarse *vr* to become enlarged
engrandecer *vt* to praise someone; to augment
grande *nmf* [64] adult; aged person
grandote *nmf* [-ote] big person

engrandecimiento *nm* enlargement
grandeza *nf* [-eza] greatness
grandilocuencia *nf* grandiloquence
grandiosidad *nf* magnificence
gran *aj* [116] great
grande *aj* [64] big
grandilocuente *aj* grandiloquent
grandioso *aj* magnificent, awe-inspiring

grano grain
desgranar *vt* to thresh
desgranarse *vr* to become threshed
granar *vt* to seed
granular *vt* to granulate
granero *nm* barn
granjero *nm* [-ero(3)] farmer
grano *nm* [2553] grain
gránulo *nm* [-culo] granule
desgranadora *nf* threshing machine
grana *nf* threshing
granja *nf* farm
granulación *nf* granulation
granulado *aj* granulated
granuloso *aj* grainy

grasa fat; grease
desengrasar *vt* to remove the fat from
engrasar *vt* to grease
engrase *nm* lubrication; greasing
grasa *nf* [1544] fat; grease
grasiento *aj* [-iento] very greasy
graso *aj* greasy; oily, referring to skin
grasoso *aj* greasy, oily

grave grave, serious
desgravar *vt* to lower a tax
gravar *vt* to charge a tax
gravitar *vi* to gravitate
gravamen *nm* obligation; tax
desgravación *nf* lowering of a tax
gravedad *nf* [2967] gravity
gravitación *nf* gravitation
ingravidez *nf* weightlessness
grave *aj* [893] grave, serious
gravitacional *aj* gravitational
gravoso *aj* heavy; costly
ingrávido *aj* weightless

gris gray
gris *nmf* [3516] gray
gris *aj* [3516] gray
grisáceo *aj* [-eo(2)] grayish

grito shout
gritar *vi* [2453] to shout
gritón,-a *nmf* one who is always shouting
gritería *nf* shouting
griterío *nm* shouting

grito *nm* [-o(1) 2482] shout
gritón *aj* [-ón(2)] always shouting

grosero rude or vulgar person
grosero,-a *nmf* rude or vulgar person
grosería *nf* [-ería(2)] rudeness; vulgarity
grosero *aj* rude; vulgar

grueso thick
engrosar *vt* to thicken
grosor *nm* thickness of liquids
grosura *nf* [-ura(1)] thickness
grueso *aj* [3632] thick

grupo group
agrupar *vt* [4297] to group
agruparse *vr* to become grouped
agrupamiento *nm* grouping process
grupo *nm* [92] group
reagrupamiento *nm* regrouping process
agrupación *nf* [-ción 1397] grouping; group
reagrupación *nf* regrouping

guante glove
guantazo *nm* [-azo(2)] hit with a glove
guante *nm* [4768] glove
guantada *nf* slap
guantera *nf* [-era] glove compartment
enguantado *aj* gloved

guapo handsome, good-looking
guapura *nf* handsomeness
guapo *aj* [3433] handsome, good-looking

guardar to keep; to save
guardar *vt* [1480] to keep; to save
guardarse *vr* to put something in its place
guarecer *vt* to protect from danger
guarecerse *vr* to protect oneself from danger
resguardar *vt* [4637] to protect or defend
something
resguardarse *vr* [4537] to protect or defend
oneself
salvaguardar *vt* to guard or protect
guarda *nmf* [-a] guard
guardabosque *nmf* forest ranger
guardacoches *nmf* parking lot attendant
guardaespaldas *nmf* bodyguard
guardafrenos *nmf* brakeman (railroad)
guardameta *nmf* [2654] goalie, goal keeper
guardarropa *nmf* person in charge of the
cloakroom
guardián,-a *nmf* guardian
guardabarros *nm* mud flap; fender
guardacostas *nm* coastguard
guardamuebles *nm* storage business
guardapelo *nm* locket to keep a lock of hair
guardapolvo *nm* dust protector
guardarropa *nm* cloakroom

resguardo *nm* security detail

guardia *nf* [2025] action of guarding; group of
  soldiers assigned to protect

retaguardia *nf* rear guard

salvaguardia *nf* safe passage

guarnición¹ garnishing, garnish

guarnecer *vt* to garnish, to adorn

guarnición *nf* garnishing, garnish

guarnición² garrison

guarnecer *vt* to garrison

guarnición *nf* garrison

guerra war

guerrear *vt* to fight a war

guerrero,-a *nmf* warrior

guerrillero,-a *nmf* guerrilla fighter

guerrilla *nf* [-illa 3341] guerrilla warfare; special
  military force or group of guerrilla fighters

aguerrido *aj* experienced in warfare; spirited

guerrero *aj* [-ero(2)] war; warlike; relating to war

guiar to guide

guiar *vt* [3447] to guide

guiarse *vr* to guide oneself

guía *nmf* [2977] guide

guía *nf* [2977] guidebook

guitarra guitar

guitarrista *nmf* [-ista 4717] guitarist

guitarreo *nm* sound of the guitar

guitarrillo *nm* 4-stringed guitar

guitarrón *nm* over-sized guitar

guitarra *nf* [2598] guitar

gusano worm

agusanarse *vr* to become filled with worms

gusanillo *nm* tiny worm

gusano *nm* worm

agusanado *aj* wormy, filled with worms

gusto pleasure

degustar *vt* to taste or to sample a food or
  drink

disgustar *vt* to displease or to upset

disgustarse *vr* to become displeased or upset

gustar *vi* [443] to please; to like (used with
  indirect object pronoun)

disgusto *nm* problem, trouble

gusto *nm* [-o(1) 1062] pleasure

regusto *nm* after-taste

degustación *nf* tasting or sampling of food or
  drink

disgustado *aj* disgusted

gustativo *aj* gustative; pertaining to the sense of
  taste

H

habilidad ability

habilitar *vt* to train; to repair; to give something
  or someone capability

inhabilitar *vt* to prevent

rehabilitar *vt* [3195] rehabilitate

rehabilitarse *vr* to become rehabilitated

habilitado,-a *nmf* person authorized to do
  something because of his ability

habilidad *nf* [-idad 2578] ability

habilitación *nf* act and effect of training a
  person or repairing a tool

inhabilidad *nf* inability

inhabilitación *nf* the act of preventing someone
  from exercising a right or privilege

rehabilitación *nf* [-ción 1775] rehabilitation

hábilmente *av* ably

hábil *aj* [4679] able

habilidoso *aj* able; capable

inhábil *aj* unable

habitación habitation

cohabitar *vi* to cohabit

deshabitar *vt* to empty a house; to remove
  belongings from where one is living

habitar *vt* [2383] to inhabit; to live in a place

habitante *nmf* [ante(2) 817] inhabitant

hábitat *nm* habitat

cohabitación *nf* cohabitation

habitación *nf* [-ción 2206] habitation; room (hotel,
  inn, etc.)

deshabitado *aj* uninhabited

habitable *aj* inhabitable; able to be lived in

inhabitable *aj* uninhabitable

inhabitado *aj* uninhabited, vacant

hábito habit

deshabituar *vt* to break a habit

deshabituarse *vr* to break one's habit

habituar *vt* to get used to

habituarse *vr* to become accustomed to

hábito *nm* [-ito(2) 2500] habit

habituación *nf* habituation; something done by
  habit

habitualmente *av* habitually

habitual *aj* [3620] habitual

hablar to speak

hablar *vti(r)* [219] to speak

hablarse *vr* to speak or to talk to each other

hablador *nmf* someone who talks too much;
  loudmouth; charlatan

hispanohablante *nmf* somebody who speaks
  Spanish

malhablado,-a *nmf* someone who curses
 frequently; blasphemer
habla *nf* the ability to speak at a particular
 moment; action of speaking
habladuría *nf* gossip, foolishness, nonsense
hablado *aj* spoken
hablador *aj* talkative
hispanohablante *aj* Spanish-speaking
malhablado *aj* blasphemous, referring to a
 person; frequently cursing

hacer to do; to make
deshacer *vt* [4413] to undo
deshacerse *vr* [4413] to become undone; to
 become dissolved
hacer *vt* [24] to do; to make
rehacer *vt* to redo
rehacerse *vr* to become redone or remade
hacedor,-a *nmf* someone who does or makes
 things
quehacer *nm* chore; something that needs done
hechura *nf* the form of the finished product
 (clothing)
hacedero *aj* possible; doable

hacienda country estate
hacendado,-a *nmf* owner of a country estate
hacienda *nf* [1112] country estate
hacendado *aj* having a country estate
hacendoso *aj* hard-working when referring to
 working at home

hallar to find
hallar *vt* [1657] to find
hallarse *vr* to find oneself in a particular state
 or situation
hallazgo *nm* [4126] find

hambre hunger
hambriento,-a *nmf* hungry man or woman
hambre *nf* [2454] hunger
hambriento *aj* [-iento] hungry

harto weary
hartar *vt* to be completely full
hartarse *vr* to completely fill oneself (with
 food, drink, situation)
harto *av* more than enough
harto *aj* weary

hebra piece of thread
desenhebrar *vt* to take out thread
enhebrar *vt* to thread
hebra *nf* piece of thread

hecho done; finished
bienhechor,-a *nmf* someone who does good
 things
malhechor,-a *nmf* someone who does bad
 things

hecho *nm* [149] fact; completed act
bienhechor *aj* referring to one who does good
deshecho *aj* undone, unmade
hecho *aj* [149] done; finished
malhechor *aj* bad, referring to one who does
 evil

herencia inheritance
desheredar *vt* to disinherit
heredar *vt* [4284] to inherit
desheredado,-a *nmf* disinherited person; person
 left without inheritance
heredero,-a *nmf* heir
heredad *nf* heredity
herencia *nf* [-encia 3770] inheritance
desheredado *aj* disinherited
heredable *aj* inheritable
heredado *aj* inherited
hereditario *aj* [-ario(2)] hereditary

herir to wound or hurt
herir *vt* [1275] to wound or hurt
herirse *vr* to hurt oneself; to become hurt
malherir *vt* to hurt badly
herido,-a *nmf* wounded person
herida *nf* [-ido(2) 1533] wound
herido *aj* [-ido(2)] wounded
hiriente *aj* wounding

hermano brother
hermanar *vt* to equalize
hermanarse *vr* to become equalized; to become
 the same as
hermanastro,-a *nmf* step-brother; step-sister
hermano,-a *nmf* [449] brother or sister
hermandad *nf* brotherhood; the brethren
hermanable *aj* brotherly

hermoso beautiful, gorgeous
hermosear *vt* to beautify
hermosura *nf* [-ura(1)] beauty
hermoso *aj* [1526] beautiful, gorgeous

héroe hero
antihéroe *nm* anti-hero
héroe *nm* [1931] hero
heroísmo *nm* heroism
heroína *nf* [-ina 4016] heroine
heroico *aj* heroic

hidalgo noble in position and character
hidalgo *nm* person noble in position and
 character
hidalgo *aj* noble in position and character;
 altruistic; of noble spirit

hielo ice
deshelar *vt* to melt
helar *vt* to freeze
helarse *vr* to become frozen

heladero,-a *nmf* person who makes or sells ice cream

deshielo *nm* slush

helado *nm* [-ado(1) 3998] ice cream

hielo *nm* [-o(1) 3517] ice

rompehielos *nm* ice pick

helada *nf* cold-spell

heladera *nf* ice cream container; freezer

heladería *nf* place where they make or sell ice cream

heladora *nf* home ice cream maker

helado *aj* [-ado(1) 3998] ice cold; freezing cold

helador *aj* freezing

hierba herb

desherbar *vt* to weed

herbívoro,-a *nmf* herb-eating animal

herbario *nm* collection of plants (by scientific category)

herbolario,-a *nmf* person who buys and sells medicinal herbs

herbicida *nf* herbicide; weed killer

herboristería *nf* medicinal herb store

hierba *nf* [3218] herb

hierbabuena *nf* mint

herbáceo *aj* herb-like

herbario *aj* relating to herbs

herbívoro *aj* [-ivoro] herbivorous

herboso *aj* herbaceous

hierro iron

aherrojar *vt* to put a ball and chain on someone

aherrumbrarse *vr* to become rusted

herrar *vt* to shoe a horse

herrador *nm* blacksmith

herraje *nm* [-aje(1)] iron made into furniture

herrero *nm* blacksmith

hierro *nm* [2384] iron

herradura *nf* spur

herramienta *nf* [3017] tool

herrería *nf* art of working iron

herrumbroso *aj* rusty

hijo son

ahijar *vt* to adopt as a godchild

hijear *vi* to sprout

prohijar *vt* to adopt a child

ahijado,-a *nmf* godson or goddaughter

hijastro,-a *nmf* step-son; step-daughter

hijo *nm* son

hijuelo *nm* [-uelo] sprout

hija *nf* daughter

hilo thread

deshilachar *vt* to remove extra threads from cloth

deshilvanar *vt* to remove temporary stitches

hilar *vt* to follow the thread of, to think, to deduce; to make thread

hilvanar *vt* to baste; to sew a stay-stitch; to sew in a temporary fashion

sobrehilar *vt* to zigzag stitch; to stitch the edge so it won't unravel

hilachos *nmpl* thread-bare clothes; rags

hilacho,-a *nmf* extra thread that is found hanging on a dress

hilado *nm* [-ado(2)] action of making thread

hilo *nm* [-o(1) 3363] thread

hilván *nm* stay-stitch; basting; sewing of fabric to prepare it for later more-permanent sewing

hila *nf* piece of thread; action of making thread

hilera *nf* line

deshilvanado *aj* with the temporary stitches removed

sobrehilado *aj* zigzagged; having the edge stitched so it won't unravel

hispanoamericano Spanish-American

hispanizar *vt* to make something Spanish; to introduce Spanish words to a language

hispanista *nmf* fan of Spanish language and culture

hispano,-a *nmf* Hispanic person

hispanoamericano,-a *nmf* Spanish-American

hispanohablante *nmf* somebody who speaks Spanish

hispanismo *nm* Spanish word used in another language

hispanoamericanismo *nm* Spanish-Americanism

hispanidad *nf* community of Spanish-speakers

Hispanoamérica *nf* Spanish America, Spanish-speaking Latin America

hispano *aj* [-ano 2488] Hispanic

hispanoamericano *aj* Spanish-American

hispanoárabe *aj* Spanish-Arab

hispanohablante *aj* Spanish-speaking

historia history

historiar *vt* to give a historical narration

historiador,-a *nmf* historian

historial *nm* personal or business history; records

historia *nf* [286] history

historieta *nf* [-eta] short story

prehistoria *nf* pre-history

histórico *aj* [-ico(2) 1212] historic

prehistórico *aj* pre-historic

hogar home

hogar *nm* [1181] home

hogareño *aj* [-eño] homey; home-loving

hoja leaf; page

deshojar *vt* to drop leaves; to defoliate

hojear *vt* to leaf through a book or magazine
hojalatero *nm* one who works with sheet metal
hoja *nf* [1841] leaf; page
hojalata *nf* sheet metal
hojalatería *nf* workshop for working with sheet metal
hojarasca *nf* pile of dried flowers fallen from a tree

holgar to do nothing
holgar *vt* to do nothing
holgazanear *vi* to be lazy; to waste time
holgazán,-ana *nmf* lazy person
holgazanería *nf* the act of wasting time; laziness
holgazán *aj* lazy

hombre man
hombrear *vi* to act "macho"; to act chauvinistic
hombre *nm* [195] man
superhombre *nm* superman
hombrada *nf* [-ada(2)] a vile "macho" act
hombría *nf* [-ería(2)] manliness

homenaje homage
homenajear *vt* [4769] to pay homage
homenaje *nm* [1888] homage

hondo deep
ahondar *vi* to go deeper; to go deeper into (water, earth, subject, situation, etc.)
hondureño *nmf* [-eño] person from Honduras
sabiondo, -a *nmf* know-it-all; person who acts as if he has deep knowledge; a presumptuous person
sabihondo,-a *nmf* know-it-all; person who acts as if he has deep knowledge; a presumptuous person
hondo *nm* [3580] deep
hondura *nf* [-ura(1)] depth
Honduras *nf* Central-American Country
hondo *aj* [3580] deep
hondureño *aj* [-eño] referring to somebody from Honduras
sabiondo, sabihondo *aj* literally, deep with knowledge; pejoratively, presumptuous

honor honor
deshonrar *vt* to dishonor
honrar *vt* [4936] to honor
honorarios *nmpl* the honorary
deshonor *nm* dishonor
honor *nm* [1039] honor
honorario *nm* [-ario(2)] honorarium
deshonestidad *nf* dishonesty
deshonra *nf* dishonor
honestidad *nf* [-idad 4718] honesty
honra *nf* honor
honradez *nf* honor (in general)

honestamente *av* honestly
deshonesto *aj* dishonest
deshonroso *aj* without honor
honesto *aj* [3902] honest
honorable *aj* honorable
honorario *aj* [-ario(2)] honorary
honrado *aj* honored
honroso *aj* respectful, honest, honorable, used to describe an act

hora hour
horario *nm* [-ario(1) 1311] schedule
deshora *nf* off-hours; time when closed or not available
hora *nf* [72] hour
ahora *av* [120] now; today

horizonte horizon
horizontalmente *av* horizontally
horizonte *nm* [4585] horizon
horizontal *aj* [-al(2)] horizontal

horror horror
horrorizar *vt* to horrify
horrorizarse *vr* to become horrified
horror *nm* horror
horrendo *aj* horrifying
horrible *aj* horrible
horripilante *aj* horrifying
horroroso *aj* horrifying

hospital hospital
hospedar *vt* to host
hospedarse *vr* to stay as a guest
hospitalizar *vt* to hospitalize
hospedaje *nm* [-aje(2)] lodging
hospicio *nm* shelter; orphanage
hospital *nm* [717] hospital
hospedería *nf* lodging, in the style of a "bed and breakfast"
hospitalidad *nf* hospitality
hospitalización *nf* hospitalization
hospitalario *aj* hospitable
inhóspito *aj* inhospitable

hostil hostile
hostigar *vt* to harass; to persecute
hostigamiento *nm* harassment; persecution
hostilidad *nf* hostility
hostil *aj* hostile

hotel hotel
hostelero,-a *nmf* manager or worker in a hostel
hotelero,-a *nmf* manager or worker in a hotel
hotel *nm* [1151] hotel
hostelería *nf* hostel
hostería *nf* inn; bed and breakfast
hotelero *aj* relating to a hotel

hueco hollow
ahuecar *vt* to make hollow
ahuecarse *vr* to become hollow
ahuecamiento *nm* hollowed-out part of
something
hueco *aj* [4566] hollow

hueso bone
deshuesar *vt* to bone; to remove the bone
hueso *nm* [2055] bone
deshuesadora *nf* a device used for pitting fruit
huesudo *aj* bony

huevo egg
aovar *vt* to make something egg-shaped
desovar *vt* to lay eggs
ovular *vi* to ovulate
huevero,-a *nmf* person who is in the business of
buying or selling eggs
huevo *nm* [2249] egg
óvalo *nm* oval
ovario *nm* ovary
óvulo *nm* ovule
huevera *nf* recipient for eggs
oval *aj* oval
ovular *aj* pertaining to oval shaped objects

huir to flee
huir *vi* [2285] to flee
rehuir *vt* to avoid; to elude
huida *nf* [-ido(2)] flight from something
huidizo *aj* fleeing

humano human
deshumanizar *vt* to dehumanize
humanizar *vt* [-izar] to humanize
humanizarse *vr* to become human
humanista *nmf* [-ista] humanist
humanismo *nm* humanism
humanitarismo *nm* humanitarianism
humano *nm* [327] human
humanidades *nfpl* humanities
deshumanización *nf* dehumanization
humanidad *nf* [-idad 2730] humanity
humanización *nf* humanization
deshumanizado *aj* dehumanized
humanístico *aj* humanistic
humanitario *aj* [4460] humanitarian
humano *aj* [327] human
infrahumano *aj* subhuman
sobrehumano *aj* super-human

húmedo humid
humedecer *vt* to moisten
humedecerse *vr* to become moist
humedad *nf* [4140] humidity
húmedo *aj* humid

humilde humble
humillar *vt* to humble
humillarse *vr* to humble oneself; to become
humble
humildad *nf* humility
humillación *nf* humiliation
humilde *aj* [3871] humble
humillante *aj* humbling

humo smoke
ahumar *vt* to smoke; to give a smoke flavor to
something
ahumarse *vr* to become smoked
humear *vi* to be smoking
sahumar *vt* to burn incense; to burn a scented
candle
ahumado *nm* smoked
humo *nm* [3364] smoke
sahumerio *nm* the act of burning incense
humareda *nf* billow of smoke; a great quantity
of smoke
ahumado *aj* smoked
humeante *aj* smoking

humor humor
humorista *nmf* humorist; comic
humor *nm* [2399] humor
humorismo *nm* humor, in a general sense
malhumor *nm* bad mood
humorístico *aj* comic; pertaining to humor or
comedy
malhumorado *aj* in a bad mood

hundir to sink
hundir *vt* [3872] to sink
hundirse *vr* to sink ("to become sunk")
hundimiento *nm* the sinking
hundible *aj* sinkable
hundido *aj* sunk

I

idea idea
idear *vt* to think of ideas
ideólogo,-a *nmf* ideologue
idea *nf* [598] idea
ideograma *nf* ideogram
ideología *nf* ideology
ideológico *aj* ideological

ideal ideal
idealizar *vt* to idealize
idealista *nmf* idealist
idealismo *nm* idealism
idealización *nf* idealization

idealmente *av* ideally
ideal *aj* [1951] ideal
idealista *aj* idealistic

idéntico identical
identificar *vti* [-ificar 1100] identify
identificarse *vr* to identify oneself; to identify with
identidad *nf* [2368] identity
identificación *nf* [-ción 3164] identification
idénticamente *av* identically
idéntico *aj* identical
identificable *aj* identifiable

idioma language
idioma *nm* [2741] language
idiomático *aj* idiomatic

ídolo idol
idolatrar *vt* idolize; to practice idolatry
idólatra *nmf* idolater
ídolo *nm* [3407] idol
idolatría *nf* idolatry
idólatra *aj* idolatrous

ignorar to be ignorant of
ignorar *vt* [2226] to be ignorant of
ignorante *nmf* [-ante(2)] ignorant person; illiterate person
ignorancia *nf* [-ancia 4819] ignorance
ignorante *aj* [-ante(2)] ignorant

igual equal
desigualar *vt* to mismatch
igualar *vt* [2022] to equal
igualarse *vr* [2022] to become equal to
igual *nm* [420] equal
desigualdad *nf* inequality
igualación *nf* equalization
igualada *nf* tie (sports)
igualdad *nf* [4225] equality
igual *av* [420] equal
igualmente *av* [2207] equally
desigual *aj* unequal
igual *aj* [420] equal
igualado *aj* equaled, matched; presumptuous
igualitario *aj* egalitarian

ilusión illusion, dream, desire
ilusionar *vt* to deceive
ilusionarse *vr* to be under the illusion
ilusionista *nmf* artist specializing in the use of illusion; magician
iluso,-a *nmf* dreamer, deceived person
ilusionismo *nm* illusionism; the use of illusion
desilusión *nf* disillusion; disappointment
ilusión *nf* [-sión 2927] illusion, dream, desire
desilusionado *aj* disillusioned; disappointed

iluso *aj* deceived
ilusorio *aj* deceiving

imagen image
imaginar *vt* [1682] to imagine
imaginarse *vr* to imagine oneself
imagen *nf* [695] image
imaginación *nf* [-ción 3669] imagination
imaginable *aj* imaginable
imaginario *aj* imaginary
imaginativo *aj* [-ivo] imaginative
inimaginable *aj* unimaginable

imitar to imitate
imitar *vt* [4418] to imitate
imitador,-a *nmf* imitator
imitación *nf* imitation
imitador *aj* imitative
inimitable *aj* inimitable

impedir to impede
impedir *vt* [929] to impede
impedido,-a *nmf* disabled person
impedimento *nm* impediment; obstacle
impedido *aj* disabled

imperio empire
imperar *vi* to act as emperor
imperialista *nmf* imperialist
emperador *nm* emperor
imperativo *nm* [-ivo] imperative
imperialismo *nm* imperialism
imperio *nm* [4128] empire
emperatriz *nf* [-triz] empress
imperativamente *av* imperatively
imperante *aj* imperative
imperativo *aj* [-ivo] imperative
imperial *aj* imperial
imperialista *aj* imperialist
imperioso *aj* imperious

ímpetu impetus
impetuosidad *nf* impetuosity
impetuoso *aj* impetuous
ímpetu *nm* impetus

implicar to implicate
implicar *vt* [1253] to implicate
implicación *nf* implication
implícitamente *av* implicitly
implícito *aj* implicit

importancia importance
importancia *nf* [-ancia 911] importance
importante *aj* [156] important

importar to import
exportar *vt* [3721] to export
importar *vti* [1188] to import
portar(se) *vt(r)* [1863] to carry

reexportar *vt* to reexport
reimportar *vt* to reimport
reportar *vt* [961] to report
transportar *vt* [2430] to transport
transportarse *vr* to be transported
exportador,-a *nmf* exporter
importador,-a *nmf* importer
portador,-a *nmf* carrier
portavoz *nmf* [1868] announcer
reportero,-a *nmf* reporter
transportista *nmf* [-ista 3480] transportation worker
portaequipajes *nm* luggage compartment
portaobjetos *nm* microscope slide
portafolios *nm* portfolio
reportaje *nm* reporting
transporte *nm* [963] transport
exportación *nf* [-ción 1614] exportation
importación *nf* [-ción 2376] importation
portaaviones *nf* aircraft carrier
exportable *aj* exportable
exportador *aj* [-dor(1) 3415] exporting
importador *aj* importing
portador *aj* carrying
portátil *aj* [-il] portable
transportador *aj* [-dor(2)] transporting

impulso impulse
impulsar *vt* [1103] to force
impulso *nm* [-o(1) 2961] impulse
impulsividad *nf* impulsivity
impulsivo *aj* impulsive

inaugurar to inaugurate
inaugurar *vt* [1892] to inaugurate
inauguración *nf* [-ción 2344] inauguration
inaugural *aj* [3165] inaugural

incidente incident
coincidir *vi* [1489] to coincide
incidir *vi* to fall into error
incidente *nm* [2062] incident
coincidencia *nf* [-encia 4091] coincidence
incidencia *nf* [-encia 3944] incidence
coincidente *aj* coinciding
incidente *aj* [2062] incidental

incitar to incite
incitar *vt* to incite
incitador,-a *nmf* one who incites or provokes
incitación *nf* incitation
incitante *aj* inciting, provoking

inclinar to lean
inclinar *vi* [3558] to lean
inclinarse *vr* [3558] to lean toward; to be inclined
inclinación *nf* inclination
inclinado *aj* leaning; inclined

incluso included, including
incluir *vt* [328] to include
inclusión *nf* [-sión 4567] inclusion
inclusivamente *av* inclusively
inclusive *av* [2672] inclusive
incluso *av* [431] including, even
incluido *aj* included
incluso *aj* [431] included

indicar to indicate
indicar *vt* [193] to indicate
indicador *nm* [-dor(2) 2682] indicator
indicativo *nm* [-ivo] indicative
índice *nm* [1248] index
indicio *nm* [-icio 4270] indication; sign
indicación *nf* [-ción 3829] indication; explanation
indicado *aj* indicated
indicativo *aj* [-ivo] indicative

indignación indignation
indignar *vt* to cause anger; to outrage
indignarse *vr* to become indignant
indignación *nf* indignation
indignidad *nf* indignity
indignado *aj* indignant
indignante *aj* outrageous; giving rise to anger
indigno *aj* unworthy

individual individual
individualizar *vt* to individualize
individualista *nmf* individualist
individualismo *nm* individualism
individuo *nm* [-uo 1431] individual
individualidad *nf* individuality
individualización *nf* individualization
individual *aj* [1851] individual
individualista *aj* individualistic

industria industry
industrializar *vt* to industrialize
industrializarse *vr* to become industrialized
industrial *nmf* [1002] owner of an industry
industria *nf* [669] industry
industrialización *nf* industrialization
industrial *aj* [1002] industrial
industrioso *aj* industrious

inexorable inexorable
exorable *aj* easily convinced
inexorable *aj* inexorable
inexorablemente *av* inexorably

infancia infancy
infante *nm* [3873] infant boy
infanticidio *nm* infanticide
infancia *nf* [-ancia 3365] infancy
infanta *nf* infant girl
infanticida *nmf* one who kills an infant

infanticida *aj* infanticidal
infantil *aj* [-il 864] infantile
infante infantryman
　infante *nm* [3873] infantryman
　infantería *nf* infantry
inferior inferior
　inferior *nmf* [3032] subordinate
　inferioridad *nf* inferiority
　inferior *aj* [3032] inferior
infierno hell, inferno
　infierno *nm* [4141] hell; inferno
　infernal *aj* infernal
infiltrar to infiltrate
　infiltrar *vt* to infiltrate
　infiltrarse *vr* to infiltrate oneself
　infiltrado,-a *nmf* intruder; infiltrator
　infiltración *nf* infiltration
influencia influence
　influir *vt* [2474] to influence
　influyente *nmf* [-ente(1)] person with influence
　influencia *nf* [-a 2131] influence (usually relating to people)
　influyente *aj* [-ente(1)] with influence
informe report
　informar *vt* [147] to inform
　informarse *vr* to become informed
　informador,-a *nmf* informer
　informe *nm* [828] report
　información *nf* [-ción 321] information
　informática *nf* information systems
　informado *aj* informed
　informativo *aj* [-ivo 2841] informative
infundir to infuse
　infundir *vt* to infuse
　infusión *nf* infusion
ingenuidad honesty and sincerity; naiveté
　ingenuo,-a *nmf* honest and sincere person; naïve person
　ingenuidad *nf* honesty and sincerity; naiveté
　ingenuo *aj* [-uo] honest and sincere; naïve
ingresar to enter; to deposit
　ingresar *vti* [1204] to enter; to deposit
　reingresar *vt* to reenter
　ingreso *nm* [-o(1) 756] deposit
　reingreso *nm* reentry
　ingresado *aj* entered; enrolled
iniciar to initiate
　iniciar *vt* [174] to initiate
　iniciarse *vr* to be initiated
　iniciado,-a *nmf* initiate, neophyte
　iniciador,-a *nmf* initiator
　inicio *nm* [-icio 689] beginning

iniciación *nf* initiation
inicial *nf* [-cial 1927] initial; first letter of a name
iniciativa *nf* [910] initiative
iniciado *aj* initiated
iniciador *aj* initiating
inicial *aj* [-cial 1927] initial
injuria insult, offense
　injuriar *vt* to insult
　injuria *nf* insult, offense
　injurioso *aj* offensive
inmenso immense
　inmensidad *nf* immensity
　inmensamente *av* immensely
　inmenso *aj* [4193] immense
inocente innocent
　inocente *nmf* [3386] innocent person; someone without malice (e.g., a young child)
　inocentón,-a *nmf* a very good person; an ingenuous person
　inocencia *nf* [-encia] innocence
　inocente *aj* [3386] innocent
　inocentón *aj* very good; ingenuous
insecto insect
　insectívoros *nmpl* insect-eating animals
　insecto *nm* [4820] insect
　insecticida *nf* insecticide
　insecticida *aj* insecticidal
　insectívoro *aj* insect-eating
insinuar to insinuate
　insinuar *vt* to insinuate
　insinuación *nf* insinuation
　insinuante *aj* insinuating, suggestive
insistir to insist
　insistir *vt* [1010] to insist
　insistencia *nf* [-encia] insistence
　insistentemente *av* insistently
　insistente *aj* insistent
instalación installation
　instalar *vt* [922] to install
　instalarse *vr* to be installed
　instalador,-a *nmf* installer
　instalación *nf* [-ción 529] installation
instante instant
　instante *nm* [-ante(1) 3581] instant
　instantáneamente *av* instantaneously
　instantáneo *aj* instantaneous
instinto instinct
　instinto *nm* instinct
　instintivamente *av* instinctively
　instintivo *aj* instinctive
instituto institute
　institucionalizar *vt* to institutionalize

instituir *vt* to institute

instituto *nm* [-uto 434] institute

institución *nf* [-ción 396] institution

institutriz *nf* [-triz] private teacher (woman)

institucional *aj* [1360] institutional

institucionalizado *aj* institutionalized

instituido *aj* instituted

instrucción instruction

instruir *vt* [4987] to instruct

instructor,-a *nmf* [4000] instructor

instrucción *nf* [-ción 2172] instruction

instructivo *aj* instructive

instruido *aj* instructed

instrumento instrument

instrumentista *nmf* person who plays a musical instrument; surgical assistant

instrumental *nm* instruments or tools of a profession

instrumento *nm* [1644] instrument

instrumentación *nf* instrumentation

instrumental *aj* instrumental

insultar to insult

insultar *vt* to insult

insulto *nm* [-o(1) 4743] insult

insultante *aj* insulting

integrar to integrate

desintegrar *vt* to disintegrate

desintegrarse *vr* to become disintegrated

integrar *vt* [546] to integrate

integrarse *vr* to become integrated

reintegrar *vt* to reintegrate

reintegrarse *vr* to become healthy; to recuperate

integrante *nmf* [-ante(2) 544] one who is part of a group; representative of a group

reintegro *nm* return of an investment (esp. lottery ticket), return of an overpayment

desintegración *nf* disintegration

integral *nf* [1637] integral (math)

integridad *nf* [-idad 3947] integrity

reintegración *nf* reintegration

íntegramente *av* completely

integral *aj* [1637] integral

integrante *aj* [-ante(2) 544] integral, integral part of a group

íntegro *aj* whole

intelectual intellectual

intelectual *nmf* [-al(2) 2742] intellectual

intelecto *nm* intellect

intelectualismo *nm* intellectualism

intelectualidad *nf* intelligentsia

inteligencia *nf* [-encia 2154] intelligence

ininteligible *aj* unintelligible

intelectual *aj* [-al(2) 2742] intellectual

inteligente *aj* [2530] intelligent

inteligible *aj* intelligible

intención intention

intentar *vt* [742] to intend; to try

malintencionado,-a *nmf* ill-intentioned person

intento *nm* [-o(1) 1583] attempt; try

intención *nf* [-ción 1012] intention

intencionadamente *av* intentionally

bienintencionado *aj* well-intentioned

intencionado *aj* intentioned

intencional *aj* intentional

malintencionado *aj* ill-intentioned

intenso intense

intensificar *vi* [-ificar 3379] to intensify

intensificarse *vr* to become intensified

intensidad *nf* [-idad 3300] intensity

intensificación *nf* intensification

intensivo *aj* intensive

intenso *aj* [1488] intense

interés interest

desinteresarse *vr* to become disinterested

interesar *vi* [783] to interest

interesarse *vr* to become interested

interesado,-a *nmf* interested party or person

desinterés *nm* disinterest

interés *nm* [471] interest

desinteresado *aj* disinterested

interesado *aj* interested

interesante *aj* [-ante(1) 1527] interesting

interior interior

interiorizarse *vr* to study a subject carefully

interior *nm* [711] interior

interioridades *nfpl* intimacies

interioridad *nf* quality of the interior

interior *aj* [711] interior

interno internal

internar *vt* to place someone in a hospital, boarding school, or concentration camp, etc.

internista *nmf* internist

interno,-a *nmf* boarding student; intern

internado *nm* [-o(1) 2289] boarding school; concentration camp

internamiento *nm* internment

internado *aj* [-o(1) 2289] referring to boarding school students, prisoners in a concentration camp, or patients in a hospital

internista *aj* internist

interno *aj* [-o(1) 656] internal

interpretación interpretation

interpretar *vt* [777] to interpret

intérprete *nmf* [1361] interpreter

interpretación *nf* [-ción 2276] interpretation

interrogar to interrogate
  interrogar *vt* [3979] to interrogate
  interrogador,-a *nmf* interrogator
  interrogante *nm* unknown
  interrogatorio *nm* interrogatory; series of
    questions
  interrogación *nf* interrogation
  interrogante *aj* interrogating
  interrogativo *aj* interrogative

interrumpir to interrupt
  interrumpir *vt* [3409] to interrupt
  interruptor *nm* [-or] interrupter; something or
    someone that interrupts
  interrupción *nf* interruption
  ininterrumpidamente *av* uninterruptedly
  ininterrumpido *aj* uninterrupted

intervenir to intervene
  intervenir *vi* [1604] to intervene
  intervencionista *nmf* interventionist
  intervencionismo *nm* interventionism
  intervención *nf* [-ción 1174] intervention
  intervencionista *aj* interventionist

íntimo intimate
  intimar *vi* to become intimate
  íntimo,-a *nmf* intimate friend or family member
  intimidades *nfpl* family secrets
  intimidad *nf* intimate friendship; intimacy
  íntimo *aj* [2370] intimate

introducir to introduce something
  introducir *vt* [1977] to introduce
  introducirse *vr* to enter; to become involved
  introductor,-a *nmf* introducer; person who
    introduces the speakers at a conference
  introducción *nf* [-ción 3228] introduction
  introductor *aj* introductory

intuición intuition
  intuir *vt* to intuit; to know by intuition
  intuición *nf* intuition
  intuitivamente *av* intuitively
  intuitivo *aj* intuitive

invasión invasion
  invadir *vt* [2237] to invade
  invasor,-a *nmf* invader
  invasión *nf* [-sión 3583] invasion
  invasor *aj* invading

inventar to invent
  inventar *vt* [3707] to invent
  inventor,-a *nmf* inventor
  invento *nm* invention
  invención *nf* invention

inventiva *nf* inventiveness
  inventivo *aj* inventive

invertir to invest; to invert
  invertir *vt* [1142] to invest; to invert
  inversionista *nmf* [-ista 2531] investor
  inversión *nf* [-sión 613] investment; inversion
  invertido *aj* invested; inverted

investigación investigation
  investigar *vt* [1347] to investigate
  investigador,-a *nmf* [1043] investigator
  investigación *nf* [-ción 394] investigation
  investigador *aj* investigating

invitación invitation
  invitar *vt* [505] to invite
  invitado,-a *nmf* invited guest
  invitación *nf* [-ción 1645] invitation
  invitado *aj* [-ado(2)] invited
  invitante *aj* inviting

ir to go
  ir *vi* [49] to go
  irse *vi* to go away, to leave

ira ire
  airar *vt* to anger
  airarse *vr* to become very angry
  ira *nm* ire
  airado *aj* angry
  iracundo *aj* [-undo] easily angered

irónico ironic
  ironizar *vt* to use irony
  ironía *nf* irony
  irónico *aj* ironic

irritar to irritate
  irritar *vt* to irritate
  irritarse *vr* to become irritated
  irritabilidad *nf* irritability
  irritación *nf* irritation
  irritable *aj* irritable
  irritante *aj* irritating

isla island
  aislar *vt* [3004] to isolate; to insulate
  aislarse *vr* to become isolated
  aislacionista *nmf* isolationist
  isleño,-a *nmf* islander; person who lives on an
    island
  aislacionismo *nm* isolationism
  aislador *nm* insulator
  aislamiento *nm* isolation
  islote *nm* small desert island
  isla *nf* [1257] island
  islote *nf* isolated rock that protrudes from the
    sea

aislacionista *aj* isolationist
aislado *aj* isolated
aislador *aj* isolating
isleño *aj* [-eño] pertaining to an island

itinerario itinerary
itinerario *nm* itinerary
itinerante *aj* itinerant

izquierdo left
izquierdista *nmf* political leftist
izquierdismo *nm* political leftism
izquierda *nf* left
izquierdista *aj* leftist
izquierdo *aj* [737] left; left-handed

J

jabón soap
enjabonar *vt* to put soap on something
jabón *nm* [4210] soap
jabonado *nmf* the act of putting soap on something
jaboncillo *nm* [-illo(1)] a small piece of soap; tailor's soap
jabonera *nf* [-era] soap dish
jabonoso *aj* soapy

jardín garden
jardín *nm* [1173] garden
jardinero,-a *nmf* [4772] gardener
jardinería *nf* the art of gardening

jaula cage
enjaular *vt* to put in a cage
jaula *nf* cage

jefe boss, chief, manager
subjefe,-a *nmf* assistant manager, supervisor
jefe *nm* boss, chief, manager
jefa *nf* female boss, chief, or manager
jefatura *nf* leadership; management group; position of leadership

Jesús Jesus
Jesuita *nmf* Jesuit
Jesucristo *nm* [4652] Jesus Christ
Jesús *nm* Jesus
Jesuita *aj* Jesuit
Jesuítico *aj* Jesuit

jinete knight, horseman
jinetear *vt* to mount a horse
jinete *nm* knight, horseman

jornada a day of work
jornalero,-a *nmf* worker

jornal *nm* day's wages
jornada *nf* [512] a day of work

joven young
rejuvenecer *vti* to rejuvenate
rejuvenecerse *vr* to become rejuvenated
joven *nmf* [215] young man or woman
jovencito,-a *nmf* very young man or woman; teenager
jovenzuelo,-a *nmf* very young man or woman; teenager
rejuvenecimiento *nm* rejuvenation
juventud *nf* [-itud 2076] youth
joven *aj* [215] young
jovencito,-a *aj* very-young; teenage
jovenzuelo,-a *aj* very-young; teenage
juvenil *aj* [-il 1154] youth; related to youth
rejuvenecedor *aj* rejuvenating

joya jewel
enjoyar *vt* to put on jewels
joyero,-a *nmf* jewelry maker or seller
joyero *nm* jewelry box
joya *nf* [3651] jewel
joyería *nf* [-ería(1) 4821] jewelry store

júbilo rejoicing
jubilar(se) *vt(r)* [2704] to retire
jubilado,-a *nmf* retired person
jubileo *nm* jubilee
júbilo *nm* rejoicing
jubilación *nf* jubilation
jubilado *aj* retired
jubiloso *aj* [-oso] rejoicing

judío Jewish
judaizar *vt* to convert to Judaism
judío,-a *nmf* Jew
judaísmo *nm* Judaism
judería *nf* Jewry
judaico *aj* Judaic
judeocristiano *aj* Judeo-Christian
judeoespañol *aj* Judeo-Spanish, especially referring to those in Spain before 1492
judío *aj* [2371] Jewish

jugar to play
jugar *vt* [259] to play
juguetear *vi* to do something for fun; also, to play around with, used pejoratively
jugador,-a *nmf* [279] player
juego *nm* [-o(1) 183] game
juguete *nm* [-ete 2872] toy
videojuego *nm* video game
jugada *nf* [1570] one play in a game (football, basketball, etc.)

juguetería *nf* [-ería(1)] toy store
juguetón *aj* [-ón(2)] overly playful

juicio judgment, considered opinion; trial
adjudicar(se) *vt(r)* [3014] to adjudicate
enjuiciar *vt* to submit to trial or judgment
juez *nmf* [918] judge
enjuiciamiento *nm* the judgment of trial or judge
juicio *nm* [-icio 1458] judgment, considered opinion; trial
adjudicación *nf* adjudication
extrajudicial *aj* extra-judicial
judicial *aj* [-cial 1363] judicial
juicioso *aj* just, judicious

junto together
adjuntar *vt* to attach
conjuntar *vt* [4558] to unite with harmony
juntar *vt* [3498] to join
juntarse *vr* [3498] to become joined to
conjunción *nf* conjunction
conjunto *nm* [-o(1) 601] set; ensemble, especially of musicians
junta *nf* [-a 1284] meeting
juntura *nf* area where two pieces are joined together
adjunto *aj* [3910] attached
conjuntivo *aj* conjunctive, joining
junto *aj* [391] together

jurar to swear
abjurar *vt* to forswear; to publicly renounce something or someone
conjurar *vi* to swear allegiance to a conspiracy or plot
conjurarse *vr* to bind oneself to others with an oath, particularly in a conspiracy or plot
juramentar *vt* to swear in
juramentarse *vr* to take an oath
jurar *vt* to swear
perjurar *vi* [-ura(2)] to perjure
conjurado,-a *nmf* participant in a conspiracy
jurado,-a *nmf* juror
jurisconsulto *nmf* a person knowledgeable in law
jurisperito *nmf* specialist in legal matters
jurista *nmf* jurist
perjuro,-a *nmf* perjurer
conjuro *nm* the act of swearing in
jurado *nm* [-ato 3724] jury
juramento *nm* oath
perjurio *nm* perjury
abjuración *nf* forswearing
conjura, conjuración *nf* conspiracy against someone or something

jura *nf* oath
jurisdicción *nf* [2734] jurisdiction
jurisprudencia *nf* jurisprudence
conjurado *aj* participating in a conspiracy
jurado *aj* [-ato 3724] jury
juramentado *aj* sworn
jurídico *aj* [1353] related to law
jurisdiccional *aj* jurisdictional
perjuro *aj* perjured

justicia justice
ajusticiar *vt* to give the death penalty; (figurative) to describe a severe penalty at home or at school
justificar *vt* [-ificar 1847] to justify
justificarse *vr* [1847] to justify oneself
juzgar *vt* [1580] to judge
ajusticiado,-a *nmf* person who receives the death penalty
justo,-a *nmf* just person
justificante *nm* a note that acts as written proof (e.g., from a parent or doctor)
juzgado *nm* a tribunal, or group of judges
injusticia *nf* [-icia 3978] injustice
justicia *nf* [-icia 603] justice
justificación *nf* [-ción 4773] justification
injustamente *av* unjustly
injustificadamente *av* unjustifiably
injustificable *aj* unjustifiable
injustificado *aj* unjustified
injusto *aj* [3456] unjust
justiciero *aj* exaggeratingly strict; following justice to the extreme
justificable *aj* justifiable
justificado *aj* justified
justificante *aj* justifying, proving
justo *aj* [1067] just

K

kilómetro kilometer
cuentakilómetros *nm* odometer
kilo *nm* thousand
kilociclo *nm* kilocycle
kilogramo *nm* [1566] kilogram
kilolitro *nm* kiloliter
kilometraje *nm* distance in kilometers, similar to mileage, but measuring kilometers
kilómetro *nm* [782] kilometer
kilovatio *nm* kilowatt
kilométrico,-a *aj* kilometric; long, measuring in kilometers

L

labio lip
labio *nm* [3380] lip
labial *aj* [-al(2)] labial
labiodental *aj* labiodental

labor labor
laborar *vi* [2115] to labor
laboratorio *nm* [-orio(1) 2459] laboratory
labor *nf* [693] labor
laboriosidad *nf* laboriousness
laboral *aj* [1104] work
laborioso *aj* laborious
laborable *aj* workable

labrador agricultural worker
labrar *vt* to cultivate
labriego,-a *nmf* agricultural worker
labrador *nm* [-dor(1)] agricultural worker
labranza *nf* [-anza] agricultural cultivation

lado side
lado *nm* [356] side
lateral *nm* [3047] street that runs parallel to a boulevard, separated only by a sidewalk
equilátero *aj* equilateral
lateral *aj* [3047] lateral
multilateral *aj* multilateral
unilateral *aj* unilateral

ladrar to bark
ladrar *vti* to bark
ladrido *nm* [-ido(2)] bark
ladrador *aj* barking

ladrillo brick
enladrillar *vt* to lay bricks
enladrillado *nm* something made of brick
ladrillo *nm* [4916] brick
enladrillado *aj* bricked; of brick

ladrón thief
ladrón,-a *nmf* [2476] thief
ladronzuelo,-a *nmf* little thief
ladronera *nf* thieves' hideout
ladrón *aj* thieving

lágrima tear
lagrimear *vt* to tear
lagrimal *nm* tear duct
lagrimeo *nm* tearing
lagrimón *nm* a big tear
lágrima *nf* [-a 3127] tear
lacrimal *aj* lachrymal
lacrimógeno *aj* tear-provoking
lagrimal *aj* lachrymal

lamentar to lament
lamentar *vt* [2558] to lament
lamentarse *vr* [2558] to be sorry
lamento *nm* lament
lamentación *nf* lamentation
lamentablemente *av* [-mente 3569] lamentably
lamentable *aj* [-able 3203] lamentable
lamentoso *aj* making sorry

lámpara lamp
relampaguear *vt* to light up with lightning
relámpago *nm* lightning
relampagueo *nm* lighting up of the sky by lightning
lámpara *nf* [4143] lamp
relampagueante *aj* lit up by lightning

lancha boat
lanchero *nmf* boat owner or skipper
lancha *nf* boat

lanzar to throw
lanzar *vt* [600] to throw
lanzarse *vr* [600] to throw oneself, to hurl oneself
lanzacohetes *nm* rocket launcher
lanzador,-a *nmf* [2970] pitcher
lance *nm* casting of a net when fishing
lanzagranadas *nm* grenade launcher
lanzallamas *nm* flamethrower
lanzamiento *nm* [-miento 2187] pitch, throw
relanzamiento *nm* re-throwing
lanza *nf* [3533] lance
lanzada *nf* hit with a lance
lanzador *aj* pitching

lápiz pencil
lapicero *nm* [-ero(1)] pencil holder; mechanical pencil
lápiz *nm* pencil

largo long
alargar *vt* [4310] to elongate, to lengthen
alargarse *vr* to become longer; to last a long time
alargamiento *nm* lengthening
largometraje *nm* [4445] long film
largura *nf* [-ura(1)] length
alargado *aj* elongated, lengthened
largo *aj* [395] long

lástima pity
lastimar *vt* [4211] to hurt
lastimarse *vr* [4211] to hurt oneself
lástima *nf* pity
lastimadura *nf* wound
lastimado *aj* hurt
lastimero *aj* [-ero(2)] painful
lastimoso *aj* [-oso] hurtful; pain-causing

latín Latin
  latinizar *vt* to Latinize a word
  latín *nm* Latin
  latinismo *nm* Latinism
  latinidad *nf* Latin culture
  latino *aj* [-ino(2) 987] Latino

lavar to wash
  deslavar *vt* to wash lightly or superficially
  lavar *vt* [1925] to wash
  lavarse *vr* [1925] to wash oneself
  lavacoches *nmf* person that washes cars
  lavabo *nm* bathroom sink and faucet
  lavadero *nm* washboard
  lavado *nm* washing
  lavamanos *nm* wash basin
  lavandero *nmf* person who washes clothes
  lavaplatos *nm* dishwasher
  lavatorio *nm* [-orio(1)] lavatory
  lavavajillas *nm* dishwasher
  lavada *nf* washing
  lavadora *nf* [-dor(2)] washing machine
  lavandería *nf* Laundromat
  lavativa *nf* enema; colonic irrigation
  lavable *aj* washable
  lavado *aj* washed

lazo lasso, rope
  desenlazar *vt* to unravel; to untie
  enlazar *vt* to tie with rope
  enlazarse *vr* to marry
  entrelazar *vt* to braid
  entrelazarse *vr* to be braided
  lazar *vt* to lasso
  desenlace *nm* finale; conclusion to a story or conference
  enlace *nm* [1810] the union or marriage of newlyweds
  lazo *nm* [-o(1) 2359] lasso, rope
  lazada *nf* slip knot; bow knot
  entrelazado *aj* woven; knitted

leal loyal
  deslealtad *nf* disloyalty
  lealtad *nf* [-tad] loyalty
  desleal *aj* disloyal
  leal *aj* [3570] loyal

lección lesson
  aleccionar *vt* to give lessons
  aleccionamiento *nm* the giving of lessons; training
  lección *nf* [3488] lesson
  aleccionador *aj* lesson-giving, said of something that teaches someone a lesson

leche milk
  lechada *nf* whitewash

leche *nf* [1241] milk
  lechería *nf* [-ería(1)] dairy store
  lechero *aj* [-ero(2) 3062] milk-producing or containing
  lechoso *aj* milky; milk-like

lector reader
  leer *vt* [871] to read
  releer *vt* to re-read
  lector,-a *nmf* [2548] reader
  lectura *nf* [-ura(2) 2155] a reading
  lector *aj* [-or] reading
  legible *aj* readable
  leído *aj* read

legal legal
  legalizar *vt* [-izar] to legalize
  legalista *nmf* legalist
  legalismo *nm* legalism
  ilegalidad *nf* illegality
  legalidad *nf* [-idad 3633] legality
  legalización *nf* legalization
  ilegalmente *av* illegally
  legalmente *av* [-mente 4492] legally
  ilegal *aj* [1913] illegal
  legal *aj* [1061] legal
  legalista *aj* legalistic

legión legion
  legionario,-a *nm* legionary
  legión *nf* legion
  legionario *aj* legionary

legítimo legitimate
  legitimar *vt* to legitimize
  legitimidad *nf* authenticity
  ilegítimamente *av* illegitimately
  ilegítimo *aj* illegitimate
  legítimo *aj* [3518] legitimate

lejos far
  alejar *vt* [1757] to move farther away; to distance
  alejarse *vr* [1757] to distance oneself
  alejamiento *nm* distance
  lejanía *nf* far distance
  lejísimos *av* very far away
  lejos *av* [1687] far away
  lejano *aj* [3117] distant

lengua tongue
  deslenguar *vt* to remove the tongue
  lingüista *nmf* linguist
  lenguaje *nm* [-aje(1) 3142] language
  lengüetada *nm* [-ada(2)] a lick
  lengua *nf* [2655] tongue
  lingüística *nf* linguistics
  deslenguado *aj* bad-mouthed
  lingual *aj* lingual

lingüístico *aj* linguistic
plurilingüe *aj* multi-lingual

lentamente slowly
lentitud *nf* [-itud] slowness
lentamente *av* [-mente 4508] slowly
lento *aj* [2246] slow

león lion
Leo *nm* [3475] Leo
león *nm* [457] lion
leopardo *nm* leopard
leona *nf* lioness
leonera *nf* lion cage

lesión lesion, wound
lesionar *vt* [879] to wound
lesionarse *vr* [879] to become wounded
lesionado,-a *nmf* wounded person
lesión *nf* [-sión 1009] lesion; wound
ileso *aj* uninjured
lesionado *aj* wounded
lesivo *aj* wounding; injuring
leso *aj* injured, used in law referring to an
   injured party

letra letter
deletrear *vt* to spell
iletrado,-a *nmf* illiterate person
letrado,-a *nmf* literate person
literato,-a *nmf* writer; person knowledgeable in
   literature
deletreo *nm* [-eo(1)] spelling
letrero *nm* sign
letra *nf* [1389] letter
literatura *nf* [-ura(2) 3310] literature
literalmente *av* literally
iletrado *aj* illiterate
letrado *aj* [-ado(1)] literate
literal *aj* literal
literario *aj* [-ario(2) 3449] literary

levantar to lift; to raise up
levantar *vt* [1006] to lift; to raise up
levantarse *vr* [1006] to get up
levantador,-a de pesas *nmf* weightlifter
levantamiento *nm* [-miento 3980] the raising
levantada *nf* act of getting out of bed
levadura *nf* leavening
levadizo *aj* [-dizo] able to raise, often said of
   drawbridges
levantado *aj* out of bed; raised

libertad liberty
liberalizar *vt* [-izar] to liberalize
liberar *vt* [2103] to liberate
liberarse *vr* [2103] to become liberated
libertar *vt* to liberate (nation, people)

librar(se) *vt(r)* [1706] to free from an obligation
   or circumstance
liberador,-a *nmf* liberator
liberal *nmf* [4703] liberal person
libertador,-a *nmf* [2823] liberator of a nation
libertario,-a *nmf* libertarian
libertino,-a *nmf* libertine
librecambista *nmf* free-trader
librepensador,-a *nmf* free-thinker
liberalismo *nm* [-ismo] liberalism
libertinaje *nm* licentiousness
librecambio *nm* free trade
librepensamiento *nm* free thinking
liberación *nf* [-ción 2489] liberation
liberalidad *nf* liberality
liberalización *nf* liberalization
libertad *nf* [-tad 794] liberty
liberalmente *av* liberally
liberado *aj* liberated
liberal *aj* [4703] liberal
libertador *aj* liberating
libertario *aj* libertarian
libertino *aj* libertine
libre *aj* [488] free
librecambista *aj* free-trading
librepensador *aj* free-thinking

libro book
librero,-a *nmf* bookseller
librero *nm* [-ero(3)] bookcase
libro *nm* [667] book
librería *nf* [-cría(1)] bookstore
libreta *nf* [-eta] small book; notebook

licenciado certified; licensed
licenciar *vt* to certify; to license
licenciarse *vr* to become certified or licensed
licenciado,-a *nmf* [2227] certified professional
licencia *nf* [-encia 2156] license
licenciatura *nf* [4918] licensure
licenciado *aj* [-ado(2)] certified; licensed
licencioso *aj* licentious

lícito licit
ilícitamente *av* illicitly
ilícito *aj* [-ito(2) 2208] illicit
lícito *aj* [-ito(2)] licit

ligado tied
ligar *vt* [3118] to tie
ligarse *vr* [3118] to become tied
ligado *nm* a tie in music; tied notes
ligamento *nm* ligament
ligadura *nf* [-dura] action of tying
ligado *aj* tied

ligero light
aligerar *vt* to lighten

aligeramiento *nm* lightening
ligereza *nf* lightness
ligeramente *av* lightly
ligero *av* [2071] light
ligero *aj* [2071] voluble or frequently-changing (of people who change their minds often)

limitar to limit
delimitar *vt* to delimit; to put limits on something
extralimitarse *vr* to go beyond the limits
limitar *vt* [1508] to limit
limitarse *vr* to limit oneself
límite *nm* [1606] limit
delimitación *nf* boundary
limitación *nf* [-ción 4018] limitation
ilimitable *aj* unlimited
ilimitado *aj* unlimited
limitado *aj* limited

limón lemon
limero *nm* [-ero(4)] lime seller
limón *nm* [1545] lemon; lemon tree
limonero *nm* [-ero(4)] lemon seller
lima *nf* lime
limonada *nf* [-ada(2)] lemonade
limonero *aj* [-ero(4)] lemon

limpiar to clean
limpiar *vt* [1395] to clean
limpiarse *vr* to clean oneself
limpiador,-a *nmf* person who cleans
limpiachimeneas *nm* chimney-sweep
limpiador *nm* rag
limpiaparabrisas *nm* windshield wipers
limpieza *nf* [-eza 1446] cleaning
limpiador *aj* cleaning
limpio *aj* [3325] clean

lindo pretty, handsome; wonderful
lindo,-a *nmf* pretty person, handsome person; wonderful person
lindeza *nf* [-eza] prettiness, handsomeness; wonderfulness
lindamente *av* prettily; in a wonderful way
lindo *aj* [3289] pretty, handsome; wonderful

línea line
alinear *vt* [4619] to put in a straight line
alinearse *vr* [4619] to form a straight line
colindar *vi* to be adjacent to
delinear *vt* to delineate
desalinear *vt* to put out of line
desalinearse *vr* to get out of a straight line
entrelinear *vt* to write between the lines
lindar *vi* to be contiguous
linde *nmf* property line

alineamiento *nm* the act of putting in a straight line; lining up
deslinde *nm* the act of placing property lines
alineación *nf* [-ción 2357] alignment (e.g., of a cars wheels)
delineación *nf* delineation
línea *nf* [581] line
alineado *aj* aligned
colindante *aj* adjacent
curvilíneo *aj* curvilinear
lineal *aj* linear

líquido liquid
licuar *vt* to liquefy
licuarse *vr* to become liquefied
liquidar *vt* [3396] to liquidate
licor *nm* [4653] liquor
licuado *nm* milkshake-like drink
líquido *nm* [-ido(1) 1813] liquid
licorera *nf* [-era] decanter
licorería *nf* [-ería(1)] liquor store
liquidación *nf* liquidation
liquidez *nf* [-ez] liquidity
liquidado *aj* liquidated
líquido *aj* [-ido(1) 1813] liquid

lírica a musical
lírico *nm* lyric
lírica *nf* a musical
lírico *aj* lyrical

liso smooth
alisar *vt* to make smooth; to make straight (e.g, hair)
alisarse *vr* to become smooth; to become straight (e.g., hair)
alisador *nm* something used to smooth (e.g., hair)
alisador *aj* smoothing; straightening (e.g., hair)
liso *aj* [4961] smooth; straight (e.g., hair)

lista list
alistar *vt* to list
alistarse *vr* to enlist
alistamiento *nm* listing
lista *nf* list
alistado *aj* listed

llama flame
lanzallamas *nm* flame-thrower
llama *nf* flame
llamarada *nf* sudden bursts of flame

llamar to call
llamar *vt* [269] to call
llamarse *vr* [269] to call oneself
llamador *nm* doorbell
llamamiento *nm* calling

llamada *nf* [-ada(2) 902]   call; telephone call
llamado *aj* called
llano plain, flatland
allanar *vt* to flatten land
allanarse *vr* to become flat (land)
llanero,-a *nmf* ranger; one who lives on a plain
allanamiento *nm* flattening of land
llano *nm* [4774] plain, flatland
llanura *nf* [-ura(1)] the plains
llave key
llavero *nm* [-ero(1)] key chain
llave *nf* [3499] key
llegar to arrive
llegar *vi* [79] to arrive
llegada *nf* [-ada(2) 945] arrival
lleno full
llenar *vt* [1773] to fill
llenarse *vr* to become full
rellenar *vt* [4900] refill; to fill with a filling
relleno *nm* [-o(1) 2331] filling
lleno *aj* [1014] full
relleno *aj* [-o(1) 2331] refilled
llevar to carry
conllevar *vt* to help bear a burden or trouble
llevar(se) *vt(r)* [87] to carry
sobrellevar *vt* to put up with, to tolerate
llorar to cry
llorar *vi* [2336] to cry
lloriquear *vi* to whine; to cry without reason or only for attention
llorón,-a *nmf* cry-baby; someone who cries a lot
llanto *nm* crying
lloriqueo *nm* whining; crying for attention only
lloro *nm* crying
llorón *aj* [-ón(2)] frequently crying
lloroso *aj* [-oso] tearful; with the appearance of having been crying
lluvia rain
llover *vt* [4060] to rain
lloviznar *vt* to rain lightly, to sprinkle
llovizna *nf* light rain, sprinkling
lluvia *nf* [1322] rain
lluvioso *aj* rainy
local local
colocar *vt* [539] to place
colocarse *vr* to be placed
descolocar *vt* to remove
dislocar *vt* to dislocate
dislocarse *vr* to become dislocated
localizar *vt* [-izar 1208] to localize; to find
locatario,-a *nmf* tenant
local *nm* [257] locale; place

colocación *nf* [-ción 3307] placing
localidad *nf* [-idad 1090] locality
localización *nf* localization
colocado *aj* placed; placed in an employment
local *aj* [257] local
loco crazy
enloquecer *vt* to drive crazy
enloquecerse *vr* to become crazy
loco,-a *nmf* crazy person
loquero,-a *nmf* caretaker of people who are mentally ill
enloquecimiento *nm* the act of becoming or going crazy
locura *nf* [-ura(1) 4385] craziness
alocado *aj* crazy-acting; without sense
enloquecedor *aj* referring to that which drives one crazy
loco *aj* [1984] crazy
lógico logical
lógico,-a *nmf* logician
lógica *nf* logic
ilógicamente *av* illogically
lógicamente *av* logically
ilógico *aj* illogical
lógico *aj* [-ico(2) 2747] logical
lograr to achieve
lograr *vt* [150] to achieve, to reach a goal
lograrse *vr* to accomplish
logro *nm* [-o(1) 2072] accomplishment
logrado *aj* [-ado(1)] accomplished, achieved
longitud longitude
longitud *nf* [-itud 4019] longitude
longitudinalmente *av* longitudinally
longitudinal *aj* longitudinal
lucha struggle
luchar *vi* [1453] to struggle
luchador,-a *nmf* [3519] struggler; fighter
lucha *nf* [-a 579] struggle
luchador *aj* [-dor(1)] struggling
lujo luxury
lujo *nm* [2815] luxury
lujosamente *av* luxuriously
lujoso *aj* [-oso] luxurious
luminoso luminous
alumbrar *vt* [2377] to put light in something; to light up
alumbrarse *vr* to become well-lit
deslumbrar *vt* to blind with bright light; to amaze
iluminar(se) *vt(r)* [4681] to illuminate
relumbrar *vi* to give off an excessive amount of light
iluminado,-a *nmf* enlightened person

alumbrado *nm* the lighting
alumbramiento *nm* birth
deslumbramiento *nm* blinding with bright light; amazement
relumbrón *nm* [-ón(1)] sudden intense flash of light
iluminación *nf* illumination
lumbre *nf* fire; light
lumbrera *nf* flame
luminaria *nf* [4939] lighting; special lamp used in the Catholic church
luminiscencia *nf* luminescense
luminosidad *nf* luminosity
alumbrado *aj* lit-up; well lighted
deslumbrador *aj* blinding; amazing
iluminado *aj* illuminated
iluminador *aj* illuminating
luminiscente *aj* luminescent
luminoso *aj* luminous

luna moon
alunizar *vt* to land on the moon
lunático,-a *nmf* lunatic
alunizaje *nm* [-aje(3)] moon-landing
lunar *nm* round mark on the skin; mole; beauty mark
lunes *nm* [634] Monday
plenilunio *nm* full-moon
luna *nf* [930] moon
lunar *aj* lunar
lunático *aj* lunatic; crazy

luto mourning
enlutar *v* to mourn
enlutarse *vr* to be in mourning
luto *nm* mourning
enlutado *aj* mourning

luz light
deslustrar *vt* to discolor; to take the shine off
elucidar *vt* to elucidate
ilustrar *vt* to illustrate
ilustrarse *vr* to enlighten; to be illustrated
lucir *vt* [907] to radiate; to shine
lucirse *vr* [907] to be a shining example; to be brilliant; to dress sharply
lustrar *vt* to shine something
traslucirse *vr* to be semi-transparent, to be "see-through"
ilustrador,-a *nmf* illustrator
lucero *nm* heavenly body that shines in the night (star, planet, comet)
lucimiento *nm* shining, brilliance
lustre *nm* the act of shining of something
trasluz *nm* light that shines through something transparent or semi-transparent

elucidación *nf* elucidation; clarification
ilustración *nf* illustration
lucidez *nf* [-ez] clarity
luciérnaga *nf* firefly
luz *nf* [606] light
deslucido *aj* dull; discolored
ilustrado *aj* illustrious; knowledgeable, well-educated
ilustrador *aj* illustrative
ilustrativo *aj* [-ivo] illustrative
ilustre *aj* famous, in the lime-light
ilustrísimo *aj* [-ísimo] most illustrious (esp., those in positions of high authority)
lucido *aj* radiating, shining, done with perfection
lúcido *aj* [-ido(1)] lucid, clear
luciente *aj* [-ente(1)] shiny, bright
reluciente *aj* [-ente(1)] very shiny, resplendent

M

madera wood
enmaderar *vt* to reface with wood
maderero,-a *nmf* woodworker
maderaje *nm* [-aje(1)] woodwork
madera *nf* [2111] wood
maderería *nf* woodworking shop or store
madero *nf* log
maderable *aj* timber-yielding; lumber-yielding
maderero *aj* [-ero(2)] pertaining to woodworking or the lumber industry

madre mother
amadrinar *vt* to act as godmother
enmadrarse *vr* to be extremely attached to one's mother
matricida *nmf* murderer of one's mother
matriarcado *nm* matriarchy
matricidio *nm* matricide
matrimonio *nm* [463] marriage
madrastra *nf* [-astro] stepmother
madraza *nf* [-aza] over-protective mother
madre *nf* [570] mother
madreperla *nf* mother-of-pearl
madrina *nf* [-ina] godmother; female sponsor of a wedding
maternidad *nf* maternity
matriz *nf* womb; uterus; headquarters
maternal *aj* maternal
materno *aj* [4317] maternal
matriarcal *aj* matriarchal

matrimonial *aj* [1822] matrimonial

prematrimonial *aj* premarital

madrugada midnight to sunrise

madrugar *vi* to get up in the early morning hours

madrugador,-a *nmf* person who gets up in the early morning hours

madrugada *nf* [1659] midnight to sunrise

madrugador *aj* early-morning rising

madurez maturity

madurar *vi* [-ura(2) 3018] to mature

prematuro,-a *nmf* premature baby

inmadurez *nf* immaturity

maduración *nf* maturation

madurez *nf* [-ez 3351] maturity

inmaduro *aj* immature

maduro *aj* [-ura(2) 4479] mature

prematuro *aj* [4801] premature

maestro master, teacher

amaestrar *vt* to train, to coach, to teach; to tame

amaestrador,-a *nmf* trainer, coach, teacher

maestro,-a *nmf* [636] master, teacher

amaestramiento *nm* mastering

maestría *nf* master's degree

amaestrado *aj* trained, coached, taught; tamed

amaestrador *aj* mastering

maestro *aj* masterly; excellent

magistral pertaining to teaching

magisterio *nm* [4020] profession of teaching

magistral *aj* pertaining to teaching

magnífico magnificent

magnificar *vt* to laud or praise

magnificencia *nf* magnificence

magnitud *nf* [-itud 3584] magnitude

magnífico *aj* [3458] magnificent

magno *aj* [4493] great; extraordinary

maíz corn

maíz *nm* [1632] corn

maizal *nm* [-al(3)] cornfield

majestad majesty

majestad *nf* [-tad] majesty

majestuosidad *nf* majesty

majestuoso *aj* majestic

mal bad

malacostumbrar *v* to develop a bad habit

malbaratar *vt* to sell below cost or value

malcomer *vti* to eat poorly

malcriar *vt* to spoil (a child)

maldecir *vti* to curse

malear *vt* to damage, to ruin

malearse *vr* to damage or ruin oneself

malgastar *vt* to misspend

malherir *vt* to hurt badly

malhumorar *vt* to put someone in a bad mood

malhumorarse *vr* to be in a bad mood

maliciar *vt* to damage, to ruin

malograr *vt* to waste; to waste an opportunity

malograrse *vr* to fail to accomplish

malquerer *vt* to wish evil on someone

maltratar *vt* to mistreat

malvender *vt* to sell below cost or value

malversar *vt* to misspend money appropriated for another purpose; to fraudulently spend; to embezzle

malvivir *vi* to be needy, to live under difficult circumstances

malandrín,-a *nmf* scoundrel

malasombra *nmf* person with brusque or poor manners

malcriado,-a *nmf* brat; spoiled child

maldiciente *nmf* [-ente(2)] one who curses

maleante *nmf* [-ante(2)] fugitive from the law; rogue; immoral person

maleducado,-a *nmf* uncouth person; one who lacks manners

malgastador,-a *nmf* spendthrift

malhablado,-a *nmf* foul-mouthed person; blasphemer; shameless person

malhechor,-a *nmf* criminal

malicioso,-a *nmf* malicious person

malintencionado,-a *nmf* ill-intentioned person

malo,-a *nmf* bad person

malpensado,-a *nmf* pessimist

malvado,-a *nmf* evildoer

malversador,-a *nmf* government official who misspends money appropriated for another purpose; embezzler

mal *nm* evil

maleficio *nm* curse; spell

malentendido *nm* misunderstanding

malestar *nm* [3948] feeling of illness

malhumor *nm* bad mood

maltrato *nm* [-o(1) 4822] mistreatment

malandanza *nf* [-anza] misfortune

maldad *nf* evil

maldición *nf* curse

maledicencia *nf* cursing

malevolencia *nf* malevolence

malformación *nf* malformation

malicia *nf* [-icia] malice

malignidad *nf* malignity

malquerencia *nf* ill-will

malversación *nf* misappropriation of funds

mal *av* bad

malamente *av* [-mente] badly

mal *aj* bad

malacostumbrado *aj* having the bad habit of

malandrín *aj* [-ín] bad, wicked, criminal; acting like a scoundrel

malcarado *aj* irritable; with an angry-looking face

malcasado *aj* separated or divorced

malcriado *aj* spoiled

maldiciente *aj* [-ente(2)] cursing

maldito *aj* damned; evil

maleante *aj* [-ante(2)] immoral; criminal

maleducado *aj* rude

maléfico *aj* damaging

malévolo *aj* malevolent

malgastador *aj* [-dor(1)] misspending

malhablado *aj* foul-mouthed; shameless; blaspheming

malhadado *aj* unfortunate person

malhechor *aj* delinquent

malhumorado *aj* ill-humored

malicioso *aj* malicious

maligno *aj* malignant

malintencionado *aj* ill-intentioned

malmirado *aj* badly thought of

malo *aj* [234] bad

malogrado *aj* failed

maloliente *aj* bad-smelling

malpensado *aj* negative thinking

malsano *aj* unhealthy

malsonante *aj* bad-sounding

maltrecho *aj* unkempt

malvado *aj* evil

malversador *aj* [-dor(1)] fraudulent; embezzling

mamá mom, mother

amamantar *vt* to breast-feed; to nurse (a baby)

mamar *vt* to suckle; to drink from breast or bottle

amamantamiento *nm* nursing

mama *nf* [-a 4988] mammary gland

mamá *nf* [967] mom, mother

mamada *nf* sucking of the breast

mamario *aj* mammary

mancha stain

manchar *vt* to stain

mancharse *vr* to become stained

mancillar *vt* to stain; to dishonor

mancillarse *vr* to become stained; to become dishonored

manchón *nm* [-ón(3)] big stain

quitamanchas *nm* stain remover

mancha *nf* [-a 2816] stain

mancilla *nf* dishonor

manchado *aj* stained

mancillado *aj* dirty; with stains; dishonored

mandar to send; to order

comandar *vt* [3334] to command

desmandarse *vr* to exaggerate; to go over the line; to lose control over oneself

mandar *vt* [1236] to send; to order

comandante *nmf* [-ante(2) 1884] commander

mandado,-a *nmf* one who is sent to carry out an order

mandatario,-a *nmf* governor

mandón,-a *nmf* one who likes to give orders; bossy person

comando *nm* [-o(1) 4503] military commando

mandado *nm* grocery shopping

mandamiento *nm* commandment

mandato *nm* [3435] mandate

mando *nm* [-o(1) 2175] authority

comandancia *nf* headquarters; office of the commander

desmandado *aj* disobedient to orders

mandón *aj* [-ón(2)] bossy

manejar to manage; to drive

manejar *vt* [883] to manage; to drive

manejarse *vr* to manage oneself

manejo *nm* [-o(1) 1335] managing; driving

manejabilidad *nf* manageability

manejable *aj* manageable

manera manner, way

manera *nf* [157] manner, way

sobremanera *av* excessively

manga sleeve

arremangar *vt* to roll up sleeves

arremangarse *vr* to roll up one's sleeves

remangar *vt* to pull up sleeves

bocamanga *nf* cuff

manga *nf* sleeve

manía mania

maníaco,-a *nmf* maniac

maníacodepresivo,-a *nmf* person with manic-depression, person with bipolar disorder

manía *nf* mania

maníaco *aj* maniacal

maniacodepresivo *aj* manic-depressive

manifestar to manifest, to show

manifestar *vt* [316] to manifest, to show

manifestarse *vr* [316] to manifest oneself, to show oneself

manifestante *nmf* [-ante(2) 2939] demonstrator

manifiesto *nm* manifesto

manifestación *nf* [-ción 1725] demonstration

manifestador *aj* demonstrating

manifiesto *aj* manifest, evident

mano hand

maniobrar *vti* to maneuver

manosear *vt* to finger; to put one's hands in something; to paw

manotear *vti* to flail; to gesticulate

manufacturar *vt* [4823] to manufacture

manicuro,-a *nmf* manicurist

manipulador,-a *nmf* manipulator

besamanos *nm* kiss of the hand (usually in a royal setting)

lavamanos *nm* sink

mango *nm* handle of a tool

manipuleo *nm* manipulation

manojo *nm* bunch

manoseo *nm* fingering; picking with hands or fingers (e.g., food); pawing

manotazo *nm* hit with the hand

manoteo *nm* exaggerated gesture; flailing

manual *nm* [4654] manual

manubrio *nm* handle

manuscrito *nm* manuscript

manicura *nf* [-ura(2)] manicure

manija *nf* tool handle; furniture handles

manilla *nf* bracelet; handle

maniobra *nf* [-a 3387] maneuver

maniobrabilidad *nf* maneuverability

manipulación *nf* manipulation

mano *nf* [299] hand

manopla *nf* mitten

manufactura *nf* manufacture

manilargo *aj* with long hands

maniobrable *aj* maneuverable

manipulador *aj* manipulating

manoseado *aj* over-handled

manual *aj* [4654] manual

manufacturado *aj* manufactured

manufacturero *aj* [-ero(2) 4704] manufacturing

manuscrito *aj* manuscript

manto cover

mantel *nm* tablecloth

manto *nm* [4989] cover

mantón *nm* shawl

salvamanteles *nm* placemat

manta *nf* [4852] blanket

mantelería *nf* table linen

manteleta *nf* [-eta] short cape for covering the shoulders

mantilla *nf* saddlecloth; scarf

mañana morning, tomorrow

mañana *nm* [335] future

mañana *nf* [335] morning, tomorrow

mañanita *nf* early morning

mañana *av* [335] in the morning

mañanero *aj* [-ero(2)] early morning

máquina machine

maquinar *vt* to work with a machine; to conspire

maquinizar *vt* to mechanize

mecanizar *vt* to mechanize

mecanografiar *vt* to type on a typewriter

maquinista *nmf* [-ista] machinist

mecánico,-a *nmf* [2135] mechanic

mecanógrafo,-a *nmf* typist

maquinismo *nm* mechanization process in general

mecanismo *nm* [-ismo 1882] mechanism

máquina *nf* [1739] machine

maquinación *nf* machination; intrigue, conspiracy

maquinaria *nf* [3143] machinery

maquinización *nf* mechanization

mecánica *nf* mechanics

mecanización *nf* mechanization

mecanografía *nf* typing

maquinal *aj* mechanical

mecánico *aj* mechanical

mar sea

amarar *vi* to land at sea (seaplane)

marear *vt* to make dizzy

marearse *vr* to become dizzy

marinero,-a *nmf* sailor

marino,-a *nmf* marine

submarinista *nmf* submarine sailor

amaraje *nm* sea landing

cazasubmarinos *nm* destroyer

mar *nm* [1459] sea

mareaje *nm* art of navigation

maremoto *nm* earthquake under the ocean floor

mareo *nm* dizziness

marisco *nm* seafood

submarinismo *nm* submarine technology

submarino *nm* submarine

ultramar *nm* overseas

marea *nf* tide

marejada *nf* high sea; swell

marina *nf* [-ina 2570] navy; coast

marinería *nf* seamanship; profession of a sailor

marisquería *nf* seafood store

mareado *aj* dizzy

mareante *aj* dizzying

marinero *aj* [-ero(3)] naval; navy

marino *aj* [-ino(2) 3811] marine; sea; seagoing

marítimo *aj* maritime

submarino *aj* submarine
ultramarino *aj* overseas

maravilloso marvelous
maravillar *v* to be marvelous
maravillarse *vr* to be surprised or amazed
maravilla *nf* [-a 3459] marvel
maravillosamente *av* marvelously
maravilloso *aj* [-oso 2600] marvelous

marcar to mark
demarcar *vt* to delimit
marcar *vt* [786] to mark
remarcar *vt* to mark again; to redial; to remark
marcador *nm* [-dor(2) 1084] marker; scoreboard
marcapasos *nm* heart pacemaker
demarcación *nf* demarcation
marca *nf* [-a 833] mark
marcadamente *av* markedly
marcado *aj* marked
marcador *aj* [-dor(2) 1084] marking; useful for marking
remarcable *aj* remarkable

marchar to march; to run (machine); to be on the move
marchar *vi* [2850] to march; to run (machine); to be on the move
marcharse *vr* [2850] to go away
marcha *nf* [-a 854] march

marco frame
enmarcar *vt* to frame
marco *nm* [392] frame

margen margin
marginar *vt* [3784] to put margins
margen *nm* [2107] margin
margen *nf* [2107] edge
marginal *aj* marginal; pertaining to the margin or edge of something

marido husband
marido *nm* [-ido(2) 2023] husband
marital *aj* marital

mármol marble
marmolista *nmf* one who works with marble
mármol *nm* marble
marmolería *nf* workshop where marble is worked; large amount of marble
marmóreo *aj* marble; of marble

martillo hammer
amartillar *vt* to hammer
martillar, martillear *vt* to hammer
martillazo *nm* [-azo(2)] hit with a hammer
martilleo *nm* hammering
martillo *nm* hammer
martinete *nm* mallet

martirio martyrdom
martirizar *vt* to martyr; to torture
mártir *nmf* [4611] martyr
martirizador,-a *nmf* one who tortures or does the killing of a martyr
martirio *nm* martyrdom
martirizador *aj* martyring; torturing

matar to kill
matar *vt* [1213] to kill
matarse *vr* to kill oneself (also, figurative); to commit suicide
matasanos *nmf* quack
matachín *nm* butcher
matadero *nm* slaughterhouse
matador *nm* [-dor(1) 4419] bullfighter
matamoscas *nm* flyswatter
matarratas *nm* rat poison
matasellos *nm* stamp used to cancel stamps; postmark
matanza *nf* [-anza 3812] massacre; slaughter
matador *aj* [-dor(1) 4419] bullfighting

matemático mathematics
matemático,-a *nmf* mathematician
matemáticas *nfpl* mathematics
matemática *nf* mathematics
matemáticamente *av* mathematically
matemático *aj* mathematical

material material
materializar *vt* to materialize, to make real
materializarse *vr* to become materialized, to become real
materialista *nmf* [-ista 4525] materialistic person
material *nm* [543] material
materialismo *nm* [-ismo] materialism
antimateria *nf* anti-matter
materia *nf* [739] matter
materialidad *nf* materiality
materialización *nf* materialization
inmaterial *aj* immaterial
material *aj* [543] material
materialista *aj* [-ista 4525] materialistic

matiz combination of colors, matching
matizar *vt* to combine colors
matiz *nm* combination of colors, matching
matización *nf* combining of colors

matricular to matriculate; to enroll; to register
matricular *vt* to matriculate; to enroll; to register
matricularse *vr* to be matriculated; to be enrolled
matrícula *nf* proof of registration or enrollment
matriculación *nf* matriculation; registration

máximo maximum
máximo *nm* [746] maximum
máxima *nf* maxim, precept
máximo *aj* [746] maximum

mayor the oldest; adult; military major
mayorista *nmf* wholesaler
mayor *nm* [114] the oldest; adult; military major
mayoral *nm* shepherd; one who looks after a flock or herd
mayorazgo *nm* [-azgo] primogeniture, rights of the firstborn
mayordomo *nm* butler
mayoría *nf* [-ería(2) 410] majority
mayúscula *nf* capital letter
mayor *aj* [114] older; bigger
mayorista *aj* wholesale
mayoritario *aj* majority
mayúsculo *aj* capital, referring to letters

medalla medal
medallista *nmf* medalist
medallón *nm* medallion
medalla *nf* [2050] medal

medicina medicine
medicar *vt* to medicate
medicarse *vr* to be medicated
medicinar *vt* to medicate
médico,-a *nmf* physician, doctor
medicamento *nm* [1803] medicine
medicación *nf* medication
medicina *nf* [1476] medicine
medicamentoso *aj* medicinal
medicinal *aj* medicinal
médico *aj* [-o(3) 343] medical

medida measure; measurement
medir *vt* [1571] to measure
altímetro *nm* altimeter
diámetro *nm* diameter
fotómetro *nm* light meter
gasómetro *nm* gas meter
metro *nm* [569] meter
metrónomo *nm* metronome
parámetro *nm* [4571] parameter
radiómetro *nm* radiometer
velocímetro *nm* speedometer
asimetría *nf* asymmetry
geometría *nf* geometry
medida *nf* [-ido(2) 369] measure; measurement
simetría *nf* symmetry
diametralmente *av* diametrically
asimétrico *aj* asymmetric
desmedido *aj* excessive; limitless
diametral *aj* diametrical
medidor *aj* measuring

métrica *aj* metric
simétrico *aj* symmetrical

medieval medieval
medievalista *nmf* medievalist
medievalismo *nm* medievalism
medievo *nm* Middle Ages
medieval *aj* medieval

medio half
mediar *vi* [2303] to arrive at the half-way point
mediante *prep* [795] through; by way of
inmediaciones *nmpl* immediate surroundings
intermediario,-a *nmf* intermediary
mediador,-a *nmf* mediator
intermediario *nm* [-ario(2) 4632] intermediary
intermedio *nm* [3509] intermission; half-time
medio *nm* [112] half
media *nf* socks that are worn at the knee; stockings
mediación *nf* mediation
medialuna *nf* half-moon shaped object
mediana *nf* medium
medianía *nf* medium position
medianoche *nf* midnight
mediocridad *nf* mediocrity
mediodía *nf* [3128] noon
entremedias *av* in between
inmediatamente *av* [-mente 2516] immediately
medio *av* [112] half; partly
inmediato *aj* [760] immediate
intermediario *aj* [-ario(2) 4632] intermediary
intermedio *aj* [3509] intermediate
mediado *aj* half-full
medianero *aj* intervening; middle; dividing
mediano *aj* [1857] medium
medio *aj* [112] half
mediocre *aj* mediocre

meditar to meditate
meditar *vti* to meditate
meditación *nf* meditation
premeditación *nf* premeditation
premeditadamente *av* premeditatedly
impremeditado *aj* unpremeditated
meditabundo *aj* [-undo] thoughtful
meditativo *aj* [-ivo] meditative
premeditado *aj* premeditated

médula marrow or pith
médula *nf* marrow, pith (also figurative)
medular *aj* pertaining to marrow or pith

mejor better
desmejorar *vi* to worsen
desmejorarse *vr* to become worse; to become sick
mejorar *vt* [642] to improve

mejorarse *vr* [642] to improve oneself; to become improved

mejoramiento *nm* [-miento 3027] improvement

mejora *nf* [-a 3211] improvement

mejoría *nf* [-ería(2) 4194] improvement

mejor *av* [94] better

inmejorable *aj* not improvable

mejor *aj* [94] better

mejorable *aj* improvable

melancolía melancholy

melancólico,-a *nmf* person suffering from melancholy

melancolía *nf* melancholy

melancólico *aj* melancholy

memoria memory

conmemorar *vt* [3413] commemorate

memorizar *vt* [-izar] to memorize

rememorar *vt* to remember, used formally

memorión,-a *nmf* memory expert; person with an excellent memory

memorándum, memorando *nm* memorandum

memorial *nm* memorial

memorión *nm* [-ón(3)] excellent memory

conmemoración *nf* commemoration

memoria *nf* [1860] memory

memorización *nf* memorization

remembranza *nf* remembrance

rememoración *nf* formal remembering

conmemorativo *aj* commemorative

desmemoriado *aj* forgetful

inmemorial *aj* immemorial

memorable *aj* [4080] memorable

memorión *aj* [-ón(3)] possessing an excellent memory

mencionado mentioned

mencionar *vt* [322] to mention

mención *nf* [-ción 2509] mention

mencionado *aj* mentioned

mendigo beggar

mendigar *vti* to beg

mendigo,-a *nmf* beggar

mendicidad *nf* begging

menos less; fewer

menoscabar *vt* to discredit

menospreciar *vt* to disdain, to scorn, to despise

menos *prep* [171] except

menor *nmf* [411] minor; youngest; younger

menos *nm* [171] minus sign

menoscabo *nm* discrediting

menosprecio *nm* disdain, scorn

menos *av* [171] less; fewer

menor *aj* [411] younger

menospreciable *aj* despicable

mensaje message

mensajero,-a *nmf* messenger

mensaje *nm* [1223] message

mensajero *aj* [-ero(3)] pertaining to messages

mente mind

mentecato,-a *nmf* fool, idiot

mentalidad *nf* [-idad 4494] mentality

mente *nf* [1557] mind

mentalmente *av* [-mente] mentally

mental *aj* [-al(2) 1814] mental

mentecato *aj* foolish

mentir to lie

desmentir *vt* [3818] to discover a lie

mentir *vi* [3696] to lie

mentiroso,-a *nmf* liar

mentira *nf* [2835] lie

mentiroso *aj* [-oso] lying

mercado market

mercadear *vi* to buy or sell; to participate in a market

mercader *nmf* merchant

mercantilista *nmf* mercantilist

hipermercado *nm* supermarket

mercado *nm* [290] market

mercantilismo *nm* mercantilism

supermercado *nm* supermarket

mercadería *nf* participation in a market

mercadotecnia *nf* marketing

mercancía *nf* [2290] merchandise

mercante *aj* merchant

mercantil *aj* mercantile

mercantilista *aj* mercantilist

meridional southern

meridiano *nm* meridian

meridiano *aj* meridian

meridional *aj* southern

mérito merit

ameritar *vt* to deserve

desmerecer *vt* to be undeserving

merecer *vti* [1668] to deserve

merecerse *vr* to be deserving of

demérito *nm* demerit

desmerecimiento *nm* undeserving

merecido *nm* just reward; just desert

merecimiento *nm* condition of being deserving

mérito *nm* [-ito(2) 3270] merit

meritocracia *nf* meritocracy

inmerecidamente *av* undeservedly

merecidamente *av* deservedly

ameritado *aj* merited, deserved

benemérito *aj* worthy of honor

inmerecido *aj* unmerited, undeserved

merecedor *aj* meriting, deserving

merecido *aj* merited, deserved
meritorio *aj* [-orio(2)] meritorious
mesa table
mesa *nf* [993] table
mesilla *nf* [-illa] small table
sobremesa *nf* after-dinner conversation
metal metal
metalizar *vt* to cover something in metal
metalista *nmf* metal worker
metalúrgico,-a *nmf* expert in metals
metal *nm* [3183] metal
metaloide *nm* metalloid; a non-metal that can form an alloy when combined with a metal
metalización *nf* covering with metal
metalurgia *nf* metallurgy
metálico *aj* [-ico(2) 3848] metallic
metalúrgico *aj* metallurgic; pertaining to metallurgy
meter to insert
entremeter *vt* to insert something between things
entrometerse *vr* to intrude; to interfere with other people's business
meter *vt* [1140] to insert
meterse *vr* [1140] to insert oneself; to go inside
someter *vt* [1333] to submit
someterse *vr* to submit oneself
entrometido,-a *nmf* busybody
sometimiento *nm* submission
entrometido *aj* meddlesome; nosy
método method
metodizar *vt* to methodize, to systematize
método *nm* [2037] method, system
metodología *nf* methodology
metódico *aj* methodical
metodológico *aj* methodological
metrópoli metropolis
metrópoli *nf* metropolis
metropolitano *aj* [3559] metropolitan
mezclar to mix
entremezclar *vt* to mix in with other things
mezclar *vt* [2585] to mix
mezclarse *vr* to be mixed; to be involved
mezclador,-a *nmf* one who mixes
mezcla *nf* [-a 1958] mixture
mezcladora *nf* [-dor(2)] mixing machine, mixer
mezcolanza *nf* strange mixture
miedo fear
amedrentar *vt* to put fear into someone, to provoke fear
medroso,-a *nmf* person who is afraid
miedoso,-a *nmf* person who is afraid
miedo *nm* [1641] fear

mieditis *nf* fear
medroso *aj* causing fear, provoking fear
miedoso *aj* fearful, afraid
miel honey
aguamiel *nm* mixture of honey and water
melaza *nf* molasses
melcocha *nf* honey-like paste made of sugar
melosidad *nf* sweetness
miel *nf* [2238] honey
melado *aj* honey-colored
meloso *aj* honey-like
mil thousand
mil *nm* [69] thousand
milenario *nm* millennium
milésimo *nm* [-ésimo] one-thousandth (fraction)
miligramo *nm* milligram
mililitro *nm* milliliter
milímetro *nm* millimeter
millar *nm* group or package of one thousand
mil *aj* [69] thousand
milenario *aj* millennial
milésimo *aj* [-ésimo] thousandth
milagro miracle
milagro *nm* [2940] miracle
milagroso *aj* [-oso] miraculous
militar to serve in the military
desmilitarizar *vt* to demilitarize
militar *vi* [571] to serve in the military
militarizar *vt* to militarize
militante *nmf* [-ante(2) 1747] militant
militarista *nmf* militarist
miliciano *nm* soldier in the militia
militar *nm* [571] soldier
militarismo *nm* militarism
desmilitarización *nf* demilitarization
milicia *nf* militia
miliciana *nf* woman soldier in the militia
militancia *nf* [-ancia 4940] militancy
militarización *nf* militarization
miliciano *aj* pertaining to the militia
militante *aj* [-ante(2) 1747] militant
militar *aj* [571] military
militarista *aj* militarist
paramilitar *aj* [4340] paramilitary
millón million
millonario,-a *nmf* millionaire
millón *nm* [106] million
millonésimo *nm* [-ésimo] one-millionth (fraction)
millonada *nf* [-ada(1)] several million
millonario *aj* [2941] millionaire
millonésimo *aj* [-ésimo] millionth
minero miner
desmineralizar *vt* to demineralize

minar *vt* to mine; to place explosive mines
mineralizar *vt* to mineralize
mineralizarse *vr* to become mineralized
minero,-a *nmf* miner; one who places explosive mines
mineral *nm* [2994] mineral
desmineralización *nf* demineralization
mina *nf* [-a 4721] mine
mineralización *nf* mineralization
mineralogía *nf* mineralogy
minería *nf* mining
minador *aj* mining
mineral *aj* [2994] mineral
mineralógico *aj* mineralogical
minero *aj* [-ero(2) 2824] pertaining to mining

mínimo minimal
miniaturizar *vt* to miniaturize
minimizar *vt* to minimize
miniaturista *nmf* miniaturist
mínimo,-a *nmf* smallest, least, or lowest of something
minusválido,-a *nmf* handicapped person
mínimo *nm* [995] minimum
miniatura *nf* miniature
minifalda *nf* miniskirt
minucia *nf* minutiae
minuciosidad *nf* meticulousness
minúscula *nf* lower-case letter
mínimo *aj* [995] minimal
minucioso *aj* meticulous
minúsculo *aj* [-culo] tiny
minusválido *aj* handicapped

ministro minister
administrar *vt* [3097] to administrate
administrarse *vr* to be administrated
administrador,-a *nmf* [3123] administrator
administrativo,-a *nmf* administrator
ministerio *nm* [770] ministry
ministro *nm* [-o(1) 897] minister
administración *nf* [-ción 467] administration
administrador *aj* administrating
administrativo *aj* [-ivo 1350] administrative
ministerial *aj* [1209] ministerial

minuto minute
minutero *nm* minute hand
minuto *nm* [-uto 200] minute

mío mine
mí *pron* me
mío,-a *pron* mine
mío *aj* [2317] mine

mira sight of a gun or instrument
admirar *vt* [2651] to admire
admirarse *vr* to be amazed

mirar *vt* [1041] to look
mirarse *vr* to look at oneself; to see oneself
remirar *vt* to review carefully
admirador,-a *nmf* [3069] admirer
mirón,-a *nmf* curious person
admirativo *nm* [-ivo] exclamation point
mirador *nm* lookout
miramiento *nm* examination; respectful dealings
admiración *nf* [-ción 4029] admiration
mira *nf* [-a] sight of a gun or instrument
mirada *nf* [2765] look
admirable *aj* admirable
admirador *aj* admiring
admirativo *aj* [-ivo] admirable; amazing
malmirado *aj* badly thought of
mirado *aj* observed
mirón *aj* [-ón(2)] curious

misa mass
misal *nm* [-al(1)] annual liturgical book of masses; missal
misa *nf* [1438] mass

miserable miserable
miserable *nmf* miserable or destitute person
conmiseración *nf* commiseration
miseria *nf* [4337] misery
misericordia *nf* mercy
miserable *aj* miserable; bad or perverse
misericordioso *aj* merciful
mísero *aj* poor, unfortunate

misión mission
misionero,-a *nmf* missionary
misión *nf* [1691] mission
misionero *aj* missionary

mismo same
mismo,-a *pron* same
mismo *av* [56] same
mismo *aj* [56] same

místico mystic
mistificar *vt* [-ificar] to mystify
místico,-a *nmf* mystic
misterio *nm* [3622] mystery
misticismo *nm* mysticism
mística *nf* mysticism
mistificación *nf* mystification
misterioso *aj* [-oso] mysterious
místico *aj* mystical

mito myth
mito *nm* [3684] myth
mitología *nf* mythology
mítico *aj* mythical
mitológico *aj* mythological

mixto mixed
mixto *nm* [4613] mixture
mixtura *nf* mixture
mixto *aj* [4613] mixed

modelo model
modelar *vt* to model
modelarse *vr* to model oneself
remodelar *vt* to remodel
aeromodelista *nmf* airplane model builder
modelista *nmf* model designer; mold maker
modelo *nmf* [-o(1) 800] model
modisto,-a *nmf* women's clothing designer
aeromodelismo *nm* airplane model building
aeromodelo *nm* airplane model
modelado *nm* model building process; clay or wax model
modelo *nm* [-o(1) 800] model
remodelación *nf* [-ción 4404] remodeling
aeromodelista *aj* pertaining to airplane model building
modelador *aj* modeling; shaping
modelo *aj* [-o(1) 800] model

moderno modern
modernizar *vt* [-izar 3849] to modernize
modernizarse *vr* to become modernized
modernista *nmf* modernist
modernismo *nm* modernism
modernidad *nf* [-idad 4827] modernity
modernización *nf* [-ción 2543] modernization
modernamente *av* modernly
modernista *aj* modern; fashionable
moderno *aj* [1660] modern
ultramoderno *aj* ultramodern

modesto modest
modesto,-a *nmf* modest person
inmodestia *nf* immodesty
modestia *nf* modesty
inmodestamente *av* immodestly
inmodesto *aj* immodest
modesto *aj* [4446] modest

modificar to modify
modificar *vt* [1723] to modify
modificación *nf* [-ción 1946] modification
modificable *aj* modifiable
modificador *aj* modifying

modo manner, way, custom
modales *nmpl* behavioral norms; manners
modo *nm* [1070] manner, way, custom
moda *nf* [2132] fashion, custom
modalidad *nf* [2885] modality, form, manner
modal *aj* pertaining to manners or customs; pertaining to grammatical modes
modoso *aj* civilized; well-behaved

molestar to bother
molestar *vt* [2836] to bother
molestarse *vr* to be bothered
molestia *nf* [2518] annoyance
molesto *aj* [2304] bothersome, annoying; annoyed, bothered

molino mill
moler *vt* [3008] to mill; to crush into tiny pieces
molturar *vt* to mill; to crush into powder
molinero,-a *nmf* mill worker
moledor *nm* cylinder used for crushing
molinete *nm* small or toy mill or windmill
molinillo *nm* hand mill
molino *nm* [-ino(1)] mill
molienda *nf* milling
molturación *nf* milling or crushing process
moledor *aj* milling
molido *aj* milled; crushed
molinero *aj* pertaining to mills or with milling

momento moment
momento *nm* [126] moment
momentáneo *aj* momentary

monarca monarch
monárquico,-a *nmf* monarchist
monarca *nm* [-arca 2150] monarch
monarquismo *nm* monarchism
monarquía *nf* monarchy
monárquico *aj* monarchic

moneda coin
monetarista *nmf* monetarist
monedero *nm* coin purse
monetario *nm* [2524] organized coin collection
monetarismo *nm* monetarism
portamonedas *nm* coin purse or container
moneda *nf* [2277] coin
monetario *aj* [2524] monetary
monetarista *aj* monetarist

monja nun
monacato *nm* monastic order
monaguillo *nm* assistant to a priest
monasterio *nm* monastery
monje *nm* monk
monja *nf* nun
monástico *aj* monastic
monjil *aj* [-il] pertaining to nuns

monstruo monster
monstruo *nm* monster
monstruosidad *nf* monstrosity
monstruo *aj* monster
monstruoso *aj* monstrous

montar to mount
desmontar *vt* to dismount

montar *vt* [1250] to mount; to climb
montarse *vr* to mount (oneself)
remontar *vr* [3698] to remount
montacargas *nm* lift; freight elevator
monta *nf* mounting
montadura *nf* saddle
montura *nf* mount; animal one mounts
montado *aj* mounted

monte mount
amontonar *vt* to pile
amontonarse *vr* to become piled up
montañero,-a *nmf* mountaineer; mountain climber
montañés *nmf* [-és] mountain man or woman
amontonamiento *nm* piling up
montañismo *nm* mountaineering; mountain climbing
monte *nm* [4480] mount; mountain
montículo *nm* small mountain
montón *nm* [4655] a large pile; a large amount
montaña *nf* [2537] mountain
amontonado *aj* piled
montañés *aj* [-és] relating to mountains
montañoso *aj* mountainous

monumento monument
monumento *nm* [3204] monument
monumental *aj* [4941] monumental

morada house, residence
morador,-a *nmf* inhabitant, resident
morada *nf* house, residence

moral moral
desmoralizar *vt* to demoralize; to corrupt
moralizar *vt* to moralize
moralista *nmf* moralist
moralismo *nm* moralism
amoralidad *nf* amorality
desmoralización *nf* demoralization
inmoralidad *nf* immorality
moral *nf* [541] moral
moraleja *nf* moral of a story
moralidad *nf* morality
moralización *nf* moralization
inmoralmente *av* immorally
amoral *aj* amoral
desmoralizador *aj* demoralizing
inmoral *aj* immoral
moral *aj* [541] moral
moralista *aj* moralistic

morder to bite
amordazar *vt* to gag
morder *vt* to bite
morderse *vr* to bite oneself
mordisquear *vt* to nibble

mordisco *nm* [-isco] nibble
mordaza *nf* gag
mordedura *nf* biting
mordida *nf* [-ido(2)] bite; bribe
mordedor *aj* [-dor(1)] biting

morir to die
amortajar *vt* to cover with a shroud
inmortalizar *vt* to immortalize
inmortalizarse *vr* to be immortalized
morir *vi* [565] to die
morirse *vr* [565] to die; to be dying to (do something, go somewhere, etc.)
mortificar *vt* [-ificar] to mortify
mortificarse *vr* to be mortified
inmortal *nmf* an immortal
mortal *nmf* [3968] mortal
muerto,-a *nmf* [784] dead person
amortajamiento *nm* act of covering with a shroud
inmortalidad *nf* immortality
mortaja *nf* shroud
mortalidad *nf* mortality
mortandad *nf* mortality rate, death rate; count of the dead in a war or other disaster
mortificación *nf* mortification
muerte *nf* [485] death
inmortal *aj* immortal
mortal *aj* [3968] mortal
mortífero *aj* [-ifero] deadly, lethal
mortuorio *aj* [-orio(2)] mortuary
muerto *aj* dead

mostrar to show
mostrar *vt* [366] to show
mostrarse *vr* [366] to show oneself
mostrador *nm* showcase
muestrario *nm* sales catalog
muestreo *nm* sampling; analytic sampling
muestra *nf* [-a 811] example; sample

motivo reason
motivar(se) *vt(r)* [2141] to motivate
motivo *nm* [-o(1) 476] reason
motivación *nf* [-ción 3981] motivation
inmotivado *aj* unmotivated

motor motor
motorizar *vt* to motorize
motorizarse *vr* to become motorized
motociclista *nmf* motorcyclist
motorista *nmf* motorist
automotor *nm* engine (railroad)
ciclomotor *nm* motorized bicycle
motocarro *nm* three-wheeled motorcycle
motociclismo *nm* motorcycling
motocross *nm* motocross

motocultivo *nm* mechanized agriculture
motor *nm* [2544] motor
motorismo *nm* motorized sport
locomoción *nf* locomotion
locomotora *nf* locomotive
moto *nf* [4338] motorcycle
motocicleta *nf* [4745] motorcycle
motonáutica *nf* motorboat racing
motonave *nf* motorized boat or ship
motora *nf* small boat with a motor
motosierra *nf* chainsaw
automotor *aj* motorized
locomotor *aj* locomotive
motonáutico *aj* pertaining to motorboat racing
motor *aj* [2544] motor
motorizado *aj* motorized

mover to move
conmover *vt* to move emotionally
conmoverse *vr* to be emotionally moved
desmovilizar *vt* to demobilize
inmovilizar *vt* to immobilize
mover *vt* [1463] to move
moverse *vr* [1463] to move oneself
movilizar *vt* [-izar 4963] to mobilize
remover(se) *vt(r)* [4364] to remove
automovilista *nmf* [-ista 2843] motorist
automóvil *nm* [1492] automobile
automovilismo *nm* motoring; automobile
  construction
movimiento *nm* [-miento 820] movement
desmovilización *nf* demobilization
inmovilidad *nf* immovability
inmovilización *nf* immobilization
movilidad *nf* mobility
movilización *nf* [-ción 2953] mobilization
automovilístico *aj* [-ico(2) 3677] pertaining to
  motoring or automobile construction
conmovedor *aj* moving (emotionally)
inconmovible *aj* imperturbable; emotionally
  unmovable
inmovible *aj* immovable
inmóvil *aj* immobile
inmovilizado *aj* immobilized; not moving
movible *aj* [-ible] movable
movedizo *aj* [-dizo] movable; easily moved;
  unstable
movido *aj* moved
móvil *aj* [-il 3652] mobile

mozo servant; entry-level worker; boy
mocerío *nm* young people
mozalbete *nm* young servant or boy
mozo *nm* servant; entry-level worker; boy
aeromoza *nf* flight attendant

mocedad *nf* youth
moza *nf* servant; maid; entry-level worker; girl
muchacho young man
muchacho,-a *nmf* [1560] young man or woman
muchachada *nf* [-ada(2)] group of boys or girls;
  immature behavior appropriate to boys or
  girls
muchachería *nf* group of boys or girls,
  especially a rebellious group; immature
  behavior appropriate to boys or girls
mucho much
mucho,-a *pron* a lot
muchedumbre *nf* [-dumbre] crowd; group of many
  people
mucho *av* [54] much
muchísimo *aj* [-ísimo] very much
mucho *aj* [54] a lot of; much
mudar to change or transform; to lose one's
  baby teeth
mudar *vti* to change or transform; to lose one's
  baby teeth
mudarse *vr* to move to another residence
muda *nf* changing or transformation; losing of
  one's baby teeth
mudanza *nf* [-anza] move to another residence
mudable *aj* [-able] changeable; transformable;
  variable
mudo mute
enmudecer *vt* to silence
enmudecerse *vr* to be silent
mudo.-a *nmf* mute
sordomudo,-a *nmf* deaf-mute
mutismo *nm* deliberate silence; intentional
  silence; forced silence
mudez *nf* muteness
mudo *aj* mute
sordomudo *aj* deaf-mute
mueble piece of furniture
amueblar *vt* to furnish
desamueblar *vt* to remove furniture
guardamuebles *nm* storage shed or warehouse
inmueble *nm* [2193] property or estate which
  cannot be moved
mueble *nm* [3120] piece of furniture; furnishing
mobiliario *nm* stage set; furniture
inmobiliaria *nf* house construction company
desamueblado *aj* unfurnished
mueble *aj* [3120] movable, referring to an object
inmobiliario *aj* pertaining to real estate
mujer woman; wife
mujeriego *nm* [-iego] philanderer
mujerío *nm* group of women
mujer *nf* [151] woman; wife

mujerona *nf* [-ón(3)] large woman
mujerzuela *nf* [-zuelo] bad woman; prostitute
supermujer *nf* superwoman
mujeriego *aj* [-iego] philandering

multiplicar to multiply
multiplicar *vt* [4547] to multiply
multiplicarse *vr* to be multiplied
multiplicador *nm* multiplier; factor in multiplication
multiplicando *nm* multiplicand; factor in multiplication
múltiplo *nm* multiple
multiplicación *nf* multiplication
multiplicidad *nf* multiplicity
múltiple *aj* [1842] multiple
multiplicable *aj* multipliable
multiplicador *aj* multiplying
múltiplo *aj* multiple

mundo world
mundano,-a *nmf* worldly person
mundial *nm* [-al(2) 230] world championship
mundillo *nm* one's personal world of acquaintances
mundo *nm* [165] world
mundialmente *av* world-wide
mundanal *aj* worldly
mundano *aj* worldly
mundial *aj* [-al(2) 230] world
tercermundista *aj* third-world

municipio municipality; city
municipalizar *vt* to convert a private service to a municipal service
municipio *nm* [178] municipality; city
municipalidad *nf* municipality
municipal *aj* [115] municipal

muñeca doll; wrist
muñeco *nm* [3830] male doll
muñeca *nf* doll; wrest
muñequera *nf* wristband

muro mural
amurallar *vt* to build a large wall
mural *nm* mural
muro *nm* [3773] wall
muralla *nf* large wall
extramuros *av* outside the city
intramuros *av* intramural
amurallado *aj* with or surrounded by large walls
mural *aj* mural; pertaining to walls

músculo muscle
músculo *nm* [-culo 3520] muscle
musculatura *nf* musculature

intramuscular *aj* intramuscular, within the muscle
muscular *aj* [3903] muscular, pertaining to muscles
musculoso *aj* muscular, having a lot of muscles

museo museum
museo *nm* [1597] museum
museología *nf* study of museums

música music
músico,-a *nmf* musician
musicólogo,-a *nmf* musicologist
musical *nm* [643] musical
música *nf* [285] music
musicalidad *nf* musicality
musicología *nf* musicology
musical *aj* [643] musical
músico *aj* musical

mutuo mutual
mutualista *nmf* member of a mutual aid organization
mutualidad *nf* mutuality
mutualista *aj* pertaining to mutuality
mutuo *aj* [-uo 4339] mutual

N

nacer to be born
desnacionalizar *vt* to denationalize
internacionalizar *vt* to internationalize
internacionalizarse *vr* to become internationalized
nacer *vi* [604] to be born
nacionalizar *vt* to nationalize
nacionalizarse *vr* to become nationalized
renacer *vi* to be reborn
nacionalista *nmf* nationalist
internacionalismo *nm* internationalism
nacido *nm* [-ido(2)] a newborn
nacimiento *nm* [-miento 1779] birth
nacionalismo *nm* [-ismo] nationalism
nacionalsocialismo *nm* national socialism
natalicio *nm* date of birth
renacimiento *nm* rebirth
Renacimiento *nm* Renaissance
desnacionalización *nf* denationalization
nación *nf* [-ción 622] nation
nacionalidad *nf* [-idad 4386] nationality
nacionalización *nf* nationalization
natalidad *nf* birth rate
natividad *nf* festivity to remember the birth of Jesus

internacionalmente *av* internationally

innato *aj* innate

internacional *aj* [253] international

multinacional *aj* multinational

nacido *aj* [-ido(2)] born; newborn

naciente *aj* [-ente(1)] new; recent

nacional *aj* [74] national

nacionalista *aj* nationalist

natal *aj* [3276] natal; native

natalicio *aj* pertaining to a date of birth

nativo *aj* [-ivo 4158] native

nato *aj* in-born; birth, esp. of qualities or defects present at birth

prenatal *aj* prenatal

nadar to swim

nadar *vi* to swim

sobrenadar *vi* to float

nadador,-a *nmf* swimmer

natación *nf* [-ción 3726] swimming

a nado *av* by swimming or floating

nariz nose

narigón,-a *nmf* big-nosed person

narigudo,-a *nmf* big-nosed person

nariz *nf* [3885] nose

narración narration

narrar *vt* [2166] to narrate

narrador,-a *nmf* narrator

narración *nm* narration

narrativa *nf* narrative

narrativo *aj* narrative

natural natural

desnaturalizar *vt* to take away the rights of citizenship

naturalizar *vt* [-izar] to naturalize

naturalizarse *vr* to become naturalized; to become a naturalized citizen

natural *nmf* [683] natural

naturalista *nmf* natural scientist; one who studies the natural sciences

naturalismo *nm* naturalism

naturismo *nm* medical philosophy that emphasizes natural means of maintaining health

desnaturalización *nf* the act of taking away the rights of citizenship

natura *nf* nature

naturaleza *nf* [-eza 1697] nature

naturalidad *nf* the quality of acting naturally or normally

naturalización *nf* naturalization

naturalmente *av* [-mente 4246] naturally

antinatural *aj* against nature, contrary to nature; not natural

connatural *aj* innate

desnaturalizado *aj* not having emotional closeness with or caring for one's family

natural *aj* [683] natural

naturalista *aj* pertaining to the medical philosophy that emphasizes natural means of maintaining health

sobrenatural *aj* supernatural

nave ship

naufragar *vi* to become shipwrecked

navegar *vt* to navigate

astronauta *nmf* astronaut

náufrago,-a *nmf* shipwrecked person

navegante *nmf* [-ante(2)] navigator

naviero,-a *nmf* seaman, especially those that sail the high seas

naufragio *nm* shipwreck

navío *nm* a very large ship

aeronáutica *nf* aeronautics

astronáutica *nf* science and technology of space voyages

astronave *nf* space ship

motonáutica *nf* motorboat racing

motonave *nf* motorboat

náusea *nf* nausea; sea sickness

náutica *nf* the art of navigation

nave *nf* [3019] ship

navegabilidad *nf* navigability

navegación *nf* navigation

aeronáutico *aj* aeronautic

aeronaval *aj* air-sea

motonáutico *aj* pertaining to motorboat racing

náufrago *aj* shipwrecked

nauseabundo *aj* [-undo] nausea-provoking

náutico *aj* nautical

naval *aj* [4798] naval

navegable *aj* [-able] navigable

navegante *aj* [-ante(2)] navigating

naviero *aj* naval

necesitar to need

necesitar *vt* [372] to need

necesitado,-a *nmf* needy person

neceser *nm* toiletry bag or case of necessary items

necesidad *nf* [-idad 453] necessity

innecesariamente *av* unnecessarily

innecesario *aj* [4610] unnecessary

necesario *aj* [294] necessary

necesitado *aj* needy

necio fool

necio,-a *nmf* fool

necedad *nf* foolishness

necio *aj* foolish

negar to deny

  denegar *vt* to deny or reject

  negar(se) *vt(r)* [830] to deny

  renegar *vi* to have a fit; to forcefully refuse

  renegado,-a *nmf* renegade; an ill-mannered person; a person who denies one's first religion and adopts another

  negativismo *nm* negativism

  reniego *nm* forceful ill-mannered refusal often using foul language; a rejection or blasphemy of God

  abnegación *nf* to put oneself at the service of others; self-denial

  denegación *nf* formal rejection

  negación *nf* denial

  negativa *nf* a negative charge

  abnegado *aj* self-denying

  innegable *aj* undeniable

  negado *aj* denied

  negativo *aj* [-ivo 1281] negative, pessimistic

  renegado *aj* renegade

negocio business

  negociante *nmf* [-ante(2)] negotiator; businessman or businesswoman

  negocio *nm* [-o(1) 595] business

  negociación *nf* [-ción 1057] negotiation

  negociable *aj* [-able] negotiable

negro black

  ennegrecer *vt* to blacken

  ennegrecerse *vr* to become black

  negrear *vt* to become black; to exploit a subordinate; to treat a subordinate cruelly

  negrero,-a *nmf* one who exploits subordinates; one who treats his subordinates cruelly

  negro,-a *nmf* dark-skinned man or woman

  negro *nm* [592] black

  negrura *nf* [-ura(1)] blackness

  negrero *aj* pertaining to black slavery; may be used to mean inhumane or cruel

  negro *aj* [592] black

  negroide *aj* Negroid

  negruzco *aj* [-usco] very dark, almost black

  renegrido *aj* very black

nervio nerve

  enervar *vt* to enervate

  neurólogo,-a *nmf* neurologist

  nervio *nm* [4656] nerve

  enervación *nf* enervation

  nerviosidad *nf* nervousness

  neurología *nf* neurology

  neurona *nf* neuron

  neurosis *nf* neurosis

  enervante *aj* enervating

  nervioso *aj* [-oso 2494] nervous

  nervudo *aj* sinewy

  neurótico *aj* neurotic

nido nest

  anidar *vi* to nest; to protect

  desanidar *vi* to leave the nest

  nidal *nm* [-al(1)] place where domesticated birds are kept; (figurative) place that one frequently goes to

  nido *nm* nest

  nidada *nf* a group of eggs in a nest that are about to hatch or have recently hatched

niebla misty cloud or fog

  neblina *nf* [-ina] fog

  nebulosa *nf* nebula

  nebulosidad *nf* cloudiness

  niebla *nf* misty cloud or fog

  nebuloso *aj* misty, foggy

nieto,-a grandchild

  biznieto,-a *nmf* great-grandchild

  nieto,-a *nmf* [2947] grandchild

  tataranieto,-a *nmf* great-great-grandchild

nieve snow, ice cream

  nevar *vi* [3933] to snow

  neviscar *vi* to snow lightly

  quitanieves *nm* snowplow

  aguanieve *nf* sleet

  Blancanieves *nf* Snow White

  nevada *nf* snowfall

  nevera *nf* ice cream container; ice chest

  nevisca *nf* snow flurry

  nieve *nf* [3342] snow, ice cream

  nevado *aj* [-ado(1)] having snow; with snow

  níveo *aj* snowy-white

niño,-a child

  aniñarse *vr* to become childlike; to act like a child

  niño,-a *nmf* [143] child

  niñada *nf* a childish action

  niñera *nf* nanny

  niñez *nf* [-ez 4318] childhood

  aniñado *aj* childlike

nivel level

  desnivelar *vt* to lean or tilt

  nivelar *vt* to level

  nivelador,-a *nmf* bulldozer

  desnivel *nm* incline, slope

  nivel *nm* [217] level

  desnivelación *nf* incline, slope

  nivelación *nf* leveling

  desnivelado *aj* leaning, inclined

  nivelador *aj* leveling

noble noble
ennoblecer *vt* to ennoble; to raise someone to the level of nobility
noble *nmf* [3423] nobleman
nobleza *nf* [-eza] nobility
noble *aj* [3423] noble

noche night
anochecer *vi* to begin the night
trasnochar *vi* to stay up all night
noctámbulo,-a *nmf* night person; night owl
trasnochador,-a *nmf* person who stays up all night
anochecer *nm* nightfall
anochecida *nf* nightfall
noche *nf* [295] night
nochebuena *nf* Christmas Eve
anoche *av* [2253] last night
anteanoche *av* night before last
nocturno *aj* [2510] nocturnal
trasnochado *aj* worn out from having stayed up all night
trasnochador *aj* having stayed up all night

nogal walnut tree
nogal *nm* [4144] walnut tree
nogueral *nm* walnut orchard
nogalina *nf* walnut color extracted from walnut shell

nombre name
denominar *vt* [1252] to denominate; to give a name to
nombrar *vt* [1928] to name to a post
nominar *vt* [2638] to nominate
denominador *nm* denominator (mathematics)
nombramiento *nm* [-miento 3302] the naming of someone to a position
nombre *nm* [262] name
nominativo *nm* nominative case
pronombre *nm* pronoun
renombre *nm* renown
sobrenombre *nm* nickname
denominación *nf* denomination
ignominia *nf* ignominy
nomenclatura *nf* nomenclature
nominación *nf* [-ción 3192] nomination
denominado *aj* denominated
denominador *aj* denominating
denominativo *aj* denominative (grammatical term)
ignominioso *aj* ignominious
innombrable *aj* unspeakable
innominado *aj* unnamed
nombrado *aj* named
nominal *aj* nominal

nominativo *aj* nominative
pronominal *aj* pertaining to a pronoun
renombrado *aj* renowned

norma norm
normalizar *vt* to normalize
normalizarse *vr* to become normal
anormalidad *nf* abnormality
norma *nf* [-a 3136] norm
normalidad *nf* normalness
normalización *nf* normalization
anormal *aj* abnormal
normal *aj* [1179] normal
normativo *aj* [-ivo 3934] normative
subnormal *aj* subnormal; below normal, often referring to intelligence
combatir *vti* [1574] to combat
combatiente *nmf* [-ente(2) 3961] combatant
combate *nm* [1081] combat
combatiente *aj* [-ente(2) 3961] combating
combativo *aj* combative
perturbar *vt* to perturb, to upset
perturbado,-a *nmf* disturbed person who does not have full use of mental faculties
perturbador,-a *nmf* disruptive person
perturbación *nf* disruption
imperturbable *aj* imperturbable
perturbado *aj* disturbed, lacking sense
perturbador *aj* perturbing, upsetting

norte north
norteño,-a *nmf* northerner
noreste *nm* [4586] north-east
noroeste *nm* [4683] north-west
norte *nm* [444] north
norteño *aj* [-eño 2861] northern

noticia news
anotar *vt* [720] to write down, to make note of
connotar *vt* to connote
denotar *vt* to denote
notar *vt* [2063] to notice
notarse *vr* to become noticed; to be apparent
notificar *vt* [3424] to notify
notario,-a *nmf* notary public
noticiero,-a *nmf* news reporter
notariado *nm* notary's office
noticiario *nm* news program
noticiero *nm* [-ero(2)] news program or report
anotación *nf* [-ción 1131] annotation
connotación *nf* connotation
denotación *nf* denotation
nota *nf* [-a 1520] note
notabilidad *nf* notability
notación *nf* notation

notaría *nf* notary, referring to the place where a notary public works

noticia *nf* [-a 1162] news

notición *nf* news flash; special news update

notificación *nf* [-ción 4548] notification

notoriedad *nf* notoriety

notable *aj* [-able 3311] notable

notorio *aj* [-orio(2) 4509] noticeable; well-known, not necessarily for negative reasons

novela novel, soap opera

novelar *vt* to novelize; to make into a novel

novelero,-a *nmf* person who loves to watch soap operas; person who loves to read novels

novelista *nmf* novelist

novela *nf* [2104] novel; soap opera

novelística *nf* novels or soap operas in general; novels or soap operas considered as a group

telenovela *nf* [992] soap opera; story made for television

novelero *aj* [-ero(2)] soap-opera loving

novelesco *aj* [-esco] pertaining to novels or soap operas

novelístico *aj* pertaining to novels or soap operas

novio groom

noviazgo *nm* [-azgo] courtship

novio *nm* groom; boyfriend

novios *npl* bride and groom; boyfriend and girlfriend

novia *nf* bride; girlfriend

nube cloud

nublar *v* to get cloudy

nublarse *vr* to become cloudy

nubarrón *nm* a big dark cloud

nublado *nm* [-ado(1)] (figurative) dark cloud (of life)

nube *nf* [4634] cloud

nubosidad *nf* cloudiness

nublado *aj* [-ado(1)] cloudy

nuboso *aj* cloudy

nuca part of the neck at the base of the skull, nape

desnucar *vt* to break the vertebrae of the neck

desnucarse *vr* to break the vertebrae of one's neck

nuca *nf* part of the neck at the base of the skull, nape

núcleo nucleus

núcleo *nm* [4588] nucleus

nuclear *aj* [3093] nuclear

nuestro our

nos *pron* [98] us

nosotros *pron* [359] we, us

nuestro,-a *pron* our

nuestro *aj* [93] our

nueve nine

diecinueve *nm* nineteen

diecinueveavo *nm* [-avo] one-nineteenth (fraction)

novecientos *nm* nine hundred

noveno *nm* [-eno 1771] one-ninth (fraction)

noventa *nm* [4510] ninety

noviembre *nm* [758] November

nueve *nm* [829] nine

diecinueve *aj* nineteen

diecinueveavo *aj* [-avo] nineteenth

novecientos *aj* nine-hundred

noveno *aj* [-eno 1771] ninth

noventa *aj* [4510] ninety

nueve *aj* [829] nine

nuevo new

innovar *vt* to innovate

renovar *vt* [2151] to renew

renovarse *vr* to become renewed

innovador,-a *nmf* innovator

novato,-a *nmf* beginner, neophyte; rookie; newcomer

renuevo *nm* renewal

innovación *nf* [-ción 3999] innovation

novatada *nf* initiation; a trick played on newcomers

novedad *nf* [3072] novelty

nueva *nf* the latest news

renovación *nf* [-ción 3249] renovation

nuevamente *av* [-mente 1471] newly

innovador *aj* innovative

novato *aj* [2485] beginner; beginning; rookie

novedoso *aj* [-oso 4854] new and different

nuevo *aj* [48] new

renovable *aj* renewable

número number

enumerar *vt* to enumerate

numerar *vt* to number

numerador *nm* numerator

numeral *nm* numeral

número *nm* [-o(1) 189] number

sinnúmero *nm* without number, countless

enumeración *nf* enumeration

numeración *nf* numbering

numeradora *nf* numerator

innumerablemente *av* innumerably

innumerable *aj* innumerable

numeral *aj* pertaining to numbers

numérico *aj* numeric

numeroso *aj* [-oso 1134] numerous

nutritivo nutritious
desnutrirse *vr* to become malnourished
nutrir *vt* [4511] to nourish
desnutrición *nf* malnutrition
nutrición *nf* [-ción 4145] nutrition
desnutrido *aj* malnourished
nutrido *aj* nourished; filled with
nutritivo *aj* [-ivo 4512] nutritious

O

obedecer to obey
desobedecer *vt* to disobey
obedecer *vti* [3327] to obey
desobediente *nmf* disobedient person
desobediencia *nf* disobedience
obediencia *nf* [-encia] obedience
desobediente *aj* disobedient
obediente *aj* obedient

obispo bishop
arzobispo *nm* [4692] archbishop
obispado *nm* office of the bishop
obispo *nm* [2318] bishop
arzobispal *aj* pertaining to the archbishop

objeción objection
objetar *vt* to object
objetor *nmf* one who objects; objector
objeción *nf* objection
objetante *aj* objecting

objeto objective
objetivo *nm* [584] objective
objeto *nm* [-o(1) 999] object
portaobjetos *nm* holder
teleobjetivo *nm* telephoto lens
objetividad *nf* objectivity
objetivo *aj* [584] objective

obligar to obligate
obligar *vt* [798] to obligate
obligarse *vr* to obligate oneself; to become
   obligated
obligación *nm* [-ción 1679] obligation
obligado *aj* obligated
obligatorio *aj* [-orio(2) 3654] obligatory

obra work
maniobrar *vt* to maneuver
obrar *vt* to work (metal, wood, etc.)
obrero,-a *nmf* [2094] worker
obrerismo *nm* [-ismo] worker class, social class of
   the worker; proletariat
maniobra *nf* [-a 3387] maneuver
maniobrabilidad *nf* maneuverability

obra *nf* [-a 211] work
maniobrable *aj* maneuverable
obrero *aj* working, referring to people

observar to observe
observar *vt* [769] to observe
observador,-a *nmf* observer
observatorio *nm* [-orio(1)] observatory
observación *nf* [-ción 3009] observation
observancia *nf* [-ancia] observance
observable *aj* observable
observador *aj* [-dor(1) 4285] observing

obsesión obsession
obsesionar *vt* to obsess
obsesionarse *vr* to become obsessed
obseso,-a *nmf* obsessive person
obsesión *nf* [-sión 4855] obsession
obsesivo *aj* obsessive
obseso *aj* obsessed

obstáculo obstacle
obstaculizar *vt* to block, to obstruct
obstinarse *vr* to become obstinate
obstruir *vt* [4775] to obstruct
obstruirse *vr* to become obstructed; to become
   blocked
obstáculo *nm* [-culo 2748] obstacle
obstinación *nf* obstinacy
obstrucción *nf* obstruction
no obstante *av* however; nevertheless
obstinado *aj* obstinate

ocasión occasion
ocasionar *vt* [1364] to cause or bring about
ocasión *nf* [-sión 303] occasion
ocasional *aj* occasional

occidente west
occidentalizar *vt* to westernize
ocaso *nm* sundown; setting of other
   astronomical object in the west
occidente *nm* [4876] west
occidental *aj* [3020] western

ocho eight
octogenario,-a *nmf* eighty-year-old person
decimoctavo *nm* [-avo] one-eighteenth (fraction)
dieciocho *nm* eighteen
ochenta *nm* [3982] eighty
ocho *nm* [561] eight
ochocientos,-as *nm* eight hundred
octágono *nm* octagon
octanaje *nm* level of octane
octano *nm* octane
octavo *nm* [-avo 1370] one-eighth (fraction)
octosílabo *nm* eight-syllable word or verse
octubre *nm* [694] October
octava *nf* octave

decimoctavo *aj* [-avo] eighteenth
ochenta *aj* [3982] eighty
ochocientos *aj* eight hundred
octagonal *aj* octagonal
octavo *aj* [-avo 1370] eighth
octogenario *aj* octogenarian
octosílabo *aj* eight-syllable

ocioso unemployed
ocioso,-a *nmf* unemployed person
ocio *nm* free-time activity, leisure time activity
ociosidad *nf* unemployment
ocioso *aj* unemployed

ocultar to hide; to conceal
ocultar *vt* [3038] to hide; to conceal
ocultarse *vr* [3038] to become hidden or concealed
ocultista *nmf* one who practices arts of the occult
ocultismo *nm* occult
ocultista *aj* pertaining to the occult
oculto *aj* [3727] belonging to the shadows; shadowed, so that it is not easily seen

ocupar to occupy
desocupar *vt* to free up
desocuparse *vr* to free up one's time
despreocuparse *vr* to be worry-free, to be carefree
ocupar *vt* [611] to occupy
ocuparse *vr* [611] to busy oneself
preocupar *vt* [1086] to cause concern or worry
preocuparse *vr* [1086] to worry
ocupante *nmf* [-ante(2) 4513] occupant
desocupación *nf* unemployment; vacancy
despreocupación *nf* state of being worry-free
ocupación *nf* [-ción 2878] occupation
preocupación *nf* [-ción 1569] worry
desocupado *aj* not busy
despreocupado *aj* not worried
ocupado *aj* busy
preocupado *aj* worried

ocurrirse to occur to oneself; to think of
ocurrirse *vr* to occur to oneself; to think of
ocurrencia *nf* an idea; a sudden thought
ocurrente *aj* witty

odio hate
odiar *vt* to hate
odio *nm* [-o(1) 3137] hate
odioso *aj* [-oso] hateful

ofender to offend
ofender *vt* [3636] to offend
ofenderse *vr* [3636] to become offended
ofensor,-a *nmf* offender
contraofensiva *nf* counter-offense

ofensa *nf* offense; insult
ofensiva *nf* offensive
inofensivo *aj* inoffensive
ofensivo *aj* [-ivo 1175] offensive
ofensor *aj* offending

oficio official
oficializar *vt* to make official
oficiar *vt* [4159] to officiate
oficinista *nmf* office-worker
oficial *nm* [-cial 415] official
oficio *nm* [-icio 2305] official
suboficial *nm* person below the rank of officer
oficina *nf* [-ina 625] office
extraoficial *aj* unofficial; unsanctioned
oficial *aj* [-cial 415] official
oficioso *aj* officious

ofrecer to offer
ofrecer *vt* [185] to offer
ofrecerse *vr* to offer oneself; to put oneself at the service of
ofrendar *vt* to make an offering
ofrecimiento *nm* [-miento 4228] offer
ofrenda *nf* offering of money

oír to hear
oír *vt* [2031] to hear
oyente *nmf* [-ente(2)] hearing
radioyente *nmf* radio listener
oído *nm* [-ido(2) 2942] ear, especially the inner ear
de oídas *av* by way of the grapevine

ojo eye
aojar *vt* to give the evil eye
anteojos *nmpl* eye-glasses
anteojo *nm* eye-glass
lavaojos *nm* container for washing out the eyes
ojo *nm* [991] eye
anteojera *nf* blinders for horses
ojera *nf* dark mark under the eyes
ojeroso *aj* having dark marks under the eyes

ola wave
oleaje *nm* waves in succession; swell
rompeolas *nm* breakwater; part of a boat that hits the waves
ola *nf* [2886] wave
oleada *nf* big wave

oler to smell
oler *vt* to smell
olfatear *vt* to sniff
olfateo *nm* sniffing
olfato *nm* sense of smell
olor *nm* [2391] smell; odor
maloliente *aj* bad-smelling
oloroso *aj* smelly; strong-smelling

olivo   olive tree
olivarero,-a *nmf*   olive farmer
olivar *nm*   olive orchard
olivo *nm* [-o(2)]   olive tree
oliva *nf*   olive
olivicultura *nf*   technique of harvesting olives
oliváceo *aj*   olive-colored
olivarero *aj*   pertaining to olive farming or selling

olvidar   to forget
olvidar *vt* [938]   to forget (in general)
olvidarse *vr* [938]   to be forgotten; to forget (in a specific instance)
olvido *nm* [-ido(2) 4247]   the forgotten
inolvidable *aj* [-able 3810]   unforgettable
olvidadizo *aj* [-dizo]   forgetful
olvidado *aj*   forgotten

onda   wave
ondear *vt*   to make waves
ondular *vt*   to make hair curly or wavy
onda *nf* [3544]   wave
ondulación *nf*   curliness
ondulado *aj*   curly, wavy
ondulante *aj*   waving
ondulatorio *aj* [-orio(2)]   wave-propagating

opaco   opaque
opacidad *nf*   opaqueness
opaco *aj*   opaque

operación   operation
cooperar *vi* [4282]   to cooperate
operar *vt* [939]   to operate
operarse *vr*   to be operated on
cooperador,-a *nmf*   one who cooperates; a cooperative person
operado,-a *nmf*   person who is operated on
operador,-a *nmf* [2688]   operator; surgeon
operario,-a *nmf*   worker that operates a machine
cooperación *nf* [-ción 2272]   cooperation
cooperativa *nf*   cooperative
operación *nf* [-ción 582]   operation
cooperativo *aj*   cooperative
inoperable *aj*   inoperable
operable *aj*   operable
operacional *aj*   operational
operado *aj*   operated on, referring to a patient
operante *aj*   operating
operativo *aj* [-ivo 839]   operative
postoperatorio *aj*   post-operative

opinión   opinion
opinar *vi* [1872]   to opine, to give an opinion
opinión *nf* [1044]   opinion
opinable *aj* [-able]   debatable

oportuno   opportune
importunar *vt*   to bother
oportunista *nmf*   opportunist
oportunismo *nm*   opportunism
oportunidad *nf* [-idad 312]   opportunity
inoportunamente *av*   inopportunely
oportunamente *av* [-mente 4684]   opportunely
importuno *aj*   bothersome
inoportuno *aj*   inopportune
oportunista *aj*   opportunistic
oportuno *aj* [2796]   opportune

opresión   oppression
oprimir *vt*   to oppress
oprimidos *npl*   the oppressed
opresor,-a *nmf*   oppressor
opresión *nf*   oppression
opresivo *aj*   oppressive
opresor *aj*   oppressing
oprimido *aj*   oppressed

optimismo   optimism
optimista *nmf* [-ista 4021]   optimist
optimismo *nm* [-ismo 4160]   optimism
optimista *aj* [-ista 4021]   optimistic
óptimo *aj* [4229]   optimal

oración   prayer
orar *vi*   to pray
orador,-a *nmf*   orator, speaker
oráculo *nm* [-culo]   oracle
oración *nf* [-ción 4359]   prayer
oratoria *nf*   oratory, art of speaking in public
oral *aj* [4022]   oral
oratorio *aj*   oratory

orbe   orb
orbe *nm*   orb
órbita *nf*   orbit
orbital *aj*   orbital

orden   order
coordinar *vt* [2214]   to coordinate
desordenar *vt*   to put in disorder
desordenarse *vr*   to become disordered
insubordinar *vt*   to disobey
insubordinarse *vr*   to become insubordinate
ordenar *vt* [1371]   to place in order; to order
reordenar *vt*   to re-order
subordinar *vt*   to subordinate
subordinarse *vr*   to subordinate oneself
coordinador,-a *nmf* [1001]   coordinator
insubordinado,-a *nmf*   an insubordinate person
subordinado,-a *nmf*   subordinate
desorden *nm* [3647]   disorder
orden *nm* [531]   order
ordenamiento *nm* [-miento 4589]   an ordering
ordenanza *nm* [-anza]   command

ordenanzas *nfpl* orders
coordenada *nf* coordinate
coordinación *nf* [-ción 1321] coordination
insubordinación *nf* insubordination
ordenación *nf* ordination
subordinación *nf* subordination
coordenado *aj* coordinated
coordinador *aj* coordinating
desordenado *aj* disordered, unorganized
insubordinado *aj* insubordinate
ordenado *aj* well-ordered
subordinado *aj* subordinate
ordinario ordinary
extraordinario *nm* [1778] special delivery
extraordinaria *nf* bonus
extraordinario *aj* [1778] extraordinary
ordinario *aj* [-ario(2) 2809] ordinary
oreja ear
orejear *vi* to move the ears, as done by animals
orejón,-a *nmf* person with big ears
oreja *nf* [2766] ear
orejera *nf* ear-coving on some hats
orejón,-a *aj* disobedient
orejudo *aj* [-udo] large-eared
orgánico organic
inorgánico *aj* inorganic
orgánico *aj* [-ico(2) 3708] organic
organismo organism
microorganismo *nm* micro-organism
organismo *nm* [-ismo 616] organism
órgano *nm* [1669] organ
organizar to organize
desorganizar *vt* to disorganize
organizar *vt* [-izar 468] to organize
organizarse *vr* to organize oneself
reorganizar *vt* to reorganize
organizador,-a *nmf* organizer
reorganizador,-a *nmf* reorganizer
organismo *nm* [-ismo 616] organism
desorganización *nf* disorganized place
organización *nf* [-ción 380] organization
reorganización *nf* re-organization
organizado *aj* organized
organizador *aj* [-dor(1) 1584] organizing
reorganizador *aj* reorganized
órgano organ
organillero,-a *nmf* player of a small portable piano
organista *nmf* organist
organillo *nm* small portable piano
órgano *nm* [1669] organ
orgullo pride
enorgullecer *vt* to make prideful

enorgullecerse *vr* to become prideful
enorgullecimiento *nm* the act of becoming prideful
orgullo *nm* [2943] pride
orgulloso *aj* [-oso 2743] prideful

oriental eastern
desorientar *vt* to disorient
desorientarse *vr* to disorient oneself
orientar *vt* [2538] to orient
orientarse *vr* [2538] to orient oneself
orientador,-a *nmf* guide
oriental *nmf* [-al(2) 3608] Oriental person, person from the Orient
oriente *nm* [1004] the east
desorientación *nf* disorientation
orientación *nf* [-ción 3277] orientation
desorientado *aj* disoriented
orientador *aj* guiding, orienting
oriental *aj* [-al(2) 3608] eastern

origen origin, birth
originar *vt* [2263] to originate, to initiate
originarse *vr* to originate, to come from
original *nmf* [1381] an original
origen *nm* [974] origin; birth
originalidad *nf* originality
original *aj* [1381] original
originario *aj* [1992] original

oscuro dark
oscurecer, obscurecer *vt* to darken
oscurecerse, obscurecerse *vr* to become dark
oscurecimiento, obscurecimiento *nm* the coming of darkness; darkening
oscuridad, obscuridad *nf* darkness
oscuramente, obscuramente *av* obscurely
oscuro, obscuro *aj* dark

ostentar to show off
ostentar *vt* [4614] to show off
ostentación *nf* ostentation
ostensible *aj* [-ible] ostensible, apparently
ostentoso *aj* ostentatious

otoño autumn, fall
otoño *nm* [4248] autumn, fall
otoñal *aj* [-al(2)] autumn, fall

otorgar to concede, allow in a formal sense
otorgar *vt* [819] to concede, allow in a formal sense
otorgante *nmf* person who concedes or allows
otorgamiento *nm* the conceding or allowing of a request, often used as a legal term

P

pacto agreement
pactar *vi* [3935] to make an agreement
pacto *nm* [-o(1) 3874] agreement

padecer to suffer from
compadecer *vt* to feel compassion for
compadecerse *vr* to show compassion for
padecer *vt* [1417] to suffer from
padecimiento *nm* [-miento 2915] suffering

padre father
apadrinar *vt* to be a godfather
expatriar *vt* to expatriate
expatriarse *vr* to be expatriated
patrocinar *vt* to sponsor
repatriar *vt* to repatriate
padres *nmpl* parents
padrinos *nmpl* godparents
apátrida *nmf* man or woman without a country
compatriota *nmf* [2410] compatriot
expatriado,-a *nmf* expatriate
papista *nmf* Papist
patriota *nmf* [4402] patriot
patrocinador,-a *nmf* sponsor, patron
patrón,-a *nmf* [2525] employer
repatriado,-a *nmf* repatriate
apadrinamiento *nm* act of being a godfather
compadre *nm* [3962] close friend; godfather and
  actual father are "compadres"
padrastro *nm* [-astro] stepfather
padre *nm* [196] father
padrenuestro *nm* prayer "our Father"; Lord's
  Prayer
padrinazgo *nm* [-azgo] act of being a godfather
padrino *nm* [-ino(1)] godfather; sponsor
papa *nm* [1135] pope
papa *nm* [1135] father, dad
papado *nm* term of papal governing
paternalismo *nm* paternalism
patriarca *nm* [-arca] patriarch
patriarcado *nm* term of patriarchal governing;
  patriarchal age; patriarchy
patrimonio *nm* [2846] patrimony
patriotismo *nm* [-ismo] patriotism
patrocinio *nm* sponsoring
patronato *nm* [-ato 3247] association for the
  purpose of charity or mutual benefit
expatriación *nf* expatriation
paternidad *nf* paternity
patria *nf* [2495] native country
repatriación *nf* repatriation
antipatriótico *aj* unpatriotic

apátrida *aj* without a country
expatriado *aj* expatriated
papal *aj* [-al(2)] papal
paternal *aj* paternal
paternalista *aj* paternalistic
paterno *aj* paternal
patriarcal *aj* patriarchal
patrimonial *aj* patrimonial
patriótico *aj* [-ico(2)] patriotic
patrocinador *aj* [-dor(1) 4590] sponsoring
patronal *aj* pertaining to the employer
repatriado *aj* repatriated

pagar to pay
pagar *vt* [304] to pay
pagador,-a *nmf* payer
pagaré *nm* I. O. U.; paper which notes a debt
pago *nm* [-o(1) 583] payment
paga *nf* payment of wages; salary
sobrepaga *nf* bonus
impagable *aj* unpayable
impagado *aj* unpaid
pagable *aj* payable
pagadero *aj* to be paid
pagado *aj* paid
pagador *aj* paying

página page
paginar *vt* to paginate
paginación *nm* pagination
página *nf* [-a 1384] page

país country
paisano,-a *nmf* [4250] countryman
país *nm* [61] country
paisaje *nm* [4249] countryside; landscape
paisanaje *nm* [-aje(1)] fellow countrymen
paisano *aj* belonging to the same country

pájaro bird
pajarear *vi* to hunt birds; to wander
pajarero,-a *nmf* person who cares for or sells
  birds
pájaro *nm* [4161] bird
pajarraco *nm* [-aco] ugly bird
pájara *nf* female bird
pajarera *nf* large birdcage
pajarería *nf* flock or multitude of birds
pajarero *aj* pertaining to birds

palabra word
apalabrar *vt* to fight with words
palabrear *vt* to chat
palabra *nf* [688] word
palabreja *nf* [-ejo] strange or ugly word
palabrota *nf* expletive or blasphemous word

palacio palace
palacete *nm* small palace, mansion
palacio *nm* [-icio] palace

pálido pale
palidecer *vi* to become pale
palidez *nf* paleness
pálido *aj* [-ido(1)] pale

palma palm
palmear *vt* to pat; to applaud
palmotear *vt* to pat
palpar *vt* to touch with the palm
palmar *nm* grove of palm trees
palmetazo *nm* hard slap
palmo *nm* hand (measurement)
palmoteo *nm* patting
palma *nf* [2466] palm of the hand; palm tree
palmada *nf* [-ada(2)] soft slap
palmera *nf* palm tree
palpación *nf* groping; feeling with the palm
impalpable *aj* impalpable
palmeado *aj* palm-shaped
palpable *aj* [-able] palpable

palo long stick or handle
apalancar *vt* to move with leverage
apalancamiento *nm* leverage
apalanque *nm* leveraging
palo *nm* [3785] long stick or handle
palanca *nf* lever
palanqueta *nf* small lever; crowbar

paloma dove
palomar *nm* place where doves live
palomino *nm* [-ino(1)] young dove
palomo *nm* male dove
paloma *nf* dove
palomilla *nf* small dove
palomina *nf* [-ina] dove droppings

palpitar to palpitate
palpitar *vi* to palpitate
palpitación *nf* palpitation
palpitante *aj* palpitating

pan bread
empanizar *vt* to bread
panificar *vt* to make bread
panadero,-a *nmf* baker
pan *nm* [576] bread
panecillo *nm* [-illo(1)] small loaf of bread
empanada *nf* turnover
empanadilla *nf* small turnover
panadería *nf* [-ería(1)] bakery
panera *nf* [-era] bread basket or box
panificación *nf* making of bread
panificadora *nf* bakery

empanado *aj* wrapped in bread
empanizado *aj* breaded

panorama panorama
panorama *nm* [2519] panorama
panorámico *aj* [-ico(2)] panoramic
pantalón *pants*
pantalonero,-a *nmf* tailor who makes pants
pantalón *nm* [2971] pants
pantalonera *nf* sweatpants

paño woolen fabric
paño *nm* woolen fabric
pañuelo *nm* [-uelo] handkerchief
pañoleta *nf* scarf for hair

papel paper
desempapelar *vt* to unwrap; to take the paper off
empapelar *vt* to wrap with paper
traspapelar *vt* to misplace a piece of paper
traspapelarse *vr* to be misplaced (piece of paper)
empapelado *nm* paper wrapping
papalote *nm* paper kite
papel *nm* [553] paper
papeleo *nm* [-eo(1)] red tape; paperwork
papiro *nm* papyrus
pisapapeles *nm* paperweight
sujetapapeles *nm* paper clip
papelera *nf* [-era] wastepaper basket; paper industry
papelería *nf* [-ería(1)] stationery store
papeleta *nf* [-eta] report card
papelero *aj* pertaining to paper
traspapelado *aj* lost among papers

par pair; even number
aparear *vt* to form a pair; to mate
aparearse *vr* to be paired with; to be mated with
desemparejar *vt* to make uneven; to mismatch
emparejar *vt* to make even; to match
apareamiento *nm* forming of a pair; mating
par *nm* [1218] pair; even number
pareja *nf* [-ejo 547] couple
paridad *nf* parity
aparejado *aj* paired; mated
desemparejado *aj* made uneven; mismatched
disparejo *aj* uneven; unequal
impar *aj* uneven
par *aj* [1218] even (numbers)
parejo *aj* [4115] even

paradoja paradox
paradoja *nf* paradox
paradójico *aj* paradoxical

paraíso paradise
paraíso *nm* [4195] paradise
paradisíaco *aj* paradisiacal; pertaining to paradise

paralelo parallel; latitude line
paralelismo *nm* parallelism
paralelo *nm* [3685] parallel; latitude line
paralelogramo *nm* parallelogram
paralelas *nfpl* parallel bars used in gymnastics
paralelamente *av* parallel
paralelo *aj* [3685] parallel

paralizar to paralyze
paralizar *vt* [-izar 4615] to paralyze
paralizarse *vr* to become paralyzed
paralítico,-a *nmf* paralytic
parapléjico,-a *nmf* paraplegic
parálisis *nm* paralysis
paralización *nf* paralysis
paraplejía, paraplejia *nf* paraplegia
paralítico *aj* paralytic
paralizador *aj* paralyzing
paralizante *aj* paralyzing
parapléjico *aj* paraplegic

parar to stop
parar *vt* [1750] to stop
pararse *vr* [1750] to stop oneself; to stand up
parado,-a *nmf* unemployed worker
parada *nm* [3851] stop; bus stop
pararrayos *nm* lightning rod
paro *nm* [3381] work stoppage; strike
paradero *nf* [3886] rest stop; whereabouts
imparable *aj* [-able 1812] unstoppable
parado *aj* stopped; not working; standing still

parcial partial
imparcialidad *nf* impartiality
parcialidad *nf* partiality
imparcialmente *av* impartially
parcialmente *av* partially
imparcial *aj* impartial
parcial *aj* [-cial 2873] partial

pardo grayish
pardo *aj* grayish
pardusco *aj* [-usco] somewhat grayish

parecer to seem; to look like
comparecer *vt* [3663] to appear before a judge
parecer *vt* [245] to seem; to look like
parecerse *vr* to look like each other
parecer *nm* [245] opinion
parecido *nm* similarity
comparecencia *nf* appearance before a judge
parecido *aj* similar to; alike; like

pared wall
emparedar *vt* to build a wall around; to prevent someone from communicating by putting them in a walled cell
emparedado,-a *nmf* person who is incommunicado
emparedado *nm* sandwich
paredón *nm* firing squad wall
pared *nf* [1227] wall
emparedado *aj* surrounded by a wall; incommunicado

pariente relative
emparentar *vi* to become relatives by marriage
pariente *nmf* [4251] relative
parentesco *nm* family relationship
parto *nm* [3919] birth
partera *nf* midwife
emparentado *aj* related by marriage

parlamento parliament
parlar *vti* to talk
parlotear *vi* to talk
parlamentario,-a *nmf* parliamentarian; member of parliament
parlante *nmf* [-ante(1)] speaker
parlamento *nm* [3545] parliament
parloteo *nm* informal chat
parlamentario *aj* [-ario(2) 2222] parliamentarian

parroquia parish
parroquiano,-a *nmf* parishioner
parroquia *nf* [982] parish
parroquial *aj* [-al(2)] parochial

participar to participate
participar *vi* [223] to participate
copartícipe *nmf* partner
participante *nmf* [-ante(1) 1319] participant
partícipe *nmf* participant
participación *nf* [-ción 404] participation
participante *aj* [-ante(1) 1319] participating
partícipe *aj* participating; sharing

particular particular
particularizar *vt* to specify
particularizarse *vr* to distinguish oneself
particular *nm* [950] specific detail
particularidad *nf* particularity
particularmente *av* [-mente 2483] particularly
particular *aj* [950] particular; private

partir to cut into pieces; to depart
compartir *vt* [955] to share
partir *vt* [331] to cut into pieces; to depart
partirse *vr* to be cut into pieces; to be divided into pieces
repartir *vt* [2056] to distribute; to deliver
partidario,-a *nmf* supporter of a party

repartidor,-a *nmf* distributor
compartimiento *nm* compartment
compartimento *nm* compartment
partidismo *nm* factionalism
partido *nm* [78] party; match or game
reparto *nm* [-o(1) 2767] distribution
parte *nf* [46] part
partición *nf* [-ción] partition
partícula *nf* particle
repartición *nf* distribution
partidario *aj* [-ario(2) 3852] factional
partidista *aj* [-ista 3522] factional
partido *aj* [78] split

pasado past
pasar *vt* [224] to pass
repasar *vt* to review
sobrepasar *vt* to surpass
traspasar *vt* to trespass
antepasado,-a *nmf* ancestor
pasajero,-a *nmf* passenger
pasadizo *nm* passageway; secret passage
pasado *nm* [122] past
pasador *nm* smuggler; hairpin
pasaje *nm* [-aje(2) 3523] passage
pasamano *nm* handrail
pasaporte *nm* [3598] passport
pasatiempo *nm* pastime
pase *nm* [1007] pass
repaso *nm* review
traspaso *nm* trespass
pasada *nf* [889] place for passing; passing
pasarela *nf* fashion parade or procession
pascua *nf* Passover; Easter
antepasado *aj* previous
pasadero *aj* passable
pasado *aj* [122] past
pasajero *aj* [-ero(2) 1919] passenger

paseo walk; excursion
pasear *vti(r)* [4287] to go for a walk or a ride
pasearse *vr* to be going for a walk or a ride; to take a trip, to go on an excursion
paseante *nmf* passerby
paseo *nm* [-eo(1) 1985] walk; excursion
pasillo *nm* [-illo(1) 4722] hallway

pasión passion
apasionar *vt* [4454] to fill with passion
apasionarse *vr* [4454] to be passionate
apasionamiento *nm* passion
compasión *nf* compassion
pasión *nf* [1993] passion
desapasionadamente *av* dispassionately
apasionado *aj* passionate

apasionante *aj* causing or creating passion; fascinating
compasivo *aj* compassionate
desapasionado *aj* dispassionate
pasional *aj* pertaining to passion

pasta pasta; paste
pastelero,-a *nmf* cake maker or seller
pastel *nm* [3073] cake
pasta *nf* [3510] pasta; paste
pastelería *nf* [-ería(1)] pastry shop; bakery specializing in pastries
pastoso *aj* pasty

pastor pastor, elder, bishop, shepherd
pastar *vi* to graze in a pasture
pastorear *vt* to shepherd
pastor *nmf* [-or 4527] shepherd
pastizal *nm* pasture
pasto *nm* grass
pastor *nm* [-or 4527] pastor, elder, bishop, shepherd
pastoreo *nm* shepherding
pastoral *aj* pastoral
pastoril *aj* pastoral

pata paw or hoof and leg of an animal; leg
patalear *vt* to repeatedly kick
patear *vt* to kick
pataleo *nm* repeated kicking
pata *nf* paw or hoof and leg of an animal; leg
patada *nf* [-ada(2)] forceful kick
patizambo *aj* bowlegged

pausa pause
pausa *nf* [-a] pause
pausado *aj* paused

pavor horror; fear
pavor *nm* horror; fear
pavoroso *aj* horrifying; frightening

paz peace
apaciguar *vt* to pacify; to calm
apaciguarse *vr* to be pacified; to be calm
impacientar *vt* to make impatient
impacientarse *vr* to become impatient
pacificar *vt* [-ificar] to pacify
pacificarse *vr* to be pacified
apaciguador,-a *nmf* person who calms or pacifies others
paciente *nmf* [972] patient
pacificador,-a *nmf* peacemaker
pacifista *nmf* [-ista] pacifist
apaciguamiento *nm* appeasement; calming; pacifying
pacifismo *nm* pacifism
impaciencia *nf* impatience
paciencia *nf* [-encia 3237] patience

pacificación *nf* pacification

paz *nf* [840] peace

impacientemente *av* impatiently

pacientemente *av* patiently

apacible *aj* peaceful

apaciguador *aj* calming; pacifying

desapacible *aj* not peaceful

impaciente *aj* impatient

paciente *aj* [972] patient

pacificador *aj* pacifying

pacífico *aj* [-ico(2) 2073] pacific

pacifista *aj* [-ista] pacifist

pecado sin

pecar *vi* to sin

pecador,-a *nmf* sinner

pecado *nm* [-o(1) 3920] sin

pecador *aj* sinful (people)

pecaminoso *aj* pertaining to sin or sinners

pecho chest

despechar *vt* to wean

despecho *nm* rancor

pechero *nm* bib

pecho *nm* [2817] chest

pechera *nf* top front part of overalls

pechuga *nf* breast of an animal

despechado *aj* filled with rancor

pectoral *aj* pectoral

peculiar peculiar

peculiaridad *nf* peculiarity

peculiar *aj* peculiar

pedagógico pedagogic

pedagogo,-a *nmf* pedagogue; teacher

pedagogía *nf* pedagogy

pedagógico *aj* pedagogic

pedazo piece

despedazar *vt* to break into many pieces

pedazo *nm* [3686] piece

pedir to ask (favor); to order or request

despedir *vt* [1457] to say good-bye when someone else is leaving; to dismiss or fire from work

despedirse *vr* [1457] to say good-bye when one is leaving

pedir *vt* [198] to ask (favor)

peticionario,-a *nmf* petitioner

despido *nm* [-ido(2) 3819] dismissal from work

pedido *nm* [-ido(2)] order; request

despedida *nf* [-ido(2) 1111] farewell

pedida *nf* petition

petición *nf* [-ción 1251] petition

pegar to hit; to stick

apegarse *vr* to become accustomed; to become attached

despegar *vt* [4696] to take off (airplane); to unstick; to take off something that is stuck

despegarse *vr* [4696] to become unstuck

pegar *vt* [1693] to hit; to stick; to glue

pegarse *vr* to become stuck

apego *nm* affection

desapego *nm* lack of affection

despegue *nm* take-off (airplane)

pegamento *nm* glue

apegado *aj* attached; accustomed

despegado *aj* unstuck

pegadizo *aj* sticky

pegado *aj* stuck; attached

pegajoso *aj* [-oso] sticky

peinar to comb

despeinar *vt* to mess up hair

despeinarse *vr* to mess up one's hair

peinar *vt* to comb

peinarse *vr* to comb one's hair

peinador,-a *nmf* hair stylist

peinado *nm* [-ado(2)] hairstyle

peinador *nm* dressing table

peine *nm* comb

peineta *nf* [-eta] ornamental comb

despeinado *aj* uncombed; disheveled

peinado *aj* [-ado(2)] combed; styled

pelear to fight

pelear *vi* [2024] to fight

pelearse *vr* to fight each other

peleonero,-a *nmf* fighter

pelea *nf* [-a 1665] fight

peleado *aj* fighting

peleador *aj* [-dor(1)] aggressive; easily provoked to fight or argue

peleonero *aj* aggressive; easily provoked to fight or argue

peligro danger

peligrar *vi* to be in danger

peligro *nm* [1157] danger

peligrosidad *nf* dangerousness

peligroso *aj* [-oso 1538] dangerous

pelo hair

pelirrojo,-a *nmf* red-haired person

pelón,-a *nmf* bald person

peluquero,-a *nmf* hair stylist; barber

pelo *nm* [2291] hair

peluquín *nm* toupee

peluquería *nf* [-ería(1)] barbershop; hair salon

pelirrojo *aj* red-haired

peludo *aj* [-udo] hairy

pena embarrassment; shame; penalty

apenar *vt* to embarrass

arrepentirse *vr* to repent

penalizar *vt* to penalize

penar *vi* to suffer; to receive a punishment

penado,-a *nmf* inmate

penalista *nmf* lawyer who specializes in criminal cases

penitente *nmf* penitent

arrepentimiento *nm* repentance

penal *nm* [875] prison

penalti, penalty *nm* penalty kick in soccer

impenitencia *nf* impenitence

pena *nf* [1301] embarrassment; shame; penalty

penalidad *nf* penalty; troublesome work

penalización *nf* penalization

penitencia *nf* [-encia] penitence

penitenciaría *nf* penitentiary

apenado *aj* filled with shame

arrepentido *aj* repentant

impenitente *aj* impenitent

penal *aj* [875] penal

penitenciario *aj* penitentiary

penitente *aj* penitent

penoso *aj* shy, timid; embarrassing

peña loose rock

peñasco *nm* large loose rock

peñón *nm* large steep rock

peña *nf* loose rock

pendiente errand; pending task

pender *vt* to hang

pendiente *nm* [1331] errand; pending task; pendant; earring (hanging)

pendiente *aj* [1331] hanging

penetrar to penetrate

compenetrarse *vr* to identify completely with each other

penetrar *vt* [2511] to penetrate

pene *nm* penis

compenetración *nf* complete identification with another person

impenetrabilidad *nf* impenetrability

penetrabilidad *nf* penetrability

penetración *nf* penetration

impenetrable *aj* impenetrable

penetrable *aj* [-able] penetrable

penetrante *aj* [-ante(1)] penetrating

península peninsula

península *nf* peninsula

peninsular *aj* peninsular

pensar to think

pensar *vt* [276] to think

librepensador,-a *nmf* freethinker

malpensado,-a *nmf* person who thinks the worst regardless of what happens

pensador,-a *nmf* thinker

librepensamiento *nm* free thought

pensamiento *nm* [-miento 1995] thought

impensable *aj* unthinkable

impensado *aj* unthought-of

librepensador *aj* freethinking

malpensado *aj* bad or evil thinking

pensado *aj* thought

pensativo *aj* pensive, thoughtful

pensión pension

pensionado,-a *nmf* retired person

pensionista *nmf* person who receives a pension

pensión *nf* [-sión 3033] pension

pensionado *aj* retired; receiving a pension

peor worse

empeorar *vi* [4817] to worsen

empeorarse *vr* [4817] to become worse

empeoramiento *nm* worsening

peor *av* [1191] worse

peor *aj* [1191] worse

pequeño small

empequeñecer *vt* to make smaller, to shrink

pequeño,-a *nmf* small person; little one, term of endearment for someone

empequeñecimiento *nm* shrinking

pequeñez *nf* [-ez] smallness

pequeño *aj* [301] small, little

percibir to perceive

percibir *vt* [2074] to perceive

imperceptibilidad *nf* imperceptibility

percepción *nf* [-ción 2831] perception

imperceptiblemente *av* imperceptibly

desapercibido *aj* unperceived, unnoticed

imperceptible *aj* imperceptible

perceptible *aj* perceptible

perceptivo *aj* perceptive

perder to lose

desperdiciar *vt* [4035] to waste

perder *vt* [210] to lose

perderse *vr* to become lost; to be lost; to miss

desperdicios *nmpl* leftovers to be thrown out

perdedor,-a *nmf* loser

desperdicio *nm* [-icio 4336] waste

perdición *nf* perdition

pérdida *nf* [-ido(2) 1138] loss

perdidamente *av* completely, blindly

perdedor *aj* [-dor(1) 3854] losing

perdido *aj* lost

perdonar to pardon

perdonar *vt* [2962] to pardon

perdón *nm* [3831] pardon

imperdonable *aj* unpardonable

perdonable *aj* pardonable

perdurar to endure, to last
  perdurar *vi* to endure, to last
  perdurablemente *av* eternally
  perdurable *aj* lasting

perecer to perish
  perecer *vi* to perish
  imperecedero *aj* not perishable
  perecedero *aj* [-ero(2)] perishable

peregrinación pilgrimage; journey
  peregrinar *vi* to make a pilgrimage; to make a journey
  peregrino,-a *nmf* pilgrim
  peregrinación *nf* pilgrimage
  peregrinaje *nf* pilgrimage
  peregrino *aj* pertaining to pilgrims or pilgrimages

pereza laziness
  desperezarse *vr* to shake off laziness
  perezoso,-a *nmf* lazy person
  perezoso *nm* [-oso] sloth
  pereza *nf* laziness
  perezosamente *av* lazily
  perezoso *aj* [-oso] lazy

perfecto perfect
  perfeccionar *vt* to perfect
  perfeccionista *nmf* [-ista] perfectionist
  desperfecto *nm* imperfection, problem
  imperfecto *nm* imperfect tense in grammar
  perfeccionamiento *nm* perfecting
  perfeccionismo *nm* perfectionism
  imperfección *nf* imperfection
  perfección *nf* [4657] perfection
  perfectibilidad *nf* perfectibility
  perfectamente *av* [-mente 3022] perfectly
  imperfecto *aj* imperfect
  perfeccionista *aj* [-ista] perfectionistic
  perfectible *aj* perfectible
  perfectivo *aj* perfective
  perfecto *aj* [1952] perfect

perfil profile
  perfilar *vt* to draw a profile
  perfilarse *vr* to show one's profile (also figurative)
  perfil *nm* [3278] profile
  perfilado *aj* profiled

perforar to perforate; to drill
  perforar *vt* to perforate; to drill
  perforador,-a *nmf* person who drills or bores holes
  perforador *nm* [-dor(2)] drill
  perforación *nf* perforation; drilling
  perforadora *nf* hole punch
  perforador *aj* [-dor(2)] perforating; drilling

perfume perfume
  perfumar *vt* to put perfume on something
  perfumarse *vr* to put perfume on oneself
  perfumista *nmf* person who makes or sells perfume
  perfumador *nm* perfume bottle
  perfume *nm* [4572] perfume
  perfumería *nf* perfume store

periódico newspaper
  periodista *nmf* [-ista 1261] newspaper reporter
  periódico *nm* [1337] newspaper
  periodismo *nm* [-ismo 4002] journalism
  periódico *aj* [1337] periodic
  periodístico *aj* [-ico(2) 4422] pertaining to newspapers or journalism

perito expert
  perito,-a *nmf* expert
  peritaje *nm* expert report
  perito *aj* [4450] expert

perla pearl
  perla *nf* pearl
  perlado *aj* pearl-colored; pearl-shaped; having pearls

permanecer to remain
  permanecer *vi* [858] to remain
  permanente *nm* [1451] permanent (hairstyle)
  permanencia *nf* [-encia 4003] permanence
  permanentemente *av* permanently
  permanente *aj* [1451] permanent

permitir to permit
  permitir *vt* [205] to permit
  permitirse *vr* to be permitted
  permiso *nm* [1387] permit
  permisión *nf* permission
  permisible *aj* [-ible] permissible
  permisivo *aj* permissive
  permitido *aj* permitted

perpetuo perpetual
  perpetuar *vt* to perpetuate
  perpetuarse *vr* to be perpetuated
  perpetuación *nf* perpetuation
  perpetuidad *nf* perpetuity
  perpetuamente *av* perpetually
  perpetuo *aj* [-uo] perpetual

perplejidad perplexity
  perplejidad *nf* perplexity
  perplejo *aj* perplexed

perro dog
  perrero *nm* [-ero(3)] dog catcher
  perro *nm* dog
  perra *nf* female dog

perrera *nf* [-era] dog pound
perruno *aj* [-uno] pertaining to dogs
persistir to persist
  persistir *vi* [3259] to persist
  persistencia *nf* persistence
  persistente *aj* persistent
persona person
  despersonalizar *vt* to depersonalize
  personalizar *vt* to personalize
  personificar *vt* to personify
  personaje *nm* [697] celebrity, famous person
  personal *nm* [-al(2) 297] personnel
  persona *nf* [67] person
  personalidad *nf* [-idad 1829] personality
  personificación *nf* personification
  personalmente *av* [-mente 3730] personally
  impersonal *aj* impersonal
  personal *aj* [-al(2) 297] personal
pertenecer to belong to
  pertenecer *vi* [1220] to belong to
  pertenencia *nf* [-encia 4919] belonging, possession
  perteneciente *aj* [1896] belonging, pertaining
pesado heavy
  apesadumbrar *vt* to weigh heavily
  contrapesar *vt* (figurative) to place a counterweight, to counterbalance
  pesar *vi* [242] to weigh
  pesarse *vr* to weigh oneself
  sopesar *vt* to weigh in one's hand; to estimate the weight of
  contrapeso *nm* counterweight, counterbalance
  pésame *nm* oral or written expression of condolence
  pesar *nm* [242] problem
  peso *nm* [125] weight
  sobrepeso *nm* excess weight
  pesa *nf* [-a 4528] weight (gym)
  pesada *nf* weight; weighing
  pesadez *nf* [-ez] heaviness
  pesadilla *nf* nightmare
  pesadumbre *nf* [-dumbre] affliction
  apesadumbrado *aj* afflicted
  pesado *aj* [-ado(1)] heavy
pescar to fish
  pescar *vt* to fish
  pescadero,-a *nmf* fishmonger
  pescador,-a *nmf* [4451] fisherman
  pescado *nm* [2338] fish (caught)
  pesquero *nm* fishing boat
  pez *nm* [4361] fish
  pesca *nf* [-a 3382] fishing
  pescadería *nf* [-ería(1)] fish market
  pesquera *nf* place for fishing

  pescador *aj* fishing; fish-catching
  pesquero *aj* pertaining to fish; fishing
pesimismo pessimism
  pesimista *nmf* [-ista] pessimist
  pesimismo *nm* pessimism
  pésimamente *av* very badly
  pesimista *aj* [-ista] pessimistic
  pésimo *aj* [3213] very bad
pestaña eyelash
  pestañear *vi* to move the eyelashes
  pestañeo *nm* moving of eyelashes
  pestaña *nf* eyelash
  pestañita *nf* nap
petróleo petroleum; oil
  petrolero,-a *nmf* petroleum merchant
  petróleo *nm* [1541] petroleum; oil
  petrolero *nm* [-ero(2) 1761] oil tanker
  superpetrolero *nm* supertanker
  petroquímica *nf* petrochemistry
  petrolero *aj* [-ero(2) 1761] pertaining to petroleum or oil
  petrolífero *aj* [-ífero] oil-producing
  petroquímico *aj* petrochemical
piano piano
  pianista *nmf* [-ista] pianist
  piano *nm* [4549] piano
  pianoforte *nm* piano
  pianola *nf* player piano
  pianísimo *av* very quietly; pianissimo
  piano *av* [4549] quietly
  pianístico *aj* pertaining to the piano
picar to bite; to sting; to chop
  picar(se) *vt(r)* [1986] to bite; to sting; to chop
  picajoso,-a *nmf* hypersensitive person
  picor *nm* bothersome burning or stinging sensation
  picadura *nf* [-dura] biting; stinging; bite; sting
  picado *aj* bitten; stung; chopped; piqued
  picajoso *aj* hypersensitive
  picante *aj* biting, stinging, hot (seasoning)
pico beak; peak
  picar(se) *vt(r)* [1986] to poke with a beak; to puncture
  picotear *vt* to be pecking
  picaflor *nm* hummingbird
  picapedrero *nm* sculptor specializing in sculpting using rock material
  picaporte *nm* door catch
  pico *nm* [-o(1) 4023] beak; peak
  picotazo *nm* forceful hit with a beak
  picoteo *nm* pecking
  zapapico *nm* pickax
  picotada *nf* forceful hit with a beak

piquera *nf* cell in a beehive
piqueta *nf* pickax
picudo *aj* [-udo] pointed

pie foot
pedalear *vt* to pedal
pedal *nm* pedal
pedaleo *nm* pedaling
pedestal *nm* pedestal
pie *nm* [844] foot
reposapiés *nm* footrest
entrepierna *nf* inner thigh, crotch
pierna *nf* [1768] leg
pedestre *aj* [-estre] pertaining to the foot

piedad piety
impío,-a *nmf* impious person
impiedad *nf* impiety
piedad *nf* [2418] piety
píamente *av* piously
impío *aj* impious
piadoso *aj* pious
pío *aj* pious
piedra *rock*
apedrear *vt* to stone (punishment); to throw rocks
desempedrar *vt* to remove rocks
empedrar *vt* to place rocks
petrificar *vt* [-ificar] to petrify
petrificarse *vr* to be petrified; to become petrified
empedrado *nm* placing of rocks; making of something with rocks; rock work
pedregal *nm* rock floor; ground covered with rock
pedrisco *nm* small avalanche; rock slide
pedrusco *nm* rock used for sculpting
picapedrero *nm* rock sculptor
pedrada *nf* throwing of a rock
pedrera *nf* rock quarry
pedrería *nf* group of precious stones
petrificación *nf* petrifaction
piedra *nf* [1413] rock
empedrado *aj* made of rocks
pedregoso *aj* rocky
pétreo *aj* rock-like; of rock; stony (also figurative)
petrificado *aj* petrified

piel skin
despellejar *vt* to remove the skin
pellejo *nm* skin of an animal
piel *nm* [1030] skin
pellejudo *aj* having a lot of skin

pila pile; battery; pool of stored water
apilar *vt* to pile

apilarse *vr* to be piled
apilamiento *nm* piling
pilar *nm* pillar
pila *nf* pile; battery; pool of stored water
apilado *aj* piled

piloto pilot
pilotar, pilotear *vt* to pilot
piloto *nmf* [1332] pilot
copiloto *nm* copilot
piloto *aj* [1332] pilot

pino pine tree
pinar *nm* [-al(3)] pine grove
pino *nm* [2606] pine tree
piñón *nm* pine nut
piña *nf* pineapple
pineda *nf* pine grove

pintar to paint; to put on makeup
despintar *vt* to remove paint from; to remove makeup
despintarse *vr* to remove one's makeup
pintar *vt* [1601] to paint; to put on makeup
pintarrajar *vt* to paint carelessly
pintarrajearse *vr* to put on makeup poorly or carelessly
pintarse *vr* [1601] to put makeup on oneself
repintar *vt* to repaint
repintarse *vr* to put on too much makeup; to reapply makeup
pintor,-a *nmf* [3337] painter
pinta *nf* [-a] stain
pintura *nf* [-ura(2) 2270] painting
pintado *aj* [-ado(1)] painted; with makeup
pinto *aj* spotted
pintoresco *aj* [-esco] picturesque

piropo flirtatious compliment
piropear *vt* to flirt
piropo *nm* flirtatious compliment

piso floor
apisonar *vt* to compact; to flatten
pisar *vt* [3587] to step on; to walk on
pisotear *vt* to trample; to step on repeatedly
pisapapeles *nm* paperweight
piso *nm* [1638] floor
pisotón *nm* hard stamping with the foot
apisonadora *nf* steamroller, road roller
autopista *nf* [4974] highway; racetrack
pisada *nf* step
pista *nf* [1698] track; clue

pistola pistol
pistolero *nm* [-ero(3)] pistol shooter; gunfighter
pistoletazo *nm* [-azo(2)] pistol shot; hit with the butt of a gun

pistola *nf* [2874] pistol
pistolera *nf* [-era] holster

placer pleasure
complacer *vt* [4299] to please
complacerse *vr* to be pleased
beneplácito *nm* approval, consent
placer *nm* [3039] pleasure
complacencia *nf* pleasing
placidez *nf* placidity, calmness, tranquility
complacido *aj* pleased
complaciente *aj* pleasing
plácido *aj* [-ido(1)] placid, calm, tranquil

plan plan
planear *vt* [1475] to plan
planificar *vt* to plan
plantear *vt* [1399] to organize or form plans
replantear *vt* to reorganize or redo plans
replantearse *vr* to reorganize one's plans
plan *nm* [614] plan
planificación *nf* planning
planeado *aj* planned

planeta planet
planetario *nm* [-ario(2)] planetarium
planeta *nf* [2503] planet
interplanetario *aj* interplanetary
planetario *aj* [-ario(2)] planetary

plano flat
aplanar *vt* to flatten
aplanarse *vr* to become emotionally flat; to become discouraged; to be flattened or squished
altiplanicie *nm* high plain; plateau
altiplano *nm* high plain; plateau
aplanamiento *nm* flattening
plano *nm* [2119] plane
aplanadora *nf* steamroller; road roller
aplanador *aj* flattening
plano *aj* [2119] flat

planta plant
implantar *vt* [4226] to implant
plantar *vt* [3599] to plant
plantarse *vr* to be planted
replantar *vt* to replant
trasplantar *vt* to transplant
trasplantarse *vr* to be transplanted
plantío *nm* planting; field of planted vegetables
transplante *nm* [4426] transplant
implantación *nf* implantation
planta *nf* [-a 818] plant
plantación *nf* [-ción] plantation
plantado *aj* planted

plata silver
platear *vt* to plate with silver

platero,-a *nmf* silversmith
plateado *nm* plated silver; plating of silver
plata *nf* [1830] silver; money
platería *nf* [-ería(1)] silversmith's shop; silversmithing; silverware
plateado *aj* plated; silver-colored

plato plate
calientaplatos *nm* hot plate, plate-warmer
lavaplatos *nm* dishwasher
platillo *nm* [-illo(1) 2064] dish
plato *nm* [2674] plate

playa beach
playa *nf* [2706] beach
playera *nf* tee shirt
playero *aj* [-ero(2) 4213] pertaining to the beach

plaza plaza, town square
desplazar *vt* [2565] to displace; to move
desplazarse *vr* [2565] to be displaced; to be moved
reemplazar *vt* [3802] to replace
desplazamiento *nm* displacement; movement from one place to another
reemplazo *nm* replacement
plaza *nf* [516] plaza, town square
plazoleta *nf* small plaza, town square
plazuela *nf* plaza, town square
desplazado *aj* displaced; moved
irremplazable *aj* irreplaceable
reemplazable *aj* replaceable

plebeyo plebeian, commoner
plebeyo,-a *nmf* plebeian, commoner
plebe *nf* plebeians, commoners
plebeyo *aj* plebeian, common

pleito fight, argument
pleitista,-a *nmf* person who is always looking for a fight
pleito *nm* [3450] fight, argument

plenitud fullness
plenitud *nf* [-itud 4748] fullness
pleno *aj* [1197] full

pluma pen; feather
desplumar *vt* to remove feathers; to pluck
emplumar *vt* to feather; to put feathers in something
cortaplumas *nm* small knife
plumaje *nm* [-aje(1)] plumage
plumazo *nm* [-azo(1)] hit with a pen
plumero *nm* feather duster
plumón *nm* color marker
pluma *nf* [3657] pen; feather
emplumado *aj* with feathers
plumoso *aj* feathery

pobre poor
empobrecer *vt* to make poor
empobrecerse *vr* to become poor
pobre *nmf* [1113] poor person
pobreza *nf* [-eza 1477] poverty
pobre *aj* [1113] poor

poco little; few
poco,-a *pron* a little; a few
poco *av* [132] little; few
poco *aj* [132] little; few

podar to prune
podar *vt* to prune
poda *nf* pruning
podadera *nf* pruning scissors; pruning knife

poder to be able to
apoderar *vr* [2803] to empower, to authorize
apoderarse *vr* to take possession of
poder *vt* [26] to be able to
apoderado,-a *nmf* person who is authorized or
   empowered
poderoso,-a *nmf* powerful person
poder *nm* [26] power
poderío *nm* authority; power
apoderado *aj* authorized
poderoso *aj* [-oso 2128] powerful
todopoderoso *aj* all-powerful

poema poem
poeta *nm* [3388] poet
poema *nf* [4431] poem
poesía *nf* [3425] poetry
poetisa *nf* poetess
poético *aj* poetic

polémica polemic, controversy
polemizar *vt* [-izar] to engage in a discussion over
   a controversial matter
polemista *nmf* person who engages in
   discussing controversy
polémica *nf* [2810] polemic, controversy
polémico *aj* polemic, polemical, controversial

policía police
policía *nmf* [-ería(2) 221] policeman; policewoman
policía *nf* [-ería(2) 221] police
policiaco, policíaco *aj* pertaining to police

político political
politiquear *vt* to engage in politics
politizar *vt* to politicize
político,-a *nmf* politician
geopolítica *nf* geopolitics
política *nf* politics
apolítico *aj* apolitical
político *aj* [129] political

pollo chicken
empollar *vi* to brood
pollero,-a *nmf* chicken farmer or merchant
pollito,-a *nmf* chick
polluelo,-a *nmf* chick
pollo *nm* [2832] chicken
polla *nf* young hen
pollera *nf* chicken coop

polvo dust
desempolvar *vt* to remove the dust from
empolvar *vt* to make dusty
empolvarse *vr* to become dusty
guardapolvo *nm* dust cover
polvo *nm* [2403] dust
polvorín *nm* [-ín] fine powder; fine gunpowder
polvareda *nf* "rain" of dust
polvera *nf* [-era] talc or powder container
pólvora *nf* gunpowder
empolvado *aj* dusty
polvoriento *aj* [-iento] very dusty

poner to put
anteponer *vt* to put in front of; to put before;
   to place with a higher priority
contraponer *vt* to oppose
contraponerse *vr* to be opposed
deponer *vt* to depose
disponer *vt* [1728] to have available
disponerse *vr* [1728] to be available or disposed
entreponer *vt* to put between two things
exponer *vt* [822] to expound on
exponerse *vr* [822] to expose oneself
imponer *vt* [862] to impose
imponerse *vr* to impose oneself; to be
   accustomed
interponer *vt* [2599] to interpose; to put
   something in between two things
interponerse *vr* to interpose oneself; to put
   oneself between others
oponer *vt* [2385] to oppose
oponerse *vr* to be opposed
poner *vt* [145] to put
posponer *vt* [3241] to postpone
predisponer *vt* to predispose
presuponer *vt* to presuppose
presupuestar *vt* to make a budget
proponer *vt* [847] to propose
proponerse *vr* to propose to oneself; to intend
reponer *vt* [4272] to replace
reponerse *vr* to recover
sobreexponer *vt* to overexpose
sobreponer *vt* to superimpose; to overlap; to
   place on top of something
sobreponerse *vr* to overcome

suponer *vt* [1575] to suppose

transponer *vt* to transpose; to move behind something else

transponerse *vr* to be behind something

yuxtaponer *vt* to juxtapose

deponente *nmf* deponent

expositor,-a *nmf* person who explains or demonstrates something

oponente *nmf* [-ente(1) 4570] opponent

opositor,-a *nmf* [3063] opponent

ponente *nmf* speaker

impuesto *nm* [679] tax

presupuesto *nm* [-o(1) 872] budget

puesto *nm* [535] post; position

repuesto *nm* replacement

supuesto *nm* [976] supposition

deposición *nf* deposition

disponibilidad *nf* [-idad 4957] availability

disposición *nf* [-ción 877] disposition

exposición *nf* [-ción 1690] exposition

indisposición *nf* indisposition

interposición *nf* interposition

oposición *nf* [-ción 1741] opposition

ponencia *nf* proposal

predisposición *nf* predisposition

propuesta *nf* [566] proposal; suggestion

puesta *nf* setting

sobreexposición *nf* overexposure

suposición *nf* [-ción] supposition

yuxtaposición *nf* juxtaposition

antepuesto *aj* placed in front of or with a higher priority

deponente *aj* deposing

disponible *aj* [-ible 2343] available

dispuesto *aj* [1164] available

expositivo *aj* expositive; explanatory

expuesto *aj* exposed

imponente *aj* imposing

impuesto *aj* [679] imposed

indisponible *aj* unavailable

indispuesto *aj* unavailable

oponente *aj* [-ente(1) 4570] opposing

predispuesto *aj* predisposed

presupuestario *aj* pertaining to a budget

presupuesto *aj* [-o(1) 872] presupposed

puesto *aj* [535] placed

sobrepuesto *aj* superimposed; overlapping; on top of something

supuesto *aj* [976] supposed

yuxtapuesto *aj* juxtaposed

popular popular

popularizar *vt* to popularize

populista *nmf* populist

populacho *nm* [-acho] town, people of a town (pejorative)

impopularidad *nf* lack of popularity

populachería *nf* local fame or popularity (pejorative)

popularidad *nf* [-idad 2545] popularity

popularmente *av* popularly

impopular *aj* unpopular

populachero *aj* pertaining to town or people of a town (pejorative)

popular *aj* [781] popular

populista *aj* populist

populoso *aj* populous

pormenor detail

pormenorizar *vt* to describe in detail

pormenor *nm* detail

portentoso portentous

portento *nm* portent

portentoso *aj* portentous

posada inn

posadero,-a *nmf* innkeeper

posada *nf* [2988] inn

poseer to possess

desposeer *vt* to dispossess

poseer *vt* [1588] to possess

posesionar *vt* to take possession of

desposeído,-a *nmf* dispossessed person

poseedor,-a *nmf* possessor

poseído,-a *nmf* possessed person

posesivo,-a *nmf* possessive person

posesión *nf* [-sión 2319] possession

poseedor *aj* possessing

poseído *aj* possessed

posesivo *aj* possessive

posible possible

imposibilitar *vt* to prevent the possibility of something

posibilitar *vt* to make possible

imposible *nm* [1667] the impossible

imposibilidad *nf* impossibility

posibilidad *nf* [-idad 448] possibility

posiblemente *av* [-mente 2851] possibly

imposibilitado *aj* unable to move; incapable of moving

imposible *aj* [1667] impossible

posible *aj* [-ible 334] possible

posición position

deposición *nf* deposition

oposición *nf* [-ción 1741] opposition

posición *nf* [671] position

transposición *nf* transposition

positivo positive

positivo,-a *nmf* positive person

positivismo *nm* positivism
positivamente *av* positively
positivo *aj* [965] positive
posterior subsequent; rear
posteridad *nf* posterity
posterioridad *nf* posteriority
posteriormente *av* [-mente 835] subsequently
posterior *aj* [2209] subsequent; rear
postrero *aj* following, next, yet-to-come
postre dessert
repostero,-a *nmf* dessert maker or seller
postre *nm* [3260] dessert
repostería *nf* dessert shop
potencia potency, power
potenciar *vt* to give power to
potentado,-a *nmf* rich or powerful person
potencial *nm* [-cial 2243] power
impotencia *nf* [-encia 4719] impotence
omnipotencia *nf* omnipotence
potencia *nf* [-encia 2757] potency, power
potencialidad *nf* [-idad] potential
potestad *nf* authority
prepotencia *nf* great power
potencialmente *av* potentially
impotente *aj* impotent
omnipotente *aj* all-powerful
potencial *aj* [-cial 2243] potential
potente *aj* [3313] potent
prepotente *aj* abusive of power
pozo well
pozal *nm* [-al(1)] pail, bucket, container used to take water out of a well
pozo *nm* [1973] well
poza *nf* spring
práctica practice
practicar *vt* [1226] to practice
practicante *nmf* medical intern
práctica *nf* [-a 899] practice
prácticamente *av* [-mente 1482] practically
practicable *aj* practicable
práctico *aj* [-ico(2) 4004] practical
pradera large meadow
prado *nm* meadow
pradera *nf* large meadow
precaución precaution
precaver *vt* to prepare
precaverse *vr* to be prepared
incauto,-a *nmf* incautious person
cautela *nf* caution
precaución *nf* [-ción 3709] precaution
incautamente *av* incautiously
incauto *aj* incautious
precavido *aj* prepared

precedente precedent
preceder *vt* to precede
precedente *nm* [-ente(1) 3512] precedent
precedencia *nf* precedence
precedente *aj* [-ente(1) 3512] preceding
precioso precious
apreciar *vt* [1535] to appreciate
depreciar *vt* to depreciate
despreciar *vt* to hate; to despise
menospreciar *vt* to have contempt for; to lack appreciation for
aprecio *nm* appreciation
desprecio *nm* hate; despising
menosprecio *nm* contempt
precio *nm* [421] price
apreciación *nf* appreciation
depreciación *nf* depreciation
preciosidad *nf* preciousness, beauty
apreciable *aj* appreciable
apreciado *aj* appreciated
apreciativo *aj* appreciative
despreciable *aj* despicable; worthless
despreciativo *aj* acting in a despicable manner
inapreciable *aj* despicable; worthless
menospreciable *aj* contemptible
precioso *aj* [-oso 4098] precious
semiprecioso *aj* semi-precious
precipitar to precipitate
precipitar *vt* to precipitate
precipitarse *vr* to be in a hurry; to be rushed
precipitación *nf* precipitation
precipitadamente *av* precipitately; hurried
precipitado *aj* precipitated
preciso precise
precisar *vt* [908] to explain carefully or precisely
imprecisión *nf* imprecision
precisión *nf* [-sión 4341] precision
precisamente *av* [-mente 1242] precisely
impreciso *aj* imprecise
preciso *aj* [2125] precise
predicar to preach
predicar *vt* to preach
predicador,-a *nmf* preacher
prédica *nf* sermon
predicación *nf* sermon
predilección predilection
predilección *nf* predilection
predilecto *aj* favorite, preferred
preferir to prefer
preferir *vt* [1146] to prefer
preferencia *nf* [-encia 2299] preference
preferentemente *av* preferably
preferiblemente *av* preferably

preferente *aj* preferable
preferible *aj* preferable
preferido *aj* preferred

pregonar to announce publicly in streets, on buses, in malls, etc.
pregonar *vt* to announce publicly in streets, on buses, in malls, etc.
pregón *nm* [-ón(1)] public announcement
pregonero *nm* announcer in streets, on buses, in malls, etc.

preguntar to ask (question)
preguntar *vt* [827] to ask (question)
preguntarse *vr* [827] to ask oneself (question); to wonder
pregunta *nf* [-a 944] question
preguntón *aj* [-ón(2)] asking many questions; overly curious

premio prize
premiar *vt* [3248] to give a prize
premio *nm* [-o(1) 573] prize
premiado *aj* prize-winning

prender to turn on; to pin
prender *vt* [3280] to turn on; to pin
prendedor *nm* switch; ignition switch; ornamental pin
prendido *aj* turned on; pinned

prensa press
impresionar *vt* to impress
impresionarse *vr* to be impressed
imprimir *vt* [4849] to print
prensar *vt* to press
reimprimir *vt* to reprint
impresionista *nmf* impressionist
impresor,-a *nmf* printer
impresionismo *nm* impressionism
impreso *nm* [3882] printed material
prensado *nm* pressing
imprenta *nf* printing shop
impresión *nf* [-sión 2871] impression
impresionabilidad *nf* impressionability
impresora *nf* printer
prensa *nf* [-a 528] press
reimpresión *nf* reprint
sobreimpresión *nf* superimposing of film
impresionable *aj* impressionable
impresionante *aj* [3543] impressive
impresionista *aj* impressionistic
impreso *aj* [3882] printed
prensado *aj* pressed

preparar to prepare
preparar *vt* [373] to prepare
prepararse *vr* [373] to prepare oneself; to be preparing

preparador,-a *nmf* preparer
preparado *nm* medicinal preparation
preparativo *nm* [3855] preparation
preparación *nf* [-ción 1158] preparation
preparado *aj* prepared
preparatorio *aj* preparatory

presa dam
presa *nf* dam
represa *nf* small dam

prescindir to omit
prescindir *vt* to omit
imprescindible *aj* indispensable
prescindible *aj* dispensable

presencia presence
presenciar *vt* [2932] to be present
presentar *vt* [108] to present; to introduce
presentarse *vr* to present oneself; to introduce oneself
representar *vt* [390] to represent
presentador,-a *nmf* presenter
representante *nmf* [-ante(2) 489] representative
presente *nm* [288] present (time); present (gift)
omnipresencia *nf* omnipresence
presencia *nf* [-a 483] presence
presentación *nf* [-ción 676] presentation
representación *nf* [-ción 1707] representation
impresentable *aj* not presentable
omnipresente *aj* omnipresent
presentable *aj* presentable
presente *aj* [288] present
representante *aj* [-ante(2) 489] representing
representativo *aj* [-ivo 2621] representative

presidente president
presidir *vt* [1594] to preside
presidente,-a *nmf* president
vicepresidente,-a *nmf* [2051] vice president
presidencia *nf* [-encia 618] presidency
vicepresidencia *nf* vice presidency
presidencial *aj* [-cial 1228] presidential

presión pressure
presionar *vt* [2202] to pressure
presión *nf* [-sión 1045] pressure
represión *nf* [-sión 4670] repression
represivo *aj* repressive
reprimido *aj* repressed

prestar to lend
prestar *vt* [1514] to lend
prestarse *vr* [1514] to volunteer
prestamista *nmf* lender
prestatario,-a *nmf* borrower
préstamo *nm* [3049] loan
prestaciones *nfpl* benefits

prestación *nf* [-ción 2566] lending
prestado *aj* lent; borrowed

prestigio prestige
  desprestigiar *vt* to cause loss of prestige
  desprestigiarse *vr* to lose prestige
  desprestigio *nm* loss of prestige
  prestigio *nm* [3752] prestige
  prestigioso *aj* prestigious

presumir to show conceit or excessive pride
  presumir *vi* [3194] to show conceit or excessive
    pride
  presumido,-a *nmf* prideful or conceited person
  presuntuoso,-a *nmf* presumptuous person
  presunción *nf* presumption
  presuntuosidad *nf* presumptuousness
  presuntamente *av* [-mente 3437] presumably,
    supposedly
  presumible *aj* presumable
  presumido *aj* prideful or conceited
  presunto *aj* [966] supposed
  presuntuoso *aj* presumptuous

pretender to desire something
  pretender(se) *vt(r)* [619] to desire something
  pretencioso,-a *nmf* pretentious person
  pretendiente,-a *nmf* one who courts another;
    pretender (throne)
  pretensión *nf* [-sión 4802] pretension; aspiration
  pretencioso *aj* pretentious
  pretendido *aj* courted
  pretendiente *aj* [-ente(2)] courting

prevalecer to prevail
  prevalecer *vi* [2996] to prevail
  prevaleciente *aj* prevailing

previo previous
  previamente *av* [-mente 3011] previously
  previo *aj* [1022] previous

primavera spring (season)
  primavera *nf* [2978] spring (season)
  primaveral *aj* spring; pertaining to spring
    (season)

primer first
  primerizo,-a *nmf* novice
  primero,-a *nmf* first one
  primeriza *nf* first-time mother
  primerizo *aj* [-izo] novice
  primer *aj* first

príncipe prince
  principado *nm* principality
  príncipe *nm* [2797] prince
  princesa *nf* [2826] princess
  principal *aj* [280] principal
  principesco *aj* pertaining to princes

prisa hurry
  apresurar *vt* [4973] to hurry
  apresurarse *vr* to be in a hurry
  prisa *nf* [4322] hurry
  aprisa *av* hurriedly, quickly
  apresurado *aj* hurried

prisión prison
  prisionero,-a *nmf* [4099] prisoner
  prisión *nf* [2120] prison

privar to deprive
  privar *vt* [644] to deprive
  privarse *vr* [644] to deprive oneself
  privación *nf* privation

privilegio privilege
  privilegiado,-a *nmf* privileged person
  privilegio *nm* [3524] privilege
  privilegiado *aj* [4288] privileged

probar to test
  comprobar *vt* [1681] to prove
  probar *vt* [1893] to test
  comprobante *nm* proof; receipt
  probador *nm* dressing room for trying on
    clothes
  comprobación *nf* proof
  improbabilidad *nf* improbability
  probabilidad *nf* [-idad 4464] probability
  probeta *nf* test tube
  problema *nf* [118] problem
  prueba *nf* [-a 599] test
  improbablemente *av* improbably
  comprobable *aj* provable
  improbable *aj* improbable
  probable *aj* probable
  probado *aj* proven
  problemático *aj* [-ico(2) 2112] problematic,
    problematical

proceder to proceed
  proceder *vi* [1307] to proceed
  procesar *vt* [3572] to process; to prosecute
  procesado,-a *nmf* accused person
  proceder *nm* [1307] behavior
  procedimiento *nm* [-miento 1356] procedure
  procesador *nm* processor
  procesamiento *nm* processing; prosecution
  proceso *nm* [-o(1) 296] process
  procedencia *nf* [-encia 3548] origin
  procesión *nf* procession
  procedente *aj* [-ente(1) 1994] originating in
  procesado *aj* processed
  procesional *aj* processional

procurar to procure; to try
  procurar *vt* [2713] to procure; to try
  procuración *nf* [-ción 4856] procurement

prodigioso prodigious
  prodigio,-a *nmf* prodigy
  prodigio *nm* supernatural phenomenon
  prodigiosamente *av* prodigiously
  prodigioso *aj* prodigious
producir to produce
  producir *vt* [426] to produce
  producirse *vr* to be produced
  reproducir *vt* [4497] to reproduce
  reproducirse *vr* to reproduce, to procreate
  coproductor *nmf* co-producer
  productor,-a *nmf* [370] producer
  producto *nm* [381] product
  subproducto *nm* by-product
  coproducción *nf* co-production
  improductividad *nf* lack of productivity
  producción *nf* [-ción 354] production
  productividad *nf* [-idad 3084] productivity
  productora *nf* film production company
  reproducción *nf* reproduction
  sobreproducción *nf* overproduction
  superproducción *nf* overproduction
  contraproducente *aj* counterproductive
  improductivo *aj* not productive
  productivo *aj* [-ivo 1302] productive
  productor *aj* productive
  reproductor *aj* reproducing; reproductive
profesor professor, teacher
  profesar *vt* to profess
  profesionalizar *vt* to make professional; to perform at a professional level
  profetizar *vt* to prophesy
  profesional *nmf* [735] professional
  profesor,-a *nmf* [919] professor, teacher
  profesionalismo *nm* professionalism
  profesorado *nm* [-ato] professorship; teaching profession
  profeta *nm* prophet
  profecía *nf* prophecy
  profesión *nf* [-sión 2631] profession
  profesionalidad *nf* professionalism
  profesionalmente *av* professionally
  profesional *aj* [735] professional
  profético *aj* [-ico(2)] prophetic
profundo profound; deep
  profundizar *vt* [-izar 4966] to explore the depths of a subject
  profundidad *nf* [-idad 3065] profundity; depths
  profundamente *av* [-mente 4832] profoundly
  profundo *aj* [-undo 1655] profound; deep
programa program
  programar *vt* [1184] to program
  programador,-a *nmf* programmer

programa *nf* [148] program
  programable *aj* programmable
  programático *aj* pertaining to a program
progreso progress
  progresar *vi* [4685] to progress
  progresista *nmf* progressive
  progresismo *nm* progressivism
  progreso *nm* [-o(1) 3230] progress
  progresión *nf* [-sión] progression
  progresivamente *av* progressively
  progresista *aj* progressive
  progresivo *aj* progressive
prohibir to prohibit
  prohibir *vt* [1744] to prohibit
  prohibicionista *nmf* prohibitionist
  prohibición *nf* [-ción 4432] prohibition
  prohibido *aj* prohibited
  prohibitivo *aj* prohibitive
prolongar to prolong
  prolongar *vt* [1718] to prolong
  prolongarse *vr* to be prolonged
  prolongamiento *nm* prolonging
  prolongación *nf* [-ción 4496] prolongation; extension
  prolongadamente *av* extensively
  prolongado *aj* prolonged
prometer to promise
  comprometer *vt* [1247] to commit; to compromise
  comprometerse *vr* [1247] to commit oneself; to compromise oneself
  prometer *vt* [1359] to promise
  prometerse *vr* to make a promise
  prometido,-a *nmf* fiancé, fiancée
  compromiso *nm* [708] commitment
  promesa *nf* [2271] promise
  comprometido *aj* committed
  comprometedor *aj* compromising
  prometedor *aj* promising
  prometido *aj* [-ido(2)] engaged
pronto soon
  pronto *av* [709] soon
  pronto *aj* [709] soon
pronunciar to pronounce
  pronunciar *vt* [2089] to pronounce
  pronunciarse *vr* to pronounce one's opinion
  pronunciamiento *nm* pronouncement
  pronunciación *nf* [-ción] pronunciation
  impronunciable *aj* unpronounceable
  pronunciado *aj* pronounced
propagar to propagate
  propagar *vt* to propagate
  propagarse *vr* to propagate, to be propagated

propagador,-a *nmf* propagator
propagación *nf* propagation
propaganda *nf* [3983] propaganda
propagador *aj* propagative
propagandístico *aj* propagandistic

propicio propitious
propiciar *vt* [2720] to originate or bring about something, to provoke
propiciatorio *aj* originating, provoking
propicio *aj* [4024] propitious, bringing about favorable circumstances

propiedad property
apropiarse *vr* to appropriate
desapropiarse *vr* to give up or lose property
expropiar *vt* to expropriate
copropietario,-a *nmf* co-owner of property
propietario,-a *nmf* property owner
copropiedad *nf* property owned by more than one person
expropiación *nf* [-ción 4701] expropriation
propiedad *nf* [921] property
copropietario *aj* co-owning
propietario *aj* [-ario(2) 1298] proprietary
propio *aj* [237] own

proporcionar to proportion; to supply
proporcionar *vt* [881] to proportion; to supply
desproporción *nf* disproportion
proporción *nf* [3658] proportion
proporcionalidad *nf* proportionality
proporcionadamente *av* proportionately
proporcionalmente *av* proportionally
desproporcionado *aj* disproportionate
proporcionado *aj* proportionate
proporcional *aj* proportional

proposición proposition
propósito *nm* [1229] proposition; proposal; purpose
proposición *nf* proposition

prosa prose
prosa *nf* prose
prosista *nf* prose writer
prosístico *aj* pertaining to prose writing

prosperar to prosper
prosperar *vti* to prosper
prosperidad *nf* prosperity
próspero *aj* prosperous

protagonista protagonist
protagonizar *vt* [-izar 1440] to perform the lead in a play, movie, etc.
antagonista *nmf* antagonist
protagonista *nmf* [1498] protagonist
antagonismo *nm* antagonism

antagónico *aj* antagonistic
antagonista *aj* antagonistic

proteger to protect
proteger *vt* [1034] to protect
proteccionista *nmf* protectionist
protector,-a *nmf* [4146] protector
proteccionismo *nm* protectionism
protector *nm* protector
protectorado *nm* protectorate
protección *nf* [-ción 935] protection
proteccionista *aj* protectionist
protector *aj* protecting
protegido *aj* protected

protesta protest
protestar *vt* [2685] to protest
protestante *nmf* [-ante(2)] protestant
protestantismo *nm* Protestantism
protesta *nf* [-a 1378] protest
protestante *aj* [-ante(2)] protestant
provecho *benefit*
provecho *nm* [4530] benefit
provechosamente *av* beneficially
provechoso *aj* good, useful, beneficial

provincia province
provinciano,-a *nmf* person who lives in a province
provincianismo *nm* provincialism
provincia *nf* [2310] province
provincial *aj* [-cial] provincial
provinciano *aj* pertaining to a province

provisional provisional
aprovisionar *vt* to stock provisions
proveer *vt* [4833] to provide
reaprovisionar *vt* to restock provisions
proveedor,-a *nmf* [2735] provider
provisiones *nfpl* provisions
providencia *nf* Providence
provisión *nf* provision
provista *nf* foreseen circumstance
providencialmente *av* providentially
provisionalmente *av* provisionally
desprovisto *aj* unforeseen
providencial *aj* [-cial] providential
próvido *aj* prepared
provisional *aj* [3353] provisional
provisto *aj* foreseen

provocar to provoke
provocar *vt* [537] to provoke
provocador,-a *nmf* provoker
provocación *nf* provocation
provocado *aj* provoked
provocador *aj* provoking

provocante *aj* provoking
provocativo *aj* provocative

próximo next
aproximar *vt* [3108] to approximate; to move toward
aproximarse *vr* [3108] to move closer to
prójimo *nm* neighbor
aproximación *nf* approximation
proximidad *nf* [-idad] proximity
aproximadamente *av* [-mente 1182] approximately
próximamente *av* [-mente 4362] soon
aproximado *aj* approximate
próximo *aj* [133] next

proyecto project
proyectar *vt* [1886] to project
proyectarse *vr* to cast a silhouette
proyectista *nmf* person who works on projects
anteproyecto *nm* preliminary study
proyectil *nm* projectile
proyecto *nm* [-o(1) 238] project
proyector *nm* projector
proyección *nf* [-ción 3427] projection

prudente prudent
imprudencia *nf* imprudence
prudencia *nf* prudence
prudencialmente *av* prudentially
prudentemente *av* prudently
imprudente *aj* imprudent
prudencial *aj* prudential
prudente *aj* prudent

psicológico psychological
psicoanalizar, sicoanalizar *vt* to psychoanalyze
parasicólogo,-a *nmf* parapsychologist
psicoanalista, sicoanalista *nmf* psychoanalyst
psicólogo,-a, sicólogo,-a *nmf* psychologist
psicópata, sicópata *nmf* psychopath
psicoterapeuta, sicoterapeuta *nmf* psychotherapist
psiquiatra, siquiatra *nmf* psychiatrist
psicoanálisis, sicoanálisis *nm* psychoanalysis
psiquiátrico, siquiátrico *nm* psychiatric hospital
parasicología *nf* parapsychology
psicología, sicología *nf* psychology
psiconeurosis, siconeurosis *nf* neurosis
psicopatología, sicopatología *nf* psychopathology
psicosis, sicosis *nf* psychosis
psicoterapia, sicoterapia *nf* psychotherapy
psique, sique *nf* psyche
psiquiatría, siquiatría *nf* psychiatry
parasicológico *aj* parapsychological
psicodélico, sicodélico *aj* psychedelic
psicológico, sicológico *aj* psychological

psicopático, sicopático *aj* psychopathic
psicosomático, sicosomático *aj* psychosomatic
psiquiátrico, siquiátrico *aj* psychiatric

público public
publicar *vt* [1008] to publish
publicista *nmf* publicist; newspaper or magazine writer
público *nm* [59] public
publicidad *nf* [-idad 2852] publicity, advertising
públicamente *av* [-mente 3984] publicly
publicable *aj* publishable
publicación *aj* [-ción 2662] publication
publicitario *aj* publishing
público *aj* [59] public

pudor shame, modesty, reserve
impudor *nm* shamelessness, immodesty, lack of reserve; cynicism
pudor *nm* shame, modesty, reserve
impúdico *aj* shameless, immodest, lacking reserve; cynical
púdico *aj* shameful, modest, reserved; decent
pudoroso *aj* having shame, modesty, reserve

pueblo town, townspeople
despoblar *vt* to depopulate
despoblarse *vr* to become depopulated
poblar *vt* to populate
poblarse *vr* to become populated
repoblar *vt* to repopulate
poblador,-a *nmf* [4726] person who lives in a town
pueblerino,-a *nmf* person who lives in a small town
republicano,-a *nmf* republican
poblado *nm* [2034] inhabited place
pueblo *nm* [559] town; townspeople
republicanismo *nm* republicanism
despoblación *nf* depopulation
población *nf* [-ción 482] population
repoblación *nf* repopulation
república *nf* [451] republic
superpoblación *nf* overpopulation
poblado *aj* [2034] populated
pueblerino *aj* from a small town
republicano *aj* [-ano 3673] republican
superpoblado *aj* overpopulated

pueril childlike in action or word
puerilidad *nf* childlike action or word
pueril *aj* childlike in action or word

puerta door; gate
portero,-a *nmf* [1484] goalie, goalkeeper in soccer; doorman
picaporte *nm* door catch
portazo *nm* [-azo(2)] door slam

portería nf [2445] soccer goal
puerta nf [842] door; gate
puerto port
aportar vti [1130] to reach port
aeropuerto nm [1163] airport
puerto nm [1176] port
portuario aj pertaining to a port
pugna fight, dispute
pugnar vi [3354] to fight, to engage in a dispute
púgil nm fighter, boxer
pugna nf fight, dispute
punto period, dot
despuntar vt to remove the point from; to break (dawn) from a point of light
puntear vt to make dots
contrapunto nm counterpoint
punteado nm making of dots
puntero nm pointer
punto nm [152] period, dot
sacapuntas nm pencil sharpener
punta nf [2429] point; end of a piece of yarn, string, hair, etc.
despuntado aj without a point
puntiagudo aj sharp, pointed, with a sharp point
puño fist
apuñalar vt to stab with dagger
empuñar vt to take hold of a dagger
puñado nm [-ada(3)] handful
puñal nm dagger
puñetazo nm [-azo(2)] hit with the fist
puño nm fist
empuñadura nf handle of a dagger or sword
puñalada nf [-ada(2)] stab with a dagger
puro pure
depurar vt to purify
expurgar vt to expurgate
purgar vt to purge
purificar vt [-ificar] to purify
purista nmf purist
puritano,-a nmf Puritan
depurativo nm purifying substance
purgante nm medicinal substance prepared to help with purging the stomach and intestinal tract
purgatorio nm [-orio(1)] purgatory
puritanismo nm Puritanism
depuración nf purification
expurgación nf expurgation
impureza nf impurity
pureza nf [-eza] purity
purga nf laxative; purging
purificación nf [-ción] purification

depurador aj purifying
depurativo aj purifying
impuro aj [-ura(2)] impure
purgante aj purging
purificador aj [-dor(2)] purifying
puritano aj puritanical
puro aj [-ura(2) 2355] pure

Q

quebrantado one who is broken-hearted
quebrantar vt to break up; to break a law, to break the heart of
quebrantarse vr to become broken (e.g., heart)
quebrar vt [3138] to break
quebrarse vr to become broken
resquebrajar vt to crack
resquebrajarse vr to become cracked
quebrado nm fraction
quebrantamiento nm the act of breaking physical objects, conceptual objects, laws, etc.
quebrantado nm one who is broken-hearted or broken in spirit
quebrantaolas nm breakwater
quebranto nm the act of breaking down or causing discouragement or pain
quebrada nf break or crack in something
quebradura nf break or crack in something
inquebrantable aj unbreakable
quebradizo aj easily broken
quebrado aj broken
quebrantado aj broken-hearted or broken in spirit
quebrantador aj heart-breaking

quejarse to complain; to groan
quejarse vr to complain; to groan
queja nf [-a 1137] complaint
quejido nm whine or groan
quejumbroso aj complaining

quemar to burn
quemar vt [2450] to burn
quemarse vr [2450] to burn oneself or itself
requemar vt to re-burn
requemarse vr literally, to re-burn oneself or itself; (figurative) to do something quickly
quemador nm a burner, computer compact-disc burner
quema nf [-a 4388] burning
quemadura nf [-dura 4686] burn
quemazón nf unbearable heat; also, the burning down (of building, forest, etc.)

quemado *aj* burned, burnt
requemado *aj* re-burned

querer to want; to love
querer *vt* [117] to want; to love
querido,-a *nmf* beloved
querer *nm* [117] to want; to love
querido *aj* [-ido(1) 1598] beloved, dear

quien who
quien *pron* who
quién *pron* who when used in a question
quienquiera *pron* whoever

quieto calm, quiet
aquietar *vt* to calm, to quiet
aquietarse *vr* to become calm, to become quiet
inquietar *vt* to upset
inquietarse *vr* to become upset
inquietud *nf* [2733] a feeling of disquiet or worry
quietud *nf* calmness, quiet, stillness
inquietante *aj* upsetting, worrisome
inquieto *aj* upset
quieto *aj* calm, quiet

químico chemical
bioquímico,-a *nmf* biochemist
químico,-a *nmf* [1501] chemist
bioquímica *nf* biochemistry
química *nf* chemistry
quimioterapia *nf* chemotherapy
químico *aj* chemical

quince fifteen
quinceañero,-a *nmf* fifteen-year-old boy or girl
quincuagenario,-a *nmf* fifty-year-old person
quintacolumnista *nmf* one who works as a member of a fifth column
quintillizo,-a *nmf* quintuplet
quince *nm* [2259] fifteen
quinientos *nm* five hundred
quinquenio *nm* five-year term; a period of five years
quinteto *nm* a musical group of five people
quinto *nm* one-fifth (fraction)
quincena *nf* [4100] fifteen days; one-half month; fortnight; two-weeks
quince *aj* [2259] fifteen
quincenal *aj* semi-monthly; every fifteen days
quincuagenario *aj* fifty-year-old
quincuagésimo *aj* [-ésimo] fiftieth
quinientos *aj* five-hundred
quinquenal *aj* five-year
quinto *aj* fifth

quitar to remove
quitar *vt* [949] to remove
quitarse *vr* [949] to remove from oneself; to take off (e.g., shirt)

quitaesmalte *nm* fingernail polish remover
quitamanchas *nm* stain remover
quitanieves *nm* snow plow

R

rabia rabies
enrabiar *vt* to give rabies; to anger
enrabiarse *vr* to get rabies; to become angry
rabiar *vt* to anger
rabia *nf* rabies
rabieta *nf* tantrum
antirrábico *aj* anti-rabies medicine
rábico *aj* rabies
rabioso *aj* rabid

radiante radiant
irradiar *vt* to irradiate
radiar *vi* to radiate
radiador *nm* [-dor(2)] radiator
irradiación *nf* irradiation
radiante *aj* radiant

radical radical
radicalizarse *vr* to become radical
radical *nm* [2853] radical
radicalismo *nm* [-ismo] radicalism
radicalmente *av* radically
radical *aj* [2853] radical

radio radio
radiografiar *vt* to give an x-ray
radio *nmf* [1066] radio
radioaficionado,-a *nmf* fan of radio
radioescucha *nmf* radio listener
radiólogo,-a *nmf* radiologist
radioyente *nmf* radio listener
radar *nm* radar
radiómetro *nm* radiometer
radioteléfono *nm* radio telephone
radiotelescopio *nm* radio telescope
radiotransmisor *nm* radio transmitter
radiación *nf* radiation
radiactividad *nf* radioactivity
radioactividad *nf* radioactivity
radiodifusión *nf* radio broadcasting
radiografía *nf* radiography
radiología *nf* radiology
radiorreceptor *nf* radio receiver
radioterapia *nf* radio therapy
radiotransmisión *nf* radio transmission
radiactivo *aj* radioactive
radioactivo *aj* radioactive

raíz root
  arraigar *vi* [4331] to sprout roots
  arraigarse *vr* [4331] to take root; to be or become rooted (also figurative)
  desarraigar *vt* to uproot
  desarraigarse *vr* to become uprooted (also figurative)
  enraizar *vi* to sprout roots
  enraizarse *vr* to take root; to be or become rooted (also figurative)
  arraigo *nm* order to remain in a jurisdiction; settlement of land
  desarraigo *nm* uprooting
  raíz *nf* [1625] root
  arraigado *aj* having roots; rooted
  desarraigado *aj* without roots; uprooted
  enraizado *aj* having roots; rooted

ramo bouquet
  ramaje *nm* [-aje(1)] collection of bouquets or branches; bouquets or branches in general
  ramo *nm* [718] bouquet
  enramada *nf* ornament made of branches or twigs; small shade-giving structure made of branches
  rama *nf* [1494] branch
  enramado *aj* interlaced (branches)

rancio rancid
  enranciar *vt* to make rancid
  enranciarse *vr* to become rancid
  rancidez *nf* rancidness
  ranciedad *nf* rancidness
  rancio *aj* rancid

rapaz rapacious
  rapacidad *nf* rapaciousness
  rapaz *nf* [-az] bird of prey; robber
  rapaz *aj* [-az] rapacious

rápido rapid
  rápido *nm* [-ido(1) 1018] rapid (river)
  rapidez *nf* [-ez 4636] rapidity
  rápidamente *av* [-mente 2460] rapidly
  rápido *av* [-ido(1) 1018] rapidly
  rápido *aj* [-ido(1) 1018] rapid

raro rare
  enrarecer *vt* to make rare; to dissipate
  enrarecerse *vr* to become rare
  rareza *nf* [-eza] rareness
  raramente *av* rarely
  enrarecido *aj* rare, uncommon
  raro *aj* [2580] rare or strange, referring to a situation

rastro sign, footprint, mark
  rastrear *vt* to look for signs or clues

rastreador *nm* investigator; one who can read signs or clues
  rastro *nm* [3075] sign, footprint, mark
  rastrojo *nm* what is left over after the harvest
  rastreo *nm* act of searching for clues or following signs

rayo ray; bolt
  rayar *vt* [4803] to shine with rays (dawn); to draw lines
  subrayar *vt* [1626] to highlight; to underline
  pararrayos *nm* lightning rod
  rayado *nm* [-ado(1)] lined
  rayo *nm* [1953] ray; bolt
  raya *nf* [-a 4363] line
  rayado *aj* [-ado(1)] lined; crossed-out

raza race
  raza *nf* [3076] race
  racial *aj* [-cial] racial

razón reason
  razonar *vti* to reason
  razonamiento *nm* reasoning
  razón *nf* [627] reason
  sinrazón *nf* unreasonableness
  razonablemente *av* reasonably
  irrazonable *aj* unreasonable
  razonable *aj* [-able 4834] reasonable
  razonado *aj* reasoned

real[1] real
  realizar *vt* [-izar 73] to realize a goal, to make real or achieve a goal or objective
  realizarse *vr* to become or develop into something
  realista *nmf* [-ista 4804] realist
  realizador,-a *nmf* [3754] producer or director of film or television
  surrealista *nmf* surrealist painter
  neorrealismo *nm* neo-realism
  realismo *nm* realism
  surrealismo *nm* surrealism
  irrealidad *nf* unreality
  realidad *nf* [-idad 665] reality
  realización *nf* [-ción 1880] realization; achieving of a goal
  realmente *av* [-mente 1118] really
  irreal *aj* unreal
  irrealizable *aj* unrealizable, unachievable
  real *aj* [534] real
  realista *aj* [-ista 4804] realistic
  realizable *aj* realizable, achievable
  surrealista *aj* surrealistic

real[2] royal
  realeza *nf* royalty
  real *aj* [534] royal

rebeldía   rebellion
   rebelarse *vr*   to rebel
   rebelde *nmf* [2211]   rebel
   rebelión *nm*   rebellion
   rebeldía *nf*   rebellion
   rebelde *aj* [2211]   rebellious

receta   recipe; prescription
   recetar *vt*   to write a prescription
   recetario *nm*   recipe book
   receta *nf* [3050]   recipe; prescription

rechazar   to reject
   rechazar *vt* [975]   to reject
   rechace *nm*   rebound of a missed shot in sport
   rechazo *nm* [-o(1) 2910]   rejection

recibir   to receive
   recibir *vt* [101]   to receive
   recepcionista *nmf*   receptionist
   receptor-a *nmf*   receiver
   receptor *nm* [-or 3261]   electrical receiver
   recibidor *nm*   entry room
   recibimiento *nm*   celebration of arrival
   recibo *nm* [2404]   receipt
   recipiente *nm* [-ente(2) 3525]   container
   radiorreceptor *nf*   radio receiver
   recepción *nf* [-ción 1418]   reception
   receptividad *nf*   receptivity
   receptivo *aj*   receptive
   receptor *aj* [-or 3261]   receiving

reciente   recent
   recién *av* [1421]   recent, newly
   recientemente *av* [-mente 1232]   recently
   reciente *aj* [670]   recent

reclamar   to reclaim
   aclamar *vt*   to acclaim
   clamar *vt*   to claim
   exclamar *vi* [4959]   to exclaim
   proclamar *vt* [3905]   to proclaim
   reclamar *vi* [1883]   to reclaim
   clamor *nm*   clamor
   aclamación *nf*   acclamation
   exclamación *nf*   exclamation
   proclama *nf*   proclamation
   proclamación *nf*   proclamation
   reclamación *nf*   complaint
   clamoroso *aj*   clamorous
   exclamatorio *aj*   exclamatory

recoger   to collect, pick up, gather
   acoger *vt*   to protect; to shelter
   acogerse *vr*   to protect oneself; to take refuge
   coger *vt*   to grasp or take in hand
   encoger *vt*   to shrink or contract
   escoger *vt* [2019]   to choose
   recoger *vt* [1954]   to collect, pick up, gather

   recogerse *vr* [1954]   to retire for the evening or go home
   sobrecoger *vt*   to take by surprise
   sobrecogerse *vr*   to be taken by surprise
   acogido,-a *nmf*   person cared for in a special place (hospice, nursing home, etc.)
   recogepelotas *nmf*   ball boy or girl
   encogimiento *nm*   shrinking
   escogimiento *nm*   choosing
   recogedor *nm*   dustpan
   recogimiento *nm*   collection
   acogida *nf*   refuge
   recogida *nf*   the act of gathering up and putting things in place
   acogedor *aj*   comfortable; enjoyable for the manner in which one is treated
   encogido *aj*   shrunk
   escogido *aj*   chosen
   recogido *aj*   collected; gathered and put in place
   sobrecogedor *aj*   surprising

recomendar   to recommend
   recomendar *vt* [1424]   to recommend
   recomendado,-a *nmf*   recommended person
   recomendación *nf* [-ción 2157]   recommendation
   recomendable *aj* [-able 4040]   recommendable
   recomendado *aj*   recommended

recordar   to remember
   recordar(se) *vt(r)* [378]   to remember
   récord *nm* [1899]   best mark; record
   recordatorio *nm*   reminder; memo
   recuerdo *nm* [1491]   keepsake or remembrance
   récord *aj* [1899]   record

recto   right, correct, straight
   rectificar *vt* [-ificar]   to rectify
   rectificador *nmf*   verifier; person who verifies
   rector,-a *nmf* [3034]   rector
   recto *nm* [3787]   rectum
   rectorado *nm*   rectorate
   recta *nf*   straight line
   rectificación *nf*   rectification
   rectitud *nf* [-itud]   rectitude; proper behavior
   rectoría *nf*   rectorate
   rectificable *aj*   rectifiable
   rectificador *aj*   rectifying
   rectilíneo *aj*   straight; in or following a straight line
   recto *aj* [3787]   right, correct, straight
   rector *aj* [-or]   governing
   rectoral *aj* [-al(1)]   relating to the rector or rectorate

recurso   recourse, resource
   recurrir *vi* [2096]   to appear before a judge as a recourse

recurso *nm* [208] recourse, resource
recurrente *aj* appearing before a judge for
   recourse
recurrible *aj* appealable; having recourse
red net, network
desenredar *vt* to untangle
desenredarse *vr* to untangle oneself; to
   untangle oneself from an amorous relationship
enredar *vt* to tangle
enredarse *vr* to become tangled
enredador,-a *nmf* person who entangles others
   in problems; gossip
enredo *nm* confusion
enredadera *nf* climbing vine
red *nf* [894] net, network
enredador *aj* gossiping
enredoso *aj* difficult; confusing; requiring
   much work to solve
redacción editing
redactar *vt* to edit
redactor,-a *nmf* editor
redacción *nf* [-ción 3166] editing
redimir to redeem
redimir *vt* to redeem
redimirse *vr* to be redeemed; to redeem oneself
redentor,-a *nmf* redeemer
redención *nf* redemption
redentor *aj* redeeming
redimible *aj* redeemable
redondo round
redondear *vt* to make round
redondearse *vr* to be round
redondez *nf* roundness
redondo *aj* [4051] round
reducir to reduce
reducir(se) *vt(r)* [715] to reduce
reducción *nf* [-ción 1817] reduction
irreducible *aj* irreducible
reducido *aj* reduced
reductible *aj* reducible
referir to refer
referir *vt* [577] to refer
referirse *vr* [577] to be referring to
referéndum *nm* referendum
referencia *nf* [-encia 1955] reference
referente *aj* [-ente(1) 2554] concerning
refinado refined
refinar *vt* to refine or purify
refinarse *vr* to become refined
refinado *nm* refining
refinamiento *nm* refined quality of a person or
   business
finura *nf* [-ura(1)] fineness

refinería *nf* refinery
entrefino *aj* somewhat fine
extrafino *aj* extra fine
fino *aj* [2499] fine
refinado *aj* refined
superfino *aj* very fine
reflejo reflection; reflex
reflectar *vi* to reflect
reflejar *vt* [1396] to reflect
reflejarse *vr* to be reflected
reflector *nm* reflector
reflejo *nm* [4181] reflection; reflex
reflectante *aj* reflecting
reflector *aj* reflecting
reflejo *aj* [4181] reflected
reflexión reflection (thought)
reflexionar *vi* [3624] to reflect with thought on
   something
reflexión *nf* [2901] reflection (thought)
irreflexivo *aj* without reflection
reflexivo *aj* with reflection; reflective; reflexive
   (grammar)
refugiar to seek refuge
refugiar *vt* [2669] to seek refuge
refugiarse *vr* [2669] to take refuge
refugiado,-a *nmf* refugee
refugio *nm* [-o(1) 2306] refuge
refugiado *aj* refugee
regalar to give a gift
regalar *vt* [1742] to give a gift
regalo *nm* [-o(1) 1365] gift
regalado *aj* given as a gift
regar to water
regar *vt* [4254] to water
regadío *nm* cultivated land
riego *nm* [-iego 1748] watering
regadera *nf* [-era] the shower
regadío *aj* cultivatable
régimen regimen
regentar *vt* to work temporarily as a governor,
   supervisor, or regent
regir *vt* [3549] to govern
reglamentar *vt* to impose a law
regente *nmf* [-ente(2)] regent
regidor,-a *nmf* member of a governing council
regionalista *nmf* regionalist
regente *nm* [-ente(2)] regent
regicidio *nm* murder of a regent or prince
régimen *nm* [1433] regimen
regimiento *nm* regiment
regionalismo *nm* regionalism
reglamento *nm* [-o(1) 1774] regulation or rule
regencia *nf* regency

regenta *nf* wife of the regent
región *nf* [330] region
regla *nf* [1639] rule; ruler
reglamentación *nf* regulation of something
regionalmente *av* regionally
antirreglamentario *aj* contrary to regulations
regente *aj* [-ente(2)] ruling
regio *aj* [4271] related to the king; luxurious
regional *aj* [662] regional
regionalista *aj* regionalistic
reglamentario *aj* [4727] required by regulation

registrar to register
registrar *vt* [310] to register
registrarse *vr* [310] to be registered
registrador,-a *nmf* registrar
registro *nm* [-o(1) 1207] registration
caja registradora *nf* cash register
registrado *aj* registered
registrador *aj* registering

regresar to return
regresar *vi* [475] to return
regreso *nm* [-o(1) 1555] return
regresión *nf* regression
regresivo *aj* [-ivo] returning

regular regular
regular *aj* [1408] regular
regularizar *vt* [-izar 3755] to regularize
irregularidad *nf* [-idad 1685] irregularity
regulación *nf* [-ción 3731] regulation
regularidad *nf* regularity
regularización *nf* [-ción 4063] regularization
regularmente *av* [-mente 4289] regularly
irregular *aj* [3092] irregular
regulable *aj* adjustable
regular *aj* [1408] regular

reír to laugh
reír *vt* [2758] to laugh
reírse *vr* [2758] to be laughing
sonreír *vi* [3562] to smile
sonreírse *vr* to be smiling
risa *nf* [2979] laughter
risita *nf* chuckle
risotada *nf* loud and strong laughter
sonrisa *nf* [2676] smile
irrisorio *aj* laughable; ridiculous
risible *aj* [-ible] laugh provoking
risueño *aj* [-eño] cheerful
sonriente *aj* smiling

reja protective bar
enrejar *vt* to put up a protective grill
enrejado *nm* latticework or protective grill
reja *nf* [3438] protective bar

rejilla *nf* grill of a window or duct system
enrejado *aj* with bars

relación relation
relacionar *vt* [909] to relate
relacionarse *vr* [909] to be related to
correlación *nf* correlation
relación *nf* [287] relation
correlativo *aj* correlative
relacionado *aj* related

relativo relative
relativista *nmf* relativist
relativismo *nm* relativism
relatividad *nf* relativity
relativista *aj* relativistic
relativo *aj* [2681] relative

relato narrative, story
relatar *vt* [3513] to relate, narrate, or tell a story
relato *nm* narrative, story

religioso religious
religioso,-a *nmf* religious person
religión *nf* [2922] religion
religiosidad *nf* religiousness
religiosamente *av* religiously
religioso *aj* [776] religious

reloj watch; clock
relojero,-a *nmf* watchmaker, watch repairman, or watch salesman
reloj *nm* [3383] watch; clock
relojería *nf* [-ería(1)] clock shop

remedio remedy
remediar *vt* to remediate
remedio *nm* [-o(1) 3242] remedy
irremediablemente *av* hopelessly
irremediable *aj* irremediable
remediable *aj* remediable

remitir to remit
remitir *vt* [2392] to remit
remitirse *vr* [2392] to use something to back up one's word; to cite or refer to another source as proof
remitente *nmf* sender
remite *nm* sender's name and address or other details

rencor rancor
rencor *nm* rancor
rencilla *nf* dispute or argument resulting in ill-will
rencilloso *aj* argumentative, quarrelsome
rencoroso *aj* [-oso] rancorous

rendir to surrender; to yield
rendir *vt* [1611] to surrender
rendirse *vr* [1611] to surrender oneself

rendimiento *nm* [-miento 2443] fatigue
rendición *nf* surrender
rendido *aj* fatigued

renta rent
arrendar *vt* to rent
rentar *vt* to rent
subarrendar *vt* to sublet
arrendatario,-a *nmf* tenant
rentero,-a *nmf* landlord or landlady
rentista *nmf* one who earns his living through rentals
subarrendatario,-a *nmf* tenant of sublet property
arrendamiento *nm* renting, leasing
subarrendamiento *nm* subletting
renta *nf* [-a 2307] rent
rentabilidad *nf* profitability
arrendatario *aj* renting, leasing
rentable *aj* profitable

renunciar to resign a position
renunciar *vt* [2362] to resign a position
renuncia *nf* [-a 2325] resignation

reñir to fight
reñir *vt* to fight
riña *nf* [2641] fight
reñido *aj* competitive

reparar to repair
reparar *vt* [2916] to repair
reparación *nf* [-ción 2799] repair
irreparable *aj* irreparable
reparable *aj* reparable

repente (de repente) suddenly
de repente *av* suddenly
repentinamente *av* suddenly
repentino *aj* [-ino(2)] sudden

repetir to repeat
repetir *vt* [1430] to repeat
repetirse *vr* to be repeated; to repeat oneself
repetidor,-a *nmf* student who is repeating a class or grade
repetidor *nm* electronic repeater
repetición *nf* [-ción 4923] repetition
repetidamente *av* repeatedly
repetido *aj* repeated
repetidor *aj* repeating

replicar to replicate
replicar *v* to replicate
réplica *nf* replica

reposo repose, rest
reposar *vi* to repose, to rest
reposarse *vr* to be resting or in a state of repose

reposacabezas *nm* headrest
reposapiés *nm* footrest
reposo *nm* repose, rest
reposado *aj* quiet, rested

reproche reproach
reprochar *vt* to reproach
reproche *nm* reproach
irreprochable *aj* irreproachable
reprochable *aj* reproachable
reprochador *aj* reproaching

repugnar to reject something for its repugnance
repugnar *vt* to reject something for its repugnance
repugnancia *nf* [-ancia] repugnance
repugnante *aj* repugnant

repulsión repulsion
repulsión *nf* [-sión] repulsion
repulsivo *aj* [-ivo] repulsive

reputación reputation
reputación *nf* reputation
reputado *aj* reputed

requerir to require
requerir *vt* [424] to require
prerrequisito *nm* prerequisite
requerimiento *nm* [-miento 3889] requirement
requisito *nm* [1920] requisite

reserva reserve
reservar *vt* [3291] to reserve
reservarse *vr* to be reserved
reserva *nmf* [-a 1532] member of military reserve
reservado *nmf* reserved or discreet person
reservista *nmf* member of military reserve
reservado *nm* reserved area
reserva *nf* [-a 1532] reserve; reservation
reservado *aj* reserved, discreet

residir to reside
residir *vi* [3368] to reside
residente *nmf* [-ente(1) 2893] resident
residencia *nf* [-encia 1124] residence; residency
residencial *aj* [-cial 3514] residential
residente *aj* [-ente(1) 2893] resident

resignar to resign
resignar *vt* to resign
resignarse *vr* to be resigned to
resignación *nf* resignation
resignadamente *av* resignedly
resignado *aj* resigned

resistir to resist
resistir *vt* [3028] to resist, to oppose

resistirse *vr* to resist, to keep oneself from
  succumbing to a temptation; to contain
  oneself
resistencia *nf* [-encia 2467] resistance
irresistible *aj* irresistible
resistente *aj* [-ente(1)] restistant

respecto a with respect to
respectar *vt* [3355] to have to do with
respecto a *nm* with respect to
respectivamente *av* [-mente 1711] respectively
respectivo *aj* [1497] respective

respeto respect
respetar *vt* [1079] to respect
respeto *nm* [-o(1) 1167] respect
respetabilidad *nf* respectability
irrespetuoso *aj* disrespectful
respetable *aj* respectable
respetuoso *aj* [-oso 4593] respectful

respirar to breathe
respirar *vi* [3906] to breathe
respiradero *nm* ventilator, vent
respiro *nm* breath
respiración *nf* respiration
irrespirable *aj* unbreathable, suffocating
respiratorio *aj* [-orio(2) 3304] respiratory

resplandor light or shine of something
resplandecer *vi* to shine, to give off light
resplandor *nm* light or shine of something
resplandeciente *aj* shiny or bright

responder to respond
responder *vt* [557] to respond
respondón *nmf* [-ón(2)] back talker
respuesta *nf* [602] answer, response

responsabilidad responsibility
responsabilizar *vt* [-izar 4065] to make responsible
  for
responsabilizarse *vr* [4065] to take responsibility
  for
irresponsable *nmf* irresponsible person
irresponsabilidad *nf* irresponsibility
responsabilidad *nf* [-idad 745] responsibility
irresponsable *aj* irresponsible
responsable *aj* [555] responsible

restaurar to restore
restaurar *vt* to restore
restaurador,-a *nmf* specialist in restoration
restauración *nf* [-ción 4835] restoration
restaurador *aj* restorative

resto the rest, the remainder
restar *vt* [4163] to subtract
resto *nm* [-o(1) 681] the rest, the remainder
restante *aj* [-ante(1) 3087] leftover

resultar to result in
resultar *vi* [477] to result in
resultado *nm* [-ado(2) 212] result
resulta *nf* [-a 1203] result
resultante *aj* resulting

resumen summary
resumir *vt* [4995] to summarize
resumen *nm* [4041] summary; resume

retirar to retire (at night)
retirar *vt* [751] to retire (at night)
retirarse *vr* [751] to go to bed for the evening
retiro *nm* [-o(1) 1815] retiring for the evening;
  retreat for prayer, meditation or study
retirada *nf* military retreat; retiring (for the
  evening)
retirado *aj* retired; distant

retórica rhetoric
retórico,-a *nmf* rhetorician
retórica *nf* rhetoric
retórico *aj* rhetorical

retrasar to turn back a clock; to delay
retrasar *vt* [3002] to turn back a clock; to delay
retrasarse *vr* [3002] to be late
retrasado,-a *nmf* slow learner
retraso *nm* [-o(1) 3130] turning back of a clock;
  delay
retrasado *aj* late; behind schedule; behind
  (clock or watch)

retrato portrait
retratar *vt* to paint or to photograph portraits
retratarse *vr* to have one's portrait made or
  taken
retratista *nmf* portrait painter or photographer
autorretrato *nm* self-portrait
retrato *nm* [-o(1) 4836] portrait
retratado *aj* photographed or painted in
  portrait form

retroceder to go back; to back up
retroceder *vt* to go back; to back up
retroceso *nm* going back; backing up

revelar to reveal; to develop (film)
revelar *vt* [1249] to reveal; to develop (film)
revelador,-a *nmf* film developer (person)
revelación *nf* [-ción 4324] revelation
revelado *aj* developed; revealed
revelador *aj* developing

revés reverse
revertir *vi* [4102] to revert
reverso *nm* reverse; back side
revés *nm* [3221] reverse
reversión *nf* reversion

irreversible *aj* irreversible
reversible *aj* reversible

revoltoso turbulent; mischievous
revoltijo *nm* disorganized mess
revuelta *nf* disorder of people
revoltoso *aj* turbulent; mischievous
revuelto *aj* scrambled; mixed-up, disorganized

revolución revolution
revolucionar *vt* to revolt, to revolutionize
revolucionario,-a *nmf* revolutionary
contrarrevolución *nf* counter-revolution
revolución *nf* [-ción 1029] revolution
revolucionario *aj* [-ario(2) 1255] revolutionary

rey king
reinar *vi* to reign
reino *nm* [-o(1) 3129] kingdom
rey *nm* [1442] king
virreinato *nm* position or office of viceroy
virrey *nm* viceroy
reina *nf* [-a 1696] queen
reinado *nf* [-ato] reign
virreina *nf* wife of the viceroy
reinante *aj* reigning

rezar to pray with repetition of words
rezar *vti* [2697] to pray with repetition of words
rezo *nm* prayer using repetition of words

rico rich
enriquecer *vt* [3868] to enrich
enriquecerse *vr* to become rich
rico,-a *nmf* rich person
enriquecimiento *nm* [-miento] enrichment
riqueza *nf* [-eza 2408] riches
ricamente *av* richly
rico *aj* [628] rich; excellent (food)

ridículo ridiculous
ridiculizar *vt* to ridicule
ridículo,-a *nmf* fool
ridiculez *nf* ridiculousness
ridículo *aj* [-culo] ridiculous

riesgo risk
arriesgar *vt* [3175] to risk
arriesgarse *vr* to take a risk
riesgo *nm* [504] risk
arriesgado *aj* at risk; risky

rígido rigid
rigidez *nf* rigidity
rígido *aj* rigid

riguroso rigorous
rigor *nm* rigor
rigurosidad *nf* rigorousness
rigurosamente *av* rigorously
riguroso *aj* rigorous

rincón corner
arrinconar *vt* to corner
arrinconarse *vr* to be cornered
rincón *nm* [2708] corner
rinconera *nf* corner piece of furniture
arrinconado *aj* isolated or set apart from the rest

río river
riachuelo *nm* small river
río *nm* [416] river

ritmo rhythm
ritmo *nm* [1323] rhythm
rítmico *aj* rhythmic

rival rival
rivalizar *vt* to rival
rival *nmf* [836] rival
rivalidad *nf* [-idad 4837] rivalry
rival *aj* [836] rival

robar to rob
robar *vt* [1314] to rob
antirrobo *nm* anti-theft system
robo *nm* [-o(1) 1278] robbery
antirrobo *aj* anti-theft

robusto robust
robustecer *vt* to make robust or stronger
robustecerse *vr* to become more robust or stronger
robustecimiento *nm* act of becoming more robust
robustez *nf* [-ez] robustness
robusto *aj* robust

roca rock
roca *nf* [4969] rock
rocoso *aj* rocky

rodar to roll
rodar *vt* [3489] to roll
rodaje *nm* [-aje(1) 3077] wheels in general
rodamiento *nm* rolling
rodada *nf* wheel rut
rodado *aj* with wheels
rodante *aj* rolling

rodear to surround
rodear *vt* [1781] to surround
rodearse *vr* [1781] to surround oneself with something
rodeo *nm* [-eo(1) 3757] rodeo; act of surrounding or encircling

rodilla knee
arrodillar *vt* to bow on a knee
arrodillarse *vr* to bow on one's knees
rodillazo *nm* [-azo(2)] a hit with the knee
rodilla *nf* [-illa 2854] knee

rodillada *nf* [-ada(2)] a hit with the knee
rodillera *nf* knee protectors or knee guards
arrodillado *aj* bowing on knees

rojo red
  enrojecer *vti* to redden
  enrojecerse *vr* to become red
  rojear *vi* to show a red coloring
  sonrojar *vt* to cause to blush
  sonrojarse *vr* to blush
  pelirrojo,-a *nmf* redhead
  rojo,-a *nmf* red one
  enrojecimiento *nm* reddening
  rojo *nm* [309] red
  sonrojo *nm* blushing
  rojez *nf* [-ez] redness
  infrarrojo *aj* infrared
  pelirrojo *aj* redheaded
  rojizo *aj* [-izo] reddish
  rojo *aj* [309] red

romano Roman
  romano,-a *nmf* Roman
  romántico,-a *nmf* [2232] romantic
  romance *nm* [3053] romance
  romanticismo *nm* romanticism
  Roma *nf* Rome
  romance *aj* [3053] romance
  románico *aj* Romanesque
  romano *aj* [-ano 2550] Roman
  romántico *aj* romantic

romper to tear; to break
  romper *vt* [1186] to tear; to break
  romperse *vr* to become torn or broken
  rompecorazones *nmf* heartbreaker
  rompecabezas *nm* puzzle
  rompehielos *nm* ship made for sailing in icy waters
  rompeolas *nm* breakwater
  rompimiento *nm* break-up; breaking
  irrompible *aj* unbreakable
  rompible *aj* [-ible] breakable

ronda rounds of vigilance
  rondar *vt* to make rounds of vigilance; to court a woman; to think of an idea not yet concrete in one's mind
  ronda *nf* [-a 1551] rounds of vigilance
  rondalla *nf* vocal and instrumental musical group, often from a school

ropa clothes
  arropar *vt* to put on heavier clothes
  arroparse *vr* to put heavier clothing on oneself
  desarropar *vt* to take off heavy clothes
  desarroparse *vr* to take off one's heavy clothes

guardarropa *nmf* cloakroom clerk
ropavejero,-a *nmf* used clothing merchant
arropamiento *nm* action of putting on heavy clothes
guardarropa *nm* closet
ropaje *nm* [-aje(1)] garments
ropero *nm* [-ero(1)] closet; wardrobe
ropa *nf* [1385] clothes

rosa rose
  sonrosar *v* to lightly blush
  rosado *nm* [-ado(1)] rose color
  rosal *nm* [-al(3)] rose bush
  rosa *nf* [2759] rose
  rosaleda *nf* [-eda] rose garden
  rosa *aj* [2759] rose
  rosáceo *aj* [-eo(2)] rose-colored; rosy
  rosado *aj* [-ado(1)] rose
  sonrosado *aj* rose-colored, referring to skin

rostro face
  arrostrar *vt* to face danger
  rostro *nm* [1786] face

rótulo announcement on a sign
  rotular *vt* to put up an announcement on a sign
  rotulador,-a *nmf* sign maker or painter
  rotulador *nm* metal-tipped pencil to make signs
  rótulo *nm* announcement on a sign
  rotulación *nf* action of putting up an announcement on a sign
  rotulador *aj* used for sign-making

rozar to touch lightly; to brush against; to give a rash to by rubbing
  rozar *vt* to touch lightly; to brush against; to give a rash to by rubbing
  rozarse *vr* to develop a rash from rubbing
  roce *nm* rubbing, friction
  rozamiento *nm* rubbing, friction
  rozadura *nf* [-dura] rash from rubbing

rubio blond
  rubio *nm* [3589] blond
  rubia *nf* blonde
  rubio *aj* [3589] blond

rubor blush, rouge
  ruborizar *vt* [-izar] to cause to blush
  ruborizarse *vr* to blush
  rubor *nm* blush, rouge

ruido noise
  ruido *nm* [3271] noise
  ruidoso *aj* noisy

ruina ruin
  arruinar *vt* to ruin
  arruinarse *vr* to be ruined
  ruina *nf* [-a] ruin

arruinado *aj* ruined

ruinoso *aj* ruinous

rumor rumor

rumorearse *vr* to be rumored

rumor *nm* [2607] rumor

rumoroso *aj* murmuring

S

sábado Saturday; Sabbath

sábado *nm* [413] Saturday; Sabbath

sabático *aj* sabbatical

sabatino *aj* [-ino(2) 4858] Saturday, Sabbath

saber to know

saber *vt* [124] to know

sabelotodo *nmf* know-it-all; person who acts as if he has deep knowledge

sabihondo,-a, sabiondo,-a *nmf* know-it-all; person who acts as if he has deep knowledge; a presumptuous person

sabio,-a *nmf* wise man or woman

saber *nm* [124] knowledge

sabiduría *nf* [-ería(2) 4838] wisdom

sapiencia *nf* wisdom

sabiendas (a) *av* knowing full well

consabido *aj* aforementioned, aforesaid

sabedor *aj* knowing

sabido *aj* known; well-known

sabihondo, sabiondo *aj* literally, deep with knowledge, but is used pejoratively to refer to someone who is presumptuous

sabio *aj* [4839] wise

sapiente *aj* wise

sabor flavor; taste

saborear *vt* to savor

sabor *nm* [1699] flavor; taste

saboreo *nm* savoring

sabrosura *nf* deliciousness

sabroso *aj* [-oso 4688] delicious

sacar to take out

entresacar *vt* to take out from a stack or collection; to cut hair in a layered manner

sacar *vt* [497] to take out; to serve, in sport

sacarse *vr* to get oneself out

sacamuelas *nmf* informal term for dentist

sacaclavos *nm* nail remover

sacacorchos *nm* corkscrew

sacapuntas *nm* pencil sharpener

saque *nm* [4551] service in sport

sacerdote priest

sacerdocio *nm* priesthood

sacerdote *nm* [1339] priest

sacerdotisa *nf* priestess

sacerdotal *aj* [-al(2)] pertaining to priests and priesthood

sacrificio sacrifice

sacralizar *vt* to consecrate; to sanctify

sacramentar *vt* to offer a sacrament

sacrificar *vt* [-ificar 3250] to sacrifice

sacrificarse *vr* to sacrifice oneself

sacramento *nm* sacrament

sacrificio *nm* [-icio 2675] sacrifice

sacrilegio *nm* sacrilege

sacristía *nf* sacristy

sacramental *aj* sacramental

sacrificado *aj* sacrificed

sacrílego *aj* sacrilegious

sacro *aj* sacred

sacrosanto *aj* sacrosanct

sacudir to shake

sacudir *vt* [4498] to shake

sacudirse *vr* to be shaking

sacudidor *nm* tool for cleaning dust; duster

sacudida *nf* [-ido(2)] shaking

sagrado sacred

consagrar *vt* [4676] to consecrate; to sanctify

consagrarse *vr* [4676] to become consecrated or sanctified

consagración *nf* consecration

sagrado *aj* [1448] sacred

sal salt

asalariar *vt* to pay a salary

desalar *vt* to remove the salt from

salar *vt* to salt

saldar *vt* to make the final payment

salpimentar *vt* to salt and pepper something

asalariado,-a *nmf* salaried employee

saladero *nm* place for salting fish

salario *nm* [-ario(2) 1225] salary

salazón *nm* salting of meats

salchichón *nm* sausage

saldo *nm* [2532] salary

salero *nm* [-ero(1)] saltshaker

salitre *nm* salt that remains after one sweats

sobresueldo *nm* extra income

sueldo *nm* [2248] salary

sal *nf* [1635] salt

saladura *nf* salting

salchicha *nf* sausage

salina *nf* salt mine

salinidad *nf* salinity

salmuera *nf* salty water

salsa *nf* [2224] salsa; sauce

asalariado *aj* salaried

salado *aj* salted
salarial *aj* [2800] pertaining to a salary
salífero *aj* [-ífero] salty
salino *aj* saline
salobre *aj* salty

sala living room
salón *nm* [1119] classroom
antesala *nf* antechamber
sala *nf* [1054] living room

saliente protruding, projecting
sobresalir *vi* [3775] to protrude; to stand out from the rest
sobresaliente *nmf* theatrical understudy; substitute bullfighter
saliente *nm* protrusion
sobresaliente *nm* highest grade in a class
salido *aj* protruding beyond the normal
saliente *aj* protruding, projecting
sobresaliente *aj* remarkable, outstanding, standing out from the rest

salir to leave
salir(se) *vt(r)* [168] to leave
salida *nf* [-ido(2) 722] exit

saltar to jump
resaltar *vt* [1865] to emphasize or to call attention to something
saltar *vi* [2571] to jump
saltarse *vr* to skip over or to jump over; to omit
sobresaltar *vt* to scare
sobresaltarse *vr* to be scared
saltador,-a *nmf* acrobat; high jumper
saltimbanqui *nmf* circus acrobat
resalto *nm* emphasizing; calling attention
saltamontes *nm* grasshopper
saltaojos *nm* peony
salto *nm* [-o(1) 3821] jump
sobresalto *nm* surprise, fright
saltador *aj* [-dor(1)] jumping
saltarín *aj* bouncing

salud health
saludar *vt* [2963] to salute
saludo *nm* [-o(1)] salute; greeting
insalubridad *nf* poor health
salubridad *nf* healthiness
salud *nf* [255] health
insalubre *aj* unhealthy
salubre *aj* healthy
saludable *aj* [3095] healthy

salvaje savage; wild
salvaje *nm* [4066] savage
salvajismo *nm* [-ismo] savagery

salvajada *nf* savagery
salvaje *aj* [4066] savage; wild

salvar to save
salvaguardar *vt* to protect; to safeguard
salvar *vt* [1578] to save
salvarse *vr* to save oneself; to be saved
salvador,-a *nmf* savior
Salvador *nm* Savior
salvaguardia *nm* guard
salvamanteles *nm* placemat
salvamento *nm* [4617] deliverance; refuge
salvavidas *nm* lifeguard
salvoconducto *nm* safe conduct
salvación *nf* salvation
salvaguardia *nf* safe conduct
salvedad *nf* the act of making an exception; qualification
salvo *av* [2902] except; outside of
salvable *aj* savable; rescuable; able to be saved
salvador *aj* saving
salvo *aj* [2902] safe

sangre blood
desangrar *vt* to remove or take blood
desangrarse *vr* to lose blood
ensangrentar *vt* to get blood on something
sangrar *vti* to bleed
sangrarse *vr* to bleed, to be bleeding
consanguíneo,-a *nmf* blood brother or sister
desangramiento *nm* blood loss
consanguinidad *nf* blood relationship
sangre *nf* [1214] blood
sangría *nf* red wine
sanguijuela *nf* leech
consanguíneo *aj* blood-related
ensangrentado *aj* bloodstained
sangrante *aj* bleeding
sangriento *aj* [-iento] bloody; bloodstained
sanguinario *aj* cruel
sanguíneo *aj* [-eo(2) 3054] pertaining to blood
sanguinolento *aj* [-lento] bloody; bloodstained

sano healthy
sanar *vti* to heal
sanear *vt* to clean up; to disinfect
sanatorio *nm* [-orio(1)] restroom, bathroom
saneamiento *nm* [-miento 2461] cleaning up; disinfecting
sanidad *nf* [-idad 4859] healthiness
insano *aj* insane
malsano *aj* unhealthy; noxious
sanable *aj* curable
sanador *aj* healing; curative
saneado *aj* cleaned-up; disinfected

sanitario *aj* [-ario(2) 1282] sanitary; clean
sano *aj* [1804] healthy
santo,-a saint
santificar *vt* [-ificar] to sanctify
santiguar *vt* to make the sign of the cross
santiguarse *vr* to make the sign of the cross on oneself
santo,-a *nmf* saint
santurrón,-a *nmf* hypocrite
Santísimo *nm* [-ísimo] Most Holy, God, Christ
santoral *nm* [-al(1)] book of the saints
santuario *nm* [4343] sanctuary
santateresa *nf* praying mantis
santidad *nf* [-idad 4752] sanctity
santificación *nf* sanctification
santurronería *nf* sanctimoniousness
santero *aj* saint-worshiping or image-worshiping (saints)
santísimo *aj* [-ísimo] most holy
santo *aj* [2714] holy
santurrón *aj* hypocritical
satisfacción satisfaction
satisfacer *vt* [3003] to satisfy
satisfacerse *vr* to be satisfied
insatisfacción *nf* dissatisfaction
satisfacción *nf* [-ción 2313] satisfaction
insatisfactorio *aj* unsatisfactory
insatisfecho *aj* unsatisfied
satisfactorio *aj* [-orio(2) 3890] satisfactory
satisfecho *aj* [2098] satisfied
sazón season
desazonar *vt* to remove the seasoning from
desazonarse *vr* to feel out of sorts; to feel unwell
sazonar *vt* [4996] to season
desazón *nf* lack of seasoning
sazón *nf* season
desazonado *aj* unseasoned
sección section
seccionar *vt* to divide into sections
sector *nm* [201] sector
intersección *nf* intersection
sección *nf* [1055] section
seco dry
desecar *vt* to dry
resecarse *vr* to dry out
secar *vt* [1246] to dry
secarse *vr* to become dry; to dry out
secadero *nm* place for drying
secador *nm* dryer; hairdryer
secano *nm* dry agricultural land
secante *nm* blotting paper; chemical agent added to paint to cause faster drying

seca *nf* drought
secadora *nf* [-dor(2)] dryer
sequía *nf* [2486] drought
reseco *aj* dried-out
secante *aj* drying
seco *aj* dry
secretario secretary
secretario,-a *nmf* [311] secretary
subsecretario,-a *nmf* [2393] undersecretary
vicesecretario,-a *nmf* assistant secretary
secretariado *nm* secretariat
secreter *nm* small desk with small drawers
secretaría *nf* [357] secretary
subsecretaría *nf* office of undersecretary
secreto secret
secretear *vi* to secret; to tell secrets to one another
secreteo *nm* act of telling secrets to one another
secreto *nm* [1700] secret
secreta *nf* secret police
secreto *aj* [1700] secret
supersecreto *aj* super-secret
secular secular
secularizar *vt* to secularize
secular *aj* secular
sed thirst
sed *nf* thirst
sediento *aj* thirsty
seda silk
sedal *nm* fishing line
seda *nf* silk
sedero *aj* of silk
sedoso *aj* silky
seducir to seduce
inducir *vt* [4938] to induce
seducir *vt* to seduce
seductor,-a *nmf* seducer
seducción *nf* seduction
inducido *aj* induced
inductor *aj* inducing
seductor *aj* [-or] seducing
seguir to continue; to follow
conseguir *vt* [440] to get
perseguir *vt* [2579] to pursue
proseguir *vt* to proceed
seguir *vt* [105] to continue; to follow
perseguidor,-a *nmf* pursuer
seguidor,-a *nmf* follower
seguimiento *nm* [-miento 2864] pursuit
persecución *nf* [-ción 3638] persecution
seguida *nf* act of following
en seguida *av* immediately, right away

seguido *av* often

consiguiente *aj* depending on something else

persecutorio *aj* persecuting

perseguidor *aj* pursuing

seguido *aj* in a row (days, weeks, etc.)

seguidor *aj* [-dor(1) 1680] following

siguiente *aj* [-ente(1) 469] next

subsiguiente *aj* subsequent

segundo second

secundar *vt* to second a motion; to help

segundo,-a *nmf* second one

segundo *nm* [-undo 102] second (time)

segundero *nm* second hand on a clock

segundón *nm* child who is not the firstborn

secundario *aj* [-ario(2) 1108] secondary

segundo *aj* [-undo 102] second

seguro sure; secure, safe

asegurar *vt* [191] to ensure; to insure

asegurarse *vr* to assure oneself

asegurador,-a *nmf* insurer

seguro *nm* [-ura(2) 548] lock; insurance

aseguradora *nf* insurance company

inseguridad *nf* [-idad 2636] insecurity

seguridad *nf* [-idad 182] security

seguramente *av* [-mente 1552] surely

seguro *av* [-ura(2) 548] sure

asegurado *aj* assured

asegurador *aj* insuring

inseguro *aj* [-ura(2)] insecure

seguro *aj* [-ura(2) 548] sure; secure, safe

seis six

sesentón,-a *nmf* person in his sixties

sexagenario,-a *nmf* sixty year old

dieciseisavo *nm* [-avo] one-sixteenth

seis *nm* [347] six

seiscientos *nm* six hundred

sesenta *nm* [3526] sixty

sesentavo *nm* [-avo] one-sixtieth (fraction)

sexto *nm* [1454] one-sixth (fraction)

séxtuplo *nm* sextuplet

dieciseisavo *aj* [-avo] sixteenth

seis *aj* [347] six

seiscientos *aj* six-hundred

sesenta *aj* [3526] sixty

sesentavo *aj* [-avo] sixtieth

sesentón *aj* sixty-year old

sexagenario *aj* sixty-year old

sexagésimo *aj* [-ésimo] sixtieth

sexto *aj* [1454] sixth

séxtuplo *aj* sextuplet

selecto select

preseleccionar *vt* to pre-select

seleccionar *vt* [1649] to select

seleccionador,-a *nmf* [4753] selector

preselección *nf* preselection

selección *nf* [585] selection; all-star team

selectividad *nf* selectivity

selectivo *aj* [4325] selective

selecto *aj* select

sello seal

sellar *vt* to seal

matasellos *nm* stamp; seal

sello *nm* [-o(1) 3096] seal

sellador *aj* sealing

semana week

semanario *nm* weekly newspaper; ring made of seven smaller rings

semana *nf* [136] week

semanal *aj* [-al(2) 3938] weekly

semanario *aj* weekly

semblante facial expression

semblante *nm* facial expression

semblanza *nf* literary self-portrait

sembrar to seed

inseminar *vt* to inseminate

sembrar *vt* [1474] to seed

sembrador,-a *nmf* [4944] person who plants seeds

sembrado *nm* field for planting seeds

semen *nm* semen

semental *nm* [-al(1)] male animal used for breeding

semillero *nm* [-ero(4)] temporary planter

inseminación *nf* insemination

sembradora *nf* machine for planting seeds

sementera *nf* planted field

semilla *nf* [-illa 2300] seed

siembra *nf* planting; sowing

simiente *nf* seed

seminal *aj* seminal

semejante similar

asemejar *vt* to make similar

asemejarse *vr* to become similar

semejar *vi* to be similar to

desemejanza *nf* [-anza] dissimilarity

semejanza *nf* [-anza] similarity

desemejante *aj* dissimilar

semejante *aj* [-ante(1) 3281] similar

sencillo simple

sencillez *nf* [-ez] simplicity

sencillo *aj* [707] simple

sentar to sit

asentarse *vr* to settle

sentar *vt* [1495] to sit

sentarse *vr* [1495] to be seated

asentamiento *nm* [-miento 4646] seating

asiento *nm* [3555] seat

asentaderas *nfpl* buttocks
sentada *nf* sitting
asentado *aj* seated
sentado *aj* seated

sentencia sentence
sentenciar *vt* [3710] to sentence
sentencia *nf* [-a 2622] sentence
sentenciado *aj* sentenced

sentido meaning; sense (of sight, hearing, etc.)
asentir *vi* [4332] to assent; to agree with; to approve
insensibilizar *vt* to desensitize
insensibilizarse *vr* to become desensitized
presentir *vt* to have a feeling about the future
resentirse *vr* to resent
sensibilizar *vt* to sensitize
sentir *vt* [164] to feel
sentirse *vr* to be feeling
insensato,-a *nmf* senseless person
resentido,-a *nmf* resentful person
sensacionalista *nmf* sensationalist
sentimental *nmf* [3343] sentimental person
asentimiento *nm* assent; agreement
presentimiento *nm* feeling about the future
resentimiento *nm* resentment
sensacionalismo *nm* sensationalism
sentido *nm* [-ido(2)] meaning; sense (of sight, hearing, etc.)
sentimentalismo *nm* sentimentalism
sentimiento *nm* [-miento 1511] feeling
sentir *nm* [164] feeling
insensatez *nf* senselessness
insensibilidad *nf* insensibility
sensación *nf* [2373] sensation
sensatez *nf* [-ez] common sense
sensibilidad *nf* [-idad 3490] sensibility; sensitivity
sensibilización *nf* sensitization
sensiblería *nf* feigned sensitivity; hypocrisy
sensualidad *nf* sensuality
hipersensible *aj* hypersensitive
insensato *aj* senseless
insensible *aj* unfeeling
resentido *aj* resentful
sensacional *aj* sensational
sensacionalista *aj* sensationalist
sensato *aj* sensible
sensible *aj* [-ible 3590] touchy; easily irritated
sensitivo *aj* sensitive
sensorial *aj* sensory; pertaining to physical senses
sensorio *aj* sensory; pertaining to physical senses
sensual *aj* [4595] sensual

sentido *aj* [-ido(2)] feeling; touchy, easily irritated
sentimental *aj* [3343] sentimental

señalar to signal
señalar *vt* [142] to signal; to sign
señalarse *vr* to distinguish oneself
señalizar *vt* to place signs
contraseña *nf* countersign; password
seña *nf* sign
señal *nf* [1745] signal
señalización *nf* placement of signs
señalado *aj* signaled; aforementioned

señor sir; Mr.
señorear *vt* to rule
señorón,-a *nmf* big shot; someone who acts self-important
señor *nm* sir; Mr.
señorío *nm* dominion
señorito *nm* son of a noble
señora *nf* married woman; madam; Mrs.
señoría *nf* lordship; formal courtesy
señorita *nf* [-ita] unmarried woman; Miss
señor *aj* having dominion
señorial *aj* noble, majestic
señorón *aj* acting self-important

separar to separate
separar *vt* [1512] to separate
separarse *vr* to separate oneself; to become separated
separatista *nmf* separatist
separador *nm* bookmark
separatismo *nm* separatism
separación *nf* [-ción 3688] separation
inseparablemente *av* inseparably
inseparable *aj* inseparable
separable *aj* separable
separado *aj* separated
separador *aj* separating
separatista *aj* separatist

sepultura tomb; grave
sepultar *vt* to entomb; to bury
sepulturero-a *nmf* cemetery worker who performs the burial
sepulcro *nm* sepulcher
sepultura *nf* tomb; grave
sepulcral *aj* pertaining to a sepulcher

serenidad serenity
serenar *vt* to calm; to fall (dew)
serenarse *vr* to calm oneself; to become calm
sereno *nm* [-o(1) 3535] quiet time during the middle of the night; dew
serenata *nf* serenade
serenidad *nf* serenity
sereno *aj* [-o(1) 3535] serene

serie series
  seriar *vt* to make a series; to serialize
  serial *nm* [2875] television or radio series
  serie *nf* [336] series
  serial *aj* [2875] serial

serpiente serpent
  serpentear *vt* to wind
  serpenteo *nm* winding
  serpentín *nm* coil
  serpentina *nf* streamer
  serpiente *nf* serpent

servir to serve
  servir *vt* [492] to serve
  servirse *vr* to serve oneself
  servidor,-a *nmf* [2451] server
  sirviente,-a *nmf* servant
  autoservicio *nm* self-service
  servicio *nm* [-icio 158] service
  servilismo *nm* servility
  servilletero *nm* [-ero(1)] napkin holder
  servidumbre *nf* group of servants
  servilleta *nf* napkin
  inservible *aj* unusable
  servible *aj* usable
  servicial *aj* helpful

severo severe
  severidad *nf* [-idad] severity
  severo *aj* [-ero(2) 2405] severe

sexo sex
  heterosexual *nmf* heterosexual
  homosexual *nmf* [4913] homosexual
  sexólogo,-a *nmf* sexologist
  sexismo *nm* sexism
  sexo *nm* [1795] sex
  transexualismo *nm* transsexualism
  homosexualidad *nf* homosexuality
  sexología *nf* sexology
  sexualidad *nf* [-idad 3803] sexuality
  sexualmente *av* sexually
  asexuado *aj* sexless
  asexual *aj* asexual
  heterosexual *aj* heterosexual
  homosexual *aj* [4913] homosexual
  sexista *aj* sexist
  sexual *aj* [1217] sexual
  sexy *aj* [3184] sexy
  transexual *aj* transsexual
  unisex *aj* unisex

siempre always
  siempreviva *nf* perennial plant
  siempre *av* [197] always
  sempiterno *aj* eternal

sierra mountain; saw
  aserrar *vt* to saw
  aserruchar *vt* to saw with a handsaw
  serrar *vt* to saw
  serrano,-a *nmf* highlander; person who lives in
    the mountains
  aserradero *nm* sawmill
  aserrado *nm* sawing; milling of wood
  aserrín *nm* sawdust
  serrucho *nm* [-ucho] handsaw
  aserradura *nf* incomplete cut
  serranía *nf* mountainous area
  serrería *nf* sawmill
  sierra *nf* [1999] mountain; saw
  aserrado *aj* having a saw-like shape
  serrano *aj* of the mountain

siete seven
  septuagenario,-a *nmf* seventy year old person
  setentón,-a *nmf* person in his seventies
  sietemesino,-a *nmf* premature baby born
    during the seventh month of pregnancy
  diecisiete *nm* seventeen
  diecisieteavo *nm* [-avo] one-seventeenth
    (fraction)
  septiembre *nm* [412] September
  séptimo *nm* [-ésimo 1550] one-seventh (fraction)
  septuagésimo *nm* [-ésimo] seventieth anniversary
  setecientos *nm* seven hundred
  setenta *nm* [3700] seventy
  setentavo *nm* [-avo] one-seventieth (fraction)
  siete *nm* [493] seven
  diecisiete *aj* seventeen
  diecisieteavo *aj* [-avo] one-seventeenth (fraction)
  séptimo *aj* [-ésimo 1550] seventh
  septuagenario *aj* seventy-year-old
  septuagésimo *aj* [-ésimo] seventieth
  setecientos *aj* seven hundred
  setenta *aj* [3700] seventy
  setentavo *aj* [-avo] seventieth
  setentón *aj* in one's seventies
  siete *aj* [493] seven
  sietemesino *aj* born prematurely during the
    seventh month of pregnancy

signo sign
  signar *vt* to sign; to make the sign of the cross
  signarse *vr* to make the sign of the cross over
    oneself
  significar *vti* [804] to mean
  signatario,-a *nmf* signatory
  significado *nm* [3305] meaning
  signo *nm* [2690] sign
  insignia *nf* insignia
  insignificancia *nf* insignificance

signatura *nf* [-ura(2)] signature
significación *nf* meaning
significativamente *av* significantly
insigne *aj* important; valued; celebrated; well-known
insignificante *aj* insignificant
signatario *aj* signatory
significado *aj* [3305] distinguished; well-known
significante *aj* significant
significativo *aj* [-ivo 2228] well-explained, clear, meaningful

silencio silence
silenciar *vt* to silence
silenciador *nm* silencer
silencio *nm* [-o(1) 2247] silence
silencioso *aj* silent

sillón large comfortable chair or couch
desensillar *vt* to remove the saddle
ensillar *vt* to saddle
sillín *nm* [-ín] bicycle or motorcycle seat
sillón *nm* [-ón(3)] large comfortable chair or couch
silla *nf* [2894] chair

símbolo symbol
simbolizar *vt* to symbolize
simbolismo *nm* symbolism
símbolo *nm* [2129] symbol
simbólico *aj* symbolic
simbolista *aj* symbolic

similar similar
asimetría *nf* asymmetry
simetría *nf* symmetry
similitud *nf* [-itud] similarity
asimétrico *aj* asymmetric
simétrico *aj* symmetric
similar *aj* [1192] similar

simpatía sympathy
simpatizar *vi* to sympathize
simpatizante *nmf* [-ante(1) 3609] sympathizer; one who sympathizes
antipatía *nf* antipathy
simpatía *nf* [4215] sympathy
antipático *aj* unsympathetic
simpático *aj* sympathetic; pleasant
simpatizante *aj* [-ante(1) 3609] sympathizing

simple simple
simplificar *vt* [-ificar] to simplify
simplón,-a *nmf* silly or foolish person; simpleton
simplismo *nm* simplicity
simpleza *nf* foolishness
simplicidad *nf* simplicity
simplificación *nf* simplification

simplemente *av* [-mente 1294] simply
simple *aj* [1603] simple
simplista *aj* simplistic
simplón *aj* very silly or foolish

simular to simulate
simular *vt* to simulate
simulacro *nm* practice exercise; simulation
simulación *nf* [-ción] simulation
simulado *aj* simulated

sincero sincere
sincerarse *vr* to be sincere
sinceridad *nf* sincerity
sinceramente *av* sincerely
sincero *aj* [-ero(2) 4466] sincere

sindicato union
sindicar *vt* to form a union
sindicarse *vr* to become part of a union
sindicalista *nmf* unionist
sindicalismo *nm* unionism
sindicato *nm* [-ato 979] union
síndico *nm* [4945] union representative
sindicación *nf* syndication
sindical *aj* [2134] union-related
sindicalista *aj* pertaining to unionism

singular singular
singularizar *vt* to single out
singularizarse *vr* to be distinguished
singular *nm* [3222] grammatical term meaning one
singularidad *nf* singular quality; uniqueness; individuality; distinct quality
singularmente *av* singularly
singular *aj* [3222] singular

síntoma symptom
síntoma *nm* [2099] symptom
sintomático *aj* symptomatic

sistema system
sistematizar *vt* to systematize
ecosistema *nm* ecosystem
sistema *nf* [252] system
sistemático *aj* systematic

situación situation
situar *vt* [2136] to situate
situarse *vr* [2136] to situate oneself; to be situated
sitio *nm* [635] site
situación *nf* [-ción 222] situation
situado *aj* situated

soberbio dominated by a feeling of superiority
soberbia *nf* feeling of superiority
soberbiamente *av* in a manner displaying a feeling of superiority

soberbio *aj* dominated by a feeling of superiority; overly proud

sobrar to be extra; to have extra
sobrar *vti* to be extra; to have extra
sobrante *nm* [-ante(1)] leftovers; extra; excess
sobra *nf* leftovers; extra; excess
sobradamente *av* excessively; extremely
sobrado *aj* [-ado(2)] excessive
sobrante *aj* [-ante(1)] extra; leftover; excess

sobriedad sobriety
sobriedad *nf* sobriety
sobrio *aj* sober

social social
disociar *vt* to disassociate
socializar *vt* to socialize
consocio,-a *nmf* associate
socialdemócrata *nmf* social democrat
socialista *nmf* [-ista 4117] socialist
socio,-a *nmf* associate
sociólogo,-a *nmf* sociologist
socialismo *nm* socialism
disociación *nf* dissociation
sociabilidad *nf* sociability
socialdemocracia *nf* social democracy
socialización *nf* socialization
sociedad *nf* [388] society
sociología *nf* sociology
socialmente *av* socially
antisocial *aj* antisocial
disociable *aj* dissociable; separable
insociable *aj* unsociable
sociable *aj* sociable
social *aj* [-cial 190] social
socialdemócrata *aj* social democrat
socialista *aj* [-ista 4117] socialist
socioeconómico *aj* socioeconomic
sociológico *aj* sociological

socorro help
socorrer *vt* to help
socorrista *nmf* paramedic; rescue worker
socorrismo *nm* emergency help
socorro *nm* help
socorrido *aj* available to offer emergency response

sol sun
asolear *vt* to sun
asolearse *vr* to bask in sunlight
solear *vt* to sun
solearse *vr* to bask in sunlight
girasol *nm* sunflower
parasol *nm* umbrella used to protect from sunlight

quitasol *nm* umbrella used to protect from sunlight
sol *nm* [1123] sun
solano *nm* east wind; warm wind from the east
asoleada *nf* over-exposure to the sun
insolación *nf* over-exposure to the sun
solana *nf* area unprotected from the sun
solanera *nf* area unprotected from the sun
solano *aj* warm and suffocating; relating to an east wind
solar *aj* [2933] solar
soleado *aj* sunny

soldado soldier
soldado *nm* [1542] soldier
soldadesca *nf* troop of soldiers
soldadesco *aj* [-esco] pertaining to soldiers

solemne solemn
solemnizar *vt* to solemnize
solemnidad *nf* solemnity
solemne *aj* solemn

solicitar to solicit
solicitar *vt* [377] to solicit
solicitador,-a *nmf* solicitor; someone who is seeking an applicant
solicitante *nmf* [-ante(2) 4924] applicant
solicitación *nf* solicitation; application
solicitud *nf* [-itud 1388] solicitude; willingness to help; application
solícito *aj* [-ito(2)] available to help; solicitous

solidaridad solidarity
solidarizar *vt* to act with solidarity
solidarizarse *vr* to be acting with solidarity
solidificar *vt* [-ificar] to solidify
solidificarse *vr* to become solidified
sólido *nm* [-ido(1) 2444] solid
solidaridad *nf* [-idad 2490] solidarity
solidez *nf* solidness
solidificación *nf* solidification
solidario *aj* pertaining to solidarity
sólido *aj* [-ido(1) 2444] solid

sólo only
solista *nmf* [-ista 3122] soloist
solo *nm* solo (music)
soltero *nm* [-ero(2) 1465] bachelor
solterón *nm* confirmed bachelor; mature bachelor
soledad *nf* [2948] loneliness
soltera *nf* bachelorette; single woman
soltería *nf* [-ería(2) 4053] bachelorhood
solterona *nf* [-ón(3)] spinster; mature unmarried woman
solamente *av* [-mente 749] only
sólo *av* only

solo *aj* unaccompanied
soltero *aj* [-ero(2) 1465] bachelor

soltar to let go; to let loose; to free
soltar *vt* [3822] to let go; to let loose; to free
soltarse *vr* [3822] to let go of one's inhibitions when performing; to gain skill at something
suelto *nm* [3877] loose coins
soltura *nf* [-ura(1)] ease of expression
suelto *aj* [3877] loose

solución¹ solution (liquid)
disolver *vt* [4699] to dissolve
disolverse *vr* [4699] to be dissolved
disolvente *nm* dissolvent, solvent
solvente *nm* solvent
disolubilidad *nf* solubility
disolución *nf* dissolution
solubilidad *nf* solubility
solución *nf* [1101] solution
disoluble *aj* soluble
disolvente *aj* dissolvent, solvent
insoluble *aj* insoluble
soluble *aj* soluble
solvente *aj* solvent

solución² solution (problem)
resolver *vt* [813] to resolve
resolverse *vr* [813] to be resolved
solucionar *vt* [1529] to solve
solventar *vt* to solve a complicated problem; to become solvent
resolución *nf* [-ción 1536] resolution
solución *nf* [1101] solution
irresoluto *aj* [-uto] irresolute
resuelto *aj* resolute

sombra shade; shadow
ensombrecer *vt* to cover with a shadow
ensombrecerse *vr* to be shadowed
sombrear *vt* to cover with shade
sombrerero,-a *nmf* hat maker
sombreado *nm* shading
sombrero *nm* [4256] hat
sombra *nf* [3106] shade; shadow
sombrerera *nf* [-era] hatbox
sombrerería *nf* [-ería(1)] hat store
sombrilla *nf* parasol; umbrella for sun; sunshade
sombrío *aj* shadowy; gloomy

sonar to sound
consonar *vt* to harmonize; to be in consonance
insonorizar *vt* to soundproof
resonar *vi* to resonate
sonar *vt* [2340] to sound
sonorizar *vt* to add the sound track to a film
consonante *nm* consonant

son *nm* pleasant sound, especially a musical sound
sonajero *nm* baby's rattle
sónar *nm* sonar
sonido *nm* [-ido(2) 2100] sound
sonsonete *nm* rhythmic sound
ultrasonido *nm* ultrasound
altisonancia *nf* high-pitched sound
consonancia *nf* [-ancia] consonance
disonancia *nf* [-ancia] dissonance
insonorización *nf* soundproofing
resonancia *nf* [-ancia] resonance
sonaja *nf* baby's rattle
sonata *nf* sonata
sonatina *nf* [-ina] short sonata
sonorización *nf* placing of a sound track to a film
altisonante *aj* high-pitched; disagreeable to the ears
consonante *aj* consonant
consonántico *aj* pertaining to consonant sounds
insonorizado *aj* soundproof
insonoro *aj* pleasant sounding
malsonante *aj* unpleasant sounding
resonante *aj* resonant
sonado *aj* well-known; frequently heard
sónico *aj* sonic
sonoro *aj* sonorous; sounding; able to sound
supersónico *aj* supersonic
ultrasónico *aj* ultrasonic

sopa soup
sopar *vt* to dip bread in a soup
sopear *vt* to scoop soup with a tortilla
sopa *nf* [3776] soup
sopera *nf* [-era] pot for making soup
sopero *aj* soup

soplo blowing
soplar *vt* to blow
soplarse *vr* to be blown (glass)
soplón,-a *nmf* prompter in theater
resoplido *nm* [-ido(2)] the act of being out of tune
soplado *nm* intestinal gas
soplador *nm* glass blowing apparatus
soplete *nm* [-ete] welding torch
soplido *nm* brusque blowing sound
soplo *nm* blowing
soplón *aj* secret-telling

soportar to tolerate
soportar *vt* [2838] to tolerate
soporte *nm* toleration
insoportable *aj* intolerable
soportable *aj* [-able] tolerable

sordo deaf
asordar *vt* to deafen
ensordecer *vt* to deafen
sordo,-a *nmf* deaf person
sordomudo,-a *nmf* deaf-mute
ensordecimiento *nm* deafness
sordera *nf* deafness
sordina *nf* [-ina] mute, in music
sordomudez *nf* deaf-muteness
ensordecedor *aj* deafening
sordo *aj* deaf
sordomudo *aj* deaf-mute

sorpresa surprise
sorprender *vt* [1127] to surprise
sorprenderse *vr* to be surprised
sorpresa *nf* [1393] surprise
sorprendente *aj* [-ente(1) 3625] surprising
sorpresivo *aj* [-ivo 4467] surprise; surprising

sosiego sense of calm
sosegar *vt* to calm
sosegarse *vr* to become calm
sosiego *nm* sense of calm
sosegado *aj* calm
sosegador *aj* calming

sospechar to suspect
sospechar *vt* to suspect
sospechoso,-a *nmf* suspect
sospecha *nf* [-a 3357] suspicion
suspicacia *nf* [-icia] suspiciousness
sospechosamente *av* suspiciously
insospechado *aj* unsuspected
sospechoso *aj* [-oso 2457] suspected
suspicaz *aj* [-az] suspicious

suave soft, smooth; cool
suavizar *vt* [-izar] to make soft or smooth
suavizante *nm* softener
suavidad *nf* softness
suavemente *av* softly
suave *aj* [2512] soft, smooth; cool

subir to go up; to get on; to board
subir *vti* [1106] to go up; to get on; to board
subirse a *vt* to go up; to get on; to board
subida *nf* going up; rise
subido *aj* strong (smell); dark (color); elevated;
   raised

sublevar to rebel; to provoke rebellion
sublevar *vt* to rebel; to provoke rebellion
sublevarse *vr* to be rebellious
sublevamiento *nm* rebellion
sublevación *nf* rebellion

sublime sublime
sublimar *vt* to exalt

sublimado *aj* exalted
sublime *aj* sublime

subsistir to subsist
subsistir *vi* to subsist
subsistencia *nf* subsistence
subsistente *aj* subsistent

suceder to happen; to occur
suceder *vi* [637] to happen; to occur
sucesor,-a *nmf* [4754] successor
suceso *nm* [2818] event, occurrence
sucesión *nf* succession
sucesivamente *av* successively
sucesivo *aj* successive

sueño dream
ensoñar *v* to daydream
soñar *vt* [2775] to dream
ensoñador,-a *nmf* daydreamer
soñador,-a *nmf* dreamer
sonámbulo,-a *nmf* sleepwalker
ensueño *nm* daydream; fantasy
sueño *nm* [-o(1) 1069] dream
ensoñación *nf* daydreaming
soñarrera *nf* act of dreaming frequently
ensoñador *aj* daydreaming
soñado *aj* dreamed of
soñador *aj* dreamy
soñoliento *aj* [-iento] sleepy

suficiente sufficient
insuficiente *nm* [2703] insufficient
autosuficiencia *nf* self-sufficiency
insuficiencia *nf* [-encia 4794] insufficiency
suficiencia *nf* sufficiency
suficientemente *av* [-mente 4424] sufficiently
autosuficiente *aj* self-sufficient
insuficiente *aj* [2703] insufficient
suficiente *aj* [790] sufficient

sugerir to suggest
sugerir *vt* [2038] to suggest
sugestionar *vt* to provoke through the power of
   suggestion
autosugestión *nf* self-suggestion
sugerencia *nf* [-encia 3856] suggestion (counsel)
sugestión *nf* suggestion (idea or thought which
   provokes change in someone's physical or
   mental state)
sugerente *aj* [-ente(1)] suggestive
sugeridor *aj* suggesting
sugestionable *aj* influenced easily
sugestivo *aj* suggestive

suicidio suicide
suicidarse *vr* to commit suicide

suicida *nmf* [-ido(2) 2477] suicide victim
suicidio *nm* [3205] suicide

sujeto subject; person
sujetar *vt* [3328] to subject, to hold
sujetarse *vr* [3328] to subject oneself; to be subjected to
sujeto *nm* [821] subject; person
sujeción *nf* subjection
sujeto *aj* [821] subjected

suma sum
sumar *vt* [1036] to add
sumarse *vr* to be added to; to unite with
sumando *nm* addend
suma *nf* [-a 1772] sum
sumadora *nf* adding machine
sumamente *av* [-mente 2934] greatly

sumergir to submerge
sumergir *vt* to submerge
sumergirse *vr* to submerge oneself
sumir *vt* [4861] to submerge something; to sink
sumirse *vr* to be sinking
sumergible *nm* submergible ship; submarine
insumergible *aj* unsinkable
sumergible *aj* submergible
sumergido *aj* submerged

superar to overcome
superar *vt* [803] to overcome; to surpass
superarse *vr* [803] to succeed, to achieve one's goals
superior,-a *nmf* superior
superación *nf* improvement
superiora *nf* mother superior in a convent
superioridad *nf* [-idad] superiority
insuperable *aj* unconquerable, invincible
superior *aj* [812] superior

superficie surface
superficialidad *nf* superficiality
superficie *nf* [1704] surface
superficial *aj* [-cial] superficial

superstición superstition
superstición *nf* superstition
supersticioso *aj* superstitious

suplicar to plead; to supplicate
suplicar *vt* to plead; to supplicate
suplicante *nmf* one who pleads
súplica *nf* [-ción] supplication
suplicante *aj* supplicating

suplir to substitute for; to replace
suplir *vt* [4640] to substitute for; to replace
suplente *nmf* [-ente(2) 4327] replacement; substitute
suplencia *nf* substitution; replacing

supremo supreme
supremacía *nf* [-ería(2)] supremacy
supremo *aj* [2559] supreme

suprimir to suppress
suprimir *vt* to suppress
supresión *nf* suppression

sur south
sureño,-a *nmf* southerner
sureste, sudeste *nm* southeast
suroeste, sudoeste *nm* southwest
sur *nm* [510] south
sureste, sudeste *aj* southeast
suroeste, sudoeste *aj* southwest
sureño *aj* [-eño] southern

surco rut or furrow
surcar *vt* to make ruts or furrows
surco *nm* rut or furrow
surcado *aj* filled with ruts or furrows

surtir to stock
surtir *vt* [4468] to stock
surtido *nm* stock
surtido *aj* well-stocked

suscitar to cause or provoke
suscitar *vt* [3675] to cause or provoke
suscitarse *vr* to take place, to occur
susceptibilidad *nf* susceptibility
susceptible *aj* susceptible

suspender to suspend
suspender *vt* [1289] to suspend
suspenso *nm* suspense
suspensión *nf* [-sión 2152] suspension
suspensivo *aj* suspensive; also used to refer to "ellipsis" as expressed in the Spanish expression "puntos suspensivos"

sustancia substance
sustanciar, substanciar *vt* to substantiate
insustancialidad, insubstancialidad *nf* insubstantiality
sustancia, substancia *nf* substance
insustancial, insubstancial *aj* insubstantial
sustancial, substancial *aj* substantial
sustancioso, substancioso *aj* substantial; valuable
sustantivo, substantivo *aj* substantive

sustentar to sustain
sustentar *vt* [4069] to sustain
sustentarse *vr* [4069] to be sustained
sustento *nm* [-o(1) 4293] sustenance
sustentación *nf* sustaining

sustituir to substitute
sustituir, substituir *vt* to substitute
sustituto,-a, substituto,-a *nmf* substitute

sustitución, substitución *nf* substitution
insustituible, insubstituible *aj* not substitutable
sustituible, substituible *aj* substitutable

sutil subtle
sutilizar *vt* to refine the details
sutileza *nf* [-eza] subtlety
sutilmente *av* subtly
sutil *aj* subtle

T

tabaco tobacco
tabacalero,-a *nmf* tobacco farmer or seller
tabaco *nm* [3401] tobacco
tabaquismo *nm* [-ismo] illness caused by the use of tobacco
tabaquera *nf* [-era] snuff box; case for tobacco
tabacalero *aj* relating to tobacco

tabla plank or board
entablar *vt* [4910] to attach planks or boards
entablillar *vt* to splint; to immobilize an injured arm or leg with a splint
tablear *vt* to make wooden planks
entablado *nm* floor or fence made of wooden planks
entablillado *nm* the placing of a splint
tablero *nm* bulletin board
tablón *nm* thick plank or board
tabla *nf* [2314] plank or board
tablilla *nf* small plank or board

talento talent
cazatalentos *nmf* business headhunter; agent
talento *nm* [1401] talent
talentoso *aj* [-oso 4499] talented

taller workshop
entallar *vt* to carve; to engrave
tallar *vt* to carve; to engrave
tallador,-a *nmf* engraver
tallado *nm* action of engraving
taller *nm* [1646] workshop
talla *nf* [4391] engraving
tallado *aj* carved

tallo stem
tallo *nm* stem
talludo *aj* [-udo] long-stemmed

tapar to cover; to put a lid on
destapar *vt* to uncover; to take a lid off
destaparse *vr* to become uncovered; to be opened
tapar *vt* [3389] to cover; to put a lid on
taparse *vr* to cover oneself

tapabocas *nm* surgical mask
taparrabos *nm* loin cloth
tapa *nf* [-a 4841] lid; cover
tapadera *nf* lid; cover
tapado *aj* covered

tapia adobe brick
tapiar *vt* to enclose using adobe brick
tapia *nf* adobe brick

tarde afternoon
atardecer *v* to set (sun)
retardar *vt* to delay
retardarse *vr* to be delayed
tardar(se) *vi(r)* [1794] to be late
atardecer *nm* sunset
retardo *nm* tardy
tardanza *nf* [-anza] late arrival; lateness
tarde *nf* [364] afternoon
tarde *av* [364] late
retardado *aj* late; behind schedule
tardío *aj* delayed
tardo *aj* slow

tarea homework; assignment; work
atarear *vt* to give work to
atarearse *vr* to be busy with assignments
tarea *nf* [1210] homework; assignment; work
atareado *aj* busy with assignments

teatro theater
anfiteatro *nm* amphitheater
teatro *nm* [727] theater
teatral *aj* [3329] of the theater; theatrical

techo roof or ceiling
techar *vt* to put a roof on
tejar *vt* to put a roof on
sotechado *nm* thatched roof; provisionally covered roof
techado *nm* roofing
techo *nm* [-o(1) 2504] roof or ceiling
tejado *nm* roof or ceiling
tejamaní *nm* roofing tile
tejamanil *nm* roofing tile
tejar *nm* factory for making brick or tile
teja *nf* tile of baked clay
techado *aj* roofed

técnica technique
técnico,-a *nmf* [277] technician
tecnicismo *nm* technical term
Tecnicolor *nm* Technicolor
microtecnología *nf* microtechnology
técnica *nf* technique
tecnología *nf* [-ería(2) 1168] technology
técnico *aj* [-ico(2)] technical
tecnológico *aj* [1150] technological

tejido   knitting; weaving
   entretejer *vt* to interweave
   tejer *vt* [2612] to knit; to weave
   tejedor,-a *nmf* one who knits; weaver
   tejido *nm* knitting; weaving
   telar *nm* weaving machine; loom
   entretela *nf* interlining
   tela *nf* [3272] cloth
   telaraña *nf* spider web
   tejedor *aj* knitting; weaving

teléfono[1]   telephone
   teledirigir *vt* to guide using remote control
   telefonear *vt* to telephone
   telegrafiar *vt* to telegraph
   televisar *vt* [1936] to televise
   radiotelegrafista *nmf* radio telegrapher
   telefonista *nmf* telephone operator
   telegrafista *nmf* telegrapher
   telespectador,-a *nmf* member of a television audience
   televidente *nmf* one who watches television
   radioteléfono *nm* radio telephone
   radiotelescopio *nm* radio telescope
   telediario *nm* news bulletin
   telefax *nm* fax machine
   teleférico *nm* sky cable car
   telefilm, telefilme *nm* film made for television
   teléfono *nm* [1258] telephone
   telégrafo *nm* telegraph
   telemando *nm* remote control system
   teleobjetivo *nm* telephoto lens
   telescopio *nm* telescope
   telesquí *nm* ski lift
   teletipo *nm* teletype machine
   televisor *nm* [2586] television
   tele *nf* television
   telecabina *nf* car or cabin suspended from an aerial wire
   telecomunicación *nf* [3244] telecommunication
   telefonía *nf* [-ería(2) 3834] telephony
   telegrafía *nf* telegraphy
   telegrama *nf* telegram
   telenovela *nf* [992] soap opera
   telepatía *nf* telepathy
   telequinesia *nf* telekinesis
   telesilla *nf* ski lift chair
   televisión *nf* [-sión 562] television
   telegráficamente *av* telegraphically
   telepáticamente *av* telepathically
   teledirigido *aj* remote-controlled
   telefónico *aj* [-ico(2) 1587] telephonic
   telegráfico *aj* [-ico(2)] telegraphic
   telepático *aj* [-ico(2)] telepathic

   telescópico *aj* telescopic
   televisivo *aj* [-ivo 2964] television

teléfono[2]   telephone
   telefonear *vt* to telephone
   telefonista *nmf* telephone operator
   fonógrafo *nm* phonograph
   gramófono *nm* gramophone
   interfono *nm* intercom
   megáfono *nm* megaphone
   micrófono *nm* [4962] microphone
   teléfono *nm* [1258] telephone
   afonía *nf* loss of voice
   fonema *nf* phoneme
   fonética *nf* phonetics
   fonología *nf* phonology
   fonoteca *nf* sound; tape or record library
   homofonía *nf* homo
   megafonía *nf* megaphone
   telefonía *nf* [-ería(2) 3834] telephony
   telegrafía *nf* telegraphy
   afónico *aj* without sound
   fonético *aj* phonetic
   fonológico *aj* phonologic
   homófono *aj* homophonic
   telefónico *aj* [-ico(2) 1587] telephonic

tema   theme, subject
   temario *nm* list of themes or subjects
   tema *nf* [209] theme, subject
   temática *nf* overall theme
   temático *aj* thematic

temblar   to tremble
   retemblar *vi* to repeatedly tremble
   temblar *vi* to tremble
   temblor *nm* earthquake
   temblón *aj* [-ón(2)] trembling
   tembloroso *aj* trembling

temer   to fear
   atemorizar *vt* to intimidate
   atemorizarse *vr* to be intimidated
   temer *vti* [2075] to fear
   temerse *vr* to be afraid; to suspect
   temor *nm* [1612] fear
   temeroso *aj* [-oso] fearful
   temible *aj* fearsome
   tímido *aj* [-ido(1)] timid; shy

temperamento   temperament
   atemperar *vt* to moderate
   atemperarse *vr* to become moderate or temperate
   temperar *vt* to temper
   temperamento *nm* temperament
   temperancia *nf* temperance
   temperamental *aj* temperamental

temporada season
  temporal *nmf* [2113] temporary worker; seasonal employee
  contratiempo *nm* mishap
  temporal *nm* [2113] storm
  tiempo *nm* [90] time; season
  intemperie *nf* outdoors
  temperatura *nf* [-ura(2) 1623] temperature
  tempestad *nf* storm; tempest
  temporada *nf* [418] season
  extemporáneo *aj* extemporaneous
  intempestivo *aj* inopportune, not at the right time
  tempestuoso *aj* tempestuous
  temporal *aj* [2113] temporary; provisional

temprano early
  temprano *av* [1521] early
  tempranero *aj* preferring things in the early morning hours; preferring things early
  temprano *aj* [1521] early

tenacidad tenacity
  tenacillas *nfpl* small tongs
  tenazas *nfpl* tongs
  tenacidad *nf* [-idad] tenacity
  tenaz *aj* [-az] tenacious

tendencia tendency
  tendencia *nf* [-encia 1837] tendency
  tendencioso *aj* tendentious

tender to spread out; to hang
  tender *vti* [1589] to spread out; to hang; to tend to
  tenderse *vr* to stretch out
  tendido *nm* action of spreading out
  tendido *aj* spread out; hanging

tenebrosidad darkness
  entenebrecer *vt* to turn dark and gloomy
  entenebrecerse *vr* to become dark and gloomy
  tenebrosidad *nf* darkness
  tenebroso *aj* dark; full of darkness

tener to have
  atenerse *vr* to rely on; to be dependent on
  contener *vt* [661] to contain
  contenerse *vr* to contain oneself
  detener *vt* [743] to detain
  detenerse *vr* [743] to stop oneself
  entretener *vt* [4737] to entertain
  entretenerse *vr* to entertain oneself
  mantener *vt* [213] to maintain
  mantenerse *vr* [213] to maintain oneself; to keep on
  obtener *vt* [254] to obtain
  retener *vt* [3356] to retain
  retenerse *vr* to restrain oneself

  sostener *vt* [594] to sustain
  sostenerse *vr* to maintain balance; to sustain oneself
  tener *vt* [21] to have
  detenido,-a *nmf* prisoner; arrested person
  tenedor,-a *nmf* possessor of something
  contenido *nm* [-ido(2)] contents
  entretenimiento *nm* [-miento 3943] entertainment
  mantenimiento *nm* [-miento 2015] maintenance
  retén *nm* reserve emergency personnel; military reserve
  sostén *nm* bra; support
  sostenido *nm* hold sign in musical notation
  sostenimiento *nm* sustenance
  tenedor *nm* fork
  detención *nf* [-ción 1470] detention
  obtención *nf* obtaining
  retención *nf* retention
  retentiva *nf* retentiveness
  tenencia *nf* [-encia 3969] possession
  detenidamente *av* slowly
  contenido *aj* [-ido(2)] contained
  detenido *aj* [-ido(1) 491] detained
  entretenido *aj* entertained
  insostenible *aj* unsustainable
  mantenido *aj* maintained
  retentivo *aj* retentive
  sostenido *aj* sustained

teniente tenant
  subteniente *nm* subtenant
  teniente *nm* [-ente(1)] tenant

tentación temptation
  tentar *vt* to tempt
  tentación *nf* [-ción 4728] temptation
  tentador *aj* tempting

teoría theory
  teorizar *vti* [-izar] to theorize
  teórico,-a *nmf* theoretician
  teorema *nf* theorem
  teoría *nf* [2650] theory
  teórico *aj* [-ico(2)] theoretical

tercero third
  terciar *vt* to divide into thirds; to do something every third day
  tercero,-a *nmf* third one
  tercero *nm* [-ero(2) 225] third party
  terceto *nm* poem or verse in which the first and third lines rhyme; trio
  tercio *nm* [1904] one-third (fraction)
  tercera *nf* third (musical interval)
  tercermundista *aj* third-world
  tercero *aj* [-ero(2) 225] third
  terciario *aj* [-ario(2)] tertiary

terminar to finish
  determinar *vt* [617] to determine
  determinarse *vr* to be determined
  terminar *vt* [239] to finish
  terminarse *vr* to be finished
  determinista *nmf* person who subscribes to the
    doctrine of determinism
  determinismo *nm* determinism
  término *nm* [771] term; end
  determinación *nf* [-ción 2480] determination
  indeterminación *nf* indetermination
  terminación *nf* termination
  terminal *nf* [-al(1) 3440] terminal
  terminantemente *av* definitely; unarguably;
    decisively
  determinado *aj* determined
  determinante *aj* [4543] determining
  determinativo *aj* determining
  determinista *aj* determinist
  indeterminable *aj* indeterminable
  indeterminado *aj* undetermined
  interminable *aj* interminable
  terminado *aj* finished
  terminal *aj* [-al(1) 3440] terminal
  terminante *aj* definite; unarguable; decisive

terror terror
  aterrar *vt* to frighten
  aterrarse *vr* to become frightened
  aterrorizar *vt* to terrorize
  aterrorizarse *vr* to become frightened
  terrorista *nmf* [-ista 1434] terrorist
  aterramiento *nm* act of frightening
  terror *nm* [4103] terror
  terrorismo *nm* [-ismo 1647] terrorism
  terrorífico *aj* [-ico(2)] full of terror
  terrorista *aj* [-ista 1434] terrorist

terso smooth
  tersura *nf* [-ura(1)] smoothness
  terso *aj* smooth

tesis thesis
  sintetizar *vt* to synthesize
  sintetizador *nm* synthesizer
  antítesis *nf* antithesis
  hipótesis *nf* hypothesis
  síntesis *nf* synthesis
  tesis *nf* [4367] thesis
  hipotético *aj* hypothetical
  sintético *aj* synthetic

tesoro treasure
  atesorar *vt* to treasure; to save as a treasure
  tesorero,-a *nmf* treasurer
  atesoramiento *nm* treasuring

  tesoro *nm* [4434] treasure
  tesorería *nf* [-ería(2) 4165] treasury
testimonio testimony
  atestiguar *vt* to testify; to act as a witness
  testar *vi* to make a will
  testificar *vti* to testify; to act as a witness
  testimoniar *vt* to give testimony
  testamentario,-a *nmf* beneficiaries of a will
  testigo *nmf* witness
  atestado *nm* affidavit
  testamento *nm* testament
  testimonio *nm* [-o(1) 3575] testimony
  atestiguación *nf* witnessing; the act of being a
    witness
  testamentaría *nf* execution of a will
  testamentario *aj* relating to a will
  testimonial *aj* testimonial

texto text
  texto *nm* [2106] text
  textual *aj* textual

tez complexion; facial skin
  atezar *vt* to make smooth or shiny
  atezarse *vr* to become tan in appearance
  tez *nf* complexion; facial skin
  atezado *aj* smooth or shiny

tienda store; tent
  tendero,-a *nmf* storekeeper; shopkeeper
  tienda *nf* [1613] store; tent
  tenderete *nm* [-ete] provisional store as in a flea
    market

tierno tender
  enternecer *vt* to make tender
  enternecerse *vr* to become tender-hearted
  enternecimiento *nm* tenderness
  enternecidamente *av* tenderly
  tiernamente *av* tenderly
  enternecedor *aj* causing tender-heartedness
  tierno *aj* [4132] tender

tierra earth; land; soil
  aterrar *vt* to bury
  aterrizar *vt* [4203] to land
  desenterrar *vt* to unbury
  desterrar *vt* to exile
  enterrar *vt* [4355] to bury
  desterrado,-a *nmf* exile
  territorio *nm* [-orio(1) 1503] territory
  extraterrestre *nmf* extraterrestrial
  terrateniente *nmf* landowner
  terrícola *nmf* human being; earthling
  aterraje *nm* [-aje(3)] touchdown point in an
    aircraft landing
  aterrizaje *nm* [-aje(3)] landing
  destierro *nm* exile

enterrador *nm* gravedigger; person who buries

entierro *nm* burial

subterráneo *nm* [3759] tunnel or cave beneath the surface of the earth

terremoto *nm* earthquake

terreno *nm* [768] terrain

territorio *nm* [-orio(1) 1503] territory

terrón *nm* dirt clod

terruño *nm* dirt clod; land of one's birth

aterrada *nf* nearness to land of a ship

terracota *nf* terra-cotta; earthen color

tierra *nf* [478] earth; land; soil

aterrada *aj* dirty

extraterrestre *aj* extraterrestrial

extraterritorial *aj* extra-territorial

subterráneo *aj* [3759] subterranean

terráqueo *aj* of planet earth, only referring to a globe of earth: "globo terráqueo"

terregoso *aj* dusty

terrenal *aj* [-al(2)] terrestrial

terrestre *aj* [-estre 4659] terrestrial

terrícola *aj* of earth, referring to people of planet earth

territorial *aj* [3788] territorial

terroso *aj* dirt-like; dusty

tímido timid

intimidar *vt* to intimidate

intimidarse *vr* to be intimidated

intimidación *nf* intimidation

timidez *nf* [-ez] timidity

tímido *aj* [-ido(1)] timid

tinta ink

entintar *vt* to fill with ink

tintar *vt* to ink

tinte *nm* dye

tintero *nm* ink bottle

tinto *nm* red wine

tinta *nf* ink

tintura *nf* dyeing

tinto *aj* dark red

típico typical

tipificar *v* [-ificar] to typify

tipificación *nf* classification by type

atípico *aj* atypical

típico *aj* [2434] typical

tiranía tyranny

tiranizar *vt* to tyrannize

tirano,-a *nmf* tyrant

tiranía *nf* tyranny

tiranización *nf* tyrannizing

tiránico *aj* tyrannical

tirar to throw away; to shoot

tirar *vt* [1379] to throw away; to shoot

tirarse *vr* to overflow; to throw or to hurl oneself

tirotear *vt* to shoot bullets into the air

tirotearse *vr* to be shooting bullets into the air

tirador *nm* [-dor(1)] gun shooter

tiro *nm* [-o(1) 1200] shot; fight

tiroteo *nm* exchange of gunfire

título title

intitular *vt* to give a title to (book, song, etc.)

subtitular *vt* to subtitle; to give a subtitle to (book, etc.)

titular *vt* [384] to title something

titularse *vr* [384] to earn licensure

titular *nmf* [384] person with a certain position

subtítulo *nm* subtitle

titular *nm* [384] person renowned for his position

título *nm* [-o(1) 766] title

titulación *nf* act of entitling

titulado *aj* licensed; titled

titular *aj* [384] possessing a title

tocar to touch

retocar *vt* to retouch

tocar *vt* [654] to touch

intocable *nmf* untouchable; person of a low caste

retoque *nm* touching up; finishing touch

tocadiscos *nm* record player

toque *nm* [2380] touch

intocable *aj* untouchable

todo all

todo *pron* [29] all

sabelotodo *nmf* know-it-all

todavía *av* [526] still; yet

todopoderoso *aj* all-powerful

tolerar to tolerate

tolerar *vt* [3711] to tolerate

intolerante *nmf* intolerant person

intolerancia *nf* [-ancia] intolerance

tolerancia *nf* [-ancia 3315] tolerance

intolerable *aj* intolerable

intolerante *aj* intolerant

tolerable *aj* tolerable

tolerado *aj* tolerated

tomar to take; to drink

tomar *vt* [128] to take (in general); to drink (in general)

tomarse *vr* to drink (at a specific time or place); to take (time, medicine)

tomavistas *nm* movie camera

toma *nf* [-a] dose; take (movies); electrical outlet

tomadura *nf* taking; pulling of someone's leg, joking

tono tone
  desentonar *vi* to be out of tune
  entonar *vt* to tune
  entonarse *vr* to be in tune
  sintonizar *vt* to tune into a radio station
  tonificar *vt* to tone up
  semitono *nm* half-tone
  sintonizador *nm* tuner knob
  tono *nm* [2326] tone
  entonación *nf* intonation
  monotonía *nf* monotone
  sintonía *nf* symphony
  sintonización *nf* tuning
  tonada *nf* tune; melody
  tonadilla *nf* short song; musical interlude
  tonalidad *nf* tonality
  tónico *nf* tonic
  atonal *aj* atonal
  átono *aj* without accent
  entonado *aj* tuned
  monótono *aj* monotonous
  tónico *aj* tonic
  tonificante *aj* invigorating

tontería foolish act
  atontar *vt* to make someone feel dizzy or woozy
  atontarse *vr* to feel dizzy or woozy
  entontecer *vt* to make someone feel dizzy or woozy
  entontecerse *vr* to feel dizzy or woozy
  tontear *vi* to do a foolish thing
  tonto,-a *nmf* foolish or silly person
  tontada *nf* foolish or silly act
  tontería *nf* foolish or silly act
  atontadamente *av* in a foolish manner
  atontado *aj* dizzy or woozy
  tonto *aj* [4368] foolish; silly

torcido twisted
  retorcer *vt* to twist even more
  retorcerse *vr* to writhe with laughter or pain
  torcer *vt* to twist
  torcerse *vr* to lose one's way
  retorcimiento *nm* twisting
  torcedura *nf* twisting
  retorcido *aj* twisted
  torcido *aj* twisted

tormenta storm
  atormentar *vt* to torment
  atormentarse *vr* to torment oneself
  atormentador,-a *nmf* tormentor
  tormento *nm* torment; torture
  tormenta *nf* [4232] storm
  atormentador *aj* tormenting; torturing
  tormentoso *aj* stormy

torno turntable; lathe
  atornillar *vt* to put in a screw
  desatornillar *vt* to take out a screw
  destornillar *vt* to take out a screw
  retornar *vi* [4116] to return
  tornar *vr* [4043] to turn
  tornarse *vr* to return; to turn (change)
  tornear *vt* to turn in a lathe
  trastornar *vt* to cause physical or mental disorder
  trastornarse *vr* to lose one's common sense or reason
  tornero,-a *nmf* lathe or turntable operator
  destornillador *nm* [-dor(2)] screwdriver
  retorno *nm* [-o(1) 3398] return; turnaround (on highway, street, etc.)
  tornasol *nm* sunflower plant
  tornado *nm* [-ado(2)] tornado
  tornillo *nm* [-illo(1)] screw
  torniquete *nm* tourniquet
  torno *nm* [-o(1) 1595] turntable; lathe
  trastorno *nm* [-o(1) 2811] loss of common sense or reason
  retornable *aj* returnable
  tornasol *aj* used to describe clothing that changes colors slightly depending on the angle of the light
  tornasolado *aj* color-changing, when referring to clothing that changes color depending on the angle of the light
  torneado *aj* lathed
  trastornado *aj* ill for having lost one's common sense or reason

toro bull
  torear *vti* to engage in bullfighting; to fight (bulls)
  toreo *nm* bullfighting
  torero *nm* [-ero(2) 3551] bullfighter
  toro *nm* [1271] bull
  torero *aj* [-ero(2) 3551] bullfighting

torpeza lack of coordination, lack of physical or mental dexterity
  entorpecer *v* to lose one's physical or mental dexterity
  entorpecimiento *nm* the act of losing one's physical or mental dexterity
  torpeza *nf* [-eza] lack of coordination, lack of physical or mental dexterity
  torpe *aj* physically or mentally uncoordinated
  torre *tower*
  torreón *nm* big tower
  torrero *nm* lighthouse keeper

torre *nf* [550] tower
torreta *nf* turret
torrente torrent
torrente *nm* torrent; torrente sanguinio: blood circulation
torrencial *aj* [-cial] torrential
total total
totalizar *vt* to total
total *nm* [428] total
totalitarismo *nm* totalitarianism
totalidad *nf* [-idad 2691] totality
total *av* [428] total
total *aj* [428] total
totalitario *aj* totalitarian
trabajo work
trabajar *vi* [181] to work
trabajador,-a *nmf* [346] worker
trabajo *nm* [-o(1) 109] work
trabajado *aj* work
trabajador *aj* working
trabajoso *aj* hard-working
tradición tradition
tradicionalista *nmf* traditionalist
tradicionalismo *nm* traditionalism
tradición *nf* [1719] tradition
tradicional *aj* [1230] traditional
tradicionalista *aj* traditionalistic
traducir to translate
traducir *vt* [3035] to translate
traductor,-a *nmf* translator
traducción *nf* translation
traductor *aj* translating
tragar to swallow
atragantarse *vr* to swallow wrong
tragar *vt* to swallow
tragarse *vr* to be swallowed up by earth or water; (figurative) to swallow (believe) something without much proof
tragón,-a *nmf* a big eater
tragadero *nm* pharynx
tragaluz *nm* skylight
trago *nm* swallow
tragón *aj* [-ón(2)] big-eating
tragedia tragedy
tragedia *nf* [2949] tragedy
tragicomedia *nf* tragicomedy
trágico *aj* [-ico(2) 3835] tragic
tragicómico *aj* tragicomic
traición betrayal
traicionar *vt* to betray
traidor,-a *nmf* traitor
traición *nf* betrayal

traicionero *aj* [-ero(2)] betraying
traidor *aj* traitorous
traje suit
trajearse *vr* to wear a suit
traje *nm* [2768] suit
trama plot
tramar *vt* to plot
trama *nf* [-a 3954] plot
tranquilo tranquil
intranquilizar *vt* to make nervous
intranquilizarse *vr* to become nervous
tranquilizar *vt* [-izar] to tranquilize; to calm
tranquilizarse *vr* to become calm; to calm down (oneself)
tranquilizante *nm* sedative; tranquilizer
intranquilidad *nf* anxiety
tranquilidad *nf* [-idad 2233] tranquility
intranquilo *aj* anxious
tranquilizador *aj* calming; tranquilizing
tranquilizante *aj* calming
tranquilo *aj* [1839] tranquil; quiet
tranquilón *aj* very tranquil, very quiet.
tránsito traffic cop; traffic
transitar *vi* [2865] to pass through
tránsito *nm* [-ito(2) 1279] traffic cop; traffic
intransitable *aj* impassable
intransitivo *aj* intransitive
transitable *aj* passable
transitado *aj* frequently traveled
transitivo *aj* transitive
transitorio *aj* transitory; temporary
transparente transparent
transparentar *vt* to make transparent
transparentarse *vr* to be transparent
transparencia *nf* [-encia 2592] transparency
transparente *aj* [-ente(1) 3292] transparent
tras after
atrasar *vt* to set your clock backward
atrasarse *vr* to get behind in
traspapelar *vt* to lose in a pile of papers
traspapelarse *vr* to be lost in a pile of papers
tras *prep* [249] after
atrasos *nmpl* past-due payments
atraso *nm* [-o(1)] late payment; the act of being late or behind in something
atrás *int* [1028] move back!
atrás *av* [1028] behind
atrasado *aj* behind
traspapelado *aj* mixed in with a pile of papers
trasladar to move something from one place to another
trasladar *vt* [4258] to move something from one place to another

trasladarse *vr* [4258] to move oneself from one place to another

traslado *nm* moving of people or things from one place to another

tratar to try

maltratar *vt* to mistreat

tratar *vt* [137] to try; to treat

tratarse *vr* to be treated; to get along with each other

maltrato *nm* [-o(1) 4822] mistreatment

tratado *nm* treaty

tratamiento *nm* [-miento 1063] treatment

trato *nm* [-o(1) 1823] relationship

intratable *aj* unsociable, hard to deal with

través (a través de) through, across

atravesar *vt* [1947] to traverse; to cross; to move through

atravesarse *vr* [1947] to move into the path of something

través (a través de) *nm* through, across

través *nm* [363] misfortune, mishap

travesaño *nm* crosspiece or crossbar

travesía *nf* cross street or road; crossing

trayectoria trajectory

trayecto *nm* [4085] the path

trayectoria *nf* [1767] trajectory

trazar to delineate

trazar *vt* [4259] to delineate

trazado *nm* act of designing a project; plan or project

trazo *nm* line in a drawing

traza *nf* design of a project

trazado *aj* designed, normally follows the words well "bien" or poorly "mal"

trepar to climb without a ladder

trepar *vt* to climb without a ladder

trepador *aj* climbing

tres three

trece *nm* [4276] thirteen

treceavo *nm* [-avo] one-thirteenth (fraction)

treinta *nm* [2776] thirty

treintavo *nm* [-avo] one-thirtieth (fraction)

tres *nm* [85] three

trescientos *nm* three hundred

tresillo *nm* three-player card game

treintena *nf* a group of thirty

trece *aj* [4276] thirteen

treceavo *aj* [-avo] thirteenth

treinta *aj* [2776] thirty

treintavo *aj* [-avo] thirtieth

tres *aj* [85] three

trescientos *aj* three-hundred

tributo tribute

tributar *vt* to give tribute

tributario,-a *nmf* [3742] tributary; one who pays tribute

tributo *nm* [-uto] tribute

tributación *nf* act of paying a tribute

tributario *aj* tributary; tribute-paying

triste sad

contristar *vt* to make sad

contristarse *vr* to become sad

entristecer *vt* to make sad

entristecerse *vr* to become sad

tristeza *nf* [-eza 2721] sadness

entristecedor *aj* saddening

triste *aj* [2137] sad

triunfo triumph

triunfar *vi* [2581] to triumph

triunfador,-a *nmf* conqueror; one who triumphs

triunfo *nm* [-o(1) 409] triumph

triunfador *aj* [-dor(1) 2950] conquering; triumphing

triunfal *aj* triumphant

trono throne

destronar *vt* to dethrone

entronizar *vt* to enthrone

destronamiento *nm* dethroning

trono *nm* throne

entronización *nf* enthroning

tropa troop

atropar *vt* to form a troop or troops

atroparse *vr* to form part of a troop

tropas *nfpl* troops

tropa *nf* [2003] troop

tropezarse to trip

tropezarse *vr* to trip

tropezón *nm* trip or fall

tropiezo *nm* stumbling block, something that causes one to trip

tropezón *aj* frequently tripping

trozo piece

destrozar *vt* to break something into pieces

destruir *vt* [1828] to destroy

destrozos *nmpl* broken pieces

destrozo *nm* breaking into pieces

destructor *nm* [-or] destroyer

trozo *nm* [-o(1) 4104] piece

destrucción *nf* [-ción 3179] destruction

destrozado *aj* broken into pieces

destructivo *aj* destructive

destructor *aj* [-or] destructing

indestructible *aj* indestructible

tubo tube

tubo *nm* [3778] tube

tuba *nf* tuba
tubería *nf* [-ería(2) 2903] plumbing
tubular *aj* tubular

tumba tomb
tumba *nf* [3576] tomb
ultratumba *av* beyond the tomb

turbar to disturb
conturbar *vt* to perturb
conturbarse *vr* to become perturbed
enturbiar *vt* to make turbid
enturbiarse *vr* to become turbid
turbar *vt* to disturb
turbarse *vr* to be disturbed
turborreactor *nm* turbine engine
turba *nf* disorderly crowd
turbación *nf* disturbance; chaos
turbina *nf* [-ina] turbine
turbonada *nf* small lightning and thunder storm
turbulencia *nf* turbulence
conturbado *aj* perturbed
turbado *aj* disturbed
turbador *aj* disturbing
turbio *aj* turbid
turbulento *aj* turbulent

turista tourist
turista *nmf* [-ista 3216] tourist
turismo *nm* [-ismo 2058] tourism
turístico *aj* [-ico(2) 2295] touristic, tourist, touristy

U

ulterior ulterior, farther, subsequent
ulterior *aj* ulterior, farther, subsequent
ulteriormente *av* subsequently

último last
ultimar *vt* to conclude, to finish
penúltimo,-a *nmf* the penultimate, the next-to-last
ultimátum *nm* ultimatum
últimamente *av* [-mente 4706] recently, lately
antepenúltimo *aj* before the next-to-last
penúltimo *aj* penultimate, next-to-last
último *aj* [113] last

uno one
desunir *vt* to separate
reunir *vt* [503] to reunite
reunirse *vr* [503] to meet; to be reunited
unificar *vt* [-ificar] to unite
uniformar *vt* [2820] to make uniform
unir *vt* [107] to unite, to join

unirse *vr* [107] to become united with, to become joined to
universalizar *vt* to generalize
uno,-a *pron* one
unificador,-a *nmf* unifier; one who unifies
universitario,-a *nmf* professor or student in a university
undécimo *nm* [-ésimo] one-eleventh (fraction)
unicornio *nm* unicorn
uniforme *nm* [-iforme 3145] uniform
unísono *nm* unison
universo *nm* [2117] universe
uno *nm* one
desunión *nf* separation
reunión *nf* [292] meeting
unanimidad *nf* unanimity
unidad *nf* [-idad 273] unity
unificación *nf* unification
uniformidad *nf* uniform
unión *nf* [549] union
universalidad *nf* universality
universalización *nf* generalization
universidad *nf* [507] university
un,-a *art* a, an, one
un *aj* [7] one
unánime *aj* unanimous
undécimo *aj* [-ésimo] eleventh
unicameral *aj* unicameral
unicelular *aj* unicellular
único *aj* [-ico(2) 365] only; unique
unido *aj* united
uniformado *aj* uniformed
uniforme *aj* [-iforme 3145] uniform
unigénito *aj* only-begotten
unilateral *aj* unilateral
unisex *aj* unisex
unitario *aj* unitary; per unit
universal *aj* [2229] universal
universitario *aj* [1233] university

uña fingernail or toenail
cortauñas *nm* nail clippers
uñero *nm* ingrown nail
uña *nf* [3909] fingernail or toenail
uno *aj* one

urbano urban
urbanizar *vt* to urbanize
suburbano *nm* one who lives in a suburb
suburbio *nm* suburb
urbanismo *nm* city planning
urbanidad *nf* urbanity, good-manners, civility
urbanización *nf* urbanization
urbe *nf* well-populated city
interurbano *aj* inter-urban

suburbano *aj* suburban
urbano *aj* [1796] urban

urgencia emergency, urgency
urgir *vi* [2664] to be urgent
urgencia *nf* [-encia 2722] urgency, emergency
urgentemente *av* urgently
urgente *aj* [-ente(1) 2341] urgent

uso use
inutilizar *vt* to make useless or worthless
usar *vt* [501] to use or to wear
usarse *vr* to be used
utilizar *vt* [-izar 362] to utilize
usuario,-a *nmf* one who uses
desuso *nm* disuse
uso *nm* [605] use
utensilio *nm* utensil
útil *nm* [2244] someone or something that is useful
utilitarismo *nm* utilitarianism
inutilidad *nf* uselessness
utilería *nf* collection of stage props
utilidad *nf* [-idad 2484] utility, usefulness; also profit from a business
utilización *nf* [-ción 3988] utilization
inutilmente *av* uselessly
desusado *aj* out of use
inútil *aj* [-il 4524] useless
usado *aj* used
útil *aj* [2244] useful
utilizable *aj* utilizable

V

vacilar to vacillate
vacilar *vi* to vacillate
vacilación *nf* vacillation
vacilante *aj* [-ante(1)] vacillating

vacío empty
vaciar *vti* [3610] to empty
vaciarse *vr* to become empty
vaciado *nm* plaster cast; technique of using a mold to duplicate a work of art
vacío *nm* [3107] emptiness
vacación *nf* [2219] vacation
vacante *nf* vacancy
vacante *aj* vacant
vacío *aj* [3107] empty
vacuo *aj* [-uo] vacuous

vagabundo vagabond
vagabundear *vi* to live the life of a vagabond
vagar *vi* to wander aimlessly

vaguear *vi* to wander around
vagabundo,-a *nmf* vagabond
vago,-a *nmf* vagrant; idler
vagabundeo *nm* the life of a vagabond
vagancia *nf* [-ancia] vagrancy
vaguedad *nf* vagueness
vagabundo *aj* [-undo] vagabond
vago *aj* vague

valer to be worth
avalar *vt* [3098] to confirm the veracity of something; to give value to something
avalorar *vt* to determine the value of something; to estimate the value
avaluar *vt* to price something; to appraise
convalidar *vt* to confirm
desvalijar *vt* to steal valuables
desvalorizar *v* to devaluate; to drop in value; to lose value
devaluar *v* to devaluate; to drop in value; to lose value
infravalorar *vt* to under-appreciate
invalidar *vt* to invalidate
revalidar *vt* to confirm; to renew the value of something; to transfer credits from a university
subvalorar *vt* to under-value
supervalorar *vt* to over-value
valer *vi* [1170] to be worth
validar *vt* [3989] to validate
valorizar *vt* [-izar] to value or appreciate; to evaluate
valuar *vt* to value; to appraise
desvalido,-a *nmf* helpless person
inválido,-a *nmf* handicapped person
desvalijamiento *nm* robbery; theft
vale *nm* bond; voucher
avaluación *nf* act of pricing
desvalorización *nf* drop in value or price
devaluación *nf* devaluation
invalidación *nf* annulment
invalidez *nf* invalidity
revalidación *nf* evaluation (e.g., of transferable credits at a university)
validez *nf* [-ez] validity
valoración *nf* determination of price; appraisal
desvalido *aj* helpless or without resources
inválido *aj* invalid; handicapped
válido *aj* [-ido(1) 3734] valid
valioso *aj* [-oso 2777] valuable

valor courage
envalentonarse *vr* to take courage; to rise to the occasion
valentón,-a *nmf* arrogant or pretentious person

valiente *nmf* [4998]   courageous or valiant person

envalentonamiento *nm*   boasting, bragging

valor *nm* [500]   courage, bravery; value

valentía *nf*   courage, bravery

valentonada *nf*   pretentious act

valientemente *av* [-mente]   courageously, valiantly

valentón *aj*   pretentious, arrogant

valeroso *aj*   courageous, brave, more often encountered in reading than in conversation

valiente *aj* [4998]   courageous, brave

vanguardia   vanguard

vanguardista *nmf*   person who is at the cutting edge (esp., in arts and letters)

vanguardismo *nm*   tendency to be at the cutting edge in arts and letters

vanguardia *nf*   vanguard

vanguardista *aj*   at the cutting edge

vano   vain

envanecer *vt*   to cause arrogance or vanity

envanecerse *vr*   to become vain

vanagloriarse *vr*   to brag or boast (usually in a religious context)

vanidoso,-a *nmf*   vain person

envanecimiento *nm*   the act of becoming conceited

vanagloria *nf*   vainglory

vanidad *nf* [-idad]   vanity

vanidoso *aj*   very vain

vano *aj*   vain

vapor   vapor

evaporar *vt*   to evaporate

evaporarse *vr*   to become evaporated

vaporizar *vt* [-izar]   to vaporize

vaporizarse *vr*   to be vaporized

vapor *nm* [4729]   vapor

vaporizador *nm*   vaporizer

evaporación *nf*   evaporation

vaporización *nf*   vaporization

vaporoso *aj*   vapor-producing; vaporous

vario   different, diverse

variar *vt* [3789]   to vary

invariabilidad *nf*   invariability; unchanging

variabilidad *nf*   variability; changing

variable *nf* [-able 4235]   variable

variación *nf* [-ción 3146]   variation

variante *nf*   variant; version

variedad *nf* [-edad 1733]   variety

invariable *aj*   invariable

variable *aj* [-able 4235]   variable

variado *aj* [-ado(1) 3462]   varied

variante *aj*   varying

vario *aj*   different, diverse

varón   man

varón *nm* [3140]   man

varonil *aj* [-il 2320]   relating to man or men

vaso   glass

envasar *vt*   to bottle

envasado *nm*   bottling

envase *nm*   container

vaso *nm* [3055]   glass

vasija *nf*   small container; jar

envasado *aj*   bottled

vasto   vast

vastedad *nf* [-edad]   vastness

vasto *aj*   vast

vecino   neighbor

vecino,-a *nmf* [519]   neighbor

vecindario *nm*   apartments or houses sharing common facilities

vecindad *nf* [-edad]   apartments or houses sharing common facilities

vecino *aj*   neighboring

vegetación   vegetation

vegetar *vi*   to vegetate

vegetariano,-a *nmf*   vegetarian

vegetal *nm* [2573]   vegetable

vegetarianismo *nm*   vegetarianism

vegetación *nf*   vegetation

vegetal *aj* [2573]   plant

vegetariano *aj* [-ano]   vegetarian

vegetativo *aj*   vegetative

vehemente   vehement

vehemencia *nf*   vehemence

vehemente *aj*   vehement

veinte   twenty

veinte *nm* [2462]   twenty

veintavo *nm* [-avo]   one-twentieth (fraction

veintena *nf*   collection of twenty; score

veinte *aj* [2462]   twenty

vela¹   candle

desvelar *vt*   to keep someone else awake at night

desvelarse *vr*   to stay up late

velar *vt*   to keep watch late at night

velero *nmf*   candle merchant

desvelo *nm*   staying up late

velador *nm*   night watchman

velatorio *nm*   place where the body of the deceased is presented for viewing

vela *nf* [-a 4309]   candle

desvelado *aj*   tired from lack of sleep

velador *aj*   that stay-up late; watchful

vela²   sail

velero *nmf*   sail maker; sailboat

vela *nf* [-a 4309] sail
  velero *aj* sailing
velo veil
  revelar *vt* [1249] to reveal
  velar *vt* to veil or to conceal
  velarse *vr* to be overexposed, to be underexposed, to be blurry
  velo *nm* veil
  velado *aj* veiled; blurred (photograph)
velocidad velocity
  velocímetro *nm* speedometer
  velódromo *nm* velodrome
  velocidad *nf* [-idad] velocity
vena vein
  desvenar *vt* to remove the veins (of chiles or vegetables)
  vena *nf* vein
  intravenoso *aj* intravenous
  venoso *aj* venous; pertaining to veins
vencer to conquer
  desvencijar *vt* to loosen; to break partially
  desvencijarse *vr* to become loosened or partially broken
  vencer *vti(r)* [638] to conquer
  vencedor *nmf* [-dor(1)] conqueror
  desvencijado *aj* loose; partially broken
  invencible *aj* invincible
  vencedor *aj* [-dor(1)] conquering
  vencido *aj* conquered
vender to sell
  revender *vt* to resell
  vender *vt* [538] to sell
  venderse *vr* to be sold
  revendedor,-a *nmf* reseller
  vendedor,-a *nmf* [1662] salesman; seller
  reventa *nf* resale; retail
  venta *nf* [382] sale
  vendedor *aj* selling
  vendible *aj* [-ible] saleable
  vendido *aj* sold
veneno venom; poison
  envenenar *vt* to poison
  envenenamiento *nm* poisoning
  veneno *nm* venom; poison
  venenoso *aj* [-oso] venomous; poisonous
venerable venerable
  venerar *vt* to venerate; to worship
  veneración *nf* veneration
  venerable *aj* venerable
vengar to avenge
  vengar *vt* to avenge
  vengarse *vr* to avenge oneself

vengador,-a *nmf* avenger
  venganza *nf* [-anza 4054] revenge
  vengador *aj* avenging
  vengativo *aj* vengeful
venir to come
  contravenir *vt* to contravene
  convenir *vi* [2487] to be convenient to or for
  prevenir *vt* [1602] to prevent
  sobrevenir *vt* to overcome
  venir *vi* [244] to come
  venirse *vr* to be coming
  contravención *nm* contravention
  porvenir *nm* future
  avenida *nf* [480] avenue
  bienvenida *nf* [3057] welcome
  prevención *nf* prevention
  venida *nf* coming
  bienvenido *aj* welcome
  desprevenido *aj* unprepared
  preventivo *aj* [-ivo 824] preventive
  proveniente *aj* [-ente(1) 2863] proceeding (from); originating (in)
  venidero *aj* coming in the future
ventaja advantage
  ventajista *nmf* person who takes advantage of a situation in a selfish way
  ventaja *nf* [900] advantage
  ventajoso *aj* advantageous
ventana window
  aventar *vt* to throw through the air
  aventarse *vr* (figurative) to dare, try, go for
  ventilar *vt* to ventilate
  ventilarse *vr* to become ventilated
  ventanal *nm* [-al(1)] very large window
  ventarrón *nm* strong wind
  ventilador *nm* fan
  viento *nm* wind
  ventana *nf* [2905] window
  ventanilla *nf* [-illa 4370] small window (in car, train, plane, etc.)
  ventilación *nf* ventilation
  ventoso *aj* [-oso] windy
ventura happiness, luck, good fortune
  bienaventurado,-a *nmf* blessed
  bienaventuranza *nf* beatitude
  buenaventura *nf* good luck
  ventura *nf* happiness, luck, good fortune
  bienaventurado *aj* blessed; fortunate
  venturoso *aj* fortunate, happy
ver to see
  averiguar *vt* to investigate
  prever *vt* [2105] to foresee
  ver *vt* [77] to see

verificar *vt* [2613] to verify
verificarse *vr* to become verified
verse *vr* to look; to appear
verificador,-a *nmf* verifier
ver *nm* [77] sense of sight
averiguación *nf* [-ción 2593] investigation
veracidad *nf* veracity
verdad *nf* [-edad 733] true
verificación *nf* [-ción 3563] verification
verdaderamente *av* [-mente 3056] truly
averiguable *aj* able to be investigated
inverosímil *aj* unbelievable
veraz *aj* [-az] true; sincere
verdadero *aj* [-ero(2) 925] true
verídico *aj* true; real
verificador *aj* verifying
verosímil *aj* believable; probable

verano summer
invernar *vi* to spend the winter
veranear *vi* to spend the summer
invernadero *nm* place where one spends the winter; greenhouse
invierno *nm* [-o(1) 1901] winter
verano *nm* [1064] summer
invernal *aj* [4850] winter
veraniego *aj* [-iego] summer

verde green
enverdecer *vi* to turn green
reverdecer *vt* to turn green again
verdear *vi* to turn green
verdulero,-a *nmf* greengrocer
verde *nm* [933] green
verdor *nm* deep green color of plants
verdulería *nf* vegetable store
verdura *nf* [-ura(1) 2787] vegetable
verde *aj* [933] green
verdoso *aj* greenish
verdusco *aj* [-usco] greenish

vergüenza shame
avergonzar *vt* to shame
avergonzarse *vr* to become ashamed
desvergonzado,-a *nmf* shameless person
sinvergüenza *nmf* person who is brazen
desvergüenza *nf* shamelessness
vergüenza *nf* [4006] shame
avergonzado *aj* [-ado(1)] ashamed
desvergonzado *aj* shameless
sinvergüenza *aj* shameless; brazen
vergonzoso *aj* shameful; causing shame

verso verse
versificar *vti* to write verse
versículo *nm* [-culo] verse of scripture

verso *nm* verse
versado *aj* well-versed

verter to pour
verter *vt* [4217] to pour
verterse *vr* to be poured
vertedero *nm* trash bin or container

vértigo vertigo
vértigo *nm* vertigo
vertiginoso *aj* vertiginous
vestido *dress*
desvestir *vt* to undress
desvestirse *vr* to undress oneself; to get undressed
revestir *v* to put on a cloak, robe, armor, etc. over other clothes
revestirse *vr* to dress oneself with a cloak, robe, armor, etc. over other clothes
vestir *vt* [721] to dress
vestirse *vr* [721] to dress oneself; to get dressed
revestimiento *nm* act of dressing oneself with a cloak, robe, armor, etc. over other clothes
vestido *nm* [-ido(2) 1630] dress
vestuario *nm* [4027] clothing; wardrobe
vestidura *nf* [-dura] dress
vestimenta *nf* vestments
vestido *aj* [-ido(2) 1630] dressed

viaje trip
desviar *vt* [2296] to detour
desviarse *vr* [2296] to take a detour; (figurative) to lose one's way
enviar *vt* [593] to send
extraviar *v* to lose one's way; to lose something
extraviarse *vr* to become lost
viajar *vi* [724] to travel
tranviario,-a *nmf* streetcar worker
viajante *nmf* [-ante(2)] traveler
viajero,-a *nmf* traveler
desvío *nm* [-o(1) 3026] detour
enviado *nm* [-ado(2)] envoy
envío *nm* [-o(1) 3453] sending; item sent for delivery
extravío *nm* act of being lost
viaje *nm* [852] trip
desviación *nf* detour
tranvía *nf* streetcar
vía *nf* [762] way; route; railroad tracks
extraviado *aj* lost
tranviario *aj* relating to streetcars
viajero *aj* [-ero(3) 3939] traveling
viario *aj* relating to railroad tracks; relating to routes

vibrar to vibrate
vibrar *vti* to vibrate

vibrador *nm* [-dor(2)] vibrator
vibración *nf* vibration
vibrante *aj* vibrating; vibrant
vibratorio *aj* [-orio(2)] capable of vibrating
vicio vice
  enviciar *vt* to involve someone in a vice
  viciar *vt* to corrupt; to pervert
  viciarse *vr* to be corrupted; to become perverted
  vicioso,-a *nmf* person who is involved in a vice
  vicio *nm* [-icio 3712] vice
  viciado *aj* corrupted
  vicioso *aj* vicious
victoria victory
  victoria *nf* [587] victory
  victoriosamente *av* victoriously
  victorioso *aj* victorious
vida life
  revitalizar *vt* to revitalize
  vitalizar *vt* to vitalize
  vitalicio *nm* [-icio] life insurance policy
  vida *nf* [-ido(2) 99] life
  vitalidad *nf* vitality
  vitamina *nf* [1631] vitamin
  vital *aj* [2332] vital
  vitalicio *aj* [-icio] lifelong
  vitaminado *aj* vitamin-enriched
  vitamínico *aj* vitamin-rich
vidrio glass
  vidriar *vt* to glaze
  vidriarse *vr* to be glazed
  vidriero,-a *nmf* person who works with glass
  vidriado *nm* technique of glazing
  vidrio *nm* [2990] glass
  vidriería *nf* [-ería(2)] glass shop
  vitrina *nf* [-ina] glass show-case
  vidrioso *aj* glass-like; glassy
viejo old
  avejentarse *vr* to grow old; to become old, often before one's time
  envejecer *vt* to grow old
  envejecimiento *nm* [-miento 4113] old age
  viejo *nm* [876] old man; informally, a husband
  vejez *nf* [-ez] old age
  vieja *nf* old woman; informally, a wife
  envejecido *aj* aging
  viejo *aj* [876] old
vigente valid
  vigencia *nf* [-encia 3891] valid status
  vigente *aj* [2541] valid
vigilar to watch over
  vigilar *vt* [1876] to watch over
  vigía *nmf* security guard; watchman

  vigilante *nmf* [-ante(2) 4532] security guard
  vigía *nf* watchtower
  vigilancia *nf* [1049] vigilance
  vigilia *nf* vigil
  vigilante *aj* [-ante(2) 4532] vigilant
vigor vigor
  vigorizar *vt* to invigorate
  vigor *nm* [3317] vigor
  vigorizador *aj* invigorating
  vigorizante *aj* invigorating
  vigoroso *aj* vigorous
vino wine
  viñador,-a *nmf* winegrower
  vinagrero,-a *nmf* person who makes or sells vinegar
  vinatero,-a *nmf* wine merchant
  vinagre *nm* [4119] vinegar
  vino *nm* [1269] wine
  viñedo *nm* vineyard
  vinagrera *nf* vinegar bottle
  vinagreta *nf* [-eta] sauce made with oil, onions and vinegar
  viña *nf* vine
  vinicultura *nf* winemaking
  vinificación *nf* process of winemaking
  vinatero *aj* relating to wine
  vinícola *aj* relating to the making of wine
  vinoso *aj* wine-like
violento violent
  violar *vt* [2547] to violate; to rape
  violentar *vt* to force
  violentarse *vr* to become violent
  violador,-a *nmf* violator; rapist
  inviolabilidad *nf* inviolability
  violación *nf* [-ción 1964] violation; rape
  violencia *nf* [-encia 1072] violence
  inviolable *aj* inviolable
  inviolado *aj* inviolate
  violento *aj* [-lento 2363] violent
  violentamente *av* violently
violeta violet
  violeta *nm* violet (color)
  violeta *nf* violet (flower)
  violetera *nf* florist that sells only violets
  violeta *aj* violet
  ultravioleta *aj* ultraviolet
virgen virgin
  desvirgar *vt* to deflower
  virgo *nm* [4598] Virgo
  virgen *nf* [2491] virgin
  virginidad *nf* virginity
  virgen *aj* [2491] virgin
  virginal *aj* virginal

viril virile
  virilidad *nf*[-idad] virility
  viril *aj* virile
virtud virtue
  desvirtuar *vt* to cause something to lose its
    virtue
  virtuoso,-a *nmf* virtuoso
  virtud *nf*[1941] virtue
  virtuosidad *nf* virtuosity
  virtuoso *aj* virtuous
visitar to visit
  visitar *vt*[801] to visit
  visitador,-a *nmf* visitor; inspector
  visitante *nmf*[-ante(2) 1195] visitor
  visita *nf*[-a 629] visit
  visitación *nf*[-ción] visitation
  visitador *aj* visiting
  visitante *aj*[-ante(2) 1195] visiting
víspera eve of an event
  antevíspera *nf* two days before an event
  víspera *nf*[2617] eve of an event
vista sight
  entrevistar *vt*[953] to interview
  entrevistarse *vr* to be interviewing
  prever *vt*[2105] to foresee
  revisar *vt*[1308] to review
  revistar *vt* to review the troops
  supervisar *vt*[3660] to supervise
  televisar *vt*[1936] to televise
  vislumbrar *vt* to glimpse; to barely see
  visualizar *vt* to visualize
  entrevistador,-a *nmf* interviewer
  invidente *nmf* blind person
  revisionista *nmf* revisionist
  revisor,-a *nmf* ticket inspector
  supervisor,-a *nmf*[4672] supervisor
  televidente *nmf* television watcher
  vidente *nmf* person who can see
  visionario,-a *nmf* visionary
  imprevisto *nm* unforeseen circumstance
  retrovisor *nm* rear view mirror
  revisionismo *nm* revisionism
  revistero *nm* magazine holder
  televisor *nm*[2586] television
  tomavistas *nm* motion picture camera
  video *nm*[1409] video
  videoclub *nm* video club
  videojuego *nm* video game
  vistazo *nm* a quick glance
  entrevista *nf*[-a 678] interview
  imprevisión *nf* lack of foresight
  previsión *nf*[-sión 3876] foresight
  revisión *nf*[-sión 1382] revision

revista *nf*[1425] magazine
supervisión *nf*[-sión 3907] supervision
televisión *nf*[-sión 562] television
visibilidad *nf*[-idad] visibility
visión *nf*[-sión 1633] vision
vislumbre *nf* glimpse; glimmer of light
vista *nf* sight
visiblemente *av* visibly
audiovisual *aj* audiovisual
imprevisible *aj* unforeseeable
imprevisto *aj* unforeseen
invidente *aj* blind
invisible *aj* invisible
previsible *aj* foreseeable
previsor *aj* farsighted
previsto *aj*[1615] foreseen
revisionista *aj* revisionist
televisivo *aj*[-ivo 2964] television
visible *aj*[-ible 4863] visible
vistoso *aj* captivating for its visual
  characteristics
visual *aj*[3824] visual

viuda widow
  enviudar *vi* to become a widow
  viudo,-a *nmf*[4071] widower; widow
  viudez *nf* widowhood
  viudo *aj* widow

vivir to live
  avivar *vt* to stimulate; to bring life to
  avivarse *vr* to wake up; to become alive with
    energy
  convivir *vi*[3171] to share experiences, food, and
    time together
  desvivirse *vr* to give of oneself completely to
    something or someone
  malvivir *vi* to be needy, to live under difficult
    circumstances
  reavivar *vt* to restimulate; to reawaken; to bring
    something back to life (situation,
    circumstance, etc.)
  revivificar *vt* to reanimate; to restrengthen
  revivir *vt*[4751] to revive
  sobrevivir *vi*[2546] to survive
  vivificar *vt*[-ificar] to animate; to encourage; to
    strengthen
  vivir *vi*[199] to live
  víveres *nmpl* provisions
  sobreviviente *nmf*[-ente(1) 4840] survivor
  vividor,-a *nmf* someone who lives life at the
    expense of others
  vivo *nmf*[-ivo 1152] living creature
  convivio *nm*[1674] get-together; sharing together
    of time, experience and food

vivero *nm* [-ero(4) 4089] nursery
convivencia *nf* [-encia 2779] get-together; sharing together of time, experience and food
supervivencia *nf* survival
vivacidad *nf* vividness
vivencia *nf* life experience
viveza *nf* [-eza] brightness of colors, eyes, and ideas
vivienda *nf* [809] place where one lives; house
viva *int* long live!
vivamente *av* with intensity
vivaz *aj* [-az] vigorous; sharp; intelligent
avivado *aj* stimulated; brought to life
sobreviviente *aj* [-ente(1) 4840] surviving
superviviente *aj* surviving
vivaracho *aj* [-acho] very awake; fun (person, personal characteristic)
vívido *aj* vivid
viviente *aj* [-ente(1)] living
vivificante *aj* animating, strengthening, encouraging
vivo *aj* [-ivo 1152] alive

volar to fly
revolotear *vt* to twirl in the air
sobrevolar *vt* to fly over something
volar *vi* [2273] to fly
volear *vt* to volley
revoloteo *nm* [-eo(1)] twirling
revuelo *nm* second flight of a bird
volador *nm* flyer person
volante *nm* [2420] flyer
voleibol *nm* volleyball
voleo *nm* [-eo(1)] volley
vuelo *nm* [-o(1) 1678] flight
volador *aj* flying
volante *aj* [2420] flying

volumen volume
volumen *nm* [2250] volume
voluminoso *aj* voluminous

voluntad will
voluntario,-a *nmf* volunteer
voluntad *nf* [-tad 1596] will
voluntariamente *av* voluntarily
involuntario *aj* involuntary
voluntario *aj* [-ario(2) 2632] voluntary
voluntarioso *aj* strong-willed; self-willed

voluptuosidad voluptuousness
voluptuosidad *nf* voluptuousness
voluptuoso *aj* voluptuous

volver to return, to go back
devolver *vt* [2328] to return, to take something back
revolver *vti* [3502] to mix; to mix up

revolverse *vr* to be mixed up
volver *vt* [323] to return, to go back
volverse *vr* [323] to be returning; to be going back
revólver *nm* revolver
devolución *nf* return of an item; return of money in exchange for an item previously purchased
devuelto *aj* returned

voto vote
votar *vti* [1621] to vote
votante *nmf* [-ante(2) 4500] voter
voto *nm* [-o(1) 799] vote
votación *nf* [-ción 2085] voting
votante *aj* [-ante(2) 4500] voting

voz voice
vocalizar *vt* [-izar] to vocalize
vocear *vt* to talk through a loudspeaker or megaphone
vociferar *vti* to vociferate
vocal *nmf* [3970] voting member of a committee
vocalista *nmf* [-ista 3158] vocalist
voceador,-a *nmf* announcer; one who sells newspapers in the street
vocero,-a *nmf* [2602] announcer; one who sells newspapers in the street
altavoz *nm* megaphone; loudspeaker
vocablo *nm* word
vocabulario *nm* [-ario(1)] vocabulary
vocalismo *nm* vowel system
vocerío *nm* loud talking, especially of a crowd
vozarrón *nm* a deep voice
vocación *nf* [3955] vocation, calling
vocal *nf* [3970] vowel
vocalización *nf* vocalization
voz *nf* [730] voice
vocacional *aj* vocational
vocal *aj* [3970] vocal
voceador *aj* announcing
vociferador *aj* boasting
vociferante *aj* boasting

vuelta lap
voltear *vt* [4182] to turn around
voltereta *nf* [-eta] flip; somersault
vuelta *nf* [946] lap

vulgar vulgar
vulgarizar *vt* to vulgarize
vulgarizarse *vr* to be vulgar
vulgarismo *nm* vulgarism
vulgaridad *nf* vulgarity
vulgarización *nf* vulgarization
vulgarmente *av* vulgarly
vulgar *aj* vulgar

Y

yacer to be lying down, to remain lying
  down
  yacer *vi* to be lying down; to remain lying
    down, most commonly used to refer to the
    sick or the dead
  yacimiento *nm* a bed of rock
  subyacente *aj* lying beneath something else
  yacente *aj* [-ente(1)] lying down

yeso plaster
  enyesar *vt* to put plaster on something or
    someone
  yesero,-a *nmf* one who works with plaster
  enyesado *nm* plastering
  yeso *nm* plaster
  yesería *nf* [-ería(2)] place where plaster is
    processed or sold
  enyesado *aj* covered with plaster
  yesoso *aj* having the texture of plaster

Z

zapato shoe
  zapatear *vti* to tap with the sole of the shoe; to
    tap dance
  zapatero,-a *nmf* shoemaker, cobbler, shoe
    repairman
  zapatazo *nm* [-azo(1)] kick
  zapateado *nm* tap-dance
  zapateo *nm* [-eo(1)] foot-tapping
  zapato *nm* [3068] shoe
  zapatón *nm* [-ón(3)] big shoe, rain boot
  zapata *nf* brake shoe
  zapatería *nf* [-ería(1)] shoe store
  zapatilla *nf* [-illa] a fine shoe, woman's dress-
    shoe; ballet slipper

zozobra the act of becoming shipwrecked
  zozobrar *vi* to become shipwrecked (also
    figurative)
  zozobra *nf* the act of becoming shipwrecked

Guide to Spanish Suffixes

This Guide contains more than 120 Spanish suffixes, chosen on the basis of their frequent recurrence throughout the Spanish language. While some endings are far more common than others, all are found in words you will encounter in everyday usage. The suffixes are arranged alphabetically and appear with their meaning; their English equivalent (when one exists); and the part(s) of speech of the words formed, followed by a short paragraph that discusses the meaning of the particular suffix, how words employing it are formed, and interesting features and/or unusual constructions characteristic of that particular ending.

Below each suffix, you will find an illustrative list of words taking that suffix. Over 4,600 examples are included in the Guide, with cross-references to the Roots Dictionary [R] and Frequency Table [number] where applicable. Each of these Spanish vocabulary entries is followed by its English equivalent, the stem to which it is related (many of which you probably already know), as well as the stem's English equivalent. For further explanation on the formation and use of this dictionary, please consult the Introduction.

-a

Meaning: *resulting object; resulting action*
English equivalent: *none*
Found in: *nouns*

There are thousands of Spanish words that end in *-a*; but what makes these words distinctive is that they are all derived from *-ar* verbs; *-er* and *-ir* verbs use different suffixes to indicate resulting actions or nouns. Also, while it may appear that these terms simply end in *-a*, upon closer inspection you will see that such nouns not only are derived from *-ar* verbs, but that when that verb is a stem-changing verb, the stem change is made in the resulting noun: *prueba* (proof; quiz) from *probar* (to prove, test); *rueda* (wheel) from *rodar* (to roll). All such nouns are feminine.

Formed Word	English Equivalent	Related to	English Equivalent
la alarma [R 4237]	alarm	**alarmar**	to alarm
la alerta [2497]	alert	**alertar**	to alert
la amenaza [R 1303]	threat	**amenazar**	to threaten
la angustia [R 4009]	anguish; distress	**angustiar(se)**	to cause anguish, distress
la apuesta [3391]	bet	**apostar**	to bet
el arma (f) [R 703]	arm (weapon)	**armar**	to arm
la aventura [R 2213]	adventure	**aventurar(se)**	to risk; to venture
la ayuda [R 677]	help; aid; assistance	**ayudar**	to aid, help, assist
la batalla [R 2035]	battle	**batallar**	to battle
la beca [2857]	scholarship; award	**becar**	to award a scholarship
la burla [R 4489]	scoff(ing); mockery; hoax	**burlar**	to mock, laugh at, hoax

Formed Word	English Equivalent	Related to	English Equivalent
la busca [R]	search; hunt; pursuit	buscar	to seek, search, look for
la captura [2783]	capture	capturar	to capture
la carga [R 1831]	charge; responsibility; burden	cargar	to charge; to make responsible; to burden
la caricia [R]	caress; stroke	acariciar	to caress, stroke, fondle, cherish
la causa [R 518]	cause; (law) case; trial	causar	to cause
la cena [R 2646]	supper; dinner	cenar	to dine, eat supper or dinner
la charla [R 3717]	chat	charlar	to chat
la cifra [R 977]	numerical digit; code, cipher	cifrar	to encode
la cita [R 1469]	appointment; quote	citar	to set an appointment; to quote
la clausura [3359]	closing session	clausurar	to close
la cocina [R 1980]	kitchen; cooking; cookery	cocinar	to cook
la compra [R 1328]	purchase; buy; buying	comprar	to buy, purchase
la condena [R 3861]	sentence (legal penalty)	condenar	to sentence, condemn
la conquista [R 3739]	conquest	conquistar	to conquer (often figurative)
la conserva [R 4110]	preserves	conservar	to preserve, maintain
la consigna [R 4539]	slogan; instruction, order	consignar	to instruct, order
la consulta [R 1721]	consultation	consultar	to consult
la copia [R 1974]	copy; duplicate	copiar	to copy, duplicate
la corona [R 1143]	crown	coronar	to crown
la cosecha [R 2648]	harvest	cosechar	to harvest
la crítica [R 2052]	criticism	criticar	to criticize
la cuenta [R 159]	bill; account; tab	contar	to count, charge
la culpa [R 2402]	fault	culpar	to blame
la danza [R 3006]	dance	danzar	to dance
la demanda [R 560]	lawsuit	demandar	to sue
la denuncia [R 870]	denunciation; accusation	denunciar	to denounce, accuse
la derrota [R 990]	defeat	derrotar	to defeat
la descarga [R 4542]	unloading; discharge; discharging	descargar	to unload; to discharge
la desgracia [R 3393]	misfortune	desgraciar(se)	to spoil; to become injured
la diferencia [R 765]	difference	diferenciar	to differentiate
la disciplina [R 1764]	discipline; scourge; whip	disciplinar	to discipline, scourge, whip
la disculpa [R 4764]	excuse	disculpar(se)	to excuse; to ask forgiveness
la disputa [R 1975]	dispute	disputar	to dispute
la distancia [R 1564]	distance	distanciar(se)	to distance oneself
la droga [914]	drug	drogar	to drug
la ducha	shower	duchar(se)	to (take a) shower
la duda [R 754]	doubt	dudar	to doubt
la encuesta [R 2046]	poll; survey	encuestar	to poll, survey
la entrega [R 691]	giving; delivery	entregar	to give, deliver
la entrevista [R 678]	interview	entrevistar	to interview
la escala [R 3060]	scale (music); stopover	escalar	to climb
la escucha [R]	listening; listening-place	escuchar	to listen (to), hear
la espera [R]	wait(ing); expectation	esperar	to wait, await, expect

Formed Word	English Equivalent	Related to	English Equivalent
la estima [R 2506]	esteem	estimar	to esteem
la estructura [R 1648]	structure	estructurar	to structure; to construct
la etiqueta [4302]	label; etiquette	etiquetar	to label
la fábrica [R 2993]	factory	fabricar	to build in a factory
la falla [1900]	failure	fallar	to fail
la falta [R 263]	absence; fault	faltar	to miss (appointment); to err
la fecha [R 319]	date	fechar	to date
la figura [R 1005]	figure	figurar	to figure
la firma [R 1076]	signature	firmar	to sign
la flecha [R 4740]	arrow	flechar	to shoot an arrow; to inspire love
la forma [R 139]	form; shape	formar	to form, shape
la fórmula [R 1738]	formula	formular	to formulate
la fractura [2616]	fracture	fracturar	to fracture
la fuerza [R 352]	strength	forzar	to force
la fuga [R 1766]	flight; escape	fugar	to flee, escape
la gira [983]	tour (performance)	girar	to turn, revolve
la gloria [R 3542]	glory	gloriar(se)	to praise; to boast
la guarda [R]	guard; care; safekeeping	guardar	to keep, guard, protect
la hipoteca	mortgage	hipotecar	to mortgage
la influencia [R 2131]	influence	influenciar	to influence
la junta [R 1284]	meeting	juntar	to meet, join
la lágrima [R 3127]	tear; teardrop	lagrimar	to weep, cry, shed tears
la liga [R 466]	league; link, rubber band	ligar	to link, join, tie together
la lucha [R 579]	struggle; fight; effort	luchar	to struggle, fight
la mama [R 4988]	mammary gland	mamar	to suck on a breast or mammary gland
la mancha [R 2816]	stain	manchar	to stain
la maniobra [R 3387]	maneuver	maniobrar	to maneuver
la maravilla [R 3459]	something marvelous	maravillar(se)	to amaze; to marvel
la marca [R 833]	mark	marcar	to mark
la marcha [R 854]	march	marchar	to march
la mejora [R 3211]	improvement	mejorar	to improve
la mezcla [R 1958]	mixture	mezclar	to mix
la mina [R 4721]	mine	minar	to mine
la mira [R]	sight; watch-tower; aim; view	mirar	to look (at), watch, gaze
la muestra [R 811]	signboard; sample; specimen	mostrar	to show
la multa [2442]	fine (penalty)	multar	to fine (penalty)
la norma [R 3136]	norm	normar	to norm, set standards
la nota [R 1520]	note	notar	to note
la noticia [R 1162]	news; news item; piece of news	noticiar	to give notice of, notify, make known
la obra [R 211]	work; piece of work; task	obrar	to work, carry out, perform
la orilla [3637]	edge; hem	orillar	to move along the edge, hem
la página [R 1384]	page	paginar	to paginate
la patrulla [2142]	patrol; patrol car	patrullar	to patrol
la pausa [R]	pause; break; stop	pausar	to pause, slow down
la pelea [R 1665]	fight	pelear	to fight

Formed Word	English Equivalent	Related to	English Equivalent
la pesa [R 4528]	weight	pesar	to weigh (intransitive)
la pesca [R 3382]	fishing	pescar	to fish
la pinta [R]	spot; mark; look	pintar	to paint, scribble, depict, draw
la plancha	iron; ironing	planchar	to iron, press
la planta [R 818]	plant	plantar	to plant
la plática [1464]	talk	platicar	to talk, chat
la práctica [R 899]	practice; training	practicar	to practice
la pregunta [R 944]	question; query; inquiry	preguntar	to ask, inquire
la prensa [R 528]	press (newspapers, etc.)	prensar	to press
la presencia [R 483]	presence	presenciar	to be present
la protesta [R 1378]	protest	protestar	to protest
la prueba [R 599]	proof; (piece of) evidence; test	probar	to prove, test, try out
la queja [R 1137]	complaint	quejar(se)	to complain
la quema [R 4388]	burning	quemar	to burn
la raya [R 4363]	line, stripe	rayar	to draw a line
la reforma [R 588]	reform	reformar	to reform
la reina [R 1696]	queen	reinar	to rule
la renta [R 2307]	rent; income; taxes	rentar	to rent, tax
la renuncia [R 2325]	resignation	reunciar	to resign
la reserva [R 1532]	reserve	reservar	to reserve
la resta [4390]	subtraction (math)	restar	to subtract
la resulta [R 1203]	result; outcome	resultar	to result, turn out, prove to be
la ronda [R 1551]	rounds (of vigilance)	rondar	to make rounds
la rueda [1836]	wheel; caster; roller	rodar	to roll, roll along
la ruina [R]	ruin; fall; downfall; wreck	arruinar	to ruin, destroy
la sentencia [R 2622]	sentence (legal punishment)	sentenciar	to sentence (legal punishment)
la sospecha [R 3357]	suspicion	sospechar	to suspect
la subasta [4639]	auction; auction sale	subastar	to auction, sell at auction
la suma [R 1772]	sum	sumar	to sum
la tapa [R 4841]	lid	tapar	to cover, place a lid on
la tizna	blackening; lampblack	tiznar	to smut, smudge, blacken
la toma [R]	taking; dose; capture	tomar	to take, have, get, gather
la tortura [4147]	torture	torturar	to torture
la trama [R 3954]	plot (story)	tramar	to plot (story, plan)
la vacuna [3527]	vaccine	vacunar	to vaccinate
la vela [R 4309]	watch; vigil; wakefulness	velar	to watch (over), keep vigil, stay awake
la visita [R 629]	visit; visitor(s); social call	visitar	to visit, call upon, search, inspect

-able

Meaning: *able to; capable of*
English equivalent: *-able*
Found in: *adjectives*

The Spanish suffix *-able* is identical to its English counterpart both in spelling and in meaning: both mean exactly what they imply, namely, "able to" or "capable of." Note below that all words taking the suffix *-able* are derived from *-ar* verbs. Another suffix, *-ible*, which performs the same function, is found in words derived from *-er* and *-ir* verbs.

Formed Word	English Equivalent	Related to	English Equivalent
acabable	that can be finished; achievable	**acabar**	to finish (off), conclude
aceptable [R 4780]	acceptable	**aceptar**	to accept
adorable [R]	adorable	**adorar**	to adore
agradable [R 2047]	pleasant	**agradar**	to please
aplacable	appeasable	**aplacar**	to appease, pacify
besable	kissable	**besar**	to kiss
calculable [R]	calculable	**calcular**	to calculate
compensable	able to be compensated	**compensar**	to compensate
conciliable	reconcilable	**conciliar**	to reconcile, conciliate, win
condenable	worthy of condemnation	**condenar**	to condemn
confiable [R 4394]	trustworthy	**confiar**	to have faith in, trust (in)
conservable	preservable	**conservar**	to preserve, conserve
considerable [R 2624]	considerable	**considerar**	to consider
contable [R 4760]	countable	**contar**	to count; to tell (a story)
criticable	open to criticism; criticizable	**criticar**	to criticize
culpable [R 2534]	guilty	**culpar**	to blame
cultivable	cultivatable	**cultivar**	to cultivate
dudable	doubtful; doubtable	**dudar**	to doubt
estimable [R 2182]	estimable	**estimar**	to esteem (vt); to esteem each other (plural) (vr)
evitable [R]	avoidable	**evitar**	to avoid
falseable	falsifiable	**falsear**	to falsify, forge, counterfeit
favorable [R 2036]	favorable	**favorecer**	to favor; to decide in favor of
imparable [R 1812]	unstoppable	**parar**	to stop (vt); to stand up (vr)
imputable	imputable	**imputar**	to impute, ascribe
indispensable [R 2455]	indispensable	**dispensar**	to dispense; to excuse or pardon
inevitable [R 4462]	inevitable	**evitar**	to avoid
inolvidable [R 3810]	unforgettable	**olvidar**	to forget
lamentable [R 3203]	lamentable	**lamentar**	to lament, be sorry (vt); to lament (vr)
mudable [R]	changeable; fickle	**mudar**	to change, move
narrable	capable of being narrated	**narrar**	to narrate
navegable [R]	navigable	**navegar**	to navigate, sail

Formed Word	English Equivalent	Related to	English Equivalent
negable	deniable	**negar**	to deny, refuse
negociable [R]	negotiable	**negociar**	to negotiate
notable [R 3311]	notable; remarkable	**notar**	to note, notice, mark
opinable [R]	questionable; debatable	**opinar**	to think, have or express opinions
organizable	organizable	**organizar**	to organize
palpable [R]	palpable; clear; obvious	**palpar**	to touch, feel, see as self-evident
pasable	passable	**pasar**	to pass
penable	punishable	**penar**	to punish, chastise
penetrable [R]	penetrable	**penetrar**	to penetrate
razonable [R 4834]	reasonable	**razonar**	to reason
reciclable [R 4484]	recyclable	**reciclar**	to recycle
recomendable [R 4040]	recommendable	**recomendar**	to recommend
soportable [R]	tolerable; supportable; bearable	**soportar**	to tolerate, bear, endure
sustentable [4131]	defensible	**sustentar**	to sustain (vt); to be sustained (vr)
variable [R 4235]	variable	**variar**	to vary
vulnerable [4044]	vulnerable	**vulnerar**	to injure

-acho; -acha

Meaning: *augmentative; deprecative*
English equivalent: *none*
Found in: *nouns, adjectives (rarely)*

Spanish words in *-acho* and *-acha* generally denote exaggeration of the root word and often carry deprecative connotations. For example, *rico* is simply a rich man, while *ricacho* is someone who is filthy rich, a "moneybags." (The filthy rich woman is *la ricacha*.) This is not a common ending, but it is a powerful one, and because of this many words ending with *-acho* and *-acha* should be used with discretion. The suffix *-acho* or *-acha* almost always is a noun ending: the only exception below is *vivaracho* (*vivaracha* when describing a feminine noun), which is an adjective. All words ending in *-acho* are masculine, while those ending in *-acha* are feminine.

Formed Word	English Equivalent	Related to	English Equivalent
la aguacha	foul water	**el agua** *nf*	water
el amigacho	chum; crony; pal	**el amigo**	friend
el barbicacho	ribbon tied under the chin	**la barba**	chin
la bocacha	great hideous mouth	**la boca**	mouth
el cocacho	rap on the head	**la coca**	(coll.) head
el dicharacho	crude, vulgar expression	**el dicho**	saying; saw
la hilacha	shred; frayed thread	**el hilo**	thread
el hornacho	furnace (for casting statues)	**el horno**	oven; kiln
el mamarracho	sissy	**la mamá**	mother; mom
el marimacho	mannish woman	*(Lat.)* **maritus**	husband
el poblacho	old, run-down town	**el pueblo**	town

Formed Word	English Equivalent	Related to	English Equivalent
el populacho [R]	mob; rabble	(Lat.) populus	people
el riacho	small, dirty river	el río	river
el ricacho	(coll.) "moneybags"	el rico	rich individual
el terminacho	(coll.) crude, vulgar expression	el término	term
el verdacho	green earth	el verde	green (color)
vivaracho [R]	(coll.) lively; spirited; frisky	vivir	to live
el vulgacho	mob; rabble	el vulgo	common people

-aco (-aca)

Meaning: *deprecative*
English equivalent: *none*
Found in: *nouns, adjectives*

The ending -*aco* is an uncommon but powerful deprecative ending. When added to the base word, it brings strong, negative connotations. When added to a noun, it remains a noun; when added to an adjective, it remains an adjective. As an adjective, the ending is -*aca* when the term describes a feminine noun.

Formed Word	English Equivalent	Related to	English Equivalent
bellaco	cunning; sly; wicked	bello	beautiful; fair
el bicharraco	revolting creature	el bicho	creature
currutaco	foppish	curro	cute; nice; showy
libraco	(coll.) wretched book; tedious tome	el libro	book
pajarraco [R]	great, ugly bird	el pájaro	bird

-ada(1)

Meaning: *group; collection; amount; flock; drove,* etc.
English equivalent: *none*
Found in: *nouns*

The suffix -*ada* can indicate a collective use or large number of its root word. It is a common ending for groups of animals as well as other goods. This ending can also denote a span of time (*la década*), approximations (*la millonada*), and groups of people (*la indiada*). All such words are feminine.

Formed Word	English Equivalent	Related to	English Equivalent
la animalada	great amount; "hell of a lot"	el animal	animal
la arañada	collection of spiders	la araña	spider
la armada [R]	navy; fleet; squadron	el arma *nf*	weapon; arm; force
la bancada [4281]	group of party members in an assembly	la banca	bench

Formed Word	English Equivalent	Related to	English Equivalent
la borregada	large flock of lambs	el borrego	young lamb
la boyada	drove of oxen	el buey	ox
la burrada	drove of asses	el burro	ass; donkey
la caballada	group of horses	el caballo	horse
la carnerada	flock of sheep	el carnero	sheep
la centenada	hundred	cien	one hundred
la cerdada	herd of swine	el cerdo	(lit., fig.) pig; hog
la cotonada	cotton good	el cotón	printed cotton
la década [947]	decade; ten years	(Gr.) deca	ten
la invernada	winter season	el invierno	winter
la mesada	monthly pay; wages	el mes	month
la millonada [R]	huge sum of money	el millón	million
la mulada	drove of mules	el mulo	mule
la novillada	drove of young bulls	el novillo	young bull
la obrada	day's work	la obra	work; piece of work; task
la otoñada	autumn season	el otoño	autumn
la palabrada	verbiage	la palabra	word
la pavada	flock of turkeys	el pavo	turkey
la peonada	gang of laborers	el peón	laborer
la perrada	pack of dogs	el perro	dog
la riñonada	dish of kidneys	el riñón	kidney
la torada	drove of bulls	el toro	bull
la uvada	glut of grapes	la uva	grape
la vacada	herd of cattle	la vaca	cow
la veranada	summer season	el verano	summer

-ada[(2)]

Meaning: *blow or strike with or from; resulting action*
English equivalent: *none*
Found in: *nouns*

In this group of words ending with -*ada*, we find many words similar to those ending in -*azo* (blow or strike with or from), in which the root noun indicates the object used for hitting. A good example is *la puñada* (punch or blow with the fist) from *puño* (fist). Also listed are several words that designate result or resulting action, generally from the root noun, e.g., *la ojeada* (glance; look) from *ojo* (eye). When the root is a verb, the ending -*ada* indicates the result of that verb, e.g., *la tirada* (throw) from *tirar* (to throw). All nouns ending in -*ada* are feminine.

Formed Word	English Equivalent	Related to	English Equivalent
la azadada	blow with a spade or hoe	la azada	spade; hoe
la badajada	stroke of the clapper	el badajo	clapper (of a bell)
la cabezada	shake of the head	la cabeza	head
la coleada	swish of a tail	la cola	tail
la corazonada [R]	hunch; presentiment	el corazón	heart
la cuchillada [R]	gash from a knife	el cuchillo	knife
la fumada	puff/whiff of smoke	fumar	to smoke

Formed Word	English Equivalent	Related to	English Equivalent
la galopada	race at a gallop	el galope	gallop
la gargantada	liquid or blood ejected from throat	la garganta	throat
la gatada	cat trick; catlike act	el gato	cat
la gaznatada	violent blow on windpipe	el gaznate	gullet; windpipe
la hombrada [R]	manly action	el hombre	man
la lengüetada [R]	lick; licking	la lengua	tongue
la limonada [R]	lemonade	el limón	lemon
la llamada [R 902]	call; knock; ring (telephone)	llamar	to call, call upon
la llegada [R 945]	arrival	llegar	to arrive
la mangonada	punch with the arm	la manga	sleeve
la mazada	blow with mace or club	la maza	mace; war club
la morrada	butting with the head	la morra	crown; top of the head
la muchachada [R]	childish prank	el muchacho	boy; lad
la nalgada	slap on or with the buttocks	la nalga	buttock
la naranjada	orange juice; orangeade	la naranja	orange (fruit)
la ojeada	glance; look	el ojo	eye
la palmada [R]	slap	la palma	palm of the hand
la palotada	stoke with a drumstick	el palote	drumstick
la panderada	stroke with a tambourine	la pandereta	tambourine
la patada [R]	kick	la pata	foot; paw
la pernada	kick with the leg	la pierna	leg
la puñada	punch; blow with the fist	el puño	fist
la puñalada [R]	stab	el puñal	dagger
la rodillada [R]	push with the knee	la rodilla	knee
la tijeretada	clip; cut with a scissors	tijeretear	to cut with scissors
la tirada	throw	tirar	to throw
la tomada	taking; capture	tomar	to take
la uñada	scratch with a fingernail	la uña	fingernail
la zancada	long stride	la zanca	shank; long leg

-ada(3); -ado

Meaning: *denotes fullness of a measure or vessel*
English equivalent: *-ful; -load*
Found in: *nouns*

The suffix *-ada* (in rare cases *-ado*) indicates fullness of the root noun, which generally is a vessel of some sort. Usually, the fullness is literal, as in *la cucharada* (spoonful); however, sometimes the meaning can be stretched a bit and done so humorously, as in *narigada* (portion of snuff; "noseful"). All words ending in *-ada* are feminine, while those ending with *-ado* are masculine.

Formed Word	English Equivalent	Related to	English Equivalent
la barcada	boatload	el barco	boat
el bocado [R]	mouthful	la boca	mouth
la bofada	lungful	el bofe	lung
la botelada	boatload	el bote	boat
la brazada [R]	armful	el brazo	arm

Formed Word	English Equivalent	Related to	English Equivalent
la calderada	cauldronful	la caldera	cauldron; boiler
la canastada	basketful	la canasta	basket; hamper
la capada	capeful; cloakful	la capa	cape; cloak
la carretada [R]	wagonload	la carreta	wagon
la carretillada	wheelbarrow-load	la carretilla	wheelbarrow
la carretonada	truckload	el carretón	truck; cart
la cazolada	panful	el cazo	pan
la cestada	basketful	la cesta	basket
la cucharada [2065]	spoonful	la cuchara	spoon
la dedada	small portion; "fingerful"	el dedo	finger
la esquifada	boatload	el esquife	skiff
la hornada	batch; "ovenful"	el horno	oven
la lanchada	lighterload	la lancha	lighter; barge
la narigada	portion of snuff; "noseful"	la nariz	nose
la palada	shovelful	la pala	shovel
la paletada	trowelful	la paleta	trowel
la panzada	bellyful	la panza	belly
la ponchada	bowlful of punch	el ponche	punch
la pulgada	inch; "thumbful"	el pulgar	thumb
el puñado [R]	handful; fistful	el puño	fist
la sartenada	frying-panful	la sartén	frying pan
la tonelada [1661]	ton; "barrelful"	el tonel	barrel
la vagonada	truckful; carload	el vagón	truck; boxcar
la zurronada	bagful	el zurrón	shepherd's pouch; leather bag

-ado⁽¹⁾ (-ada)

Meaning: *like; relating to*
English equivalent: *none*
Found in: *adjectives*

The suffix *-ado* is one of several adjectival endings meaning *like, relating to*. The examples given below all are derived from nouns. The formation of this suffix is easy: generally speaking, if the root noun ends in a vowel, drop that vowel and add *-ado*; if the root noun ends in a consonant, simply add *-ado*. As this is an adjectival ending, when describing nouns of the feminine gender, these words will end in *-ada*.

Formed Word	English Equivalent	Related to	English Equivalent
afortunado [R 4279]	fortunate	la fortuna	fortune
anisado	mixed with aniseed; aniselike	el anís	anise; aniseed
arrojado [R]	bold; fearless	el arrojo	boldness; intrepidity
avergonzado [R]	ashamed; embarrassed	avergonzar	to shame, embarrass
azafranado	saffronlike; saffron-colored	el azafrán	saffron
colorado [R]	red colored	el color	color
cruzado [R]	crossbred; crossed	la cruz	cross
cuadrado [R 2959]	square; square-shaped	el cuadro	square
enojado [R]	angry; mad	el enojo	anger
estrellado [R]	starry; cracked	la estrella	star

Formed Word	English Equivalent	Related to	English Equivalent
ferrado	plated with iron	el fierro	iron
frustrado [4399]	frustrated	frustrar	to frustrate
hadado	fateful; magic	el hado	fate; destiny
halconado	falconlike; hawklike	el halcón	falcon; hawk
helado [R 3998]	*nm* ice cream; *aj* freezing	el hielo	ice
inadecuado [R 4720]	inadequate	adecuado	adequate
inesperado [R 4384]	unexpected	esperar	to expect, wait, hope
inmaculado [4793]	immaculate	mácula	stain
irisado	rainbow-hued	el iris	rainbow
jironado	shredded; tattered	el jirón	shred; tatter
jorobado	hump- or hunch-backed	la joroba	hump
lanzado	at full tilt; rushing	la lanza	lance
leonado	lion-colored; tawny	el león	lion
letrado [R]	learned	la letra	letter
logrado [R]	successful; well-executed	el logro	gain; profit
naranjado	orange-colored	la naranja	orange (fruit)
nevado [R]	snow-covered; snowy	la nieve	snow
nublado [R]	cloudy; overcast	la nube	cloud
ovalado	egg-shaped; oval-shaped	el óvalo	oval
patronado	having a patron	el patrón	patron; protector
pesado [R]	heavy	el peso	weight
pintado [R]	spotted; mottled; speckled	la pinta	spot; mark
playado	beach-lined	la playa	beach
rayado [R]	striped; streaked	la raya	stripe
recortado [R]	(bot.) incised	el recorte	cutting; clipping
rosado [R]	rose-colored; pink	la rosa	rose; rose-color
sargado	sergelike	la sarga	serge
triangular [R]	triangular; triangle-shaped	el triángulo	triangle
variado [R 3462]	varied	variar	to vary
vomitado	(coll.) palefaced; thin	el vómito	vomit; vomiting

-ado⁽²⁾ (-ada)

Meaning: *one who; result of action*
English equivalent: *none*
Found in: *nouns*

The noun ending *-ado* can denote a person doing something or the result of an action. In either case, whether the reference is to the performer or to the action performed, such nouns ending in *-ado* all are derived from *-ar* verbs. Thus, the formation is simple: drop the *-ar* from the infinitive and add *-ado*. While all the examples listed are in the masculine form, if the resulting noun is a person and that person is female, the suffix is *-ada* (*el empleado; la empleada*). Otherwise, all nouns ending with *-ado* are masculine.

Formed Word	English Equivalent	Related to	English Equivalent
el abogado [R]	lawyer; advocate	abogar	to advocate, plead
el adobado	pickled meat (esp. pork)	adobar	to pickle (meat)

Formed Word	English Equivalent	Related to	English Equivalent
el adoptado	adopted person	adoptar	to adopt
el aficionado [R 1139]	fan (admirer); enthusiast	aficionarse	to become fond of
el aliado [R 2985]	ally	aliar	to ally
el ahijado	godchild; protégé	ahijar	to adopt, espouse
el cercado [R]	enclosure; fenced-in garden	cercar	to enclose, fence in
el constipado	cold; chill	constipar	to give a cold to
el convidado [R]	guest; person invited	convidar	to invite
la criada	maid; servant	criar	to rear, bring up
el chalado	(coll.) crazy person; nut case	chalar	to drive crazy
el decorado [R]	decoration; décor	decorar	to decorate, adorn
el delegado [R]	delegate: commissioner	delegar	to delegate
el desagrado [R]	displeasure; reluctance	desagradar	to displease
el emigrado	émigré	emigrar	to emigrate
el empleado	employee	emplear	to employ, use
el enamorado [R]	lover	enamorar	to enamor, cause to fall in love
el encabezado [2322]	headline	encabezar	to headline
el encargado [R]	person in charge	encargar	to entrust, put in charge
el enlistonado	lath-work	enlistonar	to lath
el enterrado	buried person	enterrar	to bury, inter
el enviado [R]	messenger; envoy	enviar	to send
el estado [R 42]	state; commonwealth; condition	estar	to be (in place or condition)
el granizado	iced drink	granizar	to hail down (upon)
el guisado	stew; ragout; fricassee	guisar	to cook, stew, (fig.) cook up
el helado [R 3998]	ice cream	helar	to freeze, turn to ice
el hilado [R]	spinning; yarn; thread	hilar	to spin
el invitado [R]	person invited; guest	invitar	to invite
el licenciado [R]	university graduate; lawyer	licenciar	to confer a degree upon, license
el listado [4669]	list	listar	to list
el peinado [R]	hairdo; hairstyle	peinar	to comb, do the hair of
el resultado [R 212]	result	resultar	to result
el rizado	curl	rizar	to curl
el sobrado [R]	attic; loft	sobrar	to be left over
el teclado	keyboard (piano, typewriter, etc.)	teclear	to touch upon, play chords
el tornado [R]	tornado	tornar	to turn, return, change

-aje⁽¹⁾

Meaning: *collection; set; forms abstract noun*
English equivalent: *-age*
Found in: *nouns*

When added to a root noun, the suffix *-aje* enlarges upon it; from the single *la vela* (sail), we get *velaje* (set of sails); or from *ancla* (anchor), we get *anclaje* (anchorage). In the case of the sails, we go from the specific to the collection; whereas in the case of the anchor, we go from the specific to the abstraction, idea, or purpose of the root noun. All words ending in *-aje* are masculine.

Formed Word	English Equivalent	Related to	English Equivalent
el alambraje	wiring	el alambre	wire
el almacenaje [R]	storage	el almacén	store; warehouse
el anclaje	anchorage	el ancla *nf*	anchor
el andamiaje	scaffolding	el andamio	scaffold; platform
el camionaje	trucking; truckage	el camión	truck
el caudillaje [R]	leadership; tyranny	el caudillo	chief; leader; (mil.) commander
el correaje	straps; belting	la correa	leather strap; thong
el hembraje	females in flock; "womenfolk"	la hembra	female
el herbaje	herbage	le hierba	grass; herb
el herraje [R]	hardware; ironwork	el hierro	iron
el lenguaje [R 3142]	language	la lengua	tongue
el linaje	lineage	la línea	line
el maderaje [R]	woodwork	la madera	wood
el marinaje	sailors; seamanship	el marino	sailor
el monedaje	coins; coinage	la moneda	coin
el mueblaje	furniture (in general)	el mueble	(piece of) furniture
el obraje	manufacture; handiwork	la obra	work; piece of work
el paisanaje [R]	civilian population; civilians	el paisano	civilian; peasant
el peonaje	gang of laborers	el peón	laborer
el plantaje	collection of plants	la planta	plant
el plumaje [R]	plumage; feathers	la pluma	feather
el porcentaje [R 1816]	percentage	por ciento	percent
el pupilaje	pupilage; wardship; boarding	el pupilo	pupil; ward; boarder
el ramaje [R]	mass of branches	la rama	branch
el rendaje	set of reins and bridles	la rienda	rein
el rodaje [R 3077]	set of wheels	la rueda	wheel
el ropaje [R]	clothing (in general)	la ropa	clothes; dry goods
el ultraje	outrage; affront	(Lat.) **ultra**	beyond
el varillaje	ribs; ribbing (of umbrella)	la varilla	rib (of a fan or umbrella)
el vasallaje	vassalage; servitude	el vasallo	vassal; subject
el vatiaje	wattage	el vatio	watt
el velaje	set of sails	la vela	sail
el vendaje	bandage; bandaging	la venda	band; blindfold
el ventanaje	row of windows	la ventana	window

-aje⁽²⁾

Meaning: *fee; toll; rent; dues*
English equivalent: *none*
Found in: *nouns*

Spanish words ending in *-aje* can denote the fee, toll, rent, or dues for a service rendered. The suffix *-aje* is attached to the root noun that denotes the object or service acquired. All words ending with *-aje* are masculine.

Formed Word	English Equivalent	Related to	English Equivalent
el agiotaje	agiotage; money exchange	**el agio**	agio
el almacenaje [R]	warehouse rent	**el almacén**	warehouse; store; shop
el barcaje	boat fare	**el barco**	boat
el bodegaje	warehouse dues	**la bodega**	warehouse
el caballaje	stud service	**el caballo**	horse
el cabestraje	fee paid to a drover	**el cabestro**	halter; bell-ox
el cabotaje	coasting trade	**el cabo**	cape; coast
el carneraje	tax or duty on sheep	**el carnero**	sheep
el carretaje	carting fee	**la carreta**	wagon
el castillaje	castle-toll	**el castillo**	castle
el herbaje	pasturage fee	**la hierba**	grass; herbs
el hornaje	fee for baking bread	**el horno**	oven for baking bread
el hospedaje [R]	lodging; board	**el huésped**	guest
el muellaje	dues paid on entering a port	**el muelle**	pier; dock; wharf
el pasaje [R 3523]	ticket; fare	**el paso**	passage; walk
el pasturaje	duty for grazing cattle	**la pastura**	pasture; fodder
el pedaje	toll	*(Lat.)* **pes**	foot
el pontaje	bridge-toll	**el puente**	bridge
el recuaje	duty for the passing of cattle	**la recua**	drove; strong (of mules, etc.)
el terraje	rent paid for land	**la tierra**	land
el vareaje	retail trade; selling by the yard	**la vara**	yard; yardstick
el vasallaje	vassalage; liege money	**el vasallo**	vassal; subject

-aje⁽³⁾

Meaning: *landing*
English equivalent: *none*
Found in: *nouns*

Another use of *-aje* is to denote a particular type of landing. This is not a common use of the widely used ending *-aje*. All such terms are masculine.

Formed Word	English Equivalent	Related to	English Equivalent
el alunizaje [R]	moon landing	**alunizar**	to land on the moon
el amarraje	landing on water	**amarrar**	to land a boat, moor

Formed Word	English Equivalent	Related to	English Equivalent
el arribaje	(naut.) arrival; landing	arribar	to arrive, put into harbor
el aterraje [R]	(naut.) landfall; (aer.) landing	aterrar	to land
el aterrizaje [R]	(aer.) landing	aterrizar	(aer.) to land

-ajo

Meaning: *pejorative; diminutive; result of action*
English equivalent: *none*
Found in: *nouns*

The suffix *-ajo* often holds pejorative connotations with regard to the root word. Words ending in *-ajo* are derived from either nouns or verbs: when derived from a verb, the word generally carries a specific meaning resulting from that verb's broader meaning, e.g., *espantajo* (scarecrow) from *espantar* (to scare). Note below that several words ending in *-ajo* are colloquial in their usage. All nouns ending in *-ajo* are masculine.

Formed Word	English Equivalent	Related to	English Equivalent
el arrendajo	(orn.) mockingbird	arrendar	to imitate
el bebistrajo	(coll.) rotten drink; concoction	la bebida	drink; beverage
el borrajo	embers; cinders	borrar	(fig.) to expunge, obliterate
el cintajo	rotten or tawdry old ribbon	la cinta	ribbon; tape; band
el colgajo	hanging/flapping rag or tatter	colgar	to hang, suspend
el comistrajo	(coll.) hodgepodge; concoction	la comistión	mixture (of food)
el escobajo	old broom	la escoba	broom
el escupitajo	(coll.) spit; spittle	escupir	to spit, spit at
el espantajo	scarecrow	espantar	to scare, frighten
el espumarajo [R]	ugly foam or froth	la espuma	foam; lather; froth
el estropajo	(dish) scourer; piece of rubbish	estropajear	to rub, scour
el guanajo	(coll.) simpleton	el guano	guano
el hatajo	small herd or flock	el hato	herd (of cattle)
el lagunajo	puddle; pool	la laguna	small lake; lagoon
el latinajo	(coll.) pig Latin	el latín	Latin; Latin language
el lavajo	water hole	lavar	to wash
el pingajo	rag; tatter	el pingo	rag
el sombrajo	shadow cast by another person; hut	la sombra	shade; shadow; shelter
el tendajo	small, tumbledown ship	la tienda	shop; store
el terminajo	(coll.) coarse or crude expression	el término	term
el tiznajo	(coll.) smudge; stain	la tizna	blackening; lampblack
el trapajo	old rag; tatter	el trapo	rag; cleaning rag
el zancajo	heel; heel of a shoe	el zanco	stilt

-al⁽¹⁾

Meaning: *augmentative; outgrowth; place*
English equivalent: *none*
Found in: *nouns*

The noun ending -al often signifies an enlargement of the root noun. Usually it simply indicates that something is big, as in the case of *ventanal* (large window). However, -al also can mean an extension, outgrowth, or collection of the root noun, as in *santoral* (choir book; book of saints' lives). Finally, this augmentative ending can enlarge the root so clearly as to denote an entire place, as seen in *riscal* (cliffy, craggy place), which is derived from *risco* (cliff; crag). All nouns ending in -al are masculine.

Formed Word	English Equivalent	Related to	English Equivalent
el bancal	bench cover	**el banco**	bench; pew
el cabezal	small pillow	**la cabeza**	head
el corral [R 2813]	corral	**acorralar**	to corral, surround, pin down, corner
el dedal [R]	thimble	**el dedo**	finger
el dineral [R]	fortune	**el dinero**	money
el festival [R 1263]	festival	**la fiesta**	party; feast; holiday
el lodazal	quagmire	**el lodo**	mud; mire
el manantial [4633]	source, head of a river	**manar**	to flow, stream, be plentiful
el matorral	thicket; underbrush	**la mata**	bush; shrub
el misal [R]	missal; mass-book	**la misa**	mass
el nidal [R]	(coll.) hangout	**el nido**	nest
el ojal	buttonhole	**el ojo**	eye
el ostral	oyster bed	**la ostra**	oyster
el parral	large earthen jar	**la parra**	honey jar
el pecinal	slimy pool	**la pecina**	slime
el peñascal	rocky place	**la peña**	rock; crag; boulder
el platal	great wealth; riches	**la plata**	silver; silverware; money
el portal [4616]	doorway	**la puerta**	door
el pozal [R]	covering for a well	**el pozo**	well; pit; deep hole
el ramal	branch line	**la rama**	branch
el rectoral [R]	rectory	**el rector**	rector
el riscal	cliffy, craggy place	**el risco**	cliff; crag
el ritual [4452]	ritual	**el rito**	rite
el santoral [R]	choir book; book of saints' lives	**el santo**	saint
el secadal	barren ground	**la seca**	dry season; dry sand bank
el semental [R]	stud horse; breeding animal	**el semen**	semen; sperm; seed
el soportal	portico; arcade	**el soporte**	support; stand; rest
el terminal [R 3440]	terminal	**terminar**	to finish, end
el tribunal [1329]	tribunal; court (of justice)	**el tribuno**	tribune; political orator
el varal	long pole	**la vara**	pole; rod; staff
el varganal	enclosure; stockade	**el várgano**	railing or stake (of a fence)
el ventanal [R]	large window	**la ventana**	window
el vitral	stained-glass window	*(Lat.)* **vitrum**	glass

-al$^{(2)}$

Meaning: *like; relating to*
English equivalent: *-al*
Found in: *adjectives*

The adjectival suffix *-al* is a common one both in Spanish and in English. Very broadly, it means like or relating to and is used in almost any context, including references to time periods (*semanal*), to shape (*codal*), and to color (*negral*). Many Spanish adjectives ending in *-al* are cognates of their English counterparts.

Formed Word	English Equivalent	Related to	English Equivalent
anual [R 1159]	annual	el año	year
arsenical	arsenical	el arsénico	arsenic
asnal	asinine	el asno	ass
astral [R]	astral	el astro	heavenly body; (fig.) star
central [R 672]	central	el centro	center; middle
cincuentañal	relating to/lasting 50 years	cincuenta	fifty
codal	elbow-shaped	el codo	elbow
colonial [R]	colonial	la colonia	colony
cuaresmal	relating to Lent; Lenten	la Cuaresma	Lent
disciplinal	disciplinary	la disciplina	discipline
elemental [R 4816]	elemental	el elemento	element
experimental [R 3116]	experimental	el experimento	experiment
final [R 203]	final	el fin	end; ending; aim; limit
grupal	relating to a group	el grupo	group
horizontal [R]	horizontal	el horizonte	horizon
intelectual [R 2742]	intellectual	el intelecto	intellect; understanding
labial [R]	labial; of the lips	el labio	lip; labium
marzal	relating to March	marzo	March
mental [R 1814]	mental	la mente	mind
mundial [R 230]	worldwide; world	el mundo	world; (coll.) crowd; mob
negral	blackish	el negro	black (color)
oriental [R 3608]	oriental	el oriente	orient; east
ornamental [R]	ornamental	el ornamento	ornament
otoñal [R]	autumnal	el otoño	autumn; fall
papal [R]	papal	el Papa	the Pope
parroquial [R]	parochial	la parroquia	parish
personal [R 297]	personal; characteristic	la persona	person; human being
poligonal	polygonal	el polígono	polygon
procesal	belonging to a lawsuit	el proceso	criminal case or suit; trial
sacerdotal [R]	of the priesthood; priestly	el sacerdote	priest; clergyman
semanal [R 3938]	weekly	la semana	week
suplemental	supplemental	el suplemento	supplement
terrenal [R]	earthly; mundane; worldly	la tierra	earth; land
uval	grapelike	la uva	grape
vecinal	belonging to a neighborhood	el vecino	neighbor
veinteñal	relating to the lasting 20 years	veinte	twenty

-al(3); -ar

Meaning: *field; orchard; patch; plantation; plant; tree;* etc.
English equivalent: *none*
Found in: *nouns*

This pair of suffixes is interesting in that one might first assume the unfamiliar word to be either an adjective (as are many Spanish words ending in *-al*) or an infinitive (as are most words ending in *-ar*). Nonetheless, this is a suffix with a specific chore, that of naming the type of field, orchard, etc., of the plant name to which it is attached. Note that in some cases, the root can take either suffix with no change in meaning (e.g., *manzanal; manzanar*). All such words are masculine.

Formed Word	English Equivalent	Related to	English Equivalent
el alcachofal	artichoke field	la alcachofa	artichoke
el alcornocal	plantation of cork trees	el alcornoque	(bot.) cork oak; (fig.) blockhead
el alfalfar	alfalfa field	la alfalfa	alfalfa
el almendral	almond grove	la almendra	almond
el arrozal [R]	rice field	el arroz	rice
el avenal	oat field	la avena	oat
el bananal	banana plantation	la banana	banana
el berenjenal	eggplant plantation	la berenjena	eggplant
el berzal	cabbage patch	la berza	cabbage
el cafetal [R]	coffee plantation	el café	coffee
el calabazar	pumpkin patch	la calabaza	pumpkin
el cauchal	rubber plantation	el caucho	rubber
el cebollar	onion patch	la cebolla	onion
el cerezal	cherry orchard	la cereza	cherry
el ciruelar	plum orchard	la ciruela	plum
el fresal	strawberry patch	la fresa	strawberry
el frutal [R]	fruit tree	el fruto	fruit
el guisantal	pea field	el guisante	pea
el henar	hay field	el heno	hay
el limonar	lemon grove	el limón	lemon
el maizal [R]	maize field	el maíz	maize
el majolar	white hawthorn grove	el majuelo	white hawthorn
el manzanal/ar	apple orchard	la manzana	apple
el melonar	melon patch	el melón	melon
el naranjal	orange grove	la naranja	orange
el patatal	potato field	la patata	potato
el pepinar	cucumber field	el pepino	cucumber
el peral	pear tree	la pera	pear
el pimental	pepper plantation	el pimiento	pepper
el pinar [R]	pine grove; pine forest	el pino	pine; pine tree
el platanal/ar	banana tree plantation	el plátano	banana
el rabanal	radish patch	el rábano	radish
el robledal	oak grove	el roble	oak
el rosal [R]	rosebush	la rosa	rose
el sandiar	watermelon patch	la sandía	watermelon
el tomatal	tomato field	el tomate	tomato
el trigal	wheat field	el trigo	wheat

-ancia

Meaning: *act; state of being; result of action*
English equivalent: *-ance; -ancy*
Found in: *nouns*

The Spanish suffix *-ancia*, found nearly always in cognates of their English counterparts, denotes the state, act, or result of a root verb. Note that words ending in *-ancia* are feminine and that they are derived from *-ar* verbs. To form these words, remove the *-ar* from the infinitive and add *-ancia*.

Formed Word	English Equivalent	Related to	English Equivalent
la abundancia [R]	abundance; plenty; opulence	**abundar**	to abound
la ambulancia [R 4008]	ambulance	**ambular**	to wander about, ambulate
la asonancia	assonance	**asonar**	to be assonant
la circunstancia [R 1694]	circumstance	**círculo**	circle
la consonancia [R]	consonance	**consonar**	to harmonize, rhyme, agree
la constancia [R 3897]	constancy; proof; record	**constar**	to be certain, be on record
la discrepancia	discrepancy	**discrepar**	to differ, disagree
la disonancia [R]	dissonance	**disonar**	to be dissonant
la distancia [R 1564]	distance	**distar**	to be distant, far, remote
la escancia	pouring or serving of wine	**escanciar**	to pour or serve wine
la estancia [2891]	stay; day in hospital	**estar**	to be (in a place, state, condition)
la exuberancia	exuberance	**exuberar** *(obs.)*	to be exuberant
la ganancia [R 2041]	earnings	**ganar**	to earn
la ignorancia [R 4819]	ignorance	**ignorar**	to be unaware of
la importancia [R 911]	importance	**importar**	to be important, matter
la infancia [R 3365]	infancy; childhood	*(Lat.)* **in + fari**	to not speak
la instancia [1582]	instance	**instar**	to press, urge, be urgent
la intolerancia [R]	intolerance	*(Lat.)* **in + tolerar**	to not tolerate, be intolerant
la militancia [R 4940]	militancy	**militar**	to serve in the army, militate
la observancia [R]	observance	**observar**	to observe
la perseverancia	perseverance	**perseverar**	to persevere
la relevancia	relevance	**relevar**	to emboss, make stand out
la repugnancia [R]	repugnance	**repugnar**	to disgust, nauseate
la resonancia [R]	resonance; repercussion	**resonar**	to resound, echo
la tolerancia [R 3315]	tolerance	**tolerar**	to tolerate
la vacancia	vacancy	**vacar**	to resign from a job, leave, take a vacation
la vagancia [R]	vagrancy	**vagar**	to wander, roam about
la vigiliancia	vigilance	**vigilar**	to watch, keep guard over

-ano (-ana)

Meaning: *native; native of; adherent to (a system of beliefs); like; relating to*
English equivalent: *-an*
Found in: *nouns; adjectives*

The suffix *-ano* denotes origin of birth or thought. Words taking this suffix are both nouns and adjectives: *La americana sirve café colombiano* (The American woman serves the Colombian coffee). Note that these words are not capitalized as they are in English. The ending *-ano* changes to *-ana* when denoting or describing a feminine noun.

Formed Word	English Equivalent	Related to	English Equivalent
(el) africano [2956]	African	**África**	Africa
(el) aldeano [R]	villager; relating to a village	**la aldea**	small village; hamlet
(el) alsaciano	Alsatian (native)	**Alsacia**	Alsace
(el) americano [1128]	American (native)	**América**	America
(el) australiano [2108]	Australian (native)	**Australia**	Australia
(el) boliviano	Bolivian (native)	**Bolivia**	Bolivia
(el) californiano	Californian (native)	**California**	California
(el) camboyano	Cambodian (native)	**Camboya**	Cambodia
(el) casetellano	Castilian (native)	**Castilla**	Castile
(el) centroamericano [2925]	Central American (native)	**Centroamérica**	Central America
(el) colombiano [1295]	Colombian (native)	**Colombia**	Colombia
(el) cristiano [R 1877]	Christian	**Cristo**	Christ
(el) cubano [1300]	Cuban (native)	**Cuba**	Cuba
(el) dominicano [1579]	*nmf* person from the Dominican Republic; *aj* from the Dominican Republic	**República Dominicana**	Dominican Republic
(el) ecuatoriano [3604]	*nmf* person from Ecuador; *aj* pertaining to Ecuador	**Ecuador**	Ecuador
(el) hispano [R 2488]	*nmf* Hispanic person; *aj* Hispanic	**España**	Spain
(el) jerosolimitano	(native of) Jerusalem	**Jerusalén**	Jerusalem
(el) latinoamericano [2412]	Latin American	**Latinoamérica**	Latin America
(el) luterano	Lutheran (member)	**Lutero**	Luther
(el) mendeliano	Mendelian (theorist)	**Mendel**	Mendel
(el) mexicano/mejicano	Mexican (native)	**México/Méjico**	Mexico
(el) norcoreano	North Korean (native)	**Corea del Norte**	North Korea
(el) norteamericano [996]	North American (native)	**Norteamérica**	North America
(el) paraguayano	Paraguayan (native)	**Paraguay**	Paraguay
(el) peruano [2639]	Peruvian (native)	**Perú**	Peru
(el) presbiteriano	Presbyterian (member)	**el presbítero**	presbyter; priest
(el) republicano [R 3673]	Republican; republican (native)	**la república**	republic
(el) romano [R 2550]	Roman	**Roma**	Rome
(el) siberiano	Siberian (native)	**Siberia**	Siberia
(el) siciliano	Sicilian (native)	**Sicilia**	Sicily
(el) sudamericano [2827]	South American (native)	**Sudamérica**	South America
(el) surcoreano	South Korean (native)	**Corea del Sur**	South Korea
(el) tejano [4084]	Texan	**Texas**	Texas

Formed Word	English Equivalent	Related to	English Equivalent
(el) vegetariano [R]	vegetarian	el vegetal	vegetable
(el) veneciano	Venetian (native)	Venecia	Venice
(el) venezolano [1785]	Venezuelan (native)	Venezuela	Venezuela

-ante⁽¹⁾

Meaning: *like; relating to; doing*
English equivalent: *-ing*
Found in: *adjectives*

The following words ending in *-ante* are all adjectives formed from verbs and, in describing a noun, indicate that person, place, or thing exhibits qualities relating directly to the root verb. Since the English equivalent almost always is "-ing," be careful not to confuse the English translations with the English present progressive (which ends in "-ing" as in "I am studying"). The classic ambiguous English sentence, "They are entertaining women," becomes two very different sentences in Spanish. Note that these words all come from *-ar* verbs (this suffix's counterpart is *-ente*, whose adjectives are derived from *-er* and *-ir* verbs).

Formed Word	English Equivalent	Related to	English Equivalent
abundante [R 4105]	abundant; plentiful; copious	abundar	to abound
agravante	aggravating	agravar	to aggravate
alarmante [R 4901]	alarming	alarmar	to alarm
ambulante [R 1743]	walking; ambulatory	ambular	to wander about
anticipante	anticipating	anticipar	to anticipate
aplastante	crushing	aplastar	to crush, flatten
brillante [R 2342]	brilliant; bright; sparkling	brillar	to shine, sparkle, glisten
colgante [R]	hanging	colgar	to hang, hang up
espumante	flaming; sparkling (wine)	espumar	to foam, sparkle
fascinante	fascinating	fascinar	to fascinate
fecundante	fertilizing	fecundar	to fertilize
festejante	entertaining	festejar	to entertain, feast
flagrante	flagrant; resplendent	flagrar	(poet.) to flame, blaze
flamante	flaming	flamear	to flame, blaze
instante [R 3581]	instant; urgent; pressing	instar	to press, urge
interesante [R 1527]	interesting	interesar	to interest, concern
jadeante	panting; out of breath	jadear	to pant
juzgante	judging	juzgar	to judge
madurante	maturing; ripening	madurar	to ripen, mature, mellow
mandante	commanding	mandar	to command
parlante [R]	talking; chatting	parlar	to chatter, babble
participante [R 1319]	participating	participar	to participate
penetrante [R]	penetrating	penetrar	to penetrate
plasmante	molding; shaping	plasmar	to mold, shape
restante [R 3087]	*nm* remainder; *aj* leftover, remaining	restar	to subtract
rotante	revolving	rotar	to revolve
saltante	jumping	saltar	to jump

Formed Word	English Equivalent	Related to	English Equivalent
santificante	blessing; sanctifying	**santificar**	to sanctify, hallow
semejante [R 3281]	*nmf* neighbor, fellow man; *aj* similar	**semejar**	to resemble
silbante [4291]	sibilant; hissing	**silbar**	to whistle
simpatizante [R 3609]	*nmf* sympathizer; partisan; *aj* sympathetic; partisan	**simpatizar**	to sympathize
sobrante [R]	remaining; left over	**sobrar**	to remain, be left over
sonante	sounding	**sonar**	to sound
sudante	sweating	**sudar**	to sweat
susurrante	whispering	**susurrar**	to whisper
tronante	thundering	**tronar**	to thunder
vacilante [R]	vacillating	**vacilar**	to vacillate

-ante⁽²⁾

Meaning: *one who; denotes profession*
English equivalent: *-ant; -er; -or*
Found in: *nouns*

The suffix *-ante* is one of several Spanish suffixes that mean *one who*. A unique feature of words taking this ending is that they are all derived from *-ar* verbs. This ending remains *-ante* whether the referent is male or female: *el danzante; la danzante.*

Formed Word	English Equivalent	Related to	English Equivalent
el acompañante [R 4486]	escort	**acompañar**	to accompany
el amante [R 2431]	lover	**amar**	to love
el anunciante	advertiser; announcer	**anunciar**	to advertise; to announce
el asaltante [R 4781]	*nmf* assailant; *aj* assaulting	**asaltar**	to assault
el aspirante [R 2513]	*nmf* aspirant; one who aspires to be; *aj* aspiring, desiring	**aspirar**	to aspire
el atacante [R 3264]	*nmf* attacker; *aj* attacking	**atacar**	to attack
el caminante [R]	passerby; walker	**caminar**	to walk, go, travel
el cantante [R 423]	singer	**cantar**	to sing
el celebrante [R]	celebrant (priest)	**celebrar**	to celebrate, say mass
el comandante [R 1884]	commander	**comandar**	to command
el comerciante [R 1325]	businessman; merchant	**comerciar**	to trade, deal, do business
el confesante	confessor	**confesar**	to confess
el copiante	copier; copyist	**copiar**	to copy, copy down
el danzante [R]	dancer	**danzar**	to dance
el debutante [4814]	beginner; debutante	**debutar**	to begin, make one's first appearance
el delineante	draftsman	**delinear**	to delineate, outline, draft
el dibujante [R]	drawer	**dibujar**	to draw
el donante	donor	**donar**	to donate, give
el emigrante	emigrant	**emigrar**	to emigrate
el estudiante [R 1082]	student	**estudiar**	to study
el fabricante [R 3485]	factory worker	**fabricar**	to make or manufacture

Formed Word	English Equivalent	Related to	English Equivalent
el gobernante [R 2473]	ruler	**gobernar**	to govern, rule
el habitante [R 817]	inhabitant; dweller	**habitar**	to inhabit, live in
el ignorante [R]	ignoramus	**ignorar**	to not know, be ignorant of
el informante [3366]	informant	**informar**	to inform
el inmigrante [3568]	immigrant	**inmigrar**	to immigrate
el integrante [R 544]	*nmf* one who is part of a group; representative member of a group; *aj* integral	**integrar**	to integrate
el litigante	litigant	**litigar**	to litigate
el maleante [R]	crook	**malear**	to damage, spoil, pervert, corrupt
el manifestante [R 2939]	demonstrator	**manifestar**	to manifest, to show
el mendigante/mendicante	beggar; mendicant	**mendigar**	to beg
el militante [R 1747]	militant	**militar**	to serve in the military
el navegante [R]	navigator	**navegar**	to navigate, sail
el negociante [R]	businessman; dealer; trader	**negociar**	to negotiate, deal, trade
el ocupante [R 4513]	occupant	**ocupar(se)**	to occupy, have a place (vt); to be busy, occupied (vr)
el opinante	one who gives his views	**opinar**	to express an opinion
el participante [R 1319]	participant	**participar**	to participate
el protestante [R]	protestant; Protestant	**protestar**	to protest
el representante [R 489]	representative	**representar**	to represent
el silbante [4291]	*nm* soccer referee; whistling *aj* whistling	**silbar**	to whistle
el simpatizante [R 3609]	*nmf* sympathizer; partisan; *aj* sympathetic; partisan	**simpatizar**	to sympathize
el solicitante [R 4924]	applicant	**solicitar**	to solicit, apply for
el traficante	dealer; merchant	**traficar**	to deal, trade, traffic
el veraneante	summer resident	**veranear**	to summer, spend the summer
el viajante [R]	traveler	**viajar**	to travel
el vigilante [R 4532]	guard; night watchman	**vigilar**	to watch, keep guard over
el visitante [R 1195]	visitor	**visitar**	to visit
el votante [R 4500]	voter	**votar**	to vote

-anza

Meaning: *quality; state of being; condition; process*
English equivalent: *-ance*
Found in: *nouns*

The following words ending in *-anza* are all derived from *-ar* verbs and denote the quality, state of being, condition, or process of those verbs. More simply put, a word taking the suffix *-anza* indicates the result of the action of the verb from which it is derived: from *probar* (to prove, test) we get *probanza* (proof; evidence—the result of proving or testing something). All nouns ending in *-anza* are feminine.

Formed Word	English Equivalent	Related to	English Equivalent
la acechanza	spying; watching; stalking	**acechar**	to spy on, lurk, lie in wait for
la adivinanza [R]	(coll.) prophecy; prediction; guess	**adivinar**	to guess, divine, solve
la alabanza [R]	praise; commendation; glory	**alabar**	to praise, extol
la alianza [R 1288]	alliance; wedding ring	**aliar**	to ally
la(s) andanza(s)	wandering(s); travel(s); doings	**andar**	to walk, travel, go
la añoranza	longing; sorrow; homesickness	**añorar**	to long, yearn for
la balanza [R 4949]	balance; scales; judgment	**balancear**	to balance
la cobranza	collection; receiving; recovery	**cobrar**	to collect, receive
la comparanza	comparison	**comparar**	to compare
la confianza [R 940]	confidence; trust; reliance	**confiar**	to confide, entrust
la crianza [R]	raising; rearing; nursing	**criar**	to raise, rear, bring up
la desconfianza [R 4695]	distrust; mistrust; suspicion	**desconfiar**	to distrust, mistrust, be suspicious of
la desemejanza [R]	dissimilitude; dissimilarity	**desemejar**	to change the look of
la desesperanza [R]	despair	**desesperar**	to despair, lose hope (of)
la destemplanza	inclemency (of weather)	**destemplar**	to disturb, upset the harmony of
la enseñanza [R 3150]	teaching; instruction; education	**enseñar**	to teach, train, instruct
la esperanza [R 1115]	hope; expectation	**esperar**	to hope, expect, wait (for)
la fianza [R 3842]	surety; bond; bail; guarantee	**fiar**	to guarantee, warrant
la finanzas [1391]	finances	**financiar**	to finance
la holganza	rest; leisure; idleness	**holgar**	to rest, be idea
la labranza [R]	cultivation; farming	**labrar**	to work, labor, cultivate
la malandanza [R]	misfortune	**mal + andar**	bad + to walk, travel, go
la matanza [R 3812]	killing; slaughter; butchery	**matar**	to kill
la mudanza [R]	removal; change	**mudar**	to change, remove
la ordenanza [R]	ordinance; method; order	**ordenar**	to put into order, arrange
la privanza	private life	**privar**	to deprive, forbid
la probanza	proof; evidence	**probar**	to prove, test
la pujanza	strength; force; drive	**pujar**	to push, bid up
la semejanza [R]	resemblance	**semejar**	to resemble
la sobrepujanza	great strength; exceeding vigor	**sobrepujar**	to surpass, excel
la tardanza [R]	delay	**tardar**	to take a long time
la templanza	temperance	**templar**	to temper
la usanza	use; usage; custom	**usar**	to use, wear
la venganza [R 4054]	vengeance; revenge	**vengar**	to avenge
la venturanza	happiness	**aventurar**	to venture, risk

-arca

Meaning: *ruler*
English equivalent: *-arch*
Found in: *nouns*

Spanish words ending with *-arca* denote a specific sort of ruler. Such words generally are easy to figure out, for their English counterparts often have the same base. The ending *-arca* nearly always is "-arch" in English, e.g., *el monarca* (monarch); *la matriarca* (matriarch), etc. The ending *-arca* does not change with regard to male or female referent: *el monarca; la monarca.*

Formed Word	English Equivalent	Related to	English Equivalent
el jerarca	(eccles.) hierarch; leader	*(Gr.)* **hieros**	sacred
la matriarca	matriarch	*(Lat.)* **mater**	mother
el monarca [R 2150]	monarch	*(Gr.)* **monos**	alone
el oligarca	oligarch	*(Gr.)* **oligos**	few; little
el patriarca [R]	patriarch	*(Lat.)* **pater**	father
el pentarca	pentarch; one of five	*(Gr.)* **pente**	five

-ario⁽¹⁾

Meaning: *book; bound collection; printed matter*
English equivalent: *none*
Found in: *nouns*

The use of the ending *-ario* is highly specific. The examples given all refer to a book or something printed with a particular function. One word, *diario* (diary), is unusual insofar as it is a noun in this milieu, while in the following listing of words ending with *-ario*, one finds the adjective *diario* (daily). The meaning of this term thus depends upon context. All nouns ending with *-ario* are masculine.

Formed Word	English Equivalent	Related to	English Equivalent
el abecedario	alphabet or spelling book; primer	**abecé**	(the letters) a b c
el anuario	yearbook; yearly report	*(Lat.)* **annus**	year
el calendario [2633]	calendar	**las calendas**	calends; first day of the month in Roman calendar
el confesionario [R]	treatise with rules for confession	**la confesión**	confession
el cuestionario [R]	questionnaire	**la cuestión**	question; issue; matter; subject
el devocionario [R]	prayer book	**la devoción**	devotion; piety
el diario [R 427]	diary	**el día**	day
el diccionario [R]	dictionary	**la dicción**	diction
el epistolario	epistolary; collection of letters	**la epístola**	Epistle; epistle; letter
el glosario [R]	glossary	**la glosa**	gloss; comment; footnote
el himnario	hymnal	**el himno**	hymn; anthem

Formed Word	English Equivalent	Related to	English Equivalent
el horario [R 1311]	timetable; schedule	**la hora**	hour; time
el inventario	inventory; catalogue of property	**inventariar**	to inventory, list
el noticario	newsreel; newscast	**la noticia**	news; news item; piece of news
el vocabulario [R]	vocabulary; compendium or words	**el vocablo**	word; term

-ario⁽²⁾ (-aria)

Meaning: *like; relating to; one who*
English equivalent: *-ary*
Found in: *adjectives, nouns*

The suffix *-ario* usually is an adjectival ending meaning "like" or "relating to," as do several other Spanish suffixes. In this capacity, adjectives ending in *-ario* can be related to nouns, verbs, or other adjectives. Some words ending with *-ario* can act either as a noun or an adjective, as noted below. Nouns ending in *-ario* are masculine; however, when the reference is to a person, e.g., *el millonario*, the ending changes to *-aria* when the person is female (*la millonaria*). Similarly, adjectives ending with *-ario* take the feminine form *-aria* when the term is used to describe a feminine noun.

Formed Word	English Equivalent	Related to	English Equivalent
el adversario [3602]	adversary; opponent; antagonist	**adverso**	adverse; calamitous
el aniversario [R 1244]	anniversary	**año**	year
arbitrario [R]	arbitrary	**arbitrar**	to arbitrate
bancario [R 1507]	relating to banking	**el banco**	bank
canario	of the Canary Islands	**las Canarias**	the Canary Islands
centenario [R 3537]	centenary	**ciento**	one hundred
(el) concesionario [4207]	*nmf* licensed business owner; *aj* licensed (business)	**concesión**	concession; grant; license; lease
(el) contrario [R 763]	contrary; opposite; contradictory	**contra**	opposite; opposite sense
(el) coronario	coronary; relating to the heart	**el corazón**	heart
diario [R 427]	daily	**el día**	day
el dignatario	dignitary	**digno**	worthy; fitting; decent; honest
(el) ejidatario [2004]	*nmf* person who lives in an *ejido* (small town); *aj* pertaining to an *ejido*	**ejido**	very small town
estacionario	stationary	**la estación**	station
hereditario [R]	hereditary	**heredar**	to inherit, leave property to
(el) honorario [R]	*nm* honorarium; *aj* honorary	**el honor**	honor
intermediario [R 4632]	intermediary	**intermedio**	intermediate
literario [R 3449]	literary	**la letra**	letter

Formed Word	English Equivalent	Related to	English Equivalent
lunario	lunar; relating to the moon	la luna	moon
(el) millionario	*nm, aj* millionaire	millón	million
el misionario	missionary	misionar	to preach missions, reprimand
el notario	notary; notary public	notar	to note, notice, mark
(el) ordinario [R 2809]	ordinary; ecclesiastical judge	el orden	order
(el) parlamentario [R 2222]	*nmf* member of parliament; *aj* pertaining to parliament; parliamentarian	el parlamento	parliament
(el) partidario [R 3852]	*nmf* supporter of a party; *aj* factional	el partido	party (political)
planetario [R]	planetary; relating to the planets	el planeta	planet
plenario	plenary	pleno	full; complete
primario [1183]	primary	primo	first; prime
(el) propietario [R 1298]	*nmf* property owner; *aj* proprietary	la propiedad	property
quincenario	fortnightly; every two weeks	quince	fifteen
(el) revolucionario [R 1255]	*nm, aj* revolutionary	la revolución	revolution
rutinario	routine	la rutina	routine; rut
el salario [R 1225]	salary; wage; wages; pay	la sal	salt
sanitario [R 1282]	sanitary; of health	sano	sound; healthy; fit
secundario [R 1108]	secondary	segundo	second
sedentario	sedentary	sedente	sitting; seated
el seminario [3479]	seminary; seminar	el semen	semen; sperm; seed
suplementario	supplementary	el suplemento	supplement
terciario [R]	tertiary	el tercio	third
el usuario [1149]	user; one who uses	el uso	use
(el) veterinario [4644]	*nmf* veterinarian; *aj* veterinary	la veterinaria	veterinary science
(el) visionario	*nm, aj* visionary	la visión	vision
(el) voluntario [R 2632]	*nm* volunteer; *aj* voluntary	la voluntad	will; willingness; willpower

-asma; -asmo

Meaning: *result of action; being; condition*
English equivalent: *-asm*
Found in: *nouns*

Spanish terms ending with *-asma* or *-asmo* all are derived from Greek and are masculine nouns whether they end with *-asma* or *-asmo*. Spanish words ending with the letters *-ma* are masculine when the direct derivation is Greek instead of Latin.

Formed Word	English Equivalent	Related to	English Equivalent
el entusiasmo [R 2667]	enthusiasm	(Gr.) **enthousiazein**	to be inspired or possessed by the god
el espasmo	spasm	(Gr.) **spasmos**	convulsion; spasm

Formed Word	English Equivalent	Related to	English Equivalent
el fantasma [3486]	ghost; phantom; (fig.) scarecrow	(Gr.) **phantasma**	appearance; vision
el marasmo	(med.) marasmus; stagnation	(Gr.) **marainein**	to waste away
el miasma	miasma	(Gr.) **miasma**	defilement
el orgasmo	orgasm	(Gr.) **organ**	to swell
el plasma	(biol.) plasma	(Gr.) **plasma**	anything molded or modeled
el sarcasmo	sarcasm	(Gr.) **sarkazein**	to tear flesh like dogs

-astro; -astra

Meaning: *denotes step-relations; diminutive in status*
English equivalent: *often the prefix* step-
Found in: *nouns*

The endings *-astro* and *-astra* perform two functions. The first and more common is to denote step-relations in the family, e.g., *padrastro* (stepfather) from *padre* (father). A less frequent function is to diminish the status of the base word, e.g., *medicastro* (third-rate doctor) from *médico* (doctor). Words ending with *-astro* are masculine, while those ending with *-astra* are feminine.

Formed Word	English Equivalent	Related to	English Equivalent
el camastro [R]	rickety old bed	la cama	bed
el cochastro	young sucking-boar	el cocho	(prov.) pig
la hermanastra	stepsister	la hermana	sister
el hermanastro	stepbrother	el hermano	brother
la hijastra	stepdaughter	la hija	daughter
el hijastro	stepson	el hijo	son
la madrastra [R]	stepmother; bad mother	la madre	mother
el medicastro	third-rate doctor; "quack"	el médico	doctor; physician
la nietastra	stepgranddaughter	la nieta	granddaughter
el padrastro [R]	stepfather	el padre	father
el pillastro	roguish fellow; rascal	el pillo	rogue; scamp; rascal
el pollastro	cockerel	el pollo	chicken

-ato; -ado

Meaning: *office; position; system; duty; domain*
English equivalent: *-ship; -ate*
Found in: *nouns*

The noun suffix *-ato* or, less commonly, *-ado* denotes the office or domain belonging to the root term (almost always a person) to which it is attached; *canciller* (chancellor) finds his position/domain in *cancillerato* (the chancellorship). The ending *-ato* or *-ado* implies high station, rank, or office. All words ending with either of these suffixes are masculine.

Formed Word	English Equivalent	Related to	English Equivalent
el bachillerato [R 4867]	baccalaureate	el bachiller	holder of a degree
el campeonato [R 834]	championship	el campeón	champion
el cancelariato	chancellorship (of a university)	el cancelario	chancellor (of a university)
el cancillerato	chancellorship	el canciller	chancellor
el canonicato	canonry; (coll.) sinecure	el canon	canon
el cardenalato	cardinalship	el cardenal	cardinal
el celibato	bachelorhood; celibacy	el célibe	bachelor; celibate
el clericato	clergy; priesthood	el clérigo	clergyman; cleric
el colonato	system of colonial land settlement	la colonia	colony
el comisariado [4263]	board of commissioners	el comisario	commissioner
el concubinato	concubinage	la concubina	concubine
el consulado [R 4906]	consulate; consulship	el cónsul	consul
el diaconato	deaconship	el diácono	deacon
el doctorado [R]	doctorate	el doctor	doctor
el economato	guardianship; trusteeship	el ecónomo	guardian; trustee
el generalato [R]	generalship	el general	general
el jurado [R 3724]	nmf juror; nm jury (group); aj sworn; under oath	la jura	solemn oath
el liderato	leadership	el líder	leader
el notariato/ado	notary's title, practice, profession	el notario	notary; notary public
el noviciado	novitiate; apprenticeship	el novicio	novice; beginner
el patronato [R 3247]	association for the purpose of charity or mutual benefit	el patrón	patron (of art or literature); sponsor
el procerato	high station or rank	el prócer	nobleman; grandee
el profesorado [R]	professorship; professorate	el profesor	professor
el reinado [R]	reign; kingship	el rey	king
el sindicato [R 979]	trade union	el síndico	union representative
el sultanato	sultanate	el sultán	sultan
el superiorato	office of a superior	el superior	superior

-avo (-ava)

Meaning: *denotes denominator of a fraction*
English equivalent: *-th*
Found in: *nouns*

The suffix *-avo* is used to denote the denominator of a fraction (the denomiator is the term below the line). Thus, one would say, *Yo leí un seisavo del libro* (I read one-sixth of the book) or *Yo comí una octava de la torta* (I ate one-eighth of the cake.) When *-avo* refers to a feminine noun, e.g., *la torta*, the ending changes to *-ava*.

Formed Word	English Equivalent	Related to	English Equivalent
seisavo	sixth	seis	six
octavo [R 1370]	eighth	(Lat.) octo	eight

Formed Word	English Equivalent	Related to	English Equivalent
onceavo	eleventh	once	eleven
doceavo [R]	twelfth	doce	twelve
treceavo [R]	thirteenth	trece	thirteen
catorceavo [R]	fourteenth	catorce	fourteen
quinceavo	fifteenth	quince	fifteen
dieciseisavo [R]	sixteenth	dieciseis	sixteen
diecisieteavo [R]	seventeenth	diecisiete	seventeenth
decimoctavo [R]	eighteenth	(Lat.) decem + octo	eighteen
diecinueveavo [R]	nineteenth	diecinueve	nineteen
veintavo [R]	twentieth	veinte	twenty
veintiunavo	twenty-first	veintiuno	twenty-one
veintidosavo	twenty-second	veintidós	twenty-two
veintitresavo	twenty-third	veintitrés	twenty-three
veinticuatroavo	twenty-fourth	veinticuatro	twenty-four
veinticincoavo	twenty-fifth	veinticinco	twenty-five
veintiseisavo	twenty-sixth	veintiséis	twenty-six
veintisieteavo	twenty-seventh	veintisiete	twenty-seven
veintioctavo	twenty-eighth	veinte + octo	twenty-eight
veintinueveavo	twenty-ninth	veintinueve	twenty-nine
treintavo [R]	thirtieth	treinta	thirty
cuarentavo [R]	fortieth	cuarenta	forty
cincuentavo [R]	fiftieth	cincuenta	fifty
sesentavo [R]	sixtieth	sesenta	sixty
setentavo [R]	seventieth	setenta	seventy
ochentavo	eightieth	ochenta	eighty
noventavo	ninetieth	noventa	ninety
centavo [R 2469]	hundredth; cent	cien; ciento; centavo	one hundred; cent

-az; -oz

Meaning: *full of*
English equivalent: *-cious*
Found in: *adjectives*

Spanish words ending in *-az* or *-oz* generally have English cognates ending with *-cious*. In both languages, the ending indicates that the person or thing described strongly holds the attributes referred to in the base term. These formed words relate to Spanish nouns or, at times, come directly from Latin. A good spelling aid you will find is that the suffix *-az* translates to "-acious" (*audaz*; audacious), while *-oz* generally is found in English words ending with "-ocious" (*precoz*; precocious).

Formed Word	English Equivalent	Related to	English Equivalent
atroz	atrocious	(Lat.) ater	black; dark
audaz [R]	audacious	la audacia	audacity; boldness
capaz [R 1499]	capable	la capacidad (fig.)	capacity; ability; capability

Formed Word	English Equivalent	Related to	English Equivalent
contumaz	contumacious; stubborn	**la contumacia**	obstinacy; obduracy; stubbornness
eficaz [R 3209]	efficacious	**la eficacia**	efficacy; efficiency
falaz	fallacious	**la falacia**	fallacy
feraz	fertile	**la feracidad**	fecundity; fertility; fruitfulness
feroz [R]	ferocious	**la ferocidad**	ferocity; wildness; fierceness
incapaz [R 4461]	incapable	**la incapacidad**	incapacity; incompetence; incapability
lenguaz	loquaciousness; garrulous; talkative	**la locuacidad**	loquacity; talkativeness
mendaz	mendacious; given to lying	**la mendacidad**	mendacity
mordaz	mordant; biting	**la mordacidad**	mordacity; mordant or biting nature
perspicaz	perspicacious	**la perspicacia**	perspicacity; clear-sightedness
pertinaz	pertinacious	**la pertinacia**	pertinacity; doggedness; stubbornness
precoz	precocious	**la precocidad**	precocity
pugnaz	pugnacious; quarrelsome; scrappy	**la pugnacidad**	pugnacity; quarrelsomeness
rapaz [R]	rapacious; of prey; (fig.) thievish	**la rapacidad**	rapacity; greed
sagaz	sagacious	**la sagacidad**	sagacity
salaz	salacious; wanton	*(Lat.)* **salire**	to spring, leap, jump, bound
suspicaz [R]	suspicious	**la suspicacia**	suspiciousness; mistrust
tenaz [R]	tenacious	**la tenacidad**	tenacity; tenaciousness
veloz	swift	**la velocidad**	velocity; speed
veraz [R]	veracious; truthful	**la veracidad**	veracity; truthfulness
vivaz [R]	vivacious	**la vivacidad**	vivacity; liveliness; energy; vigor
voraz	voracious	**la voracidad**	voracity; voraciousness

-aza

Meaning: *augmentative; forms abstract noun*
English equivalent: *none*
Found in: *nouns*

The ending -*aza* (like its more commonly found sister suffix -*azo*) indicates enlargement or exaggeration of the root term. At times this enlargement is no more than a physical increase in size, e.g., *la pernaza* (thick or big leg) from *la pierna* (leg); however, the ending -*aza* often also carries negative connotations, e.g., *la bocaza* (big ugly mouth) from *la boca* (mouth). All terms ending with -*aza* are feminine.

Formed Word	English Equivalent	Related to	English Equivalent
el barcaza	barge	la barca	boat
el bocaza	big ugly mouth	la boca	mouth
el carnaza	fleshiness	la carne	flesh; meat
el copaza	large wine glass; goblet	la copa	wine glass
el hilaza	yarn; fiber	el hilo	thread
el madraza [R]	doting mother	la madre	mother
el manaza	hefty hand; paw	la mano	hand
el matronaza	plump, respectable woman	la matrona	matron
el sangraza	thick, heavy blood	la sangre	blood
el terraza [3732]	terrace	la tierra	land; earth
el trapaza	fraud; trick	trapacear	to cheat; swindle

-azgo

Meaning: *office; post; dignity; relationship; tariff*
English equivalent: *-ship*
Found in: *nouns*

Added to a noun, the suffix *-azgo* usually denotes high position, office, post, or territory. In this capacity, *-azgo* is similar in meaning and function to the endings *-ato* and *-ado* (office; position; system; etc.). It also can indicate a particular relationship, e.g., *comadrazgo* (relationship between the mother and godmother), or specific tariffs or fees, e.g., *terrazgo* (land rent). All words ending with *-azgo* are masculine.

Formed Word	English Equivalent	Related to	English Equivalent
el alaminazgo	office of a surveyor/clerk	al alamín	surveyor; clerk
el alarifazgo	office of a builder	el alarife	architect; builder
el albaceazgo	executorship	al albacea	executor
el alferazgo	dignity of an ensign; ensigncy	el alférez	ensign
el alguacilazgo	office of a constable	el alguacil	constable
el almirantazgo [R]	admiralship	el almirante	admiral
el almotacenazgo	inspector's office and duty	el almotacén	inspector (or weights and measures)
el cacicazgo	dignity/territory of a political boss	el cacique	political boss; Indian chief
el comadrazgo	relationship between mother and godmother	la comadre	reciprocal name of mother and godmother
el compadrazgo	relationship between child's parents and godfather	el compadre	father or godfather (with respect to each other); mate; pal; chum
el liderazgo [2931]	leadership	el líder	leader (political)
el mayorazgo [R]	primogeniture	el mayor	the eldest (male)
el mecenazgo	patronage	el mecenas	patron (of art or literature)
el noviazgo [R]	engagement; courtship	el novio	bridegroom; groom-to-be
el padrinazgo [R]	(baptismal) sponsorship; patronage	el padrino	godfather; patron
el papazgo	papacy; pontificate	el Papa	the Pope

Formed Word	English Equivalent	Related to	English Equivalent
el pontazgo	bridge-toll	el puente	bridge
el primazgo	cousinhood	el primo	cousin
el sobrinazgo	relationship of a nephew or niece	el sobrino	nephew
el tenientazgo	lieutenantship; deputy's office	el teniente	lieutenant; deputy
el terrazgo	arable land; land-rent	la tierra	land
el vicealmirantazgo	vice-admiralship	el vicealmirante	vice-admiral
el villazgo	charter of a town	la villa	town; villa; municipal council

-azo[1]

Meaning: *augmentative*
English equivalent: *none*
Found in: *nouns*

In this group of words, the addition of *-azo* (like its sister suffix *-aza*) indicates enlargement of the base term. Usually the augmentation is physical, as in *gatazo* (big cat). However, it can be somewhat deprecative, as in *padrazo* (doting father). While this suffix is considered a noun ending, note that in one instance it works outside this milieu (see *antañazo*). All terms ending with *-azo* are masculine.

Formed Word	English Equivalent	Related to	English Equivalent
el aceitazo	thick oil	el aceite	oil
el animalazo	large hulking animal	el animal	animal
el antañazo	(coll.) way back in time	antaño *av*	in days of yore
el bigotazo	large mustache	el bigote	mustache
el bombazo [R]	great big bomb	la bomba	bomb
el copazo	large snowflake	el copo	snowflake
el exitazo	terrific success; "smash hit"	el éxito	success
el gatazo	large cat	el gato	cat
el gustazo	great pleasure; relish	el gusto	pleasure
el hombrazo	great hefty fellow	el hombre	man
el humazo	dense smoke	el humo	smoke
el maretazo	heavy surge; swell	la marea	tide; gentle sea breeze
el maridazo	doting husband	el marido	husband
el padrazo	doting father	el padre	father
el perrazo	great hefty dog or hound	el perro	dog
el platazo	platter; large helping of food	el plato	plate; dish
el playazo	long, wide beach	la playa	beach
el plumazo [R]	feather mattress or pillow	la pluma	feather
el terrazo	landscape	la tierra	land; earth
el vejazo	very old man	el viejo	old man
el vinazo	strong, heavy wine	el vino	wine
el zapatazo [R]	large shoe	el zapato	shoe

-azo⁽²⁾

Meaning: *blow or stike with or from; resulting action*
English equivalent: *none*
Found in: *nouns*

The following list of words offers a wonderful example of Spanish at its most simple and logical—and English at its least. The suffix -*azo* is commonly used in Spanish to signify a blow given by or with the root noun. As there is no English equivalent, we have to add the words *blow*, *hit*, and so on to convey the meaning found simply in the Spanish ending -*azo*. All words ending with -*azo* are masculine.

Formed Word	English Equivalent	Related to	English Equivalent
el balazo [R 4010]	shot; gunshot; bullet wound	**la bala**	bullet
el banderazo [4662]	waving of the flag in a car race	**la bandera**	flag
el batazo [4349]	hit with a bat	**el bate**	bat
el botellazo [R]	blow with a bottle	**la botella**	bottle
el botonazo	thrust with fencing foil	**el botón**	tip (of a foil in fencing)
el calabazazo	blow from a pumpkin	**la calabaza**	pumpkin
el codazo	shove with an elbow	**el codo**	elbow
el culatazo	kick of a gun	**la culata**	butt of a gun
el escopetazo [R]	gunshot wound; (fig.) thunderbolt	**la escopeta**	shotgun
el espaldarazo	back slap	**la espalda**	back (anat.)
el estacazo	blow with a stake	**la estaca**	stake; stick; bludgeon
el gatillazo	click of a trigger	**el gatillo**	trigger (of a gun)
el golpazo [R]	violent blow	**el golpe**	blow; hit
el guantazo [R]	slap with the open hand	**el guante**	glove
el latigazo	whiplash	**el látigo**	whip
el librazo	blow with a book	**el libro**	book
el martillazo [R]	hammer-stroke	**el martillo**	hammer
el palazo	blow with a shovel	**la pala**	shovel
el pelotazo	shot with a ball	**la pelota**	ball
el picazo	jab; peck	**el pico**	beak; bill
el pistoletazo [R]	pistol shot	**la pistola**	pistol
el plumazo [R]	stroke of a pen	**la pluma**	pen
el porrazo	blow; knock; fall	**la porra**	stick; nightstick
el portazo [R]	door slam	**la puerta**	door
el pretinazo	swipe with a belt; belting	**la pretina**	belt; girdle; waistband
el puñetazo [R]	blow with a fist; punch	**el puño**	fist
el rodillazo [R]	shove with the knee	**la rodilla**	knee
el tablazo	stroke with a board	**la tabla**	board
el tacazo	stroke with a billiard cue	**el taco**	billiard cue
el tijeretazo	cut with a scissors	**la tijera**	scissors
el timbrazo	sharp ring of a bell	**el timbre**	bell
el varazo	swipe with a pole, stick	**la vara**	pole; rod; staff
el ventanazo	slamming of a window	**la ventana**	window
el zapatazo [R]	blow with a shoe	**el zapato**	shoe

-cial

Meaning: *like; relating to*
English equivalent: *-cial; -tial*
Found in: *adjectives*

Spanish words ending with *-cial* generally are cognates of their English counterparts, making them easy to recognize and learn. The ending *-cial* is found in adjectives and indicates that someone or something holds characteristics of the base noun.

Formed Word	English Equivalent	Related to	English Equivalent
artificial [R 4121]	artificial; manmade	**el artificio**	workmanship; artifice; craft
comercial [R 633]	commercial; relating to trade	**el comercio**	trade; commerce
consecuente [R]	consequential; resulting	**la consecuencia**	consequence
crucial [R 4377]	crucial; cross-shaped	**la cruz**	cross
esencial [R 2653]	essential	**la esencia**	essence; scent
espacial [R 3236]	spatial	**el espacio**	space
especial [R 250]	special; particular	**la especia**	species; kind; class; sort
existencial [R]	existential	**la existencia**	existence
exponencial	(math.) exponential	**el exponente**	exponent
inicial [R 1927]	*nf* initial (letter); *aj* initial	**el inicio**	beginning
judicial [R 1363]	judicial; judiciary	**el juicio**	judgment; sense; opinion
nupcial [1439]	nuptial	**las nupcias**	nuptials
oficial [R 415]	official	**el oficio**	office (assigned position)
parcial [R 2873]	partial; biased	**la parte**	part
penitencial	penitential	**la penitencia**	penance; penitence
perjudicial	harmful; hurtful	**el perjuicio**	detriment; damage; harm
policial [3352]	(of the) police	**la policía**	police (department)
potencial [R 2243]	potential	**la potencia**	power
prejudicial	(law) requiring judicial decision	**el prejuicio**	prejudice; bias; prejudgment
presencial	relating to actual presence	**la presencia**	presence
presidencial [R 1228]	presidential	**el presidente**	president
providencial [R]	providential	**la providencia**	providence; foresight
provincial [R]	provincial	**la provincia**	province
racial [R]	racial	**la raza**	race; breed; stock
residencial [R 3514]	residential	**la residencia**	residence; domicile
social [R 190]	social	**el socio**	partner; member; fellow
superficial [R]	superficial; shallow	**la superficie**	surface; area
sustancial	substantial; solid; having body	**la sustancia**	substance; solidness; body
tangencial	tangential	**la tangente**	tangent
torrencial [R]	torrential; overpowering	**el torrente**	torrent; avalanche; rush

-ción

Meaning: *result of action; state of being; act*
English equivalent: *-tion*
Found in: *nouns*

The Spanish suffix *-ción* corresponds to the English "-tion": in both languages the suffix refers to the result of action, state of being, or attitude. Words taking this ending are related to verbs. Note below that most examples are derived from *-ar* verbs. All words ending in *-ción* are feminine and drop the accent when made plural: *la opción; las opciones.*

Formed Word	English Equivalent	Related to	English Equivalent
la acción [R 188]	action	**actuar**	to act
la aceptación [R 3023]	acceptance	**aceptar**	to accept
la actuación [R 808]	performance	**actuar**	to act
la actualización [R 3692]	updating	**actualizar**	to update
la acusación [R 1852]	accusation	**acusar**	to accuse
la adaptación [4106]	adaptation	**adaptar**	to adapt
la administración [R 467]	administration	**administrar**	to administer
la admiración [R 4029]	admiration	**admirar**	to admire
la adoración [R]	adoration; worship	**adorar**	to adore, worship
la adquisición [R 3040]	acquisition	**adquirir**	to acquire
la afición [R 2279]	hobby; interest; fondness; fans (group)	**aficionarse**	to become fond of
la afiliación [R	affiliation	**afiliar**	to affiliate
la afirmación [R 4346]	affirmation	**afirmar**	to affirm
la agrupación [R 1397]	grouping	**agrupar**	to group
la alimentación [R 1780]	feeding; nourishment	**alimentar**	to feed
la alineación [R 2357]	alignment	**alinear**	to align
la alteración [R 3124]	alteration	**alterar**	to alter
la ambición [R 4517]	ambition	**ambicionar**	to aspire to
la ampliación [R 1791]	widening or enlarging; enlargement	**ampliar**	to widen
la animación [R]	animation	**animar**	to animate
la anotación [R 1131]	annotation; note	**anotar**	to note
la anticipación [4280]	anticipation	**anticipar**	to anticipate
la aparición [R 1908]	apparition	**aparecer**	to appear
la aplicación [R 1326]	application; diligence	**aplicar**	to apply
la aprobación [R 2144]	approval	**aprobar**	to approve
la asignación [R 4600]	assigning to a post; assigning of money	**asignar**	to assign
la asociación [R 631]	association; fellowship	**asociar**	to associate
la aspiración [R 3005]	aspiration; inspiration	**aspirar**	to aspire
la atención [R 379]	attention	**atender**	to attend (to)
la atracción [R 4134]	attraction	**atraer**	to attract
la autorización [R 2274]	authorization	**autorizar**	to authorize
la averiguación [R 2593]	investigation	**averiguar**	to investigate
la bendición [R 1357]	blessing	**bendecir**	to bless
la calificación [R 2194]	grade (evaluation)	**calificar**	to grade (evaluate)
la cancelación [4352]	cancellation	**cancelar**	to cancel
la canonización [R 4334]	canonization	**canonizar**	to canonize

Formed Word	English Equivalent	Related to	English Equivalent
la capacitación [R 1686]	training	**capacitar**	to train
la captación [3564]	comprehension; understanding	**captar**	to gain (understanding)
la celebración [R 1591]	celebration	**celebrar**	to celebrate
la certificación [R 4188]	certification	**certificar**	to certify
la circulación [R 1390]	circulation	**circular**	to circulate
la clasificación [1854]	classification	**clasificar**	to classify
la colaboración [R 2018]	collaboration	**colaborar**	to collaborate
la colocación [R 3307]	placing; setting; arrangement	**colocar**	to place, position
la combinación [R 2926]	combination	**combinar**	to combine
la comercialización [R 2435]	commercialization	**comercializar**	to commercialize
la comparación [R 2162]	comparison	**comparar**	to compare
la compensación [R 4264]	compensation	**compensar**	to compensate
la complicación [R 3232]	complication	**complicar**	to complicate
la composición [R 3113]	composition	**componer**	to compose
la computación [4410]	computer science	**computar**	to compute
la comunicación [R 649]	communication	**comunicar**	to communicate
la concentración [R 2033]	concentration	**concentrar**	to concentrate
la conciliación [3991]	conciliation	**conciliar**	to conciliate
la condición [R 360]	condition; state; disposition	**condicionar**	to condition
la conducción [R 3807]	conduction	**conducir**	to drive, conduct
la confederación [R 2196]	confederation	**confederar**	to confederate
la confrontación [R 2914]	confrontation	**confrontar**	to confront
la congregación [R 4456]	congregation	**congregar**	to congregate
la conservación [R 2563]	conservation	**conservar**	to conserve
la consideración [R 2522]	consideration	**considerar**	to consider
la consolidación [4905]	consolidation	**consolidar**	to consolidate
la constitución [R 1712]	constitution	**constituir**	to constitute
la construcción [R 639]	construction	**construir**	to construct
la contaminación [1917]	contamination	**contaminar**	to contaminate
la continuación [R 2280]	continuation	**continuar**	to continue
la contracción [4092]	contraction	**contraer**	to contract
la contradicción [R 4664]	contradiction	**contradecir**	to contradict
la contratación [3308]	contracting (business)	**contratar**	to contract
la contribución [R 4170]	contribution	**contribuir**	to contribute
la conversación [R 1968]	conversation	**conversar**	to converse
la cooperación [R 2272]	cooperation	**cooperar**	to cooperate
la coordinación [R 1321]	coordination	**coordinar**	to coordinate
la corrupción [1305]	corruption	**corromper**	to corrupt
la cotización [4354]	quoting of a price; providing of an estimate	**cotizar**	to quote (price)
la creación [R 1237]	creation	**crear**	to create
la declaración [R 807]	declaration	**declarar**	to declare
la dedicación [R 4976]	dedication	**dedicar**	to dedicate
la definición [R 3403]	definition	**definir**	to define
la delegación [R 1180]	delegation	**delegar**	to delegate
la demostración [R 4171]	demonstration	**demostrar**	to demonstrate
la desaceleración [4520]	deceleration	**desacelerar**	to decelerate
la desaparición [R 2472]	disappearance	**desaparecer**	to disappear
la desesperación [R 4155]	impatience; desperation	**desesperarse**	to lose patience; to become desperate

Formed Word	English Equivalent	Related to	English Equivalent
la designación [4208]	designation	**designar**	to designate
la destrucción [R 3179]	destruction	**destruir**	to destroy
la detección [4677]	detection	**detectar**	to detect
la detención [R 1470]	detention	**detener**	to detain
la determinación [R 2480]	determination	**determinar**	to determine
la dicción [R]	diction	**dictar**	to dictate
la difamación [R]	defamation (of character)	**difamar**	to defame
la diputación [4698]	deputization; deputation; group of deputies	**diputar**	to deputize
la dirección [R 339]	direction; address	**dirigir**	to direct
la discriminación [4763]	discrimination	**discriminar**	to discriminate
la dismunición [R	diminution; lowering, lessening	**disminuir**	to diminish
la disposición [R 877]	disposition	**disponer**	to dispose
la distinción [R 4581]	distinction	**distinguir**	to distinguish
la distribución [R 1944]	distribution	**distribuir**	to distribute
la documentación [R 2858]	documentation	**documentar**	to document
la dominación [R]	domination	**dominar**	to dominate, master, command
la donación [3976]	donation; act of donating	**donar**	to donate, give
la drogadicción [4846]	drug addiction	**drogar**	to drug
la duración [R 2505]	duration	**durar**	to last
la edición [R 1277]	edition	**editar**	to edit; to publish
la elaboración [R 2793]	process	**elaborar**	to elaborate
la elección [R 551]	election	**elegir**	to elect
la eliminación [R 2898]	elimination	**eliminar**	to eliminate
la embarcación [R	embarkation	**embarcar**	to embark
la emoción [R 1705]	emotion; excitement	**emocionar**	to excite
la encarnación [R 4245]	incarnation	**encarnar**	to incarnate
la especulación [R 4872]	speculation	**especular**	to speculate
la estimación [R 4380]	esteem; estimation	**estimar**	to esteem; to estimate
la evaluación [2160]	evaluation	**evaluar**	to evaluate
la excepción [R 2423]	exception	**exceptuar**	to make an exception
la exhibición [R 2840]	exhibition	**exhibir**	to exhibit
la explicación [R 2441]	explanation	**explicar**	to explain
la explotación [R 3181]	exploitation	**explotar**	to exploit
la exportación [R 1614]	exportation	**exportar**	to export
la exposición [R 1690]	exposition	**exponer**	to expose
la expropiación [R 4701]	expropriation	**expropiar**	to expropriate
la extracción [2844]	extraction	**extraer**	to extract
la extradición [3929]	extradition	**extraditar**	to extradite
la fabricación [R 4702]	fabrication	**fabricar**	to fabricate, make
la federación [R 791]	federation	**federar**	to federate
la felicitación [R 1838]	congratulation; greeting	**felicitar**	to congratulate
la filmación [4397]	filming	**filmar**	to film
la fiscalización [R 4667]	enforcement of a law	**fiscalizar**	to prosecute
la formación [R 1653]	formation	**formar**	to form
la frustración [4037]	frustration	**frustrar**	to frustrate, thwart, foil
la fundación [R 1654]	foundation	**fundar**	to found
la generación [R 1190]	generation; graduating class	**generar**	to generate
la globalización [3299]	globalization	**globalizar**	to globalize
la gobernación [R 1825]	governing	**gobernar**	to govern, rule

Formed Word	English Equivalent	Related to	English Equivalent
la grabación [2079]	recording	grabar	to record
la habitación [R 2206]	room (hotel or large house); suite	habitar	to inhabit, live in
la identificación [R 3164]	identification	identificar	to identify
la imaginación [R 3669]	imagination	imaginar	to imagine
la importación [R 2376]	importation	importar	to import
la inauguración [R 2344]	inauguration	inaugurar	to inaugurate
la incorporación [R 4523]	incorporation	incorporar	to incorporate
la indemnización [4269]	indemnification	indemnizar	to indemnify
la indicación [R 3829]	indication	indicar	to indicate
la infección [2345]	infection	infectar	to infect
la inflación [2508]	inflation	inflar	to inflate
la inflamación [4631]	inflammation	inflamar	to inflame
la información [R 321]	information	informar	to inform
la innovación [R 3999]	innovation	innovar	to innovate
la inscripción [R 2501]	inscription	inscribir	to inscribe; to enroll
la inspiración [R 3845]	inspiration	inspirar	to inspire
la instalación [R 529]	installation	instalar	to install
la institución [R 396]	institution	instituir	to institute
la instrucción [R 2172]	instruction	instruir	to instruct
la integración [2005]	integration	integrar	to integrate
la intención [R 1012]	intention	intentar	to intend
la interpretación [R 2276]	interpretation; rendition	interpretar	to interpret
la intervención [R 1174]	intervention	intervenir	to intervene
la introducción [R 3228]	introduction	introducir	to introduce
la inundación [3434]	inundation; flood	inundar	to inundate, flood
la investigación [R 394]	investigation	investigar	to investigate
la invitación [R 1645]	invitation	invitar	to invite
la inyección [R	injection	inyectar	to inject
la justificación [R 4773]	justification	justificar	to justify
la legislación [2705]	legislation	legislar	to legislate
la liberación [R 2489]	liberation	liberar	to liberate
la licitación [3086]	bidding	licitar	to bid (on)
la limitación [R 4018]	limitation	limitar	to limit
la manifestación [R 1725]	manifestation	manifestar	to show
la mención [R 2509]	mention	mencionar	to mention
la modernización [R 2543]	modernization	modernizar	to modernize
la modificación [R 1946]	modification	modificar	to modify
la motivación [R 3981]	motivation	motivar	to motivate
la movilización [R 2953]	mobilization	movilizar	to mobilize
la nación [R 622]	nation	nacer	to be born
la natación [R 3726]	swimming	nadar	to swim
la negociación [R 1057]	negotiation	negociar	to negotiate, conduct business
la nominación [R 3192]	nomination	nominar	to name, nominate
la notificación [R 4548]	notification	notificar	to notify
la nutrición [R 4145]	nutrition	nutrir	to nourish
la obligación [R 1679]	obligation	obligar	to oblige
la observación [R 3009]	observation	observar	to observe
la ocupación [R 2878]	occupation	ocuparse	to be occupied with
la opción [1141]	option	optar	to opt, choose
la operación [R 582]	operation	operar	to operate

Formed Word	English Equivalent	Related to	English Equivalent
la oposición [R 1741]	opposition	**oponer**	to oppose
la oración [R 4359]	oration; prayer	**orar**	to pray, make a speech
la organización [R 380]	organization	**organizar**	to organize
la orientación [R 3277]	orientation	**orientar**	to orientate
la partición [R]	partition	**partir**	to part
la participación [R 404]	participation	**participar**	to participate
la pavimentación [3546]	paving	**pavimentar**	to pave
la percepción [R 2831]	perception	**percibir**	to perceive
la persecución [R 3638]	persecution	**perseguir**	to pursue
la petición [R 1251]	petition	**pedir**	to ask (for)
la planeación [2620]	planning	**planear**	to plan
la plantación [R]	plantation	**plantar**	to plant
la población [R 482]	population	**poblar**	to populate
la precaución [R 3709]	precaution	**precaver**	to take precautions
la preocupación [R 1569]	worry	**preocupar**	to cause worry
la preparación [R 1158]	preparation	**preparar**	to prepare
la presentación [R 676]	presentation	**presentar**	to present
la preservación [4321]	preservation	**preservar**	to preserve
la prestación [R 2566]	lending	**prestar**	to lend
la privatización [4197]	privatization	**privatizar**	to privatize
la procuración [R 4856]	procurement	**procurar**	to procure
la producción [R 354]	production	**producir**	to produce
la programación [3753]	programming	**programar**	to program
la prohibición [R 4432]	prohibition	**prohibir**	to prohibit
la proliferación [4495]	proliferation	**proliferar**	to proliferate
la prolongación [R 4496]	prolongation; extension	**prolongar**	to prolong
la pronunciación [R]	pronunciation	**pronunciar**	to pronounce, utter
la prostitución [4921]	prostitution	**prostituir**	to prostitute
la protección [R 935]	protection	**proteger**	to protect
la proyección [R 3427]	projection	**proyectar**	to project
la publicación [R 2662]	publication	**publicar**	to publish
la purificación [R]	purification	**purificar**	to purify
la reactivación [4857]	reactivation	**reactivar**	to reactivate
la readaptación [R 4687]	readaptation	**readaptar**	to readapt
la realización [R 1880]	realization	**realizar**	to realize
la recaudación [2223]	collection (taxes)	**recaudar**	to collect
la recepción [R 1418]	reception	**recibir**	to receive
la recomendación [R 2157]	recommendation	**recomendar**	to recommend
la reconstrucción [R 4130]	reconstruction	**reconstruir**	to reconstruct
la recuperación [1316]	recuperation (money or health)	**recuperar(se)**	to recuperate
la redacción [R 3166]	editing	**redactar**	to edit
la reducción [R 1817]	reduction	**reducir**	to reduce
la reelección [R 4899]	reelection	**reelegir**	to reelect
la reestructuración [R 4967]	restructuring	**reestructurar**	to restructure
la regulación [R 3731]	regulation	**regular**	to regulate
la regularización [R 4063]	regularization	**regularizar**	to regularize
la rehabilitación [R 1775]	rehabilitation	**rehabilitar**	to rehabilitate
la remodelación [R 4404]	remodeling	**remodelar**	to remodel
la renovación [R 3249]	renewal	**renovar**	to renew, renovate
la reparación [R 2799]	repair	**reparar**	to repair
la repetición [R 4923]	repetition	**repetir**	to repeat

Formed Word	English Equivalent	Related to	English Equivalent
la representación [R 1707]	representation	representar	to represent
la resolución [R 1536]	resolution	resolver	to resolve
la restauración [R 4835]	restoration	restaurar	to restore
la restricción [3214]	restriction	restringir	to restrict
la reubicación [3674]	the establishment of something in a new place	reubicar	to establish in a new place
la revelación [R 4324]	developing (film); revealing	revelar	to develop (film)
la revolución [R 1029]	revolution	revolver	to stir, stir up, revolve
la satisfacción [R 2313]	satisfaction	satisfacer	to satisfy
la separación [R 3688]	separation	separar	to separate
la simulación [R]	simulation	simular	to simulate
la situación [R 222]	situation; position; location	situar	to situate, locate, place
la súplica [R]	supplication; (law) appeal	suplicar	to entreat, supplicate, (law) appeal (against)
la suposición [R]	supposition; assumption	suponer	to suppose, assume
la suscripción [3953]	subscription	suscribir	to subscribe to an opinion; to sign at the bottom of a document
la sustitución [4779]	substitution	sustituir	to substitute
la tentación [R 4728]	temptation	tentar	to tempt
la transformación [R 2698]	transformation	transformar	to transform
la ubicación [3640]	placement	ubicar	to place
la utilización [R 3988]	utilization	utilizar	to utilize
la vacunación [4234]	vaccination (process)	vacunar	to vaccinate
la variación [R 3146]	variation	variar	to vary
la velación [4277]	vigil; the act of keeping watch; veiling ceremony (ecclesiastical)	velar	to keep vigil
la verificación [R 3563]	verification	verificar	to verify
la vindicación [R]	vindication	vindicar	to vindicate
la violación [R 1964]	violation; rape	violar	to violate, rape
la visitación [R]	visitation; visiting; visit	visitar	to visit
la votación [R 2085]	voting; vote (process)	votar	to vote

-culo; -cula; -ulo; -ula

Meaning: *diminutive; resulting object or person*
English equivalent: *-cule; -ule*
Found in: *nouns, adjectives (rarely)*

The suffix *-culo* and its less common variations *-cula*, *-ulo*, and *-ula* often denote something very small, e.g., *gránulo* (granule). As you will see, many of these are taken directly from Latin. Within this group is *minúsculo*, which is an adjecive (miniscule) as well as a noun (small letter); otherwise, words ending with *-culo*, *-cula*, *-ulo*, or *-ula* nearly always are nouns. Its second function is to denote result of action. These words are derived from verbs: *obstáculo* (obstacle) is something that gets in the way and comes from the verb *obstar* (to stand in the way). Note that the antepenultimate syllable is accented in words taking these endings.

Formed Word	English Equivalent	Related to	English Equivalent
el artículo [R 878]	article; item; joint	(Lat.) articulus	joint
el cálculo [R 4046]	calculation; calculus; stone (kidney, gall)	calcular	to calculate
el capítulo [2183]	chapter; heading; entry	(Lat.) capitulum	little head
la cápsula	capsule	(Lat.) capsula	little holder or container
el círculo [R 2745]	circle; ring	(Lat.) circulus	circle
el cubículo	cubicle	el cubo	cube
el discípulo [R]	disciple	(Lat.) discipulus	pupil
el edículo	small building; shrine; niche	(Lat.) aedicula	small building
el espectáculo [R 826]	spectacle; event	espectador	spectator
el folículo	follicle	(Lat.) folliculus	small bag
el glóbulo	globule	el globo	globe; ball; sphere
el gránulo [R]	granule	el grano	grain; seed; corn; pimple
(el) minúsculo [R]	small letter; miniscule	(Lat.) minusculus	somewhat small; less
el módulo [2427]	module	el modo	mode; manner; way
la molécula	molecule	(Lat.) moles	mass; bulk; pile
el músculo [R 3520]	muscle	muscular	muscular
el nódulo	nodule	el nodo	node; knot
el obstáculo [R 2748]	obstacle	obstar	to stand in the way
el oráculo [R]	oracle	orar	to pray
(el) párvulo	infant; very small	parvo	small; little; scanty
el pedículo	(bot.) pedicle; footstalk; little foot	(Lat.) pes	foot
la película [329]	film; movie	(Lat.) pellicula	small skin
el péndulo	pendulum	pender	to hang, dangle
el receptáculo	receptacle; repository; refuge	receptar	to receive, hide, shelter
(el) ridículo [R]	ridicule; ridiculous	(Lat.) ridiculus	exciting laughter
el signáculo	signet; seal	el signo	sign; mark; symbol
el tabernáculo	tabernacle	la taberna	hut
el tentáculo	tentacle	tentar	to touch, feel
el testículo	testicle	(anat.) el teste	testis
la válvula	valve; tube	(Lat.) valvae	folding doors
el vehículo [530]	vehicle	(Lat.) vehiculum	vehicle
el ventrículo	ventricle	el vientre	abdomen
el versículo [R]	small, short verse; Bible verse	el verso	verse
el vínculo [4328]	bond; tie	vincular	to tie, bind

-dizo (-diza)

Meaning: *like; relating to; tending to*
English equivalent: *none*
Found in: *adjectives*

The adjectival suffix *-dizo* is used to describe what someone or something is like or tends to do. Adjectives ending in *-dizo* are derived from verbs. Note that the *-ar* verbs retain the *a* before the suffix, just as the *-er* verbs retain the letter *e*, and the *-ir* verbs retain the *i*. From *olvidar* comes *olvidadizo*; from *llover*, *llovedizo*; from *escurrir*, *escurridizo*). As this is an adjectival ending, when you use these terms to describe feminine nouns, the suffix becomes *-diza*.

Formed Word	English Equivalent	Related to	English Equivalent
ablandadizo	soothing; easily persuaded	**ablandar**	to soften, mollify, mellow
acomodadizo	accommodating; obliging	**acomodar**	to accommodate
anegadizo	subject to flooding; easily flooded	**anegar**	to flood, inundate, submerge
apagadizo [R]	tending to go out easily	**apagar**	to turn off, extinguish
apartadizo	antisocial; standoffish	**apartar**	to separate, turn aside
apretadizo	easily bound; compressed	**apretar**	to press, tighten
arrojadizo	made for throwing	**arrojar**	to throw, hurl
asustadizo [R]	easily frightened or scared	**asustar**	to frighten, scare
bajadizo	descending; sloping gently	**bajar**	to lower, let down
bebedizo [R]	drinkable	**beber**	to drink
caedizo	ready to fall	**caer**	to fall
cambiadizo	changeable; fickle	**cambiar**	to change, alter
clavadizo	nail-studded	**clavar**	to nail
cogedizo	which can be easily collected	**coger**	to pick up, collect
enojadizo [R]	irritable; easily annoyed	**enojar**	to anger, vex, irritate
erradizo	wandering	**errar**	to wander, miss
escurridizo	slippery; tricky	**escurrir**	to slip (away), sneak away
heladizo	easily congealed	**helar**	to freeze, turn to ice, chill
levadizo [R]	that can be lifted or raised	**levantar**	to lift, raise
llovedizo	leaky	**llover**	to rain
manchadizo	easily stained or soiled	**manchar**	to stain, soil, spot
movedizo [R]	movable	**mover**	to move
olvidadizo [R]	forgetful	**olvidar**	to forget
resbaladizo [R]	slippery	**resbalar**	to slip, slide
saledizo	jutting; salient	**salir**	to go out, leave
tornadizo	fickle; changeable	**tornar**	to turn, come back

-dor$^{(1)}$ (-dora)

Meaning: *one who; denotes profession*
English equivalent: *-er; -or*
Found in: *nouns*

The following words that end in *-dor* denote persons who perform specific tasks. The task relates directly to the root verb. The formation of these terms is simple: remove the *r* from the infinitive and add the suffix *-dor*. Thus, *matar* becomes *matador*; *morder* becomes *mordedor*; *tirar* becomes *tirador*. (One exception is *veedor* from *ver*, which adds an *e*). Several Spanish suffixes indicate *one who*. Note that words ending with *-dor* often refer to persons or professions possessing or requiring physical power and strength.

Formed Word	English Equivalent	Related to	English Equivalent
el aborrecedor	hater	aborrecer	to hate
el asaltador	assailant; assaulter	asaltar	to assault
el azotador	whipper	azotar	to whip
el batallador	battler; warrior; fencer	batallar	to battle, fight, fence
el bateador	batter	batear	to bat
el batidor $^{[R]}$	beater	batir	to beat
el boxeador $^{[4409]}$	boxer	boxear	to box
el cazador $^{[R]}$	hunter	cazar	to hunt
el comprador $^{[3616]}$	buyer	comprar	to buy
el conquistador $^{[R]}$	conqueror; (coll.) lady-killer	conquistar	to conquer, win (over)
el conservador $^{[R\ 3628]}$	political rightist; conservative	conservar	to conserve
el consumidor $^{[R\ 1716]}$	consumer	consumir	to consume
el distribuidor $^{[R\ 3431]}$	distributor	distribuir	to distribute
el edificador $^{[R]}$	constructor; builder	edificar	to construct, build
el escupidor	spitter	escupir	to spit, spit at or out
el exportador $^{[R\ 3415]}$	*nmf* exporter	exportar	to export
el jaleador	cheerer	jalear	to cheer, encourage with shouts
el jugador	player (game)	jugar	to play (a game)
el labrador $^{[R]}$	laborer	labrar	to labor
el luchador $^{[R]}$	fighter; struggler	luchar	to fight, struggle
el malgastador $^{[R]}$	squanderer; spendthrift; wastrel	malgastar	to misspend, squander, waste
el malversador $^{[R]}$	embezzler	malversar	to embezzle
el matador $^{[R\ 4419]}$	killer	matar	to kill
el mordedor $^{[R]}$	biter	morder	to bite
el obrador $^{[2081]}$	working; laboring	obrar	to work
el observador $^{[R\ 4285]}$	observer	observar	to observe
el organizador $^{[R\ 1584]}$	organizer	organizar	to organize
el pateador	kicker	patear	(coll.) to kick, stamp
el patrocinador $^{[R\ 4590]}$	sponsor; patron	patrocinar	to sponsor
el peleador $^{[R]}$	fighter	pelear	to fight
el perdedor $^{[R\ 3854]}$	loser	perder	to lose
el pulverizador	pulverizer	pulverizar	to pulverize
el regidor $^{[923]}$	member of a governing council	regir	to govern
el saltador $^{[R]}$	jumper	saltar	to jump

Formed Word	English Equivalent	Related to	English Equivalent
el secuestrador	kidnapper	secuestrar	to kidnap
el seguidor [R 1680]	follower; following	seguir	to follow
el sitiador	besieger	sitiar	to besiege
el tirador [R]	shooter	tirar	to throw, shoot, fling, cast
el torcedor	twister	torcer	to twist
el toreador	bullfighter	torear	to fight bulls
el triunfador [R 2950]	nmf conqueror; one who triumphs	triunfar	to triumph
el veedor	spy; prier	ver	to see
el vencedor [R]	conqueror	vencer	to conquer
el violador	violator; rapist	violar	to violate, rape

-dor(2); -dora

Meaning: *machine; appliance*
English equivalent: *none*
Found in: *nouns*

In the previous entry you find the ending -*dor* (or -*dora*), which indicates a person who performs a specific task. In this entry you will find a list of machines and appliances that perform specific chores, each directly derived from a verb. If the origin is an -*ar* verb, that *a* is retained, e.g., *despertador* (alarm clock) from *despertar* (to wake up). If the origin is an -*er* or -*ir* verb, the *e* or *i* will be retained, respectively. Words ending with -*dor* are masculine, while those ending with -*dora* are feminine.

Formed Word	English Equivalent	Related to	English Equivalent
el abridor [3036]	opener	abrir	to open
el acondicionador [R]	air conditioner	acondicionar	to air-condition
el asador	spit; rotisserie	asar	to roast
la aspiradora [R]	vacuum cleaner	aspirar	to breathe in, aspirate
el borrador [R]	eraser	borrar	to erase, rub out
la calculadora	calculator	calcular	to calculate
la computadora [1452]	computer	computar	to compute, calculate
el congelador	freezer	congelar	to freeze, congeal
el/la contestador,-a	(telephone) answering machine	contestar	to answer, reply
el/la copiador,-a	duplicating or copying machine	copiar	to copy, duplicate
la cosechadora [R]	harvester; reaping machine	cosechar	to reap, harvest
la cultivadora	cultivating; cultivator	cultivar	to cultivate, grow
el despertador [R]	alarm clock	despertar	to awaken, rouse, wake up
el destornillador [R]	screwdriver	destornillar	to unscrew
el destripador	(seam) ripper	destripar	to rip open
el estampador	stamper	estampar	to stamp, print, imprint
el expendedora	vending machine	expender	to spend, expend, lay out
el exprimidor	squeezer	exprimir	to squeeze
la grabadora	tape recorder	grabar	to engrave, cut, tape
la grapadora	stapler; stapling machine	grapar	to staple
el humidificador	humidifier	humidificar	to humidify

Formed Word	English Equivalent	Related to	English Equivalent
el imprimador	(art) primer	imprimar	(art) to prime
el incinerador	incinerator	incinerar	to incinerate, cremate
el indicador [R 2682]	indicator	indicar	to indicate
el lavadora [R]	washing machine	lavar	to wash
el marcador [R 1084]	marker; scoreboard	marcar	to mark
el mezcladora [R]	blender; mixer	mezclar	to mix, blend
el ordeñador	milking machine	ordeñar	to milk
el perforador [R]	drill	perforar	to drill or bore (through)
el purificador [R]	purifier	purificar	to purify, cleanse
el radiador [R]	radiator	radiar	to radiate
el rallador	grater (for cheese, etc.)	rallar	to grate, vex
el refrigerador [R 4592]	refrigerator; cooler	refrigerar	to cool, refrigerate
el rociador	sprinkler	rociar	to sprinkle
el secadora [R]	dryer (for laundry)	secar	to dry
el tostador	toaster	tostar	to toast
el transportador [R]	transporter; carrier	transportar	to transport, convey
la trilladora	threshing machine	trillar	to thresh, beat
el vibrador [R]	vibrator	vibrar	to vibrate
la volador,-a	fly wheel (of an engine)	volar	to fly

-dumbre; -umbre

Meaning: *forms abstract noun*
English equivalent: *-ness*
Found in: *nouns*

The addition of *-dumbre* or *-umbre* to a base word results in an abstraction of that term. Base words can be either nouns or adjectives. As you will see, *-dumbre* and *-umbre* are not common suffixes. Words taking these endings are feminine.

Formed Word	English Equivalent	Related to	English Equivalent
la certidumbre [R]	certainty; certitude	cierto	certain; sure
la dulcedumbre	sweetness	dulce	sweet
la herrumbre	rust; irony taste	el hierro	iron
la incertidumbre [R 3104]	lack of certainty; doubt	incierto	uncertain; unsure
la mansedumbre	gentleness; meekness; mildness	manso	gentle; meek; mild; tame
la muchedumbre [R]	multitude; crowd; (fig.) masses	mucho	much; a great deal of
la pesadumbre [R]	grief; sorrow; heaviness	el peso	weight
la podredumbre	corruption; putrification	la podre	pus
la salsedumbre	saltiness	la sal	salt
la techumbre	roofing	el techo	roof

-dura

Meaning: *resulting action; resulting object*
English equivalent: *-ing*
Found in: *nouns*

The following words that end in *-dura* all are derived from verbs and indicate either the act of the verb itself, e.g., *mascadura* (chewing) from *mascar* (to chew), or the physical object directly related to that verb, e.g., *vestidura* (clothing) from *vestir* (to dress). A spelling aid is built into these formed words: Those derived from *-ar* verbs retain the *a* and thus end with *-adura*; those derived from *-er* verbs end in *-edura*; and those from *-ir* verbs end in *-idura*. Words ending with *-dura* are feminine.

Formed Word	English Equivalent	Related to	English Equivalent
la alisadura	planing; smoothing	**alisar**	to plane, smooth down
la añadidura [R]	addition; extra measure	**añadir**	to add, increase
la armadura [R]	armor; armature	**armar**	to arm
la bordadura	embroidery; embroidering	**bordar**	to embroider
la cabalgadura [R]	mount; horse; beast of burden	**cabalgar**	to go horseback riding
la cerradura [R]	locking or shutting up; lock	**cerrar**	to close, shut, lock
la escocedura	burning pain	**escocer**	to make smart or sting
la lamedura	lick; licking	**lamer**	to lick, lap
la ligadura [R]	binding; tie	**ligar**	to bind, tie
la limpiadura	cleaning	**limpiar**	to clean, cleanse
la mascadura	chewing	**mascar**	to chew
la mecedura	rocking	**mecer**	to rock
la peladura	stripping; peeling	**pelar**	to strip, peel, skin
la perfiladura	profiling; outlining	**perfilar**	to profile, outline
la picadura [R]	bite; prick; sting	**picar**	to prick, pierce
la quemadura [R 4686]	burn; scald	**quemar**	to burn, scald, scorch
la raspadura	rasping; filing; scraping	**raspar**	to rasp, file, scrape
la rociadura	sprinkling	**rociar**	to sprinkle
la rodadura	rolling	**rodar**	to roll
la rompedura	breakage; breaking	**romper**	to break
la rozadura [R]	friction; chafing; rubbing	**rozar**	to chafe, rub, scrape
la teñidura	dying; tingeing	**teñir**	to dye, stain, tinge
la vestidura [R]	clothing; vestments; dress	**vestir(se)**	to dress (one's self)

-eda; -edo

Meaning: *grove; orchard; place where something grows*
English equivalent: *none*
Found in: *nouns*

The suffix *-eda* or *-edo* generally denotes a large grouping of whatever kind of tree the root word denotes. Either ending can also indicate a place where something grows, i.e., *la cepeda* (land overgrown with heath) but nearly always refers to a collection of trees. The endings *-eda* and *-edo* are identical in the function they perform; the only difference is that -eda is always feminine, while -edo is masculine. Note that in some cases either ending is acceptable (with no change in meaning).

Formed Word	English Equivalent	Related to	English Equivalent
el/la acebedo/a	holly tree plantation	el acebo	holly tree
la alameda [R]	poplar grove	el álamo	poplar
el/la arboledo/a	grove; woodland	el árbol	tree
el arcedo	maple grove	el arce	maple tree
el/la bujedo/a	boxwood grove	el boj	box tree
el carvalledo	oak grove	el carvallo	(prov.) oak
la castañeda	chestnut grove	el castaño	chestnut tree
la cepeda	land overgrown with heath	la cepa	vinestock
la fresneda	ash grove	el fresno	ash tree
el hayedo	beech grove	la haya	beech tree
la moreda	grove of mulberry trees	el moral	mulberry tree
el olmedo	elm grove	el olmo	elm tree
la peraleda	pear orchard	el peral	pear tree
la robleda	oak grove	el roble	oak tree
la rosaleda [R]	rose garden	el rosal	rose bush
la sauceda	willow grove	el sauce	willow tree

-edad; -dad

Meaning: *state of being; forms abstract noun*
English equivalent: *-ness; -hood*
Found in: *nouns*

As most of the following words demonstrate, the addition of -edad or -dad to an adjective creates an abstract noun that relates to the qualities of that adjective. Either suffix also can be attached to a noun, denoting then the abstract collection of that noun. The more common form is -edad; but generally, if the final consonant of the root word is an *l* or *n*, the suffix is simply -dad. All words ending in -edad or -dad are feminine.

Formed Word	English Equivalent	Related to	English Equivalent
la beldad	beauty; belle	bello	beautiful; fair
la brevedad [R 4903]	briefness; brevity	breve	brief; short
la ceguedad	blindness	ciego	blind
la contrariedad [R]	opposition; annoyance; irritation	contrario	contrary; contradictory; opposite
la cortedad	smallness; (fig.) shyness	corto	short; brief; shy
la crueldad [R]	cruelty	cruel	cruel
la chatedad	flatness; shallowness	chato	flat; flat-nosed
la ebriedad [R 3385]	drunkenness; intoxication	ebrio	drunk; intoxicated
la enfermedad [R 459]	sickness; disease	enfermo	sick
la fidelidad [R]	surety; guarantee; security	fiel	faithful; loyal; true
la frialdad [R]	coldness; coolness	frío	cold; cool
la hermandad [R]	fraternity; brotherhood	(el) hermano	brother
la humedad [R 4140]	humidity; dampness	húmedo	humid; damp; moist

Formed Word	English Equivalent	Related to	English Equivalent
la humildad [R]	humility; humbleness; lowliness	**humilde**	humble; lowly; meek; submissive
la igualdad [R 4225]	equality; evenness	**igual**	equal
la impiedad [R]	impiety; impiousness	**impío**	impious; irreligious
la levedad	lightness; slightness	**leve**	light; slight; trifling
la liviandad [R]	lightness; fickleness	**liviano**	light; fickle; trivial
la mesmedad	sameness; essential nature	**mismo**	same; selfsame
la novedad [R 3072]	novelty; new thing	**nuevo**	new
la orfandad	orphanhood; neglect; dearth	**el huérfano**	orphan
la sequedad	dryness	**seco**	dry; dried-up
la seriedad [R 4326]	seriousness; earnestness	**serio**	serious; earnest
la sobriedad [R]	sobriety; frugality; moderation	**sobrio**	sober; frugal; moderate; sparing
la soledad [R 2948]	solitude; loneliness	**solo**	alone; lonely; solitary
la tochedad	rusticity; coarseness	**tocho**	rustic; uncouth; coarse
la tosquedad	coarseness; clumsiness	**tosco**	coarse; rude; clumsy
la turbiedad	turbidness	**turbio**	turbid; troubled; cloudy
la variedad [R 1733]	variety	**variado**	varied
la vastedad [R]	vastness; huge expanse	**vasto**	vast; immense; huge
la vecindad [R]	neighborhood	**el vecino**	neighbor
la verdad [R 733]	truth	**veraz**	truthful
la vialidad [1107]	highway system	**la vía**	way
la viudedad	widowhood	**la viuda**	widow
la voluntariedad	voluntariness; willfulness	**voluntario**	voluntary
la zafiedad	boorishness; cloddishness	**zafio**	boorish; uncouth; cloddish

-ejo; -eja

Meaning: *diminutive; pejorative*
English equivalent: *none*
Found in: *nouns*

The ending *-ejo* or *-eja* generally indicates physical smallness of the base term. Either ending can, however, be pejorative and denote diminished status of that object: from *el libro* (book) we get *el librejo*, which is an old, worthless book. These two suffixes are identical in function; *-ejo*, however, is the more common. Words ending with *-ejo* are masculine, while those taking *-eja* are feminine.

Formed Word	English Equivalent	Related to	English Equivalent
el anillejo	small ring	**el anillo**	ring
el animalejo	wretched, ugly creature	**el animal**	animal; creature
el arenalejo	small sandy place	**el arenal**	sandy ground; stretch of sand
el atabalejo	small kettledrum	**el atabal**	kettledrum
el azoguejo	small marketplace	**el azogue**	marketplace
el barrilejo	small barrel	**el barril**	barrel
el batelejo	small boat	**el batel**	(naut.) small vessel

Formed Word	English Equivalent	Related to	English Equivalent
el bozalejo	small muzzle	el bozal	muzzle
el caballejo	wretched little horse	el caballo	horse
el cabezalejo	tiny pillow or bolster	el cabezal	small pillow
la calleja	small street; alley	la calle	street
la canaleja	small canal	el canal	canal; channel; waterway
el castillejo	small castle	el castillo	castle
el collarejo	small collar or necklace	el collar	collar; necklace
la copleja	wretched little ballad	la copla	ballad; couplet
el cordelejo	miserable little chord	la cuerda	cord; string; rope
la cuchilleja	small knife; paring knife	el cuchillo	knife
el diablejo	scamp; little devil	el diablo	devil; demon; fiend
el librejo	old, worthless book	el libro	book
el lugarejo	wretched little village	el lugar	place; spot; village
la palabreja [R]	wretched or queer expression	la palabra	word
la pareja [R 547]	couple; team	el par	pair; equal; peer
el vallejo	small valley	el valle	valley; vale; glen
el zagalejo	young lad	el zagal	lad; youth; shepherd

-encia

Meaning: *act; state of being; result of action*
English equivalent: *-ence; -ency*
Found in: *nouns*

Spanish words that end in *-encia* nearly always are cognates of their English counterparts and denote the state, act, or result of the verb (or, occasionally, adjective) from which they are derived. Usually, these words are derived from *-er* or *-ir* verbs; however, infinitives ending with *-enciar* often have resulting nouns that end with *-encia*. Some of these formed words are derived directly from Latin infinitives. All words ending with *-encia* are feminine.

Formed Word	English Equivalent	Related to	English Equivalent
la abstinencia [R]	abstinence; forbearance; fasting	abstenerse	to abstain, forbear, refrain
la advertencia [R 3714]	warning	advertir	to warn
la afluencia [R]	affluence	afluir	to flow, flock in
la agencia [R 850]	agency; commission	agenciar	to bring about, engineer
la apariencia [R 3554]	appearance	aparentar	to give the appearance
la asistencia [R 1455]	attendance	asistir	to attend
la ausencia [R 1599]	absence	ausentarse	to be absent
la carencia [2710]	lack; deficiency	carecer	to lack
la coexistencia [R]	coexistence	coexistir	to coexist, live together
la coincidencia [R 4091]	coincidence	coincidir	to coincide
la conciencia [R 1782]	conscience	concienciar	to create awareness in
la condescendencia [R]	condescendence; condescension	condescender	to condescend
la conferencia [R 767]	conference; lecture	conferenciar	to confer, lecture
la confluencia [R 4845]	confluence	confluir	to flow, run together

Formed Word	English Equivalent	Related to	English Equivalent
la convivencia [R 2779]	get-together; sharing together of time, experience, and food	convivir	to share experiences, food, and time together
la creencia [R 3482]	belief	creer	to believe
la deferencia [R 765]	deference	deferir	to defer, yield
la deficiencia [R 2784]	deficiency	(Lat.) deficere	to fail, disappoint, desert
la delincuencia [2589]	delinquency	delinquir	to commit a crime
la dependencia [R 701]	dependency	depender	to depend on, be dependent on
la descendencia [R]	descent	descender	to descend, come down
la diferencia [R 765]	difference	diferir	to differ, be different
la dirigencia [1850]	directorship	dirigir	to direct
la divergencia [R]	divergence	divergir	to diverge, dissent
la eficiencia [R 3149]	efficiency	(Lat.) efficere	to bring about, effect, accomplish
la emergencia [1897]	emergency	emerger	to emerge
la eminencia [R]	eminence	(Lat.) eminere	to stand out, be prominent
la esencia [R 3081]	essence	esencial	essential
la evidencia [R 2149]	obviousness; certainty	evidenciar	to make evident, obvious, clear
la excelencia [R 4382]	excellence	excelente	excellent
la exigencia [R 2975]	demand	exigir	to demand
la existencia [R 1724]	existence	existir	to exist, live, have being
la frecuencia [R 1500]	frequency	frecuentar	to frequent
la herencia [R 3770]	inheritance	heredar	to inherit
la impotencia [R 4719]	impotence	impotente	impotent
la incontinencia	incontinence	incontinente	incontinent
la independencia [R 1427]	independence; privacy	in + depender	not + to depend
la indulgencia	indulgence	(Lat.) indulgere	to grant, concede, make allowance
la influencia [R 2131]	influence	influir	to influence
la inocencia [R]	innocence; guilelessness	inocente	innocent; guileless
la insistencia [R]	insistence	insistir	to insist
la insuficiencia [R 4794]	insufficiency	insuficiente	insufficient
la inteligencia [R 2154]	intelligence	inteligente	intelligent
la licencia [R 2156]	license	licenciar	to license, permit
la obediencia [R]	obedience	obedecer	to obey
la opulencia	opulence	(Lat.) opulentare	to make rich, enrich
la paciencia [R 3237]	patience	paciente	patient
la penitencia [R]	penitence; penance	penitenciar	to impose a penance on
la permanencia [R 4003]	permanence	permanecer	to remain
la pertenencia [R 4919]	belonging	pertenecer	to belong
la potencia [R 2757]	power	potente	potent
la preferencia [R 2299]	preference; priority	preferir	to prefer
la presencia [R 483]	presence	presenciar	to witness, be present at
la presidencia [R 618]	presidency; chairmanship	presidir	to preside over
la procedencia [R 3548]	origin	procedente	proceeding from
la referencia [R 1955]	reference	referir	to refer
la residencia [R 1124]	residence	residir	to reside
la resistencia [R 2467]	resistance; reluctance	resistir	to resist, withstand
la reverencia	reverence	reverenciar	to revere, reverence

Formed Word	English Equivalent	Related to	English Equivalent
la sentencia [R 2622]	sentence (legal punishment)	**sentenciar**	to sentence
la sugerencia [R 3856]	suggestion	**sugerir**	to suggest
la tendencia [R 1837]	tendency; bent; leaning	*(Lat.)* **tendere**	to be inclined, aim at
la tenencia [R 3969]	possession	**tener**	to have
la transferencia [3733]	transfer	**transferir**	to transfer
la transparencia [R 2592]	transparency	**transparentarse**	to be transparent
la urgencia [R 2722]	urgency; emergency	**urgente**	urgent
la vigencia [R 3891]	valid status	**vigente**	valid
la violencia [R 1072]	violence	**violentar**	to force

-engo (-enga)

Meaning: *like; relating to*
English equivalent: *none*
Found in: *adjectives*

This unusual suffix is one of several adjectival endings meaning "like" or "relating to." The resulting adjective indicates that someone or something holds characteristics of the base term. When the adjective describes a feminine noun, -engo becomes -enga.

Formed Word	English Equivalent	Related to	English Equivalent
abadengo	pertaining to an abbot or an abbey	**el abad**	abbot
barbiluengo	long-bearded	**la barba**	beard
luengo *(obs.)*	long; far	*(Lat.)* **longus**	long
realengo	royal; kingly	**real**	royal; real

-eno (-ena)

Meaning: *denotes ordinal number*
English equivalent: *-th*
Found in: *adjectives; nouns*

The ending -eno is a less common suffix denoting ordinal numbers (see -ésimo; -imo) or nouns (see -avo). As an adjective, you might say, *El noveno niño en la fila es mi primo* (The ninth boy in the row is my cousin). As a noun, you could say more simply, *El noveno en la fila es mi primo*. When used to describe or refer to feminine nouns, these formed adjectives or nouns take the ending -ena.

Formed Word	English Equivalent	Related to	English Equivalent
seiseno	sixth	**seis**	six
septeno	seventh	*(Lat.)* **September**	seven
noveno [R 1771]	ninth	**nueve**	nine
deceno	tenth	*(Lat.)* **decem**	ten
onceno	eleventh	**once**	eleven

Formed Word	English Equivalent	Related to	English Equivalent
doceno	twelfth	doce	twelve
treceno	thirteenth	trece	thirteen
catorceno	fourteenth	catorce	fourteen
quinceno	fifteenth	quince	fifteen
dieciocheno	eighteenth	dieciocho	eighteen
veinteno	twentieth	veinte	twenty
treinteno	thirtieth	treinta	thirty
cuarenteno	fortieth	cuarenta	forty
cincuenteno	fiftieth	cincuenta	fifty
ochenteno	eightieth	ochenta	eighty
centeno	hundredth	cien	one hundred
mileno	thousandth	mil	thousand

-ense

Meaning: *native; native of; like; relating to*
English equivalent: *none*
Found in: *nouns; adjectives*

The suffix *-ense* is one of several endings that indicate origin. It is both a noun and an adjectival ending, with its part of speech borne out in the context of the sentence: *La nicaragüense lee el periódico nicaragüense* (The Nicaraguan [woman] reads the Nicaraguan newspaper). There is no change in this ending from masculine to feminine; again, context tells you whether the referent is a masculine or feminine noun (*el canadiense; la canadiense*). Unlike their English counterparts, these words are not capitalized. Some words ending with *-ense* are adjectives only (*hortense*).

Formed Word	English Equivalent	Related to	English Equivalent
(el) abulense	(native) of Avila	Ávila	Avila
(el) ateniense	(native) of Athens	Atenas	Athens
(el) badajocense	(native) of Badajoz	Badajoz	Badajoz
(el) berlinense	(native) of Berlin	Berlín	Berlin
(el) bonaerense	(native) of Buenos Aires	Buenos Aires	Buenos Aires
(el) bracarense	(native) of Braga	Braga	Braga
(el) bruselense	(native) of Brussels	Bruselas	Brussels
(el) canadiense [2425]	(native) of Canada	Canadá	Canada
(el) cartaginense	(native) of Carthage	Cartago	Carthage
(el) costarricense	(native) of Costa Rica	Costa Rica	Costa Rica
(el) cretense	(native) of Crete	Creta	Crete
(el) escurialense	belonging to Escorial monastery	el Escorial	monastery in Spain
(el) estadounidense [353]	(native) of United States	Estados Unidos	United States
(el) gerundense	(native) of Gerona	Gerona	Gerona
hortense	pertaining to a garden or orchard	el huerto	orchard; garden
(el) lisbonense	(native) of Lisbon	Lisboa	Lisbon
(el) londinense	(native) of London	Londres	London
(el) manilense	(native) of Manila	Manila	Manila

Formed Word	English Equivalent	Related to	English Equivalent
(el) matritense	(native) of Madrid	**Madrid**	Madrid
(el) mexiquense [4061]	(native) of Mexico	**México**	Mexico
(el) nicaragüense	(native) of Nicaragua	**Nicaragua**	Nicaragua
(el) parisiense	(native) of Paris	**París**	Paris
(el) peloponense	(native) Peloponnesian	**Peleponeso**	Peleponnesia

-ente(1)

Meaning: *like; relating to; doing*
English equivalent: *-ing; -ent*
Found in: *adjectives*

The following formed words that end in *-ente* all are adjectives derived from *-er* and *-ir* verbs. These adjectives indicate that the persons, places, or things described exhibit qualities relating directly to the root verb. Since the English equivalent often is *-ing*, be careful not to confuse the Engilsh translations with the progressive mood (i.e., John is running down the street.) This suffix closely relates to *-ante*, found in adjectives derived from *-ar* verbs. These adjectives do not change with regards to gender.

Formed Word	English Equivalent	Related to	English Equivalent
absorbente	absorbing; absorbent; engrossing	**absorber**	to absorb, drink in, engross
abstinente	abstinent	**abstenerse**	to abstain, forbear, restrain
atrayente [R]	attractive; attracting	**atraer**	to attract
cedente	ceding; yielding	**ceder**	to cede, yield
competente [R 3681]	competent	**competir**	to compete
consistente [R 3862]	consistent; with consistency	**consistir**	to consist
(el) contendiente [4312]	*nmf* contender; contestant; *aj* contending	**contender**	to contend
(el) contrayente [R 2000]	*nmf* bride or groom; *aj* contracting	**contraer**	to contract
contribuyente [R 2438]	contributor; contributing	**contribuir**	to contribute
conveniente [R 2568]	convenient	**convenir**	to convene
correspondiente [R 863]	corresponding	**corresponder**	to correspond
corriente [1609]	running; current; common	**correr**	to run
(la) creciente [R 2711]	*nf* crescent moon; rising tide; *aj* growing; increasing	**crecer**	to grow
creyente [R]	believing	**creer**	to believe
(el) dependiente [R 4762]	*nmf* employee who works directly with the public; *aj* dependent	**depender**	to depend
deprimente [R]	depressing	**deprimir**	to depress, press down
diferente [R 271]	different; differing	**diferir**	to differ, be different
durmiente [R]	sleeping; dormant	**dormir**	to sleep
emergente [2321]	emergent; issuing	**emerger**	to emerge (from water)
equivalente [R 2833]	equivalent	**equivaler**	to be equivalent
existente [R 2507]	existent; existing	**existir**	to exist

Formed Word	English Equivalent	Related to	English Equivalent
inconveniente [R 4985]	inconvenient	**convenir**	to be convenient for or to
influyente [R]	influencing; influential	**influir**	to influence
leyente	reading	**leer**	to read
luciente [R]	shining; bright	**lucir**	to light, light up
mereciente	deserving	**merecer**	to deserve, merit
muriente	dying; faint	**morir**	to die
naciente [R]	nascent; incipient	**nacer**	to be born
(el) oponente [R 4570]	*nmf* opponent; *aj* opposing	**oponer**	to oppose
perteneciente	belonging; appertaining	**pertenecer**	to belong
poseyente	possessing; possessive	**poseer**	to possess, own
(el) precedente [R 3512]	*nm* precedent; *aj* preceding	**preceder**	to precede
procedente [R 1994]	originating in, arriving from	**proceder**	to proceed
proveniente [R 2863]	proceeding (from); originating (in)	**provenir**	to proceed from
queriente	willing	**querer**	to want, wish
referente [R 2554]	referring; relating	**referir**	to refer
reincidente	backsliding; relapsing	**reincidir**	to backslide, relapse
reluciente [R]	shining; glittering	**relucir**	to shine, glitter
repelente	repellent; objectionable	**repeler**	to repel
residente [R 2893]	resident; residing	**residir**	to reside
resistente [R]	resistant; resisting	**resistir**	to resist
riente	smiling; laughing	**reír(se)**	to laugh
rugiente	roaring	**rugir**	to roar
siguiente [R 469]	following	**seguir**	to follow, continue
sobreviviente [R 4840]	surviving	**sobrevivir**	to survive
sorprendente [R 3625]	surprising	**sorprender**	to surprise
sosteniente	sustaining; supporting	**sostener**	to support, hold up, sustain
sugerente [R]	suggesting; thought-provoking	**sugerir**	to suggest, hint, imply
teniente [R]	having; holding	**tener**	to have, hold
urgente [R 2341]	urgent	**urgir**	to urge
viviente [R]	living; alive	**vivir**	to live
yacente [R]	lying	**yacer**	to lie, be lying down

-ente(2); -enta

Meaning: *one who; denotes profession*
English equivalent: *-ent; -ante; -er; -or*
Found in: *nouns*

The suffix *-ente* or *-enta* is one of several Spanish endings that denote *one who*. As you will see below, all of the examples are derived from *-er* and *-ir* verbs (just as words ending with *-ante* are derived from *-ar* verbs). Most nouns ending with *-ente* are both masculine and feminine in form (e.g., *el creyente; la creyente*). Sometimes, however, the ending changes to *-enta* to denote a function typically performed by women: compare *la asistenta* and *el asistente*.

Formed Word	English Equivalent	Related to	English Equivalent
el adolescente [R 1853]	adolescent	**adolecer**	to suffer
el adquirente	acquirer; purchaser	**adquirir**	to acquire, obtain, get
el arguyente	arguer	**argüir**	to argue, dispute
la asistenta	charwoman; daily help	**asistir**	to assist, attend
el asistente [R 1042]	assistant	**asistir**	to assist, attend
el combatiente [R 3961]	combatant	**combatir**	to combat
el compareciente	person appearing in court	**comparecer**	to appear in court
el contendiente [R 4312]	contender; litigant	**contender**	to contend, litigate
el contribuyente [R 2438]	contributor; taxpayer	**contribuir**	to contribute, pay taxes
el correspondiente [R 863]	correspondent	**corresponder**	to correspond
el creyente [R]	believer	**creer**	to believe
el delincuente [3080]	delinquent	**delinquir**	to commit a crime
la dependienta	shop assistant; saleswoman	**depender**	to be the responsibility of
el dependiente [R 4762]	shop assistant; salesman	**depender**	to be the responsibility of
el dirigente [R 640]	leader; director	**dirigir**	to direct
el disidente [4714]	dissident; dissenter	**disidir**	to dissent
el distribuyente	distributor	**distribuir**	to distribute
el doliente	sufferer; mourner; one in pain	**doler**	to ache, hurt, give pain, grieve
el exponente [4048]	exponent	**exponer**	to expose
el influyente [R]	influencer; person with power	**influir**	to influence
el maldiciente [R]	curser; slanderer	**maldecir**	to curse
el oponente [R 4570]	*nmf* opponent; *aj* opposing	**oponer**	to oppose
el oyente [R]	hearer; listener	**oír**	to hear, listen
la presidenta	president; president's wife	**presidir**	to preside over, govern
el presidente [R 83]	president	**presidir**	to preside over, govern
el pretendiente [R]	claimant; suitor; wooer; boyfriend	**pretender**	to try, attempt, claim; (coll.) to court
el recipiente [R 3525]	recipient	**recibir**	to receive
el regente [R]	regent	**regir**	to rule, govern, manage, run
el residente [R 2893]	resident	**residir**	to reside
el respondiente	answerer; respondent	**responder**	to answer, reply, respond
la sirvienta	servant-girl; maid	**servir**	to serve
el sirviente	servant; server	**servir**	to serve
el sobreviviente [R 4840]	survivor	**sobrevivir**	to survive
el suplente [R 4327]	replacement; substitute	**suplir**	to supply

-eño (-eña)

Meaning: *like; relating to; native; native of*
English equivalent: *-y; usually none*
Found in: *adjectives; nouns*

Spanish words ending with *-eño* indicate a similarity to or deviation from the root noun. This suffix is often similar to several other endings that mean like or relating to. When this is the case, the formed word will be an adjective only, e.g., *roqueño* (rocky). However, when *-eño* is added to the name of a place, the formed word can act either as a noun or an adjective: *La brasileña lee el periódico brasileño* (The Brazilian [woman] reads the Brazilian newspaper). These referents to places and persons are not capitalized as they are in English. When these terms refer to a feminine noun, *-eño* becomes *-eña*.

Formed Word	English Equivalent	Related to	English Equivalent
(el) brasileño [838]	Brazilian	**Brasil**	Brazil
caleño	containing lime	**la cal**	lime
(el) caribeño [4376]	*nmf* person from the Caribbean; *aj* Caribbean	**el Caribe**	Caribbean
costeño	coastal; coasting; sloping	**la costa**	coast; shore
(el) cumbreño	(native) of the top of a mountain	**la cumbre**	summit; peak
galgueño	relating to greyhounds	**el galgo**	greyhound
(el) gibraltareño	(native) of Gibraltar	**Gibraltar**	Gibraltar
(el) guadalajareño	(native) of Guadalajara	**Guadalajara**	Guadalajara
halagüeño	flattering	**el halago**	flattery
hogareño [R]	home-loving	**el hogar**	home; hearth
(el) hondureño [R]	Honduran	**Honduras**	Honduras
(el) isleño [R]	(native) of an island	**la isla**	island
(el) limeño	(native) of Lima	**Lima**	Lima
(el) lugareño	of a village; villager	**el lugar**	place; spot; village
(el) madrileño	(native) of Madrid	**Madrid**	Madrid
marfileño	of ivory; like ivory	**el marfil**	ivory
navideño [3653]	relating to Christmas	**la Navidad**	Christmas
(el) nicaragüeño	Nicaraguan	**Nicaragua**	Nicaragua
(el) norteño [R 2861]	northerner; of the north	**el norte**	north; polestar; direction
(el) panameño [3729]	Panamanian	**Panamá**	Panama
(el) puertorriqueño [2292]	Puerto Rican	**Puerto Rico**	Puerto Rico
ribereño	relating to a riverside	**la ribera**	riverside
risueño [R]	smiling; pleasant	**la risa**	laugh; laughter
roqueño	rocky	**la roca**	rock
(el) salvadoreño	Salvadorean	**El Salvador**	El Salvador
sedeño	silken	**la seda**	silk
(el) sureño [R]	southerner; of the south	**el sur**	south
trigueño	(of) wheat color	**el trigo**	wheat

-eo[(1)]

Meaning: *resulting action*
English equivalent: *-ing*
Found in: *nouns*

This suffix, one of several that denote resulting action, is distinctive in that nouns that take the ending *-eo* are derived from verbs ending in *-ear*. Thus, when you encounter such a verb, you can most likely assume that its resulting action can be formed by replacing the *-ear* with *-eo*; and when you encounter such a noun, you can nearly always do the converse to figure out the infinitive. All nouns with the *-eo* suffix are masculine.

Formed Word	English Equivalent	Related to	English Equivalent
el barqueo	boating	**barquear**	to go about in a boat
el bateo [4732]	hitting; batting (baseball)	**batear**	to bat
el bazuqueo	shaking; stirring (of liquids)	**bazuquear**	to shake (liquids)
el besuqueo [R]	slobbery kissing	**besuquear**	to kiss slobberingly
el blanqueo [R]	whitening; bleaching	**blanquear**	to whiten, bleach
el bloqueo [R 4438]	blockade	**bloquear**	to blockade, block
el bombardeo [R 4502]	bombardment	**bombardear**	to bombard
el boxeo [2695]	boxing	**boxear**	to box
el cabeceo [R]	nod; bob; shake of head	**cabecear**	to nod, bob, shake the head
el campaneo [R]	bell-ringing; chime	**campanear**	to ring bells
el careo [R]	meeting; confrontation	**carear**	to bring face to face
el ceceo	lisping	**cecear**	to lisp
el deletreo [R]	spelling	**deletrear**	to spell
el desempleo [R 2059]	unemployment	**desemplear**	to dismiss from employment
el devaneo	nonsense; loafing	**devanear**	to talk nonsense, loaf
el empleo [R 710]	employment; use	**emplear**	to employ, use
el fisgoneo	prying	**fisgonear**	to pry (into)
el paladeo	tasting; relish	**paladear**	to taste, relish, savor
el papeleo [R]	paperwork; red tape	**papelear**	to search or rummage through papers
el paseo [R 1985]	walk; stroll; ride	**pasear**	to take a walk, stroll, ride
el pateo	(coll.) kicking; stamping	**patear**	(coll.) to kick, stamp
el recreo [R]	recreation; recess; playtime	**recrear**	to divert, amuse
el repiqueteo	pealing; ringing	**repiquetear**	to chime, ring, peal
el revoloteo [R]	fluttering	**revolotear**	to flutter about
el rodeo [R 3757]	rodeo	**rodear**	to surround
el salteo	highway assault; robbery	**saltear**	to hold up, waylay, assault
el sondeo [3952]	preliminary investigation	**sondear**	to investigate cautiously
el sorteo [3833]	drawing (raffle)	**sortear**	to raffle
el tartamudeo	stuttering; stammering	**tartamudear**	to stutter, stammer
el tecleo	fingering; touching (typewriter)	**teclear**	to touch, strike (keys)
el tijereteo	clipping; snipping noise of scissors	**tijeretear**	to cut with scissors
el traqueteo	shake; rattle; chatter	**traquetear**	to shake, rattle

Formed Word	English Equivalent	Related to	English Equivalent
el voleo [R]	volley	volear	to volley
el volteo	whirling around	voltear	to whirl around
el zapateo [R]	beating; tapping of foot	zapatear	to tap dance

-eo⁽²⁾ (-ea)

Meaning: *like; relating to*
English equivalent: *-eous*
Found in: *adjectives*

Adjectives ending with *-eo* indicate that someone or something holds characteristics of the base noun. Note below that in all cases the *-eo* is preceded by a consonant (often *r*, *n*, or *c*) and that this consonant is always preceded by an accented vowel. Many of these words deal with things found in nature (plants, minerals, etc.). When describing a feminine noun, adjectives take the feminine form *-ea*.

Formed Word	English Equivalent	Related to	English Equivalent
aéreo [R 1824]	aerial; relating to air	(Lat.) **aer**	air
arbóreo [R]	arboreal; arboraceous	el arból	tree
broncíneo	of bronze; bronzelike	el bronce	bronze
cesáreo	Caesarean; like Caesar	César	Caesar
contemporáneo [R 3646]	contemporaneous; contemporary	con + el tiempo	with + time
coriáceo	pertaining to leather	el cuero	leather
corpóreo [R]	corporeal; corporal	el cuerpo	body
etéreo	ethereal	el éter	ether
férreo [R]	ferrous; made of iron	el fierro	iron
grisáceo [R]	grayish	el gris	gray (color)
limitáneo	limitary; limitaneous; bounding	el límite	limit; bound; boundary
líneo	(bot.) linaceous; lined	la línea	line
misceláneo [4612]	miscellaneous	la miscelánea	miscellany
óseo [3336]	pertaining to bone; osseous	el hueso	bone
purpúreo	purple colored	la púrpura	purple (color)
rosáceo [R]	rosaceous	la rosa	rose
rúbeo	ruby; reddish; ruddy	el rubí	ruby
sanguíneo [R 3054]	pertaining to blood	la sangre	blood
temporáneo	temporary; transient	el tiempo	time
violáceo	violaceous; violet-colored	la violeta	(bot.) violet
virgíneo	virginal	la virgen	virgin

-era

Meaning: *container; holder*
English equivalent: *none*
Found in: *nouns*

Several Spanish words for containers end in *-era*. This is a common and useful suffix, one that will enable you to learn many terms quickly and easily as most of the root words are everyday items. This ending has a sister suffix, *-ero*, that is a bit less common than *-era* but similarly denotes a container or holder for the root object. Words ending with *-era* are feminine.

Formed Word	English Equivalent	Related to	English Equivalent
la bañera [R]	bathtub	el baño	bath
la budinera	pie plate	el budín	pie
la cafetera [R 4221]	coffeepot	el café	coffee
la cajonera	chest of drawers	el cajón	drawer
la caldera [R]	soup kettle	el caldo	broth; clear soup
la carbonera [R]	coal bin	el carbón	coal
la cartera [R 3530]	briefcase; pocketbook	la carta	letter; card
la chocolatera [R]	chocolate pot	el chocolate	chocolate
la coctelera	cocktail shaker	el cóctel	cocktail
la cucarachera	nest of cockroaches; cockroach trap	la cucaracha	cockroach
la cuchillera	knife case; scabbard	el cuchillo	knife
la ensaladera	salad bowl	la ensalada	salad
la escalera [R]	staircase; stairs	la escala	stepladder; ladder
la gasolinera [R]	gas station	la gasolina	gasoline
la guantera [R]	glove compartment	el guante	glove
la jabonera [R]	soap dish	el jabón	soap
la joyera	jewelry box	la joya	jewel
la lechera	milk pitcher	la leche	milk
la leñera	woodshed; woodbin	la leña	firewood; kindling
la licorera [R]	liquor case; liquor cabinet	el licor	liquor; liqueur
la panera [R]	bread basket	el pan	bread
la papelera [R]	wastebasket; paper case	el papel	paper
la pecera	fishbowl; aquarium	el pez	fish
la perrera [R]	dog kennel	el perro	dog
la pistolera [R]	holster	la pistola	pistol
la polvera [R]	powder case; compact	el polvo	powder; dust
la ponchera	punch bowl	el ponche	punch
la pulsera	bracelet	el pulso	pulse; pulse-beat
la ratonera	mousetrap	el ratón	mouse
la regadera [R]	watering can	el riego	irrigation; watering
la relojera	clock-case; watch-case	el reloj	clock; watch; timepiece
la salsera	gravy boat	la salsa	sauce; gravy
la sombrerera [R]	hatbox	el sombrero	hat
la sopera [R]	soup tureen	la sopa	soup
la tabaquera [R]	snuffbox	el tabaco	tobacco; snuff
la tetera	teapot	el té	tea
la tortera	baking pan; deep dish	la torta	cake; pancake; pie

-ería(1)

Meaning: *shop; store*
English equivalent: *none*
Found in: *nouns*

The suffix *-ería* is commonly used in Spanish to denote a type of shop or store. The root noun to which this ending is attached is the main item being sold, dealt in, or manufactured. Remember that this suffix takes an accent over the *i* and that all the nouns ending with *-ería* are feminine.

Formed Word	English Equivalent	Related to	English Equivalent
la barbería [R]	barbershop	la barba	beard
la botellería	bottle factory	la botella	bottle
la cafetería [R]	coffee shop; cafetería	el café	coffee
la carnicería [R]	butcher shop	la carne	meat
la droguería	drugstore	la droga	drug
la dulcería [R]	candy store	el dulce	candy
la especiería	spice shop	la especia	spice
la ferretería [R]	hardware store	el fierro	iron
la floristería [R]	florist's shop	la flor	flower
la frutería [R]	fruit shop	la fruta	fruit
la guantería	glover's shop	el guante	glove
la huevería	egg store	el huevo	egg
la joyería [R 4821]	jewelry store	la joya	jewel
la juguetería [R]	toy store	el juguete	toy
la lechería [R]	milk store	le leche	milk
la librería [R]	bookstore	el libro	book
la licorería [R]	liquor store	el licor	liquor
la mantequería	grocery store	la manteca	lard
la mueblería	furniture store	el mueble	furniture
la panadería [R]	bakery	el pan	bread
la papelería [R]	stationery shop	el papel	paper
la pastelería [R]	pastry shop; bakery	el pastel	pastry; cake
la peluquería [R]	beauty shop	el pelo	hair
la pescadería [R]	fish market	el pescado	fish
la platería [R]	silversmith's shop	la plata	silver
la pollería	poultry shop	el pollo	chicken
la relojería [R]	watchmaker's shop	el reloj	watch; clock
la ropería	clothing store	la ropa	clothing
la sombrerería [R]	hat shop	el sombrero	hat
la tabaquería	tobacco shop	el tabaco	tobacco
la tortillería	tortilla shop	la tortilla	tortilla
la vaquería	dairy store	la vaca	cow
la vinatería	wine shop	el vino	wine
la zapatería [R]	shoe store	el zapato	shoe

-ería⁽²⁾; -ría; -ía

Meaning: *forms abstract noun*
English equivalent: *-ry; -ness*
Found in: *nouns*

This suffix forms an abstract noun when added to the root noun, adjective, or verb; from *el tubo* (tube) we get *la tubería* (tubing); *zalamear* (to flatter) becomes *la zalamería* (flattery). Most commonly we find *-ería*; however, at times the root term takes on *-ría* or *-ía*. All words ending with any of these suffix forms are feminine.

Formed Word	English Equivalent	Related to	English Equivalent
la alcaldía [R 3553]	city hall; office of mayor	**el alcalde**	mayor
la alegría [R 1746]	happiness	**alegre**	happy; cheerful; sunny
la armería [R]	armory; arsenal	**el arma** *nf*	arm; weapon
la asesoría [3176]	counseling	**el asesor**	counselor
la auditoría [2957]	audit; auditing	**el auditor**	auditor
la autonomía [R 3924]	autonomy	**autónomo**	autonomous
la caloría [R 3507]	calorie	**calor**	heat
la cancillería [4887]	chancellorship; office of the chancellor	**canciller**	chancellor
la carcelería	imprisonment	**la cárcel**	jail; prison
la cercanía [R 4311]	surroundings	**cercano**	nearby
la ciudadanía [R 1035]	citizenship	**el ciudadano**	citizenship
la cobardía [R]	cowardice	**el cobarde**	coward
la cohetería	rocketry	**el cohete**	rocket
la contraloría [2180]	controllership; comptrollership; office of of the controller; office of the comptroller	**el contralor**	controller
la españolería	that which is purely Spanish	**España**	Spain
la estantería	shelving	**el estante**	shelf
la filigresía [R 3917]	parish; congregation	**el feligrés**	parishioner
la filosofía [R 3917]	philosophy	**el filósofo**	philosopher
la fiscalía [R 3201]	office of the attorney general	**fiscal**	fiscal
la fotografía [R 1473]	photography	**el fotógrafo**	photographer
la galantería [R]	gallantry	**galante**	gallant
la ganadería [R 2481]	cattle-raising	**el ganado**	cattle
la geografía [R 4629]	geography	**el geógrafo**	geographer
la gitanería [R]	gypsies; gypsydom	**el gitano**	gypsy
la golfería	loafing; hanging around	**golfear**	to loaf, hang around
la grosería [R]	grossness; rudeness	**grosero**	gross; rude; coarse
la hombría [R]	manliness	**el hombre**	man
la hotelería	hotel-keeping	**el hotel**	hotel
la ingeniería [R 3966]	engineering	**el ingeniero**	engineer
la joyería [R 4821]	jewelry store	**joya**	jewel
la mayoría [R 410]	majority	**mayor**	major
la mejoría [R 4194]	improvement	**mejor**	better
la palabrería	verbiage	**la palabra**	word

Formed Word	English Equivalent	Related to	English Equivalent
la pobrería/pobretería	poverty; beggars; wretched people	el pobre	poor person; pauper; beggar
la policía [R 221]	police	(Gr.) polis	city
la ratería	petty thieving; pilfering	ratear	to pilfer, filch
la relojería [R]	(the art of) clock making	el reloj	clock; watch; timepiece
la roñería	stinginess	la roña	(coll.) stingy individual
la sabiduría [R 4838]	wisdom; learning; knowledge	(el) sabio	sage; wise; learned (person)
la soberanía [4068]	sovereignty	el soberano	sovereign
la soltería [R 4053]	bachelorhood	el soltero	bachelor
la supremacía [R]	supremacy	supremo	supreme; final; last
la tecnología [R 1168]	technology	el técnico	technician
la telefonía [R 3834]	telephony	el teléfono	telephone
la tesorería [R 4165]	treasury	el tesoro	treasure
la trapacería	fraud; deceit	trapacear	to deceive, cheat, swindle
la tubería [R 2903]	tubing; piping	el tubo	tube
la vidriería [R]	glassware	el vidrio	glass
la villanía	meanness; lowness of birth	villano	rustic; boorish; low-class
la vinatería	vintnery; wine trade	el vino	wine
la vocería	clamor; hallooing; outcry	vocear	to yell, bawl, cry out
la yesería [R]	plasterwork	el yeso	plaster; gypsum
la zalamería	flattery; adulation	zalamear	to flatter
la zapatería [R]	shoemaker's trade	el zapato	shoe

-erizo (-eriza)

Meaning: *herder*
English equivalent: *-herd*
Found in: *nouns*

The suffix *-erizo* is very specialized, and, as a result, there are few Spanish words that take this ending. The base term is the name of the particular animal being tended to or herded, and the formed word is the name for the person doing the tending or herding. When this person is female, the suffix becomes *-eriza*.

Formed Word	English Equivalent	Related to	English Equivalent
el boyerizo	ox-herd; ox driver	el buey	ox
el caballerizo	head groom (of a stable)	el caballo	horse
el cabrerizo	goatherd	la cabra	goat
el porquerizo	swineherd	el puerco	pig; hog
el vaquerizo	herdsman	la vaca	cow
el yegüerizo	keeper of mares	la yegua	mare

-ero⁽¹⁾

Meaning: *container; holder*
English equivalent: *none*
Found in: *nouns*

The ending *-ero* is a handy suffix that will enable you to learn many new words quickly, as most of the root words are common items. This ending has a sister suffix, *-era*, that is somewhat more common than *-ero* but that performs the same function, namely, to denote a container or holder for the root term. Words ending with *-ero* are masculine.

Formed Word	English Equivalent	Related to	English Equivalent
el alfiletero [R]	pincushion; pin-case	**el alfiler**	pin
el arenillero	sandbox	**la arena**	sand
el azucarero [R]	sugar bowl	**el azúcar**	sugar
el basurero [4902]	garbage can; dump	**la basura**	refuse; rubbish; garbage; trash
el brasero	brazier; pan to hold coals	**la brasa**	live coal; red-hot coal or wood
el cenicero [4734]	ashtray	**la ceniza**	ash
el cerillero	matchbox; matchbook	**el cerillo**	wax match
el cervecero	set of beer mugs	**la cerveza**	beer
el cochero [R]	garage	**el coche**	car
el costurero	sewing room; sewing basket	**la costura**	sewing; stitching; seam
el cucharero	spoon rack	**la cuchara**	spoon
el florero [R]	vase; flowerpot	**la flor**	flower
el frutero [R]	fruit bowl or dish	**la fruta**	fruit
el gatero	cat carrier	**el gato**	cat
el gavillero	place where sheaves are collected	**la gavilla**	sheaf; (fig.) gang (of low people)
el harinero	flour bin	**la harina**	flour
el helero	glacier	**el hielo**	ice
el hormiguero	anthill	**la hormiga**	ant
el lapicero [R]	pencil-case; pencil holder	**el lápiz**	pencil
el llavero [R]	key ring	**la llave**	key
el mantequero	butter dish	**la manteca**	lard; grease; fat; pomade
el paragüero [R]	umbrella stand	**el paraguas**	umbrella
el pastillero	pillbox	**la pastilla**	pill; tablet
el pimentero	pepper shaker	**la pimienta**	pepper
el ropero [R]	wardrobe; locker	**la ropa**	clothing
el salero [R]	salt cellar	**la sal**	salt
el servilletero [R]	napkin ring	**la servilleta**	napkin
el toallero	towel rack	**la toalla**	towel

-ero(2) (-era)

Meaning: *like; relating to; able to*
English equivalent: *-y; -able*
Found in: *adjectives*

The use of this suffix *-ero* produces adjectives that refer to the properties of the root noun or verb. When derived from a noun, it means "like" or "relating to," e.g., *suertero* (lucky) from *la suerte* (luck). When derived from a verb, it means "able to," e.g., *bebedero* (drinkable) from *beber* (to drink). When the base term is a verb, a *d* is added between the infinitive stem and the suffix *-ero*. The ending *-ero* becomes *-era* when these formed words describe feminine nouns.

Formed Word	English Equivalent	Related to	English Equivalent
aduanero	relating to customs	**la aduana**	customs
algodonero [4151]	cottony; pertaining to cotton	**el algodón**	cotton
azucarero [R]	relating to sugar	**el azúcar**	sugar
bananero	relating to bananas	**la banana**	banana
bebedero [R]	drinkable	**beber**	to drink
bracero	relating to the arm	**el brazo**	arm
callejero [R 3990]	pertaining to streets; street-walking	**la calle**	street
camero	relating to the bed	**la cama**	bed
caminero	relating to a road or highway	**el camino**	road; highway
campero [R]	of the country; rustic	**el campo**	country
carbonero [R]	relating to coal or charcoal	**el carbón**	coal; charcoal; carbon
casadero [R]	marriageable	**casar(se)**	to marry
cucarachero	sneaky; sly	**la cucaracha**	cockroach
delantero [R 1235]	head; front	**adelante**	ahead
faldero [R]	of skirts or the lap	**la falda**	skirt
financiero [666]	financial	**las finanzas**	finances
guerrero [R]	warlike	**la guerra**	war
harinero	of flour	**la harina**	flour
hormiguero	pertaining to ants; feeding on ants	**la hormiga**	ant
lastimero [R]	hurtful; injurious; pitiful	**la lástima**	pity; shame
lechero [R 3062]	milk-producing or containing; pertaining to milk	**la leche**	milk
llevadero	bearable; tolerable	**llevar**	to bear, carry
maderero [R]	of wood or lumber	**la madera**	wood; timber
manufacturero [R 4704]	manufacturing	**la manufactura**	manufacturing
mañanero [R]	relating to morning	**la mañana**	morning
milagrero	miracle-working; superstitious	**el milagro**	miracle
minero [R 2824]	pertaining to mining	**la mina**	mining
noticiero [R]	news-bearing; news-giving	**la noticia**	news; news item
novelero [R]	fond of the latest fad or craze	**novel**	new; inexperienced
ovejero	relating to sheep	**la oveja**	ewe; female sheep
palabrero	wordy; talkative	**la palabra**	word
pañero	of cloth	**el paño**	cloth

Formed Word	English Equivalent	Related to	English Equivalent
pasajero [R 1919]	passing	el pasaje	passing; passage (fare)
pendenciero	quarrelsome	la pendencia	quarrel; dispute
perecedero [R]	perishable	perecer	to perish
petrolero [R 1761]	pertaining to petroleum	el petróleo	petroleum; oil
pinturero	showy; flashy	la pintura	painting; picture
placero	pertaining to the marketplace	la plaza	square; marketplace; market
playero [R 4213]	relating to the beach	la playa	beach
ranchero [3044]	relating to the ranch	el rancho	ranch
sensiblero	sentimental	sensible	sensitive; sentient
severo [R 2405]	severe; harsh	severidad	severity
sincero [R 4466]	sincere	sinceridad	sincerity
soltero [R 1465]	single; unmarried	la soltería	bachelorhood
suertero	lucky; fortunate	la suerte	luck
taquillero [4842]	relating to the box office	la taquilla	ticket window
tercero [R 225]	third (shortened form *tercer* is used before masculine nouns)	tres	three
terrero	earthy; of the earth	la tierra	earth; land
tomatero [4642]	pertaining to tomato	el tomate	tomato
torero [R 3551]	relating to bullfighting	el toro	bull
traicionero [R]	treacherous; deceptive	la traición	treason; treachery
trasero [3661]	back	tras	after
vaquero [2869]	cowboy	la vaca	cow
verdadero [R 925]	true; real; truthful	la verdad	truth
zaguero [4149]	back (sport)	zaga	rear

-ero⁽³⁾ (-era)

Meaning: *one who; denotes profession*
English equivalent: *-er; -man; -person*
Found in: *nouns*

In this group of words, the ending *-ero* combines with the root noun to name a person in a particular profession. The root noun can denote what the person works with, e.g., *el cartero* (mailman) works with *la carta* (letter), or the root noun can indicate where the person works, e.g., *el cocinero* (cook) works in *la cocina* (the kitchen). When the worker is female, the suffix becomes *-era*.

Formed Word	English Equivalent	Related to	English Equivalent
el acerero [2781]	steelworker; *nmpl* Steelers (NFL football team from Pittsburgh)	el acero	steel
el algodonero [4151]	person who picks cotton	el algodón	cotton
el arquero [2700]	archer; goalkeeper (soccer)	el arco	bow (military)
el banquero [3780]	banker	el banco	bank
el barbero [R]	barber	la barba	beard
el basurero [4902]	garbage collector	la basura	refuse; rubbish; garbage; trash

Formed Word	English Equivalent	Related to	English Equivalent
el carnerero	shepherd	el carnero	sheep
el carnicero [R]	butcher	la carne	meat
el cartero	mailman	la carta	letter
el casero [R]	landlord	la casa	house
el cervecero	brewer	la cerveza	beer
el chispero	blacksmith	la chispa	spark
el cochero [R]	driver	el coche	car
el cocinero	cook	la cocina	kitchen
el droguero	druggist	la droga	drug
el florero [R]	florist; flower-seller	la flor	flower
el fontanero	plumber	la fontana	fountain
el graffitero [4790]	graffiti writer	los graffiti	graffiti
el granjero [R]	farmer	la granja	farm
el grupero [4716]	*nmf* fans or players of *música grupera*	el grupo	group
el guerrero [R]	warrior; fighter	la guerra	war
el guerrillero [3596]	guerrilla fighter	la guerrilla	guerrilla warfare; special military force or group of guerrilla fighters
el jornalero	day laborer; journeyman	el jornal	day work; day's work
el lechero [R 3062]	milkman	la leche	milk
el librero [R]	bookseller	el libro	book
el maletero	suitcase maker or seller; porter	la maleta	suitcase
el marinero [R]	sailor	la marina	shore; seacoast
el mensajero [R]	messenger	el mensaje	message
el mesero	waiter	la mesa	table
el panadero	baker	el pan	bread
el pandillero [4896]	gang member	la pandilla	gang
el pasajero [R 1919]	*nmf* passenger; *aj* passing	el pasaje	passage
el peluquero	hairdresser	el pelo	hair
el perrero [R]	kennel-keeper; dog fancier	el perro	dog
el petrolero [R 1761]	*nm* oil tanker; *nmf* petroleum merchant	el petróleo	petroleum
el pistolero [R]	gunman; gangster	la pistola	pistol
el platero	silversmith	la plata	silver
el prisionero	prisoner	la prisión	prison
el ranchero [3044]	*nmf* person who lives on a ranch	el rancho	ranch
el relojero	watchmaker; clockmaker	el reloj	clock; watch; timepiece
el rockero [3515]	*nmf* fan of rock music; rock music singer; *aj* fond of rock music	el rock	rock (music)
el tendero	shopkeeper	la tienda	shop; store
el tesorero [2911]	treasurer	el tesoro	treasure
el tilichero	peddler	el tiliche	trinket
el torero [R 3551]	bullfighter	el toro	bull
el vaquero [2869]	cowherd; cowboy	la vaca	cow
el viajero [R 3939]	traveler	el viaje	trip; voyage; journey
el vidriero	glazier; glass-blower	el vidrio	glass

Formed Word	English Equivalent	Related to	English Equivalent
el zaguero [4149]	back (sport)	**la zaga**	rear
el zapatero	shoemaker; shoe salesman	**el zapato**	shoe

-ero⁽⁴⁾; -era

Meaning: *tree; plant; place where plants grow*
English equivalent: *none*
Found in: *nouns*

The ending *-ero*, or less commonly *-era*, is sometimes used to denote the name of a tree, a plant, or a place where it grows. The root noun usualy is the name of the fruit, nut, vegetable, or product the tree or plant produces. Generally speaking, if this root noun ends in a vowel, drop that vowel and add *-ero* or *-era*; if the root noun ends in a consonant, add the suffix directly. Words ending with *-ero* are masculine, while those ending with *-era* are feminine.

Formed Word	English Equivalent	Related to	English Equivalent
el albaricoquero	apricot tree	**el albaricoque**	apricot
el alcachofero	artichoke plant	**la alcachofa**	artichoke
el algodonero [4151]	cotton plant	**el algodón**	cotton
la avellanera	hazel tree; filbert tree	**la avellana**	hazelnut; filbert
la castañera	(prov.) area rich in chestnut trees	**el castaño**	chestnut tree
el clavero	clove tree	**el clavo**	clove
la datilera	date palm	**el dátil**	date
el fresero	strawberry plant	**la fresa**	strawberry
la higuera	fig tree	**el higo**	fig
el limero [R]	lime tree	**la lima**	lime
el limonero [R]	lemon tree	**el limón**	lemon
el melocotonero	peach tree	**el melocotón**	peach
la noguera	grove of walnut trees	**el nogal**	walnut tree; walnut wood
el pimentero	pepper plant	**el pimiento**	pepper
el semillero [R]	seedbed; seed-plot	**la semilla**	seed
el tomatero [4642]	tomato plant	**el tomate**	tomato
el vivero [R 4089]	(hort.) nursery	**el vivir**	life

-érrimo (-érrima)

Meaning: *adjectival superlative*
English equivalent: *none*
Found in: *adjectives*

The ending *-érrimo* is very uncommon and therefore often unrecognized. This is because *-érrimo* does exactly what the frequently used suffix *-ísimo* does but in a specific situation: note below that in all cases the adjectives in the "Related to" column have as their final consonant the letter *r*. This is a prerequisite for using *-érrimo*; otherwise, you will use *-ísimo*. As this is an adjectival ending, when these words describe feminine nouns, the suffix becomes *-érrima*.

Formed Word	English Equivalent	Related to	English Equivalent
acérrimo	extremely bitter	**acre**	acrid; bitter; sour
aspérrimo	extremely rough; harsh	**áspero**	rough; harsh
celebérrimo	extremely famous	**célebre**	celebrated; famous
integérrimo	most honest; upright	**íntegro**	integral; upright; honest
libérrimo	extremely free	**libre**	free; detached
lugubérrimo	extremely mournful; sad	**lúgubre**	lugubrious; mournful
misérrimo	extremely miserable, miserly	**mísero**	miserable; miserly
paupérrimo	extremely poor	*(Lat.)* **pauper**	poor
salubérrimo	most salubrious	**salubre**	salubrious; healthy
ubérrimo	very fruitful; abundant	*(Lat.)* **uber**	rich; fruitful; fertile

-és (-esa)

Meaning: *native; native of; like; relating to*
English equivalent: *-ese*
Found in: *nouns; adjectives*

The suffix *-és* is one of a number of Spanish endings that denote origin. Like these other endings, *-és* (*-esa* when denoting or describing a feminine noun) can function either as a noun or an adjective: *El japonés sirve el café francés a la barcelonesa* (The Japanese man serves the French coffee to the woman from Barcelona). Note that these terms are not capitalized, that when referring to a person you need not mention man or woman (the gender of the ending makes that clear), and that the accent in the masculine form (*-és*) is not needed in the feminine form (*-esa*).

Formed Word	English Equivalent	Related to	English Equivalent
(el) aragonés	Aragonese (native)	**Aragón**	Aragon
(el) barcelonés	(native) of Barcelona	**Barcelona**	Barcelona
(el) berlinés	(native) of Berlin	**Berlín**	Berlin
(el) bernés	Bernese (native)	**Berna**	Bern
(el) burgués [R]	(of or from) the middle class	**el burgo**	borough
(el) danés [4440]	Danish (native)	**Dinamarca**	Denmark
(el) escocés [4980]	Scottish (native)	**Escocia**	Scotland
(el) finlandés	Finnish (native)	**Finlandia**	Finland
(el) francés	French (native)	**Francia**	France
(el) groenlandés	(native) of Greenland	**Groenlandia**	Greenland
(el) hamburgués	(native) of Hamburg	**Hamburgo**	Hamburg
(el) holandés	(native) of Holland; Dutch	**Holanda**	Holland
(el) inglés	English (native)	**Inglaterra**	England
(el) irlandés [3846]	Irish (native)	**Irlanda**	Ireland
(el) japonés [2042]	Japanese (native)	**Japón**	Japan
(el) libanés	Lebanese (native)	**Líbano**	Lebanon
(el) lisbonés	(native) of Lisbon	**Lisboa**	Lisbon
(el) luxemburgués	(native) of Luxembourg	**Luxemburgo**	Luxembourg
(el) milanés	Milanese (native)	**Milán**	Milan

Formed Word	English Equivalent	Related to	English Equivalent
(el) montañés [R]	(of or from) the mountain	la montaña	mountain
(el) neocelandés	(native) of New Zealand	Nueva Zelanda	New Zealand
(el) neoescocés	(native) of Nova Scotia	Nueva Escocia	Nova Scotia
(el) nepalés	(native) of Nepal	Nepal	Nepal
(el) pequinés	Beijing (native)	Pequín	Beijing
(el) polonés	Polish (native)	Polonia	Poland
(el) portugués [3436]	Portuguese (native)	Portugal	Portugal
(el) salamanqués	(native) of Salamanca	Salamanca	Salamanca
(el) siamés	Siamese (native)	Siam	Siam
(el) tailandés	(native) of Thailand	Tailandia	Thailand
(el) vienés	Viennese (native)	Viena	Vienna

-esco (-esca)

Meaning: *in the manner or style of; relating to; resembling*
English equivalent: *-esque*
Found in: *adjectives*

In the study of Spanish suffixes, one soon learns that there are several adjectival suffixes that mean "like, relating to," etc. The suffix *-esco*, however, appears to be the strongest of these, for it often implies a capturing of the essence of the root noun. This is clearly seen in *sanchopancesco* and *quijotesco*, where the root nouns are the two famous literary characters Sancho Panza and Don Quixote. Because their personality traits are strong and focused, each can denote one characteristic, materialistic and foolishly idealistic, respectively. When such a word describes a feminine noun, the ending changes to *-esca*.

Formed Word	English Equivalent	Related to	English Equivalent
arabesco	arabesque; Arabian	Arabia	Arabia
brujesco	relating to witchcraft	la bruja	witch
bufonesco	buffoonish; farcical	el bufón	buffoon; clown; jester
burlesco [R]	burlesque; comical	la burla	hoax; mockery; scoff(ing)
caballeresco [R]	chivalrous; gentlemanly	el caballero	knight; gentleman
camaleonesco	like a chameleon	el camaleón	chameleon
carnavalesco	carnival-like	el carnaval	carnival
cervantesco	in the style of Cervantes	Cervantes	(Miguel) Cervantes
chinesco	Chinese-like	chino	Chinese
dantesco	Dantesque; nightmarish	Dante	Dante (Alighieri)
gatesco	(coll.) feline; catlike	el gato	cat
germanesco	relating to jargon	la germanía	jargon; cant; slang
gigantesco [R 4874]	like a giant; gigantic	el gigante	giant
gitanesco	gypsylike	el gitano	gypsy
goyesco	of Goya; Goyesque	Goya	(Francisco) Goya
guitarresco	(coll.) of or doing with guitars	la guitarra	guitar
hampesco	relating to the underworld	el hampa	underworld
libresco	bookish	el libro	book
marinesco	like a sailor	el marino	sailor; mariner

Formed Word	English Equivalent	Related to	English Equivalent
medievalesco	pertaining to medieval period	Edad Media	Middle Ages
monesco	apish; monkeyish	el mono	monkey
novelesco [R]	novelistic; like a novel	la novela	novel
oficinesco	clerical; bureaucratic	la oficina	office
pedantesco	absurdly pedantic	el pedante	pedant
picaresco	roguish; rascally	el pícaro	rogue; schemer
pintoresco [R]	picturesque; colorful	la pintura	painting; picture; paint
quijotesco	quixotic	Don Quijote	Don Quixote
romanesco	Roman; Romanesque	Roma	Rome
rufianesco	of pimps or scoundrels	el rufián	pimp; rascal
sanchopancesco	like Sancho Panza; materialistic	Sancho Panza	Sancho Panza
soldadesco [R]	like a soldier	el soldado	soldier
trovadoresco	like a troubadour	el trovador	troubadour
villanesco	boorish; crude; rustic	el villano	peasant; knave; scoundrel

-ésimo (-ésima); -imo (-ima)

Meaning: *denotes ordinal number*
English equivalent: *-th*
Found in: *adjectives*

To form ordinal numbers in English, generally we add "-th" to the cardinal number base (e.g., seven, seventh; ten, tenth; etc.). When you see a Spanish word with *-ésimo* or *-imo* at the end or even inside the word (e.g., *decimosexto*), you can be quite certain that you have an ordinal number and that generally it relates to the Latin name of its base number. Because ordinal numbers are adjectives, when used to describe nouns of the feminine gender, the suffix becomes *-ésima* or *-ima*.

Formed Word	English Equivalent	Related to	English Equivalent
séptimo [R 1550]	seventh	(Lat.) septem	seven
décimo [R 2179]	tenth	(Lat.) decem	ten
undécimo [R]	eleventh	(Lat.) undecim	eleven
duodécimo	twelfth	(Lat.) duodecim	twelve
decimocuarto [R]	fourteenth	(Lat.) quattuordecim	fourteen
decimoquinto [R]	fifteenth	(Lat.) quindecim	fifteen
decimosexto [R]	sixteenth	(Lat.) sedecim	sixteen
decimoséptimo [R]	seventeenth	(Lat.) septemdecim	seventeen
decimoctavo [R]	eighteenth	(Lat.) decem et octo	eighteen
decimonoveno [R]	nineteenth	(Lat.) decem et novem	nineteen
vigésimo	twentieth	(Lat.) viginti	twenty
trigésimo	thirtieth	(Lat.) triginta	thirty
cuadragésimo [R]	fortieth	(Lat.) quadraginta	forty
quincuagésimo [R]	fiftieth	(Lat.) quinquaginta	fifty
sexagésimo [R]	sixtieth	(Lat.) sexaginta	sixty
septuagésimo [R]	seventieth	(Lat.) septuaginta	seventy
octogésimo	eightieth	(Lat.) octoginta	eighty
nonagésimo	ninetieth	(Lat.) nonaginta	ninety

Formed Word	English Equivalent	Related to	English Equivalent
centésimo [R]	one-hundredth	(Lat.) **centum**	one hundred
ducentésimo	two-hundredth	(Lat.) **ducenti**	two hundred
triventésimo	three-hundredth	(Lat.) **trecenti**	three hundred
cuadringentésimo	four-hundredth	(Lat.) **quadringenti**	four hundred
quingentésimo	five-hundredth	(Lat.) **quingenti**	five hundred
sexcentésimo	six-hundredth	(Lat.) **sescenti**	six hundred
septingentésimo	seven-hundredth	(Lat.) **septingenti**	seven hundred
octingentésimo	eight-hundredth	(Lat.) **octingenti**	eight hundred
noningentésimo	nine-hundredth	(Lat.) **nongenti**	nine hundred
milésimo [R]	one-thousandth	**mil**	one thousand
dosmilésimo	two-thousandth	**dos mil**	two thousand
tresmilésimo	three-thousandth	**tres mil**	three thousand
millonésimo [R]	millionth	**un millón**	one million
billonésimo	billionth	**un billón**	one billion

-estre

Meaning: *like; relating to; denotes period of time*
English equivalent: *-estrian; -ester*
Found in: *adjectives; nouns*

The uncommon ending *-estre* usually is found in adjectives, indicating a relationship between the base term and the person or thing described. Note that while in English *pedestrian* can function either as an adjective or a noun, in Spanish, its counterpart *pedestre* is an adjective only (*el peatón* is the person walking across the street). As a noun ending, we see *-estre* as a time-marker of sorts: *el semestre* (semester) is generally half a school year. All nouns ending in *-estre* are masculine.

Formed Word	English Equivalent	Related to	English Equivalent
alpestre	alpine; Alpine	**los Alpes**	Alps; high mountains
campestre [R 1902]	country-like; rural; bucolic	**el campo**	country; field
el cuatrimestre	period of four months	**cuatro + mes**	four + month
ecuestre	equestrian	(Lat.) **equus**	horse
pedestre [R]	pedestrian	(Lat.) **pes**	foot
el semestre [2760]	semester	(Lat.) **sex + mensis**	six + month
silvestre	wild; uncivilized	**la selva**	jungle; forest; tropical forest
terrestre [R 4659]	terrestrial	**la tierra**	earth; land
el trimestre [1797]	trimester; academic quarter	(Lat.) **tres + mensis**	three + month

-eta

Meaning: *diminutive*
English equivalent: *none*
Found in: *nouns*

The suffix *-eta* is one of many Spanish word endings that act as diminutives. Its sister suffix, *-ete*, differs from *-eta* only in gender. All words ending with *-eta* are feminine.

Formed Word	English Equivalent	Related to	English Equivalent
la aleta [R]	small wing	el ala *nf*	wing
la avioneta [R]	small airplane	el avión	airplane
la barreta	small bar	la barra	bar; beam
la buseta	small bus; van	el autobús	bus
la cajeta	small box	la caja	box; case
la camioneta [R 1398]	van	el camión	truck
la camiseta [R 3187]	T-shirt; sports shirt	la camisa	shirt
la caseta [4353]	cabin	la casa	house
la cazoleta	small pan	el cazo	pan
la coleta	ponytail (hair)	la cola	tail
la cuarteta	(poet.) quatrain	el cuarto	fourth; fourth part
la cuchareta	small spoon	la cuchara	spoon
la faceta [4316]	facet; feature	la faz	face; (arch.) front
la faldeta	miniskirt	la falda	skirt
la historieta [R]	little story	la historia	story
la isleta	small isle; islet	la isla	isle; island
la lengüeta	small tongue	la lengua	tongue
la libreta [R]	bankbook; savings book; notebook	el libro	book
la manteleta [R]	mantelet; small scarf or mantle	el mantel	tablecloth; altar cloth
la opereta	operetta	la ópera	opera
la orejeta	small ear	la oreja	ear
la paleta	small shovel; fire shovel; palette	la pala	shovel
la papeleta [R]	scrap of paper	el papel	paper
la peineta [R]	curved comb; back comb	el peine	comb
la pileta	small basin	la pila	basin; water trough; font
la ropeta	short garment	la ropa	clothes; clothing
la serreta	small saw	la sierra	saw
la tarjeta [1938]	card	la tarja	visiting card
la tijereta	earwig	la tijera	scissors
la tineta	small tub	la tina	wooden vat; tub
la veleta	weathervane; pennant; streamer	la vela	sail; awning
la vinagreta [R]	vinaigrette sauce	el vinagre	vinegar
la voltereta [R]	tumble; handspring; somersault	el volteo	whirling around

-ete

Meaning: *diminutive*
English equivalent: *none*
Found in: *nouns*

The suffix *-ete* is one of many Spanish word endings that indicate smallness of the root word. It has a sister suffix, *-eta*, which differs from *-ete* in gender only. All nouns ending with *-ete* are masculine.

Formed Word	English Equivalent	Related to	English Equivalent
el anillete	small ring	el anillo	ring
el arete	small earring	el aro	hoop
el asperete	sour taste	áspero	(fig.) sour; sharp
el atabalete	small kettle-drum	el atabal	kettle-drum
el banquete [R 3806]	banquet; feast	el banco	bench; pew
el barrilete	keg	el barril	barrel; cask
el blanquete	whitening skin cosmetic; whitewash	el blanco	white (color)
el bracete	small arm	el brazo	arm
el caballete	small horse	el caballo	horse
el cañete	small tube	el caño	tube; pipe; gutter
el clarinete	clarinet	el clarín	clarion; organ-stop
el colorete [R]	rouge	el color	color; complexion; blush
el gafete	clasp; hook and eye	la gafa	hook; cramp (for holding together)
el gorrete	small cap	la gorra	cap; baseball cap
el guantelete	gauntlet	el guante	glove
el inglete	diagonal; angle of 45 degrees	la ingle	groin
el juguete [R 2872]	toy	el juego	game
el librete	small book	el libro	book
el mollete	fleshy part (of the arm)	la molla	(coll.) fat (of a person)
el ojete	eyelet-hole	el ojo	eye
el paquete [2016]	packet; parcel	la paca	bundle; bale
el sombrerete	small hat	el sombrero	hat
el soplete [R]	blowpipe; blowtorch	el soplo	blowing; blast; gust
el sorbete	sherbet	el sorbo	swallow; gulp
el templete	small temple; niche	el templo	temple; church
el tenderete [R]	(ramshackle) stall or stand	la tienda	shop
el tonelete	small cask; keg	el tonel	cask; barrel
el torete	bullock	el toro	bull

-ez

Meaning: *state of being; forms abstract noun*
English equivalent: *-ness; -ity*
Found in: *noun*

Spanish nouns ending in *-ez* denote a state of being that relates to the root word, which almost always is an adjective. Generally speaking, if the root word ends in a vowel, that vowel is dropped and *-ez* is then added; if the root word ends in a consonant, the suffix *-ez* is added directly. The ending *-ez* has a sister suffix, *-eza*, which is similar in both meaning and formation. All nouns ending in *-ez* are feminine.

Formed Word	English Equivalent	Related to	English Equivalent
la adultez	adulthood	**adulto**	adult
la amarillez [R]	yellowness	**amarillo**	yellow
la aridez [R]	dryness; aridity; aridness	**árido**	arid; dry
la azulez	blueness	**azul**	blue
la delgadez [R]	leanness; slimness	**delgado**	lean; slim
la escasez [R 3594]	scarcity	**escaso**	scarce
la estupidez [R]	stupidity	**estúpido**	stupid
la flaccidez/flacidez	flaccidity; flabbiness	**fláccido/flácido**	flaccid; flabby
la frigidez [R]	frigidity	**frígido**	frigid
la languidez	languor	**lánguido**	languid; languorous
la liquidez [R]	liquidness; liquidity	**líquido**	liquid; (com.) net amount; profit
la lividez	lividity; lividness	**lívido**	livid
la lobreguez	darkness; gloominess	**lóbrego**	dark; gloomy; murky; dingy
la lucidez [R]	lucidity	**lúcido**	lucid
la madurez [R 3351]	maturity; ripeness	**maduro**	mature; ripe; middle-aged
la magrez	thinness; leanness	**magro**	lean; thin
la marchitez	withering; fading	**marchito**	faded; withered
la matidez	dullness (of light or sound)	**mate**	mat; dull; lusterless
la mentecatez	stupidity; dim-wittedness	**mentecato**	simple; foolish
la muchachez	childhood; puerility	**el muchacho**	boy; lad; chap
la niñez [R 4318]	childhood	**el niño**	child; little boy
la nitidez	clarity; brightness; sharpness	**nítido**	clear; bright; sharply defined
la pequeñez [R]	littleness; smallness	**pequeño**	little; small
la pesadez [R]	heaviness; sluggishness	**pesado**	heavy; sluggish; sultry
la pulidez	neatness; cleanliness	**pulido**	neat; clean
la putridez	putridity; rottenness	**pútrido**	putrid
la rapidez [R 4636]	rapidity; swiftness	**rápido**	rapid; swift; fast
la robustez [R]	hardiness; robustness	**robusto**	hardy; robust
la rojez [R]	redness	**rojo**	red
la salvajez	savageness; savagery	**salvaje**	savage; barbarous; wild
la sencillez [R]	simplicity	**sencillo**	simple
la sensatez [R]	sensibleness; good sense	**sensato**	sensible; level-headed
la timidez [R]	timidity; shyness	**tímido**	timid; shy
la validez [R]	validity	**válido**	valid
la vejez [R]	oldness	**viejo**	old

-eza

Meaning: *state of being; forms abstract noun*
English equivalent: *-ness; -ity*
Found in: *nouns*

Spanish nouns ending in *-eza* denote a state of being that relates to the root word, which is almost always an adjective. Generally speaking, if the root term ends in a vowel, that vowel is dropped and the suffix is then added; if the root ends in a consonant, you add *-eza* directly. The ending *-eza* has a sister suffix, *-ez*, which is similar in both meaning and formation. All nouns ending in *-eza* are feminine.

Formed Word	English Equivalent	Related to	English Equivalent
la agudeza	acuteness; fineness; smartness	**agudo**	acute; sharp; keen
la bajeza [R]	baseness	**bajo**	base; low; short
la belleza [R 1651]	beauty; loveliness	**bello**	beautiful; lovely
la certeza [R 3860]	certainty; certitude	**cierto**	certain; sure; true
la dureza	hardness	**duro**	hard
la flaqueza [R]	thinness	**flaco**	thin
la franqueza	candor; candidness	**franco**	candid; frank
la gentileza	gentility; gentleness; grace	**gentil**	gentle; genteel; graceful
la grandeza [R]	greatness; grandeur	**grande**	great; grand; big
la guapeza	(coll.) guts; daring	**guapo**	(coll.) having guts; showy
la largueza	length; liberality	**largo**	long
la limpieza [R 1446]	cleanliness; cleanness	**limpio**	clean; clear
la lindeza [R]	prettiness; neatness	**lindo**	pretty; neat; nice
la majeza	boldness; flamboyance	**majo**	free; nonchalant; sporty
la maleza	weeds; thicket; underbrush	**malo**	bad; evil
la naturaleza [R 1697]	nature; temperament	**natural**	natural; usual
la nobleza [R]	nobility; nobleness	**noble**	noble
la pobreza [R 1477]	poverty; want; lack	**pobre**	poor
la presteza	quickness; promptitude	**presto**	quick; prompt; ready
la pureza [R]	purity	**puro**	pure
la rareza [R]	rareness; rarity	**raro**	rare
la riqueza [R 2408]	richness; wealth	**rico**	rich; wealthy
la rudeza	roughness; coarseness; crudeness	**rudo**	rough; coarse; crude
la sutileza [R]	subtlety; subtility	**sutil**	subtle
la terneza	tenderness; softness	**tierno**	tender
la tibieza	lukewarmness; coolness	**tibio**	lukewarm
la torpeza [R]	clumsiness	**torpe**	clumsy
la tristeza [R 2721]	sadness	**triste**	sad
la viveza [R]	liveliness	**vivo**	alive; lively

-fobia

Meaning: *fear*
English equivalent: *-phobia*
Found in: *nouns*

The following words ending with *-fobia* should be very easy to recognize and use because they are almost perfect cognates of their English counterparts. The *ph* in English always appears as an *f* in Spanish: *el teléfono* (telephone), *el elefante* (elephant), and so on. All words ending with *-fobia* are feminine.

Formed Word	English Equivalent	Related to	English Equivalent
la acrofobia	acrophobia; fear of heights	(Gr.) **akros**	highest
la agorafobia	agoraphobia; fear of open spaces	(Gr.) **agora**	marketplace
la androfobia	androphobia; fear and hatred of men	(Gr.) **aner**	man
la anglofobia	Anglophobia; hatred of the English	(Lat.) **Anglii**	the English
la claustrofobia [R]	claustrophobia; fear of small spaces	(Lat.) **claustrum**	confined spaces
la fotofobia	fear of light	(Gr.) **phos**	light
la hemofobia	fear of blood	(Gr.) **haima**	blood
la hidrofobia	hydrophobia; fear of water; rabies	(Gr.) **hydor**	water
la necrofobia	fear of death	(Gr.) **nekros**	dead body
la xenofobia	xenophobia; fear of strangers	(Gr.) **xenos**	stranger

-ible

Meaning: *able to; capable of*
English equivalent: *-ible; -able*
Found in: *adjectives*

The Spanish suffix *-ible* has as its English equivalents "-ible" and "-able" and means what the latter implies, namely, able to or capable of. Spanish adjectives ending with *-ible* are derived from *-er* and *-ir* verbs and rarely from *-ar* verbs (which generally are at the base of adjectives ending with *-able*). The one exception given below is *ostensible*, which comes from *ostentar*, an *-ar* verb. Generally, the suffix *-ible* simply is added to the root of the verb; however, at times, slight orthographic changes are made (e.g., *admisible* from *admitir*). Nonetheless, the formed word remains a cognate of its English counterpart, leaving such words still easy to spot and translate.

Formed Word	English Equivalent	Related to	English Equivalent
abolible	abolishable	**abolir**	to abolish
aborrecible [R]	detestable; hateful	**aborrecer**	to detest; abhor; hate
absorbible	absorbable	**absorber**	to absorb, drink in
acogible	receivable; acceptable	**acoger**	to welcome, receive
admisible	admissible; allowable	**admitir**	to admit, allow, receive

Formed Word	English Equivalent	Related to	English Equivalent
bebible [R]	drinkable	**beber**	to drink
comible	eatable	**comer**	to eat
comprensible [R]	comprehensible; understandable	**comprender**	to comprehend, understand
comprimible	compressible	**comprimir**	to compress
concebible [R]	conceivable	**concebir**	to conceive
convenible	able to be agreed upon; reasonable	**convenir**	to agree
convertible [R]	convertible	**convertir**	to convert, turn
creíble [R]	credible; believable	**creer**	to believe
decible	expressible	**decir**	to say, tell
deducible [R]	deducible; inferable	**deducir**	to deduce, infer
definible [R]	definable	**definir**	to define
discutible [R]	disputable; debatable	**discutir**	to discuss, debate
disponible [R 2343]	available	**disponer**	to dispose
imponible	taxable; dutiable	**imponer**	to impose, deposit (money in a bank)
leíble	legible; readable	**leer**	to read
movible [R]	movable; mobile	**mover**	to move
ostensible [R]	ostensible; visible	**ostentar**	to show, display, bear
permisible [R]	permissible	**permitir**	to permit, allow, enable
placible	agreeable; placid	**placer**	to please, content, gratify
posible [R 334]	possible	**poder**	to be able to
producible	producible	**producir**	to produce
risible [R]	laughable	**reír(se)**	to laugh
rompible [R]	breakable	**romper**	to break
sensible [R 3590]	sensitive, easily hurt	**sentir**	to feel
vendible [R]	salable; marketable	**vender**	to sell
visible [R 4863]	visible	**ver**	to see

-ica

Meaning: *diminutive*
English equivalent: *none*
Found in: *nouns*

The suffix *-ica*, like its sister suffix *-ico*, is among the more common Spanish diminutive endings. Usually this ending indicates physical smallness; however, it can also express endearment or familiarity, most notably at the end of a name, e.g., *Martica* (little Martha, "Marty") from *Marta* (Marta). All diminutive nouns ending with *-ica* are feminine.

Formed Word	English Equivalent	Related to	English Equivalent
la abuelica	sweet little grandmother	**la abuela**	grandmother
la avecica	small bird	**el ave**	bird
la camisica	little shirt	**la camisa**	shirt
la comidica	little meal	**la comida**	meal; food
la hermanica	little sister	**la hermana**	sister

Formed Word	English Equivalent	Related to	English Equivalent
la mañanica	daybreak; dawn; early morning	**la mañana**	morning
Martica	little Martha; "Marty"	**Marta**	Martha
la risica	giggle; titter; snicker	**la risa**	laugh; laughter
la villica	small town	**la villa**	town; municipal council

-icia; -acia

Meaning: *state of being; forms abstract noun*
English equivalent: *-ice*
Found in: *nouns*

Nearly all of the following words that end *-icia* and *-acia* are related to adjectives. The addition of either suffix usually creates an abstract noun, something that cannot be touched or seen (one exception is *la farmacia*). Spanish words ending with *-icia* or *-acia* are feminine.

Formed Word	English Equivalent	Related to	English Equivalent
la audacia [R]	audacity; boldness	**audaz**	audacious; bold
la avaricia	avarice; avariciousness	**avaro**	avaricious; miserly
la contumacia	obstinacy; obduracy; stubbornness	**contumaz**	contumacious; stubborn
la eficacia [R 4077]	efficacy; efficiency	**eficaz**	efficacious; effective; efficient
la estulticia	stupidity	**estulto**	stupid
la falacia	fallacy; deceit	*(Lat.)* **fallere**	to deceive
la farmacia [R 4934]	pharmacy; drug store	*(Gr.)* **pharmakon**	remedy; drug
la injusticia [R 3978]	injustice	**injusto**	unfair
la inmundicia	dirt; filth; filthiness; lewdness	**inmundo**	dirty; filthy; unclean; impure
la justicia [R 603]	justice	**justo**	just; fair; right
la malicia [R]	slyness; artfulness; distrust	**malo**	bad; evil; naughty; mischievous
la perspicacia	perspicacity; clear-sightedness	**perspicaz**	perspicacious
la pertinacia	pertinacity; doggedness	**pertinaz**	pertinacious
la suspicacia [R]	suspicion; mistrust	**suspicaz**	suspicious

-icio; -acio

Meaning: *result of action or attribute; forms abstract noun*
English equivalent: *-ice; -ace*
Found in: *nouns*

The addition of *-icio* or *-acio* (*-icio* is found much more frequently) to the base term forms an abstract noun, often implying a result. Such words can be derived from a verb, an adjective, or a noun. All words ending with *-icio* and *-acio* are masculine.

Formed Word	English Equivalent	Related to	English Equivalent
el alimenticio [R 3223]	nutritive	**alimentar**	to nourish, feed
el artificio [R]	artifice; workmanship; craft	**el artífice**	artificer; artist; inventor
el beneficio [R 690]	benefit; favor; utility; profit	**beneficiar**	to benefit, be good to
el desperdicio [R 4336]	waste	**desperdiciar**	to waste, squander
el edificio [R 1187]	edifice; building	**edificar**	to construct, build, edify
el ejercicio [R 948]	practice; exercise	**ejercer**	to exercise, practice, exert
el espacio [R 612]	space (all meanings)	**espaciar**	to space
el indicio [R 4270]	indication; mark; clue; sign	**indicar**	to indicate, point out, hint, suggest
el inicio [R 689]	beginning	**iniciar**	to initiate, begin
el juicio [R 1458]	judgment; sense; opinion	**juzgar**	to judge
el novicio	novice; beginner	**nuevo**	new
el oficio [R 2305]	work; occupation; job	**oficiar**	to officiate, minister
el palacio [R]	palace	*(Lat.)* **Palatium**	Palatine Hill (Rome)
el perjuicio [3478]	detriment; damage; harm	**perjudicar**	to damage, hurt, injure, impair
el precipicio	precipice; chasm; abyss	**precipitar**	to precipitate, fling headlong
el prefacio	preface	*(Lat.)* **praefari**	to say beforehand
el prejuicio	prejudice; bias; prejudgment	**prejuzgar**	to prejudge
el sacrificio [R 2675]	sacrifice; slaughter	**sacrificar**	to sacrifice, slaughter (animals)
el servicio [R 158]	service; duty; dinner set	**servir**	to serve, help
el solsticio	solstice	*(Lat.)* **sol + stare**	sun + to stand
el suplicio	torment; torture; execution	**suplicar**	to entreat, supplicate, beg
el vicio [R 3712]	vice; defect; bad habit	**viciar**	to vitiate, adulterate, falsify
el vitalicio [R]	life insurance policy	**vital**	vital; belonging to life; essential

-ico(1)

Meaning: *diminutive*
English equivalent: *none*
Found in: *nouns*

The suffix *-ico*, like its sister *-ica*, is a common Spanish diminutive ending (*-ico* is more commonly found than *-ica*). Usually this ending simply denotes smallness of the root noun, e.g., *el saltico* (small hop) from *el salto* (jump; hop). At times, this ending implies diminished status (see *el pobrecico*). Words ending with *-ico* are masculine.

Formed Word	English Equivalent	Related to	English Equivalent
el arbolico	miserable little tree	**el árbol**	tree
el gatico	little cat; kitty	**el gato**	cat
el leoncico	lion cub	**el léon**	lion
el momentico	tiny bit of time	**el momento**	moment; minute
el pedacico	small bit; small piece	**el pedazo**	piece

Formed Word	English Equivalent	Related to	English Equivalent
el pobrecico	poor little fellow, thing, etc.	el pobre	poor person; pauper; beggar
el saltico	little hop	el salto	jump; hop; leap
el santico	regular little saint	el santo	saint
el sombrerico	little hat	el sombrero	hat
el tontico	little dolt; twit	el tonto	fool; nincompoop
el vasico	small glass	el vaso	drinking glass
el villancico	Christmas carol	el villano	old Spanish melody and dance

-ico(2) (-ica)

Meaning: *like; relating to*
English equivalent: *-ic*
Found in: *adjectives*

The adjectival ending *-ico* translates into English as "-ic," and most Spanish adjectives ending with *-ico* are cognates of their English counterparts. These formed words usually are related to nouns. Generally speaking, if the root noun ends with a vowel, that vowel is dropped and *-ico* is added; if the root noun ends in a consonant, -ico is added directly. When describing feminine nouns, adjectives ending with *-ico* take the ending *-ica*. Note that in these formed words the accent is on the antepenultimate syllable.

Formed Word	English Equivalent	Related to	English Equivalent
académico [R 1848]	academic	la academia	academy
alcohólico [R 2856]	alcoholic	el alcohol	alcohol
analítico [R]	analytic	el análisis	analysis
angélico [R]	angelic	el ángel	angel
artístico [R 1215]	artistic	el arte	art
asiático [3505]	Asiatic	Asia	Asia
asmático	asthmatic	el asma	asthma
atlético [R 1827]	athletic	el atleta	athlete
automovilístico [R 3677]	pertaining to motoring or automobile construction	el automóbil	automobile
básico [R 1133]	basic	la base	base
benéfico [R 3737]	beneficial	el bien	welfare
bíblico [R]	Biblical	la Biblia	Bible
biológico [R 3679]	biological	la biología	biology
británico [1292]	British	Gran Bretaña	Great Britain
caótico [R]	chaotic; in disorder and confusion	el caos	chaos; (fig.) confusion; shambles
característico [R 1324]	characteristic; distinctive	el carácter	character
católico [R 1548]	catholic; Catholic	el católico	Catholic
científico [R 1531]	scientific	la ciencia	science
cinematográfico [R 2262]	cinematographic	el cine	cinema
cívico [R 3285]	civic	el civismo	civics
crítico [R 1403]	critic; critical (urgent or disparaging)	la crítica	criticism
crónico [R 2839]	chronic	la crónica	chronicle

Formed Word	English Equivalent	Related to	English Equivalent
cuántico [3994]	quantum	**¿cuánto?**	how much; how many
cúbico [2716]	cubic	**el cubo**	cube
democrático [R 989]	democratic	**la democracia**	democracy
diplomático [R 2334]	diplomatic	**la diplomacia**	diplomacy
discográfico [1906]	pertaining to recorded music	**la discografía**	recording industry; artist's complete collection
dramático [R 3234]	dramatic	**el drama**	drama
ecológico [2652]	ecological	**la ecología**	ecology
económico [R 220]	economic	**la economía**	economics
energético [R 2335]	power-producing; energy-producing	**la energía**	energy
enérgico [R]	energetic; vigorous	**la energía**	energy; power
enfático	emphatic	**el énfasis**	emphasis
esférico [R 3180]	spherical	**la esfera**	sphere
específico [R 1801]	specific	**la especia**	species; kind; class
estadístico [R 2048]	statistical	**la estadística**	statistic
estético [R 3977]	relating to aesthetics or the study of beauty	**la estética**	esthetics
estratégico [2330]	strategic	**la estrategia**	strategy
ético [R 2892]	ethical	**la ética**	ethics
étnico [4738]	ethnic	**la etnia**	ethnic group
evangélico [R]	evangelic; evangelical	**el evangelio**	gospel
fanático [2201]	fanatic	**el fanatismo**	fanaticism
fantástico [4137]	fantastic	**la fantasía**	fantasy
fotográfico [R 4398]	photographic	**la fotografía**	photography
frenético	frenetic; frenzied; frantic; mad	**el frenesí**	frenzy; fury; madness
futbolístico [3421]	soccer; pertaining to soccer	**el fútbol**	soccer
galáctico	galactic	**la galaxia**	galaxy
genético [R 3455]	genetic	**la genética**	genetics
geográfico [R 4459]	geographic	**la geográfia**	geography
gráfico [2937]	graphic	**la gráfica**	graphics
hidráulico [3930]	hydraulic	**la hidráulica**	hydraulics
histórico [R 1212]	historical	**la historia**	history
informático [2790]	pertaining to computer science	**la informática**	computer science
islámico [2830]	Islamic	**el Islam**	Islam
litúrgico	liturgic; liturgical	**la liturgia**	liturgy
lógico [R 2747]	logical	**lógica**	logic
mágico [3422]	magic	**el mago**	Magus; magician; wizard
metálico [R 3848]	metallic	**el metal**	metal
olímpico [1567]	Olympic	**Olimpo**	Olympus
orgánico [R 3708]	organic	**órgano**	organ
pacífico [R 2073]	pacific; peaceful; peace-loving	**la paz**	peace
panorámico [R]	panoramic	**el panorama**	panorama
patriótico [R]	patriotic	**la patria**	fatherland
periodístico [R 4422]	pertaining to newspapers or journalism	**el periódico**	newspaper
práctico [R 4004]	practical	**la práctica**	practice
problemático [R 2112]	problematic	**el problema**	problem
profético [R]	prophetic	**el profeta**	prophet

Formed Word	English Equivalent	Related to	English Equivalent
sádico	sadistic	**Marqués de Sade**	Marquis de Sade
satánico	satanic	**Satanás**	Satan
semítico	Semitic	**el semita**	Semite
técnico [R 1150]	technical	**la técnica**	technique
telefónico [R 1587]	telephonic	**el teléfono**	telephone
telegráfico [R]	telegraphic	**el telégrafo**	telegraph
telepático [R]	telepathic	**la telepatía**	telepathy
teórico [R]	theoretic	**la teoría**	theory
terapéutico [4997]	therapeutic	**terapia**	therapy
terrorífico [R]	horrific; bloodcurdling	**el terror**	terror; dread
teutónico	Teutonic	**el teutón**	Teuton
titánico	titanic	**Titán**	Titan
tóxico [4925]	toxic	**la toxina**	toxin
trágico [R 3835]	tragic	**la tragedia**	tragedy
turístico [R 2295]	tourist	**turismo**	tourism
único [R 365]	one and only	**el uno**	one (number)

-idad

Meaning: *state of being; quality*
English equivalent: *-ity*
Found in: *nouns*

When you see *-idad* at the end of a Spanish word and change *-idad* to "-ity," most likely you will have its English counterpart (or something very close to it) in front of you. The suffix *-idad* generally is attached to an existing adjective, as in all examples given below, to denote the quality or state of that adjective. This is a common suffix and appears in cognates of English words, making them easy to recognize and to translate. Words ending with *-idad* are feminine.

Formed Word	English Equivalent	Related to	English Equivalent
la absurdidad [R]	absurdity	**absurdo**	absurd
la actividad [R 260]	activity	**activo**	active
la actualidad [R 1334]	present time; *en actualidad*: nowadays	**actual**	current
la adversidad	adversity; calamity	**adverso**	adverse; calamitous
la atrocidad	atrocity; atrociousness	**atroz**	atrocious; heinous
la autoridad [R 186]	authority	**autor**	author
la capacidad [R 646]	capability	**capaz**	capable
la castidad [R]	chastity	**casto**	chaste
la casualidad [R]	chance; coincidence	**casual**	chance; coincidental
la claridad [R 3268]	clarity; brightness	**claro**	clear; bright
la comodidad [R 4471]	comfort	**cómodo**	comfortable
la competitividad [R 3793]	competitiveness	**competitivo**	competitive
la comunidad [R 350]	community; fellowship	**común**	common
la conformidad [R]	conformity; agreement	**conforme**	agreeing; in agreement
la contabilidad [R 4759]	accounting	**contable**	countable
la continuidad [R 3225]	continuity	**continuo**	continuous
la creatividad [R 3993]	creativity	**creativo**	creative

Formed Word	English Equivalent	Related to	English Equivalent
la credibilidad [R 4428]	credibility	creíble	believable
la curiosidad [R 4243]	curiosity	curioso	curious
la debilidad [R 3089]	debility; weakness	débil	weak
la densidad [R 4736]	density; thickness	denso	dense; thick
la dignidad [R 3240]	dignity	digno	worthy
la disponibilidad [R 4957]	availability	disponible	available
la diversidad [R 4112]	diversity	diverso	diverse
la efectividad [R 4266]	effectiveness	efectivo	effective
la electricidad [R 1628]	electricity	eléctrico	electric
la especialidad [2729]	specialty	especial	special
la espiritualidad [R]	spirituality	espiritual	spiritual
la estabilidad [R 2576]	stability	estable	stable
la eternidad [R]	eternity	eterno	eternal
la facilidad [R 2282]	facility (ease)	fácil	easy
la fatalidad [R]	fatality	fatal	fatal
la fecundidad [R]	fecundity	fecundo	fecund; fertile; fruitful
la felicidad [R 1895]	happiness	feliz	happy
la ferocidad [R]	ferocity; ferociousness	feroz	ferocious; savage; fierce
la finalidad [R 1420]	finality	final	final
la fragilidad [R]	fragility	frágil	fragile
la fraternidad [R]	fraternity; brotherhood	fraterno	fraternal; brotherly
la habilidad [R 2578]	ability	hábil	able
la honestidad [R 4718]	honesty	honesto	honest
la humanidad [R 2730]	humanity	humano	human
la impunidad [2968]	impunity	impune	unpunished
la incapacidad [R 4095]	incapacity	incapaz	incapable
la incorformidad	nonconformity	inconforme	nonconformist
la infinidad [R 4142]	infinity	infinito	infinite
la inseguridad [R 2636]	insecurity	inseguro	insecure
la integridad [R 3947]	integrity	íntegro	honest
la intensidad [R 3300]	intensity	intenso	intense
la irregularidad [R 1685]	irregularity	irregular	irregular
la legalidad [R 3633]	legality	legal	legal
la localidad [R 1090]	locality	local	local
la mentalidad [R 4494]	mentality	mental	mental
la modernidad [R 4827]	modernity	moderno	modern
la morbosidad	morbidity; morbidness	morboso	morbid
la nacionalidad [R 4386]	nationality	nacional	national
la necesidad [R 453]	necessity	necesario	necessary
la normatividad [3521]	laws; regulations	normativo	normative
la obesidad [3751]	obesity	obeso	obese
la oportunidad [R 312]	opportunity	oportuno	opportune
la oscuridad [4746]	darkness	oscuro	dark
la personalidad [R 1829]	personality	personal	personal
la popularidad [R 2545]	popularity	popular	popular
la posibilidad [R 448]	possibility	posible	possible
la potencialidad [R]	potentiality	potencial	potential
la probabilidad [R 4464]	probability	probable	probable
la probidad	probity; honesty; integrity	probo	upright; hones
la productividad [R 3084]	productivity	productivo	productive
la profanidad	profanity; profaneness	profano	profane
la profundidad [R 3065]	profundity; depths	profundo	profound, deep

Formed Word	English Equivalent	Related to	English Equivalent
la proximidad [R]	proximity; vicinity	próximo	near; neighboring; next
la publicidad [R 2852]	publicity	público	public
la realidad [R 665]	reality	real	real
la responsabilidad [R 745]	responsibility	responsable	responsible
la rivalidad [R 4837]	rivalry	rival	rival
la sanidad [R 4859]	healthiness	sano	healthy
la santidad [R 4752]	holiness	santo	holy
la seguridad [R 182]	security	seguro	safe, sure
la sensibilidad [R 3490]	sensibility	sensible	sensitive
la severidad [R]	severity; strictness	severo	severe; strict
la sexualidad [R 3803]	sexuality	sexual	sexual
la solidaridad [R 2490]	solidarity	solidario	pertaining to solidarity
la superioridad [R]	superiority	superior	superior; better; finer
la tenacidad [R]	tenacity; tenaciousness	tenaz	tenacious
la totalidad [R 2691]	totality	total	total
la tranquilidad [R 2233]	tranquility	tranquilo	peaceful, tranquil
la unidad [R 273]	unity	unido	united
la utilidad [R 2484]	utility; usefulness	útil	useful; serviceable; handy
la vanidad [R]	vanity	vano	vain; futile
la veracidad [R]	veracity; truthfulness	veraz	veracious; truthful
la vialidad [1107]	highway system	vial	pertaining to roads, routes, ways, tracks, etc.
la virilidad [R]	virility	viril	virile; manly
la visibilidad [R]	visibility	visible	visible

-ido⁽¹⁾ (-ida)

Meaning: *like; relating to*
English equivalent: *-id*
Found in: *adjectives*

The suffix *-ido* is a common one in Spanish: it is seen at the end of past participles of *-er* and *-ir* verbs, of adjectives, and of nouns. In the following list of formed words, all adjectives, you will find two distinct features. First, the words come directly to us from the Latin. This, however, should not trouble you in working with and learning these words, for nearly all are cognates—Latin, Spanish, and English—of one another. Secondly, the antepenultimate syllable is always accented. When these formed words describe a feminine noun, *-ido* changes to *-ida*.

Formed Word	English Equivalent	Related to	English Equivalent
ácido [2855]	acid	(Lat.) **acidus**	sharp
árido [R]	arid	(Lat.) **aridus**	dry
cálido [R 4205]	warm	(Lat.) **calor**	heat
cándido [R]	white; snowy; guileless; simple	(Lat.) **candidus**	shining
estólido	stolid	(Lat.) **stolidus**	dull; stolid; slow
estúpido [R]	stupid; dense	(Lat.) **stupidus**	stupid
fétido	fetid	(Lat.) **foetidus**	fetid

Formed Word	English Equivalent	Related to	English Equivalent
flácido, fláccido	flaccid	(Lat.) *flaccidus*	flaccid
florido [R 2257]	flowery	(Lat.) *floridus*	flower
frígido [R]	frigid; extremely cold	(Lat.) *frigidus*	frigid
gélido	gelid; frigid; icy	(Lat.) *gelidus*	gelid
grávido	gravid; laden; heavy	(Lat.) *gravidus*	heavy
hórrido	horrid	(Lat.) *horridus*	rough
insípido	insipid	(Lat.) *insipiens*	foolish
lánguido	languid	(Lat.) *languidus*	faint
límpido	limpid; crystal clear	(Lat.) *limpidus*	limpid; clear
líquido [R 1813]	liquid	(Lat.) *liquidus*	liquid
lívido	livid	(Lat.) *lividus*	bluish; black; vivid
lúcido [R]	lucid	(Lat.) *lucidus*	lucid
pálido [R]	pallid; pale; wan	(Lat.) *pallidus*	pallid
plácido [R]	placid; calm	(Lat.) *placidus*	placid
rápido [R 1018]	quick; rapid	(Lat.) *rapidus*	swift
sólido [R 2444]	solid	(Lat.) *solidus*	solid
sórdido	sordid	(Lat.) *sordidius*	dirty
tímido [R]	timid; shy	(Lat.) *timidus*	timid
tórrido	torrid	(Lat.) *torridus*	torrid
translúcido	translucent	(Lat.) *translucidus*	translucent
túmido	tumid	(Lat.) *tumidus*	tumid; swollen
válido [R 3734]	valid	(Lat.) *validus*	valid

-ido(2); -ida

Meaning: *resulting action, object, person, or sound*
English equivalent: *none*
Found in: *nouns*

Each of the following formed words, all derived from verbs, denotes the result of a particular verb's action, be it the action itself or an object, person, or sound. An unusual feature of the ending *-ido* is its frequent presence in words describing sounds that animals make, e.g., *el maullido* (meow). When the term refers to a person, e.g., *el nacido* (human being, newborn), the ending will change to *-ida* if that person is female. Words ending in *-ido* are masculine, while those ending in *-ida* are feminine.

Formed Word	English Equivalent	Related to	English Equivalent
agradecido [R 4645]	thankful; grateful	**agradecer**	to be thankful
el aparecido	ghost; specter	**aparecer**	to appear, show up
el apellido [R 3331]	surname; last or family name	**apellidar**	to call, name
el aullido	howl; howling	**aullar**	to howl
la bebida [R 1426]	drink; beverage	**beber**	to drink
el chillido	shriek; shrill sound	**chillar**	to scream, shriek, screech
el cocido [R]	stew	**cocer**	to cook, boil, bake
el cometido [R 2068]	commitment; responsibility	**cometer**	to commit
la comida [R 1097]	food; meal	**comer**	to eat
el contenido [R]	contents	**contener**	to contain, comprise, hold
la corrida [R 3481]	run; sprint	**correr**	to run

Formed Word	English Equivalent	Related to	English Equivalent
el crujido	creak; crackle	**crujir**	to rustle, crackle, creak
el desagradecido [R]	ungrateful person	**desagradecer**	to be ungrateful for
el descuido [R 4441]	neglect	**descuidar**	to neglect
la despedida [R 1111]	leave-taking; farewell; send-off	**despedir(se)**	to take one's leave, say good-bye
el despido [R 3819]	dismissal from work; firing	**despedir**	to dismiss
el detenido [R 491]	detainee; detained	**detener**	to detain
el gruñido	pig grunt; dog growl; grumble	**gruñir**	to grunt, growl, grumble
la herida [R 1533]	injury; wound; insult	**herir**	to injure, hurt, wound, offend
el herido [R]	injured or hurt person	**herir**	to injure, hurt, wound, offend
la huida [R]	flight; escape	**huir**	to flee, run away
la ida [3918]	going	**ir**	to go
el ladrido [R]	bark	**ladrar**	to bark
el marido [R 2023]	husband	**maridar**	to marry
el maullido	mew; meow	**maullar**	to mew, meow
la medida [R 369]	measurement	**medir**	to measure
la mordida [R]	bite	**morder**	to bite
el mordido	person bitten	**morder**	to bite
el mugido	moo; low; bellow	**mugir**	to moo, low, bellow
el nacido [R]	human being; newborn	**nacer**	to be born
el oído [R 2942]	ear	**oír**	to hear
el olvido [R 4247]	forgetfulness; oblivion	**olvidar**	to forget
la partida [2298]	departure; parting; deal (cards); cutting into portions	**partir**	to leave
el pedido [R]	(com.) order; request	**pedir**	to ask (for), request
la pérdida [R 1138]	loss	**perder**	to lose
el prometido [R]	fiancé; betrothed	**prometer**	to promise
el querido [R 1598]	dear one	**querer**	to love
el resoplido [R]	puffing; snort	**resoplar**	to puff, snort
el roznido	braying; crunching noise	**roznar**	to crunch, crack with teeth
el rugido	roar	**rugir**	to roar
la sacudida [R]	shake; jar; jolt	**sacudir**	to shake, jar, jolt
la salida [R 722]	exit; egress; (mil.) sortie	**salir**	to leave, go out
el sentido [R]	sense	**sentir**	to sense, feel
el silbido	whistle; hiss	**silbar**	to whistle, hiss
el sonido [R 2100]	sound; ring	**sonar**	to sound, ring
la suicida [R 2477]	*nmf* suicide victim; *aj* suicide, suicidal	**suicidar**	to commit suicide
el tañido	sound; tone	**tañer**	to play a musical instrument, ring a bell
el tronido	thunder; thunderclap	**tronar**	to thunder
el vestido [R 1630]	dress; garments; clothing	**vestir(se)**	to dress (oneself)
la vida [R 99]	life	**vivir**	to live
el zumbido	buzz; buzzing	**zumbar**	to buzz

-iego (-iega)

Meaning: *like; relating to; fond of*
English equivalent: *none*
Found in: *adjectives*

The ending -*iego* is one of the less common adjectival suffixes meaning "like" or "relating to." It can also mean "fond of," as in *mujeriego* (keen on women). Generally, words ending with -*iego* refer broadly to features of the root term. Formed words describing feminine nouns will end with -*iega*.

Formed Word	English Equivalent	Related to	English Equivalent
andariego [R]	wandering; roving	el andar	gait; pace; walking
asperiego	sour	áspero	sour
griego [3668]	Greek; Grecian	Grecia	Greece
moriego	Moorish	el moro	Moor; Mohammedan
mujeriego [R]	keen on women; womanizing	la mujer	woman
nocherniego	nocturnal	la noche	night; evening
palaciego	relating to a palace or court	el palacio	palace; mansion
pinariego	relating to pines	el pino	pine; pine tree
riego [R 1748]	watering	regar	to water
solariego	manorial; ancestral	el solar	manor house
veraniego [R]	summery	el verano	summer

-iento (-ienta)

Meaning: *inclined to: tending to; full of; like; relating to*
English equivalent: *-y*
Found in: *adjectives*

If something is covered with grease, we say that it is *greasy*, using the English suffix -*y* meaning "inclined to," "tending to," "full of," or "like." This is the function of the Spanish suffix -*iento*: it indicates that someone or something is filled with or strongly similar to the features of the base noun. One example, *amarillento*, drops the *i* from the ending to avoid an otherwise awkward pronunciation. As these are adjectives, the ending changes to -*ienta* when describing a feminine noun.

Formed Word	English Equivalent	Related to	English Equivalent
achaquiento	sickly; unhealthy	el achaque	(habitual) ailment; indisposition
amarillento [R]	yellowish	el amarillo	yellow (color)
avariento	avaricious; miserly	el avaro	miser; greedy person
calenturiento [R]	feverish	la calentura	fever
catarriento	catarrhous	el catarro	catarrh; cold
cazcarriento	(coll.) splashed; bemired	la cazcarria	splashings of mud
ceniciento	ash-colored; ashen	la ceniza	ash
gargajiento	spitting frequently	el gargajo	phlegm; spit
granujiento	pimply	el grano	pimple
grasiento [R]	greasy; oily	la grasa	grease; fat

Formed Word	English Equivalent	Related to	English Equivalent
gusaniento	wormy; maggoty	**el gusano**	worm; maggot
hambriento [R]	hungry; starving	**el hambre**	hunger
harapiento	ragged; tattered	**el harapo**	rag; tatter
holliniento	sooty	**el hollín**	soot
mugriento	grimy; filthy; greasy	**la mugre**	grime; filth; greasy dirt
polvoriento [R]	dusty	**el polvo**	dust
sangriento [R]	bloody; bloodstained	**la sangre**	blood
soñoliento [R]	sleepy; dreamy; drowsy	**el sueño**	sleep; sleepiness; dream
sudoriento	perspiring	**el sudor**	sweat; perspiration; ooze
trapiento	raggedy; in rags	**el trapo**	rag
zarriento	besmirched; bespattered	**la zarria**	dirt (on one's clothing)

-ífero (-ífera)

Meaning: *bearing; producing; yielding*
English equivalent: *-iferous*
Found in: *adjectives*

The Spanish suffix *-ífero* and its English counterpart "-iferous" both indicate that something is bearing, producing, or yielding something specific. The suffix *-ífero* is derived from the Latin *ferre*, which means "to carry or bear." Words ending in *-ífero* have at their base a noun: generally, if that noun ends in a vowel, that vowel is dropped and *-ífero* is added; if the root noun ends in a consonant, *-ífero* is added directly to the word. The ending changes to *-ífera* when these adjectives describe feminine nouns.

Formed Word	English Equivalent	Related to	English Equivalent
acuífero [3452]	water-containing	**el agua**	the water
aerífero	air-conducting	*(Lat.)* **aer**	air
coralífero	coral-bearing	**el coral**	coral
ferrífero	iron-bearing	*(Lat.)* **ferrum**	iron
florífero	flower-bearing	**la flor**	flower
frondífero	leaf-bearing	*(bot.)* **el fronde**	frond
fructífero [R]	fructiferous; fruit-bearing	*(Lat.)* **fructus**	fruit
lactífero	milk-producing	*(Lat.)* **lac**	milk
lucífero	shining	**la luz**	light
melífero	honey-producing	**la miel**	honey
metalífero	metalliferous	**el metal**	metal; brass
mortífero [R]	lethal; death-dealing	**la muerte**	death
nectarífero	nectar-bearing	**el néctar**	nectar; exquisite drink
palmífero	palm-bearing	*(bot.)* **la palma**	palm
pestífero	foul	**la peste**	plague; pestilence
petrolífero [R]	oil-bearing	**el petróleo**	petroleum; oil
plumífero	(poet.) feathered	**la pluma**	feather
salutífero	healthful; salubrious	**la salud**	health; welfare
soporífero	sleep-producing	**el sopor**	drowsiness; lethargy
sudorífero	sweat-producing	**el sudor**	sweat; perspiration; ooze

-ificar

Meaning: *to make (like)*
English equivalent: *-ify*
Found in: *verbs*

The ending *-ificar* is unusual because infinitives rarely form a specific group. The suffix *-ificar* corresponds directly to the English *-ify*, which makes these words easy to recognize and use as they nearly always are cognates. Verbs ending with *-ificar* are regular, with the single orthographic change of *c* to *qu* before *e* when conjugated: *yo clasifico* (I classify); *yo clasifiqué* (I classified).

Formed Word	English Equivalent	Related to	English Equivalent
amplificar [R]	to amplify	**amplio**	ample
beatificar	to beatify	**beato**	happy; blessed
calificar [R 1052]	to qualify	**la calidad**	quality
certificar [R 3345]	to certify	**cierto**	certain
clasificar [R 1949]	to classify	**la clase**	class; kind
cosificar	to reduce to the level of an object	**la cosa**	thing; matter
crucificar [R]	to crucify	**la cruz**	cross
cuantificar [R]	to quantify	**la cantidad**	quantity
diversificar [R]	to diversify	**diverso**	diverse
dosificar	to dose, proportion	**la dosis**	dose
electrificar [R]	to electrify	**eléctrico**	electric
especificar [R 3190]	to specify	**específico**	specific
falsificar [R]	to falsify	**falso**	false
fortificar [R]	to fortify	**fuerte**	strong; forceful
gasificar	to gasify	**el gas**	gas
glorificar [R]	to glorify	**la gloria**	glory; heaven; bliss
humidificar	to humidify	**húmedo**	humid
identificar [R 1100]	to identify *(vt)*; to identify (with) *(vi)*	**identidad**	identity
intensificar [R 3379]	to intensify	**intenso**	intense
justificar	to justify	**justo**	just; fair
mistificar [R]	to mystify	**místico**	mystic
mortificar [R]	to mortify	**muerto**	dead
osificar	to ossify	**óseo**	osseous
pacificar [R]	to pacify	**la paz**	peace
petrificar [R]	to petrify	**pétreo**	stony
purificar [R]	to purify	**puro**	pure
rectificar [R]	to rectify	**recto**	right
sacrificar [R 3250]	to sacrifice	**sacrificio**	sacrifice
santificar [R]	to sanctify, make holy	**santo**	holy; blessed
simplificar [R]	to simplify	**simple**	simple
solidificar [R]	to solidify	**sólido**	solid
tipificar [R]	to typify	**típico**	typical
unificar [R]	to unify	**unido**	united
vivificar [R]	to vivify	**vivo**	alive

-iforme

Meaning: *shaped like; in the form of; like*
English equivalent: *-iform*
Found in: *adjectives*

The Spanish ending *-iforme* and its English counterpart, *-iform*, perform the same function, making these Spanish formed words easy to recognize and translate. The English suffix *-iform*, however, is more strictly tied to meaning "shaped like," while the Spanish suffix *-iforme* can also mean "like," e.g., *carniforme* (flesh-like). Generally speaking, if the base word ends in a vowel, drop that vowel and add *-iforme*. If the base word ends in a consonant, add *-iforme* directly.

Formed Word	English Equivalent	Related to	English Equivalent
aliforme	aliform; wing-shaped	**el ala** *nf*	wing
anguiliforme	(ichth.) eel-like	**la anguila**	eel
arboriforme	shaped like a tree	**el árbol**	tree
biforme	(poet.) biform; biformed	*(Lat.)* **bis**	twice
coniforme	coniform; conical; cone-shaped	**el cono**	cone
corniforme	corniform; horn-shaped	**el cuerno**	horn
cruciforme	cruciform	**la cruz**	cross
cuadriforme	square-shaped	**el cuadro**	square
cuneiforme	cuneiform; wedge-shaped	**la cuña**	wedge
deiforme	godlike; Godlike	*(Lat.)* **deus**	god; God
dentiforme	shaped like a tooth	**el diente**	tooth
estratiforme	stratiform	**el estrato**	stratum; layer
filiforme	threadlike	*(Lat.)* **filum**	thread
fungiforme	fungiform	**el fungo**	fungus
piriforme	pear-shaped	**la pera**	pear
pisciforme	fish-shaped	*(Lat.)* **piscis**	fish
semiforme	half-formed	*(Lat.)* **semis**	half
triforme	triform	*(Lat.)* **tres**	three
uniforme [R 3145]	uniform; standard	*(Lat.)* **unus**	one

-il

Meaning: *like; relating to; concerning; capable of*
English equivalent: *-ile; -able; -ible*
Found in: *adjectives*

Words taking the adjectival ending *-il* can have as a root either a noun or a verb and, in rare cases, an adjective, e.g., *femenil* from *femenino*. When the formed adjective is derived from a noun, the meaning generally is "like" or "concerning." When the formed word traces to a verb, its meaning will be "capable of," as in *móvil* (capable of motion). As these adjectives end in a consonant, they will not change with regard to gender.

Formed Word	English Equivalent	Related to	English Equivalent
abogadil	lawyerlike; lawyerly	el abogado	lawyer
aceitunil	olive-colored	la aceituna	olive
becerril	concerning cows	el/la becerro/a	young bull/heifer
borreguil	concerning lambs	el borrego	young lamb
concejil	public; of the municipal council	el concejo	municipal council; council board
estudiantil [R 3362]	relating to students	el estudiante	student
fabril	manufacturing; industrial	la fábrica	factory; works; plant
febril [R]	feverish; febrile	la fiebre	fever
femenil [1516]	feminine; womanly	femenino	feminine
grácil	graceful	la gracia	grace
infantil [R 864]	infantile; like a child	el infante	infant
inútil [R 4524]	useless	útil	useful
juvenil [R 1154]	juvenile; youthful	joven	young
monjil [R]	nunlike; prudish	la monja	nun
móvil [R 3652]	mobile	mover	to move
mujeril	womanly	la mujer	woman
portátil [R]	portable	portar	to carry, bear
señoril	lordly; haughty; majestic	el señor	sir; lord; master
servil	servile	servir	to serve
varonil [R 2320]	manly	el varón	man; male
versátil	versatile; changeable	versar	to go round, turn
volátil	capable of flying	volar	to fly

-illa

Meaning: *diminutive*
English equivalent: *-ette; usually none*
Found in: *nouns*

The ending -*illa*, like its sister suffix -*illo*, is an extremely common diminutive. Words ending with -*illa* and -*illo* are so common that we've divided them into three groups. The first two (-*illo* and -*illa*) deal with literal (physical) diminutives, and the third (-*illo; -illa*) contains words that are diminutive in status. Most of the terms in the first group are merely names for the smaller version of the root noun, e.g., *la cocinilla* (kitchenette) from *la cocina* (kitchen). At times, however, the meaning changes significantly with the addition of -*illa*, e.g., *la rodilla* (knee) from *la rueda* (wheel; caster; roller); nonetheless, the relationship between these formed words and their respective roots generally is clear. Words ending with -*illa* are feminine.

Formed Word	English Equivalent	Related to	English Equivalent
la barbilla [R]	point of the chin	la barba	chin
la bombilla	light bulb	la bomba	lamp globe
la cadenilla	small ornamental chain	la cadena	(lit.; fig.) chain; chain-gang
la cajetilla [R]	packet of cigarettes; cigarette box	la cajeta	small box

Formed Word	English Equivalent	Related to	English Equivalent
la camilla [R]	stretcher; couch	**la cama**	bed
la canastilla [3058]	bassinet	**la canasta**	basket
la carretilla [R]	small cart; wheelbarrow	**la carreta**	wagon
la casilla [2791]	compartmentalized case; small house	**la casa**	house
la cerilla	ear wax; cold cream	**la cera**	wax; wax candles
la cocinilla	kitchenette	**la cocina**	kitchen
la colilla	cigarette butt	**la cola**	tail; tail-end; hind part
la cortinilla	small curtain	**la cortina**	curtain; screen; covering
la escobilla	small broom; whisk broom	**la escoba**	broom
la estampilla [R]	postage stamp	**la estampa**	printing stamp; engraving
la felpilla	chenille	**la felpa**	plush
las fritillas	fritters	**el frito**	fried food
la frutilla	small fruit; rosary bead	**la fruta**	fruit
la gacetilla	personal news column	**la gaceta**	gazette; political or literary newspaper
la gargantilla [R]	necklace; bead (of a necklace)	**la garganta**	throat; gullet
la gavetilla	small desk drawer	**la gaveta**	drawer (of writing desk)
la guerrilla [R 3341]	guerrilla	**la guerra**	war
la lanilla	nap (of cloth); fine flannel	**la lana**	wool; fleece
la liguilla [2354]	round-robin tournament	**la liga**	league
la manecilla	small hand; hand on a clock	**la mano**	hand
la mantequilla [3931]	butter	**la manteca**	lard; grease; fat; pomade
la mariposilla	little butterfly	**la mariposa**	butterfly
la mesilla [R]	small table; sideboard	**la mesa**	table; desk
la papadilla	fleshy part under the chin	**la papada**	double chin; dewlap
la pastilla [4723]	tablet; pill; bar (of soap, chocolate)	**la pasta**	paste; batter; pastry
la planilla [4920]	election ballot	**la plana**	sheet; page
la plumilla	small feather	**la pluma**	feather
la rodilla [R 2854]	knee	**la rueda**	wheel; caster; roller
la sabanilla	small sheet; napkin; kerchief	**la sábana**	sheet (of a bed); altar cloth
la semilla [R 2300]	seed	**el semen**	semen; sperm
la sortijilla	little ring	**la sortija**	ring
la tortilla [3132]	tortilla; pancake; omelette	**la torta**	cake; pie
la ventanilla [R 4370]	small window such as in a car, train, plane, etc.	**la ventana**	window
la zapatilla [R]	slipper; little shoe (woman's high-heeled shoe)	**el zapato**	shoe

-illo⁽¹⁾

Meaning: *diminutive*
English equivalent: *-ette; usually none*
Found in: *nouns*

In this grouping of words that end with *-illo*, this suffix indicates physical smallness. Most of the terms below are simply names for the smaller version of the root noun, e.g., *el platillo* (saucer; small dish) from *el plato* (plate; dish). All nouns ending with *-illo* are masculine.

Formed Word	English Equivalent	Related to	English Equivalent
el banquillo	small bench	**el banco**	bench
el bocadillo [R]	sandwich; snack	**el bocado**	mouthful; morsel (of food)
el bolsillo [R 4783]	pocket	**la bolsa**	purse; bag
el cachorrillo	small puppy	**el cachorro**	puppy
el caminillo	back road; path	**el camino**	road; lane; way; route
el cerquillo	small circle or hoop	**el cerco**	hoop; ring
el cervatillo	fawn	**el ciervo**	deer
el cigarillo	cigarette	**el cigarro**	cigar
el corralillo	small yard	**el corral**	enclosure; yard; barnyard
el cuentecillo	little story	**el cuento**	story; tale; short story
el dedillo	fingertip	**el dedo**	finger
el dragoncillo	little dragon	**el dragón**	dragon; flying lizard
el espejillo	little mirror; hand-mirror	**el espejo**	mirror; lookingglass
el farolillo	lantern	**el farol**	streetlamp
el halconcillo	small or young falcon or hawk	**el halcón**	falcon; hawk
el hornillo	kitchen stove	**el horno**	oven; furnace
el humillo	thin smoke; vapor	**el humo**	smoke; steam
el jaboncillo [R]	soapstone; toilet soap	**el jabón**	soap
el librillo	book of cigarette paper	**el libro**	book
el marranillo	little pig	**el marrano**	pig; swine; (coll.) filthy creature
el nudillo	knuckle	**el nudo**	joint; knot
el panecillo [R]	roll	**el pan**	bread
el pasillo [R 4722]	aisle; hallway	**el paseo**	walk; avenue
el pastelillo	small cake; meat pie	**el pastel**	cake; pastry
el pecadillo	small sin; peccadillo	**el pecado**	sin
el pececillo	little fish	**el pez**	fish
el perrillo	small dog	**el perro**	dog
el platillo [R 2064]	saucer; small dish; dish (food)	**el plato**	plate; dish
el plieguecillo	half-sheet of paper	**el pliego**	sheet of paper
el puntillo	small point; punctilio	**el punto**	point; period; dot
el torillo	little bull	**el toro**	bull
el tornillo [R]	screw	**el torno**	wheel; axletree
el trabajillo	small job; modest piece of work	**el trabajo**	work; job; labor
el versecillo	little verse	**el verso**	verse; line
el vientecillo	light wind; breeze	**el viento**	wind

-illo⁽²⁾; -illa

Meaning: *deprecative; diminutive in status*
English equivalent: *none*
Found in: *nouns*

The overall function of *-illo* and *-illa* is to denote physical diminution of the root noun to which either ending is attached. This particular grouping of words ending in *-illo* or *-illa* denotes a lessened status of the base word and thus the diminution is figurative, not literal or physical. Several of these words, especially those dealing with professions, are rather telling. Note that many of these terms have inserted the letter *c* between the root and the suffix. Those words ending in *-illo* are masculine, while those taking the suffix *-illa* are feminine. When the term refers to a female person, the ending *-illo* becomes *-illa*: a male "quack" is *el mediquillo*; a female "quack" is *la mediquilla*.

Formed Word	English Equivalent	Related to	English Equivalent
el abogadillo	third-rate lawyer	el abogado	lawyer
el amorcillo [R]	passing fancy; flirtation	el amor	love; affection
el animalillo	wretched little animal or creature	el animal	animal; creature
el autorcillo	third-rate author	el autor	author
el baratillo	heap of junk for sale	el barato	bargain; sale
el cieguillo	poor little blind person	el ciego	blind person
la cosilla	miserable little thing	la cosa	thing
el disgustillo	minor or petty upset	el disgusto	displeasure; upset
el doctorcillo	third-rate doctor; "quack"	el doctor	doctor
el escritorcillo	third-rate writer	el escritor	writer
el estanquillo	small, poor shop	el estanco	state-run shop
el estudiantillo	wretched student	el estudiante	student
el favorcillo	petty or minor favor or service	el favor	favor; good turn
la figurilla	(coll.) insignificant little person	la figura	figure; person
el geniecillo	sharpish temper	el genio	temperament; disposition; mood
la gentecilla	riffraff; rabble	la gente	people
el hombrecillo	miserable little man	el hombre	man
el ladroncillo	petty thief	el ladrón	thief
el licenciadillo	wretched lawyer; fraud	el licenciado	lawyer
el maridillo	pitiful husband	el marido	husband
el mediquillo	third-rate doctor; "quack"	el médico	doctor; physician
la mentirilla	white lie	la mentira	lie; falsehood
la mujercilla	wretched woman; slut	la mujer	woman
el pajarillo	miserable little bird; frail bird	el pájaro	bird
el papelillo	scrap of paper; cigarette paper	el papel	paper
la personilla	ridiculous little person	la persona	person
el veranillo	late or untimely summer	el verano	summer
el vinillo	weak wine	el vino	wine

-ín

Meaning: *diminutive*
English equivalent: *none*
Found in: *nouns; adjectives (rarely)*

When added to a noun, the suffix *-ín* can reduce the noun either in physical size or in status (more commonly the reduction is physical). It can also denote a lesser result of the root noun, i.e., *el serrín* (sawdust) from *la sierra* (saw). Infrequently, *-ín* is an adjectival ending; in this capacity, *-ín* still acts as a diminutive, e.g., *pequeñín*. All nouns ending with *-ín* are masculine.

Formed Word	English Equivalent	Related to	English Equivalent
el balín [R]	small-bore bullet	**la bala**	bullet
el banderín [R]	small flag	**la bandera**	flag
el batín	dressing gown	**la bata**	bathrobe
el botín	half-boot; spat	**la bota**	boot
el botiquín	medicine chest; first-aid kit	**la botica**	apothecary's shop
el cafetín	small café; "dive"	**el café**	café
el cajetín	very small box	**la cajeta**	small box
el calabacín	gourd	**la calabaza**	pumpkin
el camarín	small room; boudoir	**la cámara**	room; chamber
el camisolín	dicky; shirt front	**la camisola**	laborer's shirt; blouse
el collarín	small collar; priest's collar	**el collar**	collar
el copetín	cocktail	**la copa**	drink (usually alcoholic)
el cornetín	small bugle	**la corneta**	bugle; cornet
el espadín	small dress sword; rapier	**la espada**	sword
el fajín	small band or sash	**la faja**	sash; girdle; band; swathing-band
el faldellín	short skirt; kilt	**la falda**	skirt
el langostín	prawn	**la langosta**	lobster
el llavín	latchkey	**la llave**	key
el malandrín [R]	rascal; scoundrel	**el malandar**	wild hog
el maletín	small suitcase; satchel	**la maleta**	suitcase
el patín	small courtyard	**el patio**	court; courtyard
pequeñín *aj*	wee	**pequeño**	small; little
el pilotín	pilot's mate; second pilot	**el piloto**	pilot; mate; driver
el polvorín [R]	very fine powder	**el polvo**	powder
el serrín	sawdust	**la sierra**	saw
el sillín [R]	bicycle seat	**la silla**	chair
el verdín	pond scum; mold	**el verde**	green
el violín	violin; fiddle	**la viola**	viola; viol

-ina

Meaning: *diminutive; place where; denotes feminine name*
English equivalent: *-ine*
Found in: *nouns*

The noun ending *-ina* performs several functions. Its most common is to distinguish the physical side of the base noun, e.g., *la neblina* (fine mist; haze) from *la niebla* (fog; mist; haze). The ending *-ina* also can take on the meaning of "place where," indicating where the action of the root verb takes place, e.g., *la oficina* (office) from *oficiar* (to officiate, minister). Finally, *-ina* can denote the feminine counterpart of the masculine root noun, e.g., *la reina* (queen) from *el rey* (king). At times this ending is found in proper names, e.g., *Josefina* (Josephine) from *José* (Joseph). This suffix has a sister, *-ino*, which is similar in function but less common. All nouns ending in *-ina* are feminine.

Formed Word	English Equivalent	Related to	English Equivalent
Agustina	Augustina	**Agustín**	Augustine
la bailarina	ballerina	**el bailarín**	male ballet dancer
la cabina	cabin	**caber**	to fit, have room
Carolina	Caroline	**Carlos**	Charles
la chocolatina	small chocolate bar	**el chocolate**	chocolate
la cocina [R 1980]	kitchen	**cocer**	to cook
la cortina [3148]	curtain; screen; covering	**la corte**	(royal) court; suite; retinue
Cristina	Christine	**Cristo**	Christ
la escarlatina	(med.) scarlet fever	**la escarlata**	scarlet (color)
la filmina	filmstrip	**el filme**	film
la gallina [R]	(fig.) chicken; hen	**el gallo**	rooster
Guillermina	Wilhelmina	**Guillermo**	William
la heroína [R 4016]	heroine	**el héroe**	hero
Josefina	Josephine	**José**	Joseph
la llantina	fit of weeping	**el llanto**	crying; weeping; flood of tears
la madrina [R]	godmother	**la madre**	mother
la marina [R 2570]	shore; seacoast	**el mar**	sea
la neblina [R]	fine mist; haze	**la niebla**	fog; mist; haze
la oficina [R 625]	office	**oficiar**	to officiate; minister
la palomina [R]	pigeon dung	**la paloma**	pigeon; dove
la piscina	small swimming pool; fish pond	*(Lat.)* **piscis**	fish
la reina [R 1696]	queen	**el rey**	king
Serafina	Serafina	**el serafín**	seraph; angel (beautiful person)
la sonatina [R]	sonatina	**la sonata**	sonata
la sordina [R]	mute; damper (of a piano)	**sordo** *(aj)*	deaf; mute; noiseless
la turbina [R]	turbine	**turbar**	to upset; trouble; disturb
la vitrina [R]	glass case; showcase	*(Lat.)* **vitrum**	glass
la zarina	tsarina	**el zar**	czar; tsar

-ino(1)

Meaning: *diminutive; place where*
English equivalent: *none*
Found in: *nouns*

The noun ending -*ino* usually denotes smallness of the root noun, e.g., *el palomino* (young pigeon) from *la paloma* (pigeon). This ending, however, also can indicate the place where the action of the root verb takes place, e.g., *el molino* (mill) from *moler* (to grind). This suffix has a sister suffix, -*ina*, which is more commonly used but essentially identical in function. Nouns ending with -*ino* are masculine.

Formed Word	English Equivalent	Related to	English Equivalent
el camino [R 663]	road	**caminar**	to walk
el casino [2204]	men's club	**la casa**	house; home; business
el cebollino	onion seedling; chive	**la cebolla**	onion; onion bulb
el colino	cabbage seed	**el col**	cabbage
el molino [R]	mill	**moler**	to grind
el padrino [R]	godfather	**el padre**	father
el palomino [R]	young pigeon	**la paloma**	pigeon; dove
el pollino	young chap or fellow	**el pollo**	(fig.) chap; fellow
el vellocino	fleece	**el vello**	down; nap; soft hair; gossamer

-ino(2) (-ina)

Meaning: *like; relating to; native; native of*
English equivalent: *-ine*
Found in: *adjectives; nouns*

The adjectival suffix -*ino*, which means "like" and "relating to," also is one of several endings that denote origin. Like other endings signifying origin (e.g., -*és* or -*ano*), -*ino* in this context functions as a noun as well as an adjective: *El andino sirve el café argentino a la neoyorquina* (The Andean man serves the coffee from Argentina to the woman from New York). Note that these words are not capitalized, as they are in English, and that words ending in -*ino* take the feminine form -*ina* when denoting or describing a feminine noun.

Formed Word	English Equivalent	Related to	English Equivalent
alpino	Alpine; alpine	**los Alpes**	the Alps
ambarino	relating to amber	**el ámbar**	amber
(el) andino	(native) of the Andes	**los Andes**	the Andes
(el) argelino	(native) of Algeria	**Argelia**	Algeria
(el) argentino [293]	(native) of Argentina	**Argentina**	Argentina
azulino	bluish	**el azul**	white
blanquecino [R]	whitish	**el blanco**	white (color); blank
caballino	relating to horses; equine	**el caballo**	horse
(el) campesino [R 597]	peasant; of the country	**el campo**	country; countryside
canino	canine; relating to dogs	*(Lat.)* **canis**	dog

Formed Word	English Equivalent	Related to	English Equivalent
capitalino [1354]	pertaining to the capital city	**la capital**	capital
cochino	(coll.) filthy; rotten; vile	**el cocho**	(prov.) pig; filthy person
corderino	relating to lambs	**el cordero**	lamb
cristalino [R]	crystalline	**el cristal**	crystal
dañino [R]	harmful; destructive; noxious	**el daño**	damage; harm
elefantino	elephantine; (of) ivory	**el elefante**	elephant
esmeraldino	emeraldlike	**la esmeralda**	emerald
ferino	wild; savage; ferocious	*(Lat.)* **fera**	a wild animal
(el) filipino [3901]	(native) of the Philippines; Filipino	**Las Filipinas**	Philippines
(el) florentino	(native) of Florence; Florentine	**Florencia**	Florence
(el) granadino	(native) of Granada	**Granada**	Granada
latino [R 987]	Latino	**Latín**	Latin
marino [R 3811]	*nmf* marine; *aj* sea; seagoing	**mar**	sea
mortecino	dying	**la muerte**	death
(el) neoyorquino [4448]	(native) of New York	**Nueva York**	New York
(el) palestino [626]	(native) of Palestine	**La Palestina**	Palestine
platino [4725]	platinum	**la plata**	silver
purpurino	purplish	**la púrpura**	purple (color)
repentino [R]	sudden; unexpected	**el repente**	start; sudden movement
sabatino [R 4858]	Saturday, Sabbath	**el sábado**	Saturday, Sabbath
(el) salmantino	(native) of Salamanca	**Salamanca**	Salamanca
(el) santiaguino	(native) of Santiago	**Santiago**	Santiago
septembrino	of September	**septiembre**	September
serpentino	serpentine; snakelike	**la serpiente**	serpent; snake
(el) tangerino	(native) of Tangiers	**Tánger**	Tangiers
taurino [4425]	pertaining to bullfighting	**el toro**	bull
(el) tunecino	(native) of Tunis or Tunisia	**Túnez**	Tunis; Tunisia
zucarino	sugary	**el azúcar**	sugar

-isco (-isca)

Meaning: *like; relating to; result of action*
English equivalent: *none*
Found in: *adjectives; nouns*

The ending *-isco* is used infrequently and is found in both adjectives and nouns. As an adjectival ending, the resulting word will indicate that the person or thing described holds characteristics of the base term, usually a noun (*-isco* will change to *-isca* when the adjective describes a feminine noun). As a noun ending, the base word is a verb, and the formed word will indicate the result of that action. All nouns ending with *-isco* are masculine; those ending with *-isca* are feminine.

Formed Word	English Equivalent	Related to	English Equivalent
arenisco	sandy; gritty; like sand	**la arena**	sand; grit
arisco	churlish; surly; evasive	**ariscarse**	to become sullen, standoffish

Formed Word	English Equivalent	Related to	English Equivalent
levantisco	turbulent; restless; Levantine	**el levante**	east coast of Spain; east wind; Levant
el mordisco [R]	bite; pinch	**morder**	to bite, nip
morisco	Moorish	**el moro**	Moor

-ísimo (-ísima)

Meaning: *adjectival superlative*
English equivalent: *none*
Found in: *adjectives*

The most common superlative ending for Spanish adjectives is *-ísimo* (*-ísima* when describing feminine nouns). It can be added to most adjectives (except those whose final consonant is *r*; see *-érrimo*), and its formation is simple: if the root adjective ends with a vowel (or vowels), drop the vowel(s) and add *-ísimo*; if the root adjective ends with a consonant, add *-ísimo* directly. The exception is with base adjectives ending with *-ble*, where an *i* is added between the *b* and the *l*: *amable; amabilísimo*. The standard orthographic changes of *c* to *qu* (*rico; riquísimo*), *z* to *c* (*feliz; felicísimo*), and *g* to *gu* (*largo; larguísimo*) should be noted, because this suffix begins with the letter *i*.

Formed Word	English Equivalent	Related to	English Equivalent
amabilísimo	extremely kind	**amable**	kind
beatísimo	most holy	**beato**	blessed; pious; devout
bellísimo	extremely fair; beautiful	**bello**	fair; beautiful
bonísimo/buenísimo	extremely good	**bueno**	good
clarísimo	extremely clear	**claro**	clear
delgadísimo	extremely thin	**delgado**	thin; lean
delicadísimo	extremely delicate	**delicado**	delicate; dainty
excelentísimo	most excellent	**excelente**	excellent
feísimo	extremely ugly; hideous	**feo**	ugly
felicísimo	extremely happy	**feliz**	happy; merry; glad
ferventísimo	extremely fervent	**ferviente**	fervent
grandísimo	extremely large; huge	**grande**	big; large
guapísimo	extremely handsome	**guapo**	handsome
hermosísimo	extremely beautiful	**hermoso**	beautiful
horribilísimo	extremely horrible	**horrible**	horrible
ilustrísimo [R]	extremely illustrious	**ilustre**	illustrious
importantísimo	extremely important	**importante**	important
jovencísimo	extremely young	**joven**	young
larguísimo	extremely long	**largo**	long
limpísimo	extremely clean	**limpio**	clean
malísimo	extremely bad	**malo**	bad; evil
mismísimo	very same; selfsame	**mismo**	same
muchísimo [R]	enormous amount; very much	**mucho**	much; a lot
nobilísimo	most noble	**noble**	noble
notabilísimo	most notable	**notable**	notable

Formed Word	English Equivalent	Related to	English Equivalent
palidísimo	extremely pale; white as a sheet	**pálido**	pale
pequeñísimo	extremely small; tiny	**pequeño**	small; tiny
poquísimo	miserable little (amount)	**poco**	small (amount)
riquísimo	extremely rich; wealthy	**rico**	rich
santísimo [R]	most holy	**santo**	holy; blessed
sucísimo	extremely dirty; filthy	**sucio**	dirty; filthy
valentísimo	most valiant	**valiente**	valiant
venerabilísimo	most venerable	**venerable**	venerable

-ismo

Meaning: *system; doctrine; loyalty to; act; characteristic*
English equivalent: *-ism*
Found in: *nouns*

Though it has a number of specific meanings, the suffix *-ismo* can be reduced to one general function, that of expanding upon the particular. For example, from *el vándalo* (vandal) we get *el vandalismo* (vandalism), which encompasses all vandals and their actions. Note the expansive effect this suffix has on the base term in the following examples. Words ending with *-ismo* are masculine.

Formed Word	English Equivalent	Related to	English Equivalent
el alcoholismo	alcoholism	**el alcohol**	alcohol
el analfabetismo	illiteracy	**el alfabeto**	alphabet
el argentinismo	Argentinism	**Argentina**	Argentina
el atletismo [R 3528]	track and field	**el atleta**	athlete
el caciquismo	control by political "machine"	**el cacique**	political leader
el conservadurismo [R]	conservatism	**el conservador**	(polit.) conservative
el despotismo	despotism	**el déspota**	despot
el dogmatismo [R]	dogmatism	**el dogma**	dogma
el egoísmo [R]	egoism; selfishness	**el ego**	ego; self
el esnobismo	snobbery	**el esnob**	snob
el españolismo [R]	love or devotion to Spain	**España**	Spain
el evangelismo [R]	evangelism	**el Evangelio**	gospel
el feísmo	cult of the ugly or hideous	**feo**	ugly; nasty
el gitanismo	gypsyism; gypsy life	**el gitano**	gypsy
el hipnotismo	hypnotism	**la hipnosis**	hypnosis
el idealismo	idealism	**el ideal**	ideal
el idiotismo	ignorance	**el idiota**	idiot
el liberalismo [R]	liberalism	**el liberal**	liberal
el machismo	glorification of masculinity	**el macho**	male
el magnetismo	magnetism	**el magneto**	magnet
el materialismo [R]	materialism	**el material**	material
el mecanismo [R 1882]	mechanism	**el mecánico**	mechanic
el mejicanismo	Mexicanism	**Méjico**	Mexico
el nacionalismo [R]	nationalism	**el nacional**	nationalist
el narcisismo	narcissism	**Narciso**	Narcissus

Formed Word	English Equivalent	Related to	English Equivalent
el narcotismo	drug addition	**el narcótico**	narcotic
el obrerismo [R]	labor movement	**el obrero**	laborer
el optimismo [R 4160]	optimism	**óptimo**	optimum
el organismo [R 616]	organism	**el órgano**	organ
el paganismo	paganism	**el pagano**	pagan
el patriotismo [R]	patriotism	**la patria**	native land; fatherland
el periodismo [R 4002]	journalism	**el periódico**	newspaper
el radicalismo [R]	radicalism	**el radical**	radical
el salvajismo [R]	savagery	**el salvaje**	savage
el tabaquismo [R]	addition to cigarettes	**el tabaco**	tobacco; cigarettes
el terrorismo [R 1647]	terrorism	**el terror**	terror
el turismo [R 2058]	tourism	**el turista**	tourist
el vandalismo	vandalism	**el vándalo**	vandal
el ventajismo	(political) one-upmanship	**la ventaja**	advantage; good point
el verbalismo	verbalism	**el verbo**	word; (gram.) verb

-ista

Meaning: *one who; denotes profession*
English equivalent: *-ist*
Found in: *nouns*

Generally speaking, endings that indicate *one who* have both masculine and feminine forms (e.g., *-ero/-era; -dor/-dora*, etc.). The suffix *-ista*, however, is both masculine and feminine (*el dentista; la dentista*), and thus the gender of the person referred to is determined from context. Words ending in *-ista*, though usually derived from nouns, can be derived from verbs and adjectives as well.

Formed Word	English Equivalent	Related to	English Equivalent
el acuarelista [R]	watercolor artist	**la acuarela**	watercolor
el andinista	mountain climber	**los Andes**	the Andes
el artista [R 517]	artist	**el arte**	art
el automovilista [R 2843]	car driver	**el automóvil**	automobile
el bautista	one who baptizes; Baptist	**bautizar**	to baptize
el budista	Buddhist	**Buda**	Buddha
el capitalista [R]	capitalist	**el capital**	capital
el carterista	pickpocket	**la cartera**	pocketbook; wallet
el ciclista [R 2178]	cyclist	**el ciclo**	cycle
el cientista	scientist	**la ciencia**	science
el clarinetista	clarinet player	**el clarinete**	clarinet
el comunista [R 4265]	communist	**común**	common
el dentista [R 4154]	dentist	**el diente**	tooth
el deportista [R 2378]	sportsman	**el deporte**	sport; pastime
el economista [R 3419]	economist	**la economía**	economy
el especialista [R 1556]	specialist	**especial**	special
el espiritualista [R]	spiritualist	**el espíritu**	spirit
el extremista [R 4583]	extremist	**el extremo**	extreme
el fatalista [R]	fatalist	**fatal**	fatal

Formed Word	English Equivalent	Related to	English Equivalent
el finalista [R 4666]	finalist	**el fin**	end
el flautista	flautist	**la flauta**	flute
el florista [R]	florist	**la flor**	flower
el formalista [R]	formalist	**formal**	formal
el futbolista [2398]	soccer player	**el fútbol**	soccer; football
el guitarrista [R 4717]	guitarist, guitar player	**la guitarra**	guitar
el humanista [R]	humanist	**el humano**	human
el inversionista [R 2531]	investor	**la inversión**	(com.) investment
el licorista	liquor dealer or seller	**el licor**	liquor
el literalista	literalist; adherent to the letter	**literal**	literal
el maquinista [R]	machinist	**la máquina**	machine
el marxista	Marxist	**Marx**	Karl Marx
el materialista [R 4525]	*nmf* materialist; *aj* materialistic	**la material**	material
el mediocampista [3476]	midfielder	**el campo**	field
el mundialista [3750]	player in the World Cup (soccer)	**el mundo**	world
el optimista [R 4021]	optimist	**óptimo**	best; first-class
el pacifista [R]	pacifist	**la paz**	peace
el paisajista	landscape painter	**el paisaje**	landscape; scenery
el panista [1169]	supporter of the political party *PAN* (*Partido Acción Nacional*)	**PAN**	PAN
el partidista [R 3522]	partisan	**partido**	party
el perfeccionista [R]	perfectionist	**la perfección**	perfection
el periodista [R 1261]	journalist	**el periódico**	newspaper
el perredista [1915]	supporter of the political party *PRD* (*Partido Revolucionario Democrático*)	**PRD**	PRD
el pesimista [R]	pessimist	**pésimo**	atrocious; abominable
el pianista [R]	pianist	**el piano**	piano
el profesionista [3074]	professional	**la profesión**	profession
el realista [R 4804]	realist	**real**	real
el socialista [R 4117]	socialist	**social**	social
el solista [R 3122]	soloist	**el solo**	solo (music)
el taxista [2294]	taxi driver	**el taxi**	taxi
el tenista [3987]	tennis player	**el tenis**	tennis
el terrorista [R 1434]	terrorist	**el terror**	terror
el transportista [R 3480]	transportation worker	**el transporte**	transport
el turista [R 3216]	tourist	**el tour**	tour
el violinista	violinist	**el violín**	violin
el vocabulista	lexicographer; student of words	**el vocablo**	word; term
el vocalista [R 3158]	vocalist	**vocal**	vocal

-ita

Meaning: *diminutive*
English equivalent: *none*
Found in: *nouns*

The suffix *-ita* indicates smallness of the root noun to which it is attached. At times, the additon of *-ita* changes not only the size but also the meaning of the term itself, e.g., *la animita* (firefly) from *el ánimo* (soul; spirit). This ending has a sister suffix, *-ito*, which performs the same function. Words ending in *-ita* are feminine.

Formed Word	English Equivalent	Related to	English Equivalent
la animita	firefly	el ánimo	soul; spirit
la cajita	small box	la caja	box
la cancioncita	(delightful) little song; tune; ditty	la canción	song; tune
la caperucita	little hood or cap	la caperuza	pointed hood or cap
la chiquita	little girl	la chica	girl; lass
la cunita	little cradle	la cuna	cradle; crib
la espadita	small sword	la espada	sword
la estrellita	small star	la estrella	star
la florecita	little flower	la flor	flower
la hormiguita	tiny little ant	la hormiga	ant
la lentejita	small lentil	la lenteja	lentil
la manecita	small hand	la mano	hand
la mariquita	ladybird; (coll.) sissy	la marica	(orn.) magpie
la mosquita	small fly	la mosca	fly
la nochecita	twilight; nightfall	la noche	night
la notita	short note	la nota	note; bill; statement
la ollita	small pot	la olla	pot
la pajita	drinking straw	la paja	straw (crop)
la palabrita	brief or gentle word	la palabra	word
la patita	small foot	la pata	foot; paw
la pesita	small weight	el peso	weight
la pollita	chick; young chicken; (coll.) girl	el pollo	chicken; (fig.) young fellow
la ramita	sprig; twig	la rama	branch
la señorita [R]	Miss; young lady	la señora	Mrs.; lady; gentlewoman
la sorpresita	little surprise	la sorpresa	surprise
la sortijita	little ring; ringlet	la sortija	ring; curl (of hair)
la trencita	braid; plait	la trenza	braided hair; tresses
la vaquita	small cow	la vaca	cow
la velita	small candle; votive candle	la vela	candle
la viejecita	little old woman	la vieja	old woman
la viudita	merry little widow	la viuda	widow

-itis

Meaning: *disease; inflamation*
English equivalent: *-itis*
Found in: *nouns*

Words ending with *-itis*, in English as in Spanish, often are medical terms that indicate inflammation of the base term. Although frequently such words are not related directly to other Spanish terms, they are easy to recognize because they are cognates of their English counterparts. Spanish words ending with *-itis* are feminine.

Formed Word	English Equivalent	Related to	English Equivalent
la amigdalitis	tonsillitis	la amígdala	tonsil
la apendicitis	appendicitis	el apéndice	appendix
la artritis	arthritis	(Gr.) *arthron*	joint
la bronquitis	bronchitis	(Gr.) *bronchos*	windpipe
la celulitis	cellulitis	la célula	cell; cellule
la colitis	colitis	el colon	(anat.) colon
la conjuntivitis	conjunctivitis	(Lat.) *conjunctivus*	serving to connect
la dermatitis	dermatitis	(Gr.) *derma*	skin
la diverticulitis	diverticulitis	(Lat.) *diversticulum*	a bypath
la esplenitis	splenitis	el esplín	spleen
la estomatitis	stomatitis	(Gr.) *stoma*	mouth
la flebitis	phlebitis	(Gr.) *phleps*	vein
la gastritis	gastritis	(Gr.) *gaster*	belly
la gingivitis	gingivitis	(Gr.) *gingiva*	the gum
la glositis	glossitis	(Gr.) *glossa*	tongue
la hepatitis [R 3532]	hepatitis	(Gr.) *hepar*	liver
la laringitis	laryngitis	la laringe	larynx
la meningitis	meningitis	(Gr.) *meninx*	membrane
la nefritis	nephritis	(Gr.) *nephros*	kidney
la neumonitis	pneumonitis	(Gr.) *pneumon*	lung
la neuritis	neuritis	(Gr.) *neuron*	nerve
la oftalmitis	ophthalmitis	(Gr.) *ophthalmos*	eye
la otitis	otitis	(Gr.) *ous*	ear
la ovaritis	ovaritis	(Lat.) *ovarium*	egg
la pancreatitis	pancreatitis	el páncreas	pancreas
la pericarditis	pericarditis	(Gr.) *peri + kardia*	around + heart
la peritonitis	peritonitis	(Gr.) *peri + teinein*	around + to stretch
la queratitis	keratitis	(Gr.) *keras*	horn
la rinitis	rhinitis	(Gr.) *rhis*	nose
la sinusitis	sinusitis	el seno	(med.) sinus
la tendinitis	tendonitis	el tendón	tendon
la timpanitis	tympanitis	(Gr.) *tympanon*	drum
la vaginitis	vaginitis	la vagina	vagina

-ito⁽¹⁾

Meaning: *diminutive*
English equivalent: *none*
Found in: *nouns*

The suffix *-ito* indicates physical smallness of the root noun to which it is attached. This ending can also express endearment or familiarity, as in *Miguelito* (Mike; "Mikey") from *Miguel* (Michael). One colloquial exception is the term *adiosito* (from *adiós*), said in the same spirit as the English *ta-ta*. The ending *-ito* is a common one and has a sister suffix, *-ita*, which performs the same function. Words ending in *-ito* are masculine.

Formed Word	English Equivalent	Related to	English Equivalent
el abuelito	little grandfather; "gramps"	**el abuelo**	grandfather
adiosito *(interj.)*	ta-ta	**adiós**	good-bye
el besito	(delightful) little kiss	**el beso**	kiss
el bracito	little arm	**el brazo**	arm
el braserito	small pan to hold coals	**el brasero**	brazier; fire-pan
el burrito	(attractive or nice) little donkey	**el burro**	donkey; ass; burro
el caballito	small horse; pony	**el caballo**	horse
el cajoncito	small drawer; desk drawer	**el cajón**	drawer
el cerdito	piglet; (dear) little pig; piggy	**el cerdo**	(lit., fig.) pig; hog
el cochecito	pram; baby carriage	**el coche**	coach; carriage; car
el conejito	small rabbit	**el conejo**	rabbit
el corazoncito	dear little heart	**el corazón**	heart
el cordelito	fine, thin cord	**el cordel**	cord; thin rope; line
el corralito	playpen	**el corral**	enclosure; yard; barnyard
Danielito	little Daniel; "Danny"	**Daniel**	Daniel
despacito *av*	(coll.) very slowly; nice and slowly	**despacio** *(av)*	slowly; carefully; with attention
el dientecito	little tooth	**el diente**	tooth
el gatito	kitten	**el gato**	cat
el granito	small grain	**el grano**	grain
el halconcito	small or young falcon or hawk	**el halcón**	falcon; hawk
el huerfanito	little orphan	**el huérfano**	orphan
el jueguecito	little game	**el juego**	game
Miguelito	little Michael; "Mikey"	**Miguel**	Michael
el momentito	tiny bit of time	**el momento**	moment; minute
el palito	little stick	**el palo**	stick; pole
el patito	duckling	**el pato**	duck
el pedacito	small bit; small piece	**el pedazo**	piece; bit; lump
el perrito	puppy	**el perro**	dog
el pobrecito	poor little person or things	**el pobre**	poor person; pauper; beggar
el poquito	very small amount	**el poco**	little amount
el puentecito	small bridge; footbridge	**el puente**	bridge
el ratito	very short time; little while	**el rato**	short time; while
el regalito	small gift or present	**el regalo**	gift; present
el saltito	little hop	**el salto**	jump; spring; leap

Formed Word	English Equivalent	Related to	English Equivalent
el santito	regular little saint; image of a saint	el santo	saint
el sueñecito	nap	el sueño	sleep; sleepiness; dream
el traguito	short swig	el trago	swallow; gulp; swig; drink
el trapito	small rag	el trapo	rag
el trencito	little train; toy train	el tren	train
el viejecito	little old man	el viejo	old man

-ito(2); -ita

Meaning: *like; relating to; quality; mineral product; native; native of; one who*
English equivalent: *-ite*
Found in: *adjectives; nouns*

Spanish words ending in *-ito* or *-ita* nearly always have as their English counterparts cognates ending with *-ite* or *-yte* (those ending in *-yte* are derived from Greek). This pair of suffixes is found in adjectives as well as in nouns and can indicate several different meanings. Most words ending with *-ito* follow the usual pattern whereby the final *o* becomes *a* when denoting or describing a feminine noun; however, three examples given below, *semita* (Semite), *israelita* (Israelite), and *vietnamita* (Vietnamese), always end with *-ita*, whether masculine or feminine (*el semita; la semita*). These terms are not capitalized as they are in English and they function as both adjectives and nouns. Otherwise, all nouns ending with *-ito* are masculine, while those ending with *-ita* are feminine. Note that this is a common ending for minerals.

Formed Word	English Equivalent	Related to	English Equivalent
el acólito	acolyte; assistant	(Gr.) **akolouthos**	follower; attendant
el apetito [R 4808]	appetite	(Lat.) **appetere**	to strive after, long for
contrito	contrite	(Lat.) **conterere**	to rub away, grind
el crédito [R 752]	credit	(Lat.) **credere**	to trust
decrépito	decrepit; fallen into decay	decrepitar	to decrepitate, crackle
el depósito [R 2555]	deposit	depositar	to deposit
la dinamita [R]	dynamite	(Gr.) **dynamis**	power
emérito	emeritus	(Lat.) **emerere**	to obtain by service
erudito [R]	erudite; learned; scholarly	(Lat.) **erudire**	to free from rudeness
la estalactita	stalactite	(Gr.) **stalaktos**	oozing out in drops
la estalagmita	stalagmite	(Gr.) **stalagmos**	a dropping; dripping
exquisito [R 3782]	exquisite	(Lat.) **exquirere**	to search out
favorito [R 1194]	favorite	el favor	favor
finito [R]	finite	el fin	end
frito [4873]	fried	freír	to fry
el grafito	graphite	(Gr.) **graphein**	to write
el granito	granite	el grano	grain
gratuito [R 2140]	gratuitous	grato	pleasing; pleasant
el hábito [R 2500]	habit	habitar	to inhabit
ilícito [R 2208]	illicit; unlawful	(Lat.) **il + licet**	not + to permit
infinito [R]	infinite	in + el fin	not + end
ingénito	innate; inborn	(Lat.) **ingignere**	to implant by birth
(el) islamita	Islamic; Islamite	el islam	Islam

Formed Word	English Equivalent	Related to	English Equivalent
(el) israelita	Israelite	**Israel**	Israel
lícito [R]	licit; lawful	*(Lat.)* **licet**	it is permitted
el mérito [R 3270]	merit	**merecer**	to deserve, merit
el meteorito	meteorite	**el meteoro**	meteor
el neófito	neophyte	*(Gr.)* **neos + phytos**	new + grown
el nitrito	nitrite	*(Lat.)* **nitrum**	natron; natural soda
la pirita	pyrite	**la pira**	pyre
el pretérito	past; preterite	**preterir**	to pass over, leave out
recóndito	recondite; hidden; concealed	*(Lat.)* **recondere**	to put away, store
(el) semita	Semite	**Shem**	Shem (son of Noah)
solícito [R]	solicitous; eager to please	**solicitar**	to solicit, request, apply for
el sulfito	sulphite	*(Lat.)* **sulfur**	sulfur; sulphur
el tránsito [R 1279]	transit; traffic; passage	*(Lat.)* **transitus**	transit; a passing over or across
(el) vietnamita	Vietnamese	**Vietnam**	Vietnam

-itud

Meaning: *state of being; condition*
English equivalent: *-tude*
Found in: *nouns*

A Spanish word that ends in *-tud* is a noun that denotes the state or condition of the base word. Usually the base is an adjective: *la ineptitud* (ineptitude) indicates the state of being *inepto* (inept). Infrequently, these formed words are derived from nouns: *la actitud* (attitude) comes from *el acto* (act; deed); however, *-itud* still indicates the state or condition of that root. All words ending with *-itud* are feminine.

Formed Word	English Equivalent	Related to	English Equivalent
la actitud [R 1078]	attitude; posture; pose	**el acto**	act; deed
la amplitud [R]	amplitude; roominess	**amplio**	ample; spacious; roomy
la aptitud [R]	aptitude; fitness; ability	**apto**	able; competent; apt; fit
la beatitud	beatitude	**beato**	blessed
la decrepitud	decrepitude	**decrépito**	decrepit; fallen into decay
la esclavitud [R]	slavery; bondage	**el esclavo**	slave
la exactitud [R]	exactness; accuracy	**exacto**	exact; accurate
el excelsitud	loftiness	**excelso**	lofty; sublime
la habitud	relationship; convention; custom	**el hábito**	habit
la ilicitud	illicitness	**ilícito**	illicit
la ineptitud [R]	ineptitude; incompetency	**inepto**	inept; incompetent
la inexactitud [R]	inexactness; inaccuracy	**inexacto**	inexact; inaccurate
la inverosimilitud	unlikelihood; incredibleness	**inverosímil**	unlikely; incredible
la juventud [R 2076]	youth; state of being young	**joven**	young
la lasitud	lassitude; weariness; languor	**laso**	weary; weak; languid
la latitud	latitude; breadth; width	**lato**	broad; wide; large

Formed Word	English Equivalent	Related to	English Equivalent
la laxitud	laxness; laxity	**laxo**	lax; slack
la lentitud [R]	slowness	**lento**	slow
la longitud [R 4019]	longitude; length	**luengo** *(obs.)*	long; far
la magnitud [R 3584]	magnitude	**magno**	great
la plenitud [R 4748]	plenitude; fullness	**pleno**	full
la prontitud	promptitude; promptness	**pronto**	prompt; soon
la pulcritud	pulchritude; neatness	**pulcro**	neat; tidy; fastidious
la rectitud [R]	rectitude	**recto**	right; upright; precise
la similitud [R]	similitude; similarity	**símil**	similar
la solicitud [R 1388]	solicitude; diligence; care	**solícito**	solicitous; diligent; careful
la verosimilitud	verisimilitude	**verosímil**	likely; probable; verisimilar
la vicisitud	vicissitude	**el vicio**	vice

-ivo (-iva)

Meaning: *causing; making*
English equivalent: *-ive*
Found in: *adjectives*

Spanish adjectives ending in *-ivo* nearly always have an English counterpart ending in *-ive*. The examples given below, all derived from verbs, indicate that someone or something behaves in a manner related to the particular base verb. As with adjectives ending in *-o*, when describing a noun of feminine gender, *-ivo* becomes *-iva*.

Formed Word	English Equivalent	Related to	English Equivalent
abusivo [R]	abusive	**abusar**	to abuse
activo [R 1806]	active	**actuar**	to act
administrativo [R 1350]	administrative	**administrar**	to administer, manage
admirativo [R]	admiring; wondering	**admirar**	to admire, marvel, or wonder at
atractivo [R 1509]	attractive	**atraer**	to attract
calculativo	calculative	**calcular**	to calculate
colectivo [R 2619]	*nm* collective; shuttle; *aj* collective	**colectar**	to collect
competitivo [R 2609]	competitive	**competir**	to compete
creativo [R 3470]	creative	**crear**	to create
decisivo [R 3975]	decisive	**decidir**	to decide
declarativo	declarative	**declarar**	to declare, state; (law) to find
defensivo [R 1664]	defensive	**defender**	to defend, shield
definitivo [R 1592]	definitive	**definir**	to define
delictivo [3464]	criminal	**delinquir**	to commit a crime
descriptivo [R]	descriptive	**describir**	to describe
digestivo [4190]	digestive	**digerir**	to digest, take in
directivo [R 699]	*nf directiva*: board of governors; *aj* directive; managing	**dirigir**	to direct

Formed Word	English Equivalent	Related to	English Equivalent
educativo [R 831]	educational	educar	to educate
efectivo [R 1156]	effective	efectuar	to effect
ejecutivo [R 659]	executive	ejecutar	to execute, carry out, perform
emotivo [R 3828]	emotive; causing emotion	motivar	to motivate
evocativo	evocative	evocar	to evoke
evolutivo [R]	evolutionary; evolving	evolucionar	to evolve
excesivo [R 2806]	excessive	exceder	to exceed
exclamativo	exclamatory	exclamar	to exclaim, cry out
exclusivo [R 2061]	exclusive	excluir	to exclude
expansivo [R]	expansive	expansionar	to expand
expeditivo [R]	expeditious; prompt	expedir	to facilitate, expedite
explosivo [R 2859]	explosive	explotar	to explode
germinativo	germinative	germinar	to germinate, bud
gubernativo	administrative; governmental	gobernar	to govern, rule
ilusivo	illusive	ilusionar	to delude (vt); to have illusions (vr)
ilustrativo [R]	illustrative	ilustrar	to illustrate
imaginativo [R]	imaginative	imaginar	to imagine
imperativo [R]	imperative	imperar	to rule, reign, command
inclusivo	inclusive	incluir	to include
indicativo [R]	indicative	indicar	to indicate
informativo [R 2841]	informative	informar	to inform
legislativo [R 1198]	legislative	legislar	to legislate
meditativo [R]	meditative	meditar	to meditate (on)
nativo [R 4158]	native	nacer	to be born
negativo [R 1281]	nm photographic negative; aj negative	negar	to deny
normativo [R 3934]	normative	normar	to set standards
nutritivo [R 4512]	nutritive	nutrir	to nourish, feed
ofensivo [R 1175]	offensive	ofender	to offend, slight
operativo [R 839]	operative	operar	to operate
preventivo [R 824]	preventive	prevenir	to prevent
productivo [R 1302]	productive	producir	to produce
regenerativo	regenerative	regenerar	to regenerate
regresivo [R]	regressive	regresar	to return
representativo [R 2621]	representative	representar	to represent
repulsivo [R]	repulsive	repulsar	to rebuff, reject
significativo [R 2228]	well-explained; clear; meaningful	significar	to mean
sorpresivo [R 4467]	surprising	sorprender	to surprise
televisivo [R 2964]	television	televisar	to televise
vivo [R 1152]	alive	vivir	to live

-ívoro (-ívora)

Meaning: *tending to eat*
English equivalent: *-ivorous*
Found in: *adjectives*

Those few adjectives ending with *-ívoro* (*-ívora* when describing feminine nouns) are cognates of their English counterparts. In both languages these words indicate that some person or animal tends to eat a particular foodstuff.

Formed Word	English Equivalent	Related to	English Equivalent
carnívoro [R]	carnivorous	la carne	meat; flesh
herbívoro [R]	herbivorous	la hierba	grass; herb
omnívoro	omnivorous	(Lat.) omnis	all; every kind
piscívoro	piscivorous	(Lat.) piscis	fish

-izar

Meaning: *to make (like)*
English equivalent: *-ize*
Found in: *verbs*

When you see a verb ending with *-izar*, note that it means to make or to make like the root noun or adjective. As you will see below, many of the roots to which *-izar* is attached are cognates of English words; you therefore should find these verbs relatively easy to learn and use. Verbs ending with *-izar* are regular and when conjugated make the standard orthographic change from *z* to *c* before the vowel *e: yo organizo* (I organize); *yo organicé* (I organized).

Formed Word	English Equivalent	Related to	English Equivalent
actualizar [R 3167]	to update	actual	actual
agilizar [4090]	to do or perform quickly	ágil	agile
alfabetizar	to alphabetize	el alfabeto	alphabet
amenizar [2924]	to make pleasant, cheer	ameno	pleasant; agreeable
arborizar	to make treelike	el árbol	tree
autorizar [R 1178]	to authorize	el autor	author
bautizar [4927]	to baptize; to be baptized	bautismo	baptism
canalizar [R 3029]	to channel	canal	channel
caracterizar [R 1758]	to characterize	carácter	character
centralizar [R]	to centralize	central	central
climatizar [R]	to air-condition	el clima (artificial)	air conditioning
comercializar [R 3030]	to commercialize	comercial	commercial
especializar [1840]	to specialize	especial	special
estelarizar [3720]	to star	estelar	star
familiarizar [R]	to familiarize	familiar	familiar
fertilizar [R]	to fertilize	fértil	fertile
finalizar [R 1219]	to finalize	final	final
garantizar [R 1313]	to guarantee	garantía	guarantee

Formed Word	English Equivalent	Related to	English Equivalent
generalizar [R 3102]	to generalize	general	general
humanizar [R]	to humanize, soften	el humano	human (being)
legalizar [R]	to legalize	legal	legal
liberalizar [R]	to liberalize	liberal	liberal
localizar [R 1208]	to localize; to find	local	local
magnetizar	to magnetize	el magneto	magnet
memorizar [R]	to memorize	la memoria	memory
modernizar [R 3849]	to modernize	moderno	modern
movilizar [R 4963]	to mobilize	móvil	mobile
nasalizar	to nasalize	nasal	nasal
naturalizar [R]	to naturalize	natural	natural
neutralizar	to neutralize	neutral	neutral
organizar [R 468]	to organize	el órgano	organ; part
paralizar [R 4615]	to paralyze	la parálisis	paralysis
polemizar [R]	to engage in argument	la polémica	polemics; dispute
profundizar [R 4966]	to explore the depths of a subject	profundo	profound; deep
protagonizar [R 1440]	to perform the lead in a play, movie, etc.	protagonista	protagonist; lead
psicoanalizar [R]	to psychoanalyze	el psicoanálisis	psychoanalysis
pulverizar	to pulverize	el polvo	powder; dust
puntualizar [2264]	to make clear, describe in detail	punto	point
realizar [R 73]	to realize, accomplish	real	real
regularizar [R 3755]	to regularize, regulate	regular	regular
responsabilizar [R 4065]	to make responsible for	responsable	responsible
ruborizar [R]	to make blush	el rubor	blush; flush
satirizar	to satirize	la sátira	satire
suavizar [R]	to make smooth	suave	smooth
teorizar [R]	to theorize	la teoría	theory
tranquilizar [R]	to tranquilize	tranquilo	tranquil
utilizar [R 362]	to utilize, make use of	útil	useful
valorizar [R]	to make more valuable	el valor	value; worth
vaporizar [R]	to vaporize	el vapor	vapor
vocalizar [R]	(mus.) to vocalize, articulate	vocal	vocal; oral

-izo (-iza)

Meaning: *like; relating to; made of*
English equivalent: *none*
Found in: *adjectives*

The adjectival ending -izo is one of many Spanish suffixes meaning "like" or "relating to." However, -izo also can mean "made of": from *el cobre* (copper) we get *cobrizo* (made of copper). Adjectives ending in -izo can be derived either from nouns or from other adjectives. When used to describe feminine nouns, words ending with -izo take the ending -iza.

Formed Word	English Equivalent	Related to	English Equivalent
banderizo	factious	el bando	faction; party
castizo [R]	of noble descent; pure-blooded	casto	pure; chaste
cenizo	ash-colored	la ceniza	ash
cobrizo [R]	made of copper	el cobre	copper; brass kitchen utensils
enfermizo [R]	sickly; unhealthy	enfermo	sick
fronterizo [R 2245]	relating to a frontier or border	la frontera	frontier
hechizo	articificial; homemade	hecho	made; done; ready-made
macizo	solid; massive	la masa	mass
pajizo	made of straw	la paja	straw
plomizo	leaden; made of lead	el plomo	lead
primerizo [R]	first	primero	first; former; prime
rojizo [R]	reddish	rojo	red
suizo [2293]	Swiss	Suecia	Switzerland

-lento (-lenta)

Meaning: *like; relating to; full of*
English equivalent: *-lent*
Found in: *adjectives*

Spanish adjectives ending with *-lento* have at their base a noun and indicate that the person or thing described has characteristics of that noun. When describing a feminine noun, these adjectives take the ending *-lenta*.

Formed Word	English Equivalent	Related to	English Equivalent
corpulento [R]	corpulent; fat; fleshy	el cuerpo	body
flatulento	flatulent; windy	el flato	flatus; wind
fraudulento	fraudulent	el fraude	fraud
friolento [R]	chilly; sensitive to cold	el frío	cold; coldness; coolness
pulverulento	powdery; dusty	el polvo	powder; dust
sanguinolento [R]	bloody; dripping blood	*(Lat.)* **sanguis**	blood
suculento	succulent	el suco	sap; juice
violento [R 2363]	violent	la violencia	violence
virulento	virulent	el virus	virus

-manía

Meaning: *insane excitement; madness*
English equivalent: *-mania*
Found in: *nouns*

Spanish words ending with *-manía* are nearly perfect cognates of their English counterparts. These terms refer to madness or excitement with regard to the root term. All words ending with *-manía* are feminine.

Formed Word	English Equivalent	Related to	English Equivalent
la anglomanía	Anglomania; enthusiasm for England	*(Lat.)* **Anglii**	the English
la cleptomanía	kleptomania	*(Gr.)* **kleptes**	thief
la erotomanía	erotomania	**Eros**	Eros
la lipemanía	(med.) melancholia	*(Gr.)* **lipos**	fat
la megalomanía	megalomania	*(Gr.)* **mega**	great; mighty
la monomanía	monomania	*(Gr.)* **monos**	one; single; alone
la ninfomanía	nymphomania	**la ninfa**	nymph; young lady
la piromanía	pyromania	**la pira**	pyre
la toxicomanía	drug addiction	**el tóxico**	poison

-mano; -mana

Meaning: *one who is mad; having insane tendencies*
English equivalent: *-maniac*
Found in: *nouns; adjectives*

As nouns, Spanish words taking the suffix *-mano* refer to persons with overwhelming desires who often gratify them. These same terms also can function as adjectives and are used in describing such persons. When the referent is masculine, the ending is *-mano*; when feminine, the ending is *-mana*.

Formed Word	English Equivalent	Related to	English Equivalent
(el) anglómano	Anglomaniac; in love with England	*(Lat.)* **Anglii**	the English
(el) cleptómano	kleptomaniac	*(Gr.)* **kleptes**	thief
(el) erotómano	erotomaniac	**Eros**	Eros
(el) megalómano	megalomaniac	*(Gr.)* **megas**	great; mighty
(el) monómano	monomaniac	*(Gr.)* **monos**	one; single; alone
(la) ninfómana	nymphomaniac	**la ninfa**	nymph; young lady
(el) pirómano	pyromaniac	**la pira**	pyre
(el) toxicómano	drug addict(ed)	**el tóxico**	poison

-mente

Meaning: *forms adverbs*
English equivalent: *-ly*
Found in: *adverbs*

Just as nearly all English adverbs end in "-ly," nearly all adverbs in Spanish take -*mente* as the ending. Adverbs, which modify verbs, adjectives, and other adverbs, are derived from adjectives. Note that when the root adjective ends with the letter *o*, that *o* changes to *a* before -*mente* is added. All other adjectives simply add -*mente* to become an adverb.

Formed Word	English Equivalent	Related to	English Equivalent
abiertamente [4881]	openly	**abierto**	open
absolutamente [R 3814]	absolutely	**absoluto**	absolute
actualmente [R 536]	presently; nowadays	**actual**	present; present-day
adecuadamente [4200]	adequately	**adecuado**	adequate
afortunadamente [2724]	fortunately; luckily	**afortunado**	fortunate; lucky
altamente [R 3641]	highly	**alto**	high
ampliamente [4030]	amply	**amplio**	ample
anteriormente [R 2395]	beforehand; previously	**anterior**	previous
anualmente [4152]	annually	**anual**	annual
aparentemente [R 3015]	apparently; seemingly	**aparente**	apparent; seeming
aproximadamente [R 1182]	approximately	**aproximado**	approximate
básicamente [3469]	basically	**básico**	basic
ciegamente	blindly	**ciego**	blind
ciertamente [R 3112]	certainly	**cierto**	certain
claramente [3254]	clearly	**claro**	clear
completamente [R 2184]	completely	**completo**	complete
considerablemente [4395]	considerably	**considerable**	considerable
constantemente [R 2746]	constantly	**constante**	constant
continuamente [R 4578]	continually	**continuo**	continuous
culpablemente	guiltily	**culpable**	guilty; culpable; blameworthy
curiosamente [4713]	curiously	**curioso**	curious
debidamente [R 3704]	correctly	**debido**	correct, suitable
definitivamente [R 1911]	definitely	**definitivo**	definitive
desafortunadamente [3795]	unfortunately	**desafortunado**	unfortunate
desgraciadamente [R 3372]	unfortunately; unhappily	**desgraciado**	unfortunate; luckless
diariamente [R 2702]	daily	**diario**	daily
difícilmente [3682]	hardly	**difícil**	difficult
directamente [R 1735]	directly	**directo**	direct
económicamente [R 4475]	economically	**económico**	economic
efectivamente [R 3235]	effectively	**efectivo**	effective
enfáticamente	emphatically	**enfático**	emphatic
especialmente [R 1147]	especially	**especial**	special
específicamente [R 3996]	specifically	**específico**	specific
estupendamente [R]	extremely well; perfectly	**estupendo**	fine; great; super
evidentemente [R 4912]	evidently	**evidente**	evident
exactamente [R 3151]	exactly	**exacto**	exact
exclusivamente [R 3484]	exclusively	**exclusivo**	exclusive
fácilmente [R 2718]	easily	**fácil**	easy

Formed Word	English Equivalent	Related to	English Equivalent
felizmente	happily	**feliz**	happy
finalmente [R 734]	finally	**final**	final
finamente [4847]	finely; delicately; excellently	**fino**	fine, delicate
físicamente [R 4303]	physically	**físico**	physical
formalmente [4224]	formally	**formal**	formal
frecuentemente [R 3631]	frequently	**frecuente**	frequent
fuertemente [4417]	strongly	**fuerte**	strong
generalmente [R 2242]	generally	**general**	general
inculpablemente	blamelessly	**inculpable**	blameless; inculpable
independientemente [R 3152]	independently	**independiente**	independent
indudablemente [4914]	indubitably	**indudable**	indubitable
inicialmente [4079]	initially	**inicial**	initial
inmediatamente [R 2516]	immediately	**inmediato**	immediate
justamente [4358]	precisely; just so	**justo**	just; fair; right
lamentablemente [R 3569]	lamentably	**lamentable**	lamentable
legalmente [R 4492]	legally	**legal**	legal
lentamente [R 4508]	slowly	**lento**	slow
libremente [4797]	freely	**libre**	free
malamente [R]	in an evil manner	**malo**	bad; evil
mentalmente [R]	mentally	**mental**	mental
naturalmente [R 4246]	naturally	**natural**	natural
necesariamente [3500]	necessarily	**necesario**	necessary
neutralmente	neutrally	**neutral**	neutral
normalmente [3154]	normally	**normal**	normal
notablemente	notably	**notable**	notable
nuevamente [R 1471]	again; anew	**nuevo**	new
obviamente [2644]	obviously	**obvio**	obvious
oficialmente [2995]	officially	**oficial**	official
oportunamente [R 4684]	opportunely	**oportuno**	opportune
originalmente [4360]	originally	**original**	original
particularmente [R 2483]	particularly	**particular**	particular
perfectamente [R 3022]	perfectly	**perfecto**	perfect
personalmente [R 3730]	personally	**personal**	personal
plenamente [3547]	fully	**pleno**	full
posiblemente [R 2851]	possibly	**posible**	possible
posteriormente [R 835]	subsequently	**posterior**	subsequent
prácticamente [R 1482]	practically	**práctico**	practical
precisamente [R 1242]	precisely; exactly	**preciso**	precise; accurate; just right
presuntamente [R 3437]	presumably; supposedly	**presunto**	supposed
previamente [R 3011]	previously	**previo**	previous
principalmente [1166]	principally; mainly	**principal**	principal
probablemente	probably	**probable**	probable
profundamente [R 4832]	profoundly; deeply	**profundo**	profound; deep
próximamente [R 4362]	soon; immediately	**próximo**	next
públicamente [R 3984]	publicly	**público**	public
rápidamente [R 2460]	rapidly; fast	**rápido**	rapid; fast
realmente [R 1118]	really	**real**	real
recientemente [R 1232]	recently	**reciente**	recent
regularmente [R 4289]	regularly	**regular**	regular
relativamente [4465]	relatively; comparatively	**relativo**	relative; comparative
respectivamente [R 1711]	respectively	**respectivo**	respective

Formed Word	English Equivalent	Related to	English Equivalent
seguramente [R 1552]	surely; very likely	**seguro**	sure; secure; certain
sencillamente [4067]	simply	**sencillo**	simple
seriamente [4042]	seriously	**serio**	serious
simplemente [R 1294]	simply	**simple**	simple
solamente [R 749]	only; just	**sólo**	only
suficientemente [R 4424]	sufficiently	**suficiente**	sufficient
sumamente [R 2934]	greatly	**sumo**	highest; supreme
supuestamente [2997]	supposedly	**supuesto**	supposed
tristemente	sadly	**triste**	sad
totalmente [1373]	totally	**total**	total
tradicionalmente [4673]	traditionally	**tradicional**	traditional
usualmente	usually	**usual**	usual
últimamente [R 4706]	recently	**último**	last; most recent
únicamente [1340]	only; exclusively	**único**	only; unique
valientemente [R]	valiantly; bravely	**valiente**	valiant; brave
verdaderamente [R 3056]	truly	**verdadero**	true

-miento

Meaning: *act; state of being; result of action*
English equivalent: *-ment*
Found in: *nouns*

The suffix *-miento* marks the achievement of an action. A word ending with *miento* has as its root a verb. Infinitives ending in *-ar* retain the *a* (*tratar* becomes *tratamiento*); *-er* and *-ir* verbs take an *i* before this suffix (*envolver* becomes *envolvimiento*; *sentir* gives us *sentimiento*). All words ending with *-miento* are masculine.

Formed Word	English Equivalent	Related to	English Equivalent
el acercamiento [R 3412]	photographic or television close-up; act of moving closer	**acercar**	to draw near to
el acontecimiento [R 1238]	event	**acontecer**	to happen, occur
agradecimiento [R 4185]	gratefulness	**agradecer**	to give thanks
el agrandamiento	enlargement	**agrandar**	to enlarge
el almacenamiento [R 4186]	warehousing	**almacenar**	to store
el amillaramiento	tax assessment	**amillarar**	to assess a tax on
el aplazamiento	postponement	**aplazar**	to postpone
el aprovechamiento [R 3615]	good or profitable or wise use	**aprovechar**	to take advantage of
el aquietamiento	appeasement	**aquietar**	to appease
el asentamiento [R 4646]	settling	**asentar**	to settle
el atrincheramiento	entrenchment	**atrincherar**	to entrench
el aturdimiento	bewilderment; daze; confusion	**aturdir**	to bewilder, daze, stun
el avasallamiento	enslavement	**avasallar**	to enslave
el comportamiento [1960]	behavior	**comportar**	to behave
el confinamiento [R]	confinement	**confinar**	to confine

Formed Word	English Equivalent	Related to	English Equivalent
el **conocimiento** [R 942]	knowledge	**conocer**	to know
el **crecimiento** [R 802]	growth	**crecer**	to grow
el **cuestionamiento** [4890]	question (formal); questioning	**cuestionar**	to question (formal)
el **cumplimiento** [R 2230]	completion	**cumplir**	to complete
el **descubrimiento** [R 3963]	discovery	**descubrir**	to discover
el **embellecimiento** [R]	embellishment	**embellecer**	to embellish
el **empobrecimiento**	impoverishment	**empobrecer**	to impoverish
el **encadenamiento** [R]	enchainment	**encadenar**	to enchain
el **encantamiento** [R]	enchantment	**encantar**	to enchant
el **encarcelamiento**	imprisonment	**encarcelar**	to imprison
el **enfrentamiento** [R 1871]	confrontation	**enfrentar**	to confront
el **enriquecimiento** [R]	enrichment	**enriquecer**	to enrich
el **entendimiento** [R 4608]	understanding	**entender**	to understand
el **entrenamiento** [1610]	training	**entrenar**	to train
el **entretenimiento** [R 3943]	amusement; entertainment	**entretener**	to amuse, entertain
el **envejecimiento** [R 4113]	aging	**envejecer**	to age
el **equipamiento** [4563]	equipping	**equipar**	to equip
el **envilecimiento**	abasement	**envilecer**	to abase
el **envolvimiento**	envelopment	**envolver**	to envelop
el **esclarecimiento** [R]	enlightenment	**esclarecer**	to light up
el **establecimiento** [R 1788]	establishment	**establecer**	to establish
el **estacionamiento** [2556]	parking lot; parking place	**estacionar**	to park
el **fallecimiento** [R 4739]	death	**fallecer**	to die
el **financiamiento** [1898]	financing	**financiar**	to finance
el **fortalecimiento** [R 3783]	strengthening	**fortalecer**	to strengthen
el **fraccionamiento** [R 2053]	subdivision; neighborhood	**fraccionar**	to split up into fractions
el **funcionamiento** [R 1835]	functioning	**funcionar**	to function
el **incitamiento**	incitement	**incitar**	to incite
el **incumplimiento** [R 3945]	lack of completion	**incumplir**	to leave incomplete, unfinished
el **lanzamiento** [R 2187]	pitch, throw; launch	**lanzar**	to throw, pitch, launch
el **levantamiento** [R 3980]	raising; lifting	**levantar**	to raise
el **limpiamiento**	cleaning	**limpiar**	to clean, cleanse
el **mantenimiento** [R 2015]	maintenance	**mantener**	to maintain
el **mejoramiento** [R 3027]	improvement	**mejorar**	to improve
el **movimiento** [R 820]	movement	**mover**	to move
el **nacimiento** [R 1779]	birth	**nacer**	to be born
el **nombramiento** [R 3302]	appointment	**nombrar**	to appoint, name
el **ofrecimiento** [R 4228]	offer	**ofrecer**	to offer
el **ordenamiento** [R 4589]	ordering; act of placing things in order	**ordenar**	to order, place in order
el **padecimiento** [R 2915]	suffering	**padecer**	to suffer
el **pagamiento**	payment	**pagar**	to pay
el **pensamiento** [R 1995]	thought	**pensar**	to think
el **planteamiento** [3174]	structured plan or outline; proposal	**plantear**	to structure a plan or outline; to propose
el **procedimiento** [R 1356]	procedure	**proceder**	to proceed
el **reclutamiento**	recruitment	**reclutar**	to recruit
el **reconocimiento** [R 1254]	recognition	**reconocer**	to recognize
el **rendimiento** [R 2443]	fatigue; production	**rendir(se)**	to yield, surrender (vt); to yield (vr)

Formed Word	English Equivalent	Related to	English Equivalent
el requerimiento [R 3889]	requirement	**requerir**	to require
el saneamiento [R 2461]	cleaning up; disinfecting	**sanear**	to clean, disinfect
el seguimiento [R 2864]	pursuit; chase; continuation	**seguir**	to follow, come after, continue
el sentimiento [R 1511]	sentiment; feeling; emotion; grief	**sentir**	to sense, feel, regret
el señalamiento [2361]	appointed day; marking with signs	**señalar**	to mark out (with signs)
el sufrimiento [4405]	suffering	**sufrir**	to suffer
el tratamiento [R 1063]	treatment	**tratar**	to treat

-o(1)

Meaning: *resulting object; resulting action*
English equivalent: *none*
Found in: *nouns*

Many of the following formed words are extremely common—so common, in fact, that it is easy to overlook the properties they share. First, notice that they all come from *-ar* verbs; *-er* and *-ir* verbs generally do not produce nouns that indicate result of action in this fashion. Next, while it is obvious that they all end in *-o*, you will see upon closer inspection that such words always are the same as the verb's first-person singular (*yo*) form in the present indicative, e.g., *yo trabajo* (I work); *el trabajo* (the work). Thus, when the root is a stem-changing verb, the change will take place in the noun as well as in the verb: *yo almuerzo; el almuerzo*. All words ending in *-o* derived from *-ar* verbs are masculine.

Formed Word	English Equivalent	Related to	English Equivalent
el abandono [R 3940]	abandonment	**abandonar**	to abandon
el aborto [4485]	miscarriage; abortion	**abortar**	to miscarry; to abort
el abrazo [R]	embrace; hug	**abrazar**	to embrace, hug
el abrigo [R]	overcoat; shelter	**abrigar**	to shelter, protect, cover
el abuso [R 1821]	abuse	**abusar**	to abuse
el acuerdo [R 167]	agreement	**acordar**	to make a deal, come to an accord
el adeudo [R 2614]	debt	**adeudar**	to be in debt
el adorno [R 4576]	decoration	**adornar**	to decorate
el ahorro [R 1987]	savings	**ahorrar**	to save
el aliento [4756]	breath	**alentar**	to breathe
el alimento [R 702]	(nourishing) food; nourishment	**alimentar**	to nourish, feed
el almuerzo [R]	lunch; luncheon	**almorzar**	to eat lunch
el amparo [R 1689]	protection	**amparar**	to protect
el anuncio [R 1997]	announcement	**anunciar**	to announce
el apoyo [R 229]	to support	**apoyar**	to support
el archivo [R 524]	file (storage in office, on a computer, etc.)	**archivar**	to file
el argumento [R 2161]	argument	**argumentar**	to argue
el arreglo [R 1979]	arrangement; repair	**arreglar**	to arrange

Formed Word	English Equivalent	Related to	English Equivalent
el arresto [R 4073]	arrest	arrestar	to arrest
el arribo [R 3957]	arrival of a ship	arribar	to arrive
el asalto [R 2677]	assault	asaltar	to assault
el atajo	shortcut	atajar	to cut short, interrupt
el atraco	holdup; robbery	atracar	to hold up, rob
el atraso [R]	backwardness; delay; slowness	atrasar	to slow (down), retard
el aumento [R 857]	increase; salary raise	aumentar	to increase, augment, magnify
el auxilio [R 2848]	aid; assistance; help	auxiliar	to aid, help, assist
el aviso [R 2234]	warning	avisar	to warn
el ayuno [R]	fast; abstinence	ayunar	to fast
el baño [R 1909]	bath; bathroom	bañar	to bathe
el bateo [4732]	hitting; batting (baseball)	batear	to hit
el beneficio [R 690]	benefit	beneficiar	to benefit
el beso [R 3320]	kiss	besar	to kiss
el bloqueo [R 4438]	blocking	bloquear	to block
el bombardeo [R 4502]	bombardment	bombardear	to bombard
el boxeo [2695]	boxing	boxear	to box
el brillo [R 4810]	brilliancy; luster; shine	brillar	to shine, sparkle, glisten
el cálculo [R 4046]	calculation; calculus; stone (kidney, gall)	calcular	to calculate
el cambio [R 202]	change	cambiar	to change
el camino [R 663]	path; trail; way; highway	caminar	to walk
el canto [R 2666]	song	cantar	to sing
el cargo [R 398]	charge; responsibility; position	cargar	to charge; to place in a position of responsibility
el castigo [R 2958]	punishment; chastisement	castigar	to punish, castigate, chastise
el ciego [R 4262]	blind person; blind	cegar	to blind
el cobro [R 1845]	bill collecting	cobrar	to charge
el comando [R 4503]	commando	comandar	to command
el comercio [R 685]	commerce; business	comerciar	to engage in business
el comienzo [R 2881]	beginning	comenzar	to begin, commence
el complemento [R 4709]	complement	complementar	to complement
el cómputo [R 4109]	counting	computar	to calculate, count
el concreto [R 1967]	concrete	concretar	to specify, make concrete, firm up
el concurso [R 1652]	contest	concursar	to compete in a contest
el conjunto [R 601]	set; ensemble (esp. musicians, outfit, suit)	conjuntar	to unite with harmony
el contacto [R 1590]	contact	contactar	to contact
el contrato [R 1231]	contract	contratar	to contract
el costo [757]	cost	costar	to cost
el cuento [R 2426]	tale; story	contar	to tell (a story)
el cultivo [R 1374]	cultivation (also used figuratively)	cultivar	to cultivate
el curso [R 932]	course (often a short course or training program)	cursar	to take a course
el custodio [3767]	guard; custodian	custodiar	to take care of, guard
el daño [R 731]	damage	dañar	to damage

Formed Word	English Equivalent	Related to	English Equivalent
el dato [941]	information, data	**datar**	to date (from)
el decomiso [4622]	confiscation	**decomisar**	to confiscate
el decreto [R 2163]	decree	**decretar**	to issue a decree
el depósito [R 2555]	deposit	**depositar**	to deposit
el desafío [3188]	challenge	**desafiar**	to challenge
el desarrollo [R 235]	development; growth; expansion	**desarrollar**	to develop, expand
el desayuno [R 3071]	breakfast	**desayunar**	to eat breakfast
el descanso [R 1905]	rest; pause; break	**descansar**	to rest, pause
el descuento [R 3025]	discount	**descontar**	to discount
el descuido [R 4441]	neglect	**descuidar(se)**	to neglect (vt); to neglect oneself, let oneself go (vr)
el desecho [R 3090]	throw-away item	**desechar**	to throw away
el desempeño [R 1998]	the fulfilling of an obligation	**desempeñar**	to take out of pawn; to carry out an obligation or the duties of an office or position
el desempleo [R 2059]	unemployment	**desemplear**	to dismiss from employment
el deseo [R 1155]	desire	**desear**	to desire
el desnudo [R 3373]	nude (art object)	**desnudar**	to undress
el despacho [R 3995]	office; act of dispatching	**despachar**	to dispatch
el desperdicio [R 4336]	waste	**desperdiciar**	to waste
el desvío [R 3026]	detour	**desviar(se)**	to detour, lose one's way
el diagnóstico [2701]	diagnosis	**diagnosticar**	to diagnose
el diálogo [R 1683]	dialogue	**dialogar**	to dialogue
el dibujo [R 3361]	drawing (art)	**dibujar**	to draw
el diseño [2464]	design	**diseñar**	to design
el disparo [R 1461]	shot	**disparar**	to shoot
el divorcio [R 3840]	divorce	**divorciar**	to divorce
el documento [R 886]	document	**documentar**	to document
el egreso [3404]	graduation	**egresar**	to graduate
el ejército [R 998]	army	**ejercitar**	to exercise, practice, train, drill
el embarazo [2366]	pregnancy	**embarazarse**	to become pregnant
el embargo [R 170]	embargo	**embargar**	to embargo; to prohibit commerce
el empleo [R 710]	employment	**emplear**	to employ
el encabezado [2322]	headline	**encabezar**	to head, lead
el encuentro [R 419]	encounter; chance meeting	**encontrar**	to find
el enfermo [R 1990]	sick person; sick, ill	**enfermarse**	to become sick
el engaño [R 4715]	deceit; deception	**engañar**	to deceive
el enojo [R 4313]	anger	**enojar**	to make angry
el ensayo [R 3630]	rehearsal; essay	**ensayar**	to rehearse
el entusiasmo [R 2667]	enthusiasm	**entusiasmar**	to inspire enthusiasm
el envío [R 3453]	sending; item sent for delivery	**enviar**	to send
el escombro [3198]	debris	**escombrar**	to remove debris
el esfuerzo [R 696]	effort	**esforzar(se)**	to force; to make an effort oneself
el espacio [R 612]	space (all meanings)	**espaciar**	to space

Formed Word	English Equivalent	Related to	English Equivalent
el estímulo [R 3016]	stimulus	estimular	to stimulate
el estreno [2397]	first showing (film, theatrical performance, etc.); opening performance	estrenar	to debut, use for the first time
el estudio [R 314]	study; learning	estudiar	to study
el experimento [R 4626]	experiment; experience	experimentar	to experiment; to experience
el extremo [R 1636]	extreme	extremar(se)	to adopt an extreme attitude, go to extremes
el festejo [R 1415]	celebration	festejar	to celebrate
el fomento [2021]	strengthening; medicinal application placed on the body	fomentar	to foment, instigate
el fracaso [R 2045]	failure; collapse; flop	fracasar	to fail, be unsuccessful
el freno [4893]	brake	frenar	to brake
el fundamento [R 4176]	foundation; basis	fundamentar(se)	to place the foundation; to be founded
el gasto [R 780]	expenditure; expense	gastar	to spend (time, money, etc.)
el giro [R 2557]	complete turn; 360-degree turn; money-order	girar	to revolve
el gobierno [R 82]	government	gobernar	to govern, rule
el gozo [R]	joy; pleasure; enjoyment	gozar	to enjoy
el grito [R 2482]	shout; scream	gritar	to shout, scream
el gusto [R 1062]	taste; pleasure; liking	gustar	to be pleasing (to), like
el hado	fate; destiny	hadar	to divine, foretell, fate
el hielo [R 3517]	ice	helar	to freeze
el hilo [R 3363]	thread	hilar	to follow the thread of (conversation, investigation, etc.); to think, deduce; to make thread
el impacto [1502]	impact	impactar	to impact
el impulso [R 2961]	impulse	impulsar	to force
el incendio [2013]	fire	incendiar	to set on fire
el incremento [R 1071]	increment	incrementar	to grow incrementally
el ingreso [R 756]	income	ingresar	to enter; to deposit
el inicio [R 689]	beginning	iniciar	to initiate, begin
el insulto [R 4743]	insult	insultar	to insult
el intento [R 1583]	intent	intentar	to try
el intercambio [R 2661]	exchange	intercambiar	to exchange
el internado [R 2289]	boarding school; concentration camp	internar	to place someone in a hospital, boarding school or concen-tration camp, etc.
el interno [R 656]	boarding student; intern	internar	to place someone in a hospital, boarding school, or concentration camp, etc.
el invierno [R 1901]	winter	invernar	to winter, pass the winter

Formed Word	English Equivalent	Related to	English Equivalent
el juego [R 183]	game; play; playing; gambling	jugar	to play (a game)
el lazo [R 2359]	lasso (placed around bride and groom at weddings)	lazar	to lasso
el logro [R 2072]	gain; profit; achievement	lograr	to get, achieve
el maltrato [R 4822]	mistreatment	maltratar	to mistreat
el mando [R 2175]	authority	mandar	to send; to order
el manejo [R 1335]	management; managing; driving	manejar	to manage; to drive
el ministro [R 897]	minister	ministrar	to minister; to practice a profession
el modelo [R 800]	model	modelar	to model
el motivo [R 476]	motive; reason	motivar	to motivate
el negocio [R 595]	business	negociar	to conduct business
el número [R 189]	number	numerar	to enumerate, number
el objeto [R 999]	object	objetar	to object
el odio [R 3137]	hatred	odiar	to hate
el olvido [R 4247]	forgetfulness; oblivion	olvidar	to forget
el pacto [R 3874]	agreement, pact	pactar	to make an agreement
el pago [R 583]	payment	pagar	to pay, pay for, repay
el paseo [R 1985]	a walk; a drive; a short trip	pasear	to go for a walk, drive or ride
el paso [406]	step; gait; walk	pasar	to pass, go across
el pavimento [2656]	pavement	pavimentar	to pave
el pecado [R 3920]	sin	pecar	to sin
el pico [R 4023]	beak; peak	picar	to bite
el premio [R 573]	prize	premiar	to award a prize
el presupuesto [R 872]	budget; estimate (billing)	presupuestar	to make a budget
el proceso [R 296]	process	procesar	to process
el progreso [R 3230]	progress	progresar	to progress
el promedio [1089]	average	promediar	to average
el pronóstico [3290]	forecast; prediction	pronosticar	to predict
el proyecto [R 238]	project	proyectar	to project
el rechazo [R 2910]	rejection	rechazar	to reject
el reclamo [3051]	complaint	reclamar	to complain
el refugio [R 2306]	refuge	refugiar	to take refuge
el regalo [R 1365]	gift	regalar	to give
el registro [R 1207]	registration	registrar(se)	to register (vt); to be registered (vr)
el reglamento [R 1774]	regulation; rule	reglamentar	to regulate
el regreso [R 1555]	return	regresar	to return
el reino [R 3129]	kingdom; realm	reinar	to reign, prevail
el relevo [1547]	relief; substitute	relevar	to relieve
el relleno [R 2331]	filling	rellenar	to refill
el remedio [R 3242]	remedy; alternative course of action	remediar	to remediate
el respaldo [R 1965]	economic backing; back-up (computers); back of a chair/couch	respaldar	to back up
el respeto [R 1167]	respect	respetar	to respect
el resto [R 681]	rest (remainder)	restar	to subtract

Formed Word	English Equivalent	Related to	English Equivalent
el retiro [R 1815]	retiring for the evening; retreat for prayer, meditation, or study	**retirar**	to retire (for the evening)
el reto [1506]	challenge	**retar**	to challenge
el retorno [R 3398]	return; turnaround point on a highway	**retornar**	to return
el retraso [R 3130]	turning back of a clock; delay	**retrasar**	to turn back (clock)
el retrato [R 4836]	portrait	**retratar**	to paint or photograph portraits
el robo [R 1278]	robbery	**robar**	to rob
el rodeo [R 3757]	rodeo	**rodear**	to surround
el salto [R 3821]	jump	**saltar**	to jump
el saludo [R]	greeting; wave; salute	**saludar**	to greet, welcome, salute
el secuestro [2199]	kidnapping	**secuestrar**	to kidnap
el segmento [4423]	segment	**segmentar**	to segment
el sello [R 3096]	seal; stamp	**sellar**	to seal
el sereno [R 3535]	quiet time in middle of night; dew	**serenar**	to serenade
el silencio [R 2247]	silence; (mus.) rest	**silenciar**	to silence
el sondeo [3952]	preliminary investigation	**sondear**	to sound, test
el sorteo [3833]	drawing (raffle)	**sortear**	to raffle
el subsidio [1866]	subsidy	**subsidiar**	to subsidize
el sueño [R 1069]	dream; sleep; sleepiness	**soñar**	to dream, dream about
el suministro [3659]	supply	**suministrar**	to supply, administer, give (formal)
el suplemento [3400]	supplement	**suplementar**	to supplement
el sustento [R 4293]	sustenance; support	**sustentar**	to sustain
el techo [R 2504]	roof	**techar**	to put a roof on
el testimonio [R 3575]	testimony	**testimoniar**	to give testimony
el tiro [R 1200]	shot; fight	**tirar**	to throw away, to shoot
el título [R 766]	title	**titular**	to title; to earn a degree, to graduate
el torno [R 1595]	turntable; lathe	**tornar**	to turn; to become
el trabajo [R 109]	work; labor; job	**trabajar**	to work, labor
el tráfico [2057]	traffic	**traficar**	to traffic
el tránsito [R 1279]	traffic; traffic police	**transitar**	to conduct
el translado [3067]	transport from one place to another	**transladar**	to transport from one place to another
el trastorno [R 2811]	loss of common sense or reason	**trastornar**	to cause physical or mental disorder
el trato [R 1823]	agreement, deal	**tratar**	to try; to deal
el triunfo [R 409]	triumph	**triunfar**	to triumph
el trozo [R 4104]	piece	**trozar**	to break into pieces
el turno [1740]	turn; work shift	**turnar(se)**	to turn over to, send on (vt); to take turns (vr)
el vómito	vomit; vomiting	**vomitar**	to vomit
el voto [R 799]	vote; ballot; vow; wish	**votar**	to vote, vow
el vuelo [R 1678]	flight; flying	**volar**	to fly

-o$^{(2)}$

Meaning: *tree; plant*
English equivalent: *none*
Found in: *nouns*

Several Spanish names for trees and bushes take the suffix -o. An interesting feature of these words is that the name of the relevant fruit or nut often ends with an -a, and this suffix replaces that final letter. In other words, the plant is the masculine form of the fruit it bears: *la cereza* (cherry); *el cerezo* (cherry tree). The only exceptions below are *el cafeto* from *el café* and *el cedro* from *la cedria*. All words taking this ending are masculine.

Formed Word	English Equivalent	Related to	English Equivalent
el aceituno	olive tree	**la aceituna**	olive
el almendro	almond tree	**la almendra**	almond
el banano	banana tree	**la banana**	banana
el bergamoto	bergamot tree	**la bergamota**	bergamot
el cafeto [R]	coffee tree	**el café**	coffee
el calabazo	pumpkin plant	**la calabaza**	pumpkin; (fig.) bumpkin; clod
el canelo	cinnamon tree	**la canela**	cinnamon
el castaño	chestnut tree	**la castaña**	chestnut
el cedro	cedar tree	**la cedria**	resin from the cedar
el cermeño	pear tree	**la cermeña**	pear
el cerezo	cherry tree	**la cereza**	cherry
el ciruelo	plum tree	**la ciruela**	plum
el frambueso	raspberry bush	**la frambuesa**	raspberry
el granado	pomegranate tree	**la granada**	pomegranate
el majuelo	white hawthorn	**la majuela**	fruit of the white hawthorn
el manzano	apple tree	**la manzana**	apple
el naranjo	orange tree	**la naranja**	orange
el olivo [R]	olive tree	**la oliva**	olive; (fig.) olive branch
el sangüeso	raspberry bush	**la sangüesa**	raspberry
el toronjo	grapefruit tree	**la toronja**	grapefruit

-o$^{(3)}$ (-a)

Meaning: *one who; denotes profession*
English equivalent: *-er; -ist*
Found in: *nouns*

There are thousands of Spanish words ending in -o. What distinguishes these words, however, is that they all are derived from a science or calling of sorts and denote the person who practices it. All the examples in the "Related to" column end with -ía or -ia (with the exception of *la medicina*): from there, simply drop the -ía or -ia and add -o (an exception is *el anatómico* from *la anatomía*, which adds -ic before the suffix -o). Note that all the formed words have an accent on the antepenultimate syllable. Finally, if the person performing the action is a woman, the ending is -a: *el filósofo; la filósofa*.

Formed Word	English Equivalent	Related to	English Equivalent
el anatómico [R]	anatomist	la anatomía	anatomy
el arqueólogo	archaeologist	la arqueología	archaeology
el astrólogo	astrologist	la astrología	astrology
el astrónomo	astronomer	la astronomía	astronomy
el bígamo	bigamist	la bigamia	bigamy
el biólogo	biologist	la biología	biology
el calígrafo	calligrapher	la caligrafía	calligraphy
el cartógrafo	cartographer; mapmaker	la cartografía	cartography
el coreógrafo	choreographer	la coreografía	choreography
el craneólogo	craniologist	la craneología	craniology
el criptógrafo	cryptographer	la criptografía	cryptography
el cronólogo	chronologist	la cronología	chronology
el ecólogo	ecologist	la ecología	ecology
el filósofo	philosopher	la filosofía	philosophy
el fotógrafo	photographer	la fotografía	photography
el gastrónomo	gastronome; gourmet	la gastronomía	gastronomy
el geógrafo	geographer	la geografía	geography
el geólogo	geologist	la geología	geography
el ginecólogo	gynecologist	la ginecología	gynecology
el médico [R 343]	doctor; physician	la medicina	medicine
el microbiólogo	microbiologist	la microbiología	microbiology
el misántropo	misanthropist; misanthrope	la misantropía	misanthropy
el mitólogo	mythologist	la mitología	mythology
el monógamo	monogamist	la monogamia	monogamy
el neurólogo	neurologist	la neurología	neurology
el oftalmólogo	ophthalmologist	la oftalmología	ophthalmology
el paleontólogo	paleontologist	la paleontología	paleontology
el patólogo	pathologist	la patología	pathology
el polígamo	polygamist	la poligamia	polygamy
el pornógrafo	pornographer	la pornografía	pornography
el psicólogo	psychologist	la psicología	psychology
el radiólogo	radiologist	la radiología	radiology
el sociólogo	sociologist	la sociología	sociology
el teólogo	theologian	la teología	theology
el tipógrafo	typographer; typesetter	la tipografía	typography; typesetting
el topógrafo	topographer; surveyor	la topografía	topography
el toxicólogo	toxicologist	la toxicología	toxicology

-ón⁽¹⁾

Meaning: *denotes suddenness or intensity of an action*
English equivalent: *none*
Found in: *nouns*

One of the meanings the suffix -ón takes is that of denoting a sudden movement or action. Such words all are masculine and are derived from verbs, most of which themsleves denote intense or violent actions. When these formed words are made plural, words taking this suffix no longer require an accent mark: *el jalón; los jalones.*

Formed Word	English Equivalent	Related to	English Equivalent
el acelerón [R]	acceleration; burst of speed	acelerar	to accelerate, hasten, hurry forward
el achuchón	(coll.) squeeze	achuchar	(coll.) to squeeze
el aguijón [R]	sting; pinch; goad	aguijar	to goad, incite
el apagón [R]	blackout	apagar	to extinguish, put out, quench
el apretón [R]	sharp pressure; pain; twinge	apretar	to press, tighten, squeeze
el atracón	stuffing; gluttony	atracarse	to stuff oneself with food
el baldón	insult; blot; disgrace	baldonar	to insult, stain, disgrace
el barzón	stroll; saunter	barzonear	to saunter, loiter about
el chapuzón	(coll.) duck; ducking	chapuzar(se)	to duck
el empujón [R]	hard push; shove	empujar	to push
el encontrón	collision; clash; crash	encontrar(se)	to collide, crash
el estirón [R]	jerk; tug; sharp pull	estirar	to stretch, pull taut
el hinchazón	swelling; vanity; inflation	hinchar	to blow up, inflate, swell
el hurgón	thrust; stab	hurgar	to poke
el jalón	jerk; pull; tug	jalar	to pull, haul, tug
el lametón	hard lick; strong lick	lamer	to lick
el nevazón	snowfall	nevar	to snow
el peleón	fight; fracas; scuffle	pelear	to fight
el pregón [R]	proclamation	pregonar	to cry or proclaim publicly
el punzón	punch	punzar	to punch, puncture, prick
el rascazón	prickling; tickling; itching	rascar	to scratch, itch
el relumbrón [R]	flash; glare; tinsel	relumbrar	to shine brightly
el restregón	hard rubbing; scrubbing	restregar	to rub (hard), scrub
el retortijón	twisting; contortion	retortijar	to twist, curl
el reventón	burst; blowout	reventar	to explode
el tachón	erasure; crossing out	tachar	to cross out, strike through
el trompicón	stumbling; stumble	trompicar	to trip, trip up
el turbión	squall; heavy rain shower	turbar	to disturb, trouble, stir up
el vomitón	violent vomiting	vomitar	to vomit; (fig.) to cough up

-ón(2) (-ona)

Meaning: *(person) tending to; (person) given to*
English equivalent: *none*
Found in: *adjectives and nouns*

In this group, *-ón* can always serve as an adjectival ending, but in many of these words, this suffix also can denote a noun. Thus, one could say, though redundantly, *El preguntón es preguntón* (The nosy man is nosy). Most of these terms are derived from verbs but can also derive from nouns or other adjectives. All words ending with *-ón* are masculine; when referring to or denoting a feminine noun, these words take the suffix *-ona*. When made plural, the accent on the masculine form no longer is necessary: *el bocón; los bocones.*

Formed Word	English Equivalent	Related to	English Equivalent
abusón [R]	(coll.) given to taking advantage of	**abusar**	to misuse, take advantage
(el) adulón	fawning; groveling (person)	**adular**	to flatter, dote upon
(el) besucón	heavy kissing; necking (person)	**besucar**	to kiss, neck with
(el) bocón	wide-mouthed (person)	**la boca**	mouth
(el) burlón [R]	given to mocking (joker)	**burlar**	to mock, laugh at
(el) cabezón [R]	fatheaded; egomaniacal (person)	**la cabeza**	head
calentón	unpleasantly warm or hot	**caliente**	warm; hot
(el) cincuentón [R]	fifty years old or fiftyish (person)	**cincuenta**	fifty
(el) comilón [R]	heavy eating (big eater)	**comer**	to eat
(el) criticón	critical; faultfinding (person)	**criticar**	to criticize
(el) cuarentón [R]	forty years old or fortyish (person)	**cuarenta**	forty
gordón	(coll.) pretty fat or hefty	**gordo**	fat
gritón [R]	(coll.) vociferous; bawling	**gritar**	to shout, cry out, scream
guapetón	tall, dark, and handsome	**guapo**	handsome
holgachón	(coll.) fond of ease and little work	**holgar**	to rest, be idle, have free time
juguetón [R]	playful; frolicsome	**jugar**	to play (a game)
(el) llorón [R]	weepy (crybaby)	**llorar**	to cry, weep
(el) mandón [R]	domineering; bossy (person)	**mandar**	to order, command
(el) mirón [R]	gazing; gawking (onlooker)	**mirar**	to look at, watch
(el) narizón	big-nosed (person)	**la nariz**	nose
(el) orejón	big-eared (person)	**la oreja**	ear
peleón	given to fighting	**pelear**	to fight
politicón	keen on politics; overly polite	**político**	polite; diplomatic
(el) preguntón [R]	nosy; questioning (person)	**preguntar**	to ask (a question)
regalón	(coll.) luxury loving; spoiled	**regalar**	to give a present
replicón	(coll.) given to answering back	**replicar**	to answer back, argue back
reservón	very reserved; secretive	**reservar**	to reserve, keep secret
respondón [R]	(coll.) cheeky; saucy	**responder**	to answer, reply
temblón [R]	shaky; tremulous	**temblar**	to shake, tremble
(el) tragón [R]	greed; gluttonous (person)	**tragar**	to swallow, gulp down
vomitón	given to vomiting	**vomitar**	to vomit

-ón(3), -ona

Meaning: *augmentative; pejorative*
English equivalent: *none*
Found in: *nouns*

The suffix *ón*, or *-ona* when the referent is a feminine noun, is a common augmentative ending in Spanish. In addition to the increase in physical size, this suffix also can hold pejorative connotations, e.g., *la novela* (novel) leads to *el novelón* (long, tedious third-rate novel).

Formed Word	English Equivalent	Related to	English Equivalent
el avispón	hornet	**la avispa**	wasp
el barbón	full-bearded man	**la barba**	beard
el barcón	big boat	**el barco**	boat
el bolsón	large purse; tote bag	**la bolsa**	purse; bag; money-bag
el cajón [R]	drawer; crate	**la caja**	box; case
el calenturón	violent fever	**la calentura**	fever; temperature
el camón	large bed; portable throne	**la cama**	bed
el caserón [R]	big run-down house	**la casa**	house
el comedión	long, tedious comedy or play	**la comedia**	comedy; play
el cortezón	thick bark or rind or crust	**la corteza**	bark; peel; rind; crust
el cortinón	large curtain	**la cortina**	curtain
el culebrón	large snake	**la culebra**	snake
el gigantón	enormous giant	**el gigante**	giant
el goterón [R]	large raindrop	**la gota**	drop; raindrop
el guión [2712]	leader (of a dance)	**el guía**	guide; leader
el hombretón	hefty fellow	**el hombre**	man
el hombrón	big, lusty man; he-man	**el hombre**	man
el manchón [R]	big dirty spot or stain	**la mancha**	spot; stain
el memorión [R]	phenomenal memory	**la memoria**	memory
el moscón	big fly	**la mosca**	fly
la mujerona [R]	stout, lusty woman; hefty creature	**la mujer**	woman
el narigón	big nose	**la nariz**	nose
el novelón	long, tedious third-rate novel	**la novela**	novel
el pavón	peacock	**el pavo**	turkey
el sillón [R]	big overstuffed easy chair	**la silla**	chair
la solterona [R]	spinster	**la soltera**	unmarried woman
el tazón	basin	**la taza**	cup
el zapatón [R]	big shoe; gunboat	**el zapato**	shoe

-or (-ora)

Meaning: *one who; denotes profession or machine*
English equivalent: *-or*
Found in: *nouns*

Among the several Spanish suffixes that indicate a person who does something is the ending *-or*. This ending also can denote a machine, as in *el interruptor* (electrical switch). Such terms are derived from verbs and nearly always have as their English counterparts close cognates, which makes these terms easy to learn and use. When the referent is female, the ending is *-ora*.

Formed Word	English Equivalent	Related to	English Equivalent
el actor [R 401]	actor; performer; player	**actuar**	to act, perform
el ascensor [R]	elevator	**ascender**	to ascend, go up, rise
el auditor	judge; auditor; adviser	*(Lat.)* **audire**	to hear
el autor	author; writer; composer	*(Lat.)* **augere**	to increase, produce
el compositor	composer	**componer**	to compose
el comprensor	one who understands	**comprender**	to understand, comprehend
el compresor	compressor	**comprimir**	to compress, condense, constrain
el conductor [R]	leader; driver; conductor	**conducir**	to conduct, guide, drive (a vehicle)
el confesor [R]	confessor	**confesar**	to confess
el consultor	consultant; consultor; adviser	**consultar**	to consult
el depresor [R]	oppressor; (anat., surg.) depressor	**deprimir**	to depress; (fig.) to humiliate
el destructor [R]	destroyer	**destruir**	to destroy
el detector	detector	**detectar**	to detect, spot
el director	director; manager; chief	**dirigir**	to direct, manage, govern, control
el editor [R]	publisher	**editar**	to publish
el ejecutor	executor	**ejecutar**	to execute
el escritor	writer	**escribir**	to write
el escultor	sculptor; carver	**esculpir**	to sculpt, carve
el expositor	expounder; exhibitor	**exponer**	to expound, exhibit, expose
el eyector	ejector	**eyectar**	to eject
el impresor	printer	**imprimir**	to print, imprint, impress
el inspector	inspector	**inspeccionar**	to inspect
el instructor	instructor	**instruir**	to instruct, teach, train
el interruptor [R]	interrupter; (elec.) switch	**interrumpir**	to interrupt, discontinue
el interventor	comptroller; supervisor; auditor	**intervenir**	to audit, inspect, tap (a telephone line)
el inventor	inventor; fabricator	**inventar**	to invent, fabricate
el lector [R]	reader; teaching assistant	**leer**	to read
el mentor	mentor	*(Lat.)* **monere**	to admonish
el opositor	opponent; competitor	**oponer**	to oppose
el pastor [R 4527]	shepherd; (Protestant) clergyman	**pastorear**	to pasture, graze
el patrocinador [R 4590]	*nmf* sponsor; patron; *aj* sponsoring	**patrocinar**	to sponsor
el perdedor [R 3854]	*nmf* loser; *aj* losing	**perder**	to lose
el pintor	painter	**pintar**	to paint, depict
el profesor [R]	professor; teacher	**profesar**	to profess, practice
el receptor [R 3261]	*nm* electrical receiver; *aj* receiving	**recibir**	to receive
el rector [R]	rector; principal	**rectorar**	to attain the office of rector

Formed Word	English Equivalent	Related to	English Equivalent
el redactor	editor; copy editor	**redactar**	to edit, word, draw up
el seductor [R]	seducer; charmer	**seducir**	to seduce, allure, tempt, entice
el subdirector [3574]	assistant manager	**sub + dirigir**	under + to direct, manage, govern, control

-orio(1)

Meaning: *place where; means by which*
English equivalent: *-ory*
Found in: *nouns*

A Spanish noun ending *-orio* has two distinct meanings: (1) "place where" and (2) "means by which." In the former, we find mostly rooms and buildings whose names generally are derived from the verb expressing the action performed in them: *el lavatorio* (lavatory; washroom) comes from *lavar* (to wash). The second meaning, "means by which," indicates the thing necessary for carrying out the action denoted in the root verb: *el aspersorio* (water sprinkler) is needed in order to sprinkle (*asperjar*). All nouns ending in *-orio* are masculine.

Formed Word	English Equivalent	Related to	English Equivalent
el adoratorio	Indian temple	**adorar**	to adore, worship
el aspersorio	water sprinkler	**asperjar**	to sprinkle, spray
el auditorio [R 1586]	auditorium	*(Lat.)* **audire**	to hear
el conservatorio	conservatory	**conservar**	to conserve
el consultorio [R 4649]	medical office	**consultar**	to consult
el convictorio	students' quarters	**el convictor**	boarder; pensioner
el declinatorio	declinator (instrument)	**declinar**	to decline
el dedicatorio	dedication; inscription	**dedicar**	to dedicate
el defensorio	plea; defense	**defender**	to defend, shield
el depilatorio	depilatory	**depilar**	to depilate
el destilatorio	distillery	**destilar**	to distill
el directorio [R]	directory; directorate	**dirigir**	to direct, manage, govern
el divisorio [R]	geological divide	**dividir**	to divide
el dormitorio [R]	bedroom; dormitory	**dormir**	to sleep
el enjuagatorio	mouthwash	**enjuagar**	to rinse
el escritorio [R]	writing desk; office; study	**escribir**	to write
el laboratorio [R 2459]	laboratory	**laborar**	to labor, work
el lavatorio [R]	lavatory; washroom	**lavar**	to wash
el nalgatorio	(coll.) posterior; seat; buttocks	**la nalga**	buttock; rump
el observatorio [R]	observatory	**observar**	to observe
el ofertorio	offertory	**ofrecer**	to offer
el purgatorio [R]	purgatory	**purgar**	to purge, cleanse
el reformatorio [R]	reformatory	**reformar**	to reform, amend
el sanatorio [R]	sanatorium	**sanar**	to heal, cure
el territorio [R 1503]	territory	**la tierra**	land; earth

-orio[(2)] (-oria)

Meaning: *like; relating to*
English equivalent: *-ory*
Found in: *adjectives*

As an adjectival ending, *-orio* has two salient features. First, note below that all the examples are derived from verbs and that nearly all of them are *-ar* verbs. Second, when the derivation is an *-ar* verb, the *-ar* is replaced by *-at* before adding *-orio* (*inflamar* gives us *inflamatorio*); there is no standard formation rule for those adjectives derived from *-er* and *-ir* verbs. Words ending with *-orio* take *-oria* when describing feminine nouns.

Formed Word	English Equivalent	Related to	English Equivalent
aclamatorio	with acclaim	**aclamar**	to acclaim, applaud
aclaratorio [R]	explanatory	**aclarar**	to make clear, explain
acusatorio [R]	accusatory	**acusar**	to accuse, charge, prosecute
adivinatorio	divinatory	**adivinar**	to guess, divine, solve
aprobatorio [R]	approbatory; approving	**aprobar**	to approve
circulatorio [R]	circulatory	**circular**	to circulate
cobratorio	pertaining to collecting	**cobrar**	to collect
conciliatorio	conciliatory	**conciliar**	to conciliate, reconcile
decisorio	(law) decisive	**decidir**	to decide
declamatorio	declamatory	**declamar**	to declaim, recite
dedicatorio	dedicatory	**dedicar**	to dedicate
depilatorio	depilatory	**depilar**	to depilate, remove hair
discriminatorio	discriminatory	**discriminar**	to discriminate
eliminatorio [R 3037]	qualifying (sport)	**eliminar**	to eliminate
giratorio [R]	rotatory; revolving	**girar**	to rotate, revolve
inflamatorio	inflammatory	**inflamar**	to inflame, set afire
laudatorio	laudatory	**laudar**	(law) to give judgment on
masticatorio	chewing	**masticar**	to chew, masticate
meritorio [R]	meritorious	**merecer**	to deserve, merit
migratorio [3772]	migratory	**migrar**	to migrate
mortuorio [R]	of the dead	**morir**	to die
notorio [R 4509]	noticeable; well-known (for positive or negative reasons)	**notar**	to notice
obligatorio [R 3654]	obligatory	**obligar**	to oblige
ondulatorio [R]	undulatory	**ondular**	to undulate, rise in waves
operatorio	operative	**operar**	to operate
oscilatorio	oscillatory	**oscilar**	to oscillate, fluctuate
prohibitorio	prohibitory	**prohibir**	to prohibit
promisorio	promissory	**prometer**	to promise
purificatorio	purificatory	**purificar**	to purify
recomendatorio	recommendatory	**recomendar**	to recommend
respiratorio [R 3304]	respiratory	**respirar**	to breathe
satisfactorio [R 3890]	satisfactory	**satisfacer**	to satisfy
sublimatorio	sublimatory	**sublimar**	to sublimate
sudatorio	sudorific; pertaining to sweat	**sudar**	to sweat, perspire
vibratorio [R]	vibratory	**vibrar**	to vibrate, shake

-osis

Meaning: *condition; process; disease*
English equivalent: *-osis*
Found in: *nouns*

Words ending with *-osis*, in English as well as in Spanish, often are medical terms that denote a diseased condition. Below are listed several such terms, many of which are commonly used. As you will see, not all refer to a sickness, e.g., *la ósmosis* (osmosis). Though these words are not related directly to other Spanish terms, they are easy to recognize as cognates of their English counterparts. All words ending with *-osis* are feminine.

Formed Word	English Equivalent	Related to	English Equivalent
la acidosis	acidosis	*(Lat.)* **acidus**	sour
la alcalosis	alkalosis	**el álcali**	(chem.) alkali
la amaurosis	amaurosis	*(Gr.)* **amauros**	dim
la arteriosclerosis	arteriosclerosis	*(Lat.)* **arteria** + *(Gr.)* **skleros**	artery + hard
la cirrosis	cirrhosis	*(Gr.)* **kirrhos**	orange-colored
la endometriosis	endometriosis	*(Gr.)* **endon + metra**	within + uterus
la esclerosis	sclerosis	*(Gr.)* **skleros**	hard
la estenosis	stenosis	*(Gr.)* **stenos**	narrow
la fibrosis	fibrosis	*(Lat.)* **fibra**	fiber
la halitosis	halitosis	*(Gr.)* **halitus**	breath
la hipnosis	hypnosis	*(Gr.)* **hypnos**	sleep
la melanosis	melanosis	*(Gr.)* **melas**	black
la metamorfosis	metamorphosis	*(Gr.)* **meta + morphe**	beyond + form
la miosis	miosis	*(Gr.)* **meiosis**	diminution
la nefrosis	nephrosis	*(Gr.)* **nephros**	kidney
la neurosis	neurosis	*(Gr.)* **neuron**	nerve
la ósmosis	osmosis	*(Gr.)* **osmos**	impulse
la osteoporosis [R 3155]	osteoporosis	*(Gr.)* **osteodis**	bone
la psicosis	psychosis	*(Gr.)* **psyche**	the mind
la queratosis	keratosis	*(Gr.)* **keras**	horn
la silicosis	silicosis	*(Lat.)* **silex**	flint
la simbiosis [R]	symbiosis	*(Gr.)* **syn + bios**	with + life
la triquinosis	trichinosis	*(Gr.)* **trichinos**	hairline
la trombosis	thrombosis	*(Gr.)* **thrombos**	clot
la tuberculosis	tuberculosis	*(Lat.)* **tuberculum**	small swelling

-oso (-osa)

Meaning: *full of; having*
English equivalent: *-ous; -ful; -y*
Found in: *adjectives*

A Spanish word ending in *-oso* signifies that the person or object described possesses characteristics of the root noun. Nouns ending in a vowel generally drop that vowel and take on the *-oso* ending, while *-oso* is added directly to words ending with a consonant. In some cases, the root noun will undergo a slight spelling change (e.g., *temeroso* from *el temor*), but the root still is recognizable. Remember that as *-oso* is an adjectival ending, it will become *-osa* when the formed word describes a feminine noun.

Formed Word	English Equivalent	Related to	English Equivalent
amoroso [R 3294]	amorous; loving	**el amor**	love
carnoso [R]	fleshy	**la carne**	flesh; meat
codicioso	covetous; greedy	**la codicia**	greed
costoso [3974]	very expensive	**el costo**	cost
cuidadoso [R]	careful	**el cuidado**	care
delicioso [R 3126]	delicious	**la delicia**	delight
doloroso [R 3115]	painful; distressing	**el dolor**	pain; sorrow; regret
dudoso [R]	doubtful	**la duda**	doubt
escandaloso [R]	scandalous	**el escándalo**	scandal
espantoso [R]	frightful	**el espanto**	fright
espinoso [3869]	prickly; thorny	**la espina**	thorn
exitoso [1783]	successful	**el éxito**	success
fabuloso	fabulous	**la fábula**	fable
famoso [R 1093]	famous	**la fama**	fame
gozoso [R]	joyful	**el gozo**	joy; enjoyment
huesoso	bony	**el hueso**	bone
humoso	smoky	**el humo**	smoke
jubiloso [R]	jubilant; joyful	**el júbilo**	jubilation; joy
lastimoso [R]	pitiful	**la lástima**	pity
lloroso [R]	tearful	**el lloro**	crying; weeping
lujoso [R]	luxurious	**el lujo**	luxury
mantecoso	buttery; greasy; fatty	**la manteca**	lard; grease; fat; pomade
maravilloso [R 2600]	wonderful; marvelous	**la maravilla**	wonder; marvel
mentiroso [R]	lying	**la mentira**	lie
milagroso [R]	miraculous; marvelous	**el milagro**	miracle
misterioso [R]	mysterious	**el misterio**	mystery
mocoso	(coll.) snot-nosed; dirty-nosed	**el moco**	mucus
nervioso [R 2494]	nervous	**el nervio**	nerve
novedoso [R 4854]	new and different	**el nuevo**	new
numeroso [R 1134]	numerous	**el número**	number
odioso [R]	hateful	**el odio**	hatred; hate
orgulloso [R 2743]	proud	**el orgullo**	pride
pegajoso [R]	sticky	**la pega**	sticking; cementing
peligroso [R 1538]	dangerous	**el peligro**	danger; peril
perezoso [R]	lazy; slothful	**la pereza**	sloth
poderoso [R 2128]	powerful; mighty	**el poder**	power; might
polvoroso	dusty	**el polvo**	dust
pomposo	pompous	**la pompa**	pomp
precioso [R 4098]	precious	**el precio**	price
pulgoso	flea-ridden	**la pulga**	flea
quejoso [4483]	complaining; given to complaining	**la queja**	complaint
rencoroso [R]	spiteful	**el rencor**	spite
respetuoso [R 4593]	respectful	**el respeto**	respect
sabroso [R 4688]	tasty; delicious	**el sabor**	taste; flavor; relish
sospechoso [R 2457]	suspicious	**la sospecha**	suspicion
talentoso [R 4499]	talented	**el talento**	talent
temeroso [R]	fearful	**el temor**	fear

Formed Word	English Equivalent	Related to	English Equivalent
valioso [R 2777]	valuable	**la valía**	value; worth
venenoso [R]	poisonous	**el veneno**	poison
ventoso [R]	windy	**el viento**	wind

-ote; -ota

Meaning: *augmentative; pejoratitve; like; relating to*
English equivalent: *none*
Found in: *nouns; adjectives*

The suffix *-ote* or *-ota* serves as an augmentative that sometimes carries negative connotations; *el pajarote* is a big clumsy bird (from *el pájaro*). This ending is more commonly a noun ending but performs essentially the same function as an adjectival ending, namely, enlarging upon the root: from *feo* (ugly) we get *feote* (big and ugly). Nouns ending with *-ote* are masculine, while those ending with *-ota* are feminine. An adjective ending with *-ote* takes the ending *-ota* when describing a feminine noun.

Formed Word	English Equivalent	Related to	English Equivalent
el amigote [R]	(coll.) pal; buddy; crony	**el amigo**	friend
el angelote [R]	large figure of an angel	**el ángel**	angel
el animalote	big animal; (coll.) ignorant person	**el animal**	animal; creature
la bancarrota [R]	bankruptcy; failure	**el banco**	bank
barbarote	utterly rude; coarse	**bárbaro**	barbaric; savage
el barcote	big boat	**el barco**	boat
blancote	excessively white or pale	**blanco**	white
el bobote	great idiot or simpleton	**el bobo**	fool; dimwit
el borricote	(coll.) utter ass; plodder	**el borrico**	ass
el bravote	(coll.) bully	**bravo**	brave; valiant; manly
el caballerote	clumsy, loutish knight	**el caballero**	knight; gentleman
el camarote [R]	(naut.) stateroom	**la cámara**	chamber; room
el chicote [R]	husky youngster	**el chico**	boy; youngster; lad
feote	big and ugly	**feo**	ugly
el frailote	big, coarse friar	**el fraile**	friar; monk
francote	plainspoken	**franco**	frank; open; candid
el gatote	big cat	**el gato**	cat
grandote [R]	very big; hulking great	**grande**	big; large
guapote	(coll.) really good-looking	**guapo**	handsome
el librote	huge book	**el libro**	book
la machota	mannish woman	**el macho**	male
el machote	real he-man; tough guy	**el macho**	male
la muchachota	tomboy	**la muchacha**	girl; lass
la narizota	huge, ugly nose	**la nariz**	nose
el pajarote	big, clumsy big bird	**el pájaro**	bird
el papelote	wretched piece of paper; rubbish	**el papel**	paper
el perrote	big dog	**el perro**	dog
el pipote	keg	**la pipa**	cask
el villanote	great villain	**el villano**	villain

-sión

Meaning: *state of being; result of action; act*
English equivalent: *-sion*
Found in: *nouns*

Words ending with *-sión* are derived from verbs. Generally speaking, the *-ar*, *-er*, or *-ir* along with the final consonant of the infinitive are dropped, and then *-sión* is added. Very rarely does a Spanish word ending with *-sión* have as its English equivalent *-tion*. Only two examples are given below in which this is the case: *la contorsión* (contortion) and *la distorsión* (distortion); otherwise, the English ending is virtually always *-sion*. All words ending in *-sión* are feminine and drop the accent mark when made plural: *la decisión; las decisiones.*

Formed Word	English Equivalent	Related to	English Equivalent
la accesión	accession	**acceder**	to accede, agree, consent
la agresión [2582]	aggression	**agredir(se)**	to insult, offend, attack (vt); to fight each other (plural) (vr)
la aprehensión [2346]	apprehension	**aprehender**	to apprehend
la aspersión	aspersion: sprinkling; spraying	**asperjar**	to sprinkle
la comisión [R 265]	commission; trust	**cometer**	to commit, entrust
la compresión	compression	**comprimir**	to compress
la concesión [2436]	concession	**conceder**	to concede
la conclusión [R 2309]	conclusion	**concluir**	to conclude
la confusión [R 3085]	confusion	**confundir**	to confuse
la contorsión	contortion	**contornar**	to contour, wind around a place
la decisión [R 464]	decision	**decidir**	to decide
la depresión [R 2569]	depression	**deprimir**	to depress
la difusión [R 2610]	diffusion; diffuseness; vagueness	**difundir**	to diffuse, extend
la discusión [R 1923]	argument	**discutir**	to discuss
la distorsión	distortion; twisting; spraining	**distorsionar**	to distort, twist
la diversión [R 3465]	diversion; fun activity	**divertir(se)**	to divert, entertain (vt); to have fun (vr)
la división [R 915]	division	**dividir**	to divide
la emisión [R 2288]	emission	**emitir**	to emit
la exclusión [R 4933]	exclusion	**excluir**	to exclude
la expansión [R 4078]	expansion	**expansionar**	to expand
la explosión [R 2449]	explosion	**explotar**	to explode
la expresión [R 1802]	expression	**expresar**	to express
la expulsión [R 2883]	expulsion	**expulsar**	to expel
la extensión [R 2786]	extension	**extender**	to extend, enlarge, spread (out)
la fusión [3432]	fusion	**fusionar**	to fuse, amalgamate
la ilusión [R 2927]	illusion; dream, desire	**ilusionar(se)**	to deceive; to be under the illusion
la impresión [R 2871]	impression; printing	**impresionar**	to impress

Formed Word	English Equivalent	Related to	English Equivalent
la incisión	incision	incidir	to incise, cut into
la inclusión [R 4567]	inclusion	incluir	to include
la incursión [3468]	incursion	incursionar	to venture
la invasión [R 3583]	invasion	invadir	to invade
la inversión [R 613]	inversion; investment	invertir	to invert, reverse, invest
la lesión [R 1009]	lesion; wound; injury	lesionar(se)	to wound; to become wounded
la obsesión [R 4855]	obsession	obsesionar	to obsess
la ocasión [R 303]	occasion	ocasionar	to cause or bring about
la oclusión	occlusion	ocluir	to occlude, close
la pensión [R 3033]	pension	pensionar	to pay a pension
la percusión	percussion	percutir	to percuss, strike
la posesión [R 2319]	possession	poseer	to possess, own
la precisión [R 4341]	precision; preciseness	precisar	to specify
la presión [R 1045]	pressure; prison	presionar	to pressure; to imprison
la pretensión [R 4802]	pretension	pretender	to desire something
la previsión [R 3876]	foresight	prevenir	to prevent
la profesión [R 2631]	profession	profesar	to profess
la progresión [R]	progression	progresar	to progress
la propulsión	propulsion	propulsar	to propel, drive
la remisión [4968]	remission; forgiveness; sending (documents)	remitir	to remit
la repercusión [4806]	repercussion	repercutir	to cause repercussions, affect
la represión [R 4670]	repression	reprimir	to repress
la repulsión [R]	repulsion	repulsar	to check, rebuff, reject
la revisión [R 1382]	review; inspection	revisar	to revise
la subversión	subversion	subvertir	to subvert
la supervisión [R 3907]	supervision	supervisar	to supervise
la suspensión [R 2152]	suspension	suspender	to suspend
la televisión [R 562]	television	televisar	to televise
la transfusión	transfusion	transfundir	to transfuse, transmit, spread
la transgresión	transgression	transgredir	to transgress, sin
la transmisión [2663]	transmission	transmitir	to transmit, broadcast
la visión [R 1633]	vision	(Lat.) videre	to see

-tad; -stad

Meaning: *state of being; forms abstract noun*
English equivalent: *-ty*
Found in: *nouns*

The endings *-tad* and *-stad* are relatively uncommon in Spanish. Words taking these endings generally refer to an abstraction or intangible quality, e.g., *la lealtad* (loyalty) from the adjective *leal* (loyal). All words ending in *-tad* or *-stad* are feminine.

Formed Word	English Equivalent	Related to	English Equivalent
la amistad [R 753]	friendship; amity	**el amigo**	friend
la dificultad [R 1720]	difficulty	**difícil**	difficult
la enemistad [R]	hatred; enmity	**el enemigo**	enemy
la facultad [1310]	school; faculty; power	*(Lat.)* **facultas**	feasibility; power; means
la lealtad [R]	loyalty	**leal**	loyal; faithful
la libertad [R 794]	liberty; freedom	**libre**	free; detached
la majestad [R]	majesty	**majo**	boasting; blustering; swaggering
la voluntad [R 1596]	will; willpower; willingness	*(Lat.)* **voluntas**	will; wish; inclination

-teca

Meaning: *place where things are collected and stored*
English equivalent: *none*
Found in: *nouns*

Those few Spanish words ending in -*teca* indicate a kind of library or place where a specific object is stored. Such words are always feminine.

Formed Word	English Equivalent	Related to	English Equivalent
la biblioteca [R 2254]	library	*(Gr.)* **biblion**	book
la discoteca [3540]	discotheque; record library	**el disco**	record
la filmoteca	film library	**el filme**	film
la hemeroteca	newspaper, magazine, and periodical library	*(Gr.)* **hemero**	day
la pinacoteca	picture gallery; place where paintings are stored	**la pintura**	painting

-triz

Meaning: *denotes profession or role of female*
English equivalent: *-ess*
Found in: *nouns*

Spanish words ending with -*triz* denote an occupation or role held by a woman. In English, we usually use -*ess* to make such a distinction, although current common usage does not always distinguish between the two ("poetess" has now generally fallen out of usage). In Spanish, however, the distinction continues and -*triz* is one suffix to demonstrate it, usually by adding this ending to the stem of the root verb. As would be expected, all such terms are feminine.

Formed Word	English Equivalent	Related to	English Equivalent
la actriz [R 620]	actress	**actuar**	to act
la cantatriz	female singer	**cantar**	to sing
la emperatriz [R]	empress	**el emperador**	emperor

Formed Word	English Equivalent	Related to	English Equivalent
la fregatriz	kitchen maid	**fregar**	to scrub, scour, swab, mop (floor)
la institutriz [R]	governess	**instituir**	to instruct, teach, train, educate
la meretriz	prostitute	*(Lat.)* **merere**	to earn
la saltatriz	female ballet dancer	**saltar**	to jump, leap, spring

-ucho; -ucha

Meaning: *pejorative; diminutive (nouns); augmentative (adjectives); like*
English equivalent: *none*
Found in: *nouns; adjectives*

The ending -*ucho* or -*ucha* could be termed the "too much of a good thing" suffix. As you will see below, when -*ucho* or -*ucha* is added to the base word, the resulting word often suggests excess or something that has gotten out of hand: from *el café* we get *el cafetucho*, which is a dump, a terrible place to go for coffee. Or consider *blando* (soft) and the resulting *blanducho* (flabby). When the root word is a noun, the formed word also will be a noun; similarly, when the base word is an adjective, it will remain an adjective when this suffix is added. At times, this suffix is merely a diminutive, as in *el aguilucho* (eaglet) from *el águila* (eagle). Adjectives ending with -*ucho* are masculine, while those ending in -*ucha* are feminine.

Formed Word	English Equivalent	Related to	English Equivalent
el aguaducho	stream; stall for selling water	**el agua** *nf*	water
el animalucho	wretched, ugly little creature	**el animal**	animal
blanducho	overly soft; flabby	**blando**	soft
el cafetucho	wretched little café; dump	**el café**	café
el calducho	thin, tasteless soup or stock	**el caldo**	broth; clear soup
calentucho	revoltingly warm or hot	**caliente**	warm; hot
la camucha	wretched little bed	**la cama**	bed
el capirucho	dunce cap	**el capirote**	academic hood
la casucha	run-down house	**la casa**	house
clarucho	watery; thin	**claro**	clear
el cuartucho [R]	miserable little room	**el cuarto**	room
delgaducho [R]	overly thin; scrawny	**delgado**	thin; slim
endeblucho	very weak or flimsy	**endeble**	feeble; flimsy
enfermucho	a bit off color; groggy	**enfermo**	sick; ill
feúcho	(coll.) rather ugly; plain	**feo**	ugly
flacucho [R]	scrawny; overly thin	**flaco**	thin; lean; weak
flojucho	rather loose; on the floppy side	**flojo**	loose; slack
larguirucho	(coll.) lanky; gangling	**largo**	long
el medicucho	third-rate doctor; quack	**el médico**	doctor
el papelucho	wretched piece of paper; rubbish	**el papel**	paper
el periodicucho	tabloid; "rag"	**el periódico**	newspaper; periodical
el santucho	(coll.) hypocrite	**el santo**	saint
el serrucho [R]	handsaw	**la sierra**	saw
la tenducha	wretched little shop; "dump"	**la tienda**	shop; store

-uco; -uca

Meaning: *diminutive; endearing; deprecative*
English equivalent: *none*
Found in: *nouns*

Included among the many diminutive and deprecative suffixes in Spanish are *-uco* and *-uca*. As with many diminutive endings, the smallness can be physical, e.g., *el ventanuco* (small window) from *la ventana* (window); at times it can also be deprecative, with diminution in quality as well, e.g., *el cuartuco* (miserable little room) from *el cuarto* (room). The diminutive aspect can also express a charming quality, as in the references to animals below, e.g., *el gatuco* (cute little kitty) from *el gato* (cat). Words ending with *-uco* are masculine, while those taking *-uca* are feminine.

Formed Word	English Equivalent	Related to	English Equivalent
el abejaruco	(orn.) bee eater	**la abeja**	bee
el almendruco	green almond	**la almendra**	almond
el animaluco	cute little animal	**el animal**	animal
el becerruco	cute little bull	**el becerro**	young bull
el caballuco	cute little horse	**el caballo**	horse
la casuca	miserable house; hovel	**la casa**	house
el cuartuco	miserable little room	**el cuarto**	room
el frailuco	despicable friar	**el fraile**	friar; monk
el gatuco	cute little cat; kitty	**el gato**	cat
la gitanuca	little gypsy woman	**la gitana**	gypsy woman
el hermanuco	(contemptuous) lay brother	**el hermano**	brother
el muchachuco	cute little boy	**el muchacho**	boy; lad
la mujeruca	slovenly woman	**la mujer**	woman
la peluca	wig	**el pelo**	hair
el perruco	cute little dog; doggie	**el perro**	dog
la tierruca	small piece of land; garden bed	**la tierra**	land; earth
el ventanuco	small window	**la ventana**	window

-udo (-uda)

Meaning: *augmentative; having (a great deal of the root noun)*
English Meaning: *none*
Found in: *adjectives*

The augmentative suffix *-udo* indicates that the person or thing being described possesses a lot of the root term: *un hombre peludo* is a man with a lot of hair. As you will see below, this suffix often is attached to names of body parts. Remember that when describing a noun of feminine gender, the suffix will change to *-uda*, as in *María es narizuda* (Mary has a big nose).

Formed Word	English Equivalent	Related to	English Equivalent
barbudo [R]	full-bearded	**la barba**	beard
barrigudo	(coll.) big-bellied; pot-bellied	**la barriga**	belly; bulge (in a wall)

Formed Word	English Equivalent	Related to	English Equivalent
bigotudo [R]	heavily mustached	el bigote	mustache
bocudo	having a big mouth	la boca	mouth
cabezudo [R]	having a big head	la cabeza	head
caderudo	having large hips	la cadera	hip
cejudo	having bushy eyebrows	la ceja	eyebrow
ceñudo	frowning	el ceño	frown
cornudo [R]	horned	el cuerno	horn
dentudo	having big teeth	el diente	tooth
espaldudo	having broad shoulders	las espaldas	shoulders; back
felpudo	plushy; downy	la felpa	plush
huesudo	bony; big-boned	el hueso	bone
jetudo	snouted; big-lipped	la jeta	hog's snout; big lips
juanetudo	having bunions	el juanete	bunion
lanudo	woolly; fleecy	la lana	wool
molletudo	chubby-cheeked	la molla	(coll.) fat (of a person)
nalgudo	having big buttocks	la nalga	buttock
narizudo	having a big nose	la nariz	nose
orejudo [R]	flap-eared; long-eared	la oreja	ear
pantorrilludo	having large or thick calves	la pantorrilla	calf (of the leg)
panzudo	having a big belly	el panza	belly
papudo	having a double chin	el papo	double chin
patudo	having big feet or paws	la pata	foot; paw
peludo [R]	hairy; hirsute	el pelo	hair
picudo [R]	beaked	el pico	beak; bill
rodilludo	having big knees	la rodilla	knee
talludo [R]	grown-up; overgrown	el tallo	stem; stalk
tetuda	having large breasts; busty	la teta	breast; teat
tozudo	obstinate; stubborn; pigheaded	la toza	block of wood; stump
zancudo	having long legs	el zanco	stilt
zapatudo	wearing big shoes	el zapato	shoe

-uelo; -uela

Meaning: *diminutive*
English equivalent: *none*
Found in: *nouns*

The ending -*uelo* and -*uela* indicate smallness of the root noun. At times this smallness can be figurative, as in *el embusteruelo* (little fibber), which is derived from *el embustero* (fibber); however, most of the time it means small in the literal sense, e.g., *la hojuela* (small leaf) from *la hoja* (leaf). Note below the slight difference in meaning between *el hoyuelo* and *la hoyuela*. This pair of suffixes has sister suffixes, -*zuelo* and -*zuela*, which are similar in function. Nouns ending in -*uelo* are masculine, while those ending with -*uela* are feminine.

Formed Word	English Equivalent	Related to	English Equivalent
la abejuela	little bee	la abeja	bee
la callejuela [R]	alley	la calle	street

Formed Word	English Equivalent	Related to	English Equivalent
la cejuela	small eyebrow	la ceja	eyebrow
la chicuela	small girl	la chica	girl
el chicuelo	small boy	el chico	boy
el espejuelo	looking glass	el espejo	mirror
la habichuela	kidney bean	la haba	bean
la hachuela	hatchet	el hacha *nf*	axe
el hijuelo [R]	(bot.) shoot	el hijo	son; child; offspring
la hojuela	small leaf	la hoja	leaf; petal; sheet; blade
el hoyuelo	little hole; dimple	el hoyo	hole
la lentejuela	spangle; sequin	la lenteja	lentil
el ojuelo	small eye	el ojo	eye
la pajuela	sulfur match; short straw	la paja	straw
el pañuelo [R]	handkerchief	el paño	cloth
el patrañuelo	little story; white lie	la patraña	cock-and-bull story; yarn; lie
el polluelo	chick	el pollo	chicken
la portañuela	fly (of trousers)	la portañola	porthole
la sortijuela	little ring; ringlet	la sortija	ring; curl (of hair)
la viruela	smallpox; pockmark	el virus	virus

-undo (-unda)

Meaning: *like; relating to*
English equivalent: *-und*
Found in: *adjectives*

The suffix *-undo* is an adjectival ending implying that someone or something has characteristiccs of the root term. Many words ending in *-undo* come directly from Latin, and at times the formed word and the base term are mere translations of one another. When a Spanish root does exist, a consonant often is inserted between that root and the ending *-undo*, the most common being the letter *b*, e.g., *nauseabundo* (nauseating) from *la nausea* (nausea). When used to describe feminine nouns, words ending with *-undo* take *-unda*.

Formed Word	English Equivalent	Related to	English Equivalent
cogitabundo	pensive; musing	cogitar	to reflect, meditate
errabundo	wandering; aimless	errar	to miss, get wrong, mistake
facundo	eloquent; loquacious	(*Lat.*) **facundus**	eloquent
fecundo [R]	fecund; fertile	(*Lat.*) **fecundare**	to fertilize
furibundo [R]	furious; raging	la furia	fury; rage
gemebundo	groaning; moaning	gemir	to groan, moan, wail, whine
infacundo	ineloquent	(*Lat.*) **infacundus**	not eloquent
infecundo [R]	infertile; sterile	(*Lat.*) **in + fecundare**	not + to fertilize
inmundo	dirty; filthy; unclean; impure	(*Lat.*) **in + mundus**	not + neat; clean; nice
iracundo [R]	ireful; wrathful	la ira	ire; wrath

Formed Word	English Equivalent	Related to	English Equivalent
jocundo	jocund	*(Lat.)* **jocus**	joke
meditabundo [R]	meditative	**meditar**	to meditate
moribundo	moribund; dying	**morir**	to die
nauseabundo [R]	loathsome; nauseating	**la nausea**	nausea; seasickness
oriundo	native of; coming from	*(Lat.)* **oriundus**	descended; sprung; born
profundo [R 1655]	profound	*(Lat.)* **profundus**	deep; boundless; vast
pudibundo	modest; bashful; shy	**el pudor**	modesty; bashfulness
rotundo	rotund; round	*(Lat.)* **rotundus**	rounded; circular
rubicundo	rubicund; red; rosy	**el rubí**	ruby
segundo [R 102]	second	*(Lat.)* **secundus**	second; next; following
tremebundo	dreadful; fearful	*(Lat.)* **tremebundus**	trembling
vagabundo [R]	vagabond	**vagar**	to wander, roam

-uno (-una)

Meaning: *like; relating to; pertaining to*
English equivalent: *none*
Found in: *adjectives*

The adjectival suffix *-uno* is interesting not so much for what it does (there are several endings meaning "like" and "relating to") but instead for its specialized use in reference to animals. While this suffix is not restricted solely to the animal kingdom, it is generally the suffix of choice where animals are concerned. When used to describe a feminine noun, words ending with *-uno* take *-una*.

Formed Word	English Equivalent	Related to	English Equivalent
abejuno	pertaining to bees	**la abeja**	bee
bajuno	base; low; vile	**el bajo**	deep place
boyuno	bovine	**el buey**	ox
caballuno	pertaining to horses; equine	**el caballo**	horse
cabruno	goatish; goatlike	**el cabrón**	buck; he-goat
carneruno	pertaining to sheep; ovine	**el carnero**	sheep (ram)
cervuno	pertaining to deer	**el ciervo**	deer; stag; hart
conejuno	pertaining to rabbits	**el conejo**	rabbit
corderuno	pertaining to lambs	**el cordero**	lamb
gatuno	pertaining to cats; feline	**el gato**	cat
hombruno	mannish	**el hombre**	man
lobuno	wolfish	**el lobo**	wolf
montuno	pertaining to the mountain; wild	**el monte**	mountain
moruno	Moorish	**el moro**	Moor; Mohammedan
osuno	pertaining to bears; osine	**el oso**	bear
ovejuno	pertaining to sheep; ovine	**la oveja**	sheep (ram)
perruno [R]	pertaining to dogs; canine	**el perro**	dog
porcuno	pertaining to pigs; porcine	**el puerco**	pig; hog
vacuno	pertaining to cows; bovine	**la vaca**	cow
zorruno	foxlike	**el zorro**	fox

-uo (-ua)

Meaning: *like; relating to*
English equivalent: *-uous*
Found in: *adjectives*

Spanish adjectives ending in *-uo* nearly always correspond to English cognates ending in *-uous*. Although such words are derived from Latin, there are very few Spanish words that employ the same root. Because this is an adjectival ending, words in *-uo* take *-ua* to modify feminine nouns. Note that one term below, *el residuo*, is a noun.

Formed Word	English Equivalent	Related to	English Equivalent
ambiguo	ambiguous	*(Lat.)* **ambigere**	to wander about, waver
arduo	arduous	*(Lat.)* **arduus**	steep; high
asiduo [R]	assiduous	*(Lat.)* **assidere**	to sit near
congruo	congruous	*(Lat.)* **congruere**	to come together, agree
conspicuo	conspicuous	*(Lat.)* **conspicere**	to get sight of, perceive
contiguo [R]	contiguous; next; adjacent	*(Lat.)* **contiguus**	contiguous; near; touching
continuo [R 3556]	continuous	*(Lat.)* **continere**	to hold together
discontinuo [R]	discontinuous	*(Lat.)* **dis + continuous**	not + continuous
estrenuo	strenuous	*(Lat.)* **strenuus**	strenuous
fatuo	fatuous; conceited; foolish	*(Lat.)* **fatuus**	fatuous; foolish; inane
incongruo	incongruous	*(Lat.)* **in + congruus**	not + congruous; incompatible
individuo [R 1431]	individual	*(Lat.)* **in + dividuus**	not + divisible
ingenuo [R]	ingenuous	*(Lat.)* **ingenuus**	inborn; freeborn; noble; frank
inocuo	innocuous; harmless	*(Lat.)* **in + nocere**	not + to hurt
longincuo	distant; remote	*(Lat.)* **longe**	long; far off; distant; remote
melifluo	mellifluous	*(Lat.)* **mel + fluere**	honey + to flow
mutuo [R 4339]	mutual	*(Lat.)* **mutuus**	interchanged, mutual
oblicuo	oblique	*(Lat.)* **obliquus**	slanting; inclined
perpetuo [R]	perpetual; everlasting	*(Lat.)* **perpetuus**	continuous; throughout
perspicuo	perspicuous	*(Lat.)* **perspicere**	to look through
promiscuo	promiscuous	*(Lat.)* **promiscuus**	mixed
el residuo [4531]	residue; remainder	*(Lat.)* **residuus**	remaining
superfluo	superfluous	*(Lat.)* **super + fluere**	over + to flow
ubicuo	ubiquitous; omnipresent	*(Lat.)* **ubique**	everywhere
vacuo [R]	vacuous	*(Lat.)* **vacuus**	empty

-ura(1)

Meaning: *state of being; forms abstact noun*
English equivalent: *-ness*
Found in: *nouns*

The following words that end in *-ura* all are derived from adjectives. The addition of this suffix forms an abstract noun, an intangible that refers to the state or qualities of the root adjective. All words ending with *-ura* are feminine.

Formed Word	English Equivalent	Related to	English Equivalent
la albura	perfect whiteness; white of egg	albo	(poet.) snow white
la altura [R 1272]	height; altitude	alto	high; tall
la amargura [R]	bitterness	amargo	bitter
la anchura [R]	width	ancho	wide
la apertura [R 1172]	opening; aperture	abierto	open
la bajura	shortness; lowness	bajo	short; low
la blancura [R]	whiteness	blanco	white
la bravura [R]	courage; fierceness; manliness	bravo	brave; valiant; manly
la cobertura [2880]	coverage	cubierto	covered
la dulzura [R]	sweetness	dulce	sweet
la espesura [R]	thickness; denseness	espeso	thick; dense
la estrechura [R]	narrowness; closeness; tight spot	estrecho	tight; narrow; close
la finura [R]	fineness; delicacy	fino	fine; delicate
la flacura [R]	thinness	flaco	thin
la gordura [R]	fatness	gordo	fat; corpulent; stout; thick; big
la grosura [R]	grossness; crudeness	grosero	gross; crude; coarse
la hermosura [R]	beauty; handsomeness	hermoso	beautiful; handsome
la holgura	roominess	huelgo	room; space
la hondura [R]	depth	hondo	deep
la largura [R]	length	largo	long
la listura	smartness; quickness	listo	smart; quick
la lisura	smoothness; evenness; glibness	liso	smooth; plain
la llanura [R]	evenness; flatness	llano	even; flat
la locura [R 4385]	madness; insanity	loco	mad; crazy; insane
la negrura [R]	blackness	negro	black
la quemadura [R 4686]	burn	quemado	burned
la soltura [R]	looseness	suelto	loose
la ternura	tenderness	tierno	tender
la tersura [R]	smoothness	terso	smooth
la tiesura	stiffness	tieso	stiff; rigid; firm
la verdura [R 2787]	greenness	verde	green

-ura⁽²⁾; -uro; -urar

Meaning: *result of action; state of being; process; (to) act*
English equivalent: *-ure*
Found in: *nouns; adjectives; verbs* (-urar)

English words ending in *-ure*—which may be nouns, adjectives, or verbs—nearly always are cognates of their Spanish couterparts. Spanish words ending with *-ura*, *-uro*, or *-urar*, nearly all of which come directly from Latin, are therefore easy to recognize, use, and learn. Thus, a few tips: (1) The nouns almost always are feminine and end with *-ura* (the only masculine term below is *el futuro*). (2) Adjectives, as would be expected, end with *-uro* and take the ending *-ura* when describing feminine nouns. (3) English verbs ending with *-ure* almost always will take the verb ending *-urar* in Spanish, e.g., *fracturar* (to fracture). Verbs ending with *-urar* are regular.

Formed Word	English Equivalent	Related to	English Equivalent
la abertura [R]	opening (physical)	(*Lat.*) **aperire**	to open
la apertura [R 1172]	opening (figurative)	(*Lat.*) **aperire**	to open
la aventura [R 2213]	adventure	(*Lat.*) **advenire**	to reach, arrive
la candidatura [2415]	candidacy	(*Lat.*) **candidatus**	candidate for office
la captura [2783]	capture	(*Lat.*) **capere**	to capture
capturar [2333]	to capture	(*Lat.*) **capere**	to capture
caricatura [R]	caricature	(*Lat.*) **carricare**	to charge, overload, exaggerate
la censura	censure	(*Lat.*) **censere**	to give an opinion
censurar	to censure, censor	(*Lat.*) **censere**	to give an opinion
la criatura [R 4223]	creature	**criar**	to create, breed, foster
la cultura [R 615]	culture	(*Lat.*) **colere**	to till, cultivate
la cura [R 4075]	cure	(*Lat.*) **curare**	to care for
curar [R 3226]	to cure, heal	(*Lat.*) **curare**	to care for
la dictadura [R 4787]	dictatorship	(*Lat.*) **dictatura**	office of dictator; dictatorship
la escultura [R]	sculpture	**esculpir**	to sculpt, carve
la estatura [3900]	stature	(*Lat.*) **stare**	to stand
la estructura [R 1648]	structure	(*Lat.*) **struere**	to arrange, construct
la fractura [2616]	fracture; breaking	(*Lat.*) **frangere**	to break
fracturar	to fracture	(*Lat.*) **frangere**	to break
el futuro [R 658]	future	(*Lat.*) **futura**	future
impuro [R]	impure	(*Lat.*) **in + purus**	not + pure
la infraestructura [R 1634]	infrastructure	(*Lat.*) **infra + structura**	infrastructure
inseguro [R]	insecure	(*Lat.*) **in + segurus**	not + free from care
la lectura [R 2155]	lecture	(*Lat.*) **legere**	to pick
la literatura [R 3310]	literature	(*Lat.*) **litera**	letter (of the alphabet)
madurar [R 3018]	to mature, ripen, mellow	(*Lat.*) **maturare**	to mature, ripen
maduro [R 4479]	mature; ripe	(*Lat.*) **maturus**	ripe; seasonable
la manicura [R]	manicure	(*Lat.*) **manus + cura**	hand + care
oscuro [R 2258]	dark; obscure	(*Lat.*) **obscurus**	covered
la pastura	pasture	(*Lat.*) **pascere**	to pasture, feed
perjurar [R]	to perjure	(*Lat.*) **per + jurare**	through + to swear
la pintura [R 2270]	painting; picture; paint	(*Lat.*) **pingere**	to paint
la postura [1875]	posture	(*Lat.*) **ponere**	to place, put, posit

Formed Word	English Equivalent	Related to	English Equivalent
puro [R 2355]	pure	(Lat.) **purus**	pure
la ruptura [3758]	rupture	(Lat.) **ruptor**	breaker; violator
seguro [R 548]	secure; sure; safe	(Lat.) **securus**	without care
la signatura [R]	signature	(Lat.) **signare**	to mark
la temperatura [R 1623]	temperature	(Lat.) **temperare**	to temper, blend, regulate
la tortura [4147]	torture	(Lat.) **tortare**	to torture, torment

-usco (-usca); -uzco (-uzca)

Meaning: *like; relating to*
English equivalent: *-ish*
Found in: *adjectives*

Words ending in *-usco* and *-uzco* occur infrequently. Note that they often have names of colors as base terms. As they are adjectives, when used to describe feminine nouns, the endings become *-usca* and *-uzca*, respectively.

Formed Word	English Equivalent	Related to	English Equivalent
blancuzco [R]	whitish	**blanco**	white
negruzco [R]	blackish	**negro**	black
pardusco [R]	drab; dark brown	**pardo**	dull grayish-brown
verdusco [R]	greenish	**verde**	green

-uto; -uta

Meaning: *relating to; result of action*
English equivalent: *-ute*
Found in: *adjectives, nouns*

A Spanish word ending in *-uto* or *-uta* nearly always has an English counterpart that ends with *-ute*. Such suffixes can be found at the end of adjectives or nouns (*-uto* is a more common noun ending than *-uta*). Spanish adjectives ending in *-uto* are almost always derived from Latin, while most nouns ending in *-uto* or *-uta* have a Spanish base (at times a verb ending with *-utar*). One term below, *(el) minuto*, can perform as either a noun or an adjective; the derivation is the same for both formed words. Nouns ending with *-uto* are masculine, while those ending with *-uta* are feminine. Adjectives ending with *-uto* take the ending *-uta* when describing feminine nouns.

Formed Word	English Equivalent	Related to	English Equivalent
absoluto [R 2364]	absolute	**absolver**	to absolve, acquit
astuto	astute	(Lat.) **astutus**	shrewd; discerning
el atributo [R]	attribute	**atribuir**	to attribute
bruto [3133]	brutish; coarse; beastly; gross	(Lat.) **brutus**	dull; insensible
el bruto [3133]	brute; beast	(Lat.) **brutus**	dull; insensible

Formed Word	English Equivalent	Related to	English Equivalent
convoluto	(bot.) convolute; convoluted	(Lat.) convolvere	to roll around
disoluto	dissolute; debauched	disolver	to dissolve, break up
la disputa [R 1975]	dispute	disputar	to dispute, argue (over)
enjuto	dry	enjutar	(build.) to dry
hirsuto	hirsute	(Lat.) hirsutus	hairy
impoluto	unpolluted; spotless	(Lat.) in + polluere	not + pollute
insoluto	unpaid; insolvent	(Lat.) in + solvere	not + to free from restriction
el instituto [R 434]	institute	instituir	to institute, establish
irresoluto [R]	irresolute; unwavering	(Lat.) in + resolvere	not + to loosen
(el) minuto [R 200]	minute	(Lat.) minutus	small
poluto	polluted; soiled	(Lat.) polluere	to pollute
la prostituta	prostitute	prostituir	to prostitute
resoluto	resolute	(Lat.) resolvere	to loosen, relax
el sustituto [R 4306]	substitute	sustituir	to substitute, replace
el tributo [R]	tribute; tax	tributar	to pay (as tribute or tax)
la voluta	volute; spiral ring	(Lat.) volvere	to roll

-zuelo; -zuela

Meaning: *diminutive*
English equivalent: *none*
Found in: *nouns*

The endings -*zuela* and -*zuelo* indicate smallness of the root noun. At times this smallness can be deprecative, e.g., *el pintorzuelo* (the wretched painter), which is derived from *el pintor* (painter); however, usually it means small in the physical sense, e.g., *la cabezuela* (small head) from *la cabeza* (head). This pair of suffixes has sister suffixes, -*uelo* and -*uela*, which are similar in function. Nouns ending in -*zuelo* are masculine; those ending with -*zuela* are feminine. Note Venezuela's charming derivation.

Formed Word	English Equivalent	Related to	English Equivalent
el actorzuelo	wretched actor; ham	el actor	actor; performer
la bestezuela	small beast; creature	la bestia	beast
la cabezuela	small head	la cabeza	head
el cabezuelo	dolt; blockhead	la cabeza	head
el cantorzuelo	wretched singer	el cantor	singer; songbird
la cazuela	casserole	el cazo	pot; saucepan
la chozuela	miserable little hovel	la choza	hut; hovel
el corpezuelo	small body; carcass	el cuerpo	body
el escritorzuelo	miserable writer; hack	el escritor	writer
el garbanzuelo	small chick-pea	el garbanzo	chick-pea
el herrezuelo	scrap of iron	el hierro	iron
el ladronzuelo	petty thief; pickpocket	el ladrón	thief
la mujerzuela [R]	(coll.) prostitute	la mujer	woman
el pintorzuelo	wretched painter	el pintor	painter
el pobrezuelo	poor little wretched person	el pobre	poor person

Formed Word	English Equivalent	Related to	English Equivalent
la puertezuelo	small port	**el puerto**	port; harbor; haven
el reyezuelo	princeling; petty ruler	**el rey**	king; ruler
Venezuela	Venezuela; "little Venice"	**Venecia**	Venice
el ventrezuelo	small belly	**el vientre**	abdomen; belly
la viejezuela	little old woman	**la vieja**	old woman
el viejezuelo	little old man	**el viejo**	old man

List of Suffixes

NOUNS

Suffix	English Equivalent	Meaning
-a	none	resulting object; resulting action
-acho; -acha	none	augmentative; deprecative
-acia	-ice	state of being; forms abstract noun
-acio	-ice; -ace	result of action or attribute
-aco (-aca)	none	deprecative
-ada	none	group; collection; amount; flock; drove, etc.
-ada	none	blow or strike with or from; resulting action
-ada	-ful; -load	denotes fullness of a measure or vessel
-ado (see -ato)	-ship; -ate	office; position; system; duty; domain
-ado	-ful; load	denotes fullness of a measure or vessel
-ado (-ada)	none	one who; result of action
-aje	-age	collection; set; forms abstract noun
-aje	none	fee; toll; rent; dues
-aje	none	landing
-ajo	none	pejorative; diminutive; result of action
-al	none	augmentative; outgrowth; place
-al	none	field; orchard; patch; plantation; plant; tree; etc.
-ancia	-ance; -ancy	act; state of being; result of action
-ano (-ana)	-an	native; adherent (to a system of beliefs)
-ante	-ant; -er; -or	one who; denotes profession
-anza	-ance	quality; state of being; condition; process
-arca	-arch	ruler
-ario	none	book; bound collection; printed matter
-ario (-aria)	-ary	one who
-asma	-asm	result of action; being; condition
-asmo	-asm	result of action; being; condition
-astra	often the prefix step-	denotes step-relations; diminutive in status
-astro	often the prefix step-	denotes step-relations; diminutive in status
-ato	-ship; -ate	office; position; system; duty; domain
-avo (-ava)	-th	denotes denominator of a fraction
-aza	none	augmentative; forms abstract noun
-azgo	-ship	office; post; dignity; relationship; tariff
-azo	none	augmentative
-azo	none	blow or strike with or from; resulting action
-ción	-tion	result of action; state of being; act
-cula	-cule; -ule	diminutive; resulting object or person
-culo	-cule; -ule	diminutive; resulting object or person
-dad	-ness; -hood	state of being; forms abstract noun
-dor (-dora)	-er; -or	one who; denotes profession
-dor	none	machine; appliance
-dora	none	machine; appliance
-dumbre	-ness	forms abstract noun
-dura	-ing	resulting action; resulting object
-eda	none	grove; orchard; place where something grows
-edad	-ness; -hood	state of being; forms abstract noun
-edo	none	grove; orchard; place where something grows

Suffix	English Equivalent	Meaning
-eja	none	diminutive; pejorative
-ejo	none	diminutive; pejorative
-encia	-ence; -ency	act; state of being; result of action
-eno (-ena)	-th	denotes ordinal number
-eño (-eña)	-y; usually none	native
-ense	none	native
-enta	-ent; -ant; -er; -or	one who; denotes female profession
-ente	-ent; -ant; -er; -or	one who; denotes profession
-eo	-ing	resulting action
-era	none	container; holder
-era	none	tree; plant; place where plants grow
-ería	none	shop; store
-ería	-ry; -ness	forms abstract noun
-erizo (-eriza)	-herd	herder
-ero	none	container; holder
-ero (-era)	-er; -man; -person	one who; denotes profession
-ero	none	tree; plant; place where plants grow
-és (-esa)	-ese	native
-estre	-estrian; -ester	denotes period of time
-eta	none	diminutive
-ete	none	diminutive
-ez	-ness; -ity	state of being; forms abstract noun
-eza	-ness; -ity	state of being; forms abstract noun
-fobia	-phobia	fear
-ía	-ry; -ness	forms abstract noun
-ica	none	diminutive
-icia	-ice	state of being; forms abstract noun
-icio	-ice; -ace	result of action or attribute; forms abstract noun
-ico	none	diminutive
-ida	none	resulting action, object, or person
-idad	-ity	state of being; quality
-ido	none	resulting action, object, person, or sound
-illa	-ette; usually none	diminutive
-illa	none	deprecative; diminutive in status
-illo	-ette; usually none	diminutive
-illo	none	deprecative; diminutive in status
-ín	none	diminutive
-ina	-ine	diminutive; place where; denotes feminine name
-ino	none	diminutive; place where
-ino (-ina)	-ine	like; relating to; native; native of
-isco (-isca)	none	result of action
-ismo	-ism	system; doctrine; loyalty to; act; characteristic
-ista	-ist	one who; denotes profession
-ita	none	diminutive
-ita	-ite	native; mineral product
-itis	-itis	disease; inflammation
-ito	none	diminutive
-ito	-ite	quality; mineral product; one who
-itud	-tude	state of being; condition

Suffix	English Equivalent	Meaning
-manía	-mania	insane excitement; madness
-mano (-mana)	-maniac	one who is mad
-miento	-ment	act; state of being; result of action
-o	none	resulting object; resulting action
-o	none	tree; plant
-o (-a)	-er; -ist	one who; denotes profession
-ón	none	denotes suddenness or intensity of action
-ón (-ona)	none	person tending or given to
-ón	none	augmentative; pejorative
-ona	none	augmentative; pejorative
-or (-ora)	-or	one who; denotes profession or machine
-orio	-ory	place where; means by which
-osis	-osis	condition; process; disease
-ota	none	augmentative; pejorative
-ote	none	augmentative; pejorative
-ría	-ry; -ness	forms abstract noun
-sión	-sion	state of being; result of action; act
-stad	-ty	state of being; forms abstract noun
-tad	-ty	state of being; forms abstract noun
-teca	none	place where things are collected and stored
-triz	-ess	denotes profession or role of female
-uca	none	diminutive; endearing; deprecative
-ucha	none	pejorative; diminutive
-ucho	none	pejorative; diminutive
-uco	none	diminutive; endearing; deprecative
-uela	none	diminutive
-uelo	none	diminutive
-ula	-cule; -ule	diminutive; resulting object or person
-ulo	-cule; -ule	diminutive; resulting object or person
-umbre	-ness	forms abstract noun
-ura	-ness	state of being; forms abstract noun
-ura	-ure	result of action; state of being; process; act
-uro	-ure	state of being
-uta	-ute	result of action
-uto	-ute	result of action
-zuela	none	diminutive
-zuelo	none	diminutive

ADJECTIVES

Suffix	English Equivalent	Meaning
-able	-able	capable of; able to
-acho (-acha)	none	augmentative; deprecative
-aco (-aca)	none	deprecative
-ado (-ada)	none	like; relating to
-al	-al	like; relating to
-ano (-ana)	-an	native of; like; relating to
-ante	-ing	like; relating to; doing

Suffix	English Equivalent	Meaning
-ario (-aria)	-ary	like; relating to
-az	-cious	full of
-cial	-cial; -tial	like; relating to
-dizo (-diza)	none	like; relating to; tending to
-engo (-enga)	none	like; relating to
-eno (-ena)	-th	denotes ordinal number
-eño (-eña)	-y; usually none	like; relating to; native of
-ense	none	native of; like; relating to
-ente	-ing; -ent	like; relating to; doing
-eo (-ea)	-eous	like; relating to
-ero (-era)	-y; -able	like; relating to; able to
-érrimo (-érrima)	none	adjectival superlative
-és (-esa)	-ese	native of; like; relating to
-esco (-esca)	-esque	in the manner or style of; like; relating to; resembling
-ésimo (-ésima)	-th	denotes ordinal number
-estre	-estrian; -ester	like; relating to
-ible	-ible; -able	able to; capable of
-ico (-ica)	-ic	like; relating to
-ido (-ida)	-id	like; relating to
-iego (-iega)	none	like; relating to; fond of
-iento (-ienta)	-y	inclined to; tending to; full of; like; relating to
-ífero (-ífera)	-iferous	bearing; producing; yielding
-iforme	-iform	shaped like; in the form of; like
-il	-ile; -able; -ible	like; relating to; concerning; capable of
-imo (-ima)	-th	denotes ordinal numbers
-ino (-ina)	-ine	like; relating to; native of
-isco (-isca)	none	like; relating to
-ísimo (-ísima)	none	adjectival superlative
-ito (-ita)	-ite	like; relating to; native of
-ivo (-iva)	-ive	causing; making
-ívoro (-ívora)	-ivorous	tending to eat
-izo (-iza)	none	like; relating to; made of
-lento (-lenta)	-lent	like; relating to; full of
-mano (-mana)	-maniac	having insane tendencies
-ón (-ona)	none	tending to; given to
-orio (-oria)	-ory	like; relating to
-oso (-osa)	-ous; -ful; -y	full of; having
-ote (-ota)	none	augmentative; pejorative; like; relating to
-oz	-cious	full of
-ucho (-ucha)	none	pejorative; augmentative; like
-udo (-uda)	none	augmentative; having (a great deal of the root noun)
-undo (-unda)	-und	like; relating to
-uno (-una)	none	like; relating to; pertaining to
-uo (-ua)	-uous	like; relating to
-usco (-usca)	-ish	like; relating to
-uto (-uta)	-ute	relating to
-uzco (-uzca)	-ish	like; relating to

VERBS

Suffix	English Equivalent	Meaning
-ificar	-ify	to make (like)
-izar	-ize	to make (like)
-urar	-ure	to act

ADVERBS

Suffix	English Equivalent	Meaning
-mente	-ly	forms adverbs

Spanish Frequency Table

This index of 5,000 high-frequency words was created from a sample of over 10 million words from a daily Mexican newspaper, *El Siglo de Torreón*. The words are ordered by rank, and the first 1,000 entries are illustrated by example sentences or phrases (indicated by ■). Note also the use of □ to indicate set expression(s) and ▶ for similar word forms. Entries are also cross-referenced, where applicable, to the Root Dictionary [R] and the Suffix Guide [-suffix]. For further information on the formation and use of this dictionary, please consult the Introduction.

1 **el, la, los, las** *art* the (*la* may be used as a direct object pronoun to mean "it"; *los* and *las* may also be used as direct object pronouns to mean "them") ■ el carro azul the blue car; la pluma verde the green pen; los aviones chicos the small planes; las flores amarillas the yellow flowers

2 **de** *prep* of; from ■ Uno de ellos salió. One of them left. Ella viene de San Francisco. She comes from San Francisco.

3 **que** *conj* that, which ■ Él que escucha, aprende. He that listens, learns.
   ▶ **qué** *pron* what, how, what a . . . ■ ¿Qué es eso? What is that? ¡Qué bonita! How beautiful! ¡Qué casa tan grande! What a large house!

4 **en** *prep* in, on, at ■ La salsa está en el refrigerador. The salsa is in the refrigerator. Trabajo en la universidad. I work at the university. El vaso está en la mesa. The glass is on the table.

5 **y** *conj* and (*e* replaces *y* before words beginning with *i-* or *y-* for reasons of euphony) ■ Daniel y Fernando son hermanos. Daniel and Fernando are brothers. Maité e Isabel son hermanas. Maité and Isabel are sisters.

6 **a** *prep* to ■ Él viaja muy seguido a Puerto Rico. He travels quite often to Puerto Rico.

7 **un** *art* [R] one (*un* is used before masculine nouns) ■ un día one day; un río one river

8 **se** **1.** *pron* himself, herself, yourself, yourselves, themselves ■ La niña se cayó. The girl fell. **2.** *pers pron* him, her, you, them ■ Se lo dije. I said it to her. **3.** also used to create the passive voice ■ Se habla español. Spanish is spoken.

9 **del** *conj* of the (a compound word uniting *de* plus *el* used to indicate possession) ■ el árbol del vecino the neighbor's tree

10 **ser** *vi* to be (this verb is used for permanent conditions; the verb *estar* is used to mean "to be" when conditions are temporary) □ llegar a ser to become ■ Yo soy escultor. I am a sculptor. Felipe quiere llegar a ser astronauta. Phillip wants to become an astronaut.

11 **por** *prep* for; in place of; instead of; by; during (the preposition *para* is also often used to mean "for") □ por ejemplo for example; por la mañana during the morning ■ Él trabaja por mí. He works instead of me. Me gusta el libro escrito por Carlos Cuauhtémoc Sánchez. I like the book written by Carlos Cuauhtémoc Sánchez. Linda vive por la iglesia. Linda lives by the church.

12 **su** *aj* your, his, her, their, one's, its ■ Su desayuno está servido. Your (his, her, their) breakfast is served.

13 **con** *conj* with ■ Quiero ir con usted. I want to go with you.

14 **para** *prep* for; in order to ■ El regalo es para tí. The gift is for you. Él trabaja para mí. He works for me (not "instead of," but "for my benefit.") Para ir necesitamos una visa. In order to go we need a visa. Para navidad visitaremos Cancún. For Christmas we will visit Cancún.

15 **no** *av* no, not ■ Él no fuma. He does not smoke.

16 **al** *prep* to the (compound word uniting *a* plus *el*) ■ Fuimos al mar. We went to the sea.

17 **éste, ésta, éstos, éstas** *pron* this (one), these (ones); (*ésto* is used when gender is

neutral) ■ Ésto me ha pasado antes. This has happened to me before. Éste es el mejor. This is the best. Ésta es muy grande. This is very big. Éstos son bonitos. These are pretty. Éstas están sucias. These are dirty.

▶ **este, esta, estos, estas** *aj* this, these ■ Este libro es el mejor. This book is the best. Esta casa es muy grande. This house is very big. Estos zapatos son bonitos. These shoes are pretty. Estas cucharas están sucias. These spoons are dirty.

▶ **este** *nm* east ■ El este es más bonito. The east is prettier.

18 **haber** *v aux* to have (used as an auxiliary verb in the perfect tense) ■ Ella ha empezado. She has begun.

19 **lo** *pron* it; him; (with an adjective) what is the important thing ■ Lo sé. I know it. Lo conozco. I know him. lo importante what is important (or "the important thing"); lo interesante what is interesting (or "the interesting thing")

20 **como** *av* as, like, about ■ Santiago está caminando como si le doliera la pierna. Santiago is walking as if his leg is hurting. Ella es alta como su hermana. She is tall like her sister. He estado allí como cinco veces. I have been there about five times.

▶ **cómo** *av* how? ■ ¿Cómo está usted? How are you? ¿Cómo? How's that again?

21 **tener** *vt* [R] to have; to be (often used in expressions to indicate how one is feeling: sleepy, hungry, thirsty, hot, or cold, etc.) ■ Yo tengo una bicicleta. I have a bicycle. Yo tengo sed. I am thirsty. ¿Tiene usted frío? Are you cold?

22 **estar** *vi* [R] to be (used for temporary conditions; the verb *ser* is used to mean "to be" for permanent conditions) ■ Él está enfermo. He is sick.

23 **mas** *conj* but ■ Él hace mucho, mas cumple poco. He does a lot, but completes little.

▶ **más** *av* more; plus ■ Dos más tres son cinco. Two plus three are five. Hay más en el refrigerador. There are more in the refrigerator.

24 **hacer** *vt* [R] to do, to make (also used for the verb *to be* when referring to the weather) □ *hacer por hacer* to do things for the sake of it ■ Hace frío. It is cold.

25 **fue** *vi* (third-person preterite conjugation of the verbs *ser* "to be" and *ir* "to go") *usted fue* you were; you went; *él, ella fue* it (he, she) was; it (he, she) went ■ Usted fue el campeón de tenis el año pasado. You were the tennis champion last year. Fue ayer cuando terminé el proyecto. It was yesterday when I finished the project. Tim fue a Japón. Tim went to Japan.

26 **poder** *vt* [R] to be able to ■ Los estudiantes pueden leer. The students can (are able to) read.

27 **le** *pron* to you, to him, to her; for your, for him, for her ■ Le hablé ayer. I spoke to him (her, you) yesterday. Él le compró un regalo. He bought a gift for her (for him, for you).

28 **decir** *vt* [R] to say, to tell □ *es decir* that is to say ■ Marcos dice que va a viajar a Europa. Marcos says that he is going to travel to Europe. A mi hermano le gusta historia, matemáticas, ciencia, francés y gramática—es decir, le gusta todas las materias. My brother likes history, math, science, French, and grammar—that is to say, he likes all subjects.

29 **todo** [R] **1.** *aj* all, every, everywhere (also used in many expressions) □ *todo el mundo* everyone; *todos los días* every day; *toda la vida* all your life; all my life; *es todo uno* it's all the same ■ Hay niños en todas partes. There are children everywhere. Tienes toda la razón. You are completely right. **2.** *nmf* all, everything, everyone ■ Todos la quieren. Everyone loves her.

30 **año** *nm* [R] year □ *año escolar, año lectivo* school or academic year; *el año pasado* last year

31 **pero** *conj* but (also used to add emphasis) ■ Tengo carro, pero no tengo camioneta. I have a car, but I don't have a van. Ella me cae muy, pero muy bien. I like her very, very much.

32 **ese, esa, eso, esos, esas** *aj* that, those ■ Ese jugo es el mejor. That juice is the best. Esa mesa es muy pequeña. That table is very small. Esos calcetines están limpios. Those socks are clean. Esas galletas están ricas. Those cookies are good (tasting).

▶ **ése, ésa, ésos, ésas** *pron* that (one), those (ones) ■ Ése es el mejor. That is the best. Ésa es muy pequeña. That is very small. Ésos están limpios. Those are clean. Ésas están ricas. Those are good (tasting). Eso fue todo. That was all. Eso es lo más importante. That is the most important thing.

▶ **ese** *nf* the letter "s" ■ El nombre de la letra "s" es "ese". The name of the letter "s" is "ess."

33 **o** *conj* [R] or; either ■ tres o cuatro three or four; Me gusta o fresa o chocolate. I like either strawberry or chocolate.

34 **otro** **1.** *pron* another ■ Ella quiere otro. She wants another. **2.** *aj* other ■ el otro libro the other book

35 **¿quien?** *pron* who, whom ■ Yo sé quien fue. I know who it was.
　　▶ **quién** *pron* who?; whom? ■ ¿Quién quiere ir al parque? Who wants to go to the park? ¿Para quién? For whom?

36 **él, ella, ellos, ellas** *pron* he, she, they ■ Él camina muy rápido. He walks very fast. Ella tiene dos hermanas. She has two sisters. Ellos salen de la escuela a las tres. They leave school at three. Ellas son buenas amigas. They are good friends.

37 **dar** *vt* [R] to give ■ Dar es mejor que recibir. To give is better than to receive.

38 **si** *conj* if ■ No bajaré de peso si sigo comiendo helado. I will not lose weight if I continue eating ice cream.
　　▶ **sí** **1.** *av* yes; so ■ Sí, lo haré. Yes, I will do it. Pienso que sí. I think so. **2.** *pron* himself, herself, themselves, oneself (as a reflexive pronoun it follows a preposition) ■ entre sí among themselves

39 **ya** *av* already; enough □ *ya no* no longer; ¡Ya! That's enough! ■ Ya terminamos. We already finished. ¡Ya callense! Be quiet already! Ella ya no llora. She no longer cries.

40 **primero** [R] **1.** *nm* first day of the month ■ El primero de mayo es un día festivo. The first of May is a holiday. **2.** *nmf* first one ■ Me gusta el primero. I like the first one. **3.** *aj* first (*primer* is used before masculine singular nouns) □ *en primer lugar* in the first place ■ La primera clase del día empieza a las nueve. The first class of the day begins at nine o'clock. ¿Tienes el primer libro? Do you have the first book? **4.** *av* first ■ Tú vas primero. You go first.

41 **sin** *conj* without ■ Me gusta el té sin azúcar. I like tea without sugar.

42 **estado** [R -ado(2)] **1.** *nm* state □ *golpe de estado* coup d'état; *Estados Unidos* United States ■ Salí del estado hace tres años. I left the state three years ago. Vivo en los Estados Unidos. I

live in the United States. **2.** *vi* been (past participle of the verb *estar*) ■ ¿Cómo has estado? How have you been?

43 **deber** [R] **1.** *nm* duty; debit, expense ■ Mi deber es defender el país. My duty is to defend my country. **2.** *vt* to owe; to ought to (in the conditional tense); must ■ Debería ir. I ought to go. Debo tomar algo. I must drink something.

44 **dos** [R] **1.** *nm* two; second day of the month ■ La renta se vence el dos de cada mes. Rent is due on the second of each month. **2.** *aj* two ■ Hay dos tiendas. There are two stores.

45 **cuando** *av* when ■ Cuando ella sonríe estoy contento. When she smiles I am happy.
　　▶ **¿cuándo?** *av* when? ■ ¿Cuándo es tu examen? When is your test?

46 **parte** *nf* [R] part; place □ *partes de la oración* parts of speech ■ Parte de mi quiere ir. Part of me wants to go. Vamos a alguna parte. We're going somewhere.

47 **entre** *conj* between, among ■ Entre los Estados Unidos y México hay una frontera larga. Between the United States and Mexico there is a long border.

48 **nuevo** *aj* [R] new □ *nuevo flamante* brand-new, spanking new ■ El libro está nuevo. The book is new.

49 **ir** *vi* [R] to go □ *ir de compras* to go shopping ■ Quiero ir a Los Ángeles. I want to go to Los Angeles.

50 **donde** *av* where ■ Voy donde me gusta. I go where I like.
　　▶ **¿dónde?** *av* where? ■ ¿Dónde estudias? Where do you study?

51 **sobre** **1.** *av* above ■ Sobre todo, ella es muy amable. Above all, she is very kind. **2.** *nm* envelope ■ La carta está en el sobre. The letter is in the envelope.

52 **día** *nm* [R] day □ *día de fiesta* holiday; *en pleno día* in broad daylight, in the middle of the day; *a la luz del día* in the light of day, in broad daylight, openly ■ Trabajé todo el día. I worked all day.

53 **también** *av* also, too ■ Ella también quiere ir al cine. She also wants to go to the movies. Yo también. Me too.

54 **mucho** *av* [R] much, very much, a lot ■ Te quiero mucho. I love you very much.

55 **alguno** **1.** *pron* somebody, some ■ Algunos estudian todos los días. Some study every day.

2. *aj* some (shortened form *algún* is used with masculine singular nouns) ■ por alguna razón for some reason; Algún día volverás. Some day you will return.

⁵⁶ **mismo** *aj* [R] same (also used for emphasis) ■ el mismo lugar the same place; Ella misma hizo su vestido. She herself made her dress. Lo mismo me da. It's all the same to me.

⁵⁷ **muy** *av* very ■ Muy bien, gracias. Very well, thank you.

⁵⁸ **ciudad** *nf* [R] city ■ Vivo en la ciudad. I live in the city.

⁵⁹ **público** *nm, aj* [R] public □ *baños públicos* public bathrooms ■ El público espera. The public waits.

⁶⁰ **tanto** *aj* so much, so many ■ ¡Te amo tanto! I love you so much! Tanta gente no va a caber. That many people are not going to fit.
> **tan(to)** *av* as, so; the same as, just like □ *tan pronto como* as soon as ■ Tanto tú como yo, somos cristianos. You are just like me, in that we are both Christians. Está tan alto que no puedo alcanzarlo. It's so high that I cannot reach it.

⁶¹ **país** *nm* [R] country, nation ■ Él quiere salir del país. He wants to leave the country.

⁶² **solo 1.** *av* alone, by one's self □ *a solas* alone ■ Él vive solo. He lives alone. El niño quería cruzar la calle a solas. The boy wanted to cross the street by himself. **2.** *aj* by itself; empty Parece una casa sola. It looks like an empty house. **3.** *nm* solo performance ■ Ella cantó un solo. She sang a solo.
> **sólo** *av* only ■ El vuelo duró sólo una hora. The flight lasted only one hour.

⁶³ **cual** *aj* which, that ■ El presidente abordó al avión, el cual salió inmediatamente. The president boarded the plane, which left immediately.
> **¿cuál?** *pron* what? which? ■ ¿Cuál es tu pregunta? What is your question? ¿Cuál libro es tuyo? Which book is yours?

⁶⁴ **grande** *aj* [R] big; great (the shortened form *gran* is used before a noun) □ *Alejandro el Grande* Alexander the Great ■ El avión es grande. The airplane is large. Esa es una gran idea. That is a great idea.

⁶⁵ **porque** *conj* because ■ Corrí porque tenía miedo. I ran because I was afraid.
> **¿por qué?** *conj* why? ■ ¿Por qué llegaste tarde? Why did you arrive late?

> **porqué** *nm* reason ■ No sé el porqué. I don't know the reason.

⁶⁶ **hasta 1.** *prep* until □ *hasta mañana* until tomorrow ■ Trabajé hasta las nueve. I worked until nine. **2.** *conj* even ■ Comí la papa, hasta la cáscara. I ate the potato, even the skin.

⁶⁷ **persona** *nf* [R] person □ *buena persona* decent person; *mala persona* bad person, nasty individual; *una persona a la vez* one person at a time

⁶⁸ **mexicano,-a 1.** *nmf* Mexican (person) ■ El mexicano ganó la medalla. The Mexican won the medal. **2.** *aj* of or from Mexico, Mexican ■ ¿Te gusta la comida mexicana? Do you like Mexican food?

⁶⁹ **mil** *nm, aj* [R] thousand ■ Quiero un mil. I want a thousand. mil veces a thousand times

⁷⁰ **desde** *prep* since; from □ *desde entonces* since then ■ Viajamos desde Texas hasta California. We traveled from Texas to California.

⁷¹ **me** *pron* me, to me (used as direct or indirect object; also, first person singular of the reflexive) ■ Me dieron dinero. They gave me money. Ella me besó. She kissed me. Me cambié la ropa. I changed clothes.

⁷² **hora** *nf* [R] hour; time ■ Trabajamos una hora. We worked one hour. ¿Qué hora es? What time is it?

⁷³ **realizar** *vt* [R -izar] to complete, to bring to fruition ■ Los ingenieros realizaron su trabajo. The engineers completed their job.

⁷⁴ **nacional** *aj* [R] national ■ Ellos se conocieron en la reunión juvenil nacional. They met at the national youth meeting.

⁷⁵ **así** *av* like that, in that way, that's the way □ *así mismo* in the same way ■ Me gusta así. I like it like that. Así es la vida. That's the way life is.

⁷⁶ **vez** *nf* time (occurrence) □ *esta vez* this time; *rara vez* seldom

⁷⁷ **ver** *vt* [R] to see □ *nos vemos* see you soon; *vamos a ver* we shall see; *¿cómo ves?* how does that seem? *a ver* let's see; *ver visiones* to see things ■ Te puedo ver. I can see you.

⁷⁸ **partido** [R] **1.** *nm* party (group); game ■ El partido ganó la elección. The party won the election. El partido empezó a las tres. The game began at three. **2.** *vt* sliced, divided (past participle of the verb *partir*) ■ Ya ha

partido ella el pastel. She has already sliced the cake.

79 **llegar** *vi* [R] to arrive □ *llegar a ser* to become ■ Ella va a llegar el martes. She is going to arrive on Tuesday. ¿Qué quieres llegar a ser cuando ya seas grande? What do you want to become when you are grown up?

80 **hay** *vi* there is, there are ■ Hay una tortilla en la estufa. There is one tortilla on the stove. Hay tres excepciones. There are three exceptions.

81 **durante** *av* [R] during ■ Durante la guerra, mi abuela vivía con su hermana. During the war, my grandmother lived with her sister.

82 **gobierno** *nm* [R -o(1)] government ■ Mónica trabaja para el gobierno. Mónica works for the government.

83 **presidente** *nm* [-ente(2)] president □ *presidente municipal* mayor ■ El presidente se reunió con el embajador. The president met with the ambassador. Conocí al presidente municipal anoche. I met the mayor last night.

84 **bueno** *aj* [R] good □ *tener buena pinta* to look good ■ Eso es bueno. That is good. Es un buen libro. It is a good book. Ella es una buena muchacha. She is a good girl.

85 **tres** [R] **1.** *nm* three; third day of the month ■ Hoy es el tres de enero. Today is January third. **2.** *aj* three ■ Hay tres árboles afuera de mi casa. There are three trees outside my house.

86 **encontrar** *vt* [R] to find; to meet (by accident); to run into, to meet casually ■ Encontré las llaves. I found the keys. Nos encontramos en el centro. We ran into each other downtown.

87 **llevar(se)** *vt(r)* [R] to carry, to take with, to contain (to have in), to have (as an attribute) (vt); to get along (with each other) (vr) □ *llevar puesto* to wear ■ Juan lleva libros. John is carrying books. Ella llevó a sus nietos. She took her grandchildren (with her). Las enchiladas llevan aceitunas. The enchiladas have olives in them. La letra lleva acento. The letter has an accent. Él llevaba puesta una corbata. He was wearing a tie. Nos llevamos muy bien. We get along very well.

88 **contra** *prep* [R] against ■ Él jugó contra sus hermanos. He played against his brothers.

▶ **contras** *nfpl* political group opposing the Nicaraguan government ■ Las contras y el gobierno lucharon por más de diez años.

The *contras* and the government fought for more than ten years.

89 **equipo** *nm* team; equipment ■ En nuestro equipo hay cinco hombres y tres mujeres. On our team there are five men and three women. El equipo está en buenas condiciones. The equipment is in good condition.

90 **tiempo** *nm* [R] weather; time (to inquire about time, use *hora: ¿Qué hora es?* What time is it?) □ *el tiempo vuela* time flies; *el tiempo dirá* time will tell ■ El tiempo cambia rápidamente. The weather changes quickly.

91 **lugar** *nm* place □ *fuera de lugar* out of place; *tener lugar* to take place ■ Mi lugar favorito es la playa. My favorite place is the beach.

92 **grupo** *nm* [R] group ■ El grupo de jóvenes es grande. The youth group is large.

93 **nuestro** *aj* [R] our ■ Nuestra familia salió de vacaciones. Our family left on vacation. Nuestro carro está sucio. Our car is dirty. Nuestras hijas van a la fiesta. Our daughters are going to the party. Nuestros amigos siempre nos ayudan. Our friends always help us.

94 **mejor** *aj* [R] better; best □ *a lo mejor* perhaps ■ Mi mejor amigo vive cerca. My best friend lives nearby. Quiero comprar una mejor bicicleta. I want to buy a better bicycle. Él quiere ser el mejor de los mejores. He wants to be the best of the best. A lo mejor ella va a llegar tarde. Perhaps she is going to arrive late.

95 **mi** *aj* my ■ Mi hermana fue a Londres. My sister went to London. Quiero ver a mis amigos. I want to see my friends.

96 **ante** *av* before ■ El grupo se presentó ante la escuela. The group performed before the school.

97 **además** *av* furthermore, in addition ■ Él lavó mi carro, además de la suya. He washed my car, in addition to his own.

98 **nos** *pron* [R] us, to us (used as direct or indirect object; also first person plural of the reflexive) ■ Nos dieron chocolate. They gave us chocolate. Nos robaron. They robbed us. Nos comimos las galletas. We ate the cookies (reflexive). Nosotros nos levantamos temprano. We got up early (reflexive).

99 **vida** *nf* [R -ido(2)] life □ *vida y milagros* life and times ■ La vida es bella. Life is beautiful.

100 **después** *av* later □ *después de* after ■ Compre ahora, pague después. Buy now, pay

later. Después de la clase tomaron café. After class they drank coffee.

101 **recibir** *vt* [R] to receive ■ Laura va a recibir buenas noticias. Laura is going to receive good news.

102 **segundo** [R -undo] **1.** *aj* second (in order) ■ El premio para el segundo lugar es un carro. The prize for second place is a car. **2.** *nm* second (period of time) ■ El mesero los atenderá en un segundo. The waiter will attend to you in one second.

103 **dejar** *vt* [R] to let, to permit, to allow; to leave behind □ *dejar de* to stop ■ Déjame ir. Let me go. ¡No me dejes! Don't leave me! Ella dejó de llorar. She stopped crying.

104 **conocer** *vt* [R] to know (a person); to meet (for the first time) (the verb *saber* is used when "to know" refers to a fact) ■ La conozco. I know her. Nos conocimos en la iglesia. We met (each other for the first time) at church.

105 **seguir** *vt* [R] to follow, to come after, to be next □ *seguir adelante* to go on or ahead, press on ■ Ellos siguieron los señalamientos. They followed the signs. Ella ayudó al siguiente en la fila. She helped the next one in line.

106 **millón** *nm* [R] million ■ Roberto ahorrará un millón de dólares. Robert will save a million dollars.

107 **unir(se)** *vt(r)* [R] to unite, to join (vt); to become united with, to become joined to (vr) ■ Los niños unieron sus manos para orar. The children joined hands to pray.

108 **presentar** *vt* [R] to present, to introduce ■ Él presentó a su madre. He introduced his mother. Él va a presentar su información al grupo. He is going to present his information to the group.

109 **trabajo** [R -o(1)] **1.** *nm* work ■ El trabajo es una bendición grande. Work is a great blessing. Cuesta (mucho) trabajo. It's (very) hard. **2.** *vi* I work (first person singular of the verb *trabajar*) ■ Trabajo todos los días. I work every day.

110 **caso** *nm* case ■ El caso actual ha sido resuelto. The current case has been resolved.

111 **ayer** *av* [R] yesterday ■ Anoche dormí solamente dos horas. Last night I slept only two hours.

112 **medio** [R] **1.** *nm* half ■ Mi hija tiene un año y medio de edad. My daughter is a year and a half old. **2.** *aj* half, partly ■ El cielo está medio nublado. The sky is partly cloudy. **3.** *av* partly, somewhat ■ Me siento medio raro. I feel somewhat strange.

113 **último** *aj* [R] last, final ■ Te va a gustar el último capítulo. You're going to like the last chapter.

114 **mayor** [R] **1.** *aj* oldest; greater (in number); older □ *mayor de edad* of age ■ Cinco más cinco es mayor que nueve. Five plus five is greater than nine. Los niños mayores de diez años se van a quedar. The children older than ten are going to stay. **2.** *nmf* oldest; greater (in number); older ■ El mayor de sus hijos es niño. The oldest of his children is a boy.

115 **municipal** *aj* [R] municipal ■ El edificio de las oficinas municipales está cerrado. The municipal office building is closed.

116 **gran** *aj* [R] great ■ Esa es una gran idea. That is a great idea.

117 **querer** *vt* [R] to want; to love □ *querer más* to prefer ■ Quiero dos enchiladas. I want two enchiladas. Te quiero. I love you.

118 **problema** *nm* [R] problem ■ No hay ningún problema. There is no problem.

119 **pues** *conj* as; well, hmm (frequently used as a filler) ■ No voy a ir al mandado, pues tengo mucha comida todavía. I'm not going grocery shopping, as I still have a lot of food. Pues, no sé. Well, I don't know.

120 **ahora** *av* [R] now; today; nowadays □ *ahora mismo* right now ■ Necesito comer algo ahora. I need to eat something now.

121 **cada** *aj* each (does not change to agree in gender) ■ Te amo cada día más. I love you more each day. Cada persona votará. Each person will vote.

122 **pasado** [R] **1.** *nm* past ■ En el pasado las computadoras eran enormes. In the past computers were huge. **2.** *aj* last ■ El lunes pasado no fui a la escuela. Last Monday I did not go to school. **3.** *vti* passed (past participle of the verb *pasar*) ■ Hemos pasado por aquí muchas veces. We have passed by here many times.

123 **mes** *nm* month ■ El próximo mes voy a viajar a Italia. Next month I am going to travel to Italy.

[124] **saber** *vt* [R] to know (a fact); to know how □ *saber de cierto* to know for sure; *saberse al dedillo* to have at one's fingertips ■ Sabía la respuesta. I knew the answer. Ella sabe cocinar. She knows how to cook.

[125] **peso** *nm* [R] peso (monetary unit of several Latin American countries); weight □ *peso muerto* dead weight; *peso bruto* gross weight ■ Mi peso es de 110 libras. My weight is 110 pounds.

[126] **momento** *nm* [R] moment □ *por el momento* for the time being, for the moment ■ El niño lloró sólo por un momento. The child cried for only a moment.

[127] **agua** *nf(el)* [R] water □ *agua corriente* running water; *agua bendita* holy water ■ Ella necesita agua. She needs water.

[128] **tomar** *vt* [R] to take; to drink ■ Ellos toman limonada. They drink lemonade.

[129] **político** *aj* [R] political ■ El mundo político es muy controversial. The political world is very controversial.
 ▶ **la política** *nf politics* ■ A él le gusta la política. He likes politics.

[130] **bien** *av* [R] fine, well; very (occasionally used instead of *muy*) ■ Estoy bien. I am fine. Esta comida está bien buena. This food is very good.

[131] **esperar** *vt* [R] to wait; to hope; to expect (in Spanish the context helps communicate differences in meaning) ■ Te esperamos. We will wait for you. Espero verte pronto. I hope to see you soon. Esperamos buenas noticias de ellos. We expect good news about them.

[132] **poco** [R] **1.** *nm* a little □ *poco antes* shortly before ■ Hablo un poco de español. I speak a little Spanish. **2.** *aj* few ■ Vino poca gente. Few people came.

[133] **próximo** *aj* [R] next ■ El próximo verano visitaremos a mi hermano. Next summer we will visit my brother.

[134] **ciento** *nm, aj* [R] hundred □ *cien* one hundred ■ El tiene ciento veinte libros. He has one hundred twenty books. El necesita cien lápices. He needs one hundred pencils.

[135] **casa** *nf* [R] house □ *casa de huéspedes* boardinghouse; *casa de juego* casino; *casa flotante* houseboat ■ La casa es verde. The house is green.

[136] **semana** *nf* [R] week □ *Semana Santa* Holy Week ■ Te veré después de una semana. I will see you in one week.

[137] **tratar** *vt* [R] to treat; to try; to deal with ■ Él trata muy bien a su esposa. He treats his wife very well. Inténtalo. Try it. El estudio trata de la política. The study deals with politics.

[138] **aunque** *conj* although, even though ■ Ella vino a la escuela, aunque no se sentía muy bien. She came to school, although she did not feel very well.

[139] **forma** *nf* [R -a] form; shape ■ Ray está en buena forma. Ray is in good shape.

[140] **quedar** **1.** *vi* to remain, to have left (remaining) ■ Quedan tres limones. Three lemons remain. Nos quedan cinco días. We have five days left. **2.** *vr* to remain, to stay; to fit Me quedo aquí. I am staying here. Te queda muy bien ese vestido. That dress fits you very well.

[141] **hoy** *av* today ■ Hoy es jueves. Today is Thursday.

[142] **señalar** *vt* [R] to signal; to indicate; to point to ■ El árbitro señaló el final del partido. The referee signaled the end of the game. Este tipo de artefacto señala la presencia histórica de los maya. This type of artifact indicates the historical presence of the Mayas. El señor Pelayo señaló al reloj. Mr. Pelayo pointed to the clock.

[143] **niño,-a** *nmf* [R] child, boy, girl □ *de niño* as a child ■ El niño tiene seis años de edad. The boy is six years old.

[144] **federal** *aj* [R] federal ■ El trabaja para el gobierno federal. He works for the federal government.

[145] **poner** *vt* [R] to put ■ Laura puso sus libros en la mesa. Laura put her books on the table.

[146] **general** [R] **1.** *aj* general □ *en general, por lo general* in general ■ Por lo general a él le gustan las películas de acción. In general he likes action movies. **2.** *nm* general (military) □ *general de brigada* brigadier general ■ El general decidió avanzar contra la ciudad. The general decided to advance against the city.

[147] **informar** *vt* [R] to inform ■ El policía informó al sospechoso de sus derechos legales. The policeman informed the suspect of his legal rights.

[148] **programa** *nm* [R] program ■ El programa de la computadora es fácil de usar. The computer program is easy to use.

[149] **hecho** *nm* [R] act, deed □ *de hecho* in fact ■ El hecho de ser padre es una responsabilidad importante. The act of being a parent is an important responsibility. De hecho, es muy importante. In fact, it is very important. Del dicho al hecho, hay mucho trecho. Talk and action are two very different things. (literally, From saying to action, there is a great distance.)

[150] **lograr** *vt* [R] to achieve, to accomplish ■ Usted puede lograr sus metas. You can accomplish your goals.

[151] **mujer** *nf* [R] woman; wife □ *mujer fatal* femme fatale; *mujer de su casa* dutiful housewife ■ La mujer llevaba su bolsa. The woman was carrying her purse. Él ama a su mujer. He loves his wife.

[152] **punto** *nm* [R] point; dot; period (punctuation) □ *punto flaco* weak point ■ Él reservó el punto más importante hasta el final. He saved the most important point for last. Nuestra dirección de correo electrónico termina en "punto net". Our e-mail address ends in "dot net." Se le olvidó poner el punto al final de su frase. He forgot to put a period at the end of his sentence.

[153] **antes** *av* [R] before ■ Antes de preparar el desayuno, ella necesita ir a la tienda. Before making breakfast, she needs to go to the store.

[154] **buscar** *vt* [R] to search, to look for, to seek ■ Él está buscando una pluma. He is looking for a pen.

[155] **considerar** *vt* [R] to consider ■ Ella tiene que considerar sus opciones. She has to consider her options.

[156] **importante** *aj* [R] importante ■ Es importante estudiar. It is important to study.

[157] **manera** *nf* [R] manner, way ■ Me gusta tu manera de pensar. I like the way you think.

[158] **servicio** *nm* [R -icio] service □ *franco de servicio* off-duty (soldiers) ■ Ellos dan buen servicio. They give good service. El servicio empieza a las 9:00. The service begins at 9:00.

[159] **cuenta** *nf* [R -a] count; account; check or bill (restaurant, hotel); bead □ *ajustar cuentas* to settle accounts ■ Perdí la cuenta. I lost count. La jóven canceló su cuenta del banco. The young woman closed her bank account. Ellos pidieron la cuenta al mesero. They asked the waiter for the check. Clara tiene una colección de cuentas amarillas y negras. Clara has a collection of yellow and black beads.

[160] **ni** *conj* neither; nor □ *ni siquiera* not even ■ Ni María ni Miriam se quedaron. Neither María nor Miriam stayed. Ella ni siquiera averiguó la tarea. She did not even check the homework.

[161] **hijo,-a** *nmf* son; daughter □ *hijo de familia* minor ■ El hijo de ella tiene dos años. Her son is two years old. La hija de él estudia en Nueva York. His daughter studies in New York.

[162] **luego** *av* then; later □ *luego que* after ■ Luego comimos. Then we ate. Vamos a escribir otro libro luego que terminemos éste. We are going to write another book after we finish this one.

[163] **familia** *nf* [R] family ■ Ella viene de una familia numerosa. She comes from a large family.

[164] **sentir** [R] **1.** *vt* to feel ■ Yo puedo sentir las piedras en mis zapatos. I can feel the rocks in my shoes. Él siente mucha hambre. He feels very hungry. **2.** *vr* to be feeling ■ ¿Cómo te sientes? How are you feeling? **3.** *nm* feeling ■ Tengo este sentir de que mi hermano va a ganar la carrera. I have this feeling that my brother is going to win the race.

[165] **mundo** *nm* [R] world ■ El mundo no es tan grande. The world is not so big.

[166] **mientras** *av* meanwhile ■ Yo patinaba mientras él estaba corriendo. I was skating while he was running.

[167] **acuerdo** *nm* [R -o(1)] agreement □ *de acuerdo* agreed, in agreement ■ Tenemos un acuerdo. We have an agreement. Estamos de acuerdo. We are in agreement. ¿De acuerdo? Agreed?

[168] **salir(se)** *vt(r)* [R] to leave, to go out (vt); to overflow, to spill out (vr) □ *salir con bien* to turn out well ■ El camión sale a las ocho. The bus leaves at eight. Salimos varias veces al cine. We went out several times to the movies. Se salió el agua del lavabo. The water overflowed from the sink.

[169] **varios** *aj* various, a few ■ Mateo necesita varias herramientas. Matthew needs several tools. La niña tiene varias muñecas. The girl has a few dolls.

170 **embargo** [R -o(1)] **1.** *conj* □ *sin embargo* however, nevertheless ■ Ella está leyendo, sin embargo desea dormir pronto. She is reading, however she wants to go to sleep soon. **2.** *nm* embargo ■ El embargo duró casi un año. The embargo lasted almost a year.

171 **menos** *prep* [R] except; less; minus □ *ni mucho menos* far from it, not by a long shot ■ Él corre todos los días, menos el viernes. He runs every day except Friday. Él quiere menos sal en su comida. He likes less salt in his food. Diez menos dos son ocho. Ten minus two are eight.

172 **bajo** [R] **1.** *aj* low; short; ground □ *planta baja* ground floor ■ Los intereses son bajos. Interest rates are low. El muchacho es de estatura baja. The boy is of short stature. **2.** *av* under □ *bajo presión* under pressure; *bajo juramento* under oath

173 **colonia** *nf* [R] neighborhood; colony ■ La colonia es tranquila. The neighborhood is quiet.

174 **iniciar** *vt* [R] to initiate, to begin ■ Las clases inician el próximo lunes. Classes begin next Monday.

175 **centro** *nm* [R] center, middle; downtown □ *centro de mesa* centerpiece (for a table) ■ Hay dos personas en el centro de la foto. There are two people in the center of the photo. Voy al centro para comprar flores. I'm going downtown to buy flowers.

176 **gente** *nf* people □ *gente de bien* good, honest people, decent folk ■ Ella habla con mucha gente todos los días. She speaks with many people every day.

177 **según** *av* according to ■ El actuó según sus creencias. He acted according to his beliefs.

178 **municipio** *nm* [R] municipality ■ Es un municipio muy grande. It is a very large municipality.

179 **empresa** *nf* [R] business firm, enterprise ■ Mis amigos iniciaron la empresa. My friends started the business.

180 **director,-a** *nmf* [R] director ■ El director suele hacer ejercicios todos los días. The director usually exercises every day.

181 **trabajar** *vi* [R] to work □ *a puro trabajar* by sheer hard work ■ Él también tiene que trabajar los sábados. He also has to work Saturdays.

182 **seguridad** *nf* [R -idad] security □ *válvula de seguridad* safety valve ■ La seguridad de la familia es importante. The security of the family is important.

183 **juego** *nm* [R -o(1)] game; set (of dishes, tools, etc.) □ *juego limpio* fair play; *juego sucio* foul play ■ El juego no se ha terminado. The game has not ended. El juego de té es nuevo. The tea set is new.

184 **cuatro** [R] **1.** *nm* four; fourth day of the month ■ El cuatro es un número par. Four is an even number. **2.** *aj* four ■ Tenemos cuatro caballos en nuestro establo. We have four horses in our stable.

185 **ofrecer** *vt* [R] to offer ■ Ella vino a ofrecer sus productos. She came to offer her products.

186 **autoridad** *nf* [R -idad] authority ■ Él no tiene autoridad en esta área. He has no authority in this area.

187 **ganar** *vt* [R] to win; to earn ■ Ella ganó el premio. She earned the prize.

188 **acción** *nf* [R -ción] action ■ A él le gusta la acción. He likes action.

189 **número** *nm* [R -o(1)] number ■ El número de invitados es cien. The number of invited guests is one hundred.

190 **social** *aj* [R -cial] social □ *trabajador social* social worker ■ Ella es muy social. She is very social.

191 **asegurar** *vt* [R] to assure ■ Él nos aseguró que va a venir esta semana. He assured us that he is going to come this week.

192 **existir** *vi* [R] to exist ■ Existe la posibilidad de estudiar en Rusia. There exists the possibility of studying in Russia.

193 **indicar** *vt* [R] to indicate ■ Ellos indicaron el camino. They indicated the way.

194 **cosa** *nf* thing □ *cosa de oír, cosa de ver* thing worth hearing, thing worth seeing ■ Una cosa es cierta. One thing is certain. Eso es cosa mía. That's my business.

195 **hombre** *nm* [R] man □ *hombre faldero* ladies' man; *hombre de mundo* man of the world ■ Viktor Frankl escribió el libro *El Hombre en Busca de Sentido.* Viktor Frankl wrote the book *Man's Search for Meaning.* El hombre corrió. The man ran.

196 **padre** *nm* [R] father □ *padre de familia* head of a family; *padres nmpl* fathers, parents ■ El padre de ella se llama Tomás. Her father's

name is Thomas. **Los padres de ella son de Australia.** Her parents are from Australia.

197 **siempre** *av* [R] always ■ **Ella siempre quiere su café sin azúcar.** She always wants her coffee without sugar.

198 **pedir** *vt* [R] to ask (for), to request (*preguntar* is used to mean "to ask a question") ■ **Él pidió la mano en matrimonio.** He asked for her hand in marriage. **Pedí dos tacos.** I asked for two tacos.

199 **vivir** *vi* [R] to live □ *vivir de* to live on ■ **Él vive en Argentina.** He lives in Argentina. **Podemos vivir muy bien de nuestro sueldo.** We are able to live very well on our salary.

200 **minuto** *nm* [R -uto] minute (time) ■ **Espérame un minuto.** Wait for me one minute.

201 **sector** *nm* [R] sector ■ **La colonia se divide en dos sectores.** The neighborhood is divided into two sectors.

202 **cambio** *nm* [R -o(1)] change ■ **El cambio fue positivo.** The change was positive.

203 **final** *aj* [R -al(2)] final □ *al final* at the end, in the end ■ **La escena final fue mi favorita.** The final scene was my favorite.

204 **carrera** *nf* [R] race □ *a las carreras* in a hurry ■ **Ganó la carrera.** She won the race. **Siempre anda a las carreras.** He is always in a hurry.

205 **permitir** *vt* [R] to permit ■ **El señor González permitió salir a jugar a su hijo.** Mr. González permitted his son to go out and play.

206 **edad** *nf* age □ *mayor de edad* of age; *edad de bronce* Bronze Age; *flor de la edad* prime or bloom of youth ■ **El tiene 45 años de edad.** He is forty-five years of age.

207 **derecho** [R] **1.** *nm* right (legal or political) ■ **Tenemos nuestros derechos.** We have our rights. **2.** *aj* straight, straight ahead; right-hand □ *ser el brazo derecho de alguien* to be someone's right-hand man ■ **Sigue derecho por dos millas.** Continue straight ahead for two miles.
► **derecha** *nf* right (direction) ■ **Nuestra casa está a la derecha.** Our house is on the right.

208 **recurso** *nm* [R] recourse, option; resource □ **el departamento de recursos humanos** the department of human resources. ■ **Tuvimos pocos recursos.** We had few options.

209 **tema** *nm* [R] theme, subject, topic ■ **La política es el tema del día.** Politics is the topic of the day.

210 **perder** *vt* [R] to lose ■ **Él perdió sus llaves.** He lost his keys.

211 **obra** *nf* [R -a] work (project) □ *obra de teatro* play; *estar en obras* to be under repair; **obra maestra** masterpiece ■ **Terminaron la obra ayer.** They finished the project yesterday. **Es una maravillosa obra de teatro.** It is a great play.

212 **resultado** *nm* [R -ado(2)] result ■ **Los resultados fueron positivos.** The results were positive.

213 **mantener(se)** *vt(r)* [R] to maintain, to keep (vt); to support oneself (vr) ■ **Carla mantiene limpio su escritorio.** Carla maintains a clean desk. **Virginia se mantenía cuando estaba en la universidad.** Virginia supported herself while she was at the university.

214 **calle** *nf* [R] street □ *calle arriba* up the street; *calle abajo* down the street ■ **La calle es muy larga.** The street is very long.

215 **joven** [R] **1.** *nmf* young man or woman ■ **Los jóvenes tienen mucho entusiasmo.** The young people have a lot of enthusiasm. **Jóven, tráigame la cuenta, por favor.** Young man, bring me the check, please. **2.** *aj* young ■ **Mi hermana es más joven que yo.** My sister is younger than I am.

216 **tú** *pron* you (informal singular) ■ **Tú eres muy amable.** You are very kind.
► **tu** *aj* your ■ **Tu amiga es mi hermana.** Your friend is my sister.

217 **nivel** *nm* [R] level ■ **El nivel del agua es bajo.** The water level is low.

218 **yo** *pron* I ■ **Yo vivo cerca del centro.** I live near downtown.

219 **hablar** *vti(r)* [R] to speak ■ **Él puede hablar muy rápido.** He can speak very fast. **Mi hermana habla italiano.** Mi sister speaks Italian. **Nos hablamos ayer.** We spoke (with each other) yesterday.

220 **económico** *aj* [R -ico(2)] economic ■ **Ese restaurante es muy económico.** That restaurant is very economical.

221 **policía** [R -ería(2)] **1.** *nf* police force □ *policía municipal* city or town police ■ **La policía ya llegó.** The police already arrived. **2.** *nm* policeman ■ **El policía manejó rápidamente.** The policeman drove quickly.

222 **situación** *nf* [R -ción] situation ■ **La situación es difícil.** The situation is difficult.

223 **participar** *vi* [R] to participate ■ Ella participó en el torneo. She participated in the tournament.

224 **pasar** *vt* [R] to pass; to spend (time) □ *pasar las de Caín* to go through hell ■ Él pasó por mi casa. He passed by my house. Ella pasó el exámen. She passed her exam. Ellos pasaron tres horas esperando el tren. They spent three hours waiting for the train.

225 **tercero** *aj* [R -ero(2)] third (the shortened form *tercer* is used before masculine nouns) ■ Él es el tercero de la fila. He is third in line. Ella esperaba llegar al tercer lugar. She was hoping to come in third place.

226 **dentro** *av* [R] □ *dentro de* inside ■ Hay una sorpresa dentro de esa caja. There is a surprise inside that box.

227 **nada** *av* nothing □ *de nada* you're welcome ■ Ella no preguntó nada. She asked nothing.

228 **cinco** [R] **1.** *nm* five; fifth day of the month ■ Cinco de ellos vinieron. Five of them came. **2.** *aj* five ■ Yo tengo cinco pares de zapatos. I have five pairs of shoes.

229 **apoyo** *nm* [R] support, aid, assistance ■ Él recibe apoyo de su familia. He receives support from his family.

230 **mundial** *aj* [R -al(2)] world ■ El equipo de Brasil ganó el campeonato mundial. The team from Brazil won the world championship.

231 **señor,-a** *nmf* Sir, Ma'am; Mr., Mrs., lord, lady; Señor, Señora □ *Muy señor mío* Dear Sir (in letters) ■ El señor Flores está casado. Mr. Flores is married. El Señor es mi pastor. The Lord is my shepherd. La señora Gómez es muy activa. Mrs. Gomez is very active.
  ▶ **señorita** *nf* Miss ■ La señorita Cárdenas llegó temprano. Miss Cárdenas arrived early.

232 **dólar** *nm* dollar ■ El niño quiere un dólar. The child wants a dollar.

233 **alto** *aj* [R] tall; high; stop (similar to the English "halt") ■ Él es alto. He is tall. La montaña es muy alta. The mountain is very high. El señalamiento decía "Alto". The sign said "Stop."

234 **malo** *nm, aj* [R] bad (the shortened form *mal* is used before masculine singular nouns) □ *ser malo* to be bad or naughty; *estar malo* to be sick, feel lousy ■ Me siento mal hoy. I feel bad today. Ellos son malos. They are bad.

235 **desarrollo** *nm* [R -o(1)] development ■ Julia desarrolló su plan en dos días. Julia developed her plan in two days.

236 **fin** *nm* [R] end □ *en fin* in short; to sum up ■ El fin de la historia es muy emocionante. The end of the story is very exciting.

237 **propio** *aj* [R] own ■ tu propio carro your own car

238 **proyecto** *nm* [R -o(1)] project ■ El proyecto podría durar diez años. The project could last ten years.

239 **terminar** *vt* [R] to finish ■ Elizabeth terminó de estudiar temprano. Elizabeth finished studying early.

240 **creer** *vt* [R] to believe □ *creer a ojos cerrados* to believe blindly or implicitly, to have complete faith in ■ David no le cree a Susana. David does not believe Susana. Ella le cree a su marido a ojos cerrados. She has complete faith in her husband.

241 **aun** *av* even ■ El bombadero cumplió su responsabilidad aun con el riesgo de su vida. The firefighter fulfilled his responsibility even at the risk of his own life.
  ▶ **aún** *av* still, yet ■ Ellos hacen aún más. They do still more. El equipo aún puede calificar. The team can still qualify.

242 **pesar** *vi* [R] to weigh □ *a pesar de* in spite of ■ Pesa mucho. He weighs a lot. Él corrió a pesar de su dolor. He ran in spite of his pain.

243 **contar** *vt* [R] to count; to tell (a story) ■ Mi sobrino contó sus monedas. My nephew counted his coins. Te voy a contar una historia. I am going to tell you a story.

244 **venir** *vi* [R] to come ■ Ellos vienen todos los días. They come every day.

245 **parecer** [R] **1.** *nm* opinion ■ A mi parecer es una buena idea. In my opinion it is a good idea. **2.** *vt* to seem ■ El artículo parece interesante. The article seems interesting. **3.** *vr* to look like, to look like each other ■ Ella se parece a su padre. She looks like her father. El hombre y su mujer se parecen cada día un poco más. The man and his wife look more and more like each other every day.

246 **sino** *conj* but (rather, instead) ■ Ellos no toman café, sino té. They don't drink coffee, but rather (instead) drink tea.

247 **tipo** *nm* type; guy, man (slang) ■ No me gusta ese tipo de baile. I don't like that type

of dancing. ¿Conoces a ese tipo? Do you know that guy?

248 **ley** *nf* law ■ La ley prohibe beber mientras estás manejando. The law prohibits drinking while you are driving.

249 **tras** *prep* [R] after, following ■ José trabajó día tras día. Joe worked day after day. Tras la tormenta, viene la calma. After the storm, comes the calm.

250 **especial** *aj* [R -cial] special □ *en especial* especially ■ Gloria preparó una cena especial. Gloria prepared a special dinner.

251 **anterior** *aj* [R] previous ■ Estudié los capítulos anteriores muchas veces. I studied the previous chapters many times.

252 **sistema** *nm* [R] system ■ El sistema es complicado. The system is complicated.

253 **internacional** *aj* [R (nacer)] international ■ El vuelo internacional duró seis horas. The international flight lasted six hours.

254 **obtener** *vt* [R] to obtain ■ Él obtuvo su licencia en pocos meses. He obtained his license in a few months.

255 **salud** *nf* [R] health □ *¡Salud!* Bless you!, Cheers! ■ Ella tiene buena salud. She is in good health.

256 **agregar** *vt* [R] to add ■ Ella agrega sal, tomate y chile al huevo. She adds salt, tomato, and peppers to the eggs.

257 **local** *aj* [R] local ■ El equipo local ganó el partido ayer. The local team won the game yesterday.

258 **algo** [R] **1.** *pron* something ■ Tengo algo en el ojo. I have something in my eye. **2.** *av* somewhat ■ ¿Es interesante? Algo. Is that interesting? Somewhat.

259 **jugar** *vt* [R] to play ■ Elena sabe jugar ajedrez. Elena knows how to play chess.

260 **actividad** *nf* [R -idad] activity ■ En el parque hay mucha actividad. In the park there is a lot of activity.

261 **te** *pron* you (direct and indirect object pronoun) ■ Luis te llamará el lunes. Luis will call you Monday. ¿Te lo doy? Shall I give it to you?

▶ **té** *nm* tea ■ La hora del té es a las 4 en la tarde. Tea time is at four o'clock.

262 **nombre** *nm* [R] name □ *nombre de pila* Chistian name, given name ■ ¿Viste el

nombre de la calle? Did you see the name of the street?

263 **falta** *nf* [R -a] absence; fault ■ ¿Cuántas faltas tienes? ¿How many absences do you have? Tengo muchas faltas. I have many faults.

264 **comentar** *vt* [R] to comment ■ El participante comentó sobre sus experiencias. The participant commented on his experiences.

265 **comisión** *nf* [R -sión] commission ■ La comisión se reunió ayer. The commission met yesterday. El vendedor recibió su comisión. The salesman received his commission.

266 **abrir** *vt* [R] to open ■ El niño no puede abrir la puerta. The child cannot open the door.

267 **explicar** *vt* [R] to explain ■ Josué intentó explicar su problema. Joshua tried to explain his problem.

268 **tal** **1.** *aj* such; such and such ■ Un tal capitán estuvo aquí haciendo preguntas. One such captain was here asking questions. Nos encontraremos a tales horas. We will meet at such and such time. **2.** *av* □ *tal para cual* two of a kind; *¿qué tal?* what's up?, how?; *tal cual debe ser* that's how it should be; *tal vez* perhaps; *de tal manera (que)* in such a way; *tal como* just as; *con tal de que* on condition that ■ ¿Qué tal estuvo el concierto? How was the concert? Él ama a su esposa, tal cual debe ser. He loves his wife, and that's how it should be. Tal vez iremos al cine. Perhaps we will go to the movies. Tal como dice. Just as it says. Ella estudió de tal manera que ganó el premio. She studied in such a way as to win the prize. Te doy cinco dólares con tal de que no llores. I will give you five dollars on condition that you don't cry.

269 **llamar(se)** *vt(r)* [R] to call (vt); to call oneself (used to introduce oneself) (vr) □ *llamar la atención* to attract attention ■ ¿A qué horas me llamaste? What time did you call? Me llamo Daniel. My name is Daniel (literally, "I call myself").

270 **cumplir** *vt* [R] to complete; to turn (commonly used to refer to having a birthday) ■ Hoy ella cumple treinta y tres años. Today she turns thirty-three.

271 **diferente** *aj* [R -ente(1)] different ■ Vamos a usar un libro diferente. We are going to use a different book.

272 **destacar** *vr* [R] to stand out; to distinguish oneself ■ Rosa se destaca por ser una

bailarina ejemplar. Rosa has distinguished herself as an exemplary ballerina.

273 **unidad** *nf* [R -idad] unity ■ Gloria lucha por la unidad en su familia. Gloria strives for the unity of her family.

274 **elemento** *nm* [R] element; ingredient ■ La comunicación es un elemento importante en un buen matrimonio. Communication is an important element of a good marriage. Hay más de cien elementos químicos. There are more than one hundred chemical elements. Las fresas son el elemento principal en este pastel. Strawberries are the main ingredient in this pie.

275 **ninguno** 1. *pron* no one, nobody ■ Ninguno entendió el párrafo. Nobody understood the paragraph. 2. *aj* no (the shortened form *ningún* is used before masculine singular nouns) ■ Ningún estudiante hizo una pregunta. No student asked a question.

276 **pensar** *vt* [R] to think; to believe ■ Él piensa que puede bajar de peso. He thinks that he can lose weight.

277 **técnico,-a** [R] 1. *nmf* technician ■ Los técnicos arreglaron la máquina. The technicians repaired the machine. 2. *aj* technical ■ La carrera técnica fue corta. The technical course of study was short.
  ▶ **técnica** *nf* technique ■ Su técnica para patinar es única. Her skating technique is unique.

278 **cualquier** *aj* any, whatever, whichever ■ Él puede escoger cualquier libro. He can choose any book.

279 **jugador,-a** *nmf* [R -dor(1)] player ■ El jugador necesita un uniforme nuevo. The player needs a new uniform.

280 **principal** [R] 1. *aj* principal, main ■ La puerta principal está abierta. The main door is open. 2. *nm* principal, chief, head ■ El principal anunció su opinión. The chief announced his opinion.

281 **evitar** *vt* [R] to avoid ■ Ella quiere evitar problemas futuros. She wants to avoid future problems.

282 **frente** [R] 1. *av* front □ *frente a, al frente de* in front of ■ Ellos viven frente al parque. They live in front of the park. Ella está al frente del grupo. She is in front of the group. 2. *nf* forehead ■ Me pegué en la frente. I hit myself on the forehead.

283 **funcionario,-a** *nmf* [R] civil servant ■ Los funcionarios trabajan hasta las 3:00 de la tarde. The civil servants work until 3:00 in the afternoon.

284 **estatal** *aj* state ■ La convención estatal de medicina es en enero. The state medical convention is in January.

285 **música** *nf* [R] music □ *caja de música* music box ■ Carolina y Paulina disfrutan mucho la música. Carolina and Paulina enjoy music a lot.

286 **historia** *nf* [R] history; story ■ La historia universal me gusta. I like world history. El estudiante tiene que escribir una historia. The student has to write a story.

287 **relación** *nf* [R] relation, relationship ■ La relación entre ellos dos es muy bonita. The relationship between those two is very beautiful.

288 **presente** *nm* [R] present ■ Priscila y Lisa estuvieron presentes en la clase. Priscila and Lisa were present in the class.

289 **fútbol** *nm* soccer □ *fútbol americano* American football ■ Roberto prefiere jugar fútbol. Robert prefers to play soccer. Su amigo prefiere jugar fútbol americano. His friend prefers to play American football.

290 **mercado** *nm* [R] market ■ El mercado es enorme. The market is huge.

291 **afectar** *vt* to affect ■ El problema le afectó mucho a ella. The problem affected her very much.

292 **reunión** *nf* [R] meeting ■ La reunión inicia a las 9:30 de la mañana. The meeting begins at 9:00 a.m.

293 **argentino,-a** [-ino(2)] 1. *nmf* Argentinian person ■ Cuarenta por ciento de argentinos están debajo de los 24 años. Forty percent of Argentinians are under the age of 24. 2. *aj* Argentine ■ El equipo argentino es bien entrenado. The Argentine team is well-trained.

294 **necesario** *nm* [R] necessary, needed ■ Es necesario firmar el contrato. It's necessary to sign the contract.

295 **noche** *nf* [R] night □ *de la noche a la mañana* overnight; *Noche Buena* Christmas Eve; *mesa de noche* bedside table ■ La noche es muy bella. The night is very beautiful. De la noche a la mañana se cayeron todas las hojas del

árbol. Overnight, all the leaves on the tree fell off.

296 **proceso** *nm* [R -o(1)] process ■ Empezamos el proceso largo de adoptar un hijo hace dos años. We began the long process of adopting a child two years ago.

297 **personal** *aj* [R -al(2)] personal ■ Sus problemas personales evitaron que viniera. His personal problems prevented him from coming.

298 **amigo** *nm* [R] friend □ *amigo del alma, amigo del corazón* bosom buddy ■ Linda tiene muchos amigos. Linda has many friends.

299 **mano** *nf* [R] hand □ *hecho a mano* handmade; *de segunda mano* secondhand ■ Ruth escribe con la mano izquierda. Ruth writes with her left hand. Quería comprar regalos hechos a mano. I (you, he, she) wanted to buy handmade gifts.

300 **continuar** *vti* [R] to continue ■ Héctor planea continuar sus estudios éste verano. Hector plans to continue his studies this summer.

301 **pequeño,-a** [R] **1.** *nmf* small person; little one (term of endearment for someone) ■ Mi pequeño se llama Nathan. My little one's name is Nathan. **2.** *aj* small, little ■ El dedo pequeño me duele. My little finger hurts. La casa es pequeña. The house is small.

302 **zona** *nf* zone, area ■ La zona de construcción es muy larga. The construction zone is very long.

303 **ocasión** *nf* [R -sión] occasion ■ Hoy celebramos una ocasión muy especial. Today we celebrate a very special occasion.

304 **pagar** *vt* [R] to pay □ *pagar al contado* to pay cash (down) ■ Marcia quiere pagar sus deudas dentro de un año. Marcia wants to pay her debts within one year.

305 **aquél** *pron* that one (at a distance) ■ Me gusta aquél. I like that one.
▶ **aquel** *aj* that (at a distance) ■ Durante aquel año no pude ir de vacaciones. During that year I was unable to go on vacation.

306 **campo** *nm* [R] camp; country, area away from the city; field □ *campos Elíseos* Elysian fields ■ Él vive en el campo. He lives in the country. La pareja manejó dos horas para llegar al campo Sinaí. The couple drove two hours in order to arrive at Camp Sinai.

307 **ubicar(se)** *vt(r)* to place (vt); to find oneself, to discover one's location, to find out where one is (vr) ■ La compañía está buscando un lugar para ubicar la fábrica. The company is looking for a place to locate its factory. Después de haber estado perdido un rato, me ubiqué. After being lost for awhile, I found out where I was.

308 **convertir(se)** *vt(r)* [R] to convert, to turn (vt); to be converted (vr) ■ Eduardo convirtió sus sueños en realidad. Edward turned his dreams into reality. Pablo se convirtió en el camino a Damasco. Paul was converted on the road to Damascus.

309 **rojo** *nm, aj* [R] red □ *al rojo* red hot; *Caperucita Roja* Little Red Riding Hood ■ El vestido rojo es mi favorito. The red dress is my favorite.

310 **registrar(se)** *vt(r)* [R] to register (vt); to be registered, to register oneself (vr) ■ Debo registrar mi carro. I must register my car. Me registré en el hotel. I registered myself in the hotel.

311 **secretario,-a** *nmf* [R] secretary, governmental cabinet member or comercial board member ■ La secretaria siempre llega tarde. The secretary always arrives late.

312 **oportunidad** *nf* [R -idad] opportunity ■ Ahora tienen la oportunidad de hablar. Now you (they) have the opportunity to speak.

313 **comenzar** *vt* [R] to begin ■ El bebé ya comenzó a caminar. The baby already began to walk.

314 **estudio** *nm* [R -o(1)] study ■ Esteban disfruta el estudio del griego. Stephen enjoys the study of Greek.

315 **acompañar** *vt* [R] to accompany, to escort ■ Carlos acompañó a su madre. Carlos accompanied his mother.

316 **manifestar(se)** *vt(r)* [R] to demonstrate ■ Él manifestó su agradacimiento. He demonstrated his appreciation. Los huelguistas se manifestaron en frente de la fábrica. The strikers demonstrated in front of the factory.

317 **enfrentar** *vt* [R] to face; to come face to face with ■ La pareja joven debe enfrentar sus problemas juntos. The young couple must face their problems together. Fernando enfrentó la realidad. Fernando came face to face with reality.

318 **blanco** [R] **1.** *aj* white ■ El vestido de la novia era blanco. The bride's dress was white. **2.** *nm*

bullseye ■ El tirador le dió al blanco. The marksman hit the bullseye.

319 **fecha** *nf* [R -a] date (calendar) □ *hasta la fecha* to date ■ La fecha se acerca rápidamente. The date quickly draws near.

320 **entonces** *av* then; so □ *desde entonces* since then ■ El niño se enfermó, entonces no fue a la escuela. The boy became ill, so he did not go to school. La niña aprendió a leer, y desde entonces ha leído un montón de libros. The girl learned to read, and since then she has read a mountain of books.

321 **información** *nf* [R -ción] information ■ El escritor buscaba más información sobre el tema. The writer was looking for more information on the topic.

322 **mencionar** *vt* [R] to mention ■ Está prohibido mencionar su nombre en la casa. It is forbidden to mention his name in the house.

323 **volver(se)** *vt(r)* [R] to return, to go back (vt); to be returning, to be going back, (to do) again (vr) ■ El próximo año volveremos a la playa. Next year we will go back to the beach. La mujer se volverá a pintar el cabello en dos meses. The woman will dye her hair again in two months.

324 **escuela** *nf* [R] school ■ Justino aprovechó el tiempo en la escuela. Justin made the most of his time in school.

325 **cuánto** *av* how much, how many; how much?, how many? ■ ¿Cuántos años tienes? How old are you? ¿Cuántas cartas recibiste? How many letters did you receive?
  ▶ **cuanto** *aj* everything, as much as ■ Él se comió cuanto había en el refrigerador. He ate everything there was in the refrigerator. Él le enseñó cuanto sabía. He taught her as much as he knew.

326 **gol** *nm* goal (sport) ■ Cory metió un gol. Cory scored a goal.

327 **humano** *nm* [R] human ■ el departamento de recursos humanos the department of human resources

328 **incluir** *vt* [R] to include ■ El precio del boleto incluye una comida. The price of the ticket includes a meal.

329 **película** *nf* [-culo] film, movie ■ Timoteo está viendo una película. Timothy is watching a movie.

330 **región** *nf* [R] region, area ■ Marque el código de área primero. Dial the area code first.

331 **partir** *vt* [R] to divide, to cut ■ Nidia va a partir el pastel. Nidia is going to cut the cake.

332 **celebrar(se)** *vt(r)* [R] to celebrate (vt); to be celebrated, to have a celebration (vr) ■ José y Linda celebraron su aniversario. Joe and Linda celebrated their anniversary. La madre joven celebró la primera palabra que el bebé pronunció. The young mother celebrated the first word that her baby pronounced. La navidad se celebra el 25 de diciembre. Christmas is celebrated December 25th.

333 **base** *nf* [R] base ■ La base militar está cerca de aquí. The military base is near here.

334 **posible** *aj* [R -ible] possible ■ Ella hizo posible mi sueño. She made my dream possible.

335 **mañana** *nf* [R] morning; tomorrow □ *muy de mañana* very early in the morning; *de la noche a la mañana* overnight ■ En la mañana siempre tomo jugo de frutas. In the morning I always drink fruit juice. Tengo planes de ir mañana al librería. I have plans to go tomorrow to the bookstore. Mi esposo se levanta muy de mañana. My husband gets up very early in the morning. El clima cambió de la noche a la mañana. The weather changed overnight.

336 **serie** *nf* [R] series ■ Ellos vivieron una serie de experiencias diferentes. They lived a series of different experiences.

337 **afirmar** *vt* [R] to affirm ■ El presidente afirmó su declaración anterior. The president affirmed his previous statement.

338 **torneo** *nm* tournament ■ El torneo de verano ya se terminó. The summer tournament is already over.

339 **dirección** *nf* [R -ción] direction; address ■ Me desubiqué y fui hacia una dirección equivocada. I became disoriented and went in the wrong direction. Daniela me dió su dirección. Daniela game me her address.

340 **ahí** *av* there, over there ■ Pedro vive ahí. Peter lives over there.

341 **reconocer** *vt* [R(conocer)] to recognize ■ La maestra reconoció su error. The teacher recognized her mistake.

342 **dirigir(se)** *vt(r)* [R] to direct (vt); to direct oneself, to head to (vr) ■ La señora Castro dirigió al coro. Mrs. Castro directed the chorus. Yo me dirigí a la iglesia. I headed to the church.

343 **médico,-a** [R -o(3)] **1.** *nmf* physician, doctor □ *médico de cabecera* family doctor ■ El médico llega a las 9:00 de la mañana. The doctor arrives at 9:00 a.m. **2.** *aj* medical ■ Dr. Johnson quiere aprender los términos medicales en español. Dr. Johnson wants to learn medical terms in Spanish.

344 **hacia** *prep* toward ■ El viento sopla hacia el norte. The wind is blowing toward the north.

345 **cabo** *nm* cape (geographical landmark) □ *al fin y al cabo* after all, in the end, after all is said and done; *de cabo a cabo* or *de cabo a rabo* from head to tail, top to bottom, end to end ■ Los marineros ya pasaron el cabo. The sailors already passed the cape. Al fin y al cabo no va a trabajar. After all is said and done, he is not going to work.

346 **trabajador,-a** *nmf* [R] worker □ *trabajador social* social worker ■ Joel es un buen trabajador. Joel is a good worker.

347 **seis** [R] **1.** *nm* six, sixth day of the month ■ seis de los diez mejores tenistas six of the ten best tennis players **2.** *aj* six ■ Martina tiene seis meses viviendo en Rusia. Martina has been living in Russia for six months.

348 **respecto** *av* [R] with respect to ■ Miguel habló respecto a su problema. Miguel spoke with respect to his problem.

349 **empezar** *vti* to begin ■ La película va a empezar a las 7:00 de la tarde. The movie is going to begin at 7:00 p.m.

350 **comunidad** *nf* [R -idad] community; fellowship ■ Ray leyó *La Comunidad de los Anillos.* Ray read *The Fellowship of the Ring.*

351 **domingo** *nm* Sunday ■ El domingo es mi día favorito. Sunday is my favorite day.

352 **fuerza** *nf* [R -a] strength ■ Bárbara se quedó sin fuerzas después de la operación. Bárbara remained without strength after the operation. Rubén quería inscribirse en la fuerza aérea. Rubén wanted to enlist in the air force.

353 **estadounidense** [-ense] **1.** *nmf* person from the United States ■ Los amigos de ella son estadounidenses. Her friends are from the United States. **2.** *aj* pertaining to the United States; from the United States ■ la política estadounidense US policy

354 **producción** *nf* [R -ción] production ■ La producción del trigo aumentó este año. Wheat production increased this year.

355 **nunca** *av* never ■ Él nunca come pescado. He never eats fish.

356 **lado** *nm* [R] side ■ El ingeniero vio la máquina de un lado a otro. The engineer looked at the machine from one side to the other.

357 **secretaría** *nf* [R] secretariat ■ La Secretaría de los Naciones Unidos está ubicada en la ciudad de Nueva York. The secretariat of the United Nations is located in New York City.

358 **establecer(se)** *vt(r)* [R] to establish (vt); to be stabilized (vr) ■ Es más fácil establecer las reglas al principio. It is easier to establish the rules in the beginning. Se establecieron los precios de la bolsa. The stock-exchange prices became stabilized.

359 **nosotros** *pron* [R] we ■ Nosotros hablamos durante el vuelo. We spoke during the flight.

360 **condición** *nf* [R -ción] condition □ *a condición de que, bajo la condición de que* on (the) condition that ■ Describimos las condiciones en el contrato. We describe the conditions in the contract.

361 **fuente** *nf* source; fountain ■ ¿Cuáles son las fuentes del artículo? What are the sources for the article? Tienen una fuente en frente de su casa. They have a fountain in front of their house.

362 **utilizar** *vt* [R -izar] to utilize ■ El dentista siempre utiliza mucho equipo. The dentist always uses a lot of equipment.

363 **través** *nm* [R] mishap □ *a través de* through ■ Ignacio sufrió un través. Ignacio suffered a mishap. Ella podía ver a través de la ventana. She was able to see through the window.

364 **tarde** [R] **1.** *nf* afternoon ■ las cuatro de la tarde four o'clock in the afternoon **2.** *aj* late ■ La novia llegó tarde. The bride arrived late.

365 **único** *aj* [R -ico(2)] unique ■ Este color es único. This color is unique.

366 **mostrar(se)** *vt(r)* [R] to show (vt); to show oneself (to be) (vr) ■ Los alumnos mostraron sus tareas al maestro. The students showed their homework to the teacher. Ellas se mostraron deshonestas. They showed themselves to be dishonest.

367 **casi** *av* almost ■ Casi hemos llegado al final. We have almost arrived at the end.

368 **julio** *nm* July ■ La tienda se abrió en julio del año pasado. The store opened in July of last year.

369 **medida** *nf* [R -ido(2)] measurement □ *a medida que* while ■ La medida es la correcta. The measurement is correct. A medida que practico, mejoro. While I practice, I improve.
► **medido** *aj* measured ■ El nivel medido es más que lo del año pasado. The measured level is more than last year's.

370 **productor,-a** *nmf* [R] producer ■ El productor de la obra es mi primo. The producer of the play is my cousin.

371 **disco** *nm* disk ■ El disco está dañado. The disk is damaged.

372 **necesitar** *vt* [R] to need ■ Usted necesita descansar más. You need to rest more.

373 **preparar(se)** *vt(r)* [R] to prepare (vt); to prepare oneself, to be preparing (vr) ■ Tanya sabe preparar una lasaña muy rica. Tanya knows how to prepare a very good-tasting lasagna. Nos preparamos para un temblor. We prepared ourselves for an earthquake.

374 **decidir(se)** *vi(r)* [R] to decide (in general) (vi); to decide, to choose a specific course of action, to make a decision, to make up one's mind (vr) ■ Raúl tiene que decidir lo que va a estudiar. Raúl has to decide what he is going to study. Me decidí ir al Gran Cañón. I decided to go to the Grand Canyon.

375 **familiar** [R] **1.** *nmf* relative (family) ■ Claudia es mi familiar más cercana. Claudia is my nearest relative. **2.** *aj* family ■ Hace dos años tuvimos una reunión familiar. Two years ago we had a family reunion.

376 **cuyo** *aj* whose ■ El muchacho cuya bicicleta está aquí va a venir por ella. The boy whose bicycle is here is going to come get it.

377 **solicitar** *vt* [R] to solicit, to seek ■ Alfredo está solicitando trabajo de ingeniero. Alfredo is seeking work as an engineer.

378 **recordar** *vt* [R] to remember ■ Eduardo no podía recordar su clave. Eduardo could not remember his password.

379 **atención** *nf* [R -ción] attention □ *llamar la atención* to attract attention ■ Los niños necesitan mucha atención de sus padres. Children need a lot of attention from their parents.

380 **organización** *nf* [R -ción] organization ■ Organización es la clave del éxito. Organization is the key to success.

381 **producto** *nm* [R] product ■ El producto es muy conocido. The product is very well-known.

382 **venta** *nf* [R] sale ■ Mi hermana trabaja en la venta de teléfonos celulares. My sister works in the sale of cellular telephones.

383 **entrada** *nf* [R] entrance; inning (baseball) ■ La entrada de la casa tiene muchas flores. The entrance to the house has many flowers. Jugó seis entradas antes de lastimarse. He played six innings before injuring himself.

384 **titular(se)** *vt(r)* [R] to title (vt); to earn a degree, to graduate (vr) ■ Titularon el libro antes de escribirlo. They titled the book before writing it. Me titulé en noviembre. I earned my degree in November.

385 **cuarto** [R] **1.** *nm* room; quarter (part) □ *cuarto de costura* sewing room ■ El cuarto de los niños está limpio. The children's room is clean. **2.** *aj* one-fourth; fourth ■ Yo necesito un cuarto de taza de azúcar para hacer un pay. I need a quarter cup of sugar in order to make a pie. Jonathan está en el cuarto grado. Jonathan is in the fourth grade.

386 **acudir** *vi* to go (formal) ■ Ellos acudieron a la cita con el dentista. They went to their appointment with the dentist.

387 **entregar** *vt* [R] to give, to deliver; to give of oneself, to dedicate (oneself) ■ El mensajero entregó todos los paquetes hoy. The messenger delivered all his packages today. Deborah entregó toda su vida a la educación de sus hijos. Deborah gave her whole life to the training of her children.

388 **sociedad** *nf* [R] society ■ La sociedad actual es muy controversial. Modern society is very controversial.

389 **agente** *nmf* [R -ente(2)] agent ■ El agente hizo una investigación. The agent performed an investigation.

390 **representar** *vt* [R(presencia)] to represent ■ Ese diploma representa muchos años de estudio. That diploma represents many years of study.

391 **junto** [R] **1.** *aj* together ■ Madre e hija viven juntas. Mother and daughter live together. **2.** *av* □ *junto a* next to, near to ■ Colgué la camisa junto a los pantalones. I hung the shirt up next to the pants.

392 **marco** *nm* [R] frame ■ El marco está hecho de madera. The frame is made of wood.

393 **líder** *nm* leader ■ El líder entiende inglés. The leader understands English.

394 **investigación** *nf* [R -ción] investigation ■ La investigación se volvió complicada. The investigation became complicated.

395 **largo** *aj* [R] long ■ Ese fue un largo viaje. That was a long trip.

396 **institución** *nf* [R -ción] institution ■ Él había visitado la institución varias veces. He had visited the institution several times.

397 **amor** *nm* [R] love □ *amor propio* self-esteem, pride ■ El amor que siento por él es verdadero. The love I feel for him is true.

398 **cargo** *nm* [R -o(1)] charge; responsibility; position ■ Esta herramienta es útil para medir el cargo de las pilas. This tool is useful for measuring the charge of the batteries. El grupo de los jóvenes está a nuestro cargo. The youth group is our responsibility. (The youth group is in our charge.) Mi tío aceptó el cargo. My uncle accepted the position.

399 **novio,-a** *nmf* bridegroom, bride; boyfriend, girlfriend ■ El novio llegó a las 6:00 de la tarde. The bridegroom arrived at 6:00 p.m. La novia se veía hermosa. The bride looked beautiful. Su novio le trajo flores. Her boyfriend brought her flowers. ¿Quién es tu novia? Who is your girlfriend?

400 **aquí** *av* here ■ El orador ya está aquí. The speaker is already here.

401 **actor** *nm* [R -or] actor ■ El actor favorito de mi padre cumplió hoy 90 años. My father's favorite actor turned ninety years old today.

402 **cuerpo** *nm* [R] body □ *tomar cuerpo* to take shape ■ Nosotros debemos alimentar el cuerpo y la mente también. We must feed the body and the mind as well.

403 **cierto** [R] **1.** *aj* certain □ *saber de cierto* to know for sure; *en cierta forma* in a certain way **2.** *av* true ■ Eso no es cierto. That is not true.

404 **participación** *nf* [R -ción] participation ■ La participación del público es importante. The participation of the public is important.

405 **entrar** *vi* [R] to enter ■ Puedes entrar si quieres. You may enter if you like.

406 **paso** *nm* [-o(1)] pass; step □ *paso a paso* step-by-step, pace; *a paso de buey* at a snail's pace; *cerrar el paso* to bar or block the way ■ El paso por la montaña está cerrado. The pass over the mountain is closed. Los niños dieron un paso al frente. The children took a step forward. Puedes aprender el español paso a paso. You can learn Spanish step-by-step. A ese paso lograrás mucho. At that pace you will accomplish a lot.

407 **viernes** *nm* Friday ■ Teresa nos visitará el viernes. Teresa will visit us Friday.

408 **difícil** *aj* [R] difficult ■ El cálculo es una materia difícil. Calculus is a difficult subject.

409 **triunfo** *nm* [R -o(1)] triumph ■ Para alcanzar el triunfo hay que pagar el precio. In order to achieve triumph, one has to pay the price.

410 **mayoría** *nf* [R -ería(2)] majority ■ La mayoría del tiempo me gusta escribir. The majority of the time I like to write.

411 **menor** [R] **1.** *nmf* youngest; younger ■ El menor de mis primos tiene dos años. The youngest of my cousins is two years old. **2.** *aj* minor; younger ■ El vestido necesita un arreglo menor. The dress needs a minor repair. Margarita es menor que Andrés. Margaret is younger than Andrew.

412 **septiembre** *nm* [R] September ■ Durante septiembre llueve mucho aquí. During September it rains a lot here.

413 **sábado** *nm* [R] Saturday ■ El sábado es su día de descanso. Saturday is his day of rest.

414 **siglo** *nm* century ■ Cervantes escribió *Don Quixote* en el siglo XVII. Cervantes wrote *Don Quixote* in the seventeenth century.

415 **oficial** [R -cial] **1.** *nm* official ■ El oficial fue muy amable con nosotros. The official was very kind toward us. **2.** *aj* official ■ Estoy buscando el sitio oficial para el actor mexicano Erick Elias. I am looking for the official website of the Mexican actor Erick Elias.

416 **río** *nm* [R] river □ *río revuelto* troubled waters ■ Los estudiantes nadaron en el Río Colorado. The students swam in the Colorado River.

417 **diputado,-a** *nmf* deputy ■ El diputado tomó la decisión. The deputy made the decision.

418 **temporada** *nf* [R] season ■ Él siempre se emociona cuando empiece la temporada de beisbol. He always becomes excited when baseball season begins.

419 **encuentro** *nm* [R -o(1)] encounter; chance meeting ■ Me dio gusto nuestro encuentro inesperado. I enjoyed our unexpected encounter.

⁴²⁰ **igual** *aj* [R] equal, same □ *por igual* evenly, without discrimination ■ Son iguales. They are the same.

⁴²¹ **precio** *nm* [R] price ■ Él corrigió el precio. He corrected the price.

⁴²² **dinero** *nm* [R] money □ *dinero contante y sonante* ready cash ■ ¿Cuánto dinero tienes? How much money do you have? Poderoso caballero es don dinero. Money is power.

⁴²³ **cantante** *nmf* [R -ante(2)] singer ■ Olivia es una cantante. Olivia is a singer.

⁴²⁴ **requerir** *vt* [R] to require ■ Requieren un permiso para viajar al interior del país. They require a permit in order to travel to the interior of the country.

⁴²⁵ **usted** *pron* you (singular, formal) ■ ¿Qué piensa usted? What do you think? Pensamos como ustedes. We think like you (plural).

⁴²⁶ **producir** *vt* [R] to produce ■ La fábrica produce menos durante la temporada de la navidad. The factory produces less during the Christmas season.

⁴²⁷ **diario** [R -ario(1)] **1.** *nm* diary; daily newspaper □ *diario de navegación* logbook ■ Mi hermana escribió sus aventuras en su diario. My sister wrote her adventures in her diary. A mi abuelo le gusta leer el diario. My grandfather likes to read the daily newspaper. **2.** *aj* daily ■ Me ayuda mucho el paseo diario. My daily walk helps me a lot. **3.** *av* □ *a diario* daily ■ El atleta mejora a diario. The athlete improves daily.

⁴²⁸ **total** [R] **1.** *nm* total ■ El total de la suma son quinientos. The sum total is five hundred. **2.** *aj* total ■ El número total de empleados es cien. The total number of employees is one hundred. **3.** *av* □ *en total* in short, in sum ■ En total, tenemos que decidir. In short, we have to decide.

⁴²⁹ **aceptar** *vt* [R] to accept ■ ¿Aceptan tarjetas de crédito? Do you accept credit cards?

⁴³⁰ **actual** *aj* [R] current ■ La situación actual está mejorando. The current situation is improving.

⁴³¹ **incluso** *aj* [R] included ■ Todos fuimos al cine, incluso mi hermano. We all went to the movies, including my brother.

⁴³² **jefe, jefa** *nmf* supervisor, manager, boss, chief ■ Pedí dos días libres a mi jefe. I requested two days off from my boss.

⁴³³ **éxito** *nm* success □ *tener éxito* to be successful ■ La película tuvo mucho éxito. The film was very successful.

⁴³⁴ **instituto** *nm* [R -uto] institute ■ El instituto fue remodelado. The institute was remodeled.

⁴³⁵ **educación** *nf* [R] education ■ La educación es importante. Education is important.

⁴³⁶ **fuerte** *aj* [R] strong ■ El atleta está fuerte. The athlete is strong.

⁴³⁷ **cambiar** *vti* [R] to change ■ Me voy a cambiar la camisa. I am going to change my shirt.

⁴³⁸ **español,-a** [R] **1.** *nmf* Spanish person, Spaniard ■ Los españoles saben poco sobre la constitución de la Unión Europea. The Spanish know little about the constitution of the European Union. **2.** *nm* Spanish language ■ Quiero aprender el español. I want to learn Spanish. **3.** *aj* Spanish ■ Quiero aprender la gramática española. I want to learn Spanish grammar.

⁴³⁹ **alcanzar** *vt* [R] to reach; to catch up to ■ Ella puede alcanzar esos vasos. She is able to reach those glasses.

⁴⁴⁰ **conseguir** *vt* [R] to get, to acquire ■ ¿Puedes conseguir un permiso fácilmente? Can you get a permit easily?

⁴⁴¹ **ocurrir** *vi* to occur ■ Ocurre cada noche a la misma hora. It occurs each night at the same time.

⁴⁴² **atender** *vt* [R] to attend to ■ El deber del empleado es atender al cliente. The duty of the employee is to attend to the client.

⁴⁴³ **gustar** *vi* [R] to please, to like ■ Me gustan mucho las quesadillas. I like quesadillas very much.

⁴⁴⁴ **norte** *nm* [R] north □ *sin norte* aimless(ly) ■ La tempestad llegó del norte. The storm came from the north.

⁴⁴⁵ **listo** *aj* ready; smart ■ ¿Estás lista? Are you ready? Mi prima es muy lista. My cousin is very smart.

⁴⁴⁶ **diverso** *aj* [R] diverse ■ Nuestras habilidades son diversas. Our abilities are diverse.

⁴⁴⁷ **caer(se)** *vi(r)* [R] to fall, to suit, to like (vi); to fall down (vr) □ *dejar caer* to drop (vt) ■ ¡Me caes muy, pero muy bien! I like you very much! (You suit me very well.) El cartero se cayó afuera de la casa. The mailman fell outside the house. ¡Caíste en la trampa! You fell into the trap!

[448] **posibilidad** *nf* [R -idad] possibility ■ Hay tres posibilidades. There are three possibilities.

[449] **hermano,-a** *nmf* [R] brother, sister ■ Mi hermano vive lejos. My brother lives far away. Quiero presentar a mis hermanas. I want to introduce my sisters. Voy a visitar a mis hermanos. I am going to visit my brothers and sisters.

[450] **congreso** *nm* [R] congress ■ El congreso se reúne después de la navidad. Congress meets after Christmas.

[451] **república** *nf* [R(pueblo)] republic ■ Los fundadores de la república eran hombres valientes. The founders of the republic were brave men.

[452] **apoyar** *vt* [R -o(1)] to support ■ Nuestros senadores apoyan a los lados opuestos. Our senators support opposite sides. Sus padres le apoyaron a ella en la universidad. Her parents supported her through college.

[453] **necesidad** *nf* [R -idad] necessity ■ No tenemos que preocuparnos por las necesidades. We don't have to worry about the necessities.

[454] **campaña** *nf* campaign ■ La campaña empieza en noviembre. The campaign begins in November.

[455] **fondo** *nm* [R] bottom; depth ■ Te lo digo desde el fondo de mi corazón. I tell you from the bottom of my heart.

[456] **cantidad** *nf* quantity ■ La cantidad del tiempo que puedes pasar con tus hijos es importante. The quantity of time that you are able to spend with your children is important.

[457] **león** *nm* [R] lion ■ El Club de Leones se reúne el martes. The Lion's Club meets on Tuesday.

[458] **club** *nm* club ■ Quiero platicarte del club. I want to tell you about the club.

[459] **enfermedad** *nf* [R] sickness ■ La enfermedad me debilitó. The sickness made me weak.

[460] **miembro** *nm* member ■ Jacob es un miembro de nuestro equipo. Jacob is a member of our team.

[461] **consejo** *nm* [R] a piece of advice; advice (nmpl) ■ El consejo me ayudó mucho. The advice helped me greatly. Te quiero dar un consejo. I want to give you a piece of advice. El profesor me dió buenos consejos. The teacher gave me good advice.

[462] **concluir** *vt* [R] to conclude ■ Todos salieron cuando concluyó la junta. Everyone left when the meeting concluded.

[463] **matrimonio** *nm* [R] matrimony ■ Su matrimonio es ejemplar. Their marriage is exemplary.

[464] **decisión** *nf* [R -sión] decision ■ Mi hermana hizo una buena decisión cuando se casó con él. My sister made a good decision when she married him.

[465] **esposo,-a** *nmf* [R] husband, wife ■ Antonio quiere mucho a su esposa. Anthony loves his wife very much.
▶ **esposas** *nfpl* handcuffs ■ El preso no pudo mover las manos por las esposas. The prisoner could not move his hands because of the handcuffs.

[466] **liga** *nf* [-a] league; link; rubber band ■ Los amigos juegan basquetbol en una liga cada verano. The friends play basketball in a league every summer. ¿Seguiste la liga al nuevo sitio web? Did you follow the link to the new website? La pelirroja está usando dos ligas en su cabello. The redhead is wearing two rubber bands in her hair.

[467] **administración** *nf* [R -ción] administration ■ En enero empieza otra administración. In January another administration begins. Mi cuñada estudió administración de empresas. My sister-in-law studied business administration.

[468] **organizar** *vt* [R -izar] to organize ■ Él organizó sus libros sistematicámente. He organized his books systematically.

[469] **siguiente** *aj* [R -ente(1)] next, following ■ Dormí extra el día siguiente. I slept extra the next day.

[470] **desarrollar** *vt* [R] to develop ■ Es importante aprender a desarrollar la memoria. It is important to learn how to develop the memory.

[471] **interés** *nm* [R] interest ■ Su interés era obvio. His interest was obvious. Los intereses son bajos ahorita. Interest rates are low right now.

[472] **claro** *aj* [R] clear □ *claro que* of course ■ La explicación está muy clara. The explanation is very clear. ¡Claro que sí! Yes, of course!
▶ **clara** *nf* egg white ■ Esta receta lleva la clara de huevo. This recipe calls for egg whites.

[473] **fiesta** *nf* [R] party □ *salón de fiestas* banquet hall; *día de fiesta* holiday ■ La fiesta duró hasta las dos de la madrugada. The party lasted until two in the morning.

[474] **sufrir** *vti* to suffer ■ Ellos sufren de varias enfermedades. They suffer from several diseases.

[475] **regresar** *vi* [R] to return ■ Quiero regresar en el otoño. I want to return in the fall.

[476] **motivo** *nm* [R -o(1)] motive, reason ■ Tengo tres motivos. I have three reasons.

[477] **resultar** *vi* [R] to turn out; to prove ■ Resulta que mi hermana se va a casar. It turns out that my sister is going to marry. La operación resultó ser un éxito. The operation proved to be a success.

[478] **tierra** *nf* [R] Earth; dirt □ *tierra firme* continent ■ Dos tercios del planeta Tierra es agua. Two-thirds of planet Earth is water. La tierra está por todos lados. Dirt is everywhere.

[479] **deportivo** *aj* [R] sport, sports ■ Los uniformes deportivos son azules. The sports uniforms are blue.

[480] **avenida** *nf* [R] avenue ■ Los niños tienen que cruzar la avenida para llegar a su casa. The children have to cross the avenue in order to arrive at their house.

[481] **formar** *vt* [R] to form ■ La maestra nos pidió formar una fila. The teacher asked us to form a line.

[482] **población** *nf* [R -ción] population ■ La población del valle ha crecido mucho. The population of the valley has increased greatly.

[483] **presencia** *nf* [R -a] presence ■ Sintió la presencia de Dios. He felt the presence of God.

[484] **aplicar(se)** *vt(r)* [R] to apply (cream, medicine) (vt); to apply on oneself (cream, medicine, cream) (vr) ■ La enfermera aplicó la crema a la quemadura. The nurse applied the cream to the burn. Me apliqué el medicamento en mi herida. I applied the medicine to my wounds.

[485] **muerte** *nf* [R] death □ *estar a la muerte* to be at death's door ■ El soldado no tuvo miedo a la muerte. The soldier had no fear of death.

[486] **guerra** *nf* war □ *prisionera de guerra* prisoner of war ■ La guerra empezó hace dos años. The war began two years ago.

[487] **capital** [R] **1.** *nf* capital ■ Juan Antonio vive en la capital. Juan Antonio lives in the capital. La empresa tuvo suficiente capital. The business had sufficient capital. **2.** *aj* capital ■ En ese país solo hay una ofensa capital. In that country there is only one capital offense.

[488] **libre** *aj* [R] free (unbound), off ■ No hay casetas por la carretera libre. There are no tollbooths on the free highway. El jueves es mi día libre. Thursday is my day off.

[489] **representante** *nmf* [R(presencia) -ante(2)] representative ■ Nuestros representantes se reúnen los martes. Our representatives meet every Tuesday.

[490] **anunciar** *vt* [R] to announce ■ Ellos anunciaron la boda en el periódico. They announced the wedding in the newspaper.

[491] **detenido** [R -ido(1)] **1.** *nm* detainee ■ Los detenidos se quedaron en la cárcel. The detainees remained in jail. **2.** *aj* detained ■ Los hombres detenidos se escaparon. The detained men escaped.

[492] **servir** *vt* [R] to serve □ *servir de* to serve as, act as, be good or useful for; *servirse de* to make use of; *para servir a usted* at your service ■ Mi tía nos sirvió nieve con fresa. My aunt served us ice cream and strawberries.

[493] **siete** [R] **1.** *nm* seven, seventh day of the month ■ Siete de ellos vinieron. Seven of them came. **2.** *aj* seven ■ Mi sobrina leyó siete libros este verano. My niece read seven books this summer.

[494] **categoría** *nf* category ■ Hay tres categorías. There are three categories.

[495] **ayudar** *vt* [R] to help ■ Te quiero ayudar. I want to help you.

[496] **ejido** *nm* very small town ■ Mi primo vive en un ejido afuera de Torreón. My cousin lives in a very small town outside of Torreón.

[497] **sacar** *vt* [R] to take out, to remove; to serve (volleyball), to take out of bounds (basketball), to kick (soccer: corner kick, goal kick) ■ Saqué la basura el jueves. I took out the trash on Thursday. ¡Sácale! Throw it in! (Put the ball in play.)

[498] **área** *nf* area, territory, region ■ Me gusta vivir en esta área. I like to live in this area.

[499] **declarar** *vt* [R] to declare ■ Los combatientes declararon un cese al fuego. The combatants declared a cease-fire. Después del terremoto, el presidente declaró un estado de desastre. After the earthquake, the president declared a state of disaster.

[500] **valor** *nm* [R] courage, valor ■ El valor de ella es ejemplar. Her courage is exemplary.

[501] **usar** *vt* [R] to use; to wear (clothing) ■ Rita usa mantequilla en vez de margarina. Rita

uses butter instead of margarine. Laura usa un vestido para el trabajo. Laura wears a dress to work.

502 **cerca** [R] **1.** *nf* fence ■ El señor García construyó una cerca en frente de su casa. Mr. García built a fence in front of his house. **2.** *av* near, nearby □ *cerca de* near ■ Susana vive cerca. Susan lives nearby. La biblioteca está cerca de mi casa. The library is near my house.

503 **reunir(se)** *vt(r)* [R(uno)] to collect, to gather together (vt); to meet, to hold a meeting (vr) ■ Reuní a los padres en el salón. I gathered the parents together in the classroom. Ellos reunieron cinco mil dólares en donativos. They collected five thousand dollars in donations. Nos reunimos cada miércoles. We meet every Wednesday.

504 **riesgo** *nm* [R] risk ■ El riesgo de la proliferación de armas nucleares es preocupación de todos. The risk of nuclear arms proliferation is of concern to everyone.

505 **invitar** *vt* [R] to invite ■ Toñe invitó a su amigo a cenar. Toni invited her friend to dinner.

506 **dicho** [R] **1.** *nm* saying ■ A Alberto le encantan los dichos en español. Albert loves sayings in Spanish. Del dicho al hecho, hay mucho trecho. Talk and action are two very different things. (literally, From saying to action, there is a great distance.) **2.** *vt* said, told (past participle of *decir*) ■ Estefanía ya nos había dicho su historia. Stephanie had already told us her story.

507 **universidad** *nf* [R] university ■ La universidad está muy cerca de mi casa. The university is very close to my house.

508 **economía** *nf* [R] economy ■ La economía está mejor que hace un año. The economy is better than a year ago.

509 **añadir** *vt* [R] to add ■ "Creemos en la libertad", añadió el señor Gómez. "We believe in liberty," added Mr. Gómez.

510 **sur** [R] **1.** *nm* south ■ Ruth manejó hacia el sur. Ruth drove toward the south. **2.** *aj* south, southern, southerly ■ el Cono Sur de Sudamérica the Southern Cone of South America

511 **crear** *vt* [R] to create ■ Ester creó un nuevo proyecto. Esther created a new project.

512 **jornada** *nf* [R] work shift ■ Él trabajó dos jornadas. He worked two shifts.

513 **calidad** *nf* [R] quality (caliber) (*cualidad* is used when "quality" means "characteristic") ■ Los muebles son de buena calidad. The furniture is of high quality.

514 **foto** *nf* [R] photo (short for *fotografía*) ■ Ella cuida mucho su foto favorita. She takes good care of her favorite photo.

515 **ambos,-as** [R] **1.** *nmfpl* both ■ Daniel compró regalos para ambos. Daniel bought gifts for both. **2.** *aj* both ■ Ambas hermanas recibieron cartas de sus novios. Both sisters received letters from their boyfriends.

516 **plaza** *nf* [R] plaza; town square ■ Enrique anda con su novia en la plaza. Enrique is walking with his girlfriend at the plaza (town square). La biblioteca está cerca de la plaza. The library is near the plaza (town square).

517 **artista** *nmf* [R -ista] performer (art, music, stage, television, film, etc.) ■ A Verónica le gusta leer sobre las vidas de los artistas. Veronica likes to read about the lives of performers.

518 **causa** *nf* [R -a] cause, reason □ *a causa de* owing to, on account of, because of ■ Él no sabe la causa de mi problema. He does not know the cause of my problem.

519 **vecino,-a** *nmf* [R] neighbor ■ David es vecino de Juan. David is John's neighbor.

520 **canción** *nf* [R] song ■ Sandra está escuchando su canción favorita. Sandra is listening to her favorite song.

521 **armar** *vt* [R] to arm; to put together (puzzle or toy) □ *armar relajo* to be in disorder, to be chaotic; *armarse de valor* to pluck up courage ■ El país armó a su aliado en la guerra. The country armed its ally in the war. El niño armó su carrito. The boy put together his toy car. La clase armó relajo. The class was in chaos.

522 **ataque** *nm* [R] attack ■ El señor Montero sufrió un ataque al corazón. Mr. Montero suffered a heart attack. El ataque empezó al amanecer. The attack began at dawn.

523 **competencia** *nf* [R -encia] competition ■ Queremos ser mejores que nuestra competencia. We want to be better than our competition.

524 **archivo** *nm* [R -o(1)] file (storage, as used in an office or on a computer, etc.) ■ Buscamos la hoja en nuestros archivos. We searched for the paper in our files.

525 **nadie** *pron* nobody, anybody (with a negative) ■ Nadie de nuestro grupo fue a la reunión. Nobody from our group went to the meeting. No ví a nadie. I didn't see anybody.

526 **todavía** *av* [R] still, yet ■ Lucas todavía puede escalar montañas. Luke can still climb mountains. El bebé no puede hablar todavía. The baby does not yet know how to speak.

527 **cerrar** *vt* [R] to close □ *cerrar el paso* to bar or block the way ■ La tienda cierra a las 8 de la tarde. The store closes at 8 p.m.

528 **prensa** *nf* [R -a] press (newspapers, etc.) ■ El presidente dijo muchas cosas sobre la guerra durante la conferencia de prensa. The president said many things about the war during the press conference.

529 **instalación** *nf* [R -ción] installation ■ Ana supervisó la instalación de las computadoras. Anne supervised the installation of the computers.

530 **vehículo** *nm* [-culo] vehicle ■ La grúa tuvo que mover dos vehículos del camino. The tow-truck had to move two vehicles out of the road.

531 **orden** [R] **1.** *nm* order (orderly arrangement) □ *colocar por orden* to place in order; *hombre (mujer) de orden* law-abiding man (woman) ■ Zulema puso en orden sus libros. Zulema put her books in order. **2.** *nf* order (command or request) ■ Los soldados obedecieron las órdenes. The soldiers obeyed their orders.

532 **compañía** *nf* [R] company ■ La compañía constructora está contratando nuevo personal. The construction company is hiring new personnel.

533 **domicilio** *nm* place of residence, address ■ La recepcionista le preguntó al cliente su domicilio. The receptionist asked the client for his address.

534 **real** *aj* [R] real; royal ■ El fantasma no era real. The ghost was not real. Casi siempre hay noticias de la familia real de Inglaterra. There is nearly always news of England's royal family.

535 **puesto** [R] **1.** *nm* post, position (work, government); stand (e.g., taco stand) ■ El puesto de maestro de álgebra está vacante. The algebra teacher position is open. El puesto de burritos es muy pequeño y limpio. The burrito stand is very small and clean. **2.** *vt* placed (past participle of *poner*) ■ Ella

todavía no ha puesto la leche dentro del refrigerador. She has not yet put the milk in the refrigerator. **3.** *aj* placed, in-place ■ El transmisión consiste en una caja de cambios con levas puestas detrás del volante. The transmission consists of a gear box with levers placed behind the steering wheel.

536 **actualmente** *av* [R -mente] currently ■ Ellos actualmente viven en Canadá. They currently live in Canada.

537 **provocar** *vt* [R] to provoke, to cause ■ El exceso de sol provoca daño en los ojos de muchos que viven en el desierto. Excessive sun causes damage to the eyes of many who live in the desert.

538 **vender** *vt* [R] to sell ■ Ella quiere vender su auto. She wants to sell her car.

539 **colocar** *vt* [R] to place, to put in place □ *colocar por orden* to place in order ■ Fabián quiere colocar varios mapas en su oficina. Fabian wants to place several maps in his office.

540 **gobernador,-a** *nmf* [R] governor ■ El gobernador explicó su plan ayer. The governor explained his plan yesterday.

541 **moral** [R] **1.** *nf* morale ■ Con su mensaje el presidente quería elevar la moral de las tropas. With his message the president wanted to raise the morale of the troops. **2.** *aj* moral ■ La educación moral constituye uno de los pilares de la enseñanza. Moral education constitutes one of the pillars of learning.

542 **alrededor** [R] **1.** *av* □ *alrededor de* around ■ Ella caminó alrededor del carro. She walked around the car. **2.** *nmpl* □ *alrededores* surroundings ■ Miguel disfruta de los alrededores de esta ciudad. Michael enjoys the surrounding areas of the city.

543 **material** [R] **1.** *nm* material ■ El carpintero tiene suficiente material para hacer una mesa. The carpenter has enough material to build a table. **2.** *aj* material □ *el mundo material* the material world

544 **integrante** [R -ante(2)] **1.** *nmf* one who is part of a group; representative member of a group ■ Un integrante del grupo musical viene de Venezuela. One member of the singing group comes from Venezuela. Los integrantes del equipo van a viajar en autobús. The members of the team are going to travel by bus. **2.** *aj* integral, who form, that form (esp., part of a group) ■ Las mujeres integrantes del coro son

quince. There are fifteen women who make up the chorus.

545 generar *vt* to generate ■ La planta de energía genera suficiente electricidad para la ciudad. The energy plant generates enough electricity for the city.

546 integrar *vt* [R] to integrate, to mix ■ El paso siguiente es integrar los ingedientes. The next step is to mix the ingredients.

547 pareja [R -ejo] **1.** *nf* couple, pair (referring to living beings); partner □ *por parejas* in pairs, in twos ■ Ester es la pareja de baile de Juan. Esther is John's dance partner. **2.** *aj* even ■ Esta competencia va muy pareja. This competiton is very even.

548 seguro [R -ura(2)] **1.** *nm* lock; insurance ■ No funciona el seguro del carro. The lock on the car doesn't work. Investigamos varios planes de seguro de vida. We researched several life insurance plans. **2.** *aj* sure, certain □ *de seguro* for sure, very probably ■ Esteban está seguro de que va a pasar el exámen. Steve is sure that he is going to pass the test.

549 unión *nf* [R] union (*sindicato* is used to refer to a trade union) ■ Eliseo expuso su opinión sobre La Unión Europea. Eliseo expressed his opinion about the European Union.

550 torre *nf* [R] tower □ *torre de marfil* ivory tower ■ Nuestro hotel está ubicado cerca de la torre Eiffel. Our hotel is located near the Eiffel Tower.

551 elección *nf* [R -ción] election ■ En diciembre será la elección presidencial. The presidential election will be held in December.

552 expresar *vt* [R] to express with words, signs, etc. ■ Elena sabe expresar sus sentimientos. Elena knows how to express her feelings.

553 papel *nm* [R] paper; role (theatrical part to play) □ *papel de lija* sandpaper ■ La copiadora necesita más papel. The copy machine needs more paper. Mi actriz favorita hizo el papel de villana. My favorite actress played the role of the villain.

554 cine *nm* [R] movie theater; cinema ■ Los hermanos de Pedro fueron hoy al cine. Pedro's brothers went the movie theater today.

555 responsable [R] **1.** *nmf* responsible party ■ Gilberto es el responsable de los cambios en la empresa. Gilbert is the one responsible for the changes in the business. **2.** *aj* responsible ■ Los alumnos responsables no faltan a sus

clases. Responsible students do not miss their classes.

556 doctor,-a *nmf* [R] doctor ■ El doctor me examinó los ojos. The doctor examined my eyes. Esa fue una visita de doctor. That was a doctor's visit (a quick visit).

557 responder *vt* [R] to respond, to answer ■ El niño no pudo responder a la pregunta. The boy could not (was not able to) answer the question.

558 mayo *nm* May ■ El cumpleaños de mi esposa es el 2 de mayo. My wife's birthday is May 2.

559 pueblo *nm* [R] town; people ■ El pueblo más cercano queda a diez millas de aquí. The closest town is ten miles from here. El pueblo eligió a su alcalde. The town chose its mayor.

560 demanda *nf* [R -a] lawsuit ■ Él puso una demanda contra su jefe. He filed a lawsuit against his boss.

561 ocho [R] **1.** *nm* number eight ■ El ocho es mi número favorito. Eight is my favorite number. **2.** *aj* eight Hay ocho casas en nuestra calle. There are eight houses on our street.

562 televisión *nf* [R(vista, teléfono) -sión] television ■ El niño prendió la televisión. The child turned on the television.

563 cámara *nf* camera; chamber, house ■ Mi hermana tomó varias fotos con su cámara digital. My sister took several photos with her digital camera. El presidente habló con miembros de las dos cámaras de la legislatura. The president spoke to members of the two houses of the legislature.

564 defensa *nf* [R] defense; bumper (of a car) ■ Los abogados de la defensa se reunieron para decidir su estrategia. The lawyers for the defense met to decide their stragety. Ricardo necesita reemplazar la defensa de su carro. Richard needs to replace the bumper on his car.

565 morir(se) *vi(r)* [R] to die □ *morir de viejo* to die of old age ■ Los soldados murieron por nuestro país. The soldiers died for our country.

566 propuesta [R(poner)] **1.** *nf* proposal ■ Ellos enviaron su propuesta por correo. They sent their proposal by mail. **2.** *aj* proposed La idea fue propuesta por el comité organizador. The idea was proposed by the organizing committee.

567 ciudadano,-a *nmf* [R] citizen ■ Me preguntaron si yo era ciudadano. They asked me if I was a citizen.

568 ejemplo *nm* [R] example ■ Los hijos necesitan el ejemplo de sus padres. Children need the example of their parents.

569 metro *nm* [R] metro; meter ■ La estación del metro es enorme en México, D.F. The metro station in Mexico City is enormous. Un metro tiene cien centímetros. A meter has 100 centimeters.

570 madre *nf* [R] mother □ *madre de leche* wet nurse ■ El 10 de mayo es el día de las madres. May 10 is Mother's Day.

571 militar [R] **1.** *nm* soldier ■ Los militares se entrenan todos los días. The soldiers train every day. **2.** *aj* military ■ La base militar se ubica en las afueras de la ciudad. The military base is located on the outskirts of the city. **3.** *vi* to serve in the military; to belong to a political party; to play (team, player) ■ Milita en el PRI desde 1965. He (She) has been a member of the PRI since 1965.

572 estadio *nm* stadium ■ El estadio de fútbol tiene capacidad para veinte mil personas. The soccer stadium has a capacity of 20,000.

573 premio *nm* [R -o(1)] prize ■ El niño recibió un premio en su escuela. The child received a prize in his school.

574 color *nm* [R] color □ *color vivo* bright color; *colores claros* light colors ■ Los colores de la bandera brillan en el sol. The colors of the flag shine in the sun.

575 electoral *aj* [R] electoral ■ Varios presidentes han propuesto reformar el sistema electoral. Several presidents have proposed reforming the electoral system.

576 pan *nm* [R] **1.** bread □ *es pan comido* it's easy as pie, it's a cinch (literally, it's eaten bread) ■ El pan de trigo es buenísimo. Wheat bread is very, very good. **2.** PAN (Partido Acción Nacional) political party in Mexico ■ El PAN tiene un nuevo candidato a la presidencia. The PAN political party has a new candidate for president.

577 referir(se) *vt(r)* [R] to refer (vt); to be referring to (vr) ■ Me refiero a la reunión anterior. I´m referring to our last meeting.

578 alcalde *nm* [R] mayor ■ Hoy el alcalde dará un mensaje por televisión. Today the mayor will deliver a message on television.

579 lucha *nf* [R -a] struggle, fight, effort ■ La lucha contra la droga sigue adelante. The struggle against drugs continues.

580 efectuar(se) *vt(r)* [R] to effect, to bring about (vt); to take place (vr) ■ El gobernador efectuó muchos cambios. The governor brought about many changes. Hay varios cambios que se efectuaron en esta versión del programa. There are several changes that took effect in this version of the program. El desfile se efectuó en el centro de la ciudad. The parade took place downtown.

581 línea *nf* [R] line (geometric or commercial, as in a bus line) □ *línea de puntos* dotted line; *saltarse una línea* to skip a line ■ La línea está muy delgada. The line is very thin. La línea para entrar al cine está muy larga. The line to enter the movie theater is very long.

582 operación *nf* [R -ción] operation ■ La operación fue todo un éxito. The operation was a complete success.

583 pago *nm* [R -o(1)] payment □ *suspender el pago* to stop payment ■ El pago de los impuestos es importante. The tax payment is important.

584 objetivo *nm* [R] objective, purpose ■ ¿Cuál es el objetivo de su plan? What is the objective of your (his, her) plan?

585 selección *nf* selection; all-star team ■ Aquella selección de rocas me encanta. I love that selection of rocks. La selección argentina está entrenando muy duro. The Argentinian all-star team is training very hard.

586 aumentar *vt* [R] to augment, to increase ■ El precio de la gasolina aumentó la semana pasada. The price of gasoline rose last week.

587 victoria *nf* [R] victory ■ El equipo festejó su victoria. The team celebrated its victory.

588 reforma *nf* [R(forma) -a] reform ■ El candidato habló vigorosamente sobre las reformas políticas. The candidate spoke vigorously about political reforms.

589 dedicar(se) *vt(r)* [R] to dedicate (vt); to be dedicated to, to dedicate oneself, to devote oneself to (esp. occupation) (vr) ■ Eduardo le dedica siempre la misma canción a su mamá. Edward always dedicates the same song to his mother. Soledad se dedica a la enseñanza. Soledad is devoted to teaching.

590 adelantar *vti* [R] to move forward ■ Ulises quiere adelantar el trabajo de la próxima semana. Ulysses wants to get ahead on next week's work.

591 **evento** *nm* event ■ Su esposa organizó el evento. His wife organized the event.

592 **negro** *aj, nm* [R] black ■ Los ojos del perro son negros. The dog's eyes are black.

593 **enviar** *vt* [R] to send ■ Rebeca va a enviar el paquete mañana. Rebecca is going to send the package tomorrow.

594 **sostener** *vt* [R(tener)] to sustain, to hold; to support ■ Gabriel sostuvo a Elisa con sus dos brazos para que ella no se cayera. Gabriel held Elisa with both arms so that she wouldn't fall. Ya que estaban enfermos sus papás, Elena y Andrés los sostenían económicamente. Since their parents were ill, Elena and Andrew supported them economically.

595 **negocio** *nm* [R -o(1)] business ■ Él va a invertir en un nuevo negocio. He is going to invest in a new business.

596 **asistir** *vi* [R] to attend (an event, meeting, school, church, etc.) ■ La familia Peralta siempre asiste a los servicios de la iglesia. The Peralta family always attends church services.

597 **campesino,-a** [R -ino(2)] **1.** *nmf* peasant; one who lives in the country ■ La vida de un campesino puede ser muy difícil. The life of a peasant can be very difficult. **2.** *aj* rural, pertaining to the country ■ Mis amigos campesinos tienen una casa grande. My country friends have a large house.

598 **idea** *nf* [R] idea ■ Sandy tuvo una idea brillante. Sandy had a brilliant idea.

599 **prueba** *nf* [R -a] test; proof (may be plural in Spanish) □ *prueba de indicios, prueba de indiciaria* circumstantial evidence ■ Los alumnos pasaron la prueba fácilmente. The students easily passed the test. El teniente encontró las pruebas. The lieutenant found the proof.

600 **lanzar(se)** *vt(r)* [R] to throw, to hurl (vt); to throw oneself, to hurl oneself, to go quickly (vr) ■ El jugador lanzó el balón con mucha fuerza. The player threw the ball hard. El niño se lanzó al pasto sin lastimarse. The boy threw himself to the ground without hurting himself.

601 **conjunto** [R -o(1)] **1.** *nm* set; ensemble, especially of musicians; outfit or suit of more than one piece (*traje* is the word used for a

business suit) □ *conjunto deportivo* warm-up suit ■ El conjunto tocó música hermosa. The ensemble played beautiful music. Roberto necesita un conjunto deportivo para sus entrenamientos. Robert needs a warm-up suit for his training sessions. **2.** *aj* joined, joint ■ Las asociaciones han planeado varias actividades conjuntas. The associations have planned several joint activities.

602 **respuesta** *nf* [R] answer ■ ¿Cuál es tu respuesta? What is your answer?

603 **justicia** *nf* [R -icia] justice, fairness □ *tomarse la justicia por su mano* to take justice into one's own hands ■ Las víctimas se fueron en busca de la justicia. The victims went in search of justice. Se tomaron la justicia por su mano. They took justice in their own hands.

604 **nacer** *vi* [R] to be born ■ El bebé acaba de nacer. The baby was just born.

605 **uso** *nm* [R] use ■ Le pagamos por el uso de su estacionamiento. We paid him for the use of his parking space.

606 **luz** *nf* [R] light □ *a la luz del día* in the light of day, in broad daylight, openly ■ Ellos prefieren la luz de las velas. They prefer candle light.

607 **demostrar** *vt* [R] to demonstrate, to show ■ Los participantes pudieron demostrar sus habilidades. The participants were able to demonstrate their skills.

608 **civil** *aj* [R] civil ■ La boda civil se realizó en Virginia. The civil wedding ceremony took place in Virginia.

609 **copa** *nf* trophy; cup (formal), goblet □ *tomar una copa* to have a drink ■ El atleta ganó la copa de oro. The athlete won the gold cup. Ellos tomaron vino en copas de cristal. They drank wine in crystal wine glasses.

610 **banda** *nf* band (all meanings, except rubber band: *liga*) ■ Él necesita otra banda para la secadora. He needs another belt for the dryer. Hay varias bandas de música que me gustan. There are several (musical) bands that I like.

611 **ocupar(se)** *vt(r)* [R] to occupy, to have a place (vt); to be busy, to be occupied (vr) ■ Ella ocupa un lugar especial en mi corazón. She has a special place in my heart. Lola se ocupó toda la mañana. Lola was busy all morning.

612 **espacio** *nm* [R -icio] space (all meanings) ■ No hay suficiente espacio. There is not enough space.

613 **inversión** *nf* [R -sión] investment ■ Buscaba consejos de varios asesores de inversiones. I (you, he, she) sought advice from several investment advisors.

614 **plan** *nm* [R] plan ■ Elías desarrolló un buen plan. Elias developed a good plan.

615 **cultura** *nf* [R -ura(2)] culture ■ Cada país tiene diferente cultura. Each country has a different culture.

616 **organismo** *nm* [R -ismo] organism ■ La levadura es un organismo vivo. Yeast is a living organism.

617 **determinar** *vt* [R] to determine ■ El exámen podrá determinar su capacidad. The test will be able to determine his (her, your) ability.

618 **presidencia** *nf* [R -encia] presidency ■ Los candidatos están compitiendo por la presidencia. The candidates are competing for the presidency.

619 **pretender(se)** *vt(r)* [R] to pretend, to court (vt); to be pretending (vr) ■ Pretendí dormir. I pretended to sleep. Él la pretendió por años. He courted her for years. Me pretendí dormido. I pretended to be asleep.

620 **actriz** *nf* [R -triz] actress ■ Liz estudiará para ser actriz. Liz will study to be an actress.

621 **marzo** *nm* March (month) ■ La primavera inicia en marzo. Spring begins in March.

622 **nación** *nf* [R -ción] nation ■ La nación tiene muchas riquezas naturales. The nation has many natural resources.

623 **aparecer(se)** *vi(r)* [R] to appear (vi); to show oneself or itself (vr) ■ Apareció una ballena a 300 metros de la costa. A whale appeared 300 meters off the coast. De repente tres niños se aparecieron en la puerta. Suddenly three children appeared at the door.

624 **compañero,-a** *nmf* companion □ *compañero de trabajo* co-worker; *compañero de la escuela* classmate ■ Sus compañeras de la escuela la visitaron. Her classmates visited her. Su compañero de trabajo llegó tarde. His (her, your) co-worker arrived late.

625 **oficina** *nf* [R -ina] office; (a medical office is referred to as a *consultorio*; a law office is referred to as a *despacho*) ■ Trabajo en la oficina. I work in the office.

626 **palestino** *aj* [-ino(2)] Palestinian ■ Autoridad Palestina Palestinian Authority

▶ **Palestina** *nf* Palestine ■ Algún día espero visitar Palestina. One day I hope to visit Palestine.

627 **razón** *nf* [R] reason ■ Ella tuvo tres razones. She had three reasons. Tienes razón. You are right.

628 **rico** *aj* [R] rich; excellent (in reference to food) ■ Cuando seamos ricos, vamos a comprar una cabaña en las montañas. When we become rich, we are going to buy a cabin in the mountains. Los enchiladas son ricos. The enchiladas are excellent.

629 **visita** *nf* [R -a] visit ■ Nos disfrutó mucho su visita. We enjoyed very much your (his, her) visit.

630 **ceremonia** *nf* ceremony ■ La ceremonia de inauguración duró dos horas. The inauguration ceremony lasted two hours.

631 **asociación** *nf* [R -ción] association ■ Los ganaderos formaron una asociación. The cattle ranchers formed an association.

632 **aprovechar** *vti(r)* [R] to take full advantage of (an opportunity) ■ Ellos quisieron aprovechar la oferta. They wanted to take advantage of the sale.

633 **comercial** [R -cial] **1.** *nm* commercial ■ El comercial de automóviles salió por primera vez durante la copa mundial. The car commercial appeared for the first time during the World Cup. **2.** *aj* commercial ■ El centro comercial está a dos cuadras de su casa. The shopping center is two blocks from her house.

634 **lunes** *nm* [R] Monday ■ Empezamos las clases el lunes pasado. We began classes last Monday.

635 **sitio** *nm* [R] site, place ■ Este sitio es hermoso. This place is beautiful. ¿Te agrada nuestro sitio web? Do you like our website?

636 **maestro,-a** *nmf* [R] teacher; master □ *obra maestra* masterpiece ■ La maestra nació en Canadá. The teacher was born in Canada.

637 **suceder** *vi* [R] to happen ■ Todo sucedió en unos segundos. Everything happened in a matter of seconds.

638 **vencer** *vti(r)* [R] to conquer, to expire (vi); to become void (vr) ■ Hernán Cortez venció a los aztecas. Hernan Cortez conquered the Aztecs. La visa vence en diciembre. The visa expires in December. Se vence el pasaporte en diciembre. The passport becomes void in December.

639 **construcción** *nf* [R -ción] construction ■ Mi cuñado es un experto en construcción de casas. My brother-in-law is an expert in house construction.

640 **dirigente** *nmf* [R -ente(2)] leader, director ■ El dirigente de la excursión explicó detalladamente todo. The leader of the excursion explained everything in detail.

641 **principio** *nm* beginning ■ Me gusta mucho el principio de la historia. I like the beginning of the story very much.

642 **mejorar(se)** *vt(r)* [R] to improve (vt); to get better (health), to become improved (vr) ■ Los voluntarios mejoraron el camino histórico. Volunteers improved the historic trail. Esther se mejoró rápidamente. Esther got better quickly. Se mejoró el sistema de educación. The educational system improved.

643 **musical** *aj* [R] musical ■ El festival musical será dentro de una semana. The musical festival will take place within a week.

644 **privar(se)** *vt(r)* [R] to deprive (vt); to deprive oneself (vr) ■ Un error, a falta de un segundo para el final del partido, privó de un triunfo a nuestro equipo. One mistake, with one second left in the game, deprived our team of a victory. Jared y Caleb no se privaron de una última vista a las montañas hermosas. Jared and Caleb did not deprive themselves of one last look at the beautiful mountains.

645 **escuchar** *vt* [R] to hear; to listen (to) ■ Carl no me podía escuchar. Carl couldn't hear me. ¿Me estás escuchando? Are you listening to me?

646 **capacidad** *nf* [R -idad] capacity; capability ■ La capacidad del teatro es de 1,180 personas. The capacity of the theater is 1,180 people. Los niños tienen la capacidad de aprender rápidamente. Children have the capability of learning quickly.

647 **control** *nm* control ■ El automovilista perdió el control de su carro. The motorist lost control of his car.

648 **banco** *nm* [R] bank □ *banco de sangre* blood bank ■ El banco cierra a las 4 de la tarde. The bank closes at 4 p.m.

649 **comunicación** *nf* [R -ción] communication ■ La comunicación en el matrimonio es muy importante. Communication in marriage is very important.

650 **actuar** *vi* [R] to act ■ Ella no pudo actuar con rapidez. She was unable to act quickly.

651 **don** *nm* gift (talent); term of dignity for a man ■ La paciencia es un don. Patience is a gift. Don Ramón es el dueño del rancho. Don Ramón is the owner of the ranch.

652 **cinta** *nf* [R] tape □ *cinta de sombrero* hat band ■ La cinta de medir está en el cajón. The measuring tape is in the drawer.

653 **candidato,-a** *nmf* candidate ■ Los miembros de la prensa tenían muchas preguntas para el candidato. Members of the press had many questions for the candidate.

654 **tocar** *vt* [R] to touch; to play (a musical instrument); to knock (at the door) ■ El niño quería tocar el elefante. The child wanted to touch the elephant. Nuestra vecina sabe tocar el piano muy bien. Our neighbor knows how to play the piano very well. Ray estuvo tocando la puerta por un buen rato. Ray was knocking at the door for quite a while.

655 **departamento** *nm* [R] department; apartment ■ Mi primo trabaja como investigador en el departamento de justicia. My cousin works as an investigator for the Department of Justice. Estamos buscando un departamento de dos recámaras. We are searching for a two-bedroom apartment.

656 **interno,-a** [R -o(1)] **1.** *nmf* boarding student; intern ■ La mayoría de los internos regresan a sus casas los fines de semana. The majority of the boarding students return home on the weekends. Los directores querían contratar a varios internos este verano. The directors wanted to hire several interns this summer. **2.** *aj* internal ■ El dolor interno era intenso. The internal pain was intense.

657 **Dios** *nm* [R] God ■ ¡Que Dios te bendiga! May God bless you!
▶ **dios,-a** *nmf* god, goddess ■ Venus Williams, diosa del tenis, va a ganar Wimbledon. Tennis goddess, Venus Williams, will win Wimbledon.

658 **futuro** *nm, aj* [R -ura(2)] future ■ El futuro es incierto. The future is uncertain. Sus futuros hijos heredarán sus posesiones. Their (your, his, her) future children will inherit their (your, his, her) possessions.

659 **ejecutivo,-a** [R -ivo] **1.** *nmf* executive ■ El sistema fue diseñado para los ejecutivos de negocios. The system was designed for

business executives. **2.** *aj* executive ■ Aquellos negociantes son miembros del club ejecutivo. Those businessmen are members of the executive club.

660 **estrella** *nf* [R] star ■ Ayer vimos una estrella fugaz. Yesterday we saw a shooting star.

661 **contener** *vt* [R] to contain ■ La caja contiene varios papeles. The box contains several papers.

662 **regional** *aj* [R] regional ■ La reunión regional será en octubre. The regional meeting will be (held) in October.

663 **camino** *nm* [R -ino(1)] path, trail, way; highway □ *camino trillado* beaten track; *errar el camino* to take the wrong road, lose one's way ■ Los españoles viajaron por el Camino Real. The Spaniards traveled on the Royal Highway. Nuestros amigos nos llamaron para decirnos que están en camino. Our friends called to say that they are on the way.

664 **físico** [R] **1.** *nm* physical appearance ■ Su físico era hermoso. Her physical appearance was beautiful. **2.** *aj* physical ■ La salud física es importante. Physical health is important.
▶ **la física** *nf* physics ■ El profesor de física no ha llegado. The physics teacher has not arrived.

665 **realidad** *nf* [R -idad] reality ■ Aunque es un escritor de ficción, Andrés vive en el mundo de la realidad. Although he is a fiction writer, Andrew lives in the world of reality.

666 **financiero,-a** [-ero(2)] **1.** *nmf* financier; financial expert ■ Los financieros han escrito varios reportes sobre nuestro negocio. Financial experts have written several reports about our company. **2.** *aj* financial ■ Vemos las noticias financieras todos los días. We watch the financial news every day.

667 **libro** *nm* [R] book □ *libro de cocina* cookbook; *libro mayor* ledger ■ Arturo buscó el libro en varias librerías. Arthur searched for the book in several bookstores.

668 **asunto** *nm* subject matter, affair ■ El asunto era extremadamente complicado. The subject matter was extremely complicated.

669 **industria** *nf* [R] industry ■ Los estudiantes de administración investigaron sobre la industria hotelera. The business administration students researched the hotel industry.

670 **reciente** *aj* [R] recent ■ Paula disfrutó su reciente viaje a Italia. Paula enjoyed her recent trip to Italy.

671 **posición** *nf* [R] (physical) position; playing position (in sports) ■ Doris durmió en una posición incómoda. Doris slept in an uncomfortable position. ¿En cuál posición quieres jugar? What position do you want to play?

672 **central** [R -al(2)] **1.** *nf* main office or location; (train or bus) station ■ La central telefónica se ubica cerca del mercado. The telephone exchange (hub) is located near the market. Mis hermanos vinieron por mi a la central camionera. My brothers and sisters came for me at the central bus station. **2.** *aj* central, middle Manejé por el carril central. I drove in the middle lane.

673 **campeón,-a** *nmf* [R] champion ■ Nuestro amigo Roberto fue campeón de las olimpiadas. Our friend Robert was Olympic champion.

674 **función** *nf* [R] function (purpose); function (event) ■ La función de los riñones es vital. The functioning of the kidneys is vital. Fueron a la función de las 8 de la tarde. They went to the 8 o'clock event.

675 **diciembre** *nm* December ■ En diciembre celebramos la navidad. In December we celebrate Christmas.

676 **presentación** *nf* [R -ción] presentation, look and feel □ *tarjeta de presentación* business card ■ A mi me gusta la presentación del libro. I like the look and feel of the book. Me dio su tarjeta de presentación. He gave me his business card.

677 **ayuda** *nf* [R -a] help, assistance (note: in an emergency, the term ¡*Auxilio!* is used for "Help!") ■ Aprecio mucho su ayuda. I appreciate very much your (his, her) help.

678 **entrevista** *nf* [R -a] interview ■ La entrevista duró cincuenta minutos. The interview lasted fifty minutes.

679 **impuesto** *nm* [R] tax ■ Los impuestos son altos. Taxes are high.

680 **efecto** *nm* [R] effect ■ La medicina produce otros efectos. The medicine produces side effects.

681 **resto** *nm* [R -o(1)] rest (remainder) ■ Vamos a descansar durante el resto del día. We are

going to rest for the rest (remainder) of the day.

682 **fiscal** [R] **1.** *nmf* attorney general; district attorney; legal representative of the government responsible for the enforcement of laws and taxes ■ El fiscal leyó la declaración. The district attorney read the affidavit. **2.** *aj* pertaining to the legal representative of the government; fiscal ■ Los impuestos fiscales fueron pagados a tiempo. The fiscal taxes were paid on time.

683 **natural** *aj* [R] natural ■ Su color natural es rojo. Its natural color is red.

684 **enero** *nm* January ■ En enero es el cumpleaños de Fernando. Fernando's birthday is in January.

685 **comercio** *nm* [R -o(1)] commerce, business □ *comercio exterior* foreign trade ■ Sr. Pérez disfruta el comercio de joyas. Mr. Pérez enjoys the jewelry business.

686 **encargar(se)** *vt(r)* [R] to place in charge, to make responsible for (homework, a favor, a person, a duty), to give a task (vt); to take charge, to be in charge (vr) ■ El líder le encargó a Francisco el grupo. The leader placed Francisco in charge of the group. Cristal le encargó devolver sus libros a la biblioteca. Crystal gave him the task of returning her books to the library. Me encargué del hospedaje durante el torneo. I was in charge of hospitality during the tournament.

687 **escenario** *nm* [R] stage; set; scene ■ Los actores entraron al escenario. The actors entered the stage. El escenario parecía tener aves reales. The set appeared to have live birds. El escenario era hermoso. The scene was beautiful.

688 **palabra** *nf* [R] word □ *de palabra* by word of mouth; *palabras conciliatorias* conciliatory words; *libertad de palabra* freedom of speech ■ La palabra es difícil de pronunciar. The word is difficult to pronounce.

689 **inicio** *nm* [R -icio] beginning ■ El inicio de la clase fue emocionante. The beginning of the class was exciting.

690 **beneficio** *nm* [R -icio] benefit □ *beneficio bruto* gross profit; *beneficio neto* net profit; *no tener oficio ni beneficio* to have neither profession or means of support ■ Los beneficios de la natación son muchos. The benefits of swimming are many. Ese vago no

tiene oficio ni beneficio. That vagrant has neither profession nor any means of support.

691 **entrega** *nf* [R -a] giving, delivery ■ La entrega de regalos es una de las grandes alegrías de la navidad. The giving of gifts is one of the great joys of the Christmas season.

692 **energía** *nf* [R] energy ■ En Argentina el 31 de mayo es el Día Nacional de la Energía Atómica. In Argentina, May 31 is National Atomic Energy Day.

693 **labor** *nm* [R] labor ■ Durante su labor de parto, Marisol tuvo mucho dolor, pero después estaba llena de alegría. During labor, Marisol felt a great deal of pain, but afterward she was filled with joy. Su labor no fue en vano. His (her, your) work was not in vain.

694 **octubre** *nm* [R] October ■ Eunice nació en Octubre. Eunice was born in October.

695 **imagen** *nm* [R] image ■ Raquel no podía ver su imagen en el espejo. Racquel was unable to see her image in the mirror.

696 **esfuerzo** *nm* [R -o(1)] effort ■ Flavio hizo mucho esfuerzo para aprender a nadar. Flavio exerted great effort in learning to swim.

697 **personaje** *nmf* [R] celebrity; character in a play, movie, etc. ■ Bob Hope fue un personaje internacional. Bob Hope was an international celebrity. El personaje, Peter Pan, es muy chistoso. The character, Peter Pan, is very funny.

698 **rural** *aj* rural ■ La comunidad rural necesita agua potable. The rural community needs potable water.

699 **directivo,-a** [R -ivo] **1.** *nmf* director, member of the board of governors ■ Un directivo de la empresa es piloto. One of the members of the board of governors is a pilot. **2.** *aj* directive; managing, governing ■ El consejo directivo se reunió para elegir su presidente. The governing council met to select its chairman.
  ▶ **directiva** *nf* board of governors ■ La directiva de la universidad tuvo una junta. The board of governors of the university held a meeting.

700 **acto** *nm* [R] act, deed, action ■ El acto generoso de benevolencia maravilló a todos. The generous act of kindness amazed everyone.

701 **dependencia** *nf* [R -encia] dependence ■ En nuestro mundo la dependencia de la droga es

un peligro muy real. In our world dependence on drugs is a very real danger.

⁷⁰² **alimento(s)** *nm(pl)* [R -o(1)] food (usually referring to nourishing food); nourishment ■ Aquí los alimentos se sirven calientes. Here food is served hot. La especialidad de la enfermera es el alimento de la gente grande. The nurse's specialty is in the nourishment of elderly people.

⁷⁰³ **arma** *nf* [R -a] arm (weapon) □ *arma de fuego* firearm, gun ■ El arma estaba cargada. The weapon was loaded.

⁷⁰⁴ **favor** *nm* [R] favor □ *por favor* please ■ Juliana le pidió un favor a su padre. Juliana asked her father for a favor. ¿Me puedes ayudar, por favor? Can you help me, please?

⁷⁰⁵ **cuadro** *nm* [R] frame; square □ *en cuadro* squared ■ Los cuadros decorativos valen mucho. Decorative frames are valuable. Para ver esta página necesita un examinador que pueda mostrar cuadros. In order to see this page you need a browser that is able to display frames. El niño sabe dibujar círculos, triángulos, rectángulos y cuadros. The child knows how to draw circles, triangles, rectangles and squares.

⁷⁰⁶ **abril** *nm* April ■ En abril visitaré a mis primos. In April I will visit my cousins.

⁷⁰⁷ **sencillo** *aj* [R] simple, plain; single (scoop); one-way ■ El problema es sencillo. The problem is simple. ¿Quieres un helado sencillo o doble? Do you want a single or double scoop of ice cream? El viaje sencillo cuesta noventa dólares. One-way travel costs ninety dollars.

⁷⁰⁸ **compromiso** *nm* [R] engagement (courtship); appointment ■ Ellos anunciaron su compromiso. The couple announced their engagement. Tengo un compromiso mañana por la mañana. I have an appointment tomorrow morning.

⁷⁰⁹ **pronto** *av* [R] soon, quickly □ *hasta pronto* see you soon; *tan pronto como* as soon as ■ Llegarán pronto de su viaje. They will be arriving soon from their trip. La mesera nos sirvió pronto. The waitress served us quickly.

⁷¹⁰ **empleo** *nm* [R -eo(1)] employment ■ Mi cuñada está buscando empleo. My sister-in-law is seeking employment.

⁷¹¹ **interior** *nm* [R] interior □ *ropa interior* underwear ■ El interior del museo es

impresionante. The interior of the museum is impressive.

⁷¹² **clase** *nf* [R] class (school); class (category) □ *fumarse una clase* to skip a class; *de cualquier clase* of any kind or description ■ La clase de francés se canceló. The French class was canceled. Es más cómodo viajar en primera clase. It's more comfortable to travel in first class.

⁷¹³ **comité** *nm* committee ■ Ellos formaron un nuevo comité. They formed a new committee.

⁷¹⁴ **acabar(se)** *vt(r)* [R] to complete, to finish (vt); to run out; to have just finished, to be completed (vr) ■ Acabé la tarea. I finished the homework. Se nos acabó la leche. We ran out of milk. Se acabó el programa de televisión. The television program just finished.

⁷¹⁵ **reducir(se)** *vt(r)* [R] to reduce (vt); to be reduced, to drop, to go down (in quantity or frequency) (vr) ■ Mi abuelo está reduciendo la cantidad de sal en sus alimentos. My grandfather is reducing the amount of salt in his food. El año pasado se redujo el número de accidentes en carretera. Last year the number of accidents on the highway dropped.

⁷¹⁶ **causar** *vt* [R] to cause ■ La lluvia causó daños severos. The rain caused severe damage.

⁷¹⁷ **hospital** *nm* [R] hospital ■ El hospital necesita más voluntarios. The hospital needs more volunteers.

⁷¹⁸ **ramo** *nm* [R] bouquet; field, branch (class) ■ El ramo de rosas rojas es hermoso. The bouquet of red roses is beautiful. En el ramo de la administración hotelera es importante la capacitación. Training is important in the field of hotel management.

⁷¹⁹ **etapa** *nf* stage (of life or development) ■ La etapa de la niñez es importantísima. The childhood stage of development is extremely important.

⁷²⁰ **anotar** *vt* [R] to annotate, to cite; to write a note, to write down ■ El escritor anotó sus referencias al pie de la página. The author cited his references in footnotes. Los estudiantes anotaron lo que había en el pizarrón. The students wrote down what was on the board.

⁷²¹ **vestir(se)** *vt(r)* [R] to dress (vt); to dress oneself (vr) □ *vestirse bien* to dress properly ■ La ejecutiva debe vestir pulcramente. The

executive must dress with great attention to detail. **Me vestí de rojo para ir al teatro.** I dressed in red to go to the theater.

722 **salida** *nf* [R -ido(2)] exit; offramp ■ **La salida es por la derecha.** The exit is to the right. **La salida ocho está cerrada el día de hoy.** Offramp 8 is closed today.

723 **comarca** *nf* [R] region; shire ■ **Hay dos millones de habitantes en la comarca.** There are two million people in the region. *El Señor de los Anillos* **habla de gente de la comarca.** *The Lord of the Rings* speaks of people from the Shire.

724 **viajar** *vi* [R] to travel ■ **Este verano vamos a viajar.** This summer we are going to travel.

725 **extranjero,-a** [R] **1.** *nmf* foreigner ■ **Los extranjeros están bienvenidos.** Foreigners are welcome. **2.** *aj* foreign ■ **Tenemos monedas extranjeras.** We have (some) foreign coins.

726 **período** *nm* period (time) ■ **A Olga le gusta la música del período barroco.** Olga likes music from the baroque period.

727 **teatro** *nm* [R] theater (note: *cinema, cine* is used for movies) ■ **Fuimos a ver una obra en el teatro.** We went to see a play at the theater.

728 **alumno,-a** *nmf* [R] student ■ **El alumno ya sabe tres idiomas.** The student already knows three languages.

729 **delito** *nm* crime ■ **Queremos evitar ser víctimas de un delito.** We want to avoid being victims of a crime.

730 **voz** *nf* [R] voice ■ **La voz interna me decía lo que debía hacer.** The voice inside told me what I ought to do.

731 **daño** *nm* [R -o(1)] damage (often plural in Spanish when singular in English) □ *daños y perjuicios* damages ■ **El daño fue insignificante.** The damage was negligible. **Declararon estado de desastre en Puerto Rico debido a los daños causados por las lluvias.** They declared a disaster area in Puerto Rico because of the damage caused by the rains. **La compañía tuvo que pagar daños (y perjuicios) por el incumplimiento del contrato.** The company had to pay damages for breech of contract.

732 **febrero** *nm* February ■ **En febrero llueve mucho.** In February it rains a lot.

733 **verdad** *nf* [R -edad] truth, frequently used as an expression □ *¿Verdad?* Isn't that right? *de verdad* really, honestly ■ **Lucy le dijo toda la verdad.** Lucy told him (her, you) the whole truth.

734 **finalmente** *av* [R -mente] finally ■ **Finalmente terminamos el proyecto.** We finally finished the project.

735 **profesional** *aj* [R] professional ■ **Su actitud profesional me impresionó.** Their professional attitude impressed me.

736 **distrito** *nm* district ■ **Trabajaba para el distrito escolar cuando me embaracé.** I was working for the school district when I became pregnant.

737 **izquierdo** [R] **1.** *nm* left (direction, politics) ■ **Mi tío es izquierdo.** My uncle is left-handed. **2.** *aj* left **Su ojo izquierdo le duele.** His (her, your) left eye hurts.

738 **jueves** *nm* Thursday ■ **Tengo la clase de música los jueves.** I have music class on Thursdays.

739 **materia** *nf* [R] matter; subject ■ **El astrónomo está interesado en cuestiones sobre la materia y el origen del universo.** The astronomer is interested in matter and the origin of the universe. **Él es un experto en materia de idiomas.** He is an expert in the subject of languages.

740 **traer** *vt* to bring; to bring with ■ **Magdalena va a traer fruta al convivio.** Magdalena is going to bring fruit to the pot-luck. **Tito trae con él a su mamá a la iglesia.** Tito brings his mother with him to church.

741 **deporte** *nm* [R] sport ■ **El deporte favorito de Francisco es el fútbol.** Francisco's favorite sport is soccer.

742 **intentar** *vt* [R] to try, to attempt ■ **Cecilia intentó hablar en francés.** Cecilia tried to speak in French.

743 **detener(se)** *vt(r)* [R] to detain (vt); to stop oneself (vr) ■ **El policía detuvo al ratero.** The policeman detained the thief. **Me detuve en la tienda para ver los sombreros.** I stopped at the store to look at the hats.

744 **gracia(s)** *nf(pl)* [R] grace; thank-you □ *día de la Acción de Gracias* Thanksgiving Day ■ **El predicador habló sobre la gracia.** The preacher spoke about grace. **Gracias por tus consejos.** Thank-you for your advice.

745 **responsabilidad** *nf* [R -idad] responsibility ■ **Ser madre es una gran responsabilidad.** To be a mother is a great responsibility.

746 **máximo** [R] **1.** *nm* maximum ■ Los niños disfrutaron el campamento al máximo. The children enjoyed camp to the maximum. **2.** *aj* maximum ■ ¿Cuál es la máxima capacidad del recipiente? What is the maximum capacity of the container?

747 **recorrer** *vt* [R(correr)] to cover (distance) ■ Los viajeros recorrieron doscientas millas cada día. The travelers covered two hundred miles a day.

748 **distinto** *aj* [R] distinct, clearly different, different ■ Hay razas distintas de perros. There are distinct breeds of dogs. Lo conocí con un nombre distinto. I knew him by a different name.

749 **solamente** *av* [R -mente] only, just ■ Si solamente pudiera olvidarlo, sería feliz. If only he (you, she) could forget it, he (you, she) would be happy.

750 **citar** *vti(r)* [R] to cite a source (vi); to set or make an appointment for (vt); to set a time, to make an appointment with each other (plural only) (vr) ■ Susana citó las palabras de Cervantes. Susan cited the words of Cervantes. La recepcionista me citó a las cuatro. The receptionist made me an appointment for four o'clock. Ellos se citaron para cenar. They set a time to eat dinner (together).

751 **retirar(se)** *vt(r)* [R] to move away, to remove (vt); to withdraw, to remove oneself, to leave, to retire (at night), to go to bed for the evening (vi) ■ Nuestros vecinos retiraron su carro del callejón. Our neighbors moved their car out of the alley. El acusado retiró su confesión de culpabilidad. The accused withdrew his confession of guilt. Me retiré de la fiesta temprano. I left the party early. Cada noche, mi mamá se retira a la misma hora. Every night, my mother retires at the same time.

752 **crédito** *nm* [R -ito(2)] credit ■ ¿Usted tiene una tarjeta de crédito? Do you have a credit card?

753 **amistad** *nf* [R -tad] friendship ■ Desde la primaria ellas siempre mantuvieron su amistad. Beginning in elementary school they always maintained their friendship.

754 **duda** *nf* [R -a] doubt; question (when one is unsure of something) □ *sin duda alguna* beyond the shadow of a doubt ■ Tengo dudas en cuanto a su carácter. I have doubts concerning his (her, your) character. Tengo una duda. I have a question.

755 **concierto** *nm* [R] concert ■ El concierto me encantó. The concert captivated me.

756 **ingreso** *nm* [R -o(1)] income ■ Nuestro ingreso es suficiente. Our income is sufficient.

757 **costo** *nm* [-o(1)] cost ■ El costo de la reconstrucción es alto. The cost of reconstruction is high.

758 **noviembre** *nm* [R] November ■ Mi amiga regresará en noviembre. My friend will return in November.

759 **experiencia** *nf* [R] experience ■ Me preguntaron sobre mi experiencia. They asked me about my experience.

760 **inmediato** *aj* [R(medio)] immediate ■ La respuesta fue inmediata. The answer was immediate.

761 **demás** *nmfpl* [R] others ■ La señora Moragas siempre quiere ayudar a los demás. Mrs. Moragas always wants to help others.

762 **vía** [R] **1.** *nf* way, road, route □ vias tracks ■ Esa es la mejor vía para llegar. That is the best way to go. Cruzamos las vías del tren. We crossed the train tracks. **2.** *av* by way of, via ■ Fuimos de Monterrey a Cancún, vía Veracruz. We went from Monterrey to Cancún by way of Veracruz.

763 **contrario** *nm* [R -ario(2)] the opposite □ *al contrario* on the contrary; *ser contrario a* to be against or opposed to ■ Si yo digo una cosa, ella dice lo contrario. If I say one thing, she says the opposite. El niño no quiere dormir; al contrario, quiere jugar. The boy does not want to sleep; on the contrary, he wants to play.

764 **disfrutar** *vt* [R] to enjoy ■ Mis sobrinos disfrutaron el concierto. My nephews (and nieces) enjoyed the concert.

765 **diferencia** *nf* [R -a] difference ■ Hay diferencias grandes entre los partidos políticos. There are great differences between the political parties.

766 **título** *nm* [R -o(1)] title ■ Es importante escoger bien el título del libro. It is important to choose well the title of the book.

767 **conferencia** *nf* [R -encia] conference ■ La conferencia inició a las ocho. The conference began at eight o'clock.

768 **terreno** *nm* [R(tierra)] terrain; land (usually referring to land owned by someone) ■ Es

difícil caminar por este terreno. It is difficult to walk through this terrain. **Compramos un terreno para construir una casa.** We bought land (on which) to build a house.

769 **observar** *vt* [R] to observe ■ **Nancy quiere observar los animales del zoológico.** Nancy wants to observe the animals at the zoo.

770 **ministerio** *nm* [R] ministry ■ **El ministerio está en sus inicios.** The ministry is in its early stages.

771 **término** *nm* [R] term ■ **El maestro nos explicó los términos técnicos.** The teacher explained the technical terms to us.

772 **azul** [R] **1.** *nm* blue □ *azul celeste* sky blue; *azul turquí* indigo; *azul marino* navy blue **2.** *aj* blue ■ **Sus ojos son azules.** His (her, your) eyes are blue.

773 **accidente** *nm* [R] accident ■ **Mi amiga tuvo un accidente.** My friend had an accident.

774 **dicha** *nf* [R] joy, happiness ■ **La dicha de la vida empieza en el corazón.** The joy of life begins in the heart.

775 **entidad** *nf* entity ■ **Campos, primer director general de la entidad, quería crear una institución privada.** Campos, first general director of the entity, wanted to create a private institution.

776 **religioso** *aj* [R] religious ■ **La librería se especializa en libros religiosos.** The bookstore specializes in religious books.

777 **interpretar** *vt* [R] to interpret ■ **Es importante saber interpretar la información.** It is important to know how to interpret the information.

778 **junio** *nm* June ■ **Nos casamos en junio.** We married in June.

779 **acusar** *vt* [R] to accuse; to denounce ■ **El candidato acusó a su rival de traición.** The candidate accused his rival of treason.

780 **gasto** *nm* [R -o(1)] expense ■ **Calculamos los gastos antes de viajar.** We calculated the expenses before traveling.

781 **popular** *aj* [R] popular ■ **Aquí, la comida más popular es la comida mexicana.** Here, the most popular food is Mexican food.

782 **kilómetro** *nm* [R] kilometer ■ **La pareja camina varios kilómetros todos los días.** The couple walks several kilometers every day.

783 **interesar** *vi* [R] to interest ■ **Me interesa la política.** Politics interests me. (I am interested in politics.)

784 **muerto,-a** *nmf* [R] dead person ■ **No se sabe el número de los muertos que van a encontrar en los escombros.** It is not known the number of dead (people) that they will find in the rubble.

785 **desear** *vt* [R] to desire; to want ■ **La niña desea ir al parque.** The girl wants to go to the park.

786 **marcar** *vt* [R] to mark; to dial (telephone number) ■ **Mi compañera de cuarto marcó todas las cajas con su nombre.** My roommate marked her name on all the boxes. **Daniel marcó el número varias veces.** Daniel dialed the number several times.

787 **iglesia** *nf* church (building); church (body of believers) ■ **Nos casamos en esa iglesia.** We married in that church. **La iglesia está creciendo rápidamente.** The church is growing rapidly.

788 **crecer** *vi* [R] to grow; to grow up ■ **La ciudad creció muy rápido.** The city grew very quickly. **Carlos crece cada día más.** Carlos grows more each day.

789 **avanzar** *vi* [R] to advance, to move forward ■ **El tren no podía avanzar.** The train was unable to move forward.

790 **suficiente** *aj* [R] sufficient, enough ■ **Tengo suficiente.** I have enough. **Tuvimos suficientes jugadores.** We had enough players.

791 **federación** *nf* [R -ción] federation ■ **La federación se fundó hace diez años.** The federation was founded ten years ago.

792 **aspecto** *nm* aspect, appearance ■ **Su aspecto era muy agradable.** Her (his, your) appearance was very pleasant.

793 **oro** *nm* gold ■ **Se fueron para buscar oro en la Sierra Madre.** They went to search for gold in the Sierra Madre.

794 **libertad** *nf* [R -tad] liberty, freedom ■ **La libertad de expresión política es importante.** Freedom of political expression is important.

795 **mediante** *prep* [R] through; by way of □ *Dios mediante* God willing ■ **El guitarrista aprendió mediante la práctica.** The guitarist learned through practice. **Vamos a Europa este verano, Dios mediante.** We are going to Europe this summer, God willing.

⁷⁹⁶ **agosto** *nm* August ■ Christián iniciará su carrera en agosto. Christian will begin his (formal) studies in August.

⁷⁹⁷ **cabeza** *nf* [R] head □ *cabeza de chorlito* scatterbrain ■ Me duele la cabeza. My head hurts.

⁷⁹⁸ **obligar** *vt* [R] to obligate, to force ■ La madre obligó a su niño a decir la verdad. The mother forced her child to tell the truth.

⁷⁹⁹ **voto** *nm* [R -o(1)] individual vote; vow ■ Cada voto es valioso. Each vote is valuable. Ellos tomaron los votos del matrimonio seriamente. They took their marriage vows seriously.

⁸⁰⁰ **modelo** [R -o(1)] **1.** *nm* model ■ Teresa ha trabajado mucho en ese modelo. Teresa has worked hard on that model. **2.** *nmf* model, fashion model ■ Las modelos cambiaron de ropa rápidamente. The models changed clothes quickly.

⁸⁰¹ **visitar** *vt* [R] to visit ■ Nuestra vecina nos visitó ayer. Our neighbor visited us yesterday.

⁸⁰² **crecimiento** *nm* [R -miento] growth ■ El crecimiento constante de la ciudad es impresionante. The continual growth of the city is impressive.

⁸⁰³ **superar(se)** *vt(r)* [R] to overcome, to surpass (vt); to overcome one's difficulties (vr) ■ El joven superó la pobreza. The young man overcame poverty. El estudiante superó a todos sus compañeros del salón. The student surpassed all his classmates. Isabel se superó. Isabel overcame her difficulties.

⁸⁰⁴ **significar** *vti* [R] to mean ■ La palabra significa varias cosas. The word means various things.

⁸⁰⁵ **apenas** *av* barely, just ■ La novia apenas llegó. The bride just arrived.

⁸⁰⁶ **común** *aj* [R] common ■ Viajar en camión es común. Traveling by bus is common.

⁸⁰⁷ **declaración** *nf* [R -ción] declaration ■ Edgar cambió su declaración. Edgar changed his sworn statement.

⁸⁰⁸ **actuación** *nf* [R -ción] performance ■ Todos admiraron su actuación. Everyone admired his performance.

⁸⁰⁹ **vivienda** *nf* [R] place where one lives (house, apartment) ■ La familia Marcos está construyendo una vivienda moderna. The Marcos family is building a modern house.

⁸¹⁰ **consecuencia** *nf* [R] consequence ■ Si los estudiantes entienden las consecuencias de sus actos, es más probable que tomen buenas decisiones ahora. If the students understand the consequences of their actions, it is more likely that they will make good decisions now.

⁸¹¹ **muestra** *nf* [R -a] example; sample □ *dar muestras de* to show signs of ■ El maestro les enseñó la muestra. The teacher showed them an example. El vendedor trajo con él varias muestras. The salesman brought with him several samples.

⁸¹² **superior** *aj* [R] superior, high (level), advanced (level) ■ Mi hermano aprobó el examen para pasar a una clase de nivel superior. My brother passed the test to enter the advanced level class.

⁸¹³ **resolver(se)** *vt(r)* [R(solución)] to resolve, to solve (vt); to become resolved (vr) ■ La pareja resolvió sus problemas. The couple resolved their problems. El maestro de matemáticas resolvió la ecuación. The math teacher solved the equation. Nuestros problemas con la aduana se resolvieron en dos horas. Our problems with the customs office were resolved in two hours.

⁸¹⁴ **diez** [R] **1.** *nm* ten; tenth day of the month ■ Mi mamá llegó el diez de febrero. My mother arrived February 10th. **2.** *aj* ten ■ Tengo diez monedas. I have ten coins. Hay diez años en una década. There are ten years in a decade.

⁸¹⁵ **eléctrico** *aj* [R] electric ■ Ella quiere un abrelatas eléctrico. She wants an electric can opener.

⁸¹⁶ **advertir** *vt* to warn ■ El meteorólogo le advirtió a la gente sobre el ciclón. The weatherman warned the people about the cyclone.

⁸¹⁷ **habitante** *nmf* [R -ante(2)] inhabitant, resident ■ Aquí hay más de 200,000 habitantes. Here there are more than 200,000 residents.

⁸¹⁸ **planta** *nf* [R -a] plant ■ La planta necesita más sol y menos agua. The plant needs more sun and less water.

⁸¹⁹ **otorgar** *vt* [R] to concede, to allow in a formal sense, to approve ■ El banco le otorgó un crédito. The bank approved a line of credit for him.

⁸²⁰ **movimiento** *nm* [R -miento] movement ■ El movimiento repentino la asustó. The sudden movement frightened her.

⁸²¹ **sujeto** [R] **1.** *nm* subject, noun ■ El sujeto de la oración puede ser ubicado al final. The

subject of the sentence may be placed at the end. **2.** *nmf* person ■ El sujeto en frente de mi tía es alto. The person in front of my aunt is tall.

822 **exponer(se)** *vt(r)* [R] to expound on; to show (vt); to expose oneself (to danger) (vr) ■ Miguel quería exponer sus dibujos en la galería. Michael wanted to show his drawings at the gallery. El editor expuso sobre el papel de la prensa en una sociedad libre. The editor expounded on the role of the press in a free society. Los soldados se exponen al peligro todo el día. The soldiers expose themselves to danger all day long.

823 **ambiente** *nm* [R] environment, ambience, setting, surroundings ■ El ambiente es muy agradable. The ambience is very pleasant.

824 **preventivo** *aj* [R(venir) -ivo] preventive ■ Podemos ahorrar dinero con el mantenimiento preventiva. We can save money with preventive maintenance.

825 **construir** *vt* [R] to build, to construct ■ Vamos a construir una casita para el perro. We are going to build a dog house.

826 **espectáculo** *nm* [R -culo] spectacle, event ■ El espectáculo fue todo un éxito. The event was a complete success.

827 **preguntar(se)** *vt(r)* [R] to ask a question (vt); to ask oneself, to wonder (vr) ■ A ese niño le gusta preguntar mucho. That child likes to ask a lot of questions. Me pregunto si mañana puedo ir al gimnasio. I wonder if tomorrow I'll be able to go to the gym.

828 **informe** *nm* [R] report ■ El informe del presidente duró tres horas. The president's report lasted three hours.

829 **nueve** *nm, aj* [R] nine ■ Tengo nueve plátanos. I have nine bananas.

830 **negar(se)** *vt(r)* [R] to deny (vt); to deny oneself (vr) ■ Ella no lo pudo negar. She could not deny it. Me niego a viajar en avión. I refuse to travel by plane.

831 **educativo** *aj* [R -ivo] educational ■ ¿Cómo se puede mejorar el sistema educativo? How can the educational system be improved?

832 **corazón** *nm* [R] heart □ *corazoncito* sweetheart; *blando de corazón* softhearted; *llevar el corazón en la mano* to wear one's heart on one's sleeve ■ Escuchamos el latido del corazón del bebé. We listened to the baby's heartbeat.

833 **marca** *nf* [R -a] mark, brand ■ Prefiero esta marca. I prefer this brand.

834 **campeonato** *nm* [R -ato] championship ■ El campeonato inicia la próxima semana. The championship begins next week.

835 **posteriormente** *av* [R -mente] subsequently ■ Posteriormente, decidimos viajar más. Subsequently, we decided to travel more.

836 **rival** *nmf* [R] rival ■ Los rivales compitieron por su amor. The rivals competed for her love.

837 **arte** *nm* [R] art □ *bellas artes* fine arts; *arte manual* craft ■ Me gusta el arte renacentista. I like Renaissance art.

838 **brasileño** *nmf, aj* [-eño] Brazilian ■ Él es brasileño de nacimiento. He is Brazilian by birth.

839 **operativo** [R -ivo] **1.** *nm* operation ■ Extenderán por navidad el operativo antialcohol. The anti-alcohol operation will be extended through Christmas. **2.** *aj* operative ■ ¿Cuál sistema operativo usas? What operating system do you use?

840 **paz** *nf* [R] peace □ *dejar en paz* to leave alone ■ Muchos están buscando la paz interna. Many are searching for internal peace.

841 **comer** *vt* [R] to eat □ *quedarse sin comer* to go without one's lunch or food ■ Dan quiere comer chiles rellenos. Dan wants to eat *chile rellenos*. Me quedé sin comer todo el día de ayer. I went without food all day yesterday.

842 **puerta** *nf* [R] door; gate □ *puerta falsa* back or side door; *puerta giratoria* revolving door; *a puerta cerrada* behind closed doors ■ La puerta está abierta. The door is open. El perró se escapó por la puerta abierta. The dog escaped through the open gate.

843 **cantar** *vt* [R] to sing ■ Los mariachis cantan por muchas horas. The *mariachis* sing for many hours.

844 **pie** *nm* [R] foot ■ Me lastimé un pie. I hurt my foot.

845 **recuperar(se)** *vt(r)* to recuperate, make up (vt); to recuperate, to regain one's health (vr) ■ Debemos recuperar el tiempo perdido. We must make up the lost time. Me recuperé rápidamente después de descansar un rato. I recuperated quickly after resting a while.

846 **aprobar** *vt* [R] to approve ■ Su jefe aprobó el proyecto. His boss approved the project.

847 **proponer** *vt* [R(poner)] to propose ■ Pensamos proponer un plan. We are thinking of proposing a plan.

848 **conformar(se)** *vt(r)* [R] to form part of; to satisfy (vt); to be satisfied (vr) ■ Las mujeres conforman la mayor parte del grupo. Women form the greater part of the group. Eso me conforma. That satisfies me. Me conformo con una rebanada de pizza. I am satisfied with one slice of pizza.

849 **correr** *vi* [R] to run ■ Sylvia corrió a la tienda. Sylvia ran to the store.

850 **agencia** *nf* [R -encia] agency ■ La agencia de viajes tiene muchas promociones. The travel agency has many promotional offers.

851 **exigir** *vt* [R] to demand ■ El gerente exigió un reporte. The manager demanded a report.

852 **viaje** *nm* [R] trip ■ Estamos planeando un viaje para Cancún. We are planning a trip to Cancún.

853 **chico** [R] **1.** *nmf* boy, girl ■ El chico necesita zapatos nuevos. The boy needs new shoes. **2.** *aj* small ■ El vestido es muy chico para ella. The dress is very small for her.

854 **marcha** *nf* [R -a] march; ignition □ *en marcha* on the move ■ La marcha inició en la plaza central. The march began at the town square. No funciona la marcha del carro. The car's ignition doesn't work.

855 **ayuntamiento** *nm* municipal government ■ Las oficinas del ayuntamiento están cerca del parque. The offices of the municipal government are near the park.

856 **pasa 1.** *nf* raisin □ *ciruela pasa* prune ■ Me gusta el arroz con pasas. I like rice with raisins. Esta semana las ciruelas pasas están en oferta. Prunes are on sale this week. **2.** *vti* third person present tense of *pasar* ■ ¿Qué pasa? What's happening?

857 **aumento** *nm* [R -o(1)] gain, increase □ *ir en aumento* to increase, grow ■ Elisa recibirá un aumento en su salario. Elisa will receive an increase in her salary.

858 **permanecer** *vi* [R] to remain ■ El niño permaneció callado. The child remained quiet.

859 **abandonar** *vt* [R] to abandon ■ Es triste cuando los padres abandonan a sus hijos. It is sad when parents abandon their children.

860 **definir** *vt* [R] to define ■ El primer paso es definir el problema. The first step is to define the problem.

861 **entender** *vt* [R] to understand ■ No entiendo la tarea. I don't understand the homework.

862 **imponer** *vt* [R] to impose ■ El gobierno impuso la pena capital para los secuestradores. The government imposed the death penalty on kidnappers.

863 **correspondiente** *aj* [R -ente(1)] corresponding ■ Para encontrar más información, haz click en el hipervínculo correspondiente. To find more information, click the corresponding hyperlink.

864 **infantil** *aj* [R -il] infantile; pertaining to babies ■ Me dió pena verla actuar tan infantil. I was embarrassed to see her acting so infantile. Quiero comprar algunos juguetes infantiles. I want to buy some babies' toys.

865 **cancha** *nf* playing field or court ■ Los niños están jugando en la cancha de beisbol. The children are playing on the baseball field.

866 **aire** *nm* [R] air □ *compresor de aire* air compressor ■ Me agrada el aire puro de las montañas. I love the pure mountain air.

867 **brindar** *vt* [R] to toast (with a drink); to give, to present ■ El papá de la novia brindó por los novios. The father of the bride toasted the bride and groom. Nuestros amigos nos brindaron mucho apoyo. Our friends gave us a lot of support.

868 **plazo** *nm* period (time) before a deadline □ *terminarse el plazo* the deadline is (plus date); *de largo plazo* long term; *de corto plazo* short term; *a plazos* by installments, on the installment plan ■ Se termina el plazo el 20 de agosto. The deadline is August 20. El banquero nos preguntó si queríamos un préstamo de corto o de largo plazo. The banker asked us if we wanted a short-term or long-term loan. Mis tíos están pagando la lavadora y secadora a plazos. My aunt and uncle are paying for the washer and dryer by installments.

869 **meta** *nf* goal, objective ■ Ellos cumplirán sus metas. They will complete their goals.

870 **denuncia** *nf* [R -a] denunciation, accusation ■ La denuncia se hizo pública. The accusation was made public.

871 **leer** *vt* [R] to read ■ Sus niños ya saben leer. Their (his, her, your) children already know how to read.

872 **presupuesto** *nm* [R(poner) -o(1)] budget; estimate (billing) ■ Empezamos cada mes con

un presupuesto. We begin each month with a budget. Le pedí al mecánico un presupuesto. I asked the mechanic for an estimate.

873 **confirmar** *vt* [R] to confirm ■ El doctor confirmó nuestra sospecha. The doctor confirmed our suspicion.

874 **legislador,-a** *nmf* legislator ■ El legislador anunció su opinión. The legislator announced his opinion.

875 **penal** [R] **1.** *nm* prison; penalty kick ■ El criminal pasó varios años en el penal. The criminal spent several years in prison. El partido de fútbol terminó en penales. The game ended with penalty kicks. **2.** *aj* penal; penalty ■ El abogado estudió el código penal. The lawyer studied the penal code.

876 **viejo** *aj* [R] old ■ El sillón viejo tiene muchos hoyos. The old chair has many holes.

877 **disposición** *nf* [R -ción] disposition; disposal, service ■ Mateo tiene buena disposición. Matthew has a good disposition. Juan puso su casa a nuestra disposición. John put his house at our disposal.

878 **artículo** *nm* [R -culo] article □ *artículo definido, artículo determinado* definite article; *artículo indefinido, artículo indeterminado* indefinite article ■ Leí el artículo sobre arqueología maya. I read the article about Mayan archaeology

879 **lesionar(se)** *vt(r)* [R] to wound (vt); to become wounded, to hurt oneself (vr) ■ El terrorista lesionó muchos inocentes. The terrorist wounded many innocent people. Me lesioné la pierna. I hurt my leg.

880 **comprar** *vt* [R] to buy ■ Mi esposa fue a comprar fruta y verduras. My wife went to buy fruit and vegetables.

881 **proporcionar** *vt* [R] to proportion, to distribute; to supply, to give ■ La iglesia les proporciona comida a la gente que lo necesita. The church distributes food to those that need it. Los bomberos proporcionaron ayuda inmediata. The fire fighters gave immediate help.

882 **conducir** *vt* [R] to conduct; to drive (car) ■ Vamos a conducir un experimento. We are going to conduct an experiment. El jóven aprendió a conducir. The young man learned to drive.

883 **manejar** *vt* [R] to manage; to drive (car) ■ Ellos dos escriben su presupuesto mensual para manejar las finanzas de la familia. The two of them write their monthly budget in order to manage the family finances. Nora quiere manejar el carro a Tijuana. Nora wants to drive the car to Tijuana.

884 **empresario,-a** *nmf* [R] empresario ■ Los empresarios se reunieron para discutir el nuevo proyecto. The businessmen met to discuss the new project.

885 **fijar** *vt* [R] to pay attention to, to fix; to attach; to post ■ Fíjate bien. Pay close attention. Laura fijó su vista en el cielo. Laura fixed her sight on the sky. Esther fijó anuncios para su venta de cochera. Esther posted flyers for her garage sale.

886 **documento** *nm* [R -o(1)] document ■ El documento explica todo claramente. The document explains everything clearly.

887 **crisis** *nf* crisis ■ La crisis lo abrumó. The crisis overwhelmed him.

888 **miércoles** *nm* Wednesday □ *Miércoles de Ceniza* Ash Wednesday ■ El miércoles me saqué la lotería. On Wednesday I won the lottery.

889 **pasada** *nf* [R] path, passage, a way to arrive at another location ■ Ellos bloquearon la pasada. They blocked the path.

890 **aclarar** *vt* [R] to clarify, to clear up; to lighten the color of something ■ Tomás quiere aclarar algunas de sus dudas. Thomas wants to clear up some of his doubts. Ana aclaró su pelo. Anna lightened her hair.

891 **martes** *nm* Tuesday ■ El martes es su aniversario de bodas. Tuesday is their wedding anniversary.

892 **adquirir** *vt* [R] to acquire ■ El dueño del rancho adquirió otro terreno. The owner of the ranch acquired another piece of land.

893 **grave** *aj* [R] grave, serious ■ La situación se tornó grave. The situation turned serious.

894 **red** *nf* [R] net; network ■ Los pescadores usaron una red para capturar a los peces. The fishermen used a net to catch the fish. Las computadoras están conectadas por red. The computers are connected by a network. El programa salió por toda la red televisiva. The program appeared on the entire television network.

895 **ganador,-a** *nmf* winner ■ El ganador recibió su medalla. The winner received his medal.

896 **escribir** *vt* [R] to write ■ Timoteo escribió una carta a su mamá. Timothy wrote a letter to his mother. ¿Cómo se escribe? How do you spell it?

897 **ministro** *nm* [R -o(1)] minister ■ El ministro vive cerca de la iglesia. The minister lives close to the church.

898 **grado** *nm* [R] grade (school); degree (measurement) ■ La mayoría de los niños aprenden a leer en el primer grado. Most children learn to read in first grade. La temperatura está a 70 grados Fahrenheit. The temperature is 70 degrees Fahrenheit.

899 **práctica** *nf* [R -a] practice ■ Para aprender, la práctica es esencial. In order to learn, practice is essential.

900 **ventaja** *nf* [R] advantage ■ Hay muchas ventajas. There are many advantages.

901 **consumo** *nm* [R] consumption ■ Se prohibe el consumo de alcohol en las escuelas. The consumption of alcohol is prohibited in schools.

902 **llamada** *nf* [R -ada(2)] call (telephone); call (curtain) ■ Usted ha recibido una llamada de larga distancia. You have received a long-distance phone call. El director señaló la última llamada. The director signaled the last (curtain) call.

903 **tigre** *nm* tiger ■ Los Tigres ganaron el campeonato. The Tigers won the championship.

904 **auto** *nm* [R] auto, automobile, car ■ Quiero lavar el auto. I want to wash the car.

905 **quinto,-a** **1.** *nmf* fifth one □ *la quinta* fifth note of a triad (music) ■ Quiero la quinta. I want the fifth one. Los acordes están compuestos de la primera, la tercera, y la quinta. The chords are composed of the first, the third, and the fifth (notes of a triad). **2.** *aj* fifth ■ El quinto mes del año es mayo. May is the fifth month of the year.

906 **conductor,-a** [R] **1.** *nmf* driver; conductor ■ El conductor del taxi no es muy precavido. The taxi driver is not very cautious. El agua es un buen conductor de electricidad. Water is a good conductor of electricity. **2.** *aj* driving; conducting ■ Su amor a la familia es la fuerza conductora de su éxito. His love for his family is the driving force behind his success.

907 **lucir(se)** *vt(r)* [R] to shine, to sport (vt); to look great, to be a shining example, to be brilliant (said of a person) (vr) ■ Ella está luciendo una figura esbelta. She is sporting a slim figure. Ella se luce en su vestir. She looked great (in the way she was dressed). Ella se lució en su presentación. She was brilliant in her perfomance.

908 **precisar** *vt* [R] to explain carefully or precisely ■ El maestro necesita precisar todos los detalles. The teacher needs to explain precisely every detail.

909 **relacionar(se)** *vt(r)* [R] to relate (match), to connect (vt); to be related to (vr) ■ El detective relacionó el cabello con el crimen. The detective connected the strand of hair to the crime. El tema actual se relaciona al anterior. The current topic is related to the preceding one.

910 **iniciativa** *nf* [R] initiative ■ Ellos tomaron la iniciativa. They took the initiative.

911 **importancia** *nf* [R -ancia] importance ■ Aquí estamos para hablar de un asunto de mucha importancia. We are here to talk about an issue of great importance.

912 **incrementar** *vi* [R] to move forward incrementally, to increase incrementally ■ Para tener éxito, debemos incrementar los ingresos. In order to be successful, we must increase our income.

913 **aprender** *vt* [R] to learn ■ A ella le gusta aprender los idiomas. She likes to learn languages.

914 **droga** *nf* [-a] drug ■ La droga era abundante en ese país. Drugs were abundant in that country.

915 **división** *nf* [R -sión] dividing line; division; division (mathematical operation) ■ Esta calle es la división de las dos ciudades. This street is the dividing line between the two cities. La división del grupo fue el resultado de una mentira. The division of the group was caused by a lie. A Roberto no le gusta hacer problemas de división. Robert does not like doing division problems.

916 **canal** *nm* [R] canal; channel ■ El canal lleva agua a las granjas del valle. The canal carries water to the valley farms. El canal deportivo es muy popular. The sports channel is quite popular.

917 **corresponder** *vt* to correspond, to go to, to belong to; to feel the same way ■ A ti te corresponden tres. Three go to you. Yo

correspondo a tus sentimientos. I feel the same way as you.

918 **juez** *nmf* [R] judge □ *juez de paz* justice of the peace ■ El juez decidió rápidamente. The judge decided quickly.

919 **profesor,-a** *nmf* [R] professor, teacher ■ El profesor tiene muchos estudiantes en su clase. The professor has many students in his class.

920 **internet** *nm* Internet ■ La abuela mantiene contacto con sus nietos por medio del internet. The grandmother maintains contact with her grandchildren by way of the Internet.

921 **propiedad** *nf* [R] property ■ La propiedad se encuentra cerca del río. The property is located near the river.

922 **instalar** *vt* [R] to install ■ Él necesita instalar un programa antivirus en su computadora. He needs to install an antivirus program on his computer.

923 **regidor,-a** *nmf* [-dor(1)] member of a governing council ■ El regidor asistió a la entrevista. The member of the governing council attended the interview.

924 **festejar** *vt* [R] to celebrate with a party ■ Festejamos el día cuando pagamos la última déuda. We celebrated the day when we paid off our last debt.

925 **verdadero** *aj* [R -ero(2)] true ■ El amor verdadero dura para siempre. True love lasts forever.

926 **elevar** *vt* [R] to elevate, to raise ■ Elevaron los precios en la tienda. They raised prices in the store.

927 **asimismo** *av* in the same way, similarly, also, likewise, as well ■ Asimismo su esposa estudió intensivamente. Likewise, his wife studied intensively.

928 **firmar** *vt* [R] to sign (one's name) ■ Hay que firmar el cheque para depositarlo. It's necessary to sign the check in order to deposit it.

929 **impedir** *vt* [R] to impede, to stop ■ Armando impidió que él la golpeara. Armando stopped him from hitting her.

930 **luna** *nf* [R] moon □ *luna de miel* honeymoon; *media luna* half moon; *tener lunas* to be moody ■ Ayer hubo luna llena. Yesterday there was a full moon.

931 **tampoco** *av* neither, either ■ Tampoco yo voy a ir a París. I am not going to Paris either.

932 **curso** *nm* [R -o(1)] course (often a short course or training program) ■ Pronto terminará el curso. The course will end soon.

933 **verde** [R] **1.** *aj* green □ *uvas verdes* sour grapes ■ Mi prima prefiere el vestido verde. My cousin prefers the green dress. **2.** *nm* green ■ El verde es el símbolo de la armonía. Green is the symbol of harmony.

934 **elegir** *vt* [R] to elect; to choose ■ La gente va a elegir su presidente. The people are going to elect their president. Clara eligió su vestido de novia. Clara chose her bridal gown.

935 **protección** *nf* [R -ción] protection ■ El guardaespaldas ofrece protección. The bodyguard offers protection.

936 **vs.** *prep* vs., versus ■ En la primera vuelta hay tres partidos: Argentina vs. Uruguay, Perú vs. España y El Salvador vs. Venezuela. In the first round there are three matches: Argentina vs. Uruguay, Peru vs. Spain, and El Salvador vs. Venezuela.

937 **conflicto** *nm* [R] conflict ■ El conflicto ha durado siete años. The conflict has lasted seven years.

938 **olvidar(se)** *vt(r)* [R] to forget (vt); to be forgotten by someone (vr) ■ Ellos olvidaron sus llaves. They forgot their keys. Se me olvidó sacar la basura. I forgot to take out the trash.

939 **operar** *vt* [R] to operate ■ Ella está muy enferma y por eso decidieron operar. She is very ill and therefore they decided to operate.

940 **confianza** *nf* [R -anza] confidence, trust ■ Le tengo confianza. I trust him (her, you).

941 **dato** *nm* [-o(1)] information, data, piece of information ■ Necesito un dato importante. I need an important piece of information.

942 **conocimiento** *nm* [R -miento] knowledge ■ El conocimiento sobre la computación ha aumentado mucho. Knowledge about computers has increased greatly.

943 **balón** *nm* ball ■ Tiró el balón con todas sus fuerzas. He threw the ball with all his strength.

944 **pregunta** *nf* [R -a] question □ *hacer una pregunta* to ask a question. ■ Tengo una pregunta. I have a question. Sam me hizo una pregunta. Sam asked me a question.

945 **llegada** *nf* [R -ada(2)] arrival □ *a la llegada* on arrival ■ Ella esperaba su llegada. She was expecting your (his, her, their) arrival.

946 **vuelta** *nf* [R] turn; return; trip back □ *dar la vuelta* to turn; *darse la (una) vuelta* to go out (for a ride or a stroll, etc); *ida y vuelta* round trip, out and back ■ Dimos la vuelta en la esquina. We turned at the corner. La vuelta duró mucho menos tiempo que la ida. The trip back lasted much less time than the trip out. Carolina y yo nos dimos una vuelta en el bosque. Carolina and I went for a ride (or walk) in the forest. Quiero comprar un boleto de ida y vuelta. I want to buy a round-trip ticket.

947 **década** *nf* [-ada(1)] decade ■ Magaly trabajó en el gobierno hace más de una década. Magaly worked in the government more than a decade ago.

948 **ejercicio** *nm* [R -icio] exercise ■ Él ya hizo sus ejercicios. He already did his exercises.

949 **quitar(se)** *vt(r)* [R] to take off, to remove (vt); to take off or remove (from oneself), to move or remove (oneself) (vr) ■ Quiero quitar las cortinas para lavarlas. I want to remove the curtains in order to wash them. Al entrar a la casa me quito los zapatos. On entering the house, I take off my shoes. Me quité para que no me pegara la pelota. I moved to avoid being hit by the ball.

950 **particular** *aj* [R] private □ *la casa particular* private home ■ Esta dirección es la de una casa particular. This address is that of a private home.

951 **camión** *nm* [R] bus; truck ■ El camión de pasajeros arrived on time. The passenger bus llegó a tiempo. El camión de carga es de dieciocho ruedas. The cargo truck has eighteen wheels.

952 **víctima** *nf* victim ■ Mi hermana intentó ayudar a las víctimas del huracán. My sister tried to help the hurricane victims.

953 **entrevistar** *vt* [R] to interview ■ El reportero quería entrevistar al presidente. The reporter wanted to interview the president.

954 **factor** *nm* factor ■ Debemos considerar todos los factores. We must consider all factors.

955 **compartir** *vt* [R] to share ■ Mis hermanos comparten un cuarto. My brothers share a room.

956 **transladar** *vt* to transport; to move from one place to another, to travel ■ La Cruz Roja transladó paquetes de ayuda a las víctimas del huracán. The Red Cross transported aid packages to the victims of the hurricane. A los turistas europeos les gusta transladarse en tren. European tourists like to travel by train.

957 **analizar** *vt* [R] to analyze ■ Es importante analizar la situación. It's important to analyze the situation.

958 **detectar** *vt* to detect ■ El guardia no detectó ningún metal. The security guard did not detect any metal.

959 **grabar** *vt* to record, to make a recording ■ Los músicos quieren grabar su primer CD. The musicians want to record their first CD.

960 **adecuar** *vt* [R] to arrange or rearrange or to adapt for a purpose ■ Antes de que llegara las integrantes del club de mujeres, Delia tuvo que adecuar su casa. Before the members of the women's club arrived, Delia had to rearrange her house.

961 **reportar** *vt* [R] to report ■ Samuel reportó la pérdida de su licencia. Samuel reported losing his license.

962 **alemán,-ana** 1. *nmf* German person ■ La mayoría de los alemanes prefiere internet a la televisión. The majority of Germans prefer the Internet to the television. 2. *nm* German language ■ Este programa le ayudará a aprender alemán. This program will help you learn German. 3. *aj* German ■ Nuestro perro es un pastor alemán. Our dog is a German shepherd.

963 **transporte** *nm* [R] transport; transit ■ Los trenes operan para el transporte de turistas. The trains operate for the transport of tourists. Llamamos a la agencia de transporte rápido para verificar su horario. We called the rapid transit agency in order to verify their schedule.

964 **inglés,-a** 1. *nmf* English person ■ Los ingleses practican el criquet, el tenis, el polo y el golf. The English play cricket, tennis, polo, and golf. 2. *nm* English langauge ■ Mariela practicó mucho su inglés. Mariela practiced her English a lot. 3. *aj* English ■ Nos encontramos a una mujer inglesa en la tienda. We ran into an English woman at the store.

965 **positivo** *aj* [R] positive ■ Teresa es conocida por su actitud positiva. Teresa is known for her positive attitude.

966 **presunto** *aj* [R] alleged, supposed ■ Entrevistaron a la presunta víctima del delito.

They interviewed the alleged victim of the crime.

967 **mamá** *nf* [R] mom, mother ■ ¿Dónde nació tu mamá? Where was your mother born?

968 **animal** *nm* animal ■ Ella observa los animales a travez de la ventana. She observes the animals through the window.

969 **europeo** *aj* European (person) ■ Mi patrón tiene un carro europeo. My boss has a European car.

970 **carretera** *nf* [R] highway ■ La carretera está en construcción. The highway is under construction.

971 **carro** *nm* [R] car; chariot ■ Fuimos al lago en el carro. We went to the lake in the car. Vi una película en la cuál salieron muchos soldados romanos en sus carros. I saw a movie that showed many Roman soldiers in their chariots.

972 **paciente** [R] **1.** *nmf* patient ■ El médico cuida a sus pacientes con mucho empeño. The doctor cares for his patients fervently. **2.** *aj* patient ■ Isabel es muy paciente con sus hermanos. Isabel is very patient with her brothers and sisters.

973 **francés,-esa 1.** *nmf* French person ■ Los franceses elegirán este domingo a su presidente. The French will elect their president this Sunday. **2.** *nm* French language ■ Ellos saben hablar el francés. They know how to speak French. **3.** *aj* French ■ Su cuñado es francés. His brother-in-law is French.

974 **origen** *nm* [R] origin ■ Es de origen griego. He is of Greek origin.

975 **rechazar** *vt* [R] to reject ■ El director rechazó el proyecto inicial. The director rejected the initial proposal.

976 **supuesto** [R] **1.** *nm* hypothesis, theory, idea, case □ *por supuesto* of course ■ En el supuesto de que César no pueda terminar su contrato, Eva tomará su lugar. In the case that Cesar is unable to complete his contract, Eve will take his place. Por supuesto que sí! Yes, of course! **2.** *aj* supposed ■ Los guardaespaldas frustraron el supuesto intento de secuestro. The bodyguards thwarted the supposed kidnapping attempt. **3.** *vt* past participle of the verb *suponer* ■ La ofensiva ha supuesto la detención de 1.460 personas.

The offensive entailed the detention of 1,460 people.

977 **cifra** *nf* [R -a] numerical figure, number ■ Una cifra récord de viajeros visitaron Latino América el año pasado. A record number of travelers visited Latin America last year.

978 **corto** *nf* [R] short □ *corto de vista* shortsighted ■ El tiempo es corto. Time is short. Ella usa el pelo corto. She wears short hair.

979 **sindicato** *nm* [R -ato] trade union ■ Hay una elección del sindicato al fin del mes. There is a union election at the end of the month.

980 **disminuir** *vt* [R] to diminish, to decrease, to reduce ■ Disminuya su velocidad. Slow down.

981 **alguien** *pron* [R] someone ■ Alguien está ocupando mi asiento. Someone is sitting in my seat.

982 **parroquia** *nf* [R] parish; parish church ■ La parroquia se construyó hace doscientos años. The parish church was built two hundred years ago.

983 **gira** *nf* [-a] tour (performance) ■ Los cantantes empezaron la gira en abril. The singers began the tour in April.

984 **procuraduría** *nf* public prosecutor's office, district attorney's office ■ Mi esposa y yo fuimos a la procuraduría para declarar. My wife and I went to the public prosecutor's office to file an affidavit.

985 **completo** *aj* [R] complete ■ El documento está completo. The document is complete.

986 **depender** *vi* [R] to depend ■ La señora Hernández depende mucho de sus hijos. Mrs. Hernández depends a lot on her children.

987 **latino,-a** [R -ino(2)] **1.** *nmf* Latino ■ El gerente de la librería creó una sección para los latinos. The manager of the bookstore created a section for Latinos. **2.** *aj* Latin, Latino, Latin-American ■ Visita el sitio de talentos latinos de cine, radio y televisión. Visit the site of Latino stars of the movies, radio, and television.

988 **andar** *vi* [R] to walk; to date or to court □ *andarse por las ramas* to beat around the bush; *andar en lenguas* to be much talked about, to be the subject of gossip ■ Alex y yo andamos al centro. Alex and I walked downtown. Samuel anda con Jasmín. Samuel is dating Jasmine.

989 ■ **democrático** *aj* [R -ico(2)] democratic ■ La gente está a favor de elecciones democráticas.

The people are in favor of democratic elections.

990 **derrota** *nf* [R -a] defeat ■ Luís no está contento por la derrota de su equipo favorito. Louis is not happy with the defeat of his favorite team.

991 **ojo** *nm* [R] eye □ *¡mucho ojo!* watch out!; *no pegar ojo* not to sleep a wink ■ Me duele el ojo derecho. My right eye hurts.

992 **telenovela** *nf* [R(teléfono, novela)] soap opera ■ La telenovela empieza a las 7 de la tarde. The soap opera begins at 7 p.m.

993 **mesa** *nf* [R] table; plateau □ *centro de mesa* centerpiece (for a table); *servicio de mesa* table service ■ Luisa empezó a poner la mesa. Louise began to set the table.

994 **promover** *vt* to promote ■ Los dueños de la mueblería están pensando en promover a Paulo. The owners of the furniture store are thinking of promoting Paul.

995 **mínimo** [R] **1.** *nm* minimum ■ Necesitas un mínimo de dos años de experiencia para solicitar el empleo. You need a minimum of two years of experience in order to apply for this job. **2.** *aj* minimum ■ Elizabeth está ganando el salario mínimo. Elizabeth is earning the minimum wage.

996 **norteamericano,-a** [-ano] **1.** *nmf* North American (usually used in reference to United States citizens) ■ El señor parecía un norteamericano. The man appeared to be North American. **2.** *aj* North American ■ Los negociantes norteamericanos viajan mucho por aquí. North American businessmen travel here often.

997 **quizá(s)** *av* perhaps ■ Quizá mañana llueva. Perhaps it will rain tomorrow.

998 **ejército** *nm* [R -o(1)] army □ *ejércitos de tierra, mar y aire* armed forces ■ En el ejército se aprende sobre disciplina. In the army one learns about discipline.

999 **objeto** *nm* [R -o(1)] object ■ No pude identificar el objeto en la foto. I was unable to identify the object in the photo.

1000 **bolsa** *nf* [R] purse; pocket; sack; stock exchange ■ Se me olvidó la bolsa en la casa. I forgot my purse at the house. Puse mi cartera en la bolsa de mi pantalón. I put my wallet in my pants pocket. Llevamos tres bolsas de abarrotes. We carried three sacks of groceries.

Compramos varias acciones de la bolsa. We bought several stocks on the stock exchange.

coordinador,-a [R] **1.** *nmf* coordinator **2.** *aj* coordinating

industrial *aj* [R] industrial

apuntar *vt* [R] to note, to write down; to point

oriente [R] **1.** *nm* the East **2.** *aj* east, eastern

1005 **figura** *nf* [R -a] figure

levantar(se) *vt(r)* [R] to raise (vt); to get up, to get oneself up (vr)

pase *nm* [R] pass

publicar *vt* [R] to publish

lesión *nf* [R -sión] lesion, wound, injury

1010 **insistir** *vt* [R] to insist

defender *vt* [R] to defend

intención *nf* [R -ción] intention

estilo *nm* [R] style

lleno *aj* [R] full

1015 **descubrir** *vt* [R] to discover

corte [R] **1.** *nm* cut **2.** *nf* court (legal)

época *nf* era, age

rápido *aj* [R -ido(1)] quick, rapid

dolor *nm* [R] pain

1020 **fuego** *nm* [R] fire; cold sore □ *fuegos artificiales* fireworks; *echar leña al fuego* to add fuel to the flames

eliminar *vt* [R] to eliminate

previo *aj* [R] previous

álbum *nm* album □ *álbum de recortes* scrapbook

avance *nm* [R] advance, forward motion

1025 **doble** [R] **1.** *nmf* double (acting) **2.** *aj* double **3.** *av* double

priísta **1.** *nmf* member of the political party PRI (*Partido Revolucionario Institucional*) **2.** *aj* pertaining to PRI (*Partido Revolucionario Institucional*)

empleado,-a [R] **1.** *nmf* employee **2.** *vt* past participle of the verb *emplear*

atrás *av* [R] behind; ago □ *años atrás* years ago

revolución *nf* [R -ción] revolution

1030 **piel** *nf* [R] skin

exterior *nm* [R] exterior

allá *av* there (at a distant point not near the person being addressed)

breve *aj* [R] brief

proteger *vt* [R] to protect

1035 **ciudadanía** *nf* [R -ería(2)] citizenship

sumar *vt* [R] to add up

cubrir *vt* [R] to cover

villa *nf* village

honor *nm* [R] honor

1040 **funcionar** *vi* [R] to function, to work (mechanical objects)

mirar *vt* [R] to look □ *estar a la mira* to be on the lookout

asistente *nmf* [R -ente(2)] assistant

investigador,-a *nmf* [R] investigator

opinión *nf* [R] opinion

1045 **presión** *nf* [R -sión] pressure; prison

directo *aj* [R] direct

encabezar *vt* [R] to head, to lead

atentar *vt* to attempt to commit a crime

vigilancia *nf* [R] vigilance

1050 **bajar(se)** *vt(r)* [R] to lower (vt); to lower oneself, to get off (vr) □ *bajarse del camión* to get off the bus

acceso *nm* access

calificar *vt* [R -ificar] to grade □ *calificar de irresponsable* to call irresponsible, to stamp as irresponsible

boda *nf* wedding

sala *nf* [R] living room □ *sala de juntas* meeting room; *sala de espera* waiting room

1055 **sección** *nf* [R] section

israelí *nmf, aj* Israeli

negociación *nf* [R -ción] negotiation

surgir *vi* to appear suddenly or unexpectedly

faltar *vt* [R] to lack; to miss (a meeting, school, etc.)

1060 **error** *nm* error, mistake

legal *aj* [R] legal

gusto *nm* [R -o(1)] pleasure; taste; whim □ *mucho gusto* nice to meet you; *estar a gusto* to feel at home, to feel comfortable

tratamiento *nm* [R -miento] treatment

verano *nm* [R] summer

1065 **mitad** *nf* half; middle

radio [R] **1.** *nf* radio (apparatus) **2.** *nm* radio (industry, form of entertainment)

justo [R] **1.** *aj* just, fair, right **2.** *av* justly, fairly, rightly; tightly fitting, snugly

feliz *aj* [R] happy

sueño *nm* [R -o(1)] dream; sleep □ *tener sueño* to be sleepy; *conciliar el sueño* to woo or induce sleep; *entre sueños* half-asleep

1070 **modo** *nm* [R] manner, way, custom □ *de todos modos* in any case; *de otro modo* otherwise

incremento *nm* [R -o(1)] increment

violencia *nf* [R -encia] violence

costa *nf* [R] coast

versión *nf* version

1075 **destinar** *vt* [R] to destine

firma *nf* [R -a] signature; business firm

sede *nf* site or meeting place of an event; see, Holy See (Catholic)

actitud *nf* [R -itud] attitude

respetar *vt* [R] to respect

1080 **cobrar** *vt* [R] to charge (money) □ *cobrar un cheque* to cash a check

combate *nm* [R] combat

estudiante *nmf* [R -ante(2)] student

indio,-a *nmf, aj* Indian

marcador [R -dor(2)] **1.** *nm* marker; scoreboard **2.** *aj* marking; useful for marking □ *la aguja marcadora del velocímetro* the (marking) needle of the speedometer

1085 **policíaco** *aj* [R] police

preocupar(se) *vt(r)* [R(ocupar)] to cause worry (vt); to worry, to be worried (vr)

bulevar *nm* boulevard

golpe *nm* [R] hit □ *golpe de estado* coup d'état

promedio *nm* [-o(1)] average

1090 **localidad** *nf* [R -idad] locality

estudiar *vt* [R] to study

senador,-a *nmf* senator

famoso *aj* [R -oso] famous

caro,-a [R] **1.** *aj* expensive **2.** *nf* cara face

1095 **desaparecer(se)** *vt(r)* [R] to cause to disappear (vt); to disappear (vr)

cercano *aj* [R] near, close

comida *nf* [R -ido(2)] food

contraer(se) *vt(r)* [R] to contract (disease), to contract (shorten), to form a contract (such as a marriage contract) (vt); to contract, to become shortened (vr)

fácil [R] **1.** *aj* easy **2.** *av* easy

1100 **identificar** *vti* [R -ificar] to identify (vt); to identify (with) (vi)

solución *nf* [R] solution

adulto,-a *nmf* adult

impulsar *vt* [R] to cause to move; to push forward

laboral *aj* [R] work

1105 **cultural** *aj* [R] cultural

subir *vti* [R] to climb; to go up

vialidad *nf* [-edad] highway system

secundario *aj* secondary

▶ **secundaria** *nf* the equivalent of junior high or middle school

basura *nf* trash

1110 **carne** *nf* [R] meat; flesh □ *carne magra* lean meat

despedida *nf* [R -ido(2)] farewell □ *despedida de soltera* bridal shower

hacienda *nf* [R] country estate

pobre [R] **1.** *nmf* poor person □ *pobre de solemnidad* desperately poor person **2.** *aj* poor

antiguo *aj* [R] ancient, old

1115 **esperanza** *nf* [R -anza] hope □ *llenar la esperanza* to fulfil one's hopes

cuestión *nf* [R] question (in the sense of an issue or problem) □ *una cuestión de la ética* a question of ethics; *cuestión candente* burning question

controlar *vt* to control

realmente *av* [R -mente] really

salón *nm* [R] classroom; ballroom; salon

1120 **valer** *vi* [R] to be worth □ *vale la pena* it's worth it

parque *nm* park

serio *aj* serious

sol *nm* [R] sun

residencia *nf* [R -encia] residence

1125 **autor,-a** *nmf* author

desconocer *vt* [R] to fail to recognize or remember

sorprender *vt* [R] to surprise

americano,-a [-ano] **1.** *nmf* American **2.** *aj* American

entrenador,-a *nmf* coach, trainer

1130 **aportar** *vti* [R] to donate (vt); to reach port (vi)

anotación *nf* [R -ción] annotation; note

sesión *nf* session

básico *aj* [R -ico(2)] basic

numeroso *aj* [R -oso] numerous

1135 **papa** [R] **1.** *nf* potato **2.** *nm* pope

frío *aj* [R] cold □ *muerto de frío* frozen stiff

queja *nf* [R -a] complaint

pérdida *nf* [R -ido(2)] loss

aficionado [R -ado(2)] **1.** *nmf* fan (admirer); enthusiast **2.** *aj* fond of

1140 **meter(se)** *vt(r)* [R] to put in (vt); to go inside (vr)

opción *nf* [-ción] option

invertir *vt* [R] to invest; to invert (math)

corona *nf* [R -a] crown

denunciar *vt* [R] to denounce; to report to the authorities

1145 **papá** *nm* dad, father

preferir *vt* [R] to prefer

especialmente *av* [R -mente] especially

indígena **1.** *nmf* indigenous person (form does not change) **2.** *aj* indigenous

usuario *nmf* [-ario(2)] user, one who uses (form does not change)

1150 **tecnológico** *aj* [R -ico(2)] technological

hotel *nm* [R] hotel

vivo *aj* [R -ivo] alive □ *color vivo* bright color

abogado,-a *nmf* attorney, lawyer □ *abogado del diablo* devil's advocate

juvenil *aj* [R -il] youth

1155 **deseo** *nm* [R -o(1)] desire

efectivo [R -ivo] **1.** *nm* cash **2.** *aj* effective

peligro *nm* [R] danger □ *correr peligro* to be in danger

preparación *nf* [R -ción] preparation

anual *aj* [R -al(2)] annual

1160 **avión** *nm* [R] airplane

azteca **1.** *nmf* Aztec (form does not change) **2.** *aj* Aztec

noticia *nf* [R -a] news item □ *las noticias* the news; *noticia bomba* bombshell (news), sensational news; *agencia de noticias* news agency

aeropuerto *nm* [R] airport

dispuesto [R] **1.** *aj* inclined, available **2.** *vti* disposed (past participle of the verb *disponer*)

1165 **durar** *vi* [R] to last

principalmente *av* [-mente] principally; mainly

respeto *nm* [R -o(1)] respect

tecnología *nf* [R -ería(2)] technology

panista *nmf* [-ista] supporter of the political party *PAN (Partido Acción Nacional)*

1170 **suerte** *nf* luck □ *probar suerte* to try one's luck

involucrar *vr* to be involved in

apertura *nf* [R -ura(1)] opening; aperture

jardín *nm* [R] garden

intervención *nf* [R -ción] intervention

1175 **ofensivo** *aj* [R -ivo] offensive

puerto *nm* [R] port

beneficiar(se) *vt(r)* [R] to benefit (vt); to benefit from (vr) □ *beneficiarse de (con)* to profit from

autorizar *vt* [R -izar] to authorize

normal *aj* [R] normal

1180 **delegación** *nf* [R -ción] delegation

hogar *nm* [R] home

aproximadamente *av* [R -mente] approximately

primario *aj* [-ario(2)] primary

▶ **primaria** *nf* primary school

programar *vt* [R] to program

1185 **elaborar** *vt* [R] to elaborate; to produce through a series of steps

romper *vt* [R] to break □ *romperse la cabeza* to rack one's brains

edificio *nm* [R -icio] building

importar *vti* [R] to import (vt); to matter (vi)

ganado *nm* [R] cattle; group of domesticated animals

1190 **generación** *nf* [R -ción] generation; graduating class

peor [R] **1.** *aj* worst **2.** *av* worse

similar *aj* [R] similar

constante *aj* [R] constant

favorito,-a *nmf, aj* [R -ito(2)] favorite

1195 **visitante** *nmf* [R -ante(2)] visitor

contemplar *vt* [R] to contemplate, to think about

pleno *aj* [R] full

legislativo *aj* [R -ivo] legislative

detalle *nm* [R] detail

1200 **tiro** *nm* [R -o(1)] shot; fight

carta *nf* [R] letter (message); playing card □ *echar las cartas* to tell a person's fortune by cards; *carta blanca* carte blanche

demasiado [R] **1.** *aj* too much **2.** *av* too much

resulta *nf* [R -a] result

ingresar *vti* [R] to enroll (vt) □ *ingresar en (a)* to enroll in (at) (vi)

1205 **cáncer** *nm* cancer

dueño,-a *nmf* owner

registro *nm* [R -o(1)] register; registration

localizar *vt* [R -izar] to localize; to find

ministerial *aj* [R] ministerial

1210 **tarea** *nf* [R] homework; chore

placa *nf* plate (license); plaque

histórico *aj* [R -ico(2)] historical

matar *vt* [R] to kill □ *matar dos pájaros de un tiro* to kill two birds with one stone (shot)

sangre *nf* [R] blood □ *donante de sangre* blood donor; *a sangre fría* in cold blood; *banco de sangre* blood bank; *pura sangre* thoroughbred; *tener (mucha) sangre fría* to be cool as a cucumber; *transfusión de sangre* blood transfusion

1215 **artístico** *aj* [R -ico(2)] artistic

amar *vt* [R] to love □ *amar de corazón* to love wholeheartedly; *amar con locura* to love madly

sexual *aj* [R] sexual

par *nm* [R] pair □ *sin par* matchless, peerless

finalizar *vt* [R -izar] to finalize; to end

1220 **pertenecer** *vi* [R] to belong to

autónomo *aj* [R] autonomous, independent

disputar(se) *vt(r)* [R] to argue, to dispute, to fight (vt); to be played (vr)

mensaje *nm* [R] message

excelente *aj* [R] excellent

1225 **salario** *nm* [R -ario(2)] salary

practicar *vt* [R] to practice

pared *nf* [R] wall

presidencial *aj* [R -cial] presidential

propósito *nm* [R] purpose □ *a propósito* by the way, on purpose

1230 **tradicional** *aj* [R] traditional

contrato *nm* [R -o(1)] contract

recientemente *av* [R -mente] recently

universitario *aj* [R] university

frontera *nf* [R] border; frontier

1235 **delantero** [R -ero(2)] **1.** *nm* forward (sport) **2.** *aj* head, front □ *las luces delanteras* headlights

▶ **delantera** *nf* forward position (sport); front part

mandar *vt* [R] to send; to order □ *¿Mande?* Yes, Ma'am?, Yes, Sir?

creación *nf* [R -ción] creation

acontecimiento *nm* [R -miento] event

restaurante *nm* restaurant □ *vagón restaurante* dining car

1240 **estrategia** *nf* strategy

leche *nf* [R] milk □ *leche en polvo* powdered milk

precisamente *av* [R -mente] precisely, exactly

acerca *av* [R] *acerca de* about

aniversario *nm* [R -ario(2)] anniversary

1245 **film** *nm* film

secar *vt* [R] to dry

comprometer(se) *vt(r)* [R] to commit (vt); to commit oneself, to become engaged (vr)

índice *nm* [R] index

revelar *vt* [R] to develop (film)

1250 **montar** *vt* [R] to mount □ *montar a pelo, montar en pelo* to ride bareback

petición *nf* [R -ción] petition

denominar *vt* [R] to denominate; to give a name to

implicar *vt* [R] to implicate

reconocimiento *nm* [R(conocer) -miento] recognition

1255 **revolucionario,-a** [R -ario(2)] **1.** *nmf* revolutionary **2.** *aj* revolutionary

promoción *nf* promotion

isla *nf* [R] island

teléfono *nm* [R] telephone

beisbol *nm* baseball

1260 **derecha** *nf* [R] right (direction)

periodista *nmf* [R -ista] newspaper reporter; journalist

plantel *nm* campus

festival *nm* [R -al(1)] festival

colegio *nm* [R] secondary school

1265 **cometer** *vt* [R] to commit (crime, etc.)

ciclo *nm* [R] cycle

asumir *vt* [R] to assume (a position or responsibility)

valle *nm* valley □ *valle de lágrimas* vale of tears

vino *nm* [R] wine □ *vino tinto* red wine; *vino de Jerez* sherry; *vino de Oporto* port wine

1270 **caída** *nf* [R] fall, drop, descent

toro *nm* [R] bull □ *toro bravo, toro de lidia* fighting bull; *plaza de toros* bullring

altura *nf* [R -ura(1)] height

cuidar *vt* [R] to care for, to take care of

delgado *aj* [R] thin

1275 **herir** *vt* [R] to wound, to injure

caber *vi* [R] to fit

edición *nf* [R -ción] edition

robo *nm* [R -o(1)] robbery

tránsito *nm* [R -ito(2)] traffic; traffic police

1280 **puente** *nm* bridge; three-day week-end □ *puente colgante* suspension bridge; *puente giratorio* swing bridge; *puente levadizo* drawbridge

negativo [R -ivo] **1.** *nm* photographic negative **2.** *aj* negative

sanitario [R -ario(2)] **1.** *nm* restroom **2.** *aj* sanitary

bello *aj* [R] pretty, beautiful □ *Bella Durmiente* Sleeping Beauty

junta *nf* [R -a] meeting

1285 **reporte** *nm* report

derrotar *vt* [R] to defeat

escena *nf* [R] scene

alianza *nf* [R -anza] alliance

suspender *vt* [R] to suspend

1290 **cierre** *nm* [R] closing time; zipper

testigo,-a *nmf* witness □ *testigo presencial* eyewitness

británico *aj* [-ico(2)] British

cuidado *nm* [R] care

simplemente *av* [R -mente] simply

1295 **colombiano** *aj* [-ano] Columbian

mandatario *aj* mandatory

perro,-a *nmf* dog

propietario,-a [R -ario(2)] **1.** *nmf* property owner **2.** *aj* proprietary

asamblea *nf* [R] assembly

1300 **cubano** *aj* [-ano] Cuban

pena *nf* [R] embarrassment; shame; penalty; feeling of anguish □ *¡qué pena!* what a shame!; *vale la pena* it's worth it; *merece la pena* it's worth it

productivo *aj* [R -ivo] productive

amenaza *nf* [R -a] threat

foro *nm* forum

1305 **corrupción** *nf* [-ción] corruption

emitir *vt* [R] to emit

proceder *vi* [R] to proceed

revisar *vt* [R(vista)] to review, to check

corporación *nf* [R] corporation

1310 **facultad** *nf* [-tad] faculty; school □ *la facultad de administración* the school of administration

horario *nm* [R -ario(1)] schedule; hours (business)

tasa *nf* fee; tax levy □ *tasa de natalidad* birth rate; *tasa de mortalidad* death rate

garantizar *vt* [R -izar] to guarantee

robar *vt* [R] to rob, to steal

1315 **agropecuario** *aj* [R] pertaining to agriculture and animal farming

recuperación *nf* [-ción] recuperation (money or health)

electrónico *aj* [R] electronic

empatar *vt* to tie (games)

participante *nmf* [R -ante(1)] participant

1320 **duelo** *nm* duel

coordinación *nf* [R -ción] coordination

lluvia *nf* [R] rain

ritmo *nm* [R] rhythm

característico [R -ico(2)] **1.** *nf característica* characteristic (quality) **2.** *aj* characteristic, distinctive

1325 **comerciante** *nmf* [R -ante(2)] businessman, businesswoman

aplicación *nf* [R -ción] application; appliqué

arriba *av* up □ *de arriba abajo* from head to toe

compra *nf* [R -a] bought item; buying □ *ir de compras* to go shopping

tribunal *nm* [-al(1)] tribunal

1330 **confiar** *vi* [R] to have faith in; to trust (in) □ *confío en tí* I trust you

pendiente *nm* [R] errand; item on a "to do" list

piloto,-a *nmf* [R] pilot □ *piloto de altura* navigator

someter *vt* [R] to submit

actualidad *nf* [R -idad] present time □ *en actualidad* nowadays

1335 **manejo** *nm* [R -o(1)] management, managing; driving

concepto *nm* [R] concept

periódico *nm* [R] newspaper

bebé *nmf* [R] baby

sacerdote *nm* [R] priest

1340 **únicamente** *av* [-mente] only, exclusively

alma *nf* [R] soul

cumpleaños *nm* [R] birthday

echar *vt* [R] to throw out □ *echarse a perder* to turn bad (food); *echar la culpa* to blame

enorme *aj* [R] enormous

1345 **comentario** *nm* [R] comment

obstante *av* □ *no obstante* however, nevertheless

investigar *vt* [R] to investigate, to research

amplio *aj* [R] wide

reiterar *vt* to reiterate, to repeat for clarification

1350 **administrativo** *aj* [R -ivo] administrative

basar *vt* [R] to base

italiano,-a **1.** *nmf* Italian **2.** *nm* Italian language **3.** *aj* Italian

jurídico *aj* [R] pertaining to law

capitalino *aj* [-ino(2)] pertaining to the capital city

1355 **acordar(se)** *vt(r)* [R] to come to an agreement (vt); to remember (vr)

procedimiento *nm* [R -miento] procedure

bendición *nf* [R -ción] blessing

brazo *nm* [R] arm (body) □ *ser el brazo derecho de alguien* to be someone's right-hand man

prometer *vt* [R] to promise

1360 **institucional** *aj* [R] institutional

intérprete *nmf* [R] interpreter

análisis *nm* [R] analysis

judicial *aj* [R -cial] judicial

ocasionar *vt* [R] to cause or bring about

1365 **regalo** *nm* [R -o(1)] gift

constituir *vt* [R] to constitute

café [R] **1.** *nm* coffee; café; brown **2.** *aj* brown

convocar *vt* to convene; to call together

circular [R] **1.** *nm* bulletin, circular **2.** *aj* circular **3.** *vti* to circulate

1370 **octavo** [R -avo] **1.** *nm* eighth **2.** *nf* octave **3.** *aj* eighth; octave

ordenar *vt* [R] to order; to put in order

fase *nf* [R] phase

totalmente *av* [-mente] totally

cultivo *nm* [R -ivo] cultivation (also figurative)

1375 **democracia** *nf* [R] democracy

siquiera *av* even, at least □ *ni siquiera* not even

azúcar *nm, nf* [R] sugar (may be either masculine or feminine) □ *azúcar extrafino* powdered sugar; *azúcar en polvo* powdered sugar

protesta *nf* [R -a] protest

tirar *vt* [R] to throw away; to shoot (gun or in sport) □ *tirar un tiro* to fire a shot

1380 **comunicado** [R] **1.** *nm* written notice, memorandum **2.** *aj* easily accessed

original *aj* [R] original

revisión *nf* [R(vista) -sión] review; inspection

allí *av* there (at a distant point from the person being addressed)

página *nf* [R -a] page

1385 **ropa** *nf* [R] clothing □ *ropa interior* underwear; *ropa sucia* dirty laundry

bordo *nm* [R] edge; bump (road)

permiso *nm* [R] permission; permit

solicitud *nf* [R -itud] employment application; willingness to help

letra *nf* [R] letter (alphabet); lyrics □ *letra mayúscula* capital letter; *letra minúscula* small letter; *copiar al pie de la letra* to copy word for word; *a la letra* to the letter, literally, strictly

1390 **circulación** *nf* [R -ción] circulation

finanzas *nfpl* [-anza] finances

especie *nf* [R] species □ *la especie humana* mankind

sorpresa *nf* [R] surprise

empate *nm* tie (game)

1395 **limpiar** *vt* [R] to clean

reflejar *vt* [R] to reflect

agrupación *nf* [R -ción] grouping

camioneta *nf* [R -eta] passenger van; pick-up truck

plantear *vt* [R] to explain, demonstrate, or present a plan

1400 **bandera** *nf* [R] flag □ *alzar bandera, levantar bandera* to raise the flag; *bandera de paz* flag of truce (white flag)

talento *nm* [R] talent

diablo *nm* [R] devil □ *abogado del diablo* devil's advocate

crítico,-a [R -ico(2)] **1.** *nmf* critic **2.** *aj* critical (urgent or disparaging)

potable *aj* potable; drinkable

1405 **bosque** *nm* [R] forest; park with trees

convenio *nm* agreement

crimen *nm* [R] crime

regular *aj* [R] regular

video *nm, aj* [R] video

1410 **bravo** *aj* [R] fierce

ejercer *vt* [R] to practice a profession or position; to exercise (authority)

bastante *av* [R] enough

piedra *nf* [R] rock

destino *nm* [R] destiny

1415 **festejo** *nm* [R -o(1)] celebration

cárcel *nf* [R] jail; prison

padecer *vt* [R] to suffer from

recepción *nf* [R -ción] reception

fallecer *vi* [R] to pass away, to die

1420 **finalidad** *nf* [R -idad] finality

recién *aj* [R] recent

rock *nm* rock (music)

hectárea *nf* hectare (about 2.5 acres)

recomendar *vt* [R] to recommend

1425 **revista** *nf* [R(vista)] magazine

bebida *nf* [R -ido(2)] drink

independencia *nf* [R(depender) -encia] independence

barrio *nm* barrio, neighborhood

preso *nm* prisoner

1430 **repetir** *vt* [R] to repeat

individuo *nm, aj* [R -uo] individual

esquina *nf* [R] corner

régimen *nm* [R] regimen

terrorista *nmf, aj* [R -ista] terrorist

1435 **agrícola** *aj* [R] agricultural

alcohol *nm* [R] alcohol

estimar(se) *vt(r)* [R] to esteem (vt); to esteem each other (plural) (vr)

misa *nf* [R] mass (religious) □ *clérigo de misa* priest

nupcial *aj* [-cial] nuptial

1440 **protagonizar** *vt* [R -izar] to perform the lead in a play, movie, etc.

recinto *nm* place (formal)

rey *nm* [R] king □ *los Reyes Magos* the Magi, the Three Wise Men; *Adoración de los Reyes Magos* Epiphany

carácter *nm* [R] character

complicar(se) *vt(r)* [R] to complicate (vt); to become complicated (vr)

1445 **gas** *nm* [R] gas

limpieza *nf* [R -eza] cleaning, tidying

alternativa, -o 1. *nf* alternative **2.** *aj* alternative

sagrado *aj* [R] sacred

transmitir *vt* to transmit

1450 **contribuir** *vt* [R] to contribute

permanente *aj* [R] permanent

computadora [-dor(2)] **1.** *nm* computer **2.** *aj* computer

luchar *vi* [R] to struggle, to fight

sexto [R] **1.** *nm* sixth one **2.** *aj* sixth

1455 **asistencia** *nf* [R -encia] attendance

conectar *vt* to connect

despedir(se) *vt(r)* [R] to dismiss; to say good-bye (when the other party is leaving) (vt); to emit, to say good-bye, to bid farewell (when the person speaking is leaving) (vr)

juicio *nm* [R -icio] trial; good judgement □ *Juicio Final* Last Judgment

mar *nm, nf* [R] sea (masculine or feminine)

1460 **atacar** *vt* [R] to attack

disparo *nm* [R -o(1)] shot

clásico [R] **1.** *nm* classic **2.** *aj* classical

mover(se) *vt(r)* [R] to move (vt); to move oneself (vr)

plática *nf* [-a] talk

1465 **soltero,-a** [R -ero(2)] **1.** *nmf* bachelor, bachelorette, single person, spinster **2.** *aj* single, unmarried

ciencia *nf* [R] science

escolar *aj* [R] school □ *año escolar* school year

cadena *nf* [R] chain □ *cadena perpetua* life imprisonment

cita *nf* [R -a] appointment; date (with another person); quote □ *cita de Shakespeare* Shakespearean quote

1470 **detención** *nf* [R -ción] detention

nuevamente *av* [R -mente] again

soler *vi* to be in the habit of (used to)

fotografía *nf* [R -ería(2)] photography

sembrar *vt* [R] to sow, to plant seeds

1475 **planear** *vt* [R] to plan

medicina *nf* [R] medicine □ *medicina casera* home remedies

pobreza *nf* [R -eza] poverty

descartar *vt* discard

delegado,-a *nmf* [R] delegate

1480 **guardar** *vt* [R] to save, to keep

deuda *nf* [R] debt

prácticamente *av* [R -mente] practically

demandar *vt* [R] to sue

portero,-a *nmf* [R] goalie, goalkeeper (soccer, etc.)

1485 **golpear** *vt* [R] to hit

estación *nf* [R] station; season of the year

dama *nf* lady □ *dama de compañía* bridal attendant; *damas chinas* Chinese checkers

intenso *aj* [R] intense

coincidir *vi* [R] to coincide

1490 **gestión** *nf* [R] administration, management

recuerdo *nm* [R] keepsake; memory

automóvil *nm* [R] automobile

caminar *vi* [R] to walk

rama *nf* [R] branch □ *andarse por las ramas* to beat around the bush

1495 **sentar(se)** *vt(r)* [R] to seat (someone else) (vt); to be seated (vr)

fundamental *aj* [R] fundamental

respectivo *aj* [R] respective

protagonista *nmf* [R] protagonist

capaz *aj* [R -az] capable

1500 **frecuencia** *nf* [R -encia] frequency

químico,-a [R] **1.** *nmf* chemist **2.** *aj* chemical
▶ **química** *nf* chemistry

impacto *nm* [-o(1)] impact

territorio *nm* [R(tierra) -orio(1)] territory

género *nm* [R] genre; gender; class; genus

1505 **experto,-a** [R] **1.** *nmf* expert **2.** *aj* expert

reto *nm* [-o(1)] challenge

bancario *aj* [R -ario(2)] related to banks and banking

limitar *vt* [R] to limit

atractivo *aj* [R -ivo] attractive

1510 **dieta** *nf* [R] diet

sentimiento *nm* [R -miento] feeling

separar *vt* [R] to separate

acercar(se) *vt(r)* [R] to move (something) closer (vt); to draw near to (vr)

prestar(se) *vt(r)* [R] to lend (vt); to offer oneself, to offer one's services, to help out (vr) □ *pedir prestado* to borrow

1515 **clínica** *nf* [R] clinic

femenil *aj* [-il] women's, of women □ *reunión femenil* women's meeting

recorte *nm* [R(cortar)] detailed cutting

admitir *vt* [R] to admit

bombero,-a *nmf* firefighter

1520 **nota** *nf* [R -a] note

temprano *av* [R] early

aceite *nm* [R] oil

anillo *nm* ring

baile *nm* [R] dance

1525 **circuito** *nm* [R] circuit

hermoso *aj* [R] beautiful

interesante *aj* [R -ante(1)] interesting

semifinal *aj* [R(fin)] semifinal

solucionar *vt* [R] to solve, to resolve

1530 **academia** *nf* [R] academy

científico *aj* [R -ico(2)] scientific

reserva *nf* [R -a] reserve

herida *nf* [R -ido(2)] wound

dulce [R] **1.** *nm* candy **2.** *aj* sweet

1535 **apreciar** *vt* [R] to appreciate

resolución *nf* [R(solución) -ción] resolution

comprender *vt* [R] to understand; to grasp (a concept or idea)

peligroso *aj* [R -oso] dangerous

encima *av* [R] on top

1540 **fruta** *nf* [R] fruit □ *fruta del tiempo* fruit in season

petróleo *nm* [R] petroleum; oil

soldado *nm* [R] soldier □ *soldado raso* private soldier

divertir(se) *vt(r)* [R] to entertain (vt); to have fun (vr)

grasa *nf* [R] fat; grease

1545 **limón** *nm* [R] lemon; lime

fe *nf* [R] faith

relevo *nm* [-o(1)] relief, substitute

católico *aj* [R -ico(2)] catholic; Catholic

dormir *vi* [R] to sleep □ *Bella Durmiente* Sleeping Beauty

1550 **séptimo** *aj* [R -ésimo] seventh

ronda *nf* [R -a] rounds (of vigilance)

seguramente *av* [R -mente] surely; probably, more than likely

tarifa *nf* tariff; fee

flor *nf* [R] flower □ *flor de la edad* prime or bloom of youth; *decir flores* or *echar flores* to pay compliments; *en flor* in blossom

1555 **regreso** *nm* [R -o(1)] return

especialista *nmf* [R -ista] specialist (form does not change)

mente *nf* [R] mind

consecutivo *aj* [R] consecutive

escaso *aj* [R] scarce □ *andar escaso de* to be short of

1560 **muchacho,-a** *nmf* [R] boy, girl (usually referring to adolescents and teenagers)

cliente *nmf* [R] client, customer

cruzar *vt* [R] to cross

derivar(se) *vt(r)* [R] to derive, to come (vt); to be derived (vr)

distancia *nf* [R -a] distance

1565 **concentrar(se)** *vt(r)* [R] to concentrate (vt); to be concentrating (vr)

kilogramo *nm* [R] kilogram

olímpico *aj* [-ico(2)] Olympic

feria *nf* [R] change (coin); fair (exhibition)

preocupación *nf* [R(ocupar) -ción] worry

1570 **jugada** *nf* [R] one play in a game such as football or basketball

medir *vt* [R] to measure

cuestionar *vt* [R] to discuss a matter

clave *nf* [R] key; key note; password (computers)

combatir *vti* [R] to combat

1575 **suponer** *vt* [R(poner)] to suppose

gubernamental *aj* [R] governmental

rumbo *nm* direction, route

salvar *vt* [R] to save (rescue)

dominicano,-a [-ano] **1.** *nmf* person from the Dominican Republic **2.** *aj* referring to people or things from the Dominican Republic

1580 **juzgar** *vt* [R] to judge □ *a juzgar por* to judge by, judging from

fortalecer(se) *vt(r)* [R] to strengthen (vt); to become strong (vr)

instancia *nf* [-ancia] instance

intento *nm* [R -o(1)] intent

organizador,-a [R -dor(1)] **1.** *nmf* organizer **2.** *aj* organizing

1585 **ruso,-a** **1.** *nmf* Russian person **2.** *nm* Russian language **3.** *aj* Russian

auditorio *nm* [R -orio(1)] auditorium

telefónico *aj* [R -ico(2)] telephone □ *la cabina telefónica* telephone booth

poseer *vt* [R] to possess

tender *vti* [R] to spread out, to hang (vt); to tend to (vi)

1590 **contacto** *nm* [R -o(1)] contact

celebración *nf* [R -ción] celebration

definitivo *aj* [R -ivo] definitive

abordar *vt* [R] to board

presidir *vt* [R] to preside

1595 **torno** *nm* [R -o(1)] turntable □ *en torno* concerning, as it relates to

voluntad *nf* [R -tad] will, desire

museo *nm* [R] museum

querido,-a [R -ido(1)] **1.** *nmf* dear one **2.** *aj* dear

ausencia *nf* [R -encia] absence □ *brillar por su ausencia* to be conspicuous by one's absence

1600 **pieza** *nf* piece □ *pieza de repuesto* spare part

pintar(se) *vt(r)* [R] to paint (vt); to put on make-up, lipstick, etc. (vr)

prevenir *vt* [R(venir)] to prevent

simple *aj* [R] simple (lacking wit)

intervenir *vi* [R] to intervene

1605 **fila** *nf* [R] line (waiting); queue

límite *nm* [R] limit

aparato *nm* apparatus

captar *vt* to capture, to understand, to comprehend

corriente [-ente(1)] **1.** *nm* the actual date **2.** *nf* current (water, electricity) □ *agua corriente*

running water **3.** *aj* of poor quality; current □ *el año (mes, semana) corriente* the present year (month, week)

1610 **entrenamiento** *nm* [-miento] training

rendir(se) *vt(r)* [R] to yield (vt); to surrender (vr)

temor *nm* [R] fear

tienda *nf* [R] store, shop; tent

exportación *nf* [R -ción] exportation

1615 **previsto** *nm* [R(vista)] foreseen event

acumular *vt* [R] to accumulate

escuadra *nf* carpenter's square; squadron; squad; fleet

senado *nm* senate

boca *nf* [R] mouth □ *boca de riego* hydrant; *boca del estómago* pit of the stomach; *andar de boca en boca* to be the talk of the town

1620 **favorecer** *vt* [R] to favor; to decide in favor of

votar *vti* [R] to vote

fenómeno *nm* [R] phenomenon

temperatura *nf* [R -ura(2)] temperature

convencer *vt* [R] to convince

1625 **raíz** *nf* [R] root

subrayar *vt* [R(rayo)] to highlight; to underline

carecer *vi* to be lacking

electricidad *nf* [R -idad] electricity

arena *nf* [R] sand □ *arena movediza* quicksand

1630 **vestido** *nm* [R -ido(2)] dress

vitamina *nf* [R] vitamin

maíz *nm* [R] corn □ *harina de maíz* cornmeal

visión *nf* [R -sión] vision

infraestructura *nf* [R(estructura) -ura(2)] infrastructure

1635 **sal** *nf* [R] salt □ *sal de la Higuera* Epsom salts

extremo [R -o(1)] **1.** *nm* extreme **2.** *aj* extreme

integral *aj* [R] whole; very important; pertaining to integers (math) □ *trigo integral* whole wheat

piso *nm* [R] floor

regla *nf* [R] rule; ruler (measuring stick)

1640 **chileno** *aj* pertaining to Chile

miedo *nm* [R] fear □ *tener miedo* to be afraid (to have fear)

calentar *vt* [R] to heat, to warm up

consistir *vi* [R] to consist (of)

instrumento *nm* [R] instrument

1645 **invitación** *nf* [R -ción] invitation

taller *nm* [R] workshop

terrorismo *nm* [R -ismo] terrorism

estructura *nf* [R -a] structure

seleccionar *vt* [R] to select, to choose

1650 **ampliar** *vt* [R] to widen; to discuss more fully

belleza *nf* [R -eza] beauty

concurso *nm* [R -o(1)] contest

formación *nf* [R -ción] formation

fundación *nf* [R -ción] foundation

1655 **profundo** *aj* [R -undo] profound; deep

conservar(se) *vt(r)* [R] to conserve, to save (vt); to keep, to stay, to remain (vr)

hallar *vt* [R] to find

jamón *nm* ham

madrugada *nf* [R] early morning hours before daylight

1660 **moderno** *aj* [R] modern

tonelada *nf* [-ada(3)] ton

vendedor,-a *nmf* [R] salesman, saleswoman

criticar *vt* [R] to criticize

defensivo *aj* [R -ivo] defensive □ *estar a la defensiva, ponerse a la defensiva* to be or go on the defensive

1665 **pelea** *nf* [R -a] fight

expectativa *nf* expectation

imposible *aj* [R(posible)] impossible

merecer *vti* [R] to merit, to deserve

órgano *nm* [R] organ (of the body); organ (musical instrument)

1670 **platicar** *vti* to chat, to talk

anfitrión,-a *nmf* host, hostess

padrino,-a *nmf* godparent; sponsor

suelo *nm* floor

convivio *nm* [R] get-together, potluck

1675 **empresarial** *aj* [R] business

ruta *nf* route

trámite *nm* requirement

vuelo *nm* [R -o(1)] flight

obligación *nf* [R -ción] obligation □ *absolver de una obligación* to release from an obligation

1680 **seguidor,-a** [R -dor(1)] **1.** *nmf* follower **2.** *aj* following

comprobar *vt* [R] to prove

imaginar *vt* [R] to imagine

diálogo *nm* [R -o(1)] dialogue

independiente *aj* [R(depender)] independent

1685 **irregularidad** *nf* [R(regular) -idad] irregularity

capacitación *nf* [R -ción] training

lejos *av* [R] far

choque *nm* [R] crash

amparo *nm* [R -o(1)] protection

1690 **exposición** *nf* [R -ción] exposition

misión *nf* [R] mission

pantalla *nf* screen

pegar *vt* [R] to hit; to kick; to glue

circunstancia *nf* [R -ancia] circumstance

1695 **escrito** [R] **1.** *nm* written document **2.** *aj* written

reina [R -a] **1.** *nf* queen □ *abeja reina* queen bee **2.** *vi* he (she, it) reins (third person singular of the verb *reinar*)

naturaleza *nf* [R -eza] nature □ *naturaleza muerta* still life

pista *nf* [R] track; hint

sabor *nm* [R] flavor

1700 **secreto** [R] **1.** *nm* secret **2.** *aj* secret

contestar *vt* [R] to answer

calzada *nf* roadway which connects major avenues

enterar *vr* [R] to become aware of

superficie *nf* [R] surface

1705 **emoción** *nf* [R -ción] emotion; excitement □ *¡qué emoción!* how exciting!

librar(se) *vt(r)* [R] to free from an obligation or circumstance (vt); to be free of or from something (vr)

representación *nf* [R(presencia) -ción] representation

discutir *vt* [R] to argue

casar(se) *vt(r)* [R] to marry

1710 **diente** *nm* [R] tooth

respectivamente *av* [R -mente] respectively

constitución *nf* [R -ción] constitution

estrenar(se) *vt(r)* to use, do, or wear for the first time (vt); to be shown for the first time (vr)

rescate *nm* rescue

1715 **acostumbrar(se)** *vt(r)* [R] to be accustomed to, to be in the habit of (vt); to become accustomed (vr)

consumidor,-a [R -dor(1)] **1.** *nmf* consumer **2.** *aj* consuming

exceso *nm* [R] excess

prolongar *vt* [R] to prolong

tradición *nf* [R] tradition

1720 **dificultad** *nf* [R -tad] difficulty

consulta *nf* [R -a] consultation

escritor,-a *nmf* [R] writer

modificar *vt* [R] to modify

existencia *nf* [R -encia] existence □ *en existencia* in stock

1725 **manifestación** *nf* [R -ción] manifestation

abajo *av* [R] below □ *abajo de* below (something)

cuota *nf* payment, fee; quota

disponer(se) *vt(r)* [R] to be about to (vr) □ *disponer de* to have available, to have at your disposal (vt)

suyo *pron* his, hers, yours, theirs, its

1730 **show** *nm* show

cero *nm* zero

competir(se) *vi(r)* to compete

variedad *nf* [R -edad] variety

comunicar *vt* [R] to communicate

1735 **directamente** *av* [R -mente] directly

discurso *nm* [R] discourse, speech

disparar *vt* [R] to shoot

fórmula *nf* [R -a] formula

máquina *nf* [R] machine □ *máquina de escribir* typewriter

1740 **turno** *nm* [-o(1)] turn; work shift

oposición *nf* [R -ción] opposition

regalar *vt* [R] to give (a gift)

ambulante *aj* [R -ante(1)] able to move

prohibir *vt* [R] to prohibit

1745 **señal** *nf* [R] sign; signal

alegría *nf* [R -ería(2)] happiness □ *saltar de alegría* to jump for or with joy

militante [R -ante(2)] **1.** *nmf* militant **2.** *aj* militant

riego *nm* [-iego] watering □ *boca de riego* hydrant

grato *aj* pleasing, without problems

1750 **parar(se)** *vt(r)* [R] to stop (vt); to stand up (vr)

dañar *vt* [R] to damage

finar(se) *vi(r)* [R] to die

homicidio *nm* homicide

socio,-a *nmf* associate (person) □ *socio capitalista* financial partner

1755 **editor,-a** *nmf* [R] editor

gerente *nmf* manager

alejar(se) *vt(r)* [R] to move away (from) (vt); to move oneself away from (vr)

caracterizar(se) *vt(r)* [R -izar] to characterize (vt); to play a role, to dress up as (vr)

extender(se) *vt(r)* [R] to extend (vt); to be extended, to last (vr)

1760 **impartir** *vt* to impart

petrolero [R -ero(2)] **1.** *nm* oil tanker **2.** *nmf* petroleum merchant **3.** *aj* pertaining to petroleum or oil

chile *nm* pepper (red, green, jalapeño, etc.) ▶ **Chile** *nm* Chile

constitucional *aj* [R] constitutional

disciplina *nf* [R -a] discipline

1765 **gimnasio** *nm* gymnasium

fuga *nf* [R -a] flight, escape

trayectoria *nf* [R] trajectory

pierna *nf* [R] leg

adoptar *vt* [R] to adopt

1770 **alzar(se)** *vt(r)* [R] to raise up, to elevate, to tidy up (vt); to rise or tower (buildings, mountains), to soar (airplanes, birds), to rise up in rebellion (vr) □ *alzar velas* to hoist sails

noveno [R -eno] **1.** *nm* one-ninth (fraction) **2.** *aj* ninth

suma *nf* [R -a] sum

llenar *vt* [R] to fill; to fill out

reglamento *nm* [R -o(1)] regulation; rule

1775 **rehabilitación** *nf* [R(habilidad) -ción] rehabilitation

contratar *vt* [R] to contract

drenaje *nm* drainage

extraordinario *aj* [R] extraordinary

nacimiento *nm* [R -miento] birth

1780 **alimentación** *nf* [R -ción] feeding; nourishment

rodear(se) *vt(r)* [R] to surround (vt); to surround oneself with something (vr)

conciencia *nf* [R -encia] conscience

exitoso *aj* [-oso] successful

prioridad *nf* priority

1785 **venezolano,-a** *nmf, aj* [-ano] Venezuelan

rostro *nm* [R] face

veterano,-a *nmf, aj* veteran

establecimiento *nm* [R -miento] establishment

boleto *nm* ticket

1790 **sanción** *nf* sanction

ampliación *nf* [R -ción] widening; enlarging; enlargement

cariño *nm* [R] care

confesar *vt* [R] to confess

tardar(se) *vi(r)* [R] to take a long time; to take a certain amount of time

1795 **sexo** *nm* [R] sex □ *el bello sexo* the fair sex

urbano *aj* [R] urban

trimestre *nm* [-estre] trimester

bonito *aj* pretty, cute

cien *nm, aj* [R] hundred □ *ciento* hundred (when the quantity is more than one hundred); *ciento treinta* one hundred thirty; *por ciento* percent

1800 **enseñar** *vt* [R] to teach; to show

específico *aj* [R -ico(2)] specific

expresión *nf* [R -sión] expression

medicamento *nm* [R] medicine

sano *aj* [R] healthy

1805 **dividir** *vt* [R] to divide □ *No me puedo dividir* I can't be in two places at the same time

activo *aj* [R -ivo] active

amarillo *nm, aj* [R] yellow

corredor,-a [R] 1. *nmf* runner 2. *nm* corridor 3. *aj* running

garantía *nf* [R] guarantee

1810 **enlace** *nm* [R] the union or marriage of newlyweds

extraño *aj* [R] strange

imparable *aj* [R -able] unstoppable

líquido *nm, aj* [R -ido(1)] liquid

mental *aj* [R -al(2)] mental

1815 **retiro** *nm* [R -o(1)] retiring for the evening; retreat for prayer, meditation, or study

porcentaje *nm* [R -aje(1)] percentage

reducción *nf* [R -ción] reduction

cruz *nf* [R] cross □ *en cruz* crosswise, with arms extended; *Cruz Roja* Red Cross

hit *nm* hit

1820 **experimentar** *vt* [R] to experience; to experiment

abuso *nm* [R -o(1)] abuse

matrimonial *aj* [R] matrimonial

trato *nm* [R -o(1)] agreement, deal

aéreo *aj* [R -eo(2)] air □ *correo aéreo* airmail

1825 **gobernación** *nf* [R -ción] governing

periférico *nm* loop (highway)

atlético *aj* [R -ico(2)] athletic

destruir *vt* [R] to destroy

personalidad *nf* [R -idad] personality

1830 **plata** *nf* [R] silver

carga *nf* [R -a] charge; responsibility; burden

negociar *vi* to negotiate; to do business

arrancar *vt* [R] to pull from the root; to start a race; to start forward

fama *nf* fame

1835 **funcionamiento** *nm* [R -miento] functioning

rueda *nf* [-a] wheel; circle □ *silla de ruedas, sillón de ruedas* wheelchair

tendencia *nf* [R -encia] tendency

felicitación *nf* [R -ción] congratulatory remark or writing □ *¡felicitaciones!* congratulations!

tranquilo *aj* [R] quiet, tranquil

1840 **especializarse** *vr* [-izar] to specialize

hoja *nf* [R] leaf; page □ *hojas secas* dead leaves; *hoja de afeitar* razor blade

múltiple *aj* [R] multiple

costumbre *nf* [R] custom, habit

cerveza *nf* beer

1845 **cobro** *nm* [R -o(1)] bill collecting

contento *aj* [R] content, happy

justificar(se) *vt(r)* [R] to justify (vt); to justify oneself (vr)

académico *aj* [R -ico(2)] academic

cortar *vt* [R] to cut

1850 **dirigencia** *nf* [-encia] directorship

individual *aj* [R] individual; single

acusación *nf* [R -ción] accusation

adolescente *nmf, aj* [R -ente(2)] adolescent

clasificación *nf* [R -ción] classification

1855 **cumbre** *nf* [R] hilltop

digno *aj* [R] worthy

mediano *aj* [R] medium

abuelo,-a *nmf* grandfather, grandmother (often used in the diminutive *abuelito, abuelita;* or shortened to *abue*)

ingrediente *nm* ingredient

1860 **memoria** *nf* [R] memory

escapar(se) *vt(r)* [R] to escape

amenazar *vt* [R] to threaten

portar(se) *vt(r)* [R] to carry (vt); to behave (vr)

tenis *nm* tennis

1865 **resaltar** *vt* [R(saltar)] to emphasize; to call attention to something; to highlight

subsidio *nm* [-o(1)] subsidy

complejo [R] **1.** *nm* complex **2.** *aj* complex (difficult)

portavoz *nmf* [R] announcer

bailar *vi* [R] to dance

1870 **combinar** *vt* [R] to combine

enfrentamiento *nm* [R -miento] confrontation

opinar *vi* [R] to opine, to give an opinion

reacción *nf* [R(acción)] reaction

oferta *nf* sale (special offer)

1875 **postura** *nf* [-ura(2)] posture

vigilar *vt* [R] to watch carefully □ *vigilar de cerca* to keep a close watch on

cristiano,-a *nmf, aj* [R -ano] Christian

cuadrangular *aj* quadrangular

incorporar(se) *vt(r)* [R(cuerpo)] to incorporate (vt); to sit up or stand up (vr)

1880 **realización** *nf* [R -ción] realization

distribuir *vt* [R] to distribute

mecanismo *nm* [R -ismo] mechanism

reclamar *vi* [R] to complain

comandante *nmf* [R -ante(2)] commander □ *comandante en jefe* commander-in-chief

1885 **falso** *aj* [R] false

proyectar *vt* [R] to project

concretar(se) *vt(r)* [R] to specify, to make concrete (ideas), to firm up (vt); to speak directly to the most important aspects (vr)

homenaje *nm* [R] homage

ingeniero,-a *nmf* [R] engineer

1890 **cabildo** *nm* town council

bola *nf* [R] round object; bullet

inaugurar *vt* [R] to inaugurate

probar *vt* [R] to prove; to taste

colaborar *vi* [R] to collaborate

1895 **felicidad** *nf* [R -idad] happiness

perteneciente *aj* [R] belonging, pertaining

emergencia *nf* [-encia] emergency

financiamiento *nm* [-miento] financing

récord *nm* [R] record

1900 **falla** *nf* [-a] failure

invierno *nm* [R(verano) -o(1)] winter

campestre *aj* [R -estre] rural, pertaining to the country

chivo,-a *nmf* goat

tercio *nm* [R] one-third

1905 **descanso** *nm* [R -o(1)] rest

discográfico *aj* [-ico(2)] pertaining to recorded music

impactar *vt* to impact

aparición *nf* [R -ción] apparition

baño *nm* [R -o(1)] bath; bathroom

1910 **defensor,-a** *nmf* [R] defender

definitivamente *av* [R -mente] definitely

ecología *nf* ecology

ilegal *aj* [R] illegal

asesinato *nm* [R] murder

1915 **perredista** *nmf* [-ista] supporter of the political party *PRD (Partido Revolucionario Democrático)*

agricultura *nf* [R] agriculture

contaminación *nf* [-ción] contamination

huelga *nf* strike (labor)

pasajero,-a [R -ero(2)] **1.** *nmf* passenger **2.** *aj* passing

1920 **requisito** *nm* [R] requirement

consejero,-a *nmf* [R] counselor

agrario *aj* [R] agrarian

discusión *nf* [R -sión] argument

enemigo,-a *nmf* [R] enemy

1925 **lavar(se)** *vt(r)* [R] to wash (vt); to wash oneself (vr)

calor *nm* [R] heat

inicial [R -cial] **1.** *nf* initial (letter) **2.** *aj* initial

nombrar *vt* [R] to name (to a post or position)

consumir(se) *vt(r)* [R] to consume (vt); to be consumed (vr)

1930 **gigante** *aj* [R] giant

héroe *nm* [R] hero

reforzar *vt* [R(fuerza)] to reinforce

taza *nf* cup

barrera *nf* barrier

1935 **caja** *nf* [R] box □ *caja de música* music box

televisar *vt* [R(vista, teléfono)] to televise

consultar *vt* [R] to consult ☐ *consultar con la almohada* to sleep on it

tarjeta *nf* [-eta] card ☐ *tarjeta postal* postcard

audiencia *nf* [R] audience

1940 **once 1.** *nm* eleven; eleventh day of the month **2.** *aj* eleven

virtud *nf* [R] virtue

yarda *nf* yard (unit of measurement)

debate *nm* [R] debate

distribución *nf* [R -ción] distribution

1945 **huerto** *nm* orchard

modificación *nf* [R -ción] modification

atravesar(se) *vt(r)* [R] to traverse, to cross, to move through, to move into the path of something (vt); to be traversing, to be crossing, to be moving through, to be moving into the path of something (vr)

caballero *nm* [R] gentleman ☐ *ser todo un caballero* to be every inch a gentleman

clasificar *vt* [R -ificar] to classify

1950 **expulsar** *vt* [R] to expel

ideal *aj* [R] ideal

perfecto *aj* [R] perfect

rayo *nm* [R] ray; bolt of lightning

recoger(se) *vt(r)* [R] to collect, to pick up, to gather (vt); to retire for the evening or to go home (vr)

1955 **referencia** *nf* [R -encia] reference

atraer *vt* [R] to attract

firme *aj* [R] firm

mezcla *nf* [R -a] mixture

alcance *nm* [R] reach

1960 **comportamiento** *nm* [-miento] behavior

procurador,-a *nmf* district attorney

analista *nmf* [R] analyst

mensual *aj* monthly

violación *nf* [R -ción] rape; violation

1965 **respaldo** *nm* [R(espalda) -o(1)] economic backing; back-up (computers); back of a chair, couch, etc.

tamaño *nm* size

concreto *nm, aj* [R -o(1)] concrete

conversación *nf* [R -ción] conversation

gozar(se) *vt(r)* [R] to cause joy (vt); to feel joy (vr)

1970 **cocer** *vt* [R] to sew

consciente *aj* [R] conscious; aware

búsqueda *nf* [R] search

pozo *nm* [R] well (water) ☐ *pozo negro* cesspool

copia *nf* [R -a] copy

1975 **disputa** *nf* [R -a] dispute

inconformidad *nf* nonconformity

introducir *vt* [R] to introduce

plástico *nm, aj* plastic, rubber

arreglo *nm* [R -o(1)] arrangement; repair

1980 **cocina** *nf* [R -a, -ina] kitchen ☐ *libro de cocina* cookbook

convención *nf* convention

decena *nf* a group of ten

ámbito *nm* [R] environment, setting

loco *aj* [R] crazy ☐ *estar loco de remate* to be stark raving mad

1985 **paseo** *nm* [R -eo(1)] a walk; a drive; a short trip ☐ *dar un paseo* to take a walk

picar(se) *vt(r)* [R] to bite (insect), to poke, to burn or sting (said of hot spicy food) (vt); to become interested, to be hooked on (vr)

ahorro *nm* [R -o(1)] savings

cargar *vt* [R] to carry (a weight); to charge (electrical device, battery, etc.)

dorar(se) *vt(r)* [R] to plate with gold (vt); to cook until golden brown, to acquire a golden color (vr)

1990 **enfermo,-a** [R -o(1)] **1.** *nmf* sick person **2.** *aj* sick, ill

espíritu *nm* [R] spirit

originario *aj* [R] originally from

pasión *nf* [R] passion

procedente *aj* [R -ente(1)] originating in, arriving from

1995 **pensamiento** *nm* [R -miento] thought; thinking

agradecer *vi* [R] to give thanks

anuncio *nm* [R -o(1)] announcement

desempeño *nm* [R -o(1)] the fulfilling of an obligation

sierra *nf* [R] mountain; saw (carpentry) ☐ *sierra circular* buzz saw

2000 **contrayente** [R -ente(1)] **1.** *nmf* bride; groom **2.** *aj* contracting

fresco *aj* [R] fresh; cool

gobernar *vt* [R] to govern

tropa *nf* [R] troop

ejidatario,-a [-ario(2)] **1.** *nmf* person who lives in an *ejido* (small town) **2.** *aj* pertaining to an *ejido* (small town)

2005 **integración** *nf* [-ción] integration

masa *nf* dough; the masses; mass (physics)

ascender *vi* [R] to ascend

banca *nf* [R] bench; banking

casado *aj* [R] married

2010 **externo** *aj* [R] external

cartel *nm* [R] poster

extra *aj* extra

incendio *nm* [-o(1)] fire

jonrón *nm* home run (baseball)

2015 **mantenimiento** *nm* [R -miento] maintenance

paquete *nm* [-ete] package □ *paquete turístico* package tour

sustancia *nf* [R] substance

colaboración *nf* [R -ción] collaboration

escoger *vt* [R] to choose

2020 **ejecutar** *vt* [R] to execute (all meanings)

fomento *nm* [-o(1)] strengthening; medicinal application placed on the body □ *el fomento a la familia* the strengthening of the family

igualar(se) *vt(r)* [R] to equal, to match (vt); to become equal to (vr)

marido *nm* [R -ido(2)] husband

pelear *vi* [R] to fight, to argue

2025 **guardia** [R] **1.** *nm* guard, guard (group) **2.** *nf* guard duty

promotor,-a 1. *nmf* promoter **2.** *aj* promotive, promotional

quejar *vr* to complain

ajeno *aj* of another, belonging to someone else

esquema *nf* [R] schematic drawing; scheme

2030 **facilitar** *vt* [R] to facilitate, to make easier

oír *vt* [R] to hear

asociar *vt* [R] to associate

concentración *nf* [R -ción] concentration

poblado *aj* [R] populated; full, thick

2035 **batalla** *nf* [R -a] battle

favorable *aj* [R -able] favorable

método *nm* [R] method

sugerir *vt* [R] to suggest

virus *nm* virus

2040 **detallar** *vt* [R] to pay attention to detail

ganancia *nf* [R -ancia] earnings

japonés *aj* [-és] Japanese

vehicular *aj* vehicular

frecuente *aj* [R] frequent

2045 **fracaso** *nm* [R -o(1)] failure

encuesta *nf* [R -a] poll, survey

agradable *aj* [R -able] pleasant

estadístico *aj* [R -ico(2)] statistical

global *aj* [R] global

2050 **medalla** *nf* [R] medal

vicepresidente,-a *nmf* [R(presidente)] vice-president

crítica *nf* [R -a] criticism

fraccionamiento *nm* [-miento] subdivision, neighborhood

gastar(se) *vt(r)* [R] to spend (vt); to wear out (vr)

2055 **hueso** *nm* [R] bone □ *estar en los huesos* to be extremely thin; to be skin and bones

repartir *vt* [R(partir)] to divide (among), to hand out

tráfico *nm* [-o(1)] traffic

turismo *nm* [R -ismo] tourism

desempleo *nm* [R -eo(1)] unemployment

2060 **altar** *nm* altar

exclusivo *aj* [R -ivo] exclusive

incidente *nm* [R] incident

notar *vt* [R] to notice □ *se nota que* it's obvious that

platillo *nm* [R -illo(1)] dish (food) □ *platillo principal* main dish

2065 **cucharada** *nf* [-ada(3)] spoonful □ *cucharada cafetera* teaspoonful; *cucharada sopera* tablespoon

fan *nmf* fan

cebolla *nf* onion

cometido [R -ido(2)] **1.** *nm* commitment, responsibility **2.** *vt* committed (past participle of the verb *cometer*)

describir *vt* [R] to describe

2070 **inscribir(se)** *vt(r)* [R(escribir)] to sign up, to enroll (vt); to sign oneself up, to enroll oneself (vr)

ligero *aj* [R] light (weight)

logro *nm* [R -o(1)] accomplishment

pacífico *aj* [R -ico(2)] peaceful □ *Océano Pacífico* Pacific Ocean

percibir *vt* [R] to perceive

2075 **temer** *vti* [R] to fear

juventud *nf* [R -itud] youth (stage of life)

asesinar *vt* [R] to assassinate

difundir *vt* [R] to broadcast; to publish; to spread

grabación *nf* [-ción] recording

2080 **litro** *nm* liter

obrador *aj* [-dor(1)] working, laboring

conceder *vt* [R] to concede

desempeñar *vt* [R] to take out of pawn; to carry out an obligation or the duties of an office or position

uruguayo *aj* Uruguyan

2085 **votación** *nf* [R -ción] voting; vote (process)

duro *aj* [R] hard; difficult

escándalo *nm* scandal; commotion; disturbance

estelar *aj* stellar

pronunciar *vt* [R] to pronounce

2090 **rezagar** *vt* to leave behind

correo *nm* [R] mail

encantar *vt* [R] to enchant, to be very pleased by □ *me encanta bailar* I love to dance

femenino *aj* [R] feminine

obrero,-a *nmf* [R] worker, laborer □ *abeja obrera* worker bee

2095 **radicar** *vi* to take root; to live

recurrir *vi* [R] to recur

rubro *nm* heading, title, category

satisfecho *aj* [R] satisfied

síntoma *nm* [R] symptom

2100 **sonido** *nm* [R -ido(2)] sound

bar *nm* bar

despertar(se) *vt(r)* [R] to awaken, to wake up (vt); to wake oneself up (vr)

liberar(se) *vt(r)* [R] to free (vt); to free oneself, to become free (vr)

novela *nf* [R] novel; soap opera

2105 **prever** *vt* [R(vista, ver)] to foresee

texto *nm* [R] text

margen *nm* [R] margin

australiano *aj* [-ano] Australian

disminución *nf* [R] diminution; lowering, lessening

2110 **criterio** *nm* judgment; criterion

madera *nf* [R] wood

problemático *aj* [R -ico(2)] problematic

temporal [R] **1.** *nm* storm **2.** *nmf* temporary worker; seasonal employee **3.** *aj* temporary; provisional

enamorar(se) *vt(r)* [R] to cause to fall in love with (vt) □ *enamorarse de* to fall in love (vr)

2115 **laborar** *vi* [R] to labor

tensión *nf* tension

universo *nm* [R] universe

cielo *nm* [R] sky; heaven □ *escupir al cielo* to rail against Heaven □ *un cielo alegre* a bright sky

plano [R] **1.** *nm* plane **2.** *aj* flat, even

2120 **prisión** *nf* [R] prison

asignar *vt* [R] to assign to a post or job; to assign money

doce *nm, aj* [R] twelve

ganas *nfpl* desire □ *tener ganas de* to desire to

perspectiva *nf* perspective

2125 **preciso** *aj* [R] precise, exact; important

agredir(se) *vt(r)* to insult, to offend, to attack (vt); to fight each other (plural) (vr)

convocatoria *nf* summons to a meeting; notice of a meeting

poderoso *aj* [R -oso] powerful

símbolo *nm* [R] symbol

2130 **adicional** *aj* additional

influencia *nf* [R -a] influence □ *ejercer influencia en, ejercer influencia sobre* to exert influence on

moda *nf* [R] fashion, custom

primo,-a *nmf* cousin

sindical *aj* [R] union-related

2135 **mecánico,-a** *nmf* [R] mechanic

situar(se) *vt(r)* [R] to situate, to place (vt); to become situated, to be placed (in a place or situation) (vr)

triste *aj* [R] sad

ambiental *aj* [R] environmental; background □ *música ambiental* background music

formal *aj* [R] formal

2140 **gratuito** *aj* [R -ito(2)] free

motivar(se) *vt(r)* [R] to motivate (vt); to be motivated, to become motivated (vr)

patrulla *nf* [-a] patrol; patrol car

algodón *nm* cotton

aprobación *nf* [R -ción] approval

2145 **arrojar(se)** *vt(r)* [R] to throw forcefully (vt); to hurl oneself (vr) □ *arrojar el guante* to throw down the gauntlet

conquistar *vt* [R] to conquer

debut *nm* debut

descansar *vi* [R] to rest

evidencia *nf* [R -encia] evidence

2150 **monarca** *nmf* [R -arca] monarch

renovar *vt* [R(nuevo)] to renew

suspensión *nf* [R -sión] suspension; liquid medicine or syrup

chofer,-esa *nmf* driver, chauffeur

inteligencia *nf* [R -encia] intelligence

2155 **lectura** *nf* [R -ura(2)] reading

licencia *nf* [R -encia] license

recomendación *nf* [R -ción] recommendation

afgano *aj* Afghan

cabello *nm* [R] hair

2160 **evaluación** *nf* [-ción] evaluation

argumento *nm* [R -o(1)] argument

comparación *nf* [R -ción] comparison

decreto *nm* [R -o(1)] decree

emprender *vt* [R] to begin a job or business

2165 **inspector,-a** *nmf* inspector

narrar *vt* [R] to narrate

águila *nf* [R] eagle

alimentar *vt* [R] to feed; to nourish

completar *vt* [R] to complete

2170 **conducta** *nf* [R] conduct, behavior

enseguida *av* at once, right away (variation of *en seguida*)

instrucción *nf* [R -ción] instruction

auxiliar [R] 1. *nmf* assistant, helper 2. *vt* to help 3. *aj* assistant

detrás *av* behind

2175 **mando** [R -o(1)] 1. *nm* authority 2. *vt* I send (first person present tense of the verb *mandar*)

vial *aj* pertaining to roads, routes, ways, tracks, etc.

agenda *nf* agenda; planning book

ciclista *nmf* [R -ista] cyclist

décimo *nm* [R -ésimo] tenth

2180 **contraloría** *nf* [-ería(2)] controllership, comptrollership; office of the controller, office of the comptroller

designar *vt* to designate

estimable *aj* [R -able] estimable

capítulo *nm* [-culo] chapter

completamente *av* [R -mente] completely

2185 **distinguir(se)** *vt(r)* [R] to distinguish (vt); to distinguish oneself (vr)

evidente *aj* [R] evident

lanzamiento *nm* [R -miento] pitch, throw; launch

entrenar *vt* to train

episodio *nm* [R] episode

2190 **asesor,-a** 1. *nmf* counselor, adviser 2. *aj* counseling, advising

bomba *nf* [R] bomb; pump □ *bomba fétida* stink bomb

correcto *aj* [R] correct

inmueble *nm* [R(mueble)] property or estate which cannot be moved

calificación *nf* [R -ción] grade (evalutation)

2195 **cardenal** *nm* cardinal

confederación *nf* [R -ción] confederation

dominar *vt* [R] to dominate

ojalá *av* hopefully

secuestro *nm* [-o(1)] kidnapping

2200 **cancelar** *vt* to cancel

fanático,-a *nmf, aj* [-ico(2)] fanatic

presionar *vt* [R] to pressure

argumentar *vi* [R] to argue

casino *nm* [-ino(1)] casino

2205 **comparar** *vt* [R] to compare

habitación *nf* [R -ción] room (hotel or large house), suite

igualmente *av* [R] equally; (conversational) the same to you, I feel the same way

ilícito *aj* [R -ito(2)] illicit

posterior *aj* [R] subsequent; rear

2210 **fruto** *nm* [R] fruit (result) □ *el fruto de su trabajo* the fruit of his labor; *dar fruto* to yield fruit

rebelde [R] 1. *nmf* rebel 2. *aj* rebellious

taxi *nm* taxi

aventura *nf* [R -a] adventure

coordinar *vt* [R] to coordinate

2215 **entero** [R] **1.** *nm* whole thing, entirety, whole **2.** *aj* entire, whole

arras *nfpl* coins given by the groom to the bride in a wedding ceremony; token given in pledge

constructor [R] builder; pertaining to construction

exhortar *vt* to exhort

vacación *nf* [R] vacation

2220 **aparte** [R] **1.** *nm* an aside in theater or a speech **2.** *av* separately; in a new paragraph

bastar *vi* [R] to be enough

parlamentario,-a [R -ario(2)] **1.** *nmf* member of parliament **2.** *aj* pertaining to parliament; parliamentarian

recaudación *nf* [-ción] collection (taxes)

salsa *nf* [R] salsa; sauce

2225 **animar(se)** *vt(r)* [R] to encourage (vt); to become encouraged (vr)

ignorar *vt* [R] not to know; to lack knowledge (about); to be unaware of; to ignore

licenciado,-a *nmf* [R] term of respect applied to professionals, such as lawyers, engineers, etc. (not applied to medical doctors)

significativo *aj* [R -ivo] well-explained, clear, meaningful

universal *aj* [R] universal

2230 **cumplimiento** *nm* [R -miento] completion

fundador,-a *nmf* [R] founder

romántico,-a *nmf, aj* [R] romantic

tranquilidad *nf* [R -idad] tranquility

aviso *nm* [R -o(1)] warning

2235 **célula** *nf* [R] cell

costar *vt* [R] to cost; to require effort □ *me cuesta mucho trabajo* it requires a lot of effort (of me)

invadir *vt* [R] to invade

miel *nf* [R] honey; syrup □ *(coll.) dedada de miel* taste of honey; *miel de caña* molasses

beber *vt* [R] to drink

2240 **comedia** *nf* [R] comedy

condenar *vt* [R] to condemn □ *condenar a trabajos forzados* to sentence to penal servitude or hard labor

generalmente *av* [R -mente] generally

potencial *nm, aj* [R -cial] potential

útil *aj* [R] useful

2245 **fronterizo** *aj* [R -erizo] border; pertaining to the border

lento *aj* [R] slow

silencio *nm* [R -o(1)] silence

sueldo *nm* [R] salary

huevo *nm* [R] egg □ *huevo estrellado* fried egg (sunny side up); *huevo escalfado* poached egg; *huevo revuelto* scrambled egg; *huevo cocido* boiled egg

2250 **volumen** *nm* [R] volume

clima *nf* [R] climate; weather; atmosphere

pirata *nf* pirate

anoche *av* [R] last night

biblioteca *nf* [R -teca] library □ *biblioteca de consulta* reference library; *biblioteca circulante* lending library

2255 **compositor,-a** *nmf* [R] composer

consolidar *vt* to consolidate

florido *aj* [R -ido(1)] flowery

oscuro *aj* [R -ura(2)] dark

quince *nm, aj* [R] fifteen

2260 **alegre** *aj* [R] happy

autobús *nm* [R] bus

cinematográfico *aj* [R -ico(2)] cinematographic, film, movie

originar *vt* [R] to originate, to create, to begin

puntualizar *vt* [-izar] to make clear, to describe in detail

2265 **consumar** *vt* to consummate

esparcir(se) *vt(r)* to scatter, to spread (vt); to be scattered, to be amused or entertained (vr)

masivo *aj* massive

viento *nm* wind

fallar *vi* to fail, to stop working (device)

2270 **pintura** *nf* [R -ura(2)] paint; painting □ *capa de pintura* coat of paint

promesa *nf* [R] promise

cooperación *nf* [R -ción] cooperation

volar *vi* [R] to fly

autorización *nf* [R -ción] authorization

2275 **ceder** *vti* [R] to cede, to yield

interpretación *nf* [R -ción] interpretation; rendition

moneda *nf* [R] coin

perjudicar *vt* to harm, to injure (another)

afición *nf* [R -ción] hobby; interest; fondness; fans (group, but used in the singular)

2280 **continuación** *nf* [R -ción] continuation

expediente *nm* file, record □ *los expedientes* legal proceedings

facilidad *nf* [R -idad] facility (ease)

fibra *nf* fiber

filmar *vt* to film

2285 **huir** *vi* [R] to flee

banqueta *nf* sidewalk

costado *nm* side □ *de costado* sideways

emisión *nf* [R -sión] emission

internado [R -o(1)] **1.** *nm* boarding school; concentration camp **2.** *aj* referring to boarding school students, prisoners in a concentration camp, or patients in a hospital

2290 **mercancía** *nf* [R] merchandise

pelo *nm* [R] hair □ *ser de pelo en pecho* to be a he-man

puertorriqueño,-a *nmf, aj* [-eño] Puerto Rican

suizo,-a *nmf, aj* [-izo] Swiss

taxista *nmf* [-ista] taxi driver

2295 **turístico** *aj* [R -ico(2)] tourist

desviar(se) *vt(r)* [R] to detour (vt); to take a detour, to lose one's way (vr)

espalda *nf* [R] back (body) □ *a espaldas de alguien* behind someone's back

partida [-ido(2)] **1.** *nf* departure, parting; deal (cards) **2.** *aj* cut into portions, sliced □ *la naranja partida* sliced orange

preferencia *nf* [R -encia] preference

2300 **semilla** *nf* [R -illa] seed

auténtico *aj* [R] authentic

coronar *vt* [R] to crown

mediar *vi* [R] to arrive at the half-way point

molesto *aj* [R] bothersome, annoying; annoyed, bothered

2305 **oficio** *nm* [R -icio] occupation; official document □ *no tener oficio ni beneficio* to have neither profession nor means of support; *gajes del oficio* occupational hazards

refugio *nm* [R -o(1)] refuge

renta *nf* [R -a] rent

sustituir *vt* [R] to substitute

conclusión *nf* [R -sión] conclusion

2310 **provincia** *nf* [R] province

evaluar *vt* to evaluate

pelota *nf* ball

satisfacción *nf* [R -ción] satisfaction

tabla *nf* [R] plank or board

2315 **atribuir** *vt* [R] to attribute

exhibir *vt* [R] to exhibit

mío *pron* [R] mine

obispo *nm* [R] bishop

posesión *nf* [R -sión] possession

2320 **varonil** *aj* [R -il] men's; of or pertaining to men □ *ropa varonil* men's clothing

emergente *aj* [-ente(1)] emergent

encabezado *nm* [-ado(2)] headline

forestal *aj* forest

retomar *vt* to retake

2325 **renuncia** *nf* [R -a] resignation

tono *nm* [R] tone

abasto *nm* supply, supplying

devolver *vt* [R] to return, to take something back

espectacular [R] **1.** *nm* large banner **2.** *aj* spectacular

2330 **estratégico** *aj* [-ico(2)] strategic

relleno [R(lleno) -o(1)] **1.** *nm* filling **2.** *aj* refilled □ *chile relleno* refilled or stuffed chile

vital *aj* [R] vital

capturar *vt* [-ura(2)] to capture

diplomático,-a [R -ico(2)] **1.** *nmf* diplomat **2.** *aj* diplomatic

2335 **energético** *aj* [R -ico(2)] power-producing, energy-producing

llorar *vi* [R] to cry

maquilador **1.** *nf maquiladora* factory which imports the raw materials and exports the finished product **2.** *aj* pertaining to manufacturing

pescado *nm* [R] fish (caught)

respaldar *vt* [R(espalda)] to back up

2340 **sonar(se)** *vi(r)* [R] to sound (vi); to blow one's nose (vr)

urgente *aj* [R -ente(1)] urgent

brillante [R -ante(1)] **1.** *nm* diamond **2.** *aj* brilliant, shining, shiny

disponible *aj* [R -ible] available

inauguración *nf* [R -ción] inauguration

2345 **infección** *nf* [-ción] infection

aprehensión *nf* [-sión] apprehension

aseverar *vt* to assert

calmar(se) *vt(r)* [R] to calm (vt); to calm down (vr)

dental *aj* [R] dental

2350 **elenco** *nm* cast (performing)

equivocar *vr* [R] to make a mistake ■ *Me equivoqué.* I made a mistake.

frenar *vt* to brake; to apply the brakes

halcón *nm* falcon

liguilla *nf* [-illa] round-robin tournment

2355 **puro** [R -ura(2)] **1.** *nm* cigar **2.** *aj* pure □ *pura sangre* thoroughbred

rematar *vt* to offer at a very low price; to finish a stitch (sewing) □ *y para rematar* and to top it all off

alineación *nf* [R -ción] alignment

arreglar(se) *vt(r)* [R] to arrange, to fix (vt); to spiff up, to get ready, to fix (oneself) (vt)

lazo *nm* [R -o(1)] lasso (placed around the bride and groom at weddings)

2360 **provenir** *vi* to come from, to originate in (with *de*)

señalamiento *nm* [-miento] highway or street sign □ *señalamiento de desviación* detour sign

renunciar *vt* [R] to resign

violento *aj* [R -lento] violent

absoluto *aj* [R -uto] absolute

2365 **caballo** *nm* [R] horse □ *a caballo* on horseback

embarazo *nm* [-o(1)] pregnancy

fidecomiso *nm* a trust

identidad *nf* [R] identity

implementar *vt* to implement

2370 **íntimo,-a** [R] **1.** *nmf* close friend or relative **2.** *aj* intimate

judío,-a [R] **1.** *nmf* Jew **2.** *aj* Jewish

merienda *nf* an early dinner

sensación *nf* [R] sensation

esconder(se) *vt(r)* [R] to hide (vt); to hide oneself (vr)

2375 **frase** *nf* [R] sentence (of words); phrase

importación *nf* [R -ción] importation

alumbrar *vt* [R] to put light in something; to light up

deportista *nmf* [R -ista] sports enthusiast; athlete

gabinete *nm* cabinet

2380 **toque** *nm* [R] touch; electrical charge

felicitar *vt* [R] to congratulate

fiel *aj* [R] faithful

habitar *vt* [R] to inhabit; to live in

hierro *nm* [R] iron □ *hierro colado, hierro fundido* cast iron; *ser de hierro* to be as hard as iron or steel, tireless

2385 **oponer** *vt* [R(poner)] to oppose

reportero,-a *nmf* reporter

rescatar *vt* to rescue

afuera *av* [R] outside

clandestino *aj* clandestine

2390 **emplear** *vt* [R] to employ, to use

olor *nm* [R] odor □ *guisante de olor* sweet pea

remitir(se) *vt(r)* [R] to remit (vt); to remit, to refer (vr)

subsecretario,-a *nmf* [R(secretario)] assistant secretary

acta *nf* act, official certificate of marriage, birth, etc.

2395 **anteriormente** *av* [R -mente] beforehand, previously

dedo *nm* [R] finger □ *dedo meñique* little finger; *dedo anular* ring or third finger; *dedo cordial, dedo del corazón* middle finger; *dedo índice* index finger; *saberse al dedillo* to have at one's fingertips

estreno *nm* [-o(1)] first showing (film, theatrical performance, etc.), opening performance

futbolista *nmf* [-ista] soccer player

humor *nm* [R] humor

2400 **alterar(se)** *vt(r)* [R] to alter (vt); to lose control (emotionally) (vr)

cincuenta *nm, aj* [R] fifty

culpa *nf* [R -a] fault □ *tener la culpa* to be at fault

polvo *nm* [R] dust, powder □ *estar hecho polvo* to be wiped out, extremely tired

recibo *nm* [R] receipt

2405 **severo** *aj* [R -ero(2)] severe, harsh

arranque *nm* [R] pulling from the root; violent impulse

estacionar *vt* to park

riqueza *nf* [R -eza] wealth □ *abundar en riquezas* to abound in wealth

certamen *nm* competition, contest

²⁴¹⁰ **compatriota** *nmf* fellow countryman

eficiente *aj* [R] efficient

latinoamericano,-a *nmf, aj* [-ano] Latin American

SIDA *nm* AIDS

atleta *nmf* [R] athlete

²⁴¹⁵ **candidatura** *nf* [-ura(2)] candidacy

consenso *nm* [R] consensus

contienda *nf* fight, struggle

piedad *nf* [R] piety; pity

transformar(se) *vt(r)* [R(forma)] to transform (vt); to transform oneself, to become transformed (vr)

²⁴²⁰ **volante** *nm* [R] steering wheel

afueras *nfpl* [R] outskirts

anciano,-a [R] **1.** *nmf* old man or woman **2.** *nm* church elder

excepción *nf* [R -ción] exception

optar *vt* to opt, to choose, to select □ *optar por* to choose to, decide on

²⁴²⁵ **canadiense** *nmf, aj* [-ense] Canadian

cuento *nm* [R -o(1)] story, tale □ *cuento de nunca acabar* never-ending story; *cuento de viejas* old wives' tale

módulo *nm* [-culo] module

preparatoria *nf* preparatory school, high school (often referred to as *la prepa*)

punta *nf* [R] point; end of a piece of yarn, string, hair, etc.

²⁴³⁰ **transportar** *vt* [R] to transport

amante *nmf* [R -ante(2)] lover

zurdo *aj* left-handed

cirugía *nf* surgery

típico *aj* [R] typical

²⁴³⁵ **comercialización** *nf* [R -ción] commercialization

concesión *nf* [-sión] concession

concha *nf* shell; type of Mexican bread; common nickname (*Concepción*) □ *meterse en su concha* to go into one's shell

contribuyente [R -ente(1)] **1.** *nmf* contributor **2.** *aj* contributing

debutar *vi* to debut

²⁴⁴⁰ **compuesto** [R] **1.** *nm* chemical compound **2.** *aj* calm, composed, fixed, repaired **3.** *vt* composed (past participle of the verb *componer*)

explicación *nf* [R -ción] explanation

multa *nf* [-a] fine (penalty)

rendimiento *nm* [R -miento] fatigue; production

sólido *nm, aj* [R -ido(1)] solid

²⁴⁴⁵ **portería** *nf* [R] soccer goal

comicios *nmpl* elections

diseñar *vt* to design

entorno *nm* environment, immediate surroundings

explosión *nf* [R -sión] explosion

²⁴⁵⁰ **quemar(se)** *vt(r)* [R] to burn (vt); to burn oneself (vr)

servidor,-a [R] **1.** *nmf* servant **2.** *nm* server (computers)

crudo [R] **1.** *nm* crude oil **2.** *aj* raw

gritar *vi* [R] to shout, to scream

hambre *nm* [R] hunger □ *tener hambre* to be hungry; *matar de hambre* to starve to death; *hambre canina* ravenous hunger

²⁴⁵⁵ **indispensable** *aj* [R(dispensar) -able] indispensable

ponchar(se) *vt(r)* to cause a tire to go flat (vt); to blow or to go flat (tire) (vr)

sospechoso *aj* [R -oso] suspicious

capitán,-a *nmf* [R] captain

laboratorio *nm* [R -orio(1)] laboratory

²⁴⁶⁰ **rápidamente** *av* [R -mente] rapidly, quickly

saneamiento *nm* [R -miento] cleaning up; disinfecting

veinte *nm, aj* [R] twenty

bono *nm* bonus

diseño *nm* [-o(1)] design

²⁴⁶⁵ **ejidal** *aj* pertaining to an *ejido* or small town

palma *nf* [R] palm (hand; tree)

resistencia *nf* [R -encia] resistance

ajuste *nm* [R] adjustment

centavo *nm* [R -avo] hundredth; cent

²⁴⁷⁰ **lapso** *nm* lapse, period of time

crucero *nm* [R] crossing; ocean cruise

desaparición *nf* [R -ción] disappearance

gobernante [R -ante(2)] **1.** *nmf* governor; ruler; leader in the government **2.** *aj* governing

influir *vt* [R] to influence

²⁴⁷⁵ **poste** *nm* pole, post

ladrón,-a *nmf* [R] robber, thief

suicida [-ido(2)] **1.** *nmf* suicide victim **2.** *aj* suicide, suicidal

atreverse a *vr* to dare to

debajo de *av* beneath, under

2480 **determinación** *nf* [R -ción] determination

ganadería *nf* [R] -ería(2)] animal farming; cattle ranching

grito *nm* [R -o(1)] shout, cry, scream

particularmente *av* [R -mente] particularly

utilidad *nf* [R -idad] utility (not services such as electricity, water, etc.); bonus □ *ser de gran utilidad, ser de mucha utilidad* to be extremely useful

2485 **novato** *nm* [R] rookie, neophyte, newcomer

sequía *nf* [R] drought

convenir *vi* [R] to be convenient to or for □ *convenir en* to agree to, on, or about

hispano [R -ano] Hispanic person **2.** *aj* Hispanic

liberación *nf* [R -ción] liberation

2490 **solidaridad** *nf* [R -idad] solidarity

virgen [R] **1.** *nf* virgin □ *la Virgen* the Virgin Mary **2.** *aj* virgin

creador,-a *nmf* [R] creator

depositar *vt* [R] to deposit

nervioso *aj* [R -oso] nervous

2495 **patria** *nf* [R] native country □ *hacer patria* to boast about one's country

recesión *nf* recession

alerta *nf* [-a] alert

columna *nf* [R] column

fino *aj* [R] fine, delicate, of exquisite taste

2500 **hábito** *nm* [R -ito(2)] habit □ *tener por hábito* to be in the habit of

inscripción *nf* [R(escribir) -ción] inscription

navidad *nf* Christmas □ *¡Feliz Navidad!* Merry Christmas!

planeta *nm* [R] planet

techo *nm* [R -o(1)] roof

2505 **duración** *nf* [R -ción] duration

estima *nf* [R -a] esteem

existente *aj* [R -ente(1)] existent, existing; in stock

inflación *nf* [-ción] inflation

mención *nf* [R -ción] mention

2510 **nocturno** *aj* [R] nocturnal

penetrar *vt* [R] to penetrate

suave *aj* [R] soft, smooth; excellent (slang)

aspirante [R -ante(2)] **1.** *nmf* aspirant; one who aspires to be **2.** *aj* aspiring, desiring

espectador,-a *nmf* [R] spectator

2515 **fundar(se)** *vt(r)* [R] to found (establish) (vt); to be founded (established) (vr)

inmediatamente *av* [R(medio) -mente] immediately

jugo *nm* juice

molestia *nf* [R] bother, annoyance

panorama *nf* [R] panorama

2520 **tomate** *nm* tomato

cerebro *nm* [R] brain

consideración *nf* [R -ción] consideration

gato *nm* [R] cat □ *gato montés* wildcat; *dar gato por liebre* to sell a pig in a poke

monetario *aj* [R] monetary

2525 **patrón,-a** *aj* [R] **1.** *nmf* employer, boss **2.** *nm* pattern

poniente **1.** *nm* the West **2.** *aj* western, westerly

rebasar *vt* to pass (vehicular)

cansar(se) *vt(r)* [R] to tire (vt); to become tired (vr)

fomentar *vt* to foment, to instigate

2530 **inteligente** *aj* [R] intelligent

inversionista *nmf* [R -ista] investor

saldo *nm* [R] account balance

continente *nm* [R] continent

culpable *aj* [R -able] guilty □ *declarar culpable* to find guilty

2535 **emocional** *aj* [R] emotional

empujar *vt* [R] to push

montaña *nf* [R] mountain

orientar(se) *vt(r)* [R] to orientate, to give an orientation (vt); to orient oneself (vr)

presupuestal *aj* budgetary

2540 **ratificar** *vt* to ratify

vigente *aj* [R] valid

cultivar *vt* [R] to cultivate

modernización *nf* [R -ción] modernization

motor *nm* [R] motor

2545 **popularidad** *nf* [R -idad] popularity

sobrevivir *vi* [R] to survive □ *sobrevir a alguien* to outlive someone

violar *vt* [R] to rape; to violate

lector,-a *nmf* [R] reader

promocionar *vt* to promote

2550 **romano,-a** *nmf, aj* [R -ano] Roman

contexto *nm* context

equilibrio *nm* [R] equilibrium

grano *nm* [R] grain; pimple □ *ir al grano* to come or get to the point

referente *aj* [R -ente(1)] concerning

2555 **depósito** *nm* [R -ito(2)] deposit

estacionamiento *nm* [-miento] parking lot; parking place

giro *nm* [R -o(1)] complete turn; 360-degree turn; money-order

lamentar(se) *vt(r)* [R] to lament, to be sorry (vt); to lament (vr)

supremo *aj* [R] supreme

2560 **castigar** *vt* [R] to punish □ *castigar la vista* to strain one's sight

explotar *vt* [R] to explode; to exploit

tío,-a *nmf* uncle, aunt

conservación *nf* [R -ción] conservation

culminar *vi* to culminate

2565 **desplazar(se)** *vt(r)* [R] to displace, to move (vt); to become displaced (vr)

prestación *nf* [R -ción] lending

arribar *vi* [R] to arrive

conveniente *aj* [R -ente(1)] convenient

depresión *nf* [R -sión] depression

2570 **marina** *nf* [R -ina] navy; coast

saltar *vi* [R] to jump □ *saltar de alegría* to jump for or with joy; *saltarse una línea* to skip a line

transcurrir *vi* [R(curso)] to pass (time)

vegetal *nm, aj* [R] vegetable

abundar *vi* [R] to abound □ *abundar en riquezas* to abound in wealth

2575 **bateador,-a** *nmf* [R] batter (sport)

estabilidad *nf* [R -idad] stability

estrés *nm* stress

habilidad *nf* [R -idad] ability

perseguir *vt* [R] to pursue

2580 **raro** *aj* [R] strange □ *(coll.) bicho raro* funny guy, peculiar individual

triunfar *vi* [R] to triumph

agresión *nf* [-sión] aggression

delicado *aj* [R] weak; fragile; delicate

encaminar(se) *vt(r)* [R] to start someone down a path (vt); to head toward or for (vr)

2585 **mezclar** *vt* [R] to mix

televisor *nm* [R(vista, teléfono)] television

acceder *vt* [R] to accede; to concede, to permit □ *acceder a la petición* to accede or grant the request

cuesta 1. *nf* slope, incline □ *cuesta arriba* uphill; *cuesta abajo* downhill 2. *vti* third-person singular of the verb *costar*

delincuencia *nf* [-encia] delinquency

2590 **dominio** *nm* dominion, authority

queso *nm* cheese

transparencia *nf* [R -encia] transparency

averiguación *nf* [R -ción] investigation

bendecir *vt* [R] to bless

2595 **celular** [R] 1. *nm* celular telephone 2. *aj* cellular

cocaína *nf* cocaine

cubierto *nm* [R] cover

guitarra *nf* [R] guitar

interponer *vt* [R(poner)] to interpose

2600 **maravilloso** *aj* [R -oso] marvelous, wonderful

masculino *aj* masculine

vocero,-a *nmf* [R] announcer; one who sells newspapers in the street

bicicleta *nf* [R] bicycle

ganadero,-a *nmf* [R] cattle rancher

2605 **obsequiar** *vt* to give

pino *nm* [R] pine tree

rumor *nm* [R] rumor

cerro *nm* hill, mountain

competitivo *aj* [R -ivo] competitive

2610 **difusión** *nf* [R -sión] difusion; broadcasting

enfocar(se) *vt(r)* [R] to focus (vt); to focus oneself (vr)

tejer *vt* [R] to knit

verificar *vt* [R] to verify

adeudo *nm* [R -o(1)] debt

2615 **embajador,-a** *nmf* [R] ambassador

fractura *nf* [-a] fracture □ *fractura complicada* compound fracture

víspera *nf* [R] eve of an event

charro *nm* one who dresses in horse riding regalia

colectivo [R -ivo] 1. *nm* collective; shuttle 2. *aj* collective

2620 **planeación** *nf* [-ción] planning

representativo *aj* [R(presencia) -ivo] representative

sentencia *nf* [R -a] sentence (legal punishment)

sucio *aj* dirty

considerable *aj* [R -able] considerable

2625 **desastre** *nm* [R] disaster

recaudar *vt* to raise (money)

taquilla *nf* ticket booth, box office

tramo *nm* stretch or section of land

cómplice *nmf* accomplice

2630 **fracción** *nf* fraction

profesión *nf* [R -sión] profession

voluntario,-a [R -ario(2)] **1.** *nmf* volunteer **2.** *aj* voluntary

calendario *nm* [-ario(1)] calendar

código *nm* code

2635 **forzar** *vt* [R] to force

inseguridad *nf* [R(seguro) -idad] insecurity

manzana *nf* apple □ *manzana de Adán* Adam's apple

nominar *vt* [R] to nominate

peruano,-a *nmf, aj* [-ano] Peruvian

2640 **rato** *nm* while □ *al rato* after a while

riña *nf* [R] fight

estrellar *vt* [R] to cover with stars; to crack; to crash violently

milla *nf* mile

obviamente *av* [-mente] obviously

2645 **racha** *nf* period of time □ *racha buena* (period of) good times; *racha mala* (period of) bad times

cena *nf* [R -a] dinner □ *la Última Cena* the Last Supper

competidor,-a *nmf* [R] competitor

cosecha *nf* [R -a] harvest

narcotráfico *nm* drug traffic

2650 **teoría** *nf* [R] theory

admirar *vt* [R] to admire

ecológico *aj* [-ico(2)] ecological

esencial *aj* [R -cial] essential

guardameta *nmf* [R] goalie, goalkeeper

2655 **lengua** *nf* [R] tongue; language □ *andar en lenguas* to be much talked about, to be the subject of gossip; *de lengua en lengua* from mouth to mouth; *tener en la punta de la lengua* to have on the tip of one's tongue

pavimento *nm* [-o(1)] pavement

cama *nf* [R] bed □ *cama sencilla* single bed; *cama matrimonial* double bed

coalición *nf* coalition

corregir *vt* [R] to correct

2660 **fortuna** *nf* [R] fortune

intercambio *nm* [R(cambio) -o(1)] exchange

publicación *nf* [R -ción] publication

transmisión *nf* [-sión] transmission

urgir *vi* [R] to be very important, to be urgent

2665 **vincular(se)** *vt(r)* [-o(1)] to unite, to join together (vt); to be united, to be joined together (vr)

canto *nm* [R -o(1)] song

entusiasmo *nm* [R -asma] enthusiasm

naranja *nf, aj* orange □ *la media naranja* perfect match (spouse)

refugiar(se) *vt(r)* [R] to provide refuge (vt); to seek refuge, to take refuge (vr)

2670 **atrapar** *vt* to trap

calcular *vt* [R] to calculate

inclusive *av* [R] inclusive; including

orquesta *nf* orchestra

plato *nm* [R] plate, dish □ *plato fuerte* main dish

2675 **sacrificio** *nm* [R -icio] sacrifice

sonrisa *nf* [R] smile

asalto *nm* [R -o(1)] assault

aspirar a *vt* [R] to aspire; to inhale; to vacuum

controversia *nf* controversy

2680 **crema** *nf* cream

relativo *aj* [R] relative

indicador *nm* [R -dor(2)] indicator

anticipar *vt* to anticipate

desprender *vt* [R] to detach; to separate

2685 **protestar** *vt* [R] to protest

reanudar *vt* to begin again

estimular *vt* [R] to stimulate

operador,-a *nmf* [R] operator

reaccionar *vi* [R(acción)] to react

2690 **signo** *nm* [R] sign

totalidad *nf* [R -idad] totality

ajo *nm* garlic

ajustar(se) *vt(r)* [R] to adjust (vt); to adjust (oneself) (vr)

tren *nm* train

2695 **boxeo** *nm* [-eo(1)] boxing

gala *nf* [R] gala; celebration

rezar *vti* [R] to pray, to chant a prayer

transformación *nf* [R(forma) -ción] transformation

tricolor *aj* three-color

2700 **arquero** *nm* [-ero(3)] archer; goalkeeper (soccer)

diagnóstico [-o(1)] **1.** *nm* diagnosis **2.** *aj* diagnostic

diariamente *av* [R -mente] daily

insuficiente *aj* [R(suficiente)] insufficient

jubilar(se) *vt(r)* [R] to retire someone (from working) (vt); to retire (oneself, from working) (vr)

2705 **legislación** *nf* [-ción] legislation

playa *nf* [R] beach

renglón *nm* line (paper)

rincón *nm* [R] corner (street corner is *esquina*)

apóstol *nm* apostle

2710 **carencia** *nf* [-encia] lack, deficiency

creciente [R -ente(1)] **1.** *nf* crescent moon, rising tide □ *cuarto creciente* first quarter of the moon **2.** *aj* growing; increasing

guión *nm* [-ón(3)] hyphen □ *guión mayor* dash; *guión bajo* underscore mark

procurar *vt* [R] to try

santo,-a [R] **1.** *nmf* saint □ *santo titular* patron saint **2.** *aj* holy □ *Semana Santa* Holy Week

2715 **cartón** *nm* cardboard

cúbico *aj* [-ico(2)] cubic

enfatizar *vt* to emphasize

fácilmente *av* [R -mente] easily

maratón *nm* marathon

2720 **propiciar** *vt* [R] to originate or bring about something, to provoke

tristeza *nf* [R -eza] sadness

urgencia *nf* [R -encia] urgency; emergency

valorar *vt* to value; to appraise, to evaluate □ *armarse de valor* to pluck up courage

afortunadamente *av* [-mente] fortunately

2725 **antecedente** *nm* [R] antecedent □ *los antecedentes* past, background; personal history, person's records

cotidiano *aj* [R] daily

dictamen *nm* [R] judicial opinion or decision

ejemplar [R] **1.** *nm* example, specimen **2.** *aj* exemplary

especialidad *nf* [-idad] specialty

2730 **humanidad** *nf* [R -idad] humanity □ *las humanidades* humanities

timar *vt* to commit fraud

abarcar *vt* to take in; to include

inquietud *nf* [R(quieto)] uneasiness

jurisdicción *nf* [R] jurisdiction

2735 **proveedor,-a** *nmf* [R] provider

arrestar *vt* to arrest

astro *nm* [R] heavenly body

digital *aj* digital

dosis *nf* dose

2740 **ejecución** *nf* [R] execution

idioma *nm* [R] language

intelectual *aj* [R -al(2)] intellectual

orgulloso *aj* [R -oso] proud

acelerar *vt* to accelerate

2745 **círculo** *nm* [R -culo] circle □ *círculo vicioso* vicious circle

constantemente *av* [R -mente] constantly

lógico *aj* [R -ico(2)] logical

obstáculo *nm* [R -culo] obstacle

percatar *vr* to notice, to realize

2750 **tanque** *nm* tank

agricultor,-a *nmf* [R] farmer

ancho [R] **1.** *nf* width **2.** *aj* wide

déficit *nm* [R] deficit

editorial *nf* [R] publishing company

2755 **educar** *vt* [R] to educate

girar *vi* [R] to gyrate; to turn around

potencia *nf* [R -encia] power

reír(se) *vt(r)* [R] to laugh □ *reírse tontamente* to giggle; to titter; to snicker

rosa **1.** *nf* rose **2.** *aj* pink, rose-colored

2760 **semestre** *nm* [-estre] semester

trofeo *nm* trophy

arbitraje *nm* [R] officiating (sport); arbitration

descenso *nm* [R] descent

centrar *vt* [R] to center

2765 **mirada** *nf* [R] look

oreja *nf* [R] ear

reparto *nm* [R(partir) -o(1)] distribution

traje *nm* [R] suit (clothing) □ *traje cruzado* double-breasted suit

cadáver *nm* [R] cadaver

2770 **centímetro** *nm* [R] centimeter

flujo *nm* [R] flow

fraude *nm* fraud

paraguayo *aj* Paraguayan

rutina *nf* routine □ *por rutina* from (mere) force of habit, unthinkingly

2775 **soñar** *vt* [R] to dream □ *soñar con* to dream about

treinta *nm, aj* [R] thirty

valioso *aj* [R -oso] valuable

capacitar(se) *vt(r)* [R] to train (vt); to go through training, to improve one's skills (vr)

convivencia *nf* [R -encia] get-together; sharing together of time, experience, and food

2780 **gramo** *nm* gram

acerero *nm* [-ero(3)] steelworker □ *los acereros* Steelers (NFL football team from Pittsburgh)

calcio *nm* calcium

captura *nf* [-a] capture

deficiencia *nf* [R -encia] deficiency

2785 **doméstico,-a** [R] **1.** *nmf* domestic worker **2.** *aj* domestic

extensión *nf* [R -sión] extension

verdura *nf* [R -ura(1)] vegetable

atento *aj* [R] attentive

componer *vt* [R] to compose

2790 **informático** [-ico(2)] **1.** *nf* □ *informática* computer science **2.** *aj* pertaining to computer science

casilla *nf* [-illa] compartmentalized case

cuello *nm* [R] neck

elaboración *nf* [R -ción] process

embarazarse *vr* to become pregnant

2795 **goleador,-a** *nmf* scorer of goals

oportuno *aj* [R] opportune

príncipe *nm* [R] prince

rancho *nm* ranch

reparación *nf* [R -ción] repair

2800 **salarial** *aj* [R] pertaining to a salary

transición *nf* transition

apartar(se) *vt(r)* [R] to separate, to save (vt); to separate oneself (vr)

apoderar *vr* [R] to become owner

canciller *nm* chancellor

2805 **débil** *aj* [R] weak

excesivo *aj* [R -ivo] excessive

golear *vt* to score a goal

lidiar *vi* to fight, to struggle (against), to put up (with) (with *con* or *contra*)

ordinario *aj* [R -ario(2)] ordinary □ *de ordinario* usually

2810 **polémica** *nf* [R] polemic, controversy

trastorno *nm* [R -o(1)] loss of common sense or reason

versar(se) *vt(r)* to deal with (vt); to become versed in (vr)

corral *nm* [R -al(1)] corral

gordo *aj* [R] fat, chunky; used to describe someone or something disagreeable

2815 **lujo** *nm* [R] luxury □ *de lujo* deluxe

mancha *nf* [R -a] stain

pecho *nm* [R] chest; breast □ *ser de pelo en pecho* to be a he-man

suceso *nm* [R] event, occurrence

triple *aj* triple

2820 **uniformar** *vt* [R] to make uniform

desfile *nm* [R] parade

figurar *vi* [R] to figure

libertador,-a *nmf* [R] liberator

minero,-a [R -ero(2)] **1.** *nmf* miner; one who places explosive mines **2.** *aj* pertaining to mining

2825 **pitcher** *nm* pitcher (baseball)

princesa *nf* [R] princess

sudamericano,-a *nmf, aj* [-ano] South American

adaptar(se) *vt(r)* [R] to adapt (vt); to adapt oneself (vr)

asesino,-a *nmf* [R] assassin

2830 **islámico** *aj* [-ico(2)] Islamic

percepción *nf* [R -ción] perception

pollo *nm* [R] chicken

equivalente *aj* [R -ente(1)] equivalent

ingerir *vt* to drink

2835 **mentira** *nf* [R] lie, falsehood □ *de mentirilla(s)* in fun, for fun

molestar *vt* [R] to bother

solitario *aj* solitary

soportar *vt* [R] to tolerate

crónico *aj* [R -ico(2)] chronic

2840 **exhibición** *nf* [R -ción] exhibition

informativo *aj* [R -ivo] informative

sancionar *vt* to sanction (punish)

automovilista *nmf* [R -ista] car driver

extracción *nf* [-ción] extraction

2845 **incurrir** *vi* to incur

patrimonio *nm* [R] patrimony, inheritance

agradar *vi* [R] to please

auxilio *nm* [R -o(1)] help □ *primeros auxilios* first aid

desesperar(se) *vt(r)* [R] to exasperate (vt); to become impatient (vr)

2850 **marchar(se)** *vi(r)* [R] to march, to run (machine) (vt); to go away (vr)

posiblemente *av* [R -mente] possibly

publicidad *nf* [R -idad] publicity

radical *nm, aj* [R] radical

rodilla *nf* [R -illa] knee □ *de rodillas* on one's knees, kneeling

2855 **ácido** [-ido(1)] **1.** *nm* acid □ *ácido cítrico* citric acid **2.** *aj* acidic; sour

alcohólico,-a *nmf, aj* [R -ico(2)] alcoholic

beca *nf* [-a] scholarship (award)

documentación *nf* [R -ción] documentation

explosivo *nm, aj* [R -ivo] explosive

2860 **inspección** *nf* inspection

norteño,-a [R -eño] **1.** *nmf* northerner **2.** *aj* northern

pelotero,-a *nmf* ball boy or girl

proveniente *aj* [R -ente(1)] proceeding (from); originating (in)

seguimiento *nm* [R -miento] continuation

2865 **transitar** *vi* [R] to pass through (streets)

colección *nf* [R] collection

desierto *nm* [R] desert

increíble *aj* incredible

vaquero,-a *nmf, aj* [-ero(2)] cowboy

2870 **bloquear** *vt* [R] to block

impresión *nf* [R -sión] impression; printing

juguete *nm* [R -ete] toy □ *por juguete* jestingly

parcial *aj* [R -cial] partial

pistola *nf* [R] pistol

2875 **serial** *nm, aj* [R] serial

terrible *aj* terrible

cordial *aj* [R] cordial

ocupación *nf* [R -ción] occupation

aliviar(se) *vt(r)* [R] to lighten (vt); to recuperate, to recover, to give birth (vr)

2880 **cobertura** *nf* [-ura(1)] coverage

comienzo *nm* [R -o(1)] beginning, start

dimensión *nf* [R] dimension

expulsión *nf* [-sión] expulsion

inconforme *aj* not in agreement with, uncomfortable with

2885 **modalidad** *nf* [R] modality; form, manner

ola *nf* [R] wave

remate *nm* auction; sale at a low price; finishing stitch (sewing)

acreditar *vt* [R] to accredit; to vouch for; to guarantee; to extend credit; to give credence to

criminal *aj* [R] criminal

2890 **despensa** *nf* pantry

estancia *nf* [-ancia] den; waiting room

ético *aj* [R -ico(2)] ethical

▶ **ética** *nf* ethics

residente *nmf* [R -ente(1)] resident

silla *nf* [R] chair □ *silla de ruedas, sillón de ruedas* wheelchair; *silla de tijera* folding chair, deck chair

2895 **agotar(se)** *vt(r)* [R] to tire, to exhaust, to run out (vt); to become tired, to become exhausted (vr)

agresivo *aj* aggressive

basquetbol *nm* basketball

eliminación *nf* [R -ción] elimination

financiar *vt* to finance

2900 **musulmán,-a** *nmf* Moslem

reflexión *nf* [R] reflection

salvo [R] **1.** *aj* safe **2.** *av* except, outside of

tubería *nf* [R -ería(2)] plumbing

lobo,-a *nmf* wolf

2905 **ventana** *nf* [R] window

bienestar *nm* [R] well-being

combustible *nm, aj* [R] combustible

cualidad *nf* [R] quality (characteristic); (*calidad* is used when referring to caliber)

percance *nm* mishap, disaster

2910 **rechazo** *nm* [R -o(1)] rejection

tesorero *nm* [-ero(3)] treasurer

campus *nm* campus

carril *nm* [R] lane

confrontación *nf* [R -ción] confrontation

2915 **padecimiento** *nm* [R -miento] suffering

reparar *vt* [R] to repair

colega *nmf* [R] colleague

confundir *vt* [R] to confuse

desatar(se) *vt(r)* [R] to untie (vt); to untie oneself or one's belonging (shoes, ribbon), to become unleashed (figurative) (vr)

2920 **dictar** *vt* [R] to dictate

estricto *aj* strict

religión *nf* [R] religion

secuestrar *vt* to kidnap

amenizar *vt* [-izar] to make pleasant, to add one's charm to

2925 **centroamericano,-a** *nmf, aj* [-ano] Central American

combinación *nf* [R -ción] combination

ilusión *nf* [R -sión] illusion; dream, desire

nómina *nf* payroll

brigada *nf* brigade

2930 **ferrocarril** *nm* [R] train

liderazgo *nm* [-azgo] leadership

presenciar *vt* [R] to be present (unexpectedly)

solar *aj* [R] solar

sumamente *av* [R -mente] greatly

2935 **araña** *nf* spider

comisionar *vt* [R] to commission

gráfico *aj* [-ico(2)] graphic

hígado *nm* liver

manifestante *nmf* [R -ante(2)] demonstrator

2940 **milagro** *nm* [R] miracle

millonario,-a *nmf, aj* [R] millionaire

oído *nm* [R -ido(2)] ear; sense of hearing □ *entrar por un oído y salir por el otro* to go in one ear and out the other; *silbido de oídos* ringing in the ears

orgullo *nm* [R] pride

arteria *nf* artery

2945 **aunar** *vt* to unite, to join □ *aunado* united, joined, together (with)

batear *vt* [R] to bat (baseball)

nieto,-a *nmf* [R] grandchild

soledad *nf* [R] loneliness; common first name

tragedia *nf* [R] tragedy

2950 **triunfador,-a** [R -dor(1)] 1. *nmf* conqueror; one who triumphs 2. *aj* conquering; triumphal

cristal *nm* [R] crystal

leyenda *nf* legend

movilización *nf* [R -ción] mobilization

postal 1. *nf* postcard 2. *aj* postal

2955 **afiliar(se) a** *vt(r)* to affiliate (vt); to become affiliated (vr)

africano,-a *nmf, aj* [-ano] African

auditoría *nf* [-ería(2)] audit; auditing

castigo *nm* [R -o(1)] punishment

cuadrado *nm, aj* [R -ado(1)] square

2960 **egresar** *vi* to graduate

impulso *nm* [R -o(1)] impulse

perdonar *vt* [R] to forgive

saludar *vt* [R] to greet □ *saludar militarmente* to salute

televisivo *aj* [R(vista, teléfono) -ivo] television

2965 **arco** *nm* [R] arch

conmigo *pron* with me

gravedad *nf* [R] gravity

impunidad *nf* [-idad] impunity

ladrillero,-a *nmf* brickmaker

2970 **lanzador,-a** [R] 1. *nmf* pitcher (sport) 2. *aj* throwing

pantalón *nm* [R] pants

templo *nm* temple; church building

chino,-a 1. *nmf* Chinese person 2. *nm* Chinese language 3. *aj* Chinese

dialogar *vi* [R] to dialogue

2975 **exigencia** *nf* [R -encia] demand

extraer *vt* to extract

guía *nmf* [R] guide

primavera *nf* [R] spring (season)

risa *nf* [R] laughter □ *no es cosa de risa* it's no laughing matter

2980 **capa** *nf* [R] cape; layer □ *capa de pintura* coat of paint

contaminar *vt* to contaminate

fumar *vt* to smoke □ *fumarse una clase* to skip a class

lago *nm* lake

prieto *aj* dark (color of skin)

2985 **aliado,-a** [R -ado(2)] 1. *nmf* ally 2. *aj* allied

anular [R] 1. *vt* to annul, to cancel 2. *aj* ring-shaped □ *dedo anular* ring finger, third finger

encender(se) *vt(r)* [R] to light a fire, to turn on an electrical device (vt); to become angry quickly (vr)

posada *nf* [R] inn

recortar *vt* [R(cortar)] to cut (with attention to detail)

2990 **vidrio** *nm* [R] glass (material)

capilla *nf* [R] chapel

deterioro *nm* deterioration

fábrica *nf* [R -a] factory □ *fábrica de tejidos* textile mill

mineral *nm, aj* [R] mineral

2995 **oficialmente** *av* [-mente] officially

prevalecer *vi* [R] to prevail

supuestamente *av* [-mente] supposedly

colaborador,-a [R] **1.** *nmf* collaborator **2.** *aj* collaborating

descender *vi* [R] to descend

3000 **moderar** *vt* to moderate □ *¡Modere su velocidad!* Slow down!

nuez *nf* walnut

retrasar(se) *vt(r)* [R] to turn back a clock, to delay (vt); to be late (vr)

satisfacer *vt* [R] to satisfy

aislar *vt* [R] to isolate

3005 **aspiración** *nf* [R -ción] aspiration

danza *nf* [R -a] dance

embajada *nf* [R] embassy

moler *vt* [R] to mill; to crush into tiny pieces

observación *nf* [R -ción] observation

3010 **oeste** *nm* west

previamente *av* [R -mente] previously

velada *nf* night watch

abatir(se) *vt(r)* [R] to cause suffering, to overthrow (vt); to become discouraged (vr)

adjudicar(se) *vt(r)* [R] to confer something on someone (vt); to take for one's own, to appropriate (vr)

3015 **aparentemente** *av* [R -mente] apparently

estímulo *nm* [R -o(1)] stimulus

herramienta *nf* [R] tool

madurar *vi* [R -ura(2)] to mature

nave *nf* [R] vessel

3020 **occidental** *aj* [R] western

patio *nm* patio □ *patio de recreo* playground

perfectamente *av* [R -mente] perfectly

aceptación *nf* [R -ción] acceptance

coche *nm* [R] car

3025 **descuento** *nm* [R -o(1)] discount

desvío *nm* [R -o(1)] detour

mejoramiento *nm* [R -miento] improvement

resistir *vt* [R] to resist

canalizar *vt* [R -izar] to channel (water); to channel (communication), to direct

3030 **comercializar** *vt* [R -izar] to commercialize

evolución *nf* [R] evolution

inferior *aj* [R] inferior; lower

pensión *nf* [R -sión] pension

rector,-a *nmf* [R] rector; chancellor

3035 **traducir** *vt* [R] to translate

abridor *nm* [-dor(2)] opener □ *abridor de latas* can opener

eliminatorio *aj* [R -orio(2)] qualifying (sport)
  ▶ **eliminatoria** *nf* qualifying round in a sports tournament

ocultar(se) *vt(r)* [R] to hide, to conceal (vt); to become hidden or concealed (vr)

placer *nm* [R] pleasure

3040 **adquisición** *nf* [R -ción] acquisition

amonestar *vt* to admonish; to sanction, to punish

aplauso *nm* [R] applause

fracasar *vi* [R] to fail

ranchero,-a [-ero(2)] **1.** *nmf* person who lives on a ranch **2.** *aj* pertaining to ranches and ranching

3045 **acaso** *av* by chance, perhaps □ *por si acaso* in case

gasolina *nf* [R] gasoline

lateral *aj* [R] lateral

olimpiada *nf* Olympiad □ *las olimpiadas* the Olympics

préstamo *nm* [R] loan

3050 **receta** *nf* [R] recipe

reclamo *nm* [-o(1)] complaint

reubicar *vt* to place again

romance *nm* [R] romance

sanguíneo *aj* [R -eo(2)] pertaining to blood

3055 **vaso** *nm* [R] glass (drinking)

verdaderamente *av* [R -mente] truly

bienvenida *nf* [R] welcome

canastilla *nf* [-illa] bassinet □ *fiesta de canastilla* baby shower

chocolate *nm* [R] chocolate

3060 **escala** *nf* [R -a] scale; stopover (flight)

fungir *vi* to fill a role

lindo *nm* [R] pretty; nice □ *¡qué linda eres!* how nice you are! (you are so nice!)

3290 **pronóstico** *nm* [-o(1)] forecast; prediction

reservar *vt* [R] to reserve

transparente *aj* [R -ente(1)] transparent

ahorrar *vt* [R] to save; to put away in savings

amoroso *aj* [R -oso] amorous, loving

3295 **congelar(se)** *vt(r)* to freeze (vt); to be freezing, to become frozen (vr)

dotar *vt* [R] to give a dowry; to endow

estallar *vi* [R] to explode

fallo *nm* verdict

globalización *nf* [-ción] globalization

3300 **intensidad** *nf* [R -idad] intensity

menudo **1.** *av* □ *a menudo* often **2.** *aj* minute, tiny **3.** *nm* Mexican dish (food)

nombramiento *nm* [R -miento] the naming of someone to a position

padrón *nm* census □ *padrón electoral* list of voters

respiratorio *aj* [R -orio(2)] respiratory

3305 **significado** *nm* [R] meaning

barato *aj* [R] inexpensive, cheap

colocación *nf* [R -ción] placement

contratación *nf* [R -ción] contracting (business)

cruce *nm* [R] crossing

3310 **literatura** *nf* [R -ura(2)] literature

notable *aj* [R -able] notable

obvio *aj* obvious

potente *aj* [R] potent

prenda *nf* article of clothing; token, deposit

3315 **tolerancia** *nf* [R -ancia] tolerance

tribuna *nf* tribune

vigor *nm* [R] vigor

almacenar *vt* [R] to store

beneficiario,-a *nm, aj* [R] beneficiary

3320 **beso** *nm* [R -o(1)] kiss

corporal *aj* [R] corporal

dícese *vt* it is said (means the same as *se dice*)

equilibrar(se) *vt(r)* [R] to balance (vt); to gain one's balance or equilibrium (vr)

gemelo,-a *nmf* identical twin

3325 **limpio** *aj* [R] clean

máscara *nf* mask

obedecer *vti* [R] to obey

sujetar(se) *vt(r)* [R] to hold (vt); to be subject to, to obey (vr)

teatral *aj* [R] of the theater; theatrical

3330 **turnar(se)** *vt(r)* to turn over to, to send on (vt); to take turns (vr)

apellido *nm* [R -ido(2)] surname, last name

cerebral *aj* [R] cerebral

cheque *nm* [R] check □ *extender un cheque* to write a check

comandar *vt* [R] to command

3335 **dominical** *aj* Sunday □ *escuela dominical* Sunday school

óseo *aj* [-eo(2)] pertaining to bone, osseous

pintor,-a *nmf* [R] painter

rol *nm* roll

bronco **1.** *nm* bronco **2.** *aj* rough

3340 **compacto** *aj* compact

guerrilla *nf* [R -illa] guerrilla warfare; special military force or group of guerrilla fighters

nieve *nf* [R] snow; ice cream

sentimental *aj* [R] sentimental

balance *nm* [R] balance

3345 **certificar** *vt* [R -ificar] to certify

electo,-a [R] **1.** *nmf* person elected to office **2.** *aj* elect, elected

ergástula *nf* jail □ *ergástula municipal* city jail

estómago *nm* [R] stomach □ *boca del estómago* pit of the stomach

foco *nm* [R] light bulb

3350 **harina** *nf* flour □ *harina de maíz* cornmeal, corn flour

madurez *nf* [R -ez] maturity

policial *aj* [-cial] pertaining to the police

provisional *aj* [R] provisional

pugnar *vi* [R] to fight, to engage in a dispute

3355 **respectar** *vt* [R] to have to do with

retener *vt* [R] to retain

sospecha *nf* [R -a] suspicion

aguantar(se) *vt(r)* [R] to bear, to endure, to stand, to hold on (vt); to resist (vr)

clausura *nf* [-a] closing session; closing ceremony

3360 **deteriorar** *vi* to deteriorate

dibujo *nm* [R -o(1)] drawing (art)

estudiantil *aj* [R -il] relating to students

lechero *aj* [R -ero(2)] milk-producing; milk-containing; pertaining to milk

opositor,-a *nmf* [R] opponent; the opposition

predio *nm* property

3065 **profundidad** *nf* [R -idad] profundity; depths

terapia *nf* therapy

translado *nm* [-o(1)] transport from one place to another

zapato *nm* [R] shoe

admirador,-a [R] **1.** *nmf* admirer **2.** *aj* admiring

3070 **bando** *nm* [R] band or group of animals

desayuno *nm* [R -o(1)] breakfast

novedad *nf* [R] novelty

pastel *nm* [R] cake □ *pastelillo de fruta* tart

profesionista *nmf* [-ista] professional

3075 **rastro** *nm* [R] sign, footprint, mark

raza *nf* [R] race □ *de raza* thoroughbred

rodaje *nm* [R -aje(1)] rolling of wheels; wheels in general

bracket *nm* bracket; brace

caro *aj* expensive

3080 **delincuente** *nmf, aj* [-ente(2)] delinquent

esencia *nf* [R -encia] essence □ *por esencia* essentially

hormona *nf* hormone

panteón *nm* cemetary

productividad *nf* [R -idad] productivity

3085 **confusión** *nf* [R -sión] confusion

licitación *nf* [-ción] bidding

restante [R -ante(1)] **1.** *nm* remainder **2.** *aj* leftover, remaining

vuelto *nm* change returned after a purchase

debilidad *nf* [R -idad] weakness

3090 **desecho** *nm* [R -o(1)] throw-away item

fabricar *vt* [R] to fabricate, to build

irregular *aj* [R(regular)] irregular

nuclear *aj* [R] nuclear

proteína *nf* protein

3095 **saludable** *aj* [R -able] healthy

sello *nm* [R -o(1)] seal, stamp

administrar *vt* [R] to administer, to manage

avalar *vt* [R] to confirm the veracity of something; to give value to something

emocionar *vr* [R] to excite

3100 **entrante** *aj* [R] entering; next □ *la semana entrante* next week

estable *aj* [R] stable, steady

generalizar *vt* [R -izar] to generalize

hervir *vt* to boil

incertidumbre *nf* [R (cierto) -dumbre] lack of certainty, doubt

3105 **rollo** *nm* roll; story, tale, exaggeration □ *rollo de la cámara* roll of film; *¿qué rollo?* what's happening?

sombra *nf* [R] shade, shadow □ *tener mala sombra* to be dull or a drag, to be tireless

vacío *aj* [R] empty

aproximar(se) *vt(r)* [R] to move closer (vt); to move (oneself) closer to (vr)

conducto *nm* [R] conduct

3110 **dudar** *vt* [R] to doubt

helicóptero *nm* helicopter

ciertamente *av* [R -mente] certainly

composición *nf* [R -ción] composition

disquera *nf* disk production company

3115 **doloroso** *aj* [R -oso] painful

experimental *aj* [R -al(2)] experimental

lejano *aj* [R] distant

ligar(se) *vt(r)* [R] to tie (vt); to become tied, to become engaged (vr)

melón *nm* cantaloupe

3120 **mueble** *nm* [R] furniture

residual *aj* residual

solista *nmf* [R -ista] soloist

administrador,-a *nmf* [R] administrator

alteración *nf* [R -ción] alteration

3125 **amistoso** *aj* [R] friendly

delicioso *aj* [R -oso] delicious

lágrima *nf* [R -a] tear □ *valle de lágrimas* vale of tears; *beberse las lágrimas* to keep back one's tears

mediodía *nm* [R] noon

reino *nm* [R -o(1)] kingdom

3130 **retraso** *nm* [R -o(1)] turning back of a clock; delay

satélite *nm* satelite

tortilla *nf* [-illa] tortilla

bruto *aj* [-uto] rough

estrecho *aj* [R] narrow

3135 **fortaleza** *nf* [R] strength

norma *nf* [-a] norm

odio *nm* [R -o(1)] hate

quebrar *vt* [R] to break

recalcar *vt* to emphasize

3140 **varón** *nm* [R] man, male

editar *vt* [R] to publish

lenguaje *nm* [R -aje(1)] language

maquinaria *nf* [R] machinery

seno *nm* breast; heart (figurative) □ *en el seno de México* in the heart of Mexico

3145 **uniforme** *nm, aj* [R -iforme] uniform

variación *nf* [R -ción] variation

barco *nm* [R] ship

cortina *nf* [-ina] curtain

eficiencia *nf* [R -encia] efficiency

3150 **enseñanza** *nf* [R -anza] teaching □ *segunda enseñanza* secondary education

exactamente *av* [R -mente] exactly

independientemente *av* [R(depender) -mente] independently

irakí, iraquí *nmf, aj* Iraqi

normalmente *av* [-mente] normally

3155 **osteoporosis** *nf* [-osis] osteoporosis

paraestatal *aj* [R] semiofficial

transcurso *nm* [R(curso)] passage (of time); period (of time)

vocalista *nmf* [R -ista] vocalist

botella *nf* [R] bottle

3160 **colesterol** *nm* cholesterol

despojar *vt* to plunder, to despoil

envolver(se) *vt(r)* [R] to involve, to wrap (vt); to become involved, to wrap oneself (vr)

externar(se) *vt(r)* to express (vt); to express oneself (vr)

identificación *nf* [R -ción] identification

3165 **inaugural** *aj* [R] inaugural

redacción *nf* [R -ción] editing

actualizar *vt* [R -izar] to update

apropiar *vr* to appropriate for oneself

ascenso *nm* [R] ascent, rising, moving up

3170 **colector,-a** *nmf* collector

convivir *vi* [R] to share experiences, food, and time together

mariscal *nm* □ *mariscal de campo* quarterback (American football)

melodía *nf* melody

planteamiento *nm* [-miento] structured plan or outline; proposal

3175 **arriesgar** *vt* [R] to risk

asesoría *nf* [-ería(2)] counseling

bala *nf* [R] bullet □ *como una bala* like a shot

brote *nm* [R] sprout

destrucción *nf* [R -ción] destruction

3180 **esférico** *aj* [R -ico(2)] spherical

explotación *nf* [R -ción] exploitation

iberoamericano *aj* Ibero-American

metal *nm* [R] metal □ *el vil metal* filthy lucre

sexy *aj* [R] sexy

3185 **yanqui** *nm* Yankee

cabra *nf* [R] female goat

camiseta *nf* [R -eta] t-shirt

desafío *nm* [-o(1)] challenge

enfrente *av* [R] facing; in front

3190 **especificar** *vt* [R -ificar] to specify

mascota *nmf* pet

nominación *nf* [R -ción] nomination

predial *aj* property

presumir *vi* [R] to put on airs; to behave presumptuously

3195 **rehabilitar** *vt* [R(habilidad)] to rehabilitate

chocar *vi* [R] to crash

cola *nf* [R] tail; soft drink; line (waiting) □ *cola de caballo* ponytail; *a la cola* at the end, right at the back; *hacer cola* to line up

escombro *nm* [-o(1)] debris

espiritual *aj* [R] spiritual

3200 **eterno** *aj* [R] eternal

fiscalía *nf* [R -ería(2)] office of the attorney general

hombro *nm* shoulder

lamentable *aj* [R -able] lamentable

monumento *nm* [R] monument

3205 **suicidio** *nm* [R] suicide

adornar *vt* [R] to adorn, to decorate

consignar *vt* [R] to consign; to assign; to imprison

diabetes *nf* diabetes

eficaz *aj* [R -az] efficient

3210 **evangelio** *nm* [R] gospel

mejora *nf* [R -a] improvement

opuesto *nm* opposite

pésimo *aj* [R] very bad

restricción *nf* [-ción] restriction

3215 **sucursal** *nf* branch office of an organization

turista *nmf* [R -ista] tourist

frijol *nm* bean

hierba *nf* [R] herb

higiene *nf* hygiene

3220 **pitchear** *vt* to pitch

revés *nm* [R] reverse □ *al revés* backwards

singular *aj* [R] singular

alimenticio *aj* [R -icio] nutritive

arroz *nm* [R] rice

3225 **continuidad** *nf* [R -idad] continuity

curar *vt* [R -ura(2)] to cure, to heal

examen *nm* examination, test

introducción *nf* [R -ción] introduction

migrante *nmf, aj* migrant

3230 **progreso** *nm* [R -o(1)] progress

alternar *vt* [R] to alternate

complicación *nf* [R -ción] complication

donar *vt* to donate

dramático *aj* [R -ico(2)] dramatic

3235 **efectivamente** *av* [R -mente] effectively

espacial *aj* [R -cial] spatial

paciencia *nf* [R -encia] patience

arrastrar(se) *vt(r)* [R] to drag (vt); to drag oneself (vr)

decomisar *vt* to confiscate

3240 **dignidad** *nf* [R -idad] dignity

posponer *vt* [R(poner)] to postpone

remedio *nm* [R -o(1)] remedy; alternative course of action

sílaba *nf* syllable

telecomunicación *nf* [R(teléfono, comunicación)] telecommunication

3245 **adicción** *nf* addiction

engañar(se) *vt(r)* [R] to deceive (vt); to be mistaken, to fool oneself (vr)

patronato *nm* [R -ato] association for the purpose of charity or mutual benefit

premiar *vt* [R] to award a prize

renovación *nf* [R(nuevo) -ción] renewal

3250 **sacrificar** *vt* [R -ificar] to sacrifice

activista *nmf* [R] activist

apostar *vt* to bet

cardíaco *aj* cardiac

claramente *av* [-mente] clearly

3255 **colgar** *vt* [R] to hang; to hang up

constar *vi* [R] to be certain or evident to someone

estructural *aj* [R] structural

golf *nm* golf

persistir *vi* [R] to persist

3260 **postre** *nm* [R] dessert

receptor [R -or] 1. *nm* electrical receiver 2. *aj* receiving

acotar *vt* to mark with stakes; to stake out

acreedor,-a *nmf* creditor; deserving or worthy person

atacante [R -ante(2)] 1. *nmf* attacker 2. *aj* attacking

3265 **ave** 1. *nm* bird □ *ave de Paraíso* bird of Paradise 2. *nf* abbreviation of *avenida* (avenue)

bárbaro,-a [R] 1. *nm* barbarian 2. *aj* barbaric

barra *nf* bar

claridad *nf* [R -idad] clarity

cuarenta *nm, aj* [R] forty

3270 **mérito** *nm* [R -ito(2)] merit

ruido *nm* [R] noise

tela *nf* [R] cloth, fabric □ *tienda de telas* fabric store

abusar *vt* [R] to abuse □ *abusar de* to take advantage of, to impose upon

constatar *vt* [R] to confirm, to check, to verify

3275 **huella** *nf* footprint

natal *aj* [R] natal; native

orientación *nf* [R -ción] orientation

perfil *nm* [R] profile

pimienta *nf* pepper

3280 **prender** *vt* [R] to turn on, to switch on

semejante [R -ante(1)] 1. *nmf* neighbor, fellow man 2. *aj* similar

tecolote *nm* owl

tour *nm* tour

agravar(se) *vt(r)* to aggravate, to make worse (vt); to become worse, to charge a tax (vr)

3285 **cívico** *aj* [R -ico(2)] civic

cocinar *vt* [R] to cook

formato *nm* format

inspirar *vt* [R(espíritu)] to inspire

hilo *nm* [R -o(1)] thread

humo *nm* [R] smoke □ *cortina de humo* smokescreen

3365 **infancia** *nf* [R -ancia] infancy

informante *nmf* [-ante(2)] informant

rango *nm* range

residir *vi* [R] to reside

atropellar *vt* to run over; to trample

3370 **certificado** *aj* [R] certified

credencial *nf* [R] credential

desgraciadamente *av* [R -mente] unfortunately

desnudo [R -o(1)] **1.** *nm* nude (art object) **2.** *aj* naked, nude

ecologista *nmf* ecologist

3375 **federativo** *aj* federal □ *entidad federativa* state

filial [R] **1.** *nf* branch office of an organization **2.** *aj* filial

franja *nf* line, stripe

gota *nf* [R] drop

intensificar *vi* [R -ificar] to intensify

3380 **labio** *nm* [R] lip

paro *nm* [R] work stoppage, strike

pesca *nf* [R -a] fishing

reloj *nm* [R] watch (timepiece), clock □ *reloj de pulsera* wristwatch; *reloj de arena* hourglass; *reloj de bolsillo* pocket watch

cirujano,-a *nmf* surgeon

3385 **ebriedad** *nf* state of intoxication

inocente *aj* [R] innocent

maniobra *nf* [R -a] maneuver

poeta *nmf* [R] poet

tapar *vt* [R] to put on (a lid); to cover

3390 **apretar** *vt* [R] to squeeze □ *apretar los dientes* to grit one's teeth

apuesta *nf* [-a] bet

cineasta *nmf* [R] person that works in the film industry

desgracia *nf* [R -a] misfortune

fiebre *nf* [R] fever

3395 **IVA** *nm* value-added tax

liquidar *vt* [R] to liquidate

repunte *nm* rise in prices

retorno *nm* [R(torno) -o(1)] return; turnaround point on a highway

rudo *aj* rude

3400 **suplemento** *nm* [-o(1)] supplement

tabaco *nm* [R] tobacco

chavo,-a *nmf* young man, young girl (short form of *muchacho*)

definición *nf* [R -ción] definition

egreso *nm* [-o(1)] graduation

3405 **encerrar(se)** *vt(r)* [R] to enclose (vt); to lock oneself in (vr)

franquicia *nf* franchise

ídolo *nm* [R] idol

intercambiar *vt* [R(cambio)] to exchange

interrumpir *vt* [R] to interrupt

3410 **refresco** *nm* [R(fresco)] soda, soft drink

suegro,-a *nmf* father-in-law, mother-in-law

acercamiento *nm* [R -miento] photographic or television close-up; act of moving closer

conmemorar *vt* [R] to commemorate

dinámica *nf* [R] dynamics

3415 **exportador,-a** [R -dor(1)] **1.** *nmf* exporter **2.** *aj* exporting

aplaudir *vt* [R] to applaud

contundente *aj* convincing, unarguable

demócrata *nmf* [R] democrat

economista *nmf* [R -ista] economist

3420 **estándar** standard shift (automobile) **2.** *aj* standard

futbolístico *aj* [-ico(2)] soccer; pertaining to soccer

mágico *nm* [-ico(2)] magic

noble *aj* [R] noble

notificar *vt* [R] to notify

3425 **poesía** *nf* [R] poetry

potro *nm* colt

proyección *nf* [R -ción] projection

aledaño *aj* neighboring, bordering (pertaining to places) □ *el país aledaño* the bordering (neighboring) country

automotriz *aj* automotive

3430 **barril** *nm* barrel

distribuidor,-a *nmf* [R -dor(1)] distributor

fusión *nf* [-sión] fusion

guapo *aj* [R] handsome, good-looking

inundación *nf* [-ción] inundation, flood

3435 **mandato** *nm* [R] mandate

portugués,-esa [-és] **1.** *nmf* person from Portugal **2.** *nm* Portuguese (language) **3.** *aj* Portuguese

presuntamente *av* [R -mente] presumably, supposedly

reja *nf* [R] bar (jail or prison cell); bars (fencing; caging)

relajar(se) *vt(r)* to relax (vt); to be relaxed, to become relaxed (vr)

3440 **terminal** *nf, aj* [R -al(1)] terminal

cable *nm* cable

coraje *nm* [R] anger

corrido 1. *nm* typical Mexican song □ *tiempo corrido* running time **2.** *vti* past participle of the verb *correr* (to run)

curioso *aj* [R] strange, peculiar, interesting, curious

3445 **defecto** *nm* [R] defect

doblete *nm* double (baseball)

guiar *vt* [R] to guide

liderar *vt* to lead

literario *aj* [R -ario(2)] literary

3450 **pleito** *nm* [R] fight; fist fight

ponche *nm* punch (drink)

acuífero *nm* [-ífero] aquifer

envío *nm* [-o(1)] sending; item sent for delivery

eventual *aj* eventual; temporary

3455 **genético** *aj* [R -ico(2)] genetic

injusto *aj* [R(justicia)] unjust

lote *nm* lot, piece of land

magnífico *aj* [R] magnificent

maravilla *nf* [R -a] something marvelous

3460 **mariguana** *nf* marijuana

preservar *vt* to preserve

variado *aj* [R -ado(1)] varied

cigarro *nm* [R] cigarette; cigar

delictivo *aj* [-ivo] criminal

3465 **diversión** *nf* [R -sión] diversion, fun activity

enfermar(se) *vt(r)* [R] to make sick (vt); to become sick (vr)

gracia *nf* [R] grace □ *estar en gracia de Dios* to be in a state of grace

incursión *nf* [-sión] incursion

básicamente *av* [-mente] basically

3470 **creativo** *aj* [R -ivo] creative

dispositivo *nm* device

espejo *nm* [R] mirror □ *espejo de cuerpo entero* full-length mirror

finca *nf* country house

inédito *aj* [R(edición)] unpublished

3475 **Leo** *nm* [R] Leo (sign of zodiac)

mediocampista *nmf* [-ista] midfielder

onza *nf* ounce

perjuicio *nm* [-icio] perjury

seminario *nm* [-ario(2)] seminary; seminar

3480 **transportista** *nmf* [R -ista] transportation worker

corrida *nf* [R -ido(2)] run

creencia *nf* [R -encia] belief

estatuto *nm* statute

exclusivamente *av* [R -mente] exclusively

3485 **fabricante** *nmf* [R -ante(2)] factory worker

fantasma *nmf* [-asma] ghost

incursionar *vt* to venture

lección *nf* [R] lesson

rodar *vt* [R] to roll

3490 **sensibilidad** *nf* [R -idad] sensibility

absorber *vt* to absorb

afrontar *vt* [R] to face

balada *nf* ballad

cerdo *nm* pig

3495 **comunitario** *aj* [R] community

delante *av* [R] □ *delante de* in front of; *por delante* in front

desventaja *nf* disadvantage

juntar(se) *vt(r)* [R] to join (vt); to get together (vr)

llave *nf* [R] key; faucet □ *llave maestra* master key; *echar la llave* to lock

3500 **necesariamente** *av* [-mente] necessarily

pensionar *vt* to pay a pension

revolver *vti* [R(volver)] to revolve; to mix

sexenio *nm* six-year term

armonía *nf* [R] harmony

3505 **asiático,-a** [-ico(2)] **1.** *nmf* Asian person **2.** *aj* Asiatic

caldo *nm* [R] broth

caloría *nf* [R -ería(2)] calorie

exagerar *vt* [R] to exaggerate

intermedio *aj* [R(medio)] intermediate

3510 **pasta** *nf* [R] pasta; paste

pelar(se) *vt(r)* to peel, to shave someone's head (vt); to peel (skin), to shave one's head (vr)

precedente [R -ente(1)] **1.** *nm* precedent **2.** *aj* preceding

relatar *vt* [R] to relate

residencial *aj* [R -cial] residential

3515 **rockero,-a** [-ero(3)] **1.** *nmf* fan of rock music; rock music singer **2.** *aj* fond of rock music

gris *nm* [R] gray

hielo *nm* [R -o(1)] ice □ *punto de hielo* freezing point

legítimo *aj* [R] legitimate

luchador,-a *nmf* [R] fighter, one who struggles

3520 **músculo** *nm* [R -culo] muscle

normatividad *nf* [-idad] laws, regulations □ *la normatividad agropecuaria* farming regulations

partidista *nmf, aj* [R -ista] partisan

pasaje *nm* [R -aje(2)] passage

privilegio *nm* [R] privilege

3525 **recipiente** *nm* [R -ente(2)] container

sesenta *nf, aj* [R] sixty

vacuna *nf* [-a] vaccine

atletismo *nm* [R -ismo] track and field

bailarín,-ina *nmf* [R] ballet dancer

3530 **cartera** *nf* [R -era] wallet

coro *nm* [R] chorus

hepatitis *nf* [R -itis] hepatitis

lanza [R] **1.** *nf* lance **2.** *vt* throws (third-person singular of the verb *lanzar*)

presea *nf* prize

3535 **sereno** *nm* [R -o(1)] quiet time during the middle of the night; dew

ala *nf* [R] wing □ *dar alas* to protect, to encourage; *tomar alas* to take liberties

centenario,-a *nmf* [R -ario(2)] centenarian

contigo *pron* with you

cuadra *nf* [R] block (city)

3540 **discoteca** *nf* [-teca] discotheque

galería *nf* gallery

gloria *nf* [R -a] glory □ *sabe a gloria* it tastes heavenly

impresionante *aj* [R] impressive, amazing

onda *nf* [R] wave □ *¿qué onda?* what's going on?, what's happening?

3545 **parlamento** *nm* [R] parliament

pavimentación *nf* [-ción] paving

plenamente *av* [-mente] fully

procedencia *nf* [R -encia] origin

regir *vt* [R] to govern

3550 **sigla** *nf* acronym

torero *nm* [R -ero(2)] bullfighter

volcar *vt* to flip

alcaldía *nf* [R -ería(2)] city hall; office of mayor

apariencia *nf* [R -encia] appearance

3555 **asiento** *nm* [R] seat

continuo *aj* [R -uo] continuous

diamante *nm* diamond

inclinar(se) *vi(r)* [R] to lean (vi); to be leaning, to be inclined (vr)

metropolitano *aj* [R] metropolitan

3560 **nulo** *aj* null

software *nm* software

sonreír *vi* [R] to smile

verificación *nf* [R -ción] verification

captación *nf* [-ción] comprehension, understanding

3565 **cima** *nf* [R] top

componente *nm* [R] component

hoyo *nm* hole

inmigrante *nmf* [-ante(2)] immigrant

lamentablemente *av* [R -mente] lamentably

3570 **leal** *aj* [R] loyal

magisterial *aj* pertaining to the teaching profession

procesar *vt* [R] to process

reactivar *vt* [R(acción)] to reactivate

subdirector,-a *nmf* [-or] assistant director

3575 **testimonio** *nm* [R -o(1)] testimony

tumba *nf* [R] tomb

cantautor,-a *nmf* singer-songwriter

descuidar(se) *vt(r)* [R] to neglect (vt); to neglect oneself, to let oneself go (vr)

doler *vi* [R] to hurt □ *dolerse de* to grieve at; to feel sorrow for

3580 **hondo** *aj* [R] deep

instante *nm* [R -ante(1)] instant

interceptar *vt* to intercept

invasión *nf* [R -sión] invasion

magnitud *nf* [R -itud] magnitude

3585 **maya** *nm, aj* Mayan

migración *nf* migration

pisar *vt* [R] to walk on

ratón *nm* mouse; thief

rubio,-a *nmf, aj* [R] blond

3590 **sensible** *aj* [R -ible] sensitive, easily hurt

tiburón *nm* shark

asar(se) *vt(r)* to barbecue, to grill, to roast (vt); to be roasting (figurative) (vr) □ *asar a la parrilla* to grill

besar *vt* [R] to kiss

escasez *nf* [R -ez] scarcity

3595 **estrógeno** *nm* estrogen

guerrillero *nm* [-ero(3)] guerrilla fighter

mariachi *nm* mariachi

pasaporte *nm* [R] passport

plantar *vt* [R] to plant

3600 **tropical** *aj* tropical

acomodar(se) *vt(r)* [R] to accommodate (vt); to fix (vr) □ *acomódate el pelo* fix your hair

adversario,-a *nmf* [-ario(2)] adversary

cuchillo *nm* [R] knife

ecuatoriano,-a *nmf* [-ano] **1.** *nmf* person from Ecuador **2.** *aj* pertaining to Ecuador

3605 **exacto** *aj* [R] exact

magistrado *nm* magistrate

manteca *nf* grease □ *manteca de cacao* cocoa butter

oriental *aj* [R -al(2)] oriental

simpatizante [R -ante(1)] **1.** *nmf* sympathizer, partisan **2.** *aj* sympathetic, partisan

3610 **vaciar** *vti* to empty

ahorita *av* within a short time; right away

alias *nm, av* alias

anónimo *aj* [R] anonymous

apagar *vt* [R] to turn off, to switch off

3615 **aprovechamiento** *nm* [R -miento] good or profitable or wise use

comprador,-a *nmf* [-dor(1)] buyer

elegante *aj* [R] elegant

estratega *nmf* strategist

felino *aj* feline

3620 **habitual** *aj* [R] habitual

huracán *nm* hurricane

misterio *nm* [R] mystery

rasgo *nm* characteristic □ *los rasgos* facial features

reflexionar *vi* [R] to reflect with thought on something

3625 **sorprendente** *aj* [R -ente(1)] surprising, amazing

agresor,-a *nmf* aggressor

bañar(se) *vt(r)* [R] to bathe (vt); to bathe oneself (vr)

conservador,-a [R -dor(1)] **1.** *nmf* political rightist, conservative **2.** *aj* conservative

docente *aj* teaching

3630 **ensayo** *nm* [R -o(1)] rehearsal; essay

frecuentemente *av* [R -mente] frequently

grueso *aj* [R] thick

legalidad *nf* [R -idad] legality

leve *aj* light

3635 **menopausia** *nf* menopause

ofender(se) *vt(r)* [R] to offend (vt); to become offended (vr)

orilla *nf* [-a] edge

persecución *nf* [R -ción] persecution

semáforo *nm* traffic light

3640 **ubicación** *nf* [-ción] placement

altamente *av* [R -mente] highly

aula *nf* classroom

ausentarse *vr* to be absent

calibre *nm* caliber

3645 **catedral** *nf* cathedral

contemporáneo,-a [R -eo(2)] **1.** *nmf* contemporary **2.** *aj* contemporaneous

desorden *nm* disorder

emisor [R] **1.** *nm* transmitter **2.** *nf* emisora radio station **3.** *aj* transmitting, emitting

habitacional *aj* pertaining to housing

3650 **horno** *nm* oven □ *alto horno* blast furnace

joya *nf* [R] jewel

móvil *aj* [R -il] mobile

navideño *aj* [-eño] Christmas

obligatorio *aj* [R -orio(2)] obligatory

3655 **plaga** *nf* plague

plataforma *nf* [R] platform

pluma *nf* [R] pen

proporción *nf* [R] proportion

suministro *nm* [-o(1)] supply

3660 **supervisar** *vt* [R(vista)] to supervise

trasero [-ero(2)] **1.** *nm* bottom, buttocks **2.** *aj* back □ *la puerta trasera* the back door

barba *nf* [R] beard □ *en sus barbas* to his face

comparecer *vt* [R] to appear before a judge

contraste *nm* [R] contrast

3665 **drama** *nm* [R] drama

feo *aj* ugly

galardón *nm* prize

griego,-a [-iego] 1. *nmf* Greek person 2. *nm* Greek language 3. *aj* Greek

imaginación *nf* [R -ción] imagination

3670 **magia** *nf* magic

premier *nm* premier, prime minister

pretexto *nm* pretext, excuse

republicano,-a *nmf, aj* [R(pueblo) -ano] republican

reubicación *nf* [-ción] the establishment of something in a new place

3675 **suscitar** *vt* [R] to cause, to provoke

alcantarillado *nm* sewage system, drainage pipes

automovilístico *aj* [R -ico(2)] pertaining to motoring or automobile construction

avisar *vt* [R] to warn

biológico *aj* [R -ico(2)] biological

3680 **bronce** *nm* [R] bronze

competente *aj* [R -ente(1)] competent

difícilmente *av* [-mente] hardly

interino *aj* temporary

mito *nm* [R] myth

3685 **paralelo** *aj* [R] parallel

pedazo *nm* [R] piece

plural *aj* plural

separación *nf* [R -ción] separation

sueco,-a *nmf, aj* Swedish

3690 **súper** *aj* super

aconsejar *vt* [R] to give counsel

actualización *nf* [R -ción] updating

autógrafo *nm* autograph

despejar(se) *vt(r)* to clear, to clear up, to get rid of obstacles (vt); to clear up (vr)

3695 **globo** *nm* [R] balloon; globe

mentir *vi* [R] to lie, to tell a falsehood

postemporada *nf* postseason

remontar *vr* [R(montar)] to date from

restringir *vt* to restrict

3700 **setenta** *nf, aj* [R] seventy

afecto [R] 1. *nm* affection 2. *aj* inclined (toward), with a fondness for, fond of

cazar *vt* [R] to hunt

cómico,-a [R] 1. *nmf* comic 2. *aj* comical

debidamente *av* [R -mente] correctly

3705 **dueto** *nm* duet

explanada *nf* courtyard

inventar *vt* [R] to invent

orgánico *aj* [R -ico(2)] organic

precaución *nf* [R -ción] precaution

3710 **sentenciar** *vt* [R] to sentence (legal)

tolerar *vt* [R] to tolerate

vicio *nm* [R -icio] vice □ *de vicio* from force of habit; for the sake of it

acero *nm* [R] steel

advertencia *nf* [R -encia] warning

3715 **alegar** *vt* to discuss, to contend

basílica *nf* basilica

charla *nf* [R -a] conversation

comediante *nmf* [R -ante(2)] comedian

derramar *vt* [R] to spill; to overflow

3720 **estelarizar** *vi* [-izar] to star

exportar *vt* [R] to export

fatal *aj* [R] fatal

invicto *aj* unbeaten

jurado,-a [R -ato] 1. *nmf* juror 2. *nm* jury (group) 3. *aj* qualified 4. *vti* sworn, under oath (past participle of the verb *jurar*)

3725 **legislatura** *nf* legislature

natación *nf* [R -ción] swimming

oculto *aj* [R] hidden

oso *nm* bear □ *oso blanco* polar bear

panameño,-a *nmf, aj* [-eño] Panamanian

3730 **personalmente** *av* [R -mente] personally

regulación *nf* [R -ción] regulation

terraza *nf* [-aza] terrace

transferencia *nf* [-encia] transfer

válido *aj* [R -ido(1)] valid

3735 **ansiedad** *nf* [R] anxiety

autotransporte *aj* automobile transportation

benéfico *aj* [R -ico(2)] beneficial

cártel *nm* cartel

conquista *nf* [R -a] conquest

3740 **mero** *aj* mere, simple

plomo *nm* lead

tributario,-a [R] 1. *nmf* taxpayer 2. *aj* pertaining to taxes

barda *nf* wall

batería *nf* battery

3745 **busto** *nm* bust

culpar *vt* [R] to blame

documental *nm, aj* [R] documentary

extenso *aj* [R] extensive

galán [R] **1.** *nm* lady's man **2.** *aj* gallant

3750 **mundialista** *nmf* [-ista] player in the World Cup (soccer)

obesidad *nf* [-idad] obesity

prestigio *nm* [R] prestige

programación *nf* [-ción] programming

realizador,-a *nmf* [R] producer or director of film or television

3755 **regularizar** *vt* [R -izar] to regularize, to regulate

relevante *aj* relevant

rodeo *nm* [R -eo(1)] rodeo; indirect route

ruptura *nf* [-ura(2)] rupture

subterráneo *aj* [R(tierra)] subterranean

3760 **trascender** *vi* to transcend

trigo *nm* wheat

turco,-a 1. *nmf* Turk **2.** *nm* Turkish language **3.** *aj* Turkish

absurdo *aj* [R] absurd

borde *nm* [R] edge

3765 **callar(se)** *vt(r)* [R] to quiet (vt); to be quiet (vr)

centenar *nm* [R] one hundred

custodio [-o(1)] **1.** *nm* guard; custodian **2.** *aj* guardian □ *ángel custodio* guardian angel

decretar *vt* [R] to issue a decree

forraje *nm* food for animals

3770 **herencia** *nf* [R -encia] inheritance

lente *nm* lens □ *los lentes* glasses

migratorio *aj* [-orio(2)] migratory

muro *nm* [R] wall

ópera *nf* opera

3775 **sobresalir** *vi* [R] to protrude; to stand out from the rest

sopa *nf* [R] pasta or grain prepared with water; soup □ *estar hecho una sopa* to be wet through; to be wet to the skin

sureste *nm* [R] southeast

tubo *nm* [R] tube; pipe □ *tubo de ensayo* test tube

bacteria *nf* bacteria

3780 **banquero** *nm* [-ero(3)] banker

discapacidad *nf* incapacitation

exquisito *aj* [R -ito(2)] exquisite

fortalecimiento *nm* [R -miento] strengthening

marginar *vt* [R] to put margins; to exclude

3785 **palo** *nm* [R] long stick or handle

pronosticar *vt* to predict

recto *aj* [R] straight

territorial *aj* [R(tierra)] territorial

variar *vt* [R] to vary

3790 **aprendizaje** *nm* [R] learning

asaltar *vt* [R] to assault

bolero *nm* person who shines shoes; a type of romantic music

competitividad *nf* [R -idad] competitiveness

derribar *vt* [R] to tear down

3795 **desafortunadamente** *av* [-mente] unfortunately

examinar *vt* [R] to examine

formular *vt* [R] to formulate

informal *aj* [R(formal)] informal

lecho *nm* bed, riverbed

3800 **multitud** *nf* multitude

quiebra *nf* bankruptcy

reemplazar *vt* [R(plaza)] to replace

sexualidad *nf* [R -idad] sexuality

agarrar *vt* [R] to grab

3805 **anomalía** *nf* anomaly

banquete *nm* [R -ete] banquet

conducción *nf* [R -ción] conduction

gestionar *vt* [R] to manage a business or project

ingenio *nm* cleverness

3810 **inolvidable** *aj* [R(olvidar) -able] unforgettable

marino [R -ino(2)] **1.** *nm* marine **2.** *aj* sea; seagoing

matanza *nf* [R -anza] massacre; slaughter

soviético *aj* Soviet

absolutamente *av* [R -mente] absolutely

3815 **autódromo** *nm* [R] auto race track

cachorro *nm* puppy

colar *vt* to strain

desmentir *vt* [R] to contradict (a lie)

despido *nm* [R -ido(2)] dismissal from work, firing

3820 **round** *nm* round (sport)

salto *nm* [R -o(1)] jump □ *salto mortal* somersault

soltar(se) *vt(r)* [R] to let go, to let loose, to free (vt); to let go (of), to perform with confidence (vr)

transacción *nf* [R] transaction

visual *aj* [R] visual

3825 **asustar(se)** *vt(r)* [R] to frighten (vt); to become frightened (vr)

cereal *nm* cereal

conexión *nf* connection

emotivo *aj* [R -ivo] emotive, causing emotion

indicación *nf* [R -ción] indication

3830 **muñeco,-a** *nmf* [R] doll
▶ **muñeca** *nf* wrist

perdón *nm* [R] forgiveness, pardon

recolección *nf* [R(colección)] collection

sorteo *nm* [-eo(1)] drawing (raffle)

telefonía *nf* [R -ería(2)] telephony

3835 **trágico** *aj* [R -ico(2)] tragic

adiós *nm, intj* [R] good-bye

albergar *vr* to lodge

contentar(se) *vt(r)* [R] to make content or happy (vt); to be content or happy (vr)

desplegar(se) *vt(r)* [R] to unfold, to unroll, to spread, to extend (vt); to be unfolded, to be unrolled, to be spread out, to be extended (vr)

3840 **divorcio** *nm* [R -o(1)] divorce

equidad *nf* equity

fianza *nf* [R -anza] bail □ *bajo fianza* on bail

frontal *aj* frontal

gremio *nm* guild

3845 **inspiración** *nf* [R(espíritu) -ción] inspiration

irlandés,-esa [-és] 1. *nmf* person from Ireland 2. *aj* Irish

legendario *aj* legendary

metálico *aj* [R -ico(2)] metallic

modernizar *vt* [R -izar] to modernize

3850 **narcotraficante** *nmf* drug trafficker

parada *nf* [R] stop; bus stop

partidario,-a [R -ario(2)] 1. *nmf* supporter of a party 2. *aj* factional

payaso,-a *nmf* clown

perdedor,-a [R -dor(1)] 1. *nmf* loser 2. *aj* losing

3855 **preparativo** *nm* [R] preparation

sugerencia *nf* [R -encia] suggestion

tequila *nm* tequila

volcán *nm* volcano

acertar *vt* [R] to hit the mark; to be right

3860 **certeza** *nf* [R -eza] certainty

condena *nf* [R -a] sentence (legal penalty)

consistente *aj* [R -ente(1)] consistent; with consistency □ *consistente en* consisting of

cursar *vt* [R] to take a course

datar *vi* to date (from)

3865 **diseñador,-a** *nmf* designer

divisa *nf* foreign currency

embriagante *aj* intoxicating

enriquecer(se) *vt(r)* [R] to enrich (vt); to become rich (vr)

espinoso *aj* [-oso] prickly, thorny

3870 **golfo** 1. *nm* gulf 2. *aj* lazy

humilde *aj* [R] humble □ *de humilde cuna* of humble birth

hundir *vt* [R] to sink

infante *nmf* [R] infant

pacto *nm* [R -o(1)] agreement, pact

3875 **pizarra** *nf* chalk board, scoreboard

previsión *nf* [R(vista) -sión] foresight

suelto [R] 1. *nm* loose change 2. *aj* loose □ *estar suelto* to have diarrhea

tremendo *aj* tremendous

bloque *nm* [R] block

3880 **dengue** *nm* fussiness; dengue fever

ensalada *nf* salad

impreso [R] 1. *nm* printed material 2. *aj* printed

incumplir *vi* [R(cumplir)] to leave incomplete, to leave unfinished

interamericano *aj* inter-American

3885 **nariz** *nf* [R] nose □ *meter la nariz en* to stick one's nose in

paradero *nm* [R] rest stop; whereabouts

plantón *nm* protest, sit-in

pulso *nm* pulse □ *tomar el pulso a alguien* to take someone's pulse

requerimiento *nm* [R -miento] requirement

3890 **satisfactorio** *aj* [R -orio(2)] satisfactory

vigencia *nf* [R -encia] valid status

afán *nm* [R] effort

alberca *nf* swimming pool

brillar *vi* [R] to shine □ *brillar por su ausencia* to be conspicuous by one's absence

3895 **cantina** *nf* bar

clausurar *vi* to close (with ceremony); to hold the closing session or meeting

constancia *nf* [R -ancia] constancy, stability; letter or award of recognition □ *dejar constancia de una cosa* to leave something on record

dificultar *vt* [R] to make something difficult

eje *nf* axle; something which takes the form of an axle (such as a bus route)

3900 **estatura** *nf* [-ura(2)] stature, height

filipino,-a [-ino(2)] **1.** *nmf* person from the Philippines **2.** *aj* Filipino

honesto *aj* [R] honest

muscular *aj* [R] muscular

occiso *nm* deceased

3905 **proclamar** *vt* [R(reclamar)] to proclaim

respirar *vi* [R] to breathe

supervisión *nf* [R(vista) -sión] supervision

sustraer *vt* to subtract

uña *nf* [R] nail (finger; toe)

3910 **adjunto** *aj* [R] attached

albergue *nm* shelter, lodging

broma *nf* [R] joke, anything said in jest (*chiste* is a joke with a punch line) □ *broma pesada* nasty joke, practical joke

compensar *vt* [R] to compensate

continental *aj* [R] continental

3915 **divino** *aj* [R] divine

divulgar *vt* to divulge

filosofía *nf* [R -ería(2)] philosophy

ida *nf* [-ido(2)] going

parto *nm* [R] birth

3920 **pecado** *nm* [R -o(1)] sin

preliminar *aj* preliminary

pretemporada *nf* pre-season

aguinaldo *nm* bonus, end-of-the-year bonus

autonomía *nf* [R -ería(2)] autonomy

3925 **cansancio** *nm* [R] tiredness

complementario *aj* [R] complementary

cuerda *nf* [R] cord, rope □ *cuerda vocal* vocal cord

debilitar(se) *vt(r)* [R] to weaken (vt); to become weak (vr)

extradición *nf* [-ción] extradition

3930 **hidráulico** *aj* [-ico(2)] hydraulic

mantequilla *nf* [-illa] butter

matutino *aj* morning

nevar *vi* [R] to snow

normativo *aj* [R -ivo] normative

3935 **pactar** *vi* [R] to make an agreement

pasivo *aj* passive

rebote *nm* rebound

semanal *aj* [R -al(2)] weekly

viajero,-a *nmf* [R -ero(3)] traveler

3940 **abandono** *nm* [R -o(1)] abandonment

calabaza *nf* squash; pumpkin

comprensión *nf* [R] comprehension, understanding

entretenimiento *nm* [R -miento] entertainment

incidencia *nf* [R -encia] incidence

3945 **incumplimiento** *nm* [R(cumplir) -miento] lack of completion

indocumentado,-a [R(documento)] **1.** *nmf* undocumented alien **2.** *aj* undocumented

integridad *nf* [R -idad] integrity

malestar *nm* [R] ill feeling

pontífice *nm* pontiff, pope

3950 **prioritario** *aj* priority

quirúrgico *aj* surgical

sondeo *nm* [-eo(1)] preliminary investigation

suscripción *nf* [R(escribir) -ción] subscription

trama *nf* [R -a] plot (story)

3955 **vocación** *nf* [R] vocation

acuario *nm* [R] aquarium

arribo *nm* [R -o(1)] arrival of a ship

bote *nm* boat; container □ *bote de basura* trash container

camerata *nf* small orchestra

3960 **caña** *nf* [R] cane (plant); fishing pole □ *miel de caña* molasses

combatiente *nm* [R -ente(2)] combatant

compadre *nm* [R] close friend □ *los compadres* godfather and actual father

descubrimiento *nm* [R -miento] discovery

encarnar *vt* [R] to incarnate; to personify (often said of actors performing a role)

3965 **expedir** *vt* [R] to expedite

ingeniería *nf* [R -ería(2)] engineering

inundar *vt* to inundate

mortal *nmf, aj* [R] mortal

tenencia *nf* [R -encia] possession

3970 **vocal** *aj* [R] vocal

acá *av* here; over here

complementar(se) *vt(r)* [R] to complement (vt); to complement each other (vr)

convicción *nf* [R] conviction

costoso *aj* [-oso] very expensive

3975 **decisivo** *aj* [R -ivo] decisive

donación *nf* [-ción] donation

estético *aj* [R -ico(2)] relating to aesthetics or the study of beauty

injusticia *nf* [R(justicia) -icia] injustice

interrogar *vt* [R] to interrogate

3980 **levantamiento** *nm* [R -miento] raising, lifting

motivación *nf* [R -ción] motivation

ochenta *nf, aj* [R] eighty

propaganda *nf* [R] propaganda

públicamente *av* [R -mente] publicly

3985 **refuerzo** *nm* [R(fuerza)] reinforcement

sobrino,-a *nmf* nephew, niece

tenista *nmf* [-ista] tennis player

utilización *nf* [R -ción] utilization

validar *vt* [R] to validate

3990 **callejero** *aj* [R -ero(2)] pertaining to streets; street-walking

conciliación *nf* [-ción] conciliation

coyote *nm* coyote; person who for money smuggles people into a country (slang)

creatividad *nf* [R -idad] creativity

cuántico,-a *aj* [-ico(2)] quantum
▶ **cuántica** *nf* quantum

3995 **despacho** *nm* [R -o(1)] (attorney's) office; act of dispatching

específicamente *av* [-mente] specifically

fotógrafo,-a *nmf* [R] photographer

helado [R -ado(1)] **1.** *nm* ice cream **2.** *aj* freezing

innovación *nf* [R(nuevo) -ción] innovation

4000 **instructor,-a** *nmf* [R] instructor

melodrama *nm* melodrama

periodismo *nm* [R -ismo] journalism

permanencia *nf* [R -encia] permanence

práctico *aj* [R -ico(2)] practical

4005 **selva** *nf* jungle □ *Selva Negra* Black Forest

vergüenza *nf* [R] shame

virtual *aj* virtual

ambulancia *nf* [R -ancia] ambulance

angustia *nf* [R -a] anguish; distress

4010 **balazo** *nm* [R -azo(2)] bullet wound

diagonal *aj* diagonal

ebrio *aj* inebriated, intoxicated, drunk

elector,-a *nmf* [R] elector

fantasía *nf* fantasy

4015 **fuero** *nm* jurisdiction

heroína *nf* [R -ina] heroine

jitomate *nm* tomato

limitación *nf* [R -ción] limitation

longitud *nf* [R -itud] longitude

4020 **magisterio** *nm* [R] teaching profession

optimista [R -ista] **1.** *nmf* optimist **2.** *aj* optimistic

oral *aj* [R] oral

pico *nm* [R -o(1)] beak; peak

propicio *aj* [R] propitious, bringing about favorable circumstances

4025 **reformar(se)** *vt(r)* [R(forma)] to reform (vt); to become reformed (vr)

repertorio *nm* repertoire

vestuario *nm* [R] clothing; wardrobe

viable *aj* viable

admiración *nf* [R -ción] admiration

4030 **ampliamente** *av* [-mente] amply

antigüedad *nf* [R] antiquity; longevity in employment

brindis *nm* [R] toast (with a drink)

checar *vt* to check

curva *nf* [R] curve

4035 **desperdiciar** *vt* [R] to waste

foráneo *aj* [R] referring to outsiders or non-locals

frustración *nf* [-ción] frustration

himno *nm* hymn

maquillaje *nm* make-up

4040 **recomendable** *aj* [R -able] recommendable

resumen *nm* [R] summary

seriamente *aj* [-mente] seriously

tornar *vr* [R] to turn; to become

vulnerable *aj* [-able] vulnerable

4045 **adentro** *av* [R] inside

cálculo *nm* [R -culo] calculation; calculus; stone (kidney, gall)

campamento *nm* [R] camp

exponente *nm* [-ente(2)] exponent

pentágono *nm* pentagon; the Pentagon

4050 **preocupante** *aj* worrying

redondo *aj* [R] round

relevar *vt* to develop (film); to reveal

soltería *nf* [R -ería(2)] bachelorhood

venganza *nf* [R -anza] revenge

4055 **zaga** *nf* rear part of something; deep portion of one's territory (sport)

ángulo *nm* [R] angle

borrar *vt* [R] to erase

conejo *nm* [R] rabbit; bicep

cuenca *nf* basin (geology)

4060 **llover** *vt* [R] to rain ■ Está lloviendo a cántaros. It's raining cats and dogs

mexiquense *aj* [-ense] Mexican; pertaining to Mexico

promocional *aj* promotional

regularización *nf* [R -ción] regularization

res *nf* cow

4065 **responsabilizar(se)** *vt(r)* [R -izar] to make responsible for (vt); to take responsibility for (vr)

salvaje [R] **1.** *nm* savage **2.** *aj* savage, wild

sencillamente *av* [-mente] simply

soberanía *nf* [-ería(2)] sovereignty

sustentar(se) *vt(r)* [R] to sustain (vt); to be sustained (vr)

4070 **trío** *nm* trio

viudo,-a *nmf* [R] widow, widower

a.m. *av* a.m.

arresto *nm* [-o(1)] arrest

canela *nf* cinnamon

4075 **cura** [R -ura(2)] **1.** *nf* healing; cure **2.** *nm* priest

divo,-a *nmf* prima donna

eficacia *nf* [R -icia] efficacy, effectiveness

expansión *nf* [R -sión] expansion

inicialmente *av* [-mente] initially

4080 **memorable** *aj* [R] memorable

noria *nf* water well

porra *nf* cheer, encouragement □ *echar porras* to cheer

recabar *vt* to raise (funds)

tejano,-a *nmf, aj* [-ano] Texan

4085 **trayecto** *nm* [R] path

uva *nf* grape □ *uvas verdes* sour grapes

vaca *nf* cow □ *vaca lechera* dairy cow

Venus *nm* Venus

vivero *nm* [R -ero(4)] nursery

4090 **agilizar** *vt* [-izar] to do or perform quickly

coincidencia *nf* [R -encia] coincidence

contracción *nf* [-ción] contraction

derechohabiente 1. *nmf* one who is affiliated with a particular group and, as such, receives special benefits **2.** *aj* pertaining to one who receives special benefits because of his affiliation

freír *vt* to fry

4095 **incapacidad** *nf* [R(capacidad) -idad] incapacity

infectar(se) *vt(r)* to infect (vt); to become infected (vr)

misil *nm* missile

precioso *aj* [R -oso] precious

prisionero,-a *nmf* [R] prisoner □ *prisionero de guerra* prisoner of war

4100 **quincena** *nf* [R] fifteen days; one-half month; fortnight; two-weeks

repente *av* □ *de repente* suddenly

revertir *vi* [R] to revert

terror *nm* [R] terror

trozo *nm* [R -o(1)] piece

4105 **abundante** *aj* [R -ante(1)] abundant

adaptación *nf* [R -ción] adaptation

arancel *nm* tariff

camellón *nm* median (street, highway)

cómputo *nm* [-o(1)] counting

4110 **conserva** *nf* [R -a] preserves

conversar *vi* [R] to converse

diversidad *nf* [R -idad] diversity

envejecimiento *nm* [R -miento] aging

excepto *av* [R] except

4115 **parejo** *aj* [R] even; tied (game)

retornar *vi* [R(torno)] to return

socialista *nmf, aj* [R -ista] socialist

tira *nf* strip

vinagre *nm* [R] vinegar

4120 **almendra** *nf* almond □ *almendras garrapiñadas* sugared almonds

artificial *aj* [R -cial] artificial

calificador *aj* [R] grading

calzado *nm* footwear

encarcelar *vt* [R] to incarcerate

4125 **genio,-a** *nmf* genius

hallazgo *nm* [R] find □ *¡qué hallazgo!* what a find!

hongo *nm* mushroom; fungus

imperio *nm* [R] empire

instar *vti* to beg, to plead

4130 **reconstrucción** *nf* [R(construir) -ción] reconstruction

sustentable *aj* [-able] defensible

tierno *aj* [R] tender

aerolínea *nf* [R] airline

atracción *nf* [R -ción] attraction

4135 **balompié** *nf* soccer

colono,-a *nmf* neighbor

fantástico *aj* [-ico(2)] fantastic

filo *nm* edge for cutting

holandés,-esa 1. *nmf* person from Holland 2. *nm* Dutch language 3. *aj* from Holland

4140 **humedad** *nf* [R] humidity

infierno *nm* [R] hell; inferno

infinidad *nf* [R(fin, -idad)] infinity

lámpara *nf* [R] lamp, flashlight

nogal *nm* [R] walnut tree

4145 **nutrición** *nf* [R -ción] nutrition

protector,-a [R] 1. *nmf* one who protects, protector □ *el protector de pantalla* screensaver 2. *aj* protecting, protective

tortura *nf* [-a] torture

venado *nm* deer

zaguero *nm, aj* [-ero(3)] back (sport)

4150 **agudo** *aj* [R] pointed; sharp; high-pitched

algodonero,-a [-ero(2, 4)] 1. *nmf* person who picks cotton 2. *aj* cottony, pertaining to cotton

anualmente *av* [-mente] anually

cosechar *vt* [R] to harvest, to reap

dentista *nmf* [R -ista] dentist

4155 **desesperación** *nf* [R -ción] impatience

gladiador *nm* gladiator

mago,-a 1. *nmf* magician □ *los Reyes Magos* the Magi, the Three Wise Men; *Adoración de los Reyes Magos* Epiphany 2. *aj* magic

nativo *aj* [-ivo] native

oficiar *vt* [R] to officiate □ *oficiar de* to act as

4160 **optimismo** *nm* [R -ismo] optimism

pájaro *nm* [R] bird

plasmar(se) *vt(r)* to mold, to sign (vt); to take shape (vr)

restar *vt* [R] to subtract

siniestro 1. *nm* damage 2. *aj* left; sinister

4165 **tesorería** *nf* [R -ería(2)] treasury

tribu *nf* tribe

caos *nm* [R] chaos

cementerio *nm* cemetery

concebir *vt* [R] to conceive

4170 **contribución** *nf* [R -ción] contribution

demostración *nf* [R -ción] demonstration

dúo *nm* duo

equivaler *vi* [R] to be equivalent

erradicar *vt* to eradicate

4175 **extrañar(se)** *vt(r)* [R] to miss (vt); to be disconcerted (vr)

fundamento *nm* [R -o(1)] foundation; basis

gesto *nm* gesture

mariposa *nf* butterfly

plátano *nm* banana

4180 **preescolar** *aj* [R(escuela)] pre-school

reflejo *nf* [R] reflex; reflection

voltear *vt* [R] to turn around

zapatista *nmf* follower of revolutionary group in southern Mexico *Ejército Zapatista de Liberación Nacional (EZLN)*

abeja *nf* [R] bee □ *abeja de miel* honeybee; *abeja reina* queen bee; *abeja obrera* worker bee

4185 **agradecimiento** *nm* [R -miento] gratefulness

almacenamiento *nm* [R -miento] warehousing

celeste *nm, aj* [R] sky blue

certificación *nf* [R -ción] certification

coreano,-a 1. *nmf* Korean 2. *nm* Korean language 3. *aj* Korean

4190 **digestivo** *aj* [-ivo] digestive

egipcio,-a *nmf, aj* Egyptian

enfermero,-a *nmf* [R] nurse

inmenso *aj* [R] immense

mejoría *nf* [R -ería(2)] improvement

4195 **paraíso** *nm* [R] paradise

porcentual *aj* [R] percentage

privatización *nf* [-ción] privatization

pulir *vt* to polish

tiradero *nm* cluttered mess

4200 **adecuadamente** *av* [-mente] adequately

adverso *aj* adverse

alertar *vt* to alert

aterrizar *vt* [R] to land (plane)

box *nm* boxing

4205 **cálido** *aj* [R -ido(1)] warm

camisa *nf* [R] shirt □ *en mangas de camisa* in shirtsleeves; *camisa de fuerza* straightjacket

concesionario,-a [-ario(2)] **1.** *nmf* licensed business owner **2.** *aj* licensed □ *una empresa concesionaria* a licensed business

designación *nf* [-ción] designation

infracción *nf* infraction

4210 **jabón** *nm* [R] soap

lastimar(se) *vt(r)* [R] to injure (vt); to hurt oneself (vr)

paca *nf* bale

playero *aj* [R -ero(2)] beach
▶ **playera** *nf* t-shirt

rating *nm* rating

4215 **simpatía** *nf* [R] sympathy

vacacional *aj* vacation

verter *vt* [R] to pour

aguacate *nm* avocado

anécdota *nf* [R] anecdote

4220 **barrer** *vt* to sweep

cafetera *nf* [R -era] **1.** *nf* coffee pot; coffee machine **2.** *aj* pertaining to coffee

cardiovascular *aj* cardiovascular

criatura *nf* [R -ura(2)] creature

formalmente *av* [-mente] formally

4225 **igualdad** *nf* [R] equality

implantar *vt* [R] to implant

mosca *nf* fly (insect)

ofrecimiento *nm* [R -miento] offer, offering

óptimo *aj* [R] optimal

4230 **paje** *nm* ring bearer; page (assistant)

peatón,-a *nmf* pedestrian

tormenta *nf* [R] storm

tratador *aj* treatment □ *la planta tratadora de aguas residuales* sewage treatment plant

vacunación *nf* [-ción] vaccination (process)

4235 **variable** *aj* [R -able] variable

vencedor,-a *nmf* conqueror

alarma *nf* [R -a] alarm

amanecer [R] **1.** *nm* sunrise **2.** *vi* to greet the day

arterial *aj* arterial

4240 **celda** *nf* [R] prison or jail cell; spreadsheet cell

célebre *aj* [R] well-known, famous

comportar(se) *vi(r)* to behave (vi); to behave oneself (vr)

curiosidad *nf* [R -idad] curiosity

deleitar(se) *vt(r)* [R] to delight (vt); to be delighted, to delight oneself (vr)

4245 **encarnación** *nf* [R -ción] incarnation

naturalmente *av* [R -mente] naturally

olvido *nm* [R -ido(2)] forgetfulness; oblivion

otoño *nm* [R] autumn, fall (season)

paisaje *nm* [R] countryside; landscape

4250 **paisano,-a** *nmf* [R] fellow countryman

pariente *nmf* [R] relative

Piscis *nm* Pisces

reafirmar *vt* [R(afirmar)] to reaffirm

regar *vt* [R] to water; to spread

4255 **relevista** *aj* reserve, bench (sport)

sombrero *nm* [R] hat □ *cinta de sombrero* hat band

tope *nm* bump; speed bump

trasladar(se) *vt(r)* [R] to move something from one place to another (vt); to move oneself from one place to another, to travel (vr)

trazar *vt* [R] to delineate; to trace

4260 **villano,-a** *nmf* villain

catorce *nm, aj* [R] fourteen

ciego,-a [R -o(1)] **1.** *nmf* blind person □ *ciego de ira* blind with rage **2.** *aj* blind

comisariado *nm* [-ato] board of commissioners □ *el comisariado ejidal* town council

compensación *nf* [R -ción] compensation

4265 **comunista** *nmf, aj* [R -ista] communist

efectividad *nf* [R -idad] effectiveness

enojar(se) *vt(r)* [R] to anger (vt); to become angry (vr)

explorar *vt* to explore

indemnización *nf* [-ción] indemnification

4270 **indicio** *nm* [R -icio] indication; sign □ *prueba de indicios* circumstantial evidence

regio *aj* [R] related to the king; luxurious

reponer *vt* [R(poner)] to replace; to recover

resentir(se) *vi(r)* to resent (vi); to suffer from, to feel resentful (vr)

rotario *aj* □ *Club Rotario* Rotary Club

4275 **saturar** *vt* to saturate

trece *nm, aj* [R] thirteen

velación *nf* [-ción] vigil, the act of keeping watch; veiling ceremony (ecclesiatical)

aburrir(se) *vt(r)* [R] to bore (vt); to become bored (vr)

afortunado,-a [R -ado(1)] **1.** *nmf* fortunate person **2.** *aj* fortunate

4280 **anticipación** *nf* [-ción] anticipation

bancada *nf* [-ada(1)] group of party members in an assembly (literally, a large bench)

cooperar *vi* [R] to cooperate

fármaco *nm* [R] drug sold in pharmacies

heredar *vt* [R] to inherit; to leave as an inheritance

4285 **observador,-a** [R -dor(1)] **1.** *nmf* observer **2.** *aj* observant

onomástico *nm* saint's day celebration

pasear(se) *vti(r)* [R] to take for a walk (vt); to go for a walk or a ride, to go sight-seeing (vi, vr) □ *pasear la(s) calle(s)* to wander the streets, to stroll around

privilegiado,-a [R] **1.** *nmf* privileged person **2.** *aj* privileged

regularmente *av* [R -mente] regularly

4290 **secuestrador,-a** *nmf* kidnapper

silbante [-ante(1)] **1.** *nm* soccer referee **2.** *aj* whistling

suscribir(se) *vt(r)* [R(escribir)] to subscribe (to a belief, for example), to sign a document or agreement (vt); to subscribe (to a periodical) (vr)

sustento *nm* [R -o(1)] sustenance; support

Tauro *nm* Taurus

4295 **timonel** *nm* helmsman

abastecer(se) *vt(r)* to provide, to supply (vt); to be supplied, to be filled with provisions (vr)

agrupar *vt* [R] to group

causante *aj* [R] causing

complacer *vt* [R] to please

4300 **cotizar** *vt* to provide an estimate

equipar *vt* to equip

etiqueta *nf* [-a] tag (clothing); etiquette

físicamente *av* [R -mente] physically

porción *nf* portion

4305 **subprocurador,-a** *nmf* deputy district attorney

sustituto,-a *nmf, aj* [R -uto] substitute

textil *nm, aj* textile

tumor *nm* tumor

vela *nf* [R -a] candle; watch, vigil, wakefulness; sail □ *alzar velas* to hoist sails

4310 **alargar** *vt* [R] to lengthen

cercanía *nf* [R -ería(2)] surroundings

contendiente [-ente(1)] **1.** *nmf* contender, contestant **2.** *aj* contending

enojo *nm* [R -o(1)] anger

escorpión *nm* scorpion

4315 **estancar(se)** *vt(r)* to hold up, to hold back, to impede (vt); to become stagnant (vr)

faceta *nf* [-eta] facet

materno *aj* [R] maternal

niñez *nf* [R -ez] childhood

penalty *nm* [R] penalty

4320 **perpetrar** *vt* to perpetrate

preservación *nf* [-ción] preservation

prisa *nf* [R] hurry

reaparecer *vi* [R(aparecer)] to reappear

revelación *nf* [R -ción] developing (film); revealing

4325 **selectivo** *aj* [R] selective

seriedad *nf* seriousness

suplente *nmf* [R -ente(2)] replacement; substitute

vínculo *nm* [-culo] union, bond

volibol *nm* volleyball

4330 **agasajar(se)** *vt(r)* to indulge, to spoil (vt); to indulge (oneself) (vr)

arraigar(se) *vi(r)* [R] to sprout roots, to take root (vi); to be or become rooted or established (also figurative) (vr)

asentir *vi* [R] to assent

burlar(se) *vt(r)* to deceive (vt); to make fun of (vr)

canonización *nf* [R -ción] canonization

4335 **cónyuge** *nmf* spouse

desperdicio *nm* [R -icio] waste

miseria *nf* [R] misery

moto *nf* [R] motorcycle

mutuo *aj* [R -uo] mutual

4340 **paramilitar** [R(militar)] **1.** *nm* paramilitary soldiers **2.** *aj* paramilitary

precisión *nf* [R -sión] precision

remolcar *vt* to tow

santuario *nm* [R] sanctuary

softbol *nm* softball

4345 **zanahoria** *nf* carrot

afirmación *nf* [R -ción] affirmation

aparente *aj* [R -ente(1)] apparent

aroma *nf* [R] aroma

batazo *nm* [-azo(2)] hit with a bat

4350 **bodega** *nf* storeroom

caminata *nf* [R] walk, stroll

cancelación *nf* [-ción] cancelation

caseta *nf* [-eta] booth

cotización *nf* [-ción] quoting of a price; providing of an estimate

4355 **enterrar** *vt* [R] to bury

exótico *aj* exotic

inminente *aj* imminent

justamente *av* [-mente] exactly, precisely

oración *nf* [R -ción] prayer; sentence □ *partes de la oración* parts of speech

4360 **originalmente** *av* [-mente] originally

pez *nm* [R] fish (in its natural habitat)

próximamente *av* [R -mente] next □ *¡próximamente!* coming soon!

raya *nf* [R -a] line, stripe

remover(se) *vt(r)* [R(mover)] to move around, to stir, to remove (vt); to move (oneself) around, to stir (vr)

4365 **tamal** *nm* tamale

teletón *nm* telethon

tesis *nf* [R] thesis

tonto *aj* [R] dumb (slang, not smart), silly

urna *nf* urn; box or jar used for a raffle

4370 **ventanilla** *nf* [R -illa] small window such as in a car, train, plane, etc.

acorde *nm* [R] chord; accord

alentar *vt* [R] to encourage

apegar *vr* to be or become accustomed; to be or become attached

boricua *aj* Puerto Rican (does not change form regardless of gender)

4375 **cano** *aj* white (hair)

caribeño,-a [-eño] **1.** *nmf* person from the Caribbean **2.** *aj* Caribbean

crucial *aj* [R -cial] crucial

decorar *vt* [R] to decorate

diagnosticar *vt* to diagnose

4380 **estimación** *nf* [R -ción] esteem; estimation

etcétera *av* et cetera, etc.

excelencia *nf* [R -encia] excellence

hortaliza *nf* garden vegetable; vegetable

inesperado *aj* [R(esperar) -ado(1)] unexpected

4385 **locura** *nf* [R -ura(1)] craziness

nacionalidad *nf* [R -idad] nationality

pandilla *nf* gang

quema *nf* [R -a] burning

repercutir *vt* to cause repercussions; to affect

4390 **resta** *nf* [-a] subtraction (math)

talla *nf* [R] size; engraving

amarrar(se) *vt(r)* to tie, to tie up (vt); to tie (vr)

antro *nm* night club, restaurant-bar, discotheque

confiable *aj* [R -able] trustworthy

4395 **considerablemente** *av* [-mente] considerably

damnificado,-a **1.** *nmf* injured person **2.** *aj* damaged, injured

filmación *nf* [-ción] filming

fotográfico *aj* [R -ico(2)] photographic

frustrado *aj* [-ado(1)] frustrated

4400 **hazaña** *nf* deed, act of heroism

manipular *vt* to manipulate

patriota *nmf* [R] patriot

recital *nm* recital

remodelación *nf* [R(modelo) -ción] remodeling

4405 **sufrimiento** *nm* [-miento] suffering

activar *vt* [R] to activate

automático *aj* automatic

bordado [R] **1.** *nm* embroidery **2.** *aj* embroidered

boxeador *nm* [-dor(1)] boxer

4410 **computación** *nf* [-ción] computer science

confeccionar *vt* to make, to prepare (clothing, food)

contingencia *nf* [-encia] contingency

deshacer(se) *vt(r)* [R] to undo (vt); to become undone, to become dissolved (vr)

enfoque *nm* [R] focus

4415 **evolucionar** *vi* [R] to evolve

ficción *nf* [R] fiction

fuertemente *av* [-mente] strongly

imitar *vt* [R] to imitate

matador *nm* [R -dor(1)] bullfighter

4420 **nupcias** *nfpl* wedding

panamericano *aj* Pan-American

periodístico *aj* [R -ico(2)] pertaining to newspapers or journalism

segmento *nm* [-o(1)] segment

suficientemente *av* [R -mente] sufficiently

4425 **taurino** *aj* [-ino(2)] pertaining to bullfighting

transplante *nm* [R] transplant

contrarrestar *vt* to counteract; to resist

credibilidad *nf* [R -idad] credibility

fumador,-a *nmf* smoker

4430 **gallo** *nm* [R] rooster □ *el gallo canta* the cock crows; *tener mucho gallo* to be very cocky

poema *nm* [R] poem

prohibición *nf* [R -ción] prohibition

prórroga *nf* extension (time)

tesoro *nm* [R] treasure

4435 **arquitecto,-a** *nmf* [R] architect

barro *nm* [R] clay

batir(se) *vt(r)* [R] to beat (vt); to become beaten (food, mixture) (vr)

bloqueo *nm* [R -eo(1)] blocking

cinturón *nm* [R] belt; seatbelt

4440 **danés,-esa** [-és] 1. *nmf* Dane 2. *nm* Danish language 3. *aj* Danish

descuido *nm* [R -ido(2)] neglect

esforzar *vr* [R] to make an effort

garganta *nf* [R] throat □ *nudo en la garganta* lump in the throat

homilía *nf* homily

4445 **largometraje** *nm* [R] feature-length film

modesto *aj* [R] modest

montaje *nm* montage; mounting (photography)

neoyorquino *aj* [-ino(2)] from New York

nutriente *nm* nutrient

4450 **perito,-a** *nmf, aj* [R] expert

pescador,-a *nmf* [R] fisherman

ritual *nm* [-al(1)] ritual

ambicioso *aj* [R] ambitious

apasionar(se) *vt(r)* [R] to fill with passion (vt); to be passionate (vr)

4455 **centígrado** *aj* [R] centigrade; Celsius

congregación *nf* [R -ción] congregation

delicia *nf* [R] delight

docena *nf* [R] dozen

geográfico *aj* [R -ico(2)] geographic

4460 **humanitario** *aj* [R] humanitarian

incapaz *aj* [R(capacidad) -az] incapable

inevitable *aj* [R(evitar) -able] inevitable

mojar(se) *vt(r)* to make wet (vt); to get wet, to become wet (vr)

probabilidad *nf* [R -idad] probability

4465 **relativamente** *av* [-mente] relatively

sincero *aj* [R -ero(2)] sincere

sorpresivo *aj* [R -ivo] surprising

surtir *vt* [R] to stock

acatar *vt* to respect; to obey (law)

4470 **blanquear(se)** *vt(r)* [R] to make something white (vt); to become white (vr)

comodidad *nf* [R -idad] comfort

derrocar *vt* to defeat

discapacitado *nm, aj* disabled

duplicar *vt* to duplicate

4475 **económicamente** *av* [R -mente] economically

Eucaristía *nf* Eucharist

gene *nm* [R] gene

llanta *nf* tire

maduro *aj* [R -ura(2)] mature

4480 **monte** *nm* [R] mount

océano *nm* ocean

peatonal *aj* pedestrian

quejoso *aj* [-oso] complaining, given to complaining

reciclable *aj* [-able] recyclable

4485 **aborto** *nm* [-o(1)] miscarriage; abortion

acompañante *nmf* [R -ante(2)] escort

adherir *vr* [R] to adhere

agremiado,-a *nmf, aj* unionized

burla *nf* [R -a] joke □ *de burla* in jest; *hacer burla de* to mock, make fun of

4490 **desechar** *vt* [R] to get rid of; to eliminate

doblar *vt* [R] to fold; to double

legalmente *av* [R -mente] legally

magno *aj* [R] great; extraordinary

mentalidad *nf* [R -idad] mentality

4495 **proliferación** *nf* [-ción] proliferation

prolongación *nf* [R -ción] prolongation; extension

reproducir *vt* [R(producir)] to reproduce

sacudir *vt* [R] to shake; to dust

talentoso *aj* [R -oso] talented

4500 **votante** *nmf* [R -ante(2)] voter

bilateral *aj* bilateral

bombardeo *nm* [R -eo(1)] bombardment

comando *nm* [R -o(1)] commando

culto *nm* [R] cult; religious service

4505 **divorciar(se)** *vt(r)* [R] to divorce (vt); to become divorced (vr)

filtrar *vt* to filter

improvisar *vt* to improvise

lentamente *av* [R -mente] slowly

notorio *aj* [R -orio(2)] noticeable; well-known (for positive or negative reasons)

4510 **noventa** *nf, aj* [R] ninety

nutrir *vt* [R] to nourish

nutritivo *aj* [R -ivo] nourishing

ocupante *nmf* [R -ante(2)] occupant

oriol *nm* oriole

4515 **oxígeno** *nm* oxygen

acaparar *vt* to hoard (attention; goods)

ambición *nf* [R -ción] ambition

ángel *nm* angel □ *ángel de la guarda* guardian angel; *tener ángel* to have charm

condicionar *vt* [R] to condition

4520 **desaceleración** *nf* [R -ción] deceleration

embarcación *nf* [R] medium-sized boat

flaco *aj* [R] thin (applies to persons)

incorporación *nf* [R(cuerpo) -ción] incorporation

inútil *aj* [R -il] useless

4525 **materialista** [R -ista] 1. *nmf* materialist 2. *aj* materialistic

paquistaní *nmf, aj* Pakistani

pastor *nm* [R -or] pastor; shepherd

pesa *nf* [R -a] weight

primordial *aj* essential

4530 **provecho** *nm* [R] benefit □ *¡buen provecho!* enjoy your meal!

residuo *nm* [-uo] residue

vigilante *nmf* [R -ante(2)] guard; night watchman

aduana *nf* customs (international imports and exports)

Alzheimer *aj* Alzheimer

4535 **amparar(se)** *vt(r)* [R] to protect (vt); to protect oneself (vr)

cabellera *nf* [R] hair

Capricornio *nm* Capricorn

concurrir *vi* [R] to concur; to converge

consigna *nf* [R -a] slogan; instruction, order

4540 **coronel** *nm* colonel

deprimir(se) *vt(r)* [R] to depress (vt); to be or become depressed (vr)

descarga *nf* [R -a] unloading; discharge, discharging

determinante *aj* [R] determining

homicida 1. *nmf* murderer, murderess 2. *aj* murderous

4545 **lámina** *nf* sheet metal; illustration

morado *nm, aj* purple

multiplicar *vt* [R] to multiply

notificación *nf* [R -ción] notification

piano *nm* [R] piano □ *piano de cola* grand piano; *piano vertical* upright piano

4550 **remoto** *aj* remote

saque *nm* [R] service (sport)

secuela *nf* [R] long-term consequence

acostar(se) *vt(r)* to lay down, to put down (vt); to lie down, to go to bed (vr)

atar(se) *vt(r)* [R] to tie (vt); to tie (oneself) (vr)

4555 **boleta** *nf* card □ *boleta de calificaciones* report card

cáscara *nf* peel

chiste *nm* [R] joke, punch line; important point that makes the difference □ *no tiene chiste* there's no point

conjuntar *vt* [R] to unite with harmony

deficiente *aj* [R] deficient

4560 **diestro,-a** 1. *nmf* right-hander; matador 2. *aj* right(-handed); dexterous, skillful

distraer(se) *vt(r)* [R] to distract (vt); to be or become distracted (vr)

entusiasmar(se) *vt(r)* [R] to generate enthusiasm (vt); to become enthused (vr)

equipamiento *nm* [-miento] equipping

excluir *vt* [R] to exclude

4565 **graffiti** *nm* graffiti

hueco *aj* [R] hollow

inclusión *nf* [R -sión] inclusion

marcial *aj* martial □ *arte marcial* martial art

omitir *vt* to omit

4570 **oponente** [R(poner) -ente(1)] **1.** *nmf* opponent **2.** *aj* opposing

parámetro *nm* [R(medida)] parameter

perfume *nm* [R] perfume

rebanada *nf* slice

abdomen *nm* abdomen

4575 **abstenerse** *vr* to abstain □ *abstenerse de hacer algo* to refrain from doing something

adorno *nm* [R -o(1)] decoration

cadera *nf* hip

continuamente *av* [R -mente] continually

corporativo *aj* [R] corporate

4580 **cráneo** *nm* [R] cranium

distinción *nf* [R -ción] distinction

exigente *aj* [R] demanding

extremista *nmf, aj* [R -ista] extremist

hipertensión *nf* hypertension

4585 **horizonte** *nm* [R] horizon

noreste *nm* [R] northeast

nosocomio *nm* hospital (formal)

núcleo *nm* [R] nucleus

ordenamiento *nm* [R -miento] ordering, act of placing things in order

4590 **patrocinador,-a** [R -dor(1)] **1.** *nmf* sponsor, patron **2.** *aj* sponsoring

pulmón *nm* lung

refrigerador *nm* [R(frío) -dor(2)] refrigerator

respetuoso *aj* [R -oso] respectful

riñón *nm* kidney

4595 **sensual** *aj* [R] sensual

síndrome *nm* syndrome

trampa *nf* trap

Virgo *nm* [R] Virgo

ah *intj* ah

4600 **asignación** *nf* [R -ción] assigning to a post; assigning of money

belga *nmf, aj* Belgian

cabecera *nf* [R] headboard □ *cabecera municipal* seat of local government

cajero,-a *nmf* [R] cashier

carbón *nm* [R] coal; charcoal

4605 **corrupto** *aj* corrupt

cuartel *nm* [R] quarters, barracks

encarar(se) *vt(r)* [R] to face (vt); to be facing each other (vr)

entendimiento *nm* [R -miento] understanding

evadir *vt* to evade

4610 **innecesario** *aj* [R(necesitar)] unnecessary

mártir *nmf* [R] martyr

misceláneo *aj* [-eo(2)] miscellaneous

▶ **miscelánea** *nf* general store; miscellany

mixto *aj* [R] mixed

ostentar *vt* [R] to show off

4615 **paralizar** *vt* [R -izar] to paralyze

portal *nm* [-al(1)] main door, gateway

salvamento *nm* [R] deliverance; refuge □ *cohete de salvamento* flare

adicto,-a **1.** *nmf* addict **2.** *aj* addicted

alinear(se) *vt(r)* [R] to put in a straight line (vt); to form a straight linc (vr)

4620 **ballet** *nm* [R] ballet

cuero *nm* leather; animal skin □ *cuero cabelludo* scalp

decomiso *nm* [-o(1)] confiscation

desalojar *vt* [R] to vacate

emigrar *vi* to emigrate

4625 **exceder** *vt* [R] to exceed

experimento *nm* [R -o(1)] experiment; experience

falda *nf* [R] skirt

fluir *vi* [R] to flow

geografía *nf* [R ería(2)] geography

4630 **graduación** *nf* [R] graduation

inflamación *nf* [-ción] inflamation

intermediario,-a *nmf, aj* [R(medio) -ario(2)] intermediary

manantial *nm* [-al(1)] source, head of a river

nube *nf* [R] cloud □ *estar por las nubes* to be sky-high (price); *como caído de las nubes* out of the blue

4635 **orégano** *nm* oregano

rapidez *nf* [R -ez] speed

resguardar(se) *vt(r)* [R] to protect or defend something (vt); to protect or defend oneself (vr)

revancha *nf* revenge

subasta *nf* [-a] auction

4640 **suplir** *vt* [R] to substitute for; to replace

teñir *vt* to dye

tomatero [-ero(2)] **1.** *nm* tomato plant **2.** *aj* pertaining to tomato

tramitar *vt* to take steps to obtain something

veterinario,-a [-ario(2)] **1.** *nmf* veterinarian **2.** *aj* veterinary

4645 **agradecido** *aj* [R -ido(1)] thankful, grateful

asentamiento *nm* [R -miento] settling

cambiario *aj* pertaining to the exchange of money

concurrencia *nf* [R -encia] audience

consultorio *nm* [R -orio(1)] medical office

4650 **desarmar** *vt* [R] to disarm

epidemia *nf* epidemic

Jesucristo *nm* [R] Jesus Christ

licor *nm* [R] liquor

manual *nm, aj* [R] manual

4655 **montón** *nm* [R] large pile, heap

nervio *nm* [R] nerve

perfección *nf* [R] perfection

táctica *nf* tactic

terrestre *aj* [R(tierra) -estre] terrestrial

4660 **vacunar** *vt* to vaccinate

ahogar(se) *vt(r)* [R] to drown (vt); to drown (oneself) (vr)

banderazo *nm* [-azo(2)] waving of the flag in a car race

carnero *nm* [R] male sheep

contradicción *nf* [R -ción] contradiction

4665 **emanar** *vi* [R] to emanate

finalista *nmf* [R -ista] finalist

fiscalización *nf* [R -ción] enforcement of a law

lácteo *aj* milky

listado *nm* [-ado(2)] list

4670 **represión** *nf* [R(presión) -sión] repression

ruedo *nm* turning, rotation; bullfight arena

supervisor,-a *nmf* [R(vista)] supervisor

tradicionalmente *av* [-mente] traditionally

amargo *aj* [R] bitter

4675 **asentar** *vi* to settle

consagrar(se) *vt(r)* [R] to consecrate, to sanctify (vt); to be sanctified, to be devoted (vr)

detección *nf* [-ción] detection

escalar *vt* [R] to scale; to climb

hábil *aj* [R] able, capable

4680 **hormonal** *aj* hormonal

iluminar(se) *vt(r)* [R] to illuminate (vt); to be or become illuminated (vr)

incendiar *vt* to burn

noroeste *nm* [R] northwest

oportunamente *av* [R -mente] opportunely

4685 **progresar** *vi* [R] to progress

quemadura *nf* [R -dura] burn

readaptación *nf* [R(adaptar) -ción] readaptation

sabroso *aj* [R -oso] delicious, flavorful

abrazar(se) *vt(r)* [R] to hug (vt); to hug each other (vr)

4690 **adorar** *vt* [R] to adore, to worship

arrebatar *vt* [R] to grab forcefully; to burn too quickly (flame of a stove)

arzobispo *nm* [R] archbishop

brujo,-a *nmf* witch, warlock

contador,-a *nmf* [R] accountant

4695 **desconfianza** *nf* [R -anza] lack of confidence or faith

despegar(se) *vt(r)* [R] to remove, to unstick (vt); to take off (airplane) (vr)

despierto *aj* [R] awake

diputación *nf* [-ción] deputization, deputation; group of deputies

disolver(se) *vt(r)* [R] to dissolve (vt); to become dissolved (vr)

4700 **empeñar(se)** *vt(r)* [R] to pawn (vt); to go into debt (vr)

expropiación *nf* [R -ción] expropriation

fabricación *nf* [R -ción] fabrication

liberal *nmf, aj* [R] liberal

manufacturero *aj* [R -ero(2)] manufacturing

4705 **represalia** *nf* reprisal, retaliation

últimamente *av* [R -mente] recently

Aries *nm* Aries

autoestima *nf* self-esteem

complemento *nm* [R -o(1)] complement

4710 **confección** *nf* the making or preparation of a clothing or food product

contingente *nm, aj* contingent

cúpula *nf* dome, cupola

curiosamente *av* [-mente] curiously

disidente *nmf* [-ente(2)] dissident, dissenter

4715 **engaño** *nm* [R -o(1)] deceit; deception

grupero,-a [-ero(3)] **1.** *nmf* fans or players of *música grupera* (similar to US line dancing music) **2.** *aj* pertaining to *música grupera*

guitarrista *nmf* [R -ista] guitarist, guitar player

honestidad *nf* [R -idad] honesty

impotencia *nf* [R(potencia) -encia] impotence

4720 **inadecuado** *aj* [R(adecuado) -ado(1)] inadequate

mina *nf* [R -a] mine

pasillo *nm* [R -illo(1)] hallway

pastilla *nf* [-illa] pill, tablet (medicine)

pipa *nf* pipe (smoking); water truck

4725 **platino** *nm, aj* [-ino(2)] platinum

poblador,-a *nmf* [R] resident

reglamentario *aj* [R] required by regulation

tentación *nf* [R -ción] temptation

vapor *nm* [R] vapor

4730 **yema** *nf* yolk

aprehender *vt* to aprehend

bateo *nm* [-eo(1), -o(1)] hitting, batting (baseball)

catalogar *vt* [R] to catalog

cenicero *nm* [-ero(1)] ash tray

4735 **climaterio** **1.** *nm* period of a woman's life during which menopause and other body changes occur **2.** *aj* pertaining to this period

densidad *nf* [R -idad] density

entretener(se) *vt(r)* [R] to entertain (vt); to be entertained, to entertain oneself, to be busy about (vr)

étnico *aj* [-ico(2)] ethnic

fallecimiento *nm* [R -miento] death

4740 **flecha** *nf* [R -a] arrow

fresa *nf* strawberry

guatemalteco,-a *nmf, aj* Guatemalan

insulto *nm* [R -o(1)] insult

insumo *nm* factors of production; material used in production

4745 **motocicleta** *nf* [R] motorcycle

oscuridad *nf* [R -idad] darkness

patrullero,-a **1.** *nmf* person who is part of a patrol **2.** *nm* patrol boat, patrol plane **3.** *aj* patrol, patrolling

plenitud *nf* [R -itud] fullness

postular *vt* to nominate; to run for office; to postulate

4750 **recolectar** *vt* [R(colección)] to collect

revivir *vt* [R(vivir)] to revive

santidad *nf* [R -idad] holiness

seleccionador,-a *nmf* [R] selector

sucesor,-a *nmf* [R] successor

4755 **verbal** *aj* verbal

aliento *nm* [-o(1)] breath

allegar(se) *vt(r)* to draw someone closer (vt); to become more closely identified with, to move closer (in a relationship) (vr)

consentir *vt* [R] to coddle, to indulge

contabilidad *nf* [R -idad] accounting

4760 **contable** *aj* [R -able] countable

contralor *nm* comptroller

dependiente [R -ente(1)] **1.** *nmf* employee that works directly with the public **2.** *aj* dependent

discriminación *nf* [-ción] discrimination

disculpa *nf* [R -a] excuse

4765 **drástico** *aj* drastic

euro *nm* euro (monetary unit in Europe)

gimnasia *nf* gymnastics

guante *nm* [R] glove □ *recoger el guante* to take up the gauntlet

homenajear *vt* [R] to pay homage, to show respect

4770 **incómodo** *aj* [R(cómodo)] uncomfortable

indebido *aj* [R(deber)] incorrect; unsuitable; inappropriate

jardinero,-a *nmf* gardener

▶ **jardinera** *nf* plant stand

justificación *nf* [R -ción] justification

llano *nm* [R] plain, flatland

4775 **obstruir** *vt* [R] to obstruct

rifle *nm* rifle

Sagitario *nm* Sagitarius

senda *nf* path, trail

sustitución *nf* [R -ción] substitution

4780 **aceptable** *aj* [R -able] acceptable

asaltante [R -ante(2)] **1.** *nmf* assailant **2.** *aj* assaulting

aspirina *nf* aspirin

bolsillo *nm* [R -illo(1)] pocket □ *de bolsillo* pocket-size

cachemir *nm* cashmere

4785 **cañón** *nm* [R] canyon; cannon

cetro *nm* scepter; title (sport)

dictadura *nf* [R -ura(2)] dictatorship

divisional *aj* divisional

funcional *aj* [R] functional

4790 **graffitero** *nm* [-ero(3)] graffiti writer

incierto *aj* [R(cierto)] uncertain

infarto *nm* heart attack

inmaculado *aj* [-ado(1)] immaculate

insuficiencia *nf* [R(suficiente) -encia] insufficiency

4795 **insurgente** *nmf, aj* insurgent

jerarquía *nf* hierarchy

libremente *av* [-mente] freely

naval *aj* [R] naval

pabellón *nm* pavilion

4800 **predominar** *vt* [R(dominar)] to predominate

prematuro *aj* [R(madurez)] premature

pretensión *nf* [R -sión] pretension

rayar *vt* [R] to shine with rays (dawn); to draw lines

realista [R -ista] **1.** *nmf* realist **2.** *aj* realistic

4805 **rehén** *nmf* hostage

repercusión *nf* [-sión] repurcussion

zorro,-a 1. *nmf* fox **2.** *aj* astute, clever, foxy

apetito *nm* [R -ito(2)] appetite □ *abrir el apetito* to whet the appetite

azotar *vt* to whip

4810 **brillo** *nm* [R -o(1)] shine

bursátil *aj* pertaining to stocks and bonds

coco *nm* coconut (fruit); coconut (flavor)

condado *nm* [R] county

debutante [-ante(2)] **1.** *nf* debutante **2.** *nmf* person who is making his debut

4815 **declinar** *vi* to decline, to deteriorate

elemental *aj* [R -al(2)] elemental; elementary

empeorar(se) *vi(r)* [R] to worsen (vi); to become worse (vr)

hola *intj* hello, hi

ignorancia *nf* [R -ancia] ignorance

4820 **insecto** *nm* [R] insect

joyería *nf* [R -ería(1)] jewelery store

maltrato *nm* [R -o(1)] mistreatment

manufacturar *vt* [R] to manufacture

mellizo *nm* twin (unidentical)

4825 **micro** *nm* microwave oven; microphone; shortened form of words beginning with the prefix *micro*

milenio *nm* millennium

modernidad *nf* [R -idad] modernity

monstruo,-a *nmf* monster

nostalgia *nf* nostalgia

4830 **olla** *nf* pot (cooking)

pánico *nm* panic

profundamente *av* [R -mente] profoundly; deeply

proveer *vt* to foresee

razonable *aj* [R -able] reasonable

4835 **restauración** *nf* [R -ción] restoration

retrato *nm* [R -o(1)] portrait

rivalidad *nf* [R -idad] rivalry

sabiduría *nf* [R -ería(2)] wisdom

sabio *aj* [R] wise

4840 **sobreviviente** *aj* [R -ente(2)] surviving

tapa *nf* [R -a] lid

taquillero *aj* [-ero(2)] ticket-booth, box-office

bucal *aj* mouth

cobre *nm* [R] copper

4845 **confluencia** *nf* [R -encia] confluence

drogadicción *nf* [-ción] drug addiction

finamente *av* [-mente] finely; delicately; excellently

hincapié *nm* □ *hacer hincapié* to stress (an idea, thought, term, etc.)

imprimir *vt* [R] to print

4850 **invernal** *aj* [R(verano)] winter

macho 1. *nf* male **2.** *nf* manly

manta *nf* [R] blanket

monopolio *nm* monopoly

novedoso *aj* [R -oso] new and different

4855 **obsesión** *nf* [R -sión] obsession

procuración *nf* [R -ción] procurement □ *procuración de justicia* procurement of justice

reactivación *nf* [-ción] reactivation

sabatino *aj* [R -ino(2)] Saturday, Sabbath

sanidad *nf* [R -idad] healthiness

4860 **sindicalizado** *aj* unionized

sumir(se) *vt(r)* [R] to submerge, to sink (vt); to be sinking, to be sunken, hollow, or recessed (vr)

topar(se) *vt(r)* to bump into, to hit (vt); to meet, to bump into (vr)

visible *aj* [R -ible] visible

agitar *vt* [R] to shake; to stir; to agitate

4865 **anhelar** *vt* [R] to desire (greatly)

autoritario *aj* [R] authoritarian

bachillerato *nm* [R -ato] study at the high school or junior college level

campana *nf* [R] bell

cómodo *aj* [R] comfortable

4870 **congregar(se)** *vi(r)* [R] to congregate (vt); to congregate (oneself) with others (vr)

desemplear *vt* [R] to dismiss from employment

especulación *nf* [R -ción] speculation

frito *aj* [-ito(2)] fried

gigantesco *aj* [R -esco] gigantic

4875 **marroquí** *nmf, aj* Moroccan

occidente *nm* [R] west

raso *aj* short, low, flat □ *una cucharada rasa* level spoonful; *soldado raso* private soldier

rienda *nf* rein □ *riendas* reins

transferir *vt* to transfer

4880 **trimestral** *aj* quarterly

abiertamente *av* [-mente] openly

aeronave *nf* [R] airship

Afore *nm* financial organization responsible for retirement accounts in Mexico

apelar *vt* [R] to appeal

4885 **azar** *nm* chance □ *juegos de azar* games of chance; *el azar del destino* twist of fate

camarón *nm* shrimp

cancillería *nf* [-ería(2)] chancellorship; office of the chancellor

cemento *nm* [R] cement

conflictivo *aj* [R] conflicting

4890 **cuestionamiento** *nm* [-miento] question (formal); questioning

donativo *nm* donation

estirar(se) *vt(r)* [R] to stretch (vt); to stretch oneself (vr) □ *estirar las piernas* to stretch one's legs

freno *nm* [-o(1)] brake

lienzo *nm* linen; canvas (painting)

4895 **nazareno** *aj* Nazarene

pandillero *nm* [-ero(3)] gang member

portada *nf* cover (document)

protagónico *aj* pertaining to a protagonist

reelección *nf* [R(elegir) -ción] reelection

4900 **rellenar** *vt* [R(lleno)] to refill

alarmante *aj* [R -ante(1)] alarming

basurero *nm* [-ero(1)] dump

brevedad *nf* [R] brevity

coma *nf* coma; comma

4905 **consolidación** *nf* [-ción] consolidation

consulado *nm* [R -ato] consulate

cuñado,-a *nmf* brother-in-law, sister-in-law

decepcionar(se) *vt(r)* to disappoint (vt); to become disappointed (vr)

discreto *aj* [R] discrete

4910 **entablar** *vt* [R] to attach planks or boards; to initiate communication

esclarecer *vt* [R] to enlighten; to resolve a conflict

evidentemente *av* [R -mente] evidently

homosexual *nmf, aj* [R] homosexual

indudablemente *av* [-mente] indubitably

4915 **inyectar** *vt* to inject

ladrillo *nm* [R] brick

lata *nf* can □ *abridor de latas* can opener; *¡qué lata me das!* you're bothering me!

licenciatura *nf* [R] bachelor's degree

pertenencia *nf* [R -encia] belonging

4920 **planilla** *nf* [-illa] election ballot

prostitución *nf* [-ción] prostitution

pupilo,-a *nmf* pupil

repetición *nf* [R -ción] repetition

solicitante *nmf* [R -ante(2)] applicant

4925 **tóxico** *aj* [-ico(2)] toxic

vertical *aj* vertical

bautizar(se) *vi(r)* to baptize (vi); to be baptized (vr)

bondad *nf* [R] goodness, kindness

bota *nf* boot

4930 **carbohidratos** *nmpl* carbohydrates

cese *nm* [R] cessation

coser *vt* [R] to sew

exclusión *nf* [R -sión] exclusion

farmacia *nf* [R -icia] pharmacy

4935 **frotar** *vt* to rub lightly, to caress

honrar *vt* [R] to honor

importe *nm* amount

inducir *vt* [R] to induce

luminaria *nf* [R] lighting; special lamp used in the Catholic church

4940 **militancia** *nf* [R -ancia] militancy

monumental *aj* [R] monumental

oscilar *vi* to oscillate

refrendar *vt* to validate, to endorse

sembrador,-a *nmf* [R] person who plants seeds

4945 **síndico** *nm* [R] union representative

subcampeón *nm* [R(campeón)] runner-up, second place winner

suministrar *vt* to supply, to administer, to give (formal)

zócalo *nm* town square

balanza *nf* [R -anza] balance (scale)

4950 **bra** *nm* bra

carpeta *nf* notebook; folder

cauce *nm* river bed

circo *nm* [R] circus

corear *vt* to sing (background); to chant in chorus (such as at a sporting event)

4955 **derrumbar** *vt* to demolish

desproteger *vt* to leave unprotected; to neglect

disponibilidad *nf* [R -idad] availability

especular *vi* [R] to speculate

exclamar *vi* [R] to exclaim

4960 **frágil** *aj* [R] fragile

liso *aj* [R] smooth

micrófono *nm* [R] microphone

movilizar *vt* [R -izar] to mobilize

nocaut *nm* knock-out

4965 **prehispánico** *aj* pre-Hispanic

profundizar *vt* [R -izar] to explore the depths of a subject

reestructuración *nf* [R(estructura) -ción] restructuring

remisión *nf* [-sión] remission; forgiveness; sending (documents)

roca *nf* [R] rock

4970 **secretar** *vt* to secrete

soberano *aj* sovereign

acentuar *vt* [R] to accentuate; to accent

apresurar *vt* [R] to pressure

autopista *nf* [R] highway, freeway

4975 **biografía** *nf* [R] biography

dedicación *nf* [R -ción] dedication

deslindar *vt* to mark the limits

dibujar *vt* [R] to draw

eco *nm* echo

4980 **escocés,-esa** [-és] **1.** *nmf* Scot **2.** *aj* Scottish

fax *nm* fax

fructosa *nf* fructose

generoso *aj* [R] generous

homólogo *aj* homologous

4985 **inconveniente** *aj* [R(conveniente) -ente(1)] inconvenient

ingesta *nf* ingested food

instruir *vt* [R] to instruct

mama *nf* [R -a] mammary gland

manto *nm* [R] mantle; layer (mineral)

4990 **navaja** *nf* knife

peleador,-a *nmf* fighter

propinar *vt* to give; to hit, kick

reconstruir *vt* [R(construir)] to reconstruct

reiniciar *vt* to reinitiate

4995 **resumir** *vt* [R] to summarize

sazonar *vt* [R] to season

terapéutico *aj* [-ico(2)] therapeutic

valiente *aj* [R] valiant, brave

yugoslavo,-a *nmf, aj* Yugoslavian

5000 **agujero** *nm* hole

Alphabetical Index

This index contains over 17,000 vocabulary entries with cross-references to the Root Dictionary (full word), Suffix Guide (-ending), and Frequency Table (number). Note that cross-references are not included to the Cognate Thesaurus.

A

a 6
a.m. 4072
abadengo -engo
abajarse bajo
abajo bajo 1726
abanderado,-a bandera
abanderar bandera
abandonado abandonar
abandonar abandonar 859
abandono abandonar -o(1) 3940
abaratamiento barato
abaratar barato
abaratarse barato
abarcar 2732
abastecer 4296
abastecerse 4296
abasto 2327
abatido abatir
abatimiento abatir
abatir abatir 3013
abatirse abatir 3013
abdomen 4574
abecedario -ario(1)
abeja abeja 4184
abejaruco -uco
abejón abeja
abejorreo abeja
abejorro abeja
abejuela -uelo
abejuno -uno
abertura abrir -ura(2)
abiertamente -mente 4881
abierto abrir
abismal abismo
abismar abismo
abismo abismo
abjuración jurar
abjurar jurar
ablandadizo -dizo
ablandamiento blando
ablandar blando
abnegación negar
abnegado negar
abogacía abogado
abogadil -il
abogadillo -illo(2)
abogado abogado -ado(2)
abogado,-a 1153
abogar abogado
abolible -ible
abonado abono
abonador abono
abono abono
abordaje abordar
abordar abordar 1593
aborrecedor -dor(1)
aborrecer aborrecer
aborrecible aborrecer -ible
aborrecimiento aborrecer
aborto -o(1) 4485
abotonar botón
abotonarse botón
abovedar bóveda

abrazadera brazo
abrazar brazo 4689
abrazarse brazo 4689
abrazo brazo -o(1)
abrecartas carta, abrir
abrelatas abrir
abreviado breve
abreviar breve
abreviatura breve
abridor -dor(2) 3036
abrigado abrigo
abrigar abrigo
abrigo abrigo -o(1)
abril 706
abrillantado,-a brillante
abrillantador brillante
abrillantar brillante
abrir abrir 266
abrirse abrir 266
abrumado abrumado
abrumador abrumado
abrumar abrumado
abrumarse abrumado
absolutamente absoluto -mente 3814
absolutismo absoluto
absolutista absoluto
absoluto absoluto -uto 2364
absorbente -ente(1)
absorber 3491
absorbible -ible
abstemio,-a abstenerse
abstención abstenerse
abstencionismo abstenerse
abstencionista abstenerse
abstenerse abstenerse 4575
abstinencia abstenerse -encia
abstinente -ente(1)
abstracción abstracto
abstracto abstracto
abstraer abstracto
absurdidad absurdo -idad
absurdo absurdo 3763
abuela abuelo
abuelica -ica
abuelito -ito(1)
abuelo abuelo
abuelo,-a 1858
abulense -ense
abundancia abundante -ancia
abundante abundante -ante(1) 4105
abundar abundante 2574
aburguesarse burgués
aburrido aburrido
aburrimiento aburrido
aburrir aburrido 4278
aburrirse aburrido 4278
abusar abuso 3273
abusivo abuso -ivo
abuso abuso -o(1) 1821
abusón abuso -ón(2)
abusón,-a abuso
acá 3971
acabable -able

acabado acabar
acabar acabar 714
acabarse acabar 714
academia academia 1530
académico academia -ico(2) 1848
acallar callar
acalorado calor
acaloramiento calor
acalorar calor
acalorarse calor
acampada campo
acampanado campana
acampar campo
acanalado canal
acaparar 4516
acariciarse cariño
acariciador cariño
acariciar cariño
acarrear carretera
acarreo carretera
acaso 3045
acatar 4469
acaudalado caudal
acaudalar caudal
acaudillar caudillo
acceder ceder 2587
accesión -sión
acceso 1051
accidentado accidente
accidentado,-a accidente
accidental accidente
accidentar accidente
accidentarse accidente
accidente accidente 773
acción acción -ción 188
accionar acción
accionista acción
acebedo/a -eda
acechanza -anza
aceitar aceite
aceitazo -azo(1)
aceite aceite 1522
aceitera aceite
aceitero aceite
aceitero,-a aceite
aceitoso aceite
aceituna aceituna
aceitunado aceituna
aceitunero aceituna
aceitunero,-a aceituna
aceitunil -il
aceituno aceituna -o(2)
acelarar 2744
aceleración acelerado
acelerada acelerado
acelerado acelerado
acelerador acelerado
acelerar acelerado
acelerarse acelerado
acelerón acelerado -ón(1)
acento acento
acentuación acento
acentuado acento
acentuar acento 4972

acentuarse acento
aceptabilidad aceptar
aceptable aceptar -able 4780
aceptación aceptar -ción 3023
aceptar aceptar 429
acerado acero
acerar acero
acerca acercar 1243
acercamiento acercar -miento 3412
acercar acercar 1513
acercarse acercar 1513
acerero -ero(3) 2781
acérrimo -érrimo
acertado cierto
acertar cierto 3859
acertijo cierto
achaquiento -iento
achicado chico
achicar chico
achicarse chico
achuchón -ón(1)
ácido -ido(1) 2855
acidosis -osis
acierto cierto
aclamación reclamar
aclamar reclamar
aclamatorio -orio(2)
aclaración claro
aclarado claro
aclarar claro 890
aclararse claro
aclaratorio claro -orio(2)
aclimatable clima
aclimatación clima
aclimatar clima
aclimatarse clima
acobardar cobardía
acobardarse cobardía
acogedor recoger
acoger recoger
acogerse recoger
acogible -ible
acogida recoger
acogido,-a recoger
acólito -ito(2)
acometedor cometer
acometer cometer
acometida cometer
acometividad cometer
acomodación cómodo
acomodadizo -dizo
acomodado cómodo
acomodador cómodo
acomodar cómodo 3601
acomodarse 3601
acomodo cómodo
acompañado acompañar
acompañamiento acompañar
acompañante acompañar -ante(2) 4486
acompañar acompañar 315

agitador,-a agitar
agitar agitar 4864
agitarse agitar
aglomeración aglomeración
aglomerado aglomeración
aglomerante aglomeración
aglomerarse aglomeración
agorafobia -fobia
agosto 796
agotado agotar
agotador agotar
agotamiento agotar
agotar agotar 2895
agotarse agotar 2895
agraciado gracia
agraciar gracia
agradable gracia -able 2047
agradar gracia 2847
agradecer gracia 1996
agradecido gracia -ido(2) 4645
agradecimiento gracia -miento 4185
agrado gracia
agrandamiento -miento
agrandar grande
agrandarse grande
agrario agrícola 1922
agravante -ante(1)
agravar 3284
agravarse 3284
agredir 2126
agredirse 2126
agregación agregar
agregado agregar
agregar agregar 256
agregarse agregar
agremiados 4488
agresión -sión 2582
agresivo 2896
agresor,-a 3626
agrícola agrícola 1435
agricultor,-a agrícola 2751
agricultura agrícola 1916
agro agrícola
agronomía agrícola
agrónomo agrícola
agropecuario agrícola 1315
agrupación grupo -ción 1397
agrupamiento grupo
agrupar grupo 4297
agruparse grupo
agua agua 127
aguacate 4218
aguacero agua
aguacha -acho
aguado agua
aguador,-a agua
aguaducho -ucho
aguafiestas fiesta, agua
aguamarina agua
aguamiel miel, agua
aguanieve nieve, agua
aguantable aguantar
aguantar aguantar 3358
aguantarse aguantar 3358
aguante aguantar
aguar agua
aguarse agua
aguazal agua
agudeza agudo -eza
agudizar agudo
agudizarse agudo
agudo agudo 4150
aguerrido guerra
aguijón agudo -ón(1)
aguijonear agudo
águila águila 2167
aguileño águila
aguilucho águila
aguinaldo 3923

aguja agudo
agujerar agudo
agujereado agudo
agujerear agudo
agujero agudo 5000
agujeta agudo
agujetero agudo
agujetero,-a agudo
agusanado gusano
agusanarse gusano
Agustina -ina
aguzar agudo
ah 4599
aherrojar hierro
aherrumbrarse hierro
ahí 340
ahijado -ado(2)
ahijado,-a hijo
ahijar hijo
ahogado ahogo
ahogar ahogo 4661
ahogarse ahogo 4661
ahogo ahogo
ahondar hondo
ahora hora 120
ahorita 3611
ahorrador ahorrar
ahorrador,-a ahorrar
ahorrar ahorrar 3293
ahorrarse ahorrar
ahorrativo ahorrar
ahorro ahorrar -o(1) 1987
ahuecamiento hueco
ahuecar hueco
ahuecarse hueco
ahumado humo
ahumar humo
ahumarse humo
airado ira
airar ira
airarse ira
aire aire 866
aireado aire
airearse aire
aires aire
aíroso aire
aislacionismo isla
aislacionista isla
aislado isla
aislador isla
aislamiento isla
aislar isla 3004
aislarse isla
ajeno 2028
ajo 2692
ajustado ajustar
ajustador ajustar
ajustar ajustar 2693
ajustarse ajustar 2693
ajuste ajustar 2468
ajusticiado,-a justicia
ajusticiar justicia
al 16
ala ala 3536
alabanza alabar -anza
alabar alabar
alado ala
alambraje -aje(1)
alameda alameda -eda
alaminazgo -azgo
álamo alameda
alargado largo
alargamiento largo
alargar largo 4310
alargarse largo
alarifazgo -azgo
alarma alarma -a 4237
alarmado alarma
alarmante alarma -ante(1) 4901
alarmar alarma

alarmarse alarma
alarmista alarma
alba alba
albaceazgo -azgo
albar alba
albaricoquero -ero(4)
alberca 3893
albergar 3837
albergue 3911
albero alba
albinismo alba
albino alba
albino,-a alba
albo alba
albor alba
alborada alba
alborear alba
álbum 1023
albura -ura(1)
alcachofal -al(3)
alcachofero -ero(4)
alcalde alcalde 578
alcaldesa alcalde
alcaldía alcalde -ería(2) 3553
alcalosis -osis
alcance alcanzar 1959
alcantarillado 3676
alcanzable alcanzar
alcanzar alcanzar 439
alcohol alcohol 1436
alcohólico -ico(2) 2856
alcoholímetro alcohol
alcoholismo alcohol -ismo
alcoholizado alcohol
alcoholizar alcohol
alcoholizarse alcohol
alcohómetro alcohol
alcólico alcohol
alcornocal -al(3)
aldea aldea
aldeano aldea -ano
aldeano,-a aldea
aleccionador lección
aleccionamiento lección
aleccionar lección
aledaño 3428
alegar 3715
alegrar alegría
alegrarse alegría
alegre alegría 2260
alegría alegría -ería(2) 1746
alegrón alegría
alejamiento lejos
alejar lejos 1757
alejarse lejos 1757
alemán 962
alentado alentar
alentador alentar
alentar alentar 4372
alentarse alentar
alerta -a 2497
alertar 4202
aleta ala -eta
aletear ala
aleteo ala
alfabetizar -izar
alfalfar -al(3)
alferazgo -azgo
alfiler alfiler
alfilerazo alfiler
alfiletero alfiler -ero(1)
algo algún 258
algodón 2143
algodonero -ero(2), (3), (4) 4151
alguacilazgo -azgo
alguien algún 981
algún algún
alguno 55
alguno,-a algún
aliado alianza -ado(2) 2985

aliado,-a alianza
alianza alianza -anza 1288
aliarse alianza
alias 3612
alicaído caer
aliento -o(1) 4756
aliforme -iforme
aligeramiento ligero
aligerar ligero
alimentación alimento -ción 1780
alimentador alimento
alimentar alimento 2168
alimentario alimento
alimentarse alimento
alimenticio alimento -icio 3223
alimento alimento -o(1) 702
alineación línea -ción 2357
alineado línea
alineamiento línea
alinear línea 4619
alinearse línea 4619
alisador liso
alisadura -dura
alisar liso
alisarse liso
alistado lista
alistamiento lista
alistar lista
alistarse lista
aliviador alivio
aliviar alivio 2879
aliviarse alivio 2879
alivio alivio
allá 1032
allanamiento llano
allanar llano
allanarse llano
allegar 4757
allegarse 4757
allí 1303
alma alma 1341
almacén almacén
almacenaje almacén -aje(1), (2)
almacenamiento almacén -miento 4186
almacenar almacén 3318
almacenista almacén
almendra 4120
almendral -al(3)
almendro -o(2)
almendruco -uco
almirantazgo almirante -azgo
almirante almirante
almohada almohadón
almohadilla almohadón
almohadillado almohadón
almohadillar almohadón
almohadón almohadón
almorzar almuerzo
almotacenazgo -azgo
almuerzo almuerzo -o(1)
alocado loco
alojamiento alojamiento
alojar alojamiento
alojarse alojamiento
alpestre -estre
alpino -ino(2)
alquilar alquilar
alquiler alquilar
alrededor alrededor 542
alrededores alrededor
alsaciano -ano
altamente alto -mente 3641
altanería alto
altanero alto
altar 2060
altavoz voz, alto
alterabilidad alteración

antiquísimo antiguo
antirrábico rabia
antirreglamentario régimen
antirrobo robar
antisocial social
antítesis tesis
antojadizo antojarse
antojarse antojarse
antojo antojarse
antro 4393
anual año -al(2) 1159
anualidad año
anualmente -mente 4152
anuario año -ario(1)
anulación anular
anular anular 2986
anularse anular
anunciador anunciar
anunciador,-a anunciar
anunciante -ante(2)
anunciar anunciar 490
anunciarse anunciar
anuncio anunciar -o(1) 1997
añadido añadir
añadidura añadir -dura
añadir añadir 509
añejamiento año
añejar año
añejarse año
añejo año
año año 30
añoranza -anza
aojar ojo
aovar huevo
apacible paz
apaciguador paz
apaciguador,-a paz
apaciguamiento paz
apaciguar paz
apaciguarse paz
apadrinamiento padre
apadrinar padre
apagadizo apagar -dizo
apagado apagar
apagar apagar 3614
apagarse apagar
apagavelas apagar
apagón apagar -ón(1)
apalabrar palabra
apalancamiento palo
apalancar palo
apalanque palo
aparato 1607
apareamiento par
aparear par
aparearse par
aparecer aparecer 623
aparecerse aparecer 623
aparecido -ido(2)
aparecido,-a aparecer
aparejado par
aparentar aparecer
aparente aparecer 4347
aparentemente aparecer
-mente 3015
aparición aparecer -ción
1908
apariencia aparecer -encia
3554
apartadizo -dizo
apartado aparte
apartamento aparte
apartamiento aparte
apartar aparte 2802
apartarse aparte 2802
aparte aparte 2220
apasionado pasión
apasionamiento pasión
apasionante pasión
apasionar pasión 4454
apasionarse pasión 4454

apátrida padre
apedrear piedra
apegado pegar
apegar 4373
apegarse pegar
apego pegar
apelable apelar
apelación apelar
apelar apelar 4884
apelativo apelar
apellidar apellido
apellidarse apellido
apellido apellido -ido(2) 3331
apenado pena
apenar pena
apenas 805
apendicitis -itis
aperitivo apetito
apertura apertura -ura(1), (2)
1172
apesadumbrado pesado
apesadumbrar pesado
apetecer apetito
apetecible apetito
apetencia apetito
apetito apetito -ito(2) 4808
apetitoso apetito
apilado pila
apilamiento pila
apilar pila
apilarse pila
apisonadora piso
apisonar piso
aplacable -able
aplanador plano
aplanadora plano
aplanamiento plano
aplanar plano
aplanarse plano
aplastante -ante(1)
aplaudir aplaudir 3416
aplauso aplaudir 3042
aplazamiento -miento
aplicable aplicar
aplicación aplicar -ción 1326
aplicado aplicar
aplicado,-a aplicar
aplicar aplicar 484
aplicarse aplicar 484
apoderado poder
apoderado,-a poder
apoderar poder 2803
apoderarse poder
apolítico político
aportación aportar
aportar puerto, aportar 1130
aporte aportar
aposentamiento aposento
aposentar aposento
aposentarse aposento
aposento aposento
apostar 3252
apóstol 2709
apoyado apoyar
apoyar apoyar 452
apoyo apoyar -o(1) 229
apreciable precioso
apreciación precioso
apreciado precioso
apreciar precioso 1535
apreciativo precioso
aprecio precioso
aprehender 4731
aprehensión -sión 2346
aprender aprender 913
aprendiz,-a aprender
aprendizaje aprender 3790
apresurado prisa
apresurar prisa 4973
apresurarse prisa
apretadizo -dizo

apretado apretado
apretar apretado 3390
apretón apretado -ón(1)
apretujar apretado
apretujarse apretado
apretujón apretado
apretura apretado
aprieto apretado
aprisa prisa
aprobación aprobar -ción
2144
aprobado aprobar
aprobar aprobar 846
aprobatorio aprobar -orio(2)
apropiar 3168
apropiarse propiedad
aprovechable aprovechar
aprovechado aprovechar
aprovechamiento aprovechar
-miento 3615
aprovechar aprovechar 632
aprovecharse aprovechar
aprovisionar provisional
aproximación próximo
aproximadamente próximo
-mente 1182
aproximado próximo
aproximar próximo 3108
aproximarse próximo 3108
aptitud aptitud -itud
apto aptitud
apuesta -a 3391
apuntado apuntar
apuntador,-a apuntar
apuntar apuntar 1003
apuntarse apuntar
apunte apuntar
apuñalar puño
apurado apurar
apurar apurar
apurarse apurar
aquel 305
aquél 305
aquí 400
aquietamiento -miento
aquietar quieto
aquietarse quieto
arabesco -esco
aragonés -és
arancel 4107
araña 2935
arañada -ada(1)
arbitraje arbitrario 2762
arbitral arbitrario
arbitrar arbitrario
arbitrariedad arbitrario
arbitrario arbitrario -ario(2)
árbitro,-a arbitrario
árbol árbol
arbolado árbol
arboladura árbol
arbolar árbol
arboleda árbol
arboledo/a -eda
arbólico -ico(1)
arbóreo árbol -eo(2)
arboriforme -iforme
arborizar -izar
arbusto árbol
arcángel ángel
arcedo -eda
archiduque duque
archiduquesa duque
archivador archivo
archivador,-a archivo
archivar archivo
archivero,-a archivo
archivo archivo -o(1) 524
arco arco 2965
arder arder
ardido arder

ardiente arder
ardor arder
ardoroso arder
arduo -uo
área 498
arena arena 1629
arenal arena
arenalejo -ejo
arenillero -ero(1)
arenisco -isco
arenoso arena
arete -ete
argelino -ino(2)
argentinismo -ismo
argentino -ino(2) 293
argüir argumento
argumentación argumento
argumentar argumento 2203
argumento argumento -o(1)
2161
arguyente -ente(2)
aridecer árido
aridecerse árido
aridez árido -ez
árido árido -ido(1)
áridos árido
Aries 4707
arisco -isco
aristocracia aristocracia
aristócrata aristocracia
aristocrático aristocracia
arma arma -a 703
armada arma -ada(1)
armado arma
armadura arma -dura
armamento arma
armar arma 521
armarse arma
armería arma -ería(2)
armero arma
armero,-a arma
armonía armonía 3504
armónica armonía
armónicamente armonía
armónico armonía
armonio armonía
armonioso armonía
armonización armonía
armonizar armonía
aroma aroma 4348
aromático aroma
aromatización aroma
aromatizador aroma
aromatizar aroma
arqueología arqueología
arqueológico arqueología
arqueólogo -o(3)
arqueólogo,-a arqueología
arquero -ero(3) 2700
arquetípico arquetipo
arquetipo arquetipo
arquitecto,-a arquitecto 4435
arquitectónico arquitecto
arquitectura arquitecto
arraigado raíz
arraigar raíz 4331
arraigarse raíz 4331
arraigo raíz
arrancada arrancar
arrancado arrancar
arrancar arrancar 1833
arranque arrancar 2406
arranquen arrancar
arras 2216
arrastradizo arrastrar
arrastrado arrastrar
arrastrar arrastrar 3238
arrastrarse arrastrar 3238
arrastre arrastrar
arrebatado arrebatar
arrebatador arrebatar

arrebatamiento arrebatar
arrebatar arrebatar 4691
arrebatarse arrebatar
arrebato arrebatar
arreglado arreglar
arreglar arreglar 2358
arreglarse arreglar 2358
arreglista arreglar
arreglo arreglar -o(1) 1979
arremangar manga
arremangarse manga
arremeter arremeter
arremetida arremeter
arrendajo -ajo
arrendamiento renta
arrendar renta
arrendatario renta
arrendatario,-a renta
arrepentido pena
arrepentimiento pena
arrepentirse pena
arrestar 2736
arresto -o(1) 4073
arriba 1327
arribada arribar
arribaje -aje(3)
arribar arribar 2567
arribo arribar -o(1) 3957
arriesgado riesgo
arriesgar riesgo 3175
arriesgarse riesgo
arrinconado rincón
arrinconar rincón
arrinconarse rincón
arrocero arroz
arrocero,-a arroz
arrodillado rodilla
arrodillar rodilla
arrodillarse rodilla
arrojadizo -dizo
arrojado arrojar -ado(1)
arrojar arrojar 2145
arrojarse arrojar 2145
arrojo arrojar
arropamiento ropa
arropar ropa
arroparse ropa
arrostrar rostro
arroyar arroyo
arroyo arroyo
arroyuelo arroyo
arroz arroz 3224
arrozal arroz -al(3)
arruinado ruina
arruinar ruina
arruinarse ruina
arsenical -al(2)
arte arte 837
arteria 2944
arterial 4239
arteriosclerosis -osis
artesanal arte
artesanía arte
artesano arte
artesano,-a arte
articulista artículo
artículo artículo -culo 878
artífice arte
artificial artificial -cial 4121
artificialmente artificial
artificio arte -icio
artificioso arte
artillería artillería
artillero artillería
artista arte -ista 517
artístico arte -ico(2) 1215
artritis -itis
arzobispal obispo
arzobispo obispo 4692
asador -dor(2)
asalariado sal

asalariado,-a sal
asalariar sal
asaltador -dor(1)
asaltante asalto -ante(2) 4781
asaltar asalto 3791
asalto asalto -o(1) 2677
asamblea asamblea 1299
asambleísta asamblea
asar 3592
asarse 3592
ascender descender 2007
ascendiente descender
ascensión descender
ascenso descender 3169
ascensor descender -or
ascensorista descender
asegurado seguro
asegurador seguro
asegurador,-a seguro
aseguradora seguro
asegurar seguro 191
asegurarse seguro
asemejar semejante
asemejarse semejante
asentaderas sentar
asentado sentar
asentamiento sentar -miento 4646
asentar 4675
asentarse sentar
asentimiento sentido
asentir sentido 4332
aserradero sierra
aserrado sierra
aserradura sierra
aserrar sierra
aserrín sierra
aserruchar sierra
asesinar asesinar 2077
asesinato asesinar 1914
asesino asesinar
asesino,-a asesinar 2829
asesor,-a 2190
asesoría -ería(2) 3176
aseverar 2347
asexuado sexo
asexual sexo
así 75
asiático -ico(2) 3505
asiduidad asiduo
asiduo asiduo -uo
asiento sentar 3555
asignación asignar -ción 4600
asignar asignar 2121
asignatario,-a asignar
asimetría similar, medida
asimétrico similar, medida
asimismo 927
asistencia asistir -encia 1455
asistenta -ente(2)
asistente asistir -ente(2) 1042
asistido asistir
asistir asistir 596
asmático -ico(2)
asnal -al(2)
asociación asociación -ción 631
asociado asociación
asociado,-a asociación
asociar asociación 2032
asociarse asociación
asociativo asociación
asoleada sol
asolear sol
asolearse sol
asomar asomar
asomarse asomar
asombrado asombrar
asombrar asombrar
asombrarse asombrar

asombro asombrar
asombroso asombrar
asonancia -ancia
asordar sordo
aspecto 792
asperete -ete
aspereza áspero
asperiego -iego
áspero áspero
aspérrimo -érrimo
aspersión -sión
aspersorio -orio(1)
aspiración aspirar -ción 3005
aspirado aspirar
aspirador aspirar
aspiradora aspirar -dor(2)
aspirante aspirar -ante(2) 2513
aspirar a aspirar 2678
aspirina 4782
asterisco astro
asteroide astro
astral astro -al(2)
astro astro 2737
astrofísica físico, astro
astrolabio astro
astrología astro
astrológico astro
astrólogo -o(3)
astrólogo,-a astro
astronauta nave, astro
astronáutica nave, astro
astronave nave, astro
astronomía astro
astronómico astro
astrónomo -o(3)
astrónomo,-a astro
astuto -uto
asumir asumir 1267
asunción asumir
asunto 668
asustadizo asustar -dizo
asustado asustar
asustar asustar 3825
asustarse asustar 3825
asustón asustar
atabalejo -ejo
atabalete -ete
atacante atacar -ante(2) 3264
atacar atacar 1460
atadero atar
atado atar
atadura atar
atajo -o(1)
ataque atacar 522
atar atar 4554
atardecer tarde
atareado tarea
atarear tarea
atarearse tarea
atarse atar
atemorizar temer
atemorizarse temer
atemperar temperamento
atemperarse temperamento
atención atención -ción 379
atender atención 442
atenerse tener
ateniense -ense
atentamente atención
atentar 1048
atento atención 2788
aterrada tierra
aterraje tierra -aje(3)
aterramiento terror
aterrar tierra, terror
aterrarse terror
aterrizaje tierra -aje(3)
aterrizar tierra 4203
aterrorizar terror
aterrorizarse terror

atesoramiento tesoro
atesorar tesoro
atestado testimonio
atestiguación testimonio
atestiguar testimonio
atezado tez
atezar tez
atezarse tez
atinadamente atinar
atinado atinar
atinar atinar
atípico típico
atleta atleta 2414
atlético atleta -ico(2) 1827
atletismo atleta -ismo 3528
atmósfera atmósfera
atmosférico atmósfera
atómico átomo
atomización átomo
atomizador átomo
atomizar átomo
átomo átomo
atonal tono
átono tono
atontadamente tontería
atontado tontería
atontar tontería
atontarse tontería
atormentador tormenta
atormentador,-a tormenta
atormentar tormenta
atormentarse tormenta
atornillar torno
atracción atraer -ción 4134
atraco -o(1)
atracón -ón(1)
atractivamente atraer
atractivo atraer -ivo 1509
atraer atraer 1956
atragantarse tragar
atrapar 2670
atrás tras 1028
atrasado tras
atrasar tras
atrasarse tras
atraso tras -o(1)
atrasos tras
atravesar través (a través de) 1947
atravesarse través (a través de) 1947
atrayente atraer -ente(1)
atrever 2478
atreverse atreverse
atrevido atreverse
atrevimiento atreverse
atribución atribuir
atribuible atribuir
atribuir atribuir 2315
atribuirse atribuir
atributivo atribuir
atributo atribuir -uto
atrincheramiento -miento
atrocidad -idad
atropar tropa
atroparse tropa
atropellar 3369
atroz -az
aturdimiento -miento
audacia audacia -icia
audaz audacia -az
audible audiencia
audición audiencia
audiencia audiencia 1939
audífono audiencia
audiovisual vista, audiencia
auditivo audiencia
auditor -or
auditoría -ería(2) 2957
auditorio audiencia -orio(1) 1586

aula 3642
aullido -ido[2]
aumentado aumentar
aumentar aumentar 586
aumentativo aumentar
aumento aumentar -o[1] 857
aun 241
aún 241
aunar 2945
aunque 138
ausencia ausencia -encia
 1599
ausentarse ausencia 3643
ausente ausencia
ausentismo ausencia
austeridad austero
austero austero
australiano -ano 2108
auténtica auténtico
autenticación auténtico
autenticar auténtico
autenticidad auténtico
auténtico auténtico 2301
autentificar auténtico
auto automóvil 904
autoadhesivo adhesión
autoanálisis analizar
autobiografía biológico
autobiográfico biológico
autobús automóvil 2261
autocamión camión
autocrítica crítica
autodisciplina discípulo
autódromo automóvil 3815
autoescuela escuela,
 automóvil
autoestima 4708
autogobierno gobierno
autógrafo 3693
automático 4407
automotor motor, automóvil
automotriz 3429
automóvil mover, automóvil
 1492
automovilismo mover,
 automóvil
automovilista mover,
 automóvil -ista 2843
automovilístico mover,
 automóvil -ico[2] 3677
autonomía autónomo -ería[2]
 3924
autonómico autónomo
autónomo autónomo 1221
autopista piso, automóvil
 4974
autor -or
autor,-a 1125
autorcillo -illo[2]
autoridad autoridad -idad
 186
autoritario autoridad 4866
autoritarismo autoridad
autoritativo autoridad
autorizable autoridad
autorización autoridad -ción
 2274
autorizado autoridad
autorizar autoridad -izar 1178
autorretrato retrato
autoservicio servir
autosuficiencia suficiente
autosuficiente suficiente
autosugestión sugerir
autotransporte 3736
auxiliador auxilio
auxiliador,-a auxilio
auxiliar auxilio 2173
auxilio auxilio -o[1] 2848
avalar valer 3098
avalorar valer

avaluación valer
avaluar valer
avance avanzar 1024
avante avanzar
avanzada avanzar
avanzado avanzar
avanzar avanzar 789
avaricia -icia
avariento -iento
avasallamiento -miento
ave 3265
avecica -ica
avejentarse viejo
avellanera -ero[4]
avenal -al[3]
avenida venir 480
aventajado aventajar
aventajar aventajar
aventar ventana
aventura aventura -ura[2]
 2213
aventura aventura -a 2213
aventurado aventura
aventurar aventura
aventurarse aventura
aventurero aventura
aventurero,-a aventura
avergonzado vergüenza
 -ado[1]
avergonzar vergüenza
avergonzarse vergüenza
averiguable ver
averiguación ver -ción 2593
averiguar ver
aviación avión
aviador,-a avión
avión avión 1160
avioneta avión -eta
avisar aviso 3678
aviso aviso -o[1] 2234
avispón -ón[3]
avivado vivir
avivar vivir
avivarse vivir
ayer ayer 111
ayuda ayudar -a 677
ayudante ayudar
ayudar ayudar 495
ayudarse ayudar
ayunar desayuno
ayuno desayuno -o[1]
ayuntamiento 855
azadada -ada[2]
azafranado -ado[1]
azar 4885
azoguejo -ejo
azotador -dor[1]
azotar 4809
azteca 1161
azúcar azúcar 1377
azucarado azúcar
azucarar azúcar
azucararse azúcar
azucarera azúcar
azucarero azúcar -ero[1], [2]
azucarero,-a azúcar
azucena azúcar
azul azul 772
azulado azul
azular azul
azulez -ez
azulino -ino[2]

B

bachiller bachiller
bachillerato bachiller -ato
 4867
bacteria 3779
badajada -ada[2]

badajocense -ense
bailable baile
bailador baile
bailante baile
bailar baile 1869
bailarín,-a baile 3529
bailarina -ina
baile baile 1524
bailotear baile
bailoteo baile
baja bajo
bajada bajo
bajadizo -dizo
bajamar bajo
bajamente bajo
bajar bajo 1050
bajarse bajo 1050
bajeza bajo -eza
bajío bajo
bajista bajo
bajo bajo 172
bajuno -uno
bajura -ura[1]
bala bala 3177
balada 3493
balance balancear 3344
balancear balancear
balancearse balancear
balanceo balancear
balancín balancear
balanza balancear -anza
 4949
balazo bala -azo[2] 4010
baldón -ón[1]
balín bala -ín
balística bala
balístico bala
ballet baile 4620
balompié 4135
balón 943
bananal -al[3]
bananero -ero[2]
banano -o[2]
banca banco 2008
bancada -ada[1] 4281
bancal -al[1]
bancario banco -ario[2] 1507
bancarrota banco -ote
banco banco 648
banda 610
bandera bandera 1400
banderazo -azo[2] 4662
banderín bandera -ín
banderita bandera
banderizo -izo
bando bandera 3070
banquero -ero[3] 3780
banqueta 2286
banquete banquete -ete 3806
banquetear banquete
banquetero,-a banquete
banquillo -illo[1]
bañadero baño
bañar baño 3627
bañarse baño 3627
bañera baño -era
bañista baño
baño baño -o[1] 1909
bar 2101
baratija barato
baratillo -illo[2]
barato barato 3306
barba barba 3662
barbado barba
barbaridad bárbaro
barbarie bárbaro
barbarismo bárbaro
bárbaro bárbaro
bárbaro,-a bárbaro 3266
barbarote -ote
barbería barba -ería[1]

barbero barba -ero[3]
barbicacho -acho
barbilampiño barba
barbilla barba -illa
barbiluengo -engo
barbón -ón[3]
barbudo barba -udo
barca barco
barcada -ada[3]
barcaje -aje[2]
barcaza -aza
barcelonés -és
barco barco 3147
barcón -ón[3]
barcote -ote
barda 3743
barón barón
baronesa barón
barqueo -eo[1]
barquero barco
barra 3267
barrer 4220
barrera 1934
barreta -eta
barrigudo udo
barril 3430
barrilejo -ejo
barrilete -ete
barrio 1428
barrizal barro
barro barro 4436
barroco barroco
barroquismo barroco
barroso barro
barzón -ón[1]
basamento base
basar base 1351
basarse base
base base 333
básicamente -mente 3469
básico base -ico[2] 1133
basílica 3716
basquetbol 2897
bastante bastar 1412
bastar bastar 2221
basura 1109
basurero -ero[1], [2] 4902
batalla batalla -a 2035
batallador -dor[1]
batallador,-a batalla
batallar batalla
batallón batalla
batazo -azo[2] 4349
bate batir
bateador -dor[1]
bateador,-a batir 2575
batear batir 2946
batelejo -ejo
bateo -eo[1], -o[1] 4732
batería 3744
batidor batir -dor[1]
batiente batir
batín -ín
batir batir 4437
batirse batir 4437
bautista -ista
bautizar -izar 4927
bautizarse -izar 4927
bazuqueo -eo[1]
beatificar -ificar
beatísimo -ísimo
beatitud -itud
bebé beber 1338
bebedero beber -ero[2]
bebedizo beber -dizo
bebedor beber
bebedor,-a beber
beber beber 2239
bebible beber -ible
bebida beber -ido[2] 1426
bebido beber

bebistrajo -ajo
beca -a 2857
becerril -il
becerruco -uco
beisbol 1259
belga 4601
bellaco -aco
belleza bello -eza 1651
bellísimo -ísimo
bello bello 1283
bendecir decir 2594
bendición decir -ción 1357
bendito decir
bendito,-a decir
benedictino decir
benefactor,-a beneficio
beneficencia beneficio
beneficiado,-a beneficio
beneficiar beneficio 1177
beneficiario,-a beneficio 3319
beneficiarse beneficio 1177
beneficio beneficio -icio, -o[1] 690
beneficioso beneficio
benéfico beneficio -ico[2] 3737
benemérito mérito
beneplácito placer
benevolencia bien
benevolente bien
benévolo bien
berenjenal -al[3]
bergamoto -o[2]
berlinense -ense
berlinés -és
bernés -és
berzal -al[3]
besable -able
besamanos mano, beso
besar beso 3593
besarse beso
besito -ito[1]
beso beso -o[1] 3320
bestezuela -zuelo
besucón beso -ón[2]
besucón,-a beso
besuquear beso
besuqueo beso -eo[1]
Biblia biblioteca
bíblico biblioteca -ico[2]
bibliófilo,-a biblioteca
bibliografía biblioteca
bibliográfico biblioteca
biblioteca biblioteca -teca 2254
bibliotecario,-a biblioteca
bicharraco -aco
bicicleta ciclo 2603
bien bien 130
bienaventurado ventura, bien
bienaventurado,-a ventura, bien
bienaventuranza ventura, bien
bienestar estar, bien 2906
bienhechor hecho, bien
bienhechor,-a hecho, bien
bienintencionado intención, bien
bienvenida venir, bien 3057
bienvenido venir, bien
biforme -iforme
bígamo -o[3]
bigotazo -azo[1]
bigote bigote
bigotudo bigote -udo
bilateral 4501
billetaje billete
billete billete
billetero billete

billonésimo -ésimo
biofísica físico, biológico
biografía biológico 4975
biográfico biológico
biógrafo,-a biológico
biología biológico
biológico biológico -ico[2] 3679
biólogo -o[3]
biólogo,-a biológico
biopsia biológico
bioquímica químico, biológico
bioquímico biológico
bioquímico,-a químico, biológico
bisabuela abuelo
bisabuelo abuelo
biznieto,-a nieto,-a
Blancanieves nieve, blanco
blanco blanco 318
blanco,-a blanco
blancote -ote
blancura blanco -ura[1]
blancuzco blanco -usco
blando blando
blanducho -ucho
blandura blando
blanduzco blando
blanqueador blanco
blanqueador,-a blanco
blanquear blanco 4470
blanquearse blanco 4470
blanquecino blanco -ino[2]
blanqueo blanco -eo[1]
blanquete -ete
bloque bloque 3879
bloqueador bloque
bloquear bloque 2870
bloqueo bloque -eo[1], -o[1] 4438
bobote -ote
boca boca 1619
bocacalle boca
bocacha -acho
bocadillo boca -illo[1]
bocado boca -ada[3]
bocamanga manga
bocanada boca
bocaza -aza
bocera boca
boceras boca
bocón -ón[2]
bocudo -udo
boda 1053
bodega 4350
bodegaje -aje[2]
bofada -ada[3]
bola bola 1891
bolear bola
bolera bola
bolero 3792
boleta 4555
boleto 1789
boliche bola
bolígrafo bola
boliviano -ano
bolsa bolsillo 1000
bolsear bolsillo
bolsero,-a bolsillo
bolsillo bolsillo -illo[1] 4783
bolso bolsillo
bolsón -ón[3]
bomba bomba[1], [2] 2191
bombardear bomba[1]
bombardeo bomba[1] -eo[1], -o[1] 4502
bombardero bomba[1]
bombazo bomba[1] -azo[1]
bombear bomba[2]
bombeo bomba[2]

bombero bomba[2]
bombero,-a 1519
bombilla -illa
bonachón bueno
bonachón,-a bueno
bonaerense -ense
bondad bueno 4928
bondadoso bueno
bonísimo/buenísimo -ísimo
bonito 1798
bono 2463
boquete boca
bordado bordar 4408
bordador,-a bordar
bordadora bordar
bordadura -dura
bordar bordar
borde borde 3764
bordear borde
bordo abordar 1386
boricua 4374
borrador borrar -dor[2]
borrajear borrar
borrajo -ajo
borrar borrar 4057
borregada -ada[1]
borreguil -il
borricote -ote
borrón borrar
borronear borrar
borroso borrar
boscaje bosque
boscoso bosque
bosque bosque 1405
bosquimán,-a bosque
bosquimano,-a bosque
bota 4929
bote 3958
botelada -ada[3]
botella botella 3159
botellazo botella -azo[2]
botellería -ería[1]
botín -ín
botiquín -ín
botón botón
botonadura botón
botonazo -azo[2]
botones botón
bóveda bóveda
box 4204
boxeador -dor[1] 4409
boxeo -eo[1], -o[1] 2695
boyada -ada[1]
boyerizo -erizo
boyuno -uno
bozalejo -ejo
bra 4950
bracarense -ense
bracero -ero[2]
bracete -ete
bracito -ito[1]
bracket 3078
braserito -ito[1]
brasero -ero[1]
brasileño -eño 838
braveza bravo
bravo bravo 1410
bravote -ote
bravucón bravo
bravucón,-a bravo
bravuconada bravo
bravura bravo -ura[1]
braza brazo
brazada brazo -ada[3]
brazal brazo
brazalete brazo
brazo brazo 1358
breve breve 1033
brevedad breve 4903
breviario breve
brigada 2929

brillante brillante -ante[1] 2342
brillantez brillante
brillantina brillante
brillar brillante 3894
brillo brillante -o[1] 4810
brindar brindar 867
brindis brindar 4032
brío brioso
brioso brioso
británico -ico[2] 1292
broma broma 3912
bromear broma
bromista broma
bronce bronce 3680
bronceado bronce
broncear bronce
broncearse bronce
broncíneo -eo[2]
bronco 3339
bronquitis -itis
brotar brotar
brote brotar 3178
brujesco -esco
brujo,-a 4693
bruscamente bruscamente
brusco bruscamente
bruselense -ense
brusquedad bruscamente
bruto -uto 3133
bucal 4843
budinera -era
budista -ista
buenaventura ventura, bueno
buenazo bueno
buenazo,-a bueno
bueno bueno 84
bufonesco -esco
bujedo/a -eda
bulevar 1087
burgo burgués
burgués burgués -és
burgués,-a burgués
burguesía burgués
burla burla -a 4489
burlar 4333
burlarse burla 4333
burlesco burla -esco
burlón burla -ón[2]
burlón,-a burla
burrada -ada[1]
burrito -ito[1]
bursátil 4811
busca buscar -a
buscada buscar
buscapiés buscar
buscapleitos buscar
buscar buscar 154
buseta -eta
búsqueda buscar 1972
busto 3745

C

cabalgada caballero
cabalgadura caballero -dura
cabalgar caballero
cabalgata caballero
caballada -ada[1]
caballaje -aje[2]
caballar caballero
caballejo -ejo
caballeresco caballero -esco
caballería caballero
caballeriza caballero
caballerizo caballero -erizo
caballero caballero 1948
caballerosidad caballero
caballeroso caballero
caballerote -ote

caballete -ete
caballino -ino[2]
caballista caballero
caballito -ito[1]
caballitos caballero
caballo caballero 2365
caballuco -uco
caballuno -uno
cabecear cabeza
cabeceo cabeza -eo[1]
cabecera cabeza 4602
cabecilla cabeza
cabellera cabello 4536
cabello cabello 2159
cabelludo cabello
caber caber 1276
cabestraje -aje[2]
cabeza cabeza 797
cabezada -ada[2]
cabezal -al[1]
cabezalejo -ejo
cabezazo cabeza
cabezón cabeza -ón[2]
cabezota cabeza
cabezudo cabeza -udo
cabezuela -zuelo
cabezuelo -zuelo
cabida caber
cabildo 1890
cabina -ina
cabizbajo bajo
cable 3441
cabo 345
cabotaje -aje[2]
cabra cabra 3186
cabrerizo -erizo
cabrero,-a cabra
cabrío cabra
cabritilla cabra
cabrito,-a cabra
cabrón cabra
cabruno -uno
cacería caza
cachemir 4784
cachorrillo -illo[1]
cachorro 3816
cacicazgo -azgo
caciquismo -ismo
cada 121
cadáver cadáver 2769
cadavérico cadáver
cadena cadena 1468
cadenilla -illa
cadera 4577
caderudo -udo
caedizo -dizo
caer caer 447
caerse caer 447
café café 1367
cafeína café
cafetal café -al[3]
cafetera café -era 4221
cafetería café -ería[1]
cafetero café
cafetín -ín
cafeto café -o[2]
cafetucho -ucho
caída caer 1270
caído caer
caja caja 1935
caja registradora registrar
cajero,-a caja 4603
cajeta -eta
cajetilla caja -illa
cajetín -ín
cajita -ita
cajón caja -ón[3]
cajoncito -ito[1]
cajonera -era
calabacín -ín
calabaza 3941

calabazal -al[3]
calabazazo -azo[2]
calabazo -o[2]
calcio 2782
calculable cálculo -able
calculador cálculo
calculador,-a cálculo
calculadora -dor[2]
calcular cálculo 2671
calculativo -ivo
cálculo cálculo -culo, -o[1] 4046
caldeamiento calor
caldear calor
caldera calor -era
calderada -ada[3]
caldero calor
caldillo calor
caldo calor 3506
caldoso calor
calducho -ucho
calefacción calor
calendario -ario[1] 2633
calentador calor
calentamiento calor
calentar calor 1642
calentón -ón[2]
calentucho -ucho
calentura calor
calenturiento calor -iento
calenturón -ón[3]
caleño -eño
calibre 3644
calidad calidad 513
cálido calor -ido[1] 4205
calientaplatos plato, calor
caliente calor
calificable calidad
calificación calidad -ción 2194
calificado calidad
calificador calidad 4122
calificar calidad -ificar 1052
calificativo calidad
californiano -ano
calígrafo -o[3]
callado callar
callar callar 3765
callarse callar 3765
calle calle 214
calleja -ejo
callejear calle
callejero calle -ero[2] 3990
callejón calle
callejuela calle -uelo
calma calmar
calmante calmar
calmar calmar 2348
calmarse calmar 2348
calmoso calmar
calor calor 1926
caloría calor -ería[2] 3507
calórico calor
caluroso calor
calzada 1702
calzado 4123
cama cama 2657
camaleonesco -esco
cámara 563
camarada camarada
camaradería camarada
camarera cama
camarín -ín
camarón 4886
camarote cama -ote
camastro cama -astro
cambalachear cambio
cambiadizo -dizo
cambiante cambio
cambiar cambio 437
cambiario 4647

cambiarse cambio
cambiazo cambio
cambio cambio -o[1] 202
cambista cambio
camboyano -ano
camellón 4108
camerata 3959
camero -ero[2]
camilla cama -illa
camillero,-a cama
caminante camino -ante[2]
caminar camino 1493
caminata camino 4351
caminero -ero[2]
caminillo -illo[1]
camino camino -ino[1], -o[1] 663
camión camión 951
camionaje -aje[1]
camionero,-a camión
camioneta camión -eta 1398
camisa camisa 4206
camisera camisa
camisería camisa
camisero,-a camisa
camiseta camisa -eta 3187
camisica -ica
camisola camisa
camisolín -ín
camisón camisa
camón -ón[3]
campamento campo 4047
campana campana 4868
campanada campana
campanario campana
campanear campana
campaneo campana -eo[1]
campanero,-a campana
campanilla campana
campaña 454
campear campo
campeón,-a campeón 673
campeonato campeón -ato 834
campero campo -ero[2]
campesinado campo
campesino campo -ino[2] 597
campesino,-a campo
campestre campo -estre 1902
campiña campo
campirano campo
campista campo
campo campo 306
campus 2912
camucha -ucho
canadiense -ense 2425
canal canal 916
canaleja -ejo
canalización canal
canalizar canal -izar 3029
canalón canal
canario -ario[2]
canastada -ada[3]
canastilla -illa 3058
cancelación -ción 4352
cancelar 2200
cancelariato -ato
cáncer 1205
cancha 865
canciller 2804
cancillerato -ato
cancillería -ería[2] 4887
canción cantar 520
cancioncita -ita
cancionero cantar
candidato,-a 653
candidatura -ura[2] 2415
candidez cándido
cándido cándido -ido[1]
candor cándido

candoroso cándido
canela 4074
canelo -o[2]
canino -ino[2]
cano 4375
canon canon
canonicato -ato
canónico canon
canonización canon -ción 4334
canonizar canon
cansado cansar
cansancio cansar 3925
cansar cansar 2528
cansarse cansar 2528
cantante cantar -ante[2] 423
cantar cantar 843
cantata cantar
cantatriz -triz
cantautor,-a 3577
cantidad 456
cantina 3895
canto cantar -o[1] 2666
cantor cantar
cantor,-a cantar
cantorzuelo -zuelo
canturrear cantar
canturreo cantar
caña caña 3960
cáñamo caña
cañamón caña
cañaveral caña
cañete -ete
cañón cañón 4785
cañonazo cañón
cañonear cañón
cañonero cañón
caos caos 4167
caótico caos -ico[2]
capa capa 2980
capacidad capacidad -idad 646
capacitación capacidad -ción 1686
capacitar capacidad 2778
capacitarse 2778
capada -ada[3]
capaz capacidad -az 1499
capellán capilla
caperucita -ita
capilla capilla 2991
capirote capa
capirucho -ucho
capital capital 487
capitalino -ino[2] 1354
capitalismo capital
capitalista capital -ista
capitalización capital
capitalizar capital
capitán,-a capitán 2458
capitana capitán
capitanear capitán
capitanía capitán
capítulo -culo 2183
capote capa
capricho capricho
caprichoso capricho
caprichoso,-a capricho
Capricornio 4537
cápsula -culo
captación -ción 3564
captar 1608
captura -a, -ura[2] 2783
capturar -ura[2] 2333
capucha capa
cara cara 1094
carácter carácter 1443
característica carácter
característicamente carácter
característico carácter -ico[2] 1324

coloración color
colorado color -ado[1]
colorante color
colorear color
colorete color -ete
colorido color
colorista color
colosal colosal
coloso colosal
columna columna 2498
columnata columna
columnista columna
coma 4904
comadrazgo -azgo
comandancia mandar
comandante mandar -ante[2] 1884
comandar mandar 3334
comando mandar -o[1] 4503
comarca comarca 723
comarcal comarca
comarcano comarca
combate 1081
combatiente combate -ente[2] 3961
combatir combate 1574
combativo combate
combinación combinación -ción 2926
combinado combinación
combinar combinación 1870
combinarse combinación
combustible combustible 2907
combustión combustible
comedero comer
comedia comedia 2240
comediante comedia 3718
comedión -ón[3]
comedor comer
comensal comer
comentar comentar 264
comentario comentar 1345
comentarista comentar
comenzar comenzar 313
comer comer 841
comercial comercial -cial 633
comercialización comercial -ción 2435
comercializar comercial -izar 3030
comerciante comercial -ante[2] 1325
comerciar comercial
comercio comercial -o[1] 685
comerse comer
comestible comer
comestibles comer
cometer cometer 1265
cometido cometer -ido[2] 2068
comible -ible
comicidad comedia
comicios 2446
cómico comedia 3703
cómico,-a comedia
comida comer -ido[2] 1097
comidica -ica
comienzo comenzar -o[1] 2881
comilon comer
comilón -ón[2]
comilón,-a comer
comisaría comisario
comisariado -ato 4263
comisario comisario
comisión comisión, cometer -sión 265
comisionado comisión
comisionado,-a comisión
comisionar comisión 2936

comistrajo -ajo
comité 713
como 20
cómo 20
cómoda cómodo
cómodamente cómodo
comodidad cómodo -idad 4471
cómodo cómodo 4869
comodón cómodo
compacto 3340
compadecer padecer
compadecerse padecer
compadrazgo -azgo
compadre padre 3962
compañerismo acompañar
compañero acompañar
compañero,-a 624
compañía acompañar 532
comparable comparar
comparación comparar -ción 2162
comparado comparar
comparanza -anza
comparar comparar 2205
comparativo comparar
comparecencia parecer
comparecer parecer 3663
compareciente -ente[2]
compartimento partir
compartimiento partir
compartir partir 955
compás compás
compasión pasión
compasivo pasión
compatriota padre 2410
compenetración penetrar
compenetrarse penetrar
compensable -able
compensación compensar -ción 4264
compensador compensar
compensar compensar 3913
competencia competencia 523
competente competencia -ente[1] 3681
competer competencia
competición competencia
competidor competencia
competidor,-a competencia 2647
competir 1732
competirse 1732
competitividad competencia -idad 3793
competitivo competencia -ivo 2609
complacencia placer
complacer placer 4299
complacerse placer
complacido placer
complaciente placer
complejidad complejo
complejo complejo 1867
complementar complementar 3972
complementario complementar 3926
complementarse complementar 3972
complemento complementar -o[1] 4709
completamente completamente -mente 2184
completar completamente 2169
completo completamente 985

complicación complicado -ción 3232
complicado complicado
complicar complicado 1444
complicarse complicado 1444
cómplice 2629
componente componer 3566
componer componer 2789
componerse componer
comportamiento -miento 1960
comportar 4242
comportarse 4242
composición componer -ción 3113
compositor -or
compositor,-a componer 2255
compostura componer
compra comprar -a 1328
comprador -dor[1] 3616
comprador,-a comprar
comprar comprar 880
comprarse comprar
compraventa comprar
comprender comprender 1537
comprenderse comprender
comprensible comprender -ible
comprensión comprender 3942
comprensivo comprender
compresor -or
compresión -sión
compresor -or
comprimible -ible
comprobable probar
comprobación probar
comprobante probar
comprobar probar 1681
comprometedor prometer
comprometer prometer 1247
comprometerse prometer 1247
comprometido prometer
compromiso prometer 708
compuesto componer 2440
computación -ción 4410
computadora -dor[2] 1452
cómputo -o[1] 4109
común común 806
comuna común
comunal común
comunicable comunicar
comunicación comunicar -ción 649
comunicado comunicar 1380
comunicante comunicar
comunicar comunicar 1734
comunicarse comunicar
comunicativo comunicar
comunidad común -idad 350
comunión común
comunismo común
comunista común -ista 4265
comunitario común 3495
con 13
concebible concepto, concebir -ible
concebir concepto, concebir 4169
conceder ceder 2082
concejil -il
concentración centro -ción 2033
concentrado centro
concentrar centro 1565
concentrarse 1565
concéntrico centro

concepción concepto, concebir
concepto concepto 1336
conceptual concepto
conceptuar concepto
concertado concierto
concertar concierto
concertista concierto
concesión -sión 2436
concesionario -ario[2] 4207
concha 2437
conciencia consciente -encia 1782
concienzudo consciente
concierto concierto 755
conciliable -able
conciliación -ción 3991
conciliatorio -orio[2]
concluir concluir 462
concluirse concluir
conclusión concluir -sión 2309
concluso concluir
concluyente concluir
concretamente concreto
concretar concreto 1887
concretarse concreto 1887
concreto concreto -o[1] 1967
concubinato -ato
concurrencia concurrir 4648
concurrente concurrir
concurrido concurrir
concurrir concurrir 4538
concursante concurso
concursar concurso
concurso concurso -o[1] 1652
condado conde 4813
condal conde
conde conde
condecoración decoración
condecorar decoración
condena condenado -a 3861
condenable -able
condenación condenado
condenado condenado
condenado,-a condenado
condenar condenado 2241
condenarse condenado
condensación denso
condensado denso
condensador denso
condensar denso
condensarse denso
condesa conde
condescendencia descender -encia
condescender descender
condescendiente descender
condición condición -ción 360
condicional condición
condicionamiento condición
condicionar condición 4519
condiscípulo,-a discípulo
condolencia dolor
condolerse dolor
condominio dominar
conducción conducir -ción 3807
conducir conducir 882
conducirse conducir
conducta conducir 2170
conductibilidad conducir
conductividad conducir
conducto conducir 3109
conductor conducir -or
conductor,-a conducir 906
conectar 1456
conejera conejo
conejero conejo
conejero,-a conejo

crucifijo cruzar
crucifixión cruzar
cruciforme -iforme
crucigrama cruzar
crudeza crudo
crudo crudo 2452
cruel cruel
crueldad cruel
crujido -ido[2]
cruz cruzar 1818
cruzada cruzar
cruzado cruzar -ado[1]
cruzar cruzar 1562
cruzarse cruzar
cuadra cuatro 3539
cuadrado cuatro -ado[1] 2959
cuadragésimo cuatro -ésimo
cuadrangular 1878
cuadrante cuatro
cuadrar cuatro
cuadrarse cuatro
cuadratura cuatro
cuadrícula cuatro
cuadricular cuatro
cuadriforme -iforme
cuadrilátero cuatro
cuadrilla cuatro
cuadringentésimo -ésimo
cuadriplicar cuatro
cuadro cuatro 705
cuadrúpedo cuatro
cuádruple cuatro
cuajada cuajar
cuajado cuajar
cuajar cuajar
cual 63
cuál 63
cualidad cualidad 2908
cualitativo cualidad
cualquier 278
cuando 45
cuándo 45
cuántico -ico[2] 3994
cuantificar cuanto -ificar
cuantioso cuanto
cuantitativo cuanto
cuanto cuanto 325
cuánto cuanto 325
cuanto,-a cuanto
cuarenta cuatro 3269
cuarentavo cuatro -avo
cuarentena cuatro
cuarenteno -eno
cuarentón cuatro -ón[2]
cuarentón,-a cuatro
cuaresmal -al[2]
cuartear cuatro
cuartel cuarto 4606
cuartelero cuarto
cuarteta -eta
cuarteto cuatro
cuartillo cuatro
cuarto cuatro, cuarto 385
cuartucho cuarto -ucho
cuartuco -uco
cuatrillizo cuatro
cuatrillizo,-a cuatro
cuatrimestre -estre
cuatrimotor cuatro
cuatro cuatro 184
cuatrocientos cuatro
cubano -ano 1300
cúbico -ico[2] 2716
cubículo -culo
cubierta cubierto
cubierto cubierto 2597
cubrecama cubierto, cama
cubrecolchón cubierto
cubrir cubierto 1037
cubrirse cubierto
cucarachera -era

cucarachero -ero[2]
cucharada -ada[3] 2065
cucharero -ero[1]
cuchareta -eta
cuchillada cuchillo -ada[2]
cuchillazo cuchillo
cuchilleja -ejo
cuchillera -era
cuchillo cuchillo 3603
cuello cuello 2792
cuenca 4059
cuenta contar -a 159
cuentakilómetros kilómetro, contar
cuentarrevoluciones contar
cuentecillo -illo[1]
cuentista cuento
cuento cuento -o[1] 2426
cuerda cuerda 3927
cuerno cuerno
cuero 4621
cuerpo cuerpo 402
cuesta 2588
cuestión cuestión 1116
cuestionable cuestión
cuestionamiento -miento 4890
cuestionar cuestión 1572
cuestionario cuestión -ario[1]
cuidado cuidado 1293
cuidadoso cuidado -oso
cuidar cuidado 1273
cuidarse cuidado
culatazo -azo[2]
culebrón -ón[3]
culminar 2564
culpa culpa -a 2402
culpabilidad culpa
culpable culpa -able 2534
culpablemente -mente
culpar culpa 3746
culparse culpa
cultivable -able
cultivado cultura
cultivadora -dor[2]
cultivar cultura 2542
cultivo cultura -o[1] 1374
culto cultura 4504
cultura cultura -ura[2] 615
cultural cultura 1105
cumbre cumbre 1855
cumbreño -eño
cumpleaños cumplir, año 1342
cumplido cumplir
cumplidor cumplir
cumplimiento cumplir -miento 2230
cumplir cumplir 270
cumplirse cumplir
cúmulo cúmulo
cuna cuna
cuneiforme -iforme
cunita -ita
cuñado,-a 4907
cuota 1727
cúpula 4712
cura curar -ura[2] 4075
curación curar
curado curar
curandero,-a curar
curar curar -ura[2] 3226
curarse curar
curativo curar
curiosamente -mente 4713
curiosear curioso
curiosidad curioso -idad 4243
curioso curioso 3444
curioso,-a curioso
currutaco -aco

cursar curso 3863
cursillista curso
cursillo curso
curso curso -o[1] 932
curva curva 4034
curvar curva
curvatura curva
curvilíneo línea, curva
curvo curva
custodio -o[1] 3767
cuyo,-a 376

D

dádiva dar
dadivoso dar
dadivoso,-a dar
dado dar
dador,-a dar
dama 1487
damnificado,-a 4396
danés,-esa -és 4440
Danielito -ito[1]
dantesco -esco
danza danzar -a 3006
danzante danzar -ante[2]
danzar danzar
danzarín,-a danzar
dañado daño
dañar daño 1751
dañarse daño
dañino daño -ino[2]
daño daño -o[1] 731
dañoso daño
dar dar 37
darse dar
datar 3864
datilera -ero[4]
dato -o[1] 941
de 2
de repente repente (de repente)
deambular ambulante
debajo 2479
debate debatir 1943
debatir debatir
debe deber
deber deber 43
deberse deber
debidamente deber -mente 3704
debido deber
débil débil 2805
debilidad débil -idad 3089
debilitación débil
debilitador débil
debilitar débil 3928
debilitarse débil 3928
debilucho débil
debilucho,-a débil
debut 2147
debutante -ante[2] 4814
debutar 2439
década -ada[1] 947
decadencia decadencia
decadente decadencia
decaer decadencia, caer
decaído decadencia
decaimiento decadencia
decapitación cabeza
decapitar cabeza
deceleración acelerado
decelerar acelerado
decena 1982
deceno -eno
decepcionar 4908
decepcionarse 4908
decible -ible
decididamente decidir
decidido decidir

decidir decidir 374
decidirse decidir 374
decimal décimo
decímetro décimo
décimo décimo -ésimo 2179
decimoctavo ocho, décimo -avo, -ésimo
decimocuarto décimo -ésimo
decimonoveno décimo -ésimo
decimoquinto décimo -ésimo
decimoséptima décimo
decimoséptimo décimo -ésimo
decimosexto décimo -ésimo
decimotercero décimo
decir decir 28
decirse decir
decisión decidir -sión 464
decisivo decidir -ivo 3975
decisorio -orio[2]
declamatorio -orio[2]
declaración declarar -ción 807
declarado declarar
declarar declarar 499
declararse declarar
declarativo -ivo
declaratorio declarar
declinar 4815
declinatorio -orio[1]
decoloración color
decolorante color
decolorar color
decolorarse color
decomisar 3239
decomiso -o[1] 4622
decoración decoración
decorado decoración -ado[2]
decorador,-a decoración
decorar decoración 4378
decorativo decoración
decorazonar corazón
decorazonarse corazón
decoro decoro
decoroso decoro
decrecer crecer
decreciente crecer
decrecimiento crecer
decrépito -ito[2]
decrepitud -itud
decretar decreto 3768
decreto decreto -o[1] 2163
dedada -ada[3]
dedal dedo -al[1]
dedicación dedicar -ción 4976
dedicado dedicar
dedicar dedicar 589
dedicarse dedicar 589
dedicatoria dedicar
dedicatorio -orio[1], [2]
dedillo -illo[1]
dedo dedo 2396
deducción deducir[1], [2]
deducible deducir[1], [2] -ible
deducir deducir[1], [2]
deductivo deducir[1]
defecto defecto 3445
defectuoso defecto
defender defender 1011
defenderse defender
defendible defender
defendido defender
defendido,-a defender
defensa defender 564
defensiva defender
defensivo defender -ivo 1664
defensor defender
defensor,-a defender 1910
defensorio -orio[1]

desbocado boca
desbordamiento borde
desbordante borde
desbordar borde
desbordarse borde
descabalgar caballero
descabezar cabeza
descafeinado café
descafeinar café
descalificación calidad
descalificar calidad
descambiar cambio
descamisado camisa
descampado campo
descansadero cansar
descansado cansar
descansar cansar 2148
descanso cansar -o[1] 1905
descaradamente cara
descarado cara
descarado,-a cara
descarga cargo -a 4542
descargador,-a cargo
descargar cargo
descargarse cargo
descargo cargo
descarnado carne
descarnar carne
descaro cara
descartar 1478
descasar casa
descendencia descender
   -encia
descendente descender
descender descender 2999
descendiente descender
descendimiento descender
descenso descender 2763
descentrado centro
descentralización centro
descentralizar centro
descentrar centro
desceñir ceñido
descifrable cifra
descifrado cifra
desciframiento cifra
descifrar cifra
desclavar clavar
descolgar colgar
descolgarse colgar
descolocar local
descolonización colonia
descolonizar colonia
descoloramiento color
descolorido color
descomponer componer
descomponerse componer
descomposición componer
descompostura componer
descompuesto componer
desconcentrado centro
desconcertar concierto
desconcertarse concierto
desconcierto concierto
desconfiado fe
desconfiado,-a fe
desconfianza fe -anza 4695
desconfiar fe
desconocer conocer 1126
desconocido conocer
desconocido,-a conocer
desconocimiento conocer
desconsideración considerar
desconsiderado considerar
desconsiderado,-a considerar
desconsolado consolador
desconsolador consolador
descontar contar
descontentar contentar
descontento contentar
descorazonador corazón

descornar cuerno
descorrer correr
descorrerse correr
descorrimiento correr
descortés cortesía
descortesía cortesía
descortezar corteza
descoser coser
descoserse coser
descosido coser
descrédito creer
descreído creer
describir escribir 2069
descripción escribir
descriptible escribir
descriptivo escribir -ivo
descrito escribir
descuartizamiento cuatro
descuartizar cuatro
descubierto cubierto
descubridor,-a cubierto
descubrimiento cubierto
   -miento 3963
descubrir cubierto 1015
descubrirse cubierto
descuento contar -o[1] 3025
descuidado cuidado
descuidar cuidado 3578
descuidarse cuidado 3578
descuido cuidado -ido[2] ,
   -o[1] 4441
desde 70
desdecirse decir
desdén desdén
desdentado diente
desdeñable desdén
desdeñar desdén
desdeñarse desdén
desdeñoso desdén
desdibujado dibujo
desdibujar dibujo
desdibujarse dibujo
desdicha dicha
desdichadamente dicha
desdichado dicha
desdichado,-a dicha
desdoblamiento doble
desdoblar doble
deseable desear
deseado desear
desear desear 785
desecar seco
desechable echar
desechar echar 4490
desecho echar -o[1] 3090
desembarcadero barco
desembarcar barco
desembarcarse barco
desembarco barco
desembargar embargo
desembargo embargo
desembocadura boca
desembocar boca
desembolsar bolsillo
desembolso bolsillo
desemejante semejante
desemejanza semejante
   -anza
desempapelar papel
desemparejado par
desemparejar par
desempedrar piedra
desempeñar empeño 2083
desempeñarse empeño
desempeño empeño -o[1]
   1998
desempleado emplear
desempleado,-a emplear
desemplear emplear 4871
desempleo emplear -eo[1] ,
   -o[1] 2059

desempolvar polvo
desencadenamiento cadena
desencadenar cadena
desencadenarse cadena
desencajado caja
desencajar caja
desencajarse caja
desencajonar caja
desencantamiento encanto
desencantar encanto
desencanto encanto
desencarcelar cárcel
desenfadado enfadar
desenfadar enfadar
desenfadarse enfadar
desenfado enfadar
desenfocado foco
desenfocar foco
desenfoque foco
desengañar engañar
desengañarse engañar
desengaño engañar
desengrasar grasa
desenhebrar hebra
desenlace lazo
desenlazar lazo
desenredar red
desenredarse red
desensillar sillón
desentenderse entender
desenterrar tierra
desentonar tono
desentrañar entrañas
desenvoltura envolver
desenvolver envolver
desenvolverse envolver
desenvuelto envolver
deseo desear -o[1] 1155
deseoso desear
desequilibrado equilibrio
desequilibrado,-a equilibrio
desequilibrar equilibrio
desequilibrarse equilibrio
desequilibrio equilibrio
deserción desierto
desertar desierto
desértico desierto
desertor,-a desierto
desesperación esperar -ción
   4155
desesperado esperar
desesperante esperar
desesperanza esperar -anza
desesperanzar esperar
desesperanzarse esperar
desesperar esperar 2849
desesperarse esperar 2849
desestabilización establecer
desestabilizar establecer
desestimar estimar
desfallecer fallecer
desfallecido fallecer
desfallecimiento fallecer
desfasado fase
desfasar fase
desfasarse fase
desfase fase
desfavorable favor
desfavorecer favor
desfigurado figura
desfigurar figura
desfiladero fila
desfilar fila
desfile fila 2821
desfloración flor
desflorar flor
desfondar fondo
desfondarse fondo
desfonde fondo
desgana gana
desganado gana

desganar gana
desganarse gana
desgarrado agarrar
desgarrador agarrar
desgarrar agarrar
desgarro agarrar
desgarrón agarrar
desgastar gastar
desgastarse gastar
desgaste gastar
desgobernar gobierno
desgracia gracia -a 3393
desgraciadamente gracia
   -mente 3372
desgraciado gracia
desgraciado,-a gracia
desgraciar gracia
desgraciarse gracia
desgranadora grano
desgranar grano
desgranarse grano
desgravación grave
desgravar grave
deshabitado habitación
deshabitar habitación
deshabituar hábito
deshabituarse hábito
deshacer hacer 4413
deshacerse hacer 4413
deshecho hecho
deshelar hielo
desherbar hierba
desheredado herencia
desheredado,-a herencia
desheredar herencia
deshielo hielo
deshilachar hilo
deshilvanado hilo
deshilvanar hilo
deshojar hoja
deshonestidad honor
deshonesto honor
deshonor honor
deshonra honor
deshonrar honor
deshonroso honor
deshora hora
deshuesadora hueso
deshuesar hueso
deshumanización humano
deshumanizado humano
deshumanizar humano
desierto desierto 2867
designación -ción 4208
designar 2181
desigual igual
desigualar igual
desigualdad igual
desilusión ilusión
desilusionado ilusión
desintegración integrar
desintegrar integrar
desintegrarse integrar
desinterés interés
desinteresado interés
desinteresarse interés
deslavar lavar
desleal leal
deslealtad leal
deslenguado lengua
deslenguarse lengua
deslindar 4977
deslinde línea
desliz deslizar
deslizamiento deslizar
deslizar deslizar
deslizarse deslizar
deslucido luz
deslumbrador luminoso
deslumbramiento luminoso
deslumbrar luminoso

dignatario -ario[2]
dignatario,-a digno
dignidad digno -idad 3240
dignificante digno
dignificar digno
digno digno 1856
dilatación dilatado
dilatado dilatado
dilatador dilatado
dilatar dilatado
dilatarse dilatado
diligencia diligencia
diligenciar diligencia
diligente diligencia
dimensión dimensión 2882
dimensional dimensión
diminuto -uto
dinámica dinámico 3414
dinámico dinámico
dinamismo dinámico
dinamita dinámico -ito[2]
dinamitar dinámico
dinamitero,-a dinámico
dineral dinero -al[1]
dinerillo dinero
dinero dinero 422
dios Dios 657
diosa Dios
diploma diplomático
diplomacia diplomático
diplomado diplomático
diplomarse diplomático
diplomático diplomático
  -ico[2] 2334
diplomático,-a diplomático
diputación -ción 4698
diputado,-a 417
dirección dirigir -ción 339
direccional dirigir
directa dirigir
directamente dirigir -mente
  1735
directiva dirigir
directivo dirigir -ivo 699
directivo,-a dirigir
directo dirigir 1046
director -or
director,-a dirigir 180
directorio dirigir -orio[1]
dirigencia -encia 1850
dirigente dirigir -ente[2] 640
dirigible dirigir
dirigir dirigir 342
dirigirse dirigir 342
discapacidad 3781
discapacitado 4473
discernimiento discernir
discernir discernir
disciplina discípulo -a 1764
disciplinado discípulo
disciplinal -al[2]
disciplinar discípulo
disciplinario discípulo
discípulo -culo
discípulo,-a discípulo
disco 371
discográfico -ico[2] 1906
disconforme conforme
disconformidad conforme
discontinuidad continuar
discontinuo continuar -uo
discoteca -teca 3540
discreción discreto
discrecional discreto
discrepancia -ancia
discreto discreto 4909
discreto,-a discreto
discriminación -ción 4763
discriminatorio -orio[2]
disculpa culpa -a 4764
disculpable culpa

disculpar culpa
disculparse culpa
discursivo discutir
discurso discutir 1736
discusión discutir -sión 1923
discutible discutir -ible
discutir discutir 1708
diseñador,-a 3865
diseñar 2447
diseño -o[1] 2464
disertación disertación
disertar disertación
disfraz disfraz
disfrazar disfraz
disfrazarse disfraz
disfrutar disfrute 764
disfrute disfrute
disgregación agregar
disgregar agregar
disgustado gusto
disgustar gusto
disgustarse gusto
disgustillo -illo[2]
disgusto gusto
disidente -ente[2] 4714
disimulación disimulado
disimuladamente disimulado
disimulado disimulado
disimular disimulado
disipado disipar
disipar disipar
dislocar local
dislocarse local
disminución disminuir 2109
disminuir disminuir 980
dismunición -ción
disociable social
disociación social
disociar social
disolubilidad solución[1]
disoluble solución[1]
disolución solución[1]
disoluto -uto
disolvente solución[1]
disolver solución[1] 4699
disolverse solución[1] 4699
disonancia sonar -ancia
disparador disparar
disparar disparar 1737
dispararse disparar
disparo disparar -o[1] 1461
dispensa dispensar
dispensar dispensar
dispensario dispensar
disponer poner 1728
disponerse poner 1728
disponibilidad poner -idad
  4957
disponible poner -ible 2343
disposición poner -ción 877
dispositivo 3471
dispuesto poner 1164
disputa disputar -a, -uto 1975
disputar disputar 1222
disputarse 1222
disquera 3114
distancia distancia -a, -ancia
  1564
distanciado distancia
distanciamiento distancia
distanciar distancia
distanciarse distancia
distante distancia
distar distancia
distinción distinguir -ción
  4581
distinguido distinguir
distinguir distinguir 2185
distinguirse distinguir 2185
distintivo distinguir
distinto distinguir 748

distorsión -sión
distracción distraer
distraer distraer 4561
distraerse distraer 4561
distraído distraer
distraído,-a distraer
distribución distribución
  -ción 1944
distribuidor distribución
  -dor[1] 3431
distribuidor,-a distribución
distribuir distribución 1881
distributivo distribución
distribuyente -ente[2]
distrito 736
diurno día
divergencia diverso -encia
divergente diverso
divergir diverso
diversidad diverso -idad 4112
diversificación diverso
diversificar diverso -ificar
diversificarse diverso
diversión diverso -sión 3465
diverso diverso 446
diverticulitis -itis
divertido diverso
divertir diverso 1543
divertirse diverso 1543
dividendo dividir
dividir dividir 1805
dividirse dividir
divinidad divino
divinizar divino
divino divino 3915
divisa 3866
divisibilidad dividir
divisible dividir
división dividir -sión 915
divisional 4788
divisor dividir
divisoria dividir
divisorio dividir -orio[1]
divo,-a 4076
divorciado divorcio
divorciado,-a divorcio
divorciar divorcio 4505
divorciarse divorcio 4505
divorcio divorcio -o[1] 3840
divulgar 3916
doblaje doble
doblar doble 4491
doble doble 1025
doblegar doble
doblegarse doble
doblemente doble
dobles doble
doblete 3446
doblez doble
doce dos 2122
doceavo -avo
doceavo,-a dos
docena dos 4458
doceno -eno
docente 3629
dócil dócil
docilidad dócil
doctamente doctor
docto doctor
docto,-a doctor
doctor,-a doctor 556
doctorado doctor -ato
doctoral doctor
doctorarse doctor
doctorcillo -illo[2]
doctrina doctrina
doctrinal doctrina
doctrinario doctrina
doctrinario,-a doctrina
documentación documento
  -ción 2858

documentado documento
documental documento 3747
documentar documento
documentarse documento
documento documento -o[1]
  886
dogma dogma
dogmático dogma
dogmático,-a dogma
dogmatismo dogma -ismo
dogmatizar dogma
dólar 232
dolencia dolor
doler dolor 3579
dolerse dolor
doliente -ente[2]
dolor dolor 1019
dolorido dolor
doloroso dolor -oso 3115
doma doméstico
domador,-a doméstico
domar doméstico
domesticable doméstico
domesticación doméstico
domesticar doméstico
doméstico doméstico 2785
doméstico,-a doméstico
domicilio 533
dominación dominar -ción
dominante dominar
dominar dominar 2197
dominarse dominar
domingo 351
dominical 3335
dominicano -ano 1579
dominio 2590
don 651
donación -ción 3976
donante -ante[2]
donar 3233
donativo 4891
donde donde 50
dónde donde 50
dondequiera donde
dorado dorado
dorar dorado 1909
dorarse 1989
dormido dormir
dormir dormir 1549
dormirse dormir
dormitar dormir
dormitorio dormir -orio[1]
dos dos 44
doscientos dos
doscientos,-as dos
dosificar -ificar
dosis 2739
dosmilésimo -ésimo
dotación dote
dotado dote
dotar dote 3296
dote dote
dotes dote
dragoncillo -illo[1]
drama drama 3665
dramática drama
dramático drama -ico[2] 3234
dramatismo drama
dramatizar drama
dramaturgia drama
dramaturgo,-a drama
drástico 4765
drenaje 1777
droga -a 914
drogadicción -ción 4846
droguería -ería[1]
droguero -ero[3]
ducentésimo -ésimo
ducha -a
duda duda -a 754
dudable -able

entraña entrañas
entrañable entrañas
entrañablemente entrañas
entrañar entrañas
entrañas entrañas
entrar entrada 405
entre 47
entreabierto abrir
entreabrir abrir
entreacto acto
entrecejo ceja
entrecortado cortar
entrecortar cortar
entrecubiertas cubierto
entredicho decir
entrefino refinado
entrega entregar -a 691
entregar entregar 387
entregarse entregar
entrelazado lazo
entrelazar lazo
entrelazarse lazo
entrelinear línea
entremedias medio
entremeter meter
entremezclar mezclar
entrenador,-a 1129
entrenamiento -miento 1610
entrenar 2188
entrepierna pie
entreponer poner
entresacar sacar
entretejer tejido
entretela tejido
entretener tener 4737
entretenerse tener 4737
entretenido tener
entretenimiento tener
   -miento 3943
entrevista vista -a 678
entrevistador,-a vista
entrevistar vista 953
entrevistarse vista
entristecedor triste
entristecer triste
entristecerse triste
entrometerse meter
entrometido meter
entrometido,-a meter
entronización trono
entronizar trono
enturbiar turbar
enturbiarse turbar
entusiasmar entusiasta 4562
entusiasmarse entusiasta
   4562
entusiasmo entusiasta -asma,
   -o[1] 2667
entusiasta entusiasta
enumeración número
enumerar número
envalentonamiento valor
envalentonarse valor
envanecer vano
envanecerse vano
envanecimiento vano
envasado vaso
envasar vaso
envase vaso
envejecer viejo
envejecido viejo
envejecimiento viejo -miento
   4113
envenenamiento veneno
envenenar veneno
enverdecer verde
enviado viaje -ado[2]
enviar viaje 593
enviciar vicio
envidia envidia
envidiable envidia

envidiar envidia
envidiosamente envidia
envidioso envidia
envilecimiento -miento
envío -o[1] 3453
enviudar viuda
envoltura envolver
envolver envolver 3162
envolverse envolver 3162
envolvimiento -miento
enyesado yeso
enyesar yeso
epidemia 4651
episódico episodio
episodio episodio 2189
epistolario -ario[1]
época 1017
equidad 3841
equidistancia distancia
equidistante distancia
equidistar distancia
equilátero lado
equilibrado equilibrio
equilibrar equilibrio 3323
equilibrarse equilibrio 3323
equilibrio equilibrio 2552
equilibrismo equilibrio
equilibrista equilibrio
equipamiento -miento 4563
equipar 4301
equipo 89
equivalencia equivaler
equivalente equivaler -ente[1]
   2833
equivaler equivaler 4173
equivocación equivocar
equivocadamente equivocar
equivocado equivocar
equivocar equivocar 2351
equivocarse equivocar
eremita ermita
ergástula 3347
ermita ermita
ermitaño,-a ermita
erotomanía -manía
erotómano -mano
errabundo -undo
erradamente error
erradicar 4174
erradizo -dizo
errado error
errar error
errata error
errático error
erro error
erróneamente error
error 1060
erudición erudito
eruditamente erudito
erudito erudito -ito[2]
erudito,-a erudito
esa, esas 32
ésa, ésas 32
esbeltez esbelto
esbelto esbelto
escala escalera -a 3060
escalada escalera
escalador escalera
escalador,-a escalera
escalafón escalera
escalar escalera 4678
escalera escalera -era
escaleras escalera
escalerilla escalera
escalofriante frío
escalofrío frío
escalón escalera
escalonadamente escalera
escalonado escalera
escalonar escalera
escancia -ancia

escandalizar escándalo
escandalizarse escándalo
escándalo escándalo 2087
escandalosamente
   escándalo
escandaloso escándalo -oso
escapada escapar
escapar escapar 1861
escaparate escaparate
escaparatista escaparate
escaparse escapar 1861
escapatoria escapar
escape escapar
escarlatina -ina
escasamente escaso
escasear escaso
escasez escaso -ez 3594
escaso escaso 1559
escatimar escaso
escena escena 1287
escenario escena 687
escénico escena
escenografía escena
escenógrafo,-a escena
esclarecer claro 4911
esclarecido claro
esclarecimiento claro
   -miento
esclavitud esclavitud -itud
esclavizar esclavitud
esclavo esclavitud
esclavo,-a esclavitud
esclerosis -osis
escobajo -ajo
escobilla -illa
escocedura -dura
escocés -és 4980
escoger recoger 2019
escogido recoger
escogimiento recoger
escolar escuela 1467
escolaridad escuela
escolástico escuela
escombro -o[1] 3198
esconder esconder 2374
esconderse esconder 2374
escondidas esconder
escondite esconder
escondrijo esconder
escopeta escopeta
escopetazo escopeta -azo[2]
escorpión 4314
escribano,-a escribir
escribir escribir 896
escribirse escribir
escrito escribir 1695
escritor -or
escritor,-a escribir 1722
escritorcillo -illo[2]
escritorio escribir -orio[1]
escritorzuelo -zuelo
escritura escribir
escriturar escribir
escrúpulo escrúpulo
escrupulosamente escrúpulo
escrupulosidad escrúpulo
escrupuloso escrúpulo
escuadra 1617
escucha escuchar -a
escuchar escuchar 645
escudar escudo
escudarse escudo
escudería escudo
escudero escudo
escudo escudo
escuela escuela 324
escuetamente escueto
escueto escueto
esculpir escultura
escultismo escultura
escultor -or

escultor,-a escultura
escultura escultura -ura[2]
escultural escultura
escupidor -dor[1]
escupitajo -ajo
escurialense -ense
escurridizo -dizo
ese 32
ése 32
esencia esencial -encia 3081
esencial esencial -cial 2653
esencialmente esencial
esfera esfera
esférico esfera -ico[2] 3180
esferoide esfera
esforzado fuerza
esforzar fuerza 4442
esforzarse fuerza
esfuerzo fuerza -o[1] 696
esmeraldino -ino[2]
esnobismo -ismo
eso, esos 32
ésos 32
espaciador espacio
espacial espacio -cial 3236
espaciar espacio
espaciarse espacio
espacio espacio -icio, -o[1]
   612
espacioso espacio
espada espada
espadachín espada
espadín -ín
espadita -ita
espalda espalda 2297
espaldarazo -azo[2]
espaldilla espalda
espaldudo -udo
espantadizo espanto
espantajo -ajo
espantapájaros espanto
espantar espanto
espantarse espanto
espanto espanto
espantoso espanto -oso
español español 438
español,-a español
españolada español
españolería -ería[2]
españoles español
españolismo español -ismo
españolista español
españolizar español
españolizarse español
esparcir 2266
esparcirse 2266
espasmo -asma
especial especie -cial 250
especialidad -idad 2729
especialista especie -ista
   1556
especialización especie
especializado especie
especializarse especie -izar
   1840
especialmente especie
   -mente 1147
especie especie 1392
especiería -ería[1]
especificación especie
específicamente -mente
   3996
especificar especie -ificar
   3190
específico especie -ico[2]
   1801
espécimen especie
espectacular espectáculo
   2329

espectacularmente
espectáculo
espectáculo espectáculo
-culo 826
espectador,-a espectáculo
2514
especulación especulación
-ción 4872
especulador,-a especulación
especular especulación 4958
especulativo especulación
espejear espejo
espejillo -illo[1]
espejismo espejo
espejo espejo 3472
espejuelo -uelo
espera esperar -a
esperanza esperar -anza 1115
esperanzador esperar
esperanzar esperar
esperanzarse esperar
esperar esperar 131
espesante espeso
espesar espeso
espesarse espeso
espeso espeso
espesor espeso
espesura espeso -ura[1]
espía espía
espiar espía
espiga espiga
espigado espiga
espigar espiga
espigarse espiga
espigón espiga
espina espina
espinal espina
espinazo espina
espinilla espina
espinillera espina
espino espina
espinoso -oso 3869
espionaje espía
espiritismo espíritu
espiritista espíritu
espíritu espíritu 1991
espiritual espíritu 3199
espiritualidad espíritu -idad
espiritualismo espíritu
espiritualista espíritu -ista
espiritualmente espíritu
espléndidamente espléndido
espléndido espléndido
esplendor espléndido
esplendoroso espléndido
esplenitis -itis
espontáneamente
espontáneo
espontaneidad espontáneo
espontáneo espontáneo
esposa esposo
esposado esposo
esposar esposo
esposas esposo
esposo,-a esposo 465
espuma espuma
espumante -ante[1]
espumar espuma
espumarajo espuma -ajo
espumilla espuma
espumoso espuma
esquelético esqueleto
esqueleto esqueleto
esquema esquema 2029
esquemático esquema
esquematizar esquema
esquifada -ada[3]
esquina esquina 1432
esquinado esquina
esquinero,-a esquina
esquivar esquivar

esquivo esquivar
esta, estas 17
ésta, éstas 17
estabilidad establecer -idad
2576
estabilización establecer
estabilizador establecer
estabilizar establecer
estabilizarse establecer
estable establecer 3101
establecer establecer 358
establecerse establecer 358
establecimiento establecer
-miento 1788
estacazo -azo[2]
estación estación 1486
estacional estación
estacionamiento -miento
2556
estacionar 2407
estacionario -ario[2]
estadio 572
estadística estadística
estadístico estadística -ico[2]
2048
estadístico,-a estadística
estado estado -ado[2] 42
estadounidense -ense 353
estalactita -ito[2]
estalagmita -ito[2]
estallar estallar 3297
estallido estallar
estampa estampa
estampación estampa
estampado estampa
estampador -dor[2]
estampar estampa
estampilla estampa -illa
estancar 4315
estancarse 4315
estancia -ancia 2891
estándar 3420
estanquillo -illo[2]
estantería -ería[2]
estar estar 22
estatal 284
estatua estatua
estatuaria estatua
estatuario estatua
estatuilla estatua
estatura -ura[2] 3900
estatuto 3483
este 17
éste 17
estelar 2088
estelarizar -izar 3720
estenosis -osis
estéril estéril
esterilidad estéril
esterilización estéril
esterilizador estéril
esterilizador,-a estéril
esterilizar estéril
esterilizarse estéril
estética estético
esteticismo estético
esteticista estético
estético estético -ico[2] 3977
estilarse estilo
estilista estilo
estilística estilo
estilístico estilo
estilización estilo
estilizar estilo
estilo estilo 1013
estima estimar -a 2506
estimable estimar -able 2182
estimación estimar -ción
4380
estimado estimar
estimar estimar 1437

estimarse estimar 1437
estimulante estímulo
estimular estímulo 2687
estímulo estímulo -o[1] 3016
estirado estirar
estirar estirar 4892
estirarse estirar 4892
estirón estirar -ón[1]
estos 17
ésto, éstos 17
estólido -ido[1]
estomacal estómago
estómago estómago 3348
estomatitis -itis
estorbar estorbar
estorbo estorbar
estratega 3618
estrategia 1240
estratégico -ico[2] 2330
estratificación estratificar
estratificar estratificar
estratificarse estratificar
estratiforme -iforme
estrato estratificar
estratosfera estratificar
estrechamente estrecho
estrechamiento estrecho
estrechar estrecho
estrecharse estrecho
estrechez estrecho
estrecho estrecho 3134
estrechura estrecho -ura[1]
estrella estrella 660
estrellado estrella -ado[1]
estrellar estrella 2642
estrellarse estrella
estrellato estrella
estrellita -ita
estrellón estrella
estremecedor estremecer
estremecer estremecer
estremecerse estremecer
estremecido estremecer
estremecimiento estremecer
estrenar 1713
estrenarse 1713
estreno -o[1] 2397
estrenuo -uo
estrés 2577
estricto 2921
estrógeno 3595
estropajo -ajo
estructura estructura -a,
-ura[2] 1648
estructural estructura 3257
estructurar estructura
estudiado estudio
estudiantado estudio
estudiante estudio -ante[2]
1082
estudiantil estudio -il 3362
estudiantillo -illo[2]
estudiantina estudio
estudiar estudio 1091
estudio estudio -o[1] 314
estudioso estudio
estulticia -icia
estupendamente estupendo
-mente
estupendo estupendo
estupidez estúpido -ez
estúpido estúpido -ido[1]
estúpido,-a estúpido
etapa 719
etcétera 4381
etéreo -eo[2]
eternidad eterno -idad
eterno eterno 3200
ética ético
ético ético -ico[2] 2892
ético,-a ético

etiqueta -a 4302
étnico -ico[2] 4738
Eucaristía 4476
euro 4766
europeo 969
evadir 4609
evaluación -ción 2160
evaluar 2311
evangélico evangelio -ico[2]
evangelio evangelio 3210
evangelismo evangelio -ismo
evangelista evangelio
evangelización evangelio
evangelizador evangelio
evangelizar evangelio
evaporación vapor
evaporar vapor
evaporarse vapor
evento 591
eventual 3454
evidencia evidente -encia
2149
evidenciar evidente
evidente evidente 2186
evidentemente evidente
-mente 4912
evitable evitar -able
evitar evitar 281
evitarse evitar
evocación evocar
evocar evocar
evocativo -ivo
evolución evolución 3031
evolucionar evolución 4415
evolucionismo evolución
evolucionista evolución
evolutivo evolución -ivo
exactamente exacto -mente
3151
exactitud exacto -itud
exacto exacto 3605
exageración exagerar
exageradamente exagerar
exagerado exagerar
exagerar exagerar 3508
exaltación exaltar
exaltado exaltar
exaltado,-a exaltar
exaltar exaltar
exaltarse exaltar
examen examinar 3227
examinador examinar
examinador,-a examinar
examinar examinar 3796
examinarse examinar
excedente exceso
exceder exceso 4625
excederse exceso
excelencia excelente -encia
4382
excelente excelente 1224
excelentísimo -ísimo
excelsitud -itud
excelso excelente
excepción excepción -ción
2423
excepcional excepción
excepto excepción 4114
exceptuar excepción
excesivo exceso -ivo 2806
exceso exceso 1717
excitabilidad excitar
excitable excitar
excitación excitar
excitante excitar
excitar excitar
excitarse excitar
exclamación reclamar
exclamar reclamar 4959
exclamativo -ivo
exclamatorio reclamar

excluir exclusivamente 4564
exclusión exclusivamente -sión 4933
exclusiva exclusivamente
exclusivamente exclusivamente -mente 3484
exclusive exclusivamente
exclusividad exclusivamente
exclusivismo exclusivamente
exclusivista exclusivamente
exclusivo exclusivamente -ivo 2061
excursión excursión
excursionismo excursión
exhalación exhalar
exhalar exhalar
exhibición exhibición -ción 2840
exhibicionismo exhibición
exhibicionista exhibición
exhibir exhibición 2316
exhortar 2218
exigencia exigir -encia 2975
exigente exigir 4582
exigir exigir 851
existencia existencia -encia 1724
existencial existencia -cial
existencialismo existencia
existencialista existencia
existente existencia -ente[1] 2507
existir existencia 192
exitazo -azo[1]
éxito 433
exitoso -oso 1783
exorable inexorable
exótico 4356
expandir expansión
expandirse expansión
expansión expansión -sión 4078
expansionismo expansión
expansionista expansión
expansivo expansión -ivo
expatriación padre
expatriado padre
expatriado,-a padre
expatriar padre
expatriarse padre
expectativa 1666
expedición expedición
expedicionario expedición
expedicionario,-a expedición
expedidor,-a expedición
expediente 2281
expedir expedición 3965
expeditivo expedición -ivo
expedito expedición
expendedora -dor[2]
experiencia experiencia 759
experimentación experiencia
experimentado experiencia
experimental experiencia -al[2] 3116
experimentar experiencia 1820
experimento experiencia -o[1] 4626
expertamente experiencia
experto experiencia 1505
experto,-a experiencia
expiración espíritu
expirar espíritu
explanada 3706
explicable explicar
explicación explicar -ción 2441
explicar explicar 267
explicarse explicar

explicativo explicar
explicitar explicar
explícito explicar
explorar 4268
explosión explosión -sión 2449
explosionar explosión
explosivo explosión -ivo 2859
explotable explotar
explotación explotar -ción 3181
explotador,-a explotar
explotar explotar, explosión 2561
exponencial -cial
exponente -ente[2] 4048
exponer poner 822
exponerse poner 822
exportable importar
exportación importar -ción 1614
exportador importar -dor[1] 3415
exportador,-a importar
exportar importar 3721
exposición poner -ción 1690
expositivo poner
expositor -or
expositor,-a poner
expresado expresión
expresamente expresión
expresar expresión 552
expresarse expresión
expresión expresión -sión 1802
expresionismo expresión
expresionista expresión
expresivo expresión
expreso expresión
exprimidor -dor[2]
expropiación propiedad -ción 4701
expropiar propiedad
expuesto poner
expulsar expulsar 1950
expulsión -sión 2883
expulsor expulsar
expulsión expulsar
expurgación puro
expurgar puro
exquisitez exquisito
exquisito exquisito -ito[2] 3782
extemporáneo temporada
extender extender 1759
extenderse extender 1759
extendido extender
extensamente extender
extensión extender -sión 2786
extenso extender 3748
extenuación extender
extenuante extender
extenuar extender
extenuarse extender
exterior exterior 1031
exterioridad exterior
exteriorización exterior
exteriorizar exterior
exteriormente exterior
externamente externo
externar 3163
externarse 3163
externo externo 2010
externo,-a externo
extinción extinguir
extinguidor extinguir
extinguir extinguir
extinguirse extinguir
extinto extinguir
extintor extinguir

extra 2012
extracción -ción 2844
extradición -ción 3929
extraer 2976
extraescolar escuela
extrafino refinado
extrajudicial juicio
extralimitarse limitar
extramuros muro
extranjerismo extranjero
extranjero extranjero
extranjero,-a extranjero 725
extrañamente extranjero
extrañar extranjero 4175
extrañarse 4175
extrañeza extranjero
extraño extranjero 1811
extraño,-a extranjero
extraoficial oficio
extraordinaria ordinario
extraordinario ordinario 1778
extraterrestre tierra
extraterritorial tierra
extravagancia extravagante
extravagante extravagante
extraviado viaje
extraviar viaje
extraviarse viaje
extravío viaje
extremadamente extremo
extremado extremo
extremar extremo
extremarse extremo
extremaunción extremo
extremidad extremo
extremismo extremo
extremista extremo -ista 4583
extremo extremo -o[1] 1636
extremoso extremo
exuberancia -ancia
eyector -or

F

fábrica fábrica -a 2993
fabricación fábrica -ción 4702
fabricante fábrica -ante[2] 3485
fabricar fábrica 3091
fabril -il
fábula fabuloso
fabulista fabuloso
fabuloso fabuloso -oso
facción facción
faccioso facción
faceta -eta 4316
fácil fácil 1099
facilidad fácil -idad 2282
facilitación fácil
facilitar fácil 2030
fácilmente fácil -mente 2718
factor 954
factura factura
facturación factura
facturar factura
facultad -tad 1310
facundo -undo
faja faja
fajado faja
fajar faja
fajín -ín
fajo faja
falacia -icia
falaz -az
falda falda 4627
faldellín -ín
faldero falda -ero[2]
faldeta -eta

falla -a 1900
fallar 2269
fallecer fallecer 1419
fallecido fallecer
fallecimiento fallecer -miento 4739
fallo 3298
falseable -able
falsedad falso
falsete falso
falsificación falso
falsificador falso
falsificar falso -ificar
falso falso 1885
falta faltar -a 263
faltar faltar 1059
falto faltar
fama 1834
familia familia 163
familiar familia 375
familiaridad familia
familiarizar familia -izar
familiarizarse familia
famoso famoso -oso 1093
famosos famoso
fan 2066
fanático -ico[2] 2201
fantasía 4014
fantasma -asma 3486
fantástico -ico[2] 4137
farmacéutico farmacia
farmacéutico,-a farmacia
farmacia farmacia -icia 4934
fármaco farmacia 4283
farmacología farmacia
farmacológico farmacia
farmacólogo,-a farmacia
faro faro
farol faro
farola faro
farolillo -illo[1]
farsa farsa
farsante farsa
fascinante -ante[1]
fascismo fascismo
fascista fascismo
fase fase 1372
fastuosidad fastuoso
fastuoso fastuoso
fatal fatal 3722
fatalidad fatal -idad
fatalismo fatal
fatalista fatal -ista
fatalmente fatal
fatiga fatiga
fatigado fatiga
fatigar fatiga
fatigarse fatiga
fatigosamente fatiga
fatigoso fatiga
fatuo -uo
favor favor 704
favorable favor -able 2036
favorcillo -illo[2]
favorecedor favor
favorecer favor 1620
favorecido favor
favoritismo favor
favorito favor -ito[2] 1194
favorito,-a favor
fax 4981
faz faz
fe fe 1546
febrero 732
febril fiebre -il
fecha fecha -a 319
fechador fecha
fechar fecha
fecundación fecundo
fecundante -ante[1]
fecundar fecundo

fecundidad fecundo -idad
fecundizar fecundo
fecundo fecundo -undo
federación confederación -ción 791
federado confederación
federal confederación 144
federalismo confederación
federalista confederación
federar confederación
federativo 3375
feísimo -ísimo
feísmo -ismo
felicidad feliz -idad 1895
felicísimo -ísimo
felicitación feliz -ción 1838
felicitar feliz 2381
felicitarse feliz
felino 3619
feliz feliz 1068
felizmente -mente
felpilla -illa
felpudo -udo
femenil -il 1516
femenino feminino 2093
femineidad feminino
feminidad feminino
feminismo feminino
feminista feminino
fenomenal fenómeno
fenómeno fenómeno 1622
feo 3666
feote -ote
feraz -az
feria feria 1568
ferial feria
ferino -ino(2)
fermentación fermento
fermentar fermento
fermento fermento
ferocidad feroz -idad
feroz feroz -az
ferozmente feroz
ferrado -ado(1)
férreo ferrocarril -eo(2)
ferrería ferrocarril
ferretería ferrocarril -ería(1)
ferrífero -ífero
ferrocarril ferrocarril 2930
ferroviario ferrocarril
ferroviario,-a ferrocarril
fértil fertilidad
fertilidad fertilidad
fertilización fertilidad
fertilizante fertilidad
fertilizar fertilidad -izar
ferventísimo -ísimo
férvido fervoroso
ferviente fervoroso
fervor fervoroso
fervoroso fervoroso
festejante -ante(1)
festejar fiesta 924
festejo fiesta -o(1) 1415
festejos fiesta
festín fiesta
festival fiesta -al(1) 1263
festividad fiesta
festivo fiesta
fétido -ido(1)
feúcho -ucho
fiabilidad fe
fiable fe
fiado fe
fiador,-a fe
fianza fe -anza 3842
fiar fe
fiarse fe
fibra 2283
fibrosis -osis
ficción ficción 4416

ficticio ficción
fidecomiso 2367
fidedigno fe
fideicomiso fe
fidelidad fe
fiebre fiebre 3394
fiel fe 2382
fieles fe
fiera feroz
fiereza feroz
fiero feroz
fiesta fiesta 473
figura figura -a 1005
figuración figura
figurado figura
figurante,-a figura
figurar figura 2822
figurarse figura
figurativo figura
figurilla -illo(2)
figurín figura
fijación fijar
fijador fijar
fijamente fijar
fijar fijar 885
fijarse fijar
fijeza fijar
fijo fijar
fila fila 1605
filiación filiación
filial filiación 3376
filiarse filiación
filiforme -iforme
filigresía -ería(2)
filipino -ino(2) 3901
film 1245
filmación -ción 4397
filmar 2284
filmina -ina
filmoteca -teca
filo 4138
filosofar filosofía
filosofía filosofía -ería(2) 3917
filosófico filosofía
filósofo -o(3)
filósofo,-a filosofía
filtrar 4506
fin fin 236
finado fin
final fin -al(2) 203
finalidad fin -idad 1420
finalista fin -ista 4666
finalizar fin -izar 1219
finalmente fin -mente 734
finamente -mente 4847
financiamiento -miento 1898
financiar 2899
financiero -ero(2) 666
finanzas -anza 1391
finar fin 1752
finarse 1752
finca 3473
fingido fingir
fingimiento fingir
fingir fingir
fingirse fingir
finito fin -ito(2)
finlandés -és
fino refinado 2499
finta fingir
fintar fingir
finura refinado -ura(1)
firma firmar -a 1076
firmante firmar
firmar firmar 928
firme firme 1957
firmemente firme
firmeza firme
fiscal fiscal 682
fiscalía fiscal -ería(2) 3201
fiscalización fiscal -ción 4667

fiscalizar fiscal
fisco fiscal
fisgoneo -eo(1)
física físico
físicamente físico -mente 4303
físico físico 664
físico,-a físico
fisiología físico
fisiológico físico
fisiólogo,-a físico
fisioterapeuta físico
fisioterapia físico
flaccidez/flacidez -ez
flácido -ido(1)
flaco flaco 4522
flacucho flaco -ucho
flacura flaco -ura(1)
flagrante -ante(1)
flamante -ante(1)
flaquear flaco
flaqueza flaco -eza
flatulento -lento
flautista -ista
flebitis -itis
flecha flecha -a 4740
flechar flecha
flechazo flecha
flojucho -ucho
flor flor 1554
flora flor
floración flor
floral flor
floreado flor
florear flor
florecer flor
floreciente flor
florecimiento flor
florecita -ita
florentino -ino(2)
floreo flor
florería flor
florero flor -ero(1), (3)
floresta flor
floricultura flor
florido flor -ido(1) 2257
florífero -ífero
florista flor -ista
floristería flor -ería(1)
flota flotar
flotación flotar
flotador flotar
flotante flotar
flotar flotar
flote flotar
fluidez fluir
fluido fluir
fluir fluir 4628
flujo fluir 2771
fluvial fluir
focal foco
foco foco 3349
fogata fuego
fogón fuego
fogonazo fuego
fogonero fuego
fogosidad fuego
fogoso fuego
folículo -culo
fomentar 2529
fomento -o(1) 2021
fondeadero fondo
fondear fondo
fondo fondo 455
fonema teléfono(2)
fonética teléfono(2)
fonético teléfono(2)
fonógrafo teléfono(2)
fonología teléfono(2)
fonológico teléfono(2)
fonoteca teléfono(2)

fontanero -ero(3)
foráneo fuera 4036
forastero fuera
forastero,-a fuera
forestal 2323
forja forjar
forjado forjar
forjar forjar
forjarse forjar
forma forma -a 139
formación forma -ción 1653
formal formal 2139
formalidad formal
formalismo formal
formalista formal -ista
formalizar formal
formalizarse formal
formalmente -mente 4224
formar forma 481
formarse forma
formativo forma
formato 3287
fórmula fórmula -a 1738
formulación fórmula
formular fórmula 3797
formulario fórmula
formulismo fórmula
foro 1304
forraje 3769
fortalecedor fortaleza
fortalecer fortaleza 1581
fortalecerse fortaleza 1581
fortalecimiento fortaleza -miento 3783
fortaleza fortaleza 3135
fortificación fortaleza
fortificante fortaleza
fortificar fortaleza -ificar
fortín fortaleza
fortísimo fortaleza
fortuito fortuna
fortuna fortuna 2660
forzado fuerza
forzar fuerza 2635
forzoso fuerza
forzudo fuerza
foto fotografía 514
fotocopia fotografía, copia
fotocopiadora fotografía, copia
fotocopiar fotografía, copia
fotoeléctrico fotografía, eléctrico
fotofobia -fobia
fotogénico fotografía
fotografía fotografía -ería(2) 1473
fotografiar fotografía
fotográfico fotografía -ico(2) 4398
fotógrafo -o(3)
fotógrafo,-a fotografía 3997
fotómetro medida, fotografía
fotomontaje fotografía
fotosíntesis fotografía
fracasado fracaso
fracasado,-a fracaso
fracasar fracaso 3043
fracaso fracaso -o(1) 2045
fracción 2630
fraccionamiento -miento 2053
fractura -a, -ura(2) 2616
fracturar -ura(2)
frágil frágil 4960
fragilidad frágil -idad
fragmentación fragmento
fragmentar fragmento
fragmentario fragmento
fragmentarse fragmento
fragmento fragmento

incumplimiento cumplir
-miento 3945
incumplir cumplir 3883
incurable curar
incurrir 2845
incursión -sión 3468
incursionar 3487
indebidamente deber
indebido deber 4771
indecible decir
indecisión decidir
indeciso decidir
indefendible defender
indefenso defender
indefinible definir
indefinidamente definir
indefinido definir
indeformable forma
indelicadeza delicado
indemnización -ción 4269
independencia depender
-encia 1427
independentista depender
independiente depender
1684
independientemente
depender -mente 3152
independizar depender
independizarse depender
indescifrable cifra
indescriptible escribir
indeseable desear
indestructible trozo
indeterminable terminar
indeterminación terminar
indeterminado terminar
indicación indicar -ción 3829
indicado indicar
indicador indicar -dor[2] 2682
indicar indicar 193
indicativo indicar -ivo
índice indicar 1248
indicio indicar -icio 4270
indiferencia diferencia
indiferente diferencia
indígena 1148
indignación indignación
indignado indignación
indignante indignación
indignar indignación
indignarse indignación
indignidad indignación
indigno indignación
indio 1083
indirecto dirigir
indisciplina discípulo
indisciplinado discípulo
indisciplinarse discípulo
indiscreción discreto
indiscreto discreto
indiscreto,-a discreto
indiscutible discutir
indispensable dispensar -able
2455
indisponible poner
indisposición poner
indispuesto poner
indistintamente distinguir
indistinto distinguir
individual individual 1851
individualidad individual
individualismo individual
individualista individual
individualización individual
individualizar individual
individuo individual -uo 1431
indivisible dividir
indocumentado documento
3946
indocumentado,-a
documento

indoloro dolor
indomable doméstico
indómito doméstico
inducido seducir
inducir seducir 4938
inductor seducir
indudable duda
indudablemente -mente
4914
indulgencia -encia
industria industria 669
industrial industria 1002
industrialización industria
industrializar industria
industrializarse industria
industrioso industria
inédito edición 3474
inefectivo efecto
ineficacia eficaz
ineficaz eficaz
ineptitud aptitud -itud
inepto aptitud
inepto,-a aptitud
inequívoco equivocar
inesperadamente esperar
inesperado esperar -ado[1]
4384
inestabilidad establecer
inestable establecer
inestimable estimar
inevitable evitar -able 4462
inevitablemente evitar
inexactitud exacto -itud
inexacto exacto
inexistencia existencia
inexistente existencia
inexorable inexorable
inexorablemente inexorable
inexperiencia experiencia
inexperimentado experiencia
inexperto experiencia
inexplicable explicar
inexpresable expresión
inexpresivo expresión
inextinguible extinguir
infacundo -undo
infamar famoso
infame famoso
infamia famoso
infancia infancia -ancia 3365
infanta infancia
infante infante, infancia 3873
infantería infante
infanticida infancia
infanticidio infancia
infantil infancia -il 864
infarto 4792
infatigable fatiga
infección -ción 2345
infectar 4096
infectarse 4096
infecundidad fecundo
infecundo fecundo -undo
infelicidad feliz
infeliz feliz
inferior inferior 3032
inferioridad inferior
infernal infierno
infidelidad fe
infiel fe
infielmente fe
infierno infierno 4141
infiltración infiltrar
infiltrado,-a infiltrar
infiltrar infiltrar
infiltrarse infiltrar
infinidad fin -idad 4142
infinitamente fin
infinitesimal fin
infinitivo fin
infinitivo,-a fin

infinito fin -ito[2]
inflación -ción 2508
inflamación -ción 4631
inflamatorio -orio[2]
influencia influencia -a,
-encia 2131
influir influencia 2474
influyente influencia -ente[1]
información informe -ción
321
informado informe
informador,-a informe
informal formal 3798
informalidad formal
informalmente formal
informante -ante[2] 3366
informar informe 147
informarse informe
informático -ico[2] 2790
informático,-a informe
informativo informe -ivo
2841
informe informe 828
infortunado fortuna
infortunio fortuna
infracción 4209
infraestructura estructura
-ura[2] 1634
infrahumano humano
infrarrojo rojo
infravalorar valer
infructuosamente fruto
infructuoso fruto
infundado fundar
infundio fundar
infundir infundir
infusión infundir
ingeniar genio
ingeniarse genio
ingeniería genio -ería[2] 3966
ingeniero,-a genio 1889
ingenio genio 3809
ingenioso genio
ingénito -ito[2]
ingenuidad ingenuidad
ingenuo ingenuidad -uo
ingenuo,-a ingenuidad
ingerir 2834
ingesta 4986
inglés -és
inglés,-a 964
inglete -ete
ingobernable gobierno
ingratamente gracia
ingratitud gracia
ingrato gracia
ingrato,-a gracia
ingravidez grave
ingrávido grave
ingrediente 1859
ingresado ingresar
ingresar ingresar 1204
ingreso ingresar -o[1] 756
inhábil habilidad
inhabilidad habilidad
inhabilitación habilidad
inhabilitar habilidad
inhabitable habitación
inhabitado habitación
inhóspito hospital
iniciación iniciar
iniciado iniciar
iniciado,-a iniciar
iniciador iniciar
iniciador,-a iniciar
inicial iniciar -cial 1927
inicialmente -mente 4079
iniciar iniciar 174
iniciarse iniciar
iniciativa iniciar 910
inicio iniciar -icio, -o[1] 689

inimaginable imagen
inimitable imitar
ininteligible intelectual
ininterrumpidamente
interrumpir
ininterrumpido interrumpir
injuria injuria
injuriar injuria
injurioso injuria
injustamente justicia
injusticia justicia -icia 3978
injustificable justicia
injustificadamente justicia
injustificado justicia
injusto justicia 3456
inmaculado -ado[1] 4793
inmadurez madurez
inmaduro madurez
inmaterial material
inmediaciones medio
inmediatamente medio
-mente 2516
inmediato medio 760
inmejorable mejor
inmemorial memoria
inmensamente inmenso
inmensidad inmenso
inmenso inmenso 4193
inmerecidamente mérito
inmerecido mérito
inmigrante -ante[2] 3568
inminente 4357
inmobiliario mueble
inmodestamente modesto
inmodestia modesto
inmodesto modesto
inmoral moral
inmoralidad moral
inmoralmente moral
inmortal morir
inmortalidad morir
inmortalizar morir
inmortalizarse morir
inmotivado motivo
inmovible mover
inmóvil mover
inmovilidad mover
inmovilización mover
inmovilizado mover
inmovilizar mover
inmueble mueble 2193
inmundicia -icia
inmundo -undo
innato,-a nacer
innecesariamente necesitar
innecesario necesitar 4610
innegable negar
innombrable nombre
innominado nombre
innovación nuevo -ción 3999
innovador nuevo
innovador,-a nuevo
innovar nuevo
innumerable número
innumerablemente número
inocencia inocente -encia
inocente inocente 3386
inocentón inocente
inocentón,-a inocente
inocuo -uo
inofensivo ofender
inolvidable olvidar -able 3810
inoperable operación
inoportunamente oportuno
inoportuno oportuno
inorgánico orgánico
inquebrantable quebrantado
inquietante quieto
inquietar quieto
inquietarse quieto
inquieto quieto

inquietud quieto 2733
insalubre salud
insalubridad salud
insano sano
insatisfacción satisfacción
insatisfactorio satisfacción
insatisfecho satisfacción
inscribir escribir 2070
inscribirse escribir 2070
inscripción escribir -ción
 2501
inscrito escribir
insecticida insecto
insectívoro insecto
insectívoros insecto
insecto insecto 4820
inseguridad seguro -idad
 2636
inseguro seguro -ura[2]
inseminación sembrar
inseminar sembrar
insensatez sentido
insensato sentido
insensato,-a sentido
insensibilidad sentido
insensibilizar sentido
insensibilizarse sentido
insensible sentido
inseparable separar
inseparablemente separar
inservible servir
insigne signo
insignia signo
insignificancia signo
insignificante signo
insinuación insinuar
insinuante insinuar
insinuar insinuar
insípido -ido[1]
insistencia insistir -encia
insistente insistir
insistentemente insistir
InsIstIr Insistir 1010
insociable social
insolación sol
insoluble solución[1]
insoluto -uto
insonorización sonar
insonorizado sonar
insonorizar sonar
insonoro sonar
insoportable soportar
insospechado sospechar
insostenible tener
inspección 2860
inspector -or
inspector,-a 2165
inspiración espíritu -ción
 3845
inspirado espíritu
inspirador espíritu
inspirar espíritu 3288
instalación instalación -ción
 529
instalador,-a instalación
instalar instalación 922
instalarse instalación
instancia -ancia 1582
instantáneamente instante
instantáneo instante
instante instante -ante[1]
 3581
instar 4129
instintivamente instinto
instintivo instinto
instinto instinto
institución instituto -ción
 396
institucional instituto 1360
institucionalizado instituto
institucionalizar instituto

instituido instituto
instituir instituto
instituto instituto -uto 434
institutriz instituto -triz
instrucción instrucción -ción
 2172
instructivo instrucción
instructor -or
instructor,-a instrucción 4000
instruido instrucción
instruir instrucción 4987
instrumentación instrumento
instrumental instrumento
instrumentista instrumento
instrumento instrumento
 1644
insubordinación orden
insubordinado orden
insubordinado,-a orden
insubordinar orden
insubordinarse orden
insubstancial sustancia
insubstancialidad sustancia
insubstituible sustituir
insuficiencia suficiente -encia
 4794
insuficiente suficiente 2703
insultante insultar
insultar insultar
insulto insultar -o[1] 4743
insumergible sumergir
insumo 4744
insuperable superar
insurgente 4795
insustancial sustancia
insustancialidad sustancia
insustituible sustituir
integérrimo -érrimo
integración -ción 2005
integral integrar 1637
íntegramente integrar
integrante integrar -ante[2]
 544
integrar integrar 546
integrarse integrar
integridad integrar -idad
 3947
íntegro integrar
intelecto intelectual
intelectual intelectual -al[2]
 2742
intelectualidad intelectual
intelectualismo intelectual
inteligencia intelectual -encia
 2154
inteligente intelectual 2530
inteligible intelectual
intemperie temporada
intempestivo temporada
intención intención -ción
 1012
intencionadamente intención
intencionado intención
intencional intención
intensidad intenso -idad
 3300
intensificación intenso
intensificar intenso -ificar
 3379
intensificarse intenso
intensivo intenso
intenso intenso 1488
intentar intención 742
intento intención -o[1] 1583
interacción acción
interamericano 3884
intercambiable cambio
intercambiar cambio 3408
intercambio cambio -o[1]
 2661
interceptar 3582

intercomunicación comunicar
intercomunicador comunicar
interdecir decir
interdependencia depender
interdicción decir
interdicto decir
interés interés 471
interesado interés
interesado,-a interés
interesante interés -ante[1]
 1527
interesar interés 783
interesarse interés
interfono teléfono[2]
intergubernamental gobierno
interino 3683
interior interior 711
interioridad interior
interioridades interior
interiorizar interior
intermediario medio -ario[2]
 4632
intermediario,-a medio
intermedio medio 3509
interminable terminar
internacional nacer 253
internacionalismo nacer
internacionalizar nacer
internacionalizarse nacer
internacionalmente nacer
internado interno -o[1] 2289
internamiento interno
internar interno
internet 920
internista interno
interno interno -o[1] 656
interno,-a interno
interplanetario planeta
interponer poner 2599
interponerse poner
interposición poner
interpretación interpretación
 -ción 2276
interpretar interpretación 777
intérprete interpretación
 1361
interrogación interrogar
interrogador,-a interrogar
interrogante interrogar
interrogar interrogar 3979
interrogativo interrogar
interrogatorio interrogar
interrumpir interrumpir 3409
interrupción interrumpir
interruptor interrumpir -or
intersección sección
interurbano urbano
intervención intervenir -ción
 1174
intervencionismo intervenir
intervencionista intervenir
intervenir intervenir 1604
interventor -or
intimar íntimo
intimidación tímido
intimidad íntimo
intimidades íntimo
intimidar tímido
intimidarse tímido
íntimo íntimo 2370
íntimo,-a íntimo
intitular título
intocable tocar
intolerable tolerar
intolerancia tolerar -ancia
intolerante tolerar
intramuros muro
intramuscular músculo
intranquilidad tranquilo
intranquilizar tranquilo
intranquilizarse tranquilo

intranquilo tranquilo
intransitable tránsito
intransitivo tránsito
intratable tratar
intravenoso vena
introducción introducir -ción
 3228
introducir introducir 1977
introducirse introducir
introductor introducir
introductor,-a introducir
intuición intuición
intuir intuición
intuitivamente intuición
intuitivo intuición
inundación -ción 3434
inundar 3967
inútil uso -il 4524
inutilidad uso
inutilizar uso
inútilmente uso
invadir invasión 2237
invalidación valer
invalidar valer
invalidez valer
inválido valer
inválido,-a valer
invariabilidad vario
invariable vario
invasión invasión -sión 3583
invasor invasión
invasor,-a invasión
invencible vencer
invención inventar
inventar inventar 3707
inventario -ario[1]
inventiva inventar
inventivo inventar
invento inventar
inventor -or
inventor,-a inventar
invernada -ada[1]
invernadero verano
invernal verano 4850
invernar verano
inverosímil ver
inverosimilitud -itud
inversión invertir -sión 613
inversionista invertir -ista
 2531
invertido invertir
invertir invertir 1142
investigación investigación
 -ción 394
investigador investigación
investigador,-a investigación
 1043
investigar investigación 1347
invicto 3723
invidente vista
invierno verano -o[1] 1901
inviolabilidad violento
inviolable violento
inviolado violento
invisible vista
invitación invitación -ción
 1645
invitado invitación -ado[2]
invitado,-a invitación
invitante invitación
invitar invitación 505
involucrar 1171
involuntario voluntad
inyección -ción
inyectar 4915
ir ir 49
ira ira
iracundo ira -undo
iraki, iraquí 3153
irisado -ado[1]
irlandés -és 3846

mariachi 3597
maridazo -azo[1]
maridillo -illo[2]
marido marido -ido[2] 2023
mariguana 3460
marimacho -acho
marina mar -ina 2570
marinaje -aje[1]
marinería mar
marinero mar -ero[3]
marinero,-a mar
marinesco -esco
marino mar -ino[2] 3811
marino,-a mar
mariposa 4178
mariposilla -illa
mariquita -ita
mariscal 3172
marisco mar
marisquería mar
marital marido
marítimo mar
mármol mármol
marmolería mármol
marmolista mármol
marmóreo mármol
marranillo -illo[1]
marroquí 4875
martes 891
Martica -ica
martillar martillo
martillazo martillo -azo[2]
martillear martillo
martilleo martillo
martillo martillo
martinete martillo
mártir martirio 4611
martirio martirio
martirizador martirio
martirizador,-a martirio
martirizar martirio
marxista -ista
marzal -al[3]
marzo 621
mas 23
más 23
masa 2006
mascadura -dura
máscara 3326
mascota 3191
masculino 2601
masivo 2267
masticatorio -orio[2]
matachín matar
matadero matar
matador matar -dor[1] 4419
matamoscas matar
matanza matar -anza 3812
matar matar 1213
matarratas matar
matarse matar
matasanos matar
matasellos sello, matar
matemática matemático
matemáticamente
   matemático
matemáticas matemático
matemático matemático
matemático,-a matemático
materia material 739
material material 543
materialidad material
materialismo material -ismo
materialista material -ista
   4525
materialización material
materializar material
materializarse material
maternal madre
maternidad madre
materno madre 4317

matidez -ez
matiz matiz
matización matiz
matizar matiz
matorral -al[1]
matriarca -arca
matriarcado madre
matriarcal madre
matricida madre
matricidio madre
matrícula matricular
matriculación matricular
matricular matricular
matricularse matricular
matrimonial madre 1822
matrimonio madre 463
matritense -ense
matriz madre
matronaza -aza
matutino 3932
maullido -ido[2]
máxima máximo
máximo máximo 746
maya 3585
mayo 558
mayor mayor 114
mayoral mayor
mayorazgo mayor -azgo
mayordomo mayor
mayoría mayor -ería[2] 410
mayorista mayor
mayoritario mayor
mayúscula mayor
mayúsculo mayor
mazada -ada[2]
me 71
mecánica máquina
mecánico máquina
mecánico,-a máquina 2135
mecanismo máquina -ismo
   1882
mecanización máquina
mecanizar máquina
mecanografía máquina
mecanografiar máquina
mecanógrafo,-a máquina
mecedura -dura
mecenazgo -azgo
medalla medalla 2050
medallista medalla
medallón medalla
media medio
mediación medio
mediado,-a medio
mediador,-a medio
medialuna medio
mediana medio
medianero medio
medianía medio
mediano medio 1857
medianoche medio
mediante medio 795
mediar medio 2303
medicación medicina
medicamento medicina 1803
medicamentoso,-a medicina
medicar medicina
medicarse medicina
medicastro -astro
medicina medicina 1476
medicinal medicina
medicinar medicina
médico medicina -o[3] 343
médico,-a medicina
medicucho -ucho
medida medida -ido[2] 369
medidor medida
medieval medieval
medievalesco -esco
medievalismo medieval
medievalista medieval

medievo medieval
medio medio 112
mediocampista -ista 3476
mediocre medio
mediocridad medio
mediodía medio 3128
mediquillo -illo[2]
medir medida 1571
meditabundo meditar -undo
meditación meditar
meditar meditar
meditativo meditar -ivo
medroso miedo
medroso,-a miedo
médula médula
medular médula
megafonía teléfono[2]
megáfono teléfono[2]
megalomanía -manía
megalómano -mano
mejicanismo -ismo
mejicano -ano
mejor mejor 94
mejora mejor -a 3211
mejorable mejor
mejoramiento mejor -miento
   3027
mejorar mejor 642
mejorarse mejor 642
mejoría mejor -ería[2] 4194
melado miel
melancolía melancolía
melancólico melancolía
melancólico,-a melancolía
melanosis -osis
melaza miel
melcocha miel
melífero -ífero
melifluo -uo
mellizo 4824
melocotonero -ero[4]
melodía 3173
melodrama 4001
melón 3119
melonar -al[3]
melosidad miel
meloso miel
memorable memoria 4080
memorando memoria
memorándum memoria
memoria memoria 1860
memorial memoria
memorión memoria -ón[3]
memorión,-a memoria
memorización memoria
memorizar memoria -izar
mención mencionado -ción
   2509
mencionado mencionado
mencionar mencionado 322
mendaz -az
mendeliano -ano
mendicante -ante[2]
mendicidad mendigo
mendigante -ante[2]
mendigar mendigo
mendigo,-a mendigo
meningitis -itis
menopausia 3635
menor menos 411
menos menos 171
menoscabar menos
menoscabo menos
menospreciable precioso,
   menos
menospreciar precioso,
   menos
menosprecio precioso,
   menos
mensaje mensaje 1223
mensajero mensaje -ero[3]

mensajero,-a mensaje
mensual 1963
mental mente -al[2] 1814
mentalidad mente -idad
   4494
mentalmente mente -mente
mente mente 1557
mentecatez -ez
mentecato mente
mentecato,-a mente
mentir mentir 3696
mentira mentir 2835
mentirilla -illo[2]
mentiroso mentir -oso
mentiroso,-a mentir
mentor -or
menudo 3301
mercadear mercado
mercader mercado
mercadería mercado
mercado mercado 290
mercadotecnia mercado
mercancía mercado 2290
mercante mercado
mercantil mercado
mercantilismo mercado
mercantilista mercado
merecedor mérito
merecer mérito 1668
merecerse mérito
merecido mérito
mereciente -ente[1]
merecimiento mérito
meretriz -triz
meridiano meridional
meridional meridional
merienda 2372
mérito mérito -ito[2] 3270
meritocracia mérito
meritorio mérito -orio[2]
mero 3740
mes 123
mesa mesa 993
mesada -ada[1]
mesero -ero[3]
mesilla mesa -illa
meta 869
metal metal 3183
metálico metal -ico[2] 3848
metalífero -ífero
metalista metal
metalización metal
metalizar metal
metaloide metal
metalurgia metal
metalúrgico metal
metalúrgico,-a metal
metamorfosis -osis
meteorito -ito[2]
meter meter 1140
meterse meter 1140
metódico método
metodizar método
método método 2037
metodología método
metodológico método
métrica medida
metro medida 569
metrónomo medida
metrópoli metrópoli
metropolitano metrópoli
   3559
mexicano -ano 68
mexiquense -ense 4061
mezcla mezclar -a 1958
mezclador,-a mezclar
mezcladora mezclar -dor[2]
mezclar mezclar 2585
mezclarse mezclar
mezcolanza mezclar
mi 95

mozo mozo
muchachada muchacho
  -ada[2]
muchachería muchacho
muchachez -ez
muchacho,-a muchacho 1560
muchachota -ote
muchachuco -uco
muchedumbre mucho
  -dumbre
muchísimo mucho -ísimo
mucho mucho 54
mucho,-a mucho
muda mudar
mudable mudar -able
mudanza mudar -anza
mudar mudar
mudarse mudar
mudez mudo
mudo mudo
mueblaje -aje[1]
mueble mueble 3120
mueblería -ería[1]
muellaje -aje[2]
muerte morir 485
muerto morir
muerto,-a morir 784
muestra mostrar -a 811
muestrario mostrar
muestreo mostrar
mugido -ido[2]
mugriento -iento
mujer mujer 151
mujercilla -illo[2]
mujeriego mujer -iego
mujeril -il
mujerío mujer
mujerona mujer -ón[3]
mujeruca -uco
mujerzuela mujer -zuelo
mulada -ada[1]
multa -a 2442
multidireccional dirigir
multilateral lado
multinacional nacer
múltiple multiplicar 1842
multiplicable multiplicar
multiplicación multiplicar
multiplicador multiplicar
multiplicando multiplicar
multiplicar multiplicar 4547
multiplicarse multiplicar
multiplicidad multiplicar
múltiplo multiplicar
multitud 3800
mundanal mundo
mundano mundo
mundano,-a mundo
mundial mundo -al[2] 230
mundialista -ista 3750
mundialmente mundo
mundillo mundo
mundo mundo 165
municipal municipio 115
municipalidad municipio
municipalizar municipio
municipio municipio 178
muñeca muñeca
muñeco muñeca 3830
muñequera muñeca
mural muro
muralla muro
muriente -ente[1]
muro muro 3773
muscular músculo 3903
musculatura músculo
músculo músculo -culo 3520
musculoso músculo
museo museo 1597
museología museo
música música 285

musical música 643
musicalidad música
músico música
músico,-a música
musicología música
musicólogo,-a música
musulmán,-a 2900
mutismo mudo
mutualidad mutuo
mutualista mutuo
mutuo mutuo -uo 4339
muy 57

N

nacer nacer 604
nacido nacer -ido[2]
nacido,-a nacer
naciente nacer -ente[1]
nacimiento nacer -miento
  1779
nación nacer -ción 622
nacional nacer 74
nacionalidad nacer -idad
  4386
nacionalismo nacer -ismo
nacionalista nacer
nacionalización nacer
nacionalizar nacer
nacionalizarse nacer
nacionalsocialismo nacer
nada 227
nadador,-a nadar
nadar nadar
nadie 525
nado (a) nadar
nalgada -ada[2]
nalgatorio -orio[1]
nalgudo -udo
naranja 2668
naranjada -ada[2]
naranjado -ado[1]
naranjal -al[3]
naranjo -o[2]
narcisismo -ismo
narcotismo -ismo
narcotraficante 3850
narcotráfico 2649
narigada -ada[3]
narigón -ón[3]
narigón,-a nariz
narigudo,-a nariz
nariz nariz 3885
narizón -ón[2]
narizota -ote
narizudo -udo
narrable -able
narración narración
narrador,-a narración
narrar narración 2166
narrativa narración
narrativo narración
nasalizar -izar
natación nadar -ción 3726
natal nacer 3276
natalicio nacer
natalicio,-a nacer
natalidad nacer
natividad nacer
nativo -ivo 4158
nativo,-a nacer
nato,-a nacer
natura natural
natural natural 683
naturaleza natural -eza 1697
naturalidad natural
naturalismo natural
naturalista natural
naturalización natural
naturalizar natural -izar

naturalizarse natural
naturalmente natural -mente
  4246
naturismo natural
naufragar nave
naufragio nave
náufrago nave
náufrago,-a nave
náusea nave
nauseabundo nave -undo
náutica nave
náutico nave
navaja 4990
naval nave 4798
nave nave 3019
navegabilidad nave
navegable nave -able
navegación nave
navegante nave -ante[2]
navegar nave
navidad 2502
navideño -eño 3653
naviero nave
naviero,-a nave
navío nave
nazareno 4895
neblina niebla -ina
nebulosa niebla
nebulosidad niebla
nebuloso niebla
necedad necio
necesariamente -mente 3500
necesario necesitar 294
neceser necesitar
necesidad necesitar -idad
  453
necesitado necesitar
necesitado,-a necesitar
necesitar necesitar 372
necio necio
necio,-a necio
necrofobia -fobia
nectarífero -ífero
nefritis -itis
nefrosis -osis
negable -able
negación negar
negado negar
negar negar 830
negarse 830
negativa negar
negativismo negar
negativo negar -ivo 1281
negociable negocio -able
negociación negocio -ción
  1057
negociante negocio -ante[2]
negociar 1832
negocio negocio -o[1] 595
negral -al[2]
negrear negro
negrero negro
negrero,-a negro
negro negro 592
negro,-a negro
negroide negro
negrura negro -ura[1]
negruzco negro -usco
neocelandés -és
neoclasicismo clásico
neoclásico clásico
neoclásico,-a clásico
neoescocés -és
neófito -ito[2]
neorrealismo real[1]
neoyorquino -ino[2] 4448
nepalés -és
nervio nervio 4656
nerviosidad nervio
nervioso nervio -oso 2494
nervudo nervio

neumonitis -itis
neuritis -itis
neurología nervio
neurólogo -o[3]
neurólogo,-a nervio
neurona nervio
neurosis nervio -osis
neurótico nervio
neutralizar -izar
neutralmente -mente
nevada nieve
nevado nieve -ado[1]
nevar nieve 3933
nevazón -ón[1]
nevera nieve
nevisca nieve
neviscar nieve
ni 160
nicaragüense -ense
nicaragüeño -eño
nidada nido
nidal nido -al[1]
nido nido
niebla niebla
nietastra -astro
nieto,-a nieto,-a 2947
nieve nieve 3342
ninfómana -mano
ninfomanía -manía
ninguno 275
niñada niño,-a
niñera niño,-a
niñez niño,-a -ez 4318
niño,-a niño,-a 143
nitidez -ez
nitrito -ito[2]
nivel nivel 217
nivelación nivel
nivelador nivel
nivelador,-a nivel
nivelar nivel
níveo nieve
no 15
nobilísimo -ísimo
noble noble 3423
nobleza noble -eza
nocaut 4964
noche noche 295
nochebuena noche
nochecita -ita
nocherniego -iego
noctámbulo,-a noche
nocturno noche 2510
nódulo -culo
nogal nogal 4144
nogalina nogal
noguera -ero[4]
nogueral nogal
nombrado nombre
nombramiento nombre
  -miento 3302
nombrar nombre 1928
nombre nombre 262
nomenclatura nombre
nómina 2928
nominación nombre -ción
  3192
nominal nombre
nominar nombre 2638
nominativo nombre
nonagésimo -ésimo
noningentésimo -ésimo
norcoreano -ano
noreste norte 4586
noria 4081
norma norma -a 3136
normal norma 1179
normalidad norma
normalización norma
normalizar norma
normalizarse norma

rodillada rodilla -ada[(2)]
rodillazo rodilla -azo[(2)]
rodillera rodilla
rodilludo -udo
rojear rojo
rojez rojo -ez
rojizo rojo -izo
rojo rojo 309
rojo,-a rojo
rol 3338
rollo 3105
Roma romano
romance romano 3053
romanesco -esco
románico romano
romano romano -ano 2550
romanticismo romano
romántico romano
romántico,-a romano 2232
rompecabezas romper, cabeza
rompecorazones romper, corazón
rompedura -dura
rompehielos romper, hielo
rompeolas romper, ola
romper romper 1186
romperse romper
rompible romper -ible
rompimiento romper
ronda ronda -a 1551
rondalla ronda
rondar ronda
roñería -ería[(2)]
ropa ropa 1385
ropaje ropa -aje[(1)]
ropavejero,-a ropa
ropería -ería[(1)]
ropero ropa -ero[(1)]
ropeta -eta
roqueño -eño
rosa rosa 2759
rosáceo rosa -eo[(2)]
rosado rosa -ado[(1)]
rosal rosa -al[(3)]
rosaleda rosa -eda
rostro rostro 1786
rotante -ante[(1)]
rotario 4274
rotulación rótulo
rotulador rótulo
rotulador,-a rótulo
rotular rótulo
rótulo rótulo
rotundo -undo
round 3820
rozadura rozar -dura
rozamiento rozar
rozar rozar
rozarse rozar
roznido -ido[(2)]
rúbeo -eo[(2)]
rubia rubio
rubicundo -undo
rubio rubio 3589
rubor rubor
ruborizar rubor -izar
ruborizarse rubor
rubro 2097
rudeza -eza
rudo 3399
rueda -a 1836
ruedo 4671
rufianesco -esco
rugido -ido[(2)]
rugiente -ente[(1)]
ruido ruido 3271
ruidoso ruido
ruina ruina -a
ruinoso ruina
rumbo 1577

rumor rumor 2607
rumorearse rumor
rumoroso rumor
ruptura -ura[(2)] 3758
rural 698
ruso,-a 1585
ruta 1676
rutina 2774
rutinario -ario[(2)]

S

sábado sábado 413
sabanilla -illa
sabático sábado
sabatino sábado -ino[(2)] 4858
sabedor saber
sabelotodo todo, saber
saber saber 124
sabido saber
sabiduría saber -ería[(2)] 4838
sabiendas (a) saber
sabihondo saber, hondo
sabihondo,-a saber, hondo
sabio saber 4839
sabio,-a saber
sabiondo saber, hondo
sabiondo,-a saber, hondo
sabor sabor 1699
saborear sabor
saboreo sabor
sabroso sabor -oso 4688
sabrosura sabor
sacaclavos sacar, clavar
sacacorchos sacar
sacamuelas sacar
sacapuntas sacar, punto
sacar sacar 497
sacarse sacar
sacerdocio sacerdote
sacerdotal sacerdote -al[(2)]
sacerdote sacerdote 1339
sacerdotisa sacerdote
sacralizar sacrificio
sacramental sacrificio
sacramentar sacrificio
sacramento sacrificio
sacrificado sacrificio
sacrificar sacrificio -ificar 3250
sacrificarse sacrificio
sacrificio sacrificio -icio 2675
sacrilegio sacrificio
sacrílego sacrificio
sacristía sacrificio
sacro sacrificio
sacrosanto sacrificio
sacudida sacudir -ido[(2)]
sacudidor sacudir
sacudir sacudir 4498
sacudirse sacudir
sádico -ico[(2)]
sagaz -az
Sagitario 4777
sagrado sagrado 1448
sahumar humo
sahumerio humo
sal sal 1635
sala sala 1054
saladero sal
salado sal
saladura sal
salamanqués -és
salar sal
salarial sal 2800
salario sal -ario[(2)] 1225
salaz -az
salazón sal
salchicha sal
salchichón sal

saldar sal
saldo sal 2532
saledizo -dizo
salero sal -ero[(1)]
salida salir -ido[(2)] 722
salido saliente
saliente saliente
salífero sal
salina sal
salinidad sal
salino sal
salir salir 168
salirse 168
salitre sal
salmantino -ino[(2)]
salmuera sal
salobre sal
salón sala 1119
salpimentar sal
salsa sal 2224
salsedumbre -dumbre
salsera -era
saltador saltar -dor[(1)]
saltador,-a saltar
saltamontes saltar
saltante -ante[(1)]
saltaojos saltar
saltar saltar 2571
saltarín saltar
saltarse saltar
saltatriz -triz
salteo -eo[(1)]
saltico -cio[(1)]
saltimbanqui saltar
saltito -ito[(1)]
salto saltar -o[(1)] 3821
salubérrimo -érrimo
salubre salud
salubridad salud
salud salud 255
saludable salud -able 3095
saludar salud 2963
saludo salud -o[(1)]
salutífero -ífero
salvable salvar
salvación salvar
Salvador salvar
salvador,-a salvar
salvadoreño -eño
salvaguardar salvar, guardar
salvaguardia salvar, guardar
salvajada salvaje
salvaje salvaje 4066
salvajez -ez
salvajismo salvaje -ismo
salvamanteles salvar, manto
salvamento salvar 4617
salvar salvar 1578
salvarse salvar
salvavidas salvar
salvedad salvar
salvo salvar 2902
salvoconducto salvar, conducir
sanable sano
sanador sano
sanar sano
sanatorio sano -orio[(1)]
Sancho Panza ensanchar
sanchopancesco -esco
sanción 1790
sancionar 2842
sandiar -al[(3)]
saneado sano
saneamiento sano -miento 2461
sanear sano
sangrante sangre
sangrar sangre
sangrarse sangre
sangraza -aza

sangre sangre 1214
sangría sangre
sangriento sangre -iento
sangüeso -o[(2)]
sanguijuela sangre
sanguinario sangre
sanguíneo sangre -eo[(2)] 3054
sanguinolento sangre -lento
sanidad sano -idad 4859
sanitario sano -ario[(2)] 1282
sano sano 1804
santateresa santo,-a
santero santo,-a
santiaguino -ino[(2)]
santico -ico[(1)]
santidad santo,-a -idad 4752
santificación santo,-a
santificante -ante[(1)]
santificar santo,-a -ificar
santiguar santo,-a
santiguarse santo,-a
Santísimo santo,-a -ísimo
santito -ito[(1)]
santo santo,-a 2714
santo,-a santo,-a
santoral santo,-a -al[(1)]
santuario santo,-a 4343
santucho -ucho
santurrón santo,-a
santurrón,-a santo,-a
santurronería santo,-a
sapiencia saber
sapiente saber
saque sacar 4551
sarcasmo -asma
sargado -ado[(1)]
sartenada -ada[(3)]
satánico -ico[(2)]
satélite 3131
satirizar -izar
satisfacción satisfacción -ción 2313
satisfacer satisfacción 3003
satisfacerse satisfacción
satisfactorio satisfacción -orio[(2)] 3890
satisfecho satisfacción 2098
saturar 4275
sauceda -eda
sazón sazón
sazonar sazón 4996
se 8
seca seco
secadal -al[(1)]
secadero seco
secador seco
secadora seco -dor[(2)]
secano seco
secante seco
secar seco 1246
secarse seco
sección sección 1055
seccionar sección
seco seco
secreta secreto
secretar 4970
secretaría secretario 357
secretariado secretario
secretario,-a secretario 311
secretear secreto
secreteo secreto
secreter secretario
secreto secreto 1700
sector sección 201
secuela consecuencia 4552
secuencia consecuencia
secuencial consecuencia
secuestrador -dor[(1)]
secuestrador,-a 4290
secuestrar 2923
secuestro -o[(1)] 2199

X